WASHINGTON
HANDBOOK

WASHINGTON
HANDBOOK

INCLUDING SEATTLE, MOUNT RAINIER, AND OLYMPIC NATIONAL PARK
SIXTH EDITION

DON PITCHER

MOON
TRAVEL
HANDBOOKS

WASHINGTON HANDBOOK
SIXTH EDITION

Published by
Moon Publications, Inc.
P.O. Box 3040
Chico, California 95927-3040, USA

Printed by
Colorcraft Ltd.

© Text and photographs copyright Don Pitcher, 1999.
All rights reserved.

© Illustrations and maps copyright Moon Publications, Inc., 1999.
All rights reserved.

Some photos and illustrations are used by permission
and are the property of the original copyright owners.

ISBN: 1-56691-148-6
ISSN: 1085-2646

Editor: Asha Johnson
Production & Design: Karen McKinley, David Hurst
Cartography: Brian Bardwell and Bob Race
Index: Sondra Nation

Front cover photo: Hoh Rain Forest in Olympic National Pak, by Don Pitcher.

All photos by Don Pitcher unless otherwise noted.
All illustrations by Bob Race unless otherwise noted.

Distributed in the United States and Canada by Publishers Group West

Printed in China

Please send all comments,
corrections, additions,
amendments, and critiques to:

**WASHINGTON HANDBOOK
MOON TRAVEL HANDBOOKS
P.O. BOX 3040
CHICO, CA 95927-3040, USA
e-mail: travel@moon.com
www.moon.com**

Printing History
1st edition—1989
6th edition—June 1999

5 4 3 2 1 0

For Karen

CONTENTS

SPECIAL TOPICS

McClellan Succeeds
  at Failure *626-627*
The Rawhide Railroad *628-629*
A Nuclear Legacy *640-641*

MAPS

(continues on next page)

MAPS
(continued)

MAP SYMBOLS

EXPRESSWAY	TUNNEL	NATIONAL BOUNDARY
MAIN HIGHWAY	BRIDGE	STATE BOUNDARY
SECONDARY ROAD	PASS	COUNTY LINE
UNPAVED ROAD	STATE FERRY	OTHER BOUNDARY
FOOT TRAIL	OTHER FERRY	POINT OF INTEREST
INTERSTATE HIGHWAY	LARGE CITY	HOTEL / ACCOMMODATION
U.S. HIGHWAY	MEDIUM CITY	N. P. = NATIONAL PARK
STATE HIGHWAY	TOWN	S. P. = STATE PARK
COUNTY / OTHER ROAD	MOUNTAIN	C. P. = COUNTY PARK
WATER		CG. = CAMPGROUND
	CAMPGROUND	

WASHINGTON HANDBOOK
SECTION DIVISIONS

NORTHERN
PUGET SOUND

SAN JUAN
ISLANDS

OROVILLE

BELLINGHAM   MT. BAKER

OMAK
WINTHROP   OKANOGAN   COLVILLE

PORT ANGELES

EVERETT

OLYMPIC
PENINSULA

GRAND COULEE

SEATTLE AND
VICINITY OF SEATTLE

SEATTLE   THE   CHELAN

SPOKANE

LEAVENWORTH   EASTERN

SOUTHERN
PUGET SOUND   CASCADE   WASHINGTON

TACOMA   RANGE

WENATCHEE

ELLENSBURG

OLYMPIA   MT. RAINIER   SOUTHCENTRAL   PULLMAN

MT. ST. HELENS   YAKIMA   WASHINGTON

LONG BEACH   SOUTHWESTERN

TOPPENISH   PASCO   WALLA WALLA
RICHLAND   KENNEWICK

WASHINGTON

AND COLUMBIA GORGE   GOLDENDALE

VANCOUVER

© MOON PUBLICATIONS, INC.

0   50 mi

0   50 km

ABBREVIATIONS

B&B—bed and breakfast
CCC—Civilian Conservation Corps
d—double occupancy
F—Fahrenheit

4WD—four-wheel drive
km—kilometer
RV—recreational vehicle
s—single occupancy

CHARTS

ACCOMMODATIONS PRICE RANGES

Budget: under $35
Inexpensive: $35-60
Moderate: $60-85

Expensive: $85-110
Premium: $110-150
Luxury: $150 and up

TELL US ABOUT YOUR TRIP

Travel guides are perpetually out of date, and this one is no exception. By the very nature of the publishing business, words in print were written at an earlier time and based upon information gathered even earlier, usually just after Gutenberg invented the printing press. Things change incredibly fast in Washington, and you're bound to find places I missed, motels that are dives (but I said they were great), delightful hole-in-the-wall restaurants, new jokes about Bill Gates, incorrect phone numbers for the nudist colonies, and the names of top-secret military bases where they store all those UFOs that crashed. So send those cards, letters, and e-mails, especially if you know something offbeat that I missed. I always appreciate any hot tips, criticisms, or compliments you may wish to contribute. I try to respond, but because I'm often on the road you may have to wait awhile for a response. To reach me via email, put "Washington Handbook" in the subject heading and send messages to me care of: travel@moon.com. Send your snail-mail observations to:

Don Pitcher
Washington Handbook
c/o Moon Publications, Inc.
P.O. Box 3040
Chico, CA 95927-3040
USA

ACKNOWLEDGMENTS

Those readers who own previous editions of *Washington Handbook* will find substantial changes in this sixth incarnation. In addition to a multitude of updates, I added a number of Internet sites, changed the way lodging places are described, added many new listings, and tightened the text. This book is not simply the product of my own work, but also of a team of people from Moon Publications, including my patient editor, Asha Johnson.

Much of the information found within these pages was gleaned from employees and volunteers at Washington chambers of commerce, Forest Service and Park Service offices, and museums. In addition, a number of readers also wrote or e-mailed me with helpful comments. The following people were especially helpful for this update: Sandy Balmer, R. Lynn Barnes, Lora Bergren, Chris Boyan, Karen Breitling, Win Brickmeier, Maureen Briggs, Michelle Closson, Patricia J. Culler, Ken Dull, Pete Erben, Jeri Erickson, Chris Eubanks, Gary Fetterolf, Kristin M. Fitzgerald, Amber Geiger, Cheryl A. Grunlose, Yvonne Hall, Shana Hammett, Jean Heath, Brenda Herman, Charlotte Higgins, Eden A. Hopkins, Nancy Hubert, Kim Hughes, Tana Bader Inglima, Otto Jakubek, Jeanette Johnson, Rita Kuller, Jeffrey LeDoux, Tim Manns, Jerry McConnell, Marilyn Meechan, Sandy Meeve, Linda Miller, Mary Ann Miller, Lois Mylan, Mary Neumeyer, Judy O'Neill, Gail Ozlin, John Pettus, Cindy Pilkinton, Bernie Pineda, Suzanne Savlov, Norma Seese, Anna Sillik, Roberta H. Smith, Laurel Somerlott, Carolyn Sprague, Vladimir Steblina, Craig Tyler, Nez Thompson, Irene Thornton, Trisha Vakarcs, Jennifer Whitney, Randall W. Van Someren, and N. Zimmerman. Thanks to all for their help.

Several people deserve special commendations for their generous assistance during my research of this edition: Sue Hildreth of Seattle, Michael Smithson and Maurie Sprague of Olympic National Park, Sheri Forbes of Mt. Rainier National Park, Leah Hammer of Ravenscroft Inn, and John Warsen of Lopez Farm Cottages and Camping. Thanks to everyone! And last—but defiantly not least—a very special thank you goes to my wife Karen Shemet and our new daughter Aziza Bali, both of whom helped me through this big—and time-consuming—update.

INTRODUCTION

Americans and international travelers are discovering what locals have long known: that Washington contains some of the most diverse and fascinating country in the Lower 48. The state's forests are no secret—they don't call it the "Evergreen State" for nothing—but the abundance of other attractions is astounding. These include the city of Seattle—one of the nation's most enjoyable and sophisticated metropolitan areas; the dramatic Cascade Mountains with glacier-clad summits and active volcanoes; the arid plains, giant dams, and rolling wheat fields of eastern Washington; the long sandy beaches and rugged rocky coastline bordering the Pacific; the justly famous gorge of the mighty Columbia River; hundreds of islands of all sizes and shapes in Puget Sound; and, of course, the lush rain forests of the Olympic Peninsula for which the state is so famous. For the visitor, the state offers almost too much to see.

Travelers to Washington will quickly learn that they aren't the first to discover its wonders. The state's population has grown rapidly in the last decade and shows no signs of slowing. Part of this is due to increased jobs in high technology, but it has also been fueled by favorable publicity. More and more, the national media spotlight lands on the state, acclaiming it for cutting-edge entrepreneurship, magnificent scenery, abundant outdoor adventures, espresso coffee, and culinary treats to rival those anywhere. Washington's proclaimed "livability" has also made it a favored destination for American, European, and Asian visitors. Increased tourism has been a boon to some of the smaller towns in the Cascades and along the Olympic Peninsula, where the drastic reduction in timber harvesting has cost thousands of jobs. Tourism hasn't replaced logging and sawmill work, but it has provided new options.

Washington may be tucked away in the northwest corner of America, but it stands at the front door of the Pacific. The state's access to major Asian markets—Washington is closer to Asia than any of the contiguous states-has made it a major player in Pacific Rim trade. Boeing and Microsoft especially have major stakes here; Boeing airplanes are one of the nation's most important exports, and Microsoft's computer software programs sell to a global market—and have made Bill Gates the richest human on the planet.

THE LAND

GEOGRAPHY AND CLIMATE

A State Divided

To the surprise of many first-time visitors, who are expecting only evergreen forests, natural lakes, and lots of saltwater towered over by snowcapped mountains, Washington has a dual personality. It is divided into the dramatically different eastern and western halves by the Cascade Range, which extends 600 miles from Canada through Washington and Oregon before flattening out and disappearing in northern California. The Cascade Range has a powerful effect on the state's climate and scenery. The mountains wring moisture from the clouds, dumping rain and snow on the western flanks, but leaving little for the dry and sunny east side. Those who expect to see only the evergreen

land of the state's promotional campaigns are surprised when they travel through the broad wheat fields of eastern Washington. This country has its own beauty, and in places resembles the wide open spaces of Wyoming or Montana—not an image commonly associated with Washington.

Much smaller but with an equally dramatic silhouette, the Olympic Range is quite different from the ancient and volatile Cascades. The Olympics (the backbone of Olympic National Park) are some of the world's youngest mountains, just one or two million years old. Though not exceptionally tall (Mount Olympus is the highest at 7,965 feet), the Olympics produce dramatically varied weather. Storms spawned over the Pacific dump 70-100 inches of annual rainfall on the coastal plains, and 150 inches or more (with a record of 184 inches at Wynoochee

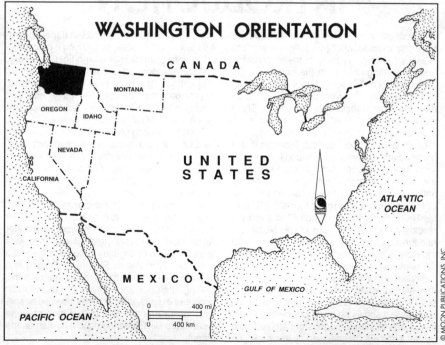

WASHINGTON ORIENTATION

© MOON PUBLICATIONS, INC.

oxbow) in the rain forests on the western and southwestern slopes—the heaviest precipitation in the contiguous United States. But on the northeast slopes of this range, Port Angeles, Sequim, Port Townsend, Whidbey Island, and the San Juans are in the driest area of western Washington, receiving only 12-20 inches annually. The most familiar example of this is Sequim, which sits in the rain shadow of the Olympics and is so dry that farmers must irrigate their crops.

Western Washington

Aside from the Olympic rain forests, most of the "wet side of the mountains" actually isn't all that wet: Seattle's annual rainfall of 38 inches is less than that of Chicago or New York. Winter snowfalls are generally light and melt quickly; a real snowstorm paralyzes the city for days due to the lack of snow-removal equipment and snow-driving expertise among natives.

Typical western Washington weather is mild and wet in the winter, warm and dry in the summer. Semipermanent high- and low-pressure systems in the North Pacific create predictable patterns of clouds and light rain beginning in October, with daytime temperatures in the 40s throughout most of the winter; December and January are the region's wettest months. In spring, the clouds give way to partly sunny days, and it's not unusual to have six weeks of cloudless skies in July and August. Summer daytime temperatures are usually in the 70s and 80s, with perhaps half a dozen 90° days each year. Thunderstorms are rare, tornadoes even more rare, and, oddly, given that Washington gets a lot of moisture, the humidity is low.

Seattle averages about an inch of snow per month in winter, though many winters are snow-free; the record snow depth is 29 inches. Mount Rainier is the place to go for snow—in the winter of 1955-56, the Paradise ranger station (elev. 5,500 feet) received 1,000 inches (83 feet) of snow. Winters with at least 70 feet are the norm. Cascade ski areas usually open in November and remain open through early spring, beginning and ending with Mt. Baker's eight-month ski season.

Western Washington's skiing may be good, but the swimming is not. Water temperatures along the Pacific Coast and in the Strait of Juan de Fuca average 45° in January, rising to 53° in July, with some secluded coves and bays getting into the 60s. Puget Sound stays around 55° year-round, though again some protected areas warm up to the mid-60s and become swimable. Most swimming and waterskiing is done in the region's numerous lakes.

Eastern Washington

Compared with western Washington, the "dry side of the mountains" has hotter summers, colder winters, more snow, and less rain. The area from the Cascade Range east across the Columbia Basin to the Palouse hills has hot, dry weather with an average of only 7-15 inches of annual rainfall. Summer daytime temperatures are in the 90s, with many days each year over 100°; the state's record high of 118° occurred at Ice Harbor Dam (near Pasco) in 1961. The bonus is that it's not humid. July and August are the driest months, often devoid of any precipitation at all; what rain they do receive generally comes packaged in thunderstorms. Winters bring 10-35 inches of snowfall and daytime temperatures in the 20s and 30s.

The Okanogan and Methow Valleys, in the north-central part of the state, are a cross-country skier's paradise. Annual winter snowfalls range 30-70 inches, beginning in November and staying on the ground through March or April. January maximum temperatures hover around 30°, with some nighttime below-zero temperatures recorded each year. In summer, the Okanogan Valley is another eastern Washington hot spot, with temperatures averaging 85-90° including several 100° days each season, plus occasional thunderstorms and hailstorms.

Much of this part of Washington, from the Columbia River east to the Spokane area and the Palouse hills south of Spokane, is technically a desert because the rainfall is less than 12 inches a year; in a few places no more than eight inches are measured. In fact, this is the northern end of the Great American Desert that runs from the Mexican border north almost to the Canadian border. Except for an occasional spot high enough to turn clouds into rainfall, the area hasn't had trees in several million years. Today it doesn't look like the Sahara or Death Valley because of the vast irrigation systems that have been built there, turning the desert into a cross-hatched garden.

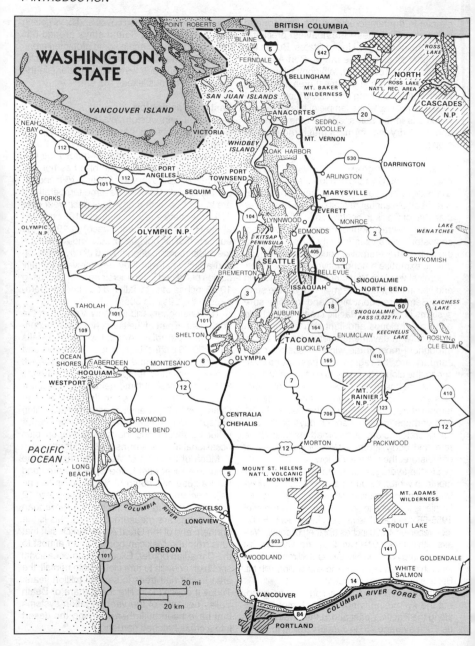

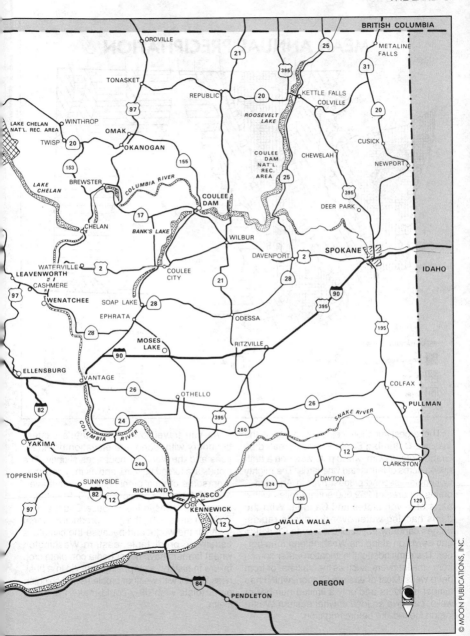

© MOON PUBLICATIONS, INC.

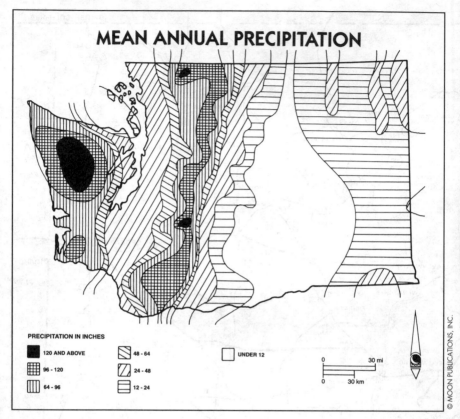

MEAN ANNUAL PRECIPITATION

PRECIPITATION IN INCHES

- 120 AND ABOVE
- 96 - 120
- 64 - 96
- 48 - 64
- 24 - 48
- 12 - 24
- UNDER 12

0   30 mi
0   30 km

The largest irrigation project, of course, is the massive **Columbia Basin Project,** created by Grand Coulee Dam, which puts water on a half-million acres of farms and vineyards. The mighty Columbia—second biggest river in America—drains an area of 259,000 square miles within parts of seven states and Canada. With the dams backing water over the river's rapids, barges can now travel all the way to Clarkston and Lewiston along the Washington/Idaho border. The remainder of the irrigation water comes from smaller rivers, such as the Yakima, or from deep wells. Most of eastern Oregon, which has almost no rivers and only a limited number of wells, can give an idea of what eastern Washington looked like before irrigation.

As you travel toward the state's eastern boundary with Idaho, the elevation gradually rises and the weather moderates slightly. The clouds are forced upward, and as they cool they drop some of their precipitation: rainfall averages 10-20 inches per year, with 20-40 inches of snow. The farms in the Palouse Country near Pullman are among the most productive wheat farms in the world, and because the climate is usually so predictable, eastern Washington wheat farmers have never had a complete crop failure in history, a surprising statistic in a business fraught with weather problems. Washington orchardists wish they could make the same claim.

Summer temperatures in central and eastern Washington are in the upper 80s and winter averages in the 30s, with a few extremes of plus 100° and minus 20° recorded every year. The

Blue Mountains in the southeast corner get up to 40 inches of precipitation, while Pend Oreille County in the northeast corner receives 28 inches of rain and 40-80 inches of snow.

FLORA AND FAUNA

Washington has a widely varied assortment of flora and fauna that reflects its richly diverse climate and geography. The Pacific Ocean and Puget Sound, the Olympic rain forest, the mountainous regions of the Cascades and Olympics, and the arid land of eastern Washington each support a unique population of birds, animals, and plants.

FLORA

The Forests

Washington's state tree, the western hemlock is widely used in the forest industry as a pulpwood species, and it and Douglas fir are two of the most abundant low-elevation trees in the state; above 3,000 feet in elevation Pacific silver fir and mountain hemlock take over. Bigleaf maples are distinguished by—you got it—their big leaves, up to a foot across. The Pacific madrone, or madrona, is characterized by waxy, evergreen leaves and peeling reddish bark that exposes a smooth underskin. Other common trees are the western red cedar, Sitka spruce, grand fir, black cottonwood, red alder, and vine maple. Northeast Washington and parts of the Cascades have other species, in-

cluding lodgepole pine, western larch, western white pine, ponderosa pine, and Engelmann spruce.

Olympic Rain Forest

At Olympic National Park, the Hoh, Queets, and Quinault River Valleys constitute the better part of the Olympic rain forest, an area unique in the world. Purists would say that 150 or more inches of annual rainfall doesn't qualify this region as a rain forest, a term usually reserved for the steamy jungle tropics. Whatever it's called, this area produces some of the world's largest trees. The largest known western hemlock and Sitka spruce grow in the Quinault Valley, the largest Douglas fir is in Queets, and the largest red alder is in the Hoh. The four major species here—the Sitka spruce, western red cedar, Douglas fir, and western hemlock—all grow very tall: trees average 200 feet, with many topping 300 feet.

The height of the trees isn't the only fascinating aspect of the rain forest: the visitor is immediately struck by how green everything is, and how pristine. These areas have never been logged; what you see is nature, pure and simple. Enormous trees spring out of the long-since-decayed "nursery logs" that gave them life, with

Hoh Rain Forest in Olympic National Park

STATE OF WASHINGTON TOURISM DIVISION

club moss eerily draping the branches; ferns and mosses cover nearly every inch of available ground in a thick carpet. Though most rainfall occurs from fall to spring, even summer days feel damp from high humidity and ocean fog. And it isn't just trees that one finds in these rain forests, but an incredible diversity of ferns, mosses, shrubs, herbs, and other plants, along with many kinds of birds, mammals, insects, and amphibians.

Old-Growth Forests

Old-growth forests are defined as being at least 250 years old, though some stands are actually far older, approaching 1,000 years. Other terms one commonly hears for old-growth forests are: mature forests (loggers prefer the term "overmature," implying that they need to be cut), or ancient forests (preferred by some environmentalists because ancient is a venerable term commonly associated with wisdom).

Because of the tall overstory trees that moderate temperatures and hold much of the snow, original forests are more stable than cutover areas and less susceptible to climatic extremes. This helps the survival of forest animals by allowing them to browse at all times of the year. It also allows for a multilayered understory of trees, bushes, and herbs that can support a larger variety of animal life. In addition, defects in the old trees and standing dead trees—called snags—provide nesting sites for birds, flying squirrels, and other animals, while the fallen trees create nutrient-rich mulch as they decay. In many old-growth forests, these fallen giants become "nursery logs" with new trees sprouting in a straight line along the trunk.

This heterogeneous structure differs markedly from the second- and third-growth tree farms where an even-aged monoculture of trees (usually Douglas fir) rises over a depauperate forest floor. Tree plantations quickly produce marketable timber, but they are a poor substitute for a more diverse natural forest where many plants and animals coexist.

rhododendron

Going, Going, Gone?

When the first Anglo settlers reached western Washington, they found immense forests that seemed to roll on forever, forests so dense that they severely slowed transportation. The wilderness represented an abundant source of wood to feed the demands of a growing society, particularly when gold lured thousands of miners to California and the Klondike. Logging was a dangerous but financially rewarding way to survive, and the cleared land created productive farmland for later settlers. After a century and a half of this, barely 15% of the original forests survive in the Pacific Northwest, and nearly half of these are within Olympic and Mt. Rainier National Parks. Most of Washington's private timberlands are operated as tree farms. On Forest Service lands, a moratorium on the logging of old-growth stands has been in effect for several years because of environmental concerns, most notably the preservation of spotted owl and marbled murrelet habitat. The closure to logging has caused major disruptions in timber-dependent communities, forcing many loggers and millworkers to look for other employment. The antigreenie sentiment runs strong in these towns. Sierra Club bumper stickers are ill-advised.

Rhododendrons

Washington's state flower—the coast rhododendron—is found from British Columbia south to northern California and east to the foothills of the Cascades. About 500 pure rhododendron species are hardy to the climate, along with several hundred more greenhouse varieties, which are combined and cross-pollinated to produce thousands of hybrids.

Rhodies are standard equipment in western Washington gardens, relatively easy to grow and beautiful to behold, in colors from yellows to pinks to bright reds and whites. The well-known rhododendron gardens on Whidbey Island, Federal Way, Bainbridge Island, Brinnon, and smaller gardens in area parks have impressive displays in spring and early summer.

MARINELIFE

Killer Whales

The orca, or killer whale, is the largest member of the family Delphinidae, a classification that includes toothed whales and dolphins. The males are significantly larger than the females of the species: up to 32 feet long, weighing five to six tons, with dorsal fins up to six and a half feet high and four feet wide and tail flukes spanning nine feet. Unencumbered by its size, the orca frequently travels at speeds upward of 30 mph. Named "killer whales" because they take warm-blooded prey, these cetaceans eat anything from harbor and ringed seals to seabirds, otters, dolphins, fish, and squid, depending on the local food supply. In Puget Sound, they generally eat only fish—mostly salmon, rockfish, and cod—and leave the other species alone.

Reports of killer whale attacks on humans and boats have been recorded as far back as 1911. In that year, H.G. Ponting, a photographer for the Scott expedition to the South Pole, was reportedly standing on ice within six feet of the water when eight whales broke through the ice and threw him into the sea. Reports such as these are so rare that one can only surmise that in those situations the orcas mistook people for marine mammals. The fact that whales and dolphins do not attack humans is one of the mysteries of nature.

Orcas are highly social, traveling in packs or "pods" of 2-40 individuals. Families stay together, protecting the young (who, at eight feet long and 400 pounds at birth, would seem to require little protection)

and mourning their dead. There are three resident pods in Puget Sound and along the Washington coast, with a total of about 100 members; other transient pods occasionally swim into the area but don't stay long. The most frequent sightings are around the San Juan Islands, especially at Lime Kiln State Park on the west side of San Juan Island—the only park in the U.S. dedicated exclusively to whalewatching.

Gray Whales

Every spring, tour boats leave the docks at Westport and a few other coastal towns for a close-up look at the migrating California gray whales. These enormous whales—ranging up to 42 feet in length and upward of 30 tons—migrate from the Bering and Chukchi seas to the warm breeding lagoons off Baja California in winter, passing the Washington coast southbound in November and December and northbound from April to June. Occasionally a group of gray whales comes into Puget Sound, and several have beached themselves and died for thus-far unknown reasons. Most, however, follow the outer coastline. After a 70-year hiatus, the Makah tribe in the far northwest corner of Washington again started hunting gray whales in 1998. They are allowed to take a maximum of five each year for food.

The gray is a baleen whale: it feeds by stirring up mud in shallow water, sucking in the water, mud, and organisms, and using its baleen—a fringelike sieve in its mouth—as a filter to trap its prey while forcing the mud and water back out. Gray whales are easily identified by their gray color, the absence of a dorsal fin, and bumpy ridges on their backs; their faces are generally covered with patches of barnacles and orange whale lice. Unconcerned with their appearance, gray whales often lift their faces out of the water

gray whale

up to about eye level in a motion referred to as "spyhopping." Although gray whales aren't aggressive and are often even friendly, whale-watchers in small boats should keep a respectful distance, since a whale may "breach," or jump completely out of the water, creating one heck of a wave as 30 solid tons splash back into the water.

Porpoises

Visitors often think that the black-and-white sea creatures riding the bow waves of their ferry or tour boat are baby killer whales, but these playful characters are Dall's porpoises. Commonly seen in the Strait of Juan de Fuca alongside the ferry *Coho* from Port Angeles to Victoria, B.C., the porpoises frequently travel south through the Admiralty Inlet and, on rare occasions, as far south as Tacoma. Dall's porpoises reach lengths of six and a half feet and weights of up to 330 pounds; they feed primarily on squid and small fish.

The harbor porpoise is Puget Sound's smallest cetacean, ranging to nearly six feet in length and 150 pounds. Although similar in appearance to the Dall's porpoise, the harbor porpoise is much more shy and rarely spotted in the wild. Accurate counts are impossible, but the population around the San Juan Islands has been estimated at fewer than 100; none live in Puget Sound, though resident populations were spotted there in the 1940s.

In summer and early fall, schools of up to 100 Pacific white-sided dolphins enter the Strait of Juan de Fuca, traveling as far inshore as Port Angeles but rarely any farther east. Reaching up to seven feet in length and 200 pounds, these dolphins are common off Japan, and along the continental shelf from Baja California to the Gulf of Alaska. They have black backs, white shoulders and bellies, and hourglass-shaped streaks that run from their foreheads to their tails; the rear halves of their dorsal fins are light gray. Like the Dall's porpoise, white-sided dolphins enjoy riding bow waves and often leap full-length out of the water alongside a boat.

Seals and Sea Lions

Harbor seals are numerous throughout Puget Sound and the Strait of Juan de Fuca, with their statewide population estimated at 7,000. They can be seen at low tide sunning themselves on rocks in isolated areas, but they will quickly return to the water if approached by humans. Though they appear clumsy on land, these 100- to 200-pound seals are poetry in motion underwater; they flip, turn, and glide with little apparent effort, staying underwater for as long as 20 minutes. (You can see harbor seals up close at the underwater viewing tank at Point Defiance Zoo in Tacoma.) Harbor seals have a bad reputation with area salmon fishermen, although studies of the seals' stomach contents and fecal material indicate that they feed primarily on flounder, herring, pollock, cod, and rockfish, as well as some mollusks and crustaceans.

The California sea lion is a seasonal visitor to the Strait of Juan de Fuca and northern Puget Sound, though on some mornings in winter and early spring their barking can be heard in shoreline communities as far south as Tacoma. These dark brown sea lions breed off the coast of California and Mexico in the early summer, and then some adventurous males migrate as far north as British Columbia for the winter. A large group of them collects just offshore from Everett, where a commercial tour boat takes visitors out for a closer look.

The lighter-colored northern sea lions are more numerous in the Puget Sound area, numbering up to several hundred in winter, primarily around Sucia Island in the northern Sound. The males of the species are much larger than the females, growing to almost 10 feet in length and weighing over a ton, while the females are a dainty six feet long and 600 pounds. Both are almost white when wet; the male has a yellow mane.

Other Marine Creatures

Puget Sound is home to the largest species of octopus in the world. Though it grows to 12 feet across the arms and weighs 25-30 or more pounds, it's not dangerous and, in fact, often plays with divers. These octopi can make themselves incredibly flat to get where they have to go: according to a local octopus legend, one of these giants slid out of its tank and under a door into its owner's bedroom.

Another peculiar Puget Sound inhabitant is the geoduck (pronounced "GOOey-duck," from the Indian *gweduck,* meaning "dig deep"). These

DIANNE BOUERICE LYONS

geoduck, the Pacific Northwest's most revolting clam

large, phallic-shaped clams can dig as deep as five feet, weighing in at four or five pounds with reports of some clams exceeding 15 pounds. The fleshy part of the body is so large that neither the entire body nor the siphon can be completely withdrawn into the shell. (Stop by Pike Place Market in Seattle to see what these creatures look like.) Geoducks are generally cut up and used in chowder, but some quality restaurants serve them as regular menu items or specials.

The horse clam is the second-largest Pacific Northwest clam, weighing up to five pounds; they can't completely withdraw their siphons, but at least their bodies fit inside their shells. Horse clams only dig about two feet deep, so they're much easier to gather and can be found in Cultus and Useless bays at the south end of Whidbey Island. Both geoducks and horse clams prefer sandy or sand-gravel beaches. For information on clamming, contact the Washington Department of Fish and Wildlife, Fish Management division, tel. (360) 902-2700,

www.wa.gov/wdfw/fish-sh.htm. Some years, the overabundant growth of microorganisms causes the clams to build up dangerous levels of toxins. So, before digging, it's always a good idea to visit the WDFW Web site or call the Shellfish Hotline at (360) 796-3215 or (800) 562-5632 for the latest on the edibility of clams.

LAND ANIMALS

Washington is home for a wide variety of land mammals, some of which have been brought back from the edge of extinction. Federal and state wildlife agencies alike have worked to preserve habitats for all forms of wildlife, and the state has become a richer place to live as a result.

Mule deer, the rare Columbia white-tailed deer, Rocky Mountain and Roosevelt elk, bighorn sheep, mountain goats, black bears (and a few grizzly bears), and a wide variety of smaller mammals, such as marmots, beaver, badgers, muskrat, nutrias, rabbits, and squirrels, are some of the animals you can expect to see, especially in the numerous wildlife refuges scattered across the state. The last remaining herd of woodland caribou in the lower 48 can be found in the Selkirk Mountains of northeast Washington. Even the timber wolf—exterminated from Washington in the 1930s—has made a comeback. The first wolf call was heard in the summer of 1990, and small numbers have now moved into the North Cascades and Selkirks from British Columbia.

Columbia White-Tailed Deer
Lewis and Clark were the first explorers to comment on this subspecies of mule deer, which evolved along the lower Columbia River between the Willamette River and the Pacific Ocean. By the time 5,200 acres were set aside for them in the 1960s, their numbers had dwindled to just 230. The population has rebounded, but they still remain endangered. These deer look very much like their larger cousins, but are smaller and have a slightly longer tail and a white underside. The Columbia White-tailed Deer National Wildlife Refuge is just west of Cathlamet on Hwy. 4. Part of it is farmland still in use on the mainland, and the remainder is a group of islands in the Columbia River, where the deer

often swim to browse on the willows and other low-growing plants.

Roosevelt Elk

Another subspecies, the Roosevelt elk live on the Olympic Peninsula, mostly inside the boundaries of Olympic National Park, and are thus given adequate protection to prevent them from being hunted to extinction. They are a subspecies of their Rocky Mountain relatives, which were almost killed off in the Cascades. They look similar to their relatives, but their antlers aren't as spectacular as those coveted by trophy hunters. Roosevelt elk are named for President Theodore Roosevelt, who was instrumental in their preservation.

Cougars

Attitudes towards these big cats have changed dramatically over the years. The bounty is long gone, and in 1996 Washington voters enacted a ban on using hounds to recreationally hunt mountain lions. Cougar populations are increasing in Washington at the same time as human developments push homes and peo-

ple onto land that was previously wild. This combination has led to an increase in cougar attacks throughout the West; of 10 fatal cougar attacks in the last century, half them have taken place in the last decade. In 1998 a cougar was shot a few blocks from Olympia city hall after preying upon pets in a residential neighborhood. More brazen was a 1998 attack near Issaquah, when a cougar killed a 50-pound Labrador and then attacked hounds sent in to track it. It was finally killed in a hollow stump where local kids played. As frightening as it is to be stalked by a big cat, wildlife experts say it is very unlikely that the cougar has mayhem in mind when following or watching humans. Like all cats, they are unusually curious animals. If you come face to face with one, maintain eye contact while backing slowly away. Try to appear larger than you are by raising your arms or by spreading a jacket or shirt. If you have children with you, pick them up. Talk loudly. But never, never run. Wildlife officials say compressed-air horns and pepper spray may ward off cougar attacks.

SLUGS

If western Washington had an official creature, it could easily be the common slug: the region is famous for them. The damp climate is just what slugs need to thrive: not too wet, because slugs aren't waterproof (they will absorb water through their outer membranes until their bodily fluids are too diluted to support them), and not too dry, because insufficient humidity makes them dry up and die. Optimum humidity for slugs is near 100%, which is why you'll see them crossing the sidewalk very early in the morning, at dusk, or on misty days.

During the dry parts of the day, they'll seek refuge under the pool cover you casually tossed onto the lawn, or under the scrap lumber piled in the back of your lot.

Slugs look like snails that have lost their shells, or little green or brown squirts of slime about three to five inches long. Though more than 300 species of slugs exist worldwide, the Northwest is home to little more than a

dozen. The native banana slug, light green or yellowish with dark spots, has been rapidly outnumbered by the imported European black slug, which is now far more common in area gardens than the native variety. Slugs can curl up into a ball to protect themselves, or flatten and elongate themselves to squeeze into tight places. They move on one long foot by secreting mucus that gets firm where the foot must grab hold and stays slimy under the part that must slide. They see (probably just patterns of light and dark) with eyes at the ends of a pair of tentacles; they have a mouth and eat primarily plants and mushrooms.

Getting rid of slugs is no easy matter. Traditional home remedies include saltshakers and beer traps; both require a strong stomach. Most residents just try to avoid stepping on them.

banana slug

FLORENCE BOUERICE

Bears

Black bears are fairly widespread in Washington, with large populations on the Olympic Peninsula and in Pend Oreille County. All of the black bears on the Olympic Peninsula are black; in other areas they may be black, brown, or honey-colored. They'll eat anything, from carpenter ants to berries to dead elk to salmon, plus anything you pack in from the supermarket. Black bears are so numerous that 400 of them are "harvested" each year in northeastern Washington.

Grizzly bears are rare in Washington, but there are a few in the North Cascades and in the Selkirk Mountains. Grizzlies once roamed throughout the western states, but now they are a threatened species with a total population of fewer than 1,000 in the Lower 48. Most of these survive in remote parts of Wyoming, Idaho, and Montana, with just a handful in Washington. A female grizzly must be 5-8 years old before reproducing, and she cares for her cubs for 2-3 years before having any more offspring, so her reproductive capacity is low. The best way to protect both the grizzly bear population and yourself is to avoid encounters with them.

Avoid unexpected confrontations with bears by letting them know you're there. If you walk with a breeze hitting your back, any bears ahead of you will know you are coming. If you're unable to see everything around you for at least 50 yards, warn any hidden animals by talking, singing, clapping your hands, tapping a cup, rattling a can of pebbles, or wearing a bell. Safety is also in numbers: the more of you hiking together, the more likely a bear is to sense you and stay away. Don't let your dog run free—it may sniff out a bear and lead it back to you. When camping in the backcountry, store all food, soaps, garbage, and clothes worn while cooking in a sack hung from a tree branch at least 10 feet up and four feet out from the tree trunk. In an established campground, keep those items in your car's trunk. Don't sleep where you cooked dinner, and keep sleeping bags and gear away from cooking odors. Stories are sometimes heard about grizzlies attacking women during their menstrual period, though nobody knows for sure if the scent actually causes an attack. Cautious women may choose to hike in grizzly country at another time.

If you do encounter a bear, here's how to identify it: a grizzly is generally lighter in color than a black bear, though color alone can't be used for identification. Look for the grizzly's shoulder hump (behind its head) and a "dish face" profile, with a distinct snout. (Black bears have no hump and a straight profile.) While you're looking for identifying marks, slowly detour out of the bear's path and stay upwind so the bear will know you're there; don't make abrupt noises or movements. While retreating, look for a tree to climb—one in which you can get at least 12 feet up and stay there until you're certain that the bear has left the area. If no tree is close, your best bet is to back slowly away. Don't try to outrun the bear—grizzlies can hit 40 mph in short bursts, and you can't beat that, no matter how scared you are. Sometimes dropping an item such as a hat or jacket will distract the bear, and talking also seems to have some value in convincing bears that you're a human. If the bear sniffs the air or stands on its hind legs it is probably trying to identify you. When it does, it will usually run away. If a bear woofs and postures, don't imitate, as this is a challenge. Keep retreating! Most bear charges are a bluff; the bear will often stop short and amble off.

If a *grizzly* bear actually does attack, curl up face-down on the ground in a fetal position with your hands wrapped behind your neck and your elbows tucked over your face. Your backpack may help protect you somewhat. Remain still even if you are attacked, since sudden movements may incite further attacks. It takes a lot of courage to do this, but often a bear will only sniff or nip you and leave. The injury you might sustain would be far less than if you had tried to resist.

Many authorities now recommend against dropping to the ground if you are attacked by a *black* bear, since they tend to be more aggressive in those situations. You're better off fighting back with whatever weapons are at hand if attacked by a black bear.

Recently, cayenne pepper sprays such as "Counter Assault" (available at camping stores) have proven useful in fending off some bear attacks. These "bear mace" sprays are effective only at close range and in non-windy conditions, and are not a cure-all or a replacement for being careful in bear country.

BIRDS

Eagles

Approximately 300 pairs of bald eagles make their year-round home in Washington, primarily west of the Cascades. In winter that number swells to over 1,600 birds, drawn to rivers throughout the state by the carcasses of spawned-out salmon. Several whitewater-rafting companies operating in the North Cascades offer midwinter Skagit float trips just for the thrill of seeing these majestic birds; see the Cascade Range chapter for more information.

In past times the bald eagle was often blamed for the deaths of sheep and other domestic animals. Actually, eagles much prefer dead and dying fish to anything running around on hooves; their common fare, aside from dead salmon, is sick or injured waterfowl or rabbits that didn't make it across the road. An aggressive bird, the eagle will often purloin the catch of an osprey or other bird in favor of finding its own.

The adult bald eagle's distinctive white head and tail make it easy to spot. But it takes four years for it to acquire distinctive markings, making the immature eagle confusing to identify, as it may show whitish markings anywhere on its body. In contrast, the somewhat similar golden eagle has distinct white patches on its tail and underwings.

Bald eagles are sensitive to disturbances in their environment; the Department of Fish and Wildlife recommends that an undisturbed circle 660 feet in diameter surround a nest during the breeding season to preserve the nest site. Their large nests, sometimes measuring over eight feet wide and 12 feet high, are often found in old-growth spruce and fir; snags are popular for

bald eagle wintering on the Skagit River

sunning, resting, and watching for their next meal.

The state's heaviest concentration of breeding bald eagles can be seen on the San Juan Islands, enjoying the warm updrafts around Mt. Constitution on Orcas Island and Mt. Findlayson and Mt. Dallas on San Juan Island, and along the Strait of Juan de Fuca. The annual "salmon festival" brings the resident and migrating birds to the inland reaches of the Skagit, Sauk, Nooksack, and Stillaguamish rivers, with some enterprising pairs seen along southern Puget Sound and the lower Columbia River.

Owls

The bird of the hour in western Washington is the northern spotted owl, which nests in old-growth forests along the Pacific Coast—forests that are filled with snags and broken trees that provide ideal nesting spots and smaller, sheltered trees for young owls who can't yet fly properly and must use their feet to climb from tree to tree. These forests are full of spotted-owl food: flying squirrels, snowshoe hares, and wood rats. Spotted owls are big eaters and quite territorial: 2,200 acres of old-growth forest will support but a single pair of owls. Because suitable forest is being greatly reduced by logging, the spotted owls' numbers are diminishing—only an estimated 2,500 pairs remain in the Pacific Northwest's old-growth forests, and researchers believe they could be gone in 30 years if logging continues at its present rate.

Other Birds

Other noteworthy birds in western Washington include the great blue heron, frequently seen along harbors or suburban lakes. The belted kingfisher is a common year-round resident of Puget Sound and the Strait of Juan de Fuca. Red-tailed hawks are often perched along I-5 and other highways, waiting for a meal. Noisy Stellar's jays, blue with a black head, are common in picnic areas and neighborhoods.

In the Cascades and east of the mountains, the beautiful mountain bluebird is sometimes spotted in snags in open areas, and the town of Bickleton in the Horse Heaven Hills of southern Washington maintains hundreds of bluebird houses that stand on fence posts, in trees, and in front of the church. East of the mountains, striking black-and-white magpies are frequently seen flitting over the highway.

HISTORY

PREHISTORY

Although Washington is one of the more recent additions to the U.S., archaeological evidence suggests that the Pacific Northwest was one of the first populated areas in North America. In recent years, animal and human remains as much as 13,000 years old have been found across the state.

In the late 1950s and early 1960s, archaeologists uncovered numerous artifacts and partial skeletons of people known as Marmes Man in a cave overlooking the Palouse River near its confluence with the Snake River. Dated at more than 10,000 years old, this is one of the earliest known human occupation sites in North America.

At Ozette in the northwest corner of the state, an ancient village was covered by a mudflow, perhaps triggered by an earthquake some 500 years ago. More than 50,000 well-preserved artifacts have been found and cataloged, many of which are now on display at the Makah Cultural and Research Center in Neah Bay. Other sites have also revealed how long people have been here: thumbnail-sized quartz knife blades found at the Hoko River site near Clallam Bay are believed to be 2,500 years old.

One of the most fascinating discoveries occurred in 1977, when Emanuel Manis, retired on a farm outside of Sequim, was digging a pond on a back corner of his land and found two enormous tusks. A Washington State University archaeological team, led by zoologist Carl Gustafson, concluded that these were 12,000-year-old mastodon tusks. The group discovered other mastodon bones, including a rib that contained the bone point of some prehistoric weapon used to kill the animal. These bones are now on display at the Sequim-Dungeness Museum in Sequim.

Native Americans

According to one theory, Native Americans originally crossed over to Alaska from Asia at the end of the last Ice Age, when the sea was 300 or more feet below present levels and the strait was a walkable passage. As these Native Americans spread throughout the Pacific Northwest, they adopted significantly different lifestyles on each side of the Cascades.

West of the mountains, salmon, shellfish, whales, and other seafood made up a large part of the Indian diet; western red cedars provided ample wood for canoes, houses, and medicinal teas and ointments. A mild climate and plentiful food allowed these coastal tribes to stay in one place for most of the year, and in fact the north coast Indians were among the wealthiest in America. They often built longhouses—wooden structures up to 100 feet long and 40 feet wide that housed several families.

Coastal tribes were skilled canoe carvers and could travel up the Columbia as far as The Dalles, where rapids prohibited further progress. Inland tribes would meet them here for an annual fair with trading, dancing, gambling, and general hell-raising. Haidas and Tlingits from Alaska and British Columbia thought nothing of paddling hundreds of miles to trade—or raid.

East of the Cascades, particularly near the Columbia River, salmon was an important part of the diet, though dependence on deer, elk, bear, squirrel, and rabbit led these tribes to live seminomadic lives. The introduction of the horse to

Totem poles such as this are common throughout Washington.

eastern Washington in the mid-1700s made hunting, especially for large bison, much easier. Indians in eastern Washington lived in caves or rock shelters while hunting, as well as in well-insulated pithouses that could hold several families.

The Pacific Northwest tribes were introduced to the by-products of white man's culture, such as knives, guns, and the deadly smallpox virus, before ever laying eyes on a white explorer. One leader in northeast Washington, Chief Charles Goosmus, went blind from crying after his twelve children all died within a month.

The Europeans' arrival was met with reactions ranging from tolerant acceptance to swift murder. Relations between the races are still strained today; the interpretation of peace treaties signed in the 1850s is being hotly debated, with many lawsuits concerning property, water, and especially fishing rights pending. Tribes have also caused considerable consternation among some local and state governmental agencies by building casinos on their reservations and earning millions of dollars each year for their members. Most Native Americans do not live on reservations, though there are 22 reservations scattered throughout Washington, the largest being the Yakima and Colville.

A NEW WORLD

The first foreigners to land on Washington's shores were Chinese and Japanese fishermen who arrived weeks or months after they were blown off course. None of the Asian nations was interested in expanding across the Pacific in those days, and nobody particularly cared about the land to the east. Records, if any, were skimpy and ignored. That was definitely not the case in southern Europe.

Spanish Explorers

In 1592, exactly a century after Columbus made his landfall in the Caribbean, a Greek explorer using the Spanish name Juan de Fuca sailed along Washington's coast and claimed to have discovered the fabled "Northwest Passage," an inland waterway crossing North America from the Pacific to the Atlantic. Later explorers did find a waterway close to where de Fuca indicat-

ed, but it led only into today's Puget Sound, not all the way to the Atlantic Ocean.

Spain, hoping to regain some of its diminishing power and wealth, sent an expedition out in the 1700s to explore the Northwest Coast. In 1774, Juan Perez explored as far north as the Queen Charlotte Islands off Vancouver Island and was the first European to describe the Pacific Northwest coastline and Olympic Mountains before being forced to turn back by sickness and storms.

In 1775, a larger Spanish expedition set out, led by Bruno de Heceta and Juan Francisco de la Bodega y Quadra. Heceta went ashore at Point Grenville, just north of Moclips on the Washington coast, and claimed all the Northwest for Spain. Farther south, Bodega y Quadra sent seven men ashore in a small metal craft for wood and water; they were quickly killed and their boat torn apart in the whites' first encounter with coastal Native Americans. The two ships sailed away without further incident; Quadra named the island Isla de Dolores (Isle of Sorrows), today's Destruction Island. Quadra continued his explorations as far north as present-day Sitka, Alaska, while Heceta sailed north to Nootka Sound. Heceta failed to note the Strait of Juan de Fuca, but he did come across "the mouth of some great river," presumably the Columbia, though the death or illness of much of his crew prevented further exploration and robbed Spain of an important claim.

Russian Voyages

Russian exploration of the Pacific Northwest began in the mid-1700s, when Vitus Bering led two expeditions to determine whether a land bridge connected Russia with North America. Bering sailed as far south as the Columbia River before turning back. The abundance of sea otters and beavers led Russian fur traders to establish posts from Alaska to northern California, which posed a serious threat to other nations hoping to stake a claim.

The Russians were quite active along the coast for several years and this led to one of the Northwest's most poignant tragedies, the result of a shipwreck near the Strait of Juan de Fuca in 1808, four years after the Lewis and Clark party had visited the Columbia estuary. The Russian ship, the *Saint Nicholas,* ran aground on Destruction Island and the crew tried to walk down the coast to Grays Harbor. Accompanying them was Anna Petrovna Bulygina, wife of Nikolai Bulygina, commander of the ship. The trip was a disaster in every way. Anna was captured, tortured, and raped; she committed suicide. Coincidentally, she was the first Caucasian woman to set foot on the West Coast. An English ship rescued the other survivors, who were signaling the boat with a kite that had twisted gut for a string.

Early English and American Exploration

England was the force to be reckoned with in the battle for the Northwest. In 1776, Captain James Cook took two ships, the *Discovery* and the *Resolution,* and 170 men on an expedition that brought him to the Hawaiian Islands, the Oregon coast, and Vancouver Island's Nootka Sound. Though he charted the coastline from Oregon to the Bering Sea, he made no mention of the Columbia River or the Strait of Juan de Fuca. Cook was killed by hostile Hawaiians in a dispute over a boat in 1779, and his crew returned to England.

Other English sailors continued in Cook's footsteps. In 1787, Charles Barkley and his wife Frances explored and named the Strait of Juan de Fuca. In 1788, John Meares named Mount Olympus and other features of the Olympic Peninsula.

An American, Robert Gray, sailed out of Boston to explore and trade along the Northwest Coast in the 1792. Stopping first at Nootka Sound—the hot spot to trade on Vancouver Island—Gray worked his way south and spent three days anchored in today's Grays Harbor. Continuing south, Gray discovered the mouth of the Columbia River and traded there with the Chinook Indians before heading home.

Best known today, however, is the expedition led by George Vancouver in 1792. His goal was to explore the inland waters and make one last attempt at finding the Northwest Passage. The names of Vancouver's lieutenants and crew members are like a list of Washington placenames: Baker, Rainier, Whidbey, Puget. (Many of the place-names were attached to curry political favor back home; almost anyone in a position of power had his name stuck on something.) The expedition carefully charted and thoroughly described all navigable waterways and named every prominent feature. When Vancouver heard of Gray's discovery of the Columbia River, he sent William Broughton upriver to a point east of Portland to strengthen England's claim on the land.

Until 1792, only the coastal areas of the Pacific Northwest had been explored. The first explorer to cross North America north of Mexico was a British trader, Alexander Mackenzie. In 1788, he traveled as far as the Arctic in search of the fabled Northwest Passage. In 1792-93, Mackenzie followed the Bella Coola River from the Canadian Rockies to just north of Vancouver Island. His two expeditions proved that there was no Northwest Passage, at least north of the 50th parallel.

Lewis and Clark Expedition

The best-known overland expedition began in St. Louis in 1804, led by Meriwether Lewis and William Clark. President Thomas Jefferson sent these men and their party to study the geology, animals, and plantlife of the 827,000 square miles acquired in the Louisiana Purchase, which extended as far west as the Rocky Mountains, and to explore and map the rivers and lands west of the Rockies that were still more or less up for grabs as the new country competed with England, Russia, and Spain for all the land between the two oceans.

Lewis and Clark's group left St. Louis in canoes and keelboats, heading north on the Missouri River to present-day North Dakota. After wintering there with the Mandan Indians, the party, whose numbers were reduced to 28 for the final push, set out again on the Missouri River, crossed the Rockies on foot, and headed down the Clearwater River to the Snake River, in search of the Columbia River they knew would lead them to the ocean. In October 1805, the party got their first view of the Columbia, and followed it downriver for many a "cloudy, rainey, disagreeable morning" until they reached the Pacific Ocean.

They built a winter camp, Fort Clatsop, south of the river and spent a cold, wet winter there, plagued by sickness. In spring they headed for home. The two leaders split up, with Lewis returning much the way they had come and Clark exploring the Yellowstone River to the south.

They met up again in North Dakota where the Yellowstone enters the Missouri and returned to St. Louis in September 1806.

Fur Traders

Wilson Price Hunt, partner in the fur-trading business with John Jacob Astor, led the second American overland expedition in 1811. His party joined others who arrived by ship—first the *Tonquin,* in 1811, and then the *Beaver,* arriving a year later—to establish Astoria, a fort on the south side of the Columbia River. Hunt was instructed to follow Lewis and Clark's route through Montana, but aggressive Blackfeet Indians changed his mind. Instead he traveled through present-day Wyoming, taking to canoes—a poor choice for the wild Snake River. One canoe was smashed and its experienced navigator killed, leading to Hunt's decision to divide the expedition into three groups and continue overland.

Donald McKenzie's team reached Astoria in January 1812; Hunt's group arrived a month later. The last third of the expedition straggled in a year after the first, in January 1813.

British overland exploration was accomplished mainly by David Thompson, a fur trader and chief cartographer for the North West Company in the early 1800s. In 1810, under Thompson's direction, Finan McDonald and Jacques Finlay built Spokane House, the first trading post in the state of Washington. Thompson traveled extensively throughout the Canadian Rockies, south into Kettle Falls and downriver to the mouth of the Columbia in 1811, where he found that the Americans had already established a fort at Astoria—Astor's men had arrived four months earlier. Though he was disappointed, Thompson's detailed maps and sketches of the Columbia were used for many years by settlers and traders.

The First White Settlers

During the time between the early exploration and the permanent settlement of the Northwest, British and American trading posts emerged to take advantage of the area's abundant supply of beaver and sea-otter pelts. Two English companies, the North West Company and Hudson's Bay Company, merged in 1821; American fur-trading outfits included many small, independent companies as well as John Astor's Pacific Fur Company and the Rocky Mountain Fur Company.

The most influential of them, the Hudson's Bay Company, built its temporary headquarters on the north side of the Columbia, 100 miles inland at Fort Vancouver, across the river from the confluence with the Willamette.

The settlers planted crops (including the apples and wheat that are so important to Washington's economy today), raised livestock, and made the fort as self-sufficient as possible. At its peak, 500 people lived at or near the fort. Fort Vancouver served as a model for other Hudson's Bay Company posts at Spokane, Okanogan, and Nisqually. When settlers began arriving in droves and the beaver population diminished in the late 1840s, the Hudson's Bay Company was crowded out and moved its headquarters north to Fort Victoria on Vancouver Island. The demise of Fort Vancouver came in large part because its chief factor, Dr. John McLoughlin, was a humane man and helped new arrivals by giving them food and seed grain for planting crops on land the Hudson's Bay Company thought should be owned by England.

Missions were another important method of establishing white settlements in the Washington Territory. The first missionary, Jason Lee, was sent by the Methodist Church in 1834 to introduce Christianity to the native peoples, but instead he spent much of his time and resources ministering to whites at Fort Vancouver.

In the 1840s, "Oregon Country" north of the 42nd parallel was jointly occupied by the U.S. and England. The westward movement gained momentum when a New York editor coined the phrase "Manifest Destiny" to symbolize the idea that all of the land west of the Rockies rightfully belonged to the United States. If you exclude trappers, prior to 1843, there were barely 40 white settlers west of the Rocky Mountains.

Between 1840 and 1860, 53,000 settlers moved west to Oregon Country to take advantage of the free land they could acquire through the Organic Act of 1843 and the Donation Land Law of 1850. Under the Organic Act of the Provisional Government, each adult white male could own a 640-acre section of land (one square mile) by simply marking its boundaries, filing a claim, and building a cabin on the land. The Donation Land Law put additional restrictions on land claims: 320 acres were awarded to white or half-white males who were American citizens and had arrived prior to 1851; another 320 acres could be claimed by his wife.

These and other restrictions effectively eliminated claims by blacks, Asians, single women, non-U.S. citizens, and Native Americans, thereby giving pioneers the legal right to take Indian land. These land grants were too large for most families to farm and prevented towns and industries from growing as quickly as they might have; people were simply too far apart. By 1855, all the land in the Willamette Valley had been claimed.

The promise of free land fueled the "Great Migration" of 1843, in which almost 900 settlers traveled to the Oregon Country, six times the number of the previous year. More pioneers followed: 1,500 in 1844 and 3,000 in 1845. Most settlers came by way of the Oregon Trail from St. Joseph, Missouri, along the North Platte River, through southern Wyoming and southern Idaho into Oregon, then north to the Columbia River. Soon the route looked like a cleared road; traces of it can still be seen where the wagon tires dug ruts in stone and where the ground was packed so hard by the wheels that grass still cannot grow. Washington's early settlers congregated around five fledgling cities: Seattle, Port Townsend, Oysterville, Centralia, and Walla Walla; other smaller communities developed at Tumwater, Steilacoom, Olympia, and Fairhaven, now part of Bellingham. In eastern Washington the major communities were Spokane and Walla Walla.

Settling the Claims

By 1846, only the U.S. and England retained claims to the Oregon Country; Spain and Russia had sold or lost their North American possessions. Negotiators brought the U.S. and England to agreement on a division at the 49th parallel from the Rockies to the main channel between Vancouver Island and the mainland, running through the center of the Strait of Juan de Fuca to the Pacific Ocean.

The unspecified "main channel" was viewed to be either the Rosario Strait or the Haro Strait, leaving the San Juan Islands in the middle of the disputed waterway. Both nations claimed the islands. The British maintained a Hudson's Bay Company fort, but American settlers began moving in and establishing farms. In 1859, one of the Americans shot and killed a British-owned pig that had repeatedly rooted in his garden, and the resulting uproar nearly started a war. The British demanded payment for the pig; the American refused, and soon both sides began bringing in soldiers and heavy weapons. Within three months the English had a force of 2,140 troops, five warships, and 167 heavy guns arrayed against the American army's 461 soldiers and 14 cannons. Fortunately, calmer heads prevailed, and no further shots were fired in the "Pig War." Soldiers of both nations remained on the islands for the next 13 years, and in 1872, Germany's Kaiser Wilhelm was chosen to conduct arbitration. He awarded the islands to the Americans and pronounced the Haro Strait the dividing channel.

In spite of all this arbitration, one small piece of real estate managed to be overlooked. A peninsula hung down from the Canadian mainland into the Strait of Georgia south of the 49th parallel, making it American land. Rather than settling the matter when it was discovered, the appendix still dangles there and is known as Point Roberts, a bit of America attached to Canada.

Growth of a New State

In 1848, President Polk created Oregon Territory and appointed Joseph Lane as the first territorial governor a year later. In the early 1840s, most Americans lived south of the Columbia River. By 1849, only 304 people lived north of the river, but in the next year that number tripled as more and more settlers ventured northward. As they moved farther away from the territorial government, the settlers felt left out of governmental matters and decided to separate from Oregon. Delegates met at the Monticello Convention in 1852 to list reasons for the proposed separation, and Congress found little opposition to the bill. Washington Territory—named, of course, for George Washington—was created in 1853. The initial territory included much of present-day Idaho and Montana. In 1863, Idaho Territory was carved off the whole, followed by Montana Territory in 1864, giving the territories much the same boundaries that the states now occupy.

When Washington became a territory, its population was under 4,000 people; by 1880 it had grown to over 125,000 and was considered a serious candidate for statehood. Washington was admitted as the 42nd state in 1889, with Olympia as its capital and a growing population of over 173,000. When the news was telegraphed to Washington officials in Olympia, they discovered one problem; the telegraph had been sent collect, and they could not read it until the cost was paid. Welcome to the United States!

Into the Twentieth Century

The 40 years between 1870 and 1910 marked a period of tremendous growth in Washington. In 1870, the territory's population was just shy of 24,000; in 1910, the new state, created with the same boundaries, had 1,142,000 residents. Much of this growth was a direct result of the arrival of the Northern Pacific and Great Northern railways in the late 1880s, bringing industry and settlers to Puget Sound and creating new towns all along their routes. Spokane saw rapid economic growth during the 1880s, outfitting miners for the gold, silver, and lead rush in Idaho.

The 1880s also spelled disaster for Spokane, Ellensburg, and Seattle, when major portions of these cities' thriving downtown areas were destroyed by fire. Though the cities were rebuilt quickly in brick, the state was hit hard by a nationwide depression, the Panic of 1893, when growth slowed on both sides of the mountains and businesses failed. A gold rush in the Yukon and the emergence of hydroelectric power helped get the state back on its feet. At the end of this period of growth, the Alaska-Yukon-Pacific Exposition of 1909 brought nationwide attention and over 3.7 million visitors to what is now the University of Washington campus in Seattle to promote the ties between Washington, the far north, and Pacific Rim countries.

The Great Depression slowed Washington's population growth to just 11% between 1930 and 1940. Seattleites were the first to call makeshift "towns" of boxes and crates "Hoovervilles," named in honor of President Herbert Hoover, whom they blamed for the nation's ills. One of the largest covered nine acres about where the Kingdome stands today.

The first and second world wars changed Washington's economy from one based largely on mining, farming, logging, and fishing to manufacturing and ship and airplane building, high-

Seattle's Space Needle, a legacy from the 1962 World's Fair

DON PITCHER

lighted by Boeing's B-17: over 13,000 of the "Flying Fortresses" were built for WW II. Boeing continues to be one of the state's largest employers and most important industries and in the 1990s became America's biggest exporter.

Seattle's 1962 World's Fair was the first such exposition to be an economic success, drawing more than 9.6 million people during its six-month run and creating a permanent addition to the city's culture with the Seattle Center. Spokane followed suit 12 years later with Expo '74, emphasizing environmental concerns and cleaning up its own Spokane River in the process.

Too Much?

Perhaps all of this self-imposed media attention was a mistake: Washington, especially west of the Cascades, continues to grow at a rate that many residents find alarming. Today, the state is rapidly approaching five million people. The trend has accelerated in the 1980s and '90s, particularly around Puget Sound. The city of Bellevue has grown from a cow-town when it was incorporated in 1953 to a booming city of almost 100,000 people today, complete with high-rise buildings, mega malls, an ever-spreading suburbia, and traffic snarls. Cities and suburbs alike are beginning to suffer from overcrowding, pollution, traffic jams, increased crime, and other big-city problems as more and more visitors are opting to stay for good, putting stress on water, refuse, and highway systems that were designed for smaller populations. Today all too many Washington towns and cities seem bent upon joining the strip-mall frenzy that is turning many places into what one book called "The Geography of Nowhere." As Washington enters the 21st century, the challenge will be to preserve the state's unsurpassed natural resources and beauty while controlling growth.

INDUSTRY AND ECONOMY

Washington's earliest industries—fishing, mining, farming, and logging—depended upon the abundant natural resources that the pioneers found here. Today only farming and logging are major industries, although logging has taken a severe hit from the spotted-owl and marbled murrelet controversy as areas are set aside from logging to preserve their habitat. Farming remains the basis for much of Washington's economy, and hydroelectric power creates jobs and low electric rates from the state's plentiful resources (but the dams have destroyed many salmon runs). Over the years, though, manufacturing, shipping, and other industries have become increasingly important to the state's economy, particularly the trio of Boeing, Microsoft, and Weyerhaeuser.

Mining

Coal was first discovered east of Bellingham in 1849, and mining began in 1855. Discoveries of coal in the Cascades in the late 1800s gave rise to a number of small mining towns (such as Black Diamond, Carbonado, Wilkeson, Newcastle, Cle Elum, and Roslyn) on both sides of the Cascades. Though coal was plentiful—geologists today believe there are 6-65 billion tons in the state—it was soft and therefore limited in its uses. Often found in steep ravines or streams, it was also difficult to extract and transport.

Washington led the country in mining disasters for many years. Here, miners at the Carbonado mining disaster of 1930.

Underground explosions and other accidents gave Washington more mining fatalities per number of miners than any other state for several years in the late 1800s. By the turn of the century, coal from the Rocky Mountains had become a cheaper and more practical fuel source, and by 1930 coal mining had virtually disappeared. Today, coal mining is seeing a minor revival: for the past several years, over five million tons of coal per year have been strip-mined near Centralia for use in a thermal-electric power plant there.

Other minerals begat industries that met with varying degrees of success. Discoveries of gold and silver in the mountains of Washington's northeastern corner caused short-lived rushes—and Indian wars, as whites crossed onto reservation lands—but outfitting miners for the gold rushes of Idaho and the Yukon yielded a better return for Seattle and Spokane. Silver, gold, and lead mines in Monte Cristo were to have been the economic basis of Everett, John D. Rockefeller's city on Port Gardner Bay, until the depression of 1893 forced him to withdraw his support. A steel mill in Kirkland, an iron refinery outside Port Townsend, and a copper mine in Holden either never got started or met with limited success. A successful silver, gold, and lead refinery in Tacoma was started in 1890 by William R. Rust; he later sold the plant to the American Smelting and Refining Company (ASARCO) for processing copper.

A gold mine still operates in Republic, and another is proposed near Oroville, but Washington's most valuable minerals are the least exotic: 60% of the money made from mineral production is derived from cement, stone, and gravel pits in the western half of the state.

Lumber

The Pacific Northwest states of Washington, Oregon, and Idaho supply about 60% of the total lumber in the United States. Washington is generally the third- or fourth-largest producer of the 50 states, with Oregon taking the lead since 1938. Douglas fir, western hemlock, and western red cedar are some of the commercially important trees native to the area west of the Cascades.

Wood and wood products have been a vital part of Washington's economy ever since the coastal Indians first began using cedar for longhouses, totem poles, canoes—they even made clothing from cedar bark. The first white settlers and missionaries used wood for construction of their forts, homes, and blockhouses, and British explorer John Meares was the first to ship lumber to the Orient in 1788. Seattle's founding fathers depended on shipments of lumber to San Francisco for much of their income; Yesler's waterfront sawmill was an important part of the city's early economy. The lumber business boomed with the cheaper transportation provided by the arrival of the railroads in Puget Sound in the late 1880s and '90s.

In 1900, Frederick Weyerhaeuser purchased 900,000 acres of prime forest land from the Northern Pacific Railroad for $6 an acre, later increasing his holdings to over two million acres by 1913. With over six million acres today, the Weyerhaeuser Corp. is now the largest lumber company in the country.

Forests cover over 23 million Washington acres, 18 million of which are commercial forests. It's difficult to look at the shaved hillsides of the Cascades and not think it offensive, but all of us use wood, the trees are replanted, and until the recent cutbacks, the logs and wood products produced $5-7 billion annually and employed a substantial number of Washington's workers.

Farming

Washington's Native Americans relied on hunting and food gathering rather than agriculture to supply their families' needs. It wasn't until Fort Vancouver was established in the 1820s that commercial agriculture took hold in Washington, as Hudson's Bay Company acquired a surplus of cattle to sell to the early settlers. Farming developed slowly west of the Cascades, as the heavily forested land first had to be cleared, and the acidic soils produced minimal yields. As settlers spread east of the Cascades, the wide-open spaces were perfect for cattle ranching, sheep herding, and grain growing.

Agriculture grew rapidly through the turn of the century due to the arrival of the railroads that created markets, irrigation projects, and the free land provided by the Organic Act of 1843 and the Donation Land Law of 1850. Agriculture flourished during the first and second world wars and quickly rebounded after the Depression when refrigeration allowed Washington farmers to compete on a national scale.

More recently, the 1952 Columbia Basin Irrigation Project opened up a half-million parched acres for farming around Ephrata and Moses Lake. Today, Washington farmers and ranchers produce more than $3.3 billion annually, over 80% of which is derived from agriculture east of the Cascades. The biggest money crop is wheat, grown on three million acres in eastern Washington, especially in the famous Palouse hills near Pullman. Nearly all the state's wheat is shipped overseas to Japan, Korea, Taiwan, the Philippines, and other Asian markets. Other important crops are hay, potatoes, livestock, apples, pears, cherries, grapes, onions, and other fruits and vegetables. Washington is one of the few states that grows cranberries; these are grown in the southeast corner in bogs near Willapa Bay.

Washington is probably best known for its apples, some 10 *billion* of which are grown annually, over half of the nation's total apple production. The center of apple growing is between Wenatchee and Chelan, but orchards can be found in many parts of the state. More than two-thirds of the apples grown in Washington are of the red delicious variety, though many other varieties are also produced.

One of the state's fastest-growing crops is wine grapes. In 1972, Washington had just six wineries; today there are almost 100, and visitors come to tour the Columbia and Yakima Valleys much as they would California's wine-producing regions. Washington is now recognized as one of the prime wine producers in the country, with many award-winning wines, and four official wine-growing regions: Columbia Valley, Yakima Valley, Walla Walla Valley, and Puget Sound. Washington boosters point out that these valleys lie at the same latitude as the France's Burgundy and Bordeaux regions (but so does South Dakota!). The state's largest producer of wines is Chateau Ste. Michelle, with wineries in both the Yakima Valley and in Woodinville.

Fishing

Fishing is one of the state's oldest industries, as the original Native Americans on both sides of the Cascades depended on Columbia River salmon and other fish for much of their diet, and

coastal Indians from the Neah Bay area were whalers. Commercial fishing, less important to the early settlers than logging and other industries, wasn't firmly established until the 1860s, when canneries, new salmon-fishing techniques, and new markets at home and abroad led to the industry's rapid expansion.

Until recently, the Pacific Northwest salmon industry harvested more than 250,000 pounds of salmon annually, worth about $100-150 million. In the 1990s, the runs collapsed due to a combination of warm oceanic currents, the destruction of spawning habitat by dams and logging, overfishing, and droughts. Ocean fishing was banned off the coast of Washington and Oregon, and except for certain tribal fisheries and a few short openings, it has remained closed. Washington's many state and private hatcheries produce all five species of Pacific salmon, but there is evidence that hatchery-grown fish are part of the problem since they compete with natural populations and are more susceptible to diseases due to a lack of genetic diversity. Also, commercial fisheries targeted on hatchery-raised fish often take large numbers of the wild fish populations at the same time. Restoring the salmon will require habitat preservation and restoration, mitigation of the devastating effects of hydroelectric dams, less emphasis on hatchery-raised fish, and stronger controls on the number of fish that can be caught.

Hydroelectric and Nuclear Power

Washington's first hydroelectric power was generated in the late 1880s in Spokane, when Spokane Falls were used to power a saw to cut wood for a local hotel. Uses multiplied to include street lighting, trolley lines, and more, and in 1899 Spokane's Washington Water Power Company was established as one of the first hydroelectric power companies in the country. Tacoma was the first major city to produce its own power when, in 1898, it took over a local utility company and later built dams on the Nisqually and Skokomish Rivers.

Franklin D. Roosevelt's New Deal paved the way for the construction of the first federally built dam on the mighty Columbia River: the Bonneville Dam, completed in 1938. It was quickly followed by the Grand Coulee Dam and others, until 14 Columbia River dams produced electricity to power much of the Pacific Northwest and California. They also provided water to irrigate much of central Washington. By the 1970s, 96% of the state's power was hydroelectric in origin.

Inexpensive hydroelectric power has been taken for granted since its inception; Tacoma City Light has been boasting for years that it offers the cheapest electric rates in the nation. But drought years in the early '90s demonstrated that even in the soggy Pacific Northwest, low electric rates are not guaranteed, and other energy alternatives must be considered. Even with the abundance of dams, the Pacific Northwest has to import energy from Canada to supply the growing demand. The other factor that has come into play is fish, or rather the lack of fish. Plummeting salmon runs have pushed some salmon populations to the brink, and much of the blame is being laid upon the dams that block the upstream migration of adults and kill young salmon heading out to sea.

Public outrage, way-over-budget construction costs, and safety concerns have made nuclear power a poor second choice. In 1968, the Washington Public Power Supply System (WPPSS, commonly called "Whoops") began work on five nuclear generators, three at the Hanford site near Tri-Cities and two at Satsop in Grays Harbor County. The $6 billion budget stretched to $24 billion, and public outcry over the inevitable rate hikes to pay for the construction resulted in approval of an initiative limiting such groups' spending and the mothballing of all but the reactor at Hanford. Customers are paying for these white elephants through the Bonneville Power Administration's substantial rate hikes, and citizens of the world will be paying for centuries to come as they grapple with the deadly waste that they create.

What's left? Coal-fired plants, such as the Centralia Steam Plant, may become more important if coal reserves can be efficiently and economically mined. Solar energy, wind farms, geothermal energy, and other alternatives will require years of research and economic support before they can become any more than token energy producers. Conservation is probably the best alternative, but cheap power has made too many folks wasteful of energy.

Aircraft Manufacturing

Washington's economy is closely tied in with the success of the Boeing Company, the state's largest employer and manufacturer of both commercial and military aircraft. Its founder, William E. Boeing, started his fledgling aircraft business in a hangar on Lake Union, then moved to a shipyard on the Duwamish River in 1916. World War I brought orders for training planes, and the company held on after the war by producing boats, furniture, and other items, plus U.S. Post Office transport planes and Army fighter planes. World War II brought over 13,000 orders for its B-17 bomber, and at the end of the war, B-29 bombers dropped the infamous atomic bombs on Nagasaki and Hiroshima.

After the war, William Allen took over as president of Boeing, and the company produced its first jet-powered passenger plane, the 707, in 1958. In the late 1960s, Boeing's 747 plant opened in Everett in the world's largest building, and Boeing was established as the world leader in aircraft manufacturing. The late '60s and early '70s were hard times for Boeing, as government contracts for the SST and other military aircraft fell through; employment fell from 110,000 to 38,000 workers. The company had to diversify to survive, so it created subdivisions in commercial aircraft, military aircraft, hydrofoils, and helicopters. In the '80s, Boeing's employment was stabilized at 68,000-80,000 workers, and the company is still the world leader in commercial aircraft production, making Boeing the country's major exporter in an era of enormous trade deficits.

The end of the Cold War hurt Boeing, but not as much as it did other defense contractors. Fortunately, Boeing relies almost entirely on sales to commercial airlines. However, as the world economy faltered in the early 1990s, Boeing had to reduce its workforce again, but not nearly as drastically as the big 1969 reduction—when someone put up a billboard reminding the last person to leave Seattle to turn out the lights. Boeing also changed its sales technique by inviting airline executives in to help design new airplanes rather than sticking to the old way of simply telling the customers what they were going to get.

Shipping

From the time Seattle's earliest settlers dropped a horseshoe on a clothesline into Elliott Bay to determine its depth, shipping has played an important role in the development of Puget Sound communities. Today, Seattle and Tacoma are among the most important seaports in the world, and other seaports and riverports along the Columbia as far inland as Clarkston helped to establish waterborne trade as one of the state's largest industries.

The first goods shipped from Seattle were logs that would be used as dock pilings in San Francisco. Lumber and wood products still account for a good portion of the area's exports, particularly from smaller ports such as Everett, Port Gamble, Port Angeles, Hoquiam, Olympia, and Bellingham. Seattle and Tacoma are important containerized shipping ports, where bulk and manufactured goods from airplanes to wheat are exported to Japan, China, Taiwan, Canada, and Australia. Telecommunications equipment, cars

and trucks, clothing, and petroleum products are the primary imports, arriving from Canada, Japan, Taiwan, and Hong Kong. Both the ports of Tacoma and Seattle continue to be national trade leaders, and the future for containerized shipping in Washington looks very bright. Oil tankers also arrive from Alaska to supply four oil refineries in Anacortes and Ferndale.

While Seattle and Tacoma get most of the shipping attention, Columbia River ports have been doing very well, thank you, especially the deep water ports of Portland, Longview, Vancouver, Kalama, which do a big business as terminals for wheat, corn, soda ash, logs, and other materials coming down the Columbia River bound for Pacific Rim nations. These same ports import massive amounts of alumina from Australia, limestone from Canada, cement from China, along with countless other products.

ON THE ROAD

RECREATION

When it comes to recreation, Washington pretty much has it covered. You can surf on a Westport beach one day, go horseback riding the next, and be on the edge of a Mt. Rainier glacier the following day. The Pacific coast has long beaches for playing in the sand, fishing, or beach-combing; the various national parks and forests offer backcountry hiking at its finest in the Olympics, Cascades, and northeast Washington; Puget Sound is a haven for sea kayaking and sailing; Columbia Gorge offers some of the finest windsurfing on the planet; anglers love the count-less lakes, reservoirs, and rivers; river rafters and kayakers head down the state's whitewater rivers throughout the summer; and cyclists dis-cover roads and trails of every description. In the winter, the options shift to snow sports, and Washington has 'em all, including skiing of all types, snowboarding, sledding, skating, and snowmobiling.

ORGANIZATIONS

The Mountaineers

Established in 1906, The Mountaineers is a 15,000-member organization of outdoor enthu-siasts with a strong environmental bent. Based in Seattle, the club organizes hiking, climbing, cy-cling, skiing, snowshoeing, sea kayaking, and many other activities and events throughout the year. They even have a singles group where you can meet others with similar interests. This is a great organization with a dedication to pre-serving the wild places; they were instrumental in the establishment of both Olympic National Park and the Alpine Lakes Wilderness. Membership is $45 per year (plus an initiation fee of $33), and members receive *The Mountaineer,* a monthly magazine listing local activities, along with 20% discounts on their many excellent books. In addi-tion to Seattle, The Mountaineers have branches in Olympia, Tacoma, Everett, and Bellingham. For more info, drop by their bookstore at 300 3rd Ave. W in Seattle, tel. (206) 284-6310. Get a catalog of the 300 books and other publications they produce by calling (800) 284-8554; many of these are available in bookstores throughout the Northwest. Find them online at www.mountaineers.org.

American Alpine Institute
The American Alpine Institute, the nation's top climbing school, is located in Bellingham at 1515 12th St., tel. (360) 671-1505. The staff includes accomplished mountain climbers and educators, and offers courses starting with the basics and going all the way to advanced monthlong mountaineering programs. Classes are taught all over the world—from the Himalayas to Alaska—with beginning mountaineering classes taught in the North Cascades.

Washington Department of Fish and Wildlife
This organization's mission is to "provide information resources to protect, restore, and enhance Washington fish and wildlife." They are a good resource for current information about fishing, hunting, and clamming as well as details about wildlife-enhancement programs. Contact them at WDFW Main Office, Natural Resources Building, 1111 Washington St. SE, Olympia, WA 98501; mailing address 600 Capitol Way N., Olympia, WA 98501-1091, tel. (360) 902-2200, fax (360) 902-2230, www.wa.gov/wdfw/. They can tell you the current game fish regulations; sporting goods or other stores that sell fishing licenses are also a good source of information. Fishing licenses cost residents $17, nonresidents $48, or $9 and $17 respectively for three-day licenses. Clamming is a very popular activity in many parts of coastal Washington, especially along the beaches near Long Beach, Westport, and Ocean Shores. The season changes each year, so check with the WDFW in Olympia for specifics. Clamming licenses are $5 for Washington residents, $20 for nonresidents. Since clams can occasionally build up toxins due to the presence of marine microorganisms, it's a good idea to call the Shellfish Hotline, tel. (360) 796-3215 or (800) 562-5632 before doing any clamming.

SNOW SPORTS

Downhill Skiing and Snowboarding
Washington's best ski and snowboard areas are stretched along the Cascades from Mt. Baker to Mt. Rainier. Snow on the western slopes of the Cascades is usually wet and heavy, but some ski areas on the eastern slopes, such as Mission Ridge, have powdery snow. The following Washington downhill ski areas are described elsewhere in this book: **The Summit at Snoqualmie** (includes Alpental, Summit West, Summit Central, and Summit East), **Ski Bluewood, Crystal Mountain, Echo Valley, 49° North, Hurricane Ridge, Loup Loup Ski Bowl, Mission Ridge, Mount Baker, Mount Spokane, Sitzmark, Stevens Pass, Leavenworth Ski Bowl,** and **White Pass.** For more info, get a copy of the *Washington State Winter Recreation Guide* from visitor centers. The larger ski areas all have Web sites; find them via www.skicentral.com.

Cross-Country Skiing
Cross-country, or Nordic, skiing is particularly popular on the eastern slopes of the mountains, in part because the snow is more powdery and the weather is usually sunny and clear. Some of the best is in the Methow Valley, where 150 km of trails are marked, the majority of which are groomed. The **Methow Valley Sports Trail Association** at provides a hotline for ski-touring information, tel. (800) 682-5787, and a brochure showing the major trails. Other popular cross-country skiing areas include Mount Tahoma Trails (near Mount Rainier National Park), Echo Valley (near Lake Chelan), Hurricane Ridge (Olympic National Park), Leavenworth Winter Sports Club, Stevens Pass Nordic Center, White Pass Nordic Center, and Ski Acres Cross-Country Center. Most of these areas groom trails for both traditional and skate-skiing.

The state maintains more than 50 **Sno-Parks** in the Cascades and eastern mountains, with nearby skiing trails (sometimes groomed, sometimes not). The permits required to park at these plowed areas are available from retail outlets throughout the state. The cost is $7 for a one-day pass, $10 for three days, or $20 for the entire winter season, with the money helping to pay for plowing, signs, trail grooming, and maintenance. The State Parks and Recreation Commission, tel. (800) 233-0321, sells Sno-Park permits and maps of groomed cross-country ski trails in the state, and offers a brochure/map showing the areas.

For the current snow avalanche danger in the backcountry, contact the Forest Service at (206) 526-6677, or www.nwac.noaa.gov.

Snowmobiling

The state maintains over 2,200 miles of groomed snowmobile trails, primarily in the Cascades and northeast corner of the state. For a map showing snowmobile trails, and a publication on snowmobile use in the state, contact Washington State Park Recreation Division, tel. (800) 233-0321.

PUBLIC LANDS

Almost 45% of Washington's 42.6 million acres are publicly held. The largest landholding agencies are the U.S. Forest Service, Bureau of Indian Affairs, National Park Service, U.S. Fish and Wildlife Service, and various branches of the military, but the state (primarily the Dept. of Natural Resources) owns almost 3.5 million acres of land.

The rules, regulations, permit requirements, and fees on public lands change constantly, especially Forest Service and Park Service lands. Before heading out, check with a local ranger station, or purchase *Washington's Backcountry Access Guide,* an excellent booklet published by The Mountaineers. It is updated annually, and details the far-too-complex regulations in each area. Find it online at www.mountaineers.org.

National Parks

Washington's three major national parks attract millions of visitors each year, and offer mustsee sights. **North Cascades National Park** covers a half-million acres of wild mountain country that includes more than 300 glaciers, hundreds of miles of hiking trails, and the 55-mile long Lake Chelan. **Mount Rainier National Park** contains the state's tallest and best summit: 14,411-foot Mt. Rainier. Hiking trails encircle the peak, and scenic mountain roads provide lingering views of the mountain meadows, sub-

alpine forests, and glaciers that make this one of the nation's crown jewels. **Olympic National Park** is famous for the lush west-side rain forests that include enormous old-growth trees, but it also has dramatic mountainous country and the incomparable Pacific coastline. In addition to these areas, the Park Service manages a small part of the **Klondike Gold Rush National Historical Park** in Seattle's Pioneer Square (the main part is in Skagway, Alaska), the **Lake Roosevelt National Recreation Area** on Lake Roosevelt in eastern Washington, **San Juan Island National Historical Park** on San Juan Island, **Ebey's Landing National Historical Reserve** on Whidbey Island, **Fort Vancouver National Historic Site** in Vancouver, and **Whitman Mission National Historical Site** near Walla Walla. All of these are described in depth elsewhere in this book. For more info, point your browser to www.nps.gov.

Forest Service Lands

United States Forest Service lands cover more than nine million acres in Washington state within seven national forests. These forests are managed for multiple uses, but the emphasis has—until recently at least—been on logging. Concerns over spotted owl survival led to a moratorium that has nearly halted timber harvesting in many areas. The National Forests of Washington also contain 24 wilderness areas that cover more than 2.5 million acres. Over half of the total acreage falls within the three largest: Glacier Peak Wilderness (576,900 acres), Pasaytan Wilderness (530,000 acres), and Alpine Lakes Wilderness (393,360 acres). The wilderness areas are described in appropriate chapters of this guide. For an excellent overview of these and other natural areas, get *Exploring Washington's Wild Areas* by Marge and Ted Mueller (Seattle: The Mountaineers). The Forest Service also manages Mount St. Helens National Volcanic Monument, and the Columbia River Gorge National Scenic Area, two of the state's most interesting natural areas.

Many Forest Service trailheads now charge user fees to help fill a gap left by a Republican-dominated Congress intent on axing recreation funding. Day use is generally $3 per vehicle per day, or pay $25 for an annual **Trail Park Pass,** which can be used in most national forests in Washington. Officially this is a test program that ends in 1999, but Congress will probably extend it. The plus side of this is that 80% of the money is used to maintain local recreation areas and trails. For details, call the headquarters offices below, or stop by a local ranger station. On the Web, find Forest Service offices at www.fs.fed.us/recreation/states/wa.html.

Colville National Forest, Colville,
    tel. (509) 684-3711
Gifford Pinchot National Forest, Vancouver,
    tel. (360) 750-5000
**Columbia River Gorge National Scenic
    Area,** Hood River, Oregon,
    tel. (541) 386-2333
**Mount St. Helens National Volcanic
    Monument,** Amboy, tel. (360) 750-3900
Mount Baker/Snoqualmie National Forest,
    Mountlake Terrace, tel. (425) 775-9702
Okanogan National Forest, Okanogan,
    tel. (509) 826-3275
Olympic National Forest, Olympia,
    tel. (360) 956-2400
Wenatchee National Forest, Wenatchee,
    tel. (509) 662-4335
Umatilla National Forest, Walla Walla,
    tel. (509) 522-6290

State Parks

The state of Washington manages more than 100 state parks covering over 232,000 acres. These are scattered in almost every corner of the state. Most are quite small, encompassing a few hundred acres or less, but some, such as Moran State Park in the San Juan Islands and Deception Pass on Whidbey Island are several thousand acres each and attract throngs of visitors each year; Deception Pass State Park is visited by more than three million folks annually. State park facilities are surprisingly diverse, including several historic forts (Fort Townsend, Fort Flagler, Fort Ebey, Fort Worden, and others), many miles of sandy ocean beaches (including Grayland Beach, Fort Canby, Long Beach, Ocean City, and Pacific Beach), one of the largest public telescopes in the region (Goldendale Observatory), a park devoted to whalewatching (Lime Kiln), a campground where Lewis and Clark spent a night (Lewis and Clark Trail), and an incredible waterfalls surrounded by desolate eastern Washington land (Palouse Falls). In addition, the state park system includes numerous historic sites, 10 environmental learning centers for school kids, and 40 marine parks, many of which are accessible only by boat. All of the developed state parks are described elsewhere in this volume; see below for a description of camping in the parks.

A fine source for state park information is the definitive *Washington State Parks* by Marge and Ted Mueller (Seattle: The Mountaineers). If you don't want to pay anything, request the helpful *Parks Guide* produced by Washington State Parks. For this publication, brochures on the parks you plan to visit, or reservation information, contact the Washington State Parks and Recreation Commission at (360) 902-8563 or (800) 233-0321. On the Web their address is: www.parks.wa.gov.

BACKCOUNTRY SAFETY

Beaver Fever

Although Washington's backcountry lakes and streams may appear clean, you could be risking a debilitating sickness by drinking untreated water. The protozoan *Giardia lamblia* is found throughout the state, spread by both humans and animals (including beaver). Although the disease is curable with drugs, it's always best to carry safe drinking water on any trip or to boil water taken from creeks or lakes. Bringing water to a full boil is sufficient to kill Giardia and other harmful organisms. Another option is to use water filters, available from backpacking stores. Note, however, that these may not filter out other organisms such as *Campylobactor jejuni,* bacteria that are just 0.2 microns in size. Chlorine and iodine are not always reliable, taste foul, and can be unhealthy.

Hypothermia

Anyone who has spent much time in the outdoors will discover the dangers of exposure to cold, wet, and windy conditions. Even at temperatures well above freezing, hypothermia—the reduction of the body's inner core temperature—can prove fatal. Hypothermia is a problem during the Northwest summers more often than winters because people often mistakenly believe that the bright, sunny morning weather is going to last. In the higher elevations of the Cascades and Olympics the weather is unpredictable, and the temperature can drop dramatically in a matter of hours or even minutes.

In the early stages, hypothermia causes uncontrollable shivering, followed by a loss of coordination, slurred speech, and then a rapid descent into unconsciousness and death. Always travel prepared for sudden changes in the weather. Wear clothing that insulates well and that holds its heat when wet. Wool and polypropylene are far better than cotton, and clothes should be worn in layers to provide better trapping of heat and a chance to adjust to conditions more easily. Always carry a wool hat, since your head loses more heat than any other part of the body. Bring a waterproof shell to cut the wind. Put on rain gear *before* it starts raining; head back or set up camp when the weather looks threatening; eat candy bars, keep active, or snuggle with a friend in a down bag to generate warmth.

If someone in your party begins to show signs of hypothermia, don't take any chances, even if the person denies needing help. Get the victim out of the wind, strip off his clothes, and put him in a dry sleeping bag on an insulating pad. Skin-to-skin contact is the best way to warm a hypothermic person, which means you'll need to also strip and climb in the sleeping bag. If you weren't friends before, this should heat up the relationship! Do not give the victim alcohol or hot drinks, and do not try to warm the person too quickly since it could lead to heart failure. Once the victim has recovered, get medical help as soon as possible. Actually, you're far better off keeping close tabs on everyone in the group and seeking shelter before exhaustion and hypothermia set in.

Frostbite

Frostbite is a less serious but quite painful problem for the cold-weather hiker; it is caused by direct exposure or by heat loss due to wet socks and boots. Frostbitten areas will look white or gray and feel hard on the surface, softer underneath. The best way to warm the area is with other skin: put your hand under your arm, your feet on your friend's belly. Don't rub it with snow or warm it near a fire. In cases of severe frostbite, in which the skin is white, quite hard, and numb, immerse the frozen area in water warmed to 99° to 104° until it's thawed. Avoid refreezing the frostbitten area. If you're a long way from medical assistance and the frostbite is extensive, it is better to keep the area frozen and get out of the woods for help; thawing is very painful, and it would be impossible to walk on a thawed foot.

Other Safety Tips

Dealing with bears and cougars is discussed under "Flora and Fauna," above. The most important part of enjoying—and surviving—the backcountry is to be prepared. Know where you're going; get maps, camping information, and weather and trail conditions from a ranger before setting out. Don't hike alone. Two are better than one, and three are better than two; if one gets hurt, one person can stay with the injured party and one can go for help. Bring more than enough food so hunger won't cause you to continue when weather conditions say stop. Tell someone where you're going and when you'll be back.

Always carry the **10 essentials:** map, compass, water bottle, first-aid kit, flashlight, matches (or lighter) and fire starter, knife, extra clothing (a full set, in case you fall in a stream), including rain gear, extra food, sunglasses—especially if you're hiking on snow.

Check your ego at the trailhead; stop for the night when the weather gets bad—even if it's 2 p.m.—or head back. Don't press on when you're exhausted—tired hikers are sloppy hikers, and even a small injury can be disastrous in the woods.

CAMPING

State Parks

Washington maintains more than 80 state parks with campgrounds, offering clean and scenic accommodations across the state. Tent sites are $10-11, RV hookups (not available in all of these) cost $15-16. Note: if you pitch a tent in a site with electricity you will be charged the RV rate. Some state parks also offer more primitive campsites for $5-7 that attract hikers and cyclists. Most park sites include a picnic table, barbecue grill, nearby running water, garbage removal, a flush toilet, plus coin-operated hot showers. Many state parks are closed Oct.-March; those that remain open often have limited winter camping facilities. Most campground gates close at 10 p.m., so get there early! The state park budget has been stretched to the limit in recent years, and there are threats that many park campgrounds may be closed; you may want to phone ahead for current conditions.

The state also maintains 17 marine state parks in the San Juan Islands and 23 in Puget Sound. Moorage occupancy is limited to 72 hours and cannot be reserved in advance. An annual moorage permit for vessels under 26 feet is $50, and nightly fees are $8; annual permits for vessels longer than 26 feet cost $80 with a nightly fee of $11. Moorage buoys cost $8 per night for all sizes. The **Cascadia Marine Trail System** includes more than 35 campsites around Puget Sound available to sea kayakers and users of other small human-powered or sailing vessels. Annual permits ($20) are available from Washington State Parks, tel. (800) 233-0321. Get maps and other information about Cascadia Marine Trail from the Washington Water Trails Association, tel. (206) 545-9161, www.eskimo.com/~wwta.

Campground reservations can be made for nearly half of the state parks, and are available as little as two days in advance, or as much as 11 months ahead of time. A $6 reservation fee is charged in addition to the first night's campground fee and can be paid by credit card or check. For the complete story on reservations, including current space availability at various state parks, call (800) 452-5687 Mon.-Fri. 8 a.m.-5 p.m. year-round. Call (800) 233-0321 for other park information, or get details on the Internet at www.parks.wa.gov.

Other Public Campgrounds

Campsites at national forests and parks are scattered across Washington, but very few of these offer showers. Some sites are free, but most campgrounds charge a $8-12. More than 40 Forest Service campgrounds are reservable for an extra fee of $9. Call (877) 444-6777 for specifics. You can also make campsite reser-

vations on the web at www.reserveusa.com. On most national forests—except along major routes—dispersed camping is allowed; simply find an off-the-road place to park for the night. A $5/night fee has been instituted for dispersed camping on some national forests; check locally for details. You cannot camp like this at all in the national parks. With a few exceptions, Park Service campgrounds are not reservable, so get there early on busy summer weekends!

Washington's Department of Natural Resources (DNR) manages millions of acres of public lands in the state, primarily on a multiple-use (some call it multiple-abuse) basis. The emphasis is on timber harvesting. Not everything has been logged, however, and campsites can be found at DNR forests throughout the state. For a helpful map showing more than 80 free public campgrounds on their land, call DNR office in Olympia at (360) 902-1000 or (800) 527-3305.

For a fairly complete listing of campgrounds in Washington, with detailed descriptions, get *Pacific Northwest Camping* by Tom Stienstra (San Francisco: Foghorn Press).

Private RV Parks

Every town of any size has at least one private RV park and so-called campground. Many of these are little more than vacant lots with sewer and electrical hookups, showers, and toilet facilities. Not great for tents, but just what the doctor ordered for the RV crowd. These private campgrounds generally charge $2-4 for showers if you're not camping there. A better deal in many towns is to use the shower in the local public swimming pool, where you get a free swim thrown in for the entrance charge. People traveling in RVs often find that they prefer the private parks since the state park reservation system can be an annoyance, and the amenities at private parks are often better.

ACCOMMODATIONS AND FOOD

LODGING

Lodging in Washington covers the complete spectrum, from five-star luxury accommodations where a king would feel pampered all the way down to seedy motels so tawdry that even the roaches think twice. The law of supply and de-

mand holds fairly true when it comes to motel rates. You'll pay the least at motels in rural areas away from the main tourist track, and the most at popular destinations in peak season. This is especially true on mid-summer weekends for such places as the San Juan Islands, Chelan, Leavenworth, Whidbey Island, or Long Beach, and for Seattle year-round. At many of the resort towns, you may need to reserve months ahead of time for the peak season, and a minimum stay of two or more nights may be required. It always pays to call ahead. If you don't smoke and can't stand the stench of tobacco in motel rooms, be sure to ask about nonsmoking rooms. Many motels and virtually all B&Bs have them. Many of the newer chain motels also now cater to business travelers, with such features as data port lines for Internet access, microwaves and fridges, conference rooms, fitness centers, free newspapers, hair dryers and irons, and suites with kitchens.

Bedfinders, tel. (800) 323-2920 (www. bedfinders.com), can help you find lodging at several hundred different Washington hotels, B&Bs, and cabins, primarily in the resort areas of Leavenworth, Long Beach, Chelan, Winthrop, and the San Juan Islands.

Throughout this book I have listed only two prices for most lodging places: one person (single, or s) and two people (double, or d). The lodging charts list peak-season prices and are arranged from least to most expensive. They do not include state tax (eight percent) and local taxes, which can sometimes be substantial. These prices are not set in concrete and will certainly head up over time. If a convention is in town or the motel is nearly full, they may rise; if the economy is tight, or it's late February at a beach resort, you may pay considerably less. Always ask to see the room before deciding to stay at one of the less expensive motels—places that I consider more than adequate may be beneath your standards. If in doubt, you may want to choose one that gets the AAA seal of approval.

For a complete listing of motels, hotels, and bed and breakfasts in Washington, request a copy of the free *Washington State Lodging & Travel Guide,* available from the Washington State Tourism Development Division, tel. (800) 544-1800. It's also available at larger visitor centers around the state, and on the Web through the state tourism page: www.tourism.wa.gov.

The annual *TourBook* for Washington and Oregon (free to members of the American Automobile Association) is a helpful guide to the better hotels and motels, offering current prices and accurate ratings. If you're looking for longerterm lodging, **Rent A Home International,** tel. (206) 789-9377, has apartments, homes, houseboats, and other lodging in Seattle, the San Juans, and other parts of Washington on a weekly basis. Find them on the Web at www.rentavilla.com.

Hostels

Hostels offer the least expensive lodging options in Washington, with bunkbed accommodations for just $10-20 per person. They are a good choice for single travelers on a budget, or anyone who wants to meet other independent travelers. Although commonly called youth hostels, these really are not just for high school and college folks; you're likely to meet adventurous people of all ages. The official versions are managed by **Hostelling International** (better known as AYH), with statewide headquarters at the Seattle hostel, tel. (206) 281-7306, www.washingtonhostels.org. In addition to Seattle, they operate hostels in Bellingham, Birch Bay, Fort Columbia (near Long Beach), Fort Flagler (near Port Townsend), Fort Worden (in Port Townsend), Elma (Grays Harbor), and Vashon Island. At these hostels, guests stay in dormitorystyle rooms, have access to a kitchen, and generally do a cleanup chore. You'll need to bring your own sleeping bag or linen, and an annual membership fee is required (nonmembers pay an introductory membership and higher overnight rates). A variety of restrictions may put a crimp in things, including that most hostels kick you out around 10 a.m. and remain closed till 5 p.m. or so, and that no alcohol is allowed. Some also have a curfew. Most have a few spaces for couples who want their own room, but you may need to reserve these in advance. The benefits of hostelling include the chance to meet fellow travelers and a sense of camaraderie and adventure that one would never get at a cheap motel. Instead of turning on the TV set, you'll meet travelers from all over the world and discover must-see sights and great out-of-the way cafes.

Private hostels are less predictable, with fewer rules. Alcohol is generally allowed, and you won't have to be back before the witching hour, but they can be more chaotic, noisy, and even downright grungy at times. These range all over the place, from the rambling old school at Bingen that is now a destination for windsurfers, to the funky Doe Bay Village Resort where the clothing-optional hot tub is filled most evenings. Seattle has several such places, and others are found in Port Angeles and south of Forks on the Olympic Peninsula, in Spokane and Republic in the northeast corner of the state, in the town of Eldon on Hood Canal, and at Ashford near Mt. Rainier. All these official and unofficial hostels are described in appropriate sections of this book. A good Web source for private (and AYH) hostel information is www.hostels.com.

Motels and Hotels

The largest cities—Seattle, Spokane, Tacoma, Bellevue, Olympia—obviously have the greatest range of accommodations. All of these cities, without exception, have very inexpensive lodging just outside city limits, so you can stay a half-hour or less away and spend the extra money having fun. If you're staying at the pricier chains, be sure to always ask about discounts such as AAA member rates, senior discounts, corporate or government rates, business travel fares, military rates, or other special deals. Try not to take the first rate quoted at these places, especially if you're calling their 800 number; these "rack rates" are what they charge if they can get away with it. Ask if they have any promotional rates. You may also get better prices sometimes by bargaining with clerks who are more likely to be able to dicker over price than the 800 number operators who work out of their room in a Texas prison. Of course, if it's a summer holiday or

festival weekend, you may have no choice.

In Seattle or Spokane, you can stay at the budget chains near the airport; in Tacoma, stay up the road in Fife. Call ahead for reservations whenever possible; the least expensive rooms fill up fast. Finding a room—any room—can be extremely difficult in summer (even on weekdays) at popular resort areas such as Lake Chelan, the San Juan Islands, the national parks, or along the ocean. Staying a half hour from the action can save you money—try the motels in Wenatchee when Lake Chelan is filled up, or stay in Forks or Port Angeles instead of at Olympic National Park lodges.

Bed and Breakfasts

Nearly 500 bed and breakfasts are scattered around the state of Washington. Some parts of the state, particularly Port Townsend, are filled with restored turn-of-the-century Victorian homes that have been converted to B&Bs. Other B&Bs are old farmhouses, lodges, cottages, or modern homes with private entrances. In most cases, a room at a B&B will cost as much as one of the better motel rooms. You may miss the cable TV (though many now have TVs in the rooms) and room service, but you'll get breakfast, a chance to spend time with a local, and peace and quiet.

Many B&Bs don't allow kids, and almost none allow pets or smoking; probably half the rooms won't have a private bath (though one is probably just a few steps away). If you plan to pay by

Ravenscroft Inn, Port Townsend

DON PITCHER

credit card, make sure they will accept it when you make reservations—many don't. B&Bs are a fine way to get acquainted with a new area and a good choice for people traveling alone, since you'll have opportunities to meet fellow travelers. Note however, that there is often little or no difference between the price a single person pays and that paid by a couple.

One problem with B&Bs is that they sometimes lack the privacy afforded by motels. I've been in ones where the owner sits by your table in the morning, feeling it his duty to hold a conversation. This may be fine sometimes, especially if you want to learn more about the local area, but not so great if you want a romantic place or just want to read the newspaper. Honeymooners or others in search of privacy may prefer B&Bs that offer separate cottages.

A Pacific Reservation Service, tel. (206) 784-0539 or (800) 684-2932, www.seattlebedandbreakfast.com, is a reservation service for more than 210 Washington B&Bs, houses, cottages, houseboats, condos, and lodges. The **Washington State B&B Guild,** tel. (800) 647-2918, will send you a brochure describing its members, or visit its Web site at www.wbbg.com. Many other B&Bs now have their own Web pages; find them through any of the Internet search engines.

FOOD AND DRINK

Restaurants
As all parts of the country do, Washington places an emphasis on certain kinds of food, an emphasis that here has gained the name "Northwest cuisine." Definitions of this vary, but "fresh" is the operative term in most of these. Fresh salmon is popular and can be found on virtually every restaurant's menu. Red snapper, halibut, and cod are also served fresh almost everywhere in western Washington. Less common are the local Olympia oysters and geoduck clams. As you head east, the seafood is generally frozen, though some restaurants pride themselves on their fresh fish. Steaks are often imported from the Midwest and are generally very good.

Farm Fresh
Western Washington is also known for its strawberries, blackberries, and various other kinds of berries. The King County Cooperative Extension Service publishes lists of U-Pick vegetable and berry farms, and the tabloid can be found at tourist information bureaus. For a detailed directory of organic farms, natural foods grocers, and organic restaurants, and a listing of farmers markets throughout the state, contact Washington Tilth, tel. (206) 527-9216.

Eastern Washington is the place to go for fresh fruit and produce. Washington apples are mostly the red and golden delicious, rome beauty, and Granny Smith varieties. Many other kinds of fruit are grown along the central corridor—cherries, peaches, apricots. The Walla Walla sweet onion is reputedly mild enough to bite into raw, like an apple, and it is sold in gift packs. Asparagus, pears, and berries of all kinds are also big eastern Washington crops.

Beer and Wine
The Pacific Northwest has the highest per capita consumption of draft beer in America, so it should come as no surprise that microbreweries are immensely popular. Today, nearly every small city in Washington seems to have at least one microbrewery, and centers such as Seattle have many. The larger ones—such as the Redhook Ale Brewery in Woodinville—offer tours and tasting.

Wine grapes are a large part of the Yakima and Columbia River Valleys' agriculture. Wineries line the highway between Yakima and the Tri-Cities and into Walla Walla; others are scattered east to Spokane. Washington wines have become world-class in just a few years, winning awards and gaining in popularity across the country. Visit at least a few wineries (western Washington also has a number of them, though the grapes are usually grown in eastern Washington), or stop by the local grocery store for a wide selection. For details on the state's 100 wineries, see the excellent *Touring the Washington Wine Country* booklet, available in visitor centers around the state, or from the **Washington Wine Commission,** tel. (206) 667-9463.

TRANSPORTATION

BY AIR

Washington's two major airports are Seattle-Tacoma International (Sea-Tac) and Spokane International, served by nearly all the major carriers and a handful of smaller airlines. Horizon Air (a subsidiary of Alaska Airlines), tel. (800) 547-9308, is the big "little" airline, connecting many Washington cities, including Seattle, Spokane, Bellingham, Lewiston, Moses Lake, Pasco, Port Angeles, Pullman, Walla Walla, Wenatchee, and Yakima.

Try for a south-side window seat (on an east-west route) when flying into or out of Sea-Tac for a spectacular close-up view of Mt. Rainier and, in the distance, Mt. St. Helens. On the north-south routes the plane usually flies within a few miles of Mt. St. Helens.

BY TRAIN

Amtrak serves Washington with three major routes. The north-south route along the West Coast is aboard the **Coast Starlight,** which has service four times a day to Seattle, Tacoma, Olympia/Lacey, Centralia, Longview/Kelso, and Vancouver, and southward to Los Angeles. The **Mount Baker International,** provides daily train connections north to Vancouver, B.C., via Edmonds, Everett, Mount Vernon, and Bellingham.

The east-west route to Chicago is on the **Empire Builder,** which has daily service to Spokane, then turns southwest to Portland with stops at Pasco, Wishram, Bingen/White Salmon, and Vancouver, or to Seattle via Ephrata, Wenatchee, Everett, and Edmonds.

For route, schedule, and fare information, phone Amtrak at (800) 872-7245. Be forewarned, though: Amtrak requires advance reservations; you can't just go down to the station and climb aboard.

BY CAR

Washington is a part of America, and as such, the car is king here. Despite their negative impacts on the environment, cars do make it easy to reach remote areas that are not served by any air, rail, or bus lines. Numerous car rental agencies operate at or near Sea-Tac and Spokane International Airports, as well as in all large cities. See the "Sea-Tac" section in the Seattle chapter for car rental tips.

From late fall to early spring, expect snow at I-90's Snoqualmie Pass (between North Bend and Cle Elum in central Washington), Stevens Pass on U.S. Hwy. 2 and White Pass on State Hwy. 12. Cayuse Pass on State Hwy. 410 and Rainy and Washington Passes on State Hwy. 20 (the North Cascades Hwy.) are closed after the first snowfall each winter.

Snow tires or chains are frequently required on the passes, which are sometimes closed during storms because of hazardous road conditions, blocking accidents, or avalanche danger. Skiers and other winter travelers passing through the Cascades should always carry a set of chains and emergency equipment (flares, shovel, blankets, and food). Before you set out, phone (206) 368-4499 or (888) 766-4636 for the Department of Transportation's **Mountain Pass Report;** they give road and weather conditions for all of the Cascade passes from October 15 through April 15. Their Web site, www.traffic. wsdot.wa.gov/sno-info, also has live cameras showing current conditions at six major Cascade passes. AAA Washington has a 24-hour recorded message on major highways within 500 miles of Seattle: tel. (206) 646-2190.

A warning to Washington newcomers: The state seems to have more cops per capita than anywhere else in the nation. They all have radar guns and aren't afraid to use them. Watch your speed! Unless otherwise posted, the speed limit on highways is 55 miles an hour.

BY BUS

Longhaul Buses
Greyhound, tel. (206) 628-5526 or (800) 231-2222, www.greyhound.com, serves most major cities in Washington, providing nationwide con-

nections. Their main routes are along I-5 from Canada to Oregon, along I-90 from Seattle to Spokane, plus I-82 from Ellensburg to Pendleton, Oregon.

Northwest Trailways (a.k.a. Northwest Stagelines) tel. (800) 366-6975, www.nwadv. com/northw, offers service along three Washington routes: Spokane to Seattle (with stops in Moses Lake, Ephrata, Quincy, Wenatchee, Skykomish, and Stephens Pass), Everett to Tacoma (via Seattle), and Spokane to Boise (with stops in Pullman and Lewiston). **Borderline Stage,** tel. (509) 684-3950, connects Colville and Spokane.

Perhaps the most unusual wheeled transportation company is **Green Tortoise Alternative Travel,** which some call a "traveling commune" or a "road show on wheels." The Green Tortoise has twice-weekly buses from Seattle to Los Angeles that take 48 hours to reach Los Angeles, including a sightseeing stop in San Francisco and a rest stop for a vegetarian feast, sauna, and entertainment at the operation's digs in southern Oregon. It also has tours all over the hemisphere, from Alaska, to Yellowstone National Park, to Costa Rica. This is a fun and inexpensive way to explore the country. Call (206) 324-7433 or (800) 867-8647 for details on all their trips. Find them on the Web at www.greentortoise.com. Green Tortoise also runs a private hostel in Seattle.

Public Transit Buses

Washington's public buses offer a remarkably comprehensive system, with low-priced service throughout all of western Washington. The coverage is less complete east of the Cascades, but still quite good. Some of these services—including Link in the Chelan and Douglas Country, Skagit Transit in Skagit County, Island Transit on Whidbey Island, and East Jefferson Transit on the Olympic Peninsula—are entirely free, paid for through local sales taxes. Most bus systems also have bike racks. The Washington State Department of Transportation publishes a helpful *Passenger Transportation Options* booklet detailing all public and private buses in the state; call (360) 586-2401 for a copy. On the Web, visit www.wsdot.wa.gov/PubTran for a complete listing of buses, trains, and other travel options. The various bus systems are described in appropriate sections of this book.

WASHINGTON STATE FERRIES

The Washington state ferry system is the largest mass transit system in the state, carrying more than 23 million passengers each year across Puget Sound. This is by far the most scenic way to see the Sound, but the system also serves many commuters who ride the ferry to work each day in Seattle, Tacoma, or Everett. Many long-time residents take rides on them, sometimes simply as a way to get away from the office for an hour with a brown-bag lunch.

The Routes

Washington has the largest ferry fleet in the United States, with 28 different vessels, ranging from a 94-foot passenger boat to jumbo-class 460-foot-long ships capable of carrying more than 200 cars and 2,500 passengers. The ferries call

ferry at San Juan Island, San Juan Islands, WA

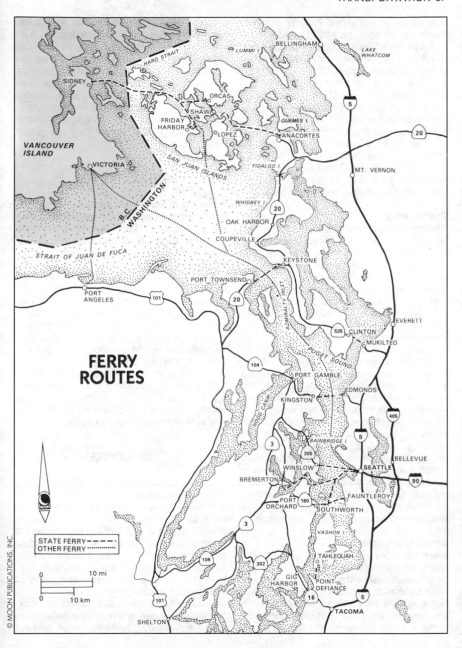

FERRY ROUTES

STATE FERRY -----
OTHER FERRY ·············

0 ——— 10 mi
0 ——— 10 km

© MOON PUBLICATIONS, INC.

at 20 different ports around Puget Sound, from Tacoma to Vancouver Island.

The best sightseeing is on the Anacortes-San Juan Islands route, which once a day continues to Sidney, British Columbia. Ferries also connect Port Townsend with Keystone (Whidbey Island); Clinton (Whidbey Island) with Mukilteo (southwest of Everett); Edmonds with Kingston (on the Kitsap Peninsula); Seattle with Winslow (Bainbridge Island) and Bremerton; Fauntleroy (southwest Seattle) with Southworth (southeast of Bremerton) and Vashon Island; and Tacoma (at Point Defiance) with Tahlequah (at the south end of Vashon Island). All of these routes are described in detail elsewhere in this book.

Practicalities

The ferry system operates on a first-come, first-served basis, with reservations available only for the routes from Anacortes to Sidney, B.C., and from Orcas Island or San Juan Island to Sidney. Ferries operate every day, including holidays. Fares range widely, depending upon your destination, whether you are on foot or in a vehicle, and the season. Senior citizens receive a 50% discount, applied only to the passenger or driver portion of the fare (not the vehicle). Credit cards are not accepted for payment of fares.

The larger ferries have food service, vending machines dispensing candy bars and junk food, and beer; the smaller boats have vending machines only. Brochure racks are usually packed with flyers from local B&Bs, real estate firms, and restaurants. Pets on leashes are allowed on the car decks or in carrying containers on passenger decks. Bikes, kayaks, and canoes are also allowed onboard for a small surcharge.

For more information about the state ferry system, along with fares and sailing schedules, call (206) 464-6400 or (888) 808-7977. Call (800) 843-3779 for automated information, or check their Web site at www.wsdot.wa.gov/ferries.

Avoiding the Crowds

Washington State Ferries are especially busy during the commute hours, when thousands of people head eastward to Seattle, Everett, and other cities each weekday morning, and back home again in the evening. Pleasure traffic increases on weekends, especially during the summer. Friday afternoons and Saturday mornings see crowded ferries heading westbound, especially to Whidbey Island and the San Juan Islands. Many of these same folks return on Sunday afternoons and evenings. Unless you don't mind waiting in long lines—up to two hours or more sometimes—avoid travel at these times (or head in the opposite direction of the crowds). Foot passengers never need to wait, but those in vehicles may find themselves watching several ferries come and go before they can get on board at peak hours.

OTHER FERRIES

A number of small Washington ferries provide service around the state, and are described elsewhere in this book. These include service to the Anderson Island, Guemes Island, and Lummi Island within Puget Sound, along with three Columbia River ferries.

Several private companies offer ferry connections to Vancouver Island. Take the MV *Coho*, from Port Angeles to Victoria, B.C., across the Strait of Juan de Fuca. From Seattle the *Victoria Clipper,* has passenger-only service to Victoria daily in summer. The *Princess Marguerite III* sails between Seattle and Victoria, offering passenger and vehicle transport.

Independent tour and charter boat companies in Seattle, Tacoma, Everett, Bellingham, the San Juan Islands, Westport, and other coastal cities offer sightseeing, fishing, and whalewatching tours throughout the year.

BY BICYCLE

Washington, and particularly Seattle, is among the most bicycle-friendly places in America. At least 10,000 persons commute to work by bicycle in Seattle. Puget Sound's numerous islands provide great scenery, some of the state's best weather, and little automobile traffic: Whidbey Island, for instance, gets only a third of the rainfall Seattle gets and offers spectacular vistas from little-traveled back roads, plus plenty of camping at the state parks.

The beauty of the San Juan Islands is best experienced on a bike, and you'll save $10 or more on the ferry toll to Friday Harbor when traveling without the cumbersome automobile. Vashon, Bainbridge, Mercer, and Camano Islands are also easy to get to and have little automobile traffic.

The urban areas have ample opportunities for cyclists. Seattle has received the blessings of *Bicycling* magazine as the "Best North American City for Bicycling," crediting the city's friendly atmosphere and the many miles of scenic and safe paths. Seattle adopted a comprehensive policy toward biking that led to more signs, more bike racks, Metro buses with bike racks, special bike lanes, and so forth. An example of this enlightened attitude toward self-propulsion is the Burke-Gilman Trail, a 14-mile paved bike path from Gasworks Park to Kenmore at the north end of Lake Washington. There, it connects with the Sammamish River Trail, which runs another 10 miles to Redmond's Marymoor Park, passing just east of Woodinville's Ste. Michelle and Columbia wineries—great places to stop for lunch with a bottle of wine.

In West Seattle, the road and bike path from Alki Beach to Lincoln Park is a popular 12-mile loop. Five Mile Drive in Tacoma's Point Defiance Park is open to cars as well, but cyclists are given a wide berth; the road passes through an impressive old-growth forest.

For information on bicycling in Washington, check with the chambers of commerce for maps of bike routes throughout their city or county.

These are available in Seattle, Bremerton, the Tri-Cities, Tacoma, Spokane, Bellevue, and Kirkland. The Washington State Department of Transportation in Olympia, tel. (360) 705-7000, publishes bicycle maps and guidelines, including a very helpful statewide map showing traffic data and road widths to help determine which roads are the safest. The Seattle Engineering Department, tel. (206) 684-7583, will send you a detailed bicycle map of Seattle.

Bike Tours

A number of companies offer cycling tours across parts of Washington. The largest is California-based **Backroads,** tel. (800) 462-2848, with trips to Whidbey Island, the Olympic Peninsula, the San Juan Islands, and the Methow Valley, along with dozens of other places worldwide. Call them for a catalog, or check their Web site: www.backroads.com. **Bicycle Adventures,** tel. (360) 786-0989 or (800) 443-6060, is an Olympia-based company with many trips throughout the Northwest, including to the Cascades, Olympics, the San Juan Islands, and Columbia Gorge. **Scenic Cycling Adventures,** tel. (541) 385-5257, has San Juan Island rides. All three companies include food, lodging, and a support vehicle in the rate. Trips start around $675 for a five-day bike-and-camping ride on the San Juans. Softer trips with lodging in B&Bs are more expensive, starting around $1,600.

INFORMATION AND COMMUNICATIONS

INFORMATION

For a free travel packet that includes the *Washington State Lodging and Travel Guide* (very helpful), along with a seasonal *Washington State Field Guide,* call the Washington State Department of Tourism at (360) 753-5601 or (800) 638-8474. Their Internet address, www.tourism.wa.gov, provides the same info online, plus comprehensive details on travel to Washington, and links to many related homepages. You can also use it to order copies of state tourism publications, or pick them up in person at the larger visitor centers around Washington, along with free

state maps. The state has six "gateway" visitor information centers at various points around its borders: Blaine, Maryhill, Oroville, Megler (across from Astoria, Oregon), Spokane, and Vancouver. The Vancouver office is open year-round; the others generally May-September.

Every city or town has a chamber of commerce. Most have offices that are filled with free brochures, maps, and information on lodging and restaurants. See "Information and Services" under each place for the chamber's address and phone. Ranger stations at the national parks and forests can sell you forest and topographic maps, campground and trail information, and other printed material.

For details on Washington's federal lands, visit the **Outdoor Recreation Information Center,** inside the Seattle REI store at 222 Yale Ave. N, tel. (206) 470-4060. It is staffed by National Park Service and Forest Service personnel, who can answer your questions on hiking trails, campgrounds, and backcountry access.

Get more specific information on your destination by phoning one of the following state offices: **Washington Department of Natural Resources,** tel. (360) 902-1000, or (800) 527-3305; **Washington State Parks and Recreation Commission,** tel. (360) 753-2027 or (800) 233-0321; **Washington Department of Fish and Wildlife,** tel. (206) 902-2200. **Washington State Department of Tourism,** tel. (800) 544-1800; and **Washington State Ferries,** tel. (206) 464-6400 or (800) 843-3779. The state homepage **http://access.wa.gov** has links to all of these and much more, including state, local, and federal agencies. You'll find everything from public libraries to the Cemetery Board here, plus photos of Washington, employment information, traffic reports, and news releases.

If you need help planning a Washington trip, try an itinerary planning service such as **Pacific Northwest Journeys,** tel. (206) 935-9730 or (800) 935-9730.

Internet Addresses

The last few years have seen an explosion in Internet homepages for governmental bodies, organizations, museums, motels, B&Bs, restaurants, and businesses of all types. A few Web addresses are included in this book, primarily those for information centers, but I have chosen to not list most other homepages since they change often, and are easy to find using a search engine such as Yahoo! or Altavista. Many Web addresses are simply the business name with .com on the end, such as www.pyramidbrew.com. For links to Washington city sites, visit **www.usacitylink.com.** Find more Washington info at **www.tourism.wa.gov** or **http://access.wa.gov.**

Money

Travelers checks (in U.S. dollars) are accepted in most stores and businesses around Washington. It's not a good idea to travel with travelers checks in non-U.S. currency, since they are only accepted at certain banks, and are a time-consuming hassle. Foreign currency can be changed at SeaTac airport or in downtown Seattle exchange bureaus. I travel primarily with an automated teller machine (ATM) card and a credit card, using a small backup stash of travelers checks in case I lose the card or the magnetic stripe is damaged. Automated teller machines are ubiquitous in Washington; see the Internet for an up-to-date listing of locations. Unfortunately, most ATMs now tack on a charge (sometimes $2 per transaction!) to your own bank's fees, making this an expensive way to get cash. If the bank imposes such a charge it will be posted on the machine; avoid these ripoff ATMs. **Washington Mutual** branches do not impose this charge; call (800) 756-8000 for their locations. Another way to avoid the fee is by making a purchase at a grocery store that accepts ATMs; just ask for extra cash back.

The major credit cards—especially Visa and Master Card—are accepted almost everywhere, even in grocery stores. For many travelers this is the easiest way to access funds while traveling, especially if you can get airline mileage credit at the same time.

COMMUNICATIONS

Post Offices

Post offices generally open between 7 a.m. and 9 a.m. and close between 5 p.m. and 6 p.m.; only a few are open on Saturday. Their outer doors are usually open, so you can go in to buy stamps from the machines. Some drug or card stores also operate a postal substation where you can buy stamps or mail packages within the U.S. (you'll have to go to a real post office for mailing to foreign addresses or other special services). Many grocery store checkout counters also sell books of stamps with no markup.

SEATTLE

By now you've probably heard all the monikers applied to Seattle: America's Most Livable City, Emerald City, Latte Land, and City of Niceness. For the last decade or so, the media have "discovered" Seattle (pop. 520,000) as a lively and enchanting place to explore and live. The obvious charms of Seattle and the Puget Sound region draw more tourists each year, many of whom come back to stay. And despite comedians' claims to the contrary, Seattle is not an old Indian term for latte, though it sometimes seems to have more espresso stands than cars.

Seattle's charm comes from its beautiful setting, its friendly and creative people, and the way the city has grown up along the shores of Puget Sound and Lake Washington. Oddly shaped towers and preserved historical districts stand alongside modern skyscrapers and the busy waterfront in a jaunty kind of disharmony. Every major event in the city's short life span, from Yesler's 1850s sawmill to the 1962 World's Fair to the 1990s high-tech boom, has left its legacy; the resulting mishmash of periods gives the city a flavor absent in showpieces of urban renewal.

History doesn't make a city livable. No one event or attraction here can ever take that credit. Rather, it's a thousand incidents, enjoyed daily: dining at the waterfront, watching the sun set behind the Olympics ás sailboats head home; reading the *Seattle P.I.* on your early-morning ferry commute, accompanied by a lively porpoise escort service; listening to a free outdoor lunchtime concert at Freeway Park; stopping for fresh vegetables or fish at Pike Place Market; cleansing your lungs with fresh, rain-rinsed air as you dodge slugs and puddles on your morning run; attending a summertime office party on a harbor tour boat; being surprised by a clear view of bashful Mt. Rainier from the highway or the QFC parking lot.

The People

A New York friend of mine who spent time in Seattle found it a difficult adjustment. The kind of things that drive aggressive New Yorkers over the edge in seconds seem to roll right off a Seattleite's back. It was the little things that stuck out: drivers waiting for other cars to pull out ahead of them, the almost total lack of horn-

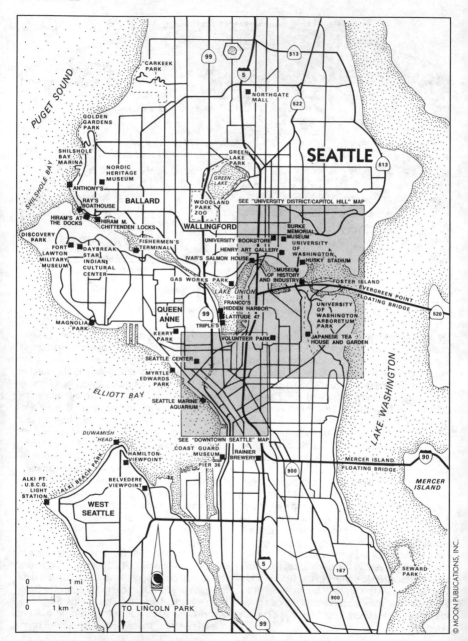

© MOON PUBLICATIONS, INC.

honking, the easy acceptance of long lines at an espresso bar, the friendly bus drivers who didn't charge for a short ride, and the pedestrians waiting for the "Walk" sign before crossing a deserted street. Sometimes this laid-back nature approaches the annoying stage—such as the times clerks stop to chat with a customer about her kids while a long queue waits patiently—but Seattleites take it all in stride. (One writer complained of being unable to get in an argument on any subject, calling it being "stoned to death with popcorn.") Maybe it's the strong Scandinavian heritage of acceptance and community; maybe it's the on-again off-again rain that teaches patience; or maybe it's something they put in the espresso. . . .

Climate

Okay, it's true. In 1898, a boy actually drowned on a downtown Seattle city street. Apparently he was trying to cross an enormous sinkhole on a raft, fell off, and couldn't swim. Despite what you may have heard, however, it doesn't normally rain enough to drown folks in Seattle. The city actually gets less annual rainfall than New York City—it just falls more slowly. Gray and drizzly skies are standard fare from October to May; when it does rain, it's frequently a who-needs-an-umbrella sprinkle. One of Seattle's oddest facts is that more pairs of sunglasses are sold there per capita than any other American city, yet umbrella and raincoat sales are no higher than other cities. The winter weather pattern remains nearly constant; storms off the Pacific coast send swirling clouds over Seattle for months, leading you to believe that the TV weather forecaster uses the same satellite photo all season.

Nearly all of the precipitation is rain; less than an inch of snow per month is the average, so plows are few . . . and generally in disrepair. When snowstorms dropped 17 inches on Seattle in November of 1985, only four of the city's seven snowplows worked. Commuters, few of whom had much experience driving on snow, relied on chains to traverse the I-5 snowfield and some actually reached their destinations; most simply abandoned their cars and turned the freeway into a disorderly parking lot. Automobile insurance companies hated that storm.

Seattle and other western Washington residents have learned to expect these three seasonal events: a windstorm on Thanksgiving that knocks out electrical power while the turkey is in the oven; floods on the Snohomish and Skagit Rivers around Christmas and New Year's that force farmers to evacuate their homes built on the floodplain; and perfect Santa Barbara weather the weekend of July 4. You could almost make a living betting on these meteorological events.

When spring arrives the clouds move more quickly; rain comes in unpredictable spurts. Summer convinces many visitors to move here: low humidity, temperatures in the high 70s to 80s, and cloudless skies; sometimes two entire months pass without a drop of rain. It makes natives restless and irritable. Then, as suddenly as it began, summer ends: clouds and smiles return, temperatures go down, and residents stockpile firewood, books, hot chocolate, and party invitations for the soggy season ahead.

Getting Oriented

See the "Seattle" map to get an idea of the major neighborhoods and thoroughfares. The city's street numbering system takes a little time to understand. Avenues run north and south, streets run east and west, but street names get more complex than this. Example: N.E. 63rd St. is in the Ravenna District east of 1st Ave. NE, and 63 blocks north of Yesler Way; 63rd Ave. SW is in West Seattle, south of Yesler Way and 63 blocks west of the Duwamish Waterway. Fortunately, the system starts to make a bit of sense after awhile, and is used throughout King County (named for Martin Luther King Jr.), making it easier to find streets in neighboring cities such as Bellevue or Renton.

As an aside, King County was originally named for William R. King, elected in 1852 as vice president under President Franklin Pierce (for whom adjacent Pierce County is named). King died just six weeks into his term of office. In the 1970s his legacy as an Alabama slave-owner made Seattleites uncomfortable, and the county was officially renamed for a more politically acceptable King, the slain civil rights leader Martin Luther King Jr. Needless to say, the name of another slave owner—George Washington—is still popular in Washington.

HISTORY

The First Inhabitants

The original settlers around present-day Seattle were the Duwamish and Suquamish tribes. They were seminomadic people who relied on salmon and other seafood for sustenance, along with seasonal plants. The Suquamish called the entire Puget Sound basin something that sounded like "Whulge," and the name stuck with early European explorers until Capt. George Vancouver named the sound for his friend, Peter Puget.

The city was named after Chief Sealth (or "Seattle"—Indian names didn't translate well into English), and both spellings are used on his tomb. The son of a Suquamish tribal leader and a Duwamish woman, Sealth became the chief of both tribes around 1810, and witnessed Capt. George Vancouver's visit in 1792. Fifty years later he befriended early settlers, encouraging a policy of peace between Indians and white newcomers. The Suquamish tribe was eventually allotted land on the Kitsap Peninsula, but the

---

AN UNLIKELY HERO

One of the most respected pioneer names in Seattle is Mercer, and one of the most famous incidents in early Seattle was engineered by Asa Shinn Mercer.

Asa Mercer graduated from Lafayette College, Pennsylvania, in 1861 and immediately set out for Seattle to join his elder brother, Judge Thomas Mercer, who was busy settling the new city. He became the first president of the University of Washington before it even existed; he helped clear the site on a hillside overlooking the village of Seattle and put up classrooms, and then he scouted the region for students. For the first two terms, he not only was president of the university, he was the entire faculty.

Asa Shinn Mercer

As he toured the region, he heard the same complaint repeatedly: not enough women. Interracial marriages were common, alcoholism was high, and morale was low. Mercer believed the area could not thrive until it had a firm family footing.

He tried to get the territorial government to subsidize female immigration, but while the men who ran the government were sympathetic, the treasury was empty. The disgruntled would-be marriage broker packed a suitcase and caught a ship back to Boston. The Civil War was creating thousands of young widows; many women of marrying age were willing to go. But when sailing time came, only 11 showed up. Mercer was probably disappointed, but it wasn't bad

for a start. They arrived in Seattle on May 16, 1864. Within only a few months all the women were married, and Mercer was a local hero.

Mercer left again in 1865, this time promising to enlist no less than President Lincoln's assistance. But when his ship arrived in New York from Panama, he found almost the entire nation hung in black crepe paper; President Lincoln had been assassinated the night before Asa's arrival.

Mercer was almost crushed by this news, but he made a quick recovery and went down to Washington, D.C., to talk to President Andrew Johnson and his cabinet. Another strikeout.

Feeling more hopeless by the minute, he took a chance and called on General Ulysses Grant and found an unlikely ally. Grant had been assigned to Fort Vancouver not too long before the war; he remembered the excruciating loneliness men suffered in the settlements that were hardly more than clearings in the dark, damp forests. He promised to do what he could.

Grant persuaded the president to donate a steamboat to Mercer's cause and ordered the quartermaster of the Army to provide it. Believing the ship was his, Mercer went on a recruiting mission all over the East Coast, speaking at churches in New York, Boston, and Washington, D.C., and in only a short time he had more than 500 women signed on.

Duwamish were relegated to land on other reservations. Many of these first residents eventually moved to Seattle.

Most Indians feared the consequences of the utterance of their names after death; historians debate whether the chief was happy that the city was to be named in his honor. Some claim it was against his will; others hold that Sealth was paid handsomely by the city's founders for his name. In any case, the name stuck, and certainly sounded better than the settlement's original name, Duwamps. Today a bronze sculpture of Chief Seattle stands at the corner of Fifth and Denny Way; his burial site, a peaceful Suquamish cemetery across the Sound, overlooks his namesake's skyscrapers.

Early Settlers

Although some white men were in the Duwamish River Valley not far from Puget Sound, David Denny and Lee Terry were the first white men to arrive at what became Seattle. Twenty-two pioneers had left Cherry Grove, Illinois, in wagons bound for Portland, Oregon; they then boarded the schooner *Exact* and sailed to Alki Point in 1851. The settlers ambitiously planned to develop "the New York of the Pacific Coast" at their landing site.

When he returned to claim his ship, there was a hitch. He could have it, but he would have to buy it at a bargain-basement price: $80,000 in cash, only one-third its value. Mercer, of course, had no money and neither did the territorial treasury. And the women began arriving in New York to sail west to matrimony.

No railroads ran coast to coast yet, but a tycoon named Ben Holladay had a stagecoach and a ship line, and he cut Mercer a deal: Holladay would buy the ship and in return he would haul 500 of Mercer's brides-to-be for a very low price.

Mercer quickly agreed, and the end finally seemed in sight. But no. The New York Herald newspaper caught up to the story and began printing accusations that Mercer was little more than a white slaver. The headlines were imaginative and painful:

HEGIRA OF SPINSTERS
PETTICOAT BRIGADE
CARGO OF HEIFERS
MERCER-NARY ADVENTURE

More than half of the women returned home and Holladay canceled his offer, but he offered to haul the remainder at the regular fare. Then Mercer saw what had really happened: it was Holladay who had planted the white-slave stories, to get the vessel at the bargain price without having to keep his end of the deal.

Still, on January 6, 1866, the Continental cast off from New York with more than 300 women aboard, bound for the frontier. It wasn't a cruise-ship crossing. By the time they reached South America, the first mate was in chains for murdering a seaman. The food was horrible; for a 17-day stretch the menu was boiled beans and tea made of saltwater.

But it wasn't such a terrible crossing that romance was impossible. Mercer fell for one young lady, who promptly rebuffed the luckless hero. So he transferred his attentions to another woman, who accepted his proposal; they were married as soon as they arrived in Seattle.

When the ship called in San Francisco it almost caused a riot. Hundreds of lonely or curious men rowed boats out for a look at the women—one really anxious fellow climbed up a rope hanging over the side, but Mercer knocked the man back into San Francisco's cold bay. Ministers and do-gooders, believing the newspaper stories that had preceded the ship, tried to talk the women into leaving.

And Ben Holladay wasn't through with his piracy—he refused to take the women on to Puget Sound. Mercer was again on the street without any money; desperately, he wired the territorial government for money and in return he received a rather long—collect—telegram of congratulations.

Everyone finally booked passage aboard the schooner Tanner, and at each stop on the way north rumors of lynch parties awaiting Mercer grew. A minister suggested that he hide in the hold of the ship and stay there until the excitement of their arrival died down.

But Mercer instead stood on the bow of the ship as it docked, and his bluff worked: everyone was too engrossed in the arrival of the brides to bother with Mercer; all except one of the women were married within months.

But the debtors caught up with Mercer, and although they didn't lynch him, they excluded him from the city's social and business community. Feeling old, cold, and very poor, Asa Mercer left Seattle shortly thereafter and showed up at various other cities around the West, his enthusiasm back at full throttle, his belief in the future of the West always strong.

Lumber was the focus of their early economy, beginning with the arrival of the *Leonesa* from San Francisco in 1852. The ship's captain had been wandering northward when he stumbled across the Alki settlement. The settlers sold the skipper 35,000 board feet of logs. Seeing an economic future in shipping lumber, the pioneers took to the waters in Indian canoes and, with the help of Mrs. Denny's clothesline and Lee Terry's horseshoes, took soundings along the Puget Sound shoreline. Discovering that the deepest waters were in today's Elliott Bay, the group relocated to Pioneer Square. Interestingly, this was the same bay about which Lt. Charles Wilkes wrote, "I do not consider the bay a desirable anchorage."

Logs were skidded down the original "Skid Road," now Yesler Way, to Henry Yesler's steam-powered sawmill. Yesler enjoyed such success that by the 1880s Yesler's Wharf was a town unto itself, with saloons, warehouses, shops, homes, and offices built on pilings extending 900 feet over the mudflats. The mill remained one of the city's economic pillars for two decades.

Women were scarce in Seattle's early years, so in the 1860s, Asa Mercer made two trips to New England to find refined, educated, single women willing to endure a little hardship to get a husband. The "Mercer Girls" (see the special topic "An Unlikely Hero") brought culture and class to the rowdy pioneer town.

Railroad

Until the 1880s, most transport to and from Seattle was by boat. Hopes for alternative methods were dashed when the Northern Pacific Railroad chose Tacoma as its Northwest terminus, citing unstable and steep terrain in Seattle. Though they received intermittent service via Tacoma by 1883, Seattleites wanted to be part of a regular, mainline route. As James J. Hill began expanding the Great Northern Line westward, rumors of a Seattle terminus resulted in a population boom and rising real estate values; the rumor became fact in 1893.

The intermittent railroad service of the '80s and highly successful lumber and coal export businesses encouraged a phenomenal population boom: from 3,500 in 1880 to 43,000 in 1890. The city's quality of life also improved rapidly, with the grading and planking of streets and sidewalks, the installation of sewer systems, electric lights, and telephones, and home mail delivery. Horse-drawn streetcars were quickly replaced by the electric variety.

Chinese workers began arriving in the 1860s; by the mid-1880s they numbered more than 500. Anti-Chinese sentiment rose as whites feared that cheap Chinese labor would cost them their jobs; the ensuing riots convinced most of the Asian laborers to flee. Judge Thomas Burke and others tried to maintain control and ultimately some Chinese remained.

The Great Fire

On June 6, 1889, 58 city blocks—the entire downtown area—were destroyed by the Great Seattle Fire. When a burning pot of glue tipped over inside a cabinet shop about 2 p.m., flames spread within minutes to an adjoining wooden liquor storeroom. Within a half-hour the entire city was threatened. Then, just when the flames were nearly under control, the hydrants abruptly dried up; firefighters tried to stop the blaze by blasting structures in the fire's path, to no avail. Jacob Levy refused to surrender his house; his 70-man bucket brigade repeatedly doused it, while a man in the street laid 10-to-one odds that the house would burn down. Levy won.

Firemen threw burning sidewalks over the cliff, ripped up roadway planking, and fought the flames with bucket brigades; the fire was finally contained by 8:30 that night. The next morning it was decreed unanimously that wooden structures would be forever prohibited in the burnt district. Business was conducted under canvas tents until the rebuilding—in brick—was completed a year later.

Seattle always had problems with drainage: streets were mudflows much of the year, and toilets backed up when the tide came in (leading some entrepreneurial souls to construct two-level toilets). While rebuilding, a clever solution was suggested: raise the sidewalks! First-floor storefronts became basements, creating Seattle's Underground.

Despite Seattle's misfortune, its pioneers were a selfless group. On May 31, only a week before the big fire, Johnstown, Pennsylvania, was struck by a disastrous flood when a dam broke above town. More than 2,000 persons, of a population of 30,000, were killed. Seattle had voted to send a gift of $558 to the survivors. After the fire was contained, the city upheld its vote to send the money, believing Johnstown was worse off.

The Klondike Gold Rush

On August 16, 1896, George Washington Carmack and two Indian friends, Skookum Jim and Tagish Charley, discovered gold deep in Canada's Yukon on a creek that fed into the Klondike River near its confluence with the Yukon River. Word reached Fortymile, an Alaska settlement on the Yukon River, and the town was almost entirely evacuated as the miners hurried to stake a claim. A year later, when the first 68 wealthy prospectors and their gold arrived in the Lower 48, the "Klondike Gold Rush" began.

The first ship to return, the *Excelsior,* arrived in San Francisco on July 15, 1897, and created some interest, but Californians knew all about gold rushes and weren't enthusiastic; the coastal steamer *Portland* arrived in Seattle two days later. Beriah Brown, a reporter on the *Seattle Post-Intelligencer,* hitched a ride on a tug and met the ship when it cleared customs at Port Townsend. He wrote that the ship was laden with "a ton of gold"; actually more than two tons left the ship in suitcases, crates, and coffee cans. Brown's words were electrifying. The rush was on: fathers left their families and even Seattle's mayor resigned to seek his fortune in the Klondike.

The Klondike trip wasn't an easy one: a 1,000-mile sea voyage to Skagway, Alaska, then an arduous hike over the snowy 33-mile Chilkoot Pass and White Pass to Lake Bennett, where would-be prospectors slapped together all manner of craft for floating down the Yukon to the Klondike. The North West Mounted Police required that each prospector carry a year's supply of food plus necessary tools and clothing, leading to the catchphrase, "a ton of gold, a ton of goods."

Erastus Brainerd, a former newspaperman, formed a publicity committee for the Seattle Chamber of Commerce and promoted Seattle as *the* place to get outfitted for the Klondike. Tacoma, Seattle, Vancouver, and Portland competed for the gold-rushers' dollars, but Brainerd ensured that Seattle received five times as much advertising as the other cities by writing feature articles, sending stacks of special newspaper editions to every postmaster in America, and encouraging citizens to write "letters to the editor" for papers worldwide.

Brainerd was enormously successful and Seattle emerged as the undisputed outfitting leader. The streets became open markets: clothing, condensed milk, dehydrated potatoes, and tools were piled high. Anything named "Klondike" was a potential big-seller, giving rise to "Klondike underwear" and "Klondike milk." Shady operators capitalized on their customers' eagerness: the Trans-Atlantic Gopher Company sold gophers allegedly trained to dig for gold. Siberian Huskies and other rugged breeds were enlisted to help pull dogsleds through the Alaskan snowfields. As the supply dwindled, families had to keep a close eye on their pets—dogs of every breed and size were stolen.

Though a handful of prospectors did strike it rich, the best claims had been staked long before most treasure-hunters arrived—leaving thousands of men worse off than when they began. Seattle emerged as the real winner, though: many of those who found gold returned to the city to establish businesses, while Seattle's "gold" was gained from outfitting the prospectors. It's said that half the $200 million in Klondike gold ended up in Seattle. More than any other event in the city's history, the Klondike Gold Rush made Seattle the major city in America's Northwest corner. From 1897 onward Seattle's future was closely allied with the north, leading one observer to say that Seattle was the only city in America to own a state (Alaska). But don't try convincing an Alaskan of that claim unless you're ready for a fight.

The Denny Regrade

One of the prominent features of Seattle is its steep hills that make walking and driving difficult. Many schemes were hatched to eliminate them, but only one ever came to fruition: the Denny Regrade project. Beginning in 1902, the city engineer directed high-pressure hoses that pumped water from Lake Union onto the steep slopes of Denny Hill in an area now called Belltown, washing the soil into Elliott Bay and creating the waterfront of today. It took eight years to complete the project, but this is now one of the few relatively level parts of this otherwise hilly city.

Modern Seattle

At the start of WW II the Boeing Airplane Company employed only about 4,000 workers, manufacturing planes on a subcontract basis for the Douglas Company of California. Orders for Boeing's B-17 bomber, developed in the mid-'30s, swelled their employment to 30,000 by 1942. Sales peaked in 1944 at $600 million, while employment figures topped 50,000.

After the war, Boeing's sales fell sharply to $14 million in 1946, when 11,000 workers were laid off. Business picked up again during the Korean conflict and the U.S./U.S.S.R. Cold War with the sale of B-47s and, later, B-52s. William M. Allen, Boeing's postwar president, sought to end this roller-coaster economy by gambling all of the company's reserves on a commercial jet-powered plane, the 707, which permanently changed civilian air travel. Later successful developments—the 727, 737, and jumbo 747—helped establish Boeing as a worldwide leader in aviation.

Civic leaders decided to throw a party to celebrate Boeing's—and, simultaneously, Seattle's—success. City Councilman Al Rochester was a leading advocate of "Century 21," the 1962 World's Fair. Rochester wanted something very special; "not just another showcase for the state seal done in corn tassels, milk cans, and steers' rears." Senator Warren G. Magnuson somehow maneuvered $9 million out of the Pentagon for the event—which became the first world's fair to show a profit.

Century 21 drew over 9.5 million people and left the entire Seattle Center—the Space Needle, Monorail, Pacific Science Center, Opera House, Coliseum, Arena, etc.—as a legacy to the event. Today, the Seattle area is vibrant and prosperous, supported in part by such major corporations as Boeing, Microsoft, and Weyerhaeuser, but also by thousands of smaller businesses.

SIGHTS

Seattle is big enough to keep an intrepid visitor busy with weeks of explorations, and even residents who have spent years here still have not ventured into all its nooks and crannies. Like most other large American cities, Seattle is a conglomeration of neighborhoods, each with an individual character that reflects both its inhabitants and its history. Because of this, you'll find sights organized respective of these neighborhoods. The attractions listed below include all of the better-known, along with several that stretch the envelope a bit. Whatever you do, try to see at least several of the following: Pike Place Market (this should be number one on every list), Pioneer Square, the Seattle Art Museum, the Seattle Aquarium, the Space Needle, Pacific Science Center, Ballard Locks, Woodland Park Zoo, the Burke Museum, and the Museum of Flight. For even more fun, add in a tour of the Rainier Brewery, the ever-popular Underground Tour in Pioneer Square, a stroll around Green Lake or through the arboretum in Volunteer Park, or a visit to one of the city's funky and delightful neighborhoods: best bets are Capitol Hill (Broadway Ave.), University District, and Fremont, all discussed within this section.

CityPass
Six of Seattle's most popular attractions—the Space Needle, Pacific Science Center, Seattle

Aquarium, the Museum of Flight, Seattle Art Museum, and Woodland Park Zoo—have gotten together to offer a half-price CityPass that provides entrance to all of these for $26 adults, $22 seniors, and $15 ages 6-13. Passes are valid for seven days, and can be purchased at any of the six attractions. This is an excellent deal for travelers.

DOWNTOWN

Downtown Seattle is a busy, almost frenetic place, with the expected mix of stuffed shirts, fashion-conscious men and women, and confused tourists. In recent years it has been transformed by the arrival of big retail operations, including Niketown, Planet Hollywood, GameWorks, and FAO Schwarz. Skyscrapers fill its center; tallest of all being the **Columbia Seafirst Center,** a sleek black structure that climbs 76 stories over downtown from the corner of 5th Ave. and Columbia Street. It dwarfs every other building in town. A glassed-in viewing deck on the 73rd floor provides a panorama of the entire region, but it will cost you $5 ($3 for seniors and kids). Ask at the information desk in the lobby for access. Also here is Metro Traffic Control, the nerve center for traffic reports on local radio stations. With a view like this, it's hard to imagine a better locale to watch the traffic. Open Mon.-Fri. 8:30 a.m.-4:30 p.m.; tel. (206) 386-5151.

Another attention-grabbing skyscraper is the **Security Pacific Tower** at 4th Ave. and University St., a surprising structure that seems to balance on the tip of an upside-down pyramid. The **Washington Mutual Tower** at 3rd and Seneca is perhaps best known as the home for a pair of nesting peregrine falcons, while the **US Bank Centre** at 5th Ave. and Union St. contains a marvelous collection of colorful glass art, including a 12-foot-high piece by Dale Chihuly.

One of the primary downtown shopping areas centers around the intersection of 4th Ave. and Pine St., the location for Westlake Center, Nordstrom, and The Bon Marché (see "Shopping," below). The central plaza here is a gathering place for musicians and the lunch-hour crowd. **Phoenix Rising Gallery,** 2030 Western Ave., tel. (206) 728-2332, is one of the finest in Seattle; it's packed with glass pieces, jewelry, gifts, and other artwork.

Built in 1929, and lovingly restored in 1995, the landmark **Paramount Theater** sits on Pine St. near 9th Avenue. Today it's one of the grandest theaters on the West Coast, providing a venue for Broadway musicals, concerts, and other productions; call (206) 292-2787 for upcoming events.

Downtown Transportation
Getting around downtown is easy—all Metro buses here are free every day between the hours of 6 a.m. and 7 p.m. The boundaries for this free area are S. Jackson St., I-5, Pine St., Battery St., and Alaskan Way. A bus tunnel runs through the center of the city, with downtown stops at Convention Place (9th and Pine), Westlake Center (4th and Pine), University Street (3rd and University), and the International District (5th and S. Jackson). The Monorail connects Westlake Center with Seattle Center.

At Sixth Ave. and Seneca over I-5, the aptly named **Freeway Park** is a solution to the blight of a freeway roaring through the heart of a city. Located just outside the Convention Center, the park was built on a lid over part of that freeway and has greenery, waterfalls, fountains, and free summertime lunch concerts.

Seattle Art Museum
The first thing you see in a visit to the Seattle Art Museum (SAM) is Jonathan Borofsky's 48-foot-high *Hammering Man* sculpture, pounding relentlessly away on the corner of University St. and 1st Avenue. Step inside the dramatically modern building to find 155,000 square feet of gallery space, a large auditorium and lecture hall, along with a gift shop and cafe. Just past the entrance, a flight of marble steps leads past Chinese statuary to three floors filled with artwork. The second level houses changing exhibits, while the two top floors feature more permanent displays. The third floor is filled with works from Asia, Africa, and Native American culture. On the fourth floor are pieces by well-known American and European artists, including one room with avant-garde works that range from the frivolously fun to the freakishly foolish.

The Art Museum is open Tues.-Sun. 10 a.m.-5 p.m., and Thursday 10 a.m.-9 p.m., (closed Monday). Admission is $6 adults, $4 seniors and students, and free for kids under 12. The first Thursday of every month is free, and your ticket gets you into both the Seattle Art Museum and the Seattle Asian Art Museum in Volunteer Park (described under "Capitol Hill" later in this chapter). Free docent-led tours of SAM are offered daily; see the information board in the lobby for the next tour. The museum also sponsors a lecture series, classes, programs on the arts, music, and films (including free family films). Pick up their quarterly program guide for specifics, or call (206) 654-3100 for recorded information on the museum and upcoming exhibitions.

Benaroya Hall
Located at 2nd Ave. and University St.—just uphill from the Seattle Art Museum—this marvelous $120-million facility is home to the Seattle Symphony. The building was completed in 1998, and is open to the public; inside you'll find a state-of-the-art 2,500-seat main auditorium, along with a 538-seat recital hall. For details, stop by the information center at 1203-B 2nd Ave., tel. (206) 515-9494; open Mon.-Fri. 10-6.

Frye Art Museum
This private museum was endowed by Charles and Emma Frye, who made some of their millions selling lard to the Germans after WW I and taking oil paintings as partial payment. The collection they amassed is—not surprisingly—heav-

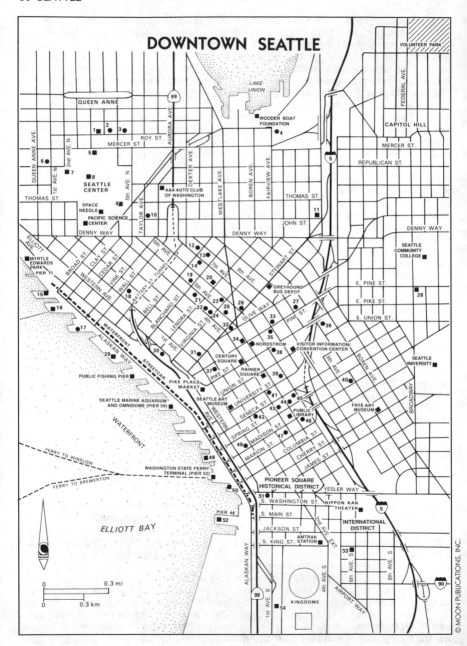

DOWNTOWN SEATTLE

© MOON PUBLICATIONS, INC.

DOWNTOWN SEATTLE

1. Bahn Thai
2. Hampton Inn
3. Hawthorn Suites Seattle Center
4. Residence Inn by Marriott
5. Opera House
6. Inn at Queene Anne
7. Key Arena
8. Children's Museum
9. Experience Music Project
10. Best Western Executive Inn
11. Recreation Equipment Inc. (REI)
12. Best Western Loyal Inn
13. Travelodge by the Space Needle
14. Days Inn Town Center
15. Spirit of Puget Sound (Pier 70)
16. Victoria Clipper to Victoria, B.C. (Pier 69)
17. Hotel Edgewater

18. Wall St. Inn
19. Ramada Inn
20. Dimitriou's Jazz Alley
21. King's Inn
22. Warwick Hotel
23. Sixth Ave. Inn
24. Claremont Hotel
25. Westin Hotel
26. WestCoast Vance Hotel
27. WestCoast Camlin Hotel
28. Egyptian Theatre
29. Odyssey Maritime Discovery Center
30. Cutter's Bay House
31. St. Regis Hotel
32. Mayflower Park Hotel
33. WestCoast Paramount Hotel
34. Monorail Terminal/Westlake Center
35. WestCoast Roosevelt Hotel
36. Westcoast Plaza Park Suites

37. Green Tortoise Backpackers Guesthouse
38. Sheraton Seattle Hotel
39. Seattle Hilton Downtown
40. Sorrento Hotel
41. Four Seasons Olympic Hotel
42. Hotel Seattle
43. Pacific Plaza Hotel
44. Hotel Vintage Park
45. Crowne Plaza Hotel
46. The Madison Hotel
47. YMCA
48. Alexis Hotel
49. Argosy Tours and Ivar's Acres of Clams (Pier 55)
50. Ye Olde Curiosity Shop
51. Best Western Pioneer Square Hotel
52. Victoria Car Ferry (Princess Marguerite) Pier 48
53. Uwajimaya
54. F.X. McRory's

ily larded with works by late 19th century German artists from the Munich School. These melodramatic oils in gilded ornate frames are a bit excessive for modern tastes, but a few works are well-known, including Alexander Max Koester's *Ducks*. Other galleries at the newly renovated and expanded Frye contain changing exhibits, and a cafe offers light meals.

The Fryes had a meat packing plant along Seattle's waterfront—but no heirs. Their wills established a trust that would fund a free public art museum; no need to leave a donation here since the trust still owns extensive and highly profitable parcels along Seattle's waterfront. Lots of free parking across the street, too. It is located near Capitol Hill at 704 Terry Ave., tel. (206) 622-9250; open Tues.-Sat. 10 a.m.-5 p.m. (Thursday till 9 p.m.), and Sunday noon-5 p.m.

PIKE PLACE MARKET

Every large city seems to have its iconographic symbols. In New York they include the Statue of Liberty and the Empire State Building, in San Francisco the Golden Gate Bridge and the cable cars, in Paris the Louvre and Eiffel Tower. For Seattle, it's the Space Needle and Pike Place Market. The Space Needle is a place to take out-of-town visitors, but Pike Place is—as more than one writer has called it—the true heart and soul of Seattle, a sensory and social statement of why the city is such a livable place. Here visitors and locals buy the freshest fish and produce in town, listen to the street musicians, enjoy the parade of humanity, and explore a myriad of shops; it's hard not to love it. Market hours are Mon.-Sat. 9 a.m.-6 p.m. and Sunday 11 a.m.-5 p.m.

History

Pike Place Market began in 1907, when the city set aside an area along the waterfront where farmers could sell their products directly to consumers, cutting out the middlemen. That first day—August 17—only a half-dozen farmers showed up, but word quickly spread, and the market was an immediate hit. By 1937, more than 600 farmers, fishmongers, and others were hawking their wares at the market. At least half of these merchants were Japanese-Americans. Consequently, when they were sent to internment camps in the 1940s, the market also suffered.

After the war, the market continued to struggle; by the late '60s the merchants had dwindled to 60 or so old-timers. Developers salivated at this piece of choice downtown real estate, promising to level the ancient buildings and construct modern high-rises and parking garages. Fortunately, the people of Seattle had more sense than this. In a 1974 election, they voted two-to-one to not only keep the market, but also to turn it into an historic district. Today, the buildings are managed by Pike Place Market Preservation and Development, and all vendors must pass a stringent set of rules that keeps the market in the hands of owner-operators, especially those offering traditional market services (unless they originated in the market, such as Starbucks). You'll never see a McDonald's here. The smaller temporary spaces are rented out on a daily basis, while the larger, more established businesses have leases with the management.

The Market

Initial appearances can be deceiving in the Pike Place Market. It's much larger than you might think, spreading over three levels in the Main Arcade, and up several blocks to include half a dozen other large buildings, each filled with additional shops. All told, the market contains more than 250 businesses covering nine acres. For a market map and newsletter, head to the **information booth** near the market entrance on the corner of Pike St. and 1st Ave.; you can also purchase half-price tickets here for concerts and

plays on the day of the show. The booth is open daily 10 a.m.-6 p.m. all year. Market hours are Mon.-Sat. 9 a.m.-6 p.m. and Sunday 11 a.m.-5 p.m. Things are pretty slow early in the morning, giving you more time to explore without having to fight your way through the crowds. Just a few feet from the info booth is **Read All About It** newsstand, where you'll find all sorts of magazines, along with papers from such diverse locations as Tulsa, Fairbanks, New Zealand, and even faraway Tacoma. Continue down this corridor to **Crêpe de France** for a quick and delicious spinach and cheese crepe, to **Pike Place Nuts** for roasted cashews, or into **DeLaurenti Market** for imported foods and wines, plus a gourmet deli.

The main focal point is beneath the famous "Public Market Center" neon sign. Enter here to meet **Rachel,** the fat bronze market pig/piggy bank that has been here since 1986. Drop a coin in to help support local charities; at last count Rachel had collected more than $35,000 for seniors, children, and the homeless. Check out the tiles covering the floor; they're imprinted with the names of those who donated money in the early 1980s to replace the worn old wooden floor. Even Ronald Reagan got a tile, though he never gave one thin dime; a local benefactor paid for his tile.

Follow the throngs of tourists to **Pike Place Fish,** right behind Rachel. You can't miss the famous flying fish (watch your head!), the raucous repartee, and the clowning around. It helps

The monorail carries passengers to and from Seattle Center and downtown.

SEATTLE/KING COUNTY CONVENTION AND VISITORS BUREAU

to be part showman to work here. Despite a competitor's complaint that "I can't see how throwing fish makes them taste any better," everything here is very fresh. For a bit less flair, but equally high quality, try one of the other three stalls selling fresh seafood in the market.

The building you're standing in is called the **Main Arcade,** and was the original market structure. Across the street are the Corner Market and the Sanitary Market buildings (the sanitary market received its name because horses were kept out). Several other buildings are also part of the market, but these are the core, and you could easily spend hours exploring their shops.

Be sure to walk downstairs in the Main Arcade to the "DownUnder Shops" that cover three less-touristy levels. You'll find all sorts of places lining the alleys: a magic shop, a comic book store, a tiny barber shop, and several antique shops, one of which sells museum-quality pieces from Asia.

Back on the main level, wander around to find **Tenzing Momo Herbal Apothecary** and **Market Spice,** or visit the **Athenian Inn,** tel. (206) 624-7166, one of the old market stalwarts and the place where several scenes in "Sleepless in Seattle" were filmed. Open since 1909, it still cranks out great red-flannel hash for breakfast and good seafood and burgers for lunch and dinner. Elliott Bay views are an added bonus. Another old-time favorite (it opened in 1908) is **Lowell's Restaurant,** where market locals still come for coffee every morning.

As you head north from here, you'll enter the **North Arcade,** where small tables are crowded with peddlers hawking artwork, jewelry, dried flowers, jams and jellies, T-shirts, fresh produce, and a myriad of other goods. More booths continue outside along the street.

The three connected buildings across the street—**Corner Market, Sanitary Market,** and **Post Alley Market**—are filled with many more shops. The **Three Girls Bakery,** in existence since 1912, is one of the market institutions, serving some of the best baked goods in town. A few other noteworthy shops in this group of buildings are: **Pike Place Market Creamery** with its old-fashioned coolers and fresh milk products; **Rasa Malaysia** with fresh and spicy Malaysian meals to go; **Milagros,** selling Mexican folk art

and handicrafts; **Sisters** with great grilled focaccia-bread sandwiches; the **Crumpet Shop** with English teas, soft crumpets, and sweet jams; **Left Bank Books** with leftist tomes strewn about; and the **Pike Place Flowers** stall that adds a splash of color to the corner of Pike and 1st.

Continue north from these buildings past Pine and Stewart Streets to the Stewart House and the Soames-Dunne Building, where the scents and sights will pull you inside. Here you'll find several delightful eating places: **Emmett Watson's Oyster Bar,** serving some of the finest oysters on the half shell; **Piroshky, Piroshky,** where you can watch them assemble delicious Russian treats; and **Cuchina Fresca,** with out-of-this-world focaccia and big square chunks of Sicilian pizza.

This sampling barely touches on the variety of shops in the market; you'll also discover a high-quality butcher shop, a Birkenstock dealer, a parrot and reptile house, a kosher deli, and even an ongoing rummage sale with old clothes and shoes.

Tours and Parking

One-and-a-half-hour **market tours** are available daily for $5 (including a continental breakfast); call (206) 682-7453 for details. It's nearly impossible to drive up Pike Place with lunch-hour pedestrians overflowing the sidewalks, and parking spaces are harder to find than a liberal Republican. Your best bet is to take the bus around town—it's free throughout downtown Seattle—but you can always find parking in the Market Parking Garage downhill from the Pike Place. Get your ticket validated at one of the market merchants.

THE WATERFRONT

Generally a sightseer's first waterfront stop, Elliott Bay's Piers 48-70 represent the main waterfront: fish and chip eateries, gift shops, museums, the aquarium, and harbor-tour departure points, connected by a sidewalk and the Waterfront Streetcar. The waterfront was made famous in Murray Morgan's *Skid Road,* written in 1951 about the docks in another era. He called it:

A good, honest, working waterfront with big gray warehouses and trim fishing boats and docks that smell of creosote and seagulls and tugs and seafood restaurants and beer joints and fish stores—a waterfront where you can hear foreign languages and buy shrunken heads and genuine stuffed mermaids . . . where you can stand at an open-air bar and drink clam nectar, or sit on a deadhead and watch the water, or go to an aquarium and look at an octopus.

Getting Around

The **Waterfront Streetcar** consists of 1927 Australian-built trolleys that run along the waterfront from Pier 70 at the north end, past the Washington State Ferry Terminal at Pier 52, through Pioneer Square, and on to the Metro tunnel station in the International District. They operate every 20 minutes; Mon.-Fri. 7 a.m.-6:30 p.m., and Sat.-Sun. 10:30 a.m.-6:30 p.m. Get a ticket for $1 ($1.25 in the commute hours) from the self-serve ticket machine at any of the nine streetcar stations along the route. It's valid for 90 minutes, and you can also use Metro passes and transfers. Call (206) 553-3000 for more information. Looking for a slower ride? **Horsedrawn carriages** line up next to Pier 56.

Park your car under the Alaskan Way Viaduct and try for a meter; as a last resort, pay the exorbitant fees at parking lots. The meters cost $1 an hour, which alone is cause enough to leave your car at a suburban park-and-ride.

Aquarium and Omnidome

A visit to Pier 59's **Seattle Aquarium,** tel. (206) 386-4320, will give you an appreciation for the incredible diversity of sealife. The traditional part of the aquarium leads you past a "touch tank" filled with various tidepool creatures, and aquariums containing everything from an octopus to an electric eel. Displays tell about the creatures and how humans are affecting their survival. A tropical coral reef exhibit makes you want to hop on a plane for Fiji. The real treat is outside, where you'll find large tanks containing harbor seals, sea otters, and northern fur seals, along with a salmon ladder and hatchery. Check the board to see when the next feeding time comes for the sea mammals and diving birds. Ducks and shorebirds occupy another noisy section, but the star feature is an underwater dome where you sit surrounded by fish from the Sound. It's as if the tables have been turned and the humans are in a giant fishbowl looking outward at salmon, skates, halibut, rockfish, and other creatures. The Seattle Aquarium is open daily 10-8 Memorial Day to Labor Day, and daily 10 a.m.-6 p.m. the rest of the year; admission is $7.75 adults, $7 seniors and disabled, $5 ages 6-18, $2 ages 3-5, and free for ages two and under. The last entrance ticket is sold an hour before closing time.

The **Omnidome,** also on Pier 59, tel. (206) 622-1868, lets you experience erupting volcanoes, outer space, foreign countries, sunken ships, and whales on their incredible 180-degree dome screen with six-channel sound. The 45-minute-long programs run continuously from 10 a.m. every day; admission is $7 adults, $6 seniors and kids, $5 for ages 3-12, and free for children under three. Get a combination pass to both the Aquarium and Omnidome for $13 adults, $11 seniors and ages 13-18, $10 for ages 6-12, and $6 for ages three to five.

More Pier Peering

On the south end of the waterfront, Pier 36 hosts the **Coast Guard Museum,** tel. (206) 217-6992, with nautical artifacts, models of Coast Guard cutters, historic photographs, and a 15-minute slide show. Open Monday, Wednesday, and Friday 9 a.m.-3 p.m., and Sat.-Sun. 1-5 p.m.; free. The Coast Guard has two 400-foot icebreakers and two 378-foot cutters that are homeported at Pier 36. They're generally open for tours on weekends 1-4:30 p.m.

Washington State Ferries depart Pier 52 for Winslow and Bremerton across the sound; see "Transportation" later in this chapter for details.

Ye Olde Curiosity Shop, a combination museum/gift shop on Pier 54, tel. (206) 682-5844, specializes in the bizarre: shrunken heads, the mummified body of "Sylvester," a two-headed calf, plus inane souvenirs and tacky curios. Very touristy, and not nearly as interesting as Marsh's Free Museum in Long Beach. Nearby is **Exclusively Washington,** tel. (206) 624-2600, a small shop filled with collectibles, books, and other Washington items.

Argosy Tours operates from Piers 55 and 56, as does Let's Go Sailing; see "Boat Tours," below, for details. Next door is **Bay Pavilion,** with an indoor carousel that is very popular with young children. Public fishing is allowed at **Waterfront Park** on Pier 57, but I wouldn't eat fish from such polluted water. The *Victoria Clipper* (see "Ferry Service," below) docks at Pier 63 between trips.

Odyssey, the Maritime Discovery Center, tel. (206) 374-4000, opened at Pier 66 in 1998, with many fun exhibits. Try your hand at loading containers onto a ship, paddle a kayak through a virtual bay, listen to vessel radio traffic from Elliott Bay, explore commercial fishing in the harvesting the sea gallery, and learn how ships move through the water. Hours are Sun.-Wed. 10 a.m.-9 p.m., Thurs.-Sat. 10 a.m.-5 p.m. Admission is $6.50 adults, $4 students and seniors, and free for kids under five.

Also at Pier 66 are a new cruise ship terminal, the Bell Harbor International Conference Center, and several shops, including the popular Bell St. Pier Fish Market. As of 2000, one of the Norwegian Line cruise ships will be departing from here on their Alaska trips. In summer, the historic tugboat *Arthur Foss* ties up at nearby Pier 69. Continue north to **Myrtle Edwards Park,** at Alaskan Way and Broad St., where a one-mile path follows the bay to Grain Terminal.

PIONEER SQUARE

Pioneer Square offers a striking clash of cultures: boutiques, art galleries, Oriental-carpet stores, and sidewalk cafes are nestled between corner missions; executives in tailored suits and young couples out for a night on the town pass Occidental Park's homeless residents. In spite of frequent complaints about the aggressiveness of the panhandlers and drunks who reside in nearby flophouses and missions (or on the street), the 20-block restored historical district along 1st Ave., Yesler Way, and S. Main St., south of downtown, is one of Seattle's most varied areas. The southern edge of the Pioneer Square area abuts the International District and the new sports stadiums; to the north are the downtown skyscrapers. Get to Pioneer Square from town center by riding one of the free buses along 1st Ave., or taking the waterfront trolley.

History
Pioneer Square itself is actually a triangle of land at the angled intersection of 1st Ave. and Yesler Way, with a beautiful turn-of-the-century **iron and glass pergola,** and a small park centered around a totem pole and a monument to Chief Seattle. The **Tlingit totem** is a replica of an original pole that was destroyed by an arsonist in 1938. The original pole was stolen on a fateful night in 1890 from Southeast Alaska's Tongass Island by a group of the city's leaders. After the original was burned, the city sent a check for $5,000 to carve a new one. The Tlingits reportedly cashed the check, and then sent a note saying, "Thanks for finally paying for the first one. A new pole will cost another $5,000." Other sights in the area include: **Waterfall Garden** at 2nd Ave. S and S. Main St., where a cascade of water provides a break from the street noise (this was the site of the first UPS office, established in 1907). Not far away is the rather depressing **Occidental Park,** a cobblestone space with several totem poles and park benches occupied by men and women who survive on the streets.

Pioneer Square is the oldest section of Seattle, although the center of activity has long since migrated north a half-mile or so. After the great fire of 1889, the area was rebuilt in brick buildings, many of which still stand here. Over the years, as businesses moved to newer places north of here, Pioneer Square became a center for cheap flophouses, drunks, and prostitutes. At its center was Yesler Ave., originally called Skid Road because it was used to drag logs to the shoreline—hence the term "skid row." By the 1960s, business leaders proposed cleaning up the mess in a massive urban renewal project that would flatten the old buildings to provide parking spaces for downtown. Fortunately, saner folks recognized the potential of the area, and in 1970 it was designated the Pioneer Square Historic District. Today the area's character is once again changing as the area moves more upscale.

Klondike Gold Rush National Historical Park
Housed in the 1901 Union Trust Annex at 117 S. Main St., tel. (206) 553-7220, this is Seattle's portion of a two-part national historical park commemorating the gold rush; the other section is in Skagway, Alaska. The center traces Seattle's

role in the 1897 gold rush with films on the event—including Charlie Chaplin's *Gold Rush*—informative exhibits, wonderful old photos, and gold rush and natural history books. During the summer, there's usually something going on: ranger talks, gold-panning demonstrations, films, and guided walks on summer weekends (assuming the budget isn't axed more). Open daily (except Christmas, New Year's Day, and Thanksgiving) 9 a.m.-5 p.m.; free. Be sure to pick up the interesting map/brochure on the gold rush, with descriptions of historic Pioneer Square buildings.

Visiting the Underground
Bill Speidel's Underground Tour is one of the city's most distinctive tours. From Doc Maynard's Public House at 1st Ave. and James St., you roam the Pioneer Square area above and below; a guide provides humorous anecdotes (often at the expense of Tacoma), along with local history. You'll learn about the speakeasies, gambling parlors, illegal lotteries, and opium dens that once occupied this section under the streets. You'll also hear how the city's tidewater location created all sorts of problems for early residents—particularly those who tried to flush toilets on an incoming tide—and how the "seamstress tax" was applied to single women working out of the Sweet Home Boarding House in the red-light district. The tour ends shamelessly in a museum/gift shop where you're encouraged to purchase such practical items as deluxe rubber rats and cockroaches. These very popular one-and-a-half-hour tours leave several times daily; $7 adults, $5 students, $6 seniors, $3 kids. Reservations recommended; phone (206) 682-4646 or (888) 608-6337.

Other Sights
The 42-story **Smith Tower** on the corner of Yesler Way and 2nd Ave. was the tallest building west of the Mississippi when completed in 1914, and remained Seattle's highest for several decades. Now dwarfed by neighboring skyscrapers, it is still an interesting place. After extensive renovation, the building is expected to reopen in 1999, with elevator rides to a 35th-floor outdoor observation deck. Another local landmark is the tall Venetian-style clock tower of Amtrak's **King Street Station** at the intersection of S. King St. and 3rd Ave. South.

Shops
Get a free map of Pioneer Square at the park office or at the cash register of almost any area merchant; it points out historical buildings in the area. The best known shop in local business is the spacious **Elliott Bay Book Company,** 101 S. Main St., tel. (206) 624-6600, with its downstairs cafe. This Pioneer Square bookstore, incidentally, is *the* quintessential place for Seattle bibliophiles. Other intriguing shops include **Merchants Cafe,** 109 Yesler Way, tel. (206) 624-1515, the city's oldest restaurant (it opened in 1890), and many nearby galleries along a pedestrian-only stretch of Occidental St. just north of the sports stadiums. Additional galleries are a block away along 1st Ave. South. Notable ones include **Foster/White Gallery,** 311 1/2 Occidental S, tel. (206) 622-2833; **Emerald City Fine Art,** 317 1st Ave. S., tel. (206) 623-1550; **Davidson Galleries,** 313 Occidental Ave. S., tel. (206) 624-7684; **Northwest Gallery of Fine Woodworking,** 101 S. Jackson St., tel. (206) 625-0542, and **Gallery Magna,** 310 Occidental Ave. S., tel. (206) 223-9563. One of the best ways to enjoy the collection of art galleries in Pioneer Square is to join the art crowd for the **First Thursday Gallery Walk** when all galleries open on the evening of the first Thursday each month.

INTERNATIONAL DISTRICT

Sometimes called "Chinatown," this part of Seattle has long been home to people from all over Asia, including those of Japanese, Korean, Chinese, Filipino, and Vietnamese ancestry. The International District is easy to reach; just catch one of the free buses and ride through the tunnel to the International District bus tunnel station, where outsized origami pieces decorate the walls.

All roads lead to **Hing Hay Park,** a small city park with a colorful pagoda-style Chinese pavilion donated by the city of Taipei. Watch out for the hundreds of pigeons that get fed here and coat the pavilion with their droppings.

The **Wing Luke Asian Museum** at 407 7th Ave. S, tel. (206) 623-5124, has artifacts from early Asian businesses, memorabilia of all types, hand-painted kites, a 35-foot Chinese dragon, plus many historic photos. The museum also displays changing exhibits of Asian art and history. Hours are Tues.-Fri. 11 a.m.-4:30 p.m., and Sat.-Sun. noon-4 p.m.; admission $2.50 adults, $1.50 seniors and students, 75 cents ages 5-12. Free on Thursdays.

King Street is the heart of the district; Chinese shops line both sides. The International District lacks the crowded intensity of San Francisco's Chinatown, but the streets are bordered with hole-in-the-wall restaurants, shops selling imported goods, and Asian grocers (some of the biggest are up the hill near the corner of S. Jackson St. and 12th Avenue). You can easily find a filling lunch for under $5. **Kobe Terrace Park,** a community garden, lines the hillside above the International District; it is capped by a concrete lantern given to Seattle by its sister city of Kobe, Japan. The historic **Nippon Kan Theater** at 628 S. Washington St., tel. (206) 467-6807, is well known for its Japanese performing arts productions.

The largest Asian supermarket in the Northwest, **Uwajimaya,** 519 6th Ave. S, tel. (206) 624-6248, sells everything from high-quality groceries to Japanese furniture. Step inside for an eye-opening venture across the Pacific, plus excellent light meals in the Japanese deli.

SEATTLE CENTER AND BELLTOWN

The flat section of land just north of downtown was originally a steep bluff, but the Denny Regrade washed the hill away, allowing for its development. Now called Belltown, the mixed commercial and residential neighborhood is rapidly becoming a funky center for the city's music and arts scene, with galleries, nightclubs, and cafes lining the streets. The biggest attraction for visitors here is Seattle Center, a 74-acre legacy of the 1962 World's Fair that is home to the Space Needle. Seattle Center is an odd mishmash of attractions, designed with the Jetson's-era architecture of the early '60s. The best way to venture into this space-age world is aboard the kitschy **Monorail,** the elevated train (of sorts) that connects trendy Westlake Center at 5th and Pine with passé Seattle Center. This strange contraption was considered a model for transportation in its day, but Seattle's is the only one to

ever make it beyond the amusement park (Disneyland has one, of course). The Monorail costs adults $1 each way for the 90-second ride; it departs every 15 minutes and is open Mon.-Fri. 7:30 a.m.-11 p.m. and Sat.-Sun. 9 a.m.-11 p.m. year-round. Call (206) 441-6038 for details.

Although it attracts many adults, Seattle Center is evolving into a favorite of children. In addition to the carnival rides and a fast trip up the Space Needle, the area includes a fantastic Children's Museum, the Pacific Science Center with hands-on displays, and the Seattle Children's Theatre. For general information about Seattle Center and upcoming events, call (206) 684-8582.

Space Needle

The Space Needle is one of Seattle's trademarks, a 605-foot tower topped by a flying saucer viewing deck and restaurant. Elevators levitate you to the top where you can walk out on the observation deck for a 360-degree view of downtown Seattle, of planes flying by, and of the Cascades, Mt. Rainier, and the Olympics on a clear day. On a rainy day you may be able to make out downtown. Detailed signboards describe the buildings and other surrounding features.

The Space Needle is privately owned and highly commercialized. Nobody is here to act as a guide or answer questions. Two mediocre restaurants are a level below, and the main observation deck is crowded with tacky gift shops, a pricey lounge, video games for the kids, penny-mashing machines, and a bland art gallery. Be sure to purchase the official soda of the Space Needle (Coke) and official film (Kodak) while here. Despite the kitsch, the spectacular view is hard to beat. The elevator ride up and back costs a sky-high $9 adults, $8 for seniors, $4 for ages 5-12, and free for younger kids. (If you have restaurant reservations, the ride is free.) Call (206) 443-2111 or (800) 937-9582 for details. The observation deck is open daily 8 a.m.-midnight.

Pacific Science Center

The Pacific Science Center, tel. (206) 443-2001, began as the U.S. Science Pavilion at the 1962 World's Fair. Distinctive white concrete arches rise over pools and fountains at this hugely popular family museum. More than 1.2 million visi-

ERIN HOGAN

The Pacific Science Center attracts almost one million people every year.

tors come each year to wander five buildings filled with hands-on exhibits. You'll find laser-light rock-music shows, virtual reality voyages, a planetarium, a ménage of memorable mechanized Mesozoic dinosaurs, a tropical butterfly house, plus fun and educational exhibits of all types. The fountains outside are filled with water toys that blast jets of water at all sorts of objects; there's even a spinning two-ton granite ball. Look for the high-rail bike demonstrations most days. The new six-story IMAX screen at Pacific Science Center uses large-format film and a 12,000-watt sound system to create unforgettably dramatic movies; their high-tech 3-D films use cordless headsets with electronic liquid crystal lenses. The Science Center also has a changing series of exhibits and special events, including a popular **Model Railroad Show** in late November and the kids-favorite **Bubble Festival** in mid-August.

Admission to the Pacific Science Center (including the IMAX or laser matinee) is $9.50 adults, $7.50 ages 6-13 and seniors, $5.50 ages

2-5, free under age two. Pacific Science Center is open daily 10 a.m.-6 p.m. mid-June through Labor Day, and Mon.-Fri. 10 a.m.-5 p.m., Sat.-Sun. 10 a.m.-6 p.m. the rest of the year. Closed only for Thanksgiving and Christmas. If you don't want to wait in long lines for the featured attractions (such as virtual reality), try to come Sunday morning or Mon.-Wed. afternoons, when things tend to be quieter.

Seattle Children's Museum

Downstairs in Center House is the delightful Seattle Children's Museum, tel. (206) 441-1768, filled with wacky and fun exhibits that manage to simultaneously educate children. Each year, 200,000 kids drag their parents through the 32,000 square feet of play space. The exhibits change all the time, but there's always something fun to do here, including hands-on workshops. Do kids like this place? The average stay is three hours; try getting any child to do anything for three hours! The gift shop sells educational toys. Open Mon.-Fri. 10-5, and Sat.-Sun. 10-6. Admission is $4 adults, $5.50 kids. Adults must accompany children under 12.

Other Sights

Recently remodeled, the **Center House** started life as an armory but was reborn as a shopping and fast-food mall for the 1962 World's Fair. Today, the interior is lined on two levels with 18 different fast-food eateries. The basement of Center House is home to the hugely successful Seattle Children's Museum (described above). A three-ton slab of the **Berlin Wall** stands inside Center House, a gift from a German businessman in 1991. **Fun Forest,** Seattle Center's amusement park, is open late spring to early autumn. Nothing special here, but kids like it; call (206) 728-1585 for details.

Basketball fans head to Seattle Center's **Key Arena,** home of the NBA's Seattle SuperSonics. Right out front is the **International Fountain,** a deceptively simple structure that never ceases to delight kids trying to escape the random jets of water, and adults laughing when the inevitable happens. The fountain erupts in an on-the-hour frenzy of action complete with music Mon.-Fri. 6-11 p.m., and Sat.-Sun. 2-11 p.m.

Seattle Center also houses the **Bagley Wright Theater** where the Seattle Repertory Theater performs; and the **Opera House,** home of the Seattle Opera, Seattle Youth Symphony, and Pacific Northwest Ballet (see "Performing Arts," later in this chapter).

Located on the southwest edge of Seattle Center, the **Experience Music Project** (www.experience.org) opened in 1999. Microsoft billionaire Paul Allen's fascination with Seattle-born Jimi Hendrix led him to bankroll much of this $60 million, 110,000-square-foot museum. Inside is a state-of-the-art interactive music and performing arts space, a 150-seat performance hall, as well as classroom and educational space. On exhibit are thousands of rock 'n' roll artifacts, including the Fender Stratocaster used to play "The Star-Spangled Banner" at Woodstock. Hendrix is buried in his family plot in Renton (see the Southern Puget Sound chapter). A statue of him also stands across from Seattle University on Capital Hill. Call (425) 450-1997 for details on Experience Music.

LAKE UNION AND VICINITY

Lake Union is a natural lake that was transformed early in this century when canals were dug linking Lake Washington, Lake Union, and Puget Sound. The Chittenden Locks provide boat access from Puget Sound into Lake Union. For many years Lake Union was treated mostly as an industrial area that floated. On the north shore stood a glum plant that manufactured gas. The south shore was dominated by boatyards and a Navy Reserve station, and parts of the east shore were (and still are) used by the federal government for its research vessels. The east shore also originally included a clutter of extremely modest cottages and shacks; to the west were boatyards and a seaplane base.

Today Lake Union is an urban neighborhood transformed. The old gas plant has become Gasworks Park, one of the most imaginative parks in America. Most of the debris has been removed from the shores, and where once you saw only greasy clutter you now see people, lots of people. The only drawback to its success is that ordinary folks and creative types, who invented the houseboat neighborhoods, can no

longer afford to live there. It has become one of the trendiest addresses in Seattle. Houseboats, some topping the $1 million price tag, have taken over most of the eastern shore and part of the northwestern end. Although it is still home to a large ship repair company, the southern end is now primarily a mix of glitzy restaurants, historical boats, kayak rentals, expensive yachts for sale, and seaplane rides, all connected by a shoreline boardwalk.

Maritime History

Run by volunteers, the **Center for Wooden Boats,** tel. (206) 382-2628, restores and maintains a fleet of historic rowboats and sailboats. Take a class here to learn about wooden boat building, or rent one of the boats to sail or row around the lake for an afternoon. The boathouse is open Wed.-Mon. 11-5; closed Tuesday. Right next door is the small **Maritime Heritage Center,** tel. (206) 447-9800, with vintage wooden boats, including the *Wawona.* Constructed in 1897, this was the largest three-masted sailing schooner built in North America and the first American ship to be listed as a National Historic Site. The restoration process is slow, partly because it is nearly impossible to get wood of the same quality; nearly all the virgin forests are gone. Pretty hard to find six by eight inch planks that are 120 feet long! The *Wawona* is open for self-guided public tours daily ($3 adults, $1.50 kids and seniors, or $6 for a family).

Chandler's Cove houses the small and free **Puget Sound Maritime Museum,** tel. (206) 938-2397, with historic maritime photos and ship models on display. Several restaurants fill the rest of the small shopping area here, including Hooters', Chandler's Clubhouse, Dukes', and Cucina! Cucina!—a popular singles' meat market. Several other restaurants are at the nearby Yale St. Landing mall.

Built on the site of a former gas plant, **Gasworks Park** at N. Northlake Way and Meridian Ave. N is the world's only industrial site conversion park. Much of the original rusting gas equipment was incorporated into the park's landscaping, including a play barn that kids (and the homeless) love. Enjoy the views of Seattle and Lake Union from the industrial equipment and fly a kite from the hills here. The paved and very popular **Burke-Gilman Trail** begins west of Gasworks, skirts Lake Washington, connects to the Sammamish River Trail, and ends in Redmond's Marymoor Park, 24 miles away.

Recreation Equipment Inc.

There aren't many places where an outdoor adventure store makes it to a must-see list of sights, but Seattle's REI is just such a place. In business since 1938, REI is America's most successful cooperatively run company, with more than 45 stores scattered across the country. Its 80,000-square-foot flagship store at 222 Yale Ave. is a favorite of locals and visitors. The building's main attraction is a 65-foot indoor climbing wall—the world's tallest—just inside the entrance. It's open to all levels of ability; ask the belay experts for help. Test hiking boots or mountain bikes on the loop trail outside, enjoy an espresso next to the waterfall, try out Gortex jackets in the rain room, plan trips with the help of Park Service or Forest Service personnel at the in-store Outdoor Recreation Information Center (see "Information and Services," below), or simply wander through the clothing and gear. REI also rents all sorts of outdoor gear, including backpacks, climbing shoes, tents, sleeping bags, ice axes, and skis of all types. The store features an auditorium where you can watch outdoor presentations and clinics most evenings. Below the store are three levels of free underground parking.

A lifetime REI membership costs $15, and entitles you to yearly rebates of around 10%. For more information on REI, call (206) 223-1944, or find them on the Web at www.rei.com. **REI Adventures,** tel. (800) 622-2236, leads treks all over the world, including such close-in places as the Olympics, San Juan Islands, and Mount Rainier.

CAPITOL HILL

Capitol Hill is a study in sharp contrasts. The hill itself is one of the most prestigious old neighborhoods in Seattle, with countless mansions and stately older homes, quite a few of which are now elaborate bed-and-breakfast inns. At one time local politicians dreamed of making this the location for Washington's capitol building—hence the name. Today the campuses of Seattle Central Community College and Seattle

University mark the southern edge while two commercial centers attract visitors: a small, fairly quiet strip along 15th Ave. E, and the busy, on-the-edge Broadway Ave. E stretch. Because of a strong gay and lesbian presence, Broadway has been likened to San Francisco's Castro District, but it could also be Berkeley's Telegraph Avenue. It's a great place to people-watch, and to catch up on the latest fashion statements for the youthful art crowd. You're guaranteed to see more black leather skirts and jackets, frenzied florescent green hair, tattoos, nose rings, and pink triangles here than anywhere else in Seattle. The center of this buzz is **Broadway Market,** a thriving set of offbeat shops with—for some reason—a big Fred Meyer store occupying the back half. Buy magazines at Bulldog News, get a glass of wheatgrass juice at the arty Gravity Bar, try on the organic hemp clothing at Fremont Hemp Company, buy half-price concert tickets at Ticket/Ticket, or get a blast of latte at B&O Espresso. Interesting artworks are displayed on the upper level. Another unusual shop is **The Pink Zone,** 211 Broadway Ave. E, tel. (206) 325-0050, with tattoos, body piercing, and out-of-the-closet t-shirts. Walk down the street in either direction and you'll discover artist Jack Mackie's amusing **Dancers Series: Steps,** bronze footprints of various dances embedded in the sidewalk.

Volunteer Park

This Capitol Hill park (enter from 14th or 15th Ave. E) has 44 acres of lawn, a concrete reservoir, and a number of interesting attractions. Completed in 1912, the park is one of many famous sites—including New York's Central Park and the University of Washington campus—that were designed by the famed Olmsted Brothers landscape architectural firm. A 75-foot brick **water tower** opens daily at 10 a.m.; climb its long spiral staircase for a grand view across the city. On the other side of the park is the glass **Conservatory,** built in 1912 and filled with colorful plants of all kinds. One room houses cacti, others contain ferns, bromeliads, and seasonal displays. The central space contains a gorgeous collection of orchids, along with a banana palm and fig tree. There's always something in bloom at the Conservatory, making this a great, steamy place to visit on a rainy winter day. It's open daily 10 a.m.-7 p.m. May to mid-September, and daily 10 a.m.-4 p.m. the rest of the year.

The centerpiece of Volunteer Park is the **Seattle Asian Art Museum,** tel. (206) 654-3100, a 1933 art-deco building. Exhibits cover two spacious wings, including rooms with Japanese folk art, Indian Mughal art, Quing dynasty Chinese art, and Korean art. Of particular interest are the beautiful Japanese screens, the bronze Buddhist sculptures, and the collection of intricate Chinese snuff bottles. The museum is open Tues.-Sun. 10 a.m.-5 p.m., and Thursday 10-9 p.m. Free tours are offered daily, or borrow an audio tape for a do-it-yourself tour. Admission costs $6 adults, $4 seniors and students, and free for kids under 12. This fee lets you in both the Asian Art Museum and the Seattle Art Museum downtown on the same day. The first Thursday of each month is free. A small gift shop sells books and other items, and the Kado Teagarden cafe serves light lunches and more than 55 different teas from around the world.

Just north of Volunteer Park is **Lakeview Cemetery,** tel. (206) 322-1582, where many of the city's early residents are buried, including Doc Maynard and the daughter of Chief Seattle. Most folks come here, however, to visit the gravesite of martial artist and actor Bruce Lee, who died in 1973. His son, Brandon Lee, also a martial artist and actor, is buried here as well. He was accidentally killed during the 1993 filming of *The Crow.*

QUEEN ANNE AND MAGNOLIA

Queen Anne is a small neighborhood crowning the tallest hill in Seattle. Given the commanding vistas from this location, it comes as no surprise that the captains of industry built mansions here at the turn of the century. Many of these spacious and pretentious old homes are still here, along with a few cobblestone streets, but alongside are other, less ostentatious homes that give Queen Anne a comfortable atmosphere. Mount Rainier, downtown Seattle, the Olympics, and the harbor can all be seen from tiny **Kerry Park** at W. Highland Dr. and 2nd Ave. W on the south slope of Queen Anne Hill. It's especially popular with photographers in search of picture-postcard shots of Seattle. The upscale **Queen Anne Thriftway,** 1908 Queen Anne N., tel. (206) 284-2530, has to be one of the friendliest grocery stores anywhere; it's hard to get down the aisles without getting a genuine smile from an employee or patron.

West of Queen Anne is the similar Magnolia neighborhood, with a wonderful shoreside route (Magnolia Dr.) along the north edge of Elliott Bay to Discovery Park. **Magnolia Park,** perched upon a high bluff, is a great place for views of Puget Sound and the Olympics and a favorite spot to watch a sunset.

Discovery Park

Located five miles northwest of downtown in the Magnolia District, the 535-acre Discovery Park juts out into Puget Sound. In Discovery—Seattle's largest city park—you'll discover an "urban wilderness" with a wild feeling that belies its location next to two million people. The park features a 2.8-mile loop trail through forest and meadow, with access to two miles of Puget Sound beaches, plus the half-mile interpretive **Wolf Tree Nature Trail.** Discovery Park's West Point is reputedly Seattle's best birding spot, with more than 150 kinds of birds, including frequent sightings of loons, grebes, cormorants, terns, and other marine birds.

Discovery Park is located on what was originally **Fort Lawton,** a defensive base begun in the late 1890s as a place to protect Puget Sound. It served mainly as a shipping center early in this century, and in WW II as a vital processing base for more than a million troops en route to the Pacific, the second busiest point of embarkation on the West Coast. At its peak, the fort contained a small city's worth of buildings, and the mess hall bragged that it could feed 12,000 troops in an hour. Things slowed down after WW II and the Korean War, and the fort was declared surplus property and given to the city of Seattle. In March of 1970, 500 Indians invaded the grounds, claiming the old fort site as a Native American cultural center. It took two battalions of Army troops and 119 arrests (including actress Jane Fonda) to quell the protest. Eventually, the city agreed to set aside 20 acres for what is now the **Daybreak Star Arts and Cultural Center,** tel. (206) 285-4425. A small collection of art is inside, but the building is mainly used for Native American events, including a salmon bake and art market the second Saturday of each month. The rest of Fort Lawton became Discovery Park in 1972. Quite a few of the fort's structures remain, including more than a dozen from the earliest days. An interesting walking tour booklet detailing the fort and its history is available at the park's visitor center, open daily 8:30 a.m.-5 p.m. all year. They offer free 90-minute Saturday nature walks at 2 p.m., along with a variety of classes and special events; call (206) 386-4236 for details.

BALLARD AND SHILSHOLE BAY

The section of Seattle called Ballard was established in the 1880s by Capt. William R. Ballard, and had grown to more than 15,000 people by the early part of this century. After a long battle over access to drinking water (Seattle had it, Ballard didn't; Seattle wanted to annex Ballard, Ballard wanted to stay independent), the citizens finally gave up and voted to join Seattle in 1907.

Ballard and nearby Shilshole Bay were the Nordic section of Seattle when immigration from Norway and Sweden peaked from 1890 to 1910. By the turn of the century, Nordic immigrants made up a quarter of Seattle's wood industry workforce and also significantly contributed to mining, farming, fishing, and shipbuilding. Sivert Sagstad established his Ballard Boat Works in Shilshole Bay four months after his arrival and built more than 300 wooden boats. Ballard still retains much of its Scandinavian heritage, although like most of the city, the ethnic lines are becoming more and more blurred. Downtown Ballard has Norwegian and Swedish flags along the street, plus several Nordic shops, including **Norse Imports Scandinavian Gift Shop,** 2016 N.W. Market St., tel. (206) 784-9420; **Olsen's Scandinavian Foods,** 2248 N.W. Market St., tel. (206) 783-8288; and **Scandie's,** 2301 N.W. Market St., tel. (206) 783-5080 (real lutefisk and Swedish pancakes). Ballard's **Syttende Mai Parade** takes place on May 17, Norwegian Constitution Day; this is the largest Syttende Mai parade outside Norway.

Nordic Heritage Museum
A turn-of-the-century red brick grade school has been transformed into the Nordic Heritage Museum, 3014 N.W. 67th St., tel. (206) 789-5707, the only museum of its kind in the nation. The first floor opens with a lengthy and educational exhibit on the "Dream of America," including the factors that pushed people to emigrate here in the 19th century. Upper levels cover the new life—in tenement slums, logging camps, and aboard fishing boats, with more exhibits on explorations by the Vikings, changing art and craft displays, and a gift shop with books on the homeland. The third floor has individual spaces for each of the Nordic countries: Norway, Sweden, Finland, Denmark, and Iceland. (Did you know Reykjavik, Iceland is a sister city to Seattle?) The museum is also home to Norwegian rosemaling classes, music, theatre, and children's programs, a research library, and the **Scandinavian Language Institute** (tel. (425) 771-5203), where you can join classes in Danish, Norwegian, or Swedish. The museum is open Tues.-Sat. 10 a.m.-4 p.m., Sunday noon-4 p.m.; admission is $4 adults, $3 seniors and students, $2 ages 6-16 years, and free for kids under six.

Come to the museum on the weekend after the Fourth of July for the **Tivoli Festival** with a pancake breakfast, food and craft booths, entertainment, and beer garden. Return on the weekend after Thanksgiving for **Yulefest,** with traditional carols, Nordic crafts, and food.

Chittenden Locks
At the west end of Ballard, on N.W. 54th St., the **Hiram M. Chittenden Locks,** tel. (206) 783-7059, connect saltwater Puget Sound with freshwater Lake Washington via Lake Union. The locks (also known as the Ballard Locks) serve various functions: as a passageway for some 90,000 ships each year, as a way to prevent saltwater intrusion into the lakes, and as a fish ladder. Built between 1911 and 1917, the locks are managed by the U.S. Army Corps of Engineers, who have a visitor center here, tel. (206) 783-7059, open daily 10 a.m.-7 p.m. June-Sept., and Thurs.-Mon. 11 a.m.-5 p.m. the rest of the year. Films are shown here every half-hour. They offer free hour-long guided tours every day at 1 p.m. and 3 p.m. in the summer, and on Saturday and Sunday at 2 p.m. in the winter months, or join the throngs and figure it out for yourself. The locks and grounds are open daily 7 a.m.-9 p.m. year-round. Chittenden Locks are one of

Seattle's most heavily visited attractions; over a million people come here each year to watch container ships, tugs, tour boats, fishing boats, and pleasure craft make the transition between salt- and freshwater. They also come to see the salmon return home to spawn via big underwater windows along the fish ladder—best time to look for the salmon is late June to early September.

On the bank overlooking the locks are the **Carl S. English Jr. Botanical Gardens,** with more than 500 species of plants that English collected from around the world, plus native Northwest species. Included are pines, palms, oaks, dawn redwood, swamp flowers and trees, and a great collection of rhododendrons. A brochure details a self-guided tour through the gardens.

Along the Water
Across the Ballard Bridge in Salmon Bay is the **Fishermen's Terminal,** a bustling marina—largest in the Northwest—packed with some 700 commercial fishing boats. Ask around to buy seafood directly from the fishermen, or head to **Wild Salmon Fish Market,** 1900 W. Nickerson St., tel. (206) 283-3366, on the water's edge.

West of the Chittenden Locks, Seaview Ave. curves north along the shore past Shilshole Bay with several popular seafood restaurants—most notably Ray's Boathouse and Anthony's Homeport—and Seattle's major pleasure boat moorage, **Shilshole Marina.** Continue north to the enormously popular **Golden Gardens Park,** with one of the Sound's best bathing beaches.

North beyond this is **Carkeek Park,** N.W. 110th St., where you'll find a beautiful picnic area and playground, enjoyable hiking trails, and walks and talks at the Environmental Education Center, tel. (206) 684-0877. Puget Sound is accessible via a footbridge over the railroad tracks. If the tide's in, chances are the beach will be out.

FREMONT

Seattle's quirkiest neighborhood, the "Republic of Fremont" has its own troll and Lenin monument, plus an official motto that proclaims the "Freedom to be Peculiar." It's a delightful place to spend an afternoon exploring the sights. The best way to reach Fremont is across the **Fremont Draw-**

bridge, according to the *Guinness Book,* the world's most active drawbridge, with over 500,000 openings. Be ready to wait; on busy weekends it often opens every 10 minutes or so.

Sights
Once you cross the bridge, you'll meet the city's most famous piece of public art, Richard Beyer's life-size group of commuters and a dog, *Waiting for the Interurban.* They are often decked out in used hats, balloons, or umbrellas contributed by passersby. Head one block east and turn up the road beneath the Aurora Bridge that towers above you. Two blocks uphill you'll meet the locally famous **Aurora Bridge Troll** in the act of devouring a VW bug. From here, walk to the official "Center of the Universe" at the corner of N. 35th St. and Evanston Ave., where a 53-foot-high **Russian rocket** prepares to blast off from one building. Inside the building you'll discover more weirdness. **Ah Nuts,** tel. (206) 633-0664, is packed with the bizarre—ghoulish dental tools, a wax version of Vincent Price, old cards, small caskets, neon lights, and all sorts of other junk. The **Almost Free Outdoor Cinema,** tel. (206) 282-5706, brings B movies and cult classics to the wall behind here on summer Saturday nights. Bring your lawn chair!

A monthly **First Saturday Art Walk,** showcases artists at work, and is one of Fremont's many attractions for art lovers. A favorite is the **Edge of Glass Gallery,** 513 N. 36th St., tel. (206) 547-6551, where you can watch students and teachers blowing glass Wed.-Sun. 11 a.m.-6 p.m.

Glamorama, 3414 Fremont Ave. N, tel. (206) 632-0287, is a must-see shop with strange and wacky toys (including voodoo dolls), retro garb, gifts, and a walk-in wedding chapel (look up for the overhead cake) for those who want a ceremony with less pomp and more weirdness. **Fremont Hemp Co.,** on the corner of Fremont Pl. and N. 36th St., tel. (206) 632-4367, has clothing, paper, and other items made from the plant that also produces marijuana. Out front stands **Lenin** in heroic pose. This statue originally stood in Slovakia till the 1989 revolution when it was toppled and sold to capitalists. Lenin is now available to the first person with $150,000 to spend. He must be spinning in his grave.

Other Fremont attractions include a big basement-level **Antique Mall** at Fremont Pl. and N. 35th St., tel. (206) 548-9140; **Tribe's** at 704 N. 34th St., tel. (206) 632-8842, with Native American arts and teas; and a fine **Puget Consumers' Co-op** market on N. 34th Street.

Breweries

In existence since 1981, **Redhook Ale Brewery** is one of the largest microbreweries in America (though Anheuser-Busch's 25% ownership makes the "micro" part a bit suspect). Stop by corporate headquarters at 3400 Phinney Ave. N in Fremont to taste their ales, check out the gift shop, or enjoy a light meal at the popular **Trolleyman Pub**, tel. (206) 483-3232. Be sure to ask here about the Fremont "brew trek" passport shared by all three local breweries. Redhook beers are no longer brewed in Fremont, but you can tour their big Woodinville brewery (see the "Vicinity of Seattle" chapter)

A much smaller operation is **Dad Watsons Restaurant & Brewery**, 3601 Fremont Ave. N, tel. (206) 632-6505. This attractive brewpub has ales on tap and an enjoyably diverse menu.

A few blocks west—and right off the bike path—is **Hale's Ales Brewery**, 4301 Leary Way NW, tel. (206) 706-1544. They crank out seven different draft-only beers, and serve meals in the cozy pub or outside on the big deck. No scheduled tours, but the staff will describe the brewing process. Open Sun.-Thurs. 11 a.m.-10 p.m., and Fri.-Sat. 11 a.m.-midnight. Hale's now has a second brewery in Berkeley, California.

WALLINGFORD AND GREEN LAKE

Wallingford consists of a busy strip of shops just west of I-5 along N. 45th Street. This attractive neighborhood is close enough to the university to have a strong student flavor, but far enough away to mix in a more upscale atmosphere. Just north of Wallingford is Green Lake, almost a mile wide and the center for recreation in the area. A small neighborhood shopping area centers around the intersection of N.E. Ravenna Blvd. and E. Green Lake Way North, with other places scattered around the shore. On the south side of the lake is the Woodland Park Zoo.

Woodland Park Zoo

Ranked among the nation's best, the Woodland Park Zoo has re-created wildlife habitats from around the world. A five-acre "African savanna" has zebras, lions, and giraffes roaming freely (but not together, to the lions' chagrin). The nocturnal house is home to bats, sloths, and other creatures of the night. Also included are a tropical Asia habitat and elephant forest where you can watch daily elephant logging demonstrations during the summer, and a Northern Trail section that leads past brown bears, river otters, bald eagles, mountain goats, gray wolves, and snowy owls, all in a relatively realistic setting (even the plants are native to Alaska). Raptor demonstrations are given on summer weekends, and the big field in the middle is a good place for a lunch break. The zoo's newest exhibit, Bug World, reveals the secret lives of singing katydids, Brazilian cockroaches, New Guinea walkingsticks, and assassin bugs.

Situated between Phinney and Aurora, N. 50th and N. 59th, tel. (206) 684-4800, the zoo is open daily 9:30 a.m.-6 p.m. from mid-March to mid-October, and daily 9:30 a.m.-4 p.m. the rest of the year. You can remain on the grounds after the gates close, but will need to be out by 7:30 p.m. Admission is $8 adults, $7.25 ages 6-17, $7.25 seniors, $3.25 ages 3-5, and free for toddlers two and under. Parking is $3.50.

Next to the zoo is the **Woodland Park Rose Garden**, tel. (206) 684-4880, with hundreds of rose varieties spread over two acres.

Green Lake

An extremely popular three-mile paved bicycle, jogging, and skating loop—watch out for errant skateboards—encompasses Green Lake, where you can also sail and swim or rent a paddleboat, canoe, kayak, sailboard, or rowboat. A kids-only fishing pier is at the east end of the lake. Crocodile hunting was popular here in 1986 when assorted reports of a lake creature took on the proportions of a Loch Ness Monster. The "monster" turned out to be a three-pound, 28-inch caiman that was shipped to a private breeder in Kansas City, and the lake was unofficially declared crocodile-free.

UNIVERSITY DISTRICT

The University District (better known as "The U District") is the center for student activity near the University of Washington's campus. The U District covers several blocks near the intersection of University Way NE ("The Ave") and N.E. 45th St., with inexpensive restaurants, CD and book stores, boutiques, coffeehouses, and other student-oriented places. This is probably the best place in Seattle to get a quick lunch or an ethnic dinner for just a few bucks. There are so many good places (especially Asian) that all you need to do is find one packed with students. Several shops are noteworthy along University, including the **Folk Art Gallery,** 4138 University Way NE, tel. (206) 632-1796, for items from around the world; the **University Bookstore,** 4326 University Way NE, tel. (206) 634-3400, for one of the largest bookstores in Washington; and **Bulldog News,** 4208 University Way NE, tel. (206) 632-6397, the biggest magazine and newspaper seller in town. The newly revamped **University Village Mall** on N.E. 45th St. at 25th Ave. NE is home to 70 shops, including a QFC market, Eddie Bauer, Gap, and Barnes & Noble, along with many small eateries and specialty shops.

University of Washington, Seattle

University of Washington

The University of Washington is the largest and best-known institute of higher education in the state and home to 35,000 students (9,000 of these are graduate students), plus some 13,000 staff and 4,000 faculty members.

The university began on a 10-acre downtown site in 1861, when Seattle was little more than a cow town. It had a fitful time at first, and closed several times before finally getting established. After statehood in 1889, the school began to grow rapidly, and the campus was relocated to the present site. (The original location on University St. downtown is still university property.) The Alaska-Yukon-Pacific Exposition of 1909 was held on the UW campus, and in exchange for use of the campus, the fair's promoters constructed several permanent buildings and landscaped the grounds, making UW one of the nation's most beautiful campuses.

Today, UW is a major center for research in the fields of Asian languages, zoology, astrono-

my, cell biology, forestry, fisheries, physics, and many other areas of study. Three UW faculty members have won Nobel Prizes in physics and medicine over the last decade, and five others have been awarded the MacArthur Foundation "genius grants." The school is highly competitive; incoming freshmen collectively have a 3.6 grade point average, and the graduate programs are widely acknowledged as some of the strongest in America. The UW library system contains more than five million volumes spread over two dozen campus libraries, making it one of the largest in the nation. The university's football and basketball teams often rank in the nation's top 20. Walk down University Way on the day of a football game, and you'll quickly learn that the team colors are purple and gold, and the mascot for the Huskies is an Alaskan malamute. (By the way, the shorthand term for the Huskies is "Dawg," but never "Dog.")

The campus is an attractive place, with tall brick buildings, a central square—**Red Square**—named for the color of its bricks, not the politics of

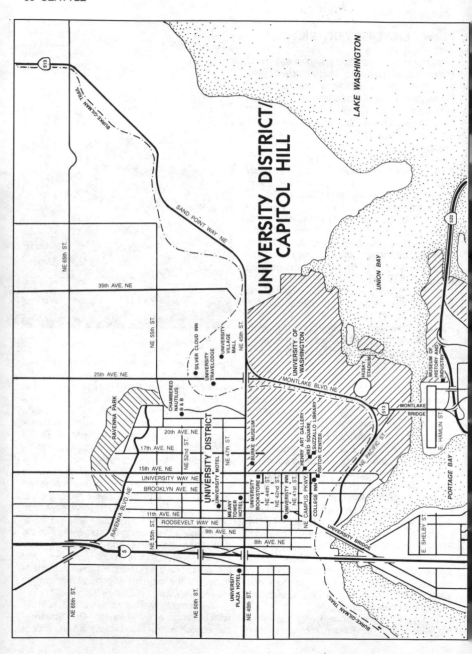

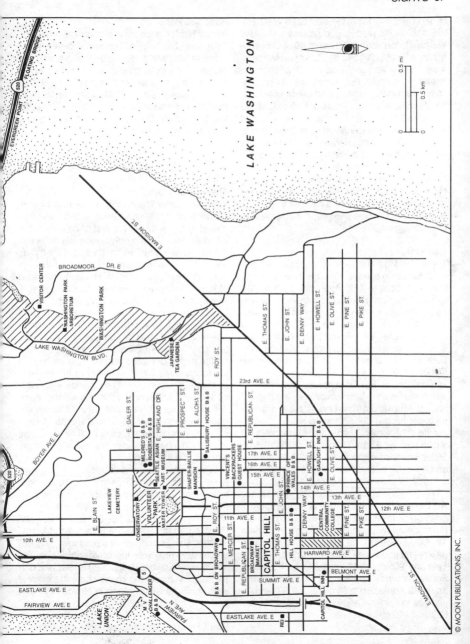

© MOON PUBLICATIONS, INC.

its denizens, fountains, views of Lake Washington, and shady, landscaped grounds. The **UW Visitors Information Center** at 4014 University Way NE, tel. (206) 543-9198, is open Mon.-Fri. 8 a.m.-5 p.m. all year. Stop here for school information, campus bus schedules, maps, upcoming sporting events, and other activities. Ninety-minute campus tours are offered Mon.-Thurs. at 2:30 p.m. and Friday at 1:30 p.m. and start from the admissions office at 320 Schmitz Hall (1410 N.E. Campus Parkway). The center of campus activity is the **Husky Union Building,** with a bookstore, newsstand, food and coffee, bowling lanes, pool tables, and more. For a taste of the good life, head to wide-open **Red Square** on a sunny spring day and join the throngs of sunseekers, Frisbee players, musicians, and brown-baggers.

Museums

The **Burke Museum** stands just inside the north entrance to the campus near the intersection of N.E. 45th St. and 17th Ave., and features an extraordinary collection of anthropological and natural-history displays. As you enter the museum you face a "treasures case" with Tlingit potlatch masks, a feathered Pomo basket, and even a ceramic horse from China's Wei dynasty. Permanent exhibits focus on Washington's geological, paleontological, and biological history, and on various Pacific cultures. The museum also features changing exhibitions, a gift shop, and totem poles out front. Downstairs is a fine little coffeehouse—it becomes a study hall during the school year. The Burke is open daily 10 a.m.-5 p.m. (till 8 p.m. Thursday), tel. (206) 543-5590. Entrance costs $5.50 adults, $4 seniors and ages 6-18, and free to kids under six as well as UW students and staff.

Washington's oldest art gallery, the **Henry Art Gallery** on the west edge of the campus, is now one of its newest. After a major expansion, the museum reopened in 1997 with more than 46,000 square feet of exhibition space. The gallery is a major facility for traveling exhibits of 19th and 20th century artists. Open Tuesday, Friday, Saturday, and Sunday 11-5, and Thursday 11-8. Admission is $5 adults, $3.50 seniors, and free to students and kids under age 13. Call (206) 543-2280 for details.

Ravenna Park

All but hidden from view in a ravine under the 15th Ave. NE bridge, Ravenna Park has 52 acres of woodlands and a babbling brook, accessible via a three-quarter-mile loop trail, plus a children's play area and soccer field, all in a most unlikely location. Douglas fir, Pacific madrone, western red cedar, big-leaf maple, and English and Pacific yew line the nature trail. A great place for a weekend stroll.

LAKE WASHINGTON AREA

The Floating Bridges

When the **Lake Washington Floating Bridge** connecting Seattle and Mercer Island was completed in 1939, it was the first of its kind in the world. Previously, the only connection between the island and mainland had been via ferry; as the ferries grew more crowded, a bridge seemed the logical solution. However, because of the 200-foot depth of the lake and the soft, mucky bottom, a conventional bridge would have been extremely expensive, if not impossible, to build. Using the concrete cell technology developed for WW I barges, the Washington Toll Bridge Authority designed a floating bridge that could withstand 90-mph winds with six-foot waves while supporting bumper-to-bumper 20-ton trucks. The bridge was supported by 25 floating concrete sections, each 350 feet long, 59 feet wide, and 14 feet high; each pontoon contains 96 watertight 14-foot-square compartments, or cells. The pontoons are cabled together and connected to stationary fixtures at either end.

When seasonal variations cause the lake level to rise or fall (as much as three feet), the pontoons attached to the stationary approaches are flooded or emptied to ensure that the rest of the pontoons maintain their flotation level. The Lake Washington (its real name is Lacey V. Murrow Floating Bridge in honor of a prominent civil engineer who also was the brother of the famed newscaster Edward R. Murrow) is now part of I-90 traffic. While being refurbished, the original sank during a winter storm in November 1990 and was then replaced. The span is just over one and a quarter mile long; the **Evergreen Point Floating Bridge,** connecting Seattle with

Bellevue and Kirkland on Route 520, is the world's longest at 1.4 miles.

Arboretum and Japanese Garden

Trees and shrubs from all over the world thrive at the 267-acre University of Washington Arboretum on Lake Washington Boulevard. A half-mile trailheads visitors past lodgepole pine, Oregon crabapple, huckleberry, Pacific dogwood, madrone, and more than 5,500 other varieties of plants. The three-quarter-mile Azalea Way path winds through cherry, Japanese maple, azalea, dogwood, and rhododendron trees and bushes; it's a gorgeous place in the spring when everything is in bloom. In the off-season, head to the Joseph A. Witt Winter Garden. The Waterfront Trail is a 1.5-mile roundtrip stroll through wooded islands and Union Bay's shores at the north end of the arboretum, passing through the largest remaining wetland in Seattle (duck sightings guaranteed). The woodchip and boardwalk trail is level, with numerous benches for resting. Pick up a nature guide at the west end, at the Museum of History and Industry, or at the arboretum visitor center. The arboretum is open daily dawn to dusk; no charge. The **Graham Visitors Center** on the north end of the park has a shop with gardening books and knick-knacks for sale. It's open daily 10 a.m.-4 p.m. Stop here for free hour-long guided tours Saturday and Sunday (Sunday only in winter) at 1 p.m.; call (206) 325-4510 for more information. A greenhouse near the visitor center sells plants propagated from the arboretum collection.

At the south end of the arboretum (near Lake Washington Blvd. E) is the 3.5-acre Japanese Tea Garden—manicured ornamental trees, a secluded pond, and an authentic teahouse (open for special tea ceremonies once a month) given to Seattle by its sister city, Kobe, in the 1960s. A very popular tea ceremony takes place on the third Saturday of each month at 1:30 p.m. The tea garden opens at 10 a.m. daily March-Nov., and closes at varying times depending upon the season. Admission is $2.50 for adults, $1.50 for kids and seniors, kids under six free; tel. (206) 684-4725.

Museum of History and Industry

Located at 2700 24th Ave. E—on the south side of Union Bay and just across the Montlake Bridge from the university—this is the city's finest historical museum, and a great place for kids. A noisy and fun exhibit on salmon fishing includes historical photos, a climb-aboard fishing boat, an "iron chink," and even an hilarious "industrial fish." Other ongoing exhibits include a walk-through 1880s Seattle street, displays on the great Seattle fire of 1889, and ornately carved figureheads from old sailing vessels. Many other exhibits change periodically. The museum is open daily 10 a.m.-5 p.m. (except Thanksgiving, Christmas, and New Year's); admission costs $5.50 adults, $3 seniors and kids (ages 6-12), $1 ages 2-5, and free for children under two. No charge on Tuesday. Call (206) 324-1126 for more information.

Other Sights

The **Northwest Puppet Center,** 9123 15th Ave. NE, tel. (206) 523-2579, is a fun place for kids, with weekend shows Oct.-May, and a puppet museum offering changing exhibits of puppets from around the globe.

Jutting into Lake Washington on a forested peninsula is **Seward Park** on Lake Washington Blvd. S and S. Juneau Street. It features trails, picnic areas, fishing, swimming, and Mt. Rainier views. A one-mile loop trail takes you past Douglas firs six feet in diameter, madrones, big-leaf maples, and the shores of Lake Washington.

WEST SEATTLE

A high bridge spans the Duwamish Waterway that separates industrial South Seattle's docks, warehouses, factories, and train tracks from quiet West Seattle. Once over the bridge you'll discover a neighborhood of simple homes and apartments with views across Puget Sound. Several shoreside parks provide places to ride bikes, walk the beaches, and enjoy the view. For photography buffs, **Hamilton Viewpoint** at California Way SW offers a panoramic view of Seattle's skyline, the Cascades, and Elliott Bay, as does **Belvedere Viewpoint** at S.W. Admiral Way and 36th Ave. SW.

For a leisurely scenic drive, head along the water on Harbor Ave. SW to Duwamish Head, then west on Alki Ave. SW to **Alki Beach Park,** a long, narrow, sandy stretch—as close to a real beach (outside Golden Gardens) as you'll find on this part of Puget Sound. In warm weather a whole beach culture emerges here—cruising cars, illegally parked vehicles, bonfires, suntan goop, the works—even though the water rarely gets above 55° F. Not far away is a Seattle classic, **Spud Fish and Chips,** 2666 Alki Ave. SW, tel. (206) 938-0606, here since 1935. Keep going on Alki Ave. to the **Alki Point Lighthouse,** tel. (206) 286-5423. Tours of the station are available weekdays by reservation.

Continue south on Beach Dr. SW to wonderful **Lincoln Park,** where you'll find great trails, playgrounds, and a long beach facing Puget Sound. A bike path follows the same scenic route. Just south of here is the **Fauntleroy** ferry dock, with connections to Vashon Island and Southworth.

SOUTH SEATTLE

The south end of Seattle is dominated by industrial developments, especially an enormous Boeing plant. The area is not especially attractive, but does contain one of Seattle's most enjoyable sights, the fabulous Museum of Flight, along with Rainier Brewery and the new football and baseball stadiums.

Museum of Flight

This world-class museum, at 9404 E. Marginal Way S, tel. (206) 764-5720, is one of Seattle's premier attractions, and the largest air and space museum on the West Coast. The main focal point is a dramatic steel and glass **Great Gallery** packed with more than 50 planes, many of which appear to be flying in formation. Everything here has been meticulously restored. Suspended overhead are a Douglas DC-3, a replica of the Wright Brothers' glider, the human-powered Gossamer Albatross II, and another 18 aircraft. An additional 40 planes sit on the tarmac below, including a Russian MiG-21, an F4C Phantom II, and the famous M/D-21 Blackbird, officially the fastest plane ever to fly. Also on the ground level is a '50s-era Aerocar III. Built by Moulton B. Taylor for the fly-and-drive crowd, the Aerocar could fly at 105 mph and convert into a car in 10 minutes. Visitors can also listen in on air traffic from busy Boeing Field at the full-size control tower exhibit here. Highly knowledgeable docents lead

tours; stop by the desk to see when the next one begins. Throughout the day, the theater screens various films about flying. Outside, visitors can walk through the first **Air Force One,** used by presidents Eisenhower, Kennedy, Johnson, and Nixon.

A second large exhibit space at the Museum of Flight is the **Red Barn,** a lovingly restored structure that was the Boeing Company's original manufacturing plant. It traces the history of flight through fascinating exhibits on two floors, including a restored 1917 Curtiss Jenny biplane and a replica of the Wright Brothers' wind tunnel. Also at the Museum of Flight are a hands-on area where kids pretend to pilot their own miniature aircraft, a Challenger Learning Center where school groups launch the space shuttle into orbit, a gift shop selling aviation paraphernalia and books, a library with an extensive collection of aviation volumes, and the Wings Cafe with light meals. More planes are arranged outside the museum. Set aside at least three hours for this extraordinary museum, especially if you're a pilot! And yes, it's okay to take photos.

Get to the museum by taking exit 158 from I-5, turning right on E. Marginal Way S, and following the signs, or by taking the No. 174 bus from downtown or the airport. The museum is open daily 10 a.m.-5 p.m., and Thursday till 9 p.m. (closed Thanksgiving and Christmas); admission is $8 adults, $7 seniors, $4 kids ages 5-17, free for kids under five. Get in free to the museum between 5 and 9 p.m. on the first Thursday of each month. On Father's Day you'll discover free admission to the museum, an outdoor barbecue, and biplane rides. Stop by during Seafair to view the Blue Angels' F/A-18 Hornets.

Sports Central

Massive changes are afoot for the area just south of Pioneer Square as the aging and disliked Kingdome (1976-2000 RIP) is being replaced by two new publicly funded stadiums. The Seattle Mariners now play baseball at the striking new **SAFECO Field,** which opened in 1999. This premier stadium seats 47,000, and has a retractable roof and real grass. Call (206) 346-4000 for details on ballpark tours.

In 1997, billionaire Paul Allen, owner of the Seattle Seahawks, persuaded King County voters to support construction of a new 67,000-seat football and soccer stadium, along with an adjacent exhibition center and parking garage. The exhibition center opened in 1999. After that, the Kingdome will be torn down and the new stadium built on the same spot. It is expected to open in 2002.

Pyramid Alehouse
Located at 91 S. Royal Brougham Way, this smoke-free microbrewery/pub is blessed with the ideal location: directly across the street from Seattle's new baseball stadium. Pyramid ales and Thomas Kemper lagers are both brewed here, and 45-minute tours and tasting ($2) are offered Mon.-Fri. at 2 and 4 p.m., and Sat.-Sun. at 1, 2, and 4 p.m. The menu includes pizzas, burgers, salmon, and shepherd's pie. Call (206) 682-3377 for more info.

Rainier Brewery
Take a free tour of Rainier Brewery, 3100 Airport Way S, tel. (206) 622-2600, Mon.-Sat. 1-6 p.m. all year. Kids must be accompanied by an adult and able to walk on their own. Take the Airport Way South exit from I-5; the brewery is on the left side. This is where they make not just Rainier ("Vitamin R"), but also many other labels of suds, including Henry Weinhard's, Black Label, Schmidt's, Heidelberg, Yakima Red, Yakima Honey Wheat, and Emerald City. Rainier was purchased in 1996 by Stroh Brewing Company. The 30-minute tour begins with a peppy 10-minute video on the company and ends in the Mountain Room, a pub (of sorts) dominated by a 12-foot wide romantic 19th-century oil painting by James Everett Stuart, *Sunset Glow—Mount Rainier.* (The gold-gilded frame alone weighs 500 pounds!) The adjacent gift shop sells beer mugs and T-shirts, but the real attraction is the beer. Visitors get three big glasses full, and can choose from nine different brands on tap; a great deal for cheapskates and boozers. The tasting room closes at 6 p.m., so folks leaving on the last tour won't get a brew unless they do their tasting before heading out. Be prepared to wait up to 45 minutes for tours in the peak tourist season.

ACCOMMODATIONS

See the "Seattle Motels and Hotels" chart for a fairly complete listing of lodging options in Seattle. Cheaper places are available, but they generally are cheap for a reason. If you're on a tight budget, stay near the airport on Pacific Hwy. S (Hwy. 99) or north of the Ship Canal on Aurora Ave. (Hwy. 99). Note that both of these "motel rows" are on heavily traveled roads with chain restaurants and ugly strip malls; try to get a room facing away from the street if you're a light sleeper. From either area it's a quick Metro bus ride to downtown. A good budget place not too far from downtown is Park Plaza Motel. Summer travelers to Seattle should make advance reservations to be sure of a room. For lodging in neighboring areas such as Bellevue, Kent, and Redmond, see the Vicinity of Seattle chapter.

In the last several years as Seattle has become an increasingly popular destination, many old downtown hotels have been totally refurbished and transformed into luxurious European-style boutique hotels. Many of the more luxurious hotels and motels offer special discount rates for business travelers or members of various organizations, so be sure to ask about them, or stop by the Convention and Visitors Bureau for a copy of the calendar of events booklet, filled with discount coupons. The bureau also offers a **Seattle Hotel Hotline,** tel. (206) 461-5882 or (800) 535-7071, through which you can make reservations at local hotels at no charge. For some reason, many of these pricey lodging places insist upon charging extra for local calls, even when you are already paying over $100 a night! Note also that parking at most downtown hotels is an extra charge, often $17 or more per day. For longer-term accommodations, check the *Yellow Pages* or local newspapers for places offering apartments and other rentals.

HOSTELS

As every young traveler knows, hostels are generally the cheapest places to stay, offering clean and safe lodging at flophouse prices. Seattle has an official hostel and several other options, including private hostels, the YMCA, and YWCA.

SEATTLE MOTELS AND HOTELS

See the text for detailed descriptions of Seattle's B&Bs and hostels. Motels and hotels are listed below from least to most expensive within each category. Rates may be lower during the winter months.

SEA-TAC AIRPORT AREA MOTELS

Note: Pacific Hwy. is also called Hwy. 99. The airport entrance is at 178th and Pacific Hwy., so addresses nearest 17800 Pacific Hwy. are closest to the airport. The numbers increase as you head south. See also the Auburn, Kent, and Federal Way chart for other nearby motels.

INEXPENSIVE

King's Arm Motel Motor Inn; 23226 30th Ave. S, Des Moines; tel. (206) 824-0300; $32-59 s, $39-65 d; outdoor pool, kitchenettes

Legend Motel; 22204 Pacific Hwy. S; tel. (206) 878-0366; $36 s or d; kitchenettes

Jet Inn Motel; 3747 S. 142nd St., Tukwila; tel. (206) 431-0085; $38-45 s or d; newer motel, fridges and microwaves

Ben-Carol Motel; 14110 Pacific Hwy. S; tel. (206) 244-6464; $38-56 s or d; kitchenettes available, local calls 30 cents, small pool, basic but clean

Tac-Sea Motel Park-Fly; 17024 International Blvd.; tel. (206) 241-6511; $40 s, $47 d; airport shuttle, AAA approved

Sea-Tac Crest Motor Inn; 18845 Pacific Hwy. S, Sea-Tac; tel. (206) 433-0999 or (800) 554-0300; $42 s, $51-62 d; airport parking, airport shuttle

Jet Motel Park 'n Fly; 17300 Pacific Hwy. S, Sea-Tac; tel. (206) 244-6255 or (800) 233-1501; $43 s, $48-53 d; outdoor pool, airport shuttle, local calls 54 cents

Continental Court All Suite Motel; 17223 32nd Ave. S, Sea-Tac; tel. (206) 241-1500 or (800) 233-1501; $45 s, $50 d; outdoor pool, airport shuttle, quiet location

New Best Inn; 23408 30th Ave. S; tel. (206) 870-1280; $45 s, $52 d

Motel 6, Sea-Tac South; 18900 47th Ave. S; tel. (206) 241-1648 or (800) 466-8356; $46 s, $52 d; outdoor pool

Motel 6, Seattle South; 20651 Military Rd. (I-5 exit 51); tel. (206) 824-9902 or (800) 466-8356; $46 s, $52 d; outdoor pool

Sea Tac Inn; 17108 Pacific Hwy. S, Sea-Tac; tel. (206) 244-1230; $46 s, $56 d; continental breakfast, airport shuttle

Motel 6, Sea-Tac Airport; 16500 Pacific Hwy. S; tel. (206) 246-4101 or (800) 466-8356; $48 s, $54 d

Spruce Motel; 14442 Pacific Hwy. S; tel. (206) 244-9930 $49 s or d; kitchenettes

Towne & Country Suites; 14800 Interurban Ave., Tukwila; tel. (206) 246-2323 or (800) 545-2323; $49-64 s, $53-64 d; country location, outdoor pool, kitchenettes available

Mini-Rate Motel; 20620 Pacific Hwy. S; tel. (206) 824-6930; $50 s, $55 d; airport shuttle

MODERATE

Howard Johnson at SeaTac Airport; 20045 Pacific Hwy. S, Sea-Tac; tel. (206) 878-3310 or (800) 872-0202; $54 s, $69 d; airport shuttle and parking, continental breakfast

Econo Lodge; 19225 Pacific Hwy. S, Sea-Tac; tel. (206) 824-1350 or (800) 223-4476; $54 s, $75 d; kitchenettes available, airport shuttle and airport parking, local calls 40 cents

Travelodge Sea-Tac Airport North; 14845 Pacific Hwy. S, Tukwila; tel. (206) 242-1777 or (800) 578-7878; $55 s, $60 d; airport shuttle, AAA approved

Silver Cloud Inn at Tukwila; 123050 48th Ave., Tukwila; tel. (206) 241-2200 or (800) 205-6941; $58-76 s, $68-86 d; outdoor pool, jacuzzi, exercise facility, continental breakfast, AAA approved

Econo Lodge-SeaTac Airport; 13910 Pacific Hwy. S, Tukwila; tel. (206) 244-0810 or (800) 553-2666; $59-69 s, $64-74 d; continental breakfast, jacuzzi, weight room, airport shuttle, airport parking, local calls 30 cents, AAA approved

Sea-Tac Airport Travelodge; 2900 S. 192nd St., Sea-Tac; tel. (206) 241-9292 or (800) 578-7878; $60 s, $66 d; sauna, airport shuttle, AAA approved

Rodeway Inn; 2930 S. 176th St., Sea-Tac; tel. (206) 246-9300 or (800) 228-2000; $60 s, $85 d; local calls 25 cents

Ramada Limited Sea-Tac; 22300 7th Ave. S, Des Moines; tel. (206) 824-9920 or (800) 272-6232; $62 s, $72 d; airport shuttle

La Quinta Inn, Sea-Tac; 2824 S. 188th St., Sea-Tac; tel. (206) 241-5211 or (800) 531-5900; $68-75 s or d; outdoor pool, jacuzzi, exercise facility, continental breakfast, airport shuttle, AAA approved

Hampton Inn Seattle Southcenter; 7200 S. 156th St., Tukwila; tel. (425) 228-5800 or (800) 476-7866; $68-100 s, $78-100 d; outdoor pool, jacuzzi, fitness center, airport shuttle, continental breakfast, AAA approved

Georgetown Inn; 6100 Corson Ave. S; tel. (206) 762-2233; $69-75 s, $79-85 d; continental breakfast, sauna, exercise room, kitchenettes available, local calls 25 cents, AAA approved

Holiday Inn Express Sea-Tac Airport; 19631 International Blvd., Sea-Tac; tel. (206) 824-3200 or (800) 465-4329; $69-99 s or d; new motel, indoor pool, sauna, jacuzzi, exercise room, airport shuttle, breakfast bar, AAA approved

Days Inn at Sea-Tac Airport; 19015 International Blvd. S, Sea-Tac; tel. (206) 244-3600 or (800) 325-2525; $74-85 s, $81-92 d; airport shuttle, continental breakfast, AAA approved

Sea-Tac Super 8 Motel; International Blvd. at 192nd St.; tel. (206) 433-8188 or (800) 800-8000; $76 s, $81-89 d

EXPENSIVE

Ramada Inn; 16838 Pacific Hwy. S, Sea-Tac; tel. (206) 248-0901 or (800) 272-6232; $78-87 s, $87-97 d; airport shuttle

Airport Plaza Hotel; 18601 Pacific Hwy. S, Sea-Tac; tel. (206) 433-0400; $80 s, $85 d; airport shuttle, local calls 40 cents, AAA approved

Comfort Inn at Sea-Tac; 19333 Pacific Hwy. S., Sea-Tac; tel. (206) 878-1100 or (800) 826-7875; $80-150 s, $85-175 d; exercise room, jacuzzi, continental breakfast, airport shuttle, AAA approved

Doubletree Inn at Southcenter Mall; 205 Strander Blvd., Tukwila; tel. (206) 575-8220 or (800) 898-4068; $89-188 s or d; outdoor pool, sauna, access to indoor pool, sauna, and jacuzzi (across the street), airport shuttle, AAA approved

Holiday Inn, Boeing Field; 11244 Pacific Hwy. S, Tukwila; tel. (206) 762-0300 or (800) 465-4329; $90 s, $98 d; outdoor pool, courtyard, airport shuttle, local calls 60 cents, AAA approved

Quality Inn SeaTac; 17101 Pacific Hwy. S, Sea-Tac; tel. (206) 246-7000 or (800) 228-5151; $90-120 s, $100-130 d; outdoor pool, sauna, exercise facility, airport shuttle, continental breakfast, AAA approved

Best Western at Southcenter; 15901 W. Valley, Tukwilla; tel. (425) 226-1812 or (800) 544-9863; $92-99 s or d; outdoor pool, sauna, jacuzzi, fitness center, airport/mall shuttle, AAA approved

(continues on next page)

SEATTLE MOTELS AND HOTELS
(continued)

WestCoast SeaTac Hotel; 18220 Pacific Hwy. S.; tel. (206) 246-5535 or (800) 426-0670; $94-102 s, $104-114 d; outdoor pool, sauna, jacuzzi, airport shuttle, AAA approved

WestCoast Gateway Hotel; 18415 Pacific Hwy. S.; tel. (206) 248-8200 or (800) 426-0670; $96 s, $106 d; fitness room, airport shuttle, local calls 50 cents

Best Western Airport Executel; 20717 Pacific Hwy. S, Sea-Tac; tel. (206) 878-3300 or (800) 648-3311; $99-129 s or d; indoor pool, exercise room, atrium, jacuzzi, sauna, continental breakfast, airport shuttle, AAA approved

Clarion Inn Sea-Tac; 3000 S. 176th St., Sea-Tac; tel. (206) 242-0200 or (800) 252-7466; $99-160 s, $109-170 d; indoor pool, jacuzzi, pass to local gym, airport shuttle

Holiday Inn, Seattle Sea-Tac; 17338 Pacific Hwy. S, Sea-Tac; tel. (206) 248-1000 or (800) 465-4329; $109 s or d; indoor pool, jacuzzi, exercise room, airport shuttle, AAA approved

PREMIUM

Courtyard by Marriott; 400 Andover Park W, Tukwila; tel. (206) 575-2500 or (800) 321-2211; $119 s or d; indoor pool, AAA approved

Hampton Inn Hotel Seattle Airport; 19445 International Blvd., Sea-Tac; tel. (206) 878-1700 or (800) 426-7866; $119 s or d; outdoor pool, exercise room, continental breakfast buffet, airport shuttle

Homewood Suites; 6955 Southcenter Blvd., Tukwila; tel. (206) 433-8000 or (800) 225-5466; $119-179 s, $129-179 d; one- and two-bedroom suites with kitchens, outdoor pool, jacuzzi, exercise facility, breakfast, airport shuttle, local calls 50 cents, AAA approved

Seattle Airport Hilton; 17620 Pacific Hwy. S, Sea-Tac; tel. (206) 244-4800 or (800) 445-8667; $125 s or d; outdoor pool, exercise room, jacuzzi, airport shuttle, local calls 65 cents, AAA approved

Wyndham Garden Hotel Seattle-Tacoma; 18118 Pacific Hwy. S, Sea-Tac; tel. (206) 244-6666 or (800) 996-3426; $129 s, $139 d; indoor pool, jacuzzi, AAA approved

Doubletree Hotel Seattle Airport; 18740 Pacific Hwy. S, Sea-Tac; tel. (206) 246-8600 or (800) 222-8733; $129-139 s, $139-149 d; outdoor pool, exercise room, concierge, airport shuttle, AAA approved

Doubletree Guest Suites Seattle; 16500 Southcenter Parkway, Tukwila; tel. (206) 246-8220 or (800) 222-8733; $149 s or d; one-bedroom suites, indoor pool, jacuzzi, sauna, racquetball courts, exercise room, airport shuttle

LUXURY

Residence Inn by Marriott-Seattle South; 16201 West Valley Hwy., Tukwila; tel. (425) 226-5500 or (800) 321-2211; $150 s or d; suites, outdoor pool, jacuzzis, kitchens, continental breakfast, airport shuttle, AAA approved

Seattle Marriott, Sea-Tac Airport; 3201 S. 176th St., Sea-Tac; tel. (206) 241-2000, (800) 643-5479, or (800) 228-9290; $154 s or d; atrium, indoor pool, sauna, jacuzzi, health club, airport shuttle, AAA approved

Embassy Suites Hotel Southcenter; 15920 West Valley Hwy., Tukwila; tel. (425) 227-8844 or (800) 362-2779; $179 s or d; large suites, outdoor pool, jacuzzi, sauna, exercise room, atrium, full breakfast, airport shuttle, local calls 75 cents, AAA approved

Radisson Hotel Seattle Airport; 17001 Pacific Hwy. S, Sea-Tac; tel. (206) 244-6000 or (800) 333-3333; $179 s or d; outdoor pool, exercise room, sauna, concierge, airport shuttle

DOWNTOWN AND VICINITY MOTELS AND HOTELS

INEXPENSIVE

Commodore Motor Hotel; 2013 2nd Ave.; tel. (206) 448-8868; $14 pp for bunk rooms (AYH card required); $39 s, $44 d for private rooms with shared baths, $49 s, $54 d private rooms with private baths; local calls 50 cents

St. Regis Hotel; 116 Stewart St.; tel. (206) 448-6366; $40 s, $47 d with bath down the hall, $50 s, $57 d with private bath; clean older hotel, no children, $7 parking

Moore Hotel; 1926 2nd Ave.; tel. (206) 448-4851 or (800) 421-5508; $44 s, $49 d; turn-of-the-century Pike Place Market area hotel, plain but clean rooms with private baths, no in-room TVs or phones, local calls 50 cents, $7 parking

Sandpiper Villas Family Motel; 11000 1st Ave. SW; tel. (206) 242-8883; $49 s, $54 d; one-bedroom suites with kitchens, outdoor pool

MODERATE

King's Inn; 2106 5th Ave.; tel. (206) 441-8833 or (800) 546-4760; $60 s, $65 d; kitchenettes $85 d

Seattle Inn; 225 Aurora Ave. N; tel. (206) 728-7666 of (800) 255-7932; $63-69 s, $79-106 d; indoor pool, jacuzzi, sundeck, game room, continental breakfast, local calls 50 cents

West Seattle Travelodge; 3512 SW Alaska St.; tel. (206) 937-9920 or (800) 578-7878; $65 s or d; kitchenettes $85 s or d, continental breakfast

Everspring Inn; 8201 Aurora Ave.; tel. (206) 789-1888 or (800) 557-7008; $65 s, $70 d; newer motel, continental breakfast, AAA approved

Eastlake Inn; 2215 Eastlake Ave.; tel. (206) 322-7726; $79 s or d; small inn near Lake Union, kitchenettes available

EXPENSIVE

Inn at Queen Anne; 505 First Ave. N; tel. (206) 282-7357 or (800) 952-5043; $79 s, $89 d; studio apartments with kitchenettes, continental breakfast, local calls 50 cents, $7 parking

Hotel Seattle; 315 Seneca; tel. (206) 623-5110 or (800) 426-2439; $80 s, $90-96 d; local calls 35 cents, $16 parking fee

Wall Street Inn; 2507 First Ave.; tel. (206) 448-0125; $85-105 s, $100-120 d; luxurious new boutique hotel, honor bars, kitchenettes available, rooftop views, full breakfast, parking fee charged

Days Inn Town Center; 2205 7th Ave.; tel. (206) 448-3434 or (800) 648-6440; $85-105 s, $89-135 d; local calls 50 cents, AAA approved

Vagabond Inn by the Space Needle; 325 Aurora Ave.; tel. (206) 441-0400 or (800) 522-1555; $89 s or d; outdoor pool, jacuzzi, continental breakfast, kitchenettes available, AAA approved

Executive Inn Express; 300 10th Ave.; tel. (206) 223-9300 or (800) 906-6226; $89-149 s or d; studios, one- and two-bedroom suites by day, week, or month, full kitchens, jacuzzi, fitness room, downtown shuttle, local calls 35 cents

Best Western Loyal Inn; 2301 8th Ave.; tel. (206) 682-0200 or (800) 238-7234; $90-102 s, $94-106 d; jacuzzi, steam room, continental breakfast, newspaper, kitchenettes available, local calls 35 cents, AAA approved

Pacific Plaza Hotel; 400 Spring St.; tel. (206) 623-3900 or (800) 426-1165; $95-125 s or d; European-style hotel, continental breakfast, local calls 50 cents, $13 parking fee, AAA approved

(continues on next page)

SEATTLE MOTELS AND HOTELS
(continued)

Inn at Virginia Mason; 1006 Spring St.; tel. (206) 583-6453 or (800) 283-6453; $98-115 s, $118-145 d; remodeled European hotel, courtyard, quiet location, local calls 35 cents, $5 parking, AAA approved

Travelodge by the Space Needle; 200 6th Ave. N; tel. (206) 441-7878 or (800) 578-7878; $99-109 s or d; outdoor pool, jacuzzi, continental breakfast, AAA approved

Ramada Inn Downtown; 2200 5th Ave.; tel. (206) 441-9785 or (800) 272-6232; $99-129 s, $109-175 d; $10 parking fee, in-room safes, AAA approved

WestCoast Camlin Hotel; 1619 9th Ave.; tel. (206) 682-0100 or (800) 426-0670; $99-175 s or d; outdoor pool, $9 parking fee

Quality Inn City Center; 2224 8th Ave.; tel. (206) 624-6820 or (800) 437-4867; $105-180 s or d; jacuzzi, sauna, exercise room, kitchenettes available, continental breakfast, newspaper, bikes available, AAA approved

Sixth Avenue Inn; 2000 6th Ave.; tel. (206) 441-8300 or (800) 648-6440; $109-120 s, $120-132 d; local calls 50 cents, AAA approved

Hampton Inn and Suites; 700 5th Ave. N; tel. (206) 282-7700 or (800) 476-7866; $109-129 s or d; new motel, breakfast buffet, exercise facility, newspaper, AAA approved

PREMIUM

Marqueen Hotel; 600 Queen Ave. N (near Seattle Center); tel. (206) 282-7407; $109-219 s, $119-229 d; new boutique hotel, rooms and suites available

WestCoast Vance Hotel; 620 Stewart St.; tel. (206) 441-4200 or (800) 426-0670; $110-120 s, $120-130 d; classic hotel, local calls 50 cents, $9 parking fee, AAA approved

Silver Cloud Inn-Seattle Downtown Lake Union; 1150 Fairview Ave. N; tel. (206) 447-9500 or (800) 551-7207 ext. 11; $110-200 s or d; new motel, indoor and outdoor pools, jacuzzis, exercise facilities, fridges, continental breakfast

Best Western Executive Inn; 200 Taylor Ave. N; tel. (206) 448-9444 or (800) 351-9444; $115-145 s, $130-165 d; jacuzzi, exercise room, downtown shuttle, local calls 50 cents, AAA approved

Holiday Inn Express; 226 Aurora Ave. N; tel. (206) 441-7222 or (800) 465-4329; $119-129 s, $129-139 d; new hotel, indoor pool, exercise room, continental breakfast

Hawthorn Suites—Seattle Center; 520 Roy St.; tel. (206) 282-2600 or (800) 527-1133; $119-144 s or d; newer hotel, studio suites, breakfast buffet, local shuttle, full kitchen, fireplaces and balconies, evening reception, three-night minimum stay in summer, weekly rates available, AAA approved

Plaza Park Suites; 1011 Pike St.; tel. (206) 682-8282; $125-340 s or d; outdoor pool, suites with kitchens and fireplaces, jacuzzi, steam room, sauna, exercise room, continental breakfast, shuttle service, valet parking $15, AAA approved

Seattle City Center Travelodge; 2213 8th Ave.; tel. (206) 624-6300 or (800) 578-7878; $129 s, $135 d; AAA approved

The Madison Hotel, A Renaissance Hotel; 515 Madison St.; tel. (206) 583-0300 or (800) 468-3571; $130-199 s or d; indoor pool, jacuzzi, health club, concierge, newspaper, parking $14, AAA approved

Residence Inn by Marriott-Seattle Downtown; 800 Fairview Ave. N; tel. (206) 624-6000 or (800) 331-3131; $130-220 s or d; suites with kitchens, indoor pool, sauna, jacuzzi, exercise room, local shuttle, newspaper, buffet breakfast, central atrium, local calls 50 cents, AAA approved

Best Western Pioneer Square Hotel; 77 Yesler Way; tel. (206) 340-1234 or (800) 800-5514; $139-149 s, $149-159 d; beautifully restored 1914 hotel on Pioneer Square, continental breakfast, local calls 40 cents, $15 parking fee, AAA approved

Sheraton Seattle Hotel & Towers; 1400 6th Ave.; tel. (206) 621-9000 or (800) 325-3535; $140-250 s or d; indoor pool, jacuzzi, sauna, concierge, parking $18, local calls 75 cents, AAA approved

WestCoast Roosevelt Hotel; 1531 7th Ave.; tel. (206) 621-1200 or (800) 426-0670; $145-180s or d; $15 parking fee, local calls 75 cents, fitness center, concierge

Tower 801 Apartments; 801 Pine St.; tel. (206) 623-8013 or (800) 447-4918; $145-225 s or d; one and two-bedroom apartments, full kitchens, outdoor pool, sauna, health club access

WestCoast Paramount Hotel; 724 Pine St.; tel. (206) 292-9500 or (800) 426-0670; $149-169 s, $169-325 d; new downtown luxury hotel, fitness center, valet parking

Hotel Edgewater; 2411 Alaskan Way (Pier 67); tel. (206) 728-7000 or (800) 624-0670; $149-235 s, $149-250 d; Seattle's only hotel on Puget Sound, parking $10, downtown shuttle, local calls 81 cents, AAA approved

LUXURY

Inn at the Market; 86 Pine St.; tel. (206) 443-3600 or (800) 446-4484; $150-325 s or d; shuttle service, health club, valet parking $17, local calls 75 cents, AAA approved

Inn at Harbor Steps; 1221 1st Ave.; tel. (206) 748-0973 or (888) 728-8910; $160-200 s or d; indoor lap pool, jacuzzi, sauna, fireplaces, wet bars, fridges, garden views, fitness facility, full breakfast

Mayflower Park Hotel; 405 Olive Way; tel. (206) 623-8700, (800) 426-5100 (U.S. and Canada), or (800) 562-4504 (in Washington); $160-350 s or d; European style hotel, $12 valet parking, AAA approved

Houseboat Hideaways; tel. (206) 323-5323; $165 d for 28-foot houseboat; $195 d for 35-foot or 40-foot houseboats; unique Lake Union accommodations with kitchenettes

Hotel Vintage Park; 1100 5th Ave.; tel. (206) 624-8000 or (800) 624-4433; $165-215 s, $180-230 d; luxury four-star hotel, valet parking $18, local calls 75 cents, health club, wine reception, concierge, in-room Internet access, AAA approved

Seattle Hilton Downtown; 6th Ave. & University St.; tel. (206) 624-0500 or (800) 542-7700 or (800) 426-0535; $165-250 s or d; parking $18, local calls 75 cents, AAA approved

Crowne Plaza Hotel Seattle; 1113 6th Ave.; tel. (206) 464-1980, (800) 521-2762; $179-199 s or d; jacuzzi, sauna, exercise facilities, valet parking $18, local calls 50 cents, AAA approved

Sorrento Hotel; 900 Madison St.; tel. (206) 622-6400 or (800) 426-1265; $190-240 s, $210-260 d; historic luxury hotel, downtown shuttle service, fitness center, concierge, parking $17, local calls 80 cents, AAA approved

Hotel Monaco; 1101 4th Ave.; tel. (206) 621-1770 or (800) 945-2240; $195-275 s, $210-295 d; new luxury hotel, fitness center evening wine reception, AAA approved

The Warwick Hotel; 401 Lenora St.; tel. (206) 443-4300 or (800) 426-9280; $200 s, $220 d; luxury hotel, indoor pool, jacuzzi, sauna, exercise facility, newspaper, parking $15, downtown shuttle, AAA approved

Alexis Hotel; 1007 1st Ave.; tel. (206) 624-4844 or (800) 426-7033; $210-220 s, $225-235 d; suites for $245-365 d (some with jacuzzi tubs); luxurious four-star European-style hotel, complimentary wine tasting, fitness club, steam room, newspaper, concierge, valet parking $18, AAA approved

The Westin Hotel, Seattle; 1900 5th Ave.; tel. (206) 728-1000 or (800) 228-3000; $210-250 s, $230-310 d; indoor pool, jacuzzi, saunas, sundeck, fitness center, newspaper, parking $15, AAA approved

Four Seasons Olympic Hotel; 411 University St.; tel. (206) 621-1700 or (800) 332-3442, (800) 268-6282 (inside Washington), or (800) 223-8772 (outside Washington); $285-325s, $325-385 d; grand luxury hotel, indoor pool, jacuzzi, saunas, health club, newspaper, valet parking, local calls 75 cents, AAA approved (five diamonds)

(continues on next page)

SEATTLE MOTELS AND HOTELS
(continued)

NORTH END MOTELS

Most of these hotels are on North Seattle's "motel row," Aurora Ave. (Hwy. 99). See the rooms first at the cheapest motels to make sure they meet your standards.

INEXPENSIVE

Park Plaza Motel; 4401 Aurora Ave. N; tel. (206) 632-2101; $35 s, $38 d; phone calls 35 cents, friendly and clean

Shoreline Motel; 16526 Aurora Ave. N; tel. (206) 542-7777; $35-45 s or d; kitchenettes available

Thunderbird Motel; 4251 Aurora Ave. N; tel. (206) 634-1213; $40 s, $46 d; kitchenettes $46 s, $52 d; local calls 20 cents

Nites Inn; 11746 Aurora Ave. N; tel. (206) 365-3216; $45 s, $55 d

La Hacienda Motel; 5414 1st Ave. S; tel. (206) 762-2460 or (800) 553-7531; $46-50 s, $50-75 d; itchenettes available, continental breakfast, local calls 25 cents, AAA approved

Marco Polo Motel; 4114 Aurora Ave. N; tel. (206) 633-4090 or (800) 295-4090; $48-52 s, $52-56 d; kitchenettes available, AAA approved

Georgian Motel; 8801 Aurora Ave. N; tel. (206) 524-1004; $50 s or d; kitchenettes available

Quest Inn; 14817 Aurora Ave. N; tel. (206) 367-7880; $55 s or d; kitchenettes available

Casabel Motel; 3938 Whitman N (off Aurora Ave.); tel. (206) 632-8200; $58-68 s or d; kitchenettes available, quiet location, local calls 50 cents

MODERATE

University Motel; 4731 12th Ave. NE; tel. (206) 522-4724 or (800) 522-4720; $57 s, $63 d; suites with kitchenettes, local calls 25 cents, AAA approved

Emerald Inn Motel; 8512 Aurora Ave. N; tel. (206) 522-5000; $60-70 s, $65-75 d; kitchenettes available, two-night minimum stay in summer, AAA approved

College Inn; 4000 University Way NE; tel. (206) 633-4441; $60-83 s, $50-72 d; historic 1909 University District hotel, bath down the hall, continental breakfast

Black Angus Motor Inn; 12245 Aurora Ave. N; tel. (206) 363-3035; $64-90 s or d; local phone calls 30 cents

Aurora Seafair Inn; 9100 Aurora Ave. N; tel. (206) 522-3754 or (800) 445-9297; $65-75 s, $70-80 d; kitchenettes available, local calls 25 cents, AAA approved

Days Inn North Seattle; 19527 Aurora Ave. N; tel. (206) 542-6300 or (800) 329-7466; $79-89 s or d; continental breakfast, kitchenettes available

University Travelodge; 4725 25th Ave. NE; tel. (206) 525-4612 or (800) 578-7878; $79-89 s or d; outdoor pool, kitchenettes available, AAA approved

EXPENSIVE

Best Western Evergreen Inn; 13700 Aurora Ave. N; tel. (206) 361-3700 or (800) 213-6308; $80-135 s, $92-135 d; continental breakfast, jacuzzi, sauna, exercise room, AAA approved

Best Western Continental Plaza; 2500 Aurora Ave. N; tel. (206) 284-1900 or (800) 238-7234; $86-120 s, $96-128 d; outdoor pool, continental breakfast, Lake Union vistas, kitchenettes available, AAA approved

Seattle Ramada Inn at Northgate; 2140 N. Northgate Way; tel. (206) 365-0700 or (800) 272-6232; $89-119 s, $99-129 d; outdoor pool, jacuzzi, exercise facility, kitchenettes available, continental breakfast, AAA approved

University Inn; 4140 Roosevelt Way NE; tel. (206) 632-5055 or (800) 733-3855; $90-125 s, $100-135 d; outdoor pool, jacuzzi, fitness room, continental breakfast, local calls 25 cents, AAA approved

Silver Cloud Inn—University District, 5036 25th Ave. NE, tel. (206) 526-5200 or (800) 205-6940; $91-132 s, $101-142 d; indoor pool, jacuzzi, exercise room, continental breakfast, kitchenettes available, AAA approved

University Plaza Hotel; 400 NE 45th St.; tel. (206) 634-0100 or (800) 203-3403; $95 s, $105 d; outdoor pool, fitness room, AAA approved

Edmond Meany Hotel; 4507 Brooklyn Ave. NE; tel. (206) 634-2000 or (800) 899-0251; $109 s, $119 d; University District 15-story hotel, exercise room, newspaper, local calls 35 cents, AAA approved

LUXURY

Claremont Hotel; 2004 4th Ave.; tel. (206) 448-8600 or (800) 448-8601; $149-209 s or d; historic luxury hotel, continental breakfast, kitchenettes available, $14 parking fee

Cavenaughs on 5th Ave.; 1415 5th Ave.; tel. (206) 971-8000 or (800) 325-4000; $170-185 s, $185-200 d; exercise room, parking $16, 75 cents for local calls; AAA approved

The **Hostelling International Seattle** is in the heart of town at 84 Union St., tel. (206) 622-5443, and just steps away from Pike Place Market. The hostel beds in 20 small dorm rooms cost $15-17 for AYH members, or $18-20 for nonmembers. A couple of private rooms cost $38 d for AYH members or $43 d for nonmembers; reserve these three months ahead for summer visits. Reservations are imperative June-Sept.; be sure to reserve at least a week or two ahead. The hostel has no curfew, though you'll need to ring the bell if you come in after 2 a.m. It has storage lockers and a full kitchen, but no alcohol is allowed. Be sure to ask about discounts to many local attractions. Travelers sometimes complain that the hostel's small rooms and bustling atmosphere give it a sterile feeling, but it is cheap, clean, and perfectly located. Parking costs $9.

American Backpackers' Hostel, 126 Broadway Ave. E, tel. (206) 720-2965 or (800) 600-2965, is a clean small hostel just off bustling Broadway Ave. in Capitol Hill. Facilities include a full kitchen and pool table, and a make-yourself continental breakfast is provided. Airport pickups are available for two or more. Dorm rooms cost $15 pp; three private rooms are $35 s or $40 d. The hostel is only open to those with an international passport or an out-of-state student ID card.

Seattle's largest private hostel, **Green Tortoise Backpacker's Guest House,** has 35 rooms right in the center of town at 1525 2nd Ave., tel. (206) 282-1222 or (888) 424-6873. It's near Pike Place, but the neighborhood also has its share of sleaze. The hostel itself is clean, well-managed, and friendly. Accommodations here are primarily for international travelers; you'll need a passport or airline ticket to stay here. Dorm rooms cost $16 pp, and private rooms go for $40 s or d; bath down the hall. The hostel has storage lockers, a full kitchen, voice mail services, and daily walking tours and videos. There is no curfew, and alcohol is okay. Parking costs $7 per day. As with other Seattle lodging places, the Green Tortoise fills up quickly in the summer; call ahead for reservations. The hostel is connected with the Green Tortoise Bus, tel. (800) 867-8647, a great and inexpensive way to explore the country; see "Transportation," below, for details.

Another relatively inexpensive lodging option is the **Downtown YMCA,** 909 4th Ave., tel. (206) 382-5000 or (800) 474-9622, where rooms for both men and women (bath down the hall) cost $41 s, or $51 d. Stay here and get free use of all the Y's facilities, including a pool, sauna, jacuzzi, and weight room. Parking costs $10 per day.

Women can stay at **YWCA of Seattle,** 1118 5th Ave., tel. (206) 461-4888, where rooms go for

$33-38 s, or $44-50 d with shared or private baths. Cooking facilities are provided, along with access to the indoor pool and health club ($5 extra). No curfew.

The **Commodore Motor Hotel,** 2013 2nd Ave., tel. (206) 448-8868, has a few dorm spaces for AYH members at $14 pp in bunk rooms. This older hotel doesn't have kitchen facilities, but parking is free.

Vincent's Backpackers Guest House, 527 Malden Ave. E, tel. (206) 323-7849, has a poor reputation and isn't always clean, but the Capitol Hill neighborhood is quiet and safe, and parking is free. The hostel has a communal kitchen, storage lockers, and no curfew. Call for airport pickups. Rules are lax, and alcohol is allowed. Beds in the three crowded dorms go for $14 pp including a make-yourself continental breakfast.

BED AND BREAKFASTS

Seattle has a number of outstanding B&Bs, particularly in the Capitol Hill neighborhood, where many of the places are historic mansions. See the *Yellow Pages* for a complete listing of local B&B reservation services. Two good ones are the **Seattle B&B Association,** tel. (206) 547-1020 (http://uspan.com/sbba); and **A Pacific Reservation Service,** tel. (206) 431-0932 (www.seattlebedandbreakfast.com). Some of the cities surrounding Seattle have less expensive B&Bs; check them out in **Vicinity of Seattle** chapter.

Seattle's B&Bs are described below by location within the city. Unless otherwise noted, all serve a full breakfast and do not allow children. If you are visiting Seattle in the summer months, make B&B reservations two months ahead.

Capitol Hill B&Bs
One of Seattle's oldest and most desirable neighborhoods, the quiet residential streets of Capitol Hill are home to more than a dozen classic bed and breakfasts. One of the most impressive is **Bacon Mansion B&B,** 959 Broadway Ave. E, tel. (206) 329-1864 or (800) 240-1864. This superb 1909 Tudor mansion sprawls over four levels, with an adjacent carriage house. Inside the mansion you'll find marble fireplaces, crystal chandelier, grand piano, and 10 guest rooms with shared or private baths. A continental break-

fast is served; $74-129 s or $84-139 d. Kids accepted.

The stately **Shafer-Baillie Mansion Guest House,** 907 14th Ave. E, tel. (206) 322-4654 or (800) 922-4654, sits along "Millionaire's Row" on Capitol Hill, with 14 attractively decorated guest rooms, most with private baths. This English-manor-style mansion was built in 1914, and is popular for weddings. A continental breakfast is served; $85-145 s or d. Kids accepted.

Built in 1904, **Salisbury House B&B,** 750 16th Ave. E, tel. (206) 328-8682, is a grand Capitol Hill home with a wrap-around porch and a flowery backyard. The public rooms are large and bright, and the five guest rooms all have private baths; $79-130 s or $89-140 d.

One of Seattle's more unusual B&Bs is **Landes House,** 712 11th Ave. E, tel. (206) 329-8781 or (888) 329-8781. The owners of this 1906 craftsman house cater to gays, but pride themselves on being "straight friendly." A continental breakfast is served, and guests can relax in the clothing-optional hot tub. Rooms are $69-110 s or d, or $180 d for a two-bedroom apartment.

Roberta's B&B, 1147 16th Ave. E, tel. (206) 329-3326, is housed in a turn-of-the-century home on a quiet tree-lined street. The five spacious guest rooms are furnished with antiques and have private baths; $90-120 s or $100-130 d.

Built in 1903, **Capitol Hill Inn,** 1713 Belmont Ave., tel. (206) 323-1955, has six guest rooms (private or shared baths) decorated in European and Asian antiques. A friendly mother-daughter team runs this old Victorian that was once a brothel. Two rooms have private jacuzzis. Three-night minimum in summer; $85-155 s or $100-165 d.

Another turn-of-century Victorian home, **Prince of Wales B&B,** 133 13th Ave. E, tel. (206) 325-9692 or (800) 327-9692, has four guest rooms with private baths. Guests discover panoramic views of downtown Seattle from the front porch; $99-125 s or d. Kids welcome. Two-night minimum in summer.

Built in 1890, **Bed & Breakfast at Mildred's,** 1202 15th Ave. E, tel. (206) 325-6072, is an attractive Capitol Hill Victorian with a wrap-around porch facing Volunteer Park. It has three guest rooms, private baths, and the living room contains a grand piano and fireplace. Kids are welcome; $105 s or $120 d.

Hill House B&B, 1113 E. John St., tel. (206) 720-7161 or (800) 720-7161, is a classic 1903 Victorian home with five tastefully appointed rooms and private or shared baths. Two night minimum on summer weekends; $80-130 s or d.

Housed in an historic 1905 home, the stately **Gaslight Inn,** 1727 15th Ave. E, tel. (206) 325-3654, is one of the larger B&Bs in Seattle, with 16 rooms (private or shared baths), a library, outdoor pool, and continental breakfast. It frequently books up far ahead, so reserve early for the summer; $68-158 s or d.

Bed & Breakfast on Broadway, 722 Broadway E, tel. (206) 329-8933 or (888) 329-8933, is a 1906 home with the original stained glass windows, oriental rugs, a fireplace, and a grand piano. The four guest rooms have private baths. A continental breakfast is served; $85-105 s or $95-115 d.

Travelers will find reasonably priced accommodations at **Capitol Hill House B&B,** 2215 E. Prospect, tel. (206) 322-1752, a nicely furnished 1932 brick home with three guest rooms, and shared or private baths; $55-75 s or d.

Capitol Hill Guest House B&B, 1808 East Denny Way, tel. (800) 281-6971, has rooms on both a short- and longterm basis. The 1908 home has been nicely decorated, and some rooms look across to the Cascades. A gourmet kitchen is available; $59-89 s or $69-99 d.

Queen Anne B&Bs

Enjoy comfortable living at **Blue Willow B&B,** housed in a 1910 foursquare home at 213 W. Comstock, high atop Queen Anne Hill. The home has three antique-furnished guest rooms with private baths, and a small garden. Kids over age three are welcome; $70-85 s or d. For details, call (206) 284-3730.

Green Gables Guesthouse, 1503 2nd Ave. W, tel. (206) 282-6863 or (800) 400-1503, consists of two craftsman homes, one built in 1904, and the second dating from 1911. Outside is a charming rose garden. The eight guest rooms are furnished with antiques, and have private or shared baths; $69-129 s or $79-139 d. Children welcome.

Queen Anne Hill B&B, 1835 7th Ave. W, tel. (206) 284-9779, is a 1907 home with English gardens and panoramic vistas. The five guest rooms have shared or private baths, and a big continental breakfast is served; $99-109 s or d.

Beech Tree Manor, tel. (206) 281-7037, is a turn-of-the-century home atop Queen Anne Hill. The inn features seven guest rooms with private or shared baths, plus English decor, a period fireplace, and wicker rockers on the shady porch. Kids over age five are welcome; $59-115 s or d.

Downtown and Lake Union B&Bs

In the heart of Pike Place Market at 1923 1st Ave., **Pensione Nichols B&B,** tel. (206) 441-7125 or (800) 440-7125, is Seattle's only downtown B&B. This European-style B&B has 10 antique-furnished guest rooms with shared baths for $60 s or $85 d, plus two suites ($160 for four people) with great views across Puget Sound. A continental breakfast is served and kids are welcome.

Seattle's most unusual B&B is the "Bunk & Breakfast" **Tugboat *Challenger,*** 1001 Fairview N, tel. (206) 340-1201. This is a retired 96-foot oceangoing tug that has been cleaned up and redecorated. Tied up permanently at the west end of Lake Union, it has eight cabins. Rates are $55 s in tiny cabins, or $80-170 d for larger rooms. The same folks offer lodging in several other boats on Lake Union, including a 1938 tugboat available for $200 d.

North Seattle B&Bs

Chelsea Station on the Park, 4915 Linden Ave. N, tel. (206) 547-6077 or (800) 400-6077, is directly across from the rose gardens at the south entrance to Woodland Park Zoo, within walking distance of Green Lake. The 1929 Federal Colonial brick home has nine guest rooms with private baths; $90-130 s or $95-135 d.

Dibble House B&B, 7301 Dibble Ave. NW, tel. (206) 783-0320, has five guest rooms with shared or private baths in a 1920s Ballard home. The owner runs a catering service, so you know the breakfasts are good. Room rates are among the lowest in Seattle: $55-65 s or d, and kids are accepted.

The Chambered Nautilus B&B, 5005 22nd Ave. NE, tel. (206) 522-2536 or (800) 545-8459, offers Cascade views on a hill within walking distance of the university. This Georgian Colonial home was built in 1915, and is the only B&B close to campus. There's a library and pleasant sun porch, and the six large guest rooms all have private baths; $84-114 s or $89-119 d. It often fills up fast, so book early.

Chez Sharon B&B, 8068 26th Ave. NW, tel. (206) 789-6660, has a quiet Ballard district suite facing a flower-filled garden. A continental breakfast is served; $85 s or d. No kids.

Other Seattle B&Bs

Scandia House B&B, 2028 34th Ave. S, tel. (206) 725-7825, is located in a distinctive modern home with panoramic views across Lake Washington. The one guest suite includes a private bath and deck; $100 s or d.

Villa Heidelberg B&B, 4845 45th Ave. SW, tel. (206) 938-3658 or (800) 671-2942, is a West Seattle craftsman home built in 1909, with a wraparound porch, six guest rooms, private or shared baths, pleasant gardens, and impressive views across Puget Sound; $70-110 s or $80-120 d. Two night minimum in summer.

Three Tree Point B&B; 17026 33rd Ave. SW, Burien; tel. (206) 669-7646 or (888) 369-7696, has a private suite with a patio offering views of Puget Sound. The fridge is stocked for a make-your-own breakfast. Guests get a day pass to a local fitness club. Rates are $125 s or d.

Near Sea-Tac Airport, **The Guest House B&B,** 1121 SW 160th, tel. (206) 439-7576, has a private two-bedroom suite with a living room, fireplace, sundeck, jacuzzi, and gardens. A continental breakfast is served; $115 s or d.

Also near the airport is **Soundview B&B,** 17600 Sylvester Rd. SW, Burien, tel. (206) 243-8687 or (888) 244-5209, a self-contained house for folks wanting privacy. Guests will love the bluff-side outdoor deck and hot tub overlooking Puget Sound and the Olympic Mountains. A continental breakfast is provided; $125 s or d.

CAMPING

There are no public campgrounds in the immediate vicinity of Seattle, but **Fay-Bainbridge State Park** has year-round campsites on Bainbridge Island, just a short ferry ride away. You'll need a car or bike to get to the park from the ferry dock (it's six miles away). Other state park campgrounds around Seattle are in Federal Way (Dash Point State Park), Enumclaw (Kanaskat-Palmer Recreation Area), and Des Moines (Saltwater State Park). See appropriate sections for complete descriptions. The closest Forest Service campgrounds are in the Cascades at least 35 miles to the east on I-90.

The closest private RV parks are: **Holiday Park Resort,** 19250 Aurora Ave. N, near Kenmore, tel. (206) 542-2760; **KOA Seattle/Tacoma,** 5801 S. 212th, in Kent, tel. (253) 872-8652 or (800) 562-1892; **Bryn Mawr Beach,** 11448 Rainier Ave. S, in Renton, tel. (206) 772-3000; **Twin Cedars RV Park,** 17826 Hwy. 99 N, tel. (800) 878-9304; **Vasa Park Resort,** 2560 W. Lake Sammamish Rd. SE in Bellevue, tel. (206) 746-3260; and **Trailer Inns RV Park,** 15531 SE 37th in Bellevue, tel. (425) 747-9181 or (800) 659-4684.

FOOD AND DRINK

The listing below is only a minuscule sampling of Seattle's food and drink options. If you are serious about your meals out, take a gander at a specific guide to Seattle dining. Three of the best are published by Sasquatch Books, the book-publishing arm of *The Seattle Weekly*. *Seattle Best Places* covers top-end restaurants, *Seattle Cheap Eats* is more practical if you aren't on an expense account, and *Offline Restaurant Guide,* has excellent descriptions of more than 500 area restaurants. You'll find the same info—in an updated form—on the Web at www.seattle.sidewalk.com. Assume all restaurants to be moderately priced for the type of food or drink offered, unless otherwise mentioned. See also "Entertainment" later in this chapter for places offering meals and fresh-brewed beer.

BREAKFAST

The team of Peter Levy and Jeremy Hardy has managed to tap into the perfect recipe for success on the Seattle breakfast scene, with three eateries scattered around town: Capitol Hill's **Coastal Kitchen,** 429 15th Ave. E, tel. (206)

322-1145; Wallingford's **Jitterbug,** 2114 N. 45th St., tel. (206) 547-6313; and Queen Anne's **5 Spot,** 1502 Queen Anne Ave. N, tel. (206) 285-7768. Each of these has its own character—Coastal Kitchen has a more varied fare and out-of-this-world pancakes, Jitterbug delivers such specials as huevos rancheros and wild mushroom omelettes, along with equally popular weekday "blunches." The 5 Spot emphasizes all-American comfort food. You will not go wrong at any of these, but be ready for a mob scene if you wake up after 9 a.m. on Sunday morning. All of these also offer down-home American cooking for lunch and dinner.

14 Carrot Cafe, 2305 Eastlake Ave. E, tel. (206) 324-1442, is located along a busy industrial street, but cranks out delicious breakfasts in a spacious atmosphere.

Not far away is **Mae's Phinney Ridge Cafe,** 6412 Phinney Ave. N, tel. (206) 782-1222, a cow-infested place complete with a "Moo Room" for milk shakes and displays of cow paraphernalia. The food is all made from scratch and includes big, sticky cinnamon rolls and scrumptious hash browns. And yes, it gets jammed on weekends.

Another great place (actually two of them) where you'll have to fend off the weekend brunch crowds is **Julia's,** 4401 Wallingford Ave., tel. (206) 633-1175, and 5410 Ballard Ave. NW, tel. (206) 783-2033. The food is tasty, with lots of vegetarian items and a lively atmosphere. On Capitol Hill, **Glo's,** 1621 E Olive Way, tel. (206) 324-2577, is a fun little place with great eggs benedict and Belgian waffles for breakfast.

Right in Pike Place Market at 1600 Post Alley is **Cafe Campagne,** tel. (206) 728-2233, the downstairs neighbor of the more ostentatious Campagne (see "French," below). The cafe serves all three meals, but their breakfasts ($7-13) are a relative bargain. Try the Provençal eggs.

COFFEE AND TEA

Latteland

If you can't find an espresso cafe within a block of any Seattle shopping district, your eyes are closed. It's hard to know where to begin when it comes to coffee in this place where coffee consumption tops that of any other American city.

With hundreds of espresso bars, carts, and drive-ups all over Seattle, you would be hard-pressed to *not* find a great cup of java. The best known, of course, is **Starbucks,** with over 40 shops scattered across the city, including the original shop in the Pike Place Market. Named for the coffee-drinking first mate in *Moby Dick,* Starbucks is considered by many the godfather of quality coffee in the Northwest. That first store opened in 1971, offering perfectly roasted beans and a commitment to quality; roasted beans more than a week old are given to charities. The employees of Starbucks also have a reputation for being very knowledgeable about coffee and can help neophytes with the intricacies of the various espresso drinks. In recent years the company has become a national phenomenon, expanding into major cities throughout the U.S. and Canada. You can even order it by phone; call (206) 447-1575 or (800) 445-3428. (Seattleites will be shocked to learn that espresso was a fixture in the Bay Area in Northern California years before it migrated north; Berkeley's Caffe Mediterraneum has been pouring the brew since the 1950s.)

After Starbucks, most of the espresso shops are small operations with just one or a handful of locations. **Cafe Septieme,** 414 Broadway E, tel. (206) 860-8858, has the charm of a Parisian cafe and is a romantic place to enjoy a big bowl of cappuccino. Four other great places to sip espresso are: **B&O Espresso,** 204 Belmont E, tel. (206) 322-5028, 401 Broadway Ave. E, tel. (206) 328-3290, and 103 Cherry St., tel. (206) 621-9372; **Uptown Espresso,** 525 Queen Anne N, tel. (206) 285-3757; **Torrefazione Italia,** 320 Occidental S, tel. (206) 624-5847, and 1310 4th Ave., tel. (206) 583-8970, and 622 Olive Way, tel. (206) 624-1429; and **Cafe Paradiso,** 1005 E. Pike St. (Capitol Hill), tel. (206) 322-6960.

Still Life in Fremont, 709 N. 35th St., tel. (206) 547-9850, is a wonderful coffeehouse with healthy sandwiches, rich soups, chocolate desserts, and espresso served in a bright and oft-crowded cafe.

A rambling old house at 50th and University Way NE contains one of the U District's classic places, **Grand Illusion Coffeehouse,** tel. (206) 523-3935. The art crowd sprawls in the funky chairs and couches, sipping coffee, reading books, and waiting for films in the adjacent arthouse theater here.

Most Seattle coffeehouses are entirely smoke-free, but the **The Last Exit,** 5211 University Way NE, tel. (206) 528-0522, violates this with a vengeance. The main room is always a dense cloud of fumes, and is jammed with a noisy mix of aging longhaired beat-generation poets, tie-dyed college kids, and frumpy street folks. The cluttered, mismatched furnishings and hippie-style art on the wall fit the crowd. The coffee is always great, and you can escape the smoke in the back room, where you're likely to meet folks playing chess or the addictive game of Magic. Last Exit on Brooklyn opened in 1967 (the first real coffeehouse in Seattle) and was on Brooklyn St. (hence the name) until a couple of years ago when it was forced to relocate. Another old favorite—it opened in 1975—is just a few blocks down: **Cafe Allegro,** 4214 1/2 University Way NE (it actually faces the alley on 15th St.), tel. (206) 633-3030. It's still a popular sit-down-and-stay-awhile espresso house with three rooms spread over two floors.

Teahouses

The **Teacup,** 2207 Queen Anne N, tel. (206) 283-5931, sells almost a hundred varieties of teas from all over the globe and always has something interesting to taste. The Chinese-style **Teahouse Kuan Yin,** 1911 N. 45th St., tel. (206) 632-2055, is connected to Wide World Books and offers a taste of Asian teas, along with light meals. For a taste of old England, don't miss **The Crumpet Shop,** tel. (206) 682-1598, in Pike Place Market, where you get delicious fresh crumpets and a steaming pot of tea.

DELIS AND LIGHT MEALS

Countless places around Seattle serve quick lunches, and the U District, Capitol Hill, and Pike Place Market are all packed with eateries for folks on the run, from pizza-by-the-slice to sushi. The better grocery market chains (PCC, QFC, and Larry's) all have excellent delis inside. Downtown, don't miss **DeLaurenti Market,** tel. (206) 622-0141, in Pike Place Market. Wander through the aisles for gourmet imported groceries and wines, or stop by the deli (Cafe Mangia Bevi) for salads and outstanding panini (grilled sandwiches). The garlic bread and eggplant dishes at

Cuchina Fresca, 1904 Pike Place, tel. (206) 448-4758, are some of the best you'll ever find. **Kosher Delight,** 1509 1st Ave., tel. (206) 682-8140, is a true Jewish deli near the Pike Place Market. Philly cheesesteak lovers will want to visit another Pike Place delicatessen, **Philadelphia's Deli,** tel. (206) 464-1899. A wonderful Italian deli with fresh pastas, breads, and salads, is **Pasta & Co.,** in University Village Mall, tel. (206) 523-8594.

AMERICAN

Looking for the best burger in town? The argument rages, but the public votes with their feet (and mouths) for **Dick's Drive-In,** 111 N.E. 45th St. (Wallingford), tel. (206) 632-5125. The food at this straight-from-the-'50s joint consists of greasy fries, fat burgers, and wonderful chocolate milk shakes. There's almost always a line out front on a summer evening. Dick's also can be found at 115 Broadway Ave. E (Capitol Hill), tel. (206) 323-1300, 9208 Holman Rd. NW (Crown Hill), tel. (206) 783-5233, and 12325 30th Ave. NE (Lake City), tel. (206) 363-7777. Another very popular place for burgers and BLTs (along with delightful breakfasts and famous cinnamon rolls) is **Hi-Spot Cafe,** 1410 34th Ave. (Madrona), tel. (206) 325-7905.

Two Bells Tavern, 2313 4th Ave., tel. (206) 441-3050, is an offbeat place jammed at lunchtime with artists, wanna-be artists, and folks on the fringe, along with the button-down set. They all come here for some of the best and biggest burgers in Seattle, served on sourdough rolls and topped with fried onions. The menu expands to include tasty soups, salads, and other well-prepared pub grub.

For "comfort food" in a no-frills setting, it's pretty hard to beat **The Bells,** 8501 5th Ave. NE (Northgate), tel. (206) 524-3100. They've been here for over 45 years and still serve the all-American favorites the way your mom made them, including meatloaf, beef stew, baked potatoes, homemade soups, and tapioca pudding.

Delcambre's Ragin Cajun, 1523 1st Ave., tel. (206) 624-2598, serves a delicious Cajun lunch or dinner of red beans and rice, spicy gumbos, sausage, and jalapeno cheese bread. For genuine soul food with a Louisiana touch, head to **Thompson's Point of View,** 2308 E. Union St., tel. (206) 329-2512. The menu includes catfish, big meaty burgers, and gumbos.

Belltown Billiards, 90 Blanchard St., tel. (206) 448-6779, is one of Seattle's newest "in" spots in the hip Belltown District near Seattle Center. The 12 custom tables attract pool sharks, and the food parade is led by pizzas, pastas, and fish.

The two **13 Coins** are Seattle's classiest 24-hour restaurants and gathering places for both the famous and the infamous. They offer more than 130 menu items in two locations: 125 Boren Ave. N (downtown), tel. (206) 682-2513; or 18000 Pacific Hwy. S, tel. (206) 243-9500, near Sea-Tac Airport (entertainment nightly here).

Metropolitan Grill, 820 2nd Ave., tel. (206) 624-3287, is one of the best places in town for steak, and it fills up with business folk at lunch. Seafood (including great clam chowder), pork, lamb, and pastas are also on the menu. Expensive. Another favorite steakhouse, Hiram's at the Locks," is described under "Dining with a View," below.

NORTHWEST CUISINE

The Painted Table in the Alexis Hotel at 92 Madison St., tel. (206) 624-3646, serves Northwest cuisine with a flair that has gained a national following and the accolades of critics. The innovative menu changes, but always includes outstanding seafood and pastas, plus unusual salads. Each place setting has handpainted plates from local artists. Dinner entrees are $17-27.

Dahlia Lounge, 1904 4th Ave., tel. (206) 682-4142, is a trendy eatery with widely varied and spicy fare created by famed chef Tom Douglas. Quite expensive, but a wonderful place for a memorable meal.

Marco's Supperclub, 2510 1st Ave., tel. (206) 441-7801, is a bright and arty Belltown place with a menu that bumps from grilled salmon to Jamaican jerk chicken to fried sage leaf appetizers (much better than it sounds). The food is always creative, and the atmosphere is relaxed. Entrees cost $12-18.

Georgian Room, in the Four Seasons Olympic Hotel at 411 University St., tel. (206) 621-7889, is an elegant dining room with a Renaissance look and Northwest cuisine. The food is very expensive but much lighter than what you might expect in a luxury hotel. The salmon, sturgeon, rabbit, lamb, veal, and steaks are cooked to a creative perfection, and the menu also includes a five-course vegetarian dinner that has garnered national praise. Expect to pay around $100 for a dinner for two with wine and dessert.

Fuller's, in the Sheraton Hotel at 1400 6th Ave., tel. (206) 447-5544, has cuisine that consistently receives national awards, including such flavorful specials as Ellensburg lamb, gorgonzola and pear stuffed beef tenderloin, and sautéed salmon. The modernistic artwork here is equally gorgeous, including glass by Dale Chihuly and a collection of paintings by Mark Tobey and Morris Graves.

SEAFOOD

Given its waterfront location, it should come as no surprise that Seattle's specialty is fresh seafood of all types. The city is jammed with seafood restaurants of all levels, from the takeaway fish-and-chips joints to luxury dining that will set you back $40 pp and more.

With five species of oysters grown in Puget Sound waters—including the native Olympia oyster—Seattle is becoming known as one of the best places to slurp fresh oysters on the half-shell. **Emmett Watson's Oyster Bar,** tel. (206) 448-7721, is one of the best of these, a relaxed little place in the Soames-Dunn Building at Pike Place Market, with reasonable prices and ultra-fresh oysters, plus great salmon soup or fish and chips. **Elliott's Oyster House & Seafood Restaurant,** Pier 56, tel. (206) 623-4340, is one of the better seafood restaurants on the waterfront, with crab, clams, and freshly shucked oysters. Expensive, but a fantastic location.

Ray's Boathouse, 6049 Seaview Ave. W, tel. (206) 789-3770, is north of the Ship Canal along Shilshoe Bay, with outstanding views over Puget Sound at sunset (be sure to reserve a window table) and perfectly prepared oysters, fish, and other fresh seafood. This large and attractive place has a slightly nautical design with wooden floors and beams like an old boat shed, and it is a bit expensive (expect a bill of $25 pp), but the seafood is great. Reservations are a must. You can save money and avoid the crowds by arriving weeknights 5-6 p.m. Upstairs is a spacious and equally popular cafe serving a lighter menu, including oysters and fish and chips.

Anthony's Homeport, 6135 Seaview Ave. W, tel. (206) 783-0780, is just up the road, with moderately priced fresh fish and a saucy cioppino; Sunday brunch, too. Delightful vistas from the windows across Lake Union. See also other members of the Anthony's family: Anthony's Pier 66 and Bell St. Diner, listed below under "Dining with a View."

For truly creative Northwest seafood cooking in a trendy setting, you will not go wrong at **Etta's Seafood,** in Pike Place Market at 2020 Western Ave., tel. (206) 443-6000. Great mixed drinks too. Another new place getting rave reviews is Belltown's **Flying Fish,** 2234 1st Ave., tel. (206) 728-8595. The food is beautifully presented, and the atmosphere is raucous. Take a seat in the bar to survey the crowd below. Expensive but worth it.

Ivar's Acres of Clams, on the waterfront at Pier 54, tel. (206) 624-6852, was folksinger Ivar Haglund's original restaurant (open since 1938). The restaurant is an unpretentious, cavernous seafood place with a take-out bar on the sidewalk that attracts lines of tourists (and some locals). The Ivar's chain now has several other locations, the most notable one being **Ivar's Salmon House** on Lake Union at 401 N.E. Northlake Way, tel. (206) 632-7223; it's located in a cedar facsimile of an Indian longhouse with historic photos and Tlingit carvings on the walls, and dugout canoes hanging from the rafters. This is a fantastic waterside location with an outside deck (summers only) looking across the lake to downtown Seattle. Unfortunately, the food at both these Ivar's is decent, but not great. A better bet may be to stop by the Whale Maker Lounge at the Salmon House for happy hour (free hors d'oeuvres Mon.-Fri. 4-6:30 p.m.), and to check out the rather intimidating (for males at least) killer whale "whalemakers." You're more likely to get a window seat here than in the restaurant.

DINING WITH A VIEW

The **Space Needle Restaurant,** tel. (206) 443-2100 or (800) 937-9582, is a top-of-the-world dining experience at 500 feet, very popular with tourists, visiting relatives, and teens on prom night. The food is mediocre and expensive (of course), but the view is unsurpassed, as the revolving restaurant completes a 360-degree turn by the time you get to dessert.

The **Cloud Room** atop the Camlin Hotel at 1619 9th Ave., tel. 292-6206, has great cityscape and Lake Union views. The Northwest cuisine is inspired and well prepared. A fine place for a romantic evening; pricey.

Cutter's Bay House, 2001 Western Ave., tel. (206) 448-4884, just up the street from Pike Place Market, has a lively bar with a long list of hors d'oeuvres; their specialties—mako shark, fresh Northwest fish, and regular pasta and prime rib dishes—are moderately priced and accompanied by an extensive wine-by-the-glass and imported beers list. This is one of Seattle's prime check-out-the-studs/babes places for the yuppie crowd. Sunsets over the Olympics are striking.

Chandler's Crabhouse, 901 Fairview Ave. N, tel. (206) 223-2722, is on the south shore of Lake Union with views north across the lake. The specialties here are crab dishes of all sorts, including a flavorful whiskey crab bisque. Dependably good seafood in a busy waterfront setting. A great place to watch the seaplanes landing and taking off.

Salty's on Alki, 1936 Harbor Ave. SW, tel. (206) 937-1600, claims to have the best view of the Seattle skyline from its Lake Union location. The overpriced menu features seafood and steaks.

Located right along the Chittenden Locks, **Pescatore,** 5300 34th Ave. NW, tel. (206) 784-1733, is a great place to watch the boats go by. Meals are a mix of pasta and seafood specials, and can be a bit uneven. The Sunday brunch is popular.

A bright and elegant waterfront place, **Anthony's Pier 66,** 2201 Alaskan Way, tel. (206) 448-6688, serves a seafood menu that includes award-winning clam chowder, fresh mahi mahi, scallops, crab fettucine, and other favorites. Dinner entrees are $20-25. Downstairs at the more casual **Bell St. Diner** the menu also focuses on fresh seafood, but prices are lower and the wine list is smaller. Both places have delightful patios overlooking Elliot Bay.

Other places with great views include Adriatica (see "Middle Eastern and Indian," below), Copacabana Bolivian Restaurant (see "South of the Border," below), and Maximilien in the Market (see "French," below). Anthony's Homeport, Ivar's Salmon House, and Ray's Boathouse are seafood restaurants (described above) with over-the-water vistas.

PIZZA

Seattle's best quick pizza place is **Pizzeria Pagliacci**, with three sit-down locations around town: 4529 University Way NE, tel. (206) 632-0421; 426 Broadway Ave. E, tel. (206) 324-0730; and 550 Queen Anne Ave. N, tel. (206) 285-1232. This is about as close as you can get to real New York style pizzas: perfect thin crusts and distinctive toppings. They always have several types of pizzas available by the slice, as well as calzones and lasagna, or order a full one with your favorite toppings. Call (206) 726-1717 for delivery.

Another pizza place with a loyal following and eight Seattle-area locations is **Romio's Pizza,** 2001 W. Dravus (Queen Anne), tel. (206) 284-6878. A special favorite are pizzas on a garlic crust. Several of the other Romio's are: 3242 Eastlake Ave. E (Eastlake), tel. (206) 322-4453; 8523 Greenwood Ave. N (near Green Lake), tel. (206) 782-9005; and 917 Howell St. (downtown), tel. (206) 622-6878.

Zeek's Pizza, 41 Dravus St. (Queen Anne), tel. (206) 285-8646, is known for its unusual pizzas and crowds of students. They also sell pizza by the slice. Another very good pizza operation is **Guido's Pizzeria,** 7900 E. Green Lake Dr. N (Green Lake), tel. (206) 522-5553, and 2108 N.E. 65th St., tel. (206) 525-3042 (Ravenna).

The **Original Pioneer Square Pizza Co.,** 614 1st Ave. (next door to Doc Maynard's), tel. (206) 343-9103, has great thin crust pizzas, including pizza by the slice. **Nicolas Pizza & Pasta,** 1924 N. 45th, tel. (206) 545-9090, is a fine Wallingford sit-down pizza place with a spacious dining area and an open kitchen.

EUROPEAN

Italian

You can have a pricey Italian feast on Pioneer Square at **Umberto's,** 100 S. King St., tel. (206) 621-0575. **Al Boccalino,** 1 Yesler Way (Pioneer Square), tel. (206) 622-7688, has one of the finest and freshest Italian meals anywhere. Especially notable are the prawns and garlic served over a bed of sautéed spinach, and the saddle of lamb. Good Italian wine list, too. Downtown, visit **Isabella Ristorante,** 1909 3rd Ave., tel. (206) 441-8281, with a splashy decor and perfect pastas, grilled meats, and wood-fired pizzas.

For an very good southern Italian eatery, visit **Salvatore Ristorante Italiano,** 6100 Roosevelt Way NE (U District), tel. (206) 527-9301. Specials include veal dishes, linguine with clams, and pasta with red hot peppers, tomatoes, capers, anchovies, and olives. They also have a fine choice of antipastos and Italian wines.

Il Terrazzo Carmine, 411 1st Ave. S, tel. (206) 467-7797, is a delightful Pioneer Square restaurant that's perfect for a romantic dinner. The pasta is cooked to perfection. Expensive, but a fine, special place.

French

For impressive French cuisine, the fairly expensive **Le Gourmand** is at 425 N.W. Market St. in Ballard, tel. (206) 784-3463. And certainly try **Crêpe de Paris,** Rainier Square, 1333 5th Ave., tel. (206) 623-4111, which was one of the first French restaurants in Seattle. It's very popular for lunch.

Campagne, 86 Pine St., tel. (206) 728-2800, is a four-star place with elegant service and a French-inspired Northwest menu. Priced to match the quality. The restaurant sits in the heart of Pike Place Market. Downstairs is the more accessible Cafe Campagne (see "Breakfast," above). Another good Pike Place restaurant with French inspirations is **Maximilien in the Market,** tel. (206) 682-7270, with views across Elliott Bay and lamb, fish, veal, and beef entrees.

Other European

For a light Greek meal, try Capitol Hill's **El Greco,** 219 Broadway Ave. E, tel. (206) 328-4604. Out in the U District, the **Continental Restaurant,** 4549 University Way NE, tel. (206) 632-4700, is a longtime favorite for inexpensive Greek meals. They also have a fine deli here. If you're just looking for a fast gyro, stop by **Mr. D's** in Pike Place Market, tel. (206) 622-4881.

For Russian meals, try **Kaleenka,** a homey, lace-curtained change of pace at 1933 1st Ave., tel. (206) 728-1278. The piroshkis, chicken Kiev, and borscht are all excellent. Not far away is **Labuznik,** 1924 1st Ave., tel. (206) 441-8899, with rich, meaty dishes from Eastern Europe. Expensive.

SOUTH OF THE BORDER

Seattle has plenty of places with standard Tex-Mex meals, along with dozens of take-away shops selling burritos, tacos, and other standard south-of-the-border fare. One of the most popular local chains is **Taco del Mar,** with a dozen places scattered around town. Their huge Mission style burritos are always good, and fish tacos are a local favorite. Another very popular local chain is **World Wraps,** with an Asia-meets-Mexico fast food menu. Try their Thai chicken wrap.

Fremont's **El Camino,** 607 N. 35th St., tel. (206) 632-7303, is a great little nouvelle Mexican place with chiles rellenos, baby back ribs, and fantastic margaritas. Good for breakfast too.

Cactus, 4220 E. Madison St., tel. (206) 324-4140, is another popular place with a blend of Spanish and Southwest dishes. You'll find a fun tapas bar, Indian fry bread, fajitas, enchiladas, and lots of more unusual dishes.

Copacabana Bolivian Restaurant, tel. (206) 622-6359, is a wonderful place on a sunny day, with a patio overlooking Pike Place Market. It's easy to find, just walk down the street through the market and look up to find folks sitting back for a beer in the sun. The spicy South American food is flavorful and hearty.

ASIAN AND MIDDLE EASTERN

Chinese

As you might guess, the International District is laden with Asian restaurants. Among the best

is **House of Hong,** 409 8th Ave. S, tel. (206) 622-7997, with dim sum, seafood, chicken, and Hong Kong barbecue (inexpensive to moderate). Things get crowded in the evening, but the dim sum carts always have something appealing on board. **Tai Tung,** 659 S. King St., tel. (206) 622-7372, is the real thing, packed with Chinese from the neighborhood and longtime Seattleites who consistently rate it an International District favorite. The food can be inconsistent, so your best bet is to look around and see what others are eating for a clue on what to order.

Sea Garden, 509 7th Ave. S, tel. (206) 623-2100, serves Cantonese meals, but the food isn't the bland chow mein you might expect. Instead, the menu offers a wide range of soups, many seafood specialties, and perfectly cooked vegetables. It's also open till midnight most nights.

For Chinese food with a difference, head to the always-crowded **Black Pearl,** 7347 35th Ave. NE (Wedgewood), tel. (206) 526-5115. Watch the busy cooks in the open kitchen, and enjoy the friendly service and distinctive dishes such as a battered eggplant fried with vegetables, or green onion and smoked salmon pancakes. But be ready for a wait most evenings. Save time and order out; they have free delivery to the north end of town. The same folks run **Pandasia,** 1625 W. Dravus St. (Magnolia), tel. (206) 283-9030.

The U District has a big cluster of cheap student-oriented places with heaping helpings of Chinese food. Just walk up University Way NE to see what looks good. A personal favorite is **Mandarin Chef,** 5022 University Way NE, tel. (206) 528-7596, with homemade noodles and dumplings for practically nothing. Good mu shu dishes too.

Japanese

Musashi's Sushi & Grill, 1400 N. 45th St. (Wallingford), tel. (206) 633-0212, is an always-crowded, friendly little place with inexpensive fresh sushi (the main attraction), chicken teriyaki, and *bento* box lunches.

HaNa Restaurant, 219 Broadway Ave. E, tel. (206) 328-1187, on Capitol Hill is another very popular place for *bento* box lunches, salmon teriyaki, sushi, sashimi, tempura, and other simple meals. Just up the street is a fine Japanese noodle house, **Kitto Japanese Noodle House,**

614 Broadway Ave., tel. (206) 325-8486, with simple but tasty bowls of *yakisoba,* teriyaki, and *udon.*

Kiku Tempura House, 5018 University Way NE, tel. (206) 524-1125, is one of the most popular student eateries on the "Ave." The tempura and teriyaki are quick and delicious, and you get huge portions. Great for a quick lunch or evening meal.

Another popular student place with made-to-order sushi and huge portions of teriyaki is **Tokyo Garden Teriyaki,** 4337 University Way NE, tel. (206) 632-2014. Order at the counter and wait for your number to be called. You'll get a big side of rice topped with teriyaki sauce, and a bowl of miso soup to go with the delicious teriyaki chicken or beef. Recommended.

Kamon on Lake Union, 1177 Fairview Ave. N, tel. (206) 622-4665, is a big place along the east side of Lake Union, with a splashy yuppified decor and excellent fresh sushi.

Out in Lake City (north of the U District) is **Toyoda Sushi,** 12543 Lake City Way NE, tel. (206) 367-7972, with some of the freshest and most succulent sushi anywhere around. This immaculately clean little shop also has excellent meat dumplings *(gyoza),* vegetable rolls, and fresh fish entrees. It gets crowded most nights.

For an upscale meal, **Nikko,** in the Westin Hotel at 1900 5th Ave., tel. (206) 322-4641, is best known for its outstanding sushi bar—considered by many to be the finest in Seattle—accompanied by a rather pricey Japanese menu that includes sukiyaki, teriyaki, tempura, and *kaiseki* dinners. Stop by earlier in the day for the *bento* box lunches.

Thai

For Thai cuisine, try the **Thai Restaurant** near the Seattle Center at 101 N. John St., tel. (206) 285-9000, **Jai Thai,** 3423 Fremont Ave. N, tel. (206) 632-7060, or **Bahn Thai,** 409 Roy St., tel. (206) 283-0444; all three are inexpensive and popular with the locals. **Bangkok Cafe/Araya Places,** 4730 University Way NE, tel. (206) 524-3220, is split into two halves, Bangkok Cafe, offering a full range of dishes, and Araya Places, cooking up vegetarian specialties from the same kitchen (but separate cooking surfaces). Prices are reasonable, and the food is artfully prepared

and excellent. They also have an all-you-can-eat lunch buffet.

Thai Thai Restaurant, 11205 16th Ave. SW, tel. (206) 246-2246, is out of the way, but well worth the drive. The food is spicy hot, with great Thai noodles, soups, and chicken angel wings.

Middle Eastern and Indian

The U District and nearby Wallingford have a corner on the market for the best in Indian and Middle Eastern restaurants. You won't go wrong at **Cedars Restaurant,** 1319 N.E. 43rd St., tel. (206) 632-7708, or the larger Cedars a few blocks away at 4759 Brooklyn Ave. NE, tel. (206) 527-5247. Great Lebanese meals (especially the falafels), plus Indian specialties and an Indian grocery at the Brooklyn location.

Chutney's 519 1st Ave. E, tel. (206) 284-6799, is one of Seattle's best Indian restaurants, a casual downtown place with spicy exotic meals in a beautiful setting. Prices are reasonable, especially for lunch. Chutney's also has restaurants in Wallingford and Capitol Hill.

Neelam's Authentic Indian Cuisine, 4735 University Way NE, tel. (206) 523-6830, lives up to its name with outstanding and very spicy East Indian meals. It has Tandoori and vegetarian specialties (but no beef), plus wonderful curries. The onion *kulcha* bread is hard to beat. Another extremely popular and reasonable U District student hangout is **Tandoor Indian Restaurant,** 5024 University Way NE, tel. (206) 523-7477.

Kabul, 2301 N. 45th St. (Wallingford), tel. (206) 545-9000, creates reasonably priced Afghan cuisine, including quite a few vegetarian dishes such as sautéed eggplant with a tomato, yogurt, and mint sauce. The food has obvious Indian influences but is distinctively different. The basmati rice spiced with saffron and pepper and topped with raisins and nuts is a treat in itself. Kabul has live sitar music on midweek evenings.

Adriatica, 1107 Dexter Ave. N, tel. (206) 285-5000, is an eastern Mediterranean restaurant on the west side of Lake Union with a great view across the lake and skyline. The food is pricey but wonderful, especially the fried calamari and the chocolate espresso soufflé. Another fine Middle Eastern restaurant is **Mediterranean Kitchen,** 366 Roy St. (Queen Anne), tel. (206) 285-6713, where the food is always packed with garlic, and the portions are enormous. Excellent and reasonable.

Other Asian

Wild Ginger, 1400 Western Ave., tel. (206) 623-4450, gets rave reviews from local food critics, and jumps all over Asia; Vietnamese, Thai, Indonesian, and Sichuan Chinese dishes all come out of this creative kitchen. Wild Ginger is best known for its *satay* bar that features skewered and grilled seafood, chicken, pork, and vegetables, but also offers delicious curries, soups, and crab. The menu changes seasonally.

Phobac Restaurant, 2815 S Hanford St. (International District), tel. (206) 725-4418, is a haven for those of us who love the Vietnamese staple, a flavorful soup called pho. It's all they serve, so you know they do it right here! In the U District, get inexpensive and tasty Vietnamese lunches at **My's Restaurant,** 4220 University Way NE, tel. (206) 634-3526. This immensely popular student eatery dishes up huge portions of pho and fried noodle specials, including several vegetarian specialties.

Rasa Malyasia is now a small chain, with six local take-away shops; the largest (and the original) is in Pike Place Market, tel. (206) 624-8388. Stop here for Malaysian noodle dishes topped with meats, shrimp, or vegetables, along with a spicy peanut sauce.

NATURAL AND VEGETARIAN FOOD

Juicebars

Ed's Juice & Java, 7900 E. Greenlake Dr., tel. (206) 524-7570, is a small shop that often has a line out front on summer weekends. Located along Green Lake, they squeeze all sorts of fresh juices and also offer espresso drinks. Another good place for smoothies and juices is **Rainbow Juice Bar,** inside Capitol Hill's Rainbow Natural Grocery at 417 15th Ave. E, tel. (206) 329-8440.

Vegetarian Restaurants

The **Gravity Bar,** 113 Virginia St. (downtown), tel. (206) 448-8826, and 415 Broadway Ave. E (Capitol Hill), tel. (206) 325-7186, has a gleaming 21st-century decor and attracts a noisy and trendy DIB (dressed-in-black) art crowd. The food is all healthy and well prepared, with fresh-squeezed juices (over 75 juice combinations offered), flavor-packed steamed veggies with brown rice, great salads, and espresso. If you're feeling adventurous, try the wheat grass shots, also available from your nearby lawnmower.

For a funkier Capitol Hill atmosphere, eat at **Globe Cafe,** 1531 14th Ave. E, tel. (206) 324-8815, a worker-owned place with simple vegan food and reasonable prices. **Bamboo Garden,** 364 Roy St., tel. (206) 282-6616, is a popular Chinese vegetarian restaurant near Seattle Center.

Cafe Flora, 2901 E. Madison St., tel. (206) 325-9100, is one of the city's best-loved vegetarian restaurants. Everything is fine, but the rustic polenta is especially notable. They also offer offbeat pizzas and portabello Wellington (grilled portabello mushrooms with pecan pâté and leeks in a puff pastry).

For more vegetarian eats, see also Julia's, described above under "Breakfast," Georgian Room, described above under "Northwest Cuisine," plus Araya Places, Kabul, Neelam's Authentic Indian Cuisine, and Wild Ginger, described above under "Asian and Middle Eastern."

MARKETS, GROCERS, AND BAKERIES

Fish Markets

Everyone knows about the fishmongers in **Pike Place Market,** where the fish are always fresh and the entertainment comes at no extra charge, but Seattle also has several other fine places to buy fresh seafood. **Mutual Fish Company,** 2335 Rainier Ave. S, tel. (206) 322-4368, has old-time service and the quality you'd expect from Japanese owners. Another place with a long heritage and excellent fresh fish, crabs, and chicken is **University Seafood & Poultry,** 1317 N.E. 47th St., tel. (206) 632-3900, in the U District.

Farmers Markets

Everyone's favorite place to buy fresh produce is **Pike Place Market** (described above), where the produce is always beautifully presented. Unfortunately, prices are not any cheaper than in the grocery stores, and many of the stalls insist upon selecting items for you. Get pesticide-free produce at the market during **Organic Farmer Days** on Sunday and Wednesday 10 a.m.-5 p.m. from mid-June through October. Another option in the summer is the **University District Farmers Market,** held Saturday 9 a.m.-2 p.m. June-Oct. on the corner of 50th St. NE and University Way NE. The **Columbia City Farmers Market,** 4801 Rainier Ave. S, is held Wednesday 3 p.m.-7 p.m. The **Fremont Sunday Market** brings a farmers market, jewelry, flea market, and live music to N. 34th St. in Fremont between late April and Christmas. During the winter months they move inside a parking garage at 400 N. 34th Street. It takes place Sunday 10 a.m.-4 p.m.

Grocers and Wineshops
As might be expected, Seattle has quite a few high-quality natural and organic grocers. The best-known is **Puget Consumers' Co-op,** a.k.a. "PCC," with seven stores around Seattle offering bulk foods, organic produce, and other healthy edibles. You don't have to be a member to shop here, though prices are a bit lower if you join this 35-plus year old cooperative. Several of the markets—notably the stores in Ravenna (6504 20th Ave. NE, tel. 525-1450) and Fremont (716 N. 34th St., tel. 632-6811)—have fine delis with both vegetarian and meat dishes. For membership information and other store locations, call (206) 547-1222. Two other excellent natural foods stores in Capitol Hill are the nonprofit **Central Co-op Grocery** at 1835 12th Ave., tel. (206) 329-1545, and **Rainbow Grocery,** 417 15th Ave. E, tel. (206) 329-8440.

Seattle has most of the major West Coast chains—Albertson's, Safeway, Red Apple, and Thriftway—along with several local grocery chains that rival Nordstrom in service and presentation of products. **QFC** stands for Quality Food Stores, and their 19 Seattle stores do indeed stress service. Another local favorite is **Larry's Markets,** a small chain with gourmet foods, artfully designed stores, big delis, and fresh breads and produce. At least one of their stores even has valet parking. **Uwajimaya,** at 519 6th St. S in the International District, tel. (206) 624-6248, is a large store selling high-quality Asian groceries. **DeLaurenti Market,** tel. (206) 622-0141, in Pike Place Market is filled with gourmet imported groceries and wines from

Europe. Other excellent places for wines include the tiny brick **Esquin Wine Merchants** shop at 1516 1st Ave. S, tel. (206) 682-7374. They are big on Italian wines but also carry Northwest varieties and offer tastings, classes, and reasonable prices. **Pike and Western Wine Merchants** at the Pike Place Market has groceries, along with a diverse choice of Northwest wines. Another noteworthy shop is **La Cantina Wine Merchants,** tel. (206) 525-4340, in the University Village Mall.

Bakeries and Sweets
When it comes to chocolates, it is pretty hard to beat **Dilettante Chocolates,** 416 Broadway E (Capitol Hill), tel. (206) 329-6463, where you'll also find a light menu of soups, salads, and sandwiches. Dilettante has three other shops scattered around Seattle.

One of the finest places for rich and rustic breads is **Grand Central Bakery,** 214 1st Ave. S, tel. (206) 622-3644. They also crank out perfect pastries and exquisite espressos.

Macrina Bakery and Cafe, 2408 1st Ave., tel. (2060 448-4032, is an absolutely wonderful Belltown bakery and cafe with earthy breads, light lunches, and perfect lattes. A fine place to hang out Seattle-style.

The Urban Bakery, 7850 E. Greenlake Dr. N, tel. (206) 524-7951, is another great spot for fresh-from-the-oven baked goods, including scrumptious chocolate cakes, cheesecakes, and pies. The espresso bar is a favorite stopping place for the Green Lake post-jogging crowd. **Honey Bear Bakery,** 2106 N. 55th St. (Wallingford), tel. (206) 545-7296, is a favorite neighborhood place for an espresso and pastry (try the white chocolate brownies) with the groovy crowd.

Great Harvest Bread Co., 5408 Sand Point Way NE, tel. (206) 524-4873, bakes deliciously seasoned whole-wheat breads and always has free slices to taste with a dollop of butter. **Three Girls Bakery,** in existence since 1912, is one of the Pike Place Market institutions, serving some of the finest croissants and sweets in town. A small inside counter offers a more relaxed setting. For something different, stop by the QFC, Larry's, or PCC markets to try a loaf of bread made by the **Spent Grain Baking Co.,** made from the sweet grains left behind in the beer brewing process at local microbreweries.

Five Loaves and Fishes, 2719 E. Madison St. (Broadmoor area), tel. (206) 726-7989, has big, dense loaves of spelt (wheatless) bread, along with more traditional breads, sweets, and healthy vegetarian lunches and vegetable juices. You'll get a dose of Seventh-Day Adventist literature with your meal; closed Saturday. Great ice cream too.

Seattle's most unusual bakers include **The Erotic Bakery,** 2323 N. 45th St. (Wallingford), tel. 545-6969, with X-rated cakes and pastries, and **Three Dog Bakery,** 106 Union St. (downtown), tel. (206) 364-9999, with freshly baked dog cakes and biscuits.

Lots of bagel places in Seattle, but my vote goes for a Berkeley import, **Noah's Bagels,** with nine Seattle area locations, including 220 Broadway E. (Capitol Hill), tel. (206) 720-2925. Other good places include **Bagel Oasis,** 2112 N.E. 65th St., tel. (206) 526-0525, and 462 N. 36th St., tel. (206) 633-2676; and **Seattle Bagel Bakery,** 1302 Western Ave., tel. (206) 624-2187.

ENTERTAINMENT AND EVENTS

In the early '90s Seattle gained a reputation as a center for alternative/grunge music, with local bands such as Nirvana, Pearl Jam, Soundgarden, Alice in Chains, and Foo Fighters gaining an international following. Seattle's music scene continues to change, and by the time you read this it will be off in a new direction. The best entertainment guides are several free papers that show up every week or two at stores or in paper boxes throughout the city. *The Seattle Weekly* has articles on politics and Seattle goings-on, along with concert information, club dates, restaurant reviews, movie, lecture, sports, dance, theater listings, phone sex ads, and page after page of singles ads. Find the same info online at www.seattleweekly.com. Another freebie, *The Stranger* (www.thestranger.com), has a gen-X edge, and is the best source for upcoming music; all the nightclubs advertise here (as do the cigarette companies in search of new smokers). Farther from the mainstream is *The Rocket,* with music reviews written from a decidedly cynical perspective. Enough teen angst to fill a bathtub. The *Seattle Times* Thursday edition and *Seattle Post-Intelligencer* Friday edition also have weekly entertainment sections packed with details on dance, dining, theater, movies, and literary events. For the latest fine arts exhibitions, pick up a copy of *Art Access* from a local gallery, or find them on the Web at www.artaccess.com.

NIGHTLIFE

Brewpubs and Hangouts

In recent years the Northwest has become a center for high quality handcrafted ales. True, most folks still swill down Rainier or Budweiser, but the microbrewed specialty beers have gained in popularity as people discover the difference between quantity and quality. Hale's Ales Brewery, Dad Watson's Brewery, and Redhook Ale Brewery are described above (**Fremont**), as is Pyramid Alehouse (**South Seattle**).

The Pike Pub & Brewery, 1415 1st Ave., tel. (206) 622-6044, is a very popular and friendly place in the heart of the market, with some of the best micros anywhere (including XXXXX Stout). Right next door is a good place for supplies to brew your own beer: **Liberty Malt Supply Company,** tel. (206) 622-1880 or (800) 990-6258, along with the small **Seattle Microbrewery Museum.**

Out in the U District is **Big Time Brewery and Alehouse,** 4133 University Way NE, tel. (206) 545-4509, with several fresh-brewed ales on tap and an 80-year-old backbar where you can enjoy the passing scene through the big front windows.

Join the loud sporting crowd at **Pacific Northwest Brewing Co.,** 322 Occidental S, tel. (206) 621-7002, near the stadiums. Good beers that change with the seasons, a trendy atmosphere, and a menu that includes sandwiches, oysters on the half shell, bratwurst, and other light meals. It really hops after football or baseball games. Another place with a similar atmosphere, but a bigger menu, is **F.X. McRory's Steak Chop & Oyster House** at 4199 Occidental Ave. S, tel. (206) 623-4800. They don't brew beer here, but they do offer 26 different Northwest microbrews on tap and fresh oysters on the half-shell.

Other pubs with on-the-premises breweries include: **McMenamins Pub & Brewery,** 200

Roy St. (Queen Anne), tel. (206) 285-4722, **Maritime Pacific Brewing Co.,** 1514 N.W. Leary Way (Ballard), tel. (206) 782-6181, and **California and Alaska St. Brewery,** 4720 California St. SW (West Seattle), tel. (206) 938-2476.

The U District's **Blue Moon Tavern,** 712 N.E. 45th St. (no phone), is one of the most famous old-time hangouts in Seattle, the sort of place that once attracted the likes of Allen Ginsberg, Jack Kerouac, and Tom Robbins. It still brings in the Deadheads on Sunday nights for a jukebox jam.

Pioneer Square Bars

Ten bars in the Pioneer Square area have banded together to charge a joint cover charge of $8 ($5 on weekdays) that lets you into all of the clubs that night. Because of this, the area is abuzz with people sampling the various acts and strolling the sidewalks. This wonderful concept fosters listening to other types of music; several places offer blues or R&B, while others have punk, funk, jazz, reggae, or retro swing. Probably the most popular places in this group are the **Fenix,** 323 2nd St., tel. (206) 467-1111, and the adjacent **Fenix Underground.** Both of these attract a young trendsetter crowd; DJ tunes below ground. Other members of the Pioneer Square shared-cover group include: **Colourbox,** 113 1st St. S, tel. (206) 340-4101, a cavernous, smoky place filled with alternative music devotees; **New Orleans Restaurant,** 114 1st St., tel. (206) 622-2563, serving up spicy Creole meals plus Dixieland jazz, R&B, and zydeco; **Bohemian Cafe,** 111 Yesler Way, tel. (206) 447-1514, and **Central Saloon** (Seattle's oldest bar), 207 1st Ave., tel. (206) 622-0209, both with great blues and reggae bands; and **Doc Maynard's,** 610 1st Ave., tel. (206) 682-4649, a restored 1890s saloon.

Other Rock Clubs

The Belltown area north of downtown has several more popular nightclubs. **Crocodile Cafe,** 2200 2nd Ave., tel. (206) 441-5611, is a great club that attracts the bigger alternative acts. It's a good place to look for rock stars passing through town. **Vogue,** 2018 1st Ave., tel. (206) 443-0673, is a center for the fringe crowd, with fetish night on Sunday, plus reggae, industrial, and alternative music or CDs other nights. **O.K. Hotel,** 212 Alaskan Way, tel. (206) 621-7903, mixes an art gallery cafe with alternative rock

and jazz music. Parts of the movie *Singles* were filmed here.

Two very popular Ballard nightclubs attracting big acts are **Ballard Firehouse,** 5429 Russell, tel. (206) 784-3516, and **Tractor Tavern,** 5213 Ballard Ave. (Ballard), tel. (206) 789-3599. Other popular live music and DJ clubs include: **Showbox,** 1426 1st Ave., tel. (206) 628-3151; **Downunder,** 2407 1st Ave., tel. (206) 728-4053; **Zasu,** 608 1st Ave., tel. (206) 682-1200; **RKCNDY,** 1812 Yale Ave., tel. (206) 860-9168; and **Lox Stock,** 4552 University Way NE, tel. (206) 634-3144.

Safari Sports Bar & Grille, 1518 11th Ave., tel. (206) 328-4250, is a gay bar with food, pool, darts, sports, and karaoke, plus hot dance tunes in the adjacent Jungle Room. **Re-Bar,** 1114 E. Howell St., tel. (206) 233-9873, is a fun dance club with DJs spinning dance music most nights; live bands on Tuesday. The city's biggest gay/lesbian dance club is **Timberline,** 2015 Boren, tel. (206) 622-6220, with a huge maple dance floor and C&W music. Drop by on Tuesday nights for free two-step lessons. Also popular is the **Romper Room,** 106 1st. Ave. N, tel. (206) 284-5003, with a music mix that romps all over the place, from alternative to dance music. One of Seattle's most unusual nightspots is **Sit & Spin,** 2219 4th Ave., tel. (206) 441-9484, a laundromat where you can watch the clothes go round while dancing, eating, or playing board games.

Jazz, Blues, and Folk

The most popular place for Seattle jazz buffs is **Dimitriou's Jazz Alley,** 2033 6th Ave., tel. (206) 441-9729, where big-time national acts and up-and-coming talent can be heard. For more live jazz, head to the **Seattle Art Museum** on the second Thursday of the month Jan.-June; tel. (206) 654-3100. Other places for jazz, blues, and folk include Belltown's **2218,** 2218 1st Ave., tel. (206) 441-2218; Greenlake's **Latona,** 6423 Latona NE, tel. (206) 525-2238; and Wedgewood's **Fiddler's Inn,** 9219 35th Ave. NE, tel. (206) 525-0752. Other downtown spots include **Larry's,** 209 1st Ave. S, tel. (206) 624-7665, and the Pioneer Square clubs described above.

Comedy Clubs

Seattle's biggest comedy club is **Comedy Underground,** 222 S. Main St., tel. (206) 622-4550, where local and national talents perform for capacity crowds. **Giggles,** another comedy club at 5220 Roosevelt Way NE, tel. (206) 526-5347, has cheap food and beer with local, smaller-time acts. **Market Theater,** in Pike Place Market, tel. (206) 781-9273, has well-known and beginning comics, along with improvisational theater performances.

Film

Seattle has earned an international reputation among filmmakers as having one of the most discriminating audiences in America. Nobody quite knows why live theater and movies are taken so seriously, but movies are sometimes tested on Seattleites before being released, and Seattle viewers have often made a little-known film a winner.

Off-the-beaten path moviehouses with art-house films include: **Grand Illusion Cinema,** 50th and University Way NE, tel. (206) 523-3935; **Egyptian Theatre,** 801 E. Pine, tel. (206) 323-4978; and **Varsity,** 4329 University Way NE, tel. (206) 632-3131. You'll also want to participate in the **Seattle International Film Festival,** held from late May to mid-June, the largest of its kind in America. It attracts more than 100,000 filmgoers. If you're just looking for a cheap flick, try the **Crest Theater,** 16505 5th Ave. NE, tel. (206) 363-6338, where all shows are only $2.

PERFORMING ARTS

Much of Seattle's cultural action—at least when it comes to live theater, classical music, opera, and ballet—centers around Seattle Center (better known as "that place with the Space Needle"). For up-to-date recording of arts events in Seattle, call (206) 447-2787. The Friday edition of both the *Seattle Times* and *Seattle Post-Intelligencer* newspapers have a complete listing of upcoming productions.

Get tickets from **Ticketmaster,** tel. (206) 628-0888. For half-price concert, comedy, and dance tickets the day of the show, stop by the **Ticket/Ticket,** booths at Pike Place Market and in Broadway Market at 401 Broadway Ave. E, tel. (206) 324-2744.

Live Theater

Nobody is quite sure why—maybe it really is the weather—but live theater has always done very well in Seattle. Consequently, if you don't see a good movie, you will have a wide choice of plays and musicals to try. Much of the action takes place in one of Seattle Center's theaters; check local papers for current activities. **Seattle Repertory Theatre** produces classic and contemporary plays Oct.-May at Seattle Center, tel. (206) 443-2222. **ACT** (A Contemporary Theatre) fills out the other half of the year, performing downtown at 700 Union St.; tel. (206) 292-7676. The **Intiman Theatre Company** has classic dramatic productions May-Nov. at Seattle Center's Intiman Theatre, tel. (206) 269-1901. The **Bathhouse Theatre,** on the shore of Green Lake in an old bathhouse, tel. (206) 783-0053, also presents a wide range of plays all year.

For multicultural productions, check out **The Group Theatre,** with performances in Seattle Center Sept.-June, tel. (206) 441-1299; and **Northwest Asian American Theatre,** 409 7th Ave. S, tel. (206) 340-1049. Also popular are offbeat and provocative productions from **Empty Space Theatre,** 3509 Fremont Ave., tel. (206) 547-7500. Two Seattle theaters provide a venue for Broadway-style musicals, the **5th Ave. Musical Theatre Company,** tel. (206) 625-1418, and the beautifully restored historic **Paramount Theater** on Pine St. near 9th Ave., tel. (206) 292-2787.

Seattle Children's Theater, tel. (206) 441-3322, is the largest (and perhaps finest) children's theater in the U.S. and is located in the impressive Charlotte Martin Theatre at Seattle Center. Productions and classes include both the silly and the serious.

Music and Dance

The **Seattle Symphony** has a sparkling new home at Benaroya Hall, located downtown at 2nd Ave. and University Street. The largest employer of artists in the Pacific Northwest, the symphony has gained international attention under conductor Gerard Schwartz, with more than 65 compact discs and 10 Grammy nominations. Performances take place in the state-of-the-art auditorium from Sept.-June, with more than 100 concerts a year. On Sunday afternoons, the "Musically Speaking" series mixes the classics with commentary about the music and the composers. For details, call the ticket office at tel. (206) 215-4747, or stop by the information center at 1203-B 2nd Avenue. Tours are available.

Seattle Center Opera House hosts the **Seattle Opera,** whose Sept.-May regular season is almost always a sellout, tel. (206) 389-7676. They present five productions annually, including Wagner's famous four-opera Ring cycle every four years; including in 1999 and 2003. The **Seattle Youth Symphony,** tel. (206) 362-2300, also plays in the Opera House several times a season.

The **Pacific Northwest Ballet,** whose season is Oct.-May., produces the traditional *Nutcracker* for Christmas; tel. (206) 628-0888. A number of contemporary dance companies help fill out the repertoire in Seattle.

Popular music aficionados won't want to miss **Summer Nights at the Pier,** with national acts performing at Pier 62/63 June-August. You might hear Ani DiFranco one night, David Grisman a few nights later, and Ziggy Marley the following week.

EVENTS

Chinese New Year is celebrated in late January or early February when the International District comes alive with parades and colorful displays; call (206) 623-8171 for info. **Fat Tuesday** is Seattle's week-long Mardi Gras celebration at Pioneer Square in February with jazz and Cajun music, arts and crafts, and a parade; tel. (206) 621-8383.

The first Saturday of May brings the **Opening Day of Boating Season** with a big parade of boats and the **Windermere Cup Races,** where top rowing teams from around the world compete on the Montlake Cut. This is the top event of its kind in the nation; call (206) 325-1000 for details. On the third weekend of May the **University District Street Fair,** tel. (206) 632-9084, attracts hundreds of artists who display their wares on University Way NE. Also here are food booths and live music. More than 6,000 musicians, dancers, and craftspeople display their talents while enormous amounts of food are consumed at the **Northwest Folklife Festival** held at Seattle Center on Memorial Day weekend; tel. (206) 684-7300. In late May the **Pike Place Market Street Festival** has free entertainment and music, a beer garden, chalk art, and a kids' area; tel. (206) 587-0351.

In June the **Pioneer Square Fire Festival** celebrates Seattle's great fire of 1889 (any excuse for a party, right?) with free activities in the park, a parade of classic firefighting equipment, contests, and free entertainment; tel. (206) 622-6235. Each June, the funky "Republic of Fremont" holds the **Fremont Fair,** with booths, live music, ethnic food and drink, and assorted street performers and residents from the fringe. More out-there performances at **artsEdge,** held in late June at Seattle Center. These are not your standard productions, but are instead visual and performance works from new artists that push the envelope. The events could be bizarre, disconcerting, funny, psychedelic, and haunting all at the same time.

The Fourth of July brings twin fireworks displays, one on Lake Union, and the other at Myrtle Edwards Park on Elliott Bay. The latter—**Fourth of Jul-Ivar's**—is sponsored by Ivar's Acre of Clams and is said to be one of the largest in America. It also features food booths and entertainment, plus a fly-over of antique and modern aircraft. Also in early July, the **Lake Union Wooden Boat Festival,** tel. (206) 382-2628, takes place at the south end of the lake, where you'll see some of the most beautiful boats on Puget Sound. In mid-July the **Bite of Seattle** comes to Seattle Center, giving restaurants, wineries, microbreweries, and coffeemakers an opportunity to show their products; tel.

(206) 684-8522. Across the way in Ballard, **Seafoodfest,** tel. (206) 784-9705, arrives on the second weekend of July, with a street festival, salmon barbecue, food and crafts booths, beer garden, and children's games.

Seattle's biggest fair of the year, **Seafair,** tel. (206) 728-0123, starts on the Fourth of July and packs in a month of crafts, parades, triathlons, ethnic festivals, music, a milk-carton boat race, ship tours, and demonstrations by the Navy's Blue Angels, culminating in the unlimited **Texaco Cup Hydroplane Races** on Lake Washington in early August. One of the more unusual events is the **Bubble Festival** held in mid-August at the Pacific Science Center. Professional bubble blowers create bubbles in every imaginable shape; tel. (206) 443-2001.

A Labor Day weekend arts extravaganza, **Bumpershoot,** brings together writers, musicians, and craftspeople for a big end-of-summer party at Seattle Center. Bumpershoot attracts more than a quarter-million visitors annually, and features internationally known musicians.

King 5 Winterfest is a five-week holiday festival with decorations, children's entertainers, choirs, an ice rink, lighting ceremony, and New Year's Eve celebration at Seattle Center.

The last festival of the year is the multi-day **Christmas Ships Parade,** a lighted flotilla that cruises Lake Washington in mid-December; call (206) 461-5840, for route and viewing information.

SPORTS AND RECREATION

Spectator Sports

Major league sports are thoroughly represented in Seattle. The American League's **Mariners,** play at brand new SAFECO Field, which opened in 1999. Call (206) 622-4487 for tickets. The NFL's **Seahawks,** tel. (206) 628-0888, frequently draw capacity crowds, and play at the Kingdome until it comes under the wrecking ball in 2000. After that they will probably play at the UW stadium until their new stadium opens in 2002. Another local favorite is the NBA's **Seattle Super-Sonics** who play at the KeyArena in Seattle Center; tel. (206) 628-0888. The Sonics are generally not sold out until the game day.

The **Seattle Thunderbirds,** tel. (206) 728-9124, play minor-league hockey Oct.-May at the KeyArena for the Western Hockey League. College sports are big here too, particularly the University of Washington's Husky football, tel. (206) 543-2200, and basketball, tel. (206) 543-2200, teams. That also applies to the women's basketball team that has been gaining in national prominence of late.

Another big Seattle-area sporting event nearly year-round is auto, drag, and motorcycle racing at **Seattle International Raceway,** 31001 144th in Kent, tel. (206) 631-1550.

The 3,000-year-old game called Go has a devoted following in Japan and on American college campuses. The **Seattle Go Center**—the only one in the nation—is at 700 N.E. 45th St., tel. (206) 545-1424.

Boating

Rent wooden rowboats and sailboats and learn about building these classics at the **Center for Wooden Boats,** 1010 Valley St., tel. (206) 382-2628, on the south end of Lake Union. Or, rent sea kayaks from **Northwest Outdoor Center,** 2100 Westlake Ave. N, tel. (206) 281-9694, on the west side of the lake. This is an outstanding place to learn about sea kayaking from the experts, with classes at all levels. They also sell kayaks and provide guided tours. Also on the south end of Lake Union, **Moss Bay Rowing & Kayak Center,** 1001 Fairview N., tel. (206) 682-2031, offers kayak rentals and lessons, plus sculling lessons and teams. Rent sailboards, surfboards, and inline skates from **Urban Surf,** 2100 N. Northlake Way, tel. (206) 545-9463. Washington's largest rafting store, **Swiftwater,** tel. (206) 547-3377, sells and rents rafts and nonmotorized inflatable boats of all types.

In the summer you can rent kayaks, rowboats, paddleboats, sailboards, and canoes to play around the warm waters of Green Lake at **Green Lake Boat Rentals,** 7351 E. Green Lake Dr., tel. (206) 527-0171.

Over on Lake Washington, head to **UW Waterfront Activities Center,** just east of the Montlake Bridge, tel. (206) 543-9433, for canoe or rowboat rentals. Take rowing, sailing, canoeing, or kayaking lessons on Lake Washington from **Mount Baker Rowing and Sailing Center,** 3800 Lake Washington Blvd., tel. (206) 386-1913.

Cycling and Running

Bikes are a favorite way to get around Seattle, even on rainy winter days. For an easy and level ride, walk, run, or skate, join the throngs at **Green Lake,** where a 2.8-mile paved path circles the duck-filled lake. On sunny spring weekends you're likely to meet hundreds if not thousands of other folks out for fun in the sun.

Get an excellent free map detailing the various cycling routes around Seattle, available from the city engineering office at 600 4th Ave., tel. (206) 684-7570. The most popular bike path is an old railroad route, the **Burke-Gilman Trail.** This 14-mile-long paved path begins in Fremont at 8th Ave. NW, cuts through Gasworks Park on the north shore of Lake Union, and then follows along Lake Washington all the way to the north end in Kenmore. From here, the 10-mile-long **Sammamish River Trail** continues to Marymoor Park in Redmond for a total of 24 miles of bike riding, rollerblading, running, or walking pleasure.

Another favorite ride is the six-mile **Alki Trail** that follows right on the shore of Puget Sound at Alki Point. It begins at the intersection of Harbor Ave. SW and S.W. Florida St., and curves around the north tip and then west to Alki Point Lighthouse.

Lake Washington Blvd. through the Arboretum and south along Lake Washington to Madrona Park makes for a very scenic bike ride, but traffic can get heavy. Other popular cycling places include Bainbridge Island, Mercer Island, Seward Park (in south Lake Washington), and Elliott Bay Trail (just northwest of downtown off Alaskan Way).

Rent bikes and rollerblades from a variety of local shops (see the *Yellow Pages*); one of the best and biggest is **Gregg's Greenlake Cycle,** 7007 Woodlawn Ave. NE, tel. (206) 523-1822.

Bike tours of the Seattle area are offered by **Terrene Tours,** tel. (206) 325-5569.

Swimming

Swimmers will find eight city-run indoor pools around town: **Ballard,** 1417 N.W. 67th St., tel. (206) 684-4094; **Evans,** 7201 E. Green Lake Dr. N, tel. (206) 684-4961; **Helene Madison,** 13401 Meridian Ave. N, tel. (206) 684-4979; **Meadowbrook,** 10515 35th Ave. NE, tel. (206) 684-4989; **Medgar Evers,** 500 23rd Ave., tel. (206) 684-4766; **Queen Anne,** 1920 1st Ave. W, tel. (206) 386-4282; **Rainier Beach,** 8825 Rainier Ave. S, tel. (206) 386-1944; and **Southwest,** 2801 S.W. Thistle St., tel. (206) 684-7440. The very popular outdoor **Colman Pool,** 8603 Fauntleroy Way SW, tel. (206) 684-7494, is open summers only with saltwater bathing. The pools at Evans, Queen Anne, and Southwest have saunas, and the Ballard and Southwest pools have jacuzzis.

Green Lake is a favorite summertime swimming hole, but the water gets a bit rank by the end of the season with algal growth. (Lots of nutrients from all the duck and goose poop.) Other beaches with lifeguards in the summer include: Madison Park, Madrona Park, Magnolia Park, Magnuson Park, Mount Baker Park, and Seward Park.

Mountaineering and Climbing

Backcountry enthusiasts should contact the **Washington Alpine Club,** tel. (206) 467-3042, in existence since 1916. Monthly meetings include slide shows and discussions, and they also offer climbing and skiing classes. A good place to practice rock climbing is the 65-foot artificial pinnacle at the REI store. Several other indoor climbing facilities are available, including America's original indoor climbing gym—**Vertical World**—at 2123 W. Elmore in Magnolia, tel. (206) 283-4497. More climbing at **The Stone Gardens** in Ballard at 2839 N.W. Market St., tel. (206) 781-9828. **Mountain Madness,** tel. (206) 937-8389 or (800) 328-5925, offers courses in rock climbing, mountaineering, and ski mountaineering, and leads technical climbs up several North Cascades peaks.

SHOPPING

Shopping Centers

Unlike most other cities around the Sound, Seattle's downtown shopping district has not died out under the pressure of surrounding suburban malls. In fact, downtown shopping is more alive than ever, with popular **Westlake Center** at 5th Ave. and Pine St., and **Century Square** at 4th Ave. and Pike Street. Top-shelf jewelry, perfume, art, leather goods, and clothing stores abound in these two small centers. Westlake is also the endpoint for the Monorail from Seattle Center, and it has an information booth with an adjacent Ticketmaster booth for discounted day-of performance tickets. Downstairs, you'll find the entrance to the bus tunnel; upstairs is a food court with plenty of quick-eat choices. Nearby is the newly opened **Pacific Place** retail and entertainment center with five levels of retail shops, three restaurants (including Stars Restaurant from famed chef Jeremiah Tower), and an 11-plex movie theater. The complex has underground parking and is connected by skywalk to Seattle's newly refurbished flagship **Nordstrom** store at 5th between Pike and Pine. Not far away is another old favorite, **The Bon Marché,** at 4th and Pine.

Another downtown shopping center with small shops—this one underground—is **Rainier Square** between 4th and 5th Avenues and Union Street. The underground concourse has bookstores and restaurants and serves as an entrance to **Eddie Bauer,** another store founded in Seattle that became global.

The **waterfront** and **Pike Place Market** are loaded with tiny wine shops, boutiques, and craft stores, plus the big, obvious produce stands and tourist traps; see "The Waterfront" and "Pike Place Market," above, for a detailed description of these areas. **Pioneer Square,** also discussed earlier, offers some of the city's finest galleries, antiques, and book and clothing stores.

Shopping malls abound in the Seattle area, the biggest being the **Northgate Shopping Mall,** seven miles north of Seattle (exit 173 from I-5). The newly refurbished **University Village Mall** near campus on N.E. 45th St. at 25th Ave. NE, is another good one. Farther away are two of the biggest: **Southcenter Mall,** down I-5 in Tukwila, and **Bellevue Square Mall** in Bellevue.

Outdoor Gear

See "Sights," above, for details on Seattle's justly famous **Recreation Equipment Inc.,** (REI) store, a place in a class of its own. **Swallows' Nest** 2308 6th Ave., tel. (206) 441-8151, is another fine outdoor and climbing shop with rental gear of all types. They often carry brands not available at REI. Other major outdoor rec places include: **The North Face,** 1023 1st Ave., tel. (206) 622-4111; **Eddie Bauer,** 1330 5th Ave., tel. (206) 622-2766; **Patagonia,** 2100 1st Ave., tel. (206) 622-9700; and **Warshal's Sporting Goods,** 1000 1st Ave., tel. (206) 624-7300. Warshal's is the most distinctive of these, an old-fashioned place that caters more to the fishing, camping, and hunting crowd than to the trendy pacesetters at North Face. They also have a big selection of photographic equipment.

Books and Magazines

Seattleites spend more money on books per capita than any other American city—almost twice the national average. Given this, you can be assured that the city has lots of choices when it comes to buying books. With more than 150,000 titles on the shelves, a comfortable atmosphere and knowledgeable staff, plus a cafe and almost nightly readings by acclaimed authors and poets, the **Elliott Bay Book Company,** 101 S. Main St., tel. (206) 624-6600, is a local legend. This Pioneer Square bookstore is *the* quintessential place for Seattle bibliophiles. Pick up their quarterly *Elliott Bay Booknotes* for detailed book reviews and articles about the craft of writing.

The **University Bookstore,** at 4326 University Way NE, tel. (206) 634-3400 or (800) 335-7323, competes with Harvard for the nation's largest university bookstore, carrying an impressive array of titles, plus office supplies, "go-Huskies" clothing, cameras, CDs, and more. Just down the block is a place at the opposite end of the spectrum, **Twice Sold Tales,** 1311 NE 45th St., tel. (206) 545-4226, with two cats and a funky collection of used books. Also on "the Ave" is **Bulldog News,** 4208 University Way NE, tel. (206) 632-6397, the largest magazine and newspaper store in town, with over 2,000 titles, including quite a few foreign magazines. Almost any night you're bound to find several dozen folks scanning the issues (and doing quite a bit of reading). Bulldog also has a smaller shop at Broadway Market on Capitol Hill. Another excellent place for magazines and out-of-town newspapers is the **Read All About It** newsstand at Pike Place Market, tel. (206) 624-0140.

For a great selection of travel books, visit **Wide World Books and Maps,** 1911 N. 45th Ave. (in Wallingford), tel. (206) 634-3453. The tea shop next door is a fine place to read about Asia while sipping fresh Chinese tea. Two Capitol Hill bookstores, **Beyond the Closet Bookstore,** 518 E. Pike St., tel. (206) 322-4609, and **Bailey/Coy Books,** 414 Broadway Ave. E, tel. (206) 323-8842, offer big selections of gay and lesbian titles. Unrepentant leftists, socialists, and radicals love **Left Bank Books** in the Pike Place Market, tel. (206) 622-0195. You can get an idea of the orientation at the collectively run **Red & Black Books,** 432 15th Ave. E (Capitol Hill), tel. (206) 322-7323, from their credo: "Capitalism is Organized Crime." Other distinctive bookstores include the appropriately named **Peter Miller Architecture and Design Books,** 1930 1st Ave., tel. (206) 441-4114, and **Cinema Books,** 4753 Roosevelt Way NE, tel. (206) 547-7667.

East West Book Shop, 1032 N.E. 65th St., tel. (206) 523-3726, is the place for the crystal, channeling, and pyramid-power crowd. For something more down to earth (literally), be sure to visit **Flora and Fauna,** 121 1st Ave., tel. (206) 623-4727, the biggest purveyor of natural history volumes in the West. Lots of other bookstore choices in town, including a big **Barnes and Noble** store in University Village Mall, tel. (206) 517-4107.

Photography
Photographers can stock up on supplies at **Cameras West,** 1908 4th Ave., tel. (206) 622-0066, or **Warshal's,** 1000 1st Ave., tel. (206) 624-7300. Professionals head to **Glazer's Camera Supply,** 430 8th Ave. N, tel. (206) 624-1100, where the shelves are stocked with lighting gear, darkroom supplies, tripods, and other supplies. A few doors down the street is **Ivey-Seright Photo Lab,** 424 8th Ave. N, tel. (206) 623-8113, the best Seattle place for professional quality processing and digital imaging classes.

INFORMATION AND SERVICES

Information
For information on Seattle attractions and events, plus maps and other assistance, contact the **Seattle/King County Convention and Visitors Bureau,** located at 800 Convention Pl. in the Washington State Convention and Trade Center, on the Galleria level (main floor); on the Web at www.seeseattle.org. They are open Mon.-Fri. 8:30 a.m.-5 p.m., Sat.-Sun. 10 a.m.-4 p.m. April-Oct.; and Mon.-Fri. 8:30 a.m.-5 p.m. the rest of the year. While here, be sure to pick up the *Seattle Visitors Guide,* a compendium of local entertainment, restaurants, shopping, and sights. Call (206) 461-5840 ahead of your visit for a big packet of Seattle information. Also in the convention center are various shops, changing displays of fine artwork along the walls, and access to **Free-way Park,** built over part of I-5, with greenery, waterfalls, and fountains. The Convention and Visitors Bureau also maintains a small summertime visitors center next to the Space Needle. At Sea-Tac Airport, the **Visitor Information Booth** (described below) has more local info and brochures.

Located inside the REI store at 222 Yale Ave. N, the **Outdoor Recreation Information Center,** tel. (206) 470-4060, has information on Forest Service and Park Service lands throughout Washington, including hiking trails, campgrounds, and backcountry access. They can't make campground or backcountry reservations, but they do sell Trail-Park Passes. Open Tues.-Fri. 10:30 a.m.-7 p.m., Saturday 9 a.m.-7 p.m., and Sunday 9:30 a.m.-6 p.m.

If you're a member, the **AAA Travel Store** at 330 6th Ave. N is a good source of maps and area information plus travel guidebooks, luggage, and other travel-related accessories.

An excellent guidebook to the area is *Seattle Access,* published by Harper Perennial and available in local bookstores. *Seattle Best Places,* published by Sasquatch Books, also details many of the finer aspects of the city.

Seattle on the Web

A good place to start your search the Web is the Seattle Public Access Network site at **www.ci.seattle.wa.us/html/visitor.** They have links to many other sites and all sorts of local information. Microsoft's **www.seattle.side-walk.com** contains detailed online info on restaurants, theaters, outdoor activities, and much more. For an up-to-date listing of Web addresses throughout the Northwest, pick up a copy of the free *Puget Sound Computer User* from racks around town; or find the list at **www.pscu.com.** Internet Seattle at **www.halcyon.com/tmend/seattle.htm** has an alphabetical listing with an amazing array of links to all sorts of Seattle sites. You'll find ATM locations, farmers markets, book clubs, webcameras, and lots more. Three other helpful sites are the *Seattle Post-Intelligencer's* **www.seattlepi.com,** the *The Seattle Weekly's* **www.seattleweekly.com,** and Yahoo's **www. seattle.yahoo.com.**

Foreign Currency Exchange

Thomas Cook, tel. (800) 287-7362, has currency exchange booths at the airport and in Westlake Center, and at 906 3rd Avenue. Other options are **American Express,** 600 Stewart St., tel. (206) 441-8622, **Wells Fargo,** 1215 4th Ave., tel. (800) 411-4932, and **Custom House Currency Exchange,** 1900 5th Ave., tel. (206) 269-6353.

Libraries

The main branch of the **Seattle Public Library** is at 1000 4th Ave., tel. (206) 625-4952, with another 23 neighborhood libraries scattered around town. Call (206) 386-4636 for their ask-anything info line. The University of Washington has collections of more than five million volumes spread in its various campus libraries, the majority of which are housed in the sprawling **Suzzallo and Allen Libraries** near the center of campus. Call (206) 543-0242 for details.

Across the street from Seattle University, **As-You-Like-It Library,** 1000 E. Madison Ave. B, tel. (206) 329-1794, is Seattle's most unusual library. This collection of 12,000 metaphysical books is open Mon.-Sat. 11 a.m.-9 p.m. Books cover the spectrum, including astrology, magic, hermetics, parapsychology, telepathy, and tarot. Anyone can come here to read, but to check out books you'll need to pay a $25 annual fee.

TRANSPORTATION

SEA-TAC AIRPORT ACCESS

Seattle's airport is 12 miles south of town and midway between Seattle and Tacoma, hence the name, Sea-Tac Airport. All the major domestic, and many international, airlines fly into Sea-Tac. Foreign travelers can change money at the Thomas Cook booth in the main terminal. Storage lockers are scattered around the airport, but you'll need to pass through security first. Another option is **Ken's Baggage and Frozen Food Storage,** tel. (206) 433-5333, located near the baggage claim area, and open daily 5:30 a.m.-12:30 a.m. Also near the baggage claim is a volunteer-staffed **Visitor Information Booth** (open daily 9:30-7:30 in the sum-

mer; brochures available at other times), along with car rentals counters and kiosks with info on Metro buses, shuttle buses, and limo services. Call (206) 431-4444 or (800) 544-1965 for updates on airport parking, weather and traffic conditions, ground transportation, and other airport services.

Getting to Seattle

The least expensive way to reach Seattle from the airport is aboard one of **Metro's** city buses. Numbers 174, 184, and 194 run between Sea-Tac and downtown Seattle about every half-hour; one-way fare is $1.25 off-peak, $1.75 peak; tel. (206) 447-4800. The buses leave from outside the lower-level baggage claim area of the domestic terminal (turn right as you exit), or catch them downtown if you're headed out. It takes approximately 50 minutes to reach downtown. Make sure you catch the bus heading north to Seattle, not south to Federal Way! Metro buses travel along the Pacific Highway and provide the cheapest access for the many motels close to the airport.

To do it the easy (and expensive) way, grab a cab on the airport's second level; they all charge the same rates—$30 one-way to downtown Seattle.

Gray Line Airport Express, tel. (206) 626-6088, has airport pick-up service to and from 10 downtown hotels every half hour 5 a.m.-11:30 p.m.; $7.50 adults, $5.50 kids. No reservations needed, just board the bus outside the baggage claim area.

Shuttle Express, tel. (206) 622-1424 or (800) 942-7433, has door-to-door van service between Sea-Tac and Seattle ($18), plus Bellevue ($21), and points north to Everett and south to Tacoma. Reserve ahead for a pickup. They also offer scheduled service to hotels in Seattle and Bellevue.

Airporter Shuttle, tel. (800) 235-5247, has connections between Sea-Tac and Marysville, Mount Vernon, Anacortes, Oak Harbor, Bellingham (including the Alaska Ferry terminal), and Blaine on the Canadian border.

Quick Shuttle Service, tel. (604) 244-3744 or (800) 665-2122, provides connections between Sea-Tac and Vancouver, B.C.; and **Olympic Bus Lines,** tel. (360) 452-3858 or (800) 550-3858, has shuttle vans to Port Angeles and Sequim.

Capital Aeroporter, tel. (253) 838-7431 or (800) 962-3579, provides connections to Tacoma, Puyallup, Olympia, and Centralia/Chehalis.

The **Bremerton-Kitsap Airporter,** tel. (206) 876-1737 or (800) 562-7948, provides connections to Bremerton, Port Orchard, Poulsbo, Gig Harbor, and northwest Tacoma. **Centralia-Sea-Tac Airport Express,** tel. (360) 786-0636 or (800) 773-9490, serves Olympia and Centralia.

TRAINS AND LONG-HAUL BUSES

Amtrak

Amtrak serves Seattle at its historic King Street Station (Third Ave. S and S. King St.), tel. (206) 464-1930 or (800) 872-7245. The **Coast Star-**light has service four times a day connecting Seattle with Tacoma, Olympia, Centralia, Kelso-Longview, Vancouver, Portland, and south to Oakland and Los Angeles. The **Empire Builder** provides daily service connecting Seattle with Edmonds, Everett, Wenatchee, Ephrata, and Spokane, and continuing to Minneapolis and Chicago. The **Mount Baker International** provides daily train connections to Vancouver, B.C., via Edmonds, Everett, Mount Vernon, and Bellingham.

Bus Service

Greyhound, tel. (206) 628-5521 or (800) 231-2222, has daily bus service throughout the lower 48 and to Vancouver, B.C., from their bus terminal at 9th and Stewart. **Northwest Trailways,** tel. (206) 728-5955 or (800) 366-6975, operates from both the Greyhound station and the Amtrak depot, with service to Everett, Tacoma, Spokane, and points between.

The most unusual bus transportation is **Green Tortoise,** tel. (800) 867-8647, a twice-weekly bus from Seattle to Los Angeles ($79). The comfortable old bus stops at Green Tortoise's creekside park in southern Oregon for a vegetarian feast and a chance to swim or enjoy the sauna. This is a fun way to travel if you don't mind sleeping on a foam pad and hanging out with youthful hostelers. Green Tortoise also runs trips all over the country, and even to Central America.

METRO TRANSIT BUSES

After years of delay, in 1996 Seattle area voters finally approved a comprehensive public transit plan that includes 25 miles of light rail, a commuter rail service, high occupancy vehicle lanes, new bus routes, and a single-ticket fare system. The light rail system itself will not be running until 2005, but at least the wheels are in motion, and the money is there to start construction. For details on Sound Transit's progress, call (800) 201-4900.

In the meantime, Seattle's Metro bus system provides efficient connections throughout the area. Metro buses run 6 a.m.-1 a.m. every day, about every 30 minutes on the city routes. Customer service offices are at 821 2nd Ave. and in the Westlake Station. Fares are $1 off-peak, $1.25 peak within the city; $1.10 off-peak or

$1.60 peak, outside city limits. For $2 on weekends, you can purchase a visitor pass that gives you unlimited rides on Metro buses and the streetcars. Get them from the bus driver when you board. Call (206) 553-3000 or (800) 542-7876 for route info and other details; their Web site is http://transit.metrokc.gov. All Metro buses carry bikes at no extra charge. Bikes are not carried within the Ride Free area of downtown.

Ride Free Zone

Downtown Metro passengers ride for free anywhere in the area bordered by S. Jackson St., I-5, Pine St., Battery St., and Alaskan Way. These buses are free between 6 a.m. and 7 p.m. Rides on the waterfront streetcars are not included in the zone.

A 1.3-mile **bus tunnel** cuts through the center of downtown along Pine St. and 3rd Ave., with stops at Convention Place (9th and Pine), Westlake Center (4th and Pine), University St. (3rd and University), and the International District (5th and S. Jackson). Buses switch from diesel outside to electric power inside the tunnel. The tunnel is decorated with several pieces of art commissioned for the project.

Waterfront Streetcar

The Waterfront Streetcar is a very popular Metro-operated trolley that follows along the waterfront and up to Pioneer Square and the International District—it costs $1 ($1.25 in commute hours).

See "The Waterfront" earlier in this chapter for a complete description.

Other Public Transit

Pierce Transit, tel. (800) 562-8109, has southern Puget Sound bus service connecting downtown Seattle with Tacoma. **Community Transit,** tel. (800) 562-1375, provides commuter bus service connecting Everett and other Snohomish County cities with downtown Seattle and the University District.

FERRY SERVICE

Washington State Ferries

One of the best ways to see Seattle is from the water, and one of the cheapest ways to do so is aboard the Washington State Ferries. Ferries operate almost continuously from before sunrise to after 1 a.m. daily, and leave from the main terminal at Pier 52 for Bainbridge Island and Bremerton. To either destination, summertime car-and-driver fares are $8 one-way; passengers and walk-ons pay only $3.60 roundtrip. A passenger-only **Seattle-Vashon Island** ferry ($3.60 roundtrip) has daily departures from Pier 50 in the summer, with Mon.-Sat. departures in the winter.

The Fauntleroy ferry dock in west Seattle serves Southworth on the Kitsap Peninsula and Vashon Island about every 20-50 minutes daily.

ferry Spokane, Puget Sound, and Mt. Olympus

DON PITCHER

Summertime car-and-driver fares to **Southworth** are $11 one-way; passengers and walk-ons pay $2.40 roundtrip; the crossing takes approximately 35 minutes. A 15-minute **Fauntleroy-Vashon Island** crossing costs $11 roundtrip for car and driver, $2.40 roundtrip for passengers and walk-ons. Get to the Fauntleroy dock by heading south on I-5 to exit 163; follow the signs from here.

There is a 60-cent surcharge to carry bikes on all these ferry runs. Fares for vehicles are lower in the off-season (mid-October to mid-May), and discounts are available for seniors, children, and people with disabilities. If you're going to be traveling a lot on the ferries, ask about frequent-user coupon books. There are no state ferry connections from Seattle to the San Juan Islands; you'll need to get to Anacortes or Sidney, B.C., to begin a San Juans trip (or take the excursion described below). For more information on Washington State Ferries, call (206) 464-6400 or (888) 808-7977. Call (800) 843-3779 for automated information.

Built in 1935, the streamlined ferry *Kalakala* plied Puget Sound until its retirement in 1962. After that, it ended up as a shore-bound crab processing plant in Kodiak, Alaska. Those of us who saw it there never believed it would float again, but in 1998, it was towed home to Puget Sound. Following restoration, it will be on display along the Seattle shoreline. Call the Kalakala Foundation for the latest; tel. (206) 632-0540 or (888) 823-1935.

Victoria and San Juan Islands Ferries

For a daylong excursion to Canada, take the *Victoria Clipper* from Pier 63 to Ogden Point in Victoria. Reservations are required for this high speed catamaran cruise, tel. (206) 448-5000 or (800) 888-2535, and it takes two hours to reach Victoria. The roundtrip cruise can be completed in one day (8:30 a.m. departure and 9:30 p.m. return) while allowing a brief stay in Olde English Victoria. Roundtrip fares for adults are $94-109 in the summer, with lower off-season rates and discounts for seniors and kids. For variety, take the *Clipper* to Victoria and fly back on Kenmore Air (see below). They also offer optional one- or two-night stays in Victoria, or a "triple play" that includes a night each in Victoria and Vancouver, plus a wide range of other tours into British Columbia. In addition, the *Clipper* of-fers service between Seattle and the San Juan Islands, and between Victoria and the San Juans. Roundtrip runs from Seattle to the San Juans costs $59 for adults; to Victoria (via the San Juans), it's $69.

The 426-foot *Princess Marguerite III* sails between Seattle and Victoria from mid-May to mid-October, offering comfortable passenger and car transport. The ferry leaves Pier 48 at 1 p.m., arriving Ogden Point, Victoria, at 5:30 p.m. From Victoria, the ferry sails at 7:30 a.m., arriving in Seattle at noon. The boat operates daily, and has a buffet, espresso bar, duty free shopping, lounge, children's play area, and gift shop on board. One-way fares are $29 for passengers, $49 for a car and driver. Bikes are an extra $5, and private day rooms are available for $29 more. Call (206) 448-5000 or (800) 888-2535 for details; reservations advised.

BY CAR

According to one recent study, Seattle's traffic was the fifth worst in the United States, and traffic jams are common. If possible, try to stay on public transit, both for your own sanity and for the environment. By all means avoid the 3-6 p.m. weekday rush hour, when I-5 and the floating bridges are often virtual parking lots. One of the more difficult aspects of Seattle city driving isn't getting there, but getting back: finding an I-5 entrance ramp can be frustrating, especially after you zigzag over and under the highway a few times. One sure cure: Head down 5th Ave. because entrances to both north- and southbound traffic are along it. Another good, although very busy, way to approach the freeway is on Mercer St.: get in the right lanes for southbound, northbound to the left.

Driving around downtown Seattle is much more difficult than walking, and is almost as expensive as flying to Portland, because at some point you've got to park the car. Parking downtown is difficult on weekdays—and costly: meters (if you can find one) are $1 an hour, and private lots cost $7-14 a day. Be warned that the vigilant meter maids seem always to be waiting for the "expired" flag to pop up so they can stick you with a $20 ticket. That can buy a lot of bus fares!

Car Rental

Seattle has all the major national car rental companies, along with several smaller operators; see the *Yellow Pages* for specifics, or call their 800 numbers. The big operators all have desks near the baggage claim at Sea-Tac. It often pays to make an initial reservation using the 800 number, and then do additional checking at the counters when you arrive. AAA or Costco members should be sure to also ask about any special discounts. The best rates are often from locations away from the airport such as Bellevue; sometimes they will pay for a shuttle van to their office. If you need a car for a week you might save $100 or more this way.

TOURS

When it comes to tours, Seattle has every possible option, from the standard drive-'em-around-in-the-bus type to the goofy, tongue-planted-firmly-in-cheek version. **Bill Speidel's Underground Tours** fall in the latter category. Guides cover the Pioneer Square area, providing humorous anecdotes (often at the expense of Tacoma residents), along with dollops of local history. See "Pioneer Square," above, for a complete description of these justifiably popular tours.

Flightseeing Tours

To see the city from about 1,500 feet, try one of **Seattle Seaplanes'** 20-minute scenic floatplane rides over Seattle; only $43 pp, two-person minimum. Longer flights are available to Mt. St. Helens, Mt. Rainier, or the San Juan Islands. Flights take off and land at Lake Union; tel. (206) 329-9638 or (800) 637-5553.

In business since 1946, **Kenmore Air,** tel. (206) 486-1257 or (800) 543-9595, has year-round scheduled floatplane flights from Lake Union or Lake Washington. Destinations include the San Juan Islands ($112-142 roundtrip), Gulf Islands ($190), Victoria ($155 roundtrip), and onward to several Vancouver Island destinations. A 24-pound baggage weight limit is in effect for these flights, with excess baggage charged at $1/pound. In addition, they offer more standard flightseeing trips over Seattle at $140 for up to three people on a quick 20-minute flight.

West Isle Air, tel. (206) 671-8463 or (800) 874-4434, has daily service from Boeing Field in Seattle to the San Juan Islands. **Scenic Air,** tel. (206) 764-1175 or (800) 995-3332, also flies out of Boeing Field, five miles south of Seattle, with flightseeing trips around Puget Sound.

One of the more distinctive ways to see Seattle is aboard a classic biplane from **Galvin Flying Service,** tel. (206) 763-9706 or (800) 341-4102. A 20-minute trip over town costs $99 for two people. They operate from Boeing Field.

See **Renton** for details on **Sound Flight** and **Northwest Seaplanes,** two companies with flightseeing trips and scheduled service to the San Juan Islands.

Bus and Van Tours

Gray Line, tel. (206) 626-5208 or (800) 426-7532, offers a number of Puget Sound tours. Their three-hour tour is highlighted by the Ballard Locks, Kingdome (as long as it stands), UW, and Pioneer Square for $24 adults, or $12 kids. A longer all-day tour of Seattle costs $33 adults, or $17 kids. Another option, Gray Line's "Trolley Tours" include eight stops scattered around downtown and Seattle Center. Riders are given a narrated tour and can get off and on at any of the stops. The cost is $14; save your money by riding the free Metro buses around downtown and let local drunks provide their own narration. A "Grapes and Hops Tour" takes you on a four-hour visit to Columbia Winery and Redhook Brewery in Woodinville for $24. Gray Line has several other sightseeing trips, including Everett's Boeing plant ($34), day trips to Mt. Rainier ($45 adults, $23 kids), and overnight trips to Mt. Rainier ($135, including lodging at historic Paradise Inn).

Several other companies offer half-day tours of Seattle for around $30-40: **Customized Tours,** tel. (206) 878-3965; **Seattle Tours,** tel. (206) 768-1234; **Stirling Pacific,** tel. (206) 767-0958; and **Show Me Seattle Tours,** tel. (206) 633-2489. Customized Tours also has trips to the Everett Boeing plant. Several other outfits offer more specialized tours. **Northwest Design Tours,** tel. (206) 824-7008 or (800) 934-4902, emphasizes interior design showrooms, and **Windsor and Haten Legal Investigators,** tel. (206) 622-0590, covers the macabre and offbeat world of private investigations. **Brew Hops**

Tours, tel. (206) 283-8460, leads suds tours of Seattle's microbreweries.

Totem Tours, tel. (206) 661-9079 or (800) 845-7291, offers bus trips to various parts of Washington throughout the year, including festivals in Leavenworth.

Scenic Bound Tours, tel. (206) 433-6907 or (888) 293-1404, takes you on all-day van trips to the wild places around Puget Sound, including both Mt. St. Helens and Mt. Rainier for $65. These tours provide a chance to explore forested hiking trails, high mountain lakes, and scenic passes.

During the summer months, **Bearfoot Backpacker Shuttle,** tel. (206) 526-0910, leads one- and two-day trips to the San Juan Islands, the Olympic Peninsula, Mt. Rainier National Park, and the Cascades. They also provide shuttle services to trailheads along with personalized tours upon request.

Boat Tours

A number of boat tours and ferry services depart from Seattle's waterfront, providing a relaxing, scenic change of pace for the foot-weary traveler. The most popular is offered by **Argosy Cruises,** tel. (206) 623-4252 (recording) or (206) 623-1445, with a fleet of eight tour and charter cruise vessels. Their one-hour informative tour of Elliott Bay and the waterfront describes the hows and whys of containerized shipping along with historical background. The tours depart daily from Piers 55 and 56; $13 adults, $12 seniors, $7 kids, and free for kids under five. No reservations necessary. Argosy also has Lake Washington cruises from Kirkland for $18 adults, $16 seniors, $9 kids, and free for kids under five; available May-September. One of their most popular tours takes you from Elliott Bay through the Chittenden Locks into Lake Union, and then back by bus. This two-and-a-half-hour narrated tour costs $23 adults, $21 seniors, $12 kids, and is free for children under five. Reservations are required. Another choice is their two-hour tour of the locks and Lake Washington. These depart daily from Lake Union and cost $18 adults, $16 seniors, $9 kids, and free for under five. Argosy also offers speedboat rides, charter fishing trips, cruises to Tillicum Village (see below), and special event cruises throughout the year, including a series of "Christmas Ship" tours with on-board choirs singing carols.

The *Spirit of Puget Sound* is a luxurious three-deck tour boat with a dance floor, a cafeteria-style dining room, and plenty of upper-deck space for fresh air. The boat has lunch cruises ($32-34), dinner cruises ($57-61), and moonlight party cruises ($18); call (206) 443-1442 for details. It departs from Pier 70, the oldest commercial pier in Seattle. Look for discount coupons at the nearby Seattle Aquarium.

Let's Go Sailing, tel. (206) 624-3931, offers 90-minute sails in the day ($20), and two-and-a-half-hour sunset sailing trips ($35) aboard a 70-foot yacht. They depart Pier 56 several times a day during the summer. Sail on Lake Union aboard a 33-foot sloop from **Sailing in Seattle,** tel. (206) 298-0094. The cost is $45 for a two-and-a-half-hour sail. And if your really serious, take weekend or evening sailing classes from the **Seattle Sailing Club,** located at Shilshole Bay, tel. (206) 782-5100.

For something different, take a guided sunset or moonlight tour of Lake Union and Ballard Locks by sea kayak. These are offered periodically in the summer by **Northwest Outdoor Center** on Lake Union, 2100 Westlake Ave. N, tel. (206) 281-9694. **Outdoor Odysseys,** tel. (206) 361-0717, offers sea kayak tours around various parts of the Sound, as well as to the San Juans and other places.

Discover Houseboating, tel. (206) 322-9157, leads specialized tours of Lake Union houseboats—from the funky to the fabulous—including the home where *Sleepless in Seattle* was filmed. Prices start at $20.

Tillicum Village Tour

This trip into history has been one of Washington's premier tours for over 35 years. Visitors ride an Argosy boat to Blake Island State Park, where they enjoy a salmon bake inside a cedar longhouse, dances, nature trails, and an Indian gift gallery. Departing from Piers 55 and 56 on the Seattle waterfront, these four-hour Tillicum Village tours are available daily from May through mid-October, with weekend-only tours the rest of the year. Fares are $50 adults, $47 seniors, $33 ages 13-19, $20 ages 6-12, $10 ages 4-5, and free for infants. Reservations are required; tel. (206) 443-1244. For those who want more time to explore Blake Island's hiking paths, the company offers six-and-a-half-hour trips on Saturday from mid-June to mid-September, plus weekdays in July and August.

Walking and Biking Tours

The best local walking tours are offered by the Museum of History and Industry on Sunday in the summer. These two-hour tours cost just $10, and offer a great way to learn local history. Call (206) 324-1126 for upcoming treks. Several private companies offer guided walking tours of Seattle on a daily basis: **Scapes Walking Tours,** tel. (206) 517-5432; **Seattle Walking Tours,**

tel. (206) 885-3173; and **See Seattle Walking Tours,** tel. (425) 226-7641.

Terrene Tours, tel. (206) 325-5569, offers custom cycling, hiking, and skiing tours in the Seattle area; they will drop off bikes and other cycling gear at your hotel. Other places to rent bikes are: **Al Young Bike & Ski,** 3615 N.E. 45th St. (U District), tel. (206) 524-2642; **Gregg's Greenlake Cycle,** 7007 Woodlawn Ave. NE (Greenlake), tel. (206) 523-1822; and **R & E Cycles,** 5627 University Way NE (U District), tel. (206) 527-4822.

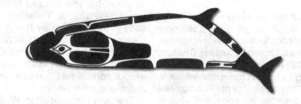

VICINITY OF SEATTLE

Lake Washington creates an eastern boundary for Seattle, separating the city from its suburban city cousins across the famous floating bridges. Completion of these bridges made it possible for commuters to live in the suburbs and work in Seattle. Now, many workers commute from homes in Seattle to high-tech jobs on the Eastside. In recent years, this area has seen an incredible population growth, fueled by high-tech industries such as Microsoft, Boeing, and Nintendo. This expansion has led Eastside to rival the Bay Area as a national technology center and has pushed cities such as Bellevue and Redmond to the bursting point with growth beyond their wildest dreams (or nightmares, depending upon your perspective). Eastside cities now contain 500,000 people, more than live in Seattle. For the traveler, these cities are not even fractionally as interesting as Seattle, but each does have something unique. And a few of the places—notably Kirkland, Edmonds, and Issaquah—are actually worth visiting.

BELLEVUE

Across Lake Washington, Bellevue (pop. 100,000) has grown from a sleepy Seattle suburb to Washington's fourth-largest city. When the city was incorporated in 1953, the surrounding land was primarily agricultural and Bellevue's downtown streets were simple gravel roads. As the home to many rapidly expanding high-tech industries, Bellevue now has its own high-rise downtown and the biggest shopping mall in the area.

Bellevue is often accused of attracting people concerned about living in the "right" neighborhood, driving the "right" automobile, sending their children to the "right" schools—in other words, Bellevue is considered, by people who don't live there, the Southern California of Puget Sound. It *is* upscale, even though the homes are often no nicer than many other Seattle suburbs. But you can add about $50,000 to the price for the pleasure of saying that you live in Belle-

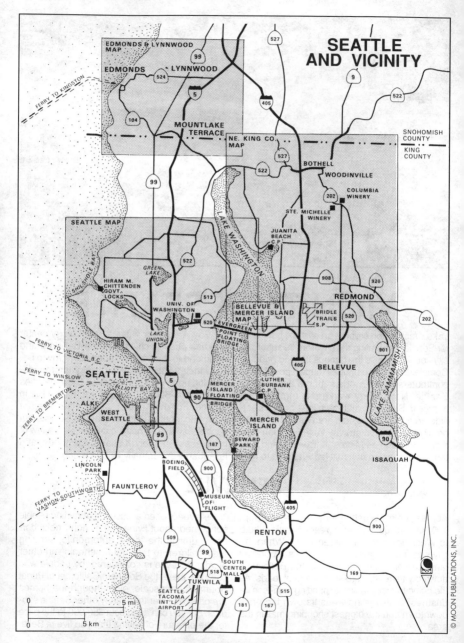

vue. Add a bit more for Bill Gate's $50-million digs; he lives just west of Bellevue on the shore of Lake Washington; the 20,000-square-foot mansion is visible from the Evergreen Point Floating Bridge. And despite Internet jokes to the contrary, the mansion does *not* contain the state of Rhode Island in the east wing, nor do the bathrooms use $100 bills for toilet paper.

SIGHTS

Bellevue's motto might be best expressed by a common bumper sticker here: "When the going gets tough, the tough go shopping." The main attraction is Bellevue Mall (see "Shopping," below). Of more interest are the museums and parks the city has to offer.

Doll Museum
Housed in an elaborate Victorian fantasy structure, the **Rosalie Whyel Museum of Doll Art,** 1116 108th Ave. NE, tel. (425) 455-1116, is home to one of the world's largest collections of dolls. Although I haven't the slightest interest in dolls, this museum is so impressive that even I found it interesting. The museum covers two expansive floors with professional presentations and more than a thousand dolls on display. Start out with a five-minute video explaining the history of doll-making, and then head upstairs to check out the diverse collection

that includes thumbnail-sized Egyptian tomb dolls and other antique dolls upstairs. Downstairs are 20th-century dolls, including mechanical dolls, authentically detailed doll houses, Barbies, GI Joes, teddy bears, and even Elvis figures. Also downstairs is a gift shop filled with dolls and doll paraphernalia. The museum is especially popular with the over-60 set—or at least older women—and bus loads roll in from senior centers all over the state. Admission costs $6 adults, $5 seniors, $4 ages 5-17, free for kids under five, and $20 for families. The museum is open Mon.-Sat. 10 a.m.-5 p.m., Sunday 1-5 p.m.

Bellevue Art Museum
Given the commercial nature of downtown Bellevue, it is perhaps fitting that the city's art museum should be located in the third-floor atrium of Bellevue Square Mall. Inside are changing exhibits of works by well-known regional artists. Open Monday and Wed.-Sat. 10 a.m.-6 p.m., Tuesday 10 a.m.-8 p.m., Sunday 11 a.m.-5 p.m.; tours are given daily at 2 p.m. Admission costs $3 adults, $2 seniors and students, and free for kids under 12; call (425) 454-3322 for details. Tuesday is free. In addition to exhibitions, the museum offers a wide range of talks, artist walks, performances, kids programs, workshops, and classes. The museum will be moving to spacious new quarters on N.E. 6th St. at Bellevue Way NE in 2000.

DON PITCHER

Bellevue

RECREATION

Parks

The 79-acre **Kelsey Creek Farm and Park,** 13204 S.E. 8th Pl., tel. (425) 455-7688, includes two enormous hip-roofed barns, an 1888 pioneer log cabin, a Japanese garden, one-mile loop trail, farmhouse, and cows, rabbits, pigs, ponies, and sheep for children to watch and pet. Open daily 7 a.m.-6 p.m.

Bellevue Botanical Garden, 12001 Main St., tel. (425) 462-2749, covers 36 acres of well-tended grounds, with a variety of display gardens within Wilburton Hill Park. The visitor center is open daily 10 a.m.-6 p.m. May-Sept., and daily 10 a.m.-4 p.m. the rest of the year; no charge. Also on the grounds is the historic Sharp log cabin.

Located along Lake Washington, both **Chism Beach Park** (off 100th Ave. SE) and **Newcastle Beach Park** (off Lake Washington Blvd. SE) have picnic areas, trails, and swimming beaches with summertime lifeguards. **Cascade Canoe and Kayak Center** tel. (425) 637-8838, offers sea kayak tours, lessons, and rentals on Lake Washington at Enatai Beach Park (108th Ave. SE at 35th Avenue).

Mercer Slough covers 320 acres of marsh habitat just south of downtown Bellevue. Here you'll discover 10 miles of trails and four miles of waterways perfect for exploring in a canoe or kayak. A fine place to watch for deer, muskrats, ducks, herons, and other critters. This entire area was underwater until 1917, when Seattle's Chittenden Locks were completed, lowering the level of Lake Washington by nine feet.

Bellevue's **Lake Hills Greenbelt,** off 156th Ave. SE, features five miles of trails through 100 acres of wetlands and pines in the heart of the city. Open to joggers, cyclists, wheelchairs, and hikers, the greenbelt trail links Larsen and Phantom lakes. A ranger station has information on the area's natural history. The **Lake to Lake Parkway Trail** is a paved cycling and running path connecting Lake Sammamish with Lake Washington.

Other Recreation

Swim at the **Bellevue pool,** 601 143rd Ave. NE, tel. (425) 296-4262, or in Lake Washington at Chism Beach and Newcastle Beach Parks (described above). **Outer Limits Kayak School,** 15600 N.E. 8th St., tel. (425) 781-6650, has river kayaking classes for all levels, from the basics to rolling and river rescue. They also offer guided river trips in the U.S. and Europe. **Cascade Canoe & Kayak Center,** 3519 108th Ave. SE, tel. (425) 637-8838, has canoe and kayak rentals and guided tours.

ACCOMMODATIONS AND CAMPING

Lodging is nearly impossible to find during the Arts and Crafts Fair in late July; book three months ahead if you're planning a visit then. The East King County Convention and Visitors Bureau (see below) can provide lodging information during the fair.

In spite of its reputation for being upscale, Bellevue has some of the most reasonably priced B&Bs in the Puget Sound region. **Bellevue Bed and Breakfast,** 830 100th Ave. SE, tel. (425) 453-1048 or (888) 453-1048, sits on a hillside overlooking Bellevue, with two guest rooms, private baths, and full breakfasts; $80 d. No young kids. **Petersen Bed and Breakfast,** 10228 S.E. 8th St., tel. (425) 454-9334, welcomes kids in their comfortable home just five minutes from Bellevue Square. Two guest rooms share a bath. A home-style breakfast and use of the hot tub on the deck are included; $70 s or $75 d. **A Cascade View B&B,** 13425 N.E. 27th St., tel. (425) 883-7078 or (888) 883-7078, is a spacious contemporary home with two guest rooms, private baths, and full breakfasts. Kids are welcome; $75-95 s or d.

Campgrounds

Although the nearest public campground is many miles away in the Cascades, Bellevue does have tent and vehicle spaces at two private RV parks: **Trailer Inns RV Park,** 15531 SE 37th (exit 11 west from I-90), tel. (425) 747-9181 or (800) 659-4684, and **Vasa Park Resort,** 2560 W. Lake Sammamish Rd. SE, tel. (425) 746-3260.

FOOD AND DRINK

Linger Longer, 10246 Main St. (Old Bellevue), tel. (425) 451-8616, is a European-style coffeehouse with the best local espresso, plus

BELLEVUE MOTELS AND HOTELS

Accommodations are arranged from least to most expensive. See the text for local B&Bs. Rates may be lower during the winter months.

INEXPENSIVE

Eastgate Motel; 14632 S.E. Eastgate Way; tel. (425) 746-4100 or (800) 628-8578; $45 s, $50-55 d; kitchenettes available

Kanes Motel; 14644 SE Eastgate Way; tel. (425) 746-8201 or (800) 746-8201; $54 s, $59 d; kitchenettes available

MODERATE

Days Inn; 3241 156th Ave. SE; tel. (425) 643-6644 or (800) 325-2525; $59-99 s, $64-99 d; jacuzzi, continental breakfast, airport shuttle, AAA approved

Bellevue Travelodge; 11011 N.E. 8th St.; tel. (425) 454-4967 or (800) 578-7878; $65 s, $70 d; outdoor pool, continental breakfast, kitchenettes available, AAA approved

Bellevue Hilton; 100 112th Ave. NE; tel. (425) 455-3330 or (800) 235-4458; $74-104 s or d; indoor pool, jacuzzi, sauna, exercise room, AAA approved

EXPENSIVE

Silver Cloud Inn; 10621 NE 12th St.; tel. (425) 637-7000 or (800) 205-6937; $88-118 s, $98-128 d; outdoor pool, jacuzzi, fridges, fitness center, kitchenettes available, AAA approved

WestCoast Bellevue Hotel; 625 116th Ave. NE; tel. (425) 455-9444 or (800) 426-0670; $90 s, $100 d; outdoor pool, exercise room, AAA approved

Fairfield Inn by Marriott; 14595 NE 29th Place; tel. (425) 869-6548 or (800) 228-2800; $109 s or d; indoor pool, jacuzzi, fitness room, continental breakfast, AAA approved

Courtyard by Marriott; 14615 NE 29th Place; tel. (425) 869-5300 or (800) 321-2211; $109 s, $119 d; indoor pool, AAA approved

Residence Inn by Marriott; 14455 29th Place NE; tel. (425) 331-3131 or (800) 331-3131; $115-190 s or d; one- and two-bedroom suites with kitchens and fireplaces, outdoor pool, jacuzzis, sports court, continental breakfast, AAA approved

Doubletree Hotel Bellevue Center; 818 112th Ave. NE; tel. (425) 455-1515 or (800) 222-8733; $120 s or d; indoor pool, kitchenettes available, AAA approved

Best Western Bellevue Inn; 11211 Main St.; tel. (425) 455-5240 or (800) 421-8193; $139-149 s, $149-159 d; outdoor pool, exercise room, local calls 60 cents, AAA approved

LUXURY

Embassy Suites Hotel; 3225 158th Ave. SE; tel. (425) 644-2500 or (800) 362-2779; $149-169 s, $174-194 d; suites, indoor pool, jacuzzi, sauna, exercise room, fridges and microwaves, full breakfast, AAA approved

Doubletree Hotel Bellevue; 300 112th Ave. SE; tel. (425) 455-1300 or (800) 547-8010; $195 s or d; large hotel, outdoor pool, jacuzzi, exercise room, AAA approved

Hyatt Regency Bellevue; 900 Bellevue Way NE; tel. (425) 462-1234 or (800) 233-1234; $199-224 s, $224-249 d; large luxury hotel, indoor pool, sauna, jacuzzi, health club, AAA approved

Bellevue Club Hotel; 11200 S.E. 6th St.; tel. (425) 454-4424 or (800) 579-1110; $210-265 s or d; new luxury hotel, indoor pool, sauna, jacuzzi, racquetball courts, tennis courts, complete athletic facility, AAA approved

delicious baked goods, salads, panini, and quiche. **Azalea's Fountain Court,** 22 103rd Ave. NE, tel. (425) 451-0426, is another notable Old Bellevue restaurant, with gourmet fare and fresh seafood from an ever-changing menu; $18-26 dinner entrees. The restaurant has outside seating for summer days, and live jazz on Friday and Saturday nights. Recommended.

Located 21 floors up in the Seafirst Building at Bellevue Place (10500 N.E. 8th St.), **Daniel's Broiler,** tel. (425) 462-4662, has good seafood chowder and steaks, and extraordinary views. The lounge here offers wines by the glass, oysters on the half shell, and a variety of light meals and desserts, plus live jazz or piano music nightly.

Jake O'Shaughnessey's in the Bellevue Square Mall, tel. (425) 455-5559, is popular for prime rib and steak. The bar has 27 different beers on tap in a convivial pub setting (if you can forget you're in a mall).

European Food

Pogacha, 119 106th Ave. NE, tel. (425) 455-5670, is certainly one of the more unusual Bellevue restaurants, with flavorful toppings on Croatian-style pizzas, and delightfully crunchy breads.

Spazzo offers impressive vistas from the top of the Key Bank Building at 10655 N.E. 4th St., tel. (425) 454-8255. The Mediterranean menu includes well-prepared food from North Africa, Turkey, and Greece. This contrasts rather sharply with the strip-mall location of **Giuseppie's,** 144 105th Ave. NE, tel. (425) 454-6868, but you'll be pleased to discover authentic Italian cooking and gourmet pizzas.

Tosoni's, 14320 N.E. 20th St., tel. (425) 644-1668, serves big portions of hearty and delicious Eastern European fare.

Asian Food

Raga Cuisine of India, 555 108th Ave. NE, tel. (425) 450-0336, offers classical Indian food, with tandoori, lamb, and vegetarian specialties, plus a popular luncheon buffet. Very good. Housed in an old IHOP building, **City Thai Restaurant,** 21 Bellevue Way NE, tel. (425) 452-8554, is a surprisingly elegant little place with friendly service and authentic Thai dishes. Lunch specials are a good bargain.

The best local Chinese restaurant is **Noble Court,** 1644 140th Ave. NE, tel. (425) 641-6011, said to have the tastiest dim sum around, along with many unusual offerings. Another favorite—especially with Chinese customers—is **Ming Chinese Seafood Restaurant,** 13200 Northup Way, tel. (425) 643-3888. For authentic Korean meals, head to **Seoul Olympic Restaurant,** 1200 112th Ave. NE, tel. (425) 455-9305. Good Japanese restaurants include: **I Love Sushi,** 11818 N.E. 8th St., tel. (425) 454-5706, and **Kampai Japanese Cuisine,** 201 106th Ave. NE, tel. (425) 451-8777.

Bellevue has the standard grocers, including two excellent upscale Larry's Markets, but one store really stands out: **Uwajimaya,** 15555 N.E. 24th, tel. (425) 747-9012. This is the other half of a two-store operation (the original is in Seattle's International District) and features fresh seafood, high-quality produce, a deli with sushi and other Japanese specialties, plus Japanese books and gifts.

EVENTS AND ENTERTAINMENT

The Bellevue Art Museum sponsors the annual **Pacific Northwest Arts Fair,** held in Bellevue Square the last full weekend of July. It is one of the state's largest such fairs, and has been going on since 1947. Many artists' careers have been helped along by the juried show and the enormous crowds. As a climatological aside, rain has fallen on the fair only once in over 50 years! For details, call (425) 454-4900.

You won't find anything approaching the Seattle scene in boring Bellevue, but **Ground Zero,** 257 100th Ave. NE, tel. (425) 452-6118, and **Daniel's Broiler,** 10500 N.E. 8th, tel. (425) 462-4662, have live bands on weekends. **Crossroads Shopping Center,** 15600 N.E. 8th Ave., tel. (425) 644-1111, has free concerts of all types on Friday and Saturday nights.

The **Bellevue Philharmonic Orchestra,** tel. (425) 455-4171, performs classical and pop concerts at various local venues, including the state-of-the-art **Meydenbauer Center** on the corner of 112th Ave. NE and N.E. 6th Street. The Meydenbauer also hosts theatrical and musical productions from a variety of Eastside companies, including the **Bellevue Chamber Chorus,** tel. (425) 881-0445, a group of 30 singers who perform Oct.-May.

SHOPPING

At N.E. 8th St. and Bellevue Way NE, **Bellevue Square** is one of the Northwest's largest shopping malls—more than 200 stores and a dozen restaurants, plus the Bellevue Art Museum, and atrium. Locals crow that this upscale shopping center attracts more visitors than Disneyland.

For a glimpse into Bellevue's past, visit the shops and galleries in **Old Bellevue's** restored business district on Main St. between 100th and Bellevue Way. These include **Cuttysark**, 10237 Main St., tel. (425) 453-1265. The store is almost a museum, with intricate old ship models, marine antiques of all sorts, and flags from around the globe. Next door is **Ming's Asian Gallery**, tel. (425) 462-4008, with antique Asian pieces.

Bellevue also is home to several surprisingly large bookstores, including: **Barnes and Noble,** 626 106th Ave. NE, tel. (425) 451-8463; **Tower Books,** 10635 N.E. 8th St., tel. (425) 451-1110; and **University Book Store,** 990 102nd Ave. NE, tel. (425) 632-9500.

INFORMATION AND TRANSPORTATION

Information
For additional information on Bellevue and the surrounding area, contact the **East King County Convention and Visitors Bureau,** 520 112th Ave. NE, Suite 101, tel. (425) 450-5640 or (800) 252-1926. Open Mon.-Fri. 8:30 a.m.-5 p.m., plus some summer weekends. Bellevue's modern **Public Library,** at 11501 Main, tel. (425) 455-6889, is the largest in King County.

Transportation
Metro Transit, tel. (800) 542-7876, has several buses serving Bellevue from Seattle, plus numerous local routes. The main stop is the Bellevue Transit Center, on N.E. 6th St. downtown. **Shuttle Express,** tel. (425) 622-1424 or (800) 487-7433, provides door-to-door service between Bellevue hotels and Sea-Tac Airport.

VICINITY OF BELLEVUE

MERCER ISLAND

Mercer Island (pop. 21,000) is primarily an upper-middle-class Seattle suburb, connected to the city at its north end by I-90's floating bridge. The island has stringent growth regulations that help preserve its rural character and severely limit both the size of its commercial district and the height of buildings. Partly because of these limitations, the cost of a home has approached stratospheric levels; the average home on Mercer Island sells for over $500,000! A great place to check out the BMW/Lexus/Mercedes crowd. Mercer's most famous resident is also its richest: Microsoft billionaire Paul Allen has a mansion along the southwest shore.

Sights
Mercer Island is approximately five miles long and two miles wide, with scenic roads that make for delightful bike tours. Parks cover 475 acres on the island. **Luther Burbank Park** at 2040 84th Ave. SE is the island's best waterfront park, with a beach, hiking trails, a picnic area, and fishing in Lake Washington. Start here for a 15-mile loop bike tour of the island: first go east on N. Mercer Way, then south on E. Mercer Way to the island's southern tip, then back up north on W. Mercer Way. At S.E. 68th St. and Island Crest Way, **Pioneer Park** has equestrian and hiking trails in a natural, wild setting (no restrooms), including a three-quarter-mile interpretive nature trail.

Accommodations
Mercer Island Travelodge, 7645 Sunset Hwy. (exit 9), tel. (206) 232-8000 or (800) 255-3050, has rooms for $49 s or $61 d, including a jacuzzi. Homier accommodations can be found in one of several island B&Bs. **Duck-In B&B,** 4118 100th Ave. SE, tel. (206) 232-2554, has a romantic two-bedroom 1920s cottage ($125 for up to four) with a big grassy lawn right on the shore of Lake Washington. A continental breakfast is served, and kids are welcome.

Ceda's LakeView B&B, 4220 Crestwood Pl., tel. (206) 230-0653 or (800) 825-4866, is an impressive contemporary home with a balcony overlooking Lake Washington. A continental breakfast is served, and kids are welcome. Four guest rooms have shared or private baths; $75-125 s or d. **Tree House B&B,** tel. (206) 230-8620, is a contemporary home with three guest rooms (shared or private bath), a huge deck facing the lake, lush gardens, and a full breakfast. No kids under 10, and a two-night minimum; $115-145 s or d.

Other Practicalities

Mercer's small business district is located on the north end of the island and just off I-90. Here you'll find most of life's necessities: chocolates, espresso, bagels, books, booze, bike repairs, and Thai food. In fact there are actually two very good Thai restaurants here: **Pon Preom Restaurant,** 3039 78th Ave. SE, tel. (206) 236-8424, and the more Americanized **Thai on Mercer,** 7691 S.E. 27th St., tel. (206) 236-9990. For food from the European continent, head to **Cucina! Presto!,** 7807 S.E. 27th St., tel. (206) 236-6888.

Visit **Mercer Island Chamber of Commerce,** "downtown" at 7601 S.E. 27th, tel. (206) 232-3404, for local information. The main annual event is **Summer Celebration,** held in mid-July, with a street fair, fireworks, concerts, and more fun. Swim at the **Mercer Island Pool,** 8815 S.E. 40th, tel. (206) 296-4370, or in the lake at **Clarke Beach** on the southeast end of the island.

Getting There

The only way to drive to Mercer Island is to take I-90 over the Mercer Island (Lacey V. Murrow) Floating Bridge. The bridge was built in honor of a prominent civil engineer who also was the brother of the famed newscaster Edward R. Murrow. While being refurbished, the original bridge sank during a winter storm in November 1990 and was then replaced. The span is just over one and a quarter miles long.

Metro Transit, tel. (206) 553-3000 or (800) 542-7876, has regular service to the island from either Seattle or Bellevue, along with a number of on-island routes. **Shuttle Express,** tel. (206) 622-1424 or (800) 487-7433, provides frequent direct service to Sea-Tac Airport.

KIRKLAND

Kirkland (pop. 42,000) is a gentrified bedroom community that has managed to retain much of its original charm in spite of the boutiques, art galleries, cafes, and condos lining Lake Washington. A waterfront business development called **Carillon Point** is a centerpiece along the shore, with six carillons ringing every half hour. The city also houses the corporate headquarters for the Seattle Seahawks football team and Costco.

History

The oldest city on the east side of Lake Washington, Kirkland was founded in 1888 and incorporated in 1905. Surprisingly enough, Peter Kirk wasn't Kirkland's founding father—that honor

belongs to Leigh Smith Jones Hunt. Hunt persuaded Kirk to build his steel mill, originally slated for Tacoma, in his town instead and offered to change the name to "Kirkland" as an added incentive. Kirk hoped to build the "Pittsburgh of the West"; fortunately or not, he never succeeded.

One of the most monumental of the places built in Kirkland's early days is the **Marsh Estate,** a Tudor-style mansion built in 1929 that faces Lake Washington. It is privately owned, but worth a gander from the outside; find it at 6604 Lake Washington Blvd. NE.

City Parks

A cluster of city parks provide much-needed open space on the shore of Lake Washington. **Marina Park** and **Waverly Beach Park** are right downtown, and provide great across-the-lake views. Just north of downtown along Lake Washington is **Juanita Bay Park,** an old golf course now transformed with scenic hiking trails and guided walks in the summer (call 425-828-1217. Continue north around the bay to **Juanita Beach Park,** with an impressively long pier, picnic tables, and one of the area's best swimming beaches. Northwest of Juanita, **Denny Park,** Holmes Point Dr., has a small beach, picnic area, and hiking trail leading to King County's largest Douglas fir; standing 255 feet high and eight feet in diameter, it's estimated to be 585 years old.

Fine Arts

Downtown Kirkland is sprinkled with fun public sculptures, including "Cow and the Coyote" on Central Way. **Kirkland Arts Center,** tel. (425) 822-7161, has exhibits and classes in the historic Peter Kirk Building (1891) at 620 Market Street. Another dozen galleries are right downtown on Central Way NE and Park Lane. Three of the best are **Berozkina Gallery,** 9 Lake St., tel. (425) 803-5032; **Foster/White Gallery,** 126 Central Way, tel. (425) 822-2308; and **Lakeshore Gallery,** 15 Lake St., tel. (425) 827-0606. The second Thursday of each month, the galleries open for **Art Walk,** featuring artist receptions and shows 6-9 p.m.

Bridle Trails State Park

This immensely popular park covers 482 acres off 116th Ave. NE, with 28 miles of equestrian

Bridle Trails State Park

and hiking trails (more horses than hikers). The **Bridle Crest Trail** continues on to Redmond's Marymoor Park. The park is also a favorite place for riding shows throughout the summer months. No camping.

St. Edward State Park

Head farther north on N.E. 145th St. to St. Edward State Park, tel. (425) 296-2970, a 316-acre retreat from civilization. This quiet piece of property was part of a Catholic seminary until 1977; when the seminary closed, the diocese sold the land to the state and the park opened the following summer. Saint Edwards boasts three-quarters of a mile of forested, undeveloped Lake Washington shoreline and five miles of hiking and mountain biking trails, plus picnic areas, a gymnasium, and an indoor pool. tel. (425) 296-2970. The separate St. Thomas Center nearby is still owned by the archdiocese and is used as a conference center and for various recovery programs.

Bed and Breakfasts

Shumway Mansion, 11410 99th Place NE, tel. (425) 823-2303, a 23-room B&B, is a three-minute walk from Juanita Beach. The antique-furnished inn was built in 1909; it was bought in 1982 and moved down the hill to its present location on spacious grounds overlooking Juanita Bay. This is a favorite place for weddings. The eight elegant guest rooms have private baths,

and a buffet breakfast is served. Guests also have access to a health club; $70-105 s or d.

Set on 3.5 wooded acres with a pond and gazebo, **Cottage Creek Inn B&B,** 12525 Avondale Rd. NE, tel. (425) 881-5606, is a Tudor-style home with four guest room, private baths, and full breakfast; $89-115 s or d. No kids under 12.

Hotels and Motels

The **Woodmark Hotel,** 1200 Carillon Pt., tel. (425) 822-3700 or (800) 822-3700, doesn't look that impressive from the outside but is actually one of the finest lodging places in the area, with every possible amenity (grand piano, stocked minibars, terry robes, TV in the bathroom, and full breakfast) and rooms overlooking Lake Washington. This is the only hotel on the shores of the lake, and rates are commensurate with the amenities: $185-230 s or $200-245 d.

Other Kirkland lodging places include the following. **Best Western Kirkland Inn,** 12223 NE 116th St., tel. (425) 822-2300 or (800) 332-4200, has an outdoor pool, jacuzzi, and continental breakfast; $81-92 s or $83-94 d. **Clarion Inn at Totem Lake,** 12233 N.E. Totem Lake Way, tel. (425) 821-2202 or (800) 252-7466, is similarly set up, with an outdoor pool, jacuzzi, sauna, exercise room, library bar, and continental buffet breakfast; $115-175 s or $115-185 d. **La Quinta Inn,** 10530 N.E. Northup Way, tel. (425) 828-6585 or (800) 531-5900, has an outdoor pool, continental breakfast, and health club access; $75-82 s or d. **Silver Cloud Inn,** 12202 N.E. 124th St., tel. (425) 821-8300 or (800) 205-6933, charges $72-87 s or $82-97 d, including an outdoor pool, jacuzzi, exercise room, continental breakfast, and airport shuttle. The least expensive local place is **Motel 6,** 12010 120th Pl. NE, tel. (425) 821-5618 or (800) 466-8356, for $55 s or $61 d, including an outdoor pool.

Food and Drink

Kirkland is blessed with a mix of quick eateries and fine restaurants, many of which are right downtown. A good breakfast place is **Hector's Restaurant,** 112 Lake St., tel. (425) 827-4811, with home-style breakfasts and a tasty lobster bisque at lunch.

Third Floor Fish Cafe, on the marina at 205 Lake St. S, tel. (425) 822-3553, is a yuppified place specializing in seafood. Great seafood and dramatic Lake Washington views. Another place with lake vistas and seafood specials is **Yarrow Bay Grill and Beach Cafe,** 1270 Carillon Point, tel. (425) 889-9052.

Coyote Creek Pizza Co., 228 Central Way NE, tel. (425) 822-2226, bakes distinctive and inspired pizzas and calzones.

The **Ristorante Paradiso,** 120 A Park Lane, tel. (425) 889-8601, offers outstanding nouvelle cuisine with an Italian twist, including fresh seafood, lamb chops, and veal. **Cafe Juanita,** 9702 N.E. 120th Place, tel. (425) 823-1505, is another fine Italian restaurant with dependably great meals and an extraordinary choice of Italian wines.

La Provençal, 212 Central Way, tel. (425) 827-3300, is the oldest French restaurant operating in a single location in the Puget Sound area; it's owned by Philippe Gayte, who learned to cook in his native Rhone Valley. Very expensive, but outstanding.

Izumi, in the Totem Lake West Shopping Center, tel. (425) 821-1959, has very good Japanese sushi, tempura, teriyaki, and other specialties. Another treat is the extremely popular **Shamiana,** 10724 N.E. 68th St., tel. (425) 827-4902, is a great place for Indian and Pakistani food, including a number of vegetarian specials. **City Thai Restaurant,** 134 Parkplace Center, tel. (425) 827-2875, is the place to go if you can't afford a visit to Thailand. **Santori Greek Grill,** 106 Central Way, tel. (425) 822-0555, is a good place for Greek fast food, including huge gyros and falafels.

Join the raucous, upscale crowd at the **Kirkland Roaster and Ale House,** 111 Central Way, tel. (425) 827-4400, to sample the 19 microbrews on tap, including several of Hale's Ales made in the adjacent brewery. The menu covers quite a range, from fresh fish to nachos. But the featured attraction is a huge spit where they roast chicken, lamb, and other meats.

Events

Kirkland Arts & Craft Festival, the second weekend in July, attracts crowds of people for local arts and crafts; call (425) 822-7161 for details. In late September, **Taste Kirkland** is another very popular fair with food booths lining the main thoroughfare and live music at Marina Park.

Entertainment

Waldo's Tavern, 12657 N.E. 85th St., tel. (425) 827-9292, is a big place with live rock bands on weekends and pool tables all the time. **Kirkland Roaster and Ale House,** 111 Central Way, tel. (425) 827-4400, also has live music on weekends. More music and dancing at **Davinci's,** 89 Kirkland Ave., tel. (425) 889-9000, and **Dynamite Lounge,** 15 Lake St., tel. (425) 822-3474; and **The Shark Club,** 52 Lakeshore Plaza, tel. (425) 803-3003.

Shopping

The **Kirkland Antique Gallery** is a collector's paradise. Located at 151 3rd St., this antique mall has 80 shops filled with collectibles. **Eastside Trains,** 217 Central Way, tel. (425) 828-4098, is a surprisingly large place where 40-something men play with model trains and pretend to be kids again (or pretend to be buying trains for their kids).

Information

For maps and a limited amount of other information, drop by the **Kirkland Chamber of Commerce** (www.kirkland.net), upstairs in Parkplace Mall, tel. (425) 822-7066. Open Mon.-Fri. 9 a.m.- 5 p.m. year-round.

Recreation and Tours
Argosy Cruises, tel. (425) 623-4252 (recording) or (425) 623-1445, offers scenic 90-minute boat tours of Lake Washington, departing from Kirkland's Marina Park daily May-September. These take place onboard the historic MV *Kirkland,* a 110-foot wooden ferry built in 1924, and feature the lake and surrounding sights (including homes of the rich and famous). The cost is $18 adults, $16 seniors, $9 kids, and free for under five. **Upper Left-Hand Corner Kayak Tours,** tel. (425) 828-4772, leads sea kayaking tours of Lake Washington.

Transportation
Metro Transit, tel. (425) 447-4800 or (800) 542-7876, provides daily bus service to Kirkland, Bellevue, Seattle, and other points in King County.

   Shuttle Express, tel. (425) 622-1424 or (800) 487-7433, has door-to-door connections between Kirkland and Sea-Tac Airport.

REDMOND

Redmond began as a boat landing along the Sammamish Slough, the slow-moving stream that links Lake Washington and Lake Sammamish. Foot travel in pioneer days was virtually impossible due to the dense forests and extensive marshland, so most inland travel was accomplished via river. Today the city is the self-proclaimed bicycle capital of the Northwest, holding regular bicycle races at its Velodrome in Marymoor Park.

   In recent years, rapid growth has transformed the city of Redmond from a Seattle suburb to a city in its own right—with traffic jams and ugly strip malls to match. A number of large companies now call Redmond home, including Nintendo, Eddie Bauer, and software giant Microsoft. The Microsoft campus now encompasses almost two million square feet of office space in Redmond, and has additional facilities in Bothell, Bellevue, and Kirkland. Redmond has no real downtown, just a series of shopping malls strung together in what now passes for a town of 40,000.

   The striking **Ling Shen Ching Tze Temple,** 17012 N.E. 40th Ct., tel. (425) 882-0916, is the largest and most impressive Buddhist temple in

Washington. Open Mon.-Sat. 9:30 a.m.-6 p.m., with meditations on Saturday at 8 p.m.

Parks and Recreation
Marymoor Park on the West Lake Sammamish Pkwy. has 533 acres of open space on Seattle banker James Clise's 1905 estate. Half of the furnished 28-room mansion is now the **Marymoor Museum,** tel. (425) 885-3684, featuring photos and exhibits of local history; open Tues.-Thurs. 11 a.m.-4 p.m., and Sat.-Sun. 1-5 p.m.; donation. The other half is used for wedding receptions and other gatherings. Marymoor Park is better known for its **Velodrome,** a banked 400-meter bike-racing track that draws competitors from across the United States. This is one of the only such facilities in the nation. Bike races are held Friday evenings April-Nov.; tel. (425) 389-5825. The park also features a one-mile interpretive trail, soccer fields, tennis courts, a model airplane field, dog training grounds, and picnic shelters.

   Idylwood Park is south of Marymoor Park along the west shore of Lake Sammamish, with a swimming beach and picnicking grounds.

   Sixty-eight-acre **Farrel-McWhirter Park,** 10400 192nd Ave. NE, has horse and hiking trails, picnicking, a barnyard zoo, and horse arena. Charlotte's Trail is a paved path that extends the length of the park.

   Swim at the **Redmond Pool,** 17535 N.E. 104th, tel. (425) 296-2961. For horseback rides, contact **Lori's Sammamish Stables,** tel. (425) 868-5299. **The Balloon Depot,** 16138 N.E. 87th St., tel. (425) 881-9699, lifts off with hot air balloon rides most mornings and evenings.

Sammamish River Trail
The paved 13-mile Sammamish River Trail begins in Marymoor Park and follows the river through Redmond, Woodinville, and on to Kenmore. There it connects with Seattle's Burke-Gilman Trail, which continues all the way to Fremont, a total distance of approximately 27 miles. This immensely popular path provides Mt. Rainier and Lake Washington views and passes the Chateau Ste. Michelle and Columbia wineries, favorite stopping places. The **Puget Power-Redmond Trail** is a three-mile gravel path (great for mountain bikes) that connects the Sammamish River Trail to Farrel-McWhirter Park.

Lodging and Camping

Cottage Creek Inn B&B, tel. (425) 881-5606, is a Tudor-style manor home in an attractive country setting. **Lilac Lea Christian B&B**, 21008 N.E. 117th St., tel. (425) 851-1898, has a comfortable and attractive cottage suite with a Christian emphasis (no alcohol allowed) that may put some folks off. A continental breakfast is served; no kids. $85 s or d.

Surrounded by 10 acres of old-growth forest four miles from downtown, **Aurora's La Residencia B&B**, 5355 204th Pl., tel. (425) 836-4696, is a luxurious Swiss chalet-style home. The three guest rooms have private baths, and a gourmet breakfast is served. $150-195 d.

Local motels include the following. **Silver Cloud Inn**, 15304 N.E. 21st St., tel. (425) 746-8200 or (800) 205-6934, is a new motel with rooms for $77-97 s or $87-107 d, including an indoor pool, jacuzzi, exercise facility, and continental breakfast. **Redmond Inn** 15304 N.E. 21st St., tel. (425) 883-4900 or (800) 634-8080, features an outdoor pool and jacuzzi; $79-89 s or $89-99 d. **Inn on the River Trail,** tel. (206) 285-0810, is a 22-room country inn right along the Sammamish River Trail. All rooms include view balconies and most have king-size beds. A light breakfast is served; $95-175 s or $115-200 d.

Food

For the best local breakfasts, visit **Village Square Cafe**, 16150 N.E. 85th, tel. (425) 885-7287. **Cornerstone Coffee Bar,** on the corner of Cleveland and Leary Way, tel. (425) 883-3871, is a pleasant little place with coffees and sweets in an historic brick building. Famous locally for their espresso shakes. **Mikie's Brooklyn Bagel Deli,** 16640 Redmond Way, tel. (425) 881-3344, has fresh-baked breads and deli meats from New York; locals call their bagels the most authentic on the Eastside.

Kikuya, 8105 161st Ave. NE, tel. (425) 881-8771, is a wonderful small Japanese restaurant with friendly service and high-quality food. Don't come here on a weekend evening unless you're ready to wait. **Peking Chinese Restaurant,** 16875 Redmond Way, tel. (425) 883-2681, has some of the finest Mandarin and Sichuan food on the Eastside.

il Bacio, 16564 Cleveland St., tel. (425) 869-8815, has delicious and authentic Italian cuisine. Next door is **Delicious World Bistro & Deli,** tel. (425) 883-4443, with food from Turkey, Bulgaria, Italy, Russia, and other places. Get homemade pizzas and calzones at **Big Time Pizza,** 7824 Leary Way, tel. (425) 885-6425.

Redmond Brewing Company, 7950 164th Ave. NE, tel. (425) 883-9835, is a big downtown restaurant and brewery with live music on weekends.

The **Redmond Saturday Market** brings fresh veggies, flowers, crafts, fruit, honey, and more to 7730 Leary Way. It's held downtown May-Oct. on Saturday 8 a.m.-2 p.m.; tel. (425) 882-5151.

Events

Head to Marymoor Park on the Fourth of July weekend for the very popular annual **Heritage Festival,** tel. (425) 296-2964, with arts and crafts, music, ethnic dancing, and food booths. It's followed by fireworks next to the Redmond High School.

The **Derby Days Festival** in mid-July is a major cycling event with street criterion bike races, a carnival, an antique car show, parades, arts and crafts, and plenty of food. It has been going on since 1939. Call (425) 885-4014 for details. The **Evergreen Classic Horse Show**—one of the top 10 equestrian shows in the nation—is held at Marymoor Park each September.

Information and Shopping

The **Greater Redmond Chamber of Commerce,** 16210 N.E. 80th St., tel. (425) 885-4014, www.redmondchamber.org, has local information, and is open Mon.-Fri. 9 a.m.-5 p.m. year-round. Swim at the **Redmond Pool,** 17535 N.E. 104th, tel. (425) 296-2961.

The **Antique Connection,** 16701 Cleveland St., tel. (425) 882-3122, has 65 antique dealers under one roof. For more antiques, try **Days Gone Bye Antique Mall** on the lower level of the Ethan Allen Bldg., 2207 N.E. Bel-Red Road.

Transportation

Metro Transit, tel. (800) 542-7876, has daily bus service around Redmond, on to Seattle and Bellevue, and throughout King County.

Shuttle Express, tel. (425) 622-1424 or (800) 487-7433, provides frequent direct service from Redmond's Silver Cloud Inn and Redmond Inn to Sea-Tac Airport.

ISSAQUAH

At the foot of the "Issaquah Alps," Issaquah (ISS-a-kwa, pop. 9,000) offers an escape to country-fresh air in a fast-growing town loaded with history. Just two exits east of Renton on I-90, Issaquah's hills are within a half-hour drive of Seattle and Tacoma. These are very old, worn-down mountains; their lower elevation keeps them mostly snow-free—and hikeable—virtually year-round. The town itself is a pleasant place to enjoy the blend of old and new; but get here soon, because gross condos, shopping malls, and suburbs are quickly devouring the remaining open space.

HISTORY

Members of the Snoqualmie tribe inhabited the land around present-day Issaquah for centuries, subsisting on the rich fish resources in Lake Sammamish, Lake Washington, and nearby rivers. They called this place "Squak," after the sound made by the thousands of ducks and cranes that passed through each spring and fall. To the whites, the Indian word sounded something like "Issaquah." The earliest Anglo settlers arrived here in the 1860s, opening coal mines, logging the dense evergreen forests, and starting farms. Coal discoveries brought a flood of miners to the area, and coal remained the economic mainstay till the 1920s. The town was a rough place at first: rioters sent Chinese workers fleeing for their lives, and the state militia was later brought in to shut down a coal strike by union activists from the Wobblies. Nearly every one of the first 70 town ordinances enacted dealt with liquor, misconduct by public officials, and out-of-control animals.

The coal mines closed in the 1920s, but lumber mills replaced them as loggers stripped away the surrounding forests. Issaquah puttered along for the first half of this century, but completion of the Lake Washington Floating Bridge in 1940 and the opening of Interstate 90 in the 1970s made commuting easy. This sudden influx of new people has led to the construction of many new homes and businesses, transforming this once-sleepy burg into a bustling place. Today, the largest local employers are high-tech industries: Boeing Computer Services, Siemens Medical Systems, Egghead Software, and Microsoft. But there still are vestiges of the farming past: the creamery in town produces all the Darigold yogurt sold in the Northwest.

SIGHTS AND TOURS

Museums
The **Gilman Town Hall Museum,** 165 S.E. Andrews, tel. (425) 392-3500, is open Monday 10:30 a.m.-2:30 p.m., and Saturday noon-4 p.m.; free. Built in the 1890s, this building served as the original town hall, back when Issaquah was known as Gilman. Railroad tools, children's toys, a pioneer kitchen and grocery store, artifacts, and many historical photographs are on display inside. Out back is the old two-cell town jail. **Issaquah Train Depot Museum,** in the restored 1889 train depot at Front and Sunset Streets, tel. (425) 392-2322, also has historical photos and artifacts. Open Saturday 11 a.m.-3 p.m.

Gilman Village
Issaquah's Gilman Village is a collection of 40 or so turn-of-the-century homes, all moved and restored to form a quaint cluster of boutiques selling clothing, crafts, gifts, kitchenware, and jewelry. If you're into lacy frou-frou, you'll love these boardwalk-linked places. Several shops do offer something more substantial, including a number of restaurants listed below. Be sure to drop by **Evolution,** tel. (425) 392-6963, an artists cooperative that sells high quality works, including many pieces made from recycled products. The **Chukar Cherries** shop sells their delicious sweet cherry concoctions, with free samples for the tasting. They also have a mail-order catalog, tel. (800) 624-9544.

In historical downtown Issaquah, the **Issaquah Gallery** has paintings, photography, stained glass, pottery, and prints by Northwest artists at 49 N. Front St., tel. (425) 392-4247. **Northwest Basketry,** 38 Front St., tel. (425) 557-

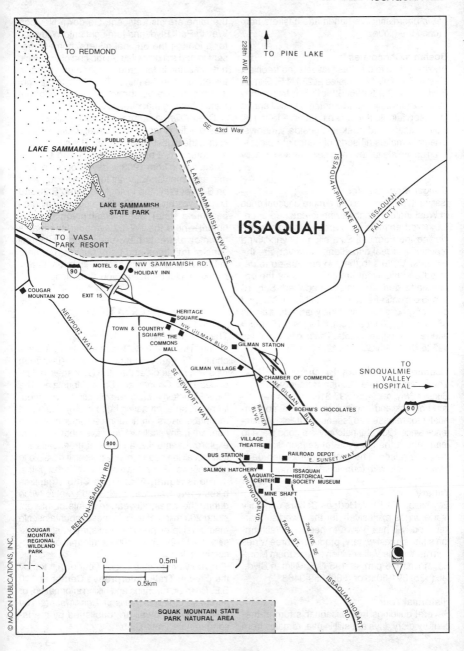

6559, has distinctive handmade baskets from around the globe.

Boehm's Chocolates
Another place to purchase sweets (no freebies, alas) is Boehm's Chocolates at 255 N.E. Gilman Blvd., tel. (425) 392-6652, offering free candy factory tours July to mid-September; call ahead for reservations. If you can't get on a tour, just walk outside and peek in the side windows. Boehm's makes all sorts of chocolate pieces, even chocolate turkeys and dolphins. Open daily 9 a.m.-6 p.m.

Cougar Mountain Zoo
Issaquah's zoo is one of the more unusual ones in Washington, emphasizing threatened or endangered animals from around the globe, including the Formosa Sika elk and hyacinthine macaw. The real attractions, however, are the cougars. Visitors to the zoo are treated to detailed and highly informative tours by the docents and staff. The zoo is open Wed.-Sun. 10 a.m.-5 p.m. mid-February to mid-November, and only for groups the rest of the year. Admission is $5.50 adults, $4 for seniors, $4 ages 4-15, $2.50 ages 2-3, and free for tots. The zoo is located at 19525 S.E. 54th St.; tel. (425) 391-5508.

Issaquah State Salmon Hatchery
The Issaquah State Salmon Hatchery, 125 W. Sunset Way, tel. (425) 392-3180, raises five million chinook and one million coho salmon annually for release into Issaquah Creek. In existence since 1936, the hatchery is a good place to learn about the life cycle of salmon and how they are raised. The grounds are open daily dawn to dusk, with tours in late summer.

Winery
Established in 1987, **Hedges Cellars** originally made wines exclusively for the Swedish market. Today it has grown to become Washington's fifth-largest winery, producing three wines from its Yakima Valley winery. Taste them Mon.-Sat. 11 a.m.-6 p.m. at 195 N.E. Gilman Blvd., tel. (425) 391-6056 or (800) 859-9463.

Historical Tour
Several buildings from Issaquah's turn-of-the-century glory days are still in use; remains from the mine are also evident. Go down Newport Way to Park Blvd. and turn right onto Wildwood for a look at the original miners' homes, preserved and still occupied. At the end of the block, a depression in the ground near a grove marks the entrance to the mine's first shaft; to the right is the concrete bulkhead used to anchor the mine's hauling machinery.

Downtown, a number of historically significant buildings face Front Street. **Odd Fellows Hall** is the oldest, built in 1888. The second-oldest commercial building is the **Grand Central Hotel**, dating from 1903; today it houses offices and apartments. Adjacent to the railroad tracks on Sunset Way, the lovingly restored **Railroad Depot** was built in 1889 (the year Washington became a state), out of Washington Territory timber—note the "W.T." symbol. Issaquah's downtown streets have been planted with all sorts of fruit trees and berry bushes; get here in late summer to pick apples, cherries, pears, plums, or blueberries as you stroll along.

RECREATION

The Issaquah Alps
As the "Trailhead City," Issaquah takes pride in a chain of nearby mountains—the "Issaquah Alps"—a range older than the Cascades that includes Tiger, Cougar, and Squak Mountains. The Tiger Mountain area is Washington's most popular hiking area, attracting hundreds of hikers and mountain bikers on a sunny summer day. Also here are many shallow talus caves that are fun to explore. Eventually, a series of greenbelts will connect all the nearby parks, making it possible to head out from downtown onto a myriad of paths.

The **Issaquah Alps Trails Club** organizes hikes every Saturday and Sunday, plus twice during the week, all year, to points of interest along 200 miles of trails in these mountains. No membership or previous registration is necessary. Call (425) 328-0480 for information on upcoming hikes.

If you want to step out on your own, stop by the city-run **Trails Interpretive Center** at 110 S.E. Bush St. for maps and hiking information, or purchase *Guide to Trails of Tiger Mountain* by William K. Longwell Jr., published by the Issaquah Alps Trails Club.

Tiger Mountain State Forest covers 13,500 acres of forested lands and is capped by 3,004-foot **East Tiger Mountain,** the highest peak in the range. The hike up East Side Rd. to the summit provides spectacular views of the surrounding country. To reach the trailhead, take I-90 exit 25; go right onto Hwy. 18 and drive three miles to a dirt road on the right; proceed to the power line and park. Start your seven-mile hike on the uphill road under the power line.

Tiger Mountain is also home to one of the more unique local parks, **Fraternity Snoqualmie Nudist Park,** tel. (425) 392-NUDE, a 40-acre family place to let it all hang out, so to speak. This is the oldest (in existence since 1931) and largest nudist park in the Northwest. They sponsor a clothing-optional "Bare Buns Fun Run" in early July, followed in mid-August, by a summer music festival—called, what else, **Nudestock.** Thousands of nudists show up. Fun for the whole naked family.

Cougar Mountain Regional Wildland Park encompasses second-growth forests surrounding this 1,595-foot peak, with well-marked trails climbing past an old mining camp and waterfalls.

Squak Mountain State Park covers 613 acres of forested land just south of Issaquah and contains a maze of poorly maintained trails. Access is a bit tricky; ask locally for directions. No camping at Squak Mountain.

Horseback Riding

Even if you've had no prior experience, riding a horse along wooded trails can be a relaxing, enjoyable way to view the scenery. **Tiger Mountain Stables,** 132nd Ave., tel. (425) 392-5090, offers guided three-hour trips in Tiger Mountain State Forest. **High Country Outfitters,** 23836 S.E. 24th, tel. (425) 392-0111, leads trail rides and overnight trips into the Cascades.

On the Water

A mile and a half northwest of Issaquah, **Lake Sammamish State Park** is one of the more popular Puget Sound area parks, attracting over 1.5 million visitors each year. Facilities include a big sandy beach for sunbathing and swimming, a swimming float, bathhouses, boat ramps, picnic tables, hiking trails, and a concession stand selling fast food. The area is popular with boaters and water-skiers. Get here on a sunny weekend morning and you'll find long traffic jams at the boat launch. Call (425) 455-7010 for more information. No camping. **Klub Kayak,** tel. (425) 453-5363 or (888) 765-2925, offers sea kayak tours, lessons, and rentals on Lake Sammamish in the summer.

Owners of smaller motorboats, canoes, and rafts may prefer **Pine Lake,** a county park off 228th SE with a five-mph speed limit on the lake.

ACCOMMODATIONS

Lodging

Standard, inexpensive motel rooms are available at **Motel 6,** 1885 15th Pl. NW at I-90 exit 15, tel. (425) 392-8405 or (800) 466-8356, for $52 s or $58 d, including an outdoor pool. You'll find more luxurious accommodations at **Issaquah Holiday Inn,** 1801 12th Ave. NW, tel. (425) 392-6421 or (800) 465-4329. Amenities include a salmon-shaped outdoor pool, sauna, and jacuzzi; $86 s or $89 d.

Water's Edge B&B, 2736 222nd Ave. SE, tel. (425) 392-7727, has a private suite with a patio facing Pine Lake. Visitors can use the canoe and row boat, and kids are welcome. A continental breakfast is served; $100 s or d.

Campgrounds

Although there are no public campgrounds near Issaquah, you can camp in comfort at the 120-acre **Issaquah Highlands Camping Club,** 10610 Renton-Issaquah Rd. SE, tel. (425) 392-2351. Other private campgrounds include: **Issaquah Village RV Park,** 50 1st Ave. NE, tel. (425) 392-9233 or (800) 258-9233; **Blue Sky RV Park,** 9002 302nd Ave. SE, tel. (425) 222-7910; and **Vasa Park Resort,** on the west side of Lake Sammamish at 3560 W. Lake Sammamish Rd., tel. (425) 746-3260.

FOOD

Issaquah has a wide diversity of restaurants serving everything from fast food to gourmet fare. Several of the best are in Gilman Village, where the lovingly restored old buildings add to the ambiance. Notable Gilman Village eateries include the following. **Tantalus Restaurant,** tel. (425) 391-6090, has Greek specialties, and **Ristorante Nicolino Italiano,** tel. (425) 391-8077, makes deliciously authentic southern Italian dinners. For lunch, join the crowds at **The Sweet Addition,** tel. (425) 392-5661, where the salads and sandwiches are always well prepared, and the decadent cakes, truffles, and pies are a real temptation. Not recommended if you're on a diet. Also good for breakfast and lunch is **Snow Goose Cafe,** tel. (425) 391-4671.

Fine restaurants can also be found elsewhere in Issaquah. Housed in the Village Theatre building at 303 Front St. N, **Stage Right Cafe,** tel. (425) 392-0109, is a delightful, airy cafe with fresh soups, quiche, sandwiches, desserts, and espresso. Very popular with the brunch and after-theater crowds.

The Chinese food is tasty—but the atmosphere is rather plain—at **Mandarin Garden,** 40 E. Sunset Way, tel. (425) 392-9476.

Head down an alley way off the main street to find **Pizzuto's Cafe,** 157½ Front St. N, tel. (425) 557-6753, a quaint little place with delicious Italian meals. **Jay-Berry's Gourmet Pizza & Pasta & Lounge,** 385 N.W. Gilman Blvd., tel. (425) 392-0808, bakes the best pizzas in town, and the lounge overlooks quiet Issaquah Creek.

Issaquah Brewhouse, 35 W. Sunset Way, tel. (425) 557-1911, has 10 or so brewed-on-the-premises beers on tap, and a surprisingly good pub menu that includes salads and sandwiches, Cajun gumbo, and Thai grilled chicken.

American Eats

Looking for an all-American meal? Look no farther than **The Roost Restaurant,** 120 N.W. Gilman Blvd., tel. (425) 391-8077, for thick steaks and spicy ribs. The **XXX Drive-In,** 98 N.E. Holly St., tel. (425) 392-1266, is a real old-time favorite, with burgers, shakes, and the best root beer around. On summer weekends, their parking lot fills to overflowing with dozens of vintage cars.

Markets and More

The **Issaquah Public Market,** tel. (425) 837-3321, located in the Pickering Barn off 10th Ave., attracts shoppers on Saturday 9 a.m.-3 p.m. from mid-April through September. In addition to fresh produce, the market features all sorts of handicrafts.

Get quality cuts of meat and fresh smoked salmon at **Fischer's Meats & Seafoods,** 85 Front St. N, tel. (425) 392-3131, in existence since 1910. **Suncrest Whole Grain Bread Co.,** 1175 N.W. Gilman Blvd., tel. (425) 392-8983, bakes earthy and delicious fat-free breads, cinnamon rolls, and muffins using organically grown wheat.

ENTERTAINMENT AND EVENTS

Theater

The semiprofessional **Village Theatre** at 120 Front St. N puts on first-rate productions in their modern 488-seat theater (complete with a soundproof room for screaming babies). Theatrical productions are generally on the light side, with a heavy dose of musical favorites. For upcoming events and tickets, call (425) 392-2202.

Events

Issaquah's **Down Home 4th of July Parade** is fun for everyone, with all the usual events. Every fall, salmon return to their birthplace at the state salmon hatchery, and Issaquah doesn't miss the opportunity for a celebration. The two-day **Issaquah Salmon Days** comes around the first weekend in October with a parade, kids fair, 350 arts and crafts booths, live music, a pancake feed, fun run, and hatchery tours. More than 200,000 people crowd downtown Issaquah for the festival. **Santa's Raindeer Festival** takes place at Cougar Mountain Zoo in December, with thousands of twinkling lights, plus Santa and his herd of raindeer.

INFORMATION AND TRANSPORTATION

For maps and information contact the **Issaquah Visitor Information Center,** 155 N.W. Gilman Blvd., tel. (425) 392-7024; www.issaquah.org. Open daily 9 a.m.-5 p.m.

You can get to and from Seattle, Bellevue, and other points in King County via **Metro Transit,** tel. (425) 447-4800 or (800) 542-7876. **Shuttle Express,** tel. (425) 622-1424 or (800) 487-7433, provides direct service from Issaquah to Sea-Tac Airport.

NORTH FROM SEATTLE

WOODINVILLE

Woodinville (pop. 10,000), barely far enough from Seattle to have its own identity, is a rapidly growing suburban town that was just incorporated in 1993. It has stables and bridle trails and is becoming a very popular cycling destination, with easy access from Seattle via the Burke-Gilman and Sammamish River trails that pass right by several wineries and a big brewery. This is also the destination of the Spirit of Washington dinner train, described below. Unfortunately, this rural character is rapidly disappearing under an avalanche of asphalt and concrete as business parks, apartment complexes, and parking lots replace pasture land.

Chateau Ste. Michelle Winery

Woodinville is home to the state's largest winery, Chateau Ste. Michelle, off Hwy. 202 at 14111 N.E. 145th St., tel. (425) 488-1133. Established in 1934 as the National Wine Company—shortly after the end of Prohibition—and renamed Ste. Michelle Vintners in 1965, it has come to represent the Washington wine industry across the country. Though the wine grapes are grown (and most of the wine is produced) in eastern Washington, this winery is among the nicest to visit.

The original 1912 residence—once owned by Seattle lumber baron Fred Stimson—is surrounded by 87 acres of manicured grounds that include experimental vineyards, an arboretum, and trout ponds. The amphitheater is home to the **Summer Festival on the Green,** a full summer of music and arts events with picnics on the lawn; get tickets from Ticket Master, tel. (425) 292-2787. The crowds gather at the impressive French-chateau winery building, built in 1976. Very informative cellar tours and free tastings are offered every half-hour daily 10 a.m.-4:30 p.m., except Christmas and New Year's Day. Avoid the summer mob scene by visiting on Monday or Tuesday; weekends can get pretty hectic. Those who take the tours can taste four different wines, but if you don't take a tour you can sample a wider variety. The gift shop sells wines, books, cheese, and more. By the way, Chateau Ste. Michelle is owned by U.S. Tobacco Co.—the "smokeless chew" company—a fact they aren't likely to tell you on the tour.

Columbia Winery

A modern Victorian-style building directly across the road from Chateau Ste. Michelle houses the

Chateau Ste. Michelle Winery

DON PITCHER

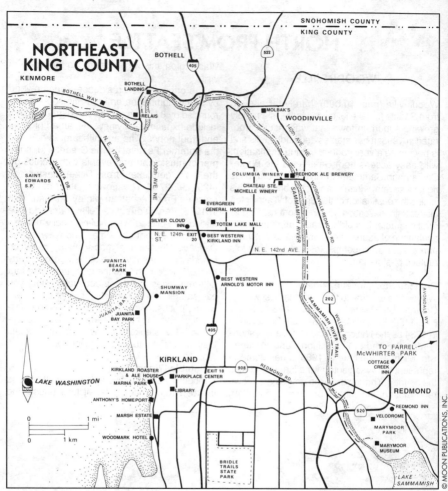

NORTHEAST KING COUNTY

Columbia Winery, tel. (425) 488-2776. This is Washington's oldest winery, founded in 1962 by 10 friends—six of whom were University of Washington professors. Columbia produces award-winning chardonnay, semillon, cabernet sauvignon, merlot, among others. The tasting room is open daily 10 a.m.-7 p.m. (except holidays), with tours on weekends 11 a.m.-5 p.m. Sample five regular wines for free, or five of their reserve wines for $5 (a bargain). The winery gets very crowded during the visits of the Spirit of Washington train (described under **Renton**); avoid visiting on Saturday 1:30-2:30 p.m., or Sunday 12:30-1:30 p.m., unless you want to join the throngs in the dining room. The best time to visit is during the grape crush each September and October. **Gray Line,** tel. (206) 626-5208 or (800) 426-7532, offers a summertime four-hour "Grapes and Hops Tour" from Seattle that includes a visit to Columbia Winery and Redhook Brewery for $24.

Redhook Ale Brewery

Right next door to the Columbia Winery is Redhook Ale Brewery, tel. (425) 483-3232. This large facility is one of three owned by Redhook (the others are in Portsmouth, New Hampshire and the Fremont district of Seattle). Forty-minute tours ($1 including the glass) are offered Mon.-Fri. at 2 p.m. and 4 p.m., and Sat.-Sun. every hour noon-5 p.m., and include a sampling of four brews. The immensely popular pub, **Forecasters Public House,** has a half-dozen beers on tap, a menu of light and tasty meals, plus live jazz on Monday, and blues on Friday and Saturday nights. The patio is very popular with weekend cyclists.

More Beer and Wine

A much smaller brewery, **Seattle Brewing Company/Aviator Ale,** 14316 N.E. 203rd St., tel. (425) 487-0717, is open for tours Mon.-Fri. at 10 a.m., noon, and 2 p.m.

Two small wineries are also located in Woodinville. **Silverlake Winery,** 17721 132nd Ave. NE, tel. (425) 486-1900, is open Mon.-Fri. noon-5 p.m. **Facelli Winery,** 16120 Woodinville-Redmond Rd., tel. (425) 488-1020, is a small family operation with a tasting room that's open Sat.-Sun. noon-4 p.m.

Nursery

Molbak's, an impressive nursery at 13625 N.E. 175th St., tel. (425) 483-5000, is far larger than it looks—more than 2,000 varieties of indoor and outdoor plants, cut flowers, garden tools, trees, bulbs, and a conservatory/aviary fill the numerous greenhouses here. Molbak's is as popular with browsers as serious gardeners; an espresso bar and gift shop add to the fun. Open daily 9 a.m.-6 p.m.

Outdoor Recreation

For a bit of fresh Woodinville air try the **Tolt Pipeline Trail,** an 11-mile hiking and horse trail that passes through town and extends to Snoqualmie Valley near Duvall. Find the trailhead just around the corner from Chateau Ste. Michelle. The paved **Sammamish River Trail** (see **Redmond,**) passes through on the other side of Ste. Michelle on its way north and west to Bothell and Seattle, or south to Redmond. For horseback rides, contact **Serenity Ranch,** tel.

(425) 702-9373. Hot air ballooning is a popular attraction in Woodinville; contact **Over the Rainbow,** tel. (425) 364-0995, for details.

Lodging

A Big Red Barn, 16560 140th Place NE, tel. (425) 806-4646 or (888) 400-2276, has four guest rooms (shared or private baths) in a renovated 1939 dairy barn on the north end of Lake Washington. The main loft includes spacious living room with a 17-foot ceiling, a massive wood burning fireplace and a 12-foot picture window; $79-119 s or d. **By the Creek B&B,** 20232 N.E. 148th St., tel. (425) 885-0639, also has local accommodations.

Food

Woodinville has a wide variety of dining experiences, including the Forecasters Public House at Redhook Ale Brewery, described above. At **Armadillo Barbecue,** 13109 N.E. 175th St., tel. (425) 481-1417, you may not find armadillo on the menu, but you will find real Texas-style barbecued ribs, chicken, baked beans, and more, plus wine and beer in a fun atmosphere; open for lunch and dinner daily.

Feast on Mexican food at **Las Margaritas,** 13400 N.E. 175th, tel. (425) 483-5656. **Chin's Palace,** 13317 N.E. 175th St., tel. (425) 486-6252, serves Mandarin, Sichuan, and Cantonese dishes. Good pizzas, pasta, and veal at **Italianissimo,** 17650 140th Ave. NE, tel. (425) 485-6888.

Out in the nothing place called Maltby (approximately five miles northeast of Woodinville on Hwy. 522), is **Maltby Cafe,** tel. (425) 483-3123, where the outstanding breakfasts and lunches are well worth the trip.

The **Woodinville Farmers Market** comes to city hall 13209 N.E. 175th on Saturday 9 a.m.-4 p.m. from April to mid-October; tel. (425) 485-1042.

Events

Local events include the bizarre **All Fool's Day Parade and Basset Bash** in late March, and the very popular **Woodinville Wine Festival** in August or September. **Summer Concerts on the Green** are staged in the amphitheater at Chateau Ste. Michelle. Contact the winery at (425) 488-1133 for information; or get tickets from Ticket Master, tel. (425) 292-2787.

Other Practicalities

Get local information from the **Woodinville Chamber of Commerce,** inside city hall at 13203 NE 175th St., tel. (425) 481-8300, www. woodinvillechamber.org. Behind city hall is an indoor pool at the **YMCA,** tel. (425) 489-6378. **Metro Transit,** tel. (800) 542-7876, has daily bus service to Seattle and environs from Woodinville.

BOTHELL

Bothell (pop. 25,000) was founded in 1884 by David Bothell and his family. Apparently without competition, they logged the area, built a hotel, platted the town, and sold lots to pioneers who wanted to get away from the bustle of the city. Northeast of Lake Washington on the Sammamish River, Bothell is about a half hour from Seattle. The town straddles the line separating King and Snohomish counties, creating an odd political situation for local elections. It is also home to a large Microsoft campus.

The featured attraction is **Bothell Landing,** 18120 N.E. Bothell Way, where a park, small shopping complex, and the **Bothell Historical Museum** mark the original steamboat berth. The museum, tel. (425) 486-1889, housed in the 1893 William Hannan cabin, is open Sun. 1-4 p.m. March to mid-December. Cross the footbridge behind the museum to pick up the **Sammamish River Trail** and follow it east to Marymoor Park in Redmond, or head west on the **Burke-Gilman Trail** to Seattle.

Country Village, between Bothell Landing and I-405 at 23730 Bothell Hwy. SE, has 48 antique, food, jewelry, clothing, restaurants, and gift shops.

Swim at the **Northshore Pool,** 9815 N.E. 188th St., tel. (425) 296-4333.

Accommodations and Campgrounds

Comfort Inn, 1414 228th St. SE, tel. (425) 402-0900 or (800) 228-5150, has an indoor pool, jacuzzi, and continental breakfast, with rooms for $55-115 s, $60-120 d. **Wyndham Garden Hotel,** 19333 North Creek Parkway, tel. (425) 485-5557, has rooms for $95 s or $105 d, including an outdoor pool, jacuzzi, and exercise room. Luxury accommodations are found at **Res-idence Inn by Marriott,** 11920 N.E. 195th St., tel. (425) 485-3030 or (800) 331-3131, where two-bedroom suites go for $140-170 s or d, including an outdoor pool and jacuzzi.

Open year-round, **Lake Pleasant RV Park,** 24025 Bothell-Everett Hwy., tel. (425) 483-9436, has lakeside RV pads and campsites.

Food and Events

Bothell's best restaurant is **Relais,** an elegantly classic French restaurant in a remodeled home at 17121 N.E. Bothell Way, tel. (425) 485-7600; open for dinner only, Tues.-Sun. evenings. Exquisite meals, but very expensive.

Local events include an **Arts and Crafts Fair** in August, and **Music in the Park** on Friday evenings in July and August. Country Village has all sorts of minor festivals and open houses that draw in shoppers throughout the year. Bothell's **Fourth of July** celebration is also a fun event.

Information and Services

Get information at **Northshore Chamber of Commerce,** 10410 Beardslee Blvd., tel. (425) 486-1245, www.northshorecc.org. Swim at the **Northshore Pool,** 9815 N.E. 188th St., tel. (425) 296-4333, or the **Northshore YMCA,** 11811 N.E. 195th St., tel. (425) 485-9797.

Transportation

Metro Transit, tel. (800) 542-7876, has bus service between Seattle and Bothell. Once in Bothell you can travel to Lynnwood, Edmonds, or Everett on **Community Transit,** tel. (800) 562-1375.

Shuttle Express, tel. (800) 487-7433, provides frequent direct service from Bothell to SeaTac Airport. **Kenmore Air,** tel. (206) 486-1257 or (800) 543-9595, has floatplane service from the nearby town of Kenmore on the north end of Lake Washington. They fly to Victoria, B.C., and the San Juan Islands on a daily basis.

LYNNWOOD AND MOUNTLAKE TERRACE

The run-together towns of Lynnwood (pop. 32,000) and Mountlake Terrace (pop. 20,000) have little of note, unless you're in a shopping mood. Enormous **Alderwood Mall** on the east

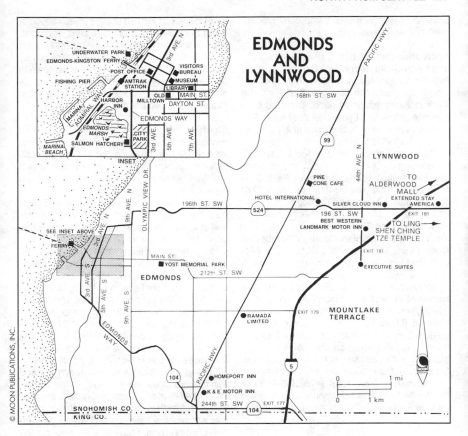

EDMONDS
AND
LYNNWOOD

side of Lynnwood hosts The Bon Marché, Nordstrom, JCPenney, Sears, Lamonts, and many smaller stores; the mall is surrounded by other, smaller shopping plazas. More cheesy developments, discount megamarts, car dealers, condos, fast food joints, cheap motels, and strip malls line busy Hwy. 99. For a taste of a slower era, drop by **Keeler's Korner,** at 164th and Hwy. 99, where you'll find two old gas pumps in front of a classic gas station that is now a video repair shop. The building is on the National Register of Historic Places.

Lodging and Food

Lodging is available in a dozen local motels; the info center (see below) has specifics. Fine dining

is at a minimum in Lynnwood and Montlake Terrace; a cow thrown in any direction would hit a fast food burger joint. Despite this, a pair of local places are worth a visit. **Thai Terrace,** 21919 66th Ave. W, tel. (425) 774-4556, is the standout, with surprisingly authentic and delicious Thai meals.

A longtime favorite, **Pine Cone Cafe,** 18929 Hwy. 99, tel. (425) 776-0788, serves generous portions of all-American fatty foods at a not-so-fat price, and your coffee cup never runs dry. You'll get a patty melt here without the waitress wrinkling her nose, and you'll get hash browns so crunchy and tasty that you'll almost forget the country sausage and squeeze-bottle of ketchup. They'll cook anything they have on the menu anytime of day. Warning: if you don't smoke, don't bother coming here.

Recreation and Events

The **Lynn-Swim Recreation Center,** tel. (425) 670-6288, has a sauna, plus an indoor pool that opens up during the summer. **Scriber Lake Park** includes this small pond, encircled by a half-mile nature trail. Lynnwood also has an **REI** store with all sorts of outdoor gear at 4200 194th St. SW, tel. (425) 774-1300.

Mountlake Terrace features a recreation pavilion housing an Olympic-size pool, weight room, and racquetball courts. **Ballinger Park Golf Course,** 23000 Lakeview Dr., tel. (425) 774-4940, is also in Mountlake Terrace.

Information and Transportation

The **South Snohomish County Chamber of Commerce,** 3400 188th St. SW, tel. (425) 774-0507, has local info; open Mon.-Thurs. 8 a.m.-5 p.m., and Friday 8 a.m.-4 p.m. year-round.

Headquarters for the **Mt. Baker-Snoqualmie National Forest** is in Mountlake Terrace at 21905 64th Ave. W, tel. (425) 775-9702; open Mon.-Fri. 8 a.m.-4:30 p.m. year-round, plus Saturday 8 a.m.-4:30 in summer. Stop by for information on this 1.7-million-acre national forest that covers the west side of the Cascades from Snoqualmie Pass to the Canadian border.

Community Transit, tel. (425) 353-7433 or (800) 562-1375, has bus connections to other parts of Snohomish County, and on to Seattle.

EDMONDS

Edmonds, 15 miles north of Seattle on Puget Sound, is a small, florally enhanced city (pop. 31,000) surrounded by rolling hills and pine forests. In spite of its spurt of growth in the last decade, downtown Edmonds has retained its small-town appearance, and if you live there you can walk to everything, including the auto mechanic. The town is best known as the gateway to the Olympic Peninsula; the state ferry shuttles constantly between Edmonds and Kingston on the Kitsap Peninsula.

The first white settlers found the shores of Puget Sound crowded with dense forests. By the turn of the century, Edmonds was at the center of the action with 10 shingle mills working at full tilt along the waterfront. The trees, of course, didn't last forever, and when the last mill closed in 1951, Edmonds was gradually transformed into a suburb of Seattle. Today, downtown is filled with trendy gourmet shops, and a walk along Edmonds' mile-and-a-half waterfront makes a pleasant afternoon outing.

Sights

A good way to see Edmonds is to begin with a stroll on the half-mile-long **Sunset Avenue** with its Victorian homes and views of Puget Sound and the Olympic Mountains. If the tide is out you can walk back along the beach.

At the foot of Dayton St., **Olympic Beach Park** has a life-size bronze sculpture of a father and children looking at sea lions. The park has picnic tables and a small beach. Two restaurants, a deli, and a fish market adjoin the park.

A 950-foot lighted public **fishing pier** runs out into the Sound, where anglers cast for salmon and bottom fish and jig for squid. Walkers and joggers like the boardwalk that runs a quarter of a mile along the Port of Edmonds marina. The marina itself is home to 1,000 boats, including the largest charter fishing fleet on Puget Sound. It is only a short walk down to the small **Edmonds Marina Beach Park,** a perfect place to fly kites, cook a dinner over a beach fire, and watch ferries crossing the sound into the sunset.

A dozen or more shops and restaurants in a former automobile agency remodeled into old-time atmosphere make up **Old Milltown** at 5th Ave. S and Dayton. Step inside to check out the historic photos of Edmonds. For a more modern flavor, try **Harbor Square's** boutiques and galleries near the waterfront on W. Dayton.

The **Edmonds Historical Museum,** 118 5th Ave. N, tel. (425) 774-0900, has a working shingle mill model, historical photos, a marine room, model trains, and other displays depicting Edmonds's past. Open Wed.-Sun. 1-4 p.m. year-round. No charge.

The shoreline drive north from Edmonds along Olympic View Dr. leads through comfortable neighborhoods, and eventually reaches **Picnic Point County Park,** approximately seven miles north of town. This is a popular place for a beach picnic, with Puget Sound and the Olympics as a backdrop. Access is a bit quicker from Hwy. 99; go west on Shelby Rd. for 1.3 miles, bear right onto Picnic Point Rd. at the "Y," and continue another 1.5 miles to the park. A closer place is **City Park** on 3rd Ave. S at Pine Street. The park has picnic shelters and a bandstand for summertime concerts. Just south of here is a small king salmon hatchery run by a group of local anglers.

Outdoors and Underwater
Just two blocks from downtown is the **Edmonds Marsh,** a haven for wildlife of all kinds. It's an amazing little piece of the natural world where blackbirds, herons, ducks, and crows feed in an enclave surrounded by a boatyard, abandoned oil tanks, an athletic club, and creeping development. A boardwalk overlooks the marsh.

Off the shoreline of Brackett's Landing (the little beach next to the ferry dock) is the 27-acre **Underwater Park.** It was the first underwater park in Washington and is used by scuba divers year-round to explore the 300-foot DeLion dry dock, sunk there in 1935 to serve as a breakwater and marinelife habitat. Since then, other underwater structures—including old tires, steel shelving, a model of the Evergreen Point Floating Bridge, and two tugboats—have been added for the enjoyment of both fish and diver, resulting in one of the Pacific Northwest's most popular underwater parks. From the shore, you'd never know anything was down there. You can rent diving equipment, learn to dive, or find a dive buddy at **Underwater Sports,** 264 Railroad Ave., tel. (425) 771-6322, two blocks south across the street from the Amtrak depot.

If you aren't into scuba diving, try the swimming pool in **Yost Memorial Park** at Bowdoin and 96th Ave. W. Call (425) 775-2645 for details.

Accommodations
Built in 1922, **Hudgens Haven B&B,** 9313 190th St. SW, tel. (425) 776-2202, sits on a half-acre of land surrounded by apple trees. The single guest room is a very reasonable $55 s or $60 d, including a continental breakfast.

Dayton House B&B, 522 Dayton, tel. (425) 778-3611, is a private upstairs apartment with a view deck. A continental breakfast arrives each morning; $95 d ($85 d without breakfast).

Maple Tree B&B, two miles north of Edmonds at 18313 Olympic View Dr., tel. (425) 774-8420, is an older restored home on a bluff, and is notable for the fine views of the Olympics. The single guest room has a private bath, and a light breakfast is served; $60 d.

Enchanted Garden B&B, 1030 A Ave., tel. (425) 771-4721, features a spacious guest suite with private balcony overlooking Puget Sound. A full breakfast is served; $80 d. No kids.

Andy's Motel, 22201 Hwy. 99, tel. (425) 776-6080, has standard rooms for $40 s or $42 d; kitchenettes are available. Stay at **Golden West Motel,** 23916 Hwy. 99, tel. (425) 771-3447, for $42 s or $45 d. **K & E Motor Inn,** 23921 Hwy. 99, tel. (425) 778-2181, charges $47-52 s or $52-57 d, including a continental breakfast. **Travelodge Seattle North,** 23825 Hwy. 99, tel. (425) 771-8008 or (800) 771-8009, charges $57 s or d, including a jacuzzi and continental breakfast.

Ramada Limited, 22127 Hwy. 99, tel. (425) 776-0200 or (800) 272-6232, is a new motel with rooms for $59-79 s or $69-89 d, including a jacuzzi and continental breakfast. **Edmonds Harbor Inn,** 130 W. Dayton St., tel. (425) 771-5021 or (800) 441-8033, has large rooms for $66 s or $76 d, including a continental breakfast.

Food
Brusseau's, 5th and Dayton, tel. (425) 774-4166, is Edmonds's trendiest restaurant, with Lycra-clad cyclists at the outdoor tables on weekend mornings. Outstanding breads and pastries—including marionberry cobbler—or try the omelettes, soups, salads, quiche, or sandwiches for lunch. Highly recommended.

Enjoy Northwest seafood for lunch, dinner, or Sunday champagne brunches at **Arnie's,** 300 Admiral Way, tel. (425) 771-6533, two blocks south of the ferry terminal beside the city park. Their popular end-of-the-day bar overlooks the marina and is a great place to watch the ferries come in.

Provinces Asian Restaurant & Bar, upstairs inside Old Milltown (201 5th Ave. S), tel. (425) 744-0288, serves up a diverse and eclectic selection of Asian cuisine, plus daily lunch specials.

El Puerto Mexican Restaurant, 423 Main St., tel. (425) 672-2469, has quality south-of-the-border meals. **Chantrelle,** 316 Main St., tel. (425) 774-0650, is a popular downtown bistro and espresso place, with three dependably fine meals a day.

A pair of restaurants offer marina-side dining. **Anthony's Homeport Restaurant,** tel. (425) 771-4400, is the old standby, but **Anthony's Beach Cafe** next door has a more creative menu, less pretensions, and lower prices.

Edmonds has a good French restaurant, **Cafe de Paris,** 109 Main St., tel. (425) 771-2350, near the ferry landing, with entrees in the $13-19 range. Popular for Sunday brunch too. For Italian meals and pizza, you won't go wrong at **Ciao Italia,** 5133 25th Ave. NE, tel. (425) 524-6989.

The popular **Edmonds Museum Summer Market** takes place Saturday 9 a.m.-3 p.m. on Bell St. between 5th & 6th, July-September; tel. (425) 775-5650

Shopping

Edmonds has several large antique and collectibles stores, including the **Waterfront Antique Mall,** inside an antique Safeway building at 190 Sunset Ave. S, tel. (425) 670-0770, and **Old Milltown Mall** with dealers on the upper level at Dayton and 5th, tel. (425) 771-9644. The Waterfront Antique Mall is the better of the two. **Gallery North,** an artists' cooperative inside Old Milltown, tel. (425) 774-0946, is the finest local gallery. Edmonds has three good bookstores, including **The Savvy Traveler,** 107 5th Ave. S, tel. (425) 744-6076, a great source for travel books of all types.

Events and Music

Local events of note include the **Edmonds Art Festival** on the third weekend of June, with a juried art show, artists in action, arts and crafts booths, and live music. The old-fashioned **Fourth of July** brings the usual parades, a chicken barbecue, fireman's water fights, live music, and fireworks. The **Taste of Edmonds Festival** on the second weekend of August is a very popular street fair with ethnic foods, cooking demonstrations, a carnival, music, and beer garden. **Concerts in the Park** are held at city park on Sunday afternoons during July and August.

Cascade Symphony, a 90-piece orchestra in existence for more than 30 years, features winter concerts; tel. (425) 778-4688.

Information and Services

The friendly folks at the log cabin **Edmonds Visitors Bureau,** 120 5th Ave. N, tel. (425) 776-6711, will be happy to provide you with maps and current information. The office is open Mon.-Fri. 9 a.m.-4 p.m., and Saturday 11 a.m.-3 p.m. in the summer, and Mon.-Fri. 9 a.m.-4 p.m. winters.

Transportation

Community Transit, tel. (425) 353-7433 or (800) 562-1375, provides bus connections to other parts of Snohomish County and on to Seattle.

Take the **Washington State Ferry** from Edmonds to Kingston, the Olympic Peninsula's drop-off point. The crossing takes 30 minutes and leaves Edmonds about every 40 minutes during the day. Summer fares are $8 one-way car and driver, $3.60 for passengers or walk-ons; tel. (425) 464-6400 or (888) 808-7977 for details; or (800) 843-3779 for automated info.

Amtrak's **Empire Builder** heads south to Seattle and east to Spokane and Chicago. The **Mt. Baker International** provides daily train connections to Vancouver, B.C., via Everett, Mount Vernon, and Bellingham. For information on Amtrak, call (425) 778-3213 or (800) 872-7245. The train station is at 211 Railroad Avenue.

NORTHERN PUGET SOUND

EVERETT

Everett (pop. 82,000) is a largely industrial city best known as the place where Boeing's big 747, 767, and 777 jets are assembled. Located on Puget Sound 27 miles north of Seattle, it could be a sister city to Tacoma in terms of geography, distance from Seattle, and industrial base. And like Tacoma, the city is undergoing something of a rebirth as buildings in the historic downtown core are restored and the streets are spruced up. Unfortunately, the main commercial drag, Evergreen Way (Hwy. 99) offers another side to the city; here you'll find used car lots, pizza joints, tire and auto parts dealers, storage lockers, fast-food and discount stores of all types, and mile after mile of stoplights, backed-up traffic, and exhaust fumes. Progress.

The Setting
Everett is flanked by distant mountains, with Mt. Baker to the north, Mt. Rainier to the south, and 5,324-foot Mt. Pilchuck to the east. Puget Sound's Port Gardner Bay is at its front door, and the view across the Sound includes Whidbey Island, Gedney Island, and Camano Island. The Snohomish River curves north on the edge of town and creates a maze of islands and sloughs before emptying into Puget Sound.

Coupled with its waterfront location, Everett is surrounded by recreational opportunities, as well as more indoor fun than most cities its size. It is close to the skiing at Stevens Pass—the Cascades begin virtually at the city's back door—the rivers and lakes have excellent boating and fishing, and the Sound is speckled with small boats during salmon runs.

HISTORY

Everett is one of the few Puget Sound areas that prompted Capt. George Vancouver to get off his boat. After coming ashore in 1792, Vancouver named the area "New Georgia" for King George III, and the English claim to this land lasted for more than 50 years.

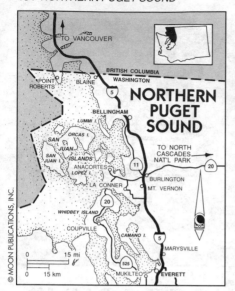

the "New York City of the West," and based their dreams on the expectation that the Great Northern Railroad would make Port Gardner its western terminus, and that the nearby Monte Cristo mines would bring unparalleled wealth. Instead, Seattle was chosen as the end point for the railroad, and the gold and silver mines never lived up to expectations. In addition, the Silver Panic of 1893 led to a devastating national depression that lasted until the Klondike gold rush of 1898 helped lift the nation out of its financial doldrums.

It was Charles Colby who named the town—in honor of his infant son Everett—but downtown streets also bear the names of the others whose financing got the city started: Rockefeller, Wetmore, and Hewitt. The new town was aided significantly by the Monte Cristo mines, and a smelter was built to serve them. However, the ore did not last, and it was eventually timber that guaranteed the city's success.

Lumber Years

As much or more influential than Rockefeller in Everett's development was a man named Frederick Weyerhaeuser. Born in Germany in 1834, he immigrated to the U.S. in 1852, where he worked in an Illinois lumber mill and married a German woman, Elizabeth Bloedel. Weyer-

Eastern Money

The city of Everett was established in 1891 in boomtown fashion by a group of influential East Coast promoters that included John D. Rockefeller, Charles Wetmore, Henry Hewitt Jr., and Charles Colby. They envisioned it as

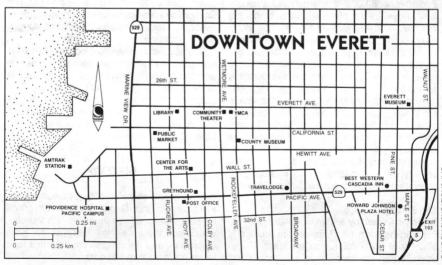

747-400s await final assembly at Boeing's Everett factory.

haeuser was so hardworking and thrifty that he was able to buy the mill a few years later, and then expanded his operation westward. His main Pacific Coast lumber mill was built in Everett in 1903, becoming—and long remaining—the city's most important industry. When he died, Weyerhaeuser's lumber company was the biggest in the country. Weyerhaeuser is now headquartered in Tacoma, and a big Kimberly-Clark mill operates along the shoreline.

By the early 1900s, lumber, paper, and shingle mills—along with other factories producing everything from nails to barges—had given Everett the moniker, "the city of smokestacks." Everett was also known for its labor unrest during the first two decades of this century, and the Industrial Workers of the World (Wobblies) congregated in Everett with their then-radical ideas that included worker ownership of factories. The worst fears of all were realized on November 5, 1916, when two boatloads of Wobblies arrived from Seattle. The Everett Massacre that followed resulted in the deaths of at least seven men.

BOEING PLANT

More than 30,000 people work for Boeing in their massive Everett factory. A tour of Boeing's astounding 747-767 assembly plant is *the* highlight of a visit to the Everett area, and for many technology and aviation buffs, it's the highlight of a visit to the whole state. The plant itself—11 stories high—has the largest capacity of any building in the world, containing 291 million cubic feet and covering an incredible 62 acres. (For trivia buffs, the largest building by floor surface is the West Edmonton Mall in Canada; the Boeing assembly plant comes in second.) A total of eight 747s or 767s can be assembled at one time, and it takes eight months to complete each plane. They roll outside through football-field sized doors. Boeing's new 777s are assembled in another Everett building (not generally open to the public), while their 737s are put together in the Renton facility.

Tours

Ninety-minute tours of the Everett Boeing plant are available hourly in the summer months, Mon.-Fri. 9 a.m.-3 p.m., and at least twice a day (9 a.m. and 1 p.m.) on winter weekdays. No kids under 50 inches tall, and no tours on holidays or late December. The tours begin with three short films (including the star attraction, where a 777 is assembled in a few brief moments). Then you head out, take a shuttle to the building, and get a guided tour of the plant. No bathrooms are along the way, so make a pit stop before departing. No still or video cameras are permitted, and the tours are offered on a first-come, first-served basis; reservations are available only for groups of 10 or more. No charge, except for large groups. For details, call (425) 544-1264 or (800) 464-1476.

Because of their popularity, get to the Boeing Tour Center two or three hours ahead of time during the mid-summer peak season, and be sure to arrive before 11 a.m. to make sure of getting on a tour that day. (Tips: Try arriving by 7:30 a.m. since Boeing sometimes offers an 8 a.m. tour that is less crowded. The least crowded days are Tues.-Thurs.) Avoid the wait entirely by plunking down $35 for a three-hour tour that leaves Seattle daily in the summer. These are offered by **Gray Line,** tel. (206) 626-5208 or (800) 426-7532; **Customized Tours,** tel. (206) 878-3965 or (800) 770-8769; and **Bledsoe's NW Excursions,** tel. (206) 526-7996.

The Tour Center—where you begin and end your visit—has all sorts of aircraft-related gifts, perfect for any pilot friends. Call (425) 342-4801 for a recording with more details on the Boeing tours. To reach the Tour Center, take I-5 exit 189 west onto Hwy. 526 and follow the signs.

OTHER SIGHTS

Museums and Art

The **Snohomish County Museum and Historical Association** at 2817 Rockefeller Ave., tel. (425) 259-2022, has historical photos and artifacts from throughout the county; no charge. A museum store sells local history books. Open Wed.-Sat. 1-4 p.m. At the 13th St. dock, look through the windows at a collection of firefighters' equipment in the small **Firefighters Museum.**

The **Everett Center for the Arts** at 1507 Wall St., tel. (425) 259-8380, in the historic Monte Cristo Hotel, exhibits works of regional artists and includes a permanent collection of Dale Chihuly glass. Open Mon.-Fri. 10 a.m.-5 p.m., and Saturday 11 a.m.-3 p.m.

The **Children's Museum in Snohomish County,** 3013 Colby, tel. (425) 258-1006, has fun children's exhibits, including a 19th-century Snohomish homestead and a magic school bus. Open Mon.-Sat. 10 a.m.-3 p.m.; $2.

Additional Sights

In its early years, Everett was home to some of the timber industry's most successful entrepreneurs. These lumber barons built elaborate mansions in the north end of town on Grand and Rucker Avenues, many of which still stand. The visitor center has more info on these historic homes.

Naval Station Everett is home port to the aircraft carrier **USS *Abraham Lincoln*** and its six support ships. Call (425) 304-5665 to see which ships are available for tours.

Paine Field is home to the **Museum of Flight Restoration Center,** tel. (425) 745-5150, where aircraft are restored for this outstanding Seattle museum. The restoration center is located in Building C-72, and is open Tues.-Sat. 9 a.m.-5 p.m.; no charge. Get here from the Boeing Tour Center by returning to Hwy. 526 eastbound,

Everett's lumber barons lived in exquisite mansions.

DIANNE BOUERICE LYONS

and taking the first exit (Airport Rd.). Head south on Airport Rd. for a mile, and turn right onto 100th St. SW. Building C-72 is on the right side.

Parks

Located on Alverson Blvd., **American Legion Park** features a par course, tennis courts, and baseball field. **Forest Park** on Mukilteo Blvd. has a popular summertime children's animal farm and an indoor public pool. **Howarth Park,** just west of Forest Park on Mukilteo Blvd., has tennis courts and a fine view of Possession Sound from an observation tower.

The best-known local park is **Jetty Island,** just off the mouth of the Snohomish River. This two-mile long narrow stretch of sand is composed of spoils from dredging the harbor and river mouth and is very popular with birders, sea mammal watchers, or people just out for a picnic and a bit of beachcombing. The island has two miles of walking trails, and the shallow water warms to 70° in August, making it a popular swimming spot. It is served by a free passenger ferry that runs every half-hour from July to mid-September from Marina Park. For information call (425) 257-8300.

ACCOMMODATIONS AND CAMPING

Bed and Breakfasts

Harbor Hill Inn, 2208 Rucker Ave., tel. (425) 259-3925 or (888) 572-3925, is a grand 1908 mansion with five large guest rooms, private baths, an outdoor pool, exercise room, hot tub, and full breakfast; $65-95 s or d.

Gaylord House B&B, 3301 Grand Ave., tel. (425) 339-9153 or (888) 507-7177, a 1910 craftsman home, has five luxurious guest rooms with antiques, private baths, and gourmet breakfasts. Kids are accepted; $85-175s or d.

Campgrounds

Located south of town at 11621 W. Silver Lake Rd., **Silverlake RV Park,** tel. (425) 338-9666, has swimming and fishing in addition to the tent sites and RV hookups. **Lakeside RV Park,** 12321 Hwy. 99 S, tel. (425) 347-2970 or (800) 468-7275, is on a three-acre lake with all hookups and facilities.

FOOD

Breakfast and Lunch

Start the day at **The Sisters Restaurant,** 2804 Grand Ave. (inside the Everett Public Market), tel. (425) 252-0480, a friendly place with great breakfast specials and espresso coffees. Lunches include great soups (especially the chilled tomato and avocado), salads, veggie burgers, and homemade ice cream. The **O'Donnell's Food and Drink,** 1510 41st St., tel. (425) 259-3838, also makes good home-cooked breakfasts, as well as gourmet burgers and salads for lunch. The magician-owner performs most evenings during dinner.

A classy downtown place is **Wylde Thyme Cafe,** 1509 Wall St., tel. (425) 347-6995. Lunch and dinner entrees include such delectables as Jamacian prawns, roasted red pepper penne pasta, and Greek lemon chicken. If you're down on the marina, find lunchtime panini sandwiches and other tasty light meals at **Meyer's Cafe,** 1700 W. Marine View Dr., tel. (425) 259-3875. **Kira's City Cafe,** 2801 Colby Ave., tel. (425) 259-5090, makes good sandwiches on home-baked bread.

American

Everett Marina Village has a couple of popular waterfront restaurants with views to match the food. **Anthony's Homeport,** tel. (425) 252-3333, has fresh Northwest and imported seafood flown in fresh daily, plus tasty fish-and-chips for a simpler meal. **Confetti's,** tel. (425) 258-4000, serves steak, prime rib, pasta, and seafood.

Alligator Soul, 2013 Hewitt Ave., tel. (425) 259-6311, is a fun place with heaping helpings of old-South and Cajun favorites, including seafood gumbo and smoked ribs.

Pubs

Sporty's Beef & Brew, 6503 Evergreen Way, tel. (425) 347-1733, has burgers and beer, plus three large-screen televisions for sports fans. Two local restaurants offer full-menu dining in a brewpub atmosphere: **Flying Pig Brewing Co.,** 2929 Colby, tel. (425) 339-1393, and **Scuttlebutt Brewing Co.,** on the waterfront at 1524 W. Marine View Dr., tel. (425) 257-9316.

EVERETT MOTELS AND HOTELS

Accommodations are arranged from least to most expensive. Rates may be lower during the winter months.

INEXPENSIVE

FarWest Motel; 6030 Evergreen Way; tel. (425) 355-3007; $37-40 s, $40-44 d; kitchenettes available, AAA approved

Topper Motel; 1030 N. Broadway Ave.; tel. (425) 259-3151; $39-45 s or d; kitchenettes available

Welcome Motor Inn; 1205 N. Broadway Ave.; tel. (425) 252-8828; $39-45 s, $44-52 d; kitchenettes available, AAA approved

Waits Motel; 1301 Lombard Ave.; tel. (425) 252-3166; $40 s, $42 d; kitchenettes available

Royal Motor Inn; 952 N. Broadway Ave.; tel. (425) 259-5177; $42 s, $44-52 d; outdoor pool

Motel 6; 224 128th St. SW; tel. (425) 353-8120 or (800) 466-8356; $47 s, $53 d

Motel 6; 10006 Evergreen Way; tel. (425) 347-2060 or (800) 466-8356; $47 s, $53 d; outdoor pool

Travelodge; 3030 N. Broadway Ave.; tel. (425) 259-6141 or (800) 255-3050; $54 s or d; AAA approved

Sunrise Motor Inn; 8421 Evergreen Way; tel. (425) 347-1100; $56 s or d

MODERATE

Travelodge Everett Mall; 9602 19th Ave. SE; tel. (425) 337-9090 or (888) 454-9090; $57 s, $67 d; outdoor pool, jacuzzi, kitchens available, continental breakfast, AAA approved

Days Inn; 1122 N. Broadway Ave.; tel. (425) 252-8000 or (800) 845-9490; $59 s, $66 d; jacuzzi, continental breakfast, kitchenettes available, AAA approved

Comfort Inn Everett Mall; 1602 S.E. Everett Mall Way; tel. (425) 355-1570 or (800) 228-5150; $64-69 s, $69-74 d; jacuzzi, continental breakfast

Quality Inn; 12619 4th Ave. W; tel. (425) 347-9099 or (800) 228-5151; $75 s or d; outdoor pool, AAA approved

EXPENSIVE

Marina Village Inn 1728 W. Marine View Dr.; tel. (425) 259-4040 or (800) 281-7037; $87-195 s or d; very nice rooms facing Gardiner Bay, private jacuzzis, continental breakfast, telescopes, AAA approved

Best Western Cascadia Inn; 2800 Pacific Ave.; tel. (425) 258-4141 or (800) 822-5876; $89-99 s, $99-109 d; outdoor pool, jacuzzi, exercise room, continental breakfast, AAA approved

Holiday Inn Hotel & Conference Center 101 128th St. SE; tel. (425) 337-2900 or (800) 221-9839; $89-119 s or d; indoor pool, jacuzzi, exercise room, business center, game room, local shuttle, AAA approved

The Inn at Port Gardner; 1700 W. Marine View Dr.; tel. (425) 252-6779 or (888) 252-6779; $89-195 s or d; new inn, luxurious rooms, marina-side location, ISDN lines, continental breakfast

PREMIUM

Howard Johnson Plaza Hotel; 3105 Pine St.; tel. (425) 339-3333 or (800) 556-7829; $109 s, $119 d; indoor pool, sauna, jacuzzi, exercise room, airport shuttle, AAA approved

International

For very good pasta and pizza, head to **Gianni's Ristorante Italiano,** 5030 Evergreen Way, tel. (425) 252-2435. **Bella Rosa,** 2803 Colby Ave., tel. (425) 258-8028, creates southern Italian lunches and dinners.

Find authentic Mexican meals and a friendly atmosphere at **Tampico Restaurant,** 2303 Broadway, tel. (425) 339-2427.

Spice of Thai, 607 Everett Mall Way SE, tel. (425) 290-7900, is one of those unexpected gems. Located in a strip mall, this small restaurant cranks out great curries, Thai eggplant, and other specialties. Find more good Thai food at **Orchid Thai Cuisine,** 9506 19th Ave. SE, tel. (425) 338-1064.

Bakeries and Markets

Pave Specialty Bakery, 2613 Colby, tel. (425) 252-0250, has earthy breads and European pastries. Everett's **QFC** markets are the best places to shop, and have very complete delis.

The **Everett Farmers Market,** takes place at Port Gardner Landing in the marina on Sunday 11 a.m.-4 p.m., June-Sept.; tel. (425) 347-2790.

EVENTS

Held on the first weekend in June, **Salty Sea Days** features a parade, Navy ship tours, hydroplane races, an arts show, live music, plus outrigger canoe races. Everett's **Freedom Festival U.S.A.** blasts into town for the Fourth of July weekend, with a parade, fireworks, and ship tours.

A summer-long recreational event from July to September sponsored by the parks department, **Jetty Island Days** includes free ferry rides to the island departing from the Marina Village Visitors Dock, guided nature walks, sailing and rowing regattas, concerts, and campfire programs, as well as picnicking, beachcombing, and birdwatching on a saltwater beach. For details, call (425) 259-0300.

Return to Everett on the second and third Saturday of December for the **Christmas Boat Parade** around Port Gardner Bay.

ARTS AND ENTERTAINMENT

The Arts

Theatrical performances are held throughout the year in the new showpiece **Performing Arts Center,** 2710 Wetmore, tel. (425) 259-8888. The theater features touring musicals, concerts, and regional performing arts groups. The building houses the excellent **Arts Council Gift Gallery.** Another fine gallery is **Sheldon James Gallery,** 1724 W. Marine View Dr., tel. (425) 252-6047.

The **Everett Symphony** performs at the Everett Civic Auditorium on Oct.-June; call (425) 257-8382 for more information. For something less formal, the **Music in the Parks** program brings live music to local parks on Sunday afternoons June-Aug.; tel. (425) 259-0300.

Nightlife

Everett has a disproportionate number of dancing and drinking establishments for a city this small. The sprawling **Club Broadway,** 1611 Everett Ave., tel. (425) 259-2756, has seven dance floors, with music on Friday and Saturday nights for all tastes: an underage (16-20) room with DJ tunes, more top-40 discs in another room for adults, a rhythm & blues room, techno music in another, plus a sports bar with pool tables, darts, and classic rock bands. **McCabe's American Music Cafe,** 3120 Hewitt Ave., tel. (425) 252-3082, has country music, while **Alligator Soul,** 2013 Hewitt Ave., tel. 9425) 259-6311, has jazz music.

Other places with live music include: **Filibeck's Chuck Wagon Inn,** 6720 Evergreen Way, **Petosa's on Broadway,** 3121 Broadway, tel. (425) 258-1544, and **The Everett Underground,** 1212 California, tel. (425) 339-0807.

SPORTS AND RECREATION

The San Francisco Giants' Class-A farm team, the **Everett Aquasox,** plays at Everett Memorial Stadium from mid-June to September. Call (425) 258-3673 for schedule information.

The **Everett Marina** is the second largest in Puget Sound and a fun place to watch the boating action. Swim or sunbathe at popular **Silver Lake,** where a lifeguard is on duty between late June and Labor Day, or enjoy the saltwater and two miles of sandy beach at **Jetty Island.** Local swimming pools include the summer-only **McCollum Park Pool,** 600 128th St. SE, tel. (425) 337-4408, or the year-round **Forest Park Swim Center,** tel. (425) 259-0300. **Paine Field Recreation Center,** at Paine Field on the south side of Everett, tel. (425) 353-4944, has basketball, racquetball, tennis, volleyball, and weightlifting facilities, plus a sauna.

Health-conscious vacationers may be interested in a one-day membership at the **Everett YMCA,** 2720 Rockefeller, tel. (425) 258-9211, with a rooftop track, racquetball and squash courts, weight room, jacuzzi, and indoor pool.

Rent bikes from **Bicycle Center,** 4718 Evergreen Way, tel. (425) 252-1441. In the summer, you can rent canoes, rowboats, sailboats, and paddleboats from **Everett Parks and Recreation Dept.** at Silver Lake, tel. (425) 337-7809.

Local public 18-hole golf courses include **American Legion Memorial Course,** 144 W. Marine View Dr., tel. (425) 259-4653, and the **Walter E. Hall Golf Course,** 1226 W. Casino Rd., tel. (425) 353-4653.

SHOPPING

The area's largest shopping center is **Everett Mall,** with over 140 small shops, giant department stores including The Bon Marché, Mervyn's, and Sears. Along the bay at **Everett Marina Village** is an 1890s-style waterfront marketplace with restaurants, gift shops, and clothing stores, to name a few.

The **Everett Public Market,** 2804 Grand Ave., has more than 100 antique dealers, plus fresh fish and produce, the Sisters Restaurant, and the Everett Underground nightclub.

For discount shopping, it's hard to beat Evergreen Way (Hwy. 99), where all the big stores can be found, complete with acres of paved parking spaces. Not the most attractive place, but it serves the purpose. A surprising number of thrift stores cluster around Evergreen at 52nd St., including Value Village, St. Vincent de Paul's, Salvation Army, and Children's Hospital Thrift Store. Great for cheapskates.

INFORMATION AND SERVICES

For maps and brochures, stop by the **Snohomish County Visitor Information Center,** 101 128th St. SE (I-5 exit 186). They're open daily 9 a.m.-5 p.m. with extended summer hours; tel. (425) 348-5802 or (888) 338-0976. Find them on the Web at www.snohomish.org. For more info, head to **Everett Area Chamber of Commerce,** on the first floor of the historic Weyerhaeuser office building at 1710 W. Marine View Dr., tel. (425) 252-5181; www.snobiz.org. Open Mon.-Fri. 8:30 a.m.-5 p.m. year-round.

TRANSPORTATION AND TOURS

Bus Service

Everett Transit's buses provide local transportation; call (425) 257-8803 for details. To get out of town, **Community Transit** goes south to Edmonds and Seattle, north to Stanwood and Darrington, and east to Snohomish, Lake Stevens, and Granite Falls; call (425) 778-2185 or (800) 562-1375 for information.

Northwestern Trailways, tel. (800) 366-6975, and **Greyhound,** tel. (425) 252-2143 or (800) 231-2222, have bus connections throughout the Northwest, stopping in Everett at 1503 Pacific.

If you're flying into Sea-Tac airport, **Shuttle Express,** tel. (425) 622-1424 or (800) 942-7433, has door-to-door van service between Sea-Tac and Everett; reservations required.

Train Service

Amtrak trains serve the Everett area from their 2900 Bond St. station; tel. (425) 258-2458 or (800) 872-7245. The **Empire Builder** heads south to Seattle and east to Spokane and Chicago. The **Mt. Baker International** provides daily train connections to Vancouver, B.C., via Mount Vernon and Bellingham.

Ferries and Tours Boats

See **Mukilteo** for local ferry connections. The **Mosquito Fleet,** 1724-F W. Marine View Dr., tel. (425) 252-6800 or (800) 325-6722, offers year-round all-day boat tours that take travelers through Deception Pass to Friday Harbor on San Juan Island. There, you can spend several hours enjoying the sights, or stay on board to watch for whales (a highlight of most trips) before returning to Everett. Take your bike along for no extra charge. Fares are $79 adults, $74 seniors, or $39 kids.

VICINITY OF EVERETT

SNOHOMISH

The charming town of Snohomish (pop. 6,500) is a delightful surprise, especially if you last stopped in damn-the-torpedoes Monroe. The attractive downtown has a classic small-town feel and a real sense of the past. Early Indians called Snohomish something like "Sdob-dwahlb-bluh," meaning "Indian Moon." The town was settled in 1859 along the banks of the Snohomish and Pilchuck Rivers, making it one of Washington's oldest communities. The first settler was a merchant named E.C. Ferguson, who set up shop with some goods to sell, believing a military road between Fort Steilacoom and Fort Bellingham would soon come through. The road never arrived, but other people did because the Snohomish River was the natural transportation corridor for boats and log rafts. There's still an active and noisy sawmill right downtown, but the past has become the focal point for most visitors in the form of old homes (some from the 1870s) and antique shops. There's something for every taste in Snohomish; it sure beats a shopping mall.

Sights

The **Blackman Historic Museum,** 118 Ave. B, tel. (360) 568-5235, is an 1878 mansion built by a lumberman as a proud display of his cedar shingles; today it's filled with area artifacts and Victorian furniture. Open Wed.-Sun. noon-4 p.m.; $1 adults, 50 cents seniors or children. For more history, head to the **Pioneer Village Museum** at 2nd and Pine Streets (next to Rite Aid Pharmacy), tel. (360) 568-5235. Here are six historic structures and a tiny graveyard. Open daily noon-4 p.m. Memorial Day to Labor Day; $1.50 adults, $1 children or seniors. The free **Ollie Winston Shuttle** ferries folks all over Snohomish and out to Pioneer Village on weekends.

Antiques

Snohomish calls itself "Antique Capital of the Pacific Northwest." Antique shops of all sorts line Main St., including ones specializing in old toys, Victorian furnishings, realistic models of sailing ships, Persian rugs, and clocks. The biggest of all is **Star Center Antique Mall** at 829 2nd St., where 150 dealers have small booths inside. **Upper Case Books,** 121 Glen Ave., tel. (360) 568-5987, is a big shop with thousands of used, out-of-print, and rare books.

Lodging Places

The comfortable **Inn at Snohomish,** 323 2nd St., tel. (360) 568-2208 or (800) 548-9993, has deluxe rooms for $58 s or d, including a jacuzzi.

a Snohomish
street scene

DON PITCHER

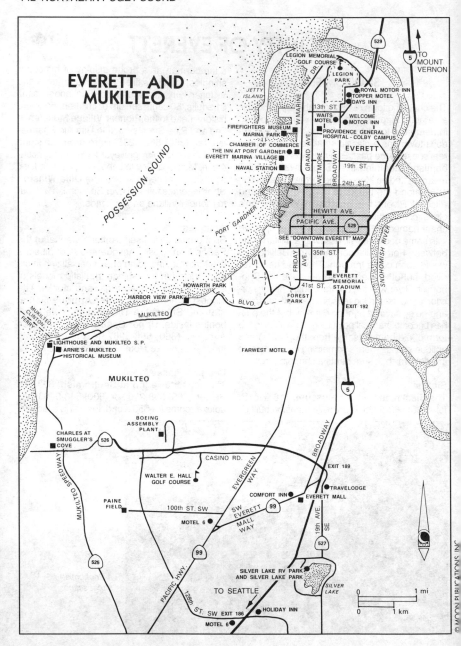

EVERETT AND MUKILTEO

POSSESSION SOUND

JETTY ISLAND

TO MOUNT VERNON

Legion Memorial Golf Course

Legion Park

Royal Motor Inn

Topper Motel

Days Inn

13th ST.

Waits Motel

Welcome Motor Inn

Firefighters Museum

Marina Park

Chamber of Commerce

The Inn at Port Gardner

Everett Marina Village

Naval Station

Providence General Hospital - Colby Campus

EVERETT

19th ST.

24th ST.

GRAND AVE.

WETMORE

BROADWAY

W. MARINE VIEW DR.

PORT GARDNER

HEWITT AVE.

PACIFIC AVE.

529

SEE "DOWNTOWN EVERETT" MAP.

FRIDAY AVE.

35th ST.

41st ST.

Everett Memorial Stadium

Forest Park

EXIT 192

SNOHOMISH RIVER

Howarth Park

Harbor View Park

MUKILTEO BLVD.

MUKILTEO CLINTON FERRY

LIGHTHOUSE AND MUKILTEO S.P.

ARNIE'S / MUKILTEO HISTORICAL MUSEUM

MUKILTEO

FARWEST MOTEL

BOEING ASSEMBLY PLANT

CHARLES AT SMUGGLER'S COVE

526

MUKILTEO SPEEDWAY

CASINO RD.

WALTER E. HALL GOLF COURSE

EVERGREEN WAY

EXIT 189

TRAVELODGE

COMFORT INN

EVERETT MALL

PAINE FIELD

100th ST. SW

SW EVERETT MALL WAY

99

MOTEL 6

525

99

19th AVE. SE

BROADWAY

527

SILVER LAKE RV PARK AND SILVER LAKE PARK

SILVER LAKE

PACIFIC HWY.

TO SEATTLE

128th ST. SW EXIT 186

HOLIDAY INN

MOTEL 6

0   1 mi

0   1 km

MOON

© MOON PUBLICATIONS INC.

Countryman's B&B, 119 Cedar, tel. (360) 568-9622 or (800) 700-9622, has three rooms with private baths on the second floor of an historic Queen Anne Victorian home; $75 d, with a continental breakfast. Kids okay.

Nita's on Ninth St. B&B, 425 9th St., tel. (360) 568-7081, is in a carefully restored 1884 Victorian hilltop estate with an outdoor pool and gourmet breakfasts. The rooms offer comfortable, homey accommodations and panoramic mountain vistas; $85-95 s or d. No kids.

Redmond House B&B, 317 Glen Ave., tel. (360) 568-2042, is a quaint Victorian home built in 1890, and within walking distance of downtown. The home is furnished with period antiques, and has a fireplace, hot tub, and full breakfast; $85-100 s or d.

Two miles south of town, **Snohomish Grand Valley Inn B&B,** tel. (360) 568-8854, is a farm home with five guest rooms and a full breakfast. $60-85 s or d. Kids okay.

Campgrounds

Ferguson Park, on Blackman Lake in Snohomish, tel. (360) 568-3115, is a city park with a picnic area, lake access, camping ($10 tents, $15 RVs), and showers. Open mid-May through October, this is a fun place to feed the ducks and geese. See **Monroe** for info on two nearby county parks where you can camp: Flowing Lake Park and Lake Roesiger Park.

Food and Wine

Silver King Cafe, 1101 1st St., tel. (360) 568-4589, specializes in steak and seafood, including Hood Canal oysters. For coffee or a light snack, the **Rivers Edge Cafe,** 1011 1st St., tel. (360) 568-5835, has a comfortable, historic feeling and tasty breakfasts. On the edge of town at 102 Ave. D, **City Deli & Wine,** tel. (360) 568-0369, has great sandwiches, desserts, and deli cheeses, plus a big choice of wines.

Jordan's, 920 1st St., tel. (360) 568-2020, serves inexpensive light lunches, plus pastries, breads, espresso, and milkshakes. Also of note is **Oxford Saloon & Eatery,** 913 1st St., tel. (360) 568-3845, with pub grub and live music. Built in 1889, it is said to be haunted by a former policeman. **Mardini's,** 1001 1st St., tel. (360) 568-8080, has well-prepared

pasta, seafood, chicken, and steaks in a romantic setting.

For inexpensive Chinese food, try **Peking Duck,** 1208 2nd St., tel. (360) 568-7634. Open for breakfast, lunch, and dinner daily, the **Cabbage Patch Restaurant,** tel. (360) 568-9091, offers sandwiches, salads, pasta, beef, and seafood plus homemade desserts in an old home at 111 Ave. A.

For fresh fruits and veggies, baked goods and crafts, head to the **Snohomish Farmers Market,** (425) 347-2790, held downtown on Thursday 5-9 p.m. mid-May to late September.

Quilceda Creek Vintners, 5226 Old Machias Rd., tel. (360) 568-2389, is a small family-run operation producing just 1,500 cases per year of highly regarded cabernet sauvignon. Open by appointment.

Sports and Recreation

The town's indoor **swimming pool** is on the corner of Pine Ave. and 3rd Street. **Centennial Cycle,** 511 Maple Ave., tel. (360) 568-1345, rents mountain bikes. **Airial Hot Air Balloon Co.,** tel. (360) 485-3658, offers hot air balloon rides, and **Snohomish Parachute Center,** at Harvey Airfield, (360) 569-5960 or (8800) 338-5867, will give you a thrill with their tandem dives for beginners. Take a scenic flight over Snohomish from **Snohomish Flying Service,** tel. (360) 568-1541.

Information, Events, and Transportation

The **Snohomish Chamber of Commerce,** tel. (360) 568-2526, is right next door to the museum and is open daily noon-4 p.m. in the summer, and Mon.-Fri. 9:30 a.m.-4 p.m. in the winter. Pick up a self-guided tour brochure for the town's elegant Victorian-era homes (part of the Snohomish National Historic District), or see inside during the annual **Historic Homes Tour & Vintage Car Show** in late September. The town's biggest event is **Kla Ha Ya Days** (Snohomish for "welcome") on the third week of July. Activities include a carnival, parade, frog jump, criterium cycling race, arts and crafts, and entertainment.

Community Transit, tel. (360) 778-2185 or (800) 562-1375, has daily bus service throughout Snohomish County.

MUKILTEO

The name Mukilteo (muck-il-TEE-o) comes from an Indian term meaning "good meeting place"; for centuries the site served as a location for councils and potlatches. In 1855, this was where the Point Elliott Treaty was signed, in which the leaders of 22 Indian tribes handed over their land to white settlers. (Tribal chiefs were unaware that they were trading all their lands for tiny reservations that they wouldn't see for many years.) The first Anglos settled here three years later, and by 1861 Mukilteo had been designated the county seat, a title it later lost to Everett. In the 1920s, Mukilteo was home to the Puget Sound and Alaska Powder Company, a manufacturer of dynamite. The plant blew up in 1930, at the same time the local lumber mill was shutting its doors. Since then, Mukilteo (pop. 13,000) has gradually become an attractive suburb of Everett, with a perfect little lighthouse, views across Puget Sound to Whidbey Island, and a the busiest ferry terminal in Washington. Travelers or commuters frequently find themselves stuck in long lines of traffic waiting to board.

Sights
Adjacent to the ferry terminal, **Mukilteo State Park** has a large picnic area, a popular beach for sunbathing (but the water can be treacherous), and a boat launch with excellent fishing in Possession Sound; open for day use only. Because of consistent winds, the park is a favorite with kite flyers and windsurfers. Not far away is the wooden **Mukilteo Lighthouse,** built in 1905 and still functional. It's open for free tours April-Sept., Sat.-Sun. noon-5 p.m.; call (425) 355-4141 for details.

Behind the Rosehill Community Center at the corner of 3rd St. and Lincoln Ave., the tiny **Mukilteo Historical Museum,** tel. (425) 355-2514, has photos, artifacts, and rotating exhibits on local history. Open Saturday 1-3 p.m., Oct.-March only; free.

Other historical structures in town include two churches that face off against each other at 3rd and Loveland: the **First Presbyterian Church** (1907) and the **St. John Catholic Church** (1919). Head up Mukilteo Blvd. for a scenic drive through older residential neighborhoods along the water, and past a string of parks as you head into Everett, including Edgewater Park, Harbor View Park (excellent views), Howarth Park, and Forest Park.

Lodging and Food
By the Bay B&B, 821 4th St., tel. (425) 347-4997, has a guest room in a 1914 home with a porch and patio; $75 d, including a continental breakfast.

Get an espresso in the flower-filled courtyard of **Mukilteo Coffee Co. Cafe,** 619 4th Ave., tel. (425) 348-4825; a great place to relax on sunny mornings.

Mukilteo has one of the Ivar's chain of seafood restaurants, but you're better off heading uphill to **Arnie's,** 714 2nd St., tel. (425) 355-2181, for water views from two levels. Enjoy very good lunches and dinners of salmon and other seafood, along with chicken, steaks, and a Sunday champagne brunch. Dinner entrees cost $12-23.

For quite good Indian fare, head to **Marco Polo,** 204 Lincoln Ave., tel. (425) 290-7627. **Riley's Pizza/Eagle Brewing,** 625 Lincoln Ave., tel. (425) 348-8088, has a tiny brewery in the basement and pizzas, calzones, and sandwiches upstairs.

A bit out of the way, **Charles at Smuggler's Cove,** 8310 53rd Ave. W (just west of the intersection of Highways 525 and 526), tel. (425) 347-2700, serves highly praised French dinners in pretentious surroundings. The name comes from its original owners, including the 1920s gangster Al Capone, who distilled whiskey in this big brick mansion with water views, shipping it out via a tunnel that led to the waterfront. Dinner entrees are $18-25; the three-course fixed-price lunch is $19.

Events and Recreation
Held at the state park downtown, the mid-August **Mukilteo Lighthouse Festival** has a pancake breakfast, parade, salmon barbecue, fishing derby, arts and crafts display, and country music and dancing.

Swim at the **Mukilteo YMCA,** 9600 Holly Dr., tel. (425) 290-5834, or **Kamiak High,** 10801 Harbour Pointe Blvd., tel. (425) 356-6620. Mukilteo is home to the **Harbour Pointe Golf Course,** 11817 Harbour Pointe Blvd., tel. (425) 355-6060 or (800) 233-3128.

Transportation

The **Washington State Ferry** has service between Mukilteo and the town of Clinton on the south end of Whidbey Island every half-hour from 5 a.m. to 1 a.m. Fares are $5.50 one-way for car and driver, $2.40 roundtrip for passengers or walk-ons, 60 cents extra for bicycles. You only pay on the westbound leg of the trip (leaving Mukilteo). For details, call (425) 355-7308 or (888) 808-7977. Call (800) 843-3779 for automated information.

Community Transit covers nearly all of Snohomish County, with service south to Seattle, and east as far as Snohomish and Darrington; call (425) 778-2185 or (800) 562-1375 for information.

MARYSVILLE

Founded in 1872, Marysville (pop. 15,000) grew up on logging and farming. Both remain economic mainstays—along with manufacturing enterprises and gambling jobs at the nearby Tulalip Casino—but the city is best known for its strawberry, raspberry, and blueberry farms. Marysville has experienced rampant growth in recent years, due in part to its proximity to Everett and the relative affordability of homes here. The unfortunate result is that the old farms are now malls; Marysville is car central today, with a this-could-be-anywhere (or nowhere?) atmosphere.

Sights

In addition to nature trails, a duck pond, and a petting zoo (tel. 360-659-8581; open daily 11 a.m.-7 p.m. from mid-May to mid-August), the 50-acre **Jennings Memorial Park/Jennings Nature Park** at 6915 Armar Rd., tel. (360) 659-3005, is home to the Gehl House Historical Museum. **Mother Nature's Window** is a unique private park on 100th St. NE on 55th Ave. NE, with an outdoor amphitheater and various carved objects amid a second-growth forest.

Tulalip

Learn the rich history of the Tulalip (too-LAY-lip) tribe along the 1.5-mile-long **Walk with the Ancestors Interpretive Trail** that begins at St. Anne's Church in the village of Tulalip (five miles

west of Marysville). St. Anne's is on the site of the oldest Catholic mission on Puget Sound.

Operated by the Tulalip Tribes, **Tulalip Casino**, off I-5 at exit 199, has keno, bingo, blackjack, craps, roulette, baccarat, poker, and pull-tabs. For information, call (360) 651-1111 or (888) 272-1111.

Accommodations

The **Best Western Tulalip Inn** has moderately priced luxury at 6128 33rd Ave. NE (exit 199), tel. (360) 659-4488 or (800) 528-1234, with an indoor pool, jacuzzi, free airport shuttle, and rooms for $99-109 s or d. **Village Motor Inn,** 235 Beech St., tel. (360) 659-0005, charges $55 s or $60 d, including a continental breakfast. **Holiday Inn Express,** 6311 33rd Ave. NE, tel. (360) 658-1339 or (800) 465-4329, has rooms for $63 s or $69 d, also with a continental breakfast. Get budget lodging at **City Center Motel,** 810 State Ave., tel. (360) 659-2424.

Recreation and Campgrounds

Twelve miles north of Marysville, **Wenberg State Park,** tel. (360) 652-7417, on Lake Goodwin has

MARYSVILLE AND LAKE STEVENS

© MOON PUBLICATIONS, INC.

a very popular swimming beach, excellent fishing for rainbow and cutthroat trout, water-skiing, a concession stand for fishing supplies and snacks, plus campsites ($11; $16 with hookups) on 46 acres. Open year-round. Get here early on summer weekends to find a space, or call (800) 452-5687 for reservations ($6 extra).

Covering 650 acres, **Kayak Point County Park,** approximately 15 miles west of Marysville on Marine View Dr., is home to a popular swimming beach, picnic area, and boat launch. Camp here year-round for $10 tents, or $15 RVs. No showers, and the bathrooms are closed in the winter months.

Nearby is the 18-hole **Kayak Point Golf Course,** tel. (360) 652-9676 or (800) 562-3094, considered one of Washington's finest public courses.

Food

Marysville's **Village Restaurant,** 220 Ash St., tel. (360) 659-2305—in business since 1937—is famous for its "mile-high" meringue pies and other all-American fare.

The best place to eat in Marysville is **Fanny's Restaurant,** 505 Cedar St., tel. (360) 653-8164, where the diverse and eclectic menu includes international and vegetarian dishes. For Italian food and pizza, head to **Conto's,** 314 State Ave., tel. (360) 659-9222.

Get great espresso coffees at the friendly **Ed'spresso** stand, tel. (360) 659-8665, inside the Sno-Co Berry Pak Building at 4th and Cedar Streets. During June and July, you can purchase fresh raspberries and strawberries here, though most of the packing is for wholesale customers.

Henry's Lady, in the Best Western Tulalip Inn, 6128 Ave. NE, tel. (360) 659-4488, has a popular Sunday brunch that features omelettes, Belgian waffles, and strawberry desserts.

Entertainment and Events

Stop by Jennings Memorial Park on Friday evenings during July and August for live concerts of all sorts. The third week in June brings the **Strawberry Festival,** the town's tribute to one of its major crops. This is the area's biggest summer event, with parades, a carnival, car show, art and food booths, and adult trike races. The festivities last 10 days; call (360) 659-7664 for details. The second weekend of July brings

Sights and Bites, with an art show, demonstrations by artists, gourmet foods, and live music. It is followed by the **Homegrown Arts & Crafts Fair,** held the first weekend of August. On the first Saturday in December, Santa Claus heads down festively adorned State Ave. for a torchlight **Christmas Parade.**

Information and Transportation

The **Marysville-Tulalip Visitor Information Center,** is at 6128 33rd Ave. NE, tel. (360) 653-2634. **Community Transit,** tel. (425) 353-7433 or (800) 562-1375, offers bus service to other parts of Snohomish County, and on to Seattle. **Airporter Shuttle,** tel. (800) 235-5247, offers direct service between Marysville and Sea-Tac.

LAKE STEVENS

The settlement of Lake Stevens (pop. 4,200) borders the north shore of this attractive lake located five miles east of Everett and acts as a bedroom community for that city. The town centers around Frontier Village Shopping Mall. Stop by the small **Lake Stevens Historical Museum** at 1802 124th Ave. NE, tel. (425) 334-3944, for a glimpse of the past. Open Fri.-Sat. 1-4 p.m.

Lundeen Park covers eight acres of shoreline just west of town, with a roped-off swimming beach, playground, picnic tables, and grand views across the water to the Cascade Range. Another Snohomish County park—**Wyatt Park**—occupies the west shore of Lake Stevens with a dock, boat launch for fishermen and water-skiers, picnic area, plus a sandy beach for sunbathing and swimming. No camping at either of these parks.

Scenic Drive

The drive northwest from Lake Stevens on Hwy. 92 to Granite Falls cuts through a big open valley created by the Pilchuck River. Enjoy the old farm homesteads with junk-covered yards, the U-pick berry farms, horse pastures, and tree farms while you can; it won't be long before the rapidly encroaching city pushes Wal-Marts, 7-Elevens, and split-level homes over all of this. See the Cascade Range chapter for details on the scenic "Mountain Loop" that begins in Granite Falls.

Practicalities

The main event in Lake Stevens is **Aquafest,** held on the last weekend of July, featuring a parade, arts and crafts, music, food, and a race. Get information from the **Lake Stevens Chamber of Commerce,** 9327 4th NE, tel. (425) 334-0433.

Community Transit, tel. (425) 353-7433 or (800) 562-1375, offers bus service to other parts of Snohomish County.

ARLINGTON

Just three miles from busy I-5, quiet Arlington (pop. 4,400) offers a delightful slice of small town America without the shopping-"mall-itis" blighting so much of the Puget Sound area. Downtown is a healthy mix of clothing stores, auto parts stores, and restaurants.

Sights

Stillaguamish Valley Pioneer Museum, 20722 67th Ave. NE, tel. (360) 435-7289, contains historical displays. Open Sunday, Monday, and Wednesday 1-3 p.m.; $1. **U.S. Marine** (Bayliner) just outside of town has tours Wednesday at 2 p.m. of the largest pleasure boat manufacture in the world, tel. (425) 435-5571.

Enjoy a picnic lunch at **Two Rivers Park** along the South Fork of the Stillaguamish River just east of town. America's **tallest chestnut tree** (106 feet high) stands in a field approximately eight miles east of town on Hwy. 530. It is located one mile east of the bridge over the North Fork Stillaguamish River on the north side of the road.

Lodging

Smokey Point Motor Inn, 17329 Smokey Point Dr. at Arlington exit 206 off I-5, tel. (360) 659-8561, has rooms for $44 s or $49 d, plus an outdoor pool, jacuzzi, and kitchenettes. The **Arlington Motor Inn,** 2214 Hwy. 530 (exit 208), tel. (360) 652-9595, charges $46-48 s or $51-53 d, and has a jacuzzi. **Crossroads Inn,** 5200 172nd St. NE, tel. (360) 403-7222 or (877) 856-3751, is a new motel with a jacuzzi, weight room, and continental breakfast; $59-79 s or d.

Campgrounds and RV Parks

Year-round camping ($10; no hookups) is available at **River Meadows County Park,** tel. (360) 435-3441, several miles east of town on the South Fork of the Stillaguamish River. Drive east on Hwy. 530 for three quarters of a mile, turn right onto Arlington Heights, and continue two miles. Turn right on Jordan Rd., and drive another three miles to the park. River Meadows Park also offers enjoyable hiking trails, picnic grounds, and a mile of river shoreline for fishing. The surrounding area is filled with farms with all sorts of critters, from longhaired Scottish cattle to Peruvian horses. Lots of horses are pastured around here, and Byle's Tit Farm (hey, I don't name these places) makes a great place to pose for a comical photo.

Smokey Point RV Park, 17019 28th Dr. NE, tel. (360) 652-7300 or (800) 662-7275, has RV spaces.

Food

Amazingly enough, Arlington has none of the national fast food chains; hopefully they won't arrive any time soon. **Islands Bakery,** 19224 62nd Ave. NE, tel. (360) 435-2100, has delicious fresh-baked breads and pastries. For espresso and live music, take a break at **Gimme A Break Coffeehouse,** 3405 172nd St. NE, tel. (360) 653-7427. **La Hacienda,** 210 W. Division, tel. (360) 435-9433, serves authentic Mexican cooking.

The Bistro, 231 N. Olympic, tel. (360) 403-9341, is where locals go for lunches and lattes, along with Northwest dinners of seafood, steak, chicken, pasta, and vegetarian specials. Dinner entrees are $13-28. It is run by the Love Israel commune, who put on the annual garlic festival.

Events and Entertainment

Arlington's airport is the third largest general aviation facility in Puget Sound and calls itself the world's largest ultralight airport. On the second weekend of July, it is home to the **Northwest Experimental Aircraft Association Fly-In,** America's third biggest fly-in. It includes experimental planes, military aircraft, hot air balloons, and an air show. Call (360) 403-9352 for details. The weekends around the Fourth of July bring **Arlington Festival,** the town's annual celebration, with parades, an auto show, triathlon, and rubber duck race. Each August, more than 20,000 people descend on Love Israel Ranch, seven miles northeast off Arlington for the annual **Garlic Festival,** with everything from garlic beer to garlic jellies. (The ranch is headed by "Love Israel" and is one of the few communes left in the state.) Be sure to return to Arlington in December to see a Santa parade, and to discover why they call it the "Christmas tree city."

Information and Transportation
Stop by the **Arlington Chamber of Commerce,** tel. (360) 435-3708, in the trailer on N. Olympic Ave. for local information; open Mon.-Fri. 9 a.m.-5 p.m. year-round.

Community Transit, tel. (425) 353-7433 or (800) 562-1375, has bus service throughout Snohomish County.

STANWOOD

Founded in 1865, Stanwood started as a center for the transport of logs floated down the Stillaguamish River. Located just east of the bridge to Camano Island, this compact farming village of 2,000 people prides itself on having as its chief employer the largest independent frozen-pea processor in the world: Twin City Foods. The town hosted the world's shortest railroad—seven-eighths of a mile—until it shut down in 1938.

Sights
Many of Stanwood's early residents were Scandinavian, a heritage that is still apparent in the Norwegian rosemaling (floral designs) on a handful of local buildings. Visit the **Scandia Bakery-Lefse Factory,** tel. (360) 629-2411, where you'll find fresh potato lefse and other treats.

The **Pilchuck Glass School** east of Stanwood was begun in 1971 by Dale Chihuly, now recognized as one of the world masters in the creation of glass sculptures. The school occupies a 64-acre wooded campus where both students and faculty live during their intensive May to September sessions. Today Pilchuck has 25 teachers and attracts artists from all over the world. Public tours are given only during an early August open house; call (360) 445-3111 for more information.

The **D.O. Pearson House Museum,** on the corner of 102nd Ave. NW and 271st St. SW, tel. (360) 629-3352, houses local historical items in a home built in 1890; open Sunday 2-5 p.m.

For an delightful country drive, head southeast from Stanwood on the road to the tiny burg called **Silvana.** Along the way, you'll wind along wooded Prestliens Bluff, overlooking big dairy farms, haystacks, and aging barns.

Practicalities
Sunday Lake B&B, 2100 Sunday Lake Rd. (five miles east of Stanwood), tel. (360) 629-4356, has one guest room with a private bath and full breakfast; $55 s or d. No kids.

Park RVs at the Stanwood Fairgrounds, where the **Stanwood-Camano Community Fair** is held in late July and early August; tel. (360) 445-2806. More RV parking at **Cedar Grove Shores RV Park,** 16529 Lake Goodwin Rd., tel. (360) 652-7083, south of town along Lake Goodwin.

Eat at **Cafe Bistro** for Italian fare, or **Jimmy's Pizza,** tel. (360) 629-6565, for surprisingly good pizzas. Get fresh produce at the **Stanwood Farmers Market,** tel. (360) 653-9356, Saturday 9 a.m.-2 p.m., May-September. The **Silvana Farmers Market** takes place on Saturday 10 a.m.-4 p.m. from late April to early October.

For local information, drop by the **Stanwood Chamber of Commerce,** 8705 271st St. NW, tel. (360) 629-4912.

Community Transit, tel. (425) 353-7433 or (800) 562-1375, provides bus connections to other parts of Snohomish County. **Airporter Shuttle,** tel. (800) 235-5247, has daily service between Stanwood and Sea-Tac.

CAMANO ISLAND

Primarily a residential island of vacation homes separated from the mainland by the shortest of bridges, Camano Island was originally inhabited by the Kikialos and Snohomish Indians and later, in the mid-1850s, by European loggers and settlers. Like Whidbey Island to the west, Camano receives fewer than 20 inches of rain annually because of the Olympic rain shadow effect. It is a quiet, bucolic place that attracts many artisans. The **History of the World, Part IV Gallery** displays some of these pieces, including an annual showing from the nearby Pilchuck Glass School each summer. Find them on the south end of Camano Island at 3325 S. East Camano Dr., tel. (360) 387-5225. Also of interest is **Alpaca de la Patagonia,** 332 N.E. Camano Dr., tel. (360) 387-9356, where you'll see upwards of 400 alpacas at pasture.

Camano Island State Park

Located 14 miles southwest from Stanwood, this state park covers 134 acres along Saratoga Passage. The picnic tables on the park's west side provide striking views of Whidbey Island and the Olympics. Hiking trails, including a half-mile interpretive loop, wind through 600-year-old Douglas firs with possible sightings of bald eagles, deer, raccoon, and opossum. Other activities here include fishing from the Point Lowell boat launch and sunbathing along the cliff-backed beaches. The park's two camping areas have tent sites ($10; no hookups) and coin-operated showers. Open year-round.

Lodging and Food

The **Inn at Barnum Point B&B,** 464 S. Barnum Rd., tel. (360) 387-2256 or (800) 910-2256, has three spacious guest rooms with private baths in a modern Cape Cod-style home overlooking the water. This is a fine place for a quiet and romantic getaway; $99-185 s or d, including a full breakfast. Kids accepted.

A newly remodeled turn-of-the-century hotel, **Camano Island Inn B&B,** 1054 S.W. Camano Dr., tel. (360) 387-0783 or (888) 718-0783, has six waterfront guest rooms with private baths, a wrap-around deck, and full breakfast; $120-160 s or d. Guests can borrow kayaks, and kids are welcome.

Get excellent seafood, steaks, and lamb at **Renee's Northwest Cuisine,** 170 E. Cross Island Rd., tel. (360) 387-0671. Open for lunch and dinner; entrees are $18-22.

Transportation

Community Transit, tel. (425) 353-7433 or (800) 562-1375, offers bus service from Camano Island to other parts of Snohomish County. The **Camano Island Visitor Center** (staffed in the summer) is visible as you come onto the island. Call (360) 387-2542 for additional info.

MOUNT VERNON AND BURLINGTON

The rich bottom land of the Skagit (SKAJ-et) Valley near Mount Vernon produces peas, potatoes, cabbage, cauliflower, broccoli, cucumbers, strawberries, raspberries, spinach, corn, vegetable seeds, and the area's best-known crops: daffodils, tulips, and irises. More than half the world's cabbage and spinach seeds are grown in the valley.

With a fast-growing population of more than 22,000, the city of Mount Vernon is largest in the county, and in spring is certainly among the prettiest: tulips and daffodils are *everywhere,* from fields to yards to gas stations. The attractive downtown features brick-fronted buildings, planters filled with flowers, and a prosperous mixture of stores. Unfortunately, just a mile to the north, the city shows another side—the shop- ping frenzy of Skagit Mall and other car-infested commercial havens.

Downtown Burlington (pop. 5,000) is a few minutes north of Mount Vernon, so close that it's difficult to tell where the borders are. It's hard to come up with any reason to spend much time in Burlington, unless you're heading to the shopping malls, a cheap motel, or home to suburbia.

The Skagit River is the second largest in the western U.S.; only the mighty Columbia River has more water. The Skagit reaches all the way to Manning Provincial Park in British Columbia and was an important access route into the Cascades during the early years of settlement. Today the river's main attraction is not transportation but recreation, including whitewater rafting and float trips down upper reaches of the river. Several large dams on the upper Skagit provide large amounts of power to the Pacific Northwest.

VICINITY OF MOUNT VERNON

© MOON PUBLICATIONS, INC.

History

Mount Vernon was named after George Washington's plantation, both to honor him and because the town was founded on his birthday in 1877. It was established along a big bend in the Skagit River where an enormous log jam prevented the upstream passage of steamships. Settlers were forced to stop here to portage around the jam before continuing overland or upstream in smaller boats. After the logjam was finally cleared in 1879, Mount Vernon became a refueling stop on the way upriver. In 1884 it was chosen as the county seat, and by 1900 its population exceeded that of neighboring La Conner. Construction of a lumber mill, and the arrival of the railroad, followed by the routing of old Hwy. 99 and modern-day I-5, helped establish Mount Vernon as a crossroads city.

SIGHTS

Flowers

With its rich loamy soil and mild weather, the Skagit Valley is Washington's primary bulb-growing region and home to Washington Bulb Co., the largest producer of bulbs in America. From late

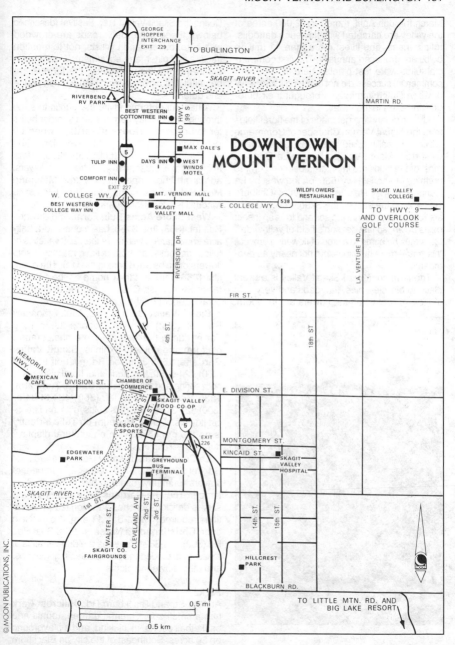

DOWNTOWN MOUNT VERNON

March through April, more than 2,000 acres of the valley are carpeted with flowering daffodils, tulips, irises, and lilies; more than 41 million bulbs are produced annually. The first commercial tulips were test-planted here in 1908, but commercial success did not come until after WW II, when Dutch immigrants brought their bulb-growing skills to the valley.

After mid-January, get maps of the floral fields from the Mount Vernon Chamber of Commerce Office or by calling (360) 428-5959. Or, just head west from Mount Vernon toward La Conner; most of the fields are in an area bounded on the north by Memorial Hwy. 536, on the west by La Conner-Whitney Rd., on the south by Chilberg Rd., and on the east by the Skagit River. Crops are rotated to preserve the soil and to keep insect pests down, so last season's field of yellow daffodils may be home to a crop of flowering broccoli this year—more nutritious, but not nearly as photogenic.

The farm country of Skagit Valley is a great place to bicycle—nice, flat roads and very little traffic—except when the flowers are in bloom.

DIANNE BOUERICE LYONS

daffodil fields

During the Skagit Valley Tulip Festival (described below), these same back roads are crowded with cars, buses, and cyclists, not to mention tractors and other farm equipment. Weekends in early April are insanely busy; the flowers are beautiful, but bicyclists won't have much peace and quiet.

A handful of farms invite the public to stroll through their display gardens and to order bulbs for fall delivery. **RoozenGaarde** (owned by Washington Bulb Co.), 1587 Beaver March Rd., tel. (360) 424-8531 or (800) 732-3266, offers retail and mail-order bulb sales, fresh-cut flowers, and a gift shop; open daily March-May, and Mon.-Sat. the rest of the year. The Dutch-style windmill is a local landmark.

West Shore Acres Bulb Farm, 956 Downey Rd., tel. (360) 466-3158, has a one-and-a half-acre show garden with more than 200 varieties of tulips, daffodils, and other flowers; they'll ship flowers or bulbs anywhere in the U.S. The beautiful 1886 Gardner family home on the grounds faces Swinomish Channel on one side and a floral splendor on the other.

Skagit Valley Bulb Farms, 1502 Bradshaw Rd., tel. (360) 424-8152, opens "Little Tulip Town" during the festival, with a photographic platform and nursery exhibits. **Skagit Valley Gardens,** 1695 Johnson Rd. (just off I-5), tel. (360) 424-6760, has additional floral displays in both spring and fall. **LeFeber Bulb & Turf Farm,** 1335 Memorial Hwy., tel. (360) 424-6234 or (800) 524-3181, also sells bulbs, gifts, and fresh-cut flowers. A small **Museum on Tulip Industry** is on the premises, with agricultural displays during the Tulip Festival.

La Conner Flats Display Garden, 1598 Best Rd., tel. (360) 466-3190, has an assortment of flowers (primarily roses) in bloom March-September. The **The Gardens at La Conner Flats** serves delicious lunches and high tea (reservations required) Tues.-Sat. 11 a.m.-4 p.m. Next door, **Christianson's Nursery,** 1578 Best Rd., tel. (360) 466-3821, features the 600 varieties of roses, plus rhododendrons, azaleas, dogwoods, and other flowering plants.

Parks

At 13th St. and Blackburn Rd., **Hillcrest Park** has a small zoo, Oriental garden, tennis and basketball courts, picnicking, and a playground on 30 acres. Southeast of the city on Blackburn

Rd. W, the 927-foot **Little Mountain** affords fine views of the Olympics, San Juan Islands, and Skagit Valley farmland with 490 forested acres surrounding the summit observation area; to get there, follow Blackburn Rd. to Little Mountain Road.

Eight miles west of Burlington on Padilla Bay, **Bay View State Park,** tel. (360) 757-0227, is small—25 acres—but has an abundance of campsites, along with a well-kept picnic area and sunbathing beach with broad views of the bay and Hat and Saddlebag Islands.

Located in the Padilla Bay National Estuarine Research Reserve, the **Breazeale Interpretive Center,** tel. (360) 428-1558, has natural history and marine displays, hands-on exhibits for kids, and a range of programs. Borrow a trail guide from the center for a three-quarter-mile nature hike through the upland cedar forest and fields, where you might see bald eagles, herons, ducks, or geese. The interpretive center is open Wed.-Sun. 10 a.m.-5 p.m.; free. Find it just north of Bay View State Park on Bay View-Edison Road.

ACCOMMODATIONS

Local motels and B&Bs fill up fast for the Tulip Festival; be sure to make reservations at least a month ahead if you plan to visit at that time.

Bed and Breakfasts
Unless otherwise noted, all the B&Bs below serve a full breakfast and do not allow young children. **Colonial Manor B&B,** 1556 McLean Rd., tel. (360) 424-3237 or (800) 893-1022, is a very nice 1907 Colonial Revival with five guest rooms, private baths (two with jacuzzi tubs), and an outdoor jacuzzi; $95-135 s or d.

Three miles northwest of Burlington in farming country, **Benson Farmstead B&B,** (360) 757-0578 or (800) 685-7239, is a beautifully restored 1914 home with four antique-filled guest rooms and private baths. Guests can relax in the hot tub, and kids are welcome; $75-85 s or d.

Fulton House B&B, 420 Fulton St., Mount Vernon, tel. (360) 336-2952, is a 1908 Victorian with three guest rooms and private baths; $85 s or d.

Snuggled in the midst of 250 wooded acres three miles south of Mount Vernon, **Whispering Firs B&B,** tel. (360) 428-1990 or (800) 428-1992, is a large, modern home with shaded seclusion. Three guest rooms have private baths, and a large hot tub is on a deck; $65-95 d. Kids are welcome.

Barnhouse B&B, 1501 Avon Allen Rd., tel. (360) 424-4099, is a contemporary hip-roofed home with two guest rooms and private baths; $65-85 s or d.

Thirteen Firs B&B, five miles southeast of Conway, tel. (360) 445-3571, is a large contemporary home on Lake McMurray with one guest room, a sun deck, and continental breakfast; $85 s or d.

Dutch Treat on Big Lake, 1777 W. Big Lake Blvd., tel. (360) 422-5466, is a modest home on a sandy shore of Big Lake with a canoe, rowboat, and sailboat for guests; $60 s or d.

Motels
Accommodations are arranged by price. **Sterling Motor Inn,** 866 S. Burlington Blvd. in Burlington, tel. (360) 757-0071, has rooms for $37 s or $42 d. **Mark II Motel,** 805 Goldenrod Rd. in Burlington, tel. (360) 757-4021, charges $38 s or $43-46 d.

Rooms are $40 s or $45-50 d at **West Winds Motel,** 2020 Riverside Dr. in Mount Vernon, tel. (360) 424-4224. **Days Inn,** 2009 Riverside Dr. in Mount Vernon, tel. (360) 424-4141 or (800) 882-4141, has an outdoor pool and jacuzzi; $40-55 s or d. **Hillside Motel,** 2300 Bonnie View Rd. in Mount Vernon, tel. (360) 445-3252, has kitchenettes for $43 s or d. **Tulip Valley Inn,** 2200 Freeway Dr. in Mount Vernon, tel. (360) 428-5969 or (800) 599-5969, charges $49 s or $55-68 d. **Cocusa Motel,** 200 W. Rio Vista in Burlington, tel. (360) 757-6044 or (800) 628-2257, has an outdoor pool and rooms for $58 s or d.

Best Western CottonTree Inn, 2300 Market Place in Mount Vernon, tel. (360) 662-6886 or (800) 662-6886, charges $59-69 s or $75-85 d, including an outdoor pool and continental breakfast. **Best Western College Way Inn,** 300 W. College Way in Mount Vernon, tel. (360) 424-4287 or (800) 528-1234, has an outdoor pool, jacuzzi, and continental breakfast; $60-70 s or $65-75 d. **Comfort Inn,** 1910 Freeway Dr. in Mount Vernon, tel. (360) 428-7020 or (800) 228-5150, charges $69 s or d, including an indoor pool, jacuzzi, fitness pass, and breakfast buffet.

CAMPING

Eight miles west of Burlington on Padilla Bay, **Bay View State Park,** tel. (360) 757-0227, has year-round campsites for $11 ($16 RVs) across Bay View-Edison Rd. from the waterfront. Call (800) 452-5687 for reservations ($6 extra).

Conway County Park, below the bridge over Skagit River in Conway (just off I-5), has campsites open June to mid-October. **Skagit County Fairgrounds** on the corner of Hazel and Virginia in Mount Vernon has additional public campsites.

Private RV parks include **Burlington KOA,** 646 N. Green Rd., tel. (360) 724-5511; **Riverbend Park,** 305 W. Stewart Rd. (off I-5 exit 227), tel. (360) 428-4044; **Mt. Vernon RV Park,** 1229 Memorial Hwy., tel. (360) 428-8787; and **Big Lake Resort,** 1785 W. Big Lake Blvd., tel. (360) 422-5755. The latter also rents boats and has a swimming beach.

FOOD

Mount Vernon is blessed with more than its share of excellent places to eat, from the oddball (**Chuck Wagon Drive-In,** 800 N. 4th St., tel. 360-336-2732, has to be seen to be believed) to elegant establishments offering some of the finest meals in the region.

American

Mt. Vernon's favorite breakfast place is **Calico Cupboard Cafe and Bakery,** 121B Freeway Dr., tel. (360) 336-3107. For an espresso in an enjoyable downtown location, stop by **Same Ol' Grind,** 508 S. 1st St., tel. (360) 336-5632.

Get all-American steak and seafood at **Gentleman Gene's,** 1400 Parker Way, tel. (360) 424-4363. The pub has over a hundred beers. **Max Dale's Restaurant,** 2030 Riverside Dr., tel. (360) 424-7171, serves fine steak, seafood, and prime-rib, with entertainment and dancing on weekends.

Enjoy moderately priced fresh seafood, delicious baked goods, and other creative preparations at **Wildflowers Restaurant,** located in a 1934 house with gardens at 2001 E. College Way, tel. (360) 424-9724. A fine place for a romantic gourmet dinner.

Skagit River Brewing Co., 404 S. 3rd St., tel. (360) 336-2884, has fresh-brewed beer on tap, pub grub on the menu, plus jazz, blues, or world beat bands most Saturday nights.

International

Pacioni's Pizzeria, 606 S. 1st St., tel. (360) 336-3314, bakes outstanding thin-crust, crunchy pizzas with tasty toppings, along with calzone and panini. Also of note is **Cascade Pizza,** 1825 Riverside Dr., tel. (360) 428-0200, with pizzas and Italian dishes.

Cocina del Rio, 602 W. Division, tel. (360) 336-1011, is a nice place with good Mexican food. Another noteworthy south-of-the-border eatery (great margaritas and *chile verde* dishes) is **Mexico Cafe,** 1320 Memorial Hwy., tel. (360) 424-1977.

Fortune Mandarin, 1617 Freeway Dr., tel. (360) 428-1819, serves good Chinese food.

Produce and More

Skagit Valley Food Co-op, 202 S. 1st. St., tel. (360) 336-3886, has a wide selection of bulk foods, locally baked bread, wine and beer, fresh produce, plus an all-natural deli (Deli Next Door) for a take-out lunch or dinner. This is the best and most nutritious quick meal deal in town. On Friday evenings, they offer a very reasonable all-you-can-stuff-in spaghetti or burrito feed. Open till 7 p.m.

Another place for fresh produce (and flowers, of course) is the **Mount Vernon-Skagit Valley Farmers Market,** held in downtown Mount Vernon Saturday 9:30 a.m.-1:30 p.m. between early June and late September. At other times, stop by Burlington's **Country Farms Produce Market,** 101 Orange Ave., tel. (360) 755-0488, for fresh locally grown fruits and vegetables.

SKAGIT VALLEY TULIP FESTIVAL

The 10-day county-wide Tulip Festival, held annually in early April, corresponds with the blooming of the tulip and daffodil fields and includes bus tours, Skagit River trips, bike rides, street fairs, foot races, llama hikes, antique shows, a salmon bake, volleyball tournaments, and art shows. Tour buses dump hundreds of sightseers on the area, and many more drive up from Seattle to photograph the colorful fields. Daily

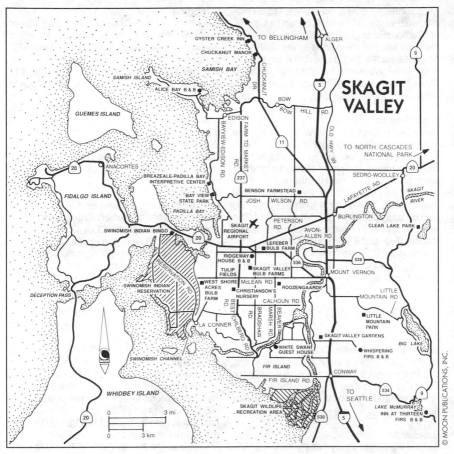

bus shuttles help alleviate some of the congestion, but with several hundred thousand visitors, it still gets crazy, especially on weekends between 11 a.m. and 4 p.m. Be sure to stop at the visitor's booths for a map of local bike lanes if you're pedaling around during the festival. Kodak sponsors an official photo platform at **Little Tulip Town,** 1502 Bradshaw Rd., tel. (360) 424-8152, along with music, art, pony rides, kite flying, espresso coffee, cut flowers, and refreshments. In addition, RoozenGaarde, West Shore Acres, and Skagit Valley Gardens all have paths that wind through flower gardens. You can purchase cut flowers or buy bulbs at these or other local places. Call (360) 428-5959 for a detailed map and description of the fields and Tulip Festival activities.

In Mount Vernon itself, the Tulip Festival action centers on a downtown **Street Fair** that includes more than 130 art and craft vendors, plus live entertainment and food.

Festival Transportation
During the first two weeks of April, the *Victoria Clipper,* tel. (360) 448-5000 or (800) 888-2535, offers a special 12-hour voyage to La Conner from Seattle's Pier 69. This includes the cruise and a guided bus tour of the tulip fields for $38-48 adults, $27-37 seniors, or $19-24 children.

On weekdays during the festival, **Tulip Transit** buses, tel. (360) 678-4211, depart La Conner, Mt. Vernon, Burlington, and Conway on two-to-four hour tours of the valley's flower fields. The cost is $8 adults, $4 kids, and free for children under three. Weekends bring out the $2 **Skagit Transit** buses that loop through the valley; tel. (360) 428-5959.

Other Events

Berry Dairy Days the third weekend of June celebrates Burlington's agricultural roots, with a big parade, carnival, arts and crafts, salmon barbecue, music, and plenty of strawberry shortcake. In early July, the **Highland Games & Scottish Fair** comes to Mt. Vernon, with a parade, dancing, competitions, food, fireworks, and enough bagpipe music to drive you batty. The second weekend of August brings the **Skagit County Fair** to the fairgrounds on the southwest side of Mount Vernon off Blackburn Road. Fair activities include live entertainment, agricultural exhibits, food, and lots more.

OTHER PRACTICALITIES

Arts

Historic **Lincoln Theatre Center,** 712 S. 1st St., tel. (360) 336-2858, is the place for films, plays, and musical productions throughout the year. The original Wurlitzer organ—used for silent films and vaudeville shows in the 1920s—still works.

Recreation

Swim at the **Skagit Valley Family YMCA,** 215 E. Fulton St., tel. (360) 336-9622. Six miles east of Mount Vernon on Hwy. 9, **Overlook Golf Course,** tel. (360) 422-6444, is a nine-hole course with views of Big Lake.

Shopping

Browse through the shops in downtown Mount Vernon, particularly 1st Street's bakeries, gift and clothing stores, and cafes. You'll also discover four different bookstores here, including the spacious **Scott's Bookstore,** at 120 N. 1st St., tel. (360) 336-6181, a great place to linger.

If you prefer to shop in a mall, Mount Vernon and Burlington have several to choose from, including **Cascade Mall,** with Sears, JCPenney, Bon Marché, and Emporium, and **Burlington Outlet Center,** 234 Fashion Way, tel. (360) 757-3549, with more than 50 outlet stores.

Information

For maps, brochures, and festival information, contact the **Mount Vernon Chamber of Commerce,** 117 N. 1st St., tel. (360) 428-8547. Hours are Mon.-Fri. 8:30 a.m.-5 p.m., Saturday 9 a.m.-4 p.m., Sunday 10 a.m.-4 p.m., in the summer; or Mon.-Fri. 8:30 a.m.-5 p.m., and Saturday 9 a.m.-4 p.m. the rest of the year.

Transportation

Skagit Transit (SKAT), tel. (360) 757-4433, offers *free* daily bus service throughout Skagit Country, including Mt. Vernon and Burlington.

Amtrak, tel. (800) 872-7245, provides daily train connections from Mount Vernon north to Vancouver, B.C., and south to Seattle.

The **Airporter Shuttle,** tel. (800) 235-5247, has connections to Sea-Tac. **Greyhound,** tel. (360) 336-5111 or (800) 231-2222, has long-haul bus service from the Mount Vernon terminal at 1101 S. 2nd Street.

Skagit Eagle Air, tel. (360) 757-1036 or (800) 542-7600, has flightseeing tours over the tulip fields from Skagit Regional Airport.

LA CONNER AND VICINITY

West of Mount Vernon, the broad Skagit Valley is carpeted with fields of vegetables and flowers, with a sprinkling of old barns and homesteads. This nearly level country is a favorite place for a spring or summer bike ride, especially when the tulips are blooming. After all this farmland, La Conner comes as quite a surprise; you might think you'd stumbled upon a transplanted Vermont town. The operative term here is cute, with more frills and lace than a Victoria's Secret catalog. La Conner is the most touristy town in Skagit County—too much so to suit the locals. But there's no denying it's a fun place to visit. Park your bike or car and browse the old buildings, shops, restaurants, and bakeries all jammed into a tiny downtown area along the saltwater Swinomish (SWIN-o-mish) Channel. You probably won't be alone. Crowds are likely on summer weekends and during the Tulip Festival, when La Conner looks like a California beachfront tourist trap in July, with standing traffic, cyclists, mobs of pedestrians, full parking lots, and sidewalk hot-dog stands. If you're driving here, don't bother looking for a space downtown on such days; just head north up 2nd St. to the big parking lot.

HISTORY

The Swinomish

The Swinomish Indians—Skagit River Valley's original inhabitants—spent their winters in villages dominated by long cedar houses with central firepits, and their summers in temporary structures made from cattail reeds. They lived off the bounty of this verdant land, eating from the abundant natural larder of fish, fowl, and game. As with many other tribes, introduced diseases brought by early European explorers—especially smallpox—quickly spread through the villages, killing nearly everyone in their path. Only a single Swinomish family survived, and their descendants alone represent the Swinomish tribe of today. When white settlers moved into the Skagit Valley, only a fraction of the native people

were still alive, and, as elsewhere, they were increasingly marginalized and forced to sign away their land in the Point Elliott Treaty of 1855. Today, the **Swinomish Indian Reservation** occupies less than 5,000 acres of land on Fidalgo Island just across Swinomish Channel from La Conner.

From Trading Post to Tourist Central

The oldest town in Skagit County, La Conner's first white settlers arrived shortly after the Civil War. They built dikes to tame the annual floods on the Skagit River and planted crops in the fertile soil that proved to be some of the most productive in the world. The town grew up along Swinomish Channel—the protected slough that separates the mainland from Fidalgo Island. In 1876, John Conner purchased a trading post and named the site after his wife, Louisa A. Conner (L.A. Conner eventually became La Conner).

La Conner flourished as a fishing and shipping port—by the turn of the century more than 1,000 people lived here—but overfishing and the Depression of the 1930s combined to send it into decline. Fortunately, the area's beauty began attracting artists looking for an interesting but inexpensive place to live. Guy Anderson was one of the first to arrive. Others followed, and as a group, they came to be known as the Skagit Valley School. Sometime in the 1970s, Seattle art critic Tom Robbins moved here and began writing novels. Locals started promoting the town as a quaint place to escape city life, and the tourists have been flooding in ever since.

Today La Conner is home to barely 700 people but is one of Washington's most loved destinations. More than 160 local buildings in La Conner are on the National Register of Historic Places. Its galleries, gift shops, restaurants, museums, and 19th-century homes make for enjoyable exploring, and the bright-orange **Rainbow Bridge,** crossing the Swinomish Channel, is a good spot for photographers to get a shot of the La Conner waterfront with a Mt. Baker backdrop.

LA CONNER

TO ANACORTES

MARINA

PUBLIC PARKING

STATE

CENTRE

TO HWY 20

LA CONNER WHITNEY RD

SWINOMISH

LA CONNER CHANNEL LODGE

CHAMBER OF COMMERCE

TILLINGHAST SEED COMPANY

RAINBOW INN B & B

INDIAN

MUSEUM OF NORTHWEST ART

LA CONNER COUNTRY INN

MORRIS

LIBRARY

THE HERON INN

THE WILD IRIS INN

RESERVATION RD

LIGHTHOUSE INN

WASHINGTON

KATY'S INN

TALBOT

TO CONWAY AND I-5

RESERVATION

SKAGIT COUNTY HISTORICAL MUSEUM

ART'S PLACE

RAINIER

LAUREL

HOTEL PLANTER

BENTON

CALHOUN

MYRTLE

GACHES MANSION

MAPLE HALL

TOWN HALL

DOUGLAS

HILL

MAPLE AVE.

SWINOMISH CHANNEL

PARK ST

RAINBOW BRIDGE

CALEDONIA

PIONEER PARK

SHERMAN

SCALE NOT AVAILABLE

© MOON PUBLICATIONS, INC.

SIGHTS AND SHOPS

Museums

Housed in a beautiful award-winning building in the center of town, the outstanding **Museum of Northwest Art,** 121 S. 1st St., tel. (360) 466-4446, features paintings and sculptures by well-known regional artists. This is the only museum to exclusively showcase Northwest art, and it includes a permanent collection of works upstairs. Downstairs are contemporary art exhibits, including a room on glassmaking. Open Tues.-Sun. 10 a.m.-5 p.m. year-round. Entrance costs $3 adults, free for kids under 13.

Skagit County Historical Museum, 501 4th St., tel. (360) 466-3365, sits high on a hill, with a panoramic view from the observation deck across the fields and farms of Skagit Valley. Inside are pioneer artifacts from the days of mining, logging, and fishing, historical photos, horse-drawn carriages, Indian baskets, and even a moonshine still from the 1930s. Watch the video for a taste of local history, or stop by the gift shop for books and crafts. Open Tues.-Sun. 11 a.m.-5 p.m. all year (longer hours during the Tulip Festival); admission is $2 adults, $1 seniors and kids ages 6-12, $5 families, and free for under five.

Constructed in 1891, the majestic **Gaches Mansion** at 2nd and Calhoun was lovingly restored after a 1973 fire gutted the structure. The first floor contains turn-of-the-century furnishings, while the upstairs houses the **La Conner Quilt Museum,** tel. (360) 466-4288, with changing exhibits and a small gift shop selling locally made quilts. Open Wed.-Sun. 11 a.m.-5 p.m.; $3. Just around the corner from the Gaches Mansion at 2nd and Commercial, you'll find an 1869 log cabin that was moved here from the Skagit River. Nearby are the old brick city hall from 1886 and historic **Maple Hall** used for theatrical and music performances.

The little **Fireman's Museum** on 1st St. contains a horse-drawn handpump that was used to put out fires in San Francisco following the 1906 earthquake. It was later used by the La Conner Fire Department; peek in the window to see it.

Pioneer Park, is a quiet riverside place for a picnic beneath tall Douglas fir trees next to Rainbow Bridge. No camping. **Skagit Wildlife Recreation Area,** a refuge south of La Conner on Fir Island, is a good place to look for wintering snow geese and trumpeter swans.

Shopping

The most fun way to shop in La Conner is to simply meander through downtown, stopping for lunch or a beer and heading out again. Art galleries, gift shops, antique dealers, espresso and sweets places, and restaurants line 1st and Morris Streets. Most of these sell cloyingly dolled-up tourist crap, but there are several notable exceptions. **The Stall,** 712 1st St., tel. (360) 466-

3162, sells unusual folk art imports from all over the globe. More distinctive imports at **Inside Out,** 711 E. Morris St., tel. (360) 466-3144, where you'll find gargoyles and other architectural statuary. **Bowman Bay Company,** 608 S. 1st St., tel. (360) 466-1900 or (888) 356-3866, is a fine-arts shop with paintings and local crafts. **The Next Chapter Books,** 721 S. 1st St., tel. (360) 466-2665, is a great little shop on the east end of 1st Street.

Established in 1885, the **Tillinghast Seed Company,** 623 E. Morris St., tel. (360) 466-3329 or (800) 320-3329, is the oldest operating retail seed store in the Northwest, with flower and vegetable seeds and plant paraphernalia of all types. Even brown thumbs will enjoy this shop! Each October they have a big pumpkin and scarecrow contest.

ACCOMMODATIONS

La Conner is blessed with a number of delightful inns and historic B&Bs. See **Mount Vernon and Burlington** for additional places (often cheaper) just a few miles east of La Conner.

Bed and Breakfasts

Unless otherwise noted, all B&Bs listed below serve a full breakfast and do not allow young children.

For country lodging at its best, stay at **White Swan Guest House B&B,** 15872 Moore Rd.

DIANNE BOULERICE LYONS

Gaches Mansion

on Fir Island, tel. (360) 445-6805, a beautiful 1898 farmhouse with three guest rooms (shared baths), and a large English-style garden; $80 s or d. A vegetarian breakfast is served. A separate cottage has its own bath, kitchen, and sundeck; $150 s or d.

For another taste of the past, **Katy's Inn B&B,** 503 S. 3rd, tel. (360) 466-3366 or (800) 914-7767, is an 1876 Victorian farmhouse facing Swinomish Channel with a wraparound porch, gazebo, and jacuzzi. Inside are five luxurious guest rooms with shared baths; $72-120 s or d.

Built in 1928, **Ridgeway Farm B&B,** 1292 McLean Rd., tel. (360) 428-8068 or (800) 428-8068, stands near the tulip fields midway between La Conner and Mount Vernon. This antique-filled yellow-brick farmhouse is surrounded by a flower-filled lawn and orchard, and has five guest rooms, shared or private baths, and a separate cottage. A hot tub sits in the rose garden; $75-155 s or d.

Another restored old farmhouse next to the tulips has been turned into **Rainbow Inn B&B,** 1075 Chilberg Rd., tel. (360) 466-4578 or (888) 266-8879. Guests enjoy the gourmet breakfast, explore the surrounding floral bouquet, or just relax in the jacuzzi. It has eight guest rooms and shared baths; $75-100 s or d.

The Parsonage on Pleasant Ridge, 1754 Chilberg Rd., tel. (360) 466-1754, is another historic 1894 country farmhouse that originally served as a parsonage for the Swedish Lutheran church. Now on the National Register of Historic Places, the home has one guest suite, plus a newer carriage house. A continental breakfast is served; $95 s or d.

Not far away atop Pleasant Ridge, you'll find **Valentine House B&B,** 1842 Valentine Rd., tel. (360) 466-3079 or (888) 466-3079, another classic Victorian. The three spacious guest rooms have private baths; $75-120 s or d.

Also in the same vicinity is another turn-of-the-century, **Storyville B&B,** 1880 Chilberg Rd., tel. (360) 466-3207 or (888) 373-3207, with five guest rooms an private or shared baths; $90-125 s or d. A jacuzzi is outside.

Skagit Bay Hideaway, 1740 B Goldenview, tel. (360) 466-2262 or (888) 466-2262, is a luxurious contemporary home across the Rainbow Bridge with a rooftop jacuzzi and a breakfast basket each morning. $195 d.

Art's Place, 511 E. Talbot, tel. (360) 466-3033, is a modern two-story home with a balcony bedroom, spiral staircase, and jacuzzi tub. A continental breakfast is served; $60 s or d. Kids accepted.

Hotels and Motels

The **Hotel Planter,** 715 1st St., tel. (360) 466-4710 or (800) 488-5409, has quaintly decorated rooms in a 1907 building, with a hot tub and gazebo in the garden courtyard. No kids on weekends. $75-120 s or d.

The Heron Inn, 117 Maple St., tel. (360) 466-4626, is a Victorian-style country inn with a jacuzzi and continental breakfast; $69-135 s or d. Next door, the same folks run **Wild Iris Inn,** tel. (360) 466-1400 or (800) 477-1400, a luxurious 20-room Victorian-style inn with view suites, jacuzzis, fireplaces, outside decks, and a breakfast buffet; $115-180 s or d. No kids under 12 in either place.

La Conner Channel Lodge, 205 N. 1st St., tel. (360) 466-1500, is a waterfront hotel with gas fireplaces, small balconies, jacuzzis, and a continental breakfast; $96-106 s or d. **La Conner Country Inn,** 107 S. 2nd St., tel. (360) 466-3101, has two-bedroom units with gas fireplaces and a continental breakfast; $131-176 s or d.

Lighthouse Inn, 512 S. 1st St., tel. (360) 466-3147, has an upstairs guest room with a private deck; $80 s or d. **Esteps' Residence in La Conner,** 1st St., tel. (360) 466-2116, is an in-town condominium with deck overlooking Swinomish Channel; $135 d.

Campgrounds

Bay View State Park, eight miles north of La Conner, has year-round campsites for $11 ($16 RVs). Call (360) 757-0227 for details, or (800) 452-5687 for reservations ($6 extra).

Head south to Fir Island for **Blakes RV Park & Marina,** 1171-A Rawlins Rd., tel. (360) 445-6533.

FOOD

Breakfast and Lunch

Start your day at **Calico Cupboard Cafe & Bakery,** 720 S. 1st St., tel. (360) 466-4451, for great homemade country breakfasts, plus wonderful pastries and healthy lunches and dinners.

Arrive early to avoid a lengthy wait on summer weekends. Get the best local sandwiches, salads, and soups in the bright and airy **Hungry Moon Delicatessen,** 110 N. 1st St., tel. (360) 466-1602, located on the north end of town, away from the hordes. **La Conner Pub,** 702 S. 1st St., tel. (360) 466-9932, serves burgers and wonderful baskets of fish and chips.

Dinner

La Conner Seafood & Prime Rib House, 614 1st St., tel. (360) 466-4014, has waterfront dining emphasizing—as might be expected given the name—seafood and prime rib; $10-20 entrees.

Palmer's Restaurant & Pub, 416 Myrtle St., offers an extensive wine list to complement its outstanding Northwest and French cuisine. Open for lunch and dinner; call (360) 336-9699 for reservations. Dinner entrees are $15-26. Palmer's hilltop location and romantic interior make it a popular place to watch the sun go down. The same owners run **Adiamo Ristorante Italiano,** 501 S. 1st, tel. (360) 466-9111, a pleasant two-level restaurant with delicious contemporary Italian cuisine. Lunches are your best bet if you're on a budget; dinner entrees cost $14-23.

In business since 1939, **Hope Island Inn** serves eclectic cuisine (especially seafood), and offers waterside dining on the deck. Located northwest of town on Sneeoosh Rd., tel. (360) 466-3221.

La Conner Brewing Co., 117 S. 1st. St., tel. (360) 466-1415, has five kinds of brewed-on-the-premises beer, along with tasty wood-fired pizzas, oysters, soups, and salads. The outside patio is very popular in the summer.

Produce

In the summer, be sure to stop at the **Hedlin's Farm Fruit Stand** on the east edge of town for fresh corn, tomatoes, peas, honey, strawberries, and other produce from their nearby farm.

EVENTS

The event season kicks off each year with an early February **Smelt Derby.** La Conner's main event is also Mount Vernon's: the **Skagit Valley Tulip Festival** each April. It attracts thousands of folks to town, especially on festival weekends. Head to La Conner on the **Fourth of July** for a big fireworks display over Swinomish Channel. In mid-July the **Puget Sound Painters** are out in force, producing artwork that can be purchased at the museum. The season winds down with the **Art's Alive!** celebration in early November featuring demonstrations by painters, jewelers, potters, and others, and the **Christmas Boats Parade** up the Swinomish Channel each December.

RECREATION AND ENTERTAINMENT

Recreation

The Swinomish Channel is a peaceful body of water for paddling or rowing; rent a sea kayak from **La Conner Kayaks,** tel. (360) 466-5516. Whale-watching trips are becoming increasingly popular from La Conner, with two companies offering a variety of cruises: **Mystic Sea Charters,** tel. (800) 308-9387, and **Viking Cruises,** tel. (360) 466-2639. Several other companies offer charter fishing trips; see the chamber of commerce for specifics.

La Conner Kayaks, tel. (360) 466-5516, has sea kayak rentals and tours.

Rent bikes from **Boater's Discount Center,** 601 N. Dunlap St., tel. (360) 466-3540. Take a hot air balloon ride with **Vagabound Balloons,** tel. (360) 466-1906 or (800) 488-0269.

Gambling

Swinomish Casino and Bingo has gambling—including bingo, craps, roulette, blackjack, poker, and sic bo—at their casino just across the Hwy. 20 bridge on Fidalgo Island; call (360) 293-2691 or (800) 877-7529 for details. A gift shop here sells native arts and crafts, the cabaret has live music, and the restaurant features a seafood and prime rib buffet.

INFORMATION AND TRANSPORTATION

For local info, visit the **La Conner Chamber of Commerce** at 4th and Morris, tel. (360) 466-4778 or (888) 642-9284, open Mon.-Fri. 9:30 a.m.-3:30 p.m., and Sat.-Sun. 10 a.m.-4 p.m. April-October. The rest of the year, hours are

Mon.-Fri. 9:30 a.m.-3:30 p.m., and Sat. 10 a.m.-4 p.m. Find them on the Web at www.laconner-chamber.com.

Skagit Transit (SKAT), tel. (360) 757-4433, has *free* daily bus service throughout the county, from Anacortes to Concrete. **Rainbow Van Service,** tel. (360) 466-5324 or (800) 733-5320, has service to Sea-Tac Airport.

CHUCKANUT DRIVE

Heading north up the coast from the Skagit Valley, you enter one of the most scenic stretches of highway in the state—Chuckanut Drive. This 11-mile portion of Hwy. 11 was the first route designated a scenic drive by the state. Built as part of the now-extinct Pacific Highway, it leaves I-5 just north of Burlington and heads straight as a cue stick across the black, flat soil of the Skagit Valley, passing the **Rhododendron Cafe** at the Bow-Edison intersection. The cafe serves good food, and is populated on weekends by bicyclists and weekend-drive aficionados. The tiny towns of **Bow** and **Edison** have recently begun attracting artists, and several studios are open for weekend visits. **Harrah's Skagit Valley Casino** in Bow, tel. (360) 724-7777, has blackjack, craps, roulette, keno, bingo, and more ways to suck your wallet dry. Harrah's also has three restaurants and live music nightly. **Blau Oyster Co.** 919 Blue Heron Rd., tel. (360) 766-6171, grows fresh oysters; in business since 1935. The dinky place called Alger (just off I-5), is home to **Skagit Speedway,** tel. (360) 568-2529, with auto racing between mid-April and late September.

A short distance north of Bow, the highway runs head-on into the mountains that hover over Puget Sound; it's here that the fun begins. The road doesn't have a straight stretch for seven miles as it swoops and swerves along the face of the cliff with grand views across to Anacortes, Guemes Island, and, farther north, the San Juan and Lummi Islands. With no shoulder, a narrow strip of pavement, and tight corners, its a bit dicey for bikes, but the views are stunning.

As you drive north, you'll pass three good places to eat. Overlooking Sammish Bay and the San Juans at 302 Chuckanut Dr., **Chuckanut Manor Restaurant and B&B,** tel. (360) 766-6191, at the southern end of the drive, spe-cializes in fresh seafood and continental dishes ($10-25 entrees), Friday night smorgasbord, and Sunday champagne brunch. The bar has the best and usually quietest seats in the house and serves 26 different single malt scotches. The oyster-sized **Oyster Bar,** 240 Chuckanut Dr., tel. (360) 766-6185, is a cozy and expensive place clinging to the side of the mountain; it serves oysters (of course) and has a limited, mostly seafood menu. Every table overlooks the San Juan Islands. Specializing in Northwest food and wine, **Oyster Creek Inn,** 190 Chuckanut Dr., tel. (360) 766-6179, serves seafood, chicken, lamb, and other dishes. This is a must-stop place right in the trees and ferns overlooking a cascading creek. Head a half-mile down the canyon to the shoreline and **Taylor Shellfish Farm,** tel. (360) 766-6002, for locally raised fresh oysters, clams, scallops, mussels, and Dungeness crabs (cooked while you wait).

Accommodations

Both Chuckanut Manor and Oyster Creek Inn have overnight accommodations, and although the restaurants are some distance apart, their lodgings are only yards away. **Chuckanut Manor,** tel. (360) 766-6191, has a two-room suite upstairs over the restaurant with a spa and private deck. Nearby is a cottage with a hot tub, antique furnishings, a private deck, and kitchen. Both of these are $100 d including a continental breakfast and champagne.

Oyster Creek Inn, tel. (360) 766-6179, has a small Japanese-style cabin just south of Chuckanut Manor overlooking the bay; $115 s or d, including champagne and breakfast.

Alice Bay B&B, 982 Scott Rd. on Sammish Island just west of Edison, tel. (360) 766-6396 or (800) 652-0223, has a two-story cottage where you can soak in the hot tub on the deck overlooking Alice Bay, take the rowboat out, or borrow a bike; $95 s or d, including a full breakfast. Kids welcome.

Samish Point by the Bay, 447 Samish Point Rd., tel. (360) 766-6610 or (800) 916-6161, has four guest rooms with private baths in a secluded Cape Cod home facing Samish Bay. Outside, you'll find a jacuzzi and extensive gardens. Two night minimum; $175 s or d for the entire house. The kitchen is stocked for a make-your-own breakfast.

Parks and Beaches

Seven miles south of Bellingham on Chuckanut Dr., **Larrabee State Park,** tel. (360) 676-2093, was the state's first, created in 1923 when Charles Xavier Larrabee's family donated 20 acres in his honor. The park contains a popular campground with tent ($11) and RV ($16) sites, plus coin-operated showers. Open year-round. Call (800) 452-5687 for reservations ($6 extra). Now covering more than 2,500 acres of mountainous land, the park borders Samish Bay, with a boat launch, a sandy beach for sunning, and tidepools for marine explorations. Nine miles of hiking trails include the southern end of the **Interurban Trail** connecting the park with Bellingham. Other trails lead to scenic Fragrance and Lost Lakes for trout fishing, and to dramatic vistas from the 1,941-foot summit of **Chuckanut Mountain** (also accessible via a gravel road).

Continue north from Larrabee State Park to **Teddy Bear Cove,** located at the foot of the cliff just before you enter the Fairhaven District. For many years it was an unofficial nude beach, but the county purchased the land and started fining the au naturel crowd $125 in 1997. The prudes strike again.

BELLINGHAM

With a population of more than 61,000, Bellingham is no longer a town, but it still maintains a friendly small-town feel. The city is an almost perfect blend of the old and the new, with stately homes and extraordinary museums, an abundance of cultural events, plus many fine shops and restaurants. Bellingham has managed to hold onto both its blue-collar paper mill jobs and white-collar university positions, while attracting increasing numbers of tourists. The city is also a jumping-off point for northbound travelers aboard the Alaska Marine Highway's ferries; the terminal is in the historic Fairhaven section.

HISTORY

The original inhabitants of what is now Bellingham—the Lummi Indians—lived in wooden houses built of cedar planks that were placed seasonally around a permanent frame. They lived off the land, harvesting shellfish, fish, wild plants, deer, and other game animals. When Capt. George Vancouver sailed into Puget Sound in 1792, he found a community of nearly 3,000 native people living along these productive shores. He named it Bellingham Bay for Sir William Bellingham, the British Admiralty controller who provided Vancouver with supplies for his explorations.

European Settlement

Captain Henry Roeder and Russell V. Peabody established the first permanent settlement here in 1852; they came north from San Francisco in search of a sawmill site to supply their hometown's growing demand for lumber. When Roeder and Peabody met Lummi Chief Cha-wit-zit in Olympia, they asked him if he knew of any place with "falling water all the time from a high hill."

a sidewalk scene in Fairhaven

DON PITCHER

INSET 2

5

Maple St.

Villa Motel
Cascade Motel
Coachman Inn
Bay City Motor Inn
Motel 6

Aloha Motel

Abbott St.
Otis St.
Laurel St.

Ramada Inn

Samish Way

Park Motel
Consolidation

34th St.

36th St.

Evergreen Motel

Samish Way

5

32nd St.

EXIT 254

Iowa St.

Sportsplex
Bellingham Aquatic Center
Joe Martin Stadium
A Secret Garden B & B

Lakeway Dr.

Best Western Lakeway Inn

Lincoln St.

5

Convention and Visitors Bureau
Val-U Inn Motel

EXIT 253

EXIT 252

Samish Way
See Inset 2

Macs Motel
See Inset 2

State St.

Shangri-La Downtown Motel

Maple St.

Laurel St.

Garden St.

Travelodge

Sehome Hill Arboretum

Macdonald Pkwy.

College Dr.

24th St.

Old Fairhaven Pkwy.

Holly St.

Chestnut St.

Maritime Heritage Center

Georgia Pacific Corporation

Cornwall Ave.

South Bay Trail

State St.

Western Washington University

Knox Ave.

The Castle

Harris St.

11

Fairhaven Park

14th St.

INSET 1

Cornwall Ave.

Unity St.

N. Commercial St.

Lottie St.

Dupont St.

Central Ave.

Library

Mindport

Grand

Prospect

Post Office

Children's Museum
Northwest

Whatcom Museum of History and Art

Flora St.

Mt. Baker Theatre

Champion St.

Magnolia St.

Holly St.

Bus Terminal

Old Town Cafe

BELLINGHAM BAY

FAIRHAVEN

Alaska Marine Ferry Terminal
Amtrack Depot/
Bus Station

© MOON PUBLICATIONS, INC.

Cha-wit-zit apparently understood the Americans' broken English and, speaking in kind, suggested "at Whatcom, noise all the time." With the aid of Lummi tribe members, Roeder and Peabody built a mill at the foot of Whatcom Falls in 1853 that produced lumber until it burned down in 1873.

William H. Prattle, another of Bellingham's earliest settlers, responded to Native American tales of local coal outcroppings by opening a marginally successful coal mine in the settlement called Unionville in 1853. The same year, San Francisco investors opened the Sehome Mine, adjacent to the Whatcom settlement, and it became one of the two largest employers in the area until the mine was flooded in 1878. Coal mining ceased until the Bellingham Bay Co. opened the largest mine in the state in the city's north end in 1918; it operated until 1951, when decreased demand led to its closure.

The 1850s also brought to Bellingham the aborted Fraser River Gold Stampede. About 10,000 people, most of whom had traveled north from California, came to Whatcom to await the opening of a trail to British Columbia's newfound gold. The trail was never completed, and an order from Vancouver Island's governor James Douglas that all gold diggers obtain permits in Victoria before entering the province further squelched the would-be gold rush. One remnant from the gold boom is a brick building on E St.; the first brick building in the territory, it first served mercantile purposes and later was the Whatcom County Courthouse for 25 years.

Fairhaven

The boomtown of Fairhaven grew to prominence in the late 1880s when rumors circulated that it would be the western terminus for the Great Northern Railroad. At its peak, the town hummed on 35 hotels and boardinghouses, seven saloons, an opera house, and 11 real estate offices. Despite the large number of hotels, many men were forced to sleep in tents along the beach.

The selection of Tacoma as the Great Northern's terminus sent Fairhaven into a tailspin, but the arrival of a smaller line—the Fairhaven and Southern Railroad—brought service from Skagit Valley. Men working on the railroad would follow the tracks back to 9th St. for an evening's

entertainment; rowdy bars and hotels such as "Miss Reno's" provided much more than just a bed for their patrons—Fairhaven had quite a hot reputation. One unidentified man romanced himself into a state of exhaustion and dropped dead while walking up 9th Street. Another, John Moore, had a few too many at the Gilt Edge Saloon and decided to sleep it off on the tracks—poor John never heard the 2:30 a.m. train pulling into town.

Growing Up

In 1903, the cluster of four towns—Whatcom, Sehome, Bellingham, and Fairhaven—was consolidated to form Bellingham, but only after a long battle between the two main rivals, Fairhaven and Whatcom; residents of each demanded that theirs be the new town's name. Eventually the name Bellingham was chosen as a compromise. The town prospered with eight saw- and shingle-mills and four salmon-packing plants. Today the unpretentious city runs on a wide variety of businesses, including a large Georgia-Pacific tissue manufacturing mill, fishing, agriculture, tourism, and Western Washington University. The Alaska Marine Highway also uses Bellingham as its southern terminus, attracting a considerable number of travelers to town, especially in the summer.

SIGHTS AND TOURS

Fairhaven

Today Fairhaven is considerably more sedate than its original incarnation, though the recently revitalized section of town now attracts so many visitors that parking can be a real headache, especially when the Alaska ferry is in port. You can see its old buildings and Victorian homes by taking a walking tour of the Fairhaven Historic District; maps are available from the visitors bureau, 904 Potter St., tel. (360) 671-3990, and various Fairhaven shops and restaurants.

Several interesting shops and galleries can be found in the district. **Good Earth Pottery,** 1000 Harris Ave., tel. (360) 671-3998, has fine ceramics; the cooperatively owned **Artwood,** 1000 Harris Ave., tel. (360) 647-1628, sells handcrafted woodworking; and **Gallery West,** 1300 12th St., tel. (360) 734-8414, has paintings, sculpture, pottery, weavings, and jewelry. **Working Art Center** 1010 Harris St., tel. (360) 715-3099, has drawing, painting, raku, and other art classes throughout the year.

One of the most popular places in Fairhaven, or in all of Bellingham for that matter, is **Village Books,** 1210 11th St., tel. (360) 671-2626 or (800) 392-2665, and its companion, **Colophon Cafe,** sharing space on both floors. Village Books usually has Sunday book readings, a good time to meet authors. A fine shop selling used titles is **Eclipse Bookstore,** 915 Harris Ave., tel. (360) 647-8165.

Western Washington University

This 189-acre campus has five colleges and two schools for 10,000 students. It began as the State Normal School in 1893, and became a full-fledged university in 1977. The campus is also known for its 22 sculptures in the **Outdoor Sculpture Garden.** Contact the Admissions office, tel. (360) 650-3861, for campus tours. **Viking Union** includes a bookstore, deli and other food options, a post office, and information desk.

Overlooking Bellingham Bay and accessible via a footpath from the university, the **Sehome Hill Arboretum** provides splendid views of the San Juans and Mt. Baker, plus 70 acres of tall Douglas firs, wildflowers, and big-leaf maples preserved in their natural state. The 3.5 miles of paved trails provide views of Bellingham and the San Juans, along with Mt. Baker.

Museums

Located on a high bluff overlooking Bellingham Bay, the outstanding **Whatcom Museum of History and Art,** 121 Prospect St., tel. (360) 676-6981, is housed in old city hall, an ornate red-brick building capped by a four-corner cupola and a tall clock tower. Built in 1892 as the New Whatcom City Hall, it remained in use until 1939. Today, the museum has grown to include the old city hall, along with three nearby structures. Hours for all but the Children's Museum are Tues.-Sun. noon-5 p.m. year-round, and a donation is requested.

The main building contains historical displays, changing exhibits, Victorian clothing, woodworking tools, toys, and contemporary art. Also here is a small gift shop with unusual items from around the globe. The **Syrie Education Center,** 201 Prospect, right next to old city hall, features many beautiful native baskets, bentwood boxes, reed mats, and even a Chilkoot blanket, plus a large number of stuffed birds. Also here are fascinating displays on the early days of Northwest logging—including the famous Darius Kinsey collection of images. These and thousands of other historical photographs make the archives one of the finest in Washington.

Two nearby structures house separate collections that are also part of the Whatcom Museum "campus." The **Arco Exhibits Building,** across the street at 206 Prospect, houses changing fine-art and historical exhibits. The **Children's Museum Northwest,** 227 Prospect St., tel. (360) 733-8769, has many participatory exhibits for kids of all ages, including an infant/toddler exploration center and puppet theater. Open Sunday, Tuesday, and Wednesday noon-5 p.m., Thurs.-Sat. 10 a.m.-5 p.m.; $2.

Make it a point to visit **Mindport,** a free creative center that will amuse, fascinate, and educate both kids and adults. The exhibits are mostly made from reused old junk, with a touch of whimsy thrown in. Great fun. Find them a block from the Whatcom Museum at 111 Grand Ave., tel. (360) 647-5614. Open Wed.-Sun. 10 a.m.-5 p.m.

Something Fishy

Bellingham's **Maritime Heritage Center,** 1600 C St., tel. (360) 676-6806, is an urban park where you can fish for salmon and steelhead on Whatcom Creek, watch salmon spawning in mid-October, and learn about hatchery operation. Admission is free; open dawn to dusk. Kids will enjoy the marinelife touch tank where they can pet intertidal creatures. It's located inside the Harbor Center Mall at Squalicum Harbor off Roeder Avenue.

Tours

Maps of historic walking tours are available from the visitors bureau at 904 Potter Street. These include tours of stately Victorian mansions in the **Eldridge** and **Sehome** districts, and of **Fairhaven,** with its 1880s mansions and old brick storefronts. The **Squalicum Harbor** tour is along the two-mile promenade past pleasure and commercial boats and ships. This is the second-

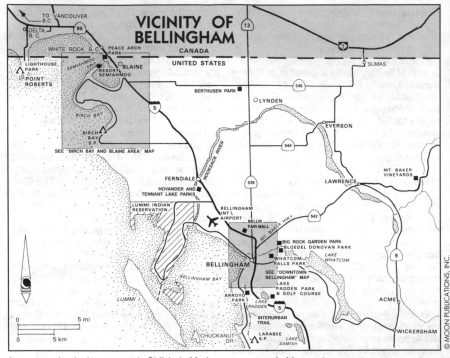

© MOON PUBLICATIONS, INC.

largest marina in the state; only Shilshole Marina in Seattle is bigger. The **Outdoor Art Walk,** takes you past works in downtown and on the Western Washington University campus. Held quarterly, the **Uptown Gallery Walks** occur when about 10 galleries open new shows on the same night. Call (360) 676-8548 for dates.

PARKS

Whatcom County has one of the best collections of city and county owned parks. In Bellingham alone there are more than 35 places that qualify as parks, including green belt areas, fitness areas, and trails. These parks range from less than half an acre to over a thousand acres.

A test site for the American Rose Society, **Fairhaven Park Rose Garden** is the highlight of the 16-acre manicured Fairhaven Park at 107 Chuckanut Dr., which also has picnic areas, a playground, hiking trails, and tennis courts. Best time to see it is July, when a hundred varieties of roses are in bloom at once.

Beautiful **Samish Park,** at I-5 exit 246 south of Bellingham, tel. (360) 733-2362, is a 39-acre county park along Lake Samish with swimming, fishing, boating, picnicking, hiking, and a children's play area. Rent canoes, paddleboats, rowboats, sailboats, or sailboards.

Whatcom Falls Park, near Lake Whatcom at 1401 Electric Ave., has hiking trails, tennis courts, a playground, a picnic area, and a state fish hatchery on 241 acres. With 12 acres on the lake itself, **Bloedel Donovan Park** has a swimming beach, boat launch, playground, and picnic area at 2214 Electric Avenue.

Lake Padden Park, 4882 Samish Way, has over 1,000 acres of hiking and horse trails, a golf course, picnic areas, and a playground, plus swimming, fishing, and nonmotorized boating on the lake.

Thirty-eight acres of practically untouched canyon wilderness is yours for the hiking at **Arroyo Park** on Old Samish Rd., with nature and horse trails and creek fishing.

Overlooking Lake Whatcom, **Big Rock Garden Park** includes hundreds of varieties of rhododendron and azaleas, along with dozens of Japanese maples. Surrounded by suburban sprawl, this is an oasis of tranquillity, with forests, and outdoor sculptures. The park is located at 2900 Sylvan Street.

SPORTS AND RECREATION

Hiking
Stop by the visitors bureau for descriptions of more than 20 hiking trails in and around Bellingham, including trails in Whatcom Falls Park and Sehome Hill Arboretum. Another 2.6 miles of paths circle Lake Padden Park.

The **Interurban Trail** is a six-mile path that follows a former railroad bed from Old Fairhaven Parkway south to Larrabee State Park. A great place for a jog or bike ride.

Equipping for the Outdoors
Rent sea kayaks, rowboats, and sailboats in summer from **Fairhaven Boatworks,** near the Bellingham Cruise Terminal at 501 Harris Ave., tel. (360) 647-2469. **Bellingham Boat Rentals,** 3034 Silvern Ln., tel. (360) 676-1363, has canoes and pedal boats for rent on Lake Whatcom; open May-August. **Klub Kayak,** tel. (888) 765-2925, rents sea kayaks on Lake Padden in the summer.

Brenthaven, 1059 N. State St., tel. (360) 733-5608 or (800) 803-7225, sews and sells high-quality day packs, shoulder bags, and soft luggage. **The Great Adventure,** 201 E. Chestnut, tel. (360) 671-4615, rents all sorts of outdoor gear, from climbing boots and backpacks to skis. Rent bikes, skis, and snowboards from **Fairhaven Bike & Mountain Sport,** 1103 11th St., tel. (360) 733-4433.

Climbing
Bellingham is home to the **American Alpine Institute,** the nation's preeminent center for mountaineering education. Located at 1515 12th St., tel. (360) 671-1505, the school has a staff that includes accomplished mountain climbers and educators, and courses from the basics to advanced month-long programs. Classes are taught all over the world, with beginning moun-

taineering courses in the North Cascades. Prices start at $115 pp/day. They also rent outdoor equipment.

Learn to climb indoors at **Leading Edge Rock Climbing Wall,** 1409 Fraser St., tel. (360) 733-6969.

Swimming and Skating
The **Bellingham Aquatic Center,** 1414 Potter St., tel. (360) 657-7665, has an indoor pool and water slide. A second pool is available at the local **YMCA,** 4600 Guide Meridian, tel. (360) 671-4378. In the summer months you can also swim at **Lake Padden Park** at 4882 Samish Way, tel. (360) 676-6985; **Lake Samish,** 673 N. Lake Samish Dr., tel. (360) 733-2362; and **Bloedel Donovan Park,** 2214 Electric Ave., tel. (360) 676-6985.

Sportsplex 1225 Civic Field Way, tel. (360) 733-9999, has indoor ice skating in fall and winter, and in-line skating the rest of the year.

Golf
Local public golf courses include: **Lake Padden Golf Course,** 4882 Sammish Way, tel. (360) 676-6989; **New World Pro Golf Center,** 5022 Guide Meridian, tel. (360) 398-1362; and the semi-private **Sudden Valley Golf & Country Club,** 2145 Lake Whatcom Blvd., tel. (360) 734-6435.

On the Water
The visitors bureau has a complete listing of local sailing and fishing charter operators, and cruises. **Moondance Sea Kayaking Adventures,** tel. (360) 738-7664, offers guided sea kayak tours from Bellingham.

Island Mariner Cruises, No. 5 Harbor Esplanade, tel. (360) 734-8866, has all-day whale-watching cruises on weekends in the summer for $55 adults, $45 seniors, and $35 kids. Two-and-a-half-hour narrated historical voyages are offered on Thursday evenings from July-Aug. for just $15.

The *Snow Goose* is a 65-foot fully equipped research vessel operated by two local marine biologists. They offer a range of trips, from four hours to five days. On all of these you'll get a firsthand look at marinelife and how researchers work in Puget Sound. Call (360) 733-9078 for details on this unique opportunity.

ACCOMMODATIONS

The **Bellingham and Whatcom County Convention and Visitors Bureau,** 904 Potter St., tel. (360) 671-3990 or (800) 487-2032 (recorded message), keeps track of local lodging availability during the summer months. Stop here for brochures on local places, discount coupons, or to check out their books with photographs of local B&Bs.

Hostels
Bellingham has a friendly and cozy 10-bed **AYH Hostel** at 107 Chuckanut Drive in historic Fairhaven. Dorm spaces cost $12-15; sorry, no private rooms. Like most hostels, it is closed during the day (9:30 a.m.-5 p.m.). Call (360) 671-1750 for advance reservations (strongly advised in the summer). The hostel has no curfew, though the common areas—including the kitchen—are locked after 11 p.m. A pancake breakfast is served each morning ($1). Closed Dec.-January.

Bed and Breakfasts
Several of Bellingham's B&Bs offer classic accommodations. Call **Whatcom County B&B Guild,** tel. (360) 676-4560, for details on the finest local B&Bs, or **BAB's Reservation Service,** tel. (360) 733-8642, for local B&B reservations. Unless otherwise noted, all B&Bs listed below serve a full breakfast and do not allow young children.

North Garden Inn, 1014 N. Garden St., tel. (360) 671-7828, (800) 922-6414 (U.S.), or (800) 367-1676 (Canada), is an ornate four-story Queen Anne Victorian home overlooking Bellingham Bay with a grand piano in the sitting room. The 10 guest rooms have private or shared baths; $64-79 s or $69-84 d.

More fine views from **A Secret Garden B&B,** tel. (360) 671-5327 or (800) 671-5327, a gorgeous turn-of-the-century Victorian home with two guest rooms, private baths, and a grand piano. Kids are welcome; $65-85 s or d.

The Castle, 1103 15th St., tel. (360) 676-0974, is a unique place with old-world grandeur and four antique-furnished rooms. This is not your usual B&B. The century-old hilltop mansion could pass for the Addams Family home, and the owners have a delightfully offbeat way of doing things; $45-95 s or d.

DeCann House B&B, tel. (360) 734-9172, is a 1902 home adorned with stained glass, etchings, family heirlooms, and fine views of the San Juan Islands. The two guest rooms have private baths. $64-74 s or d.

Stratford Manor B&B, 1416 Van Wyck Rd., tel. (360) 715-8441, is a classic Tudor-style mansion on 30 acres of parklike grounds. The three luxurious guest rooms have jacuzzi baths, fireplaces, and access to a solarium-covered hot tub; $125-165 s or d.

Fairhaven B&B, 1714 12th St., tel. (360) 734-7243 or (888) 734-7243, began as a 1908 bungalow, and was converted in 1970 into a striking Victorian-style home with two guest rooms, private baths, a hot tub, antique pool table, and continental breakfast; $75-95 s or d.

Big Trees B&B, tel. (360) 647-2850 or (800) 647-2850, is a 1907 craftsman home three miles east of town. The home sits amid tall trees with a big veranda overlooking Lake Whatcom, and a stone fireplace inside. The three guest rooms ($90-110 s or d) have private baths.

South Bay B&B, 4095 S. Bay Dr., tel. (360) 595-2086, is a large craftsman home on the south shore of Lake Whatcom. The five guest rooms have jacuzzi tubs, fireplaces, a sunroom, and private patios; $150 s or d.

Mark James Manor B&B, 2925 Vining St., tel. (360) 738-4919, is a graciously distinctive home on two acres right in town, with a single luxurious guest room complete with wet bar and sauna. Outside is a solarium with hot tub. A full breakfast and high tea are served. $95 s or d.

Above Lake Whatcom and surrounded by tall evergreens is the modern **Schnauzer Crossing,** 4421 Lakeway Dr. (three miles east of Bellingham), tel. (360) 734-2808 or (800) 562-2808. You'll find luxurious and spacious accommodations in the house and a separate cottage, plus a gourmet breakfast, a jacuzzi, and one and a half acres of gardens. Two night minimum on weekends, and kids accepted. $120-200 s or d. Friendly owners too.

CAMPING

The closest public campsites ($11 tents, $16 RVs) are seven miles south of Bellingham at **Larrabee State Park.** Call (800) 452-5687 for reservations ($6 extra). See "Chuckanut Drive," above, for details on the park. Additional campsites are 14 miles north in **Birch Bay State Park,** 5105 Helwig Rd. with year-round tent sites ($11) and RV hookups ($16) in the trees. Call (360) 371-2800 for information, or (800) 452-5687 for reservations ($6 extra). Private RV parks include **Sudden Valley Resort,** on Lake Whatcom at 2145 Lake Whatcom Blvd., tel. (360) 734-6430, and **Bellingham RV Park,** 3939 Bennett Dr., tel. (360) 752-1224 or (888) 372-1224.

FOOD

Bellingham has an amazing variety of creative eating establishments. Head to Fairhaven and just walk around to see what looks interesting, or check out the places below.

Breakfast
Great breakfasts and lunches at **Old Town Cafe,** an earthy place where the waitress is likely to have a nose ring and the queue of customers is out the door on a weekend morning. The atmosphere is laid-back and noisy. Another popular downtown place is **Cafe Toulouse,** 114 W. Magnolia St., tel. (360) 733-8996, with a diverse breakfast and Sunday brunch menu.

A completely different dining experience can be found at **The Little Cheerful Cafe,** a minuscule place with a counter plus a handful of tables at 133 E. Holly, tel. (360) 738-8824. The cook has barely enough room to turn around. Be prepared to wait a long time if you get here after 10 a.m. on weekends.

Espresso
Many Bellingham places have espresso, but one stands out: **Tony's Coffee & Teas,** 1101 Harris Ave. (Fairhaven), tel. (360) 733-6319, where the smell of roasting coffee wafts through the air. They have another location downtown, but Fairhaven is the hangout for the long-hair and leather-jacket crowd. Read the newspaper,

sample the carrot cake, play a chess game, or just lean back and enjoy the scene. This is as close to Berkeley as you'll get this far north. Stop in on Sunday mornings for live jazz.

Lunch
Don't bother with all the standard fast-food grease pits; head instead to **Wok 'n' Roll Restaurant,** right across from the visitors bureau at 1400 King St., tel. (360) 733-0503. This friendly little cafe has American breakfasts and pastries, and very good Asian lunches. Another place with healthy quick eats at reasonable prices is **Casa Qué Pasa,** 1415 Railroad Ave., tel. (360) 738-8226, where the burritos are the best in town.

Swan Cafe inside the Community Food Co-Op at 1059 N. State, tel. (360) 734-8158, serves hearty salads and sandwiches. This is a fine place for an inexpensive downtown lunch.

If you're in Fairhaven and want great sandwiches, bagels, quiche, or just a scoop of Ben & Jerry's, drop by **Colophon Cafe** inside Village Books at 1210 11th St., tel. (360) 671-2626. Also great for huge slices of carrot cake. Get here early at lunch or be ready to wait. Another justifiably popular Fairhaven lunch place is **Skylark's Fountain & Mercantile,** 1308B 11th St., tel. (360) 715-3642. Good ice cream and espresso here too.

Located across the street from the museum at 114 Prospect St., **Wild Garlic,** tel. (360) 671-1955, is a quiet little place for lunch or a date. The food ranges from burgers and salads to filet mignon and gourmet pizzas; all well prepared.

Italian and Pizza
Pastazza, in Barkley Village, tel. (360) 714-1168, is an excellent place for homemade pastas and wonderful desserts. **Il Fiasco,** 1309 Commercial, tel. (360) 676-9136, is another recommended Italian place. A bit expensive, but outstanding food.

For pizzas, **Stanello's Restaurant,** 1514 12th St. (Fairhaven), tel. (360) 676-1304, is the place to go; in business for more than two decades. **Lucci's Bayshore Pizzeria,** 2615 S. Harbor Loop, tel. (360) 733-7100, has a great harborside deck and gourmet pizzas, plus pasta, chicken, and steak.

Other International
Fairhaven's **Dos Padres,** 1111 Harris Ave., tel. (360) 733-9900, has an extensive menu of Mex-

BELLINGHAM MOTELS AND HOTELS

Accommodations are arranged from least to most expensive within each category. Rates may be lower during the winter months. See the text for descriptions of local B&Bs and the hostel. In addition to the places listed, a new boutique hotel—Fairhaven Village Inn—was opening as this book went to press.

INEXPENSIVE

Macs Motel; 1215 E. Maple; tel. (360) 734-7570; $30 s or d

Lions Inn Motel; 2419 Elm; tel. (360) 733-2330; $30 s or d; kitchenettes available, local calls 25 cents

Evergreen Motel; 1015 Samish Way; tel. (360) 734-7671 or (800) 821-0016; $35 s, $38 d; quiet motel near Lake Padden, fridges, airport and ferry shuttle, kitchenettes available

Shangri-La Downtown Motel; 611 E. Holly St.; tel. (360) 733-7050; $32 s, $37-39 d; kitchenettes available

Aloha Motel; 315 N. Samish Way; tel. (360) 733-4900; $38 s, $44 d; fridges, kitchenettes available, good budget place

Motel 6; 3701 Byron St.; tel. (360) 671-4494 or (800) 466-8356; $38-45 s,

$44-50 d; outdoor pool, avoid noisy freeway side

Bay City Motor Inn; 116 N. Samish Way; tel. (360) 676-0332 or (800) 538-8204; $39 s, $45 d; continental breakfast, AAA approved

Villa Inn; 212 N. Samish Way; tel. (360) 733-4060 or (888) 714-1996; $40 s, $42 d; outdoor pool, sauna, jacuzzi

Cascade Inn; 208 N. Samish Way; tel. (360) 733-2520; $40-60 s or d; kitchenettes available

Rodeway Inn; 3710 Meridian St.; tel. (360) 738-6000 or (800) 728-7230; $40-65 s, $46-73 d; jacuzzi, AAA approved

Coachman Inn; 120 N. Samish Way; tel. (360) 671-9000 or (800) 962-6641; $45-65 s or d; outdoor pool, jacuzzi, sauna, continental breakfast, AAA approved

Travelodge; 101 N. Samish Way; $48 s, $54 d; tel. (360) 733-8280 or (800) 732-1225; jacuzzi, sauna, continental breakfast

ican dishes with a Southwest twist. They're locally famous for margaritas and nachos. Come here for lunch when prices are lower. Another very good Mexican restaurant—with more traditional fare—is **Gloria's,** 3040 Northwest, tel. (360) 647-1534. Some of the area's best Southwestern-style meals can be found at **Pepper Sisters,** 1055 N. State St., tel. (360) 671-3414. Recommended.

India Grill, 1215 Cornwall Ave., tel. 9360) 714-0314, is *the* place for Indian lunches and dinners, including tandoori and vegetarian specials. Several local places have good Thai food; one of the best is **Busara Siamese Cuisine,** 324, 36th St., tel. (360) 734-5111. **Oriento Restaurant,** 2500 Meridian, tel. (360) 733-3322, has a big Chinese menu that includes Mandarin, Sichuan, and Cantonese favorites along with

vegetarian dinners.

American and Eclectic
Dirty Dan Harris' in the Fairhaven District at 1211 11th St., tel. (360) 676-1011, has prime rib, steaks, and fresh seafood dinners in an 1800s-style saloon. It's named for Daniel Jefferson Harris, a feisty eccentric best known for his bathing habits—or lack thereof—who platted the town's streets, built a dock, and sold lots to the thousands of folks who rolled into Fairhaven in 1883. He made a small fortune in the process.

If you aren't looking for the gourmet variety burger, **Boomer's Drive In,** 310 N. Samish Way, tel. (360) 647-2666, has the best anywhere around.

Traveler's Inn; 3570 Meridian St.; tel. (360) 671-4600 or (800) 633-8300; $49 s, $57 d; outdoor pool, jacuzzi, AAA approved

Val-U Inn Motel; 805 Lakeway Dr.; tel. (360) 671-9600 or (800) 443-7777; $50-55 s, $55-60 d; jacuzzi, continental breakfast, airport and ferry shuttle, AAA approved

Travelers Lodge; 202 E Holly St.; tel. (360) 733-8280 or (800) 367-2250; $54 s, $59 d; fridges, AAA approved

Holiday Inn Express; 4160 Guide Meridian; tel. (360) 671-4800 or (800) 465-4329; $55-89 s or d; indoor pool, jacuzzi, continental breakfast, airport and ferry shuttle, AAA approved

MODERATE

Comfort Inn; 4282 Meridian St.; tel. (360) 738-1100 or (800) 228-5150; $56-71 s, $61-76 d; indoor pool, jacuzzi, sauna, exercise room, continental breakfast, airport and ferry shuttle, AAA approved

Days Inn; 125 E. Kellogg Rd.; tel. (360) 671-6200 or (800) 831-0187; $55-70 s, $60-80 d; outdoor pool, jacuzzi, continental breakfast, kitchenettes available, AAA approved

Quality Inn Baron Suites; 100 E. Kellogg Rd.; tel. (360) 647-8000 or (800) 900-4661; $60-90 s, $70-100 d; outdoor pool, jacuzzi, exercise room, business center, kitchenettes available, breakfast buffet, airport and ferry shuttle, AAA approved

Hampton Inn; 3985 Bennett; tel. (360) 676-7700 or (800) 426-7866; $69-74 s or d; outdoor pool, fitness room, continental breakfast, airport and ferry shuttle, AAA approved

Best Western Heritage Inn; 151 E. McLeod Rd.; tel. (360) 647-1912 or (800) 528-1234; $69-89 s or d; outdoor pool, jacuzzi, airport shuttle, continental breakfast, AAA approved

Best Western Lakeway Inn; 714 Lakeway Dr.; tel. (360) 671-1011 or (888) 671-1011; $79-99 s or d; indoor pool, exercise room, jacuzzi, sauna, continental breakfast, airport shuttle, AAA approved

EXPENSIVE

Ramada Inn; 215 N. Samish Way; tel. (360) 734-8830 or (800) 368-4148; $75 s, $85 d; outdoor pool, continental breakfast buffet, AAA approved

The Pacific Cafe, downtown at 100 N. Commercial, tel. (360) 647-0800, serves moderately priced "East-meets-West/Northwest" cuisine including steak, seafood, pasta, and teriyaki dishes in a warm atmosphere. Very good.

From the Sea
The Breakwater, 2625 Harbor Loop, tel. (360) 671-2030, faces the sailboats of Squalicum Harbor, and features salmon, halibut, and oysters, plus steak and prime rib. Classy atmosphere, and jazz on weekends.

The Marina, 985 Thomas Glenn Dr., tel. (360) 733-8292, also has a terrific harbor view, indoor-outdoor lounge, and reasonably priced meals. You'll find some of the best local fish and chips here. **Barnacles,** in Fairhaven at the Ferry Terminal, tel. (360) 647-5072, is a simple shoreside place with tasty clam chowder, soups, burgers, and sandwiches; low prices too.

Microbreweries and Pubs
Orchard St. Brewery, 709 W. Orchard Dr., tel. (360) 647-1614, seems perpetually crowded, and with good reason. Great fresh brews, and a surprisingly sophisticated restaurant that goes far beyond pub-grub fare, with filet mignon, king salmon, spot prawns, stone-oven pizzas, and other superb dishes. Reasonable prices, too. **Boundary Bay Brewing Co.,** 1107 Railroad Ave., tel. (360) 647-5593, features seven beers on tap and a limited pub menu.

Located in Fairhaven downstairs at 1212 10th St., **Anchor's Ale House,** tel. (360) 647-7002, is an English-style pub with an antique oak bar, 10 microbrews on tap, a dart board, and no smoking. The menu includes deep-dish pizza by the slice, vegetarian specials, and British pasties (decidedly not vegetarian).

Grocers and Bakeries
Bellingham's **Community Food Co-Op,** 1059 N. State, tel. (360) 734-8158, is a spacious natural foods market, and home to the Swan Cafe (described above). **Haggen Foods** has three large gourmet markets at 210 36th, 2814 Meridian St., and Barkley Village, with fine delis offering Chinese food, pizza by the slice, sandwiches, and a salad bar. A good deal for fast and tasty meals.

Fairhaven's **European Pastry Shop & Cafe,** 1307 11th St., tel. (360) 671-7258, bakes elegant French pastries, and is popular for lunchtime salads and sandwiches.

The **Bellingham Farmers Market** is held in the parking lot at Chestnut St. and Railroad Ave. from early April to late October. It runs Sat.-Sun. 10 a.m.-3 p.m.; tel. (360) 647-2060. Over in Fairhaven at 11th and McKenzie, the **Wednesday Farmers Market** takes place 3 p.m.-7 p.m., June-Sept.; tel. (360) 738-1574.

ARTS AND ENTERTAINMENT

The Arts
The **Whatcom Museum of History and Art** (see "Sights and Tours," above) is recognized as one of the finest regional museums on the West Coast with changing exhibits of regional history and contemporary art, plus occasional evening lectures and performances.

Western Washington University hosts a number of musical and theatrical groups in its auditorium, and the campus features 22 outdoor sculptures from the whimsical to the monumental. The **Performing Arts Center** series on campus features local productions as well as internationally known performing companies.

The historic **Mt. Baker Theatre**—built in 1927 as a vaudeville and movie palace—hosts the **Whatcom Symphony Orchestra,** tel. (360) 734-6080, plus many other musical and theatrical performances at 106 N. Commercial. Don't miss the weekly double features—shown on the

largest screen in the Northwest. The two-week-long **Bellingham Festival of Music** each August brings world-class classical and jazz musicians to town, and the **Brown Bag Music Series** features concerts on the public library lawn each Friday mid-June through August; tel. (360) 676-6985.

Staffed and performed entirely by local volunteers, the **Bellingham Theatre Guild** produces five plays a year from fall to spring in the old Congregational Church building at 1600 H St.; for ticket information call (360) 733-1811. More plays are presented in the **Theatre Arts** series at Western Washington University; call (360) 650-6146 for tickets.

Galleries
At 2940 New Market (Barkley Village), **Hamann's Gallery,** tel. (360) 733-8898, displays original artwork, etchings, and limited-edition prints. **Chuckanut Bay Gallery,** south of Fairhaven at 700 Chuckanut Dr., tel. (360) 734-4885, is also of note, featuring the works of potter Don Salisbury. The **Blue Horse Gallery,** 301 W. Holly St., tel. (360) 671-2305, has high quality works from 20 regional artists. A few blocks away at 700 W. Holly St. is **Pacific Marine Gallery,** tel. (360) 738-8535, where all the pieces reflect the marine environment. **Mark Bergsma Photographer Gallery,** 1306 Commercial St., tel. (360) 671-6818, displays multi-panel landscape photographs. Other galleries are found in Fairhaven, described above.

Nightlife
For live jazz on weekends, drop by **Calumet Restaurant,** 113 E. Magnolia, tel. (360) 733-3331, the local jazz hangout (good food too). **Russell's,** 1313 E. Maple, tel. (360) 733-2430, and **Anna's Kaddy Shack,** 1114 Harris Ave., tel. (360) 671-6745 both feature blues and rock bands. **Doublewide Tavern** 1226 N. State St., tel. (360) 734-1881, is *the* place for up and coming rock bands, with live music Friday and Saturday nights, and DJ tunes other evenings. More dance tunes at **The Royal,** 208 E. Holly, tel. (360) 738-3701, and **Downtown Johnny's,** 1408 Cornwall Ave., tel. (360) 733-2579. **Elephant & Castle Pub & Restaurant,** at Bellis Fair Mall, tel. (360) 671-4545, has comedy, dancing, and karaoke.

EVENTS

Bellingham's **Ski to Sea Race,** held Memorial Day weekend, tests the physical endurance and athletic skills of its participants over an 85-mile course that includes a downhill skiing, running, bicycling, canoeing down the Nooksack River, and sailing across Bellingham Bay to the finish in the Fairhaven District. In existence for over 25 years, the race is the highlight of a weeklong festival that includes parades, a street fair with crafts, live music and dancing, food, and a beer garden on Sunday after the race. For specifics, call (360) 734-1330.

In August, Western Washington University is the home of the two-week **Bellingham Festival of Music,** where outstanding classical and jazz musicians perform. Call (360) 676-5997 for ticket info. Around the same time, the **Bellingham Chalk Art Festival** attracts a wide range of talent, from kids to serious artists. Great fun as everyone gets to draw on the city's sidewalks and not get arrested. Call (360) 676-8548 for details.

Like other Puget Sound cities, Bellingham sponsors a Christmas **Lighted Boat Parade** in Bellingham Bay in mid-December; tel. (360) 733-7390.

SHOPPING

The Fairhaven District (described above) is Bellingham's most enjoyable place to stroll and shop. Massive **Bellis Fair Mall** (I-5 exit 256B), was built mainly for Canadian shoppers, and has over 150 shops, a food court, and a six-plex theater. Keep going out Meridian St. to enjoy the frenzy of shopping even more; here you'll find all the big discount chain stores, fast-food joints, new motels, and hundreds of B.C. license plates. Another 50 shops can be found at **Burlington Outlet Center** at exit 229 off I-5.

Antiques

Whatcom County has a number of antique shops and malls. In Bellingham proper, **Bellingham Antiques,** 202 W. Holly St., tel. (360) 647-1073, has a wide selection of collectibles from 20 dealers. **Bay City Furniture and Antiques,** 310 W. Holly St., tel. (360) 715-0826, has small collectibles and hundreds of new books on an-

tiques. Several other antique shops are located along W. Holly Street.

INFORMATION AND SERVICES

For maps, brochures, and general information, contact the **Bellingham and Whatcom County Convention and Visitors Bureau,** 904 Potter St. (exit 253 off I-5), tel. (360) 671-3990 or (800) 487-2032 (recording). Find them on the Web at www.bellingham.org. The office is open daily 8:30 a.m.-5:30 p.m. all year. A second visitor kiosk can be found inside Bellis Fair Mall; open daily. In the summer, the Bellingham Cruise Terminal (where the Alaska ferry docks) also has an information booth that opens around the ferry schedule on Thursday and Friday.

TRANSPORTATION

By Car

Downtown Bellingham makes up for its relatively small size with odd street intersections that send you off in the opposite direction you intended. It's as if someone laid out a grid, and then took the central (downtown) section and twisted it at a 45-degree angle. Newcomers are guaranteed to get lost at least once.

By Ferry

The **Bellingham Cruise Terminal,** located several blocks downhill from Fairhaven, is where you can catch ferries to the San Juans, Victoria, and Alaska. The terminal has reservation and ticketing booths for the **Alaska Marine Highway,** which provides passenger and vehicle ferry service to Prince Rupert and Southeast Alaska destinations. Alaska ferries usually depart on Friday evenings year-round; call (360) 676-8445 or (800) 642-0066 for details and a schedule. The terminal is open Thursday and Friday each week, in time for Alaska ferry arrivals and departures, and has a gift shop, storage lockers, and a fine little seafood cafe.

Victoria-San Juan Cruises, 355 Harris Ave., tel. (360) 738-8099 or (800) 443-4552, offers ferry service between Bellingham and Victoria from late May to mid-October. You'll sail aboard the *Victoria Star,* a 300-passenger

The Alaska Marine Highway ferry system docks its ships in Bellingham.

SEATTLE/KING COUNTY CONVENTION AND VISITORS BUREAU

boat; the cost is $79 RT adults, or $39 RT kids.

San Juan Island Shuttle Express, tel. (360) 671-1137 or (888) 373-8522, operates a passenger ferry—the *Red Head*—connecting Bellingham with Orcas, Lopez, Island and San Juan Island. Roundtrip fares are $33 adults, $29 seniors, and $27 students. Bikes are $5 extra. The ferry runs daily late May-September. They also provide three-hour whalewatching cruises for $60 adults, or $45 students.

By Train

Amtrak, tel. (800) 872-7245, provides daily train connections north to Vancouver, B.C., and south to Mount Vernon, Everett, Edmonds, and Seattle aboard the Mt. Baker International. Trains stop at the Fairhaven depot, just a short walk from the ferry terminal.

By Air

Horizon Air and **United Express** have service from **Bellingham International Airport** to Seattle and other West Coast cities. Many Canadians use the airport because they can get more convenient flights to some U.S. destinations, cheaper tickets, and the parking, $1 a day, is a big savings, too. **West Isle Air,** tel. (360) 671-8463 or (800) 874-4434, has scheduled service to the San Juan Islands, plus charter flights and flightseeing trips. **Aviation Northwest,** tel. (360) 733-3727, also flies from Bellingham to the San Juans.

If you're flying into Sea-Tac Airport and can't make good connections, **Airporter Shuttle** offers daily van service, tel. (360) 733-3600 or (800) 235-5247. **Quick Shuttle,** tel. (800) 665-2122, has shuttle service to Vancouver and Seattle destinations, including Sea-Tac.

By Bus

Locally, **Whatcom Transit,** tel. (360) 676-7433, provides bus service Mon.-Sat. to Bellingham, Ferndale, Lynden, Blaine, and the Lummi Indian Reservation. **Greyhound,** tel. (360) 733-5251 or (800) 231-2222, provides nationwide bus connections from the Amtrak depot in Fairhaven.

NORTH TO CANADA

LUMMI ISLAND AND RESERVATION

Lummi (pronounced "LUM-ee," as in "tummy") is only an eight-minute ferry ride from the mainland, but since it is some distance from the other islands (the San Juans), it doesn't get a lot of attention or heavy automobile traffic. The peanut-shaped island's southern end is a steeply wood-ed mountain that slopes down abruptly to more or less level land on the north end, which is where nearly all the residents live. Most of the is-land is private property with no public access, but you can ride the roads to a few public areas.

Lummi Indians were the first inhabitants of the island, but they abandoned it after northern Indians raided their village to capture slaves. By the time the first Anglos arrived in the 1870s, the Lummi had moved to the mainland. Today

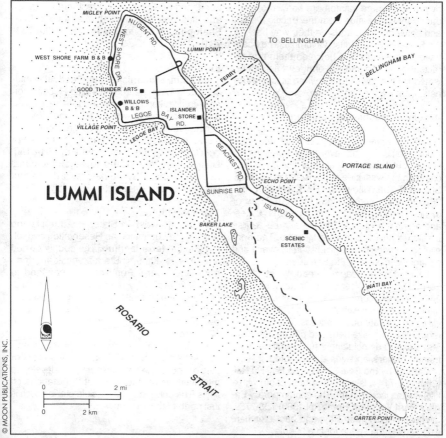

3,100 people live in scattered homes on the 13,000-acre Lummi Reservation at Gooseberry Point.

Touring the Island

Lummi is a quiet island, home primarily to artists, weekenders, and a few salmon fishermen, some of whom fish with reef-nets in the style of the original Indians. This ingenious way of fishing is unique to this area, and the state of Washington issues only about 50 commercial reef-fishing licenses. You can see the reef boats on the western shore along Legoe Bay. Basically, two reef boats, which aren't much more than small barges, are anchored side by side over a reef where salmon are known to swim during their migration from the Pacific Ocean and between the islands on their way back to the Fraser River in British Columbia. The boats have a net suspended between them that directs the salmon into the end, and fishermen watch from a tower to tell when to close the nets, trapping the fish.

Accommodations and Camping

Lummi Island has a church, school, library, grocery store, espresso joint, post office, and community hall. It has no taverns, gas stations, or motels, but it does have several nice B&Bs. Located on the west side of the island at 2579 W. Shore Dr., **The Willows Inn B&B,** tel. (360) 758-2620, has accommodations for $110-235 s or d, including rooms in the inn, a cottage, suites, and a guest house. All include a three-course breakfast, private baths, and jacuzzi. The honeymoon cottage provides additional privacy and a magnificent view of the San Juans.

Located on a 21-acre spread, **West Shore Farm B&B,** 2781 West Shore Dr., tel. (360) 758-2600, offers accommodations in an octagonal handcrafted home with sweeping Georgia Strait views and private beach access. The two guest rooms with king-size beds and private baths are $80 s or $90 d, including a full breakfast. Very friendly owners, and kids are accepted.

Cottage by the Sea, 3869 Legoe Bay Rd., tel. (360) 758-7144, is a two-bedroom cabin with a kitchen and jacuzzi bath. The contemporary **Eagle's Bluff Vacation Home,** tel. (360) 758-7789, overlooks Bellingham Bay, and has a kitchen, woodstove, and space for five people.

The Washington Department of Natural Resources maintains a small kayak-accessible campground on the east side near the south end of the island. This is the only camping place on Lummi Island.

Food and Shopping

Just south of the ferry dock, the **Islander Store** tel. (360) 758-2190, sells beer, pop, ice cream, and other necessities of life; open daily. North of the dock is **Beachstore Cafe,** tel. (360) 758-2233, with an eclectic choice of meals, along with fresh baked breads and pastries.

Good Thunder Arts, on Centerview Rd., tel. (360) 758-7121, has handcrafted pottery, sculptures, and other art work. Fresh crab, shrimp, and scallops are available at **Leo's Live Seafoods,** on Legoe Bay Rd., tel. (360) 758-7318.

Events

The **Lummi Stommish Water Festival** in mid-June is held on the Lummi Indian Reservation and features competitive war-canoe races over a five-mile course, with up to 11 people in a canoe. Other activities include arts and crafts sales, Indian dancing, and a salmon bake. For details, call the tribal office at (360) 734-8180. Local artists offer **studio tours** on Memorial Day and Labor Day weekends, and the first weekend of December; call (360) 758-7121.

Transportation

From I-5, go west on Slater Road to Haxton Way on the Lummi Indian Reservation and follow it to the **ferry landing.** The county-owned ferry makes eight-minute trips back and forth from Gooseberry Point on the mainland to Lummi Island every hour from 6 a.m. to midnight (more frequently during the commute period). Roundtrip cost is $2 for cars, $1 for passengers (free for kids). For information call (360) 676-6692.

Because Lummi is nearly all in private hands, access is quite limited. You can ride bikes or cars on the island's roads, but the undeveloped mountainous southern end of the island is off limits. The only readily accessible public beach is just north of the ferry dock.

FERNDALE

The fast-growing and prosperous town of Ferndale (pop. 8,000) sits on the west side of the Nooksack River north of Bellingham. High bluffs over the river provide fine views of the rich farmland, the Cascades, and Mt. Baker. In addition to agriculture, the town is supported by Arco and Tosco oil refineries, plus an enormous Intalco aluminum reduction plant—third largest in the world—which employs more than 1,200 people. The bauxite ore arrives by ship from Australia and is processed into aluminum ingots for shipment to other mills. Aluminum production uses prodigious amounts of electricity (supplied by the Columbia River dams) since the anodes must be kept at 2,100° F for two weeks(!).

Parks

Pioneer Park, two blocks south of Main on 1st Ave., contains an extraordinary collection of a dozen hand-hewn log buildings. Many of these date from the late 19th century and were made with massive cedar logs—evidence of the trees that once stood here. This is one of the finest collections of log structures in Washington. Several of the cabins contain historical exhibits, including everything from postal relics to historical photos and a Linotype machine. The two-story Shields house, built in 1885, is the most elaborate. The cabins were moved here from the surrounding country by the Old Settlers Association, who recognized their value even in the 1930s. Tours of the buildings are available Tues.-Sun. 11:30 a.m.-4:30 p.m. mid-May to mid-September.

Head south from town on Hovander Dr. to **Hovander Homestead Park** where you'll find a restored turn-of-the-century Victorian home and farm on the Nooksack River, a big red barn, milk house, treehouse, children's petting zoo, flower gardens (including 30 varieties of dahlias), fruit orchard, hayfields, and antique farm equipment. Bring your picnic basket for a lunch along the river. Now a National Historic site, the park is open daily, but the homestead is open only on summer weekends. Admission is $3 per car. Tours are available in the summer Thurs.-Sun. 12:30-4:30 p.m.; call (360) 384-3444 for details.

Take a walk around a bog and displays at **Tennant Lake Natural History Interpretive Center,** at the end of Nielsen Rd. (just south of the turnoff to Hovander Homestead), tel. (360) 384-3444. This 200-acre park is an interpretive center for Tennant Lake, with a system of trails, a half-mile boardwalk along the marsh, and a birdwatching tower. One of the park's highlights is the **Fragrance Garden,** designed so that people who are visually impaired, and anyone else, can experience more than 60 varieties of plants by scent.

Lake Terrell Wildlife Preserve, four miles west of Ferndale, tel. (360) 384-4723, covers 11,000 acres and is operated by the state. It has restrooms, picnic areas, trails, fishing, and three boat launches.

Accommodations

The **Slater Heritage House B&B,** 1371 W. Axton, tel. (360) 384-4273 or (800) 815-4273, has beautifully landscaped grounds and four guest rooms with private baths in a restored 1904 Victorian home. Lodging, including a jacuzzi and full breakfast, is $60-85 s or d. Children welcome.

Scottish Lodge Motel, 5671 Riverside Dr., tel. (360) 384-4040, has an outdoor pool and rooms for $30 s or $34 d. The **Best Western Voyager's Landing All Suites,** 5370 Barrett Rd., tel. (360) 380-4600 or (888) 665-4600, has new rooms for $99-129 s or d, including an indoor pool, jacuzzi, exercise room, and continental breakfast.

Campgrounds

Public tent ($11) and RV ($16) sites are just a few miles northwest of Ferndale at **Birch Bay State Park.** Call (800) 452-5687 for reservations ($6 extra). The privately run **Cedars RV Resort,** 6335 Portal Way, tel. (360) 384-2622, has full hookups, showers, and laundry facilities.

Food

Popular with locals are **Cedar's Cafe,** 2038 Main St., tel. (360) 384-1848, and **Ferndale Bakery,** 5686 3rd Ave., tel. (360) 384-1554. The best local meals can be found at **Pacific Prime Rib,** 2254 Douglas Rd., tel. (360) 384-5111, where the menu also includes pasta, seafood, and steaks. **Haggen Foods,** 1815 Main St., tel. (360) 380-6353, has a big deli.

Events

Ferndale has several of the county's best festivals. The **Scottish Highland Games** take place in early June, with bagpipe music, Highland dancing, dog trials, and the caber toss. In early August the **Hot Air Balloon Festival and Civil War Re-enactment** takes place at Hovander Homestead, and includes balloons, music, staged battles, and arts and crafts. In August, the **International Folk Dance Festival** arrives at the park, with dancers of many nationalities, plus an arts and crafts fair, food, music, and hot air balloon rides. Call (360) 384-3444 for details on these very popular events, both of which are held in Hovander Homestead Park. Then comes the **Whatcom County Old Settlers Picnic** at Pioneer Park on the last weekend of July. More than an old-timers picnic, this century-old festival includes country music, dancing, parades, and a carnival; call (360) 384-1866 for more info.

Information and Services

The **Ferndale Chamber of Commerce,** 5640 Riverside Dr., tel. (360) 384-3042, is the place to go for local info; open Mon.-Fri. 10 a.m.-5 p.m. all year, plus Sat.-Sun. 10 a.m.-5 p.m. in the summer. Play golf at **Riverside Golf Club,** 5799 Riverside Dr., tel. (360) 384-4116.

Whatcom Transit, tel. (360) 676-7433, provides bus service Mon.-Sat. to Bellingham, Lynden, Blaine, and the rest of Whatcom County.

LYNDEN

Immaculate Lynden (pop. 6,500) is the sort of town where dense pots of flowers hang from store eaves, kids ride bikes down wide, shady streets, and the big events are parades and old-time threshing bees. Ignore the snow-capped summits of Mt. Baker and the Cascade Range east of town and it's easy to imagine yourself in a small Dutch town. Originally settled by people from Holland, Lynden still counts half its residents as from the "Old Country." The flat, green pastures surrounding town—some are just two blocks from town center—are dotted with dairy cattle so fat they look as if they've overindulged

in their own products. (This means, of course, that the odor of manure sometimes wafts through downtown.) Farmers also raise large quantities of strawberries and raspberries, along with hops, potatoes, and—borrowing from the town's Dutch heritage—bulbs.

Little Holland

Add Lynden to the growing list of small towns in Washington that attract tourists by redecorating themselves to reflect an ethnic or historical heritage. Since most of its settlers were dairy farmers from The Netherlands, Lynden turned itself into a Dutch treat for people driving on Hwy. 539 between Bellingham, 12 miles south, and British Columbia, three miles north.

Quite a few downtown buildings have been outfitted with Dutch false fronts painted caramel, chocolate, cheese yellow, or sea blue. Front Street, the main drag, is dominated by a four-story, 72-foot-tall windmill that is part of the Dutch Village Mall, which also has a 150-foot indoor "canal," a theatre, and shops along a simulated Dutch cobblestone street. Many of these are cloyingly sweet, with places selling fudge, books, cards, kitchenware, knickknacks, and heart-shaped doormats.

The Dutch theme includes provincial flags flapping in the breeze, Dutch food and gifts (yes, wooden shoes) sold in stores, and costumed clerks on special holidays such as Holland Days (the first weekend in May). Residents in costumes sweep the immaculate streets that are normally clean anyway—just like in Holland.

Lynden is very conservative and religious; the Christian rest home and school are two of the largest local employers, and the 30 local churches are busy on Sunday. The town has an unofficial ban on Sunday business, and a town ordinance prohibits dancing wherever drinks are sold—leading to Saturday-night 12-mile pilgrimages to Bellingham's hot spots. Be careful while driving busy Hwy. 539 on weekends.

Lynden Pioneer Museum

Lynden is home to one of the finest small museums in Washington, the Lynden Pioneer Museum at 217 W. Front St., tel. (360) 354-3675. On the main floor is a re-created turn-of-the-century Lynden town and a collection of Indian artifacts. The basement is a must-see, centering around 40 or so buggies, wagons, sleighs, carts, and other horse-drawn vehicles, plus antique tractors and farm machinery, and a big antique car and truck collection. The museum is open Mon.-Sat. 10 a.m.-4 p.m.; $3 adults, $2 seniors or students.

Berthusen Park

This gorgeous city park is a great place to pitch a tent; get there by heading a mile west of town to Guide Meridian (Hwy. 539), then north to W. Main Road. Follow the signs to the park, located in a tall stand of old-growth Douglas fir and western red cedar. The park has picnicking, camping, a small fishing stream, and walking trails, but it is best known for its enormous barn (built in 1913) that contains old boats, sleds, and other memorabilia; outside are antique steam-powered tractors, along with the farming equipment they pulled or operated.

Accommodations

Spend a night in a windmill at the **Dutch Village Inn,** 655 Front St., tel. (360) 354-4440. Six hotel rooms (three are in the windmill and two have hot tubs) feature Dutch furnishings, antiques, and a Dutch-style breakfast for $69-110 s or d. The modern **Windmill Inn Motel & RV Park,** 8022 Guide Meridian, tel. (360) 354-3424, has rooms for $35-39 s or $39-49 d. Hook up RVs outside. **Homestead Sports Cabanas** tel. (800) 354-1196, are full apartments next to the golf course at 115 E. Homestead Blvd.; $99-149 s or d.

Century House B&B, 401 South B.C. Ave. (13th St.), tel. (360) 354-2439 or (800) 820-3617, has four elegant guest rooms with private or shared baths, a fireplace, bay windows, and chandeliers in an 1888 home, plus a full breakfast; $65-95 s or d.

Near the town of Everson is **Kale House B&B,** 201 Kale St., tel. (360) 966-7027 or (800) 225-2165, features a downstairs bedroom and upstairs suite, both with private baths. A full breakfast is served; $65 s or d. No kids.

Three miles north of the little town of Everson (pop. 1,700), **Wilkins Farm B&B,** 4165 S. Pass Rd., tel. (360) 966-7616, has the least expensive B&B accommodations in the state: just $22 s or $35 d in a grand old farmhouse built in 1875, and surrounded by cattle pastures. Three

DON PITCHER

guest rooms share a bath, and a full breakfast is served. Kids are okay, too.

Campgrounds

Berthusen Park, tel. (360) 354-2424, about a mile north on Guide Meridian, has shady campsites under the tall Douglas fir trees; $10 tents or $15 RVs. RV hookups are available at **Lynden KOA,** three miles east of Lynden, tel. (360) 354-4772 or (800) 562-4779, and **Hidden Village RV Park,** 7062 Guide Meridian, tel. (360) 398-1041 or (800) 843-8606. In addition, the **Northwest Washington Fairgrounds** are open to RV parking with full hookups; call (360) 354-4111.

Food

The **Koffee Loft** serves three meals a day (except Sunday of course), but is best known for flavorful skillet breakfasts along with lunchtime sandwiches and wraps. Find them at 444 Front St., tel. (360) 354-5222. **Hollandia,** 655 Front St., tel. (360) 354-4133, is Lynden's fine dining establishment, with a Dutch chef and such specials as schnitzel Hollandia and cordon bleu.

Closed Sunday and Monday. You'll find Dutch specialties, and country-style dinners at **Dutch Mothers Restaurant,** 405 Front St., tel. (360) 354-2174. **Lynden Dutch Bakery,** tel. (360) 354-3911, is a great place for sandwiches and pastries, including excellent Dutch apple pie. The best steaks and other mesquite-grilled meats can be found in nearby Everson at **Black Forest Steakhouse,** tel. (360) 966-2855.

Events

For such a small town, Lynden has an abundance of unusual events. The Queen Juliana Theatre in Dutch Village Mall is home to productions by the Lynden Performing Arts Guild Oct.-May. Call (360) 354-4425 for upcoming plays.

Holland Days, held the first weekend of May, brings wooden shoe races, Klompen dancing, and costumed Lyndenites scrubbing down Front Street. A parade and draft horse plowing show are the highlights of Lynden's **Farmer's Day Parade,** held the first weekend of June. In early August, an old-time **Antique Tractor & Machinery Show** attracts visitors to view the puffing steam engines and old farm equipment at nearby Berthusen Park. Mid-August brings the largest event: more than 240,000 people come to the **Northwest Washington Fair,** with farm animal exhibits, carnival rides, a tractor pull, demolition derby, and musical entertainers. The **Harvest Festival** in mid-October brings rows of scarecrows, hayrides, a huge maze made from bales of hay, and other fun activities. The **Dutch Sinterklaas Celebration** in early December is a Christmas parade with lighted farm equipment, antique vehicles, horses, and floats, plus Sinterklaas (Santa Claus) atop a white horse.

Information and Services

The **Lynden Chamber of Commerce,** tel. (360) 354-5995 or (888) 354-5995, is upstairs in the back of the Delftst Mall at 444 Front St.; open Mon.-Fri. 10 a.m.-4 p.m. Find them on the Web at www.lynden.org. **Homestead Golf & Country Club,** tel. (800) 354-1196, is an elaborate place where one hole sits on a small island.

Whatcom Transit, tel. (360) 676-7433, provides bus service Mon.-Sat. to Bellingham, Ferndale, Blaine, and the rest of Whatcom County.

SUMAS

The bustling border town of Sumas (SOO-mass) is right on Hwy. 9 and is one of the main crossing points in Washington. You'll find plenty of cheap gas stations where Canadians can sneak across the border for a tankful, a couple of gallons of milk, and a pull-tab or two from the minimart—the border crossing is open 24 hours a day. Also here are big grocers and duty-free shops.

The name Sumas comes from the Cowichan Indian word, "Sm-mess," meaning land without trees—a reference to the surrounding prairie country.

Food, Lodging, and Entertainment

Stay at the modern **Sumas Mountain Village,** 819 Cherry St., tel. (360) 988-4483, for $50-115 s or d. The food is quality all-American, including homemade pies. Mexican meals can be found at **El Nopal Dos,** 120 Front St., tel. (360) 988-0305. More lodging at **B&B Border Inn Motel,** 121 Cleveland, tel. (360) 988-5800, where rooms are $35 s or $40-48 d. **J.J. Fryes,** 625 Cherry St., tel. (360) 988-3797, has a DJ or rock bands on weekends.

Events and Information

Sumas Community Days the last Saturday of June has a bed race (part of which is down a local creek), a car show, and fireworks. The **Sumas Junior Rodeo** on Labor Day weekend in September features bucking bulls at a "bullarama." Call the Sumas City Hall, tel. (360) 988-5711, for other local information.

BIRCH BAY

Birch Bay (pop. 2,000) is one of western Washington's oldest resort towns, the kind of place families go for generations, always renting the same cabin. The "Bay Area" has managed to keep its calm in spite of numerous housing and condominium developments going on nearby, and its only street is designed for pedestrians instead of cars. Most of the places along the main street are modest beach cabins, and many are owned by Canadians; they constitute half the population here on a summer day.

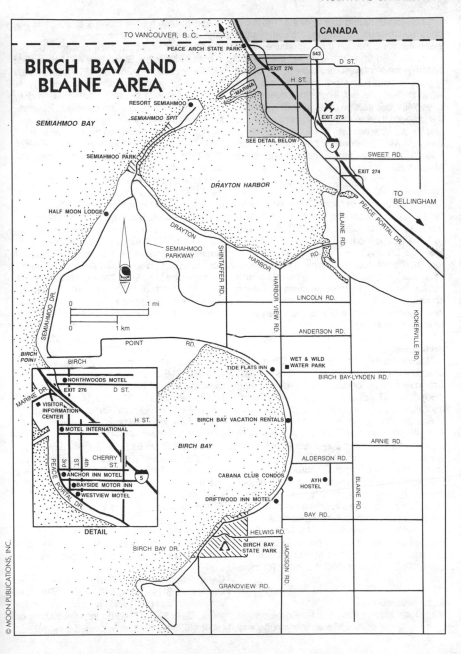

BIRCH BAY AND BLAINE AREA

TO VANCOUVER, B.C.

CANADA

PEACE ARCH STATE PARK

543

D ST.

EXIT 276

H ST.

MARINA

RESORT SEMIAHMOO

SEMIAHMOO SPIT

EXIT 275

SEMIAHMOO BAY

SEMIAHMOO PARK

SEE DETAIL BELOW

5

SWEET RD.

DRAYTON HARBOR

EXIT 274

TO BELLINGHAM

HALF MOON LODGE

DRAYTON

SEMIAHMOO PARKWAY

SHINTAFFER RD.

HARBOR

BLAINE RD.

PEACE PORTAL DR.

SEMIAHMOO DR.

HARBOR VIEW RD.

LINCOLN RD.

0   1 mi

0   1 km

ANDERSON RD.

KICKERVILLE RD.

POINT   RD.

BIRCH POINT

BIRCH

TIDE FLATS INN

WET & WILD WATER PARK

BIRCH BAY-LYNDEN RD.

MARINE DR.

NORTHWOODS MOTEL

EXIT 276   D ST.

VISITOR INFORMATION CENTER

H ST.

BIRCH BAY VACATION RENTALS

ARNIE RD.

MOTEL INTERNATIONAL

PEACE PORTAL DR.

3rd ST.

4th ST.

CHERRY ST.

5

BIRCH BAY

ALDERSON RD.

ANCHOR INN MOTEL

BAYSIDE MOTOR INN

WESTVIEW MOTEL

CABANA CLUB CONDOS

AYH HOSTEL

BLAINE RD.

DRIFTWOOD INN MOTEL

BAY RD.

DETAIL

HELWIG RD.

BIRCH BAY DR.

BIRCH BAY STATE PARK

JACKSON RD.

GRANDVIEW RD.

The moon-shaped bay is one of the most shallow in the area, and during the summer the water heats up enough for comfortable swimming. It's said to be the warmest and safest beach on the Northwest Pacific coast. The beach is popular with clammers and crabbers, and when the tide goes out, it goes for a quarter of a mile. Volleyball nets go up as the tide goes out, the Frisbees fly, the sunscreen lotion comes out, and the sandcastles rise. Not far to the south is the giant ARCO refinery with its eternal flame towering above the timber, and 50 enormous fuel tanks. Farther south is a Tosco refinery.

Recreation
The main attraction, of course, is the long sandy beach, but kids also love **Wet N' Wild Waterpark,** 4874 Birch Bay-Lynden Rd., tel. (360) 371-7500; open daily 10:30 a.m.-7:30 p.m. Memorial Day to Labor Day. The park has a 60-foot "hydrocliff, four giant waterslides, lots of other kiddie slides, plus a volleyball court and hot tub for oldsters. Entrance costs $11 ages six and up, $8 for ages 3-5, $7.50 seniors, and free for kids under age two. **Pioneer Valley Railroad** 4620 Birch Bay-Lynden Rd., tel. (360) 371-7700, has miniature train rides and go-karts in the summer.

Golfers may want to try out **Sea Links Golf Club,** 7878 Birch Bay Dr., tel. (360) 371-7933; **Grandview Golf Course,** 7738 Portal Way, tel. (360) 366-3947; or **Dakota Creek Golf & Country Club,** 3258 Haynie Rd. (Custer), tel. (360) 366-3131.

At the west end of Helwig Road, the very popular 193-acre **Birch Bay State Park** follows the mile-long waterfront on Birch Bay, with campsites in the trees. The main attraction here is the beach, a favorite place for swimming, kite flying, windsurfing, clamming, and volleyball. Other facilities include an underwater park, fishing (though there's no boat launch), a picnic area, and the half-mile Terrell Marsh nature trail through an estuary that is home to beavers, opossums, muskrats, and great blue herons. Call (360) 371-2800 or (800) 452-5687 for more info.

Accommodations
Many local lodging places can also be rented by the week or month. Make reservations well ahead of time for the months of July and August, especially on weekends.

At the bottom of the price category, but not in popularity, is the **Birch Bay AYH-Hostel,** at 467 Gemini St., tel. (360) 371-2180. Dorm beds are $10-12, and couples can stay in private rooms for $22-24 d. The hostel is closed daily 9:30 a.m.-5 p.m., and October-May. Reservations are advised if you're arriving in the summer months. A full kitchen is on the premises.

B&D Rentals, 4837 Fir Tree Lane, tel. (360) 371-2084, rents three two-bedroom houses near the water for $125/night.

Bev's Beach Resort, 8126 Birch Bay Dr., tel. (360) 371-2756, has studio and two-bedroom units with kitchens for $95-150/night.

Cabana Club Condos, 7503 Birch Bay Dr., tel. (360) 371-2511, has a range of units that sleep up to eight for $100-300. All have fireplaces and kitchens, and access to an outdoor pool, jacuzzi, and sauna. Three-night minimum.

Driftwood Inn Motel, 7394 Birch Bay Dr., tel. (360) 371-2620 or (800) 833-2666, has motel units, apartments, and rustic cottages, with an outdoor pool, kitchenettes, and canoe rentals; $75 for four people. Three-night minimum.

Tide Flats Inn, 8124 Birch Bay Dr., tel. (360) 371-7800 or (800) 972-2586, has attractive studios, and one- and two-bedroom units, all with full kitchens; $95-175 s or d.

Water's Edge B&B, is a bright and spacious beachside home at 7379 Birch Bay Dr., tel. (360) 371-2043. The bedroom ($80 d) and suite ($130 d) both have king-size beds, private baths, and a gourmet breakfast.

Sleepy Hollow B&B, 8068 Birch Bay Dr., tel. (206) 329-9288, is a separate house with a big sundeck and kitchenette. $70 s or d includes a make-your-own breakfast.

At the top of the spectrum is **Birch Bay Vacation Rentals at Jacobs Landing,** 7825 Birch Bay Dr., tel. (360) 371-7633, which has one and two-bedroom condominium units on the beach, with an indoor pool, jacuzzi, plus tennis and racquetball courts; $95-120 d. Two-night minimum.

Campgrounds and RV Parks
Birch Bay State Park, 5105 Helwig Rd., has year-round tent ($11) and RV ($16) sites in the trees. Call (360) 371-2800 for information, or (800) 452-5687 for reservations ($6 extra).

Local places to park RVs include: **Ball Bay View RV Park,** 7387 Jackson Rd., tel. (360) 371-0334; **Beachside RV Park,** 7630 Birch Bay Dr., tel. (360) 371-5962 or (800) 596-9586; and **Richmond Resort,** 8086 Birch Bay Dr., tel. (360) 371-2262.

Food

The restaurant options in Birch Bay are limited; locals head across the border to White Rock for the best regional cooking. Get sandwiches and pizza from the summer-only **C Shop,** Alterson Rd. at Birch Bay Dr., tel. (360) 371-2070. **Tide Flats Restaurant,** 8124 Birch Bay Dr., tel. (360) 371-7800, is a friendly place featuring home-cooked Cajun and Creole cuisine. They also serve filling breakfasts and seafood specials.

Events

Birch Bay Discovery Days is the main summer event, with a "clampetition" clamming contest, parade, golf tournament, and arts and crafts show. It's held in mid-July; call (360) 371-0334 for details. For something different, come here on January 1 for the annual **Polar Bear Swim** with other hardy fools. The Birch Bay area also has monthly **sandcastle contests** all summer.

BLAINE

Known to most travelers as the town at the international border and the site of the Peace Arch, Blaine (pop. 2,900) faces out onto protected Drayton Harbor. It is just 35 miles from Vancouver, British Columbia. I-5 cuts through town, bringing 70,000 folks a day, and traffic sometimes backs up for several miles. Unless you're crossing into Canada, be prepared to turn off I-5 before the main part of Blaine. Traffic is worst on the Dominion Day/Independence Day weekend in July, when it can take you three hours to cross. Not surprisingly, Blaine depends upon all this cross-border traffic, though a small fishing fleet also provides jobs. Many of the town's post office boxes belong to Canadians who use them for business in the States. Blaine has cheap gas, grocery stores, a shopping mall, duty-free shops, five banks, and a couple of pretty good seafood restaurants. For some reason, it also has not just one, but two psychic readers.

Gasoline is considerably cheaper in the U.S. than in Canada, so thousands of Canadians drive across the border to Blaine each day just to fill their tanks. Many continue to Bellis Fair Mall in Bellingham, although the gap between U.S. and Canadian prices is narrowing. There was a time when the garbage cans at the last rest area before Blaine would be filled to overflowing with old clothes Canadians had worn to the U.S., then discarded when they put on their new clothing to wear across the border and avoid paying duty.

History

The original peoples inhabiting this corner of Washington were the Semiahmoo Indians. Anglo settlers began arriving in the 1850s during the Fraser River gold rush, and the town of Blaine was platted in 1884 by James Cain. He named his town for James G. Blaine, the Republican candidate for president that year (he lost to Grover Cleveland), and future Secretary of State. The town grew up on fishing, logging, and cross-border trade and served as a major shipping port for lumber.

Peace Arch

Open for day use only, the 40-acre **Peace Arch State Park** at the Canadian border has beautifully landscaped grounds and gardens surrounding the Peace Arch, a symbol of friendship between the U.S. and Canada that stands with one "foot" in each country. The park was constructed in 1921 by American and Canadian volunteers and funded by Washington and British Columbia schoolchildren, who contributed from one to 10 cents each for the project. A piece of the *Mayflower* along with the Hudson's Bay Company steamer *Beaver* are included in the monument. The facade is dominated by the inscription "Children of a Common Mother" on one side and "Brethren Dwelling Together in Unity" on the other. Facilities include a picnic area, playground, and impressive floral displays, with rhododendrons and azaleas starring in late spring, and dahlias the featured attraction in late summer. Get to the Peace Arch by heading north on 2nd St. into the parking lot; they don't like folks stopping at customs to enter the park.

East of town is one of the more vivid statements about the relationship between the U.S.

Peace Arch at the U.S.-Canada border

DON PITCHER

and Canada. As you drive east toward Sumas and Lynden, you can turn north off the main road and follow it until it makes a sharp right turn to the east again. Here you will notice two, two-lane blacktop highways running east and west, side by side, with a ditch separating them. That ditch is the international boundary between Canada and America. That is all the international boundary is for more than 3,000 miles, the longest unprotected boundary in the world. When the boundary goes through forests, a swath is kept cleared by crews from both countries. But in Washington, it is separated from British Columbia by a ditch that any child can toddle across.

Semiahmoo Area

Head out the 1.5-mile-long Semiahmoo Spit to **Semiahmoo County Park,** where you'll find restored salmon cannery buildings, a gift shop and art gallery, plus a museum that depicts early fishing and cannery operation; open Wed.-Sun. 1-5 p.m., March through Labor Day; Wed.-Sun.

1-4 p.m. in the fall; closed mid-December through February. The park itself is open daily year-round. Call (360) 371-5513 for details. The Raven-Salmon Woman Totem Pole stands outside. A paved bike path parallels the road along Semiahmoo Spit.

Located at the end of a long sandspit guarding Drayton Harbor, **The Resort Semiahmoo** is a planned community for the elite—don't even think about moving in if you're a commoner. The Inn at Semiahmoo is a part of this massive development with elaborate facilities such as a 300-slip marina, athletic club, indoor/outdoor pool, hot tub, racquetball and tennis courts, steam room, an 18-hole championship golf course designed by Arnold Palmer, restaurants, lounges, and plenty of Puget Sound beachfront. The old buildings from the Alaska Packers Association cannery—in business till 1965—have been restored and developed into a conference center. The entire complex is not my cup of tea; it's one of those places with lots of flash (and cash) but absolutely no soul.

The **M.V.** *Plover* was built in 1944 as a ferry for cannery workers at Semiahmoo. Today the 32-foot boat has been lovingly restored, and serves as a free passenger and bike ferry. It operates between the harbor at Blaine and the Inn at Semiahmoo Fri.-Sat. noon-9 p.m., and Sunday 10 a.m.-6 p.m. summers only. Call (360) 332-5742 for details.

Accommodations and Campgrounds

See **Birch Bay** for nearby public and private campgrounds. The following motels and lodges are arranged by price. In addition to those listed, quite a few lodging places can be found just across the border in White Rock, British Columbia.

Westview Motel, 7080 Peace Portal Dr., tel. (360) 332-5501, charges $30-40 s or d. **Bayside Motor Inn,** 340 Alder, tel. (360) 332-5288, has an outdoor pool, and rooms for $32-46 s or d. **Anchor Inn Motel,** 250 Cedar St., tel. (360) 332-5539, is a nice place with rooms for $37 s, $40 d. **Northwoods Motel,** 288 D. St., tel. (360) 332-5603, has an outdoor pool; rooms are $37-40 s or $40 d.

Motel International, 758 Peace Portal Dr., tel. (360) 332-8222, charges $40 s or $48 d. **Harbor House B&B,** 5157 Drayton Harbor Rd., tel. (360) 371-9060, has a private suite with its own entrance, plus a full breakfast and outdoor hot tub. $65 s or $75 d.

Half Moon Lodge at Semiahmoo, Semiahmoo Dr., tel. (360) 371-2256, is a three-bedroom waterfront log house with a 500-square-foot master bedroom, jacuzzi, fireplace, sauna, and kitchen. A one-week minimum is required June-August ($900), and a two-night minimum the rest of the year, when the price is $150 d.

The Inn at Semi-ah-moo, 10 miles west of Blaine, tel. (360) 371-2000 or (800) 770-7992, is an elaborate coastal resort with an indoor/outdoor pool, athletic club, sauna, jacuzzi, steam room, jacuzzi, racquetball and tennis courts, and golf course; $169-378 s or d.

Food and Entertainment
Get breakfasts from **Cafe International,** 758 Peace Portal Dr., tel. (360) 332-6035. Also here is Players' Club, a popular place for poker and blackjack. The most popular local restaurant is **Harbor Cafe,** 295 Marine Dr., tel. (360) 332-5176, where you'll find oyster stew, cod fish and chips (big servings; go for the half-order), and clam chowder.

215 Dockside Bar & Grill, 215 Marine Dr., tel. (360) 332-6006, has great harbor views from the outside deck, and a lunch and dinner menu of old fashioned favorites like roast turkey sandwiches, meatloaf, and baron of beef.

The best local burgers are at **Nicki's Restaurant,** 1700 Peace Portal Dr., tel. (360) 332-7779. More burgers and seafood, plus "health-conscious" dinners at **Maritime Inn,** 1830 Peace Portal Dr., tel. (360) 332-3663. They also have excellent prime rib on Friday and Saturday nights.

Out on the end of Semiahmoo Spit, the Inn at Semiahmoo, tel. (360) 371-2000, has a formal restaurant, **Stars,** featuring expensive Northwest cuisine, plus the less pretentious **Oyster Bar,** with delicious fish and chips.

Lots more restaurants (including Thai and Greek places) in the pretty town of White Rock, just across the border. **Clancy's Tea Cosy,** 15223 Pacific Ave. in White Rock, tel. (604) 541-9010, is a fun place to relax with tea and a scone.

Recreation and Shopping
The **Peace Arch Factory Outlets** are located just off I-5 at exit 270, six miles south of the border. Here you'll find 30 outlet stores open daily. **Peace Arch Equestrian Center,** tel. (360) 366-4049, has horse and pony rides near the outlet shops. Blaine also has three antique shops.

Events
The **Semi-Ah-Moo Dixieland Jazz Weekend** takes place each April at the resort. The annual **Hands Across the Border Peace Arch Celebration,** held the second Sunday in June, brings together veterans and boy and girl scouts from the U.S. and Canada to celebrate our friendly relations. Return on the first Friday of December for **Christmas Lighting Ceremony,** when Santa visits the Peace Arch.

Information and Services
The **Blaine Visitor Information Center,** 215 Marine Dr., tel. (360) 332-4511 or (800) 624-3555, is open daily 9 a.m.-5 p.m. April-Sept., and Mon.-Sat. 9 a.m.-5 p.m. the rest of the year. Across the street is a killer whale sculpture that is popular with kids.

Whatcom Transit, tel. (360) 676-7433, provides bus service Mon.-Sat. to Bellingham, Ferndale, Lynden, and the rest of Whatcom County. **Airporter Shuttle,** tel. (800) 235-5247, has direct bus service between Blaine and Sea-Tac.

Crossing into Canada
Citizens of the U.S. crossing the Canadian border generally have little trouble; all you need is a driver's license or birth certificate. Because of Canada's sane gun laws—in sharp contrast to America's anything-goes attitude—you aren't allowed to bring in firearms. Pitted fruits are also prohibited, though they aren't likely to be used as a weapon. If you're planning to make any large purchases, pick up a brochure describing what you can bring back without being charged extra duties. Americans are entitled to refunds on the seven percent GST tax paid in British Columbia; save your receipts. Be prepared for a long wait, especially when coming into the U.S.; you may be in line for two hours on weekends. Avoid the madness by getting there early in the morning. Change greenbacks at **UnBank Currency Exchange,** 545 Peace Portal Dr., tel. (360) 332-5264. Open Sunday, too.

POINT ROBERTS

Bounded on three sides by water and on the fourth by British Columbia, it's only by political accident that Point Roberts belongs to the United States. Nobody knew this appendix of land dangled below the international boundary when it was drawn at the 49th parallel. Rather than giving it to Canada, as it should have been, the U.S. kept Point Roberts and now everyone is glad. The local population is just 900 year-round, but in the summer months it swells to 4,500 as Vancouverites come down to enjoy summer homes along the beach and the boating from the protected marina.

Most businesses at Point Roberts discount Canadian dollars even though the signs claim prices are "at par." The border itself is open 24 hours a day. You'll find the highway to Point Roberts clogged almost continually by Canadians driving down for cheap gasoline (sold by the liter), booze, cigarettes, and other American

goods. Point Roberts also serves as a shipping point for Canadians, who maintain cross-border mailboxes at Point Roberts, as they do in Blaine, Sumas, and other border towns. Several businesses offer UPS and FedEx drop-offs. (By the same token, some American couples arrange to have their children born in Canada because it is cheaper, even for aliens, and the children will have dual citizenship until the age of 18, and access to Canada's almost-free health-care system.) Americans living in Point Roberts year-round like the steady income.

There isn't a lot to see here, but the shoreline is lined with summer homes. You'll find a smattering of restaurants, shops, gas stations, and other businesses, but Point Roberts is primarily a rural parcel of land with a slow-paced country feel.

The Border

Monument Park at the north end of Marine Dr. marks the 49th parallel that separates the U.S. and Canada. Not much here, just a small obelisk

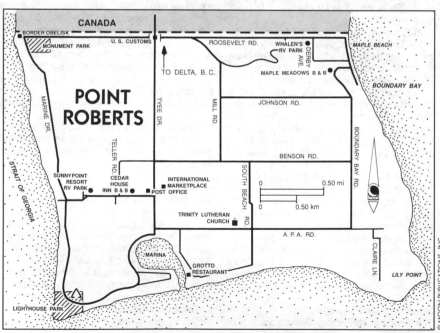

(border monument number one) erected in 1861 inscribed with the latitude and longitude at the westernmost point along the border. The road makes a sharp right here so you can't drive across, but Canadian homes are inches from the unguarded border, marked by a shallow ditch.

The border has had incidents that would cause wars between less friendly people. Several years ago a bulldozer owner from one side of the border did some work on the other side, and when he sent the bill, the recipient of his labor refused to pay. So the dozer owner cranked up his dozer, drove it across the border, and proceeded to demolish the work he had done. This upset the client, who fired shots at the dozer, which lumbered back across the border. Authorities on both sides of the border discussed the matter, took it under advisement, and apparently decided that justice had already been done; the incident faded into legal obscurity.

Parks, Recreation, and a Church
Located on the southwest tip of Point Roberts, Whatcom County's **Lighthouse Park** has 22 acres and a half-mile beach, highlighted by a boardwalk with a 30-foot lookout platform. This is a great place to watch the white British Columbia ferries crossing the Strait of Georgia to Vancouver Island, and to look for killer whales (orcas) in the summer. The boat launch here sees a lot of use, with some of the Puget Sound's finest salmon fishing right off the point. The beach is a favorite place to build sandcastles, dig clams, fly kites, or enjoy the sunset. The park is open all year and charges a day-use fee.

On the point's east side, the beaches on Boundary Bay have some of the warmest water on the West Coast as the tide comes in over a square mile of sand bars, providing safe fun for kids and waders. The **Point Roberts Marina** was carved out of the peninsula as a protected harbor with 1,000 slips filled with Canadian yachts and powerboats.

Built in 1913, the little New England-style white **Trinity Lutheran Church** stands on A.P.A Rd.; it's still used.

Accommodations
Maple Meadows B&B, 101 Goodman Rd., tel. (360) 945-5536, is a restored 1910 farmhouse in an open pasture with horses and cattle. The four guest rooms have shared or private baths, a jacuzzi, and a full breakfast for $75-125 d. No kids.

Cedar House Inn B&B, 1534 Gulf Rd., tel. (360) 945-0284, is a comfortable home with six guest rooms, shared baths, and a full breakfast; $36 s or $49 d. Other lodging places can be found just across the border in Delta, British Columbia.

Campgrounds
Camp at **Lighthouse Marine Park** ($12; no RV hookups); open all year. Call (360) 945-4911 for reservations. Both **Sunnypoint Resort RV Park & Campground,** on Gulf Rd., tel. (360) 945-1986, and **Whalen's RV Park & Campground,** near Maple Beach, tel. (360) 945-2874, have tent and RV spaces.

Food and Shopping
Grotto Restaurant, 713 Simundson Dr. (next to the marina), tel. (360) 945-2425, has casual fine dining with seafood, filet mignon, and other specials. Good food for reasonable prices. Right next door, the **Dockside Cafe,** tel. (360) 945-1206, makes fish and chips, sandwiches, burgers, and tacos. The **South Beach House,** 725 South Beach Rd., tel. (360) 945-0717, also specializes in seafood, especially bouillabaisse. Their Mongolian barbecue is fun to watch in action. The busy town of Delta, B.C., sits just across the border and offers many other culinary options.

The big store on Point Roberts, **International Marketplace,** 480 Tyee Dr., tel. (360) 945-0237, has groceries and a deli.

Entertainment and Events
The Breakers, 531 Marine Dr., tel. (360) 945-2300, has music and line dancing on weekends. **Kiniski's Reef Tavern,** 70 Gulf Rd., tel. (360) 945-4042, also has dancing sometimes, plus pool tables and big-screen TVs. The **Fourth of July** at Point Roberts brings bike and foot races, a parade, salmon barbecue, and games for kids.

Information
Check with the **Point Roberts Chamber of Commerce,** tel. (360) 945-2313, for info. Pamphlets describing Point Roberts are available from a kiosk near International Marketplace.

Getting There

Point Roberts is 23 road miles from the rest of Washington state. Access is via I-5 to the Canadian border at Blaine, then north on Hwy. 99 to Delta, and south on Hwy. 17 to the B.C. town of White Rock and the American settlement at Point Roberts. The Tsawwassen ferry terminal is just a few miles from here, providing a **British Columbia Ferries** link to Sidney on Vancouver Island; call (604) 669-1211 for a schedule. No reservations are available for this ferry, but there's always room for walk-on passengers.

WHIDBEY ISLAND

INTRODUCTION

The longest island in the lower 48 states—New York's Long Island was declared a peninsula by a U.S. Supreme Court ruling in 1985—Whidbey Island encompasses 208 square miles in its 45-mile length, no spot of which is more than five miles from the water. The island is one of western Washington's biggest tourist attractions, with attendance at Deception Pass State Park rivaling that of Mount Rainier. Also popular are the quaint towns of Coupeville and Langley, along with the quiet shoreline of Ebey's Landing National Historical Reserve.

WHIDBEY ISLAND

FERRY TO SAN JUAN ISLANDS AND SIDNEY, B.C.

ANACORTES

TO VANCOUVER, B.C.

MT. VERNON

FIDALGO ISLAND

DECEPTION PASS

DECEPTION PASS S.P.

WHIDBEY

20 ISLAND

5

JOSEPH WHIDBEY S.P.

OAK HARBOR

SEE COUPEVILLE AREA MAP

FORT EBEY S.P.

PENN COVE

STRAIT OF JUAN DE FUCA

COUPEVILLE

EBEY'S LANDING

KEYSTONE FERRY LANDING

FORT CASEY S.P.

525

ADMIRALTY BAY

GREENBANK

FERRY TO PORT TOWNSEND

MEERKERK RHODODENDRON GARDENS

SOUTH WHIDBEY S.P.

LANGLEY

FREELAND

BAYVIEW

EVERETT

DOUBLE BLUFF

CLINTON

USELESS BAY

FERRY

MUKILTEO

POSSESSION PT.

TO SEATTLE

0   5 mi

0   5 km

© MOON PUBLICATIONS, INC.

History

When the first European explorers reached Whidbey Island, they found it one of the most densely populated places in the Northwest. The original inhabitants, the Salish Indians, depended upon the rich resources of both the sea and the land and used fire to keep the prairies open. The prairies in southern Whidbey attracted settlers in the 1850s, who took advantage of the Homestead Act to carve out farms.

Credit for the 1792 "discovery" of Whidbey Island goes to Joseph Whidbey, master of George Vancouver's flagship, the HMS *Discovery*. Whidbey explored the island in a small vessel, although he apparently wasn't the first one there: while exploring the island's west side, Whidbey stumbled upon the rotted remains of another ship, too weather-beaten to identify.

Today, Whidbey Island's economy is supported by the Whidbey Island Naval Air Station in Oak Harbor, tourism, and farming. It is also increasingly a home for Everett commuters; hence all the vanpool vehicles you'll see crowding the ferries.

Seeing the Island

Whidbey is a perfect destination for a day-trip or a weekend outing, with lots to explore and a wide variety of places to stay. The island is also a great place for cyclists, with many miles of quiet back roads; get maps from the Langley Chamber of Commerce. One nice aspect of

Whidbey is that its picturesque towns of Langley and Coupeville are natural; the charm of the two towns is a result of their history, not a theme created to attract tourism.

For a fast day tour, take the Mukilteo-Clinton ferry to the south end of the island followed by a leisurely drive up the island, with stops in each town and park. To really see Whidbey right you'll need more than a hurried day-trip. Take the time to explore the many natural areas and historic sites, camping out in one of the excellent state parks or staying in a local B&B. Be warned, however, that lodging rates can approach the stratosphere, and that reservations are needed for summer weekends. If you're on a budget, your best bet is to camp out. Oak Harbor has the least expensive motel rooms, but is also the least interesting city on the island. Call **Island County Visitor Information** at (888) 747-7777 for information and brochures on Whidbey, or search the Web at www.whidbey.net.

Getting There
To drive onto Whidbey Island, you've got only one option: the Deception Pass Bridge at the island's north end. To get there, go west on Hwy. 20 from I-5. Otherwise, you'll have to go by **Washington State Ferry** from Mukilteo or Port Townsend.

The Mukilteo ferry leaves for Clinton about every half-hour 5 a.m.-2 a.m. The 20-minute crossing costs $2.40 roundtrip for passengers or walk-ons, 60 cents extra for bikes, and $5.50 one-way for car and driver. Busiest times are during the weekday commute periods, Saturday mornings, and Sunday evenings (particularly during the summer).

From the Olympic Peninsula, board the ferry in Port Townsend to arrive at the Keystone landing next to Fort Casey State Park approximately 30 minutes later. These ferries operate about every 45 minutes between 7 a.m. and 10 p.m. in the summer, and one-way fares are $1.80 for passengers (30 cents extra one-way for bikes), and $8 for car and driver. Be ready for a two-hour wait on summer weekends. For details on the state ferry system, call (206) 464-6400 or (888) 808-7977. Call (800) 843-3779 for automated information.

Getting Around
Island Transit, tel. (360) 678-7771 or 321-6688, is a free bus system that offers Mon.-Sat. service all across Whidbey Island, from Clinton on the south to Deception Pass on the north. All buses have bike racks. **Backroads,** tel. (800) 462-2848, has cycling tours of Whidbey Island during the summer, offered as either camping trips or rides where you stay at local inns and B&Bs. A sag-wagon carries your gear.

CLINTON

Clinton (pop. 2,100) sits on the bluff looking south across Possession Sound to Mukilteo and Everett. The ferry traffic lines up for as much as a mile on Sunday and at the end of holiday weekends. For most folks, Clinton—named for Clinton, Michigan—is a get-through-it place with a handful of restaurants, coffeehouses, grocers, and other commuter services. The town does, however have several nice places to stay.

Driving or biking around Clinton's rural, wooded back roads provides fresh air and great views. Take Deer Lake Rd. (watch the signs—the road takes 90-degree turns without notice) to **Deer Lake Park** for swimming, boating, and fishing in a secluded, wooded area. From Hwy. 525, go left onto Campbell Rd., then left again on Maxwelton Rd. to **Dave Mackie County Park,** where you'll find the island's best Dungeness crabbing, along with shallow water for swimming. **Possession Beach County Park** covers just two acres at the southern tip of Whidbey Island, but is a fine place to enjoy the views. At **Cultus Bay Nursery and Garden,** 4000 E. Baily Rd., tel. (360) 579-2329, a Victorian style home is surrounded by unusual perennials, vines, herbs, and drought-tolerant shrubs.

Accommodations
Ocean View B&B, 3493 E. French Rd., tel. (360) 579-2494 or (888) 799-5979, is a large modern home with a fourth floor dormer suite ($125 s or d including a continental breakfast) and a first-floor two-bedroom flat that is perfect for families ($200 for up to six people).

Home by the Sea Cottages, tel. (360) 321-2964, has two luxurious places to stay ($165-175 d); both with a continental breakfast. A restored 1918 cottage sits amid vineyards and has a jacuzzi tub and wrap-around deck. The second cottage faces Useless Bay and features an outdoor jacuzzi, woodstove, and sea kayaks. **Sweetwater Cottage,** 6111 S. Clutus Bay Rd., tel. (360) 341-1604, is a secluded two-bedroom cottage with a kitchen, woodstove, and sauna on 22 forested acres. Kids are welcome; $115 s or d. **Sunset Cottage,** tel. (360) 579-1590, is a two-bedroom cottage with a king-size bed and full kitchen. $85 d.

Other Practicalities

Whidbey CyberCafe & Bookstore, tel. (360) 341-5922, has Internet access, espresso, and books. Next door is **La Paz!,** with fish and shrimp tacos, homemade tamales, and chowder.

The state ferry departs Clinton for Mukilteo approximately every half-hour throughout the day. See "Getting There," for specifics. **Island Transit,** tel. (360) 321-6688, offers free bus service Mon.-Sat. throughout Whidbey Island.

LANGLEY

This town of 1,000 is six miles from the Clinton ferry landing, and a world away in style. The ritzy shops lining the streets of this tiny waterfront artists' community make for good browsing, and several of its lodging establishments have views across Saratoga Passage to Camano Island and beyond. You'll find an abundance of gourmet restaurants, boutiques, B&Bs, bookstores, and art galleries.

History

Langley is probably the only Washington town founded by a teenager. In 1880, an ambitious 15-year-old German immigrant, Jacob Anthes, settled here. Because he was too young to file for a homestead, Anthes spent $100 to buy 120 acres of land, adding to his holdings with a 160-acre homestead claim when he reached 21. He later built a store and post office and teamed up with Judge J.W. Langley to plat the new town.

Sights

The main attraction in Langley is simply the attractive town itself with its setting right along Puget Sound. A favorite downtown stopping place for photos is the life-size bronze *Boy and Dog,* by local sculptor Georgia Gerber. The 160-foot fishing pier offers great views and a chance to pull out your fishing pole, and the beach here is a popular place for picnicking and swimming. **South Whidbey Historical Museum,** has local memorabilia in a century-old building at 312 2nd Street. Open Sat.-Sun. 1-4 p.m.; tel. (360) 579-4696. Children love the **wooden castle** located near in the community park on the south end of town.

Tiny Langley is home to nine galleries, including several noteworthy ones. The two best are **Museo,** 215 1st St., tel. (360) 221-7737, and **Childers/Proctor Gallery,** 302 1st St., tel. (360) 221-2978, both with unusual and highly creative pieces. Also of note is **Lowry-James Fine Antiques,** with a fine collection of old natural history engravings and lithographs. Langley's galleries open for evening **Art Walks** on the first Saturday of every month.

Whidbey Island Vineyard and Winery, 5237 S. Langley Rd., tel. (360) 221-4941, is a family operation, producing wines from estate-grown vinifera grapes, along with surprisingly good rhubarb wines. The tasting room is open Thurs.-Sun. noon-5 p.m. Stop for a picnic overlooking the adjacent vineyard and apple orchard. Their wines are only available here or in local stores and restaurants.

A good downtown Langley place is **Moonraker Books,** 209 1st St., tel. (360) 221-6962, with a fine selection of regional titles. **North Star Trading Co.,** 602 2nd St., tel. (360) 221-6707, produces ultra-soft sheepskin slippers and hats.

Accommodations

The chamber of commerce has details on all the local B&Bs and inns and keeps track of vacancies; call them at (360) 221-5676. Take a tour of Whidbey B&Bs on the first Sunday of December during the **Deck the Halls Holiday B&B Tour.** Unless otherwise noted, all B&Bs listed below serve a full breakfast and do not allow young children.

Bed and Breakfasts

Langley's many B&Bs are arranged below by price.

A classic Langley home, **The Maine Stay B&B,** 619 1st St., tel. (360) 221-8173, has three guest rooms with private baths, and serves a continental breakfast; $65-95 s or d.

Perched over Saratoga Passage, **Pine Cottage & Chalet,** 3827 McKeay Dr., tel. (360) 730-1376, has a modern small home ($150 s or d) with a fireplace, plus a tiny cottage ($85 s or d) with a wood stove. Both have kitchens, and a continental breakfast.

The rambling **Twickenham House B&B Inn,** 5023 Langley Rd., tel. (360) 221-2334 or (800) 874-5009, is one of the more distinctive local places, with a country location, six guest rooms with private baths, plus ducks and chickens. A gourmet breakfast is served; $85-120 s or d.

Stay in one of two guest rooms at **Heron Haven B&B,** 513 Anthes Ave., tel. (360) 221-9121, a charming older home surrounded by beautiful gardens. $90 s or d.

The Angel Cottage, tel. (360) 321-5749, is a fully equipped cottage with a new age atmosphere, fine views across Saratoga Passage, and a continental breakfast; $95 s or d.

Villa Isola B&B Inn, 5489 S. Coles Rd., tel. (360) 221-5052 or (800) 246-7323, sits in the country two miles from Langley, and features spacious grounds (including a lawn bowling court), bikes, and three guest rooms with private baths. A continental breakfast is served; $95-130 s or d.

Island Tyme B&B Inn, 4940 S. Bayview, tel. (360) 221-5078 or (800) 898-8963, is a new Victorian-style home on 10 acres. Inside, you'll find a pool table and five guest rooms with private baths, fireplaces, and outside decks. Children are accepted; $95-140 s or d.

For downtown lodging at its best, stay at **Garden Path Inn B&B,** 111 1st St., tel. (360) 321-5121, where the two suites include a continental breakfast; $95-175 s or d.

Eagles Nest Inn B&B, 4680 E. Saratoga Rd., tel. (360) 221-5331, is a custom four-story octagonal home offering magnificent views across Saratoga Passage. Relax in the jacuzzi. Four guest rooms have private baths; $95-125 s or d.

Log Castle B&B, 3273 E. Saratoga Rd., tel. (360) 221-5483, is a unique waterfront log home with open beam ceilings, a big stone fireplace, and four guest rooms with private baths. A gourmet breakfast is served, and guests can use the canoe or rowboat. $95-120 s or d.

Country Cottage B&B, 215 6th St., tel. (360) 221-8709 or (800) 713-3860, is a 1920s home with five guest rooms, two of which have jacuzzis and private decks; $105-159 s or d.

Gallery Suite B&B, 301 1st St., tel. (360) 221-2978, is a small waterside unit with a kitchenette and make-your-own breakfast; $110 s or d. Two-night minimum on weekends.

Whidbey Inn B&B, 106 1st St., tel. (360) 221-7115, includes three downstairs rooms with a big sundeck, and three upstairs suites with fireplaces. A continental breakfast is served; $110-160 s or d.

Boatyard Inn, 200 Wharf St., tel. (360) 221-5120, has modern beachfront studio or loft units with kitchens, fireplaces, and decks; $120-195 s or d. The same owners operate the **Inn at Langley,** 400 1st St., tel. (360) 221-3033, where each room has a private patio overlooking Saratoga Passage, a jacuzzi tub, and a fireplace. A continental breakfast is served; $179-279 s or d. Both places have a two-night minimum on weekends.

Lone Lake Cottage B&B, 5206 S. Bayview Rd., tel. (360) 321-5325, has two cottages and a tiny paddlewheel houseboat along Lone Lake. Guests can use the canoes, bikes, and rowboat. An aviary is on the property, and a continental breakfast is served; $125-140 s or d. Two-night minimum on weekends.

A new Cape Cod style lodge, **Saratoga Inn,** 201 Cascade Ave., tel. (360) 221-5801, features spacious rooms and a continental breakfast for $125-175 s or d. A separate cottage ($275) with fireplace and sundeck is a favorite honeymoon suite.

Primrose Path B&B, 3191 E. Harbor Rd., tel. (360) 730-3722, is a 1928 cottage in the woods with a path to the beach, and a relaxing hot tub. A make-your-own breakfast is in the kitchen; $145 s or d.

Probably the most elaborate local B&B is **Galittoire Contemporary Guest House,** 5444 S. Coles Rd., tel. (360) 221-0548. Designed by the owner-architect, this beautiful Japanese-style home sits on 11 acres and is very popular for summer weddings. The two guest suites have everything you might want: king-size beds, jacuzzi tubs, an exercise room, sauna, and gazebo, plus gourmet breakfasts and evening hors d'oeuvres; $155-265 s or d. Two-night minimum on weekends.

Edgecliff Cottage B&B, tel. (360) 221-8857 or (800) 243-5536, is another of the island's luxury spots. This romantic penthouse cottage has its own jacuzzi and fine views of Saratoga Passage. A stairway leads to a private beach; $195 s or $235 d.

Cottages and Homes

The simplest Langley lodging is **Drake's Landing,** 203 Wharf St., tel. (360) 221-3999, where the single room costs $65 s or d. **Inverness Inn,** 2479 E. Hwy. 525, tel. (360) 321-5521, has six duplex cottages with kitchenettes; $75-90 for up to four.

Sharron's Cottage, tel. (360) 221-5494, is a newly built cottage in the woods with a king-size bed, fireplace, cathedral ceiling, and kitchen; $125 s or d.

The same owners manage three cottages located on six acres of gardens and ponds overlooking Saratoga Passage: **Dove House** ($200 d), **Chauntecleer House** ($225 d), and **The Potting Shed** ($175 d). All have private hot tubs and fireplaces; call (360) 221-5494 or (800) 637-4436.

Tara Vacation Rentals, tel. (360) 331-6300 or (206) 624-3951, has furnished homes, condos, and cottages all over the island available on a daily or weekly basis. Other furnished lodging places include: **Sea Breeze,** 5122 S. Bayview Rd., tel. (360) 321-5900, a three-bedroom beachfront home; and **The Beach Cabin,** 325 Wharf St., tel. (360) 221-3960.

Campgrounds

Camp at **South Whidbey State Park** (described under **Freeland**) for $10. **Island County Fairgrounds,** 819 Camano Ave., tel. (360) 321-4677, has year-round tent sites and RV hookups. Coin-operated showers are at the marina.

Food

Langley is blessed with an abundance of fine and surprisingly reasonable restaurants. It's almost a challenge to get a bad meal in this town! Get delicious light breakfasts and lunches—plus espresso drinks and fresh juices—at **Sapori,** 197 2nd St., tel. (360) 221-3211. **Langley Village Bakery,** tel. (360) 221-3525, bakes out-of-this-world breads and sweets.

A personal favorite, **Star Bistro,** serves burgers, soups, fish and chips, salads, pasta, and more upstairs at 201 1/2 1st St., tel. (360) 221-2627. Downstairs, the **Star Store** has gourmet and imported items.

Down the street a bit at 113 First, **Cafe Langley,** tel. (360) 221-3090, has a big local following, and great Greek and Middle Eastern dishes. Less pretentious, but noteworthy nonetheless, is **Village Pizzeria,** right across the street at 108 1st St., tel. (360) 221-3363, where they use all sorts of distinctive toppings.

Located on a hilltop on the south edge of town, **510 Bar & Grill,** 510 Cascade Ave., tel. (360) 221-6959, is Langley's most elegant restaurant, with perfectly prepared seafood, meats, and vegetarian specials. Even here, the most expensive entree is under $20. Big windows and a patio offer 180-degree views of Saratoga Passage and the Cascades.

Near the intersection of Hwy. 525 and Langley Rd. turnoff is **Trattoria Giuseppe,** tel. (360) 341-3454, with delicious Italian food and seafood in a romantic, white-linen setting. Classical piano music Wednesday and Saturday.

Dog House Tavern and Backdoor Restaurant, tel. (360) 221-9996, at 1st and Anthes, is nothing fancy—just a fun and funky place to have burgers, fish and chips, or chili, or perhaps just a drink while enjoying the view.

Whidbey Island Brewing Co., 630 2nd St., tel. (360) 221-8373, has a tasting room open daily noon-6 p.m., plus hot dogs, pretzels, and focaccia on the menu.

The **South Whidbey Tilth Farmers' Market** offers organic fruits and vegetables, plus flowers, baked goods, and seafood Saturday 10 a.m.-1 p.m. early May-October. It's held at 2780 Marshview; tel. (360) 730-7013.

Arts and Events

The **Whidbey Island Center for the Arts,** 565 Camano Ave., tel. (360) 221-8268 or (800) 638-7631, features concerts and plays throughout the year. In late February, several thousand people converge on town to search out the culprit in the annual **Langley Mystery Weekend.** Langley's popular **Choochokam Festival of the Arts** is held the second weekend of July with a juried arts festival, food, crafts, music, and dancing; call (360) 221-7494 for details. Don't miss Langley's **Island County Fair,** a four-day event in late August that includes a logging show, carnival, parade, music, and 4-H exhibits. Call (360) 221-4677 for details.

Recreation and Entertainment

South Whidbey Island was seemingly designed for biking. The rolling hills, clean air, and beautiful weather are inspiring enough, but occasional whale and eagle sightings add to the pleasure. Rent a bike from **Velocity Bikes,** 5603½ S. Bayview Rd., tel. (360) 321-5040.

A local theater group performs regularly in the old-fashioned theater on the short main drag. The **Clyde Theatre** on 1st St., tel. (360) 221-5525, is the only place to watch first-run movies on the south end of Whidbey Island.

Information and Services

Langley Chamber of Commerce is located at 208 Anthes St., tel. (360) 221-6765, www.whidbey.com/langley. Open daily 10 a.m.-5 p.m. all year.

Island Transit, tel. (360) 321-6688, is a free bus system that offers Mon.-Sat. service.

FREELAND

Freeland (pop. 1,700) was founded in 1900 by a utopian group of socialists. They formed a cooperative, the Free Land Association, and each contributed $10 toward five acres of land; the balance was to be paid off through cooperative labor. Their experiment didn't last long, but the name stuck. One reminder of that era is the classic wooden **Freeland Hall,** built in 1914, and still visible along the shore north of town.

Today Freeland has a handful of businesses, including the Nichols Brothers Boat Builders. Many other folks commute to Everett for work. A boat launch and small sunny picnic area are found at **Freeland Park** on Holmes Harbor, about two streets over from "downtown" Freeland—just look for the water. The beach is popular with clammers. **Double Bluff Point,** three miles south of Freeland, is an interesting place to explore and a good place to find big chunks of soft coal that eroded from the cliff.

South Whidbey State Park

Easily the island's most underrated park, South Whidbey State Park on Smuggler's Cove Rd. (halfway between Greenbank and Freeland) has outstanding hiking and picnicking, plus clamming and crabbing on a narrow sandy beach, campsites, and striking Olympic views. The 85 acres of old-growth Douglas fir and red cedar protect resident black-tailed deer, foxes, raccoons, rabbits, bald eagles, ospreys, and pileated woodpeckers.

Be sure to hike **Wilbert Trail,** a 1.5-mile path that circles through these ancient forests; it starts directly across from the park entrance.

Get to the park by heading east from Freeland on Bush Point Road; it becomes Smugglers Cove Road and continues past the park, a distance of seven miles.

Accommodations

For the ultimate in luxury, stay at **Cliff House B&B,** 5440 Windmill Rd., tel. (360) 331-1566, where the stunning modern home sits atop a cliff over Admiralty Inlet, and has a jacuzzi, king-size bed, stone fireplace, and gourmet kitchen. A light breakfast is in the fridge. $410 d. Also on the 13 acres of wooded land is **Seacliff Cottage,** with equally grand vistas for $165 d.

Harbour Inn Motel, 1606 E. Main St., tel. (360) 321-6900; has rooms for $50-66 s, $56-72 d, including some kitchenettes.

Mutiny Bay Resort & Motel, 5856 S. Mutiny Bay Rd., tel. (360) 331-4500, has cabins ($65 s or d) with kitchenettes and shared bath, and chalets ($125 s or d) with kitchenettes and fireplaces; kids welcome.

Mutiny Bay Hideaway, 5939 S. Mutiny Bay Rd., tel. (360) 331-6010 or (800) 262-3308, has quiet homey accommodations with fireplaces, a garden-side deck, and mountain bikes. The two guest rooms have jacuzzi tubs. No kids; $100-120 s or d.

Island Getaway, 397 Cardinal Way, tel. (360) 331-7707, has a luxurious penthouse suite with a deck and hot tub overlooking the water ($149 s or d), and a continental breakfast. A separate two-bedroom cottage with private hot tub is $135 for up to four. Two-night minimum on weekends.

Bush Point Wharf, 229 E. Main St., tel. (360) 331-0405 or (800) 460-7219, is a beachfront house with two guest suites, private baths, a deck, and jacuzzi; $95-195 s or d.

The Bungalow at Baby Island, tel. (360) 221-5121, has a two-bedroom cottage with woodstove and kitchen for $110; kids welcome.

Seaside Cottage, 213 E. Sandpiper Rd., tel. (360) 331-8455; has a cottage with water views ($110 for up to four), plus a one-bedroom suite with a deck for $75 d. Both places have kitchens and make-your-own-breakfasts.

Camping

Camp at **South Whidbey State Park,** tel. (360) 331-4559, for $10; no RV hookups. Open late February to October. Call (800) 452-5687 for reservations ($6 extra). Park RVs at **Mutiny Bay Resort,** 5856 S. Mutiny Bay Rd., tel. (360) 331-4500.

Food

Main Street's **Island Bakery,** tel. (360) 331-6282, has breads, espresso, cookies, pastries, and deli lunches. **Freeland Cafe,** 1642 E. Main St., tel. (360) 331-9945, is an old-time establishment with breakfast served anytime. Very popular with locals.

Information and Services

Freeland Chamber of Commerce at Harbor and Main, tel. (360) 331-1980, is open summer weekends. Play golf at the 18-hole **Holmes Harbor Golf Course,** 50232 Harbor Hills Dr., tel. (360) 331-2363.

GREENBANK

Don't be surprised if you never see Greenbank center—the turn-of-the-century general store, restaurant, and post office are easy to miss—but you can't miss the big red barn marking **Whidbey Island Greenbank Farm,** tel. (360) 678-7700, once the largest loganberry farm in the world. After the owners closed it down in 1996, local citizens organized to keep the area from being turned into a housing development, and persuaded the county to purchase it in 1997. New loganberry vines are being planted, and grape wine from Hoodsport Winery is bottled here; this has to be one of the few taxpayer-supported wineries anywhere! The gift shop is open daily 10 a.m.-5 p.m. in summer, and Mon.-Wed. noon-4 p.m., and Thurs.-Sun. 11 a.m.-5 p.m. the rest of the year. A **Farmer's Market** takes place here Sat.-Sun. 11 a.m.-3 p.m., mid-April through October.

Meerkerk Rhododendron Gardens

This delightful garden boasts more than 1,500 varieties of rhododendron species and hybrids on a 53-acre site just south of Greenbank off Resort Road. Begun by Max and Anne Meerkerk in the 1960s, the gardens are now maintained by the Seattle Rhododendron Society, and are a major tourist attraction. Peak season for "rhodies" is in late April and early May. The gardens are open daily 9 a.m.-4 p.m. $3 adults; free for children. Call (360) 321-6682 for details.

Accommodations

Set amid 25 wooded acres, **Guest House B&B Cottages** 3366 S. Hwy. 525, tel. (360) 678-3115, has four-star lodging with a homey feel. Accommodations include a log home ($285 d) and five cottages ($110-210 d) with continental breakfasts. All have access to the outdoor pool, jacuzzi, and exercise room. Two-night minimum and no kids.

Smugglers Cove Haven B&B, 3258 Smugglers Cove Rd., tel. (360) 678-7100 or (800) 772-7055, has an apartment and carriage house, fireplace, kitchen, and a make-yourself breakfast; $95-150 s or d. Kids okay.

Situated on five secluded acres, **The Yoga Lodge,** 3475 Christie Rd., tel. (360) 678-2120, is a peaceful place to spend a peaceful night surrounded by gardens and trees. The three guest rooms are $75 s or $120 d, including a yoga lesson, continental breakfast, and wood-fired sauna. Kids are welcome.

Other Practicalities

At **Whidbey Fish Market and Cafe,** 3078 Hwy. 525, tel. (360) 678-3474, you won't find white linen tablecloths, but the fish is as fresh as it gets. Stop here on Monday and Saturday for their popular and filling all-you-can-eat fish feeds. Reservations advised.

Greenbank's **Loganberry Festival** the third weekend of July features a pie-eating contest, along with arts and crafts, live music, and food stands; call (360) 678-7700.

Island Transit, tel. (360) 321-6688, has free bus service around Whidbey Island.

FORT CASEY STATE PARK

Fort Casey State Park—an historic Army post three miles south of Coupeville next to the Keystone ferry dock—has two miles of beach, an underwater park, a boat ramp, hiking trails, picnic areas, spectacular Olympic views, and campsites, plus good fishing in remarkably clear water.

History
Fort Casey was one of the "Iron Triangle" that guarded the entrance to Puget Sound and the Bremerton Naval Shipyard at the turn of the century. This deadly crossfire consisted of Fort Casey, plus Fort Worden at Port Townsend and Fort Flagler on Marrowstone Island; fortunately, the guns were never fired at an enemy vessel. Fort Casey's big weapons were the ingenious 10-inch disappearing carriage guns; the recoil sent them swinging back down out of sight for reloading, giving the sighter a terrific ride. By 1920, advances in naval warfare had made them obsolete, so they were melted down. During WW II, Fort Casey was primarily a training site, although anti-aircraft guns were mounted on the fortifications. The fort was closed after the war and purchased by Washington in 1956 for a state park.

Sights
If you're arriving on Whidbey Island by ferry from Port Townsend, get to Fort Casey by taking an immediate left onto Engle Rd. as soon as you exit the ferry terminal. Much of the fort is open for public viewing, including ammunition bunkers, observation towers, underground storage facilities (bring your flashlight), gun catwalks, and the main attraction—two disappearing guns. Because the originals were long gone, these were brought here in 1968 from an old American fort in the Philippines.

Be sure to visit the **Admiralty Point Lighthouse Interpretive Center,** where you can learn about coast artillery and the 1890 defense post. The lighthouse itself has not been used since 1927, but you can climb to the top for a view of Puget Sound and the Olympic Mountains. Open Thurs.-Sun. 10 a.m.-4 p.m.

Many of the fort's old buildings are now used as a conference center run by Seattle Pacific

University, and the turn-of-the-century officers' quarters have been turned into Fort Casey Inn B&B. Also nearby is shallow **Crockett Lake,** a good place to look for migratory and resident birds. The **Crockett Blockhouse,** one of four remaining fortifications built in the 1850s to defend against Indian attacks, stands on the north shore of the lake. An offshore underwater park is popular with divers. Northeast of Crockett Lake is Outlying Landing Field, used by Navy pilots to simulate aircraft carrier landings.

Campgrounds
The small and crowded campground ($11) at Fort Casey is open year-round, and has showers, but no RV hookups. Get here early to be assured of a site on summer weekends; a better bet may be to head to Fort Ebey State Park (see **Coupeville**) instead. A couple of pleasant hiking trails lead through the wooded grounds of the fort.

EBEY'S LANDING NATIONAL HISTORICAL RESERVE

Ebey's Landing, two miles southwest of Coupeville center, has easily the most striking coastal view on the island; no wonder portions of *Snow Falling on Cedars* were filmed here. As the roads wind through acres of rich farmland, the glimpses of water and cliff might remind you of the northern California or Oregon coastline; the majestic Olympics add to the drama.

Managed by the National Park Service and covering 17,400 acres, the Ebey's Landing National Historical Reserve helps keep this land rural and agricultural through scenic easements, land donations, tax incentives, and zoning. Approximately 90% of the land remains in private hands. Created in 1978, this was America's first national historical reserve. Headquarters are located at 908 N.W. Alexander St. in Coupeville, tel. (360) 678-6084.

History
The native Skagit Indians were generally friendly toward the white settlers, but their northern neighbors were considerably less forgiving of the invaders. Alaska's Kake tribe of Tlingit Indi-

Ebey's Landing

DIANNE BOUERICE LYONS

ans had a fierce reputation as exemplified by the following incident recorded by Richard Meade (1871):

In 1855 a party of Kakes, on a visit south to Puget Sound, became involved in some trouble there, which caused a United States vessel to open fire on them, and during the affair one of the Kake chiefs was killed. This took place over 800 miles from the Kake settlements on Kupreanof Island. The very next year the tribe sent a canoe-load of fighting men all the way from Clarence Straits in Russian America to Whidby's Island in Washington Territory, and attacked and beheaded an ex-collector—not of internal revenue, for that might have been pardonable—but of customs, and returned safely with his skull and scalp to their villages. Such people are, therefore, not to be despised, and are quite capable of giving much trouble in the future unless wisely and firmly governed.

The man so beheaded was Col. Isaac Ebey, the first settler on Whidbey Island; his head was eventually recovered and reunited with his body before being buried at Sunnyside Cemetery. To fend off further attacks (which never came), the pioneers built seven blockhouses in the 1850s, four of which still stand.

The Anglo settlers were attracted to this part of Whidbey Island by the expansive prairies and fertile black soil. These prairies occupy the sites of shallow Ice-Age lakes; when the water dried up, the rich, deep soil remained. Indian burning helped keep them open over the centuries that followed, and the white settlers simply took up residence on this prime land.

Sights

The main attraction at Ebey's Landing National Historical Reserve is simply the country itself: bucolic farmland, densely wooded ridges, and steep coastal bluffs. Pick up an informative tour brochure describing a detailed tour of Ebey's Landing at the Coupeville museum.

For a very scenic bike ride or drive, turn onto Hill Rd. (two miles south of Coupeville) and follow it through the second-growth stand of Douglas fir trees. It emerges on a high bluff overlooking Admiralty Inlet before dropping to the shoreline at tiny **Ebey's Landing State Park.** From the small parking area at the water's edge, hike the 1.5-mile trail along the bluff above **Parego Lagoon** for a view of the coastline, Olympics, and the Strait of Juan de Fuca that shouldn't be missed. The lagoon is a fine place to look for migratory birds. Return along the beach, or continue northward to Fort Ebey State Park (three miles from Ebey's Landing). Along the way, keep your eyes open for gem-quality stones such as agate, jasper, black and green jade, plus quartz and petrified wood.

Another trail leads 1.4 miles from Ebey's Landing to **Sunnyside Cemetery,** where you can look north to snowcapped Mt. Baker and south to Mt. Rainier on a clear day. The cemetery is also accessible from Cook Rd. (see "Coupeville Area" map). The **Davis Blockhouse,** used to defend against Tlingit and Haida attacks, stands at the edge of the cemetery; it was moved here in 1915. Colonel Isaac Ebey is buried here.

COUPEVILLE

The second oldest town in Washington, the "Port of Sea Captains" was founded and laid out in 1852 by Capt. Thomas Coupe, the first man to sail through Deception Pass. The protected harbor at Penn Cove was a perfect site for the village that became Coupeville (pop. 1,600), and timber from Whidbey was shipped from here to San Francisco to feed the building boom created by the gold rush. Today, modern businesses operate from Victorian-era buildings amidst the nation's largest historical preservation district. Downtown has an immaculate cluster of false-fronted shops and restaurants right on the harbor and a long wharf that was once used to ship local produce and logs to the mainland. This is a cat-friendly town; perhaps half the downtown business have one inside.

Historical Sights
The **Island County Historical Society Museum** at Alexander and Front Streets, tel. (360) 678-3310, has pioneer relics, including a shadow box with flowers made from human hair, an interesting video on local history, and changing exhibits. Out front is a garden with drought-tolerant plants. The museum is open daily 10 a.m.-5 p.m. May-Sept.; Fri.-Mon. 11 a.m.-4 p.m. the rest of the year. Entrance is $2 adults, $1.50 seniors, students, and military personnel, $4.50 families, and free for kids under six.

While at the museum, pick up their brochure describing a walking tour of the town's beautiful Victorian buildings. It lists some 40 buildings in Coupeville that are of historical significance and tells the family histories of many owners. Ninety-minute guided tours are offered Saturday and Sunday at 1:30 p.m. May-Sept., departing from the museum.

One of the original Whidbey Island fortifications, the **Alexander Blockhouse,** built in 1855, stands outside the museum, along with a shelter housing two turn-of-the-century Indian racing canoes. Also out front are attractive gardens with herbs and drought-tolerant plants. Additional blockhouses can be found at the Sunnyside Cemetery, just south of town, and near Crockett Lake.

Chief Snakelum's Grave, in a grove two miles east of Coupeville, commemorates the chief of the Skagit Tribe and one of the town's last Indian residents.

For something with a longer history, head south from downtown on Main St. to the house-sized boulder. Called a glacial erratic, this enormous rock was deposited here by the Vashon Glacier during the last ice age.

Penn Cove
For a very scenic drive, head northwest from Coupeville along Madrona Way, named for the Pacific madrone (a.k.a. madrona) trees whose distinctive red bark and leathery green leaves line the roadway. Quite a few summer cottages and cozy homes can be found here, along with the one-of-a-kind Captain Whidbey Inn. Offshore are dozens of floating pens where mussels grow on lines hanging in Penn Cove. On the northwest corner of Penn Cove, Hwy. 20 passes scenic **Grasser's Hill** where hedgerows alternate with open farmland. Development restrictions prevent this open country from becoming a mass of condos. Just north of here are the historic **San de Fuca schoolhouse** and Whidbey Inn.

Fort Ebey State Park
Fort Ebey State Park, tel. (360) 678-4636, southwest of Coupeville on Admiralty Inlet, has campsites, a large picnic area, three miles of beach, and two miles of hiking trails within its 644 acres. The fort was constructed during WW II, though its gun batteries were never needed. The concrete platforms remain, along with cavernous bunkers, but the big guns have long since been removed. Due to its location in the Olympic rain shadow, the park is one of few places in western Washington where cactus can be found; it also has stands of second-growth forests and great views across the Strait of Juan de Fuca.

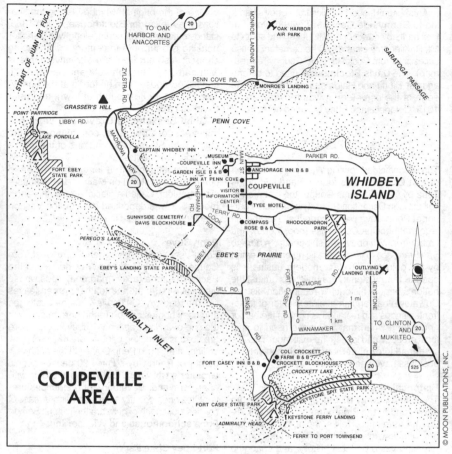

© MOON PUBLICATIONS, INC.

Although not as well known as other parks on Whidbey, it is still a favorite summertime spot. Much of Fort Ebey's popularity stems from tiny **Lake Pondilla,** formed by a glacial sinkhole—a bass-fisherman's and swimmer's delight. Follow the signs from the north parking lot for a two-block hike to the lake; half a dozen picnic tables and a camping area are reserved for hikers and bicyclists. Other trails lead along the bluffs south from here, and down to the beach. Adventurous folks (after consulting a tide chart and with a bit of care) can continue all the way to Fort Casey State Park, eight miles away.

Accommodations

Coupeville is blessed with many historic buildings, several of which have been turned into delightful B&Bs and inns. Unfortunately, they are priced accordingly, and equally likely to be full on summer weekends. Be sure to make advance reservations. Unless otherwise noted, all B&Bs listed below serve a full breakfast and do not allow young children.

One of the most striking places is **Compass Rose B&B,** 508 S. Main St., tel. (360) 678-5318 or (800) 237-3881, a Queen Anne Victorian home built in 1890 and packed with antiques. Two guest rooms share a bath; $85 s or d. Friendly owners, too.

The Inn at Penn Cove B&B, 702 N. Main, tel. (360) 678-8000 or (800) 688-2683, spreads across two lovingly restored Victorian homes built in 1887 and 1891. Inside each are three guest rooms with private or shared baths and fireplaces; $60-125 s or d. Kids accepted.

The Victorian B&B, 602 N. Main St., tel. (360) 678-5305, is another beautiful two-story home from the same era. Stay in a separate cottage or one of the two guest rooms in the house; $80-100 s or d.

Also of note is **Colonel Crockett Farm B&B,** 1012 S. Fort Casey Rd., tel. (360) 678-3711, an 1855 farmhouse with a large lawn and flower beds overlooking Admiralty Bay. The renovated home is furnished with antiques, and five guest rooms have private baths; $75-105 s or d.

Right next to Fort Casey State Park, **Fort Casey Inn B&B,** tel. (360) 678-8792, consists of 10 restored Georgian revival homes that served as officers' quarters during WW I. These large two-story homes are divided into two duplex units each, with full kitchens and private baths. The basements were built to be used as bomb shelters in case of attack, and some still have the original steel-shuttered windows. A continental breakfast is served, and kids are welcome. $75-125 s or d.

Captain Whidbey Inn, 2072 W. Captain Whidbey Inn Rd., tel. (360) 678-4097 or (800) 366-4097, has rooms inside this classic two-story inn built in 1907 from madrone logs, plus modern cottages and houses. Rates are $95-225 s or d. The expansive wooded grounds (with Pacific madrone trees) face onto Penn Cove. Even if you aren't staying here, be sure to stop and take in the scenery or sip a drink in the bar. The lodge also operates a 52-foot wooden ketch, the *Cutty Sark,* with regularly scheduled sailing trips.

Anchorage Inn B&B, 807 N. Main St., tel. (360) 678-5581 or (800) 843-3779, charges $75-95 s or d for the five guest rooms (private baths) in a large and luxurious Victorian-style inn.

Captain Kinney House, 207 N.E. Front St., tel. (360) 678-3415 or (800) 505-3800, is an historic 1872 two-bedroom house along the water; $109 for up to four people.

Garden Isle Guest Cottages B&B, 207 N.W. Coveland St., tel. (360) 678-5641, features two cottages with kitchens and a continental breakfast; $85-95 s or d.

Old Morris Farm B&B, 105 W. Morris Rd., tel. (360) 678-6586 or (800) 936-6586, is a comfortable home on 10 forested acres, with a hot tub, four guest rooms, and private baths; $80-125 s or d.

The **Coupeville Inn,** 200 N.W. Coveland St., tel. (360) 678-6668 or (800) 247-6162, has modern rooms with waterside views of Penn Cove, and serves a continental breakfast; $60-105 s or d. **The Crow's Nest,** 180 N.W. Coveland St., tel. (360) 678-6186, is a one-bedroom flat with fine views from the deck. Rooms are $75 s or d. **Tyee Motel,** 405 S. Main St., tel. (360) 678-6616, has basic rooms for $46 s or d.

DON PITCHER

Compass Rose B&B

Campgrounds

Camp year-round at **Fort Casey State Park,** three miles south of Coupeville, for $11 (no RV hookups). **Fort Ebey State Park,** approximately five miles west of Coupeville, has campsites ($11; no RV hookups) and a camping area reserved for hikers and bicyclists ($5); open late February to October. Call (800) 452-5687 for reservations ($6 extra).

Rhododendron Park, a Department of Natural Resources-managed park, is two miles east of Coupeville on Hwy. 20. It's easy to miss; look for the small blue camping sign on the highway. Here you'll find free in-the-woods campsites in a second-growth stand of Douglas fir trees, with an understory that includes blooming rhododendrons each April and May.

Food

Great Times Waterfront Coffee House, 12 N.W. Front St., tel. (360) 678-5860, has a delightful patio right on the water, plus good espresso and sweets. Get good homemade soups, fresh-baked breads, and enormous cinnamon rolls at the unpretentious **Knead & Feed Bakery Restaurant,** downstairs at 4 N.W. Front St., tel. (360) 678-5431.

For well-prepared seafood, burgers, chicken, and other American fare, it's hard to beat **Penn Cove Restaurant,** 11 N.W. Coveland, tel. (360) 678-5474. Get dependably good pub grub—including fish and chips, Reubens, and mussel chowder—at **Toby's Tavern,** 8 N.W. Front St., tel. (360) 678-4222. The 1884 red building *is* a bar, so no kids allowed.

Captain Whidbey Inn, 2072 W. Captain Whidbey Inn Rd., tel. (360) 678-4097 or (800) 366-4097, has a pricey restaurant emphasizing local seafood, especially Penn Cove mussels. Reservations required.

The **Coupeville Farmers Market** is held Saturday 10 a.m.-2 p.m. at 8th and Main Streets April to mid-October; tel. (360) 678-6757. Buy ultra-fresh mussels, clams, or oysters from **Penn Cove Shellfish,** 1900 Penn Cove Rd., tel. (360) 678-4803.

Events

Lots of events take place in tiny Coupeville, starting with the **Penn Cove Mussel Festival** the first weekend of March. Events include scavenger hunts, arts and crafts, and mussel cooking competitions. The **Penn Cove Water Festival** in early May includes Indian canoe races, arts and crafts, kayak events, and entertainment. The **Coupeville Arts and Crafts Festival** on the second weekend in August features a juried art show that attracts participants from across the Northwest, plus arts and crafts exhibits, food, music, and entertainment.

On Sunday in July and August, **Concerts on the Cove** are held in the Town Park pavilion, featuring a wide variety of music; call (360) 678-4684 for dates and tickets. If you're here the second weekend in October, don't miss the **Harvest Festival,** with music, food booths, a giant pumpkin contest, scarecrows, art and antique auction, and flea market. The first weekend of November brings **Bonanza Days,** a combination scavenger hunt and dance event. On the first Saturday of December, the **Greening of Coupeville** is a popular craft bazaar and tree-lighting festival.

Information and Services

The **Central Whidbey Chamber of Commerce,** 302 N. Main St. (across from the Catholic church), tel. (360) 678-5434, is open Sun.-Mon. 11 a.m.-6 p.m. and Tues.-Sat. 10 a.m.-6 p.m. all year. It is unstaffed, but the friendly owner of Rita's Rainbow next door may be able to answer a question or two. **Coupeville Arts Center,** tel. (360) 678-3396, teaches a wide range of first-rate workshops throughout the year, from photography to watercolor to calligraphy.

Transportation

Island Transit, tel. (360) 678-7771, has free bus service Mon.-Sat. throughout Whidbey. **Whidbey Scenic Flights,** tel. (360) 678-8384, offers airplane flights over the island. Rent sea kayaks and inflatable boats from **Whidbey Water Works,** tel. (360) 678-9301, located at the Captain Whidbey Inn.

OAK HARBOR

Settled first by sea captains, then the Irish, and at the turn of the century by immigrants from Holland, Oak Harbor (pop. 19,000) takes its name from the many ancient Garry oak trees that grew here; those remaining are protected by law. The city was founded by three men in the early 1850s: a Swiss named Ulrich Freund, a Norwegian named Martin Tafton, and a New Englander named C.W. Sumner. The arrival of the military during WW II transformed this town, making it a busy place.

The city's historic downtown faces the water and retains a bit of local character, but the main drag—Hwy. 20—is yet another disgusting example of the malling of America. This is the only place on the island where you'll find burger joints, shopping malls, traffic jams, and noise. It's on a far smaller scale than many Puget Sound cities, but comes as a rude shock if you've just driven in from genteel Coupeville and Langley. One good aspect of this, however, is that Oak Harbor has the cheapest gas on the island. Be sure to fill up.

Whidbey Island Naval Air Station
The largest naval air base in the Northwest was placed here in 1942 because the area has some of the best flying weather in the U.S.: it gets only 20 inches of annual rainfall, is out of the path of commercial flight routes, and has little electrical interference. The Whidbey Naval Air Station just outside Oak Harbor is home to electronic warfare squadrons of EA-6B carrier-based jets, and employs 8,000 military personnel. For tour information, call (360) 257-2286. Watch planes landing from the CPO Club (open to the public) on Ault Field Rd. along the north side of the base.

Parks
City Beach Park on Beeksma Dr., has a sandy beach with piles of driftwood, sheltered picnic tables, swimming and wading pools, a gazebo, tennis and baseball facilities, campsites, and a Dutch-style windmill. There's a nice view of the peaceful and protected harbor from here, and a great kiddie playground. Look for ducks along the shore. **Smith Park** at Midway Blvd. has a fine collection of old Garry oak trees and a large boulder left behind by the last Ice Age.

Joseph Whidbey State Park, just south of the Naval Air Station on Swantown Rd., is largely undeveloped, with picnic tables, pit toilets, and a few trails. The real attraction here is the long and scenic beach, one of the finest on the island.

Holland Gardens, between S.E. 4th and S.E. 6th Avenues, has shrub and flower gardens surrounding its big white and blue windmill—one of three in town. **Hummingbird Farm,** 2319 Zylstra Rd., tel. (360) 679-5044, has extensive display gardens, a nursery, and garden shop.

Accommodations
Oak Harbor has some of the least expensive lodging places on Whidbey Island. **Queen Ann Motel,** 450 S.E. Pioneer Way, tel. (360) 675-2209, features an indoor pool and jacuzzi; $47-52 s or $50-56 d. **Acorn Motor Inn,** 31530 State Route 20, tel. (360) 675-6646, charges $48-58 s or $52-64 d.

Auld Holland Inn, 33575 State Route 20, tel. (360) 675-2288 or (800) 228-0148, is a Dutch-style motel with an outdoor pool, jacuzzi, sauna, tennis court, exercise room, and lawn games; $55-85 s or d. **Coachman Inn,** 32959 State Route 20, tel. (360) 675-0727 or (800) 635-0043, has an outdoor pool, exercise room, fridges, and continental breakfast; $60-100 s or d. **Best Western Harbor Plaza,** 33175 State Route 20, tel. (360) 679-4567 or (800) 927-5478, charges $89-99 s, $99-119 d, including an outdoor pool, jacuzzi, fitness center, microwaves, fridges, and continental breakfast.

The friendly **Inn at the Bay B&B,** nine miles north of Oak Harbor, tel. (360) 679-8320, has a suite with private bath on a wooded hill near Deception Pass. A full breakfast is served, no kids allowed; $80 s or d.

Harbor Pointe B&B, 720 W. Bonnie View Acres Rd., tel. (360) 675-3379 or (800) 668-1110, is a large contemporary home with a private beach, four guest rooms, shared or private baths, and a full breakfast; $95-155 d. Kids accepted.

Camping
City Beach Park at the end of Beeksma Dr., tel. (360) 679-5551, has tent and RV sites along the lagoon for $15. RVers head to **North Whidbey RV Park,** 565 W. Cornet Bay Rd., tel. (360) 675-9597, or nearby **Sunrise Resort,** 550 W. Comet Bay Rd., tel. (360) 675-6575.

Food and Entertainment
As might be expected given the strong military presence in Oak Harbor, most eating places fall

in the traditional American food groups: McDonald's, pizza joints, and steak houses. A better bet is **Kasteel Franssen** at the Auld Holland Inn, 33575 State Route 20, tel. (360) 675-2288 or (800) 228-0148, where they specialize in seafood, European cuisine, and excellent desserts. Try to ignore the faux-Dutch trappings. Get authentic Mexican fare—including delicious chiles rellenos and margaritas—at **Lucy's Mi Casita Mexican Restaurant,** 31359 State Route 20, tel. (360) 675-4800.

Oak Harbor Pub & Brewery, 32295 State Route 20, tel. (360) 675-7408, is a nice little place with unusual beers (including a blackberry ale), and a menu of burgers, soups, sandwiches, and fish tacos. No smoking

The **Oak Harbor Public Market** is held Thursday 4-7 p.m., June to late September next to the visitor center; tel. (360) 675-3397.

Events

Whidbey Playhouse, 730 S.E. Midway Blvd., tel. (360) 679-2237, has plays throughout the year. The last weekend in April, Oak Harbor's Dutch roots appear as it hosts **Holland Happening**—a carnival, arts and crafts show, Dutch dinner, and tulip show in Holland Gardens. The **Fourth of July** includes a parade and fireworks, followed in mid-July by **Whidbey Island Race Week,** one of the top 20 yachting regattas in the world; tel. (360) 675-1314. In early December, the **Christmas Boat Parade** departs from Oak Harbor, proceeding around Penn Cove to the Coupeville Wharf and back.

Recreation

Swim at City Beach Park in the summer, or the indoor pool at 85 S.E. Jerome St., tel. (360) 675-7667, all year. The latter facility includes a sauna, two jacuzzis, and a wading pool. The city is home to the 18-hole **Gallery Golf Course** on Crosby Rd., tel. (360) 257-2295. Rent kayaks from **Adventure Marine,** on Hwy. 20 near Arby's, tel. (360) 675-9395.

Information and Transportation

The **Oak Harbor Visitor Center,** 32630 Hwy. 20, tel. (360) 675-3535, is open Mon.-Sat. 9 a.m.-5 p.m. all year.

Island Transit, tel. (360) 321-6688 or (800) 240-8747, has free bus service throughout

Whidbey Island. **Harbor Air,** tel. (800) 359-3220, offers daily service from Oak Harbor's Ault Field to Sea-Tac, the San Juan Islands, Port Angeles, Astoria, and Portland. **Airporter Shuttle,** tel. (800) 235-5247, has direct bus service from Oak Harbor to Sea-Tac.

DECEPTION PASS STATE PARK

Washington's most popular state park, Deception Pass, has facilities that rival those of national parks: swimming at two lakes, four miles of shoreline, 28 miles of hiking trails, fresh- and saltwater fishing, boating, picnicking, rowboat rentals, boat launches, viewpoints, an environmental learning center, and several hundred campsites. The park, nine miles north of Oak Harbor on Hwy. 20, covers almost 3,600 forested acres on both sides of spectacular Deception Pass Bridge.

History

When Capt. George Vancouver first sighted this waterway in 1792, he called it Port Gardner. But when he realized the inlet was actually a tidal passage between two islands, he renamed it "Deception Pass." Because of the strong tidal currents that can reach nine knots twice a day, the passage was avoided by sailing ships until 1852, when Capt. Thomas Coupe sailed a fully rigged three-masted vessel through the narrow entrance. Others quickly followed, and his namesake town—Coupeville—became a major shipping port.

Deception Pass Bridge

Completed in 1935, Deception Pass Bridge, a steel cantilever-truss structure, links Fidalgo, Pass, and Whidbey Islands. Much of the work was done by the Civilian Conservation Corps (CCC), who also built many other structures in the park. The bridge towers 182 feet above the water. It's estimated that each year more than 3.5 million people stop at the bridge to peer over the edge at the turbulent water and whirlpools far below, or to enjoy the sunset vistas.

Other Sights

Bowman Bay is just north of the bridge on the west side of the highway and has campsites, a

THE MAIDEN OF DECEPTION PASS

The Samish Indians told the story of the beautiful Maiden of Deception Pass, Ko-Kwal-Alwoot. She was gathering shellfish along the beach when the sea spirit saw her and was at once enamored; as he took her hand, Ko-Kwal-Alwoot became terrified, but the sea spirit reassured her, saying he only wished to gaze upon her loveliness. She returned often, listening to the sea spirit's declarations of love.

One day a young man came from the sea to ask Ko-Kwal-Alwoot's father for permission to marry her. Her father, suspecting that living underwater would be hazardous to his daughter's health, refused, despite the sea spirit's claim that Ko-Kwal-Alwoot would have eternal life. Miffed, the sea spirit brought drought and famine to the old man's people until he agreed to give his daughter away. There was one condition: that she return once every year so the old man could be sure she was properly cared for.

The agreement was made, and the people watched as Ko-Kwal-Alwoot walked into the water until only her hair, floating in the current, was visible. The famine and drought ended at once.

Ko-Kwal-Alwoot kept her promise for the next four years, returning to visit her people, but every time she came she was covered with more and more barnacles and seemed anxious to return to the sea. On her last visit her people told her she need not return unless she wanted to; and since that time, she's provided abundant shellfish and clean spring water in that area. Legend has it that her hair can be seen floating to and fro with the tide in Deception Pass.

Today this Samish legend is inscribed on a story pole on Fidalgo Island. To get there, follow Hwy. 20 to Fidalgo Island; go west at Pass Lake, following the signs for Bowman Bay and Rosario Beach, and hike the trail toward Rosario Head.

boat launch, and a fishing pier, plus a **Civilian Conservation Corps Interpretive Center** inside one of the attractive structures they built. Three rooms contain displays on the CCC and the men who worked for it in the 1930s. You may find one of the original CCC workers on duty, ready to talk about the old times. Open Thurs.-Mon. summers only.

Rosario Beach, just north of Bowman Bay, features a delightful picnic ground with CCC-built stone shelters. A half-mile hiking trail circles Rosario Head, the wooded point of land that juts into Rosario Bay (technically this is part of the 75-acre Sharpe County Park). The shoreline is a fine place to explore tidepools. The **Maiden of Deception Pass** totem pole commemorates the tale of a Samish Indian girl who became the bride of the water spirit. The Walla Walla College Marine Station is adjacent to Rosario Beach, and an underwater park offshore is very popular with scuba divers.

A mile south of the Deception Pass bridge is the turnoff to Coronet Bay Road. This road ends three miles out at **Hoypus Point,** a popular place to fish for salmon or to ride bikes. Great views of Mt. Baker from here.

Lakes and Hikes

Only electric motors, canoes, or rowboats are allowed on the park's lakes. You can observe beaver dams, muskrats, and mink in the marshes on the south side of shallow **Cranberry Lake,** which also hosts a seasonal concession stand. Good fishing for trout here, and the warm water makes a favorite swimming hole. North of the bridge is **Pass Lake,** another place to fish or paddle.

A 15-minute hike to the highest point on the island, 400-foot **Goose Rock,** provides views of the San Juan Islands, Mt. Baker, Victoria, and Fidalgo Island, and possibly bald eagles soaring overhead. The trail starts at the south end of the bridge, heading east from either side of the highway; take the wide trail as it follows the pass, then take one of the unmarked spur trails uphill to the top. Other hiking trails lead throughout the park, ranging from short nature paths to unimproved trails for experienced hikers only.

Campgrounds

Lots of places to camp at Deception Pass. The primary campground along Cranberry Lake has year-round sites ($11 tents; $6 bikes) with hot showers and trailer dump stations, but no RV hookups or reservations. This is one of the finest campgrounds in this part of Washington, with tall Douglas fir trees and a gorgeous lakeside setting. Unfortunately, it's also one of the most popular; be ready for a multitude of fellow visitors.

More campsites (summers only) at Bowman Bay, just north of the bridge. Call (360) 675-2417 for additional park information. Call (800) 452-5687 for reservations ($6 extra).

ANACORTES

Many visitors know Anacortes (ah-nah-KOR-tez) only as the jumping-off point for the San Juan Islands, but this city of 13,000 is far more than a ferry dock on the tip of Fidalgo Island. It is one of the more pleasant cities of that size in the Puget Sound basin and has a casual end-of-the-road atmosphere. Recent years have seen the town take pride in its heritage as buildings are renovated to house new shops.

Although it's hard to believe, Anacortes is legally on Fidalgo Island; Sammamish Slough cuts a sluggish, narrow swath from the La Conner area around the hills known as Fidalgo Head. The slough is kept open for boaters, and it is spanned by a beautiful curving arc of a bridge.

HISTORY

Anglos first resided on the island in the 1850s, but William Munks, who called himself "The King of Fidalgo Island," claimed to be the first permanent settler and opened a store in 1869. A geologist named Amos Bowman tried to persuade the company he worked for, the Canadian Pacific Railroad, to establish their western terminus at Fidalgo—despite the fact that Bowman had never seen the island. When they refused, Bowman came down to check out the property himself, bought 168 acres of it, and opened a store, a wharf, and the Anna Curtis Post Office—

named after his wife—in 1879. Bowman was so determined to get a railroad—any railroad—into Anacortes, that he published a newspaper, *The Northwest Enterprise,* to draw people and businesses to his town.

He was so convincing that the population boomed to more than 3,000 people, even though, by 1890, the town's five railroad depots had yet to see a train pull up. The Burlington Northern Railroad eventually came, and residents found financial success in salmon canneries, shingle factories, and lumber mills. Anacortes grew to prominence as a shipping and fishing port; by its heyday in 1911 it was home to seven canneries and proclaimed itself "salmon canning capital of the world." Workers were needed for all these plants, and Anacortes became a major entry point of illegal laborers from China and Japan; several outlaws made a prosperous living smuggling in both workers and opium. Anacortes' title as salmon canning capital of the world has long since been lost as salmon stocks dwindled in Puget Sound due to

DIANNE BOULERICE LYONS

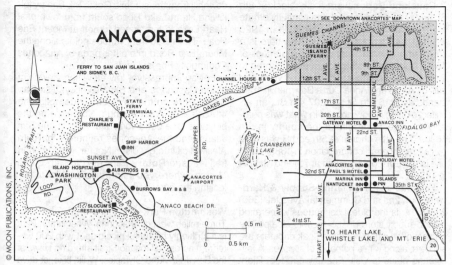

overfishing (and particularly the use of fish traps), but the city still maintains a strong seaward orientation.

Anacortes Today

The city of Anacortes relies on its Texaco and Tesoro oil refineries, the large Dakota Creek shipyard, two seafood processing plants (including the Trident Seafoods plant where they process Alaskan pollack for fish burgers used by Burger King and Long John Silver's), and tourists en route to the San Juan Islands. A fleet of gillnetters and seiners supplies salmon for local markets, and many of the boats here head north to Alaska each summer. In recent years the city has experienced growth as retirees move in to enjoy the mild and relatively dry weather, and as tourism increases in importance.

SIGHTS AND TOURS

Museums and Historic Buildings

At 1305 8th St., the **Anacortes Museum,** tel. (360) 293-1915, has local historical exhibits, photographs, and period furniture. Open Thurs.-Mon. 1-5 p.m. all year; donation. Get another taste of the past in a walk around Anacortes to see almost 50 (mostly small) **historic murals** on local buildings. The visitor center has descriptions of each, including the mural of Anna Curtis across the street from the center.

Other remnants of earlier days are scattered throughout town, including the historic sternwheeler **W.T. Preston**—now a National Historic Landmark—on display at 7th St. and R Ave. (next to the marina). The *Preston* operated as a snagboat for the U.S. Corps of Army Engineers from 1914 till she was finally retired in the 1970s and given to the city of Anacortes; she was the last sternwheeler operating on Puget Sound. The *Preston* kept the waterways clear of debris by towing off snags, logs, and stumps that piled up against bridge supports. Entrance to the *Preston* is $2 for adults, $1 for kids and seniors, and free for kids under eight. Open weekends 11 a.m.-5 p.m., tel. (360) 293-1916.

Right next to the *Preston* is the 1911 Burlington Northern Railroad Depot at 7th and R, now the Depot Arts Center.

Speaking of railroads, don't miss the **Anacortes Railway.** Over a 20-year period, long-time resident Tommy Thompson restored a 1909 narrow-gauge steam locomotive that pulls three passenger cars from the depot on a three-quarter-mile scenic train ride Sat.-Sun., mid-June to Labor Day. Rides cost $1; call (360) 293-2634 for more info.

Causland Park covers a city block at 8th St. and N Ave.; its colorful and playfully ornate mosaic walls and gazebo were built in 1920 with stones from area islands. Also here is a small amphitheater. Nearby are a number of 1890s homes and buildings, many restored to their original splendor. The home owned and built by Amos and Anna Curtis Bowman in 1891 stands at 1815 8th St.; at 807 4th St., an architect's office is now housed in what was probably the finest bordello in the county in the 1890s. The little church at 5th and R was built by its Presbyterian congregation in 1889; still in use is the Episcopal Church at 7th and M, built in 1896.

Founded in 1913, **Marine Supply & Hardware Co.,** 2nd and Commercial Ave., tel. (360) 293-3014, is the oldest continuously operating marine supply store west of the Mississippi. The original oiled wood floors and oak cabinets are still here, along with a potpourri of supplies. A fascinating place to visit. Friendly cat, too. Right across the street is the large **Dakota Creek Shipyard.**

Viewpoints

Five miles south of Anacortes, 1,270-foot **Mt. Erie** is the tallest "mountain" on Fidalgo Island. The steep and winding road leads 1.5 miles to a partially wooded summit where four short trails lead to dizzying views of the Olympics, Mt. Baker, Mt. Rainier, and Puget Sound. Don't miss the two lower overlooks, located a quarter mile downhill from the summit. Get to Mt. Erie by following Heart Lake Road south from town past Heart Lake to the signed turnoff at Mount Erie Road. Trails lead from various points along the Mount Erie Road into other parts of Anacortes Community Forest Lands.

For an impressive, low-elevation viewpoint of the Cascades and Skagit Valley, visit **Cap Sante Park** on the city's east side, following 4th Street to West Avenue. Scramble up the boulders for a better look at Mt. Baker, the San Juans, and the Anacortes refineries that turn Alaskan oil into gasoline. Not far away, a short trail leads to **Rotary Park** next to Cap Sante Marina, where you'll find picnic tables overlooking the busy harbor.

Washington Park

Three miles west of Anacortes, Washington Park is a strikingly beautiful picnic spot with 200 waterfront acres on Rosario Strait affording views of the San Juans and Olympics. Walk, bike, or drive the 2.3-mile paved scenic loop, and pull into one of many waterfront picnic areas. Other facilities include a popular boat launch, several miles of hiking trails offering views of the San Juans and the Olympics, a playground, and crowded campsites. The original park acreage was donated by one of Fidalgo Island's earliest pioneers, Tonjes Havekost, who said, "Make my cemetery a park for everybody." His grave stands on the southern edge of the park, overlooking Burrows Channel. Additional acreage was bought by the

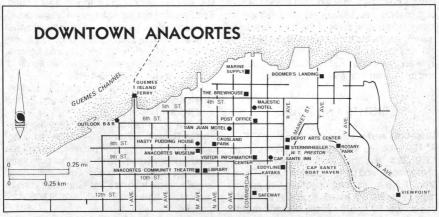

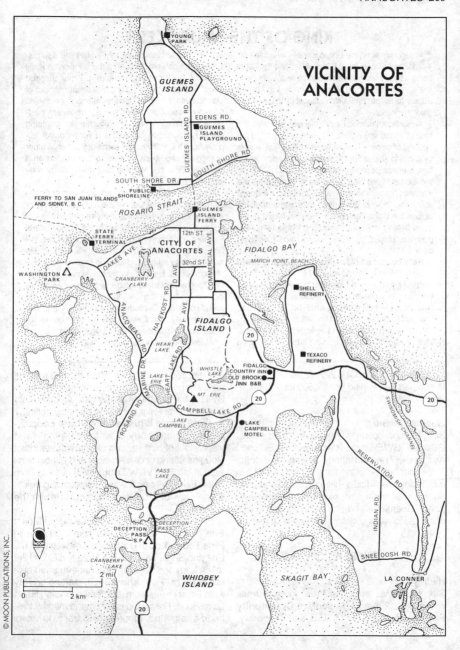

VICINITY OF ANACORTES

KING OF THE SMUGGLERS

Smuggling along the United States-Canadian border has always been a fact of life, and the items being transported back and forth have always been the same: liquor (particularly during the United States' foray into prohibition), illegal drugs, and illegal immigrants.

An Irishman named Larry Kelly was probably the best of all the smugglers. He even managed to die outside of prison. Kelly arrived in America simply by jumping ship in New Orleans and heading as far from there as possible. He fought in the Civil War on the Confederate side, but it wasn't long after the war that he arrived in Seattle because he heard about the "hole in the fence," meaning smuggling across the Canadian border. He also heard of the good fishing in Puget Sound for "bottle fish, poppies, and chinks," or liquor, opium, and Chinese laborers.

Kelly bought an old sailboat in 1872 and sailed north to Guemes Island, where he set up shop and learned it was easy to hide from the revenue cutters because they ran on a set schedule. Kelly made a nice profit smuggling opium, which he bought at $15 a pound in Britain and sold for $45 in the U.S.

The opium was packed in watertight tin cans, and to each can Kelly tied a chunk of salt as a sinker in case he was caught—after the salt dissolved, the can would float to the surface so Kelly could go back out and retrieve it. Kelly charged about $50 for smuggling a Chinese laborer out of Canada into the United States. Although he denied he ever killed one, other smugglers weren't adverse to chaining all of them together and dumping them overboard to drown if a revenue cutter approached. It is likely he did some of the things other smugglers did, such as putting them down on a beach in British Columbia and telling them they were in America.

Kelly was caught in 1882 with 40 cases of Canadian whiskey, and fined. He wasn't caught again for another four years, but that time he had 567 tins of opium. For this he was sent to McNeil Island Federal Penitentiary. And in 1891 he was caught for the final time, on a train with opium in his traveling bag. He was put away again, and while in prison decided to change his life. He wrote to the Louisiana Chapter of the Daughters of the Confederacy to see if any of his old friends from the Civil War were still alive. He found some in a Confederate old soldiers' home in New Orleans, and it was there he went on his release from prison, never to smuggle again.

At least he was never caught at it.

Anacortes Women's Club in 1922 from the sale of lemon pies—they paid just $2,500 for 75 beachfront acres.

Guemes Island

Skagit County operates ferry service to residential Guemes (GWEE-mes) Island from 6th St. and I Ave.; see "Transportation," below, for details. Take your bicycle along for a scenic tour of this rural island. You'll find a mile-long public shoreline on the southwest end, plus two small county parks. Guemes Island Resort on the north end of the island has a country store and boat rentals.

RECREATION

Hiking

Stop by the visitor center for a guide to trails within the 2,200-acre **Anacortes Community Forest Lands** around Mt. Erie and Cranberry, Whistle, and Heart Lakes. More than 25 miles of trails are here, with mileage, elevation, and highlights. Many of these paths can be linked into loop hikes for folks of varying physical ability.

The 3.5-mile **Whistle Lake Shore Loop** circles this small body of water, offering water views, lots of birdlife, and old-growth stands of Douglas fir and cedar. An easy and almost-level path is the **Erie View Trail,** which departs from Heart Lake Rd. and follows a seasonal creek to a fine view of Mt. Erie a mile out. Return the same way.

From the trailhead at the intersection of Mount Erie and Heart Lake Roads, hike the half-mile **Pine Ridge Loop Trail,** for more views of Mt. Erie and Sugarloaf. This moderately difficult hike takes from one to two hours. Another short hike is the 1.6-mile **Sugarloaf Trail,** starting on Ray Auld Dr. six miles from its intersection with Heart Lake Road. Follow the trail from the marshy trailhead straight up, ignoring side trails, to views to the west of Port Townsend, the San Juan Islands, and the Strait of Juan de Fuca, and north to Bellingham.

The Cranberry Lake area also has a number of hiking paths, including the mile-long **John M. Morrison Loop Trail** that starts at the end of 29th Street. This easy loop hike provides blufftop views of Cranberry Lake and old-growth Douglas fir forests, where some trees are seven feet wide.

Biking and Boating

Rent bikes from **Ship Harbor Bicycle Rental** near the ferry terminal at Ship Harbor Inn, tel. (360) 293-5177 or (800) 852-8568. You can roll them aboard the ferry and head out as soon as you get to the San Juan Islands. (Bikes are also available for rent on the three main islands.)

One of the nation's largest sea kayak manufacturers, Eddyline, has a factory in nearby Burlington. Learn about kayaking at the **Eddyline Watersports Center** along the Anacortes marina at 1019 Q Ave., tel. (360) 299-2300. You can take boats out for a test paddle, rent a kayak, try on the hi-tech clothing, or join classes or tours. Several companies offer powerboat or sailboat charters; see the visitors center for a listing.

Other Recreation

Scimitar Ridge Ranch, 527 Miller Rd., tel. (360) 293-5355 or (800) 798-5355, has horseback riding, camping, and other family adventures. **Similk Beach Golf Course,** tel. (360) 293-3444, has a nine-hole course with Puget Sound vistas.

ACCOMMODATIONS

Anacortes is blessed with an abundance of cozy B&Bs and fine hotels; several of the nicest are also described below. Make reservations far ahead for the summer months; some places fill up by March for the peak summer season (July and August). Unless otherwise stated, all B&Bs below serve a full breakfast and do not allow young children.

Within walking distance to downtown and the Cap Sante waterfront, the **Hasty Pudding House,** 1312 8th St., tel. (360) 293-5773 or (800) 368-5588, is an elegantly restored 1913 craftsman home furnished in antiques and lace. Four

guest rooms have private baths and a cozy fireplace; $75-89 s or d. The Hasty family also owns **Nantucket Inn,** 3402 Commercial Ave., tel. (360) 293-6007 or (888) 293-6007, a 1925 Cape Cod home with seven antique-filled rooms, most with private baths. A jacuzzi sits on the deck; $75-125 s or d.

Another home from the same era is **Blue Rose B&B,** 1811 9th St., tel. (360) 293-5175 or (888) 293-5175, a 1910 craftsman home in a quiet neighborhood. The B&B has three guest rooms with private baths; $87-111 s or d.

Albatross Bed and Breakfast, 5708 Kingsway W, tel. (360) 293-0677 or (800) 484-9507, is a well-kept 1927 home with marina views. The four guest rooms have private baths and kids are accepted; $90 s or $95 d.

A Burrows Bay B&B, 4911 Macbeth Dr., tel. (360) 293-4792, is a contemporary B&B with a luxury suite that features a fireplace, library, and a private deck with views of the San Juans. A large continental breakfast is served; $120 s or d.

Channel House, 2902 Oakes Ave., tel. (360) 293-9382 or (800) 238-4353, is a 1902 home overlooking the San Juans. The four guest rooms have private baths; outside is a hot tub and a cottage with two additional rooms; $59-95 s or $69-105 d.

Outlook B&B, 608 H Ave., tel. (360) 293-3505 or (888) 634-5844, is a 1910 craftsman home with a flower-filled yard overlooking Guemes Channel and the San Juans. Inside, find two guest rooms (one with jacuzzi tub), private baths, and a woodstove; $89 s or d.

Old Brook Inn, 530 Old Brook Ln., tel. (360) 293-4768 or (800) 503-4768, is a modern home with fine views of Fidalgo Bay; nearby, find trails through nine acres of forest along with a stocked pond. The two guest rooms have private baths, and kids are welcome. A continental breakfast is served. $80-90 s or d.

Sunset Beach B&B, 100 Sunset Beach, tel. (360) 293-5428 or (800) 359-3448, provides sweeping views of the San Juan Islands from its beachfront location. The three guest rooms have private baths, shorefront docks, and a hot tub; $89-109 s or d.

The Shannon House B&B, 2615 D Ave., tel. (360) 299-3876 or (800) 828-1474, was built in 1915, and has three guest rooms with shared or private baths; $80-110 s or d.

ANACORTES MOTELS AND HOTELS

Accommodations are arranged from least to most expensive. Rates may be lower during the winter months. Bed and breakfasts are listed in the text.

INEXPENSIVE

Paul's Motel; 3100 Commercial Ave.; tel. (360) 293-3108; $30-50 s or d

San Juan Motel; 1103 6th St.; tel. (360) 293-5105 or (800) 533-8009; $40-60 s or d; kitchenettes available

Gateway Motel; 2019 Commercial Ave.; tel. (360) 293-2655 or (800) 428-7583; $40-65 d; kitchenettes available

Lake Campbell Motel & Apartments; 1377 Hwy. 20 (four miles south); tel. (360) 293-5314; $43 s or d in motel; $52-64 s or d in two- or three-bedroom units with kitchenettes

Holiday Motel; 2903 Commercial Ave.; tel. (360) 293-6511; $50 s, $55 d

MODERATE

Marina Inn; 3300 Commercial Ave.; tel. (360) 293-1100 or (800) 231-5198; $59-75 s, $65-75 d; attractive new motel, kitchenettes available, jacuzzi, continental breakfast, AAA approved

Cap Sante Inn; 906 9th St.; tel. (360) 293-0602 or (800) 852-0846; $60 s, $64 d; AAA approved

---

In addition to these places, **Guemes Island Resort,** 325 Guemes Island Rd., tel. (360) 293-6643 or (800) 965-6643, has a store, swimming pool, boat rentals, and waterfront cabins and houses for $105-220; five-night minimum in mid-summer.

CAMPING

Three miles west of Anacortes, the city-run **Washington Park,** tel. (360) 293-1918, has crowded campsites in the woods year-round ($12 tents, $15 RVs), with showers and boat launches. Two popular state parks with campsites are within 20 miles of Anacortes: Deception Pass State Park (see above), and Bay View State Park (see **Mount Vernon and Vicinity**).

Park RVs at **Fidalgo Bay Resort,** 1107 Fidalgo Bay Rd., tel. (360) 293-5353 or (800) 727-5478; **Lighthouse RV Park,** 1900 Skyline Way, tel. (360) 293-4584; **Pioneer Trails Campground,** 527 Miller Rd., tel. (360) 293-5355 or (888) 777-5355; and **Scimitar Ridge Ranch,** south of town at 527 Miller Rd., tel. (360) 293-5355 or (800) 798-5355. Scimitar Ridge even has covered wagons for family camping.

FOOD

Breakfast, Bakeries, and Lunch

Start your day at the smoke-free **Calico Cupboard Cafe & Bakery,** 901 Commercial Ave., tel. (360) 293-7315, for great homemade country breakfasts and healthy lunches. Save room for dessert; the fudge pecan pie and apple dumplings are legendary. Get there early, or be ready for a wait on weekends.

Fidalgo Bay Roasting Co., 710 Commercial Ave., tel. (360) 293-0243, is the place to go for fresh-roasted coffee or to relax with an espresso (or is that a contradiction in terms?).

La Vie en Rose French Bakery, 418 Commercial Ave., tel. (360) 299-9546, has wonderful French pastries and breads, plus delicious soups and sandwiches for lunch. If you're heading out on the ferry, have them put together a box lunch special. Get wraps, smoothies, and fresh-squeezed juices next door at **Star Bar and Solé Luna Cafe,** tel. (360) 299-2120. For take-out food or casual eat-in dining—including sandwiches, salads, soups, and homemade desserts—stop by **Gere-a-Deli,** 502 Commercial Ave., tel. (360) 293-7383.

Anacortes Inn; 3006 Commercial Ave.; tel. (360) 293-3153 or (800) 327-7976; $60-65 s, $65-70 d; outdoor pool, fridges and microwaves, kitchenettes available, AAA approved

Ship Harbor Inn; 5316 Ferry Terminal Rd.; tel. (360) 293-5177, (800) 852-8568 (U.S.), or (800) 235-8568 (Canada); $60-70 s, $60-80 d; cabins and lodge, fireplaces, continental breakfast, kitchenettes available, AAA approved

Islands Inn; 3401 Commercial Ave.; tel. (360) 293-4644; $70-105 s or d; outdoor pool, jacuzzi, full breakfast

Fidalgo Country Inn; 1250 Highway 20; tel. (360) 293-3494 or (800) 244-4179; $71-86 s, $81-96 d; new motel with large rooms, outdoor pool, jacuzzi, continental breakfast, AAA approved

Anaco Inn; 905 20th St.; tel. (360) 293-8833 or (888) 293-8833; $69 s or $74-99 d; jacuzzi, jetted tubs, full breakfast

EXPENSIVE TO PREMIUM

The Majestic Hotel; 419 Commercial Ave.; tel. (360) 293-3355 or (800) 588-4780; $98-225 s or d; historic European-style country inn, guest rooms and suites with antiques, some with view decks, private baths, continental breakfast, rooftop cupola with views

Troll House; 197 Rosario Rd.; tel. (360) 293-5750; $125 s or d; guest cabin with hot tub overlooking San Juan Islands

Town Cottages; 1219 18th St., tel. (360) 293-1252; $550/week for turn-of-the-century cottages (sleep two) with kitchens, $795/week for two-bedroom condos (sleep four) with kitchens

Surf and Turf

On the waterfront at 209 T Ave., **Boomer's Landing,** tel. (360) 293-5108, specializes in lobster, steak, and seafood. **Charlie's Restaurant,** next to the ferry terminal, tel. (360) 293-7377, has a moderately priced menu with water and dock views; it's a convenient place to stop for a drink while you're waiting for your ship to come in.

Pubs

Anacortes two best drinking establishments are both smoke-free. You won't go wrong with a lunch or dinner at **Anacortes Brewhouse,** 320 Commercial Ave., tel. (360) 293-3666, where the menu includes seafood, pastas, wood-fired pizzas, and fresh ales from the on-the-premises brewery. Just down the street at 412 Commercial Ave. is **Brown Lantern Ale House,** tel. (360) 293-2544, where the burgers and halibut fish and chips are noteworthy.

Fine Dining

La Petite, 3401 Commercial Ave., tel. (360) 293-4644, serves some of the best dinners in Anacortes, plus a hearty Dutch breakfast. Be ready to drop $30 per person or more for dinner.

The Majestic Hotel's **Salmon Run,** 419 Commercial Ave., tel. (360) 299-2923, has a gorgeous garden setting and serves excellent but pricey fresh seafood, from mahi mahi and swordfish to Penn Cove mussels. The English-style Rose and Crown pub serves the same menu.

Bella Isola Ristorante Italiano, 619 Commercial Ave., tel. (360) 299-8398, has classic Italian pastas, plus pizzas, steak and seafood. It's packed most nights. Dinner entrees are $12-17. Recommended.

Markets and Produce

The **Depot Farmers Market,** tel. (360) 293-3663, takes place at 7th St. and R Ave. on Saturday 10 a.m.-2 p.m. from mid-May to mid-October. For fresh seafood, stop by two longtime favorites: **Thibert's Crab Market,** 697 Stevenson Rd., tel. (360) 293-2525, or **Knudson's Crab Market,** 2610 Commercial Ave., tel. (360) 293-3696. Get smoked salmon and other treats from **Seabear Smokehouse,** 30th St. and T Ave., tel. (360) 293-4661.

ENTERTAINMENT AND EVENTS

The Arts

The **Depot Arts Center,** tel. (360) 293-3663, houses Northwest Departures Gallery, showcasing a wide range of locally produced art, plus the **Vela Luka Croatian Dancers,** a local group that performs all over the world. You can see them perform during the Skagit Valley Tulip Festival, and at several other times during the year. This is the most obvious example of Anacortes' active Croatian community; a quarter of the local population is of Croatian descent.

The **Anacortes Community Theatre,** tel. (360) 293-6829, stages plays and musicals, plus annual Christmas performances at 10th and M. Meet regional authors during book and poetry readings at **Watermark Book Co.,** 612 Commercial Ave., tel. (360) 293-4277. Both **Anacortes Brewhouse** and **The Salmon Run** (described above) have live weekend music.

Festivals

Held the first three weekends in April in Anacortes, La Conner, and Mount Vernon, the ever-popular **Skagit Valley Tulip Festival,** tel. (360) 293-3832, includes everything from boat rides to fireworks; see **Mount Vernon and Vicinity** earlier in this chapter for details. The **Anacortes Waterfront Festival,** held at Cap Sante Boat Haven the weekend before Memorial Day each May, celebrates the city's maritime heritage with a food court and beer garden, craft booths, farmers and seafood market, boat show and regatta, and art show.

Anacortes, like every other town in America, has a parade and fireworks on the **Fourth of July.** The last weekend in July brings the self-explanatory **An-O-Chords Annual Barbershop Concert and Salmon Barbecue.**

The **Anacortes Arts and Crafts Festival,** held the first weekend of August, attracts more than 50,000 people and includes a juried fine art show, high-quality arts and crafts booths, a children's fair, ethnic foods, antique cars, and plenty of live music and entertainment; call (360) 293-6211 for details. If you missed this one, shoot for the **World's Largest King Salmon Barbecue** on the third weekend of August. Catch the holiday spirit, Puget-sound style: watch for the annual **Lighted Ships of Christmas Boat Parade,** held the second Saturday in December.

INFORMATION AND SERVICES

For maps, brochures, and up-to-date information, drop by the **Anacortes Tourism and Information Center,** 819 Commercial Ave., tel. (360) 293-3832. Open Mon.-Fri. 9 a.m.-5 p.m. and Sunday 10 a.m.-3 p.m. May to mid-Sept.; and Mon.-Fri. 9 a.m.-5 p.m., and Saturday 10 a.m.-3 p.m. the rest of the year. Across the street is a mural of Anna Curtis, for whom the town was named. Find more on the Web at www.anacorteschamber.com.

TRANSPORTATION

Ferry Service

To reach the San Juan Islands via state ferry, you have no choice but to leave from Anacortes—and ferry traffic keeps a good portion of local businesses in business. Be prepared for a lengthy wait on summer weekends. Avoid the waits by leaving your car in the free lot and walking aboard; there's always space for walk-on passengers. The Anacortes ferry terminal is four miles west of downtown on Oakes Ave. (12th St.) and has a small cafe with espresso, along with two nearby restaurants. For fares and other vital information see **San Juan Islands** or phone the Washington State Ferry System at (360) 293-8166 in Anacortes, or (888) 808-7977. Call (800) 843-3779 for automated information. Tune your radio to **AM 1340** for broadcasts of the current ferry status, including any backups or other problems. Reservations are recommended for ferry service between Anacortes and Sidney, B.C.; call (206) 464-6400 or (888) 808-7977 for details.

Skagit County operates a small ferry to residential **Guemes Island** from 6th St. and I Avenue. The five-minute crossing costs $6.25 roundtrip for car and driver, and $1.25 roundtrip for passengers or walk-ons. The boat departs daily on the hour or better, from 6:30 a.m. most days to at least 6 p.m. Call (360) 293-6356 for details.

Island Taxicat, tel. (360) 293-1157, is a fast catamaran that delivers people, kayaks, and camping gear anywhere on the San Juans at an hourly rate. Very useful for families and small groups looking to get off the main ferry routes quickly.

By Air
Departing from Anacortes Airport, **West Isle Air,** tel. (360) 293-4691 or (800) 874-4434, offers commuter flights year-round to San Juan Islands, plus flightseeing trips and air charters.

By Bus
Airporter Shuttle, tel. (800) 235-5247, has daily shuttles between Anacortes and Sea-Tac. **Skagit Transit,** tel. (360) 299-2424, has free daily bus connections from Anacortes to Mt. Vernon, La Conner, and other parts of Skagit County.

SAN JUAN ISLANDS

Nestled between the Washington mainland and Vancouver Island, the San Juan archipelago consists of 172 named islands. In actuality, there are more than 786 at low tide and 457 at high tide. Four of the largest—Orcas, Lopez, Shaw, and San Juan—are served by state ferry and are home to approximately 12,000 people. These numbers swell to 30,000 at the peak of summer tourism. The pace is slow and the dress is casual, so leave your ties at home, but don't forget your binoculars (for watching whales and birds), camera, and bike.

More than any other part of Washington, the San Juans will give you a sense of being *away.* When the ferry pulls away from the Anacortes dock, it is almost like departing on a cruise ship. The islands have become one of the state's favorite places to get away, and each summer more visitors arrive, and the demand for facilities goes higher. In recent years the numbers have approached two million ferry passengers, along with many more folks who arrive by plane.

It isn't just tourists who travel to the San Juans. In the last two decades they have been discovered as a place to escape the fast pace of city liv-

ing, and as a retirement haven. But any land deals are long gone. Anyone wanting to buy shoreline property will soon discover that the going rate is $1,000 a foot! San Juan County has an assessed per-capita property valuation more than three times the state average. Another measure of the importance of land is this: there are 30 different real estate dealers on the islands, one for every 333 residents!

An oddity of the islands is that all of the three islands with heavy population manage to have their distinct personalities. Generally speaking (very generally), Lopez Island attracts low-key people who care less than most about an extravagant lifestyle, people who are comfortable alone or in a small community. San Juan is the county seat so that's where the lawyers and promoters and political hangers-on go. Friday Harbor is a hotbed of environmentalists vs. developers, a struggle that has been going on for decades. Fortunately, the **San Juan Preservation Trust,** a local nonprofit organization, has been able to protect a considerable amount of the remaining open space on San Juan Island through conservation easements.

Orcas is something of the Kiwanis Club of the islands. Several industrialists have built homes there, including members of the Kaiser family and several Northwest industrial powers. The island also continues to attract those with less cash, particularly artists and writers.

CLIMATE

The San Juans do most of their tourist business between Memorial Day and Labor Day when the weather is warm—rarely above 85°—and sunny, but for the locals September and October are the nicest months of the year: the tourists are gone, and the weather is still warm and dry, with highs in the 60s and lows in the 40s or 50s, and the salmon are running. Because the islands are shielded by the Olympic and Vancouver Island mountains, rainfall amounts to less than 25 inches per year; December is the wettest month, with 4.5 inches of rain on the average and temperatures in the low 40s. The sun shines an average of 247 days a year on the islands, much of that during the mostly dry summer months. It rarely snows in the San Juans, and when it does it lasts but a few days.

Water—or the lack thereof—is a serious problem on the islands, particularly during the all-too-frequent drought years. There are few permanent creeks and even fewer lakes on the islands, but there's heavy demand due to increasing development. Most B&Bs and other lodging places use low-flow showerheads and other means to conserve water. Do your part by not wasting a drop. This means avoiding long showers, not leaving the water running while brushing your teeth, and not flushing the toilet as often.

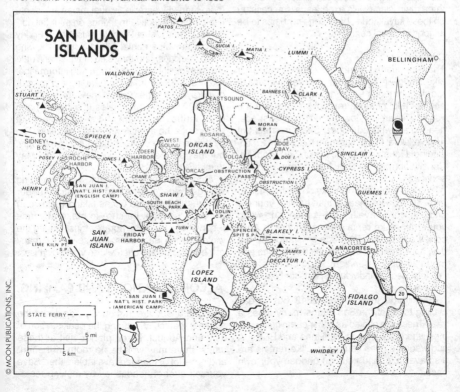

© MOON PUBLICATIONS, INC.

SPORTS AND RECREATION

The San Juans abound with outdoor pleasures of all kinds: cycling, sea kayaking, camping, hiking, scuba diving, sailing, windsurfing, whalewatching, and fishing to name a few. Specifics on these are listed in descriptions for the various islands below.

Sea Kayaking

The protected waters, diverse landscapes, rich wildlife, and a myriad of bays and coves make the San Juans a marvelous place to explore in a sea kayak. This is one of the finest ways to see the islands, as more and more folks are discovering each year. A number of companies offer such trips, and several will also rent kayaks to you. Kayaking companies are listed below under the "Sports and Recreation" headings for the three main islands. No experience is necessary on these kayak tours, but it certainly helps to be in good physical condition.

Cycling

The San Juans seem to have been made for bike riding—mild weather, a wide diversity of terrain, gorgeous scenery, excellent facilities, and not a lot of traffic (except on San Juan). If you have a family in tow or aren't in great shape, head to slow-paced Lopez; Shaw is small but fun to explore; Orcas has more rugged terrain (including a tough ride to the top of 2,409-foot Mt. Constitution); while San Juan offers the most services.

You can bring your own bike on the ferry for an extra $2.90, a lot cheaper than hauling your car and you won't have to wait—or rent one when you arrive. Bike rentals are available in Anacortes and on the three major islands by the day, hour, or week. Most shops rent touring and mountain bikes, panniers, child carriers, and helmets. See the individual islands for bike rental companies.

Backroads, tel. (800) 462-2848, has six-day cycling tours of the San Juans many times a year. These are offered as either camping trips or trips where you stay at local inns and B&Bs. A sag-wagon carries your gear. Bike rentals are also available, and you can choose your own pace.

Whalewatching

The waters around the San Juans are famous for the whales that come here during the summer months, so it's no surprise that the movie *Free Willy II* was filmed here. The most exciting of these are the orca, or "killer" whales that pursue migrating salmon and seals. What some visitors think are baby orcas are actually full-grown black-and-white Dall's porpoises. Other marine mammals commonly seen around the islands include minke whales, harbor porpoises, harbor seals, and even elephant seals.

Watching whales is a favorite activity around the San Juans, with daily tours offered from both San Juan and Orcas Islands throughout the summer. Most trips last five to six hours. Three resident pods, or families, of orcas are frequently spotted along these trips, along with a few strays. The whales are here in pursuit of migrating salmon. They have been extensively studied for more than 25 years; individual males are identifiable from distinctive markings on their tall dorsal fin. The excellent Whale Museum in Friday Harbor has a pamphlet with drawings showing these markings, and they also maintain a **Whale Hotline** for sightings and stranding information: (800) 562-8832. If you're heading out in your own kayak or other vessel, be sure to stay at least 100 yards from whales (it's the law) and even farther from seal and sea lion haul-out areas since the animals are easily spooked. The best time to see orcas is mid-June to mid-July, but they are periodically visible from mid-May to mid-September.

For local companies offering whalewatching voyages, see "Sports and Recreation" under San Juan Island and Orcas Island (below). In the peak season, be sure to make advance reservations for these popular trips. During the winter—when the whales are elsewhere—many of these companies offer wildlife viewing cruises.

ACCOMMODATIONS AND CAMPING

The San Juans are immensely popular in the summer, particularly during the peak season of July and August. If you plan a visit at these times, there may well be no room in the inn, and not a lot of mangers available either. Save yourself a lot of headaches by making reservations far in advance. At the older and more established B&Bs this means calling at least four months ahead of time for a mid-summer weekend reservation! If you're looking for space on Memorial Day, the Fourth of July, Labor Day, or during the Jazz Festival in late July, make reservations up to a year in advance. Do *not* arrive in Friday Harbor on a July Saturday afternoon expecting to find a place; you won't. Many of the resorts, inns, and cottages also offer weekly rates and require a minimum summertime stay of at least two nights (sometimes a week). Also note that most B&Bs on the San Juans cater almost exclusively to couples and do not allow kids. Families may want to head instead to Birch Bay (see the Northern Puget Sound chapter), where the facilities are lower-key and more kid-proof.

There are not a lot of motels on the San Juans—and none of the big motel chains; most places on the islands have just a few rooms, so space is at a premium. It also costs a premium, and only a few lodges cost less than $80 d. Hostel accommodations are available at Doe Bay Village Resort on Orcas Island. Several real estate companies on the islands offer weekly and monthly home rentals. Check the Seattle newspapers or the two local weekly papers—*The Journal of the San Juan Islands* and *The Islands' Sounder*—for vacation rentals.

In the winter months you'll find fewer fellow travelers, lower lodging rates (often 30% less), and less of a problem getting a room, but the weather won't be quite as inviting and things won't be as green. Winter holidays (especially Christmas to New Year's) are likely to be booked well in advance. See the accommodations charts for complete listings of places to stay on the three main islands. **San Juan Central Reservation,** tel. (360) 378-8773 or (888) 999-8773, is a good source for reservations, with dozens of B&Bs, vacation homes, and other lodging on the three main islands. Find them on the Web at www.fridayharbor.com.

Public campsites are most abundant on Orcas Island, but even these fill up; San Juan Island has only a handful, and they are generally completely reserved by the end of May (though private RV parks often have space).

INFORMATION AND SERVICES

Each of the three main islands has its own chamber of commerce office. For maps and other information before you arrive, call the **San Juan Islands Visitor Information Service** at (360) 468-3663 or (888) 468-3701, or look for them on the Web at www.guidetosanjuans.com. Another good online source is **www.islandcam.com** where you'll find live webcam images, up-to-date info, and links to other Web sites.

Two books by Marge and Ted Mueller are also useful: *The San Juan Islands Afoot & Afloat* and *The Essential San Juan Islands Guide.* Both are published by The Mountaineers (Seattle).

All phone calls among the various San Juan islands are local calls. The three main islands all have ATMs if you run short on greenbacks.

Fuel and Food

If you're driving around the islands, be sure to fill your tank in Anacortes before getting on the ferry. Because of the extra cost of shipping fuel here (and because they can get away with it) gas stations on the islands charge at least 30% more for gas than on the mainland. Similarly, prices for food are also higher. Save by stocking up in Anacortes.

FERRY SERVICE

If you can only take one ride aboard a **Washington State Ferry,** the trip from Anacortes to the San Juans should be the one. The scenery is so beautiful that even amateur photographers can get spectacular sunset-over-the-islands shots. In the summer, ferries leave Anacortes at least a dozen times a day 4:30 a.m.-12:20 a.m. stopping at Lopez, Shaw, Orcas, and Friday Harbor, in that order; it takes roughly two hours from Anacortes to Friday Harbor. Not every ferry stops on each island, but nearly all of them stop at Friday Harbor on San Juan Island. Ferries between Anacortes and Sidney, B.C., run twice a day in the summer and once a day the rest of the year. (Vehicle reservations are *required* for service between the San Juans and Sidney.) The ferries have food and booze onboard, and a duty-free shop can be found on ferries heading to British Columbia. For more information, call (360) 293-8166 in Anacortes, (206) 464-6400 in Seattle, or (888) 808-7977 statewide. Call (800) 843-3779 for automated information. In Victoria, call (604) 381-1551.

When to Travel

During the peak summer season for travel to the San Juans, it's wise to arrive at least two hours early on weekends, or an hour early on weekdays. On holiday weekends you may find yourself in line for up to five hours! Free parking is available at the Anacortes ferry terminal if you're heading over on foot or by bike. Both San Juan and Orcas Islands have excellent bus services, so you really don't need a car there anyway. The terminal usually has information on current campsite availability at parks on the San Juans (meaning they often say none are available) to help in planning where to stay that night. Avoid the crowds by traveling in midweek, early in the morning, late in the evening (except Friday evenings), or better yet, by foot, kayak, or bike.

The ferry system operates on a first-come, first-served basis, with reservations available only for the routes from Anacortes to Sidney, B.C., and from Orcas Island or San Juan Island to Sidney. No reservations for travel to the San Juans; just get in line and wait like everyone else. In Anacortes, tune your radio to **AM 1340** for broadcasts of current ferry status, including any backups or other problems.

Fares

Peak season fares to Friday Harbor, the last American stop, are $5.10 passengers, $21.75 car and driver. Bikes are $2.90 extra, and kayaks cost $7 more. Car-and-driver fares to the other islands from Anacortes are a few dollars less. Interisland ferries are free for passengers and bikes, and $9.25 for cars and drivers. Rates are lower in the off-season.

Ferry travelers are only charged in the westbound direction; eastbound travel within the San Juans or from the islands to Anacortes is free. (The only exception to this is for travelers leaving from Sidney, B.C.). If you're planning to visit all the islands, save money by heading straight to Friday Harbor, and then working your way back through the others at no additional charge.

Once a day, a ferry continues on from Orcas and Friday Harbor to Sidney, B.C.; fares are $4 passengers or $20.50 car and driver.

Private Ferries

The *San Juan Explorer,* tel. (360) 448-5000 or (800) 888-2535, is a popular way to reach the islands from either Seattle or Victoria. The passenger-only boat departs from Seattle's Pier 69 on daily cruises to the San Juans in the summer, less frequently the rest of the year. Roundtrip adult fares are $59 to Friday Har-

state ferry Evergreen State *at Friday Harbor, San Juan Island*

DON PITCHER

bor (San Juan Island), and $67 to Rosario Resort (Orcas Island). Get your tickets 14 days ahead to save on these rates. Transportation between Friday Harbor and Victoria is $44 roundtrip. A variety of travel-and-lodging packages are also available for trips to the islands on the *Explorer*. Discounts are available for seniors and kids.

San Juan Island Shuttle Express, tel. (360) 671-1137 or (888) 373-8522, operates a passenger ferry—the *Red Head*—connecting Bellingham with Orcas, Lopez, and San Juan Islands. Roundtrip fares are $33 adults, $29 seniors, and $27 students. The ferry runs daily late May-September. They also offer whalewatching cruises from Friday Harbor.

Emerald Sea Taxi, tel. (360) 378-2772, is a 30-foot boat that transports up to six passengers between the islands or to the mainland. **Island Transport Ferry Service** has private water-taxi service to all the San Juan Islands aboard a landing craft; call (360) 293-6060 for details.

P.S. Express, tel. (360) 385-5288, provides passenger-only service between Port Townsend and Friday Harbor. The boat leaves Port Townsend daily, April-Oct., and stays in Friday Harbor long enough for a quick three-hour visit, or you can overnight there and return to Port Townsend later. The charge is $49 roundtrip, bikes and kayaks $12.50 extra.

OTHER TRANSPORTATION

Boat Tours

The San Juans are famous as a boater's paradise, with relatively protected waters, good wind conditions, an abundance of coves and shoreline to explore, numerous state parks only accessible by boat, and gorgeous scenery. Many sailing charters and motorboat charters operate from the San Juans; see the specific islands for details. In addition, you'll find boat tours of the San Juans from Bellingham and Anacortes; see visitor centers in these cities for specifics.

The **Mosquito Fleet,** tel. (206) 252-6800, has day tours from Everett to San Juan Island; see **Everett** for details.

One of the more interesting cruise boats is the *Snow Goose,* a Bellingham-based 65-foot research vessel operated by two marine biologists. They offer a range of trips, including five-day voyages around the San Juans where you'll get a firsthand look at marinelife and how researchers study life in Puget Sound. Call (360) 733-9078 for details.

Catalyst Cruises offers luxurious six-day cruises of the San Juans and eight-day cruises of the San Juans and Gulf Islands. These take place aboard the 59-foot motor yacht *Sacajawea.* It carries up to eight passengers and offers more personalized trips than the larger tour boats. Fares are $250 pp/day double occupancy, including all meals. Trips depart from Seattle or Anacortes; call (253) 537-7678 or (800) 670-7678 for details.

By Air

Kenmore Air, tel. (206) 486-1257 or (800) 543-9595, has scheduled floatplane flights from Lake Union in Seattle and Lake Washington in Kenmore to Friday Harbor and Roche Harbor on San Juan Island, to Fisherman Bay on Lopez Island, and to Rosario Resort and West Sound on Orcas Island. Kenmore Air also offers charter service to other destinations in the San Juans and flightseeing trips.

West Isle Air, tel. (360) 293-4691 or (800) 874-4434, has daily wheeled-plane flights from Seattle or Bellingham to most of the San Juan Islands. They also offer flightseeing trips over the San Juans from Bellingham. **Aviation Northwest,** tel. (360) 733-3727, also flies from Bellingham to the three main islands.

Harbor Air, (360) 675-6666 or (800) 359-3220, offers frequent scheduled wheeled-plane service from Sea-Tac and Oak Harbor to Friday Harbor and Orcas Island.

Charter service and flightseeing is offered by **Aeronautical Services Inc.,** tel. (360) 378-3110 or (800) 378-5566, out of San Juan Island Airport. If several folks are flying together, this may be your least expensive air-travel option.

Sound Flight, (425) 255-6500 or (800) 825-0722, provides service between Renton and the San Juans. **Northwest Seaplanes,** tel. (425) 277-1590 or (800) 690-0086, also flies out of Renton, with daily service to the San Juans, including Rosario, West Sound, Friday Harbor, and Roche Harbor.

SAN JUAN ISLAND

The largest island in the archipelago, San Juan Island is about 20 miles long and seven miles wide, covering 55 square miles. Friday Harbor, the only incorporated town in the chain, is also the county seat, the commercial center of the San Juans, and home to half of the island's 5,300 residents. Picturesque Friday Harbor sits along the west side, its marina protected by Brown Island. This is a U.S. Customs port of entry, as is Roche Harbor on the other side of the San Juan Island.

PIG WAR SIGHTS

In one of the stranger pieces of history, the killing of a pig by an American settler nearly set off a war between the U.S. and Britain; see the special topic for details on this bizarre incident. Fortunately, conflict was averted and the San Juan Islands were eventually declared American territory. One doesn't have to look far to find how similar minor incidents set off dramatic consequences: in

THE PIG WAR

Because of vague wording in the Oregon Treaty of 1846—the document that established the boundary between the U.S. and Canada—the San Juan Islands were not only the subject of a territorial dispute, but also the stage for an international incident commonly referred to as the "Pig War." Britain's claim to the islands came in 1791 when Capt. George Vancouver sailed into Puget Sound; Capt. Charles Wilkes did the same for America in 1841. The Oregon Treaty noted that the boundary would extend "to the middle of the channel which separates the continent from Vancouver's Island." Simple enough one might think, but there were actually two channels. Rosario Strait went between the mainland and the San Juans, while Haro Strait separated the San Juans from Vancouver Island. Both sides saw the islands as theirs.

The Hudson's Bay Company established a salmon-curing station on San Juan Island in 1850, followed by a sheep ranch three years later. American settlers began moving onto the island about the same time, and by 1859 around 25 of them occupied land here. The relationship between the two sides was strained, since both considered the other to be there illegally.

Porker Trouble

In June of 1859 one of the American settlers, Lyman A. Cutler, got tired of a Hudson's Bay Company-owned hog rooting in his potato patch, so he shot and killed it. English authorities insisted that Cutler pay for the porker, and when he refused, insisted that he be brought to trial in Victoria. This was the spark that almost set off a war. The American settlers asked for military protection and received a company of soldiers under Capt. George E. Pickett—the man who later gained fame as the Confederate general who led the charge up Cemetery Ridge during the Battle of Gettysburg. The British responded quickly, and by the end of August that year they had a force of 2,140 troops, five warships, and 167 heavy guns arrayed against the American army's 461 soldiers and 14 cannons.

Fortunately, cooler heads prevailed and the pig was the only casualty. President James Buchanan sent the head of the army, Gen. Winfield Scott, to seek a peaceful settlement, and both sides agreed to leave just a token force of men while negotiations proceeded. The British built a stockade and encampment about midway on the west side of the island in beautiful Garrison Bay, while the Americans established their camp at the very southern tip on the most windy, exposed part of the island. The soldiers, bored most of the time because no shots were fired, gradually turned down the animosity level and took turns entertaining the other side. The troops remained there until the matter was settled by arbitration 12 years later by Kaiser Wilhelm I of Germany, who gave the San Juans to the United States.

Both the English and American camps are now part of the San Juan Islands National Historic Park.

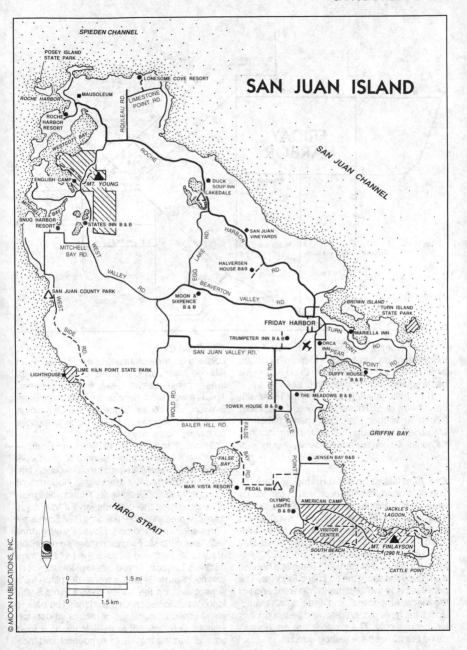

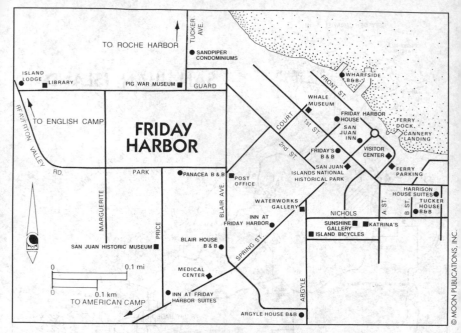

1854 an emigrant's cow was butchered near Wyoming's Fort Laramie by a Miniconjou Indian; when he refused to surrender to the U.S. Army, a battle ensued that left 29 soldiers dead.

The small, privately run **Pig War Museum,** on the corner of Tucker and Guard, tel. (360) 378-4830, is open Mon.-Sat. noon-6 p.m. from Memorial Day through Labor Day. Admission is $4 adults, $3 seniors and students, free for kids under five.

San Juan Island National Historical Park
The sites where the American and British forces were based are now part of the San Juan Island National Historical Park, with headquarters on Spring St. in Friday Harbor, tel. (360) 378-2240. Open daily 8 a.m.-5 p.m. Memorial Day through Labor Day, and Mon.-Fri. 8:30 a.m.-4:30 p.m. the rest of the year. The office houses a small exhibit about the so-called Pig War. The park itself is in two sections on different ends of the island: American Camp and English Camp. Both sites have picnic areas and beach access for day use only. The grounds are open year-round but do not have campgrounds.

American Camp
Located on the southeast corner of San Juan Island, American Camp sits on a windswept grassy peninsula six miles from Friday Harbor. This is a wonderful place on a sunny summer afternoon, with both the Cascades and Olympics in view. It's a deliciously lonely place to explore on a rainy winter day.

Two buildings remain at American Camp—an officer's quarters and a laundress' quarters—along with a defensive fortification (redoubt) that was constructed by Henry M. Roberts, of *Roberts' Rules of Order* fame. A long white picket fence circles the grounds, and a trail leads downhill past the old Hudson's Bay Company Farm site on Grandma's Cove. Other nature trails take off to Mt. Finlayson (hardly a mountain at just 290 feet) and through the forests along **Jackle's Lagoon,** or you can explore driftwood-jammed **South Beach,** a wonderful place for a sunset walk on the sandy shores. This is the longest public beach on the island. The park is also home to thousands of rabbits whose ancestors were brought to the islands as a food source, but the inevitable happened and they keep multiplying. Birders come to American Camp to see the only nesting **Eurasian skylarks** in the U.S.; they were introduced to Vancouver Island early in this century and a small number ended up here.

The **American Camp Visitor Center** is open daily 8 a.m.-5 p.m. in the summer, and Thurs.-Sun. 8:30 a.m.-4:30 p.m. in winter. It houses historical exhibits.

The tip of the peninsula is **Cattle Point Interpretive Area,** where you'll find a picnic shelter housed in an old powerhouse, and trails to a nearby lighthouse and beach.

English Camp
Ten miles from Friday Harbor on the northwest side of the island, English Camp (also known as British Camp) includes a restored hospital, a picturesque reconstructed blockhouse right on the water's edge, commissary, an impressive formal garden, and a small white barracks. The blockhouse and barracks are open daily 8:30 a.m.-4:30 p.m. in the summer, but closed the rest of the year. The location is a beautiful one, with protected waters on both sides of Bell Point—a sharp contrast to American Camp—and spreading maple trees overhead. The mile-long **Mt. Young Trail** leads from English Camp to the old British cemetery where six Royal Marines are buried, and then up through second-growth forests to 650-foot Mt. Young with fine vistas of the archipelago from the top. An almost-level nature path also heads a mile out to the tip of **Bell Point.**

OTHER SIGHTS

Museums
The Whale Museum, 62 1st St. N in Friday Harbor, tel. (360) 378-4710, has whale and porpoise displays including the genealogy of Puget Sound orcas, full skeletons of a baby gray whale, plus adult killer and minke whales. Watch a fine video on orcas, learn about snoring whales, examine whale fetuses, learn how whales use echolocation, and how they mate. You can also "adopt" one of the hundred or so local orcas. The museum is open daily 9 a.m.-6 p.m. Memorial Day through September, and daily 10 a.m.-6 p.m. the rest of the year. Admission costs $5 adults, $4 seniors, $2 ages 5-18 and students;

free for under age five. There's also a gift shop in the museum with games, T-shirts, and jewelry. If you spot a whale anywhere around the San Juans, swimming or stranded, call the museum's 24-hour **Whale Hotline:** tel. (800) 562-8832.

San Juan Historical Museum, 405 Price St. in Friday Harbor, tel. (360) 378-3949, is open Thurs.-Sun. 1-4 p.m. May-Sept., and Tuesday and Thursday 10 a.m.-2 p.m. the rest of the year. Housed in an 1890s farmhouse, the museum includes fascinating antiques, old photos, and historical artifacts, plus old farm equipment outside. Also on the property are the first county jail, a log cabin, and other historic buildings. Entrance is $2 adults, $1 kids.

Roche Harbor Resort
Located on the north end of San Juan Island, Roche Harbor Resort is a delicious step into the past. In 1886, John S. McMillin established the Roche Harbor Lime & Cement Co., mining lime deposits from 13 hillside quarries and processing the lime in brick-lined kilns along the shore. By the 1890s this was the largest lime works west of the Mississippi and required 4,000 acres of forest just to keep the kilns running (each kiln burned 10 cords of wood every six hours!). McMillin built a company town for his employees, had warehouses that extended hundreds of feet into the bay, and operated a general store on the wharf. His Hotel de Haro began as a log bunkhouse, but later grew into the distinctive three-story wood structure of today. It was twice visited by President Theodore Roosevelt, in 1906 and 1907, and his signature can still be seen on the guestbook. The limestone quarries operated till 1956, when they were essentially mined out. The beautiful white-clapboard hotel has been restored and is fronted by a formal garden with rose trellises. McMillin's home is now a waterside restaurant, facing the protected harbor filled with sailboats. The old general store is still in use, the remains of several kilns are visible, and the simple cottages of McMillin's employees are now rented out to guests. The only affronts to this slice of living history are the ugly condos that have sprouted nearby.

Take some time to explore the area around the hotel (now on the National Register of Historic Places), and the little New England-style Our Lady of Good Voyage Chapel—built in 1892, and the only privately owned Catholic church in the nation. The bizarre family **mausoleum** ("Afterglow Vista" no less) is approximately a mile from the hotel. Located north of the cottages and a quarter-mile hike up a dirt side road, the mausoleum's centerpiece is a stone temple packed with Masonic symbology, and containing the family's ashes in chairs around a limestone table. There's even a broken column symbolizing the "unfinished state" of life, but the planned bronze dome was never added to this once-grandiose mausoleum. Step out of the past at the fly-in aviation community nearby, with planes taxiing down Cesna Ave. and parked in hangers next to nearly every house.

Lime Kiln Point State Park

A good spot to watch for whales is from Lime Kiln Point State Park along Haro Strait on the island's west side; it's the only park in the country dedicated exclusively to whalewatching. Sit here long enough on a summer day (it may be quite a while) and you're likely to see killer whales (orcas), and possibly minke and pilot whales, Dall's porpoises, or harbor porpoises. Rangers are usually at the park in the summer and fall and can answer your questions. The small white lighthouse was built in 1914 and has a foghorn that announces its presence constantly. Researchers use the lighthouse to watch for whales and to determine if boats are affecting their behavior. If there aren't any whales to watch, you can just take in the vistas that stretch to Victoria. No camping is available at the park. Call (360) 378-2044 for more information.

Bald eagles live on the island year-round; look for them between Eagle Cove and Cattle Point on the island's east side.

Winetasting

San Juan Vineyards, tel. (360) 378-9463, is housed in a century-old schoolhouse three miles out Roche Harbor Road. The vineyards here should start producing in 2000, so wines they sell now are all made from eastern Washington grapes. Stop by for wine tasting daily noon-7 p.m.

No vineyards at **The Island Wine Company,** next to the ferry dock in Friday Harbor, tel. (360) 378-3229 or (800) 248-9463, but you can sample wines bottled under their San Juan Cellers label. Open daily 10 a.m.-6 p.m.

SPORTS AND RECREATION

Bikes and Moped Rentals

Although many folks bike around San Juan Island, it isn't as bike-friendly as slower-paced Lopez. Be ready for narrow roads and speeding cars; skinny-tire bikes are probably not a good idea for most folks here. Rent bikes to cruise around San Juan Island from **Island Bicycles,** 380 Argyle St., tel. (360) 378-4941. **Island Scooter & Bike Rentals,** across from the ferry landing in Friday Harbor, tel. (360) 378-8811, rents both bikes and mopeds. **Suzie's Mopeds** above the ferry parking in Friday Harbor, tel. (360) 378-5244 or (800) 532-0087, rents mopeds March to October.

Sea Kayaking

A number of very reputable companies lead one-day and multi-day sea kayaking tours from San Juan Island: **Elakah! Expeditions,** tel. (360) 734-7270 or (800) 434-7270; **Northwest Outdoor Center,** tel. (206) 281-9694 or (800) 683-0637; **Outdoor Odysseys,** tel. (360) 378-3533; **San Juan Kayak Expeditions,** tel. (360) 378-4436; and **Sea Quest Expeditions,** tel. (360) 378-5767. Several of these also lead trips elsewhere in Puget Sound and even off Baja.

In addition to the above companies, several local outfits also depart San Juan Island on one-day sea kayak tours: **Crystal Seas Kayaking,** tel. (360) 378-7899; **Leisure Kayak Adventures,** tel. (360) 378-5992 or (800) 836-1402; **San Juan Excursions,** tel. (360) 378-6636 or (800) 809-4253; and **Roche Harbor Marine Activity Center,** tel. (360) 378-2155 or (800) 451-8910. Expect to pay around $60 for an all-day tour. Do-it-yourselfers can rent sea kayaks from **Emerald Seas Aquatics,** Spring St. Landing, tel. (360) 378-2772.

Whalewatching

The best time to look for whales around the San Juans is during the summer months, especially in June and July. Local companies that provide scheduled whalewatching trips from Friday Harbor include: **Bon Accord Charters,** tel. (360) 378-5921 or (800) 677-0751; **San Juan Boat Tours,** tel. (360) 378-3499 or (800) 232-6722; **San Juan Excursions,** tel. (360) 378-6636 or

(800) 809-4253; **San Juan Island Shuttle Express,** tel. (360) 671-1137 or (888) 373-8522; and **Western Prince Cruises,** tel. (360) 378-5315 or (800) 757-6722. Whalewatching trips generally cost around $45 for a four-hour trip.

Roche Harbor Marine Activity Center, tel. (360) 378-2155 or (800) 451-8910, offers whale-watching trips out of Roche Harbor.

Sailing and Fishing Charters

Sailing charters are available in Friday Harbor from **Charters Northwest,** tel. (360) 378-7196; **Friday Harbor Yacht Sales & Charters,** tel. (360) 378-4047 or (800) 742-6061; and **Sails Aloft,** tel. (360) 378-8333 or (888) 588-7245. The *Arequipa* is a classic 65-foot wooden yacht that departs Mariella Inn's dock on day cruises; call (360) 378-6868 or (800) 700-7668 for details. Two companies with historic motor-yacht cruises are **Classic Passages Northwest,** tel. (360) 378-3012, and **Island Navigator,** tel. (360) 301-3000.

For fishing and other boat charters from Friday Harbor, contact: **Trophy Charters,** tel. (360) 378-2110, or **Buffalo Works,** tel. (360) 378-4612.

Additional fishing charters—and day-trips to Victoria—are available through **Roche Harbor Marina,** tel. (360) 378-2155 or (800) 451-8910, the largest marina in the San Juans, and a U.S. Customs port of entry for boaters coming in from Canada. Facilities here include permanent and guest moorage, showers and laundry, plus a store, restaurant, bar, and full-service resort. Motorboats, canoes, kayaks, and paddle-boats are available for rent.

Diving

Emerald Seas Aquatics, Spring St. Landing, tel. (360) 378-2772, is a full-service dive center with dive boat charters, training, equipment, and scuba tank filling. Locals claim that the San Juans offer the finest cold water diving on earth, and note that Jacques Cousteau called them his second-favorite place to dive.

Other Sports and Recreation

San Juan Llama Encounters, tel. (360) 378-4869, offers llama hikes from Lakedale Resort near Roche Harbor. The **San Juan Golf & Country Club,** 2261 Golf Course Rd., tel. (360) 378-2254, is a nine-hole public course.

Fitness fanatics might want to take advantage of one-day memberships ($10) for **San Juan Fitness and Athletic Club,** 435 Argyle Ave., tel. (360) 378-4449. Facilities include racquetball, handball, and squash courts, aerobics and strength-training equipment, a sauna, steam room, jacuzzi, and juice bar.

ACCOMMODATIONS

During the summer it's a good idea to make reservations several months ahead of time to be

SEATTLE/KING COUNTY CONVENTION AND VISITORS BUREAU

Sailboats provide photographic opportunities in the San Juans.

assured of a bed, particularly on weekends. **San Juan Central Reservations,** tel. (360) 378-8773 or (888) 999-8773, (www.fridayharbor.com), is an excellent source for up-to-date lodging information. They make reservations for dozens of local B&Bs, inns, resorts, and vacation homes. Call the **Bed & Breakfast Association of San Juan Island** hotline at (360) 378-3030 for lodging availability at a dozen of the finest local establishments; find them on the Web at www.san-juan-island.net. The **San Juan Island B&B Guild,** tel. (360) 378-8383, makes reservations for five local B&Bs.

Many of San Juan Island's resorts, inns, and cottages also offer weekly rates, and many require a minimum summertime stay of at least two nights (sometimes a week). For additional places with weekly rates, contact: **San Juan Island Vacation Rentals,** (360) 378-5060 or (800) 992-1904, or **Windermere Real Estate,** tel. (360) 378-3600 or (800) 262-3596.

B&Bs and Inns

Bed and Breakfasts are listed below alphabetically, and unless otherwise noted, all serve a full breakfast and do not allow young children.

Arbutus Lodge B&B, 1827 Westside Rd. N, tel. (360) 378-8840, contains two guest rooms with private baths in a new home on six acres along the west side of the island. $110-130 s or d. Professional massage is available.

Built in 1910, **Argyle House B&B,** 685 Argyle St. in Friday Harbor, tel. (360) 378-4084 or (800) 624-3459, is a craftsman home just a short distance from downtown. Located on an acre of land, the B&B has three guest rooms with private baths ($85-125 d), a private honeymoon cottage ($145 d), and a hot tub.

Blair House B&B, 345 Blair Ave. in Friday Harbor, tel. (360) 378-5907 or (800) 899-3030, is a beautifully restored 1909 home on wooded grounds with antique furnishings, an outdoor pool, and hot tub. Guests can stay in seven rooms in the house or in a separate cottage (kids okay here); $85-155 d. Kids okay in the cottage.

The 1926 Tudor-style **Duffy House B&B,** 760 Pear Point Rd. in Friday Harbor, tel. (360) 378-5604 or (800) 972-2089, overlooks the Olympics and the Strait of Juan de Fuca from its lonely location along Griffin Bay. There's a

private beach and even a resident bald eagle nest tree that is active most summers. The five guest rooms all have private baths; $95-125 s or d. Two-night minimum on summer weekends.

Friday's B&B, 35 First St., tel. (360) 378-5848 or (800) 352-2632, is one of the newer places to stay, but it's in one of Friday Harbor's oldest buildings (built in 1891). Great if you want to be close to the restaurants and shops, but it can be a bit on the noisy side at times. The 11 guest rooms have shared or private baths and continental breakfasts; $90-175 s or d. Kids are welcome.

Gaia's Grace, 6040 Yacht Haven (near Roche Harbor), tel. (360) 378-3732, is a rustic two-bedroom cabin with woodstove and kitchen; $125 s or d. Two-night minimum in summer.

Halvorsen House B&B, 1165 Halvorsen Rd. in Friday Harbor, tel. (360) 378-2707 or (888) 238-4187, is a contemporary home with three guest rooms, private baths, plus a luxury suite with a kitchen and jacuzzi; $99-130 s or d. Kids accepted.

Right in town, **Harrison House Suites B&B,** 235 C St. in Friday Harbor tel. (360) 378-5587 or (800) 407-7933, offers privacy in the form of four nicely appointed suites for $125-195. They sleep 4-10 people each, and are a good deal for families. A jacuzzi is available for guests, and kids are welcome. Two-night minimum on summer weekends.

Hillside House B&B, 365 Carter Ave. in Friday Harbor, tel. (360) 378-4730 or (800) 232-4730, a spacious contemporary home with seven guest rooms and private baths, is notable for its full-flight aviary and fine harbor views. The home sits on an acre of wooded land just a half-mile from town; $75-175 s or d. Two-night minimum in summer.

Jensen Bay B&B, Jensen Bay Rd., tel. (360) 378-5318, is a 1920s one-bedroom home on five acres of land. The entire house (sleeps four) is rented for $165, including a make-your-own breakfast. Kids are welcome.

Longhouse B&B, 2387 Mitchell Bay Rd., tel. (360) 378-2568, is an eclectic home with two bedrooms ($100-110 d), private baths, and full breakfasts. A rustic cottage ($110 for four) has a kitchen (no breakfast here) with a deck along Mitchell Bay. Kids okay in the cottage.

Mariella Inn & Cottages, tel. (360) 378-6868 or (800) 700-7668, sits on nine gorgeous acres overlooking Friday Harbor. The elegantly restored 1902 home contains 11 guest rooms and suites—all with private baths—for $125-275 d. Also here are 12 immaculate cottages (from tiny studios to two-bedrooms) for $175-375 d. Kids are welcome in cottages, and all guests have access to the hot tub. Bikes, kayaks, and sailboats are available for rent. A buffet breakfast is served.

The Meadows B&B, tel. (360) 378-4004, is an 1892 farmhouse out in the country three miles east of Friday Harbor. The two large guest rooms share a bath. $85 s or d.

The **Moon & Sixpence B&B,** 3021 Beaverton Valley Rd., tel. (360) 378-4138, is a turn-of-the-century farmhouse on 15 acres. Two guest rooms have private baths ($90 s or d), and a three-level water tower ($125 d) has been converted into a cozy space. All rooms include private baths and a continental breakfast. The home has an arty feeling supplemented by the adjacent weaver's studio. Kids accepted; two-night minimum in summer.

Out in the open fields near American Camp, **Olympic Lights B&B, tel. (360) 378-3186,** is an 1895 Victorian farmhouse with Olympic Mountains views, five guest rooms, and shared or private baths. $70-105 s or $75-110 d. Two-night minimum in summer.

Panacea B&B, 595 Park St. in Friday Harbor, tel. (360) 378-3757 or (800) 639-2762, is a 1907 craftsman bungalow with four guest rooms, plus private baths and entries; $135-165 s or d.

San Juan Inn B&B, 50 Spring St., tel. (360) 378-2070 or (800) 742-8210, just a half block from the ferry, has been in the lodging business since 1873 and still retains its original Victorian charm. The nine guest rooms and two suites have shared or private baths, a central garden with a hot tub, and continental breakfasts; $85-195 d.

States Inn B&B, tel. (360) 378-6240, is a country home on a working horse, sheep, and alpaca ranch seven miles northwest of Friday Harbor. The 10 guest rooms have private baths, and kids are accepted; $85-125 s or d.

Tower House B&B, 1230 Little Rd., tel. (360) 378-5464 or (800) 858-4276, is a Queen Anne-style country home on 10 acres. Two guest suites have private baths, and a vegetarian breakfast is served; $95-120 s or d.

Trumpeter Inn B&B, a mile west of Friday Harbor, tel. (360) 378-3884 or (800) 826-7926, is a large contemporary home on five acres of pastoral land with a pond. The five guest rooms have private baths and a garden hot tub; $95-135 s or d.

Tucker House B&B, 260 B St. in Friday Harbor, tel. (360) 378-2783 or (800) 965-0123, within walking distance from the ferry, is a quaint 1898 Victorian home with three upstairs rooms ($85 s or $95 d), plus three cottages ($125-150) with private baths and woodstoves. Guests can use the hot tub, and kids are welcome in the cottages.

For a real waterfront room, **Wharfside B&B,** tel. (360) 378-5661, has two staterooms aboard the 60-foot sailing vessel *Jacquelyn,* docked at the Friday Harbor Marina; kids are welcome. $95 d. Two-night minimum in summer

Resorts

The classic 19th century **Roche Harbor Resort/Hotel de Haro** in Roche Harbor, tel. (360) 378-2155 or (800) 451-8910, has a range of lodging options, including rooms with shared baths ($79-84 d), suites with private baths ($89-135 d), and cottages with kitchens ($130-195 d). Avoid their condos that have destroyed the view in this historic harbor. Guests wanting to sleep where Roosevelt slept should book room 2A in the hotel. Facilities at the resort include a restaurant, tennis courts and an Olympic-size outdoor pool, plus motorboat, canoe, kayak, and paddle-boat rentals. The lounge has live music and dancing on summer weekends. See "Sights," above, for more on this historic resort.

A favorite of the just-married set is **Lonesome Cove Resort,** nine miles north of Friday Harbor, tel. (360) 378-4477. Here are six pretty little waterfront cabins with kitchens, delightful scenery, and plenty of private space. No phones or TVs; $95 d to $150 for six people. Kids are accepted. Five-night minimum in summer.

Snug Harbor Resort, tel. (360) 378-4762, is a cozy resort along Mitchell Bay on the west side of the island. A variety of lodging is available, including studio units with kitchenettes ($99-125 d), a treehouse cabin ($189 d), two-bedroom cabins ($185 for four people), and even a RV

($89 d). All of these are on the water, and guests can borrow a rowing skiff or canoe. Boat and kayak rentals are available.

Located along three small lakes in the center of the island, **Lakedale Resort,** tel. (360) 378-2350 or (800) 617-2267, has six attractive two-bedroom lakeside log cabins with kitchens and shared bath houses. Rates are $190 d ($15 pp for additional people). Other amenities include a hot tub, continental breakfast basket, rowboats, canoes, and paddleboats.

Mar Vista Resort, 2005 False Bay Dr., tel. (360) 378-4448, has beachfront one-, two- and three-bedroom cabins on 20 acres. All contain kitchens and have access to the private beach; $125 s or d. Open mid-April to mid-October.

Inns and Other Lodging
Discovery Inn, 1016 Guard St. in Friday Harbor, tel. (360) 378-2000 or (800) 822-4753, charges $99-110 s or d for motel rooms, some with kitchenettes. A hot tub is available.

Friday Harbor House, 130 West St., tel. (360) 378-8455, charges $187-277 s or d, and features fireplaces, jacuzzi tubs, fridges, windows on the harbor, a continental breakfast, and two-night minimum on weekends.

The Inn at Friday Harbor, 410 Spring St., tel. (360) 378-3031 or (800) 752-5752, has an indoor pool, sauna, jacuzzi, exercise room, fridges and microwaves; $104-185 d. The same folks also run **The Inn at Friday Harbor Suites,** a few blocks away at 680 Spring Street. One- or two-bedroom suites here with fridges and microwaves are $120-240 d. Guests staying at the suites can use the pool and other facilities at the inn.

Harmony Cottage, seven miles west of town, tel. (360) 378-5283, is a dramatically situated private cottage near Lime Kiln Lighthouse. Inside is a full kitchen and an upstairs loft bedroom; $225 for up to six people.

Orca Inn; 700 Mullis St. in Friday Harbor, tel. (360) 378-2724 or (888) 541-6722, has the cheapest rooms around: $39-79 s or d. Basic, but clean and comfortable.

Sandpiper Condominiums, 570 Jenson Alley, Friday Harbor, tel. (360) 378-5610, has studio and one-bedroom apartments with kitchenettes; $65-85 s or d. No phones.

CAMPING AND RV PARKS

Pitch a tent at the 12-acre **San Juan County Park,** a mile north of Lime Kiln State Park along West Side Rd., for $16; open year-round. (The 1998 film *Practical Magic* was filmed here.) Because this is the only public campground on the island, you'll need to make reservations ahead if you plan a summer visit. Call (360) 468-4413 for reservations not less than seven days in advance and not over two months ahead of time. You may find space on a summer weekday, but weekends are almost always fully reserved, especially in August. The park has a boat ramp and drinking water, but no showers or RV hookups. It is located along **Smallpox Bay,** so-named when a ship left two sailors with the disease on the island to prevent them from contaminating the rest of the crew. When they were helped by local Indians who had no immunity to the disease, smallpox spread quickly across San Juan Island. The feverish victims jumped into the bay to cool off and died of pneumonia. The few survivors fled the island.

Park that RV or pitch a tent at the spacious **Lakedale Resort,** 2627 Roche Harbor Rd., tel. (360) 378-2350 or (800) 617-2267, with secluded waterfront tent, bike, and RV sites, plus rentals of bikes, boats, and camping gear. It's located 4.5 miles from Friday Harbor, and open mid-March to mid-October. Cyclists can pedal in to **Pedal Inn,** 1300 False Bay Dr. (five miles from Friday Harbor), tel. (360) 378-3049, where wooded campsites around a pond are just $5. Open May-Oct., with showers, a small store, and a laundromat. No cars allowed.

More campsites and RV hookups are available at **Snug Harbor Marina Resort,** 2371 Mitchell Bay Rd., tel. (360) 378-4762, plus rentals of skiffs, fishing tackle, and crab pots. A small store has supplies and dive tank refills. **Town and Country Mobile Home Park,** 595 Tucker Ave. N (one mile from Friday Harbor), tel. (360) 378-4717, has tent sites and RV hookups, with showers and a laundry. Coin-operated showers are also available at the **Friday Harbor Marina** and **Roche Harbor Resort Marina.** During the Jazz Festival, RVs can park in the fairgrounds parking lot (fee charged).

FOOD

Given the enormous numbers of visitors to Friday Harbor, it comes as no surprise that the town has a wide range of restaurants and eateries, including some real gems. Head up almost any street and you're likely to find something of interest. Unless otherwise noted, all the restaurants listed below are located in Friday Harbor.

Breakfast and Lunch
Front Street Cafe, 101 Spring St., tel. (360) 378-2245, is *the* hangout place in town, with a fun atmosphere, espresso and pastries, and a ferry-side location. This is one of the best local places for breakfast, and their lunches (homemade soups, salads, sandwiches, and more) are also dependable.

Fat Cat Cafe, 1 Nichols St. Walk, tel. (360) 378-8646, is a very popular breakfast and lunch stop with outside tables for summertime al fresco dining. Next door is **Gray Matter,** an espresso cafe with Internet access.

Madelyn's Bagel Bakery & Espresso, tel. (360) 378-4545, has a perfect location on A St. above the ferry parking area. Slip out of your vehicle for a fresh bagel and cream cheese, or a Starbucks latte and cinnamon roll.

Seafood
Springtree Cafe, Spring St., tel. (360) 378-4848, serves a varied menu that includes fresh seafood and vegetarian specials in a simple setting with checked tablecloths and a heated patio. Open daily for lunch, dinner, and Sunday brunch (in summer).

Duck Soup Inn, five miles north of Friday Harbor on Roche Harbor Rd., specializes in superbly done local seafood, along with a constantly changing and eclectic menu with an international flavor. The country setting adds to the relaxed and romantic atmosphere. This is where locals go for a celebration night. Dinner entrees are $20-26; open summers only. Call (360) 378-4878 for reservations.

The Place Next to the Ferry Cafe, tel. (360) 378-8707, gets the nod from locals who come here for a creative seafood-rich menu. It changes periodically; dinner entrees are $14-20. The restaurant has a great location: on the marina next to the ferry dock.

Westcott Bay Seafood Farm, 4071 Westcott Dr. (a mile east of Roche Harbor), tel. (360) 378-6388, supplies local restaurants with gourmet oysters and clams; get them at the source for the freshest available.

American
One of the most popular eating establishments on San Juan Island is **Friday's Crabhouse,** directly across from the ferry. Open summers only, this is the place for finger-lickin' fish and chips, shrimp cocktails, or grilled crabcakes. Service is fast, making this a fine last-minute stop while waiting for your ship to come in.

If you're simply in search of a great all-American burger, fries, and shake, head to **Vic's Drive Inn,** 25 2nd St., tel. (360) 378-2120.

The **Front St. Ale House,** 1 Front St., tel. (360) 378-2337, sits next door to San Juan Brewing Company, and their ales are all on tap here. The huge menu includes burgers, fish and chips, pasta, steak, and other crowd-pleasing favorites. Very popular for lunch and dinner.

Katrina's, tel. (360) 378-7290, is a bit away from the downtown mob scene in a cozy house at 135 2nd Street. Open for lunch, dinner, and Sunday brunch, the meals are reasonably priced and always good.

International
Roberto's Italian Restaurant, 205 A St., consistently cranks out distinctive and delectable homemade Italian dishes, including some with a very spicy kick (notably the "pasta from hell"). Reasonable prices; reservations required: tel. (360) 378-6333.

For very good pizzas, big salads, and Italian food where everything is under $10, try **The Friday Harbor Bistro** at 35 1st St.; tel. (360) 378-3076. Outside dining, too.

Amigo's, 40 B Spring St., tel. (360) 378-5908, serves reasonably priced Mexican meals in a nothing-fancy atmosphere. Eat on the patio on a sunny day, but don't bother showing up in the winter; the owners are in Mexico.

Markets
A **farmers market,** tel. (360) 378-4874, is held on summer Saturdays 10 a.m.-1:30 p.m. at the

county courthouse, with lots of organic fruits, vegetables, berries, and flowers.

Giannagelo Farms, on the north end of the island, grows impressive produce and makes herbal vinegars, dried herbs, and other natural treats.

Waterfront Deli & Market, on the corner of Front and Spring, tel. (360) 378-8444, has good sandwiches and salads to go. The island's largest grocer is **King's Market,** 160 Spring St., tel. (360) 378-4505, with fresh meats and fish, a fine deli, fishing tackle, and sportswear.

EVENTS

Jazz Festival
Each year thousands of people crowd into Friday Harbor for the main event—the Dixieland Jazz Festival. Held the third weekend in July, it features a dozen different bands and begins with a Thursday night street dance, and Friday morning promenade down Spring Street. Concerts are held at four locations in Friday Harbor and Roche Harbor, with shuttle bus service among the sites. If you plan to attend, make lodging reservations many months ahead of time (up to a year ahead for the fanciest B&Bs), and leave your car in Anacortes. Entrance to these concerts isn't cheap: around $50 for all three days. Call (360) 378-5509 for details on this year's Jazz Festival events.

Other Events
The **Fourth of July** brings a variety of fun events, including a parade, pig barbecue contests with celebrity judges, a 10-km race, music, dancing, plus evening fireworks to Friday Harbor. (The best local Fourth of July fireworks, however, are over at Roche Harbor Resort.) The season ends with more fun at the four-day **San Juan County Fair** in mid-August, featuring a sheep-to-shawl race, chicken and rabbit races, music, livestock judging, and, of course, carnival rides. Each **Memorial Day** Friday Harbor has a popular parade with speeches.

THE ARTS

San Juan Community Theatre & Arts Center, 100 2nd St., tel. (360) 378-3211, is the cen-

ter for local performing arts. **Summerfest** takes place here every Wed.-Sun. evening from early July to Labor Day, with classical music, plays, drama, and folk music. Watch first-run films at **Royal Theatre,** 209 Spring St., tel. (360) 378-4455.

Galleries and Books
Sunshine Gallery, 85 Nichols St., tel. (360) 378-5819, is a cooperatively run gallery with excellent local artwork. A large, contemporary gallery, **Waterworks Gallery,** 315 Argyle, tel. (360) 378-3060, has paintings, prints, watercolors, and sculpture by island and international artists. **Annikin,** 165 1st St., tel. (360) 378-7286, is another good contemporary art gallery. **The Garuda & I,** 60 1st St., tel. (360) 378-3733, is a unique gallery with ethnic artifacts, beautiful jewelry, and a large cage filled with chirping zebra finches.

Friday Harbor has three good bookstores: **Boardwalk Books,** upstairs from Front St. Cafe, tel. (360) 378-2787; **Griffin Bay Bookstore,** 40 1st St., tel. (360) 378-5511; and **Harbor Bookstore,** in Cannery Landing, tel. (360) 378-7222.

INFORMATION AND SERVICES

The **San Juan Island Chamber of Commerce Visitor Centre** is directly across from the ferry terminal in the Friday's Marketplace complex, tel. (360) 378-5240. Open daily in the summer for local info; closed winters. Find them on the Web at www.sanjuanisland.org. **San Juan Information Center,** at Cannery Landing next to the ferry dock, tel. (360) 378-8887 or (800) 887-8387, operates the San Juan Transit buses and tours. They also stock local brochures, and can arrange whalewatching trips, boat and kayak rentals, scenic flights, and fishing charters.

Store bags in the coin-operated **lockers** opposite the ferry terminal next to Friday's. You can do your laundry at **Sunshine Coin-Op Laundry,** 210 Nichols Street.

TRANSPORTATION

Warning: Friday Harbor has a big parking problem in the summer, and the city *strictly* enforces a two-hour downtown parking limit. Get back to your car three minutes late and you'll probably have a ticket pasted on the windshield.

By Ferry

The **Washington State Ferry** stops right in Friday Harbor on San Juan Island; tel. (360) 378-4777 or (888) 808-7977. Call (800) 843-3779 for automated info. See "Ferry Service," above, for details on ferry service and fares to the islands, including the private ferries.

Buses and Tours

You don't need a car on San Juan Island. **San Juan Transit,** tel. (360) 378-8887 or (800) 887-8387, operates shuttle buses around the island April-September. Service is daily in mid-summer; weekends only till mid-May. The cost is $7 roundtrip or $10 for an all-day pass, and buses can carry bikes and luggage. Their office is next to the Friday Harbor ferry in the Cannery Landing Building.

Soul of the Islands tel. (360) 378-2942, leads half-day historic tours. **Island Girl Tours** offers walking tours of Friday Harbor; tel. (360) 378-2219.

Car Rentals and Taxis

Rent cars from **Inn at Friday Harbor,** tel. (360) 378-3031; **M&W Auto Rentals,** tel. (360) 378-2886; and **West Isle Rent A Car,** tel. (360) 378-2440. Call **San Juan Taxi,** tel. (360) 378-3550, or **San Juan Limo Service,** tel. (360) 378-6777 for local rides year-round. On-the-water service is provided by **Fairweather Water Taxi and Tours,** tel. (360) 378-8029 in Roche Harbor.

ORCAS ISLAND

Known as "The Gem of the San Juans," Orcas Island is considered the chain's most beautiful island. It is definitely the hilliest—drive, hike, or bike to the top of 2,409-foot Mt. Constitution for a panoramic view from Vancouver, B.C., to Mt. Rainier. Orcas's most prominent mansion, Rosario Resort, regularly graces the pages of national travel magazines and employs almost 200 people, making it San Juan County's largest private employer. The island—named by a Spanish explorer in 1792 for the viceroy of Mexico, not for the orca whales common in neighboring waters—is home to 3,200 people.

Towns

The ferry docks at the cluster of cafes and gift shops called **Orcas Village,** located on the south end of this horseshoe-shaped island. The tiny settlement of **West Sound** is eight miles northwest of the ferry landing, and has a large marina, along with a couple of stores. Approximately four miles west of here is another little gathering place, **Deer Harbor,** with a handful of resorts and B&Bs, a couple of restaurants, charter sailboats, and kayak rentals. It's appropriately named for the many black-tailed deer in the area and throughout the San Juans. Orcas Island is almost cut in half by East Sound, and the town of **Eastsound** sits at its head. This is the main village on the island, and the place to go for groceries, gas, and a wide choice of gift shops, cafes, and galleries.

SIGHTS

Moran State Park

Near Eastsound, 4,605-acre Moran State Park is most popular for its steep paved road to the 2,407-foot summit of **Mt. Constitution,** where you'll discover a 52-foot stone tower constructed by the Civilian Conservation Corps in the 1930s. This is the highest point on the San Juans and offers a commanding view in all directions, from Mt. Rainier to British Columbia. If you've ridden to the top by bike, it's an exciting ride back down. Another popular attraction is **Cascade Falls,** where Cascade Creek drops into a deep pool 100 feet below. A quarter-mile path leads to the falls, and you can continue uphill to two less impressive falls.

The park has more than 30 miles of other hiking trails, from easy nature loops to remote and rugged out-of-the-way hikes. Get a park map for details on all of these. A four-mile loop trail circles Mountain Lake, offering a chance to see black-tailed deer, particularly in the morning and early evening. You can climb to the summit of Mt.

ORCAS ISLAND

POINT LAWRENCE

DOE ISLAND STATE PARK

MORAN STATE PARK

MOUNTAIN LAKE

CASCADE FALLS

DOE BAY VILLAGE RESORT

DOE BAY RD.

OBSTRUCTION PASS COUNTY PARK

BUCK BAY FARM B & B

OBSTRUCTION PASS

LIEBER HAVEN MARINA RESORT

MT. CONSTITUTION (2,407 ft.)

SAND DOLLAR INN

ORCAS ISLAND ARTWORKS

OLGA

SPRING BAY INN

BARTWOOD LODGE

SANDCASTLE GUEST HOUSE

BUCKHORN FARM BUNGALOW

HORSESHOE HWY.

CASCADE LAKE

OTTER'S POND B&B

WONDER O' THE WIND

CASCADE HARBOR INN

ROSARIO RESORT

EAST SOUND

DOLPHIN BAY RD.

EASTSOUND

NORTH BEACH

SMUGGLER'S VILLA RESORT

KANGAROO HOUSE B & B

MT. BAKER RD.

ENCHANTED FOREST RD.

DOUBLE MT. B & B

3 mi

3 km

CHESTNUT HILL INN B&B

HORSESHOE HWY.

BEACH HAVEN RESORT

WEST BEACH RESORT

WALKING HORSE COUNTRY FARM

CROW VALLEY SCHOOL MUSEUM

TURTLEBACK FARM INN

CROW VALLEY RD.

WEST SOUND

OLD TROUT INN B&B

WEST SOUND B&B

WINDSONG B&B

HAZELWOOD B&B

LIBERTY CALL B&B

ORCAS HOTEL

ORCAS

FERRY LANDING

FERRY TO SHAW AND LOPEZ ISLANDS.

HARBOR RD.

KINGFISH INN B&B

DEER HARBOR INN B&B

DEER HARBOR

DEER HARBOR RD.

CABINS-ON-THE-POINT

THE PLACE AT CAYOU COVE B&B

DEER HARBOR RESORT

WEST SOUND

HARNEY CHANNEL

FERRY TO SAN JUAN ISLAND.

© MOON PUBLICATIONS, INC.

Constitution from Mountain Lake on a 3.7-mile path, or save your legs by catching a ride to the top and hiking downhill instead.

Moran State Park has several lakes that are popular for fishing, motorless boating, and swimming in the cold water. Rent rowboats and paddleboats (summers only) at the largest of these, Mountain and Cascade Lakes, where you'll find good trout and kokanee fishing. Both also have boat ramps and fishing supplies. Cascade Lake has a roped-off swimming area in the summer, and the park is one of the most popular camping places in the state; see below for details.

Magnificent **Rosario Resort**—described below—is near the park and worth a visit.

Museums
Located in a cluster of six pioneer log buildings, the **Orcas Island Historical Museum** on North Beach Rd. in Eastsound, tel. (360) 376-4849, has a collection of relics from 1880s pioneer homesteads, Chinese immigrants, and philanthropist Robert Moran. Of particular note are the Indian artifacts that includes carvings and baskets. Open Mon.-Sat. 1-4 p.m. June-Sept., Fri.-Sat. in May and the first half of October; closed mid-October through April.

The small **Crow Valley School Museum,** tel. (360) 376-4260, three miles southwest of Eastsound on Crow Valley Rd., is open Thurs.-Sat. 1-4 p.m. from Memorial Day to Labor Day. Built in 1888, this classic one-room school has old desks, a great school photo collection, report cards, school clothes, toys, and other pieces from a bygone era. No Internet access here.

SPORTS AND RECREATION

Bike and Moped Rentals
Rent bikes to cruise around Orcas Island from **Dolphin Bay Bicycles** in Orcas Landing, tel. (360) 376-4157, or **Wildlife Cycles** in Eastsound, tel. (360) 376-4708.

Sea Kayaking
Shearwater Adventures, tel. (360) 376-4699, is a long-established company offering kayak tours departing from Rosario Resort, Deer Harbor Resort, and Doe Bay Resort. In addition, they have seminars and multi-day classes. Stop by their store in Eastsound for kayak and camping gear, along with natural history books.

Osprey Tours in Eastsound, tel. (360) 376-3677, is a distinctive company that uses hand-built traditional Aleutian-style kayaks and offers half-day and all-day tours. **Black Fish Paddlers,** tel. (360) 376-4947, is a small kayak tour company run by a local marine biologist.

Rent single or double kayaks in Eastsound from **Crescent Beach Kayaks,** tel. (360) 376-2464, or **Orcas Kayak Rental,** tel. (360) 376-3767. If you're planning on launching your own kayak, be forewarned that you may be subject to a launching fee ($5 at Deer Harbor) if you aren't on public lands.

Whalewatching
Local companies that provide scheduled whale-watching trips from Orcas Island include: **Deer Harbor Charters** in Deer Harbor, tel. (360) 376-5989 or (800) 544-5758; **Navigator,** at Orcas Hotel, tel. (360) 376-4300; and **Orcas Island Eclipse Charters** in Orcas Landing, tel. (360) 376-4663 or (800) 376-6566. Expect to pay around $45 for a four-hour whalewatching cruise. Be sure to bring your binoculars, camera, and warm clothes.

Boat Charters
Deer Harbor is the main center for skippered sailboat charters on Orcas Island, with four companies: **Amante Sail Tours,** tel. (360) 376-4231; **Deer Harbor Charters,** tel. (360) 376-5989 or (800) 544-5758; and **Eclipse Charters,** tel. (360) 376-4663. Deer Harbor Charters also rents skiffs. Skippered sailing charters (and bareboat charters) are available from **Valkyrie Sailing Charters** in Eastsound, tel. (360) 376-4018. **Quarter Moon Cruises,** tel. (360) 376-2878, has day excursions and multi-night cruises aboard a classic 55-foot motor yacht based in Deer Harbor.

Other Recreation
Walking Horse Country Farm, tel. (360) 376-5306, offers guided trail rides on their distinctive Tennessee walking horses, as well as carriage rides. The **Orcas Island Country Golf Club,** tel. (360) 376-4400, is a nine-hole public course on the Horseshoe Hwy. southwest of Eastsound.

ACCOMMODATIONS

During the summer it is a good idea to make reservations several months ahead of time to be assured of a space, particularly on weekends. Call the Orcas Island Chamber of Commerce **lodging hotline** at (360) 376-8888 for availability. It's updated on a daily basis in the summer.

Many of the resorts, inns, and cottages also offer weekly rates, and many require a minimum summertime stay of at least two nights (sometimes a week). For additional homes available by the week ($400-1,200), contact **Lindholm Real Estate,** tel. (360) 376-2202, or **Windermere Real Estate,** tel. (360) 376-2262.

For classic lodging, stay at beautiful **Orcas Hotel,** a three-story turn-of-the-century hotel overlooking the ferry landing. In addition to these, the **Camp Moran Vacation House** inside Moran State Park sleeps 10 people; call (360) 902-8600 for details.

Bed and Breakfasts

Unless otherwise noted, all B&Bs listed below serve a full breakfast and do not allow young children. They are listed alphabetically.

Buck Bay Farm B&B in Olga, tel. (360) 376-2908, is a farmhouse on five acres with four guest rooms and a jacuzzi; $85-115 s or d. Kids by arrangement.

Located near Rosario Resort, **Cascade Harbor Inn,** tel. (360) 376-6350 or (800) 201-2120, has new studio, one- and two-bedroom units, all with private waterfront balconies. Larger units contain full kitchens and are ideal for families. Rates are $90-270 s or d, including a continental breakfast. Two-night minimum in summer.

Chestnut Hill Inn B&B, Orcas, tel. (360) 376-5157, is a grand Victorian-era country farmhouse. The five guest rooms ($145-195 s or d) have fireplaces and private baths. Also here is a private cottage for $125 s or d (no breakfast). Massage is available.

Deer Harbor Inn B&B, tel. (360) 376-4110, is a contemporary log lodge surrounded by an old apple orchard. The eight guest rooms ($99-115 s or d) contain private baths. Three private cottages ($169-189 s or d) have fireplaces and a two-night minimum in summer. Kids are accepted in cottages. All rooms include a continental breakfast and access to the jacuzzi.

Double Mountain B&B, west of Eastsound, tel. (360) 376-4570, is a contemporary home atop a 600-foot hill with amazing vistas of the San Juans from the deck. The three guest rooms have private baths; $85-135 s or d.

A contemporary hilltop home on 12 acres, **Hazelwood B&B,** Victoria Valley Rd., tel. (360) 376-6300 or (888) 360-6300, offers impressive vistas of the Olympics and Puget Sound. The three guest rooms have private baths and a big

Orcas Hotel,
Orcas Island

DON PITCHER

continental breakfast. Two-night minimum in summer; $95-125 s or d. Kids accepted.

The **Kangaroo House,** north of Eastsound Village, tel. (360) 376-2175, was built in 1907 and bought in the '30s by a sea captain, Harold Ferris, who picked up a young female kangaroo on one of his Australian voyages. The kangaroo is long gone, but the name remains in this attractive old home with a big fireplace, period furnishings, decks, a garden hot tub, and friendly owners. The five guest rooms have private or shared baths; $75-125 d.

Kingfish Inn B&B, tel. (360) 376-4440, has three guest rooms with private baths for $125-135 d. Breakfast is served downstairs in the Westsound Cafe. Kids okay.

L'Aerie B&B, on the east end of the island, tel. (360) 376-4647, is a modern hillside home with impressive views. The two guest rooms have private baths and decks; $100 d.

Liberty Call B&B, tel. (360) 376-5246, is a turn-of-the-century home near the ferry terminal at Orcas Landing. The comfortable home sits on two acres, and is a good place to see deer in the evenings or to feed the pygmy goats. Two suites offer waterfront views and private baths. Kids are welcome and rates are reasonable: $85 d.

The Old Trout Inn B&B, tel. (360) 376-8282, offers a number of luxurious lodging options, including three suites ($125-165 d) in the elegant country home, a private cottage ($175 d) on a pond, and three townhouse units (a.k.a. Anchorage Inn; $165 d) with private decks and their own beach. All of these have hot tubs.

Otter's Pond B&B, near Moran State Park, tel. (888) 893-9680, a romantic country home on a 20-acre pond, features an enclosed hot tub and five guest rooms with private baths; $75-150 d.

The Place at Cayou Cove B&B, tel. (360) 376-3199 or (888) 596-7222, has a private cottage (kids okay) and two guest rooms in a 1913 home at Deer Harbor. Guests have access to a private beach and tennis court. Rates are $150 d in the home, and $195 d in the cottage.

Sandcastle Guest House, tel. (360) 376-2337, is a one-bedroom waterside home on the north end of the island with a private beach and continental breakfast. Two-night minimum; $95-105 s or d. Kids are welcome.

Sand Dollar Inn, tel. (360) 376-5696 or (877) 376-5696, near the ferry landing and once owned by a ferry boat captain, is an historic home with four large upstairs rooms offering good views of Buck Bay. Private baths; $125 s or d.

Spring Bay Inn B&B, near Obstruction Pass, tel. (360) 376-5531, is a new shoreside lodge on 60 acres with five guest rooms, private baths, fireplaces, a hot tub, and free kayak tours; $175-225 s or d. Kids accepted. Two-night minimum in summer.

Situated on 80 acres in the shadow of Turtleback Mountain, **Turtleback Farm Inn,** on Crow Valley Rd., tel. (360) 376-4914, has 11 guest rooms in two buildings—all with private baths. It's a comfortable farmhouse atmosphere; $80-210 d. Two-night minimum in summer.

An historic 1917 schoolhouse on three acres, **Windsong B&B** in West Sound, tel. (360) 376-2500, features three large guest rooms with shared or private baths and fireplaces; $115-140 s or d. Two-night minimum in summer.

Resorts

See the chart for a complete listing and prices at Orcas Island resorts. Two of the most interesting places are described below.

Rosario Island Resort & Spa, tel. (360) 376-2222 or (800) 562-8820, is a nationally known getaway five miles south of Eastsound, and the largest resort on the islands. It's well worth a look even if you can't afford to stay here. This perfect island setting makes it a very popular outdoor wedding location. The resort is housed in a turn-of-the-century mansion that once belonged to shipbuilder and Seattle mayor Robert Moran. Moran wasn't blessed with musical talent, so he played the 1,972-pipe organ like a player piano and none of his guests were the wiser; organ concerts are still held frequently. The historic building—on the National Register of Historic Places—has been beautifully restored, offering fine dining, an indoor pool, jacuzzi, sauna, fitness facility, and massage (extra fee). Rooms cost $175-388 s or d.

Located on a 50-acre spread, the wonderfully funky **Doe Bay Village Resort** in Doe Bay (20 miles from ferry terminal); tel. (360) 376-2291, stands alone on the San Juan Islands, a throwback to the '70s with its rustic cabins, yurts, tent-cabins, and hostel set on scenic Doe Bay.

ORCAS ISLAND RESORTS AND LODGES

Accommodations are listed from least to most expensive. Rates are often lower during the winter months. Bed and breakfasts are described in the text.

BUDGET TO INEXPENSIVE

Doe Bay Village Resort; Doe Bay (20 miles from ferry terminal); tel. (360) 376-2291; $16 pp in dorm, $45-100 s or d in other rooms; see text for full description

MODERATE

Outlook Inn; Eastsound; tel. (360) 376-2200 or (888) 688-5665; $74-230 s or d rooms or suites with shared or private baths in beautifully restored 1888 hotel, period furnishings, bay views, AAA approved

Orcas Hotel; Orcas; tel. (360) 376-4300 or (800) 672-2792; $79-105 d for modest rooms with shared baths; $120-180 d with private baths; beautifully restored Victorian inn, package tours available

North Beach Inn; Eastsound; tel. (360) 376-2660; $80 s or d; $115-145 for four people; very private beachfront cottages on a beautiful beach, fireplaces, kitchens, kids okay, seven-day minimum stay in July and August, two-day minimum rest of year, closed December to mid-February, reserve far ahead

EXPENSIVE

The Beach House; Westsound; tel. (360) 376-6720 or (800) 956-6722; $85-125 s or d; three guest rooms in 1904 waterfront home, comfortable decor, two-night minimum in summer.

Beach Haven Resort; Enchanted Forest Rd.; tel. (360) 376-2288; $85-200 for up to six in 16 rustic log cabins and apartments with kitchens, along beach with old-growth forest, one-week minimum stay in summer, rowboat and canoe rental, kid-friendly

Bartwood Lodge; tel. (360) 376-2242; $89-179 s or d; waterfront lodge, tennis court, private dock, fishing charters

Lieber Haven Marina Resort; near Olga; tel. (360) 376-2472; $90-110 for up to four; cottages and apartments with kitchens, protected bay, kayak and boat rentals, fishing charters, kids okay

---

No dolled-up rooms, pseudo-Victorian architecture, or antique vases here! There are even treehouses for the really adventurous. Most accommodations use a central shower house and communal kitchen. $16 pp in dorm, $45-100 s or d in other rooms.

Doe Bay emphasizes relaxation, with a friendly new-age atmosphere that brings couples and families back again and again. What other place would decorate its cafe with lava lamps? Featured attractions are the sauna and creekside mineral-spring jacuzzis ($6 for those who are not staying here), both decidedly clothing-optional. You can sit inside the wood-fired sauna with its octagonal stained-glass windows, and then head to one of three mineral baths with sulfurous water pumped from the ground.

The restaurant (open daily in summer, weekends in winter) cooks vegetarian and seafood meals three times a day, but service can be slow and haphazard. Tent and RV hookups are available. Sea kayak tours ($40 for three hours) and bike rentals are also available; ask about renting a bike here and dropping it off at the ferry (or vice versa). Professional massage is also available.

CAMPING

Orcas Island's finest campsites are at **Moran State Park,** with four different campgrounds along Cascade and Mountain Lakes, plus a separate bike-in area. Tent sites are $11 with showers; no RV hookups. Due to the park's popular-

Deer Harbor Inn; eight miles southwest of ferry terminal; tel. (360) 376-4110; $99-115 s or d; modern log house, decks overlooking Deer Harbor, indoor pool, continental breakfast, no kids, AAA approved

Buckhorn Farm Bungalow; near Eastsound; tel. (360) 376-2298; $100 s or d; restored country cottage, full kitchen, woodstove, in-the-orchard setting. Kids welcome, two-night minimum.

PREMIUM

Landmark Inn; Eastsound; tel. (360) 376-2423; $130-160 s or d; condo units, private decks, kitchenettes, two-night minimum in summer, AAA approved

West Beach Resort; two miles west of Eastsound; tel. (360) 376-2240 or (877) 937-8224; $130-160 for up to four; two-bedroom beachside cottages, kitchens, woodstoves, boat rentals, one-week minimum stay in July and August

Cascade Harbor Inn; near Rosario Resort; tel. (360) 376-6350 or (800) 201-2120; $110-130 s or d in standard rooms; $180-320 for for 4-6 people in one- and two-bedroom suites with fireplaces and kitchens; all rooms with private decks and continental breakfast in summer

LUXURY

Cabins-on-the-Point; Eastsound; tel. (360) 376-4114; $175-195 s or d for four romantic beachfront cabins (two with hot tub), full kitchens, woodstoves, sea kayak, two-night minimum, kids okay; $195 d for a large two-bedroom house with full kitchen

Rosario Island Resort & Spa; five miles south of Eastsound; tel. (360) 376-2222 or (800) 562-8820; $175-388 s or d; see text for full description

Smuggler's Villa Resort; Eastsound; tel. (360) 376-2297 or (800) 488-2097; $195-210 for up to four people in condos with Haro Strait views, outdoor pool, two hot tubs, sauna, fireplaces, kitchens, tennis and basketball courts, private beach, kids welcome

Deer Harbor Resort; 200 Deer Harbor Rd.; tel. (360) 376-4420 or (888) 376-4480; $199-399 d; waterfront cottages with kitchenettes and private hot tubs, outdoor pool, boat rentals, continental breakfast, two-night minimum in summer

Walking Horse Country Farm; West Beach Rd.; tel. (360) 376-5306; $200 for four people; spacious contemporary two-bedroom home, antiques furnishings, 27 acres of pastures, horse rides available, kitchen

---

ity, reservations are required in the summer months. All sites are pre-assigned, so check in at the pay station across from Cascade Lake when you first arrive. Call (800) 452-5687 for reservations ($6 extra). The campground is open year-round.

Obstruction Pass County Park is a tiny place with a boat ramp, a beach, and several walk-in campsites a half-mile from the road. No reservations or water. The park is located at the end of Obstruction Pass Rd., 2.5 miles southeast of Olga.

The decidedly funky **Doe Bay Village Resort,** near Olga, tel. (360) 376-2291, has tent and RV sites.

West Beach Resort, three miles west of Eastsound, tel. (360) 376-2240, has campsites and RV hookups (reservations accepted) along a scenic beach. Also here is a marina with boat rentals, sea kayak tours, fishing and scuba supplies, and groceries.

FOOD

The "big city" on Orcas—Eastsound—has the best choice of food on the island, though you'll find a scattering of fine restaurants and cafes elsewhere.

Orcas Landing and Deer Harbor

When you step off the ferry at Orcas, the grand old **Orcas Hotel** faces you. Inside is an excellent little cafe and bakery for light meals, pastries, and espresso, along with a larger dining room/pub for sumptuous seafood dinners and other fare. Open for all three meals; call (360) 376-4300 for today's specials.

Deer Harbor Inn, at Deer Harbor (of course), tel. (360) 376-4110, is a spacious place with a comfortable atmosphere and outstanding meals. You can get something as simple as freshly baked bread and homemade soups, or choose a full dinner from the blackboard listing today's specials. There's always something from the sea and a vegetarian entree.

Eastsound Area

Comet Cafe, tel. (360) 376-4220, is a very popular breakfast and lunch hangout, with outside tables to enjoy a big pastry and espresso on a sunny day.

For Mexican food, **Bilbo's Festivo,** tel. (360) 376-4728, is something of a local legend. They're open daily for lunch and dinner, with distinctive handcrafted furniture, tasty Mexican/Southwest fare, mesquite grilled meats, seafood, and fresh-fruit margaritas. Outside dining is available in the courtyard. Dinner entrees are $8-15.

Get inexpensive but well-prepared traditional Italian meals and Northwest seafood ($10-18 dinner entrees) at **La Famiglia Ristorante,** tel. (360) 376-2335, and good pizzas at **Portofino Pizzeria,** tel. 376-2085.

Ship Bay Oyster House, a short ways east of Eastsound, tel. (360) 376-5886, may be the best place to get fresh oysters in the San Juans. A recent expansion has turned this old farmhouse overlooking Ship Bay into a spacious place that attracts both visitors and locals. The restaurant cooks up a variety of fresh-from-the-sea daily specials, and the appetizer list always includes fresh oysters from Buck Bay. Dinner entrees are $15-19.

Enjoy excellent Northwest cuisine at **Christina's** in Eastsound, tel. (360) 376-4904, located upstairs and directly behind the gas station. The menu changes daily, and there's a patio out back overlooking East Sound. Dinner entrees are $22-28; stop by at lunch for lighter and more reasonably priced meals.

The East End

Cafe Olga, inside the Orcas Island Artworks building south of Moran State Park, has inex-pensive and delicious home-style lunches. The food covers a broad spectrum: sandwiches, vegetarian dishes, quiche, pasta, ethnic dishes, espresso, and their justly famous blackberry pie. Guaranteed to please. You also won't want to miss the adjacent cooperative gallery. For more vegetarian meals, head to **Doe Bay Art Cafe** in Doe Bay Village, tel. (360) 376-2291; see "Accommodations," above, for more on this unique place.

Rosario Resort & Spa, five miles south of Eastsound, tel. (360) 376-2222 or (800) 562-8820, has spectacular views and fine dining nightly ($18-25 entrees), plus a very popular Friday night seafood buffet and Sunday champagne brunch. Reservations required.

Markets

For groceries, film, and other essentials, stop by the **Island Market** in Eastsound. This is the largest grocery store in the islands, with an in-store bakery and deli.

The **Orcas Island Farmers Market** is held at Eastsound's Village Square Saturday 10 a.m.-3 p.m., April to October. Come here for local produce, flowers, crafts, and clothing. More fresh organic produce is available on Wednesday near the ferry landing in Orcas Village. **Homegrown Market** in Eastsound, tel. (360) 376-2009, has natural foods and a deli with daily specials and salads.

EVENTS AND ENTERTAINMENT

Eastsound—like nearly every small town in the U.S.—has a fun parade on the **Fourth of July,** followed by boat races, music, and fireworks. The town also features **sailboat races** on Friday nights in the summer. Every Thursday at noon during July and August, head to Emmanuel Episcopal Church in Eastsound for a free **Brown Bag Concert.**

The **Orcas Theatre & Community Center,** which was built entirely with donated funds, hosts a variety of events nearly year-round in Eastsound, from concerts by nationally known musicians to theatrical performances and productions for kids. For ticket and schedule info, phone (360) 376-2281. Check out the latest movies at **Sea View Theatre,** tel. (360) 376-5724, in Eastsound.

SHOPPING

Orcas has a number of craft shops and galleries kept well supplied by the artists and craftspeople who live there. Olga's artist co-op is **Orcas Island Artworks,** tel. (360) 376-4408, with an assortment of locally made arts and crafts in an old barn at the junction of Horseshoe Hwy. and Doe Bay Rd. (south of Moran State Park). Upstairs is **Temenos Books & Music,** where the emphasis is on contemplative volumes.

Darvill's Rare Print Shop in Eastsound, tel. (360) 376-2351, sells prints from the 18th and 19th centuries, plus limited-edition prints by contemporary Northwest artists. **The Right Place** in Eastsound, tel. (360) 376-4023, has an assortment of local crafts, from pottery to blown glass. Next door is **The Naked Lamb,** tel. (360) 376-4606 or (800) 323-5262, where you'll discover hand-spun yarns, one of the largest selections of dyed-in-the-wool yarns in the nation, plus hand-knit sweaters, socks, and other goods. Not far away is **Orcas Island Pottery,** tel. (360) 376-2813, the oldest pottery studio in the Northwest. **Crow Valley Pottery,** is housed in an 1866 log cabin between Orcas Landing and Eastsound, and features the works of more than 50 artists, with pottery, paintings, jewelry, and other locally produced pieces; tel. (360) 376-4260.

INFORMATION AND SERVICES

Request local info from the **Orcas Island Chamber of Commerce** at (360) 376-2273. You'll find local brochures inside Eastsound's **Pyewacket Books,** tel. (360) 376-2043; while you're here check out the new and used books. **Darvill's Bookstore** in Eastsound, tel. (360) 376-2135, has a big choice of books on the San Juans. **Airport Center Self Service Laundry** is located at the southwest end of the airport and just north of Eastsound, tel. (360) 376-2478.

TRANSPORTATION

By Ferry
The **Washington State Ferry** docks at Orcas Landing on the south end of the island; call (360) 376-2135 or (888) 808-7977. Call (800) 843-3779 for automated info. For fare and schedule information see "Ferry Service" at the beginning of this chapter.

Other Transport and Tours
Cascade Auto Rental, tel. (360) 376-4176, has rental cars on the island. **Orcas Island Taxi and Car Rental,** tel. (360) 376-8294, offers cab service and rental vehicles. **Gem Island Taxi,** tel. (360) 376-5883, is the other local cab company.

Magic Air Tours, tel. (360) 376-2733, has scenic biplane tours from Eastsound Airport. See "Sports and Recreation," above, for bike and moped rentals on Orcas.

LOPEZ ISLAND

Because of its gently rolling hills and lack of traffic, Lopez (pop. 1,500) is very popular with cyclists; views of the surrounding islands and mountains to the east and west poke out from every turn. Despite being one of the largest San Juan islands, Lopez is probably the friendliest—waving to passing cars and bicycles is a time-honored local custom, and failure to wave will label you a tourist as surely as a camera around your neck and rubber thongs.

The business center for the island is **Lopez Village,** where you'll find a scattering of cafes, shops, a museum, stores, and especially real estate offices—which should tell you something about the island's newfound popularity. A few more businesses can be found along pretty Fisherman Bay—filled with sailboats and other craft—but the rest of the island is essentially undeveloped.

SIGHTS

Lopez's main attraction is its rural, pastoral countryside. The long stretches of hills, pastures, orchards, and woods might just as well be New England. Cows and sheep are a common sight, including some exotic long-haired breeds at **Cape St. Mary Ranch** on the southeast end of the island. Also of interest are the bright fields of daffodils, tulips, lilies, gladiolus, and delphiniums at **Madrona Farms,** near the intersection of Richardson and Davis Bay Roads. Bucolic Lopez Island is a delightful place to explore; unfortunately many of the beaches are privately owned and closed to the public.

Lopez Island Vineyards on Fisherman Bay Rd., tel. (360) 468-3644, is a small family winery that grows organic grapes and produces wines from these, along with grapes from eastern Washington. Open summers Wed.-Sun. noon-5 p.m., and Mon.-Fri. noon-5 p.m. in fall and spring; closed Christmas to mid-March.

A Taste of History

Lopez Historical Museum on Weeks Rd. in Lopez Village, tel. (360) 468-2049, is open Wed.-Sun. noon-4 p.m. during July and August; and Fri.-Sun. in May, June, and September. Closed the rest of the year. The museum contains local flotsam and jetsam: the first car driven on the island, old farm equipment, and historical photos. Outside, find a reef net boat and an aging tractor.

A couple of other buildings are worth a gander on the island. The **Lopez Library** is housed in a bright red and white 19th century schoolhouse

Fisherman's Bay, Lopez Island

ARCHIE SATTERFIELD

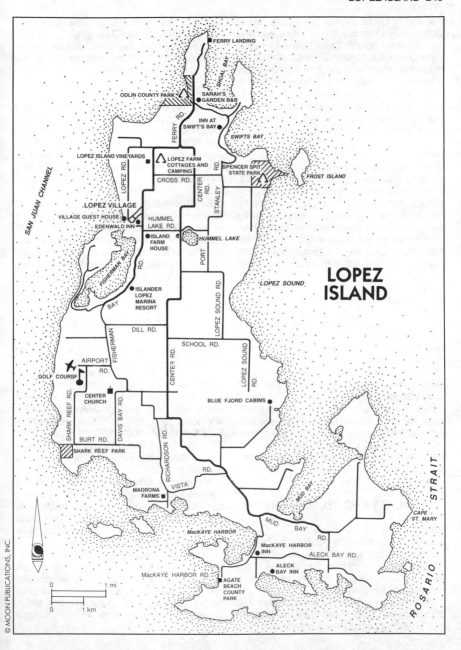

just east of Lopez Village. The **Lopez Island Community Church** in Lopez Village was built in 1904 and is notable for its steeple that splits into four cupolas. **Center Church,** built in 1887, is a simple white wood structure surrounded by a picket fence and next to a hilltop cemetery. The church is home to both Catholics and Lutherans (what would Martin Luther think of this?) and is approximately two miles south of Lopez Village on Fisherman Bay Road.

Parks

On the east side of the island, the 130-acre **Spencer Spit State Park,** tel. (360) 468-2251, has a mile-long beach for good year-round clamming, beachcombing, hiking, and picnicking. Also here are seasonal campsites, mooring buoys, and an RV dump station. A brackish lagoon frequently has ducks and shorebirds, and black-tailed deer are a common sight in the evening. Call (800) 452-5687 for campsite reservations ($6) extra.

Other campsites and a boat launch are available at **Odlin County Park** at the north end of the island, just a mile from the ferry landing.

Very few of Lopez's beaches are open to the public. One exceptional exception is **Agate Beach,** located on the south end of the island at the end of MacKaye Harbor Road. This little park provides access to a beach filled with colorful wave-rounded stones. Another fine small park is **Shark Reef Recreation Area,** located at the south end of Shark Reef Rd. on the southwest side of the island. An easy half-mile path takes you through one of the few old-growth stands of trees left on Lopez to the rocky coastline. This is a good place to look for harbor seals, sea lions, and bald eagles.

SPORTS AND RECREATION

Biking

A favorite local activity is pedaling the 30-mile loop around Lopez Island. Once you get beyond the steep initial climb from the ferry dock, the rest of the island consists of gently rolling hills, a perfect place for families.

Bike rentals and tours are available from **The Bike Shop on Lopez,** in Lopez Village, tel. (360) 468-3497, and **Lopez Bike Works,** along Fish-

erman Bay just south of Lopez Village, tel. (360) 468-2847. **Cycle San Juans,** tel. (360) 468-3251, also guides bike tours, and will deliver rental bikes to you at the ferry terminal or your lodging place for a small fee.

Sea Kayaking

Lopez Kayaks, tel. (360) 468-2847, has sea kayak rentals and tours from Fisherman Bay. Inquire at Lopez Bicycle Works on Fisherman Bay Road. They can deliver the kayak to you anywhere on the island. **MacKaye Harbor Inn,** MacKaye Harbor Rd., tel. (360) 468-2253, also rents kayaks.

Other Recreation

Harmony Charters, tel. (360) 468-3310, has a luxurious 63-foot motor yacht available for $200 pp/day including meals and crew. **Kismet Sailing Charters,** tel. (360) 468-2435, has a 36-foot sailboat available. **Lopez Island Golf Club,** tel. (360) 468-2679, is a nine-hole public course on Airport Road.

ACCOMMODATIONS

During the summer it is a good idea to make reservations a month or more ahead of time to be assured of a space, particularly on weekends. Many of the resorts, inns, and cottages also offer weekly rates. For furnished homes with weekly rates, contact: **Island House Realtors,** tel. (360) 468-3401; **Coldwell Banker Real Estate,** tel. (360) 468-3311 or (800) 472-3311; or **Village Guest House** tel. (360) 468-2191. Expect to pay $750-2,000 per week in the summer months.

Aleck Bay Inn B&B, tel. (360) 468-3535, has a sundeck overlooking Aleck Bay. Other amenities include a hot tub, pool table, and private beach, plus kayak and mountain bike rentals. A full breakfast is served and dinners are available. The four guest rooms are $89-169 d.

Blue Fjord Cabins, tel. (360) 468-2749 or (888) 633-0401, has two modern cabins with full kitchens in a wooded setting. Spectacular views of Jasper Bay from the gazebo, and a fine place to relax and soak up the quietude; $95 d. Three-night summer minimum. This is not a B&B.

Surrounded by floral gardens, **Edenwild Inn B&B,** tel. (360) 468-3238, is a contemporary Victorian-style inn right in Lopez Village. The eight rooms have private baths; $100-155 s or d. A full breakfast is served and kids are welcome.

Located a mile south of the ferry, the **Inn at Swifts Bay,** tel. (360) 468-3636, is a Tudor-style home with five guest rooms and three suites, (private or shared baths) plus a private beach, hot tub, and sauna. A gourmet breakfast is served; $95-175 d. No kids.

It isn't a B&B, but **Island Farm House** Hummel Lake Rd., tel. (360) 468-2864, has two rooms with private baths on a 12-acre farm; $50-75 d. Kids are welcome.

Islander Lopez Marina Resort, Fisherman Bay Rd., tel. (360) 468-2233 or (800) 736-3434, $89-259 s or d, has motel-style units and three-bedroom suites. Also here are an outdoor pool, jacuzzi, and marina. Kids okay.

For delightful in-the-country lodging, stay at **Lopez Farm Cottages and Camping,** Fisherman Bay Rd., tel. 468-3555 or (800) 440-3556. The four immaculate new cottages come with kitchenettes, fireplaces, continental breakfast, and a jacuzzi; $125 s or d. The adjacent pasture has several friendly sheep.

MacKaye Harbor Inn, tel. (360) 468-2253, is a stately 1904 farmhouse on the south end of the island. The five rooms have shared or private baths, and are just a stone's throw from the water, where you can rent kayaks to explore protected MacKaye Harbor. A separate carriage house has two suites, and is popular with families. A full breakfast is served, and guests can borrow a bike to explore the island. Rates are $99-175 d. Two-night minimum in summer.

CAMPING

Campsites ($10-15) are available at **Odlin County Park,** just a mile south of the ferry landing. Call (360) 468-4413 for reservations, available up to two months ahead; two-night minimum. No RV hookups, but the park does have a boat ramp. Open year-round.

Spencer Spit State Park, five miles from the ferry landing on the east end of Baker View Rd., tel. (360) 468-2251, has campsites for $11; no RV hookups, showers, or reservations. Open late Feb.-Oct., this very popular campground seems perpetually filled in the summer. Get here early to be assured of a place on a mid-summer weekend.

Lopez Farm Cottages and Camping, Fisherman Bay Rd., tel. 468-3555 or (800) 440-3556, has 10 walk-in campsites in the woods ($28 d) with showers. Open May-October. These are perfect for cyclists; no RVs.

Coin-operated showers are available at the public restrooms near the Lopez Village Market and at Fisherman Bay Marina.

FOOD

Gail's Restaurant in Lopez Village, tel. (360) 468-2150, has good breakfasts (served all day), fresh-baked muffins, and other treats, and a deli for lunch sandwiches. During the summer, Gail's has a full dinner menu that changes weekly. Much of the produce comes from their own organic garden. A few outside seats are available on the patio.

Holly B's Bakery in Lopez Village, tel. (360) 468-2133, is the place to go for great breads, cookies, scones, and cinnamon rolls. Open summers only. Next door is **Caffe Verdi,** where you can sip espresso at tables out front. **Lopez Island Pharmacy** on Village Rd. in Lopez Village, tel. (360) 468-2616, has an old fashioned soda fountain. **South End Cafe,** tel. (360) 468-3198, has good pizzas.

The Bay Cafe in Lopez Village, tel. (360) 468-3700, is Lopez Island's four-star restaurant, with Northwest cuisine that includes seafood and grilled meats. Open only for dinner; entrees are $14-26. Reservations are essential at this very popular place.

Not as expensive, but still very good is **Bucky's Lopez Island Grill,** also in Lopez Village, tel. (360) 468-2595. Great fish and chips, plus burgers, barbecued ribs, salads, and chicken.

The **Galley Restaurant and Lounge,** tel. (360) 468-2713, on Fisherman Bay, is best known for its enormous omelettes, prime rib, and abalone. This is where locals go to shoot the breeze and smoke cigarettes.

Groceries and Produce

Get groceries from **Village Market** in Lopez Village, tel. (360) 468-2266. Closed on Sunday, so stock up ahead of time or eat in a restaurant. The **Lopez Island Farmers Market** is open Wednesday 2-5 p.m. and Saturday 10 a.m.-2 p.m. in Lopez Village June-September. Stop by for fresh garden produce and flowers, along with arts and crafts. In the summer months, get fresh-cut flowers, jams, and jellies at the **Madrona Farms** stand on the south end of the island at the corner of Richardson and Davis Bay Rds., tel. (360) 468-3441.

OTHER PRACTICALITIES

The big event in Lopez Village is—not surprisingly—the **Fourth of July,** where you'll find a parade, fun run, barbecue, and fireworks.

Don't miss **Chimera** in Lopez Village, tel. (360) 468-3265, a cooperatively run gallery with unusual blown glass pieces, sweaters, pottery, and jewelry.

Information
Call the **Lopez Island Chamber of Commerce,** tel. (360) 468-3800, for local information, or pick up a free *Map and Guide of Lopez Island* from the museum or local real estate offices. Wash laundry at **Keep it Clean** on Fisherman Bay Rd., a mile north of Lopez Village; tel. (360) 468-3466, and get books from **Panda Books** in Lopez Village, tel. (360) 468-2132.

Transportation
The **Washington State Ferry** docks at the north end of Lopez Island, approximately four miles from Lopez Village. Call (360) 468-2252 or (888) 808-7977 for a real person, or (800) 843-3779 for recorded info. See "Ferry Service" at the beginning of this chapter for details on service and fares to the San Juan Islands. There are no buses on Lopez Island, but **Angie's Cab Courier,** tel. (360) 468-2227, offers taxi service.

OTHER ISLANDS

In addition to the three main islands, the San Juans contain a myriad of smaller ones. Shaw Island is served by the ferry system but has limited services. None of the others are visited by the ferries, and of the remaining islands, only Blakely Island has a store and marina. The rest are either marine state parks, part of the San Juan Islands National Wildlife Preserve, or private property.

SHAW ISLAND

The least visited of the ferry-served islands, Shaw (pop. 190) is primarily residential and known mostly for the nuns who operate the ferry dock and general store, **"Little Portion."** The four nuns are members of the Franciscan Sisters of the Eucharist, a Catholic order that takes vows of chastity, poverty, and obedience. Tours are available by appointment, and you are welcome to see the beautiful little chapel—with a nautical theme—where mass is held each Sunday. A half-dozen other nuns from the cloistered Benedictine order live at Our Lady of the Rock, where they operate a big dairy farm on the island.

Shaw Island remains essentially undeveloped, with second-growth forests covering most of the land. Access to all but a few beaches is limited by No Trespassing signs. You won't find any B&Bs, cottage industries, or bike rental places on the island; by law, the Little Portion store is the only business allowed. The store itself sells groceries, along with beer, wine, and chocolate for decadence.

Sights
The **Shaw Island Historical Museum** is housed in a small log cabin at the intersection of Blind Bay and Hoffman Cove Roads. It's open Tuesday 2-4 p.m., Thursday 10 a.m.-noon, and Saturday 2-4 p.m. (the same hours as the adjacent library). Out front is a reef-netting fishing boat similar to those still used to fish for salmon in the San Juans. Across the way is the **Little Red Schoolhouse,** one of the few one-room schools still in use.

South Beach County Park, two miles south of the ferry landing, has a dozen in-the-trees campsites ($13), a picnic area, boat launch, and limited drinking water. No reservations or showers. Get here early for a space on summer weekends since there are no other camping or lodging options on Shaw. The 65-acre park is best known for its long beach where you'll often find sand dollars.

The University of Washington's **Cedar Rock Biological Preserve** is a quiet off-the-beaten-path place on the south end of Hoffman Cove Road. A trail leads through fields, woods, and past small coves.

ISLAND STATE PARKS

A number of the smaller islands in the San Juan archipelago are preserved as marine state parks, accessible only by private boat and largely undeveloped. The parks have primitive campsites, no drinking water (bring plenty with you), and no garbage collection. Sea kayaks are a popular island-hopping mode of transportation, but since some of the smaller islands are several miles out, be careful not to overestimate your ability. Sailboats and motorboats can tie up at mooring buoys in these marine parks for a fee. The parks listed below all have camping. In addition, many other islets are open to day use, but islands within the San Juan Islands National Wildlife Refuge are off limits to protect nesting birds and other animals. For information on the marine parks and the wildlife refuge, talk with folks at Lime Kiln State Park on San Juan Island, tel. (360) 378-2044.

Blind Island State Park
This three-acre grassy island just north of Shaw Island in Blind Bay is a great place to watch the ferries pass by. The shoebox-sized park has mooring buoys and four primitive campsites ($5).

Doe Island State Park
Located just southeast of Orcas Island, Doe Island has five primitive campsites ($5) on a small, secluded island with a rocky shoreline. No mooring buoys, but just a short kayak paddle from the hot tubs at Doe Bay Village Resort.

James Island State Park
Less than a half-mile east of Decatur Island and just four miles from the Anacortes ferry terminal, James Island has 13 primitive campsites ($5) on a small, cliff-faced and forested island with sunny beaches on the Rosario Strait. The is-

land also has short hiking trails, mooring buoys, and a dock.

Clark Island State Park
Two miles northeast of Orcas Island, this island park has eight primitive campsites ($5), and beautiful beaches on the south end for walking, sunbathing, fishing, or diving offshore. Nearby is privately owned Barnes Island, plus a cluster of rocky islets called The Sisters; they are frequently crowded with seabirds.

Matia Island State Park
This marine park is three miles northeast of Orcas Island, with six primitive campsites ($5) near the dock and a large population of nesting puffins and other seabirds on a nearby rocky island. Most of Matia Island is managed as part of the San Juan Islands National Wildlife Refuge. It was also once home to a hermit who got a regular workout rowing the three miles to Orcas and walking another two miles to Eastsound to buy his groceries. On his last trip in 1921, he headed out from Eastsound in rough seas and was never seen again.

Sucia Island State Park
Covering 564 acres, Sucia Island State Park is the largest and most popular marine state park, and with good reason. The U-shaped park sits three miles north of Orcas Island and contains numerous protected anchorages, 50 mooring buoys, 55 primitive campsites ($5), and six miles of trails. The shoreline has delightful sandy beaches for sunbathing, exploring, clamming, and crabbing, plus bizarre water-carved sandstone formations. Offshore, you can scuba dive on sunken wrecks. Don't expect to be the only visitor on Sucia Island; on a summer weekend the waters around the island are jam-packed with U.S. and Canadian vessels of all description.

Patos Island State Park
Patos is northernmost of the San Juans, located six miles north of Orcas Island and two miles northwest of Sucia Island. The park has two mooring buoys, four primitive campsites ($5), and a trail that circles the forested island. You'll find great beaches to explore on the north side, good salmon and bottom fishing offshore, and a

lighthouse (built in 1908 and now automated) at the northwest tip of the island.

Jones Island State Park

One of the most overused of the San Juan state marine parks, this 188-acre island is just a mile west of Orcas Island near Deer Harbor. The park has 10 primitive campsites ($5), seven mooring buoys, and a public dock. Hiking trails cross the island, passing places where a 1990 storm knocked down magnificent old-growth trees.

Turn Island State Park

Turn Island, just a quarter-mile from San Juan's east shore and within easy kayaking distance of Friday Harbor, is a very popular place for picnickers and campers. It features 10 primitive campsites ($5), three mooring buoys, two beaches, and three miles of wooded hiking trails.

Posey Island State Park

This pinprick of an island covers just one acre and is located a quarter-mile north of San Juan Island's Roche Harbor. Shallow waters and a single primitive campsite ($5) make this a favorite spot for folks on kayaks and canoes in search of their own little island.

Stuart Island State Park

Stuart Island, five miles northwest of Roche Harbor, has two well-protected harbors for boats and 19 primitive campsites ($5) with drinking water. The park covers only a small portion of this 3.5-mile-long island; much of the rest is private. A county road leads past a number of homes, an airstrip, and a white one-room schoolhouse now used as a library. A newer school

building is nearby, along with a small cemetery. Also worth checking out is **Turn Point Lighthouse,** built in 1936, a seven-mile roundtrip hike from the park. Great views from here across to Vancouver Island and the nearby Gulf Islands in British Columbia.

PRIVATE ISLANDS

The rest of the San Juan Islands are home to a few hundred individuals. Some islands have only a single home, others a few dozen residences occupied seasonally. None have more than 80 or so people. Privacy is closely guarded on most of these islands, and visitors are not appreciated.

As the state ferry heads west from Anacortes to the San Juans, it threads its way between two privately owned islands, **Blakely** and **Decatur.** Blakely Island has a public marina with a store, post office, fuel, laundry, and showers on the north end, but the rest of the island is private and off limits. Decatur is even more private, with no stores or other facilities.

Located north of San Juan Island, tiny **Spieden Island** covers just 480 acres, and is home to a wild game farm with various species of exotic deer, wild goats, and antelope. The animals were brought here in the 1970s with the intention of attracting hunters; now they attract folks who just want to see them.

Waldron Island, northwest of Orcas, is nearly all private land, though Cowlitz Bay on the west side contains 273 acres of Nature Conservancy land with public access for day use only; this is primarily a bird refuge. Much of the island is flat and marshy, though the north end rises to 600 feet near Point Disney.

SOUTHERN PUGET SOUND
TACOMA

Washington's third largest city, Tacoma (pop. 184,000), is a city in transition from an industrial past to a diversified future. No longer simply the "papermill town 30 miles south of Seattle," Tacoma is undergoing a true renaissance that even snobbish Seattleites are starting to notice. The air is much cleaner since the Weyerhaeuser mill cleaned up its act, a striking new girder-span bridge crosses Thea Foss Waterway, and downtown has a vibrancy from the newly added Washington State History Museum and campus of the University of Washington. The old warehouses are becoming artists lofts, an International Glass Museum is in the works, and a vibrant theater district has been created. Add to this a diverse 700-acre city park with a world-class zoo, a rambling public market, top-quality hotels and waterfront restaurants, and a spruced up shoreline. Tacoma sure isn't the same dowdy city of just a few years back!

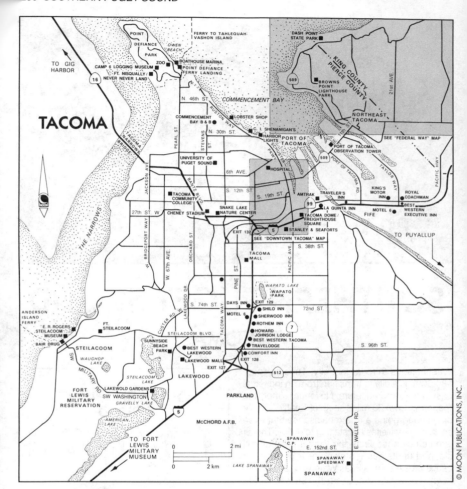

HISTORY

English sea captain George Vancouver and his entourage first stumbled across the Puget Sound area in 1792 when Peter Puget, under Vancouver's orders, sailed by Point Defiance and the Narrows. Members of Hudson's Bay Company later came along and built Fort Nisqually in 1833, which has since been reconstructed at Point Defiance Park. Another sea captain, Charles Wilkes, surveyed the Sound in 1841 and gave his starting point the name it still bears: Commencement Bay. Tacoma's name comes from the Indian term for Mt. Rainier, "Tahoma" or "Takhoma," meaning "Mother of Waters." The mountain for which the city is named rises prominently over the southeastern skyline.

Boom and Bust

The first Anglo settler, Nicholas Delin, built Tacoma's first sawmill and cabin in 1852. He was

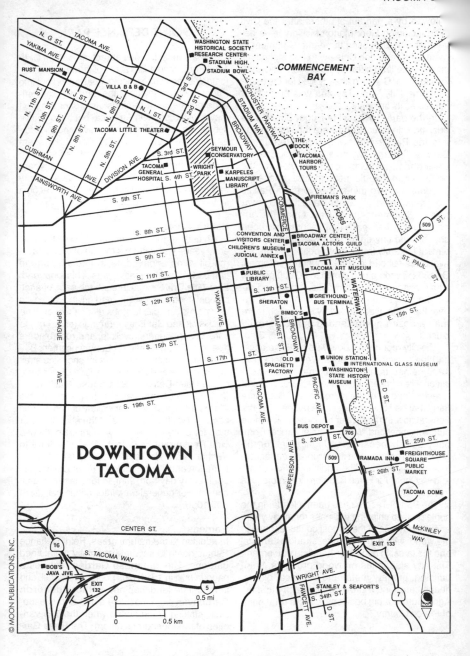

COMMENCEMENT
BAY

N. G ST.
TACOMA AVE.
YAKIMA AVE.
RUST MANSION
N. 11th ST.
N. J ST.
N. 10th ST.
N. 9th ST.
N. 8th ST.
N. 6th ST.
VILLA B & B
N. 6th ST.
N. I ST.
N. 2nd ST.
N. 3rd ST.

WASHINGTON STATE
HISTORICAL SOCIETY
RESEARCH CENTER
STADIUM HIGH
STADIUM BOWL

SCHUSTER PARKWAY

TACOMA LITTLE THEATER
N. 5th ST.
DIVISION AVE.
CUSHMAN
AINSWORTH AVE.

S. 3rd ST.
SEYMOUR
CONSERVATORY
WRIGHT
PARK
KARPELES
MANUSCRIPT
LIBRARY

BROADWAY

STADIUM WAY

THE
DOCK
TACOMA
HARBOR
TOURS

TACOMA
GENERAL
HOSPITAL
S. 4th ST.

S. 5th ST.

FIREMAN'S PARK

FOSS

509 ST.

S. 8th ST.

COMMERCE ST.

CONVENTION AND
VISITORS CENTER
CHILDREN'S MUSEUM
JUDICIAL ANNEX

BROADWAY CENTER
TACOMA ACTORS GUILD

E. 11th ST.

ST. PAUL ST.

S. 9th ST.

YAKIMA AVE.

PUBLIC
LIBRARY
S. 13th ST.
SHERATON
BIMBO'S

TACOMA ART MUSEUM

GREYHOUND
BUS TERMINAL

WATERWAY

E. 15th ST.

S. 11th ST.

S. 12th ST.

MARKET ST.

BROADWAY

S. 15th ST.

S. 17th ST.

OLD
SPAGHETTI
FACTORY

UNION STATION
INTERNATIONAL GLASS MUSEUM
WASHINGTON
STATE HISTORY
MUSEUM

E D ST.

SPRAGUE
AVE.

S. 19th ST.

TACOMA AVE.

PACIFIC AVE.

BUS DEPOT
705
S. 23rd ST.

JEFFERSON AVE.

509

RAMADA INN

E. 25th ST.

FREIGHTHOUSE
SQUARE
PUBLIC
MARKET

E. 26th ST.

TACOMA DOME

DOWNTOWN
TACOMA

CENTER ST.

McKINLEY
WAY

EXIT 133

16

S. TACOMA WAY

7

BOB'S
JAVA JIVE
EXIT
132

5

WRIGHT AVE.
FAWCETT AVE.
STANLEY & SEAFORT'S
S. 34th ST.
D ST.

0   0.5 mi
0   0.5 km

MOON

© MOON PUBLICATIONS, INC.

~lowed by a handful of others after the Civil
War, including Gen. Morton McCarver—a developer who proposed the name Commencement City—and Job Carr—who had staked his
claim to the land a few years earlier. McCarver
was too late, Carr had already filed for the name
"Tacoma City," and Tacoma was born; Carr
served as its first mayor.

In the early 1870s all of Puget Sound was
buzzing with rumors on where the first railroad
into the Pacific Northwest would terminate.
Seattle, Tacoma, Olympia, Mukilteo, Everett,
Bellingham, and Steilacoom all vied for the
honor, since it would mean instant prosperity.
Tacoma had two things the Northern Pacific
Railroad wanted: cheap land and the deep waters of Commencement Bay. Once the an-
nouncement was made that Tacoma had been
chosen, the tiny settlement was transformed
almost instantly into a metropolis, and the arrival of the railroad in 1873 brought boom times.
By 1892, Tacoma had grown to 50,000 people,
with growth fueled by sawmills, a gold and silver smelter, flour mills, and coal mines. However the boom went suddenly bust when more
than a dozen overextended banks abruptly
closed.

The city rebounded slowly from this setback,
and the arrival of Frederick Weyerhaeuser in
1900 helped transform Tacoma—and Washington. His company purchased 900,000 acres of
forested land from the railroads for $6 an acre
(land that had been given to the railroads by the
Federal government), later buying a million more
acres of timberland. Weyerhaeuser Timber Company quickly became the focal point for the
growth of Tacoma, and its corporate headquarters are still nearby. The addition of Fort Lewis
and McChord Air Force Base brought more jobs
to Tacoma,

The Port of Tacoma has been a leader in the
containerized shipping business for many years
and is today one of the largest container ports in
the world, with gantry cranes, straddle carriers,
and the latest in container-handling equipment.
The city also relies on wood products, shipbuilding, primary metal and chemical plants,
health care, and a growing high-tech industry.
Agriculture is a big business in more rural parts
of Pierce County.

POINT DEFIANCE PARK

Tacoma's most famous attraction is Point Defiance Park, almost 700 acres of gardens, forests,
footpaths, and shady picnic areas jutting out into
Puget Sound at the tip of the narrow Point Defiance peninsula. It reminds visitors of the best
metropolitan parks in America, but once you've
seen it, the cliff setting with its views and thick forest will make most other similar parks seem
modest. This is a great place, with an amazing
array of attractions to please almost anyone.
The park was originally set aside as a military
reservation, but was given to the city of Tacoma
in 1888 for use as a public park.

Natural Areas

Much of the park's wild nature remains from the
early years, visible from a myriad of hiking paths
(no bikes on unpaved trails) and a loop road
that passes all the main sights. This loop road,
Five-Mile Drive winds through the park, offering
a popular jogging, cycling, and driving route with
viewpoints and picnic stops along the way. The
road is closed Saturday mornings (till 1 p.m.) to
cars, giving joggers, cyclists, and rollerbladers
free rein. **Owen Beach** on Commencement Bay
offers summer sun or a pleasant shoreline stroll
any time of year. Rent a boat with a small motor
at the Point Defiance **Boathouse Marina,** tel.
(253) 591-5325; the water off the point is always
littered with fishermen, particularly during salmon
season. Get fishing tackle at the shop here, or
stop for a meal at the very popular Boathouse
Grill Restaurant next door. The state ferry to
Vashon Island docks here as well (see "Transportation and Tours," below). Point Defiance is
open every day from sunrise to a half-hour past
sunset. For general park information call (253)
305-1000.

Gardens

In addition to the natural areas, Point Defiance
Park is home to several beautifully maintained
gardens. The **Japanese Garden** features a
pagoda built in 1914, plus pools, a waterfall, and
immaculate landscaping. A **Rhododendron
Garden** covers almost five acres and is especially striking in the spring when the 115 varieties of rhododendrons bloom. The **Rose Gar-**

den contains a rustic gazebo and some 1,500 rose bushes that flower June through September. Other featured gardens at Point Defiance are the **Iris Garden,** the **Dahlia Trial Garden** (best time to see these is August), and the **Northwest Native Garden** with plants from all six biotic zones in the Northwest.

Zoo and Aquarium
The biggest attraction at Point Defiance is the excellent Zoo and Aquarium—one of the finest zoos on the West Coast—home of beluga whales, polar bears, sharks, walrus, red wolves, elephants, and much more. The real attractions here are the ocean exhibits. You'll discover a tropical reef filled with brilliantly colored fish, a huge cold-water aquarium with fish, jellyfish, eels, and other critters from the Puget Sound area, and the main event: a large tank where you can come face to face with more than 30 sharks, reaching up to 10 feet long. (Get here on Sunday and Thursday at 11 a.m. to watch the feeding frenzy.) Fascinating displays describe the lives of sharks, stingrays, and skates, and you will even get to see shark egg cases with living embryos. The Rocky Shores exhibit includes tufted puffins, harbor seals, Pacific walrus, beluga whales, and playful sea otters. Another favorite attraction is the polar bear area, which features a deep pool where you can watch them swimming from behind a thick glass wall.

The zoo has cafes and gift shops. In August and September, the Friday evening **Zoosounds** concerts are fun for the whole family. In December, come in the evening to see the twinkling animal **Zoolights.** Admission is $7 adults, $6.55 seniors, $5.30 ages 4-13, and free for kids under four. Open daily 10 a.m.-7 p.m. Memorial Day to Labor Day, and daily 10 a.m.-4 p.m. the rest of the year; closed Thanksgiving and Christmas. Call (253) 591-5335 for recorded info, or (253) 591-5337 for the office.

Fort Nisqually
Fort Nisqually Historic Site, on the southwest side of Point Defiance Park, has a half-dozen historic and reconstructed buildings inside log bastions. Fort Nisqually was a Hudson's Bay trading post in the mid-1800s and was originally located 17 miles to the south on the Nisqually delta near present-day Fort Lewis. The build-

ings were moved here in the 1930s and carefully restored. Of particular interest is the working blacksmith shop where you can learn how tools and hardware were fabricated for trade. Also on the grounds is the factor's house, a trade store, and a storehouse originally built in 1851. This is considered the oldest standing building in Washington. The staff is clad in period costumes from the 1850s and offers living history demonstrations on everything from spinning to black powder shooting. Come here in May to celebrate Queen Victoria's birthday, in August for a mountain man encampment, or in October for a candlelight tour. Entrance to the fort costs $1.50 adults, or 75 cents for kids. Hours are daily 11 a.m.-6 p.m. Memorial Day to Labor Day, and Wed.-Sun. with varying hours the rest of the year. Call (253) 591-5339 for more information.

Never Never Land
The strangest sight at Point Defiance is Never Never Land, where 10 acres of woods are sprinkled with 32 life-size scenes from favorite children's stories: Humpty-Dumpty, Hansel and Gretel, Goldilocks and the Three Bears, Peter Rabbit, and Mother Goose. Costumed characters delight the kids with these and other tales. Never Never Land is open daily 11 a.m.-6 p.m. May-Aug., and weekends only in April and September. Closed Oct.-March. Entrance is $3 adults, $2 kids, and free for kids under two. Call (253) 591-5845 for details. Older children have fun at the go-kart track in another part of Point Defiance Park.

Camp 6 Logging Museum
Camp 6 is a reconstructed logging camp with steam equipment from the late 1800s and early 1900s, when most Northwest logging was done from railroads. Featured attractions (everything still runs) include a 90-ton logging locomotive specially built to handle steep grades and sharp curves, a steam-powered 1887 Dolbeer Donkey engine that was used to yard logs, and various high lead, skidders, and other logging equipment from the heyday of timber harvesting in the Northwest. Also here are loggers' bunkhouses, including turn-of-the-century bunkhouses on rails that could be moved as the trees were cut. The bunkhouses contain photos and artifacts from life in the logging camps.

Kids love the 1929 steam-powered **P.D.Q. & K. Railroad,** which includes log cars, cabooses, speeders, and other railcars. It offers rides on weekend afternoons April-September. There's also a special **Santa Train** the first three weekends of December. Camp 6 is open Wed.-Sun. 10 a.m.-4 p.m.; closed Nov.-Jan.; tel. (253) 752-0047.

OTHER SIGHTS

Historical Museums

Tacoma is now home to the impressive **Washington State History Museum.** This 100,000 square-foot building sits next to historic Union Station, and repeats its rounded design in a series of three gracefully vaulted arches. Visitors walk through a maze of exhibits that include a Salish Indian plank house and Native basket collection, dioramas of mining and logging towns, exhibits on the arrival of the railroad and the effect of Depression and WW II, and a theater with an educational video about the Columbia River. Given the importance of high-tech industries in Washington, it comes as no surprise to find lots of interactive displays. Upstairs are galleries with temporary exhibits. The museum is joined to the restored Union Station by a scenic courtyard and amphitheater, a fine place for a lunch break. Also inside is a cafe and museum store. Located at 1911 Pacific Ave., tel. (253) 593-2830 or (888) 238-4373, the museum is open Sunday 11 a.m.-6 p.m., and Mon.-Sat. 10 a.m.-6 p.m. (Thursday till 8 p.m.) Memorial Day to Labor Day; and Sunday 11 a.m.-5 p.m., Tues.-Sat. 10 a.m.-5 p.m. (Thursday till 8 p.m.) the rest of the year. Admission is $7 adults, $6 seniors, $5 ages 13-17, $4 ages 6-12, and free for under age six.

The **Washington State Historical Society Research Center,** 315 N. Stadium Way, tel. (253) 597-3642, houses a research library with thousands of historic photos, old posters (including many ship bills from the Klondike gold rush), and other archives. The rooftop patio provides a fine view of Stadium High School, the city of Tacoma, and Mt. Rainier.

Historic Buildings

Completed in 1911, Tacoma's copper-domed **Union Station** was designed by the same firm that built New York's Grand Central Station and has a similar sense of grandeur. The depot originally served as the terminus of the Northern Pacific's rail line and was later used by the Great Northern and Union Pacific railroads before falling into disuse. A massive restoration in 1989 transformed the distinctively domed building into a federal courthouse for all of western Washington—its magnificent central space is filled by the works of the renowned Tacoma-born glass artist, Dale Chihuly. An 18-foot cobalt-blue chandelier hangs from the high center, and many other pieces provide bright accents. Union Station is open Mon.-Fri. 10 a.m.-4 p.m.; closed weekends. No charge.

Old City Hall, on the corner of S. 7th St. and Pacific Ave., is another distinctive downtown building. Patterned after an Italian town hall, the dominant feature is a tall free-standing clocktower. The building was built in 1905 and is now used for commercial offices. A new $85-million campus of the **University of Washington** opened in Tacoma in 1997, spread through 22 restored historic downtown buildings.

Tacoma Art Museum

In recent years Tacoma has undergone something of an artistic renaissance as old warehouses are transformed into studios and galleries. A focal point is the Tacoma Art Museum, 1123 Pacific Ave., tel. (253) 272-4258, a four-story building that is best known for its paintings and other pieces from 19th- and 20th-century artists, and its permanent exhibitions of Dale Chihuly glass. New exhibits come to the museum almost monthly, and there are frequent lectures and other activities, plus a fine museum shop with gifts, art books, and jewelry. Hours are Sunday noon-5 p.m., and Tues.-Sat. 10 a.m.-5 p.m. (Thursday till 7 p.m.). Admission is $4 adults, $3 students and seniors, free under age 12. No charge on Tuesday. A brand new Art Museum is expected to open in 2002.

International Glass Museum

Tacoma's newest gem is slated to open in 2001, covering two acres along the downtown waterfront. This $59 million project will feature galleries and a workshop amphitheater where you can watch as glass art is created. A 600-foot-long "Bridge of Glass" created by native son

Dale Chihuly will connect it with the history museum. Call (253) 572-9310 for the current status.

For the Kids

The **Children's Museum of Tacoma,** 936 Broadway, tel. (253) 627-6031, is a fun and educational place for kids, with changing exhibits. The museum is open Tues.-Fri. 10 a.m.-5 p.m., Saturday 10 a.m.-4 p.m., and Sunday noon-4 p.m., Admission is $3.75 adults or kids.

Tacoma Dome

Completed in 1983, this blue, geometric-patterned structure off I-5 is one of the largest wood-domed structures in the world. Spanning 530 feet in diameter, and 115 feet tall (as high as a 15-story building), the Dome is owned by the city and is used for various sporting and musical events, as well as trade shows. It can seat up to 22,000 persons, and its concert seating can go up to 28,000. For upcoming events at the Dome, call (253) 572-3663. Tours are not available, but a small museum of local sports history is open during events.

Stadium District

One of Tacoma's most historic sections is the Stadium District, located near **Stadium High School** on Tacoma Avenue. Built on the top of a hill in the style of a French chateau, this extraordinary high school was begun in 1891 and was intended to be a grandiose seven-story railroad hotel. The depression of 1893 left it vacant for several years until it was transformed into a high school in 1906. Next door is the Stadium Bowl, the West Coast's first stadium, and the site of visits by three presidents (Theodore Roosevelt, Warren Harding, and Franklin Delano Roosevelt), along with such sports legends as Babe Ruth and Jack Dempsey. More than 100 turn-of-the-century mansions and stately homes can be found in the area around the stadium, including several of the city's best B&Bs. Be sure to see the **Rust Mansion** at 1001 N. I St., a Classical Revival structure built in 1905.

Wright Park at S. 3rd and G Streets is a shady place with gardens, paved paths, stone lions, lawn bowling greens, and a delightful surprise: the **W.W. Seymour Botanical Conservatory.** Built in 1908 and on the National Register of Historic Places, this Victorian-style conservatory—one of just three on the West Coast—hosts a bright array of tropical plants and cacti beneath 12,000 panes of glass. This is a great place to visit on a rainy winter day (or any time for that matter). The conservatory is open daily (except Christmas and Thanksgiving) 10 a.m.-4:30 p.m.; no charge. The small gift shop has botanical gifts, and the friendly cat will come up to greet you; call (253) 591-5330 for more information.

One of Tacoma's strangest sights is the **Karpeles Manuscript Library Museum,** 407 S. G St. (across from Wright Park), tel. (253) 383-2575. Located in an old Carnagie Library, the museum displays changing exhibits of rare and unique documents from all over the world, from D-Day defense plans signed by Adolf Hitler to letters written by Charles Manson. Open Tues.-Sun. 10 a.m.-4 p.m.; free.

Yet More Sights

If you're in Tacoma on a semi-clear day, there are few places you can be without a view of 14,411-foot **Mt. Rainier.** It dominates the landscape with its permanent whitecap and looks particularly dramatic from the Cliff House parking lot (6300 Marine View Dr. at Browns Point in Federal Way), the 11th St. bridge, Ruston Way, and Gig Harbor.

For a view of the action at the Port of Tacoma, head to the **observation tower** just off E. 11th St., where signs describe the port's history. Continue north to **Browns Point Lighthouse Park,** a sunny spot for picnicking, ship-watching, or launching your own boat. Here you've got a great view of downtown Tacoma and Point Defiance, Vashon and Maury Islands, the Olympics, and of course, the Sound. The trick is to find it (see the maps "Tacoma" and "Federal Way"). The lighthouse is open on weekends and contains an exhibit on the building of a Coast Guard boat; free. Call (253) 925-1111 for details.

Tacoma's **University of Puget Sound** has an attractive campus with older brick buildings on wooded grounds. The small Museum of Natural History, room 337 Thompson Hall, houses specimens in cases, but no exhibits. Cheap eats at the Student Center cafeteria.

Connecting Tacoma with the Olympic Peninsula, the **Tacoma Narrows Bridge** is the second bridge to cross the sound at this location, and the

DISASTER OVER THE SOUND

The windy Tacoma Narrows presented an obstacle to the linking of Tacoma with Kitsap Peninsula. During the buildup to WW II, the link became more crucial, since the shipyards of Bremerton were just 20 miles north on the peninsula. The ferry service was being overworked, and after many attempts backers finally got the 5,939-foot-long bridge built; in 1940 it was the third-longest suspension bridge in the world.

It was quite an undertaking, and the construction process was exciting for sidewalk superintendents from both shores. The towers stood 500 feet above the swift currents below, and more than 19,000 miles of wire were wound into the cables that supported the roadbed.

When it was finished in 1940, the workmen reported that the roadbed didn't behave properly; it rippled. A professor of engineering at the University of Washington, F. Bert Farquarson, was commissioned to make wind-tunnel tests, and he urged a much more comprehensive study. His warnings went barely heeded, and the insurance agent who sold the bridge insurance pocketed the premium—after all, who had ever heard of a new bridge falling?

In the meantime, the bridge earned its nickname of Galloping Gertie from its great rippling effect, and motorists in search of a thrill could pay their toll on a windy day, drive onto the bridge, and watch the car ahead completely disappear in the ripples.

It all ended on the morning of November 7, 1940, when a strong wind came up and held steady at about 40 mph. The bridge began a corkscrew twist so severe that it was closed. But Leonard Coatsworth, editor for the Tacoma *News Tribune,* was driving across at the time with his cocker spaniel, Tubby. Coatsworth found that he couldn't drive.

Before I realized it, the tilt from side to side became so violent that I lost control of the car . . . I jammed on the brakes and got out of the car, only to be thrown onto my face against the curb. I tried to stand and was thrown again. Around me I could hear concrete cracking. I started back to the car to get the dog, but was thrown before I could reach it. The car itself began to slide from side to side of the roadway.

On hands and knees most of the time, I crawled 500 yards to the towers. . . . My breath was coming in gasps; my knees were raw and bleeding, my hands bruised and swollen from gripping the concrete curb. . . . Finally my breath gave out completely and I lay in the roadway clutching the curb until I could breathe again, and then resumed my progress. Toward the last I risked rising to my feet and running a few yards at a time. . . . Safely back at the toll plaza, I saw the bridge in its final collapse and saw my car plunge into the Narrows.

On that same morning a college student named Winfred Brown walked out onto the bridge a short distance, but returned when the bridge twisted so far that he seemed to be looking straight down at the water.

Professor Farquarson had heard of the contortions and drove down from Seattle to film the event. He went out onto the bridge to try to save Tubby but wasn't able to walk upright, so he retreated to the shore.

The twisting became worse; lampposts began snapping off and chunks of concrete were flying. Finally, about 100 feet of roadway with Coatsworth's car and Tubby fell into the Narrows. Soon most of the roadway was gone. The towers that had been supporting the concrete snapped back toward each shore until the cables stopped them, humming in the wind, and finally the whole twisted mess fell into Puget Sound.

The Narrows was without a bridge for almost exactly a decade while engineers designed—and redesigned—a new bridge that did not act like a sail every time a gale blew through. The new $14 million bridge was opened on October 14, 1950.

In 1992 the remains of Galloping Gertie were added to the National Register of Historic Places to protect her from salvagers. Only fish, marine mammals, and scuba divers visit her now.

fifth largest suspension bridge in the world. The first was the famous "Galloping Gertie" (see the special topic "Disaster over the Sound").

Other Parks
Fireman's Park is a small downtown park at S. 8th and A Sts. with an Alaskan totem pole, outstanding views of Mt. Rainier and the harbor, and great whiffs of the pulp mill.

A two-mile cycling and jogging path runs along Ruston Way, good for a breezy post-lunch or -dinner walk. Follow Ruston to Tacoma's best known park, Point Defiance (described above), or stop at two smaller beachfront parks on the way: **Commencement Park,** with a fishing pier and large sundial, and **Marine Park,** a long narrow strip of shoreline with open grassy areas, picnic tables, a fishing pier, bait shop, and snack stand. Fishing may not be such a smart idea, however, since Commencement Bay is one of Puget Sound's "hot spots," where the bottom fish and even salmon have shown unhealthy levels of toxins.

Tucked away where you'd least expect it is the **Nature Center at Snake Lake,** 1919 S. Tyler St., tel. (253) 591-6439. The 54 acres of marshland and evergreens are just a stone's throw from busy 19th St. but this is a fine place to watch ducks and other birds. There are two miles of self-guiding nature trails for the do-it-yourselfers. Don't let the name scare you off—the lake was named for its shape, not its inhabitants. Trails are open daily from 8 a.m. until dark; the interpretive center (filled with hands-on exhibits) is open Mon.-Sat. 8 a.m.-5 p.m. yearround. No charge.

Wapato Lake is a good practice pond for novice rowboaters. Located at S. 72nd St. and Sheridan Ave., the park also has picnic tables, some small flower gardens, and boat rentals.

ACCOMMODATIONS AND CAMPING

Lodging
Many of Tacoma's motels are strung along Pacific Hwy. Southwest/South Tacoma Way/Pacific Hwy. East; this is essentially a continuation of the same route with changing names. More motels are located near the various I-5 exits and along Pacific Ave. (east of I-5). South Tacoma Way/Pacific Hwy. Southwest is not the most inviting place to stay, but it does provide fast food, 7-Elevens, Chinese restaurants, strip malls, strip joints, and plenty of used car dealers. The Tacoma area has some of the least expensive motel rates in Washington, but not all of these budget places may be acceptable. I've eliminated the worst ones, but for the cheapest of these you may still want to check the rooms to make sure they meet your standards.

Bed and Breakfasts
For reservations at local B&Bs, give a call to the **B&B Association of Tacoma and Mt. Rainier,** tel. (253) 593-6098 or (888) 593-6098; or **Greater Tacoma B&B Reservation Service,** tel. (253) 759-4088 or (800) 406-4088. Unless otherwise noted, all B&Bs listed below serve a full breakfast and do not allow young children.

Commencement Bay B&B, 3312 N. Union Ave. in North Tacoma, tel. (253) 752-8175, is an elegant large home built in 1937 and overlooking the bay. Three guest rooms have private baths, and guests have access to the deck, secluded hot tub, and game room. $90-120 s or d.

Built in 1911 and on the National Register of Historic Places, the elegant Colonial-style **Devoe Mansion B&B,** 208 E. 133rd St., tel. (253) 539-3991 or (888) 539-3991, is situated on one and a half acres. The mansion was the home of Emma DeVoe, a turn-of-the-century suffagate whose efforts gave Washington women the right to vote. The four guest rooms have antiques and private baths. Guests can soak in the garden hot tub; $85-110 s or d.

An 1889 Queen Anne Victorian in the historic Stadium District, **Chinaberry Hill B&B,** 302 N. Tacoma Ave., tel. (253) 272-1282, is one of the finest B&Bs in Tacoma. The home has a wraparound front porch, period furnishings, stained glass windows, and a separate carriage house for families or couples looking for privacy. Five guest rooms have private baths, and suites contain jacuzzi tubs; $95-175 s or $105-195 d. Kids are accepted.

Also in the Stadium District, **Villa B&B,** 705 N. 5th St., tel. (253) 572-1157, is a grand Mediterranean-style mansion built in 1925. The Villa features four large guest rooms, verandas, and gardens; $80-135 s or d.

TACOMA AREA MOTELS AND HOTELS

Lodging places listed include Tacoma, Lakewood, and Fife, arranged from least to most expensive. At the least expensive motels, see the rooms first to make sure they are up to your standards. See the text for descriptions of local bed and breakfasts.

BUDGET

Bay Motel; 1220 Puyallup Ave., Tacoma; tel. (253) 272-7720; $27 s, $34 d; kitchenettes

Golden Lion Motel; 9021 S. Tacoma Way, Tacoma; tel. (253) 588-2171; $31 s or d

Nights Inn; 9325 S. Tacoma Way, Tacoma; tel. (253) 582-7550; $32 s or d; kitchenettes available, AAA approved

Vagabond Motel; 10005 S. Tacoma Way, Tacoma; tel. (253) 581-2920; $32-42 s or d

INEXPENSIVE

Fort Lewis Motel; 12215 Pacific Hwy. SW, Tacoma; tel. (253) 588-7226; $35 s or d; kitchenettes available

Hometel; 3520 Pacific Hwy. E, Fife; tel. (253) 922-0555; $35 s, $40 d; outdoor pool

Stagecoach Inn; 4221 Pacific Hwy. E, Fife; tel. (253) 922-5421; $35 s, $40 d

Madigan Motel; 12039 Pacific Hwy. SW, Tacoma; tel. (253) 588-8697; $35-45 s or d; kitchenettes available

Calico Cat Motel; 8821 Pacific Ave. S, Tacoma; tel. (253) 535-2440; $35-54 s or d; kitchenettes available, airport shuttle

Morgan Motel; 7301 Pacific Ave., Tacoma; tel. (253) 472-5962; $37 s or d

King's Motor Inn; 5115 Pacific Hwy. E, Fife; tel. (253) 922-3636 or (800) 929-3509; $37 s, $39 d; kitchenettes available

Traveler's Inn; 3100 Pacific Hwy. E, Fife; tel. (253) 922-9520 or (800) 633-8300; $37 s, $44 d; outdoor pool, AAA approved

Redwood Motel; 17023 Pacific Hwy., Spanaway; tel. (253) 531-0355; $38 s or d; kitchenettes available

Home Motel; 11621 Pacific Hwy. SW, Tacoma; tel. (253) 584-1717; $40 s or d; kitchenettes available

Motel 6, 5201 20th St. E, Fife; tel. (253) 922-1270 or (800) 466-8356; $40 s, $44 d; outdoor pool

Days Inn; 3021 Pacific Hwy. E, Fife; tel. (253) 922-3500 or (800) 325-2525; $40-55 s, $45-60 d; outdoor pool, kitchenettes available, AAA approved

Budget Inn; 9915 S. Tacoma Way, Tacoma; tel. (253) 588-6615; $42-55 s or d; kitchenettes available

Econo Lodge; 3518 Pacific Hwy. E, Fife; tel. (253) 922-0550 or (800) 424-4777; $44 s, $48 d; AAA approved

Motel 6, 1811 S. 76th St., Tacoma; tel. (253) 473-7100 or (800) 466-8356; $44 s, $50 d; outdoor pool

Rothem Inn; 8602 S. Hosmer, Tacoma; tel. (253) 535-0123; $40 s, $45 d; new motel with kitchenettes

Comfort Inn; 5601 Pacific Hwy. E, Fife; tel. (253) 922-2301 or (800) 228-5150; $46-65 s, $55-69 d; jacuzzi, exercise facility, continental breakfast, kitchenettes available, AAA approved

---

Built in 1892, **Austrian B&B,** 723 N. Cushman, tel. (253) 383-2216, is a spacious and quiet home. The three suites have private baths and are furnished with Austrian antiques; $75 s or d. Kids welcome and German is spoken.

Victorian Inn B&B, 3320 N. Union, tel. (253) 756-9044 or (888) 756-9044, is an exquisitely restored 1890 Queen Anne Victorian mansion in the Proctor District. Surrounded by beautiful gardens, the home is furnished with antiques.

MODERATE

King Oscar Motel; 8820 S. Hosmer, Tacoma; tel. (253) 539-1153 or (888) 254-5464; $57-62 s, $62-67 d; outdoor pool, jacuzzi, airport shuttle, continental breakfast, kitchenettes available, AAA approved

Sherwood Inn Travelodge Hotel; 8402 S. Hosmer, Tacoma; tel. (253) 535-2800; $54-59 s, $59-64 d; outdoor pool, continental breakfast, airport shuttle, AAA approved

Royal Coachman Motor Inn; 5805 Pacific Hwy. E, Fife; tel. (253) 922-2500 or (800) 422-3051; $59-65 s, $65-73 d; jacuzzi, kitchenettes available, AAA approved

Best Western Lakewood Motor Inn; 6125 Motor Ave. SW, Lakewood; tel. (253) 584-2212 or (800) 238-7234; $62-72 s, $69-79 d; continental breakfast, AAA approved

Corporate Suites; 3571 B St. E, Tacoma; tel. (253) 473-4105 or (800) 255-6058; $65 s or d; one-room suites, kitchens, jacuzzi tubs, two-night minimum

Best Western Tacoma Inn; 8726 S. Hosmer St., Tacoma; tel. (253) 535-2880 or (800) 305-2880 $69-89 s or d; outdoor pool, jacuzzi, exercise room, playground, kitchenettes available, AAA approved

Howard Johnson Express Inn; 8702 S. Hosmer, Tacoma; tel. (253) 535-3100 or (800) 446-4656; $69 s or d; outdoor pool, continental breakfast, kitchenettes available, AAA approved

Quality Inn; 9920 S. Tacoma Way, Lakewood; tel. (253) 588-5241 or (800) 228-5151; $70 s, $75 d; fridges, continental breakfast, kitchenettes available, AAA approved

Ramada Inn Tacoma Dome; 2611 East E St.; tel. (253) 572-7272 or (800) 755-1547; $71 s, $77 d; sauna, exercise room, jacuzzi

La Quinta Inn; 1425 E. 27th St., Tacoma; tel. (253) 383-0146 or (800) 531-5900; $74-81 s or d; outdoor pool, jacuzzi, exercise room, continental breakfast, AAA approved

Days Inn Tacoma South; 6802 Tacoma Mall Blvd., Tacoma; tel. (253) 475-5900 or (800) 325-2525; $75 s, $80 d; outdoor pool, AAA approved

Holiday Inn Express; 3501 Pacific Hwy. E; tel. (253) 926-1000 or (800) 465-4329; $75 s or d; AAA approved

EXPENSIVE

Best Western Executive Inn; 5700 Pacific Hwy. E, Fife; tel. (253) 922-0080 or (800) 938-8500; $79-129 s, $89-139 d; indoor pool, jacuzzi, sauna, exercise room, lounge, restaurant, airport shuttle, AAA approved

Shilo Inn; 7414 S. Hosmer, Tacoma; tel. (253) 475-4020 or (800) 222-2244; $79-99 s or d; indoor pool, jacuzzi, sauna, exercise room, kitchenettes available, continental breakfast, AAA approved

Holiday Inn Express; 8601 Hosmer, Tacoma; tel. (253) 539-2020 or (800) 465-4329; $89 s or d; indoor pool, jacuzzi, sauna, exercise room, continental breakfast

PREMIUM

Sheraton Tacoma Hotel; S. 1320 Broadway Plaza, Tacoma; tel. (253) 572-3200 or (800) 845-9466; $113-124 s, $120-132 d; jacuzzi, sauna, honor bars, airport shuttle, AAA approved

Two guest rooms offer sound and mountain views and private baths; $135 s or d. Kids accepted.

Keenan House B&B, near the University of Puget Sound at 610 N. Warner, tel. (253) 752-0702, is a 1910 Tudor home with four guest rooms and private or shared baths; $60-70 s or d. Children accepted.

The Green Cape Cod B&B, 2711 N. Warner, tel. (253) 752-1977, is a cozy 1929 Cape Cod

DeVoe Mansion B&B

DON PITCHER

antique-furnished home in north Tacoma where three guest rooms have private baths; $95 s or d.

Bay Vista B&B, 4617 Darien Dr., tel. (253) 759-8084, is a private two-bedroom suite with fireplace, kitchen, and a patio offering sweeping views of Mt. Rainier. $85-95 s or d.

Oakes St. Barn B&B, 5814 S. Oakes St., tel. (253) 475-7047, has two guest rooms (shared bath) in a large contemporary home with a hot tub; $65 s or d.

Campgrounds

Camping is not allowed at Point Defiance Park, but head north to the city of Federal Way for **Dash Point State Park** with year-round sites for both tents ($10) and RVs ($15). More campsites are located at **Kopachuck State Park,** 12 miles northwest of Tacoma and **Penrose Point State Park,** approximately 20 miles west of Tacoma on the Key Peninsula. Call (800) 452-5687 for reservations ($6 extra)

Local RV parks include **Karwan Village,** 2621 84th St., Tacoma, tel. (253) 582-1197; and **Majestic Manor RV Park,** 7022 River Rd. E, tel. (253) 845-3144 or (800) 348-3144.

FOOD

Breakfast, Lunch, and Coffee

Start out at **Knapps Restaurant** 2707 N. Proctor St., tel. (253) 759-9009, in the Proctor District, where you'll find the best breakfasts in Taco-

ma, from pancakes to eggs Benedict. **Grounds for Coffee,** 764 Broadway, tel. (253) 627-7742, is a sprawling and comfortable downtown coffeehouse with a limited menu of sandwiches, bagels, salads, and soup. A good place to read the newspaper or hang out with friends.

Located in north Tacoma near Point Defiance Park, the **Antique Sandwich Company,** 5102 N. Pearl, tel. (253) 752-4069, seems a throwback to the early '70s. The atmosphere is earthy; the menu includes good soups, clam chowder, salads, espresso, and sweets. Come back in the evening for live acoustic or folk groups.

American and Northwest Cuisine

Fife City Bar & Grill, 3025 Pacific Hwy. E, tel. (253) 922-9555, gets kudos from Tacoma locals for its highly creative meals at surprisingly low prices. Open for three meals a day. The menu includes a wide diversity of lunch and dinner choices.

Yankee Diner, 6812 Tacoma Mall Blvd. (south Tacoma), tel. (253) 475-3006, serves three solid all-American meals a day, including huge portions of pot roast and a turkey dinner served year-round. Another place to fill yourself is **Southern Kitchen,** 1716 6th Ave., tel. (253) 627-4282, where the menu of home-cooked meals includes catfish, pork chops, collard greens, barbecued ribs, and sweet potato pie. This is a longtime Tacoma favorite. **Roof-n-Doofs,** 754 Pacific Ave., tel. 9253) 572-5113, serves genuine Louisiana-style Cajun and Creole cooking and features a popular Wednesday lunch buffet and jazz on Friday nights.

Pubs

The Swiss, 1904 S. Jefferson, tel. (253) 572-2821, is a friendly pub with 37 beers on tap, splendid Dale Chihuly glass art, and surprisingly good sandwiches and pasta. The back room has pool and darts, plus live music on weekends. Drop by on the third Sunday of the month for a brunch with live polka tunes. **Harmon Pub and Brewery,** right across from the museum at 1938 Pacific Ave., tel. (253) 383-2739, is a big bustling place with brewed-on-the-premises ales and porter, good pub grub (fish and chips, burgers, pizza, and pasta), and live jazz on weekends.

Ram American Restaurant & Big Horn Brewery, 3001 Ruston Way, tel. (253) 756-7886, is a family restaurant with a waterfront location and homemade pizzas, gourmet burgers, and Tex-Mex specialties. The bar is a very popular place to watch sports.

Established in 1913, **The Spar Tavern,** 2121 N. 30th, tel. (253) 627-8215, has great pub grub: burgers, sandwiches, chili, and homemade soups, but it is a bar, so no kids. **Katie Downs Tavern,** 3211 Ruston Way, tel. (253) 756-0771, sits on a pier and attracts a good-sized crowd with a big selection of beer and wine, deep-dish pizza, a jeans-and-sneakers atmosphere, with outdoor seating in the summer; over age 21 only.

Located in a turn-of-the-century firehouse **Engine House No. 9,** 611 N. Pine, tel. (253) 272-3435, stocks nearly 50 local and imported beers and features a pub menu of pizza, tacos, soups, and salads.

Seafood

The **Lobster Shop Dash Point,** 6912 Soundview Dr. NE, tel. (253) 927-1513, sister to the Lobster Shop South across the bay on 4015 Ruston Way. tel. (206) 759-2165, is the original, more rustic version, where the steaks, seafood, and wine list are reliably good. Great waterside views, too. Open for dinner only; reservations advised. The Lobster Shop South is open for lunch and dinner, and it serves a substantial Sunday brunch.

Located right on the water at 2761 Ruston Way, **Harbor Lights,** tel. (253) 752-8600, is a

Tacoma tradition, with giant steaks, four-poun buckets of clams, tasty fish and chips, and moderate prices. Also good for drinks.

Johnny's Ocean Fish Co., 2201 Ruston Way, tel. (253) 383-4571, in Old Town right alongside the fishing pier, is a friendly market with fresh and smoked seafood of all kinds. A good place to pick up fish recipes, too.

For the View

If you want a sweeping Sound view, try the old-time **Cliff House,** 6300 Marine View Dr. at Browns Point, tel. (253) 927-0400. The steak and seafood are very good—though not cheap; be ready to spend $30 pp or more. The downstairs lounge offers the same view and a sandwich menu.

Overlooking the Dome and busy I-5 is **Stanley and Seafort's Steak, Chop, and Fish House** at 115 E. 34th, tel. (253) 473-7300, with another view that gets better as the sun goes down. Part of a small chain of similar restaurants, Stanley and Seafort's is one of those dependably good places with fine meats, seafood, and desserts.

C.I. Shenanigan's, 3017 Ruston Way, tel. (253) 752-8811, is a spiffy waterside restaurant with outdoor seating, a seafood menu, and long waits on weekends. Reservations advised.

Located atop the Sheraton Hotel at 1320 Broadway Plaza, **Altezzo Ristorante,** tel. (253) 591-4155, has excellent Italian meals and window views of Commencement Bay and Mt. Rainier.

Asian

For ultra-fresh Japanese sushi, head downtown to **Fujiya,** 1125 Court C, tel. (253) 627-5319. Tacoma has a big Vietnamese community, and a number of authentic restaurants. Three of the best are: **Wendy's Vietnamese Restaurant** inside Freighthouse Square, 430 E. 25th, tel. (253) 572-4678; **Vien Dong Vietnamese,** 3801 S. Yakima Ave., tel. (253) 472-6668; and **East & West Cafe,** 5319 Tacoma Mall Blvd., tel. 9253) 475-7755.

Mandarin on Broadway is a fine downtown Chinese restaurant, at 1128 Broadway Plaza, tel. (253) 627-3400; or pig out at the all-you-can-eat buffet aboard the **Emerald Queen Casino,** 2102 Alexander Ave., tel. (888) 831-7655.

Italian

Simbo's, 1516 Pacific Ave., tel. (253) 383-5800, has been serving old-time Italian specialties at this location for over 75 years—the food's still great, but the run-down locale leaves something to be desired. **Luciano's,** 3327 Ruston Way, tel. (253) 756-5611, has a much nicer location—right on the water—with trendier Italian fare. A good place for a romantic evening.

Rock Pasta, 1920 Jefferson Ave., tel. (253) 272-1221, is the place to go for gourmet wood-fired pizzas and pasta and a big choice of microbrews. Another excellent pizza place—one reader called it the best he ever tasted—is **Cloverleaf Pizzas,** 6430 6th Ave., tel. (253) 565-1111. An upscale (albeit formulaic) place with fine northern Italian cuisine is **Trattoria Grazie,** 2301 N. 30th St., tel. (253) 627-0231.

Ravenous Restaurant, 785 Broadway, tel. (253) 572-6374, is a fine little downtown bistro that makes surprisingly good Italian and Northwest cuisine. Popular with the business lunch crowd.

Mexican

La Fondita, inside Freighthouse Square, tel. (253) 627-7326, has fresh Mexican food for reasonable prices. Two other of the city's best Mexican restaurants are **Moctezuma's,** 4102 S. 56th St., tel. (253) 474-5593, and **La Costa,** 928 Pacific Ave., tel. (253) 272-0300.

Groceries and Produce

Out in the Proctor District, the **Queen Anne Thriftway,** 2420 N. Proctor, tel. (253) 761-3663, is a great gourmet grocery store with imported and specialty foods and a fine deli.

The **Tacoma Farmers Market,** tel. (253) 272-7077, comes to 9th and Broadway ("Antique Row") every Thursday 10 a.m.-3 p.m. June through mid-September. Stock up on fresh fruits and vegetables, along with arts and crafts. Another farmers market is held in Proctor at 4001 N. 26th St. Saturday 9 a.m.-2 p.m., June-Aug.; tel. (253) 756-8901.

EVENTS

Kick the year off in a nonalcoholic way at Tacoma's **First Night** celebration, with all sorts of events: theater, gallery openings, live music, comedy, mimes, and more. Activities start at noon on December 31; call (253) 591-7205 for details. For three days in mid-February, **Wintergrass,** is the largest indoor bluegrass festival in the world, with 30 bands on five stages around Tacoma.

The **Daffodil Festival** in mid-April features a parade of floral floats through downtown Tacoma, a marine parade with daffodil-decorated boats, plus live entertainment and other events.

Tacoma's big **Seafirst Freedom Fair** on the Fourth of July includes arts and cultural events, and live entertainment along the waterfront. A huge fireworks display is the feature when dusk arrives, but the main attraction is the airshow—one of the largest in the nation—featuring both civilian and military aircraft over Commencement Bay. The **Taste of Tacoma** takes place at the same time, with dozens of local restaurants providing food, two concert stages with live music and entertainment, and a beer garden.

Several weekend **Salmon Bakes** are held July through September at Owen Beach in Point Defiance Park; call (253) 756-7336 for dates. The zoo in Point Defiance Park has periodic summertime concerts—**"Zoo Sounds"**—and a holiday **"Zoo Lights"** for fun; tel. (253) 591-5358.

ENTERTAINMENT AND THE ARTS

Nightlife

There's plenty of nightlife in Tacoma. For an exhaustive listing, pick up one of the free *Tacoma City Paper* or *Tacoma Reporter* newspapers in racks around town, or check the Web at www.tacoma.net. The clubs are in an almost constant state of change, but the following places are a starting point. For rock, blues, reggae, and pop bands, try **Drake's,** 734 Pacific, tel. (253) 572-4144; **The Central Tavern,** 3829 6th Ave., tel. (253) 756-0424; **Planet Hot Rod,** 7403 Pacific Hwy. in Fife, tel. (253) 926-3599; **The Swiss,** 1904 S. Jefferson, tel. (253) 572-2821; and **Christie's** at the Executive Inn in Fife (5700 Pacific Hwy. E) tel. (253) 922-0080. **The Mothership,** 7404 Pacific Hwy. in Fife, tel. (253) 922-1930, is where nationally known groups play.

Country music fans should head to **Baldy's Roadhouse**, 2501 Milton Way E, tel. (253) 927-9943, or **McCabes**, 2611 Pacific Ave., tel. (253) 272-5403.

Kellys Restaurant, 1101 Tacoma, tel. (253) 627-6425, is the main jazz venue, and the **Antique Sandwich Co.**, 5102 N. Pearl St., has jazz on weekends in a no-alcohol setting.

If gambling fits your idea of fun, head to **Emerald Queen Casino**, 2102 Alexander Ave., tel. (888) 831-7655, a New Orleans-style riverboat, with blackjack, roulette, craps, poker, and more, plus live music and a restaurant.

Taverns

A neighborhood favorite is the distinctive **Bob's Java Jive**, 2102 S. Tacoma Way, tel. (253) 475-9843, a teapot-shaped bar on S. Tacoma Way with a neon-decorated handle and spout. Inside is a jukebox with classics from the '60s, and all-American meals. Built in 1927, this place is a classic inside and out.

The **Ale House Pub & Eatery**, 2122 Mildred West, tel. (253) 565-9367, has one of the largest selections of draught beer in the state, with an incredible 63 different beers on tap. The menu is reasonable and good (especially the ribs), and the big-screen TV is popular for sporting events. See also "Pubs" under "Food," above for more places with booze and food.

Theater

Tacoma's **Broadway Center for the Performing Arts** contains a trio of outstanding theaters downtown near the intersection of 9th and Commerce Streets. The newest is the state-of-the art **Theater on the Square**, a 302-seat theater that is home to the nationally acclaimed **Tacoma Actors Guild**, who perform through the winter season; tel. (253) 272-2145. An adjacent spot of green contains a **waterfall park**, a fine place on a hot summer day. Also nearby are bronze performance masks representing various cultures.

Two lovingly restored 1918 buildings, the **Pantages Theater** and **Rialto Theater** offer a taste of Tacoma's glory days in the Broadway district. Pantages is a large and ornate vaudeville palace where there's always something going on—plays, acrobats, concerts. Get tickets early because many events sell out. The Beaux-Arts style Rialto is used for films, concerts, lectures, and touring troupes. Call (253) 591-5894 to see what's on the agenda for both of these. Also check the 1,650-seat **Temple Theatre** at 47 St. Helens, tel. (253) 272-2042, for more theatrical events, including Broadway plays, comedy shows, and concerts. Built in 1926, the Temple is one of the grandest halls in the Northwest.

In existence for more than 75 years, the **Tacoma Little Theater**, 210 N. I St. in the Stadium District, claims to be the oldest continuously performing theater west of the Mississippi. For upcoming programs, call (253) 272-2281.

Music and Dance

The **Tacoma Philharmonic**, tel. (253) 272-0809, plays at the Pantages Theater five times a year. The **Tacoma Symphony**, tel. (253) 756-3396, brings in several guest artists each year; enjoy classical music in the theater and free pops in the parks during the summer. **Tacoma Musical Playhouse**, tel. (253) 565-6867, features mystery dinners and other musicals all year. The **Tacoma Youth Symphony**, tel. (253) 627-2792, has 250 school musicians performing several concerts each year. The **Tacoma Master Chorale**, tel. (253) 565-6867, performs a series of Christmas and folk concerts each winter.

BalleTacoma offers several performances each year, including the annual *Nutcracker;* call (253) 272-9631 for more information. The **Tacoma Opera**, tel. (253) 627-7789, has English-language performances at the Pantages Theater. Call the **Arts Hotline** at (253) 383-9000, for upcoming events around Tacoma.

SPORTS AND RECREATION

Point Defiance Park (described above) has many of Tacoma's best recreation opportunities, particularly on Saturday mornings when the roads are closed to cars. For outdoor gear, head to **Backpackers Supply & Outlet**, 5206 S. Tacoma Way, tel. (253) 472-4402, where you can also rent all sorts of outdoor supplies, including kayaks and canoes. This is the place to find out about **Tahoma Outdoor Pursuits**, tel. (253) 474-8155, a group that offers classes and tours in kayaking, canoeing, rock climbing, mountaineering, and other recreation.

Spectator Sports
The Pacific Coast Baseball League is represented by the **Tacoma Rainiers,** a AAA farm club for the Oakland A's that plays at Cheney Stadium, 2525 Bantz Blvd. (off Hwy. 16), and sometimes outdraws the Seattle Mariners. For information, call (253) 752-7707. The **Tacoma Rockets** are a Western Hockey League franchise; their season is Sept.-March, and they play in the Tacoma Dome, tel. (253) 627-3653.

Swimming
Tacoma has five public swimming pools: **Eastside Community Pool,** 3424 E. L St., tel. (253) 591-2042; **People's Center Pool,** 1602 Martin Luther King Jr. Way, tel. (253) 591-5323; **South End Pool,** 402 E. 56th St., tel. (253) 474-3821; **The Centre at Norpoint,** tel. (253) 591-5504; and **Titlow Pool,** 8355 6th Ave., tel. (253) 564-4044. South End and Titlow are outdoor pools open only in the summer months.

Public swimming beaches can be found at **Titlow Park,** just south of the Narrows Bridge, and **Wapato Lake Park,** where a lifeguard is present in the summer. **American Lake Park,** south of Tacoma near Fort Lewis, also has swimming.

Golf
Local public golf courses include: **Allenmore Golf Course,** 2125 S. Cedar, tel. (253) 627-7211; **Meadow Park Golf Course,** 7108 Lakewood Dr. W, tel. (253) 473-3033; **North Shore Golf & Country Club,** 4101 North Shore Blvd. NE, tel. (253) 927-1375 or (800) 447-1375; **Brookdale Golf Course,** 1802 Brookdale Rd. E, tel. (253) 537-4400; **Classic Country Club,** 4908 208th St. E in Spanaway, tel. (253) 847-4440; and **Ft. Steilacoom Golf Course,** 8202 87th Ave. SW, tel. (253) 588-0613.

SHOPPING

Freighthouse Square on 25th and East D (a block north of Tacoma Dome) is Tacoma's version of Pike Place Market, though it isn't nearly as successful. More than 70 small shops and restaurants can be found inside the turn-of-the-century Milwaukee/St. Paul Railroad freighthouse. You can get everything from pet supplies to clothes to fettuccine here. It's worth a look if you're in town, and a couple of the ethnic cafes are quite good. Open daily. A great place to explore for used books is not far away, the **Tacoma Book Center,** 324 E. 26th St., tel. (253) 572-8248.

Downtown Tacoma has more than 20 fine art galleries, along with several antique shops along **"Antique Row"** on Broadway between 7th and 9th Sts. in downtown Tacoma.

One of the most enjoyable browsing sections in Tacoma is a mostly upscale cluster of shops and boutiques called the **Proctor District** along the 2700 block area of N. Proctor. Some of the more interesting ones include the **Proctor District Antique Mall** with more than 40 dealers, and the **Pacific Northwest Shop,** which stocks only goods produced in the region. Also here is **Bulldog News,** with a great selection of magazines.

All the major national and regional stores can be found at local shopping malls. The biggest are: **Tacoma Mall** with 135 stores, and **Lakewood Mall** with 160 stores.

INFORMATION AND SERVICES

For information on Tacoma and the surrounding area, head to **Tacoma-Pierce County Visitor and Convention Bureau** 1001 Pacific Ave., Suite 400 (entrance is on 10th St.), tel. (253) 627-2836 or (800) 272-2662. Open Mon.-Fri. 8:30 a.m.-5 p.m. year-round. A second visitor center is inside the State History Museum at 1911 Pacific Ave.; open daily. Get more info on the Web at www.tpctourism.org.

The main **Tacoma Public Library,** tel. (253) 591-5666, is at 1102 Tacoma Ave. South. Be sure to head upstairs to the Northwest Room to check out the stained glass dome ceiling. Tacoma's main **post office,** at 1102 S. A St., tel. (253) 471-6122, has a small museum with a mail sleigh and other philatelic memorabilia, along with historic stamps.

TRANSPORTATION AND TOURS

Bus Service
Pierce Transit, tel. (253) 581-8000 or (800) 562-8109, has daily bus service to Puyallup, Gig

Harbor, Lakewood, Steilacoom, Spanaway, Fife, Buckley, and every other town in Pierce County, along with commuter service to Seattle and Olympia. Find them on the Web at www.ptbus.pierce.wa.us.

The bus station is located at 1319 Pacific Avenue. **Greyhound,** tel. (253) 383-4621 or (800) 231-2222, has bus service throughout the nation, including along the I-5 corridor, connecting Tacoma with Portland, Seattle, and Vancouver. **Northwestern Trailways,** tel. (800) 366-6975, connects Tacoma with Seattle and Everett.

Train Service
Amtrak, tel. (800) 872-7245, serves Tacoma from its passenger station at 1001 Puyallup Ave., between the tide flat area and I-5 in the eastern part of the city. The Coast Starlight provides four-times-a-day service to the Puget Sound area from Portland, San Francisco, and Los Angeles.

Ferry Service
The **Washington State Ferry** system is a heavily used method of everyday transportation around the Puget Sound region. From Tacoma, however, it can only get you to Tahlequah on Vashon Island. Ferries depart from Point Defiance; summer fares are $2.40 roundtrip for passengers and walk-ons, $11 roundtrip for car and driver. Fares are collected only on the way to Vashon, not when you return. For information on the ferry system, call (425) 355-7308 or (888) 808-7977. Call (800) 843-3779 for automated information.

Seattle-Tacoma International Airport
If you're flying into Tacoma, you'll probably arrive at the Seattle-Tacoma International Airport. As the name suggests, it's about halfway between Seattle and Tacoma. For information, call (206) 431-4444 or (800) 544-1965. **Super Shuttle,** tel. (800) 487-7433, and **Capital Aeroporter,** tel. (206) 754-7113 or (800) 962-3579, offer door-to-airport service.

VICINITY OF TACOMA

PARKLAND/SPANAWAY, LAKEWOOD, AND FORT LEWIS

Technically separate towns, but in reality an extension of the Tacoma metropolitan area, the Parkland, Spanaway, and Lakewood area hosts a few good restaurants and a beautiful park. Fort Lewis and McChord Air Force Base reside in neighboring Lakewood, appropriately named for its three lakes: American, Gravelly, and Steilacoom. Established in 1917 when the citizens of Tacoma passed a bond measure to donate land for a military post, Fort Lewis was a vital training center during WW I. Today, it is still one of the Army's largest permanent posts, with 20,000 rangers, Special Forces, and other soldiers, along with the Madigan Army Medical Center, a recently opened $200 million facility that is the largest on the West Coast. Nearby McChord Air Force Base has been here since 1938, and today employs more than 6,600 personnel in a variety of military and civilian roles.

Sights
Lakewood Gardens, 12317 Gravelly Lake Dr., tel. (253) 584-3360 or (888) 858-4106, is a 10-acre collection of rare plants, including blue poppies from Tibet. The gardens feature one of the largest collections of rhododendrons and Japanese maples in the Northwest and were designed by noted landscape architect Thomas Church. A lovely Georgian-style brick home on this country estate is also open to the public. Hours are Thurs.-Mon. 10 a.m.-4 p.m. (Friday noon-8 p.m.), April-Sept., and Fri.-Sun. 10 a.m.-3 p.m. the rest of the year. Admission is $6 adults, $5 seniors and kids under 12. Get in on Saturday for $6 per carload.

Take exit 120 from I-5, 16 miles south of Tacoma, to the **Fort Lewis Military Museum,** tel. (253) 967-7206, located in a 1918 Swiss-style building originally used as a Salvation Army center. The museum emphasizes Northwest military history, including displays of the dress uniforms from various eras, the history of the I Corps, and such oddities as Gen. Norman Schwartzkopf's jeep (he was base commander here in the early 1980s). Obtain a pass at the vis-

'tors office on the east side of the freeway near the main gate. Open Wed.-Sun. noon-4 p.m.; free.

Another military collection is the **McChord Air Museum,** tel. (253) 984-2485, one mile east on exit 125. The museum contains several aircraft, flying gear, uniforms, and other Air Force memorabilia from the 1930s through the 1960s. Open Tues.-Sun. noon-4 p.m., closed holidays. Free.

One of Spanaway's main summertime attractions is the **Spanaway Speedway,** which has racing on Sunday afternoons, plus Wednesday, Friday, and Saturday nights March to October. The speedway is located at 159th and 22nd Ave. E; call (253) 537-7551 for events.

Located off Pacific Ave., **Spanaway County Park** is an ideal place to take a walk, go for a swim, or take out the boat. Back to back with Spanaway Lake Golf Course, the park has a beach, trails, lots of trees, and picnic areas.

Accommodations and Food

See the "Tacoma Area Motels and Hotels" chart for Lakewood area motels.

Thornewood Castle B&B, 8601 N. Thorne Ln. SW, tel. (253) 589-9052, is a magnificent 1910 Tudor mansion on American Lake, with a half-acre sunken English garden. Inside you'll find 16th-century stained glass and other ornate furnishings. Five guest rooms have private baths, and a full breakfast is served; $150-200 d. No kids.

Maxey's Restaurant, 10727 Pacific Hwy. SW, tel. (253) 588-5503, serves breakfast 365 days a year from 6 a.m. on. **La Palma,** at Lakewood Mall, tel. (253) 582-8349, has authentic Mexican dishes. **Marzano's,** 516 Garfield S, tel. (253) 537-4191, is a wonderful little restaurant with perfectly prepared Italian meals.

Events and Information

Lakewood's main summer event is **Summerfest** at Lakewood Mall in late July, where the streets are taken over by arts and crafts vendors, food vendors, live entertainment, a beer garden, and amusement park rides. Call (253) 584-6191 for details.

The **Lakewood Area Chamber of Commerce,** 9523 Gravelly Lake Dr. SW, tel. (253) 582-9400, has local info.

STEILACOOM

The state's second oldest incorporated town (after Tumwater) had established itself as the busiest port on Puget Sound by 1854. Today the quaint town of Steilacoom (STILL-a-cum) still clings to and respects its historic heritage. More than 30 local buildings are on the National Register of Historic Places, including the state's first jail (1858), first Protestant church (1853), and first library north of the Columbia River (1858).

Sights

Bair Drug and Hardware, at 1617 Lafayette, tel. (253) 588-9668, is an 1895 shop with a sampling of historic items on display and a 1906 soda fountain where you can still get a soda or sundae, along with something you wouldn't find in 1906, espresso coffees. Great baked goods and pies here as well. Open Mon.-Thurs. 9 a.m.-4 p.m., Friday 6-9 p.m., and Sat.-Sun. 8 a.m.-4 p.m.

The **Steilacoom Town Hall and Museum,** tel. (253) 584-4133, focuses on the town's pioneer period. Pick up their *Guide to Historic Steilacoom* for a walking tour. Located downstairs in the white New England-style Town Hall on Main and Lafayette, the free museum is open Tues.-Sun. 1-4 p.m. March-Oct., and Fri.-Sun. 1-4 p.m. in November, December, and February; closed January.

The Historical Society also owns the **Nathaniel Orr Home and Orchard,** 1811 Rainier St., tel. (253) 584-4133, a two-story clapboard home built by its owner, who constructed wagons, coffins, and cabinets. The well-tended orchard includes apple, cherry, and plum trees. Open Sunday 1-4 p.m. April-October.

Located in a turn-of-the-century Congregational Church building, **Steilacoom Tribal Cultural Center and Museum,** 1515 Lafayette St., tel. (253) 584-6308, documents the history of the Steilacoom tribe with exhibits that feature the prehistory of the Tacoma Basin, historical artifacts, and contemporary artistry. The Steilacoom were one of the eight Washington tribes that were never allotted a reservation. The gift shop sells native crafts, and the snack bar serves light breakfasts and lunches. Open Tues.-Sun.

10 a.m.-4 p.m. year-round; admission is $2 adults, $1 seniors and kids, children under six free, and $6 families.

East from the town of Steilacoom is **Fort Steilacoom,** tel. (253) 584-2368, right next to the massive Western State Hospital (a mental institution). Four small frame houses remain from this fort, established in 1849. One of the buildings has an interpretive center and small museum open for summertime tours on Saturday 1-4 p.m.

Fort Steilacoom County Park on Steilacoom Blvd. has a trail that circles Waughop Lake (drive down Dresdon Lane, then park by the barns). **Sunnyside Beach Park** off Lafayette St. and **Salters Point Park** off 1st St. are both small waterfront parks with picnic facilities.

Food

Crystal chandeliers, antiques, and a wonderful Queen Anne Victorian home overlooking the Sound provide an elegant setting for some of the best food around Puget Sound, at **E.R. Rogers,** 1702 Commercial, tel. (253) 582-0280. The prime rib and seafood entrees are pricey, but well worth the money. If you can't get reservations, at least have a drink in the cozy, upstairs-bedroom bar with a couple of outside tables. Open daily for dinner only, plus a very popular Sunday brunch.

Less ostentatious—and considerably cheaper—is **Bair Drug and Hardware** (see above) where the old soda fountain has sundaes, ice cream sodas, and fresh pies and sweets from the bakery. They also serve Friday night dinners.

Events

The **Steilacoom Fourth of July** includes a parade and street fair with food vendors, art booths, and live entertainment. Other events include a popular **Salmon Bake** on the last Sunday in July, and the **Apple Squeeze Festival** in early October. Call (253) 584-4133 for details.

Ferry Service

Pierce County operates the small **Anderson Island-Steilacoom Ferry,** which leaves Steilacoom Dock about every two hours 6 a.m.-6 p.m. Roundtrip summer fares are $11.40 for car and driver, $2.70 for passengers and pedestrians. Call (253) 798-7250 for more information. The ferry also visits tiny Ketron Island (no public facilities). A separate ferry takes corrections officers and prisoners to McNeil Island, home of a state prison.

ANDERSON ISLAND

Miles of roads and rural bike paths are the primary attractions to draw mainlanders to quiet Anderson Island. The restored **Johnson Farm,** founded by John Johnson in 1881, has tours weekend afternoons in the summer. Also here is the pilothouse from the *Tahoma,* the island's ferry from 1943 to 1954. **Anderson Island Historical Museum,** tel. (253) 884-2135, has local historical items on display. Open Sat.-Sun. noon-4 p.m. summers only.

Lodging

There are two places to stay on the island. **The Inn at Burg's Landing B&B,** 8808 Villa Beach Rd., tel. (253) 884-9185, is a modern log home featuring views of Mt. Rainier, a private beach, jacuzzi, and full breakfast. The four rooms are $75-110 s or d. Kids welcome. Another fine place is **Anderson House on Oro Bay,** 12024 Eckenstam-Johnson Rd., tel. (253) 884-4088 or (800) 750-4088, a beautiful 1920s farmhouse at the head of Oro Bay. Stay in one of four rooms for $98 s or d, including a full breakfast and private baths. No kids. A separate three-bedroom house with kitchen and deck sleeps six (kids accepted) and costs $240/night.

Ferry Service

The **Anderson Island-Steilacoom ferry,** tel. (253) 798-7250, leaves Steilacoom Dock about every two hours from 6 a.m. to 6 p.m. on a 20-minute run to the island. Roundtrip fares are $11.40 for car and driver, and $2.70 for passengers and people on foot.

GIG HARBOR

Just across the Narrows Bridge from Tacoma, the prosperous town of Gig Harbor (pop. 6,400) definitely warrants a visit. The harbor is one of the finest and most scenic on Puget Sound, with hundreds of sailing and fishing boats, tall pine trees, and a circle of seaside houses, all against

Kopachuck State Park

the picture-perfect backdrop of Mt. Rainier—a photo that graces many calendars and magazine covers.

Gig Harbor was named by Commander Charles Wilkes who sent out a captain's gig (a small boat) for a survey of the area. When a sudden storm blew up, the protected waters—almost entirely circled by land—proved an excellent harbor for his gig. Today, Gig Harbor is home to many commercial fishing and pleasure craft. Boatbuilding was an important part of Gig Harbor's history, and hundreds of purse seiners, gill netters, tenders, yachts, and other vessels were constructed here over the decades. Early inhabitants were mostly from Sweden and Croatia. Today, the town attracts tourists with upscale shops, galleries, good restaurants, and at least one great tavern.

Sights and Shopping
The **Gig Harbor-Peninsula Historical Society Museum** is housed in a new building at 4218 Harborview Dr., tel. (253) 858-6722, and is open Tues.-Sat. 10 a.m.-4 p.m ; free. Inside is a nice small collection of exhibits on fishing and boat building, plus local artifacts and more than 2,500 historical photos.

Downtown Gig Harbor is strung out along the water, with shops and restaurants luring browsers. Head to the head of the harbor for **Ebb Tide Gallery & Gifts,** tel. (253) 851-5293, a cooperative gallery with the works of local artists, and **Gallery Row,** tel. (253) 851-6020, both at 8825 N. Harborview Drive.

Kopachuck State Park
You'd never expect so much solitude so close to a major city. Located 12 miles northwest of Tacoma off Hwy. 16 (just follow the signs), Kopachuck has a campground and picnic areas. The 103-acre park is shaded by skyscraping pines and has a beach for swimming, clamming, and fishing. It is also one of Puget Sound's most beautiful parks, and even includes the small (5.5 acres) Cutts Island, which is a marine park only a short distance offshore with mooring buoys. Scuba divers come here to explore an underwater park with a sunken barge. For more information, call (253) 265-3606.

Fox Island
Fox Island is five miles southwest of Gig Harbor and is connected by a bridge over Hale Passage. The **Fox Island Historical Society and Museum,** tel. (253) 549-2239, is open Monday and Saturday 1-4 p.m., and Wednesday 1-3 p.m.; $1.

Several Fox Island B&Bs provide cozy lodging choices. The **Beachside B&B,** 679 Kamus Dr., tel. (253) 549-2524, is a gorgeous waterfront home with fireplace, kitchen, beach, and buoy for boaters. A continental breakfast is served and kids are allowed; $95 s or d. **Island Escape B&B,** 210 Island Blvd., tel. (253) 549-2044, is a contemporary suite with a king-size bed, jacuzzi bath, and private deck affording a view of the Sound. No kids; $95 s or $115 d. **The Brambles B&B,** 1077 12th Ave., tel. (253) 549-4959, contains a suite with king size bed, private bath, and full breakfast; $70 s or $80 d.

Olalla
Several B&Bs can be found in the rolling pasture lands around tiny Olalla, on the shore of Colvos

Passage north of Gig Harbor. **Childs House B&B,** tel. (253) 857-4252 or (800) 250-4954, has three guest rooms in a large three-story home with a wrap-around porch for $65-95 d. **Still Waters B&B,** tel. (253) 857-5111, has three guest rooms in a plantation home with a hot tub for $55-65 d. **Olalla Orchard B&B,** tel. (253) 857-5915, has a single guest room with a jacuzzi bath and porch for $85 d. **Eagleview House,** tel. (253) 857-2822, is a private waterfront suite with its own beach for $115 d.

Gig Harbor B&Bs

Gig Harbor has a number of bed and breakfast establishments and motels. Other nearby places are listed above under "Fox Island" and "Olala." Unless otherwise noted, all B&Bs listed below serve a full breakfast and do not allow young children.

Peacock Hill Guest House B&B, 9520 Peacock Hill Ave., tel. (800) 863-2318, is an open contemporary home near the marina with one guest room ($85) and a spacious suite ($115), both with private bath.

Sunny Bay Cottage, 50 Raft Island, tel. (253) 265-6987 or (800) 410-6987, is a charming and secluded cottage with a full kitchen, woodstove, and hot tub; $115 s or d.

Rosedale B&B, 7714 Ray Nash Dr., tel. (253) 851-5420, is a contemporary Victorian-style home right along the shore, with a spacious guest suite and private bath, fireplace, and deck. Kids are welcome; $95 s or d.

Mary's B&B, 8212 Dorotich St., tel. (253) 858-2424, has three guest rooms with private baths in a charming old waterfront home filled with family heirlooms. A good place to watch sunsets; $85 s or d.

Harborside B&B, 8708 Goodman Dr. NW, tel. (253) 851-1795, is a new suite with full kitchen and private entrance for $120 s or d. Next door is **Water's Edge B&B,** tel. (253) 851-3890, where the suite includes an outside hot tub and boat dock; $130 s or d.

The Pillars B&B, 6606 Soundview Dr., tel. (253) 851-6644, offers a plantation-style home with views of Mt. Rainier, plus an indoor pool and jacuzzi. Stay in one of three guest rooms, all with private baths; $95 s or $125 d.

The Fountains B&B, 926 120th St. NW, tel. (253) 851-6262, is an elaborate three-story home

in the country north of Gig Harbor. The guest suite has a private bath and entrance, and a fine view; $115 s or d.

Twelve miles north of Gig Harbor on Glen Cove at 9418 Glencove Rd., the **Old Glencove Hotel,** tel. (253) 884-2835, built in 1897 and now on the National Register of Historic Places, has been restored and transformed into a waterside bed and breakfast. Inside are four guest rooms with shared or private baths; $65-85 s or d. Kids are accepted.

Westbay, tel. (253) 265-3033 or (800) 420-3033, is a beautiful waterfront home on Wollochet Bay with a deck, boat dock, and porch facing the water. Rates are $150 d (sleeps six). This is not a B&B, but it does have a full kitchen and hot tub.

Gig Harbor Motels

Located in an attractive wooded setting, **Gig Harbor Motor Inn,** 4709 Pt. Fosdick Dr. NW, tel. (253) 858-8161, has rooms for $50-70 s or d (some with kitchens). **Westwynd Motel-Apartments,** 6703 144th St. NW, tel. (253) 857-4047 or (800) 468-9963, has apartments (some with kitchens) for $48-72 s or d. **The Maritime Inn,** 3212 Harborview Dr., tel. (253) 858-1818, has rooms right in town for $75-130 s or d. **The Inn at Gig Harbor,** 3211 56th St. NW, tel. (253) 858-1111 or (800) 795-9980, is a large new hotel with rooms and suites for $89-199 s or d, including an exercise facility, jacuzzi, and continental breakfast. **Best Western Wesley Inn,** 6575 Kimball Dr., tel. (253) 858-9690 or (888) 462-0002, is another attractive new hotel with rooms and suites for $99-159 s or d, including an outdoor pool, jacuzzi, and continental breakfast.

Campgrounds

Camp in the tall pines at **Kopachuck State Park** (described above), seven miles northwest of Gig Harbor, tel. (253) 265-3606. Tent spaces are $11; no RV hookups; open from late April to early October. Call (800) 452-5687 for reservations ($6 extra). The private **Gig Harbor RV Resort,** 9515 Burnham Dr., tel. (253) 858-8138 or (800) 526-8311, has RV and tent sites.

Food

At the immensely popular **Tides Tavern,** 2925 Harborview in Gig Harbor, you can arrive by car or boat, and they've got a small deck for outdoor drinking and boat-watching. Besides burgers, the Tides offers pizza, sandwiches, and the best local fish and chips, plus live music on weekends. No kids.

Harbor Inn Restaurant, 3111 Harborview Dr., tel. (253) 851-5454, has a great view of the harbor on three levels and serves lunch and dinner every day and breakfast on Sunday.

Get fiery hot Chinese food at **Harbor Monsoon Restaurant,** 4628 Pt. Fosdick Dr. NW, tel. (253) 858-9838.

Harbor Bread Co., 8812 N. Harborview Dr., tel. (253) 851-4181, bakes wonderful earthy breads and tasty pastries. The bakery is hidden behind Finholm's Market and Grocery at the head of the harbor. **Suzanne's Bakery & Deli,** 3411 Harborview Dr., tel. (253) 853-6220, is a fine stop for sandwiches, sweets, and espresso.

Marco's Ristorante, 7707 Pioneer Way, tel. (253) 858-2899, has Italian fare with flair, along with an adjacent Italian deli. The same folks run another favorite of locals and visitors: **The Green Turtle,** 2905 Harborview Dr., tel. (253)·851-3167, where the menu ventures eastward, with distinctively creative Thai and Chinese-inspired meals. Both of these are recommended, but reservations are a good idea.

Spiro's Pizza & Pasta, 3108 Harborview Dr., tel. (253) 851-9200, makes very good from-scratch pizzas, pasta, subs, and salads.

For the freshest local produce, baked goods, and crafts, head to the **Gig Harbor Farmers Market,** tel. (253) 884-2496, held on Saturday 9 a.m.-3 p.m. May-Oct. at the Pierce Transit Park & Ride on Kimball Street.

Events
Gig Harbor events include a **Maritime Gig** on the first weekend of June, and a couple of arts and crafts fairs: the **Gig Harbor Art Festival** in mid-July features a parade, kids' fest, art fair, fun run, live music, and a salmon dinner. Gig Harbor's **Lighted Boat Parade** the second Saturday of December is another enjoyable event. For information, call (253) 851-6865.

Arts and Entertainment
Gig Harbor's **Performance Circle Theater** has productions in Celebrations Meadow during the summer months and at Burton Park Theater on winter weekends. Celebrations Meadow is on the left side of Peacock Hill Ave., about one-half mile up from Harborview; the Burton Park theater is at the extreme north end of 38th Ave. NW. For information, call (253) 851-7529.

Tides Tavern, 2611 Harborview Dr., tel. (253) 858-3982, has live rock or blues bands on the weekends.

Information and Services
The **Gig Harbor/Peninsula Area Chamber of Commerce,** 3302 Harborview Dr., tel. (253) 851-6865, can provide you with local brochures and info. Open Mon.-Fri. 10 a.m.-5 p.m., Saturday 10 a.m.-3 p.m. and Sunday 11 a.m.-2 p.m. June to Labor Day, and Mon.-Fri. 10 a.m.-5 p.m. the rest of the year.

Rent powerboats, jet skis, skippered sailboats, sea kayaks, pedal boats, and other on-the-water vessels from **Rent-a-Boat & Charters,** 8827 N. Harborview Dr., tel. (253) 858-7341. **Gig Harbor Kayak Center,** 8809 N. Harborview Dr., tel. (253) 851-7987 or (888) 429-2548, has sea kayak rentals and tours.

Transportation
Pierce Transit, tel. (253) 581-8000 or (800) 562-8109, has daily service from Gig Harbor, Fox Island, Key Center and Longbranch to Tacoma and other parts of Pierce County. The **Bremerton-Kitsap Airporter,** tel. (253) 876-1737 or (800) 562-7948, offers shuttle bus connections to Sea-Tac Airport. Or, you can fly there aboard **Harbor Air,** tel. (253) 851-2381.

KEY PENINSULA

West of Gig Harbor and across Carr Inlet is another fingerlike appendage reaching into the southernmost end of Puget Sound: Key Peninsula. The peninsula has a small commercial center called **Home,** but is essentially a haven for retirees and commuters. Find a collection of local memorabilia at the **Key Peninsula Historical Museum** in Vaughn, tel. (253) 884-4538, open Thurs.-Sat. 1-4 p.m. The big summertime event is the **Key Peninsula Pioneer Days Festival** in early August.

Parks

Penrose Point State Park covers 152 acres of shoreline two miles south of Home. No RV hookups, but the park has tent spaces in the trees for $11; open late April through Labor Day. Also here are a couple miles of hiking trails and a boat dock. Call (253) 884-2514 for more information, or (800) 452-5687 for reservations ($6 extra). More camping ($10; open year-round) at the 170-acre **Joemma State Park,** tel. (253) 884-1944, two miles south of Home along Whitman Cove. The park has a fun beach and a big dock.

Purdy Spit, located at the head of Henderson Bay (the upper end of Carr Inlet), is bisected by Hwy. 302 and is a favorite place to beachcomb, dig for clams, and windsurf.

VASHON ISLAND

Vashon Island is not the place to go if you're expecting a hot time on the ol' town; cows and horses probably outnumber humans. This rural, slow-paced, homey environment is fine for bike tours but not bar-hopping. There are no McDonald's, Burger Kings, or Wendy's here. Vashon's residents are a mix of commuting yupsters, post-hippie artisans, retirees, and power-politics farmers.

Vashon Island was one of the many islands encountered in 1792 by Capt. George Vancouver, who, having named enough things after himself, decided to give this one to his Navy buddy, James Vashon. Maury Island, the piece of land east of Vashon, is connected to it by a natural sandbar and lots of manmade fill (and therefore is not an island at all). Maury was separately named and identified by a member of the Wilkes survey party in 1841. The Vashon piece is 12.5 miles north to south and a maximum four miles wide; Maury is only 5.5 miles long and, at most, two miles wide. Vashon is only 15 minutes by ferry from Tacoma and about the same from West Seattle. In the early years of this century, Vashon was heavily logged over, and fruit orchards and berry crops covered large areas. Today, the trees are slowly returning in many areas, and the main crop seems to be homes.

Farm Products

Gourmet fruits and vegetables are a specialty of Vashon Island. Every Saturday 9 a.m.-3 p.m., March through mid-October, the **Vashon Farmers Market** in downtown Vashon is as much a social gathering as a place to buy food and artwork from islanders; tel. (206) 463-6557. **Wax Orchards,** 22744 Wax Orchard, tel. (206) 463-9735, offers fresh cider and homemade fruit syrups; and **The Country Store and Farm,** on Vashon Hwy. SW at S.W. 204th St., tel. (206) 463-3655, sells island food, natural fiber clothing, herbs, and flowers. Next door is **Maury Island Farm General Store,** tel. (206) 463-5617 or (800) 356-5880, selling locally made preserves, jams, marmalades, and other berry products. Across the highway stands a favorite Vashon restaurant, **Sound Food** (described below). For an odd scene, walk 100 feet north of the restaurant and across a tiny creeklet. Here you'll find a child's bike deeply embedded in a two-foot diameter Douglas fir. Nobody knows exactly how the bike got there.

Maury Island's **TailorMade Farm,** tel. (206) 463-9816, raises angora goats and Lincoln sheep—a long-haired English breed—and uses the wool in lamb fleeces and hand-woven rugs. There are at least seven **llama farms** on Vashon; check with the chamber of commerce for specifics, and also for local U-pick strawberry and raspberry farms. One of Vashon's best-known residents is farmer and Republican sugar daddy, Tom Stewart. His Misty Isle Farms estate/cattle ranch remains a favorite of national GOP leaders who appreciate Stewart's fundraising abilities (despite a 1997 conviction and $5 million fine for illegal contributions).

Other Attractions

The roasting plant for **Seattle's Best Coffee** can be found at Valley Center. The collection of historic coffee-roasting machinery is fun to explore in this funky old building; be sure to check out the "items found in the beans" collection. Half-hour tours of the roasting and tasting facilities are available by calling (206) 463-9335 at least one day ahead. Established in 1968 as Stewart Brothers Coffee, SBC officially changed the company name in 1989 after becoming better known for the SBC initials used on their signs. Fresh whole-bean or ground coffee is available

VASHON ISLAND

SOUTHWORTH FERRY

SEATTLE AND FAUNTLEROY FERRIES

99

103 AVE. SW

104 AVE SW

BETTY MacDONALD FARM COTTAGE

106 SW AVE. SW

107 AVE SW

VASHON ISLAND HWY.

123 AVE. SW

MIMI'S COTTAGE BY THE SEA

ARTIST'S STUDIO LOFT

VASHON ISLAND RANCH / AYA HOSTEL

COVE RD.

SW 168 ST.

OLD TJOMSLAND HOUSE B&B

BANK RD.

SW 176 ST.

VASHON

CHAMBER OF COMMERCE

SOJOURN HOUSE

VAN GELDERS RETREAT B&B

VASHON ISLAND

SBC COFFEE

BLUE HERON CENTER FOR THE ARTS

SW CEMETERY RD.

BOULDER LODGE

KVI BEACH

SW 204 ST.

SOUND FOOD

TRAMP HARBOR INN B&B

111 AVE. SW

OLD MILL COTTAGES B&B

SW 220 ST.

91 AVE. SW

PARADISE VALLEY FARM B&B

PEABODY'S B&B

SEA LOTUS DAY SPA AND B&B

SW 232 ST.

MAURY ISLAND

WAX ORCHARDS

BACK BAY INN B&B

BURTON ACRES PARK

PT. ROBINSON LIGHTHOUSE

SW 240 ST.

75 PL. SW

SWALLOW'S NEST GUEST COTTAGES

DOCKTON RD

TAYLORMADE FARM

131 AVE. SW

ANGELS OF THE SEA B&B

CASTLE HILL B&B

TAHLEQUAH RD.

131 AVE. SW

TAHLEQUAH

ALL SEASONS'S WATERFRONT

TACOMA FERRY

MOON

0   1 mi

0   1 km

© MOON PUBLICATIONS, INC.

at the plant, in Seattle-area stores, or by calling (800) 962-9659. A block or so north of the SBC building is the **K-2** ski and snowboard manufacturing plant; no tours.

The **Blue Heron Center for the Arts,** mid-island at Vashon Island Hwy. and 196th St. SW, tel. (206) 463-5131, has a small gallery with high quality arts and crafts, and a central space for concerts, classes, and plays. Closed Sunday and Monday. Two other fine places for artwork are **Silverwood Gallery,** 24927 Vashon Hwy. SW in Burton, tel. (206) 463-1722, and **Emerald City Gallery,** 17508 Vashon Hwy. SW, tel. (206) 463-6468.

Quiet downtown Vashon is the home of **Vashon Hardware Co.,** tel. (206) 463-9551, one of Washington's finest old-time hardware stores. A collection of antique tools lines the walls. Another place worth a look is **Oberton's Wonderful Store,** tel. (206) 463-6621, on S.W. 178th Street. Oberton's bills itself as an antique and curio shop, but is best known for the collection of vintage radios.

There are very few parcels of public land on Vashon Island, meaning that much of the shoreline is posted with No Trespassing signs. One exception is **Point Robinson Lighthouse** on the easternmost end of Maury Island. Built in 1893, it is open for tours Sat.-Sun. noon-4 p.m.

A pleasant place for an evening stroll is the pebbly, driftwood-strewn beach and marsh on land owned by radio station KVI. Get to **KVI Beach** by heading east out S.W. Ellisport Rd. and then turning left (north) where it hits the shoreline.

Burton Acres Park faces out onto Quartermaster Harbor and Maury Island and has hiking trails. The local school district has some 500 acres of undeveloped land out on S.W. Bank Road. Although some of it has been logged recently, there are other second-growth forested areas with trails cutting through that are popular with those afoot or on horseback. The school land is at the south end of 115 Ave. SW not far from the hostel.

Recreation

Cyclists love the quiet roads of Vashon Island. You can carry bikes aboard all state ferries (including the passenger one to Vashon from Seattle) for an extra 60 cents roundtrip. Metro buses all have front bike racks that you can use if your legs poop out while riding around the island, or for getting to the Fauntleroy terminal from Seattle. Rent bikes from **Vashon Island Bicycles,** 17232 Vashon Hwy. SW, tel. (206) 463-6225. **Eastlyshire Hayrides,** 16309 Crescent Dr. SW, tel. (206) 567-4146, offers hay wagons pulled by their distinctive Shire horses.

A summer-only outdoor **swimming pool** is at the high school on S.W. Ellisport Rd. tel. (206) 463-3787. **Vashon Island Kayak,** tel. (206) 463-9257, rents sea kayak and leads tours from Burton Acres Park.

Hostel

The least expensive place to stay on the island is unique **Vashon Island Ranch and Summer Hostel,** 12119 Cove Rd., tel. (206) 463-2592. Owner Judy Mulhair has created an amusing Western-theme hostel with teepees, covered wagons, a log bunkhouse, and barn. The ranch sits on 10 acres of meadows and woods. The lodge houses two dorms ($10-13 pp), and a full kitchen. Guests can also stay in the covered wagons and teepees (same rate), or pitch their own tent for the same price. In addition, couples can stay in a private room with separate bath for $35-45 d. The hostel is open May-Oct. only.

Guests can borrow the old one-speed bikes and rent sleeping bags or lockers. A free do-it-yourself pancake breakfast, volleyball and horseshoe games, barbecue grill, and the evening campfire provide chances to trade tales with fellow travelers. This is a very popular place for adventurous travelers from all over the globe, with 50 or so visitors on busy summer nights. The owner picks up folks at the Vashon Thriftway grocery store on weekdays or at the ferry terminal on weekends, but call ahead so she can meet you.

Bed and Breakfasts

Vashon Island has a number of delightfully romantic B&Bs and guest cottages, making this a great weekend get-away place. Unless otherwise noted, all B&Bs listed below serve a full breakfast and do not allow young children. **Castle Hill B&B Lodging and Reservations,** tel. (206) 463-5491, is a very helpful reservation service for most of Vashon Island's B&Bs. They also have a nicely furnished turn-of-the-century apartment with a kitchen for $85 s or d; kids accepted. Other B&Bs are listed alphabetically below.

Angels of the Sea B&B, Dockton Harbor, tel. (206) 463-6980 or (800) 798-9249, has three guest rooms in a converted country church (built in 1917) with a shared and private bath. Guests are treated to live harp music during breakfast. Kids are welcome. $75-125 s or d.

Set on five acres with flower gardens and ponds, **Artist's Studio Loft,** 16529 91st SW, tel. (206) 463-2583, has three private suites with separate entrances, a jacuzzi, woodstove, and a big continental breakfast; $85-105 s or d. Two-night minimum on weekends.

Back Bay Inn B&B, 24007 Vashon Hwy. SW, tel. (206) 463-5355, is a turn-of-the-century country inn with four guest rooms, private baths, and European antiques. $98-113 s or d.

Betty MacDonald Farm, 12000 99th Ave. SW, tel. (206) 567-4227, was the home of this well-known children's author; she wrote *The Egg and I* and many others. MacDonald died in 1958, and her Vashon Island farm is now a tastefully romantic B&B just a few blocks from the ferry dock. The big old barn sits on six acres atop a bluff facing Mt. Rainier, and has a spacious upper loft with kitchen and woodstove. A separate cottage is popular with families. Both go for $108-115 s or d. The fridges are well stocked for a make-your-own breakfast.

Boulder Lodge, 13320 108th Ave. SW, tel. (206) 567-0999 (evenings), is a cozy two-bedroom log cabin with a full kitchen, fireplace and a deck facing the water; $85 s or d. Kids accepted, and two-night minimum.

Harbor Inn B&B, 9118 SW Harbor Dr., tel. (206) 463-6794, is a custom-designed waterside English Tudor home with a luxurious suite and guest room. Breathtaking views, and the suite includes a jacuzzi tub; $125-185 s or d.

One of the nicer places on Vashon is **Harbor Hideaway,** 11709 252nd Ln. SW, tel. (206) 463-3476, located right on the water. The grounds are popular for weddings, and the two-bedroom apartment includes a full kitchen and continental breakfast; $125 s or d. Kids accepted.

Run by the same folks who own the Vashon Hostel, **Lavender Duck B&B,** 16503 Vashon Hwy. SW, tel. (206) 463-2592, is a century-old farmhouse facing Mt. Rainier. Inside are four comfortable guest rooms with private baths. Kids are welcome, and a pancake breakfast is served. Rates are $55 s or d ($45/night for two nights). This is the best deal on the island for couples.

Surrounded by 10 acres of parklike grounds, **Old Mill Cottage B&B,** 4603 Old Mill Rd. SW, tel. (206) 463-1670, is a pretty two-story cottage in the woods with an upstairs bedroom and soaking tub. A continental breakfast is provided. $100 d.

Old Tjomsland House B&B, 17011 Vashon Hwy. SW, tel. (206) 463-5275, is an historic 1890 farmhouse with two upstairs guest rooms ($65 s or d; shared bath), and a separate cottage ($85 s or d; private bath). Children accepted and two-night minimum.

Paradise Valley Farm, 21831 107th SW, tel. (206) 463-9815, is a large two-bedroom luxury apartment on a 30-acre farm. A make-your-own-breakfast is provided, and kids are welcome. $65 s or $110 d.

A 1910 waterfront farmhouse, **Peabody's B&B,** 23007 64th SW, tel. (206) 463-3506, offers sweeping views of the sound. Guests can stay in a guest room or suite with private baths, and will enjoy the hot tub on the wrap-around porch. $100 s or d. Kids accepted.

Rose Cottage, tel. (206) 463-1463, is a luxurious two-bedroom cottage on the water with a full kitchen and woodstove. The kitchen is stocked for a make-your-own breakfast; $125 d.

Sea Lotus Day Spa and B&B, 10823 Vashon Hwy. SW, tel. (206) 567-5565, has a romantic waterfront cottage with kitchenette and continental breakfast for $105 d. A range of relaxing services are offered (extra charge), including massage, steam baths, refloxology, and aromatherapy.

Van Gelder's Retreat B&B, tel. (206) 463-3684, has three efficiency units, each with private bath and kitchen. Outside find gardens, a jacuzzi, and seasonal pool; $90-100 s or d with continental breakfast.

Guest Cottages and Homes

All Seasons Waterfront, 12817 SW Bachelor Rd., tel. (206) 463-3498, is a beautiful waterfront cabin with large deck and views, fireplace, and full kitchen; $95 s or d. Two-night minimum.

Sojourn House, 18211 Vashon Hwy. SW, mailing address 27415 94th SW, tel. (206) 463-5193, is a furnished four bedroom house that sleeps eight. Rates start at $125 d. Two-night minimum.

Swallow's Nest Guest Cottages, 6030 SW 248th St., tel. (206) 463-2646 or (800) 269-6378, has seven comfortable cottages scattered around the island; $75-180 s or d.

Food
The ever-popular **Vashon Farmers Market** is described above under "Farm Products." Several downtown Vashon restaurants pull in both locals and out-of-towners.

Bob's Bakery, 17506 Vashon Hwy. SW, tel. (206) 463-5666, has sweet-tooth victuals. **Express Cuisine Restaurant,** tel. (206) 463-6626, is a favorite lunch and dinner spot with moderate prices and a casual order-at-the-counter atmosphere. The menu cuts across the spectrum, from chicken chimichangas to *pad Thai.*

The Malt Shop & Charbroiler, tel. (206) 463-3740, is a wonderful little place for charbroiled burgers, sandwiches, and 18 flavors of ice cream. Everything is made from scratch, so don't expect fast food. It's downtown just off the main drag at 17635 100th Ave. SW.

Sound Food Restaurant and Bakery, mid-island on the Vashon Island Hwy., has a homey atmosphere and tasty breakfasts, lunches, and dinners, along with a fine bakery and natural foods grocery.

Events
Vashon's biggest summertime event is the two-day **Strawberry Festival** in mid-July. Parades, music, food, and crafts highlight the event; ferry traffic will be heavy, so it's a good idea to arrive early. Local art galleries open to the public with **open studios** the first two weekends of May and December.

Information
The **Vashon-Maury Island Chamber of Commerce,** tel. (206) 463-6217, can be found in the main village of Vashon at 17633 Vashon Hwy. SW, and on the Web at www.vashonisland. com/chamber. Open Mon.-Fri. 10 a.m.-4 p.m. all year, plus Saturday 11 a.m.-3 p.m. April-September. Vashon Island is a local phone call from Seattle.

Getting There
The **Washington State Ferry** has auto and passenger service to both the north and south ends of Vashon Island. The return trip is always free (roundtrip fare is charged on your way to the island), so you can arrive or depart from either end for the same price. There are four departure points for the island. To reach Heights Dock on the north end, you can take the half-hour passenger-only ferry from downtown Seattle's Pier 50 for $3.60 roundtrip. This ferry operates Mon.-Sat., but not on Sunday or holidays, and generally runs from 5:30 a.m. to after midnight.

By car or bus, you can take the frequent ferries from West Seattle's Fauntleroy terminal for $8 roundtrip. This rate includes the car and driver; passengers and walk-ons are $3.60 roundtrip; winter fares are lower. Ferries also connect Heights Dock with the Southworth ferry terminal on the Kitsap Peninsula, and the Tahlequah dock on the south end of Vashon Island with Tacoma's Point Defiance ferry terminal. Both of these ferry runs have the same rate schedule as from Fauntleroy. For ferry system details, call (425) 355-7308 or (888) 808-7977. Call (800) 843-3779 for automated information.

Getting Around
The main town of Vashon is five miles from the ferry landing. **Metro Transit,** tel. (206) 553-3000 or (800) 542-7876, has Mon.-Sat. bus service around the island, and direct buses to and from downtown Seattle. The bus also connects to the south end of Vashon, where you can catch the ferry to Tacoma. **Karma Kab,** tel. (206) 463-3684, has island service. **Island Air,** tel. (206) 567-4994, has flightseeing trips over Puget Sound from Vashon Municipal Airport.

PUYALLUP

Puyallup (pyoo-AL-up; pop. 25,000) sits less than a dozen miles southeast of Tacoma in the scenic, nearly level Puyallup Valley. Spring is a pretty time in the valley, with fields of flowers backdropped by Mt. Rainier. The city of Puyallup grew up on agriculture, and by 1890 it was one of the most important hops producing areas in the country. Unfortunately, an 1891 infestation of hop lice destroyed the crop, forcing farmers to switch to other crops, especially berries and flower bulbs. Agriculture is still a big part of the local economy, but industries have moved in (including a big Matsushita semiconductor plant), along with an all-American suburban sprawl that is rapidly crowding out the farms with shopping malls and homes. Today, many folks commute to work in nearby Tacoma or other cities.

Sights

Furnished in 1890s style, the 17-room **Ezra Meeker Mansion** was built by the city's founder and first mayor. The original stained glass pieces, ceiling artwork, six inlaid fireplaces, and a grand staircase offer a taste of life for the elite in this carefully restored Victorian mansion. As a hugely successful hop grower and broker, Meeker earned the moniker "Hop King of the World" and was for a time the richest man in the Pacific Northwest; he once earned more than $500,000 in a single year. The double whammy of the financial panic of 1890 and an infestation of hop lice nearly drove him into bankruptcy. Meeker lived through a fast-changing era: he drove a team of oxen over the Oregon Trail, later rode the route in a train, drove it in an automobile, and flew over it in an airplane. His fascination with the Oregon Trail led to the erection of markers along the route and the preservation of the historic trail. Located at 312 Spring St., tel. (253) 848-1770, Meeker's Victorian mansion is today a National Historic Site. It is open for tours Wed.-Sun. 1-4 p.m. March through mid-December; admission $4 adults, $3 teens and seniors, and $2 kids.

VanLierop Bulb Farms, 13407 80th St. E (two miles east of Puyallup), tel. (253) 848-7272, was created by Simon VanLierop, a Dutch immigrant from a family with a long history of bulb growing. VanLierop helped establish the bulb industry in the Puyallup area in the 1930s, and the farm is still a family operation, now producing more than 20,000 bulbs each year. Each spring these fields glow with the colors of 150 different varieties of crocus, daffodils, hyacinths, tulips, and other flowers. You can have them shipped or take them with you. The flower shop is open daily 10 a.m.-4:30 p.m. February to June and mid-September through October. Best time to see the flowers in bloom is mid-March to mid-April.

The Tacoma Astronomical Society's **Pettinger-Guiley Observatory,** 6103 132nd St. E, tel. (253) 537-2802, contains a 15-inch Swanson Refractor—the largest amateur refracting telescope in the Northwest. The scope is open to the public twice a month (except August), providing a great opportunity to view the moon, planets, and other celestial treats.

Accommodations

Two local B&Bs offer homey accommodations. **Tayberry Victorian Cottage B&B,** 7406 80th St. E, tel. (253) 848-4594, is a modern Victorian-style home on the edge of town with three guest rooms, private baths, and a full breakfast; $65-85 s or d. **Country House B&B,** 10 miles south in

Daffodil Princesses surrounded by Puyallup in bloom

Graham, tel. (253) 846-1889, is a contemporary country home with a guest room and loft, hot tub, and full breakfast. Kids welcome; $60 s or d. **Motel Puyallup,** 1412 S. Meridian, tel. (253) 845-8825, has standard rooms for $40 s or $44 d. **Northwest Motor Inn,** 1409 S. Meridian, tel. (253) 841-2600 or (800) 845-9490, charges $45 s or $49 d, including a jacuzzi. **Best Western Park Plaza,** 9620 S. Hill Place E, tel. (253) 848-1500 or (800) 238-7234, has the nicest rooms in town, plus an outdoor pool, jacuzzi, exercise facility, and continental breakfast; $84-94 s or $89-99 d.

Camping
Local RV parks include **Majestic Mobile Manor,** 7022 River Rd., tel. (253) 845-3144, and **River Road Motor Home Court,** 7824 River Rd. E, tel. (253) 848-7155.

Food
Start out your day with a hearty breakfast at **Mr. A's Restaurant,** 816 E. Meridian, tel. (253) 927-5119. The deck is popular for summertime lunches. Another favorite for American food three meals a day is **Anton's Restaurant,** 3207 E. Main St., tel. (253) 845-7569. At lunch, try **Lonzos,** 109 S. Meridian, tel. (253) 770-0150, serving specialty sandwiches, soups, and espresso.

The small, family run **Balsano's Restaurant,** 127 15th St. SE, tel. (253) 845-4222, features tasty homemade Italian specialties and fresh seafood in a fun atmosphere. For more Italian fare—and the best local pizzas—try **Casa Mia,** 505 N. Meridian, tel. (253) 770-0400. **Mazatlan Restaurant,** 215 15th SE, tel. (253) 848-8550, or 13018 Meridian, tel. (253) 770-8702, has Mexican food.

The fanciest place around is **Iron Gate Restaurant,** 1806 River Rd., tel. (253) 845-8854, with a supper club setting (live country music and a big screen TV in the lounges) and locally famous prime rib.

The popular **Puyallup Farmers Market,** tel. (253) 845-6755, features fresh local produce May through Labor Day. The market is held downtown next to Pioneer Park on Saturday 9 a.m.-2 p.m. At other times, head out River Rd. to find the produce stands, or stop by the chamber of commerce for a list of local places.

Taste honey ales at **Kelley Creek Brewing Co.,** 20123 Old Buckley Hwy. in Bonney Lake (six miles east of Puyallup), tel. (253) 862-5969. This in-the-country microbrewery sells through a number of local taverns. Open for tours Wed.-Sunday.

Events
Puyallup is famous as the home of the **Puyallup Fair,** officially known as the Western Washington Fair. One of the nation's 10 largest, the fair runs for 17 days in September (starting the Friday after Labor Day) and attracts a crowd of more than 1.3 million fairgoers to its top-flight concerts, livestock displays, a PRCA rodeo, carnival rides, and refreshments. Don't miss the justly famous raspberry scones. The fairgrounds are located at the intersection of Meridian St. and 9th Ave. Southwest.

The **Spring Fair and Daffodil Festival** is another of Puyallup's well-known attractions. Sponsored by the region's bulb farms, and in existence since 1934, it's a two-week series of events throughout Pierce County: the Grand Floral Parade (the third-largest parade of flowers in the nation) heads through Puyallup, Tacoma, Sumner, and Orting. For information, call (253) 627-6176.

Yet another fair in the Puyallup Valley is the **Pierce County Fair,** held in Graham at 218th and Meridian (Hwy. 161) the second weekend of August. Highlighted by the infamous cow-chip-throwing contest, there are also floral and photo exhibits, livestock displays, and a five-km race. For information call (253) 843-1173 before, or (253) 847-4754 during, the fair. Other popular fairground events include the **Scandinavian Days Festival** in early October, and the **Victorian Country Christmas,** in late November and early December. The latter features more than 450 booths and dozens of stage shows. All vendors are dressed in Victorian period costume, and a living nativity and strolling musicians add to the Christmas spirit. For a complete listing of upcoming events at the fairground, call (253) 845-1771.

A big summer event is the outdoor production of *Jesus of Nazareth* in Puyallup's open-air amphitheater at 14422 Meridian S, performed at 8 p.m. every Friday and Saturday from the third weekend in July through Labor Day. One of seven major passion plays in the country, the cast of hundreds is assisted by horses, cows, sheep, pigeons, and a donkey. For ticket information call (253) 848-3411. For something a bit more secular, try the free **Concerts in the Park** on Tuesday and Thursday during July; tel. (253) 841-5457. Late June brings the **Meeker Days Hoedown and Bluegrass Festival,** with entertainment, arts and crafts booths, a mountain man rendezvous, and street dance.

Information and Shopping

The **Puyallup Area Chamber of Commerce,** 322 2nd St. SW, tel. (253) 845-6755 or (800) 634-2334, is open Mon.-Fri. 9 a.m.-4:30 p.m. year-round. **South Hill Mall** has over 150 stores at the intersection of Hwy. 512 and South Meridian.

Transportation

Pierce Transit, tel. (253) 581-8000 or (800) 562-8109, has daily service to Tacoma and other parts of Pierce County, along with Seattle and Olympia. **Capital Aeroporter,** tel. (253) 754-7113 or (800) 962-3579, operates shuttle vans between Puyallup and Sea-Tac Airport.

SUMNER

The town of **Sumner** (pop. 8,000)—just three miles east of Puyallup—is a charming settlement with sturdy brick downtown buildings and older homes surrounded by dairies, berry farms, fields of daffodils, tulips, and irises. Hothouse rhubarb is another specialty product from this rich farming land. First called "Stuck Junction," Sumner was settled by whites in the early 1850s. Hops production brought a measure of prosperity that led to the building of stately Victorian-era homes.

Sights

Taste German wines at **Baron Manfred Vierthaler Winery,** tel. (253) 863-1633, a Bavarian-style hilltop chalet just east of Sumner on Hwy. 410. The wine tasting room is open daily 11 a.m.-10 p.m.; be sure to try their port and dessert wines. The adjoining restaurant serves traditional German-Bavarian dishes, and has a dining room overlooking the Puyallup Valley. **Tapps Brewing,** 15625 Main St., tel. (253) 863-8438, is a small microbrewery with handmade and bottled ales, porters, and seasonal brews.

Ryan House Museum, 1228 Main St. in Sumner, tel. (253) 863-8936, showcases a Victorian farmhouse from 1875, with tall backyard trees and regional history displays. Named for the first mayor of Sumner—who lived here for many years—the home is open April-Oct., and December only; hours are Sat.-Sun. 1-4 p.m.

Practicalities

Bavarian Chalet Motel, 15007 Main St., tel. (253) 863-2243, has basic accommodations for $38 s or $42 d. Much better is **Rodeway Inn;** 15506 E. Main St., tel. (253) 863-3250 or (800) 228-2000, with very nice rooms for $50-62 s or $55-62 d. **Vierthaler Winery Restaurant,** is described above.

Pierce Transit, tel. (253) 581-8000 or (800) 562-8109, has daily service to throughout Pierce County, along with Seattle and Olympia.

SOUTHWEST KING COUNTY

The southern end of King County encompasses several rapidly growing suburbs and industrial areas, with Sea-Tac Airport as a central focal point, A maze of highways, shopping malls, and towns fill the American dream of escaping from the cities. Unfortunately, this escape has transformed rich farmland into yet more development. This part of Washington has little to offer the traveler, other than cheap lodging and food, though each town has something of interest.

FEDERAL WAY

Just north of Tacoma, over the line into King County, is Federal Way. This recently incorporated city of 75,000 people received its name many years ago when some federal land was sold and the proceeds were used to build a school. The land was next to Highway 99, then known as the Federal Highway. The town of Federal Way was incorporated in 1989 as an antidote to the uncontrolled growth that King County was permitting in the area. It is still one of America's fastest growing communities, but the local government tries to keep order to the development.

Amusements

For a commercial form of entertainment, Wild Waves and Enchanted Village, sister enterprises at 36201 Enchanted Parkway, will keep the whole family amused. **Wild Waves** offers 400 feet of whitewater rapids on their Raging River Ride, four giant water slides, a "beach" with artificial five-foot waves for bodysurfing, and scaled-down versions of the adult attractions for the kiddies. All the water is heated so don't worry about the weather. Neighboring **Enchanted Village,** has 16 rides (including a 1906 carousel), bumper boats, a free-flight bird aviary, pony rides, children's museum, petting zoo, and other attractions. Call (253) 661-8000 for details. Both Enchanted Village and Wild Waves are open summers only.

Gardens and Parks

The Rhododendron Species Foundation Garden on Weyerhaeuser Way displays over 2,100 varieties of wild rhododendrons from around the world in a 24-acre garden. This is the world's largest such collection, and something is in bloom Mar.-September. Admission costs $3.50 adults, $2.50 students and seniors, under 12 free. Open Fri.-Wed. 10 a.m.-4 p.m. March-May, and Sat.-Wed. 11 a.m.-4 p.m. the rest of the year. Call (253) 661-9377 for more information. The garden is operated by the nonprofit Rhododendron Species Foundation, which also offers workshops, classes, and tours for members.

Just south of the Rhododendron Garden is **Pacific Rim Bonsai Collection,** tel. (253) 924-5206, operated by the Weyerhaeuser Corporation; corporate headquarters is just up the way. The collection contains more than 50 bonsai trees; some more than 500 years old. Go three-quarters of a mile east from exit 142A, then a half-mile north on Weyerhaeuser Way. By the way, the correct pronunciation for bonsai—Japanese for "a tree in a pot"—is "bone-sigh." Admission is free, and hours are the same as the rhodie garden. Classes on growing bonsai trees are taught throughout the year.

Saltwater State Park, two miles south of Des Moines on Marine View Drive S, is one of the most popular summer spots around; get here early on summer weekends or you may have to wait at the gate to enter. The sandy beach is very popular for swimming, scuba diving, and sea kayaking, and a two mile path loops through the forest. Also here are picnic tables, a refreshment stand, and campsites ($11 tents, no RV hookups). The park is open year-round for day use, and late April to early September for camping. Showers are available. Call (253) 764-4128 for information.

Dash Point State Park is five miles northeast of downtown Tacoma on Puget Sound, on Hwy. 509, a.k.a. Dash Point Road. The wooded camping area on the east side of the road has tent ($10) and RV ($15) sites on 397 acres. Open year-round. On the west, or sound, side of the park, are a beach (the water here is warm

FEDERAL WAY

enough for swimming—or at least wading—in summer), picnic tables, and trails that lead to the water. Call (253) 593-2206 for more info, or (800) 452-5687 for reservations ($6 extra).

On the northern edge of Federal Way, also on the sound, is the community of **Des Moines.** The city marina is one of the largest in the area. Nearby is a 670-foot fishing pier that provides great views of the mountains for fishermen and strollers. To the north of the pier is the **Des Moines Beach Park,** a 20-acre park with Des Moines Creek, to which salmon return each year.

Lodging
Palisades B&B at Dash Point, 5162 S.W. 311th Pl., tel. (253) 927-1904 or (888) 838-4376, is a private three-room suite along the water. Guests can enjoy the deck that overlooks the harbor,

and the private sandy beach. A full breakfast is served; no kids. $195 d.

Best Western Federal Way Executel, 31611 20th Ave. S, tel. (253) 941-6000 or (800) 346-2874, has rooms for $89-149 s or $99-159 d, including an outdoor pool and jacuzzi. **Holiday Inn Express,** 34827 Pacific Hwy. S., tel. (253) 838-3164 or (800) 465-4329, charges $75 s or $84 d, including an outdoor pool and continental breakfast.

Other local motels with standard accommodations include the following: **New Horizon Motel,** 33002 Pacific Hwy. S, tel. 927-2337; **Ridge Crest Motel,** 1812 S. 336th, tel. 874-9161; **Roadrunner Motel,** 1501 S. 350th St., tel. (253) 838-5763 or (800) 828-7202; **Siesta Motel,** 35620 Pacific Hwy. S, tel. 927-2157; and **Super 8 Motel,** 1688 S. 348th, tel. 838-8808 or (800) 800-8000.

Camp at Dash Point State Park and Saltwater State Park, described above.

Food

Redondo, just west of Federal Way on Puget Sound, has a fishing pier, boat launch, and one of the area's best restaurants: **Salty's at Redondo.** Primarily a seafood restaurant, Salty's has one of the best sunset views around, and you can drink or dine outdoors on the pier in the summer months.

A good place for a light meal is **Lolli's Broiler & Pub,** 32925 1st Ave. S (in the Quad), a restaurant/tavern that serves huge burgers and good sandwiches, along with an extensive selection of beers on tap (32 at last count).

Recreation

Several public swimming pools are in the area, but the star attraction is the **King County Aquatic Center,** 650 S.W. Campus Dr., tel. (253) 296-4444, constructed to host the 1990 Goodwill Games and used for other national swimming meets. You don't have to be a hotshot to swim here, or to try out the diving boards. The **North Shore Golf & Country Club,** 4101 North Shore Blvd. NE, tel. (253) 927-1375, is an 18-hole public course.

Shopping and Entertainment

The **Sea-Tac Mall** on the south side of S. 320th St. has over 100 stores. Also in Federal Way is an **REI** store with camping and backpacking supplies at 2565 S. Gateway Center Plaza (I-5 at 320th St.), tel. (253) 941-4994.

The **Federal Way Philharmonic,** tel. (253) 838-0565, performs Sept.-April at St. Theresa's Church at S.W. 331st St. and Hoyt Road.

Information and Transportation

The **Greater Federal Way Chamber of Commerce,** 34004 16th Ave., tel. (253) 838-2605, can help you out with maps and other area information. Open Mon.-Fri. 9 a.m.-5 p.m. year-round.

Metro Transit, tel. (253) 447-4800 or (800) 542-7876, provides bus service to Seattle and other parts of King County. **Pierce Transit,** tel. (253) 581-8000 or (800) 562-8109, has service to Tacoma and other parts of Pierce County, along with Seattle and Olympia.

KENT AND AUBURN

The city of Auburn (pop. 35,000) began as an agricultural settlement in the White River Valley and was originally named Slaughter, for an Army lieutenant who was killed in an Indian battle nearby. Later settlers decided Slaughter wasn't a particularly appealing name for the town, and so they renamed it Auburn. Because of periodic flooding, settlers rerouted the White River southward from its original course into the Stuck River, thus removing the river from the valley it had created. Today Auburn and neighboring Kent (pop. 44,000) are small cities that are rapidly becoming links in the chain of urban growth that continues almost without a break from Seattle to Olympia.

Sights and Attractions

Auburn's newly renovated **White River Valley Historical Museum,** 918 H St. SE, tel. (253) 939-2783, has artifacts from the early days in the valley, including old photos, a one-room schoolhouse, country store, and farm machinery. The museum is open Thurs.-Sun. 1:30-4:30 p.m. year-round. No charge. Ask here for directions to the majestic **Neely Mansion** built in 1894.

The **Auburn Avenue Dinner Theater** at 10 Auburn Ave., tel. (253) 833-5678, has fun musical productions and plays. It's Washington's oldest and largest dinner theater. Gamblers can try their luck at blackjack, craps, roulette, or poker at **Muckleshoot Indian Casino,** 2402 Auburn Way S, tel. (253) 939-7484 or (800) 804-4944. Also here are two restaurants and a lounge.

Located on the north side of Auburn, **Emerald Downs,** tel. (253) 288-7000 or (888) 931-8400, is the Seattle area's thoroughbred horse racing center, with races April-September.

Shoppers head to the enormous **SuperMall of the Great Northwest,** with over 140 outlet and "rack" stores located just off Hwy. 167 at 15th St. Southwest.

Lodging and Campgrounds

For a relaxing stay, **Rose Arbor Inn B&B,** 514 A St. NE, tel. (253) 931-8564, has a cozy, old-fashioned home with three guest rooms and shared or private baths; $60-90 s or d. A full jetarian breakfast is made each morning, and assage is available.

Park RVs or pitch a tent in Kent at **KOA Kampground,** 5801 S. 212th St., tel. (253) 872-8652 or (800) 562-1892. This is one of the few RV parks in the Seattle area.

Food
Nothing's stellar on the local restaurant scene, but several places are worth a visit. For breakfast, head to **Sun Break Cafe,** at 1st St. SE and A St. SE in Auburn, tel. (253) 939-5225, or **Trotter's Restaurant,** 825 Harvey Rd. in Auburn,

---

AUBURN AND KENT MOTELS AND HOTELS

Lodging places are arranged from least to most expensive. See the text for descriptions of local bed and breakfasts.

INEXPENSIVE

Auburn Motel; 1202 Auburn Way S in Auburn; tel. (253) 833-7470; $40 s or d; local calls 25 cents

New Best Inn; 23408 30th Ave. S in Kent; tel. (425) 870-1280; $45 s, $52 d; kitchenettes available

Nendel's Inn Auburn; 102 15th St. NE in Auburn; tel. 833-8007 or (800) 547-0106; $48 s or d; continental breakfast

Microtel Inn & Suites, 16th and B in Auburn; tel. (253) 833-7171 or (888) 643-7171; $49-69 s, $54-74 d; new motel, kitchenettes available

MODERATE

Valu-U Inn; 9 14th Ave. NW in Auburn; tel. 735-9600 or (800) 443-7777; $55 s, $60 d; jacuzzi, continental breakfast, newspaper, AAA approved

Comfort Inn; 1 16th St. NE in Auburn; tel. (253) 833-2222 or (800) 228-5150; $55-70 s; $63-78 d; indoor pool, exercise room, jacuzzi, continental breakfast

Val-U Inn; 22420 84th Ave. in Kent; tel. (253) 872-5525 or (800) 443-7777; $60 s or d; jacuzzi, continental breakfast, newspaper, airport shuttle

Howard Johnson Inn; 1521 D St. NE in Auburn; tel. (253) 939-5950 or (800) 446-4656; $68-82 s or d; outdoor pool, sauna, jacuzzi, fridges

Howard Johnson Inn; 1233 N. Central in Kent; tel. (253) 852-7224 or (800) 446-4656; $68-82 s, $71-86 d; outdoor pool, sauna, jacuzzi, exercise facility

Days Inn; 1711 W. Meeker St. in Kent; tel. (253) 854-1950 or (800) 329-7466; $69 s or $73 d; outdoor pool, continental breakfast.

Best Western Choice Lodge; 24415 Russell Rd. in Kent; tel. (253) 854-8767 or (800) 835-3338; $69-99 s, $79-109 d; sauna, jacuzzi, exercise room, continental breakfast, airport shuttle

EXPENSIVE

Comfort Inn; 22311 84th Ave. S in Kent; tel. (253) 872-2211 or (800) 228-5150; $75-90 s; $85-105 d; new motel, indoor pool, continental breakfast

Holiday Inn Hotel & Suites; 22218 84th Ave. S in Kent; tel. (253) 395-4300 or (800) 465-4329; $99-139 s or d; outdoor pool, jacuzzi, continental breakfast, airport shuttle

LUXURY

Hawthorne Suites; 6329 S. 212th in Kent; tel. (253) 395-3800 or (800) 527-1133; $149-169 s or d; studio suite, full kitchen, fireplace, patio, full breakfast buffet, weekday meals, outdoor pool, jacuzzis, fitness center, tennis court, airport shuttle

tel. (253) 833-2323. Get Indian cuisine, including a Tues.-Sat. lunch buffet, at **India Bazaar,** 20936 108th SE in Kent, tel. (253) 850-8906. **Triple Crown,** 2041 Auburn Way N in Auburn, tel. (253) 288-2070, is the best place for upscale meals.

The **Kent Farmers Market** takes place Saturday 9 a.m.-4 p.m. and Sunday 10 a.m.-3 p.m., April-Oct. at Smith St. and 4th Ave.; tel. (253) 813-6976.

Events and Entertainment

Auburn events include a fun **Fourth of July Parade,** and the **Good Ol' Days Community Celebration,** held the last weekend of August. The later includes a parade, square dancing, quilts, vaudeville, and food and crafts. On the first Saturday of December, Auburn's **Christmas Parade** brings Santa to town. Also popular are auto and motorcycle racing at **Seattle International Raceway,** 31001 144th in Kent, tel. (253) 631-1550. **Radens,** 1815 Howard Rd., tel. (253) 833-7980, is the place to go for live bands on Sunday nights.

Information and Recreation

Get local info from the **Auburn Area Chamber of Commerce,** 228 1st St. NE, tel. (253) 833-0700; open Mon.-Fri. 9 a.m.-5 p.m.

Auburn's **swimming pool** is located next to the high school at 516 4th NE, tel. (253) 939-8825, while Kent has pools at 25316 101st Ave. SE, tel. (253) 296-4275, and 18230 S.E. 240th, tel. (253) 296-4276.

Transportation

Metro Transit, tel. (253) 553-3000 or (800) 542-7876, has bus service to Auburn, Kent, and the rest of King County. **Super Shuttle,** tel. (253) 622-1424 or (800) 487-7433, provides direct service to Sea-Tac Airport, along with door-to-door connections.

TUKWILA, SEATAC, AND BURIEN

This trio of urban and industrial sprawl occupies the southwestern corner of King County, with Seattle to the north, and Tacoma and Federal Way to the south. The main "attractions" are **Sea-Tac International Airport** in SeaTac (pop. 23,000), and **Southcenter Mall,** located south of

the intersection of I-5 with I-405 in Tukwila (pop. 15,000). Major department stores here include The Bon Marché, Nordstrom, JCPenney, and Sears (the company's "flagship store"), plus 150 other stores.

Practicalities

Because of the proximity to Sea-Tac Airport, Tukwila and SeaTac have literally dozens of motels and hotels of all types, especially along motel row (Pacific Hwy. South/Hwy. 99).

Not surprisingly, you can find all the standard fast and not-so-fast eating places in the cities. Worth a visit is **Grazie Ristorante Italiano,** 16943 Southcenter Parkway, tel. (206) 575-1606, for dinners. The **SeaTac Farmers Market,** tel. (206) 248-9346, takes place Saturday 10 a.m.-3 p.m. June-Aug. at 4424 S. 188th.

Information and Events

For a handful of local brochures, drop by **Southwest King County Chamber of Commerce,** 16400 Southcenter Parkway, Suite 210, tel. (206) 575-1633.

Tukwila has a popular **Summer Festival** each July, while nearby Burien (pop. 28,000; just west of the airport) is home to the **Strawberry Festival** each June, along with a fun **Fourth of July Parade.** SeaTac's Angle Lake Park features a **Music in the Park** series in the summer. For live music, head to **21 Club Sports Bar & Casino,** 14101 Pacific Hwy. S, tel. (206) 248-1224.

RENTON

Renton was born when coal was mined in the area before the turn of this century but is now home to a massive Boeing plant where 737s are assembled. As you would expect from its ties with Boeing, the city has an excellent airport as well as a large floatplane base, named the **Will Rogers-Wiley Post Seaplane Base** because it was the place from which those two men launched the flight that ended in their deaths outside Nome, Alaska, on August 7, 1935. A monument commemorates their fateful trip.

Today, with a population of 45,000, Renton is fast becoming just another mass of spreading suburban growth, and most visitors are en route to the Southcenter Mall in nearby Tukwila or other centers of rampant consumer spending. But rock music fans will know that Renton is where Jimi Hendrix is interred.

Sights

The simple grave of **James M. "Jimi" Hendrix** can be found in Greenwood Memorial Park, located east of town on N.E. 3rd at Monroe. Find the ground-level grave marker by heading toward the sundial and then turning right. Born in Seattle in 1942, Hendrix died in 1970 from a drug-related suffocation. Hundreds of people of all ages still make the pilgrimage to his grave each year, leaving behind tokens of all sorts, from flowers to pinwheels to McDonald's "valued customer" coupons. Be sure to stop by the office near the cemetery entrance to sign in the guest book, and to read comments from visitors who arrive from around the globe. Seattle's newly built Experience Music Project has much more on this rock legend; see the Seattle chapter for details.

Most of the town's history is told in the **Renton Historical Museum** at 235 Mill Ave. S, tel. (425) 255-2330. It has a nice collection and professional quality exhibits of pioneer, coal mining, and Indian artifacts. Open Tuesday 9 a.m.-4 p.m., and Wed.-Sun. 1-4 p.m.; donation.

Dinner Train

The ever-popular **Spirit of Washington Dinner Train** leaves Renton Depot year-round, pulled by a 1935 diesel engine, and continues along Lake Washington to the Columbia Winery in Woodinville, 45 miles to the north. There you are given a tour of the winery and a chance to sample several wines before returning to Renton three and a half hours later. A gourmet meal is served along the way; the cost is $59 for the parlor car, or $69 for the dome car. Call (425) 227-7245 or (800) 876-7245 for more information and reservations.

Accommodations

The most luxurious local place is **Holly Hedge House,** 908 Grant Ave. S, tel. (425) 226-2555, where the entire cottage is reserved for one couple (no kids), including a private jacuzzi, outdoor pool, and English-country-style furnishings. A full breakfast is served; $125-140 d. Three-night minimum.

Maple Valley B&B, 10 miles southeast of Renton in Maple Valley, tel. (425) 432-1409, is a distinctive contemporary home on five acres with a wildlife pond. Inside are two guest rooms that share a bath; a full breakfast is served. Rates are $85 s or d, and kids are accepted.

The following motels also have space. For other nearby options, see the "Seattle Motels and Hotels" chart. **Don-a-Lisa Motel,** 111 Meadow N, tel. (425) 255-0441, has inexpensive rates ($38 s or $43 d), and is notable for an amusing clown collection in their lobby. **Traveler's Inn,** 4710 Lake Washington Blvd., tel. (425) 228-2858 or (800) 633-8300, charges $43 s or $50 d, and has an outdoor pool. **West Wind Motel,** 110 Rainier Ave. S, tel. (425) 226-5060, charges $48-55 s or d. **Nendel's Inn Renton,** 3700 E. Valley Rd., tel. (425) 251-9591 or (800) 547-0106, costs $58 s or d, including a jacuzzi and continental breakfast. **Silver Cloud at Renton,** 1850 Maple Valley Hwy., tel. (425) 226-7600 or (800) 205-6936, has a jacuzzi, exercise room, and kitchenettes; $68-73 s or $78-83 d. **Holiday Inn Select,** 1 S. Grady Way, tel. (425) 226-7700 or (800) 521-1412, has an outdoor pool and airport shuttle; $109 s or $119 d.

Campgrounds

Campers and RVers will enjoy the amenities at **Aqua Barn Ranch,** 15227 Renton-Maple Valley Hwy., tel. (425) 255-4618. The RV and tent sites come with an indoor pool, horse rentals, a big-screen TV, and movies. **Riverbend RV Park,** 17410 Maple Valley, tel. (425) 255-2613, has adults-only tent sites on 12 acres.

Food

The atmosphere is similar to a slightly upscale Denny's, but the food—especially the steaks and homemade pies—are impressive in **All City Diner,** 423 Airport Way, tel. (425) 228-7281. Quite popular for breakfast.

Whistle Stop Ale House, 340 Burnett Ave. S, tel. (425) 277-3039, is right across from the downtown train station. It's a friendly little smoke-free bar and eatery with microbrews on tap and good sandwiches. Get good Italian food at **Armondo's Cafe Italiano,** downtown at 919 S. 3rd, tel. (425) 228-0759.

Rainier Ave. is the city's commercial strip, lined with fast- and slow-food restaurants. Mexican food fanciers will appreciate **Torero's,** 431 Rainier Ave. S, tel. (425) 228-6180. **Royal Orchid Thai Cuisine,** 104 Rainier Ave. S, tel. (425) 271-4219, has authentic Thai food.

Shopping

For a surprisingly complete selection of Western garb, be sure to tie up at the state's largest cowboy shop, **Renton Western Wear,** 724 S. 3rd, tel. (425) 255-3922 or (800) 886-3922. Antique lovers will have fun wandering through the downtown antique shops along Wells Ave. S near 3rd.

Events

Renton River Days in early August is the main local event, with parades, live music, games, food and craft vendors, and more. Each December Ivar's Acres of Clams puts up an amusing set of colorful **"Clam Lights"** at Coulon Beach Park.

Information and Services

The **Renton Chamber of Commerce,** 300 Rainier N, tel. (425) 226-4560, is open Mon.-Fri. 8:30 a.m.-5 p.m. Behind them on the airport tarmac you'll see new Boeing 737s and 757s in the finishing stages before delivery. Swim at the **Renton Pool,** 16740 128th Ave. SE, tel. (425) 296-4335.

Transportation

Renton Urban Shuttle, tel. (425) 277-5555, has free bus service around town. **Metro Transit,** tel. (425) 447-4800 or (800) 542-7876, provides daily bus service to Seattle and other parts of King County. **Super Shuttle,** tel. (425) 622-1424 or (800) 487-7433, has van service to Sea-Tac Airport.

   Sound Flight at the Renton Airport offers flightseeing tours over Seattle, Mt. Rainier, the San Juan Islands, and north to Vancouver Island. They also provide scheduled service to the San Juan Islands ($170 roundtrip), the Gulf Islands ($145 roundtrip), and Victoria ($180 roundtrip), along with other destinations on Vancouver Island. For details, call (425) 255-6500 or (800) 825-0722. **Northwest Seaplanes,** tel. (425) 277-1590 or (800) 690-0086, also has scheduled service to the San Juans from Renton Airport.

ENUMCLAW AND BUCKLEY AREA

Enumclaw (pop. 7,500; pronounced "EE-numclaw") occupies a low plateau surrounded by dairy farms. The views of Mt. Rainier are outstanding from just about anywhere in town. Although housing developments are starting to move in, much of the surrounding country still retains its rural charm, and 50 or so dairies still survive. The distinctive "eau de Enumclaw" from these farms hangs in the air on many summer days, and one local entrepreneur even offers cans of "DairyAir" for a whiff of the Enumclaw's best-known aerial export.

History

Enumclaw ("Thundering Mountain") was established in 1885 and named for a nearby mountain where local Indians were once frightened by a severe thunderstorm. The town was platted shortly after the Northern Pacific Railroad arrived in 1885. Dense forests here provided lumber and shingles for many years, and the logged-over land was transformed into productive dairy farms.

Sights

Enumclaw itself doesn't have a lot to offer in the way of attractions for the traveler, but do stop by **MacRae's Indian Bookstore,** 1605 Cole St., tel. (360) 825-3737, where you'll find a remarkable collection of books on the original inhabitants of this land. It's said to be the largest bookstore of its kind anywhere; a mail order catalog is available. For a taste of farming life, head to the **Enumclaw Sales Pavilion,** 22712 S.E. 436th St., tel. (360) 825-3151, on Wednesday or Saturday for auctions of cattle, horses, and other animals.

   For an especially pretty drive, head south from Enumclaw through Buckley and then on to minuscule Kapowsin, where the winding road takes you past small lakes, old dairy barns, and newer homes on a tree-draped valley floor. Get a taste of the Enumclaw Plateau's rich farming land by heading north from town toward Black Diamond on Hwy. 169. Lots of cows and horses along the way, including Rainier Stables, home to thoroughbred racehorses.

   Mud Mountain Dam Park, seven miles southeast of Enumclaw off Hwy. 410, tel. (360) 825-

3211, contains one of the nation's highest earth and rock flood-control dams, a 430-foot-high structure. The park features 10 miles of hiking trails, a wading pool, playground, picnic areas, and overlooks.

Federation Forest State Park

Eighteen miles southeast of Enumclaw on Hwy. 410, Federation Forest State Park, tel. (360) 663-2207, has 619 acres of old-growth forest along the White River. This is one of the only patches of virgin timber left in the area. An interpretive center (open Wed.-Sun. 10 a.m.-5 p.m. in the summer; closed winters) houses displays on plants and animals in the forest. The park contains 11 miles of hiking trails, including two short interpretive paths and remnants of the historic Naches Trail—a pioneer trail that connected eastern Washington with Puget Sound. Federation Forest is also popular for fishing and picnicking. No camping in the park.

Green River Gorge

A dozen miles northeast of Enumclaw on Hwy. 169, **Green River Gorge Conservation Area** is a 14-mile-long protected area that includes narrow gorges, whitewater rapids, wildflowers, fossils, and caves along the Green River. Several state parks have been developed along the river, the most dramatic being the **Hanging Gardens Area,** where a trail leads to the fern-covered cliffs lining the river. Access is via S.E. 386th St. (Franklin-Enumclaw Rd.); ask locally for specific directions.

Flaming Geyser State Park occupies several big bends in the Green River four miles southeast of Black Diamond on Flaming Geyser Road. Old coal-mining test holes produced two geysers, one burning an eight-inch flame and the other sending methane gas bubbling up through a stream. Enjoy hiking, picnicking, fishing, boating, and a playground; no camping. This is a takeout point for kayakers and rafters floating the Green River Gorge, and the quiet waters below here (at least in the summer) are very popular with inner tubers. No camping at Flaming Geyser State Park.

Eleven miles northeast of Enumclaw on Farman Rd., **Kanaskat-Palmer State Park** is a popular play area on the Green River with fishing (especially for steelhead in the winter), camp-

ing, and trails through the riverside forests. Several access points in the park are used by river rafters and kayakers heading down the gorge. Because of several Class III-IV stretches, this part of the river is not for beginners; see below for rafting companies able to offer a safer trip.

Nolte State Park, six miles northeast of Enumclaw, is a favorite hangout for picnicking, swimming, and fishing. The main attraction is Deep Lake, and the 1.4-mile trail that offers a pleasant stroll around this 39-acre lake. Closed October to mid-April.

Green River Rafting

The Green River Gorge is a 14-mile stretch of river north of Enumclaw rated Class III-IV, including many well-known rapids with names like Nozzle, Pipeline, and Ledge Drop. The river has a short spring season, generally March and April, since a dam holds the water back for Tacoma's water supply the rest of the year. Expect to pay $60-75 for a half-day excursion. Contact one of the following companies for more info: **Blue Sky Outfitters,** tel. (800) 228-7238; **Downstream River Runners,** tel. (800) 234-4644; **Northern Wilderness River Riders, Inc.,** tel. (800) 448-7238; **River Recreation,** tel. (800) 464-5899; **Wild & Scenic River Tours,** tel. (206) 323-1220; and **Wildwater River Tours,** tel. (800) 522-9453.

Buckley

The town of Buckley (pop. 3,600; motto: "Below the snow, above the fog") lies just four miles south of Enumclaw, on the south side of the White River. This plateau country was originally densely forested, but loggers took care of that problem, and the rich soil was turned into agricultural land. A large Weyerhaeuser lumber mill still provides many local jobs.

Buckley is home to the **Buckley Foothills Historical Society Museum,** tel. (360) 829-1289, with memorabilia from the early part of this century spread across both sides of River Avenue. Open Wed.-Thurs. noon-4 p.m. and Sunday 1-4 p.m. in the summer, and Wed.-Thurs. noon-4 p.m. the rest of the year. **Main St. Antiques and Collectibles,** 712 Main St., tel. (360) 829-2624, is a small mall housing 20 different antique shops.

Black Diamond

The spread-out town of Black Diamond (pop. 1,500), seven miles north of Enumclaw, is named for the coal that is still mined here. The first mines were underground; now the John Henry No. 1 Mine strip-mines 200,000 tons of coal a year just outside town. The small **Black Diamond Museum,** tel. (360) 886-1168, houses various pieces of mining equipment, along with a model of a coal mine, a blacksmith shop, and the old town jail. Out front is a 1920s caboose. The museum is open Thursday 9 a.m.-4 p.m., and Sat.-Sun. noon-3 p.m.

Lodging

The White Rose B&B Inn, 1610 Griffin Ave., tel. (360) 825-7194 or (800) 404-7194, is an elegant 1922 colonial mansion with a rose garden and four guest rooms with private baths. Full breakfasts are served and kids are accepted; $85-95 s or d. **King's Motel,** 1334 Roosevelt Ave. E, tel. (360) 825-1626, has rooms for $52 s or $62 d, including an outdoor pool. **Best Western Park Center Motel,** 1000 Griffin, tel. (360) 825-4490 or (800) 528-1234, charges $68-88 s or d, including a jacuzzi, exercise room, and courtyard patio.

Over in Buckley, stay at **West Main Motor Inn,** 466 W. Main St., tel. (360) 829-2400; $40 s or $50 d. Also in Buckley, the **Mountain View Inn,** 29405 Hwy. 410 E, tel. (360) 829-1100 or (800) 582-4111, has an outdoor pool, jacuzzi, and sauna, plus a continental breakfast; $55 s or $60 d.

Campground

Eleven miles northeast of Enumclaw on Farman Rd., **Kanaskat-Palmer State Park,** tel. (360) 886-0148, has tent ($11) and RV ($16) sites on the Green River. Showers and boat rentals are also available. Open all year, but with limited winter facilities. Call (800) 452-5687 for reservations ($6 extra).

Food

Charlie's Cafe, 1335 Roosevelt, tel. (360) 825-5191, is a very popular spot for breakfast, serving blueberry pancakes, home fries, and big omelettes. In Buckley, be sure to stop by **The Sweet Shoppe, Etc.,** 760 Main, tel. (360) 829-2229, for sandwiches, soups, salads, and wonderful homemade pies.

The best all-round dinner place is **Loading Dock Restaurant & Lounge,** 1502 Railroad, tel. (360) 825-6565, where marinated steaks and fresh steamer clams are the house specialties. **Cynthia's Pony Express Cafe,** 1239 Griffin Ave., tel. (360) 825-2055, is a great down-home place with lots of food for the money.

Over in Buckley, **D'Jon's Restaurant & Steakhouse,** 720 Main St., tel. (360) 829-2127, cranks out the best local steaks, prime rib, and seafood. Also in Buckley is **Wally's White River Drive-In,** 282 Hwy. 410 N, tel. (360) 829-0871, with real old-fashioned burgers and fries.

Head north to Black Diamond for **Black Diamond Bakery & Deli,** 32805 Railroad Ave., tel. (360) 886-2741, where many kinds of bread emerge from their wood-fired oven, along with apple-cinnamon wheat rolls, cookies, and other goodies. A deli and espresso cafe next door serve delicious breakfasts and lunches.

Get fresh produce, flowers, arts and crafts at the **Enumclaw Country Market,** tel. (253) 939-1707, at Railroad St. and Griffin Ave., Saturday 9:30 a.m.-3 p.m., late April to mid-October.

Events and Entertainment

The oldest county fair in the state, **King County Fair,** is held the second and third week of July at Enumclaw's fairgrounds. A rodeo, live music (including top names), 4-H exhibits, food, crafts, racing pigs, and a logger's show highlight this popular event. Another big summertime activity at the fairgrounds is the **Pacific Northwest Highland Games,** held the last weekend in July. In addition to the tests of brute strength that are the main attraction, the games include bagpipe and dance competitions, animal exhibits, and vendors selling Scottish crafts, clothing, and foods. That same weekend brings the **Enumclaw Street Fair** with a children's art festival, street dancing, and a food court. In early December, Enumclaw's **Christmas Parade and Tree Lighting** are also very popular.

See loggers in action at the **Buckley Log Show** on the last full weekend of June. Other Buckley events of note are the **Antique Rod and Car Show** in August, and **Clarence Hamilton Day** with a horseback parade and Western art show each September. In the little place called Wilkeson (four miles south of Buckley), the **National Handcar Races** are held in mid-June each year. In addition to the railroad handcar races, an Indian powwow, parade, antique show, and arts and crafts festival provide diversions.

True Grit Saloon, 23525 S.E. 436th in Enumclaw, tel. (360) 825-5648, is a fun place with bar stools made from old saddles.

Recreation

Rent bikes and skis from **Enumclaw Ski and Mountain Company,** 414 Roosevelt E, tel. (360) 825-6910, and swim at Enumclaw High School's **indoor pool,** 226 Semanski S, tel. (360) 825-1128.

Information and Services

The **Enumclaw Visitor's Center,** 1421 Cole St., tel. (360) 825-7666, is open Mon.-Fri. 8 a.m.-5 p.m., Saturday 9 a.m.-3 p.m. and Sunday 10 a.m.-2 p.m. in summer; and Mon.-Fri. 8 a.m.-

4:30 p.m. the rest of the year. Get tourist brochures in Buckley inside the liquor store (!) at 691 Main Street.

The Mt. Baker-Snoqualmie National Forest's **White River Ranger District,** 857 Roosevelt Ave. E in Enumclaw, tel. (360) 825-6585, has information on nearby hiking trails. Open Mon.-Fri. 8 a.m.-4:30 p.m., plus Saturday 8 a.m.-4:30 p.m. in winter. Unfortunately, much of the Forest Service and private land in this area has been heavily logged, and a checkerboard ownership pattern makes for difficult access. The two small wilderness areas—Clearwater Wilderness and Norse Wilderness (see **Vicinity of Mt. Rainier**)—get very heavy use.

Transportation

Metro Transit, tel. (425) 447-4800 or (800) 542-7876, provides daily bus service to Seattle and all of King County. **Pierce Transit,** tel. (206) 581-8000 or (800) 562-8109, has daily service to Tacoma and Pierce County.

OLYMPIA

Washington's state capital, Olympia is surprisingly small and still has the friendly feel of a town that doesn't yet realize it has become a city of 39,000 people. It's a fits-like-a-shoe, comfortable place with tall shade trees, attractive older housing areas, and turn-of-the-century mansions. The location, at the southern end of Puget Sound, offers outstanding views, and the quietly beautiful Capitol Campus gives Olympia a distinctively elegant flavor. But there is more here, including the nearby Olympia Brewery, an abundance of art galleries, a great farmers market, creative restaurants, and three colleges.

Much of Olympia's economy runs on government jobs; in fact, 44% of Thurston County workers are employed in the public sector. Things really hum during the legislative session. Being at the southernmost end of Puget Sound would presumably mean an active shipping industry, but Olympia's port is primarily a log-moving convenience, as lumber from the forests of the Olympic Peninsula is shipped to its destination. The Olympia Brewery in nearby Tumwater is among the area's biggest businesses; oysters, berries, and mushrooms provide agricultural jobs.

HISTORY

Among the oldest of Washington's cities, Olympia was settled in 1846 by Edmund Sylvester and Levi Smith, who filed claims of 320 acres each under the Oregon Land Law. The town was named Smithfield until Smith died, leaving his share to Sylvester, who platted the new town. In 1851 Col. Isaac Ebey (who was later beheaded in a Whidbey Island Indian raid) persuaded the town to change its name to Olympia, which he took from a book, *Life of Olympia.*

When Washington became a territory in 1853, Governor Isaac Stevens named Olympia the capital, and Edmund Sylvester donated land for a town square (now Sylvester Park) and for the new capitol building. He then turned to selling lots from his other holdings. For the next 40 years, Olympia fought Seattle, North Yakima, Vancouver, Port Townsend, Ellensburg, Centralia, and other growing cities to retain the title. Some, such as Ellensburg, even built capitol buildings in anticipation of the event. A bill was actually passed in 1861 moving the capital to Vancouver,

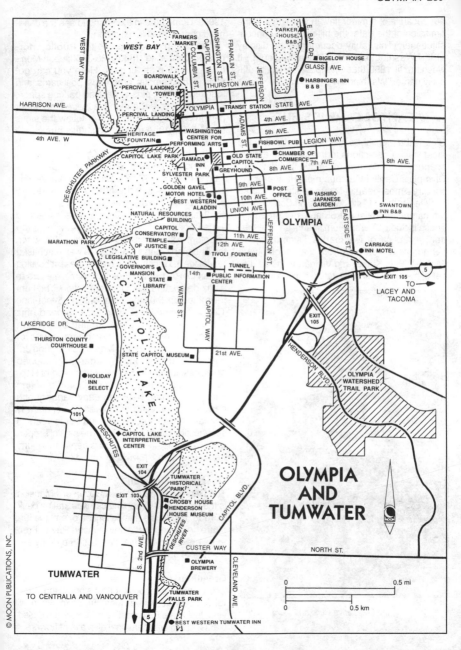

OLYMPIA
AND
TUMWATER

but because of a minor flaw in wording and the omission of the date, the bill was ruled unconstitutional. (This faulty document is on display at the Washington State Capital Museum.) It wasn't until 1890 that Olympia was finally officially named Washington's state capital.

CAPITOL CAMPUS SIGHTS

Clearly the highlight of the city—and one of the most visited attractions in the state—the landscaped grounds and majestic buildings of Olympia's Capitol Campus make it one of the country's most beautiful state capitals. Located between 11th and 14th Avenues off Capitol Way, the campus consists of 55 acres of greenery. These include an arboretum, a sunken rose garden, a replica of Denmark's Tivoli fountain, memorials to veterans from the various wars (WW I, WW II, Korea, and Vietnam), and a number of historical buildings dating back to the early

the Legislative Building

1900s. Come here in the spring to see the Japanese cherry trees in full bloom.

The best place to start is the **Public Information Center,** tel. (360) 586-3460; open Mon.-Fri. 8 a.m.-5 p.m. all year. Here you can get maps of the campus, brochures, post cards, and tour information, plus a metered parking space. All of the on-street parking is leased, so either park in one of the visitor lots or follow the signs from I-5 exit 105A to the free shuttle bus.

Legislative Building
The imposing Legislative Building (the Capitol) is hard to miss: its 287-foot dome was completed in 1928, and it is still the fifth-largest masonry domed building in the world. It shows a strong resemblance to the U.S. Capitol. This is the third state capitol building. The first—a simple log structure—stood on this site until 1903, when the Thurston County Courthouse was purchased to replace it. Construction on the present building began in 1921, but it took seven more years to gain adequate funding for completion. The central rotunda is the focal point, with a 25-foot-long Tiffany chandelier suspended overhead (this was the last major piece created by Comfort Tiffany), enormous bronze doors, busts of George Washington and Martin Luther King Jr., Belgian marble steps, and gargoyle-capped draperies. Enter the Senate and House of Representatives gallery chambers from the fourth floor. Come here between early January and early March on even-numbered years, or early January to mid-April on odd-numbered years to see the legislators in session. The capitol is open daily, with free 45-minute tours departing hourly from 10 a.m. to 3 p.m. year-round.

Governor's Mansion
The Georgian-style red brick Governor's Mansion is the oldest building on the campus, dating back to 1908. Inside is a fine collection of antique furniture, including pieces by Duncan Phyfe. Free tours are given Wednesday 1-2:45 p.m. by appointment only; call (360) 586-8687.

Greenhouse
One of the most popular tourist stops is the **Capitol Conservatory,** open Mon.-Fri. 8 a.m.-4 p.m. all year. Inside are 500 varieties of tropical and desert plants, along with seasonal displays of flowers.

DIANNE BOULERICE LYONS

State Library and Supreme Court

In addition to state and federal publications, the State Library, on the south side of the Capitol, houses a collection of murals, mosaics, paintings, and sculpture by Northwest artists. It's a nice place to sit inside on a rainy day (a common occurrence in Olympia).

The Temple of Justice is not a sequel to *Indiana Jones and the Temple of Doom,* though it may mean doom for certain individuals. Instead, this is where the State Supreme Court meets. Open Mon.-Fri. 8 a.m.-5 p.m. year-round for self-guided tours. Also inside is the Washington State Law Library.

Other State Buildings

A few blocks off the campus at 211 W. 21st Ave., the **Washington State Capital Museum,** tel. (360) 753-2580, houses permanent exhibits that include a marvelous collection of Indian baskets, and a hands-on Indian house with smoked salmon hanging from overhead racks. See lots more on the political and cultural history of Washington, including pioneer settlements and the early history of Northwest publishing, plus rotating exhibits, lectures, and programs. The building itself is historical, built in 1920 as a 32-room California mission-style mansion for banker C.J. Lord. After his death, it was deeded to the state as a museum. Open Tues.-Fri. 10 a.m.-4 p.m., and Sat.-Sun. noon-4 p.m. year-round. Entrance is $2 adults, $1.75 seniors, $1 kids, free for under age seven.

Also off campus, at Legion Way and Franklin St., the **Old State Capitol Building,** tel. (360) 753-6740, was constructed in 1891 as the Thurston County Courthouse and served as the state capitol from 1903 until the completion of the current Legislative Building in 1928. Today the flamboyant turreted building—complete with gargoyles—houses the State Department of Public Instruction. The Old Capitol is open Mon.-Fri. 8 a.m.-5 p.m. for self-guided tours, and has historical exhibits in the hallways.

The **Washington State Archives,** on the corner of 12th and Washington, tel. (360) 586-1492, are a good source for genealogy research. Open Mon.-Fri. 8:30 a.m.-4:30 p.m.

OTHER SIGHTS

Pick up self-guided tour brochures describing Olympia's historic neighborhoods from the chamber of commerce office. The gingerbread-decorated **Bigelow House** located on Glass Ave. just off East Bay Dr. overlooks Budd Inlet and is one of the oldest frame buildings in Washington. It was built in 1854 by Daniel and Ann Bigelow and is still owned by their descendants. Open Thurs.-Fri. by appointment; tel. (360) 753-1215. $3 adults, $1 kids.

Washington's state flower is displayed in force at **Zabel's Rhododendrons,** a four-acre park where 1,200 rhodies and azaleas are yours to behold from early May through Memorial Day. No pets or picnicking. To get there, go east on San Francisco Ave. from E. Bay Dr., then go north on N. Bethel St. and follow the signs to 2432 N. Bethel Street.

Olympia is home to **Evergreen State College,** a liberal arts institution with a beautiful campus and a reputation for eclecticism. This alternative school was founded in the 1960s, and has as its mascot the geoduck clam. Even the commencement ceremonies (Super Saturday) are always offbeat.

Olympia's **Hands On Children's Museum,** 108 Franklin NE, tel. (360) 956-0818, has kids exhibits—including a chance to explore the ocean floor. It's a fun space for play. Open Tues.-Sat. 10 a.m.-5 p.m. year-round; $2.50 per person.

PARKS AND RECREATION

Parks

Located at the north end of Capitol Lake at 5th Ave. and Water St., **Capitol Lake Park** shows off with cherry blossoms in April, and swimming, sunbathing, sailing, hiking, biking, and picnicking the rest of the year. It also makes a fine reflecting pool for the Legislative Building. Each fall, the Capitol Lake fish ladder is used by hundreds of king salmon returning home to spawn in the Deschutes River.

Heritage Park is the newest Olympia park, and will eventually follow the shore of Capitol

Lake from downtown to the State Capitol. The main attraction is **Heritage Fountain** at 6th Ave. and Water St., where the jets of water are splashing great fun for kids. Closed Monday.

Downtown at 7th Ave. and Capitol Way, **Sylvester Park**—named for city founder Edmund Sylvester—hosts concerts in the gazebo in July and August on Friday at noon, and Wednesday evenings. Directly behind the park is the Old Capitol Building (described above).

The **Olympia Japanese Garden** on Plum St. near Union Ave., tel. (360) 753-8380, was built in cooperation with Olympia's sister city of Yashiro, Japan. This small and peaceful park has a main gate built without nails, a garden lantern of cut granite, a bamboo grove, and an 18-foot pagoda. The central feature is a pond and waterfall. Open daily 10 a.m. to dusk; no charge.

Percival Landing Tower sits at the north end of a 1.5-mile shoreline boardwalk along Budd Inlet. Climb the tower (open daylight hours only) for a panoramic view of the yacht-filled harbor with the Capitol behind, the Olympic Mountains, and freighters loading logs for Asian markets.

Located a mere mile and a half north of downtown Olympia on East Bay Dr., **Priest Point Park** has 253 wooded acres that include picnic areas, a wading pool, and a playground, plus access to Budd Inlet, and excellent trails—including a fine three-mile loop that circles Ellis Cove. No overnight camping. The main attraction of **Olympia Watershed Park** along Henderson Blvd. is its two-mile hiking trail through woods, marsh, and streams. Six miles north of Olympia on Boston Harbor Rd., **Burfoot County Park** has an interpretive trail, hiking trails, a saltwater beach, a playground, and an open, grassy picnic area.

A six-mile cycling and walking trail leads from Martin Way in town north to Woodard Bay along an old railroad track. Eventually this will continue south six more miles to Offutt Lake. At Woodard Bay, the Dept. of Natural Resources has purchased 190 acres of land, managed as the **Woodard Bay Natural Resources Area.**

Recreation

Follow Capitol Blvd. south to the **Trails Arena** at 7824 Trails End Dr. SE (technically in Tumwater), where horse shows of various types are held several times a week, as well as an occasional circus and BMX race. Entry to the lower arena is generally free.

Local public pools can be found at the campus recreation center at **Evergreen State College,** tel. (360) 866-6000; **Tanglewilde Pool,** 414 Wildcat SE, tel. (360) 491-3907 (summers only); and the **YMCA,** 510 Franklin St. SE, tel. (360) 357-6609. Practice your rock climbing skills at **Capital City Climbing Gym,** 215 7th Ave. SW, tel. (360) 705-1585.

Motocross fans and four-wheelers may want to try out the 150-acre **ORV Sports Park,** located 16 miles west of Olympia off Hwy. 8, tel. (360) 495-3243. Camping sites and showers are also available here.

ACCOMMODATIONS AND CAMPING

Several local B&Bs offer more personal accommodations. Built in 1910, **Harbinger Inn B&B,** tel. (360) 754-0389, is a classy three-story brick mansion right on Budd Inlet with wide balconies, a hidden tunnel to the street, a waterfall, and antique furnishings. The five guest rooms have shared or private baths, and a continental breakfast; $60-125 s or d. No kids.

Also along Budd Inlet, **Parker House B&B,** 1919 East Bay Dr., tel. (360) 357-7988, is a private craftsman bungalow built in 1917. Rates are $105 s or $120 d, including a continental breakfast. No kids.

Swantown Inn, 1431 11th Ave. SE, tel. (360) 753-9123, is an 1893 Victorian mansion with four guest rooms, private baths, and gourmet breakfasts for $75-115 s or d. No kids.

Puget View Guesthouse, 7924 61st Ave. NE, tel. (360) 459-1676, is a romantic cottage near Tolmie State Park, with views across Puget Sound. Guests can borrow a canoe to explore the peaceful Nisqually Reach. A light breakfast is served, and kids are accepted; $89 s or d.

Nisqually Birder B&B, 5440 Beverly Dr. NE, tel. (360) 943-0107, has two rooms ($55 s or d with full breakfast) in a home near Nisqually Refuge. The owners are birders who also offer nature tours of the area. Outside decks overlook Puget Sound.

Forest Haven B&B, tel. (360) 956-7800, is a new alpine-style home on 10 acres of forest 20 miles east of Olympia. The three guest rooms include antiques and fireplaces. A full breakfast is served; $85-100 s or d.

OLYMPIA, TUMWATER,
AND LACEY MOTELS AND HOTELS

Accommodations are arranged from least to most expensive. Rates may be lower in the winter months. See the text for descriptions of local B&Bs.

BUDGET

Holly Motel; 2816 Martin Way, Olympia; tel. (360) 943-3000; $32 s or d; old furnishings, local calls 25 cents, see rooms first

INEXPENSIVE

Ranchotel Motel; 8819 Martin Way E., Olympia; tel. (360) 491-5410; $35 s, $40 d

Bailey Motor Inn; 3333 Martin Way, Olympia; tel. (360) 491-7515; $37 s or d; local calls 25 cents

Motel 6; 400 W. Lee St., Tumwater; tel. (360) 754-7320 or (800) 466-8356; $38 s, $44 d; outdoor pool

Shalimar Suites; 5895 Capitol Blvd. S, Tumwater; tel. (360) 943-8391; $39 s or d; studios, one- and two-bedroom suites, kitchens, four-night minimum stay, weekly and monthly rates

Golden Gavel Motor Hotel; 909 Capitol Way, Olympia; tel. (360) 352-8533; $43 s, $48 d; AAA approved

Super 8 Motel; 4615 Martin Way, Lacey; tel. (360) 459-8888 or (800) 800-8000; $50 s, $55 d; indoor pool

Carriage Inn Motel; 1211 S. Quince, Olympia; tel. (360) 943-4710; $50 s, $56-60 d; outdoor pool, microwaves and fridges, AAA approved

Days Inn/Capital Inn Motel; 120 College SE, Lacey; tel. (360) 493-1991 or (800) 282-7028; $58-65 s or d; sauna, exercise room, fridges, microwaves, continental breakfast, AAA approved

Tyee Hotel; 500 Tyee Dr., Tumwater; tel. (360) 352-0511 or (800) 386-8933; $59-79 s or d; wooded grounds, outdoor pool, tennis and basketball courts, AAA approved

MODERATE

Best Western Tumwater Inn; 5188 Capitol Blvd., Tumwater; tel. (360) 956-1235 or (800) 367-7771; $66-74 s, $71-78 d; outdoor pool, saunas, jacuzzi, exercise room, microwaves and fridges, continental breakfast, local calls 25 cents, AAA approved

Best Western Aladdin Hotel; 900 Capitol Way, Olympia; tel. (360) 352-7200 or (800) 367-7771; $66-86 s, $71-91 d; outdoor pool, AAA approved

Comfort Inn; 4700 Park Center Ave. NE, Lacey; tel. (360) 456-6300 or (800) 221-2222; $69-79 s or d; indoor pool, jacuzzi, exercise room, contintal breakfast, AAA approved

Holiday Inn Express; 4704 Park Center Ave. NE, Lacey; tel. (360) 412-1200 or (800) 551-8500; $69-79 s or d; indoor pool, continental breakfast, AAA approved

King Oscar Motel; 8200 Quinault Way NE, Lacey; tel. (360) 438-3333 or (888) 254-5464; $70-75 s or d; indoor pool, jacuzzi, sauna, fitness center, continental breakfast, AAA approved

Holiday Inn Select; 2300 Evergreen Park Dr., Olympia; tel. (360) 943-4000 or (800) 551-8500; $80 s or d; hilltop hotel with views of the Capitol and Cascades, outdoor pool, jacuzzi, volleyball court, AAA approved

EXPENSIVE

Ramada Inn Governor House Hotel; 621 S. Capitol Way; tel. (360) 352-7700 or (800) 228-2828; $89-124 s, $99-134 d; eight-story hotel overlooking Sylvester Park and Capitol Lake, outdoor pool, jacuzzi, sauna, exercise room, kitchenettes available, AAA approved

Campgrounds

The closest public camping can be found at **Millersylvania State Park,** 12 miles south of Olympia, off I-5 (exit 95). Tent ($11) and RV ($16) sites are available year-round. Call (360) 753-1519 for details, or (800) 452-5687 for reservations ($6 extra). **Capitol Forest,** approximately 20 miles southwest of Olympia, has an abundance of primitive campsites (free; no water). Call the Dept. of Natural Resources at (360) 902-1234, or (800) 527-3305 in Washington, for details and a map. **Showers** are available at East Bay Marina in Olympia.

Olympia has an abundance of RV parks, including several just a few miles from the center of town. These include: **Alderbrook Estates,** 2110 54th Ave., tel. (360) 357-9448; **American Heritage Campground,** 9610 Kimmie St. SW, tel. (360) 943-8778; **Black Lake RV Park,** 4325 Black Lake-Belmore Rd. SW, tel. (360) 357-6775; **The Coach Post,** 3633 7th Ave. SW, tel. (360) 754-7580; **Columbus Park,** 5700 Black Lake Blvd., tel. (360) 786-9460; **Olympia Campground,** 1441 83rd Ave. SW, tel. (360) 352-2551 or (800) 943-8778; **Riverbend Campground,** 1152 Durgin Rd. SE, tel. (360) 491-2534; and **Salmon Shores Resort,** 5446 Black Lake Blvd., tel. (360) 357-8618.

FOOD AND DRINK

Olympia is an eating-out town, with restaurants, cafes, and coffeehouses filling the downtown core. Walk a few blocks and you're bound to find a place that appeals.

Breakfast and Lunch

For an all-natural breakfast, lunch, or dinner, try the **Urban Onion** at the corner of Legion and Washington, tel. (360) 943-9242. Their wholesome cuisine—salads, soups, sandwiches, Mexican meals, and vegetarian specials—is served daily 7 a.m.-midnight. Try the open-face shrimp and cheese haystacks at lunch, or the *huevos rancheros* for breakfast.

More healthy food at **J-Vee Health Foods & Cafe,** a longtime natural foods store at 3720 Pacific Ave. SE, tel. (360) 491-1930.

Coffeehouses and Bakeries

Olympia has discovered espresso in a big way, and it's hard to find any cafe that doesn't have an espresso machine. **Batdorf and Bronson Roaster,** next to the Farmers Market at 513 Capitol Way S, tel. (360) 786-6717, sells freshly-roasted-on-the-premises coffee beans. Watch the roasting through the windows. Open Wed.-Sun. 8:30 a.m.-4:30 p.m.

Get fresh bagels and espresso from **Otto's,** 111 Washington NE, tel. (360) 352-8640, located just a few doors down from **Dancing Goats Espresso Co.,** 124 4th Ave. E, tel. (360) 754-8187, a relaxed place to meet the hip Olympia set over a tempting dessert.

Get some of the best pastries in southern Puget Sound at **Wagner's European Bakery & Cafe,** 1013 Capitol Way S, tel. (360) 357-7268, where they also serve soups, salads, and sandwiches for lunch, as well as light breakfasts. Be prepared for a line of state workers on weekdays at lunchtime.

San Francisco Street Bakery, 1320 San Francisco St. NE, tel. (360) 753-8553, bakes wonderful earthy breads (using organic grains), plus pastries and bagels.

On the Water

Waterfront and view restaurants aren't as common in Olympia as in other Puget Sound cities, but they do exist. **The Whale's Tale,** on Percival Landing dock at 501 N. Columbia St., tel. (360) 956-1928, has light breakfasts and lunches (including soup in a breadbowl), along with espresso, ice cream, and Italian sodas.

Genoas on the Bay, 1525 Washington St. NE, tel. (360) 943-7770, is an elegant steak, chicken, pasta, and seafood restaurant overlooking Budd Bay. They also have a Sunday champagne brunch. Located in a gorgeous Victorian home at 1205 W. Bay Dr., **Seven Gables Restaurant,** looks across Budd Bay to the Olympic Mountains. The food is equally attractive, with an emphasis on fresh seafood with a Northwest twist.

Budd Bay Cafe at Percival Landing, 525 Columbia St. NW, tel. (360) 357-6963, is open for lunch and dinner daily and has a very popular Sunday brunch buffet, with outdoor dining in summer featuring a marina view. This and Genoas are good places to sample the famous Olympia oysters on the half shell.

American and Seafood

Get Olympia oysters, geoduck clams, and other perfectly prepared seafood at **Gardner's Seafood and Pasta,** 111 W. Thurston St., tel. (360) 786-8466. Reservations advised.

Spar Cafe & Bar, 114 4th Ave. E, tel. (360) 357-6444, is a family place serving solid all-American breakfasts, lunches, and dinners. In business since the 1930s, the Spar has a decor to match: classic Northwest logging photos line the walls.

Ben Moore's Cafe, 112 W. 4th Ave., tel. (360) 357-7527, serves reasonably priced Northwest seasonal dishes, along with steaks, oysters, and prawns. Also try **Bristol House,** 2401 B Bristol Court, tel. (360) 352-9494, for great steaks and seafood.

International

Meet legislators and lobbyists on expense accounts at **La Petite Maison,** 2005 Ascension Ave. NW, tel. (360) 943-8812, a France-meets-Northwest restaurant with an emphasis on seafood and game. **Sweet Oasis,** 507 Capitol Way, tel. (360) 956-0470, has Middle Eastern specialties and a $6 lunch buffet.

Saigon Rendez-Vous, 117 5th Ave. W, tel. (360) 352-1989, is one of the best local Asian restaurants, with Vietnamese and Chinese menus, and vegetarian specialties. **China Town Restaurant,** 213 E. 4th Ave., tel. (360) 357-7292, is a very popular Chinese restaurant with happy hour specials Mon.-Fri. 4-6 p.m. Get quick and reasonable meals at either location of **Happy Teriyaki:** downtown at 530 Capitol Way S, tel. (360) 705-8000, and over in West Olympia at 2915 Harrison Ave. NW, tel. (360) 786-8866. Two good Thai places are **Thai Garden Restaurant,** 270 Capitol Mall, tel. (360) 786-1959, and **Thai Pavilion,** 303 E 4th Ave., tel. (360) 943-9093.

For Mexican meals, head to **La Palma Restaurant,** 523 S. Sound Center, tel. (360) 459-9805, with a big menu with all the favorites, including fajitas and seafood dishes.

Pizza and Italian

Get distinctive pizzas at **Jo Mamas,** 120 Pear St. NE, tel. (360) 943-9849, where the atmosphere is funky and the pizzas are thick whole-wheat-crust versions with healthy toppings. **Capitale,** 609 Capitol Way S., tel. 9360) 352-8007, is a fine little downtown place with pasta, pizza, and other creative dishes. **Casa Mia,** 716 Plum St., tel. (360) 459-0440, is another good Italian restaurant.

Pubs

Fishbowl Pub & Cafe, 515 Jefferson St. SE, tel. (360) 943-6480, offers a surprising contrast to Olympia's better known brew. Located downtown, this small brewery and pub produces seven different beers, all with such fishy names as "Trout Stout" and "Fish Tale Ale." Get a pizza or sandwich from the cafe and enjoy it in this friendly lounge-around place. Highly recommended.

Markets

Located in big new building on the north end of Capitol Way, the very popular **Olympia's Farmers Market,** tel. (360) 352-9096, is Washington's second largest (after Pike Place Market). In addition to the expected fresh fruits and veggies, you'll discover all sorts of handcrafted items, plants, meats and seafood, baked goods, and wonderful ethnic foods. The market has festivals throughout the summer, and is open Thurs.-Sun. 10 a.m.-3 p.m. April-Oct., and Sat.-Sun. 10 a.m.-3 p.m. Nov.-December.

For natural foods at other times, visit the **Olympia Food Co-op,** 921 Rogers NW, tel. (360) 754-7666, and 3111 Pacific Ave. SE, tel. (360) 956-3870. Get fresh-squeezed apple cider, U-bake apple pies, eggs, honey, and more at **Lattin's Country Cider Mill,** 9402 Rich Rd. SE, tel. (360) 491-7328. They are located just a short ways south of the Amtrak station in East Olympia.

ENTERTAINMENT AND THE ARTS

Nightlife

Olympia has an active music scene. The **Capitol Theater,** 206 E. 5th, tel. (360) 754-5378, is the biggest alternative rock venue. Other downtown bars with music include: **Club Infinity,** 311 4th Ave., tel. (360) 352-2375; **Fishbowl Pub,** 515 Jefferson St. SE, tel. (360) 943-3650; **All That Jazz,** 325 E. 4th Ave., tel. (360) 534-9212; and **The Spar,** 114 4th Ave., tel. (360) 786-1823. The gay-friendly **Thekla,** 116 E. 5th Ave., tel. (360) 352-1855, is a very popular dance club.

Performing Arts

Olympia's **Washington Center for the Performing Arts** is a state-of-the-art facility with seating for 987 people and hundreds of activities throughout the year—from ballet to rock concerts. Located at 512 Washington St. SE, tel. (360) 753-8586, featured performances (Oct.-April) include nationally renowned artists, along with many local groups. Both the **Olympia Symphony Orchestra,** tel. (360) 753-0074, and the **Masterworks Choral Ensemble,** tel. (360) 491-3305, perform at the Washington Center for the Performing Arts. See "Events," below, for other artistic activities.

 Capitol Playhouse '24, located in the historic Capitol Theatre at 206 E. 5th Ave., tel. (360) 754-5378, produces plays from December to May as well as a summer Shakespeare Festival, consisting of three plays, from June through August. The Capitol Theater also hosts a film festival in November. The **Olympia Little Theater,** 1925 Miller Ave. NE, tel. (360) 786-9484, is the place for light comedies.

Galleries

Downtown Olympia has a number of art galleries and boutiques on 4th and 5th Avenues. Three good ones are: **State of the Arts Gallery,** 500 Washington St., tel. (360) 705-0317; **Terra Gallery,** 418 Washington St., tel. (360) 754-8776; and **Artists' Co-Op Gallery,** 610 Columbia St. SW, tel. (360) 357-6920.

EVENTS

Don't miss the **Olympia Arts Walk** on the third weekend of April, with performances, literary and art events, and tours of local galleries. Many downtown businesses—even furniture stores—open their windows for budding artists. The unique and whimsical **Procession of the Species** is the main event, with magically bizarre creatures and plants of every shape and form. Call (360) 753-8380 for details on this fun event. A second Arts Walk (sans procession) takes place the first weekend of October.

 The **Wooden Boat Festival,** tel. (360) 357-3370, held in mid-May at Percival Landing, includes a regatta and wooden boats open for public viewing. The first Saturday in June, Evergreen State College's **Super Saturday** features hundreds of arts and crafts booths, food, and entertainment for all ages; phone (360) 866-6000, for information.

 The city's biggest summer festival is **Lakefair,** held the third weekend of July, tel. (360) 943-7344. Activities include a twilight parade, fireworks, carnival, food and craft vendors, and crowning of the Lakefair queen. From mid-July through August, Sylvester Park has **Music in the Park** events at noon on Wednesday; tel. (360) 943-2375. In August, the **Shakespeare Festival/Renaissance Faire** at Sylvester Park brings out costumed performers of all types, and performances of Shakespeare's classics in the nearby Capitol Theater.

 Summer's end brings the **Harbor Days Festival** to Percival Landing over Labor Day weekend, highlighted by a regatta and vintage tugboat races in the sound; call (360) 754-4567 for information. December means the **Parade of Lighted Ships,** put on by the Olympia Yacht Club; tel. (360) 357-6767.

SHOPPING

Given that this is a government/college town, you'd expect to find good bookstores in Olympia. Biggest is **Orca Books,** 509 4th Ave. E, tel. (360) 352-0123, open late most nights for browsers. **Going Places,** 515 Washington SE, tel. (360) 357-6860, has travel books, maps, and outdoor recreation guides. **Bulldog News,** 116 4th Ave. E, tel. (360) 357-6397, has a big choice of foreign magazines and newspapers.

Capital Mall, 9th Ave. SW and Black Lake Blvd., is the area's largest shopping center with nearly 100 shops and restaurants, including The Bon Marché, JCPenney, and Lamonts. Just up Black Lake Blvd. is another shopping plaza, Capital Village, with grocery, drug, and hardware stores plus a sprinkling of fast-food restaurants. **Shipwreck Beads,** 2727 Westmoor Court SW, tel. (360) 754-2323, claims to have the world's largest selection of beads for sale, numbering in the billions.

INFORMATION AND SERVICES

Information
For maps and general information stop by the **Olympia/Thurston County Chamber of Commerce,** 521 Legion Way SE, tel. (360) 357-3362; www.olympiachamber.com. Open Mon.-Fri. 9 a.m.-5 p.m. all year. At the Capitol Campus, head to the **Public Information Center,** tel. (360) 586-3460; open daily 8 a.m.-5 p.m. yearround. The headquarters office for **Olympic National Forest** is in Olympia at 1835 Black Lake Blvd. SW, tel. (360) 956-2300.

TRANSPORTATION

Trains and Planes
Amtrak, tel. (800) 872-7245, serves Olympia along its north-south **Coast Starlight** route from Seattle to Los Angeles. The Amtrak station is in east Olympia at 6600 Yelm Highway.

There are no scheduled passenger flights to Olympia; take a van to Sea-Tac instead. **Capital Aeroporter,** tel. (360) 754-7113 or (800) 962-3579, and **Centralia-SeaTac Airport Express,** tel. (360) 786-0636 or (800) 773-9490, both serve Olympia.

Bus Service
Intercity Transit has daily service to Olympia, Tumwater, and most of Thurston County. They operate two **free shuttles** that serve downtown, the farmers market, and the Capitol Campus area weekdays 11 a.m.-2 p.m. All buses have bike racks. For details, call (360) 786-1881 or (800) 287-6348, or stop by the Olympia Transit Center on State St. between Franklin and Washington Streets.

Pierce Transit, tel. (206) 581-8000 or (800) 562-8109, offers an express bus between Olympia and Tacoma, where you can catch another express bus to downtown Seattle.

Greyhound, tel. (800) 231-2222, connects Olympia to Seattle, Tacoma, Portland, and other cities along its north-south I-5 corridor. The bus station is located at Capitol and 7th.

VICINITY OF OLYMPIA

LACEY AREA

A few miles northeast of Olympia right off I-5, the fast-growing city of Lacey (pop. 27,000) is primarily a suburban shopping area and retirement village. The area has been settled for well over a century, but Lacey was not incorporated until 1966. Just east and slightly north of Lacey proper is the Nisqually Delta, preserved wetlands geographically identical to Tacoma's industrial tideflat area.

Sights

The small **Lacey Museum** at 829 Lacey St., tel. (360) 491-0857, is open Thurs.-Sat. 10 a.m.-4 p.m. year-round. The town is also home to **St. Martin's College,** founded in 1895 by Catholic Benedictine monks. Today the school has 1,000 students, and strong programs in education and engineering. Its basketball team is called—fittingly enough—the St. Martin's Saints.

Parks

Just off I-5 at exit 114, **Nisqually National Wildlife Refuge,** tel. (360) 753-9467, is a protected home for 300 species of wildlife, including great blue herons, bald eagles, and red-tailed hawks, as well as a resting area for over 20,000 migrating ducks and geese each spring and fall. This is one of the largest surviving estuaries in the state of Washington. Several hiking trails provide a chance to stretch your legs on portions of the 3,870-acre refuge, and photo blinds assist you in your birdwatching. Be sure to bring binoculars and a field guide! Visitors are welcome at the refuge seven days a week during daylight hours; $3 per family. No jogging, bicycling, motorbikes, pets, fires, or camping. The **Twin Barns Education Center** here is open Sat.-Sun. 10 a.m.-2 p.m. (Saturday only in winter).

Managed by the Audubon Society, the **Nisqually Reach Nature Center,** 4949 D'Milluhr Rd. NE at Luhr Beach, tel. (360) 459-0387, has marine animals and birds, a museum, fishing dock, boat launch, picnic area, guided tours, and raft trips. Open Wednesday and Sat.-Sun. noon-4 p.m. (closed Wednesdays in winter); no charge.

Tolmie State Park, five miles from exit 111, has 1,800 feet of waterfront on Nisqually Reach with swimming, fishing, 3.5 miles of hiking trails, and an underwater park with an artificial reef created by the intentional sinking of three wooden barges. Open for day use only (no camping), the park also provides an outdoor shower for swimmers and divers near the lower restroom. The park was named for Dr. William Frazer Tolmie, who spent 16 years at Fort Nisqually as physician, surgeon, botanist, and fur trader for Hudson's Bay Company. Tolmie also studied the languages of the Northwest people—his communication skills proved invaluable for negotiations during the Indian Wars of 1855-56.

Accommodations and Food

See the chart "Olympia, Tumwater, and Lacey Motels and Hotels" for a complete listing of local lodging choices.

Meconi's Italian Subs, 5225 Lacey Blvd. SE, tel. (360) 459-0213, is the best and most authentic sub shop in the Olympia area—very popular with state workers. Good pizzas at **Brewery City Pizza,** 4354 Martin Way, tel. (360) 491-6630. Next door, **O'Blarney's Pub,** 4411 Martin Way, has Irish music on Tuesday.

Events

The **Thurston County Fair,** held the first full weekend in August at the County Fairgrounds in Lacey, is a five-day festival with entertainment, food, and booths. Call (360) 786-5453. Lacey is also home for the **Capital Food & Wine Festival** in March, with food from local restaurants and wine from Washington wineries.

Information and Services

The **Lacey-Thurston Chamber of Commerce,** 7 South Sound Center, tel. (360) 491-4141. Open Mon.-Fri. 9 a.m.-5 p.m.

Swim at **North Thurston High School,** 600 Sleater-Kinney Rd. NE, or **Timberline High School,** 6120 Mullen Rd. SE, tel. (360) 491-

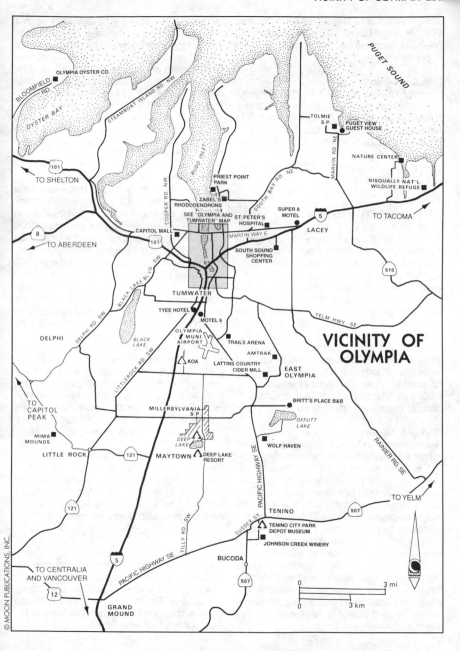

VICINITY OF OLYMPIA

0857. The 18-hole **Meriwood Golf Course,** 4550 Meriwood Dr., tel. (360) 412-0495 or (800) 706-1881, is considered one of the finest in the Puget Sound area.

Transportation

Intercity Transit, tel. (360) 786-1881 or (800) 287-6348, has daily bus service in Olympia, Tumwater, and most of Thurston County. Both **Centralia-SeaTac Airport Express,** tel. (360) 773-9490 or (800) 773-9490, and **Capital Aeroporter,** tel. (360) 754-7113 or (800) 962-3579, provide direct shuttle service between Lacey and Sea-Tac Airport.

TUMWATER

The home of Olympia beer was Washington's first community—then named New Market—settled in 1845 along the Deschutes River at the end of one branch of the Oregon Trail. Starting at Independence, Missouri, the families in the Wagon Train of 1844 endured 19 months of cold, rain, and wearying travel en route to their final destination above Tumwater Falls. Members of Hudson's Bay Co., who had been stationed at Fort Nisqually since 1833, provided the settlers with the makings for the first sawmill north of the Columbia and traded Army supplies for wood shingles. Tumwater is now home to 12,000 people and acts as both a suburb of Olympia and a small city in its own right.

Olympia Brewery

Heading down I-5 toward Tumwater, you can't miss the Olympia Brewery immediately adjacent to Tumwater Falls Park (see below) at exit 103. Olympia began as Capital Brewing Co., established in 1895 by a beer maker from Montana, Leopold F. Schmidt. Over the years, the company acquired Hamm's and Lone Star, before being taken over itself by Pabst Brewing Co. in 1983. The mergers continued, and Pabst is now owned by S&P Holding, a California real estate company! The sign out front still says Olympia Brewing Company, but they also make Pabst, Buckhorn, Hamm's, Olde English malt liquor, and dozens of other brands, including contract-brewed beer for some microbreweries (Oly is a microbrewery?).

Tours of the brewery have always been a major tourist draw for the area, but because of cost-cutting under new management they are only offered in the summer. The gift shop and tasting room are open Mon.-Sat. 9 a.m.-4:30 p.m. all year, and you can watch a video on beer making. Call (360) 754-5177 for tour details. The real treat at Oly is their incredible collection of more than 250 antique beer steins, including one that holds 32 quarts, and a tankard made from elephant ivory that once belonged to President Theodore Roosevelt.

Other Sights

The 15-acre privately owned **Tumwater Falls Park** (free) is the site of the first American settlement in the Puget Sound region, founded in 1845. The neatly landscaped grounds include picnic areas, a boat launch into the Deschutes River, hiking trails, and lots of hungry ducks. Nearby, the **Henderson House Museum,** 602 Deschutes Way, tel. (360) 754-4163, has photographic exhibits depicting life along the Deschutes River during the late 1800s and recent photos of Tumwater's people and events; open Sunday 1-3 p.m. and Thursday noon-3 p.m. year-round; free.

The **Crosby House,** adjacent to Tumwater Falls Park at Deschutes Way and Grant St., tel. (360) 943-9884, is Tumwater's oldest home; it was built in 1860 by Bing Crosby's grandfather, Capt. Nathaniel Crosby III, who came around the Horn to the Oregon Territory in 1847 and inspired the whole Crosby clan to follow him out West. Open for tours Thursday 12:30-2:30 p.m.; free.

Accommodations and Campgrounds

See the "Olympia, Tumwater, and Lacey Motels and Hotels" chart for a complete listing of local lodging choices. See "Accommodations and Camping" in the Olympia section above for nearby campgrounds and RV parks.

Food

In front of the Olympia Brewery and overlooking Tumwater Falls, **Falls Terrace Restaurant** has moderately priced dinners that feature chicken, steak, seafood, and veal. They also offer a Sunday brunch. The lounge features an outside deck, a favorite place to drop by for a drink. Reservations highly recommended.

The **Mason Jar,** 478 Cleveland Ave. SE, tel. (360) 754-7776, is a favorite Tumwater lunch spot with homemade soups, freshly baked breads, and sandwiches. The best burgers in the Olympia area come from **Big Tom Drive Inn** at 303 Cleveland Ave. SE, tel. (360) 352-7711. Big Tom and his son Little Tom both work here.

Louisa, 205 Cleveland Ave., tel. (360) 352-3732, is the most creative local restaurant, with an inviting atmosphere, Northwest-inspired Italian food and good salads.

Recreation
Swim at **Tumwater Valley Pool,** 4801 Tumwater Valley Dr. SE, tel. (360) 943-1040. Open to the public, the 18-hole **Tumwater Valley Golf Course,** 4611 Tumwater Valley Dr. SE, tel. (360) 943-9500, has a driving range, pro shop, and lessons.

On Deschutes Way, butting up against the brewery, you'll find **Tumwater Falls Park,** where you may see king salmon heading up the fish ladders late August through October. They spawn in nearby pens. Paths lead to the falls.

Other Practicalities
In mid-July, the **Southern Puget Sound Air Show,** comes to the Olympia Airport in Tumwater.

Find the **Tumwater Area Chamber of Commerce** at 488 Tyee Dr. (next to the Tyee Hotel), tel. (360) 357-5153. Open Mon.-Fri. 9 a.m.-5 p.m.

Intercity Transit, tel. (360) 786-1881 or (800) 287-6348, has daily bus service in Olympia, Tumwater, and most of Thurston County. Both **Centralia-SeaTac Airport Express,** tel. (360) 786-0636 or (800) 773-9490, and **Capital Aeroporter,** tel. (360) 754-7113 or (800) 962-3579, offer shuttle vans between Tumwater and Sea-Tac Airport.

TENINO AND YELM

From downtown Olympia, follow Capitol Blvd. S onto Old Hwy. 99 to Tenino, a quiet old town with stone-fronted buildings lining the main street. These stones came from Tenino's sandstone quarry, now a popular swimming hole. The name Tenino (ten-NINE-oh) has a handful of possible origins, from the Indian name for a fork or junction, to the more colorful Engine Number 1090 (ten-nine-oh) that ran on the Kalama-Tacoma railroad line in the 1870s. Yelm is located 14 miles east of Tenino on Hwy. 507, and is home to "psychic channeler" J.Z. Knight who considers herself the reincarnation of a 35,000-year-old warrior named Ramtha. You can't miss her ranch; the fence is topped with a string of copper pyramids.

Wolf Haven
This 80-acre wolf refuge is home to two dozen

wolves that were taken in for a variety of reasons; some were no longer needed by researchers, some were mistreated or unwanted by zoos and refuges, and others were family "pets" who grew predictably wild. The sanctuary offers hourly guided tours and "howl-ins" on Friday and Saturday 6:30-9:30 p.m. during the summer. Wolf Haven is at 3111 Offutt Lake Rd., north of Tenino just off Old Hwy. 99, tel. (360) 264-4695 or (800) 448-9563; open Wed.-Sun. 10 a.m.-4 p.m. May-Sept., and Wed.-Sun. 10 a.m.-3 p.m. the rest of the year. Tours are $5 adults, $2.50 ages 5-12, free under age four; howl-ins $6 adults, $4 ages 5-12.

Parks and Museum
One block off Sussex St., **Tenino City Park,** tel. (360) 264-4620, has overnight camping and picnic areas, plus the **Tenino Depot Museum,** 399 W. Park St., tel. (360) 264-4620, an original sandstone train station housing a collection of historical artifacts. Open Fri.-Sun. noon-4 p.m. mid-April to mid-October.

Millersylvania State Park, 842-acres of forested land on the north shore of Deep Lake, is less than four miles off I-5 at exit 95. The park has impressive stone picnic shelters and bathhouses constructed between 1933 and 1939 by the Civilian Conservation Corps. Other facilities include two swimming beaches and an environmental learning center for school groups. Enjoy fishing for rainbow trout and boating on Deep Lake. Campsites ($11) and RV sites ($16) are available, along with showers. The campground is open year-round. Call (360) 753-1519 for details, or (800) 452-5687 for reservations ($6 extra).

Deep Lake Resort, tel. (360) 352-7388, has cabins and RV sites along the shore of the lake, plus a swimming beach with floats, mini-golf, rowboats, and canoes.

Lodging and Food
7C's Guest Ranch B&B, 11123 128th St. SE in Rainier, tel. (360) 446-7957, has three guest rooms (shared or private baths) in a ranch home on 10 acres, plus a hot tub in the gazebo. A full farm breakfast is served, and kids are welcome; $35 s, $45-100 d.

A turn-of-the-century farmhouse five miles south of Tenino houses **Alice's Restaurant,** with locally famous five-course country-style meals. Call (360) 264-2887 for reservations. **Arnold's Country Inn** 717 Yelm Ave. E in Yelm, tel. (360) 458-3977, is another noteworthy restaurant with steaks, seafood, and pasta.

Events
Tenino's **Old Time Music Festival** on the third weekend of March features a fiddle musicians from all over. The fourth weekend in July brings all kinds of commotion to quiet Tenino with the **Oregon Trail Days,** including a parade, arts and crafts, entertainment, and a muzzle-loading camp. In early December, **Winterfest in Historic Tenino** features wagon rides, living history demonstrations, a gingerbread house competition, a quilt contest, and 1880s arts and crafts. **Yelm Prairie Days** the last weekend of July has food and craft booths, carnival rides, and games. The **Lighter than Air Hot Air Balloon Festival** takes place in Yelm in mid-July.

Other Practicalities
The **Tenino Chamber of Commerce** is located at 149 N. Ritter St., tel. (360) 264-5075. Find the **Yelm Chamber of Commerce** at 701 Prairie Park Ln., tel. (360) 458-6608.

Red Wind Casino, 12819 Yelm Hwy., tel. (360) 456-3328, has gambling action daily and

cheap breakfast specials. Tenino's swimming pool is an abandoned sandstone quarry; open mid-June to early September; tel. (360) 264-2368. Rent canoes to float the peaceful Black River from **Black River Canoe Trips,** in Littlerock (west of I-5), tel. (360) 273-6369.

Intercity Transit, tel. (360) 287-6348 or (800) 287-6348, has Mon.-Sat. bus service to Tenino, Yelm, Rochester, Olympia, and most of Thurston County.

ROCHESTER AND OAKVILLE

Heading west from I-5, Hwy. 12 follows the winding Chehalis River through Christmas tree farms, second- and third-growth forests, and dairy farms. You'll meet a constant parade of logging trucks. The don't-blink-or-you'll-miss-it town of Rochester has a few businesses, and Oakville is home to antique shops in old frame buildings and a popular soda fountain. Just west of here is the entrance to Capitol Forest, managed by the Dept. of Natural Resources. Highway 12 joins Hwy. 8 at Elma and continues westward to Aberdeen and Grays Harbor.

Mima Mounds
Eight miles south of Tumwater is the **Mima Mounds Interpretive Area,** tel. (360) 753-2449, a registered national landmark with nature walks, an interpretive center, and picnic area. These grass-covered mounds, ranging in height up to eight feet, are also scattered throughout southern Thurston County, parts of China, and Alaska. They're often referred to as "mysterious" because no one really knows how they got there; theoretical origins range from glaciers to giant gophers, although the latter is mainly from the same folks who brought you the "jackalope." Indians burned these areas to keep them open and productive, but today Douglas fir trees are gradually spreading across the hilly mounds.

Capitol Forest
From Mima Mounds continue north on Waddell Creek Rd. to Capitol Forest, a multiuse "working" forest (look out for logging trucks) in the Black Hills. The hills received their name when early Anglo settlers found the entire area had been charred by a forest fire. Free primitive

campsites are available for tents and RVs at nine locations within the forest; many miles of hiking and horseback riding trails are clustered at the south end of the forest, while trailbikes may use those in the north end. The **McLane Creek Nature Trail** is a mile-long route that circles a beaver pond and meadow; call the Dept. of Natural Resources at (360) 902-1234, or (800) 527-3305 in Washington, for directions. To get a panoramic view of the area, follow the marked dirt road from Waddell Creek Rd. to 2,658-foot Capitol Peak, the highest point in the Black Hills.

Practicalities

The **Lucky Eagle Casino,** tel. (360) 273-2000 or (800) 720-1788, sits on the **Chehalis Indian Reservation** between Rochester and Oakville and has blackjack, craps, roulette, keno, and other gambling. Also here are a restaurant and lounges with live music and comedy.

Rochester's **Maharaja Cuisine of India,** 19712 Old Hwy. 99, tel. (360) 273-2442, has northern Indian dishes, including tandoor oven and vegetarian specialties.

Built in 1931, **Country Rose B&B,** 18010 Anderson Rd. SW in Rochester, tel. (360) 273-6213, is a 1931 farmhouse with three guest rooms, private or shared baths, and a full breakfast. Kids accepted; $55-70 s or $64-79 d.

Outback RV Park, 19100 Huntington St. SW, tel. (360) 273-0585, has tent and RV spaces.

Rochester's main summer event is the **Black Hills Wranglers Rodeo.**

Intercity Transit, tel. (360) 287-6348 or (800) 287-6348, has Mon.-Sat. bus service to Tenino, Yelm, Rochester, Olympia, and most of Thurston County.

CENTRALIA AND CHEHALIS

Washington's "Twin Cities" of Centralia and Chehalis lie halfway between Seattle and Portland (about 85 miles each way) and are accessible from five different I-5 exits. The two small cities are four miles apart, but the route connecting them is lined with retail businesses as they gradually grow together.

Because it is considerably larger and has a more dramatic history, Centralia gets more attention than Chehalis, even though the latter is the Lewis County seat. Centralia's population of more than 13,000 makes it nearly twice as big as Chehalis.

The economy of the Twin Cities depends primarily upon a mix of dairy farms, Christmas tree farms, logging, coal mining, power generation, and food processing, but it also has a strong retail focus with its antique malls and discount outlet shops.

CENTRALIA

Centralia is approximately 25 miles south of Olympia, and just east from busy I-5. The town has a rich and interesting history and is becoming a center for antiques in the region.

History

Centralia is the only city in Washington founded by an African-American man. George Washington—born of a mulatto slave father and a white mother—was the slave of James C. Cochran, a Missourian who, in 1850, filed a claim on the land where Centralia now sits. Cochran set him free and adopted Washington as his son. It was illegal then for a black person to own property, so the claim rested in Cochran's name until the Washington Territory was created. (Its laws forbade slavery and placed no restrictions on ownership.)

Cochran returned the land to Washington, who insisted that Cochran take $3,200 for it. Then he platted a town, sold lots, built a home, and donated a parcel of land for the development of George Washington Park. Within 15 years, Washington had sold 2,000 lots, throwing in an extra one to anyone who built a house. He named the thriving town "Centerville." It wasn't long before the Post Office Department discovered there were two towns of the same name in the territory, so the name was changed to Centralia.

During the depression that followed the crash of 1893, Washington hauled supplies up from Portland for his neighbors, offered interest-free

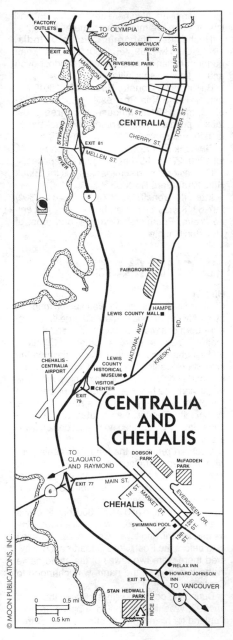

loans, found work for Centerville's residents, and saved the town from economic disaster. Though a respected businessman, not everyone liked him: someone once tried to kill him by putting carbolic acid in his wine. But Washington lived to be 88, when he died from being thrown from a buggy.

The "Wobbly War"

Centralia is the site of one of the state's most notorious lynchings. Others occurred from time to time, but none was so immortalized as that of Wesley Everest. The Marxist-oriented Industrial Workers of the World (IWW) strongly urged its members not to enlist when the U.S. declared war on Germany in WW I. Their stance drew fire from the *L.A. Times* and others, who claimed that IWW stood for "I won't work" and "I want whiskey." The IWW, or "Wobblies," wanted to abolish the wage structure and sometimes resorted to violent means. In September 1918, 100 Wobbly leaders were convicted of obstructing the war effort, and the Wobblies were finished as a major labor force.

American Legionnaires began attacking the IWW hiring halls throughout the West, and rumors had circulated for weeks that the Legionnaires planned an attack in Centralia; both sides were armed. On Armistice Day, 1919, the worst of the fighting began. An American Legion-led parade went past the union hall once, and those inside thought they had escaped. But then the parade turned around and started back. At this point, the stories clash. Supporters of the Legionnaires claimed they were fired upon from inside as they marched past peacefully. IWW members said they were simply defending themselves from an attack. In the melee that followed, four Legionnaires were shot and killed.

Wesley Everest, an IWW member, emptied his rifle magazine into the attacking Legionnaires and then ran out the back with the mob following. He had a pistol to keep them far enough behind, then ran to the river. He reached waist-deep water, then turned and fired to keep them from rushing him. He offered to surrender to a policeman, but none stepped forward. The mob attacked, dragged him from the river, and deposited him in the jail. That night, during a blackout, a mob rushed the jail, and the guard simply stood aside while they hauled

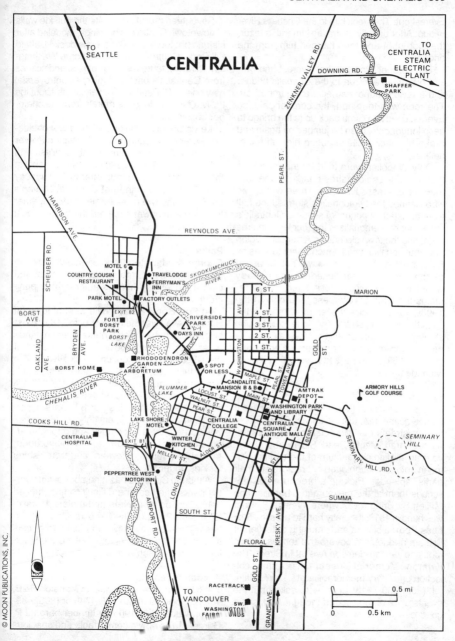

CENTRALIA

rest out. They took him to the Chehalis River bridge. After brutally castrating him with a razor, the mob shot and then hanged him from the bridge.

The coroner reported that Everest had broken out of jail and run to the Chehalis bridge, tied a rope around his neck, and jumped off. The rope was too short, the coroner said, so Everest used it to climb back up to the bridge to get a longer one. Then he jumped off again and broke his neck while shooting himself full of holes.

Only Wobblies were tried for the massacre that left four Legionnaires dead; no one was tried for Everest's lynching. Three witnesses who claimed the Legionnaires stormed the hall were arrested for perjury. A statue in Centralia's town square memorializes the four legionnaires slain, and the town still has an American Legion post, but you won't find a monument to Wesley Everest or the IWW. The case was not discussed by the community for decades, and nobody would give interviews about it. Even today it remains a source of bitterness, and only in the 1990s was the incident even mentioned in the local historical museum. The American Legion still wants the story go away. When a Centralia mural depicting the labor movement was completed in 1997, they passed a resolution strongly condemning it.

Sights

Take exit 81 off I-5, then follow Mellen St. west for one-quarter mile to the Chehalis River bridge. On the streets that Mrs. George Washington named—Iron, Maple, Pearl, Silver, and First—you can still find elegant turn-of-the-century Victorian homes, though often not restored to their earlier splendor. Pick up a brochure that describes them at the museum in Chehalis. The Mellen St. Bridge was where Wesley Everest was hung in 1919. It's pretty hard to miss the **5 or Less Spot;** a bizarre and amusing collection of flotsam and jetsam covers the fences, walls, roof, and yard on Harrison Ave. at M Street. The **Veterans Memorial Museum,** has a small collection of military memorabilia at 712 W. Main; tel. (360) 330-7913. Stop by to ask about the events of 1919; on second thought, that isn't a good idea.

Seventeen **murals** decorate the outside walls of downtown Centralia's buildings, modeled after historic photographs. The murals depict Buffalo Bill Cody, Centralia's founder George Washington, railways, ferries, sternwheelers, and scenes from Centralia's past, including a controversial new one on S. Pearl and Tower streets about the IWW. Get a guide to the murals from the chamber of commerce.

Lewis County is the largest producer of electric power in the state, thanks to **Pacific Power and Light Co.,** a coal-fired plant 12 miles north of town. Call (360) 736-9901 to reserve a spot in their two-hour guided tour, offered on Tuesday only. The coal is mined at Centralia Mining's open-pit mine two miles farther north; together the mine and power plant are the biggest local employers.

Parks

George Washington Park, downtown between Pearl and Silver Streets, was donated by the city's founder and houses a library and playground.

At **Fort Borst Park,** a mile west of town off Harrison Ave., visit the reconstructed 1852 Borst blockhouse, which was a bulwark against Indian attacks, originally built at the confluence of the Chehalis and Skookumchuck Rivers. The house that Joseph Borst, an early Centralia settler, built for his young bride Mary in 1857 still stands here; Borst boasted that the house was so well built it would last for 80 years! Open Sat.-Sun. 1-4 p.m. summers only; tel. (360) 736-7687. The park is open daily and offers an arboretum, rhododendron garden, playground, racquetball courts, showers, and trout fishing for kids under 14.

Although Centralia has a number of noteworthy parks, they can be difficult to find, tucked behind shopping centers and motels. **Rotary-Riverside Park,** on the Skookumchuck River, has a large grassy play and picnic area, plus tent and RV spaces, hidden behind the Huntley Inn on Harrison Avenue.

Accommodations

The 6,500-square-foot **Candalite Mansion B&B,** 402 N. Rock, tel. (360) 736-4749 or (800) 489-4749, was built in 1903 by lumber baron J.P. Gurrier and is now a comfortable and spacious

B&B with a Christian-oriented atmosphere. Inside are five guest rooms (shared or private baths), a pool table, and fireplace. A full breakfast (continental during the week) is served; $50-65 s or d. No kids.

In addition to the motels listed below, McMenamins Olympic Club plans to open a combination hotel and hostel in their historic building; call (360) 736-5164 for the latest.

Get budget-priced lodging at **Motel 6,** 1310 Belmont Ave., tel. (360) 330-2057 or (800) 466-8356: $33 s or $39 d, with an outdoor pool. **Peppertree West Motor Inn & RV Park,** 1208 Alder St., tel. (360) 736-1124, charges $35-39 s or $38-41 d. **Park Motel** 1011 Belmont, tel. (360) 736-9333, has rooms for $36 s or $42 d.

Days Inn, 702 Harrison Ave. E, tel. (360) 736-2875 or (800) 325-2525, has rooms for $44-59 s or d, including an outdoor pool and continental breakfast. **Ferryman's Inn Motel,** 1003 Eckerson Rd., tel. (360) 330-2094, has an outdoor pool, jacuzzi, exercise facility, and continental breakfast for $45 s or $48 d. **Knights Inn,** 1325 Lake Shore Dr., tel. (360) 736-9344 or (800) 600-8701, sits along Plummer Lake and has a grassy area for picnics; $54-58 s or d. **Travelodge** 1049 Eckerson Rd., tel. (360) 736-1661 or (800) 578-7878, is a new motel with an outdoor pool, jacuzzi, and continental breakfast; $60 s or d.

Campgrounds

Pitch a tent or park that RV at the city-run **Rotary-Riverside Park** along the Skookumchuck River, tel. (360) 330-7688. Private RV parks are **Peppertree RV Park,** 1208 Alder St., tel. (360) 736-1124, and **Harrison RV Park,** 3312 Harrison Ave., tel. (360) 330-2167.

Food

Centralia and Chehalis are not known as centers of *haute cuisine,* but you can find inexpensive and decent meals. Centralia has all the standard fast food places strung out around exit 82 from I-5. The best lunch place is **Winter Kitchen,** 827 Marsh, tel. (360) 736-2916, in a small forest-green home decorated with icicles. The menu includes salads, soups, sandwiches on freshly baked bread, and other tasty fare.

At 1054 Harrison Ave., the **Country Cousin,** tel. (360) 736-2200, is a corny family place with three solid meals a day, including a filling breakfast and meat-and-potatoes dinners. The place is always busy, especially for their Tuesday chicken and ribs buffet.

Head out to the golf course where **Back Nine Bistro** serves casual lunches or dinners of pizza, pasta, steak, or seafood; tel. (360) 736-5967.

Built in 1908, **McMenamins Olympic Club,** 112 N. Tower Ave., tel. (360) 736-5164, still has the Tiffany chandeliers, card room, and the sign proclaiming "Ladies patronage not solicited." The bar is now part of a chain of more than 40 McMenamins brewpubs, and has fresh ales on draft and a fine sandwich, burger, and fish and chip menu. Nearby on Tower Ave. is **Centralia Pharmacy,** where you'll find a 1903 soda fountain that still serves shakes, malts, and banana splits.

The **Lewis County Farmers Market,** tel. (360) 785-3101, is held Friday 9:30 a.m.-1 p.m., and Saturday 11 a.m.-3:30 p.m. late April-Oct. on Pine St. at Railroad Avenue. You'll find handicrafts, plants, flowers, and baked goods in addition to fresh fruits and veggies.

Events and Entertainment

On July 4th weekend, Centralia comes alive with **Summerfest,** featuring a parade, fireworks, and a demolition derby. Since 1909, the **Southwest Washington Fair** has been one of the largest summer festivals in the state, attracting crowds of over 125,000 on the third weekend in August. The fairgrounds are at the south end of town on Gold Street. **Evergreen Playhouse,** 226 W. Center St., tel. (360) 736-8628, has live community theater.

Recreation

For a taste of the old days, head to the **Rollerdrome** at 216 W. Maple, tel. (360) 736-7376, to rent skates and circle the ancient wooden floors. Swim at **Centralia Community Pool,** 910 Johnson Ave., tel. (360) 736-0143, where you'll also find an exercise room, sauna, and jacuzzi.

Three golf courses serve the area: **Centralia Public Golf Course,** 1012 Duffy, tel. (360) 736-5967; **Newaukum Valley,** 3024 Jackson Hwy., in Chehalis, tel. (360) 748-0461, and **Riverside Golf Course,** 1451 N.W. Airport Rd. in Centralia, tel. (360) 748-8182.

Shopping

Downtown's **Centralia Square Antique Mall,** 201 S. Pearl St., tel. (360) 736-6406, is an antique collector's paradise, with more than 80 dealers displaying estate jewelry, furniture, and other collectibles; open daily till 5 p.m. Other large antique places include **Duffy's Antique Decorators Mall,** 310 N. Tower Ave., tel. (360) 736-7572, **Antique Market,** 120 S. Tower, tel. (360) 736-4079, and at least nine other shops.

Centralia's big **Factory Outlet,** just off I-5, has 50 stores. A pair of local businesses at the outlet mall are more interesting: **Northwest Factory Co-Op,** sells clothing, jewelry, art, foods, and other items handcrafted in the Northwest, and **The Original Mt. St. Helens Volcanic Ash Glass Factory** tel. (360) 736-3590, produces blown-glass products using ash from the 1980 eruption. Stop by to watch the glassblowers making Christmas tree ornaments and other colorful pieces.

Information and Services

Get local info from a small **visitor information center** next to the Avia factory outlet store off Lum Rd., tel. (360) 736-7132. Open daily 10 a.m.-5 p.m. in the summer, and daily 10 a.m.-4 p.m. winters.

Transportation

Amtrak, tel. (360) 736-8653 or (800) 872-7245, serves Centralia from Union Depot, located on Railroad Avenue. Call (800) 831-5334 for details on special two-for-one shopper fares.

Twin Transit, tel. (360) 330-2072, has daily bus service connecting Centralia and Chehalis. Long distance bus service is provided by **Greyhound,** tel. (360) 736-9811 or (800) 231-2222, with service along I-5 from the Texaco station at exit 81 (1232 Mellen St.).

Centralia-SeaTac Airport Express, tel. (800) 773-9490, and **Capital Aeroporter,** tel. (360) 754-7113 or (800) 962-3579, offer direct van service between Centralia and Sea-Tac Airport.

CHEHALIS

Chehalis (pop. 7,000) is an unpretentious place with a downtown of attractive brick buildings. It's a blue-collar place where folks make a living mining coal or processing food. The Darigold plant in Chehalis is the world's second largest producer of powdered milk. Chehalis is about four miles south of Centralia. Driving south from Seattle, you'll know you're near Chehalis when you see the Hamilton Farms billboard, proclaiming a bombastic right wing political message. You gotta wonder about these folks.

History

When Northern Pacific Railroad built a line north to Puget Sound from Kalama on the Columbia River in 1873, it built a warehouse on the bank of the Chehalis River, and gradually a settlement grew up around this warehouse. The warehouse was called Saundersville in honor of S.S. Saunders, on whose land the town was founded. Later the name was changed to Chehalis, a Native American word meaning "Shifting Sands." It became the Lewis County seat in 1872. Logging quickly became the major industry, and the area was settled by Scandinavians and British. As the valleys were cleared, dairy-farming became a major industry, along with fruit and vegetable packing and coal mining. It is this rich deposit of coal that made the Pacific Power and Light steam plant possible.

Sights

The **Lewis County Historical Museum,** 599 N.W. Front St., tel. (360) 748-0831, is in a former railroad depot, with freight trains rolling past at all hours. The museum has several fine Native baskets, a diorama of an Indian longhouse, and a big collection of pioneer goods, logging equipment, and farm tools. Also here are displays on the Armistice Day Riot of 1919 (but no artifacts). Out front is a surprisingly small WW I tank. Pick up walking tour brochures here describing historic sites in Chehalis. Open Tues.-Sat. 9 a.m.-5 p.m. and Sunday 1-5 p.m. Entrance is $2 adults, $1 kids, or $5 for the family.

The **McFadden Log Home,** 475 W. Chehalis Ave., built in 1859, is the oldest continuously lived-in home in the state, (a home in Port Gamble also claims the title). Another historic footnote is the **McKinley Stump,** located at Recreation Park on 13th Street. This was where President McKinley gave what was literally a stump speech in 1903. (The stump originally stood next to the Chehalis Depot.)

DIANNE BOULERICE LYONS

Rainbow Falls State Park

The **Claquato Church** is all that remains from the town of Claquato. Built in 1857, it is the oldest Protestant church still at its original location in the Pacific Northwest, and is also noteworthy for its crown-of-thorns octagonal steeple. Get here by heading west on Hwy. 6 (exit 77 off I-5) for two miles, then right on Chilvers Rd., left on Stearns Rd., and another left onto Water Street.

For a bit of whimsy, head to **Winlock,** a little place off I-5 exit 63 southwest of Chehalis. In the 1960s the town was famous for its egg hatcheries that produced 2.5 million chicks a year. Commemorating this momentous piece of history is a big concrete egg, located three miles west of town. The **Egg Days** celebration each June includes a parade, street fair, pancake breakfast, horse show, and free egg salad sandwiches.

Parks
Chehalis has several small city parks, the most interesting being **Stan Hedwall Park,** located on Rice Rd. just west of I-5 (take exit 76). The park borders the Newaukum River and has camping spaces, a swimming area, hiking trails, ornamental gardens, and the usual picnic spaces and athletic fields.

Sixteen miles west from Chehalis on Hwy. 6, you come upon the 125-acre **Rainbow Falls State Park,** where the mist from a minor waterfall creates sunny day rainbows. Pitch a tent in the tall Douglas fir and hemlock trees, hike the seven miles of forest trails, and try your luck at fishing in the river. A fun stone-and-log supported suspension footbridge built by the CCC in the 1930s crosses the Chehalis River. Call (360) 291-3767 for more info on the park. Open April-Sept. and on weekends and holidays the rest of the year.

Steam Railroad
Take a ride on the **Centralia/Chehalis Steam Railroad** from Chehalis out and back to a railroad junction called "Ruth" in the Boistfort Valley. The train—pulled by a 1917 Boldwin locomotive—operates on Saturday in the summer. Fares are $11 adults, $9 ages 4-16, and free for kids under three. Shorter trips to Milburn are available on weekends, and a special dinner train runs several times a summer; call (360) 748-9593 for details.

Accommodations
Relax Inn, 550 S.W. Parkland Dr., Chehalis, tel. (360) 748-8608 or (800) 843-6916, charges $40 s or $49 d, including a continental breakfast. **Howard Johnson Inn,** 122 Interstate Ave. (exit 76), tel. (360) 748-0101 or (800) 547-0106, has rooms for $59 s or d, including an outdoor pool, jacuzzi, and continental breakfast. See the "Centralia Accommodations" above for other local motels.

Campgrounds
Campsites are available at **Stan Hedwall Park** on Rice Rd. just off I-5 at exit 76, tel. (360) 748-0271 for reservations. More camping at **Rainbow Falls State Park,** 16 miles to the west on Hwy. 6, tel. (360) 291-3767. The campground ($10; no RV hookups) is open April-Sept. and has showers. Park RVs at **I-5 KOA,** 118 Hwy. 12, tel. (360) 262-9220 or (800) 562-9120.

Food and Shopping

Mary McCrank's Restaurant, four miles south of Chehalis at 2923 Jackson Hwy., tel. (360) 748-3662, is one of the oldest dinner houses in the state, in business since 1935. The food is dependably good, featuring such favorites as iron skillet chicken, meat loaf with gravy, and pork chops.

Sweet Inspirations, 514 N. Market Blvd., tel. (360) 748-7102, the best place for lunch in Chehalis, offers burgers, sandwiches, vegetarian specials, espresso, and desserts. **Spiffy's Restaurant,** 110 N. Hwy. 12, tel. (360) 262-3561, has an all-American menu, but is best known for their huge slices of pie, including peanut butter pie. Get tasty barbecue ribs at **The Old Brickyard,** 1587 N. National Ave., tel. (360) 740-1032.

Matrix Coffeehouse, 434 N.W. Prindle, tel. (360) 740-0492, has espresso, plus folk music some evenings. **Red Dawg Brewpub,** 492 N. Market Blvd., tel. (360) 740-8072, is one of the state's smallest microbreweries. They also serve sandwiches, soups, pizzas, and have music some weekends.

Get authentic Mexican food at **Plaza Jalisco,** 1340 N.W. Maryland, tel. (360) 748-4298, and fresh sushi and teriyaki at **Paradise Teriyaki,** 337 N.W. Chehalis Ave., tel. (360) 748-7513.

Recreation and Events

Swim at the summer-only outdoor pool in **Recreation Park** on the east side of Chehalis at 13th St. and William Avenue. Call (360) 748-0271 for details. Also here are picnic tables, a community kitchen, and shady grounds. **Dobson** and **McFadden** parks provide almost 50 acres of undeveloped hillside country with hiking trails and fine views of Mt. Rainier.

The popular **Chehalis Music & Art Festival** takes place in late July.

Information and Shopping

For local info, head to the **Centralia & Chehalis Chamber of Commerce Visitor Center,** 500 N.W. Chamber of Commerce Way (just west of exit 79 from I-5), tel. (360) 748-8885 or (800) 525-3323. Open Mon.-Fri. 8 a.m.-5 p.m. year-round.

Most of the shopping attractions are in Centralia, but Chehalis has its share, including the **Lewis County Mall** halfway between the two at 151 N.E. Hampe Way.

Transportation

Twin Transit, tel. (360) 330-2072, has daily bus service connecting Centralia and Chehalis. **Capital Aeroporter,** tel. (360) 754-7113 or (800) 962-3579, goes farther, with van service between Chehalis and Sea-Tac Airport.

OLYMPIC PENINSULA

Washington's Olympic Peninsula juts up like a thumb hitchhiking a ride from Canada. The 6,500-square-mile peninsula covers an extraordinary diversity of terrain, from remote rocky beaches to glacier-faced mountains. It is one of the most beautiful parts of Washington and seems to capture the spirit of the Evergreen State. At the core of the peninsula is Olympic National Park, one of the nation's crown jewels, recognized as a Man and the Biosphere Reserve by UNESCO. Much of the Olympic Peninsula is in private and tribal hands, where the emphasis is on logging rather than preservation. Virtually all land outside the park and Olympic National Forest has been cut at one time or another, and much of it is managed as tree farms with perpetual rotations of trees in varying stages of growth. Get ready for some of the most massive clearcuts you've ever seen.

Highway 101 follows three sides of the peninsula and joins Highways 8 and 12 to provide a fine circular route that accesses all the sights. Excellent public transit service means that you can also catch buses to many points along the way, and complete the entire loop for just a few bucks.

Rain Forests

Precipitation varies greatly on the peninsula: from Sequim, where only 17 inches fall in a typical year, to the eastern slopes of the Olympic Mountains, where more than 160 inches (that's over 13 feet!) of rain drop to earth. They don't call this the rain forest for nothing. These temperate rain forests are the best-known vegetation on the peninsula. Not much remains of the original old-growth stands, but parts of the Queets, Hoh, and Quinault river drainages still have examples of these forests. The distinguishing features are (in addition to the rain): the presence of Sitka spruce, abundant mosses, clubmosses, and lichens, nurse logs (fallen trees where seedlings grow), colonnades of trees that got their start on nurse logs, trees growing on stilts (they began as seedlings on stumps that later decayed away), and the presence of big leaf or vine maples. Other common trees are Douglas fir, western red cedar, and western hemlock. You aren't likely to remember all these features, but you'll know when you are in an old-growth rain forest. The lush profusion of moss-carpeted trees and dense understory of salal, rhododendron, huckleberry, and other plants give it an unforgettably verdant feeling.

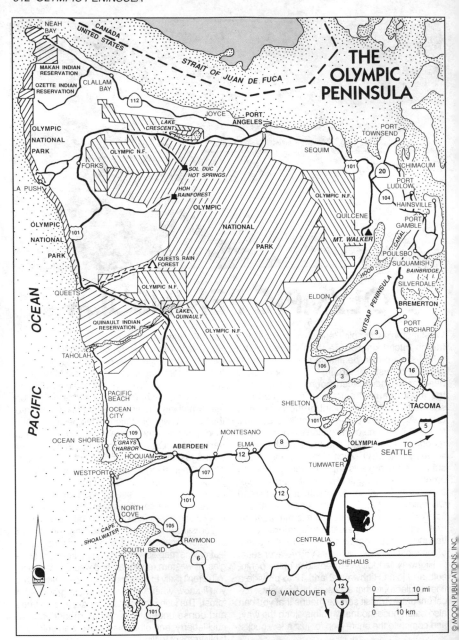

THE
OLYMPIC
PENINSULA

© MOON PUBLICATIONS, INC.

KITSAP PENINSULA

The Kitsap Peninsula is an appendage to the Olympic Peninsula; in fact, visitors and locals alike sometimes confuse the two, thinking that anything west of Seattle must be the Olympic Peninsula. Not true: The Kitsap is separated from the Olympic Peninsula by Hood Canal. This separation has helped prevent the peninsula from being developed as rapidly as the Seattle side of Puget Sound. For those living on the eastern side, the peninsula retains an air of remoteness, similar to that of Whidbey Island, a short ferry ride across Admiralty Inlet from Port Townsend. There are Christmas tree farms, second-growth stands of timber, and boat-filled marinas, but things are changing fast. Rapid growth in some parts of the Kitsap has brought the predictable housing subdivisions, chain restaurants, megamart shopping centers, and traffic congestion that people moving here are fleeing. The Kitsap has a number of places that are particularly notable, including the towns of Port Gamble, Port Orchard, and Poulsbo, the marvelous Naval Undersea Museum in Keyport, and the naval ships in Bremerton.

The Kitsap is readily accessible by ferry from Seattle and Edmonds, and its many back roads are favorite cycling destinations. Bainbridge Island is especially popular because of the easy access, diverse country, lack of traffic, and abundance of fine cafes and B&Bs. For a helpful map of recommended bike routes—plus all sorts of other local info—contact the **Kitsap Peninsula Visitor & Convention Bureau** in Port Gamble, tel. (360) 297-8200 or (800) 416-5616. Find them on the Web at www.visitkitsap.com.

BREMERTON

The blue collar city of Bremerton (pop. 38,000)—the largest settlement on Kitsap Peninsula—offers sweeping views of both the Cascades and the Olympics, and has a waterfront crowded with mothballed Navy ships. The city has long suffered in the glare of attention paid to its across-the-sound neighbor, Seattle, and the comparison has not improved with time. The run-down city center resembles a dying Massachusetts milltown; one could easily imagine that Bremerton had been hit by an errant missile from one of the destroyers anchored offshore. Many of the businesses have fled to suburban strip malls or to the booming patches of real estate around Belfair and Silverdale. The city does, however, have several interesting historical sights, including famous battleships and a naval museum, as well as good restaurants and inexpensive housing.

With all the water around it and the deep harbor at its doorstep, Bremerton is an ideal location for the **Puget Sound Naval Shipyard,** the city's economic mainstay since 1891. Today the facility is where nuclear ships and subs are overhauled and deactivated. It is the second largest industrial employer in Washington (after Boe-

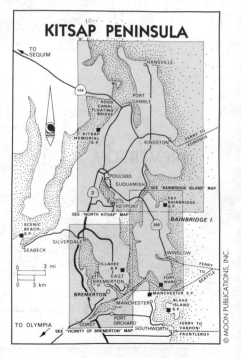

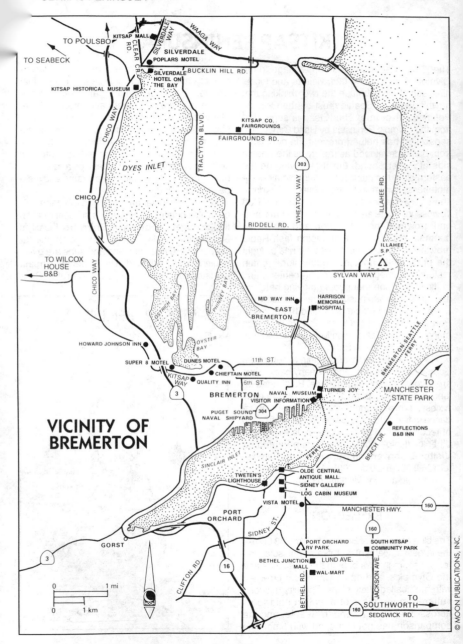

VICINITY OF BREMERTON

ing), with 9,200 civilian workers and over 10,000 military personnel. Other nearby military facilities include the Naval Hospital and Naval Supply Center in Bremerton, the Naval Undersea Warfare Center in Keyport, and the Naval Submarine Base in Bangor. Both the USS *Nimitz* and the USS *Midway* aircraft carriers are home-ported in Bremerton. Recent moves to downsize the Navy have hit Bremerton hard and will continue to affect the local economy in the future.

Sights

A number of mothballed Navy ships—including the USS *New Jersey* and the USS *Oriskany*—sit at anchor in varying states of disrepair. They aren't open to the public, but **Kitsap Harbor Tours,** tel. (360) 377-8924, offers 45-minute boat tours around the ships several times a day mid-May through September, and on weekends in October. The narrated tours are $8.50 adults, $7.50 seniors, and $5.50 ages 5-12. Get tickets on the boardwalk at Ship's Store.

The destroyer USS **Turner Joy** was one of the ships involved in the Gulf of Tonkin Incident in 1964 that led to the escalation of the Vietnam War. During the shelling of Chu Lai later that year, one of her guns jammed and an ensuing explosion killed three men. The destroyer was decommissioned in 1982 and opened to the public in 1988 for self-guided tours. If you haven't been aboard a Navy ship before, a tour of the USS *Turner Joy* will be an education, with its tight sleeping quarters and an impressive array of weaponry. The 418-foot ship is open daily 11 a.m.-4 p.m. mid-May through September, and Thurs.-Sun. 11 a.m.-4 p.m. the rest of the year. Admission is $6 adults, $5 seniors, and $4 ages 5-12. For information call (360) 792-2457. Tickets are sold in the **Ship's Store,** tel. (360) 792-1008, a fine nautical gift shop on the boardwalk. They also offer combination harbor-and-ship tours.

The excellent **Bremerton Naval Museum,** 130 Washington Ave., tel. (360) 479-7447, has American and Japanese naval artifacts, highly detailed models of the USS *Nimitz* and other Navy ships, plus naval memorabilia of all types. Open Tues.-Sat. 10 a.m.-5 p.m. and Sunday 1-5 p.m.; donation.

The **Kitsap County Historical Museum,** 280 4th St., tel. (360) 479-6226, shows historical items from the Bremerton area. Open Tues.-Sun. 10 a.m.-5 p.m.; donation.

Parks and Recreation

Illahee State Park, three miles northeast of Bremerton on Hwy. 306, has campsites on 75 acres, with swimming beaches, a short but steep hiking trail, a boat launch, and a pier for fishing and lolling in the sun.

Hikers will enjoy the two-mile trek to the summit of 1,700-foot **Green Mountain** for spectacular views of Kitsap Peninsula, Puget Sound, and the Seattle skyline. Take Seabeck Hwy.

DON PITCHER

Memorial, Bremerton

NW for two miles, turn left (west) on Holly Rd., then take a left onto Tahuyeh Rd. for 1.25 miles to Gold Creek Rd.; turn left onto Gold Creek and follow it for 1.5 miles to the trailhead on the left, before Gold Creek Bridge. Be sure to wear proper footwear since the trail is rocky and often wet.

Swim at **Wildcat Lake,** approximately five miles west of Bremerton, where a seasonal lifeguard is on duty. Also here are bathhouses, picnic areas, and a playground.

Accommodations

Bremerton's lodging options are arranged below from least to most expensive.

Chieftain Motel, 600 National Ave. N, tel. (360) 479-3111, charges $40 s or d including an outdoor pool. **Super 8 Motel,** 5068 Kitsap Way, tel. (360) 377-8881 or (800) 800-8000, has rooms for $47 s, $51-55 d. **Dunes Motel,** 3400 11th St., tel. (360) 377-0093 or (800) 828-8238, has rooms with a jacuzzi and continental breakfast for $50 s or d. **Flagship Inn,** 4320 Kitsap Way, tel. (360) 479-6566 or (800) 447-9396, charges $55 s or $60 d, including an outdoor pool and continental breakfast. **Oyster Bay Inn,** 4412 Kitsap Way, tel. (360) 377-5510, costs $55-60 s or d, including a continental breakfast.

Rooms at **Mid Way Inn,** 2909 Wheaton Way, tel. (360) 479-2909 or (800) 231-0575, are $62 s or d, including a continental breakfast. **Quality Inn at Oyster Bay,** 4303 Kitsap Way, tel. (360) 405-1111 or (800) 776-2291, charges $69-100 s or $74-150 d, including an outdoor pool, jacuzzi, exercise room, and continental breakfast.

Highland B&B, 622 Highland Ave., tel. (360) 479-2295, has two upstairs bedrooms in an elegant 1901 home for $55-65 d, or stay in a charming cottage for $95 d. A full breakfast is served.

Howard Johnson Inn, 5640 Kitsap Way, tel. (360) 373-9900 or (800) 422-5017, is one of the nicer places in Bremerton, with rooms for $95-109 s or d, including an indoor pool and hot tub.

Situated on a six-acre wooded site along Puget Sound, **Illahee Manor B&B,** 6680 Illahee Rd. NE, tel. (360) 698-7555 or (800) 693-6680, has six suites with private baths, most with fireplaces and jacuzzi baths. The eclectically furnished and comfortable house was built in 1929. A full breakfast is served, and families can stay in the beach house; $95-275 d.

Campground

Illahee State Park—three miles northeast of Bremerton—has camping ($10, no RV hookups) and showers year-round. Call (360) 478-6460 for information. Showers are also available at the Bremerton marina.

Food

Christophe's Waterfront Cafe, 112 Washington Ave., tel. (360) 792-1603, is a popular lunch spot with delicious homemade soups, salads, sandwiches, and espresso. Get nachos, fresh seafood, steaks, pasta, sandwiches, or salads over the water at the **Boat Shed,** at 101 Shore Dr., tel. (360) 377-2600. Find distinctive Sichuan cuisine at **Panda Inn on the Bay,** 4180 Kitsap Way, tel. (360) 377-7785, where the windows face scenic Oyster Bay.

Events

The third weekend of May brings an **Armed Forces Festival & Parade,** the largest celebration of its type in the nation. Call (360) 479-3579 for details. In late August the **Kitsap County Fair and Rodeo,** tel. (360) 692-3655, comes to the Kitsap County Fairgrounds five miles north of Bremerton. Highlighted by a PRCA rodeo, the fair also includes a carnival, circus, and other entertainment. Join the late August end-of-summer party at the **Blackberry Festival** on the boardwalk with arts and crafts, food, music, a classic car show, and fun run.

The Arts

The **Bremerton Symphony Orchestra,** tel. (360) 373-1722, performs concerts throughout the winter season. **Bremerton Community Theatre,** 599 Lebo Blvd., tel. (360) 373-5152, has comedy, drama, and musical theatrical events. Free **Concerts on the Boardwalk** take place on Friday evenings mid-July to mid-August.

Two notable fine art galleries are **Collective Visions,** 331 Pacific Ave., tel. (360) 377-8327, and **Amy Burnett Gallery,** 412 Pacific Ave., tel. (360) 373-3187. The latter is said to be the largest art gallery in the Northwest.

Information

The folks at the **Bremerton Area Chamber of Commerce,** 301 Pacific Ave., tel. (360) 479-3579, can answer most of your questions. Open

Mon.-Fri. 9 a.m.-5 p.m. year-round. Find them on the Web at www.bremertonchamber.org. They also have an information booth next to the ferry terminal.

Ferries and Tours

From the Seattle waterfront you can take a 60-minute trip to Bremerton on the **Washington State Ferries.** Ferries depart about every 70 minutes for Bremerton. Summertime fares are $8 one-way for car and driver, $3.60 roundtrip for passengers, and 60 cents extra for bikes. A passenger-only ferry (same rates) sails from Seattle five times a day and makes the run in 50 minutes. Call (360) 842-2345 or (888) 808-7977 for details; or (800) 843-3779 for automated information. You'll probably end up paying $3 if you want to park anywhere near downtown because so many folks from the Kitsap park here and ride the ferry to Seattle.

Horluck Transportation Co. Inc., tel. (360) 876-2300, is the oldest operating ferry in the state, providing service across the Sinclair Inlet between Bremerton and Port Orchard for foot traffic and bikes only. The 10-minute crossing costs $1.10 one-way; available daily 6 a.m.-midnight.

Kitsap Harbor Tours, tel. (360) 377-8924, offers tours of the mothball fleet along with tours to Blake Island on summer weekends.

Other Transportation

Kitsap Transit, tel. (360) 373-2877 or (800) 501-7433, has daily bus service throughout the peninsula and meets all state ferries. All buses have bike racks. **Bremerton-Kitsap Airporter,** tel. (360) 876-1737 or (800) 562-7948, offers shuttle buses to Sea-Tac Airport.

PORT ORCHARD

Across the Sinclair Inlet from Bremerton, Port Orchard—the Kitsap County seat—shows a split personality. The prosperous waterfront section faces the marina with covered walkways, colorful murals, antique shops, and cozy cafes. This contrasts sharply with the standard Kmart-and-fast-food section sprawling outward on the south end. Port Orchard still keeps a small fishing fleet, and boat sheds fill the harbor, but it is

primarily a bedroom community for Seattle and Tacoma, and for Bremerton military workers.

Port Orchard was named for H.M. Orchard, the clerk on Captain Vancouver's 1792 expedition who first discovered this bay. The town was founded in 1886 and became the county seat seven years later. Today it is home to 6,600 people.

Sights

From downtown, head two blocks uphill on Sidney Ave. to the **Sidney Art Gallery,** tel. (360) 876-3693. The lower floor contains a gallery with imaginative paintings and ceramic pieces; upstairs is a small but well-presented collection of historical displays representing various turn-of-the-century shops and industries. (Sidney was the original name for Port Orchard.) Housed in a 1913 pioneer log home, the quaint **Log Cabin Museum**—two blocks farther at 416 Sidney—has exhibits of local history. Open Saturday 11 a.m.-4 p.m. and Sunday 1-5 p.m.; free.

Parks and Recreation

Follow Beach Dr. from Port Orchard for a scenic approach to **Manchester State Park,** tel. (360) 871-4065, six miles away at the entrance to Sinclair Inlet. The park's 111 acres include campsites, hiking and interpretive trails, plus swimming, fishing, and scuba diving in Rich Passage. The main attractions here are various turn-of-the-century military structures, built to protect the Bremerton Naval Shipyard from attack. These include a brick warehouse once used to store underwater mines (now it's an oversized picnic shelter), and a control center where the mines could be set off remotely if enemy warships intruded. Fortunately, the mines were never deployed, and the fort was abandoned and turned into a state park. The park is open from late April to early September.

The 200-acre **South Kitsap Community Park** at the intersection of Jackson and Lund Rds., two miles southwest of downtown, has hiking trails and a picnic area, plus kiddie steam trains (free) daily 11 a.m.-4 p.m. from June to mid-September. Swim or boat at **Long Lake,** approximately four miles south of Port Orchard. For indoor swimming, head to the high school on Mitchell St., tel. (360) 876-7385. Two 18-hole golf courses in the vicinity are **Horseshoe Lake**

Golf Course, 15932 Sidney Rd. SW, tel. (360) 857-3326, and **McCormick Woods Golf Course,** 5155 McCormick Woods Dr. SW, tel. (360) 895-0130. The latter is considered one of the finest in the Northwest.

Accommodations

Port Orchard's newest motel is **Holiday Inn Express,** 1121 Bay St., tel. (360) 895-2666 or (800) 465-4329, with rooms for $73 s or $79 d. **Vista Motel,** 1090 Bethel Ave., tel. (360) 876-8046, charges $42 s, and $46 d; kitchenettes are $60 d.

Northwest Interlude B&B, 3377 Sarann Ave. E, tel. (360) 871-4676, has three guest rooms for $55-75 d, including a gourmet breakfast. Great views across Sinclair Inlet from the decks.

Reflections B&B, 3878 Reflection Ln. E, tel. (360) 871-5582, is a large two-story home with four guest rooms, a hot tub, gazebo, and full breakfast. Rooms offer views of Port Orchard Passage; $60-95 s or d. No kids.

Laurel Inn B&B eight miles east of Port Orchard near Manchester State Park, tel. (888) 888-9661, is a contemporary home filled with family heirlooms, three guest rooms, and a full breakfast; $53-83 s or $58-88 d. No kids.

Campgrounds

Pitch a tent at **Manchester State Park** (described above) for $10; no RV hookups. Open late April to early September. Call (800) 452-5687 for reservations ($6 extra). Park RVs in the trees at the city-owned **Orchard RV Park** southwest of town on Bethel Rd. at Lund Ave., a quarter mile south of the Safeway. Amazingly, they don't allow tents, even though it is a wooded area with no electrical hookups or facilities. Local cops take pleasure in rousting campers in the middle of the night.

Food

A very good breakfast, lunch, and espresso place is **Pot Belly Deli and Baking Co.,** 724 Bay St., tel. (360) 895-1396. Great breads too. They also have acoustic music on Sunday afternoons. For outside dining with a semi-scenic view of the Bremerton shipyards, try **Tweten's Lighthouse Restaurant,** on the water at Bay St. and Port Orchard Blvd., tel. (360) 876-8464. Enormous cinnamon rolls show up at breakfast, and the Monday night seafood buffet and Sunday brunch are especially popular.

Myhre's Terrace Room, 739 Bay St., tel. (360) 876-9916, offers marina views while you taste the reasonably priced steaks, prime rib, and fresh seafood. For ethnic eats, head to **Green Valley Chinese Restaurant,** 691 Bethel Rd., tel. (360) 895-4109, which has a lunch buffet; and the popular **Puerto Vallarta,** tel. (360) 876-0788, near the intersection of Bethel Rd. and Lund Avenue.

Bay Street Ale House, 807 Bay St., tel. (360) 876-8030, has 16 beers on tap, distinctive pizzas, and other pub meals, all in a smoke-free environment.

The **Port Orchard Farmers Market** takes place behind Peninsula Feed Store on Bay St. on Saturday 9 a.m.-3 p.m., May-Oct.; tel. (253) 876-8632. This is one of the largest markets in the state and features more than 100 vendors offering homegrown fruits and veggies, homemade crafts, and ethnic foods. A winter market takes place at the community center.

Shopping

Port Orchard's many antique, craft, and gift shops generally cater to an audience that appreciates lots of lace, schlocky junk, and sickly sweet smells. Cute is the operative term, although revolting also comes to mind. Try the **Victorian Rose Tea Room,** 1130 Bethel Ave., tel. (360) 876-5695, to see for yourself. It's a favorite of the doll-and-teddy-bear crowd. Two big antique malls are filled with pieces of the past: **Olde Central Antique Mall,** 801 Bay St., tel. (360) 895-1902; and **Side Door Mall,** 701 Bay St., tel. (360) 876-8631. **Jomar Books,** 713 Bay St., sells used and out of print titles. The real gem for shoppers in Port Orchard is the Sidney Gallery, described in "Sights," above.

Events and the Arts

Port Orchard's most peculiar event is the **Seagull Calling Contest,** held on the Saturday before Easter. Contestants in goofy costumes attempt to see who can call in the most gulls. The **Fathoms O' Fun Carnival**—Port Orchard's premier summer festival and one of the state's oldest—is held from the last Saturday in June through the Fourth of July. Highlights include a big parade, carnival, a fun run, fireworks, and various contests. Then comes the **Chris Craft Rendezvous** that attracts more than a hundred vintage boats in mid-July. The **Peninsula Jazz Festival** is a two-day event at the end of July; call (360) 846-1979 for details. The **The Cruz** comes to Port Orchard on the first Sunday of August, and Bay St. is closed off to display more than 1,000 custom cars and hot rods, plus juried arts and crafts, food booths, live music, dancing, and games.

The **Bay Street Playhouse**, 820 Bay St., tel. (360) 876-6610, is home to the Performing Arts Guild of South Kitsap, a group that puts on plays, musicals, and kid's shows throughout the year.

Information and Services

Get information at **Port Orchard Chamber of Commerce**, 839 Bay St., tel. (360) 876-3505 or (800) 982-8139. Open Mon.-Fri. 10 a.m.-5 p.m., and Sat. 10 a.m.-2 p.m. year-round. Be sure to stop here to check out the beautifully crafted seven-foot-long wooden model of the *Virginia V*.

Ferry Service

Catch the **Washington State Ferry** from the Fauntleroy dock in West Seattle for the 35-minute ride to Southworth on the southeast side of the Kitsap Peninsula near Port Orchard. Summertime fares are $8 one-way for car and driver, $3.60 roundtrip for passengers and walk-ons, and 60 cents extra for bikes. You can also catch a ferry from Southworth to Vashon Island every hour and a half for $2.40 roundtrip for passengers, $11 roundtrip for vehicle and driver, and 60 cents extra for bikes. Call (360) 842-2345 or (888) 808-7977 for details or (800) 843-3779 for automated information.

Horluck Transportation Co. Inc., tel. (360) 876-2300, has the oldest operating ferry in the state, providing ferry service across the Sinclair Inlet between Bremerton and Port Orchard for foot traffic and bikes only. The company has five small vessels, including the *Carlisle II*, the last of the working "Mosquito Fleet" that once plied the waters of Puget Sound. The 10-minute crossing costs $1.10 one-way and is available daily 6 a.m.-midnight. (It's a seven mile drive around the head of Sinclair Inlet to Bremerton if you drive there instead.)

Other Transportation

Kitsap Transit, tel. (360) 377-2877 or (800) 501-7433, provides daily bus service throughout the Kitsap Peninsula and Bainbridge Island, and meets all Southworth ferries. **Bremerton-Kitsap Airporter,** tel. (360) 876-1737 or (800) 562-7948, offers shuttle buses to Sea-Tac Airport.

BLAKE ISLAND

Accessible only by boat, Blake Island has 476 acres of state park land with year-round camping ($10); sandy beaches for swimming, sunbathing, and clamming; fishing and scuba diving; a three-quarter-mile loop nature trail; and 12 miles of other hiking trails. The main attraction is Tillicum Village, where Indian dances, a salmon bake, and crafts are offered daily. To reach the island from the Kitsap, rent a boat from Manchester Boatworks in Port Orchard, or check with local chambers of commerce for charter operators.

Tillicum Village

This native-style village can be visited as part of a full-day trip offered by Argosy Cruises that includes a salmon bake in the cedar longhouse, traditional dances, nature trails, Indian artifacts, and a gift shop. See the Seattle chapter for details on Tillicum Village trips departing from Piers 55 and 56. **Kitsap Harbor Tours,** tel. (360) 377-8924, offers tours to Blake Island from Bremerton on Friday and Saturday evenings May-October.

SILVERDALE

The unincorporated town of Silverdale has a beautiful setting with some of the best views across Dyes Inlet, but much of what you see today is far less attractive. The Navy's Trident Nuclear Submarine Base has brought prosperity, turning Silverdale into the prime shopping area for the whole peninsula. A busy four-lane road leads through the new parts of town, bordered by a jumble of new homes and condos, shopping plazas, restaurants, and the massive Kitsap Mall—largest on the Olympic Peninsula. **Waterfront Park,** has a pier jutting into Dyes Inlet.

Accommodations

Cimarron Motel, 9734 N.W. Silverdale Way, tel. (360) 692-7777, charges $48 s or d, including kitchenettes. The **Poplars Motel,** 9800 Silverdale Way, tel. (360) 692-6126 or (800) 824-7517, has quality rooms for $58 s or $63-66 d, with an outdoor pool and jacuzzi. A step up in price, **Silverdale Hotel on the Bay,** 3073 N.W. Bucklin Hill Rd., tel. (360) 698-1000 or (800) 544-9799, is a resort with two- and three-bedroom units for $75-95 s or $85-105 d. Amenities include an indoor pool, sauna, jacuzzi, exercise room, private balconies, putting green, and tennis courts.

Heaven's Edge B&B, 7410 NW Ioka Dr., tel. (360) 613-1111 or (800) 413-5680, has a suite with a patio facing Hood Canal, private entrance, and full breakfast. Two-night minimum on summer weekends and no kids; $115-130 d.

Food

Waterfront Old Town Bakery & Cafe, next to the park on N.W. Byron, tel. (360) 698-2991, makes fresh baked goods and espresso, plus deli lunches. Two ethnic restaurants offer authentic Asian food: **Hakata,** 10876 Myhre Pl., tel. (360) 698-0929, has the best sushi on the Kitsap; while **Bahn Thai,** 98811 Mickelberry Rd., tel. (360) 698-3663, has spicy Thai meals.

For substantial and delicious seafood and pasta, served on the outdoor deck in good weather, head to **Yacht Club Broiler,** 9226 Bayshore Dr., tel. (360) 698-1601. The big **Silver City Brewing Co.,** next to Kitsap Mall at 2799 N.W. Myhre Rd., tel. (360) 698-5879, offers fresh-brewed ales and lagers on tap in a lively atmosphere, plus a big menu of gumbo, halibut and chips, burgers, pizzas, and weekend prime rib.

Shopping and Events

Kitsap Mall, just south of the junction of Highways 305 and 3, has over 115 stores, including Sears, Lamonts, Barnes & Noble Books, and The Bon Marché. **Silver Bay Herb Farm,** south of Silverdale at 9151 Tracyton Blvd., tel. (360) 692-1340, is a tranquil place with herb gardens, classes, plants, seeds, and a gift shop.

Silverdale's **Whaling Days Festival,** held the last weekend of July, is the town's biggest event, with a parade, live music, arts-and-crafts displays, hydroplane races, a carnival, and fireworks.

Information and Transportation

For local information, contact the **Silverdale Chamber of Commerce,** 3100 Bucklin Hill Rd., tel. (360) 692-6800; www.silverdalechamber .com.

Kitsap Transit, tel. (360) 377-2877 or (800) 501-7433, provides daily bus service throughout Kitsap Peninsula and Bainbridge Island, and meets all Southworth ferries. **Bremerton-Kitsap Airporter,** tel. (360) 876-1737 or (800) 562-7948, offers shuttle buses to Sea-Tac Airport.

SEABECK

The small town of Seabeck occupies a point of land west of Silverdale on the east shore of Hood Canal, with dramatic panoramic views of the Olympic Mountains. It has a marina and a few restaurants and grocers, and is a favorite of anglers. The oldest outdoor theater in the Northwest, **Mountaineers' Forest Theater** holds productions near Seabeck late May through June. The amphitheater's terraced log seats are beautifully backdropped by rhododendrons, Douglas firs, and hemlocks; be prepared for a one-third-mile hike from your car to the theater. For tickets and information call (206) 284-6310.

Scenic Beach State Park

Scenic Beach State Park has forested campsites ($11; no RV hookups), salmon fishing, oyster gathering in season, and Olympic Mountain views on Hood Canal. The 88-acre park is particularly pleasant when the spring rhododendrons are in bloom. The park is open for day-use year-round, but the campground is only open from late April to late September. Call (360) 830-5079 for more info, or (800) 452-5687 for reservations ($6 extra).

Accommodations

Once the private residence of Colonel Julian Willcox and built in 1936, the 10,000-square-foot waterfront **Willcox House,** on the Hood Canal south of Seabeck, tel. (360) 830-4492 or (800) 725-9477, was described as "the grand entertainment capitol of the Canal region." Every room is angled to capture a water view, and the house is filled with marble and copper fireplaces, with luxurious period furnishings. Outdoors, a 300-foot pier can accommodate guests' boats. Clark Gable once stayed in the room that now bears his name. Five rooms are available with private baths, a pool, and gourmet breakfast. A two-night minimum is required. No kids; $149-189 d.

Located on 10 acres of woods, meadows, and ponds, **La Cachette B&B,** 10312 Seabeck Hwy., tel. (360) 613-2845 or (888) 613-2845, overlooks Hood Canal. The four luxury suites feature private baths, king-size beds, fireplaces, and antiques. A gourmet breakfast is served; $120-190 s or d. No children.

KEYPORT

Keyport is home to the top-secret **Naval Undersea Warfare Center,** a place that sounds like something out of a James Bond film. This is where much of America's torpedo research is conducted, gaining it the moniker "Torpedo Town." Just west of Keyport in Bangor is the **Naval Submarine Base,** where the fleet of eight Trident nuclear submarines is headquartered, and where some 1,600 nuclear warheads are stored—more than in France, China, and Great Britain combined! The base is also home to 5,000 military personnel.

Naval Undersea Museum
For visitors, this marvelous museum offers a less-secretive look at the world of undersea warfare. One of the most unique museums in Washington, it houses fascinating exhibits on the history of undersea warfare and exploration, from scale models of Navy subs, to underwater archaeology, to mines. A large globe details the mountainous floor beneath the oceans. Some of the most interesting items are the torpedoes—including such oddities as a 19th century wind-up torpedo and a WW II Japanese version with space for a kamikaze human driver—plus a half-scale model of an undersea rescue vehicle that appeared in the movie *Hunt for Red October.* The museum is open daily 10 a.m.-4 p.m. June-Sept., and Wed.-Mon. 10 a.m.-4 p.m. the rest of the year; tel. (360) 396-4148. Free. Out front is

the blimp-like Trieste II, which reached the bottom of the Marianas Trench—the deepest point on earth—in 1960. The bulk of this cumbersome, 88-ton sub was filled with aviation fuel; the two men were suspended below it in a tiny chamber.

Practicalities
Continental Inn, on Hwy. 308 in Keyport, tel. (360) 779-5575 or (800) 537-5766, has rooms, kitchenettes, and suites for $44-79 s or d.

Island Lake, halfway between Keyport and Silverdale, has a swimming beach and bathhouse. **Lange's Ranch** tel. (360) 779-4927, just south of Keyport, has a big outdoor pool and other recreational facilities.

Kitsap Transit, tel. (360) 377-2877 or (800) 501-7433, provides daily bus service throughout the peninsula.

POULSBO

The quaint town of Poulsbo (pop. 6,000) occupies the head of Liberty Bay, and could pass for a tourist village on the coast of Maine. The main street is crowded with antique shops—11 at last count—along with cafes, galleries, high quality craft boutiques, a chocolate shop, and a wonderful quilt shop. Sailboats bob in the busy marina just a few feet away, and old-fashioned lamps brighten the evening sky. Locals jokingly call the town "Viking Junction," and it doesn't take much to see that Poulsbo loves to play up its Norwegian heritage.

History
Credit for the establishment of Poulsbo goes to Jorgen Eliason, a Norwegian who rowed across the sound from Seattle in 1883 and was reminded of the mountains, fjords, and valleys of his homeland. His relatives quickly followed, scratching out a farm at the head of Dogfish Bay. Other Norwegians arrived, and for many years more than half the residents were from Norway; anyone speaking English was likely an outsider. In 1886, Ivar Moe named the town Paulsbo—Norwegian for Paul's Place—but the postmaster general couldn't read his handwriting and listed it instead as Poulsbo. Over the years, Poulsbo survived on logging, farming, and fishing. A fleet of Bering Sea schooners sailed north

DON PITCHER

a Poulsbo street

to Alaska each summer and back home in the fall with cargo holds filled with salted cod. The town's insularity was broken by the arrival of WW II as military personnel moved in to protect the vital naval base at Bremerton. (A long anti-submarine net was stretched across Port Orchard Bay.)

In the early 1960s, Poulsbo was a complacent community in need of an attraction, so they went to the University of Washington for ideas. A survey showed strong support for a "Little Norway" theme, and the concept quickly took hold, just in time for the 1962 World's Fair in Seattle. Scandinavian architecture and festivals perpetuate the culture of "Little Norway's" first immigrants; many of the downtown buildings have Scandinavian decor and sell some Scandinavian products. And yes, there is a **Sons of Norway Hall** on Front St. in Poulsbo. Unfortunately, Poulsbo is developing something of a schizophrenic personality, with a quaint old downtown, and a strip of RV dealers, real estate offices, and fast food places up the hill.

Sights

You can get friendly with sea cucumbers, starfish, sea anemones, and barnacles in the saltwater touch-tank, watch a jellyfish flotilla, examine a gray whale skeleton, and learn about other Puget Sound sea creatures and problems facing the ocean at the fascinating **Marine Science Center,** right next to the marina, tel. (360) 779-5549. Open daily 11 a.m.-5 p.m. all year. Admission is $4 adults, $3 seniors and youths, $2 kids under 12.

Stroll down the 600-foot shoreside boardwalk that connects **Liberty Bay Park** to the small arboretum at **American Legion Park.** Both parks have picnic areas, restrooms, and water access. Head uphill to the corner of 4th Ave. and Lincoln Rd. for the **Fordefjord Lutheran Church,** built in 1908.

Sea Kayaking

Poulsbo's **Olympic Outdoor Center,** 18791 Front St., tel. (360) 697-6095, is a great place to learn sea kayaking and whitewater kayaking. Classes include the basics, special ones for kids, kayak rescue courses and roll clinics, and comprehensive four-day sea kayak courses. The center also leads sea kayak trips and sells and rents kayaks if you want to head out on your own.

Accommodations

Be sure to make reservations well ahead for summer weekends; some rooms are booked up a year in advance.

Poulsbo Inn, 18680 Hwy. 305, tel. (360) 779-3921 or (800) 597-5151, charges $55-70 s or d; on-site are an outdoor pool, jacuzzi, and playground. **Holiday Inn Express,** 19801 N.E. 7th, tel. (360) 697-4400 or (800) 465-4329, has rooms for $69-99 s or d, including an outdoor pool and continental breakfast.

Murphy House B&B, 425 N.E. Hostmark, tel. (360) 779-1600 or (800) 779-1606, offers in-town lodging, with five very comfortable guest rooms, private baths, and a full breakfast for $69-98 s or d. No kids.

The impressive and luxuriously furnished **Manor Farm Inn,** a B&B at 26069 Big Valley Rd. NE, tel. (360) 779-4628, sits on 25 acres of land. It is run as a "gentleman's farm" with a sprinkling of critters and has a hot tub (no cows allowed in the hot tub). The B&B pampers guests

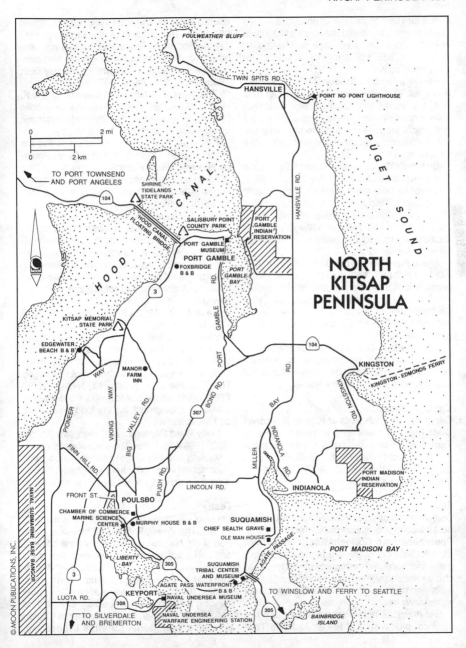

FOULWEATHER BLUFF

TWIN SPITS RD.

HANSVILLE

POINT NO POINT LIGHTHOUSE

PUGET SOUND

0   2 mi

0   2 km

TO PORT TOWNSEND
AND PORT ANGELES

104

HOOD CANAL FLOATING BRIDGE

HOOD   CANAL

SHRINE
TIDELANDS
STATE PARK

SALISBURY POINT
COUNTY PARK

PORT GAMBLE
MUSEUM

PORT GAMBLE

FOXBRIDGE
B & B

PORT
GAMBLE
BAY

PORT GAMBLE
INDIAN
RESERVATION

HANSVILLE RD.

MOON

3

KITSAP MEMORIAL
STATE PARK

EDGEWATER
BEACH B & B

MANOR
FARM
INN

PORT GAMBLE RD.

BOND RD.

307

104

KINGSTON

KINGSTON - EDMONDS FERRY

NORTH
KITSAP
PENINSULA

PIONEER WAY

VIKING WAY

FINN HILL RD.

BIG VALLEY RD.

PUGH RD.

MILLER BAY RD.

INDIANOLA RD.

KINGSTON RD.

LINCOLN RD.

INDIANOLA

PORT MADISON
INDIAN
RESERVATION

FRONT ST.

POULSBO

CHAMBER OF
COMMERCE

MARINE SCIENCE
CENTER

MURPHY HOUSE B & B

SUQUAMISH

CHIEF SEALTH GRAVE

OLE MAN HOUSE

LIBERTY BAY

305

AGATE PASSAGE

PORT MADISON BAY

NAVAL SUBMARINE BASE BANGOR

3

LUOTA RD.

KEYPORT

308

TO SILVERDALE
AND BREMERTON

SUQUAMISH TRIBAL CENTER
AND MUSEUM

AGATE PASS WATERFRONT
B & B

NAVAL UNDERSEA MUSEUM

NAVAL UNDERSEA
WARFARE ENGINEERING STATION

305

TO WINSLOW AND FERRY TO SEATTLE

BAINBRIDGE
ISLAND

© MOON PUBLICATIONS, INC.

with a leisurely three-course breakfast. Seven guest rooms with private baths are $120-170 d. No kids. Four- and six-course dinners are an option for $35 pp, and are available for nonguests as well. Farther away is **Foxbridge B&B,** 30680 Hwy. 3 NE, tel. (360) 598-5599, located a half mile from the Hood Canal floating bridge. This two-story home sits on five wooded acres with a panoramic view. Three guest rooms have private baths, and a full breakfast is served. $75 s or d; no kids.

Built in 1929, **Edgewater Beach B&B,** 26818 Edgewater Blvd., tel. (360) 779-2525 or (800) 641-0955, is three miles northwest of town along Hood Canal. It includes three guest rooms in a large home with a deck, plus gardens and a small pond for $95-145 s or $105-155 d. A full breakfast is included, and bald eagles nest nearby. Kids are welcome.

Agate Pass Waterfront B&B, tel. (360) 779-7727 or (800) 869-1632, is an impressive custom home (with lighthouse!) southeast of Poulsbo. The beautiful grounds front a beach along Port Orchard Narrows. Three guest rooms are available for $75-125 s or d, including a make-your-own breakfast.

Liberty Place Guest House, tel. (360) 779-4943, sits on Liberty Bay, two miles from Poulsbo, and is a one-bedroom home with a full kitchen and deck; $95 for the house.

Campgrounds

Campers can pitch tents at **Kitsap Memorial State Park,** six miles north of town on Hwy. 3. Tent sites on 58 acres are $10 (showers, but no RV hookups). Call (360) 779-3205 for info. **Cedar Glen RV Park,** tel. (360) 779-4305 is three miles south of Poulsbo.

Food

Despite its small size, Poulsbo has one of the best collections of eating places on the Kitsap. **Poulsbohemian Coffeehouse,** 19003 Front St., tel. (360) 779-9199, is a friendly and funky gathering place, with espresso, giant chocolate chip cookies, cozy couches and chairs, art on the walls, and ongoing arts events of all sorts. Great water views too.

Get delicious homemade soups and other lunches, plus a spot of tea at **Judith's Tea-**

rooms & Rose Cafe, on Front St., tel. (360) 697-3449. This is also the place to get pickled herring and other Scandinavian offerings. Another recommended lunchtime place with inexpensive sandwiches is **Poulsbo Country Deli,** 18937 Front St., tel. (360) 779-2763.

The New Day Seafood Eatery, 325 N.E. Hostmark St., tel. (360) 697-3183, overlooks Liberty Bay and serves tasty fish and chips made from fresh fish caught by their own boat.

Perhaps the best known Poulsbo food is Poulsbo Bread, originally baked at **Sluys Poulsbo Bakery,** 18924 Front St. NE, tel. (360) 779-2798. The Poulsbo bread sold in grocery stores is now made elsewhere, but Sluys still bakes excellent pastries, Norwegian lefse, and coarse-grained European breads.

That's a Some Italian Ristorante, 18881 Front St. NE, tel. (360) 779-2266, has the traditional red checked tablecloths, but the Italian food and pizzas have West Coast influences, including an Anaheim chili penne. Get huge thick-crust pizzas at **Poulsbo Pizzaria,** 19559 Viking Way, tel. (360) 779-9812.

Casa Luna, 18830 Front St. NE, tel. (360) 779-7676, is one of the more distinctive Mexican-inspired restaurants in the Puget Sound area. The menu isn't the same old mashed beans and colored rice. Everything is made to order in the open kitchen and packed with flavor. **Aroydy Thai Cuisine,** 225 Lindvig Way NW, tel. (360) 779-4888, is just north of town in the basement of a small shopping mall, but the food is authentic and exceptional.

Molly Ward Gardens 27462 Big Valley Rd., tel. (360) 779-4471, is Poulsbo's splurge place, emphasizing fine Northwest seafood, along with fresh salads and herbs from their beautiful gardens. The menu changes seasonally. Expensive.

Festivals

Poulsbo's summer season is packed with ethnic events. The **Viking Fest** in mid-May celebrates Poulsbo's Norwegian heritage with a parade, arts and crafts show, pancake breakfast, food booths, and fun run. The **Scandia Midsommarfest** in June brings Scandinavian food, music, and Norwegian folk dancers, and pole dancing for a solstice celebration. On the third Saturday of October, the First Lutheran Church puts on a **Traditional Lutefisk Dinner** with

Swedish meatballs for the wimps. The holiday season brings the **Yule Fest,** in late November or early December, featuring Norwegian folk dancers, lighting of the Yule log, and a guest appearance by Santa Claus by boat. A **Lighted Boat Parade** follows in mid-December.

Information and Services
For information, visit the **Greater Poulsbo Chamber of Commerce,** 19131 8th Ave. NE, tel. (360) 779-4848. Open Mon.-Fri. 9 a.m.-5 p.m.; www.kitsapedc.org. If you're downtown, drop by the small visitor center inside Poulsbohemian Coffeehouse, open daily. Pick up a walking tour of Poulsbo's historic buildings at either place.

The **North Kitsap Community Swimming Pool,** 1881 N.E. Hostmark St., tel. (360) 779-3790, has lap swimming and open swim hours.

Poulsbo is home for the **Northwest College of Art,** located in an old brick mansion south of town on Hwy. 305, tel. (360) 779-9993.

Two good downtown bookshops are **Liberty Bay Books,** tel. (360) 779-5909, for new volumes, and **Book Stop,** 18954-A Front St. NE, tel. (360) 779-9773, with a big choice of used books, including many offbeat titles.

Transportation and Tours
Kitsap Transit, tel. (360) 377-2877 or (800) 501-7433, provides daily bus service around the peninsula. **Bremerton-Kitsap Airporter,** tel. (360) 876-1737 or (800) 562-7948, offers shuttle buses to Sea-Tac Airport.

BAINBRIDGE ISLAND

Just a 35-minute ferry ride from downtown Seattle, Bainbridge Island offers a comfortable escape from the hordes, a place where yupster commuters retreat to rural waterside homes and retirees enjoy a peaceful escape from the workaday world. Over 18,000 folks call Bainbridge home today, and more move here every week.

History
When Vancouver sailed through Puget Sound in 1792, he didn't realize that Bainbridge Island was an island. Then in 1841 Charles N. Wilkes found Agate Pass, the waterway separating the island from the Kitsap Peninsula. Wilkes named the island for Capt. William Bainbridge, a Naval hero from the USS *Constitution.* Within 15 years of its charting, Bainbridge Island was home to one of Puget Sound's greatest lumber mills, and soon thereafter its ports were world renowned. Port Blakely had the biggest sawmill in the world, employing more than 1,000 men, and the shipyard there built the largest sternwheeler at that time in the Pacific Northwest, the *Julia.*

Today the four- by 12-mile island is almost entirely privately owned by politicians, doctors, artists, many stockbrokers, a few fishermen, and a lot of ordinary folks, 70% of whom commute by ferry to Seattle-area jobs. Although the entire island is officially incorporated, there is only one real town: **Winslow,** located along Eagle Harbor where the ferry docks. Winslow is a genuine—albeit gentrified—town with Volvos crawling the streets, yachts in the marina, and classical music in the cafes. Several other small settlements are scattered around Bainbridge, including Lynwood Center and Island Center.

If you're arriving by ferry from Seattle, you'll find Winslow an easy place to explore by foot. Start on the shoreline footpath that heads west from the ferry to **Eagle Harbor Waterfront Park,** a fine place for a sunny-day picnic. If you're arriving by car, parking can be a real problem on weekends, and no on-street overnight parking is allowed.

Bainbridge Island Historical Museum
The history of former mill towns Port Madison and Port Blakely (once home to the largest lumber mill in the world) is preserved in exhibits and displays at the Bainbridge Island Historical Museum in Strawberry Hill Park. The building itself offers a blast from the past; it's a charming little red schoolhouse. Open Saturday 11 a.m.-4 p.m. in the summer, closed winters; admission is free.

Fay-Bainbridge State Park
This park covers a mere 17 acres but has campsites in the trees ($11 tents; $16 RVs), hot showers, plus beach access with scuba diving and boating facilities at the island's northeast end. This is the closest public campground to Seattle —just a ferry ride and short drive or bus ride away—so it is very popular in the summer months. The views are fine too, with over-the-water vistas of the Cascades and the twinkling

BAINBRIDGE ISLAND

TO SUQUAMISH →

PUGET SOUND

CASINO
SUQUAMISH TRIBAL
CENTER AND MUSEUM ◆

TO
POULSBO
305

KITSAP
PENINSULA

MONROE POINT

BLOEDEL
RESERVE

W. PORT
MADISON

MADISON BAY

PORT
MADISON

FAY - BAINBRIDGE
STATE PARK

PHELPS RD.

OUR COUNTRY
HAUS B & B

MANZANITA
PARK

MANZANITA BAY

DAY RD. W.

MANZANITA

305

N. MADISON AVE.

SUNRISE RD.

BATTLE
POINT
STATE
PARK

WILLIAMS LN.

ARROW PT.
DR.

BATTLE PT. DR.

MILLER RD.

THE GRAND
FOREST

VALLEY RD.

SUMMER HILL
FARM B&B

FLETCHER BAY

ISLAND
CENTER

NEW BROOKLYN RD.

YAQUINA AVE.

BAINBRIDGE INN

STRAWBERRY
HILL PARK

SPRING RIDGE RD.

BAINBRIDGE ISLAND
HISTORICAL
MUSEUM

HIGH SCHOOL/
SWIMMING POOL

THE WOODSMAN B & B

HERB COTTAGE B&B

HIGH SCHOOL RD.

STUDIO D

MADISON AVE.

ISLAND COUNTRY INN

WINSLOW INN

WINSLOW

WYATT WAY

BAINBRIDGE
ISLAND WINERY

CAPTAIN'S
HOUSE B & B

WATERFRONT PARK

EAGLE HARBOR

THE BEACH
COTTAGE

EAGLE

SEATTLE FERRY

HARBOR DR.

MARY'S
FARMHOUSE

ROCKAWAY BEACH
GUEST HOUSE

CRYSTAL
SPRINGS DR.

BAKER HILL RD.

LYNWOOD
CENTER

OLD MILL

BLAKELY AVE.

CEDAR
MEADOW
B & B

THE
BOMBAY
HOUSE
B & B

RD.

PORT
BLAKELY

WATERFRONT B & B

BLAKELY HARBOR

PLEASANT
BEACH DR.

FT. WARD HILL RD.

RICH PASSAGE

FORT WARD
STATE PARK

0   1 mi

0   1 km

KITSAP PENINSULA

MANCHESTER STATE PARK

© MOON PUBLICATIONS, INC.

lights of Seattle. A delightful place to escape the city. The park is open for day-use year-round, and for camping from mid-April to mid-October. Call (206) 842-3931 for details.

Fort Ward State Park
Located six miles from the Winslow ferry terminal at the island's south end, Fort Ward State Park has 137 acres for day-use picnicking, bird-watching, boating, and scuba diving on a mile-long beach. No camping, but a one-mile path loops through the park. Like many of the state parks surrounding Puget Sound, this one began as a military fort. Established in 1891 to protect the Bremerton Naval Yard, it and Fort Manchester (now Manchester State Park) faced each other across Rich Passage. Underwater nets were placed offshore during WW II to snag any Japanese subs that might stray into these waters, but none did.

Gardens
The 150-acre **Bloedel Reserve** contains many native plants from Washington, a bog, pond, Japanese garden, moss garden, and spacious lawns, plus the old Bloedel home, now used as a visitor center. The reserve is especially popular in the spring when the rhododendrons are in bloom, but the 15,000 cyclamen plants are also an attraction. Get here by heading six miles west from Winslow on Hwy. 305, then following the signs another mile to the entrance. It's open Wed.-Sun. 10 a.m.-4 p.m. all year, but reservations are necessary because they only let in 200 people a day; call (206) 842-7631. Entrance is $6 adults, $4 seniors and kids, free for children under five.

Bainbridge Gardens is an historic nursery with unusual trees, theme gardens, and a nature trail. The cafe has wood-fired oven cuisine and espresso. Find them on the west side of the island at 9415 Miller Rd. NE, tel. (206) 842-5888.

Other Parks
Pick up a map of hiking trails on Bainbridge from the chamber of commerce office. The largest parcel of public land—280 acres—contains second-growth forests managed by the Dept. of Natural Resources. Called **Grand Forest**, it's near the center of the island off Mandus Oldon

Rd. and has two miles of paths. **Manzanita Park** is a 120-acre parcel with a two-mile hiking and equestrian trail through woods and wetlands. The park is on Day Rd. on the northwest side of the island.

Wineries
Family-operated **Bainbridge Island Winery,** one-quarter mile from the ferry terminal at 682 Hwy. 305 in Winslow, tel. (206) 842-9463, is the only place to buy their limited-run wines made from grapes grown on Bainbridge Island. The outdoor picnic area is a refreshing spot for a lunch break, and the antique wine glass collection is worth a gander. Tours and tastings are held Wed.-Sun. noon-5 p.m.

Rich Passage Winery, 7869 N.E. Day Rd. W, is a small family operation producing pinot noir, chardonnay, and fumé blanc wines. The winery is generally open for tastings, but call (206) 842-8199 to be sure someone is there.

Accommodations
See **Fay-Bainbridge State Park** (above) for camping on Bainbridge Island. The island has 13 fine B&Bs and one motel. A number of other places offer multi-day stays; see the chamber of commerce for details. Unless otherwise noted, all B&Bs listed below serve a full breakfast and do not allow young children. Lodging places are listed by price.

The Captain's House, 234 Parfitt Way NE, tel. (206) 842-3557, is a turn-of-the-century B&B overlooking Eagle Harbor with rowboats, tennis courts, and an old-fashioned porch swing. The two guest rooms have private baths; $45-70 s or d.

Marys Farmhouse, 5129 McDonald Rd. NE, tel. (206) 842-4952, is a 1904 restored farmhouse on five acres. Inside are two guest rooms sharing a bath, a grand piano, and continental breakfasts. Kids are welcome; $50 s or $60 d.

Cedar Meadow B&B, 10411 Old Creosote Hill Rd., tel. (206) 842-5291, is a beautiful older home on six acres with grazing sheep, flower gardens, two grand pianos, and friendly hosts. The four guest rooms have private or shared bath. Kids are welcome; $50-80 s or d.

The charming turn-of-the-century **Bombay House,** 8490 Beck Rd. NE, tel. (206) 842-3926 or (800) 598-3926, overlooks Rich Passage and has country antiques, flower gardens, a gazebo, and a widow's walk. The four guest rooms include antiques, and private or shared baths; $59-149 s or d.

Bainbridge Island's only hotel, **Island Country Inn,** 920 Hildebrand Ln. NE, tel. (206) 842-6861 or (800) 842-8429, has deluxe guest rooms and suites, an outdoor pool, jacuzzi, and continental breakfast; $63-129 s or $73-139 d.

Waterfront B&B, 3314 Crystal Spring Dr. NE, tel. (206) 842-2431, charges $70 s or d for a waterside cottage with a private entrance and continental breakfast. Popular with honeymooners.

The Woodsman B&B, 7700 Spring Ridge Rd. NE, tel. (206) 842-7386 or (888) 799-6637, is a Dutch Colonial home on five acres with a fireplace, library, and hot tub. The single guest room has a private bath, and kids are welcome; $75 s or d.

Herb Cottage B&B, tel. (206) 842-2625, is on the west side of Bainbridge Island near the water. The single guest room has a private entrance and garden; $75 s or d.

Winslow Inn B&B, 366 Morrill Place NE, tel. (206) 842-9604, contains a private one-bedroom apartment with separate entry and full kitchen; $85 s or d.

Rockaway Beach Guest House B&B, 5032 Rockaway Beach Rd., tel. (206) 780-9427, has a master suite and guest room (both with private bath) in a modern beachfront home with stunning views, an outdoor hot tub, and continental breakfast. Kids accepted; $85-125 s or d.

Our Country Haus B&B, 13718 Ellingsen Rd. NE, tel. (206) 842-8425, is a private carriage house on two acres with gardens and pond, private bath and kitchen; a continental breakfast is served; $90 s or d.

Bainbridge Inn B&B, 9200 Hemlock St., tel. (206) 842-7564, is a two-bedroom apartment with kitchen, hot tub, and private entry. A continental breakfast is served and kids are welcome; $100 s or d.

Bainbridge House B&B, 5257 Lynwood Center Rd. NE, tel. (206) 842-1599, is a furnished guest apartment with a make-your-own breakfast. Kids are welcome. $125 s or d.

For a vacation from the kids, try the gorgeous and tranquil **Beach Cottage,** 5831 Ward Ave. NE, tel. (206) 842-6081, right on Eagle Harbor with Olympic and Cascade views. The kitchen has ingredients for a cook-it-yourself breakfast. $135 s or d

Food

Streamliner Diner, 397 Winslow Way, tel. (206) 842-8595, is famous for its hearty breakfasts that include wonderful home fries and omelettes. It's popular with both locals and tourists, so be ready for a wait most mornings. For something lighter, get fresh baked goods and espresso coffees at **Bainbridge Bakers,** 140 Winslow Way W, tel. (206) 842-1822, or head to the historic brick building at 131 Parfitt Way that houses **Pegasus Coffee House and Gallery,** tel. (206) 842-6725. This is a fun place to enjoy a relaxing light lunch and espresso. Live music on Saturday nights. More live music on weekends at **Winslow Way Cafe,** 122 Winslow Way E, tel. (206) 842-0517, an elegant place with a menu that includes gourmet pizzas, pastas, fresh seafood, plus a popular Sunday brunch.

Blue Water Diner, 305 Madison Ave., tel. (206) 842-1151, is a beautifully restored slice of Americana that has been restored with an interior of Formica and chrome. The menu emphasizes traditional favorites too—from steak and eggs to meatloaf—all of it well prepared.

Harbour Public House, 231 Parfitt Way SW, tel. (206) 842-9037, has tasty on-the-water eats, including fish and chips and burgers, plus a dozen microbrewed beers. The best fast meals are at **Chili Cosmo's** stand at 100 Winslow Way, tel. (206) 780-9053, where the burritos are huge, filling, and tasty.

Ruby's on Bainbridge, 4569 Lynwood Center Rd., tel. (206) 780-9303, is a neighborhood bistro with inspired Northwest cuisine, including pasta, chicken, and lamb—all perfectly prepared. Dinner entrees are $12-18.

Noted for serving some of the best Southwestern food in the Northwest is the **San Carlos Restaurant,** two blocks from the Winslow ferry terminal at 279 Madison N, tel. (206) 842-1999. Open for lunch Tues.-Fri. and dinner daily.

For Thai cooking, head to **Sawatdy Thai Cuisine,** 8780 Fletcher Bay Rd., Island Center, tel. (206) 780-2429.

Winslow's **Town & Country Thriftway** 343 Winslow Way, is a big gourmet grocery with a fine wine cellar (in the cellar, of course); tel. (206) 842-3848. The **Bainbridge Farmers Mar-**

ket comes to the municipal parking lot at 200 Madison Ave. on Saturday 9 a.m.-1 p.m. May-Sept. and includes flowers, organic fruits and vegetables, handicrafts, and ethnic foods; tel. (206) 297-8906.

Events
In February, Puget Sound's cycling season kicks off with the popular **Chilly Hilly** bicycle marathon. More than 4,000 riders pedal around Bainbridge. The island's most unique event is one you're likely to miss, the **Scotch Broom Parade,** held on the spur of the moment sometime in June, whenever local folks decide to put it on. The **Fourth of July** brings a two-day street fair and parade to Winslow. No fireworks, but Bainbridge offers a fine view of Seattle's fireworks show. **Concerts in the Park** take place at Waterfront Park in Winslow on Wednesday evenings in July and August, and an **Outdoor Music Festival** brings more performers to Waterfront Park in August.

Recreation
Bainbridge Island Boat Rentals, tel. (206) 842-9229, has sea kayak, canoe, sailboat, and rowboat rentals and tours from the Winslow waterfront. **B.I. Cycle Rentals,** 195 Winslow Way, tel. (206) 842-6413, rents mountain bikes. **Exotic Aquatics,** 100 Madison Ave. N, tel. (206) 842-1980, guide scuba dives in nearby waters and rent sea kayaks.

Shopping
Downtown Winslow is jammed with gift and import shops, including several inside Winslow Green, the little strip mall in town. Two fine bookshops are in the center of town. **Eagle Harbor Books,** tel. (206) 842-5332, with new titles, plus an espresso cafe in the back. Head across the street for a great choice of used and out-of-print books at **Fortner Books,** tel. (206) 780-2030. Also downtown is **Bainbridge Arts and Crafts,** tel. (206) 842-3132, an excellent non-profit gallery with local works.

Information and Services
The **Bainbridge Island Chamber of Commerce Visitor Center,** 590 Winslow Way E, tel. (206) 842-3700, is open Mon.-Fri. 9 a.m.-5 p.m. and Saturday 10 a.m.-3 p.m. year-round. It's at the top of the hill as you exit the ferry, or on the Web at www.bicomnet.com. An information kiosk at the ferry terminal is open daily 10 a.m.-6 p.m. May-Oct., and weekends the rest of the year. Swim at the **indoor pool** at the high school.

Transportation and Tours
The **Washington State Ferry,** tel. (206) 842-2345 or (888) 808-7977, provides service between downtown Seattle and Winslow on Bainbridge Island every 50 minutes throughout the day. The crossing takes 35 minutes and in summer costs $8 one-way for car and driver, $3.60 roundtrip for passengers, and 60 cents extra for bikes. The Seattle-Bainbridge route is the busiest ferry run in Washington—over six million riders each year. Be ready for long delays—especially in the summer—if you're traveling on Friday evenings from Seattle to Bainbridge, and on Sunday evenings back to Seattle. Avoid the waits by leaving your car behind and taking the bus.

Kitsap Transit, tel. (206) 373-2877 or (800) 501-7433, provides daily service around Bainbridge Island and the Kitsap Peninsula, and meets all state ferries in Winslow. All buses have bike racks.

Tours of Bainbridge and surrounding areas are offered by **WeatherVane Tours,** tel. (206) 780-5003, and **Taxis & Tours,** tel. (206) 698-7660.

SUQUAMISH

The name "Suquamish" came from the Indian word D'suq'wub (apparently after much mispronunciation), meaning "Place of Clear Salt Water." The Suquamish were a peaceful people, and as the white man took over they were forced to surrender their own culture: children were sent to Tacoma schools, where boys learned trades and girls provided cheap kitchen labor, while the Suquamish men went to work at Port Madison lumber mills. Today they run the keno, craps, roulette, poker, and bingo operations at the local moneymaker, **Suquamish Clearwater Casino,** tel. (360) 598-6889 or (800) 375-6073. The casino has live music, cabaret, or comedy acts most nights.

Historical Sights

The **Suquamish Museum,** tel. (360) 598-3311, off Hwy. 305 just beyond the Bainbridge Island bridge, is a good place to start a tour of Suquamish and the Port Madison Indian Reservation. Chief Seattle, his Suquamish descendants, and Pacific Northwest history come to life in this shoreline museum with exhibits on the history of the people and commercial fishing, plus historical photos and a slide presentation narrated by Suquamish elders. Open daily 10 a.m.-5 p.m. May-Sept., and Fri.-Sun. 11 a.m.-4 p.m. the rest of the year; admission is $2.50 adults, $2 seniors, and $1 kids under 13. The gift shop has a few handmade baskets and books for sale.

Chief Sealth's Grave overlooks Puget Sound with a glimpse of Seattle's skyscrapers in a small, peaceful cemetery on the Port Madison Indian Reservation. It's not hard to tell which grave is his; black and red canoes are positioned high above the headstone to honor this leader of the Suquamish Nation and friend to the early settlers for whom Seattle was named. Follow the signs to find the graveyard.

A cedar longhouse 500 feet long and 60 feet wide—the communal home of eight Suquamish chiefs (including Chief Sealth) and their families—stood at the waterfront site now called "Ole-Man-House" until 1870, when federal agents torched it in a subtle effort to discourage this form of accommodation. Today a Washington State Heritage site, a small historical display marks the location of the original longhouse on a lot surrounded by housing developments at the west end of Agate Passage. After seeing the slide show and displays at the Suquamish Museum depicting the peaceful everyday Suquamish life, this minuscule historical remembrance will break your heart.

Practicalities

Once in a While B&B, tel. (360) 598-2212, has a single guest room with a deck overlooking Puget Sound for $70 s or d, including a continental breakfast.

Chief Seattle Days, an annual weekend affair held the third week in August at the downtown Suquamish waterfront park, has been going strong since 1911 with canoe racing, arts and crafts, a powwow with traditional Native American dancing, and a salmon bake.

KINGSTON

Kingston (pop. 2,000) is a pleasant little town toward the northern tip of the Kitsap Peninsula that is best known as the ferry landing directly across the sound from Edmonds. It is mostly a residential community with a cluster of shops near the ferry landing.

Accommodations

Smiley's Colonial Motel, 11057 Hwy. 104, tel. (360) 297-3622, has rooms for $40-50 s or d. **Kingston House B&B,** 26117 Ohio Ave. NE, tel. (360) 297-8818 or (800) 624-9480, is a cozy historic bungalow just three blocks from the ferry. The spacious suite has a king-size bed and continental breakfast; $85 s or d.

Food and Events

The historic **Kingston Hotel Cafe,** tel. (360) 297-8100, at 1st and Washington, has a deck overlooking the water and outstanding breakfasts, lunches, and dinners. The weekend brunch attracts people from all over the peninsula. Live music on Saturday nights. Also popular is **Dickinson's Restaurant,** at the ferry dock, tel. (360) 297-8566, where the attraction is tableside flambé cooking and scenic vistas.

The **Kingston Farmers Market,** tel. (360) 297-2876, takes place at Marina Park Wednesday 3 p.m.-7 p.m. (mid-June through Sept.), and Saturday 9 a.m.-2 p.m., (May to mid-October). This is a great place to look for handmade clothing and crafts, fresh produce, and baked goods.

Kingston's old fashioned **Fourth of July** includes a parade, music, food booths, dancing in the streets, logging competitions, fireworks, and the speedy slug races.

Transportation

The **Washington State Ferry** system has service between Edmonds and Kingston approximately every 40 minutes during the day. The crossing takes 30 minutes. Summertime fares are $8 one-way for car and driver, $3.60 roundtrip for passengers, and 60 cents extra for bikes. Call (360) 842-2345 or (888) 808-7977 for details. A word to the wise: If you're returning late from the Olympic Peninsula on the Edmonds ferry, be sure to check the ferry schedules because the Edmonds-Kingston ferry shuts down a couple of hours earlier than the Bainbridge-Seattle ferries. Also note that you can expect delays if you're heading to Kingston on a Friday evening or east to Edmonds on a Sunday evening in the summer.

Kitsap Transit, tel. (360) 373-2877 or (800) 501-7433, provides daily bus service throughout Kitsap Peninsula, and meets all Kingston ferries.

HANSVILLE

The **Hansville Recreation Area** occupies the northernmost tip of the Kitsap Peninsula, northeast of Port Gamble and the Hood Canal Bridge. This is the place to catch salmon in Puget Sound—most fishing is done quite close to shore, rarely more than a half mile out. The facilities here are all geared toward fishermen: the accommodations are sparse and the lone restaurant isn't fancy.

The squat **Point No Point Lighthouse** occupies a parcel of land just west of Hansville. It was named by the Wilkes expedition of 1841 because the point that was visible from one approach disappeared from the other. The light station—established in 1879—is open Sat.-Sun. noon-4 p.m. May-Sept., or by appointment only in winter; call (360) 286-5420. The beach here provides good views of Hood Canal, Admiralty Inlet, and Whidbey Island and is a favorite place to dig for clams. Just south of Hansville is tiny **Buck Lake,** which has picnic areas, bathhouses for swimmers, a boat launch, fishing, and a playground.

For something a bit more out of the ordinary, you aren't likely to miss the ship-shape home located on the road to Point No Point; it's one of the most distinctive in the state. For more weirdness, check out the "world's largest rocking chair" at the turnoff to Hansville on Hwy. 104 (west of Kingston).

Captain's Landing, tel. (360) 638-2257, has rustic cabins with kitchenettes ($75 for up to four people), and an RV park. **The Guest House at Twin Spits,** tel. (360) 638-1001, has panoramic water vistas and a suite with kitchen for $75 d.

PORT GAMBLE AREA

A native of East Machias, Maine, Capt. William Talbot founded a sawmill at Port Gamble in 1853 and modeled the settlement after his hometown, complete with traditional New England-style homes and imported trees from back East. The Pope and Talbot sawmill survived until 1995 when it closed for good and everything was sold off in an auction. The mill building was totally destroyed in two subsequent fires, and the site is now used for chipping logs. Olympic Resource Management still owns the entire town, plus another 3,000 acres of surrounding land. The homes—restored in the 1960s—are all on the National Register of Historic Places, and the town is preserved as an historic district. Walking down these quiet streets past the neat houses and the steeply steepled church while shuffling through the fallen leaves, you'd swear you were in Maine. Many other Washington towns have put on false fronts that turn them into European or wild-west towns, but Port Gamble is the real thing. So far, the village maintains its undeveloped charm, but another sawmill property owned by the company—Port Ludlow—was transformed into a lavish resort. It will be a sad day if Port Gamble becomes yet another hangout of nouveau-riche Seattle commuters.

Sights

Start out in the **Kitsap Peninsula Visitor & Convention Bureau** housed in one of the old homes. It's open daily 9 a.m.-5 p.m. all year; tel. (360) 297-8200 or (800) 416-5616, www.visitkitsap.com. Port Gamble's two museums are housed in the charming 1914 **General Store,** where you can purchase groceries, sandwiches, and ice cream cones. Head upstairs to discover two levels of seashells in the **Of Sea and Shore Museum.** This is one of the largest shell collections in the country, with more than 25,000 species—only a fraction of which are on display—plus a variety of other oddities such as gargantuan beetles and other insects from hell. Books and shells of various kinds are offered for sale to help support the museum. Open Tues.-Sun. 11 a.m.-4 p.m. from mid-May to mid-September, and Sat.-Sun. 11 a.m.-4 p.m. the rest of the year; free.

The **Port Gamble Historic Museum,** on the back side of the General Store, tel. (360) 297-3341, houses exhibits from the timber company, original rooms from hotels and houses, sailing ship interiors, and a "Forest of the Future" display. Open daily 10 a.m.-4 p.m. from Memorial Day to Labor Day; $1 adults, 50 cents for seniors and students, free for kids under age six. Closed during the winter months.

Pick up a walking tour of Port Gamble's historic sites at the museum. The rest of the town consists of more than two dozen 19th-century homes, including the **Thompson House,** said to be the oldest continuously lived-in home in Washington (the McFadden home in Chehalis also lays claim to this title). The scenic hilltop **cemetery** has the grave of Gustave Englebrecht, the first U.S. Navy man to die in action in the Pacific. He was killed in 1856 during an Indian raid.

Hood Canal Nursery

The Hood Canal Nursery, on the edge of town off Hwy. 3 (follow the signs), tel. (360) 297-7555, was established in 1976 to grow more than three million trees annually on Pope and Talbot lands. Tours of the facility include a look at four greenhouses, a water reservoir, pump house, tree shade house, and a film about tree growing; free.

Parks

Located four miles south of Port Gamble on Hwy. 3, **Kitsap Memorial State Park** has saltwater swimming, hiking, fishing, oyster- and clam-gathering, boating, picnicking, scuba diving, and campsites ($10 tents; no RV hookups) on 58 acres. Call (360) 779-3205 for information. The park's sturdy log hall and kitchen shelters were built by the Work Progress Administration in the 1930s. Open year-round. Additional campsites can be found at **Salisbury Point County Park,** right next to the Hood Canal Floating Bridge, and just across the bridge at **Shine Tidelands State Park.**

HOOD CANAL AND VICINITY

The Kitsap Peninsula is separated from the Olympic Peninsula by a 1.5-mile-wide channel of saltwater, the 65-mile-long Hood Canal. Highway 101 follows the west side of the "Canal Zone," providing a delicious tidewater drive through second-growth forests with countless vistas of the waterway from every possible angle. The road hugs the canal, tucking in and out of various inlets along the way. Much of the route between Quilcene and Union is only minimally developed, though a few towns provide the essentials, and scattered resort estates dot the shoreline. Several places sell freshly shucked oysters along the way. At the southwest corner of Hood Canal, the waterway makes a sharp bend, angling northward and nearly turning the Kitsap Peninsula into an island. South from this elbow is the largest town in the area, Shelton, and at the head of the canal is the fast-growing region around Belfair.

In addition to the fine vistas along Hood Canal, you'll discover camping and hiking at two state parks and on nearby Olympic National Forest and Olympic National Park lands, plus out-

standing scuba diving and fishing. Lake Cushman is a popular fishing and summer recreation spot, just east of the Staircase entrance to Olympic National Park, and the dam at the lake's southeast end produces some of Tacoma's electricity.

History

Like many other features in Washington, Hood Canal received its name from Capt. George Vancouver during his 1792 exploration of Puget Sound. He called it "Hood's Channel," after a British naval hero, Lord Hood, but a printer's error in Vancouver's report changed the word channel to canal. Hood Canal is *not* a canal, but actually a long, glacially carved fjord. The waters of Hood Canal are more susceptible to pollution than other parts of Puget Sound because of limited tidal flushing. At the head of the canal in Belfair, it takes upwards of six years for a complete change of water. Rapid development around the southern end of Hood Canal has led to increasing concerns over water pollution, and several beaches have been closed to shellfish gathering in recent years.

Hood Canal Bridge

Hood Canal is spanned at only one point along its entire length, the 6,471-foot-long **Hood Canal Floating Bridge** that connects the Kitsap and Olympic Peninsulas near Port Gamble. The world's third-longest floating bridge (the longest over tidewater) was opened in 1961 and served the peninsulas well until February 13, 1979, when a violent storm with 100-mph gales broke off and sank nearly a mile of the western portion of the bridge. In a remarkable feat of driving, a trucker in his 18-wheeler backed the semi at almost full throttle off the bridge when it began to sink. To prevent another sinking, the center span of the rebuilt bridge is now opened when wind conditions are severe. Call (800) 419-9085 to check on the current bridge status. You can cast a line for salmon or bottom fish from the fishing pontoon; there's a special anglers' parking lot at the Kitsap end of the bridge. Keep your eyes open for subs; the Navy's Trident fleet often passes through en route to or from the Bangor submarine base. Just north of the bridge, **Salsbury Point County Park** has a boat launch and camping.

ARCHIE SATTERFIELD

Hood Canal

SHELTON

The peaceful blue-collar town of Shelton (pop. 7,700) occupies the head of Oakland Bay on the southwest toe of Puget Sound. It is both the Mason County seat and the only incorporated city in the county. Put on your plaid shirt and baseball cap to blend in. It's easy to see the importance of timber here: a sprawling yellow Simpson Timber Co. lumber and plywood mill dominates the town, and the surrounding land is filled with tree farms in varying stages of regrowth. Also here are the Rayonier Research Center, where the chemistry and manufacture of pulp is studied, and a maximum-security state prison. Downtown has wide streets and a friendly atmosphere, but up the hill you'll find homogenized America, with a McDonald's, Wal-Mart, and Super 8 Motel.

Mason County is one of the nation's largest Christmas tree-producing areas; every year, over two million trees are shipped worldwide. Originally named Sheltonville, the town was founded in 1855 by David Shelton, although its plat wasn't officially recorded until 1884. Forestry and oystering were, and still are, the primary industries here, beginning in 1878 when the first shipment of highly prized Olympia oysters left Kamilche.

Olympia Oysters

These tiny and sweet-tasting oysters—approximately the size of a silver dollar—were found at one time all the way from San Francisco Bay to Alaska, but overfishing, pollution, and parasites blighted the population. Today, Olympia oysters survive only in the southernmost reaches of Puget Sound in beds within Big Skookum, Little Skookum, Oyster, and Mud Bays. In the mid-1920s the average annual harvest peaked at about 48,000 bushels, but it went into a tailspin due to overharvesting and toxic wastewater from a Shelton pulp mill. The oyster population dwindled still further in the 1930s, when the importation of Japanese oysters began.

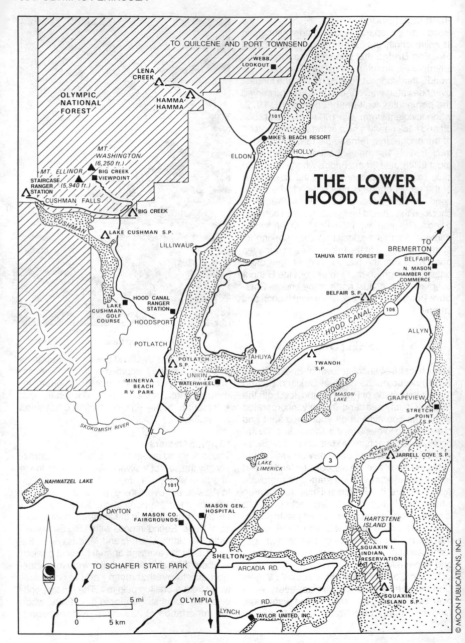

THE LOWER HOOD CANAL

These oysters brought with them two pests: the Japanese oyster drill and the Japanese flatworm, harmful only to smaller oysters like the Olympia. Although the pulp mill closed in 1957, it has taken 40 years for the water quality to improve enough to support the oysters again. Biologists are optimistic now that within a few years the southern Puget Sound population will be approaching their original levels.

To see how Olympia oysters are raised, visit the largest and oldest producer (in business since 1876), **Olympia Oyster Co.,** S.E. 1042 Bloomfield Rd., tel. (360) 426-3354. The plant is located halfway between Olympia and Shelton along Totten Inlet. **Taylor United, Inc.**—the biggest producer of clams in the nation—grows and harvests shellfish from more than 3,000 acres of tidelands around the southern Puget Sound. Visit their oyster sheds and clam hatchery at S.E. 130 Lynch Rd., three miles south of Shelton. The shop sells fresh clams and oysters; call (360) 426-6178 to arrange a tour.

Other Sights

The **Mason County Historical Museum** in the old library building at 5th St. and Railroad Ave., tel. (360) 426-1020, emphasizes the importance of logging in Shelton's history with displays on railroad logging, historical photos, and artifacts. Open Tues.-Fri. noon-5 p.m., Saturday noon-4 p.m. year-round; no charge.

"**Tollie,**" the locomotive in downtown Shelton between 2nd and 3rd on Railroad Ave., is a 90-ton Shay logging engine that saw most of the country in its heyday. Behind it sits a red caboose housing the visitor center. Downtown Shelton also has a number of antique shops scattered along Railroad Avenue.

The **Bronze Works** is a newly opened foundry and gallery four miles south of town on Hwy. 101. This is the only bronze foundry in Washington, and visitors can tour the facility and view finished pieces in the gallery. Open Mon.-Fri. 8 a.m.-5 p.m., Saturday 10 a.m.-6 p.m.; bronze is poured most Thursdays. Six-week workshops are available, and a **Mother's Day Arts Fair** attracts dozens of artisans. Call (360) 427-3857 or (888) 821-0372 for details.

Tour the Dept. of Wildlife's **Shelton Trout Hatchery** on Eells Hill Rd., approximately eight miles north of Shelton, tel. (360) 426-3669;

Tollie and Caboose 700

open daily 8 a.m.-5 p.m. Continue up the road, turning right at the sign marking Denny Ahl Seed Orchard, and cross over the 440-foot-high **Steel Arch Bridge** that spans the Skokomish Gorge.

Accommodations

Super 8 Motel, 6 Northview Circle, tel. (360) 426-1654 or (800) 843-1991, has rooms for $49 s or $54 d. **Shelton Inn Motel,** 628 Railroad Ave., tel. (360) 426-4468 or (800) 451-4560, charges $43 s or $48 d, including an outdoor pool and kitchenettes. **City Center Motel,** 128 E. Alder, tel. (360) 426-3397 or (888) 771-2378, costs $33-36 s or $38-41 d.

Twin River Ranch B&B, tel. (360) 426-1023, is a 1918 farmhouse six miles north of Shelton along Oakland Bay. The home sits on a 140-acre hay farm, and has two guest rooms, shared baths, a big stone fireplace, and full breakfasts; $64 s or d. No kids.

Rest Full Farm B&B, five miles west of Shelton, tel. (360) 426-8774, has two rooms that share a bath in a country home. A full breakfast is served and kids are accepted; $60 s or d.

Parks and Campgrounds

Jarrell Cove State Park, along a small cove on the north end of Hartstene Island, has campsites ($10; no RV hookups) and is open April-October. Call (360) 426-9226 for information. Get here by heading seven miles northeast of Shelton on Hwy. 3, crossing the bridge to Hartstene Island, and then following the signs another five miles to the park. The 43-acre park is primarily used by boaters and is a fun place to explore in a kayak. **Jarrell Cove Marina,** E. 220 Wilson Rd., tel. (360) 426-8823, has RV spaces, a marina, groceries, and gas.

You'll need a boat to get to tiny **Stretch Point State Park** (12 miles north of Shelton next to the town of Grapeview), which has no camping, showers, toilets, or drinking water, but has one of the best sandy beaches around Puget Sound. Grapeview itself has vineyards, a country store, marina, and a sometimes-open museum.

Lake Nahwatzel Resort, 10 miles west of Shelton, tel. (360) 426-8323, features cabins, RV spaces, a couple of tent sites, and a restaurant on the shores of this 280-acre spring-fed lake in the foothills of the Olympics. More RV parking at **We & You RV Park,** S.E. 261 Craig Rd., tel. (360) 426-3169.

Food

A good place to start the day is **Pine Tree Restaurant,** 102 S. 1st, tel. (360) 426-2604, a family place with big breakfasts served all day, plus seafood and steak for dinner. For lunch, head to **Chez Constance at Tea & Crumpets,** tel. (360) 427-1681, an elegantly furnished historic brick building at 203 W. Railroad. The food includes quiche, sandwiches, and salads for lunch, or seafood, sirloin, and pasta for dinner. Sunday brunch is very popular.

Owned by Taylor United and managed by Xinh Dwelley—a fine Vietnamese chef and former oyster-shucking champ—**Xinhs Clam & Oyster House,** delivers such treats as hot and spicy seafood soup, oysters sautéed in black bean sauce, and grilled halibut. Recommended.

For traditional American favorites such as steak, roast beef, and turkey, head to **Timbers Restaurant,** 6th and Railroad, tel. (360) 426-9171. They also have a salad bar. **El Sarape,** 318 W. Railroad, tel. (360) 426-4294, is the place for authentic Mexican food.

Get produce at the **Shelton Farmers Market,** on 2nd and Railroad, tel. (360) 427-4555, open Sat.-Sun. 10 a.m.-3 p.m. May to mid-October.

Events

Early June's **Mason County Forest Festival** includes two Paul Bunyan parades (one for kids), a carnival, musical entertainment, an arts-and-crafts show, and logging competition in such events as skidder driving, speed climbing, ax throwing, and log-rolling.

Mason County Fair is held the last weekend in July at the fairgrounds. Highlights include live entertainment, and traditional county fair favorites such as 4-H exhibits and cake and preserve competitions. Return to the fairgrounds in early August for a **Polynesian Luau and Heritage Fair,** which features traditional dancing, food, and crafts from the South Pacific.

The **West Coast Oyster Shucking Championship and Seafood Festival,** a.k.a. "OysterFest," is held annually on the first full weekend of October at the fairgrounds. The main event, high-speed oyster shucking, lasts less than three minutes; the national record, set here in 1984, is held by Diz Schimke, who shucked 24 oysters in 2:41.31 minutes. Surrounding the competition are two days of wine tasting, an oyster cook-off, food booths, art and boating exhibits, dancers, bands, and magicians.

The holiday season brings Santa to Shelton during the annual **Christmas Parade and Bazaar,** held the first weekend in December with a parade by land and by sea.

Entertainment and Recreation

Little Creek Casino in Kamilche (five miles south of Shelton), tel. (360) 427-7711 or (800) 667-7711, has poker, blackjack, keno, and other games, plus inexpensive buffet dining and a surprisingly good cafe. Both **PJ's Runway Cafe,** 11880 Hwy. 101, tel. (360) 426-3073, and **Doo Wop Diner,** S.E. 843 Hwy. 3, tel. (360) 427-8755, have live entertainment on weekends.

Swim at the **Shelton High School pool** on Shelton Springs Rd., tel. (360) 426-4240.

Information and Transportation

For maps and festival information, contact the **Shelton-Mason County Chamber of Commerce,** located in the caboose on Railroad Ave., tel. (360) 426-2021 or (800) 576-2021. Open Mon.-Fri. 9 a.m.-6 p.m. and Sat.-Sun. 9 a.m.-3 p.m. June-Sept., and Mon.-Fri. 10 a.m.-5 p.m. the rest of the year.

Mason County Transit, tel. (360) 427-5033 or (800) 374-3747, has free bus service throughout the county, and onward to Olympia. Bike racks are on all buses. **Olympic Air,** tel. (360) 426-1477, offers scenic flights over the area.

UNION

The scattered settlement of Union occupies land near the "elbow" where Hood Inlet angles abruptly to the northeast. Summer and weekend homes crowd the highway, providing a contrast to the from-another-era **waterwheel,** built by Edwin J. Dalby in 1923 and still operational (albeit unused). A few miles to the west is the **Skokomish Indian Reservation,** near the intersection of Highways 101 and 106. You can tell you're on the reservation by all the fireworks stands that clutter the highway. The tribal center houses a small museum with arts and crafts.

Twanoh State Park
Seven miles east of Union on Hwy. 106, Twanoh State Park is a very popular spot for picnicking beneath tall trees, and swimming and waterskiing on Hood Canal. The 182-acre park also has several miles of hiking trails along scenic Twanoh Creek, sturdy CCC-constructed structures from the 1930s, a tennis court, a concession stand with snacks and groceries, bathhouses, and camping in tent ($11) and RV ($16) sites with coin-operated showers. Open late April to early September. Call 275-222 for more information.

Practicalities
Union's elaborate **Alderbrook Resort** was purchased by conservative Christa Ministries in 1997, and the bar was immediately closed, followed by most other public facilities. Christianity at work! The 18-hole golf course remains open, along with the marina and pool; call (360) 898-2200 or (800) 622-9370.

Robin Hood Village, tel. (360) 898-2163, has four cottages with hot tubs and kitchenettes. Couples can stay in the smaller and older ones for $75-85 d; the larger ones are $100-185 and sleep six. Tent and RV sites are also available.

Victoria's, E. 6791 Hwy. 106, tel. (360) 898-4400, has wonderful meals, including prime rib,

pasta, and seafood specialties. Great desserts too. **Union Country Store,** tel. (360) 898-2641, has a fine small deli.

Mason County Transit, tel. (360) 427-5033 or (800) 374-3747, provides free bus service throughout the county.

BELFAIR AND ALLYN

Located at the end of Hood Canal, the sprawling town of Belfair (pop. 18,000 at last count, but higher by the time you read this) is one of the fastest growing places in Washington. The waterside location and proximity to Tacoma, Bremerton, and Seattle make it a favorite of folks fleeing crime and looking for a suburban setting to raise kids or retire. In the summer months, Belfair triples in size as tourists roll in.

Parks
Sixty-three-acre **Belfair State Park,** three miles southwest of Belfair on Hwy. 300, has year-round camping ($11 tents, $16 RVs), swimming in a protected lagoon, and fishing on the north side of Hood Canal. Call (360) 275-0668 for information, or (800) 452-5687 for reservations ($6 extra).

The **Thieler Wetlands** cover 135 acres of open space behind the Mary E. Thieler Memorial Community Center off Hwy. 3. Nearly four miles of level nature trails take you through the saltwater and freshwater marshes with natural history exhibits and a rich diversity of wildlife.

North of Belfair is **Tahuya State Forest,** covering 23,100 acres of relatively flat multiple-use land. The emphasis here is on logging, but hikers and mountain bikers will find a number of trails and campsites. For a map, contact the Dept. of Natural Resources, tel. (360) 825-1631, or (800) 527-3305.

In the tiny waterside village of **Allyn,** three miles south of Belfair, you'll find a pleasant park with a covered gazebo, picnic tables, boat dock, and boat launching ramp. It is a center for oyster growers and Christmas tree suppliers.

Accommodations and Campgrounds
Belfair Motel, 23322 Hwy. 3, tel. (360) 275-4485, is a clean and modern place with rooms for $47 s or $51 d.

Selah Inn at Hood Canal, N.E. 130 Dulalip Landing, tel. (360) 275-0916, is an elegant new waterside B&B with four guest bedrooms, private baths, and gourmet breakfasts. $80-125 s or d. **Country Garden Inn,** N.E. 2790 Old Belfair Hwy., tel. (360) 275-3683, has comfortable B&B accommodations in a country home with three guest rooms (private baths). A hot tub is on the patio. $75 s or d, including a full breakfast.

On the north side of Hood Canal and west of Belfair, the little dot of a place called Tahuya is home to **Summertide Resort & Marina,** tel. (206) 925-9277. Also here is a store, restaurant, and RV park. **Cady Lake Manor B&B** is 13 miles west of Belfair, tel. (360) 272-2673. This large new home sits on a 53-acre estate and has its own catch-and-release trout fishing lake. Rates are $125-185 d in the four guest rooms with private baths and full breakfasts. Kids accepted.

See above for camping in nearby state parks. Park RVs at **Snooze Junction RV Park,** N.E. 621, Gladwin Beach, tel. (360) 275-2381, or **Sherwood Hills RV Park,** near Belfair State Park, tel. (360) 275-6767.

Food

Clifton Town Deli & Bakery, N.E. 23690 Hwy. 3, tel. (360) 275-4986, has homemade soups, baked goods, salads, sandwiches, and good breakfasts. **Leonard Kay's** in Allyn, tel. (360) 275-2954, serves three meals a day, with good pizzas, steaks, and burgers. **Belfair Farmers Market** takes place across from Theiler Center on Saturday 9 a.m.-3 p.m., May-Oct.; tel. (360) 275-2032.

Events

Belfair's **SummerFest** on the last weekend in June includes food, games and competitions, craft booths, and entertainment. Call (360) 275-5548 for details. **Allyn Days** in late July features a pancake breakfast, music, a parade, and a big salmon bake; tel. (360) 275-5002.

Information and Transportation

Get info on Belfair and northern Mason County at the **North Mason Visitor Info Center** located in the community center at E. 22871 Hwy. 3, tel. (360) 275-5548. Open daily 8 a.m.-4 p.m. year-round. Mason County Transit, tel. (360) 427-5033 or (800) 374-3747, has free bus service throughout the county.

HOODSPORT AREA

The town of Hoodsport is the largest along the west side of Hood Canal and can provide most of your travel needs. This is the place to get Forest Service and Park Service information and to stock up on food before heading north. Hoodsport's lodging places cater to scuba divers, particularly small groups who come to explore the deep, clear waters just offshore where the creatures are amazingly diverse. The lack of strong currents and only minor tidal fluctuations help make this a good place for beginning divers. Visibility is best in the winter—to 50 feet—when fewer plankton are in the water. Other people come to water-ski, sail, windsurf, or to catch shrimp, fish, and crabs. The **Hood Canal Hatchery** is right in town.

Five miles north from Hoodsport is the village of **Lilliwaup,** with a general store and motel, an RV park, and a pair of restaurants. The little burg of **Potlatch** is two miles south of Hoodsport on Hwy. 101.

Potlatch State Park

Enjoy camping, diving, clamming, crabbing, and fishing in Hood Canal at Potlatch State Park, three miles south of Hoodsport on Hwy. 101. Have a picnic on the water, or explore the underwater park with scuba gear. The campground ($10 tents, $15 RVs) is open April-Oct. and year-round for day-use. Call (360) 877-5361 for information.

Lake Cushman Area

Lake Cushman was a popular resort area at the turn of the century, offering fishing, hiking, and hunting. By the 1920s, the two lakeside resorts had shut down and the city of Tacoma built a dam on the Skokomish River. When completed, the dam increased the lake's size tenfold to 4,000 acres. Though private summer homes are springing up around the lake, the area still has a decidedly remote feel, thanks in part to its protected neighbor, Olympic National Park, about 10 miles up the road. Call (360) 383-2471 to arrange a tour of the **Tacoma Public Utilities dam** and power plant.

Lake Cushman State Park, seven miles west of Hoodsport, is a popular spot with anglers: cutthroat, Kokanee, and rainbow trout inhabit the lake. Hikers will enjoy the four miles of hiking trails, leading from lake's edge to deep woods. Others come to swim, waterski, and, in winter, cross-country ski. Camp in one of the two campgrounds ($11 tents; $16 RVs). Open early March through September. Call (360) 877-5491 for information, or (800) 452-5687 for reservations ($6 extra).

Cushman Lake Resort, tel. (800) 588-9630, has rustic cabins ($75-90) with kitchens and baths, canoe, jet ski, and boat rentals, a convenience store, plus tent and RV sites.

Follow Lake Cushman Rd. to a "T" at road's end; go left and follow the lake's edge to 70-foot **Cushman Falls,** near the lake's northwest end, about 11 miles from Hoodsport. Or, turn right at the "T," then turn left in another 1.5 miles onto Big Creek Rd. 2419 for six miles to **Big Creek Viewpoint** for a sweeping view to the east. The **Mt. Ellinor Trail** leaves Rd. 2419 at the five-mile point; the trail heads up one mile for a view over Lake Cushman. Trailheads on Olympic National Forest now require a $25 annual **Trail Park Pass,** or a $3 daily parking fee.

The Forest Service's **Big Creek Campground** ($8; open May-Sept.) is nine miles up State Route 119. The road ends after a total of 16 miles at **Staircase Campground,** just west of the lake below the Staircase Rapids of the North Fork of the Skokomish River. This Olympic National Park site has year-round camping for $10. A $10 entrance fee is collected for access to the park May-September.

Hiking trails lead into Olympic National Park from Staircase Trailhead at the head of Lake Cushman, providing a range of hiking options. The **Flapjacks Lake** area is accessed by hiking up the North Fork Skokomish Trail, and then turning up the four-mile side route to the lake. For longer hikes, you can continue up the North Fork Trail, which connects to others, providing a number of lengthy loop-trip options. A steep and challenging three-mile trail switchbacks from the campground to **Wagonwheel Lake** gaining over 3,200 feet en route.

Wonder Mountain Wilderness
The tiny **Wonder Mountain Wilderness** covers just 2,349 acres abutting the southern edge of Olympic National Park. It has no developed trails and is not readily accessible. Wilderness permits are not required. Call the Forest Service office at (360) 877-5254 for more information.

Hoodsport Winery
This small family-run operation produces wine from Puget Sound fruits and berries, and is especially well-known for its rhubarb wine. They also have varietal grape wines, including a surprising cabernet sauvignon. The tasting room is open daily 10 a.m.-6 p.m. Call (360) 877-9894 or (800) 580-9894 for details.

Recreation
Rent dive gear, get air refills, and take classes from **Hood Sport 'N Dive,** a mile north of Hoodsport, tel. (360) 877-6818, or **Mike's Dive Center,** tel. (360) 877-9568. Hood Sport 'N Dive also rents dive kayaks and sea kayaks. Golfers can enjoy the summer sunshine at the **Lake Cushman Golf Course,** four miles west of Hoodsport, tel. (360) 877-5505.

Accommodations
Glen-Ayr Canal Resort, 1.5 miles north of Hoodsport, tel. (360) 877-9522 or (800) 367-9522, is the most elaborate and largest local place, with motel rooms and suites for $58-90 s or d. Two-night minimum on summer weekends. Also here are a jacuzzi, recreation room, and marina. Glen-Ayr primarily attracts retirees—especially the RV crowd—and does not allow kids or tents.

Sunrise Motel and Resort, 24520 Hwy. 100 on the north side of Hoodsport, tel. (360) 877-5301, is a favorite of scuba divers and has rooms for $54-63 d, and dorm spaces for $50 pp for two nights and three days, including free air tank refills.

The old-fashioned **Lilliwaup Motel** in the village of Lilliwaup, tel. (360) 877-5375, charges $45-60 s or d. **Canal Side Resort** in Potlatch, tel. (360) 877-9422, has motel rooms for $45 s or d, and a cabin (sleeps six) with kitchen for $90 d.

Campgrounds
See "Potlatch State Park" and "Lake Cushman Area," above, for public campgrounds near Hoodsport, or stop by the Forest Service office for a complete listing of nearby sites. Several private RV parks are also in the area: **Glen-Ayr**

RV Park, in Hoodsport, tel. (360) 877-9522; **Sunrise Resort,** in Hoodsport, tel. (360) 877-5301; **Canal Side Resort** in Potlatch, tel. (360) 877-9422; **Minerva Beach RV Park,** four miles south of Hoodsport, tel. (360) 877-5145; and **Rest-A-While RV Park,** three miles north of Hoodsport, tel. (360) 877-9474. Rest-A-While also rents dive gear and has a marina.

Food
Hoodsport Inn, tel. (360) 877-6720, has good food three meals a day, with a big choice of local seafood and steal. The similarly named **Hoodsport Marina & Cafe** has an extensive dinner menu, but is best known for their fish and chips and fresh oysters. The waterside location is a real plus.

Other Practicalities
The main summer event is **Celebrate Hoodsport Days,** with a street fair, food, kids' parade, and fireworks on the first full weekend of July. The **Hoodsport Inn,** tel. (360) 877-5526, has live music on weekends.

Stop by the **Hood Canal Ranger Station** in Hoodsport for Olympic National Forest and Olympic National Park info. Hours are Mon.-Fri. 8 a.m.-4:30 p.m. all year, plus Sat.-Sun. 8 a.m.-4:30 p.m. from mid-May to mid-September. Call (360) 877-5254 for details.

Mason County Transit, tel. (360) 427-5033 or (800) 374-3747, has free bus service along Hood Canal and throughout the county.

ELDON TO BRINNON

Not much to Eldon—just a cafe, gas station, shellfish farms, and a diver's resort. The Hamma Hamma River enters Hood Canal here, and a paved road leads to two Forest Service campgrounds on the edge of Olympic National Park. In the winter, bald eagles gather along the banks of the Hamma Hamma to feed on spawning salmon. Brinnon isn't much bigger than Eldon, but this stretch of Hood Canal has a number of interesting attractions. Note: trailheads on Olympic National Forest now require a $25 annual Trail Park Pass, or a $3 daily parking fee.

Sights
In Brinnon, **Whitney Gardens & Nursery,** tel. (360) 796-4411, has seven acres of display gardens that include more than 3,000 rhododendrons, azaleas, and other flowering plants. It is especially stunning from mid-May to mid-June, but you'll find something in bloom all summer. Open daily 9 a.m.-dusk; $1. They also ship plants all over the country; get their mail-order catalog for $4.

Learn how oysters, mussels, and clams are raised at Brinnon's **Shellfish Interpretive Center,** tel. (360) 796-4601, run by the Washington Dept. of Fisheries. In Eldon, the **Hamma Hamma Oyster Farm Seafood Store,** tel. (360) 877-5811, sells fresh oysters.

Dosewallips State Park
A half-mile south of Brinnon on Hwy. 101, Dosewallips State Park covers 425 acres at the base of the Olympic Mountains, offering both fresh- and saltwater activities at the confluence of Hood Canal and the Dosewallips River. Enjoy camping ($10 tents, $15 RVs; open year-round) and fishing for salmon and steelhead in the river, but avoid the clams and oysters—seal poop has contaminated the beaches. Six miles of hiking trails provide access to the forested west end of Dosewallips. Call (360) 796-4415 for information, or (800) 452-5687 for reservations ($6 extra).

Two miles south of Brinnon, **Pleasant Harbor State Park** has a protected dock adjacent to a private marina; but no camping, boat launch, or swimming facilities.

Hamma Hamma Recreation Area
Hamma Hamma Rd. begins two miles north of Eldon and continues to the edge of the Mt. Skokomish Wilderness (see below). **Hamma Hamma Campground** ($8; open May to mid-November) is six miles up the road; continue another two miles to **Lena Creek Campground** ($8; open mid-May through September). **Lena Lake Campground** is a free walk-in campground at this pretty lake, a three mile hike from the Lena Creek Campground. Built by the CCC in the 1930s, the historic **Hamma Hamma Cabin** can be rented for $40. It sleeps six; call the Forest Service at (360) 877-5254 for details.

Webb Lookout is a popular high spot, although it offers no Olympic views, just a broad shot of the canal. Take Hamma Hamma Rd. and turn right on a logging road at about 2.5 miles and follow the signs. Park along the road and hike the half-mile trail to the lookout.

Mount Skokomish Wilderness

Covering a little more than 13,000 acres, the Mt. Skokomish Wilderness occupies steep terrain bordering the western edge of Olympic National Park. The **Putvin Trail** starts from Forest Rd. 25, approximately four miles beyond Lena Creek Campground on Hamma Hamma Rd., and climbs steeply, rising more than 3,700 feet in less than four miles. The trail ends at rock-rimmed Lake of the Angels, just inside the park boundary. The Mt. Skokomish Wilderness is managed by Olympic National Forest, tel. (360) 877-5254. Wilderness permits are not required.

Dosewallips Recreation Area

Scenic Dosewallips Rd. (Forest Rd. 2610) heads west from Brinnon, following the Dosewallips River into the heart of the Olympics, and ending 15 miles later at Dosewallips Campground within Olympic National Park. Look for elk along the way. Approximately three miles up is **Rocky Brook Falls.** The turnoff isn't marked, but look for the bridge and small hydro plant on the right side. It's a short walk to the 80-foot falls, but use care since water levels can change quickly.

The Forest Service's **Elkhorn Campground** ($8; open May-Sept.) is 10 miles up Dosewallips Rd. and has sites right along the river. **Dosewallips Falls** cascades over enormous boulders just inside the Olympic National Park boundary, and the Park Service's **Dosewallips Campground** ($10; open mid-June through September) is another mile up. A trailhead here provides access to the park backcountry via the West Fork and Main Fork Dosewallip trails.

Duckabush Recreation Area

Duckabush Rd. (Rd. 2519) heads west from Hwy. 101 four miles south of Brinnon, providing access to both the Brothers Wilderness and Olympic National Park. Four miles up Duckabush Rd. is the rustic **Interrorem Ranger Cabin,** built in 1907 as headquarters for Olympic National Forest. Today the Forest Service rents this historic four-person cabin for $30; call (360) 877-5254 for details. Two short trails—the **Interrorem**

Nature Trail and **Ranger Hole Trail**—provide access to the densely forested country near the cabin. Another mile up Duckabush Rd. is **Collins Campground** ($8; open May-September). Continue a short distance up Duckabush Rd. to Forest Rd. 2530, and follow it 1.3 miles. From here, **Marhut Falls Trail** climbs three-quarters of a mile to this picturesque waterfall.

Brothers Wilderness

This 16,682-acre wilderness lies within Olympic National Forest and occupies a blip of land on the eastern flank of Olympic National Park. Wilderness permits are not required in the Brothers Wilderness. Only a few developed trails exist in the wilderness, the primary one being the **Duckabush River Trail,** which begins a mile up from the Collins Campground (described above). The trail climbs six miles to the park boundary, with a fine view from Big Hump rock. Once inside the park, you can connect to a maze of other routes through the high country. From Lena Lake Campground on Hamma Hamma Rd., a hiking trail leads uphill to Lena Lake on the edge of the wilderness, and then on to **Upper Lena Lake** inside Olympic National Park. This is a fine overnight backcountry trip. For more information on the wilderness, call (360) 877-5254.

Accommodations

Mike's Beach Resort, 38470 Hwy. 101 (two miles north of Eldon), tel. (360) 877-5324 or (800) 231-5324, is a fun and friendly place with a variety of accommodations, including dorm beds in a hostel with a full kitchen for $20 per person. Cabins with kitchens are $70 d. Tent and RV hookups are also available, and divers can fill tanks at the air station. Great scuba diving at an artificial reef just offshore; ask about the eight-foot octopus.

Bayshore Motel, 31503 Hwy. 101, tel. (360) 796-4220 or (800) 488-4230, has large and comfortable rooms for $42 s or $45-50 d, and a six-person apartment with a full kitchen for $71.

Houseboats for Two, tel. (800) 966-5942, is a newly built barge boat in Pleasant Harbor near Brinnon. The accommodations are luxurious, and include a jacuzzi, fireplace, and pool. A favorite honeymoon spot for $195 d.

Elk Meadows B&B, tel. (360) 796-4886, is a big ranch-style home three miles up Dosewallips Rd. in the heart of elk country. Two guest suites have private baths and a full breakfast; $85 d. No young kids.

Campgrounds

A number of public campgrounds are described above. In addition to these, the Forest Service's **Seal Rock Campground** ($12; open May-Sept.) is just north of Brinnon. **Cove RV Park,** tel. (360) 796-4723, has RV hookups three miles north of Brinnon.

Food

Brinnon's **Half Way House Restaurant,** tel. (360) 796-4715, has a gourmet chef and very reasonable prices on seafood, steak, burgers, and lighter fare. Their Tuesday night five-course dinners are legendary, but be sure to make advance reservations. This is also the place to go for a homemade breakfast (but the smoke can get thick). The **Geoduck Tavern** in Brinnon, tel. (360) 796-4430, is popular for burgers and sometimes has live music on weekends.

Events and Transportation

Brinnon's **Hood Canal ShrimpFest** on the third Saturday of May—the start of the shrimping season—includes an art fair, street dance, boat show, farmers market, and shrimp cooking contests; call (360) 796-4886 for details.

    Jefferson Transit, tel. (360) 345-4777 or (800) 833-6388, has bus service connecting Brinnon with Port Townsend, Sequim, and Poulsbo. **Mason Transit,** tel. (360) 427-5033 or (800) 374-3747, has free bus service south to Shelton and other parts of Mason County.

QUILCENE AREA

Tiny Quilcene has a rough-at-the-edges country feeling reminiscent of Northern California. The compact town has simple homes and trailers, piles of split wood in the yards, and smoke curling from the chimneys. Chainsaw carving is considered high art, and the surrounding cutover landscape looks like a bad haircut. Two miles south is the **Quilcene National Fish Hatchery,** tel. (360) 765-3334, open daily. The small **Quilcene Historical Museum,** is open Fri.-Mon. noon-5 p.m. late April to late September.

Buckhorn Wilderness

Covering 44,258 acres, the Buckhorn Wilderness occupies barren ridges and peaks topping 7,000 feet within Olympic National Forest and bordering on the extensive wilderness within Olympic National Park. The **Mt. Townsend Trail** begins from Forest Rd. 2760 off Rd. 27, northwest of Quilcene. This six-mile route climbs to the top of 6,280-foot Mt. Townsend, providing incredible vistas in all directions. **Big Quilcene Trail** starts at the three-sided shelter 10 miles up Forest Rd. 2750 from Quilcene, and follows the Big Quilcene River into the high country before switchbacking to the summit of Marmot Pass at 6,000 feet. From here, you can continue into Olympic National Park via the Constance Pass Trail. The Big Quilcene is famous for the multitudes of rhododendrons that bloom here in early summer. Call (360) 765-3368 for more information on the Buckhorn Wilderness.

Mount Walker

The most popular viewpoint along Hood Canal is 2,804-foot **Mt. Walker,** five miles south of Quilcene. A narrow gravel road leads to the summit, or you can hike up via a two-mile path through tall Douglas fir forests and a lush understory of huckleberry and rhododendron. The trail (or road) emerges onto a ridge with panoramic views of Seattle, Mt. Rainier, and the Cascades to the east, and the Olympics to the northwest. Bring a lunch to enjoy at the summit picnic area.

Food and Lodging

Prime rib, roast beef, and seafood (including ultra-fresh local oysters) distinguish the **Timber House,** restaurant on Hwy. 101 one-half mile south of Quilcene, tel. (360) 765-3339. Good food, but the service can be very slow.

    Quilcene's **Maple Grove Motel,** tel. (360) 765-3410, charges $40-50 s or d, and has some kitchenettes. The historic **Old Church Inn,** 130 Randolph St., tel. (360) 732-7552, is perfect for families, with room for eight, including a full kitchen. Only $95 for the entire church (sleeps eight).

Campgrounds

Quilcene County Park has in-the-trees tent spaces (no RV hookups) on the south side of

Quilcene. Additional campsites can be found at **Lake Leland Recreation Area** six miles north of Quilcene. The Forest Service's very popular **Falls View Campground** ($10; open May-Sept.) is 3.5 miles south of Quilcene. The half-mile **Falls View Canyon Trail** drops down to the Big Quilcene River from the campground.

Events and Information
The **Olympic Music Festival** is an annual summertime concert series held weekends late June to early September in a turn-of-the-century barn located 10 miles west of Hood Canal Bridge, off Hwy. 104. Concerts feature chamber music in a unique setting: patrons sit on hay bales in the barn or enjoy picnics outside with mountain (and cow) vistas. The Philadelphia String Quartet and guest artists perform these "Concerts in the Barn" one-quarter mile south of Hwy. 104 on Center Road. For tickets and upcoming concerts, call (206) 527-8839.

The Olympic National Forest **Quilcene Ranger District,** 20482 Hwy. 101, tel. (360) 765-3368, has maps and information on local camping and hiking options on both Forest Service and National Park lands.

PORT TOWNSEND AND VICINITY

Standing on the northern tip of Quimper Peninsula—a point off the northeast corner of the Olympic Peninsula—Port Townsend (pop. 7,700) is best known for its generous helping of Victorian architecture. It has more authentic remnants of this period than any other town north of San Francisco, including some 70 buildings on the National Register of Historic Places. Wealthy merchants of the late 1800s built these beauties, many of which have been restored and are located in one of the town's two national historic districts. Behind town rise the perpetually snow-covered Olympic Mountains; out front lies the ship-filled Strait of Juan de Fuca.

Given its Victorian opulence, one might expect Port Townsend to be solely focused on tourism, but this is still a genuine town with much to see and explore. Many folks consider it one of the most interesting and beautiful towns in Washington.

HISTORY

As the main port of entry to Puget Sound and the first townsite on the Olympic Peninsula, Port Townsend started off with a bang. Platted in 1852, by the late 1880s the town prospered as a busy seaport; more than a few men made their fortunes here. As the official port of entry for the Pacific Northwest, Port Townsend hosted consulates and agencies from Chile, Sweden, Norway, Germany, France, Great Britain, and Hawaii during its prime. It was supposed to become the New York City of the Pacific Northwest, and elaborate, ostentatious Victorian mansions sprouted atop the hills. Considerably less grandiose accommodations and businesses lined the waterfront, including more than a few saloons and bordellos.

The cornerstone of this speculative boom was the anticipation that Port Townsend would be the end point for the Union Pacific's transcontinental railroad; its location was far better than the Seattle area for sailing ships—the wind seems to be always blowing. The dream went bust when the advent of steamships made travel in Puget Sound easier, allowing the railroad to opt for a shorter Tacoma terminus. History seemed to pass Port Townsend by, as Seattle and Tacoma siphoned off most of the town's shipping, and a financial depression gripped the nation, causing many of the beautiful mansions to be abandoned. Eventually they were converted into rooming houses and apartments, and only later rescued.

Over the years, military bases and a pulp and paper mill restored Port Townsend's economic stability; the largest employer is still the Port Townsend Paper Company Mill at Glen Cove (call 360-379-2064 for tours). The away-from-it-all location attracted a hippie crowd in the 1970s, and today tourism accounts for much of Port Townsend's prosperity. This tourism is fed by a gorgeous setting that features commanding views over Admiralty Inlet and the nearby Olympic Mountains, by the abundance of Victorian mansions that have been transformed into

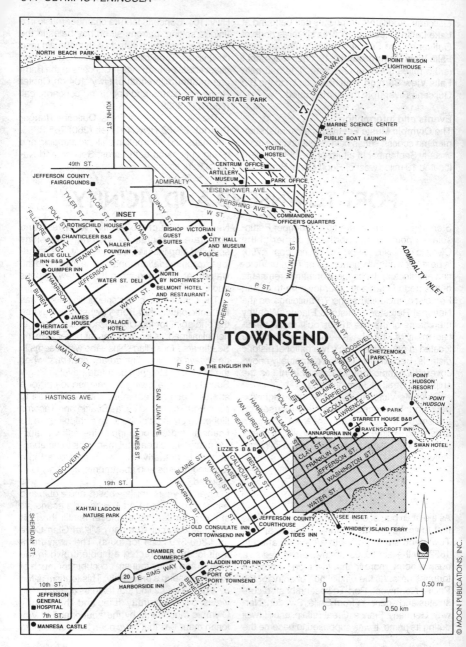

PORT TOWNSEND

NORTH BEACH PARK

POINT WILSON LIGHTHOUSE

DEFENSE WAY

FORT WORDEN STATE PARK

KUHN ST.

MARINE SCIENCE CENTER

PUBLIC BOAT LAUNCH

49th ST.

YOUTH HOSTEL

JEFFERSON COUNTY FAIRGROUNDS

CENTRUM OFFICE

TAYLOR ST.

POLK ST.

QUINCY ST.

ADMIRALTY

ARTILLERY MUSEUM

PARK OFFICE

EISENHOWER AVE.

PERSHING AVE.

W ST.

COMMANDING OFFICER'S QUARTERS

ADMIRALTY INLET

INSET

FILLMORE ST.

TYLER ST.

POLK ST.

ADAMS ST.

QUINCY ST.

ROTHSCHILD HOUSE

CHANTICLEER B&B

CLAY

FRANKLIN

HALLER FOUNTAIN

BISHOP VICTORIAN GUEST SUITES

CITY HALL AND MUSEUM

BLUE GULL INN B&B

QUIMPER INN

WALNUT ST.

POLICE

WATER ST. DELI

NORTH BY NORTHWEST

P ST.

VAN BUREN ST.

HARRISON ST.

JEFFERSON ST.

WATER ST.

BELMONT HOTEL AND RESTAURANT

JAMES HOUSE

HERITAGE HOUSE

PALACE HOTEL

UMATILLA ST.

CHERRY ST.

JACKSON ST.

ROOSEVELT ST.

CHETZEMOKA PARK

F ST.

THE ENGLISH INN

TAYLOR ST.

ADAMS ST.

MADISON ST.

MONROE ST.

POINT HUDSON RESORT

HASTINGS AVE.

SAN JUAN AVE.

HAINES ST.

TYLER ST.

POLK ST.

FILLMORE ST.

HARRISON ST.

VAN BUREN ST.

PIERCE ST.

QUINCY ST.

BLAINE

GARFIELD

LINCOLN ST.

LAWRENCE ST.

POINT HUDSON

PARK

STARRETT HOUSE B&B

ANNAPURNA INN

RAVENSCROFT INN

DISCOVERY RD.

BLAINE ST.

KEARNEY ST.

WALKER ST.

SCOTT ST.

CASS ST.

CALHOUN ST.

BENTON ST.

LIZZIE'S B&B

CLAY ST.

FRANKLIN ST.

JEFFERSON ST.

WASHINGTON ST.

WATER ST.

SWAN HOTEL

19th ST.

KAH TAI LAGOON NATURE PARK

SHERIDAN ST.

SEE INSET

JEFFERSON COUNTY COURTHOUSE

OLD CONSULATE INN

PORT TOWNSEND INN

TIDES INN

WHIDBEY ISLAND FERRY

CHAMBER OF COMMERCE

20 E. SIMS WAY

ALADDIN MOTOR INN

PORT OF PORT TOWNSEND

HARBORSIDE INN

10th ST.

JEFFERSON GENERAL HOSPITAL

7th ST.

MANRESA CASTLE

0   0.50 mi

0   0.50 km

MOON

© MOON PUBLICATIONS, INC.

lavish B&Bs, and by the plentiful galleries, shops, and gourmet restaurants. Today the citizens of Port Townsend are a blend of blue-collar mill-workers, post-hippie new agers, and wealthy newcomers and retirees. Visitors will be pleased to discover a fascinating real town, not a Victorian-era Disneyland.

Parking can be a nightmare on summer weekends; avoid the hassles (and parking tickets) by parking at the Park & Ride stop on the south side of town and hopping aboard the free **People Mover** shuttle buses that cruise downtown.

SIGHTS

Port Townsend's main attractions are its historic late 19th-century homes and businesses, along with impressive Fort Worden State Park. Downtown's main boulevard, Water St., consists of stout brick buildings filled with fine galleries, restaurants, and shops selling antiques, books, clothing, wines, and gifts.

One of the more distinctive town sights is the **Haller Fountain,** which features a bronze, scantily clad maiden emerging from a shell that is supported by water-spraying cherubs and fish. Created for the Mexican exhibit at the 1893 Chicago Exhibition, the fountain was later donated to the city by Theodore N. Haller "in memory of early pioneers."

Port Townsend is still very much a seafaring town. Its Port Hudson Harbor is jammed with yachts, and quite a few boatbuilding businesses are based nearby. Of particular note is the **Northwest School of Wooden Boatbuilding,** 251 Otto St., tel. (360) 385-4948, where several-day classes and six- and nine-month programs develop skills through intensive classes and hands-on projects.

Historic Tours
Stop by the chamber of commerce (2437 E. Sims Way) to pick up a tour map of historic downtown and other parts of Port Townsend. Guided tours of the waterfront, saloons, and historic homes are also available from **Sidewalk Tours,** 820 Tyler St., tel. (360) 385-1967, and **Kathy Hill Step On Tours,** tel. (360) 385-4356.

Historic Home Tours are held the third weekend in September; owners of private Victorian

residences open their doors to the public. Call the visitor information center for tickets; tel. (360) 385-2722.

Uptown
A second section of historic Port Townsend, "Uptown," covers a block or so of Lawrence St. near Taylor St. and is where you're more likely to meet people who actually live in town. It was originally created as a turn-of-the-century shopping district for the genteel ladies living in the hilltop mansions, a place to avoid the bawdy waterfront shopping district ("the most wicked city north of San Francisco" in the 1880s). Today, uptown's mansions are elaborate B&Bs, and a collection of offbeat stores caters to the Birkenstock-and-tie-dyed generation. You'll discover great views across Admiralty Inlet from a tiny park at Monroe and Clay Streets.

Museums
Housed in the city's 1891 City Hall Complex, **Jefferson County Historical Society Museum,** 210 Madison St., tel. (360) 385-1003, this excellent museum rambles over three floors of boat exhibits and models, intricate Indian baskets, button and bottle collections, a Victorian bedroom, and even two buffalo-horn and bearskin chairs from an old photo studio. Downstairs is the old (and cold) city jail, used until the 1940s. The museum is open Mon.-Sat. 11 a.m.-4 p.m. and Sunday 1-4 p.m. year-round; $2 adults, or $5 families.

There's also a small museum inside the lobby of the **post office** at 1322 Washington Street. During the 1880s, this imposing stone building served as the Customs House, the port of entry for all international traffic into Puget Sound.

Another building of interest is the **Jefferson County Courthouse** standing high on a hill at Jefferson and Walker Streets. Built in 1892, this red brick building is one of Washington's oldest courthouses and is notable for the 100-foot-tall clocktower that serves as a beacon to mariners. **Bergstrom's Antique and Classic Automobiles,** 809 Washington St., tel. (360) 385-5061, has a showroom filled with classic cars.

Rothschild House State Park
The Rothschild House on Franklin and Taylor Streets was built in 1868 by D.C.H. Rothschild, a

Port Townsend merchant and a distant relative of Germany's famous Rothschild banking family. Notable for its simplicity—in contrast to Port Townsend's many flamboyant Victorian-era homes—the house belonged to the family for nearly 90 years. The last remaining son, Eugene, donated it to the state in 1959. Now restored, with much of the original furniture, wallpaper, and carpeting, the house is surrounded by herb and flower gardens and is open to the public daily 10 a.m.-5 p.m. April-Oct., and weekends 10 a.m.-5 p.m. in November (closed Dec.-March). Entry is $2; call (360) 385-2722 for more information on this, Washington's smallest state park.

Manresa Castle

The Manresa Castle is an 1892 mansion at 7th and Sheridan that began its life as a home to Port Townsend's first mayor, Charles Eisenbeis. A native of Prussia, Eisenbeis made a fortune supplying crackers and bread for sailing ships and spent a small fortune building this sumptu-

DON PITCHER

Manresa Castle

ous hilltop home in the style of a medieval European castle. After his death in 1902, his wife remarried and moved away. In 1925, the Jesuits purchased the castle, added a new wing, and used it as a training college called Manresa Hall (the name came from Manresa, Spain, where the Jesuit order originated). The Jesuits departed in 1968, and the building was turned into a hotel. Originally, Manresa had only one bathroom per floor, but when the film *An Officer and a Gentleman* was being shot, the Hollywood crew ran out of rooms at other hotels and motels. Their contracts called for a bathroom for each room, so the studio made a deal with Manresa's owner: they advanced him money against the rent, and it was used to build the 43 bathrooms of today. Tours of the castle are free. A restaurant and lounge are on the premises, and an attractive rose and rhododendron garden provides a quiet place to enjoy the vista of Port Townsend and Admiralty Inlet.

City Parks

Chetzemoka Park on Admiralty Inlet at Jackson and Roosevelt Streets remembers Chief Chetzemoka, friend to the town's earliest settlers (he was also known, inexplicably, by the name "Duke of York"). Today the small, shady park offers eight flower gardens, picnicking, a bandstand, and beach access. The wooden arbor is covered with some 25 varieties of roses. Birdwatchers may be interested in **Kah Tai Lagoon Nature Park** at 12th St. near Sims Way. It encompasses 85 acres of wetlands, grasslands, and woodlands, plus 2.5 miles of trails.

Ann Starrett Mansion

Easily the most opulent Victorian structure in Port Townsend, the Ann Starrett Mansion is a National Historic Landmark and a favorite B&B. Take a tour ($2 adults, $1 kids), available daily noon-3 p.m., or stay here to enjoy the luxury up close. Step inside this stunning 12-room mansion to learn how it was built in 1889 as George Starrett's wedding present for his new wife, Ann. The rooms are furnished with period antiques and offer outstanding views, but the real treat is the three-story circular staircase capped by a domed ceiling. Dormer windows in the dome admit light that illuminates a different red ruby stone for each season of the year. Behind is a carriage house that has also been converted into B&B accommodations. Call (360) 385-3205 or (800) 321-0644 for information on the mansion or B&B reservations.

Old Fort Townsend State Park

Four miles south of town, 377-acre Old Fort Townsend State Park, tel. (360) 385-3595, has campsites and seven miles of hiking trails through tall firs, sloping down to a 150-foot cliff along Port Townsend Bay. The park is open mid-April to mid-September only. A fort was established here in 1856 to guard against possible Indian attacks, and in 1859 troops were sent from the fort to assist in the San Juan Island boundary dispute commonly known as "The Pig War." Fort Townsend saw sporadic activity throughout the 1800s until a fire—started by an exploding kerosene lamp—destroyed the barracks in 1895. The fort was decommissioned but was used during WW II as an enemy munitions defusing station. In 1958 it was turned over to the State Parks Commission. A short self-guided historical walk starts at the display board near the park entrance.

FORT WORDEN STATE PARK

History

Capping Point Wilson—the peninsula separating the Strait of Juan de Fuca from Admiralty Inlet—Fort Worden State Park served as one of the "Iron Triangle" of forts protecting the entrance to Puget Sound. All three forts (the others were Fort Flagler on Marrowstone Island, and Fort Casey on Whidbey Island) were built at the turn of the century as a first line of defense for the vital Bremerton Naval Ship Yard and the cities of Puget Sound. Fort Worden is named after John L. Worden, the Union commander during the Monitor-Merrimac battle on March 9, 1862; it's the only Army fort named for a Navy man.

Fort Worden's guns were never fired in battle, and advances in military technology made them obsolete almost as soon as they were in place. Many of the guns were pulled out and shipped to Europe during WW I, and in WW II the fort served as the command center to monitor any Japanese submarine activity in Puget Sound and to coordinate coastal defenses. After the army left in 1953, Fort Worden served as a state detention center before becoming a state park in 1973.

Fort Worden Today

Fort Worden is on the National Register of Historic Places and houses a collection of turn-of-the-century homes, historical Army barracks, a dozen massive gun emplacements (the big guns are long gone), and hidden bunkers. Its modern facilities include a campground, boat launch, tennis courts, underwater scuba-diving park, rhododendron garden, hiking trails, refurbished officers' homes, and a hostel. If the place seems familiar, it may be because much of the movie *An Officer and a Gentleman* was filmed here.

The fort's old barracks and command buildings line the north side of a central parade ground, and the more comfortable officer's row homes form a picket fence to the south. The **Commanding Officer's House** is nearest the shoreline and contains Victorian furnishings representing the way its inhabitants lived. It's open daily 10 a.m.-5 p.m. April-October 15, and by special appointment the rest of the year. Take a self-guided tour on weekend afternoons for $1.

Fort Worden has a large conference center and a fine restaurant, but its most popular civilian role is as home for the **Centrum Foundation,** a nonprofit center for the arts housed in one of the old barracks.

One of the old barracks buildings now houses the **Coast Artillery Museum,** tel. (360) 385-0373, where you'll learn how the enormous gun batteries out on the coastal bluffs worked. Displays include a scale model of one of the batteries, photos of the big guns in action, old military uniforms, and various WW I and WW II artifacts. The museum is open daily 11 a.m.-4 p.m. in July and August; and Sat.-Sun. 11 a.m.-4 p.m. Sept.-Aug. and March-June (closed December and January). No charge.

Also at the park is the **Port Townsend Marine Science Center,** tel. (360) 385-5582, located on the dock. "Wet tables" offer intimate, hands-on relationships with local sea creatures; beach walks, evening slide shows and lectures are also offered. Hours are Tues.-Sun. noon-6 p.m. from mid-June to early September, and weekends only noon-4 p.m. early Sept.-Oct. and April to mid-June (closed Nov.-March).

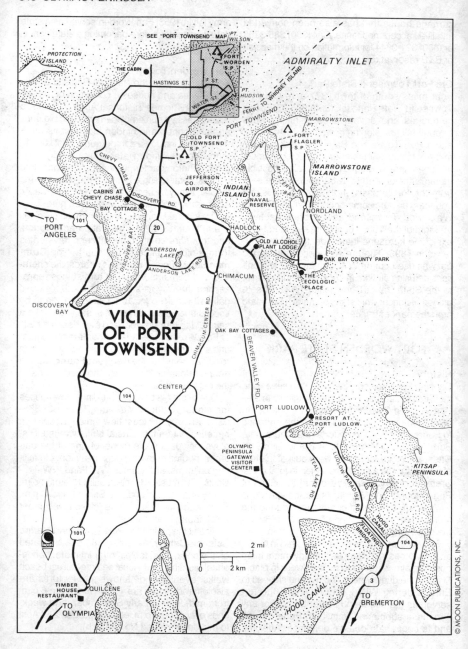

Lighthouse and Gun Batteries

Built in 1917, the **Point Wilson Lighthouse** (closed to the public) stands on a sandy spit of land jutting into the Strait of Juan de Fuca. The beach here makes for wonderful sunup or sundown strolls, with dramatic Mt. Baker seeming to rise directly across the water, and a constant parade of ship traffic in between. Several old gun emplacements and a watchtower are near the lighthouse, but the most interesting are atop **Artillery Hill.** Get here by walking up the gated road that begins behind the noncommissioned officers homes, or by walking uphill behind the beachside campground. A series of roads lead through the fascinating old gun emplacements and bunkers; get a walking tour brochure at the park office before heading uphill.

ACCOMMODATIONS AND CAMPING

Port Townsend has some of the finest (and most expensive) lodging choices in the state, most notably the plethora of old Victorian homes that have been turned into luxurious bed and breakfasts, along with a dozen or so motels and hotels, and an equal number of cabins and guest houses. Port Townsend is an extremely popular place to visit, and reservations are advised, especially in the summer and on weekends; popular B&Bs may book up months ahead during festival weekends. The chamber of commerce, tel. (360) 385-2722, keeps track of local accommodations and can tell you who has rooms available.

See "Sights" (above) for information on the must-see **Manresa Castle.** For a piece of Hollywood trivia, stay at **Tides Inn,** where parts of *An Officer and a Gentleman* were filmed. Room 10 is the luxury suite where you can pretend your partner is (take your pick) Richard Gere or Deborah Winger. Of considerably less appeal may be room 12, where the shower hanging scene was filmed. The **Palace Hotel** is a beautifully restored boutique hotel with antique furnishings and an old-world charm.

Hostel

The **Olympic Port Townsend AYH Hostel,** tel. (360) 385-0655, is located in a former barracks building at beautiful Fort Worden. In addition to the dorm facilities, the 28-bed hostel has kitchen facilities, a common room, and five couples rooms. It's located right in the midst of the summer festival action at Fort Worden and has all-you-can-eat pancake breakfasts. Reservations are strongly advised in summer months, especially for the couples' rooms. The hostel is open year-round, but guests must be out 9:30 a.m.-5 p.m. Rates are $12-15 pp in dorms, $32-38 d in couples rooms.

Bed and Breakfasts

While some towns have a few old homes turned into B&Bs, Port Townsend seems to burst at the seams with wonderful homes from its late 19th-century glory days. Many of these have been lovingly restored and filled with antiques. Unless otherwise noted, all B&Bs listed below serve a full breakfast and do not allow young children. One of the most impressive of these, **Ann Starrett Mansion,** 744 Clay St., tel. (360) 385-3205 or (800) 321-0644, has nine rooms ($80-175 s or d) in the 1889 mansion and two in a separate cottage ($165-225 s or d). Gourmet breakfasts are served.

Another lovely Victorian B&B, **The Old Consulate Inn,** 313 Walker St., tel. (360) 385-6753 or (800) 300-6753, overlooks Port Townsend from atop a high bluff, providing panoramic mountain and water views in comfortably elegant surroundings. The inn was built in 1889 by F.W. Hastings, son of Port Townsend's founding father Loren B. Hastings, and served as the office of the German Consul (hence the "Old Consulate" name) in the early part of this century. Enjoy the fireplaces in two parlors, hone your skills in the large billiard and game room, or play the grand piano and antique organ. A gazebo encloses the jacuzzi. Eight guest rooms all have private bath. A gourmet breakfast is served; $96-195 s or d.

Three short blocks from downtown, the elegant **Ravenscroft Inn,** 533 Quincy St., tel. (360) 385-2784 or (800) 782-2691, features a wide verandas with sound and mountain views in a custom-built B&B. The eight guest rooms have private baths, and two suites with fireplaces and soaking tubs. Owner Leah Hommel creates elegant gourmet breakfasts in this great getaway place. $50-158 s or $67-175 d.

James House, 1238 Washington St., tel. (360) 385-1238 or (800) 385-1238, a Victorian

PORT TOWNSEND MOTELS AND HOTELS

Accommodations are arranged from least to most expensive. Rates drop 20% or so in the winter months, and some places have lower weekday rates. See the text for descriptions of Port Townsend's hostel and bed and breakfasts.

INEXPENSIVE

Ginger's Guest House; 841 K St.; tel. (360) 385-1587; $37 s, $46 d; one guest room with private entrance

North Beach Rental; 510 56th St.; tel. (360) 385-1621; $50 s or d; apartment unit with kitchenette

Point Hudson Resort; Pt. Hudson; tel. (360) 385-2828 or (800) 826-3854; $49-79 s or d; family place, spartan rooms (some with shared baths), beachside location, no phones, a few TVs

The Water Street Hotel; 635 Water St.; tel. (360) 385-5467 or (800) 735-9810; $50-125 s or d; nicely renovated 1889 hotel, continental breakfast, AAA approved

Belmont Hotel and Restaurant; 925 Water St.; tel. (360) 385-3007; $59-79 s or d; 1885 Victorian inn

MODERATE

Harborside Inn; 330 Benedict St.; tel. (360) 385-7909 or (800) 942-5960; $64-84 s or d; outdoor pool, jacuzzi, continental breakfast, harbor views, kitchenettes available, AAA approved

Palace Hotel; 1004 Water St.; tel. (360) 385-0773 or (800) 962-0741; $65-149 s or d (some rooms with shared bath); gorgeous 1889 inn with antique-furnished rooms, continental breakfast, microwaves and fridges, AAA approved

Manresa Castle; 7th and Sheridan; tel. (360) 385-5750 or (800) 732-1281 (Washington); $70-175 s or d; unique 1892 castle-hotel, antique furnishings, bay views, continental breakfast, AAA approved

Ft. Worden Recreation Housing; Ft. Worden State Park; tel. (360) 385-4730; $74-312 for historic Officer's Row homes (1-11 bedrooms)

mansion built in 1889, was the first B&B in the Northwest (opened in 1973) and is still going strong. Several of the 12 antique-furnished guest rooms offer commanding views of the town, and most have private baths; rates are $60-100 s or $75-165 d. There's also a secluded bungalow with two beds for $165 d.

Built in 1888, **Quimper Inn B&B,** 1306 Franklin, tel. (360) 385-1060 or (800) 557-1060, is a distinctive three-story home with a two-level porch and five elaborately furnished guest rooms with shared or private baths; $80-140 s or d.

Holly Hill House, 611 Polk St., tel. (360) 385-5619 or (800) 435-1454, built in 1872, has been beautifully renovated to provide five guest rooms, each with a private bath. The home is surrounded by tall holly and elm trees; $76-125 s or d.

The English Inn, 718 F St., tel. (360) 385-5302 or (800) 254-5302, is a large, edge-of-town Italianate Victorian home built in 1885. This very nice B&B stands on a hill, with a garden, gazebo, and outdoor jacuzzi on the patio. All five guest rooms have small private baths, and even Internet terminals; $85-105 s or d.

Annapurna Inn, 538 Adams, tel. (360) 385-2909 or (800) 868-2662, is a combination B&B and retreat center close to the far-more-elaborate Ann Starrett Mansion. The house (built in 1881) has cozy but unpretentious rooms. A sauna/steam bath is included, along with a vegetarian breakfast. Many guests also take advantage of the foot reflexology, cranio/sacral massage, and yoga (extra fee for these). Room rates are $80-128 s or d. Their two-night retreat packages are $250-385 s or $420-556 d, including massage, yoga, and reflexology.

A Victorian B&B, **Lizzie's,** 731 Pierce St., tel. (360) 385-4168 or (800) 700-4168, has seven

Studio Loft; 913 L St.; tel. (360) 385-5027; $75 s or d; studio apartment, Olympic Mt. views

Aladdin Motor Inn; 2333 Washington St.; tel. (360) 385-3747 or (800) 281-3747; $80 s or d; continental breakfast, microwave and fridge

EXPENSIVE

Bishop Victorian Guest Suites; 714 Washington St.; tel. (360) 385-6122 or (800) 824-4738; $89-99 s, $89-139 d; kitchens, continental breakfast, AAA approved

SalmonBerry Farm; 2404 35th St.; tel. (360) 385-1517; $90 for up to six; three-room suite in the country, make-your-own breakfast, kids welcome

Discovery Gardens Cottage; 2607 Haines; tel. (360) 385-4313; $95 s or d; cottage in pastoral location, bicycles, make-your-own breakfast, kids welcome

The Cabin B&B; 839 N. Jacob Miller Rd.; tel. (360) 385-5571; $95 d, cozy and fun cabin in the woods, private beach, kitchen, hot tub, champagne and make-yourself breakfast, no children

Bay Cottage; 4346 S. Discovery Rd. (six miles west of Port Townsend); tel. (360) 385-2035; $95 s or d; two oceanside cottages, private beach, kitchens, children welcome

Morgan Hill Guest Cottage; 608 Roosevelt; tel. (360) 385-2536; $100 for up to four; modern cottage with loft, kitchenette, make-your-own breakfast

Port Townsend Inn; 2020 Washington St.; tel. (360) 385-2211 or (800) 216-4985; $68-98 s or d; dockside location, large indoor pool and jacuzzi, continental breakfast, kitchenettes available, AAA approved

The Cabins at Chevy Chase; 3710 S. Discovery Rd.; tel. (360) 385-0704; $75-130 s or d; cabins near golf course, swimming pool, some rooms with fireplaces and kitchens

Tides Inn; 1807 Water St.; tel. (360) 385-0595 or (800) 822-8696; $75-135 s or d; used in scenes from *An Officer and a Gentleman,* some private docks and jacuzzis, kitchenettes available

The Swan Hotel; 222 Monroe St.; tel. (360) 385-1718 or (800) 776-1718; attractive and cozy cottages ($90-100), suites ($105-135), and a penthouse units ($275-350); fridges in rooms

---

guest rooms, all with private bath. Enjoy the two parlors with fireplaces, leather sofas, library, and grand piano; $70-135 s or d.

Chanticleer B&B, 1208 Franklin St., tel. (360) 385-6239 or (800) 858-9421, is an 1876 Victorian home with five guest rooms offering private baths. $90-140 s or d.

An 1868 Victorian Gothic home is now the **Blue Gull Inn B&B,** 1310 Clay St., tel. (360) 385-6944 or (888) 700-0205, with six guest rooms and private baths; $85-175 s or d.

Another enjoyable place is **The Commander's Guest House,** 400 Hudson St., tel. (360) 385-1778 or (888) 385-1778, a 1934 Colonial Revival style home at Point Hudson Resort. The three guest rooms with private baths are $90-135 s or d.

Bowen's Inn B&B, 1110 Jackman St., tel. (360) 379-1999 or (800) 586-8583, is a spacious contemporary home with panoramic views. The

five guest rooms all have private baths, and a gourmet breakfast is served; $124-151 s or d.

Officers' Quarters

An interesting alternative lodging—especially for families and groups—is to rent one of the former homes of officers and noncommissioned officers in Fort Worden. Most of the 32 houses have been completely refurbished with reproductions of Victorian furniture, brass headboards, Tiffany lamps, and new carpeting. All of these have full kitchens and a wonderful in-the-park location, but no TVs. Meals are available at the cafeteria by prior arrangement. Rates begin at $74 per night for a one-bedroom apartment unit and go up to $312 for an 11-bedroom barracks. Because of their popularity—especially during summer festivals—reservations for these houses should be made far in advance; call (360) 385-4730 for details.

James House (1881) was the Northwest's first bed and breakfast.

DIANNE BOULERICE LYONS

Campgrounds

Fort Worden State Park has 50 year-round beachside campsites and another 30 near the conference area. All sites have electricity, sewer, and water hookups, so even folks in tents get charged $16; showers are available. Reservations ($6 extra) are available by mail or in person: call the park at (360) 385-4730 for details.

Four miles south of town, **Old Fort Townsend State Park,** tel. (360) 385-3595, has shady campsites ($10 tents, $15 RVs) under tall firs along Port Townsend Bay. It also has showers. The campground is open mid-April to mid-September only. See **Fort Flagler State Park** for another camping option.

RVers can park at the private **Point Hudson Resort** on the beach, tel. (360) 385-2828 or (800) 826-3854, or the **Jefferson County Fairgrounds,** tel. (360) 385-1013.

FOOD

It's hard *not* to find a good meal in Port Townsend; just walk along Water St. till something strikes your fancy. It's all there, from pizza-by-the-slice to gourmet Northwest cuisine.

Breakfast and Lunch

Coho Cafe, 1044 Lawrence St., tel. (360) 379-1050, is a tiny Uptown place serving an eclectic breakfast, lunch, and dinner menu of vegetarian specials, black bean chili, frittatas, and fruit blasts. **Salal Cafe,** 634 Water St., tel. (360) 385-6532, is a simple down-home eatery with a post-hippie flavor. Come here for the outstanding omelettes and blintzes, as well as earthy lunches. **McKenzie's** 221 Taylor, tel. (360) 385-3961, is another downtown spot for quick lunches and baked goods.

Stop by **Sea J's Cafe,** 2501 Washington St., tel. (360) 385-6312, for the best fish and chips in town. Great sub sandwiches to go at **Jordini's,** 924 Washington St., tel. (360) 385-2037, and the best local burgers are at **Jake's Original Grill,** 600 Simms Way, tel. (360) 385-5356.

Bakeries, Sweets, and Espresso

Bread & Roses Bakery, 230 Quincy, tel. (360) 385-1044, cranks out delicious pastries, along with espresso and from-scratch breads, soups, and salads. **Elevated Ice Cream,** 627 Water St., tel. (360) 385-1156, has Italian ices, chocolates, and homemade ice-cream. A few blocks away, **Nifty Fifty's,** 817 Water St., tel. (360) 385-1931, is a fun waterside malt-shop with all-American ice cream sodas, malts, and sundaes. The 1952 jukebox plays Elvis hits. Jump ahead 40 years to **Cafe Internet,** 2021 E. Sims Way, tel. (360) 385-9773, where Internet access (for a fee) comes with your cappuccino.

Northwest Cuisine

Sandwiched between a laundromat and a Radio Shack store at 2330 Washington St., **Lonny's Restaurant,** tel. (360) 385-0700, is a big surprise. Step inside to find an elegant atmosphere, gourmet pasta, and charbroiled seafood and meats. Dinner entrees are $15-19. Highly recommended.

Fountain Cafe, 920 Washington St., tel. (360) 385-1364, serves natural foods, pastas, and oysters in a tiny backstreet location. It's a very popular place, so be ready to wait for a table on summer weekends; open for lunch and dinner daily.

Silverwater Cafe on the corner of Washington and Taylor Streets, tel. (360) 385-6448, is well known for fresh and reasonably priced pasta, vegetarian entrees, and seafood served in a bright and airy space. Dinner entrees are $9-15. Out at Fort Worden, Blackberries, tel. (360) 385-1461, is also popular for Northwest cuisine. Open May to mid-September.

International Eats

If you're a fan of spicy Thai food, beat tracks to Khu Larb Thai, 225 Adams St., tel. (360) 385-5023. Prices are reasonable, and the food—including a dozen vegetarian dishes—is delicious and authentic.

Lanza's Ristorante/Pizzaria, uptown at 1020 Lawrence St., tel. (360) 385-6221, has several kinds of excellent pizzas, plus outstanding home-cookin' in the form of antipasto and pastas. A simpler—but surprisingly good—choice is to get a slice and a Coke at Waterfront Pizza, 951 Water St., tel. (360) 385-6629. A good place to hang out with local high schoolers. For a fast and massive south-of-the-border fix (made by Asian owners) hop over to Burrito Depot, 609 Washington St., tel. (360) 385-5856.

Markets

Whole Foods Grocery Coop, on Lawrence St. in Uptown, is a throwback to the '60s with quality organic and natural foods. On the opposite side of the street, but just a short distance away, is Aldrich's Grocery, 940 Lawrence St., tel. (360) 385-0500. There's a small-town country store feel here, but you'll also find gourmet specialties and a big wine selection. The deli here (Sally's) makes fantastic baked goods and the best soups anywhere around.

Find fresh fish and other seafood at Key City Fish Co., tel. (360) 385-7841 or (800) 617-3474, right next to the ferry terminal. They'll pack your fish in ice to take home aboard the ferry.

Get baked goods, organic produce, crafts, and flowers at the Port Townsend Farmers Market, held downtown every Saturday 9:00

a.m.-1 p.m., mid-April through October. A second farmers market takes place Uptown on Wednesday 5:30-8:30 p.m. May-August.; tel. (360) 379-4939.

ENTERTAINMENT AND EVENTS

Centrum Foundation

Port Townsend's calendar is jam-packed with activities, many of which are sponsored by the nonprofit Centrum Foundation, located at Fort Worden State Park. Founded in 1976, Centrum organizes major festivals and events each year both downtown as well as at the performing arts pavilion (an old balloon hanger) at the fort. These events permit you and thousands of other guests to see and hear performances by some of the country's finest jazz, bluegrass, blues, and classical musicians, along with folk dance festivals, plays, and seminars, plus readings by well-known authors. For a schedule of upcoming events, contact Centrum Foundation at (360) 385-3102 or (800) 733-3608.

Events

The Rhododendron Festival (third week in May) features a big Saturday parade, dances, antique and art shows, a carnival, rhododendron displays, and the crowning of the Rhododendron Queen, whose handprint and signature are captured in the cement sidewalk downtown. The Port Townsend Blues Festival comes to town on the last weekend of June. July is a particularly busy month, with the Port Townsend Writers' Conference (a mid-July Centrum event), the Festival of American Fiddle Tunes (fourth weekend of July), and Jazz Port Townsend (last weekend in July). The jazz festival is a Centrum event that attracts nationally acclaimed performers.

The second weekend in August is reserved for the Jefferson County Fair, the old-fashioned kind with livestock shows, 4-H displays, and a mud race. Then comes the Marrowstone Music Festival (last three weekends in August), and the Wooden Boat Festival (second weekend in September), an educational affair with displays, lectures, and classes.

Early October brings the Kinetic Sculpture Race to Port Townsend; human-powered me-

wooden boats at Port Townsend

PAUL BOYER

chanical sculptures race over land *and water* to the finish. If you're in town on the first Saturday in December, you'll be able to join the fun as Santa arrives by ferry, and people gather to sing carols on Water St. and watch the **tree lighting ceremony.**

Live Music and Theater

The Public House Grill & Ales, 1038 Water St., tel. (360) 385-9708, has live music on weekends, and good pub food, especially for lunch. For C&W or rock tunes, try the **Hilltop Tavern,** 2510 Sims Way, tel. (360) 385-0101.

Rose Theatre 385 Taylor St., tel. (360) 385-1089, is a delightful and lovingly restored old-time moviehouse with nightly showings. The **Key City Players** put on plays at 419 Washington St. throughout the year, tel. (360) 385-7396. The **Port Townsend Orchestra,** tel. (360) 732-6898, gives four performances between October and May.

RECREATION

On the Water

Kayak Port Townsend, tel. (360) 385-6240, offers sea kayak rentals and trips locally, along with longer tours to the San Juans and Nootka Sound. The 1913 schooner *Adventuress* sails on voyages of all lengths throughout the summer and fall; call (360) 379-0438 for their schedule of trips. **Brisa Charters,** tel. (360) 376-3264, offers day and sunset sails.

Anderson Lake State Park, south of Port Townsend on Anderson Lake Rd. off Hwy. 20, is an isolated lake surrounded by trees. No camping or swimming, but it's a popular place to fish for cutthroat and rainbow trout. The public **swimming pool** is at Walker and Blaine Streets, tel. (360) 385-7665.

Other Recreation

Rent mountain, touring, and tandem bikes from **P.T. Cyclery,** 100 Tyler St., tel. (360) 385-6470. You can also rent bikes, sea kayaks, and camping gear from **Sport Townsend,** 1044 Water St., tel. (360) 379-9711. **Port Townsend Athletic Club,** 229 Monroe St., tel. (360) 385-6560, has exercise and weight rooms, racquetball courts, yoga and aerobic classes, and a sauna and jacuzzi.

Local golf courses include **Chevy Chase Golf Club,** 7401 Cape George Rd., tel. (360) 385-0704, and the nine-hole **Port Townsend Golf Club,** 1948 Blaine St., tel. (360) 385-0752.

SHOPPING

Water St. houses numerous art galleries, antique shops, cafes, trendy gift shops, and an import toy store. **Ancestral Spirits Gallery,** 921 Washington St., tel. (360) 385-0078, features an impressive blend of modern and traditional Indian and Eskimo art, masks, and jewelry. Another gallery emphasizing Native arts—especially baskets and masks—is **Northwest Native Expressions,** 637 Water St., tel. (360) 385-4770. **Earthenworks Gallery,** 1002 Water St., tel. (360) 385-0328, is a bit glitzy, but sells high quality, creative works—especially ceramics. **Gallery Walks** are held the first Saturday of each month, 5:30-8 p.m. March-Dec., during which galleries hang new works, serve refreshments, and often have artists on hand.

FairWinds Winery, 1984 Hastings Ave. W., tel. (360) 385-6899, is a tiny family operation producing cabernet sauvignon, gewürztraminer, and merlot. The tasting room is open Sat.-Sun. 1-5 p.m.

INFORMATION AND TRANSPORTATION

For local info and a ton of brochures, head to the **Port Townsend Chamber of Commerce Tourist Information Center,** 2437 E. Sims Way, tel. (360) 385-2722 or (888) 365-6978. They're open Mon.-Fri. 9 a.m.-5 p.m., Saturday 10 a.m.-4 p.m., and Sunday 11 a.m.-4 p.m. all year. **Port Townsend Public Library,** 1220 Lawrence St., tel. (360) 385-3181, is one of the many Carnagie Libraries built early in this century.

Bus Service
Jefferson Transit, tel. (360) 385-4777 or (800) 773-7788, serves Port Townsend and Jefferson County, with service to Polsbo where you can connect with Kitsap Transit, and to Sequim for connections to Clallam Transit. Bike racks are on all buses. Unfortunately, there is no service to Marrowstone Island. **Pennco,** tel. (360) 452-5104 or (888) 673-6626, has van service connecting Port Angeles with Sea-Tac Airport.

Ferry Service
Port Townsend is served directly by the **Washington State Ferry** from Keystone on the southwest side of Whidbey Island. The ferries depart downtown about every 50 minutes, and in summer cost $1.80 one-way for passengers and walk-ons, $8 one-way for car and driver, 30 cents extra for bikes. Call (206) 842-2345 or (888) 808-7977 for details, or (800) 843-3779 for automated information.

P.S. Express, tel. (360) 385-5288, provides passenger-only service between Port Townsend and Friday Harbor on San Juan Island. The boat leaves Port Townsend daily, April-Oct., and takes you through Admiralty Inlet and the Strait of Juan de Fuca where you're likely to see seals, sea otters, and orcas. They stay in Friday Harbor long enough for a quick three-hour visit, or you can overnight there and return to Port Townsend later. The charge is $49 roundtrip, bikes and kayaks $12.50 extra. **Front St. Water Taxi,** tel. (360) 379-3258, has passenger service along the waterfront daily in the summer; $5 roundtrip from the city dock to the fuel dock.

Air Service
Port Townsend Airways, tel. (360) 385-6554 or (800) 385-6554, has direct service to Sea-Tac Airport, Victoria, and the San Juan Islands, and scenic half-hour flights around Port Townsend.

PORT HADLOCK AREA

The tiny towns of Port Hadlock, Irondale, and Chimacum make up the so-called "Tri-Area" (not to be confused with the Tri-Cities!). Each of these has a cluster of businesses and a number of fascinating historic homes, including **Hadlock Manor** on Curtiss St. in Hadlock, built in the 1890s by a Swedish sea captain. For local info, head to **Port Hadlock Chamber of Commerce,** 23 Colwell St., tel. (360) 385-1469.

Accommodations
The Old Alcohol Plant Lodge, tel. (360) 785-7030 or (800) 785-7030, stands just east of town on the way to Indian and Marrowstone Islands. Built in 1911 by the Classen Chemical Co., this large building produced alcohol from sawdust for just two years before the company

went bankrupt. It stood abandoned for the next 65 years, but a $4 million revamping has turned it into a most unusual lodge and restaurant. Hotel rooms go for $80-89 d; split level suites for $130, and condos and the penthouse suite for $225 d. The reasonable steak and seafood restaurant provides fine harbor views, and has a popular Sunday brunch. The bar has live music on weekends.

Windridge Cottage, 2804 W. Valley Rd., tel. (360) 732-4575, has a modern cedar cabin out in the country along Beausite Lake. There's a full kitchen, fireplace, and bath; $115 for four. **Oak Bay Cottages,** tel. (360) 437-0380 or (800) 727-4706, has two large furnished houses (one can sleep 10) located between Port Hadlock and Port Ludlow on Oak Bay Road; $95-150 d.

Port Hadlock Cottages, 311 Lower Hadlock Rd., tel. (360) 698-2460, charges $200 per weekend for cozy cottages with kitchens.

Food

Ferino's Pizzeria, in Port Hadlock, tel. (360) 385-0840, bakes outstanding gourmet pizzas and pizzas by the slice. Also in Port Hadlock is **Ajax Cafe,** tel. (360) 385-3450, with the best steaks in the area, plus a variety of creative Northwest seafood and chicken dishes. They also have live music nightly. **Chimacum Cafe,** in Chimacum, tel. (360) 732-4631, another locals' favorite, makes all-American steaks, chicken, burgers, and chocolate malts.

MARROWSTONE ISLAND

Quiet Marrowstone Island is off the beaten path but offers wooded country, attractive summer homes, and a fascinating historic fort. The only real business on the island is **Nordland General Store,** which pretty much makes up the entire town of Nordland. The historic store maintains a wonderful charm and friendliness, and is a great place to get a cup of coffee and sit in the back by the woodstove while reading the paper. They also rent sea kayaks.

Upper Oak Bay Jefferson County Park, on the southwest corner of Marrowstone Island, has fine views east across Puget Sound. Summer-only camping is available, and no hookups or showers.

Tiny **Mystery Bay State Park,** just north of Nordland, has a picnic area, beach, pier, boat moorage, and protected waters for small boaters, along with striking Olympic views, but no camping. The park's name came from the seemingly mysterious disappearance of boats belonging to Prohibition-era booze-smugglers who brought liquor here from Canada. (The smugglers used the tall overhanging trees here to hide their skiffs.)

Fort Flagler State Park

Marrowstone Island's biggest attraction is Fort Flagler State Park, at the northern tip of Marrowstone Island and surrounded by water on three sides. Boating, picnicking, crabbing, salmon and bottom fishing, wooded hiking trails, and camping at beach sites are available in this 783-acre park. Since it is in the Olympic rain shadow, the park gets lots of sun and only 17 inches of rain per year.

With Fort Worden and Whidbey's Fort Casey, Fort Flagler formed what old-timers called the Iron Triangle, the trio of forts—the others were Fort Worden and Fort Casey—guarding the narrow Admiralty Inlet between Port Townsend and Whidbey Island against attack of Puget Sound. They were equipped with 10-inch "disappearing rifles," the cannons you can see today at Fort Casey. When these cannons were fired, the recoil would cause them to swing down out of sight behind the cement walls for reloading, giving the gun sighter a wild ride and often a shiner from being repeatedly struck by the eyepiece. The Iron Triangle forts also had enormous mortars that were proven impractical at the first test: the concussion was so great that windows were broken, pictures fell off walls, and foundations cracked.

Fort Flagler was built in the late 1890s and served as a training center during the two world wars, but its guns were never fired in anger. The fort was closed in 1955 and later became a state park. Nine gun batteries remain, and two three-inch guns (obtained from the Philippines) have been installed at Battery Wansboro facing out onto Admiralty Inlet. From here you can watch the ships, barges, sailing boats, and fishing vessels cruise past; it's pretty easy to see why a fort was built on this strategic bottleneck.

Today, Fort Flagler is on the National Register of Historic Places. The spacious green parade grounds are bordered by barracks and gracious old officers quarters. Several trails cut through wooded sections of the park, including the "Roots of the Forest" interpretive trail. Other activities include camping, clam digging, scuba diving in an adjacent underwater park, and boating. The **Marrowstone Point Lighthouse** (closed to the public) stands on the northeast edge of the fort, with massive Mt. Baker creating an attractive photographic backdrop. There's also a small U.S. Fish and Wildlife Service **Fishery Research Center** here; tel. (360) 385-1007. Several of the fort's old buildings are now used for a state Environmental Learning Center, tel. (360) 385-3701, used primarily by school groups. Two historic buildings are rented out as vacation homes; call (360) 902-8600 for details.

The campground (actually two separate areas) is open late February through October only and costs $11 tents or $16 RVs; showers are available. Call (360) 385-1259 for information, or (800) 452-5687 for reservations ($6 extra).

Accommodations

The **Fort Flagler AYH Hostel,** tel. (360) 385-1288, is in one of the barracks of the old fort, and is open mid-March through September. It has a common kitchen and lounge and rental bikes. Lodging is $11-14 pp in the dorms; there's also one couples' room for $28-34 d. The hostel is closed 10 a.m.-5 p.m.

The Ecologic Place, 10 Beach Dr. in Nordland, tel. (360) 385-3077 or (800) 871-3077, has 11 rustic cabins with Oak Bay and Olympic views for $65-90 d. Each comes with complete kitchen and bath facilities, plus a woodstove; minimum is two nights.

PORT LUDLOW

The Resort at Port Ludlow dominates Port Ludlow. Once a major sawmill and shipping town, the sawmill closed and shipping went with it, and the town diminished until the resort arrived. Port Ludlow offers the utmost in luxury: large heated outdoor and indoor pools, jacuzzi, saunas, squash and tennis courts, paved bike paths, a 27-hole championship golf course, a 300-slip marina on Port Ludlow Bay complete with rental sailboats. A wide variety of rooms are available, from standard rooms for $99 d to four-bedroom suites that sleep eight for $445. Call (360) 437-2222 or (800) 732-1239 for reservations.

On the waterfront, the sprawling **Inn at Ludlow Bay,** tel. (360) 437-0411, charges a whopping $168-450 s or d. Luxurious facilities include jacuzzi tubs, fireplaces, continental breakfasts, mountain views, and a wrap-around veranda

The Cottage on Mats Mats Bay, three miles north of Port Ludlow, tel. (360) 437-0366, is actually a two-bedroom home along a beautiful little bay; $135 for four.

Nantucket Manor B&B, 941 Shire Rd. (south of Port Ludlow), tel. (360) 437-2676, is a newly built bed and breakfast with five guest rooms, three of which face the water. A four-course breakfast is served. Outside, find a gazebo and pleasant gardens; no kids. $155-185 d.

Shine Tidelands State Park has a few campsites jammed together below the north end of the Hood Canal Bridge; $7 all year, but no drinking water.

Food

Ludlow Bay Cafe, tel. (360) 437-0144, serves good breakfasts and lunches, plus espresso. **Harbormaster Restaurant** in the Resort at Port Ludlow serves breakfast, lunch, and dinner, with entertainment most nights in the lounge. The outside deck is a favorite place for a romantic evening meal.

The **Port Ludlow Farmers Market** comes to town on Saturday in the summer; tel. (360) 437-0996.

Information and Transportation

The **Olympic Peninsula Gateway Visitor Information Center,** on the corner of Hwy. 104 and Beaver Valley Rd. (four miles north of the Hood Canal Bridge), tel. (360) 437-0120, is open daily 9 a.m.-4 p.m. in the summer. Stop here for local information and brochures.

Jefferson Transit, tel. (360) 385-4777 or (800) 773-7788, serves all of Jefferson County, with connections to Port Angeles via Clallam Transit or the Kitsap Peninsula via Kitsap Transit.

SEQUIM

As storms pass over the Olympic Peninsula, they split in two; one part clings to the Olympics and the other is blown along by the strait's air currents, bypassing Sequim (pronounced "skwim") like an island in the stream. The result is Sequim's famous "blue hole." The 17 inches of rain that fall here are less than fall on Los Angeles, and a typical year has 299 days of sun. The pleasant climate has transformed this town of 3,800 into a booming retirement community, with more than 25,000 people spread across the surrounding Dungeness Valley. Although there are a number of enjoyable spots in the area, the town itself is a line of businesses strewn haphazardly along the heavily trafficked Hwy. 101. Unfortunately, this unchecked development threatens to connect Sequim and Port Angeles in one long stretch.

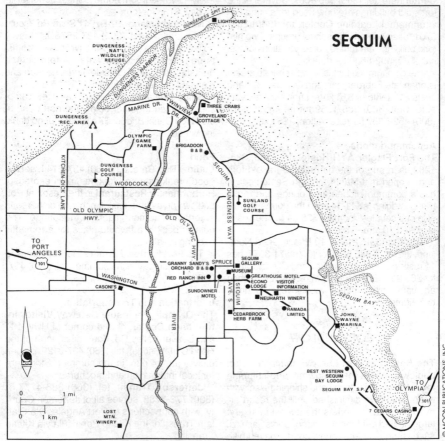

© MOON PUBLICATIONS, INC.

History

The first Anglo settlers in the Dungeness Valley found an arid landscape of grasses and cacti bisected by the mountain-fed waters of the Dungeness River. The first irrigation ditches were dug by hand in 1886, allowing water from the river to transform the prairies into highly productive dairies and farms. Produce from the valley supplied food for the booming city of Victoria, British Columbia, across the Strait of Juan de Fuca. Today, ditches reach for almost 100 miles and irrigate some 12,000 acres.

The village of Sequim grew up as a farm center and mill town and was originally called "Seguin" (till a postal service employee changed it to Sequim). The term was somehow derived from the S'Klallam word "Such-e-kwi-ing," meaning "quiet water." The town was officially incorporated in 1913 and has been a retirement haven for the past thirty years. With each passing year, more and more farms are being transformed into suburban homes, paved roads, golf courses, and other developments. And everywhere you look are more "For Sale" signs. Kiss it all goodbye.

SIGHTS

Museum and Arts Center

One block north of Hwy. 101 at 175 W. Cedar St., the Museum and Arts Center, tel. (360) 683-8110, was built to store the 12,000-year-old tusks, bones, and artifacts unearthed at Sequim's famous Manis Mastodon Site, discovered in 1977 by Emanuel Manis, a retired farmer. Archaeologists discovered a prehistoric spear point in the rib cage of one of the mastodons, some of the earliest evidence that humans hunted these elephantine beasts. Other displays include several fine old cedar bark baskets, pioneer farming displays, and timber exhibits. Open Mon.-Sat. 9 a.m.-4 p.m. and Sunday 1-4 p.m., year-round; donation.

Dungeness Spit

The word "Dungeness" means "sandy cape," a fitting description for this 5.5-mile long stretch of sand that creates Dungeness Bay. The **Dungeness National Wildlife Refuge** here provides habitat for 250 species of birds on the nation's longest natural sandspit. As many as 30,000 birds rest at this saltwater lagoon during their migratory journeys. Admission to the refuge is $3 per group; call (360) 457-8451 for further info.

Built in 1857, the **New Dungeness Lighthouse** at the tip of the spit is managed by volunteers and offers tours, but you'll have to hike a total of 11 miles out and back to see it. It's a good idea to check the tide charts before starting out. For an overview of the area, hike the half-mile trail from the parking lot to a bluff overlooking Dungeness Bay. Clamming, fishing, and canoeing are permitted in this protected wildlife refuge, but no camping, dogs, firearms, or fires. The spit is closed to horses on weekends and holidays from April 15 to October 15.

Wineries

Two local wineries produce wines from eastern Washington grapes. **Olympic Cellars,** tel. (360) 683-9652, is housed in a century-old cedar barn along Hwy. 101 just west of Sequim. Stop by to sample cabernet sauvignon, merlot, or riesling and other wines in their tasting room; open daily 9:30 a.m.-5:30 p.m. **Lost Mountain Winery,** 3174 Lost Mountain Rd., tel. (360) 683-5229, makes robust red wines; open by arrangement or chance. They have an open house the last week of June and the first week of July when the new wines are released.

Cuddly Critters

The **Olympic Game Farm,** tel. (360) 683-4295 or (800) 778-4295, a vacation and retirement home for Hollywood stars, is a 90-acre preserve where Gentle Ben and over 200 other animals of TV and movie fame can be visited. Many of the Walt Disney nature specials were filmed here, along with parts of many feature movies. Hour-long guided walking tours are available daily mid-May to early September for $7 adults, $6 seniors and ages 5-12, free for kids under five; the park is open all year for driving tours for the same prices. Follow the signs from Sequim five miles northwest to Ward Road.

Other Attractions

One of the oddest local sites is **Bandy's Troll Haven,** a private residence crowded with dozens of fairy-tale creatures. Get here by heading east from Sequim on Hwy. 101 to Gardiner, and turning onto Gardiner Beach Road.

John Wayne loved the Northwest because he could visit the area and not be hounded by autograph seekers, and he especially loved the Strait of Juan de Fuca. The Duke liked it so much he bought land on Sequim Bay and donated it for a marina. The **John Wayne Marina** has 422 slips, a landscaped park and picnic area, and a bronze statue of the Duke as he appeared in the 1949 flick *She Wore A Yellow Ribbon.* Rent boats here at **The Bosun's Locker,** tel. (360) 683-6521. They also sell John Wayne souvenirs.

Dungeness Valley's mild climate is perfect for growing herbs, and it is now one of only two places in the world where lavender oil is produced (the other being France). At least eight small farms grow lavender locally; get a list from the visitor center. Gourmet cooks will enjoy a visit to Washington's first herb farm, **Cedarbrook Herb Farm,** 986 Sequim Ave. S, tel. (360) 683-7733, where 200 varieties of herbs, teas, and flowers are organically grown.

The **Dungeness Fish Hatchery,** four miles up Taylor Cutoff Rd. along the Dungeness River, raises 350,000 coho and 300,000 chinook salmon each year. Open for tours daily 8 a.m.-4:30 p.m.

The enormous **7 Cedars Casino,** tel. (360) 683-7777 or (800) 458-2597, at the minuscule settlement of Blyn near the head of Sequim Bay has bingo, blackjack, craps, keno, poker, and roulette, and is run by the Jamestown S'Klallam Tribe. Inside, the Salish Room Restaurant serves buffet dinners and regional specialties. Also here is **Northwest Native Expressions Gallery,** tel. (360) 681-4640, with masks, paintings, jewelry, and weaving.

A couple more miles east from Sequim on Hwy. 101 is **Wild Birds Unlimited,** a fun place to visit if you are a birder or just like to feed birds.

The cooperatively run **Blue Whole Gallery,** downtown at 129 W. Washington St., tel. (360) 681-6033, features quality pieces by local artists.

ACCOMMODATIONS

Bed and Breakfasts

Unless otherwise noted, all B&Bs listed below serve a full breakfast and do not allow young children. They are listed by price.

Brigadoon B&B, four miles north of Sequim at 62 Balmoral Ct., tel. (360) 683-2255 or (800) 397-2256, is a 1920 country home filled with English antiques. It has three guest rooms and a jacuzzi; $50-90 s or $80-95 d.

Glenna's Guthrie Cottage B&B, 10083 Old Olympic Hwy., tel. (360) 681-4349 or (800) 930-4349, is an historic farmhouse with four guest rooms, a hot tub, private baths and entrances; $60-90 s or d.

Groveland Cottage, five miles north of Sequim at 4861 Sequim-Dungeness Way, tel. (360) 683-3565 or (800) 879-8859, is a turn-of-the-century house with a large lawn and pond. Inside are five guest rooms with private or shared baths; $70-95 s or d. Two night minimum.

Margie's Inn on the Bay B&B is five miles east of Sequim at 120 Forrest Rd., tel. (360) 683-7011 or (800) 730-7011. This contemporary home has a spectacular waterside location and five guest rooms with private baths; $75-140 s or d.

Diamond Point Inn B&B, in the woods at Diamond Point (east of Sequim), (360) 797-7720 or (888) 797-0397, has rooms in a house and two cottages for $75-115 s or d.

A 1920s farmhouse on an iris farm, **Granny Sandy's Orchard B&B,** 405 W. Spruce, tel. (360) 683-5748 or (800) 841-3347, has two guest rooms with private baths. Children are welcome; $85 s or d.

For great views, it's hard to beat **Dungeness Panorama B&B,** seven miles north of Sequim, tel. (360) 683-4503, where the decks front on the Strait of Juan de Fuca. The two large suites have private baths, and an authentic French country breakfast is served; $85-110 s or d.

Normandie Farm B&B, 1223 Atterberry Rd., tel. (360) 681-0184, sits in the foothills just west of Sequim, and has comfortable rooms for $88-98 s or d, including a vegetarian breakfast. French is spoken.

Greywolf Inn B&B, 395 Keeler Rd., tel. (360) 683-5889 or (800) 914-9653, is a country estate with dramatic vistas and a jacuzzi. The five guest rooms have private baths; $85-120 s or d.

BJ's Garden Cafe B&B, six miles north of Sequim, tel. (360) 452-2322 or (800) 880-1332, is a newly built Victorian-style B&B with five guest rooms, each with fireplaces and some with jacuzzi tubs; $130-165 s or d.

Motels

The following Sequim motels are arranged by price. **Sequim Bay Resort,** three miles east of Sequim, tel. (360) 681-3853, has the cheapest local accommodations: $29-42 s or d for cabins with kitchenettes. **Greathouse Motel,** 740 E. Washington (Hwy. 101 E), tel. (360) 683-7272 or (800) 475-7272, charges $45-79 s or d including a continental breakfast. **Sundowner Motel,** 364 W. Washington, tel. (360) 683-5532 or (800) 325-6966, charges $59 s or d, and has kitchenettes. **Sequim West Inn,** 740 W. Washington St., tel. (360) 683-4144 or (800) 528-4527, has rooms with microwaves and fridges for $66-73 s or d.

Econo Lodge, 801 E. Washington, tel. (360) 683-7113 or (800) 488-7113, has rooms for $69 s or $79 d, including microwaves, fridges, and a continental breakfast. **Red Ranch Inn,** 830 W. Washington St., tel. (360) 683-4195 or (800) 777-4195, charges $75 s or d, and has a nine-hole putting course.

Dungeness Bay Motel, 140 Marine Dr., tel. (360) 683-3013 or (800) 484-5829 ext. 3013, is five miles north of town along the bay, and has five cottages with full kitchens on a private beach for $75-90 s or d. **Best Western Sequim Bay Lodge,** three miles east of town at 1788 Hwy. 101 E, tel. (360) 683-0691 or (800) 622-0691, charges $77-145 s or $87-145 d, including an outdoor pool and jacuzzi.

Near Blyn (east of Sequim) is **Sunset Marine Resort,** tel. (360) 681-4166, where six-person cabins with kitchens are $85-125. **Ramada Limited,** 1095 E. Washington St., tel. (360) 683-1775 or (800) 683-1775, charges $89-119 s or d, including an indoor pool, jacuzzi, microwaves, and fridges.

Seven miles north of Sequim are **Juan de Fuca Cottages,** tel. (360) 683-4433, with six fully equipped housekeeping cottages overlooking Dungeness Spit. A jacuzzi is available; $115 s or d. Two-night minimum on weekends.

Campgrounds

Dungeness Recreation Area, tel. (360) 683-5847, a 216-acre Clallam County park at the base of the refuge, has camping Feb.-Oct. ($10) with showers, beach access, and a picnic area. **Sequim Bay State Park,** just east of Sequim on Hwy. 101, has wooded tent sites ($10), hookup sites ($15), a boat launch, scuba diving, hiking, tennis courts, and superb views of Sequim Bay. Open year-round. Call (800) 452-5687 for reservations ($6 extra). More campsites can be found at **South Sequim Bay Recreation Area** east of town along the bay and just off Hwy. 101.

The Forest Service has two campgrounds ($8; open late May to early September) in the mountains south of Sequim. **Dungeness Forks Campground** is 11 miles south via Forest Roads 2909 and 2958; **East Crossing Campground** is 13 miles south via Forest Roads 28 and 2860. Contact the Quilcene Ranger Station, tel. (360) 765-3368, for details.

Sequim's private RV parks include **Sunshine RV Park,** four miles west of town, tel. (360) 683-4769, **Idle Wheels Mobile Home Court,** 530 W. Washington, tel. (360) 683-4276; and **Rainbow's End RV Park,** 261831 Hwy. 101, tel. (360) 683-3863.

FOOD

Start out the day at **Oak Table Cafe,** 292 W. Bell, tel. (360) 683-2179, where the breakfasts are filling and delicious (try the wonderful soufflé-style baked apple pancakes).

Housed in an historic white church at 134 S. 2nd Ave., **Jean's Deli,** tel. (360) 683-6727, is the best lunch spot in town, with delightful pastries, sandwiches, and espresso.

The Three Crabs, tel. (360) 683-4264, has served Dungeness crab and other local seafood specialties for nearly 30 years at their waterfront location on Three Crabs Rd.; they also have a retail seafood market. The crabs are well prepared, but the rest of the rather pricey menu isn't noteworthy. The **Oyster House** in Discovery Bay (18 miles east of Sequim), tel. (360) 385-1785, has a fine seafood and pasta menu, featuring—of course—fresh oysters.

Nummie's, tel. (360) 683-2487, downtown at 120 W. Washington St., has espresso and bagels, plus ice cream, malts, and shakes. **Khu Larb Thai II,** 120 W. Bell St., tel. (360) 681-8550, is owned by the same folks who run the acclaimed Khu Larb in Port Townsend, so you know the food will be both authentic and flavorful, especially the garlic prawns.

Another place for fast and well-prepared lunches is **Hiway 101 Diner,** 392 W. Washington, tel. (360) 683-3388, a "fabulous fifties" family diner with the biggest local burgers. Popular for breakfast.

The **Dungeness Inn,** tel. (360) 683-3331, overlooking the Dungeness Golf Course at 491A Woodcock Rd., specializes in prime rib, steak, and seafood. **Tarcisio's,** 609 W. Washington, tel. (360) 683-5809, is the place to go for from-scratch pizzas.

Fans of Mexican food will enjoy two local eateries: **Las Palomas,** 1085 E. Washington, tel. (360) 681-3842, and **El Cazador,** 537 W. Washington, tel. (360) 683-4788. The latter has a pleasant outside deck.

Sequim's **Open Aire Market,** tel. (360) 683-9446, takes place Saturday 9 a.m.-2 p.m. late May through October at 2nd and Cedar.

OTHER PRACTICALITIES

Events

Established a century ago and still going strong—it's the state's oldest festival—the **Sequim Irrigation Festival** celebrates the beginning of Dungeness Valley agriculture thanks to the hand-dug ditch that first brought water from the Dungeness River in 1896. The first festival (May 1, 1896) was a picnic in a shady grove; today parades, art and flower shows, a carnival, fireworks, logging show, and a bizarre chainsaw carving contest (second largest in America!) commemorate the annual event, held on the first full week of May each year. In early August, the **Celebrate Lavender Festival** features tours of local lavender farms, and an open air market offering food, music, and demonstrations. Also popular is a mid-August **Salmon Bake.**

Entertainment

Red Ranch Restaurant, 830 W. Washington St., tel. (360) 683-6622, has prime rib and a big salad bar, plus a lounge with live bands on weekends. **Town Tavern,** 735 W. Washington, tel. (360) 683-1013, has pool tables, darts, shuffleboard, pub grub, and "the biggest beer can collection on the peninsula."

Recreation

Recreation in the Sequim area focuses on the protected waters inside the inner harbor of Dungeness Bay, a favorite place for windsurfers and sea kayakers. The six-mile path to the lighthouse on Dungeness Spit is a very popular place for a seaside walk or horseback ride. **Dungeness Bay Touring Co.,** tel. (360) 681-3884, leads beginners on sea kayak trips around the bay. Whale watching trips are offered by **Sequim Bay Tours & Charters,** tel. (360) 681-7408.

Mountain bike rentals and tours of the nearby foothills are available from **D&G Cyclery,** 551 W. Washington, tel. (360) 681-3868. The **Sequim Aquatic Recreation Center,** 610 N. 5th, tel. (360) 683-3344, has two swimming pools, a gym, racquetball courts, exercise equipment, and a sauna.

Two 18-hole public golf courses in the area are the **SunLand Golf Course,** tel. (360) 683-6800, just north of Sequim at 109 Hilltop Dr., and the **Dungeness Golf Course,** tel. (360) 683-6344, adjacent to the Dungeness Inn Restaurant, north of Carlsborg on Woodcock Road.

Information

For maps, brochures, and lots of local information drop by the helpful **Sequim-Dungeness Valley Chamber of Commerce Visitor Information Center,** 1192 E. Washington, tel. (360) 683-6690 or (800) 737-8462. The office is open daily 9 a.m.-5 p.m. year-round.

Transportation

Clallam Transit, tel. (360) 452-4511 or (800) 858-3747, connects Sequim with Port Angeles, Forks, and Neah Bay. **Jefferson Transit,** tel. (360) 385-4777, has transportation east to Port Townsend and Polsbo.

Olympic Bus Lines, tel. (360) 452-3858 or (800) 550-3858, has a daily shuttle to Sea-Tac Airport. **Evergreen Express Airways,** tel. (360) 683-7597, offers scenic flights and air service to Sea-Tac.

PORT ANGELES

Port Angeles is the largest city on the northern Olympic Peninsula and the gateway to many of its pleasures. Its busy harbor, protected by the strong sandy arm of Ediz Hook, is visited daily by logging ships, fishing boats, and the Victoria ferry MV *Coho*. The view from the Port Angeles city pier is breathtaking: rocky Hurricane Ridge, made more ominous by a wispy cloud cover, seems to rise straight out of the turbulent waters of the Strait of Juan de Fuca, creating an overwhelming contrast of land and water, height and depth. Two of the biggest local employers are the big Daishowa pulp mill (where they make phone book paper), and the large K-Ply mill which produces plywood. Because of its location as an entry point to both Vancouver Island (via the ferry) and to nearby Olympic National Park, Port Angeles is a very busy place during the summer. Parking downtown can be a nightmare on a July weekend.

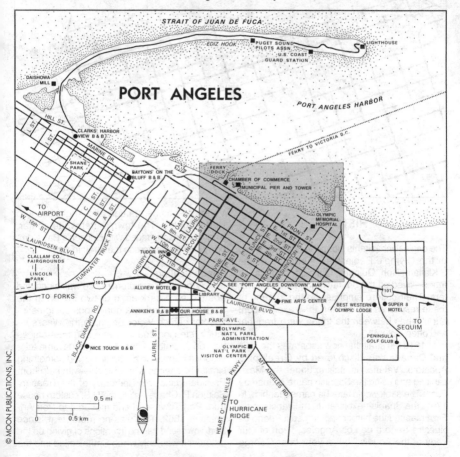

© MOON PUBLICATIONS, INC.

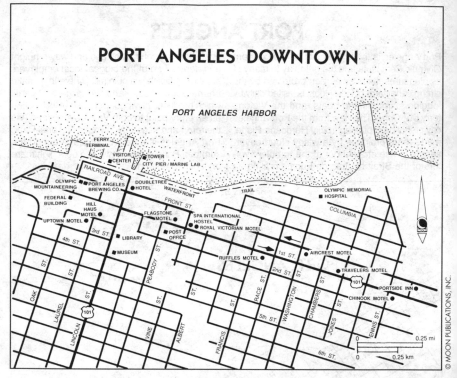

PORT ANGELES DOWNTOWN

PORT ANGELES HARBOR

FERRY TERMINAL
VISITOR CENTER
TOWER
CITY PIER / MARINE LAB
RAILROAD AVE.
OLYMPIC MOUNTAINEERING
PORT ANGELES BREWING CO.
DOUBLETREE HOTEL
WATERFRONT
FRONT ST.
TRAIL
OLYMPIC MEMORIAL HOSPITAL
FEDERAL BUILDING
HILL HAUS MOTEL
FLAGSTONE MOTEL
SPA INTERNATIONAL HOSTEL
ROYAL VICTORIAN MOTEL
COLUMBIA
UPTOWN MOTEL
3rd ST.
LIBRARY
POST OFFICE
4th ST.
MUSEUM
RUFFLES MOTEL
1st ST.
AIRCREST MOTEL
2nd ST.
TRAVELERS MOTEL
PORTSIDE INN
CHINOOK MOTEL
5th ST.
6th ST.
ST.
OAK
LAUREL
LINCOLN
VINE
ALBERT
FRANCIS
PEABODY ST.
RACE ST.
WASHINGTON
CHAMBERS ST.
JONES
ENNIS ST.
101

0   0.25 mi
0   0.25 km

© MOON PUBLICATIONS, INC.

HISTORY

The original inhabitants along the northern shore of the Olympic Peninsula—members of the S'Klallam, Hoh, Quinault, Quileute, and Makah tribes—lived off the bounty of the land and waters. Their culture emphasized the sharing of these resources rather than their exploitation, but clashes between the tribes were frequent and often violent.

In 1610 the strait that now separates the U.S. and Canada was discovered by Greek pilot Apostolos Valerianus, sailing under the Mexican flag and using the Spanish name of Juan de Fuca. The strait would later be named for him. In 1791, the Spanish explorer Juan Francisco de Eliza mapped the harbor and named it Puerto de Nuestra Señora de Los Angeles, "Port of Our Lady of the Angels," but a year later George Vancouver came through and Anglicized it to Port Angeles. The town's first white settler, Angus Johnson, traded with Hudson's Bay Company in Victoria across the strait in 1857.

Shady Dealings

Port Angeles' rise to prominence was aided and abetted by a dark deed or two involving the town's true founder, a duplicitous customs inspector named Victor Smith. In the West's infancy, stealing county seats and post offices was on an entertainment par with daytime television. It happened all the time, and something similar happened when Smith—with help from President Lincoln's Secretary of the Treasury Salmon P. Chase—stole the U.S. custom house from Port Townsend and moved it to Port Angeles in 1862. This was no mean feat, since Port Townsend had no intentions of giving up the records; it was only when Smith sailed into the harbor aboard a warship and pointed the guns at the city that the citizens relented. He later added insult to injury by returning to force the hospital patients and staff out of Port Townsend and onto his ship, which became a floating hospital till a new one could be completed in Port Angeles. These deeds brought no happiness to either Smith or Chase. Chase had to resign from the Cabinet in disgrace and Smith was lost at sea. But Port Angeles is still the county seat.

The same year that Smith stole the courthouse, he also persuaded President Lincoln to name Port Angeles and Ediz Hook as military reservations. Port Angeles was the second townsite (after Washington, D.C.) to be planned by the federal government; President Lincoln called it the "second National City," in case Washington, D.C. fell to the Confederate Army, even though the town's population at the time was only 10. The real reason for creating a national city was to provide money from land sales to support the war effort, but that effort was a decided failure. With all the free land in surrounding areas, the government finally gave up in 1891, opening the town for settlement.

Later Years
Port Angeles—like Seattle—both benefitted from and suffered from its seaside location, and in both cases the downtown had to be built up to raise it above the tideline. In 1914, Peabody Creek was diverted away from town, fill dirt was washed down from nearby hillsides, and the streets were raised a level using walls and pilings, turning two-story buildings into one-story structures. The resulting "underground" is still visible in places around town.

A strong military influence held on for decades here, as parts of the Pacific Fleet anchored in Port Angeles every summer in the 1920s and '30s, providing the town with 30,000 eligible bachelors and attracting unattached women from all over for a little summer fun. Long a major lumber town, the city is becoming more reliant on tourists; it feeds, shelters, and entertains many of Olympic National Park's three million annual visitors. In recent years the local economy has been hit by a double whammy of declining salmon runs that have devastated commercial and sport fishing, and the 1997 closing of the big Rayonier pulp mill.

SIGHTS

Municipal Pier and Marine Laboratory
The best part of Port Angeles—outside of its proximity to Olympic National Park—is clearly the city pier. An observation tower at pier's end provides 360-degree views of the city, harbor, and majestic Olympic mountains, while a sandy beach with picnic area is available for day use. Also located on the pier near the *Coho* ferry dock, the **Arthur D. Feiro Marine Laboratory,** operated by Peninsula College, has hands-on displays and exhibits of the area's sealife; volunteers will answer questions. More than 80 species are here, including sea slugs, eels, octopuses, starfish, and sea urchins. Open daily 10 a.m.-8 p.m. in the summer, and Sat.-Sun. noon-4 p.m. the rest of the year. Admission is $2 adults, 50 cents for kids ages 6-12, and free for younger children. For specific hours or a guided tour call (360) 417-6254.

Municipal Pier and observation tower

DIANNE BOULERICE LYONS

Walking Tour

Stop by the downtown visitor center for a walking tour brochure that leads you through the historical sights of Port Angeles. The city's **Waterfront Trail** is a delightful six-mile paved path that follows the downtown shoreline and continues out to the Coast Guard base on **Ediz Hook**—a three-and-a-half-mile-long natural sandspit protecting the Northwest's deepest harbor. Along the way you're treated to views across to Vancouver Island and back toward town with the snowcapped Olympics in the background. Watch as freighters are guided in, or take out your own boat for fishing or sightseeing. Picnicking and beachcombing are also popular activities. The U.S. Coast Guard Air Station occupies the far end of the spit and has the cutter *Active* docked at the city pier when she isn't out on rescue missions or drug searches. Located a short distance from the Coast Guard base, the Puget Sound Pilots Association assigns a pilot to each commercial ship passing this point to steer it on its way through Puget Sound. Another place offering fine vistas across to Vancouver Island is from the top of the Laurel St. stairs, two blocks uphill from the *Coho* ferry dock.

Art Center

The **Port Angeles Fine Arts Center,** 1203 E. 8th St., tel. (360) 457-3532, is a bit out of the way, but well worth the side trip. Located on a hill, the building's enormous picture windows face north to Vancouver Island, offering panoramic vistas that pull your eyes away from the art on the walls. Walk outside to discover a small forest with gardens and a path leading to additional viewpoints. The Fine Arts Center features changing exhibits by prominent Northwest artists and is open Thurs.-Sun. 11 a.m.-5 p.m.; free.

Olympic National Park Visitor Center

Located a mile out of town at 3002 Mt. Angeles Rd., this is often the first stopping place for visitors to Olympic National Park, and very popular Hurricane Ridge, 17 miles south of town. The center includes a large panoramic map, exhibits about the park, a Discovery Room for kids, and a 12-minute slide show that introduces visitors to the Olympics. Nature trails lead through the forest to park headquarters, a block away. The visitor center is open daily year-round. Call (360) 452-0330 for more information. Get backcountry info from the summer-only **Wilderness Information Center** directly behind the visitor center. Call them at (360) 452-0300. Also here is the Beaumont log cabin, built in 1887 and moved here in 1962.

ACCOMMODATIONS

Because of the popularity of Port Angeles in the summer months, it's a good idea to make reservations ahead of your visit. Stop by the visitor center to check the board for space availability at local motels, B&Bs, and RV parks, or to use their phone to make reservations. Many places offer free transport from the airport or ferry terminal upon request.

Hostel

Port Angeles has a delightful private hostel, **The Spa International Hostel,** downtown at 511 E. First St., tel. (360) 452-3257. The dorm has six beds, plus mattresses for others, and guests are served an organic breakfast in the English-style tearoom. Rates are $15 pp, or $40 d in the couples room. Open year-round. The hostel is closed 9 a.m.-5 p.m., and almost always has space. Steam baths and massage are also available.

Bed and Breakfasts

Unless otherwise noted, all B&Bs listed below serve a full breakfast and do not allow young children. They are listed (more or less) by price.

A Nice Touch B&B, two miles south of Port Angeles, tel. (360) 457-1938 or (800) 605-6296, is a contemporary country home with five guest rooms, and private or shared bath; $59-110 s or $69-120 d.

Clarks' Harbor View B&B, 1426 W. 4th St., tel. (360) 457-9891, is a new home with a deck overlooking the harbor, a pool table, and a single guest room; $60 s or $65 d;

You'll discover panoramic water views from **Baytons' On-The-Bluff B&B,** 824 W. 4th St., tel. (360) 457-5569 or (888) 400-5569, a 1920s home on a quiet street. The two guest rooms share a bath. $60-65 s or d.

PORT ANGELES HOTELS AND MOTELS

Accommodations are arranged from least to most expensive. Rates may be lower during the winter months. See the text for local bed and breakfasts.

INEXPENSIVE

Point Hudson Resort; Pt. Hudson; tel. (360) 385-2828 or (800) 826-3854; $49-79 s or d; family place, spartan rooms (some with shared baths), beachside location, no phones, a few TVs

Point Hudson Resort; Pt. Hudson; tel. (360) 385-2828 or (800) 826-3854; $49-79 s or d; family place, spartan rooms (some with shared baths), beachside location, no phones, a few TVs

Royal Victorian Motel; 521 E. 1st St.; tel. (360) 452-2316; $35-55 s, $40-70 d; microwaves and fridges, AAA approved

Travelers Motel; 1133 E. 1st St.; tel. (360) 452-2303; $38 s, $42 d; microwaves and fridges, very reasonable off-season rates

All-View Motel; 214 E. Lauridsen Blvd.; tel. (360) 457-7779; $39-46 s, $41-48 d; kitchenettes available

Fairmont Motel; 1137 Hwy. 101 W (one mile west of Port Angeles); tel. (360) 457-6113; $40 s, $45 d

The Pond Motel; 196 Hwy. 101 W (two miles west of Port Angeles); tel. (360) 452-8422; $42 s, $45-49 d; attractive rural location with pond, kitchenettes available, AAA approved

Ruffles Motel; 812 E. 1st St.; tel. (360) 45-7788; $42 s, $47 d; kitchenettes available, see rooms first

Aircrest Motel; 1006 E. Front St.; tel. (360) 452-9255 or (800) 825-9255; $44 s, $54 d; jacuzzi, AAA approved

Flagstone Motel; 415 E. 1st St.; tel. (360) 457-9494; $45-50 s, $52-58 d; indoor pool, sauna, continental breakfast, AAA approved

MODERATE

Chinook Motel; 1414 E. 1st St.; tel. (360) 452-2336; $50 s, $60 d; outdoor pool, kitchenettes available, see rooms first

Hill Haus Motel; 111 E. 2nd St.; tel. (360) 452-9285 or (800) 421-0706; $55-95 s or d; panoramic views, AAA approved

Super 8 Motel at 2104 E. 1st St.; tel. (360) 452-8401 or (800) 800-8000; $60 s, $67 d

Portside Inn; 1510 E. Front St.; tel. (360) 452-4015 or (800) 633-8300; $62 s, $69 d; outdoor pool, jacuzzi, AAA approved

Uptown Motel; 101 E. 2nd St.; tel. (360) 457-9434 or (800) 858-3812; $69-129 s or d; excellent hilltop motel with harbor and mountain views, jacuzzi, continental breakfast, microwaves and fridges, AAA approved

EXPENSIVE

Doubletree Hotel; 221 N. Lincoln; tel. (360) 452-9215 or (800) 222-8733; $89-109 s or d; outdoor pool, jacuzzi, waterfront location, AAA approved

Best Western Olympic Lodge; 140 Del Guzzi Dr.; tel. (360) 452-2993 or (800) 600-2993; $129-179 s or d; impressive setting, outdoor pool, continental breakfast, large rooms, mountain views, jacuzzi, exercise room, free airport and ferry shuttle, AAA approved

Ocean Crest B&B, (360) 452-4832, a mile west of Port Angeles on the waterfront, has two bedrooms with private baths; kids accepted. $65-85 s or d.

Blue Mountain Lodge B&B, sits half-way between Port Angeles and Sequim, tel. (360) 457-8540. Guests stay in a cottage with a full kitchen and continental breakfast; kids welcome. An outdoor pool and trout pond are on the land; $65-85 s or d.

Klahhane B&B, 1203 E. 7th St., tel. (360) 417-0260 or (888) 552-4263, is an award-winning contemporary home with four guest rooms, king-size beds, and private or shared baths; $65-85 s or $75-95 d. Two-night minimum on summer weekends.

The SeaSuns B&B is a gorgeous 1926 Dutch Colonial home on spacious grounds at 1006 S. Lincoln, tel. (360) 452-8248. Inside are four guest rooms, shared or private baths, and period furnishings; $75-105 s or 85-115 d.

Hurricane Hills B&B two miles east of town, tel. (360) 452-7974, is a new country home with mountain views, and two guest rooms with private baths and patios. Guests enjoy a jacuzzi. Open May-Sept. only; $79-89 s or d.

Maple Rose Inn B&B, 112 Reservoir Rd. (south of town), tel. (360) 457-7673 or (800) 570-2007, is a large contemporary home with mountain views. The five very nice rooms all have private baths, plus access to the jacuzzi and large deck. Kids are accepted; $79-149 s or d.

Tudor Inn B&B, 1108 S. Oak, tel. (360) 452-3138, is a 1910 English Tudor home containing five antique-filled guest rooms with mountain and water views and private baths; $80-115 s or $85-125 d.

Bavarian Inn B&B, 1126 E. 7th, tel. (360) 457-4098, is a chalet-style home with harbor views, four guest rooms, and private baths; $80 s or $85-110 d.

The Haven B&B, 1206 W. 10th St., tel. (360) 452-6373 or (800) 794-8913, is a ranch-style home with four guest rooms, shared or private baths, and a full breakfasts. Kids accepted; $85-95 s or d.

Located halfway between Port Angeles and Sequim, **Domaine Madeleine,** tel. (360) 457-4174, is an elegant waterfront estate overlooking the Strait of Juan de Fuca. The four guest rooms and a separate cottage (perfect for honeymooners) are luxuriously appointed, and a multicourse epicurean breakfast starts your day; $135-165 s or d. Two-night minimum on summer weekends. French is spoken.

Colette's B&B, 339 Finn Hall Rd., tel. (360) 457-9197, is a luxurious 10-acre seaside estate with flower gardens, jacuzzi baths, king-size beds, fireplaces, and goumet breakfasts; $150-165 s or d. Two-night mininum in summer.

Other local B&Bs include **The Inn Transit,** 1405 W. 5th St., tel. (360) 452-1207; and **Northwest Manor B&B,** 1320 Marie View, tel. (360) 452-5839 or (888) 229-7052.

Campgrounds

The Park Service's **Heart O' the Hills Campground** ($10; open year-round unless closed by heavy snow) is five miles south of Port Angeles on Hurricane Ridge Road. Near the airport at W. Lauridsen Blvd. and Bean Rd., **Lincoln Park's** authentic pioneer cabins and an Indian longhouse accompany tennis courts, baseball diamond, campsites ($8; no hookups), nature trails, picnic area, and children's fishing pond at this 144-acre park. Campers can use the showers at the local swimming pool (225 E. 5th St.) or the boat harbor.

Nearby private RV parks include **Al's RV Park,** three miles east of Port Angeles, tel. (360) 457-9844 or (800) 357-1553; **Arney's Dam RV Park,** five miles west of Port Angeles, tel. (360) 452-7054; **Conestoga Quarters RV Park,** seven miles east of Port Angeles, tel. (360) 452-4637 or (800) 808-4637; **KOA Kampground,** seven miles east of Port Angeles, tel. (360) 457-5916 or (800) 562-7558; **Peabody Creek RV Park,** 127 S. Lincoln, tel. (360) 457-7092 or (800) 392-2361; and **Welcome Inn RV Park,** 1215 Hwy. 101 W, tel. (360) 457-1553.

FOOD

Because of its location as a jumping off point for Olympic National Park and Vancouver Island, Port Angeles is packed with high quality eateries of all persuasions.

Breakfast and Lunch

The acclaimed **First Street Haven,** 1st and Laurel, tel. (360) 457-0352, serves hearty breakfasts, along with reasonable sandwiches, quiche, pastas, and salads for lunch. The location is tiny, but the food is hard to beat. The same owners run the equally popular **Chestnut Cottage Restaurant,** 929 E Front St., tel. (360) 452-8344, featuring creative egg dishes for breakfast, plus salads, pastas, fajitas, and burgers for lunch. The setting is cozy and friendly.

Another fine breakfast and lunch spot is **Cafe Garden,** 1506 E. 1st St., tel. (360) 457-4611, where the menu covers the spectrum from Belgium waffles for breakfast to Asian stir-fries and deli sandwiches for lunch.

For a well-prepared traditional American breakfast—including 64 different omelettes—head to **Pete's Pancake House,** 110 E. Railroad Ave., tel. (360) 452-1948. Good breakfasts, along with the best local fish and chips, can be found just across the street at **Landing Restaurant,** 115 E. Railroad Ave., tel. (360) 457-6768.

American
Get the best burgers and fries anywhere around at **Frugals,** 1520 E. Front St., tel. (360) 452-4320. No seating; just drive up or walk up to order. **Rosewood's Family Buffet,** 1936 E. 1st, tel. (360) 457-1400, has inexpensive one-price dining for lunch and dinner, and is popular with families.

A popular steak and seafood restaurant overlooking the water is **Downriggers Restaurant,** 115 E. Railroad, tel. (360) 452-2700. **The Bushwacker Restaurant,** 1527 E. 1st, tel. (360) 457-4113, specializes in fresh seafood and prime rib, but also has a good salad bar. Open for dinners only.

International
For delicious, reasonably priced, and authentic south-of-the-border meals, be sure to visit **Chihuahua Mexican Restaurant,** 408 S. Lincoln St., tel. (360) 452-8344. Housed in a cozy Victorian-era home, **Toga's International Cuisine,** 122 W. Lauridsen Blvd., tel. (360) 452-1952, specializes in upscale German and Hungarian dinners, but also includes Northwest seafood. Very nice, but expensive.

Four miles east of Port Angeles, **C'est Si Bon,** tel. (360) 452-8888, prepares delicious local seafood with a French accent. The Olympics

and rose garden views add to the luxurious ambiance; open for dinner only with $20-24 entrees.

Located downstairs from an organic grocery, **Bella Italia,** 117B E. 1st St., tel. (360) 457-5442, blends traditional Italian cooking with a natural foods sensibility. The result is easily Port Angeles' finest Italian restaurant. Great desserts too.

Coffeehouses and Bakeries
If you're waiting for the ferry to come in, a good hangout spot is **Coffee House Gallery & Restaurant,** 118 E. 1st St., tel. (360) 452-1459. They have light vegetarian meals and espresso, plus acoustic music most nights.

Bonny's Bakery, 215 S. Lincoln St., tel. (360) 457-3585, bakes from-scratch French pastries, Danish rolls, all-American pies, and wonderful cookies. Housed in an old church, **Gina's Bakery,** 710 S. Lincoln St., tel. (360) 457-3279, has many more sweets, including "sinful cinnamon rolls" and other favorites. Good lunches too.

Beer and Wine
Port Angeles Brewing Co., 134 W. Front St., tel. (360) 452-6013, is a fine addition to the local food scene. Half-a-dozen fresh ales are on tap, and the menu includes gourmet pizzas, burgers, and sandwiches (including a delicious grilled eggplant and portabella version). Nice atmosphere too.

Camaraderie Cellars, tel. (360) 452-4964, just west of Port Angeles at 165 Benson Rd., specializes in cabernet sauvignon and sauvignon blanc and is open by appointment only.

Produce and Grocers
Get the freshest local fare at **Port Angeles Farmers Market,** held Feb.-Dec. near the corner of 8th and Chase Streets. The market is open Saturday 9 a.m.-4 p.m.; tel. (360) 683-7089. **Sunny Farms Country Store,** tel. (360) 683-8003, has a large produce stand located halfway between Port Angeles and Sequim. Also sold here are everything from hanging plants to homemade pizzas.

The Country Aire, 117 E. 1st St, tel. (360) 452-7175, has big selection of natural and organic foods. For the freshest local seafood—along with canned and smoked specialties—stop by **Hegg & Hegg** at 801 Marine Dr., tel. (360) 457-3344, or on Hwy. 101 E, tel. (360)

457-1551. They also have a small gift shop in the Landing Mall (where the ferry docks), tel. (360) 457-3733.

RECREATION

Playing Around

Rent mountain and road bikes along with kayaks from **Pedal 'n Paddle,** 120 E. Front St., tel. (360) 457-1240.

Swim at the **William Shore Memorial Pool,** 225 E. 5th St., tel. (360) 457-0241. For lake swimming, head a dozen miles west of town to **Lake Sutherland,** where the water gets quite warm by late summer.

Hurricane Ridge, 17 miles south of Port Angeles within Olympic National Park, is very popular with cross-country and downhill skiers and snowboarders. See "Olympic National Park" below for details.

Olympic Mountaineering, 140 W. Front St., tel. (360) 452-0240, has outdoor gear for sale, along with all sorts of rental gear, including backpacks, water filters, tents, stoves, cross-country skis, snowshoes, and ice axes. They also guide hiking and rock climbing trips in the Olympics. Also here is **Climb On Inn Climbing Gym,** a good place to hone your rock climbing skills.

From early April to mid-October, **Port Angeles Speedway,** tel. (360) 452-4666, six miles east of Port Angeles on Hwy. 101, has stock- and hobby-car races on Saturday nights, plus go-kart rentals at other times.

ENTERTAINMENT AND EVENTS

Nightlife

Dance to rock and roll in town at **Smitty's,** 536 Marine Dr., tel. (360) 457-1952, or drive six miles west to the only blues club on the peninsula, **Junction Tavern,** tel. (360) 452-9880. For relaxed listening, the **Coffee House Gallery,** 118 E. 1st St., tel. (360) 452-1459, has live jazz, classical, or other acoustic tunes on weekends.

Check out the big screen at **Lincoln Theater,** 132 E. 1st St., tel. (360) 457-7997, for the latest flicks.

Performing Arts

The **Port Angeles Symphony Orchestra** performs six concerts during the winter months; for tickets and other information, call (360) 457-5579. The **Port Angeles Light Opera Association** produces a musical each July; call (360) 457-6626 for tickets and information. The **Port Angeles Community Concert Association,** tel. (360) 457-5052, offers a series of concerts throughout the year. Live theater performances are given by **Port Angeles Community Players** year-round at the playhouse on Lauridsen Blvd. and Liberty Street. Call (360) 452-6651 for a schedule.

Each Memorial Day weekend, the **Juan de Fuca Festival** features a wide range of music, dance, comedy, kids' activities, arts and crafts, food, and more; call (360) 457-5411 for details. For something a bit less formal, free **Concerts on the Pier,** tel. (360) 452-2363, take place every Thursday evening between mid-June and mid-September.

Other Events

The **Fourth of July** brings music at the pier, kids' events, and a big fireworks show off the beach. The **Clallam County Fair** comes to Port Angeles the third weekend of August, with a carnival, rodeo, horse shows, farming exhibits, and a crowd-pleasing smash-'em-up demolition derby. Another popular event is the **Storytelling Festival,** which attracts tale-tellers from the U.S. and Canada on the third weekend of September. End the year in style with a visit to the **Christmas Crafts Fair** on the first weekend of December, where local artisans display their works.

SHOPPING

Arts and Crafts

Port Angeles's downtown shopping district is centered on 1st St., where you'll find shops, restaurants, galleries, and movie theaters. Of note is **Dragon's Hoard Art Gallery** 126 W. 1st, tel. (360) 452-5250, where you'll find handmade jewelry, bronze sculptures, and pottery and a museum of sorts with rocks and dinosaur bones. Other galleries worth a look include **Clallam Art Gallery,** at the Landing Mall, tel. (360) 452-8165; **Olympic Stained Glass,** 112 N. Laurel, tel. (360) 457-1090, and **North Light Gallery,** 120 N. Laurel, tel. (360) 452-4262. For something completely different, head to **Pacific Rim Hobby,** 124-A W. 1st St., tel. (360) 457-0794, for a voyage to model railroad heaven. The big HO-scale railroad village makes for fun gawking; look for such details as the giant insect attacking villagers.

Books

Port Angeles also has three good bookstores: **Odyssey Bookshop,** 114 W. Front St., tel. (360) 457-1045; **Port Book and News,** 104 E. 1st, tel. (360) 452-6367 (an expansive choice of magazines here too); and **Olympic Stationers,** 122 E. Front St., tel. (360) 457-6111.

INFORMATION AND SERVICES

For maps, brochures, and more local information, contact the **Port Angeles Chamber of Commerce Visitor Center,** 121 E. Railroad Ave., tel. (360) 452-2363; www.cityofpa.com. Open daily 8 a.m.-9 p.m. Memorial Day to mid-Sept.; and daily 10 a.m.-4 p.m. the rest of the year.

Just a few steps away is the **Port Angeles-Victoria Tourist Bureau,** tel. (360) 452-1223, open daily 7 a.m.-5 p.m. year-round. Here the focus is on travel, motel, and B&B reservations for southwest British Columbia—particularly nearby Vancouver Island—but they can also make motel reservations for Port Angeles. Tons of B.C. maps and brochures are free for the taking. Both the chamber of commerce and the tourist bureau are exceptionally helpful. Another source of information is the **North Olympic Peninsula Visitor and Convention Bureau,** tel. (800) 942-4042; www.olympus.net/olympic-peninsula.html.

The **Olympic National Park Visitor Center,** 3002 Mt. Angeles Rd., tel. (360) 452-0330, can give you sightseeing, hiking, camping, and other park info.

Campers and backpackers will appreciate **Peabody Street Coin Laundry** after getting back to nature in Olympic National Park; open seven days a week, 24 hours a day, at 212 S. Peabody. **The Spa,** 511 E. 1st St., tel. (360) 452-3257 or (800) 869-7177, has been around since 1928, with Finnish style steam rooms, massage, herbal body wraps, and a juice bar and tea room. (The hostel is also here.)

TRANSPORTATION AND TOURS

Ferries to Victoria

Port Angeles is a major transit point for travelers heading to or from Victoria, B.C., just 18 miles away across the Strait of Juan de Fuca. The MV *Coho* leaves Port Angeles for Victoria four times daily in summer (mid-May through October), and twice daily the rest of the year. One-way fares for the one-and-a-half-hour crossing are $27.25 for car and driver, $6.75 for passengers, $3.40 for kids 5-11, free under age five, and $10 for bicycle and rider. For specific departure times, contact the Black Ball ferry terminal at the foot of Laurel St. in Port Angeles, tel. (360) 457-4491. Vehicle space is at a premium on summer weekends and no reservations are accepted; get there very early to be assured of passage. Another option is to park your car in one of the lots near the ferry terminal ($7/day) and take the *Victoria Express* over. The *Coho* is out of service for maintenance from early January to early March.

The *Victoria Express,* a passenger-only ferry, makes the same run in an hour, two or three times a day from late May to early October. Roundtrip fares are $25 adults, $10 ages 5-11, free for children under age five. Bicycles are $3 extra. The ferry departs the Landing Mall terminal in Port Angeles; call (360) 452-8088 or (800) 633-1589 for details. Advance reservations are advised July-Labor Day.

By Air

Horizon Airlines, tel. (800) 547-9308, provides daily commuter service to Victoria, B.C., and Sea-Tac Airport from Fairchild International Airport on the city's west side. **Harbor Air,** tel. (800) 359-3220, also flies to Sea-Tac.

Buses and Tours

Public bus service now extends throughout the Olympic Peninsula, making it possible to reach all the towns for a minimal fare on any of the four different public transit systems. **Clallam Transit,** tel. (360) 452-4511 or (800) 858-3747, provides Mon.-Sat. service around the Olympic Peninsula to Forks, Neah Bay, La Push, and Olympic National Park's Sol Duc Hot Springs and Lake Crescent. The buses have bike racks. They also connect with **Jefferson Transit,** tel. (360) 385-4777 or (800) 773-7788, in Sequim for Port Townsend and other Jefferson County points, and with **Grays Harbor Transit** in Queets for points to the south.

Both **Olympic Bus Lines,** (360) 452-3858 or (800) 550-3858, and **Pennco,** tel. (360) 452-5104 or (888) 673-6626, offer van service connecting Port Angeles with Seattle and Sea-Tac Airport. Olympic also offers a variety of day trips in the summer, including Hurricane Ridge, Hoh Rain Forest, and a "see-it-all" park tour. In addition, they provide backpacker trailhead shuttles.

Rite Bros. Aviation, tel. (360) 452-6226, and **Olympic Aviation,** tel. (360) 417-0645, both have flightseeing and charter flights over the Olympics from Port Angeles.

OLYMPIC NATIONAL PARK

The diversity of climate and geography in Olympic National Park's 908,720 acres of wilderness is one reason it was among the 100 parks in the world named a "World Heritage Park" by the United Nations in 1981. The park has a central core covering the heart of the Olympic Mountains, and a separate narrow strip that follows the western coast for over 62 miles. These disconnected units offer an extraordinary range of habitats, from sea level beaches to mossy rain forests to rugged glaciated peaks. There's something for everyone here, and together these disparate elements provide some of Washington's most spectacular (and most photographed) scenery. The beauty contrasts sharply with surrounding timber-company lands where economics rule and the trees fall, leaving behind a bleak landscape of stumps and tree farms.

Paved roads only skirt the park, with spurs leading a short ways into the mountains, allowing the largest old-growth coniferous forest in the Lower 48 to remain the undisturbed home of 200 species of birds and 70 species of mammals, including Roosevelt elk (named for Theodore Roosevelt), black bear, deer, bald eagles, and Olympic marmots. Noticeably absent are the grizzly bear, pika, porcupine, ptarmigan, and other species common to the Cascade Range. The reason for this difference between the ranges dates back to the Pleistocene Ice Age, when a Canadian glacier isolated the Olympics from the rest of Washington. It's taken 11,000 years for the porcupine to advance to the park's southern boundary. Mountain goats native to the Cascades were artificially introduced to the Olympics in the 1920s and are now found in the park's interior. The National Park Service captured and removed a number of goats from the park because they were causing so much damage to the plantlife. The park service has also talked about shooting many of the goats, which has fed the flames of this controversial issue.

Olympic National Park is famous for the lush rain forests that carpet the western flanks of the mountains. The best known and most visited is Hoh Rain Forest, but the others—Quinault and Queets—are equally interesting, and visitors are more likely to have a more personal experience. Visitor centers have pamphlets describing the locations of "record trees" in or around Olympic National Park, including the largest western hemlocks, western red cedar, Sitka spruce, subalpine fir, and Alaska cedar remaining in the nation.

Only 15% of old-growth stands remain in the Pacific Northwest, and nearly half of these are within Olympic and Mount Rainier National Parks. Nearly all private lands are operated as managed forests; the trees viewed as an agricultural crop to be planted, thinned, and harvested. These tree farms are usually planted with a monoculture of Douglas fir trees and lack the heterogeneity and species richness of a natural forest. On Forest Service lands within Olympic National Forest, logging of old-growth stands has been essentially halted for the last several years because of environmental concerns, most notably the preservation of spotted owl and marbled murrelet habitat. This has caused immense controversy, especially in timber-dependent communities around the Olympic Peninsula, where jobs are at stake.

History

When English sea captain John Meares first sighted **Mt. Olympus** from aboard ship in 1788, he reputedly said, "If that be not the home where dwell the gods, it is certainly beautiful enough to be, and I therefore will call it Mt. Olympus." He seemed to have forgotten (or never knew) that Juan Perez already named the four peaks "Sierra Nevada de Santa Rosalia" in 1774. George Vancouver used Meares's name for the mountain, following a trend of waning Spanish influence in the Northwest.

Although Indians hunted in and traveled through these mountains for centuries, the central

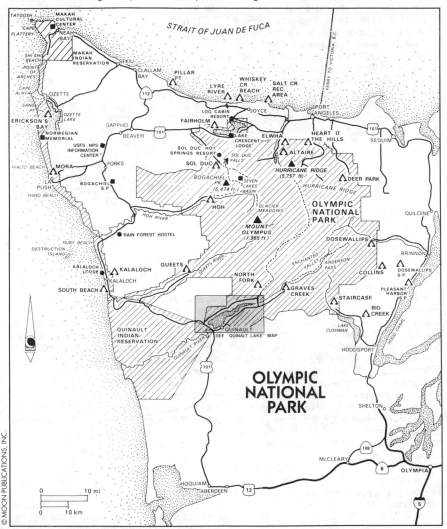

portion of the Olympics remained unexplored by westerners until late in the 19th century. The first substantiated exploration of the area came in 1885 when a small group of soldiers from the Vancouver Barracks got as far as Mt. Anderson on the eastern flank of the mountains.

The most famous exploration came in the winter of 1889-90, when a group of six men headed into the mountains, funded by the *Seattle Press* newspaper. Led by James Christie, the "Press Expedition" picked a bad time to start: December of 1889, one of the snowiest winters ever recorded. They ended up spending the winter exploring the Elwha River valley, and finally headed across the mountains in early May, reaching the coast almost six months after they began. One result of their trip is that many peaks in the Olympics are named for newspaper publishers and editors of that era.

The following summer, Mt. Olympus was climbed by members of a group of military men and scientists who cut a mule trail across the range. The leader, Lieutenant Joseph O'Neil, noted in his report: "In closing I would state that while the country on the outer slope of these mountains is valuable, the interior is useless for all practicable purposes. It would however, serve admirably for a national park. There are numerous elk—that noble animal so fast disappearing from this country—that should be protected." (John Muir and Judge James Wickersham both pushed for creating a national park here earlier.)

Seven years later, Congress created the Olympic Forest Reserve (later called Olympic National Forest), including much of the Olympic Peninsula. In 1909 President Theodore Roosevelt, in one of his last acts, issued a proclamation that created Mount Olympus National Monument to protect elk habitat. Washington congressman Monrad C. Wallgren and another President Roosevelt—FDR this time—were instrumental in making the monument a national park in 1938. The 62-mile coastal strip was added to the park in 1953.

Today Olympic National Park sees over four million visitors a year. Because of its enormous size and preserved interior, it's not hard to find peaceful solitude on its lakes and trails.

Climate

Weather in Olympic National Park is as varied and unpredictable as its geography. Rain is an ever-present threat, particularly on the western "wet" side, although three-quarters of the park's precipitation falls Oct.-March. In summer, park temperatures may be in the 80s—or the 60s; at sea level mild temperatures prevail, summer 70s to winter 40s.

Practicalities

A $10 park entrance fee, good for seven days, is charged for vehicles, or $5 for those on foot or bikes. Annual passes cost $20, and seniors can get a Golden Age Passport to all the parks for a one-time charge of just $10. Entrance fees are collected at Elwha, Hurricane Ridge/Heart O' the Hills, Hoh, Sol Duc, and Staircase entrance stations. See "Information and Services," below, for visitors centers and ranger stations in the park. Backcountry users should be sure to request a copy of the *Olympic Wilderness Trip Planner* from the Wilderness Information Center in Port Angeles, or call (360) 452-0300.

INTERIOR SIGHTS

The main portion of Olympic National Park occupies the mountainous interior of the Olympic Peninsula. Highway 101 circles the park, with paved or dirt roads leading to attractions around the park's periphery. The park is open year-round, although some roads may be closed in winter. The eastern side of Olympic National Park along Hood Canal is accessible from various points between Quilcene and Hoodsport; for details, see **Hood Canal.**

Hurricane Ridge

One of the park's most scenic and most visited areas, Hurricane Ridge rises over 5,200 feet seemingly straight up from the Strait of Juan de Fuca, providing an awesome contrast from sea level and breathtaking 360-degree views. The paved road starts at Race St. in Port Angeles, becoming Mt. Angeles Rd. and then Hurricane Ridge Rd. as it snakes up mountainsides for 17 miles at an easy seven percent grade; frequent turnouts allow for photo breaks. At the top, the **Hurricane Ridge Visitor Center** provides a

ARCHIE SATTERFIELD

Hurricane Ridge,
Olympic National Park

must-stop location to peer across a meadow-and-mountain landscape that might have been imported straight from the Swiss Alps. This is one of the park's best areas for spotting wildlife; black-tailed deer often bound across the parking lot, marmots are found in nearby slopes, and black bears are occasionally visible from a distance. The ridge's name isn't without basis in fact: the first lodge at the summit lost its roof in a strong winter blast. The weather can change quickly up here; tune in to AM 530 in Port Angeles for weather and other park information.

Hurricane Ridge Visitor Center provides food service, a gift shop, winter ski rentals, and ski-tow service. It is usually open daily May-Sept., and on weekends only during October and mid-December through April. Park naturalists offer summertime walks and talks plus wintertime snowshoe treks. Clallam Transit, tel. (360) 452-4511 or (800) 858-3747, has direct bus service between Port Angeles and Hurricane Ridge.

If the drop-offs and absence of guardrails on Hurricane Ridge Rd. made your palms sweat, you're in for a real treat on **Obstruction Point Road.** Starting from the Hurricane Ridge parking lot, this narrow gravel road (no RVs) follows the ridge for eight miles without a rail or fence, providing spectacular views for the strong-hearted. The road, constructed in the 1930s by the Civilian Conservation Corps, went as far as it could until a steep talus slope prohibited any further roadmaking.

Campgrounds: No camping or overnight lodging is available at Hurricane Ridge, but **Heart O' the Hills Campground,** five miles south of Port Angeles on Hurricane Ridge Rd., has year-round camping for $10. Campfire programs are offered July through Labor Day.

Deer Park Campground sits at the end of a narrow 18-mile gravel road on the eastern edge of the park (no RVs, and not accessible from the Hurricane Ridge area). Located at an elevation of 5,400 feet, the campground is $8 and open mid-June to late September.

Hiking: A number of trails begin at Hurricane Ridge, including 1.5-mile **Hurricane Hill Trail,** a paved walk to the top of 5,757-foot Hurricane Hill that passes picnic areas, marmot colonies, and spectacular vistas. A longer hike, the **Klahanee Ridge Trail,** follows the ridge's summit for four miles after leaving the paved trail near the marmot colonies. It continues downhill to Heart O' the Hills Campground, or you can return back to Hurricane Ridge.

In addition to these, visitors to Hurricane Ridge will find three other short paved trails through the flower-filled meadows with views of the Olympics. Longer paths lead downhill to the Elwha Valley and along the Little River. From Obstruction Peak, additional trails provide access into the heart of the Olympics.

Winter Activities: Between late December and late March, Hurricane Ridge is a popular winter destination for sightseeing, cross-country and downhill skiers, snowboarders, and tubers.

A small ski area, tel. (360) 417-0259, has two rope tows and a Poma lift. It's open on weekends and during the Christmas-New Year's holiday. Ski rentals, including cross-country and Telemark packages, are also available, along with ski lessons. Clallam Transit, tel. (360) 452-4511 or (800) 858-3747, provides a ski bus between Port Angeles and Hurricane Ridge. Backcountry skiers will discover a wealth of open country at Hurricane Ridge—check avalanche conditions before heading out.

Park Service naturalists offer guided snowshoe walks on weekends and other times in the winter; call (360) 452-0330 for information and reservations. Snowshoes are provided ($2 donation suggested). The visitor center—where you can warm up—and cafeteria are open winter weekends. The road to the top is open Sat.-Mon. 9 a.m.-dusk, and is closed overnight or during storms. Entrance fees are charged on weekends. Call (360) 452-0329 for current road and weather conditions, and always come prepared for the worst. No overnight parking at the summit.

Elwha Area

Take Olympic Hot Springs Rd. south from Hwy. 101 just west of Port Angeles into the Elwha River watershed, an area that has been the focus of controversy. The river is dammed by the Elwha and Glines Canyon dams, providing power for the Daishowa paper mill in Port Angeles. The dams—built early in this century before the park was created—devastated salmon runs in the river by raising water temperatures, blocking upstream and downstream migration (neither has a fishpass), and damaging or inundating spawning habitat. The high water temperatures have contributed to salmon kills, and many environmentalists have pushed to have these dams removed. Supporters of the dams point to their economic value in powering the paper mill. A Park Service study proposed that the dams be demolished to restore the Elwha, and there is hope that at least one of them will be removed in the next few years. Pitch your tent at the Elwha and Altaire campgrounds ($10) along the road north of Lake Mills (created by Glines Canyon Dam).

Nearly everyone in Washington knows of Sol Duc Hot Springs, but less well known are **Olympic Hot Springs,** located at the end of Boulder Creek Rd., off Elwha River Road. The springs were once the site of a large resort, but today they are essentially undeveloped. A 2.5 mile trail leads to shallow rock-lined pools where the water varies from lukewarm to 138° F. The Park Service discourages bathing and prohibits nudity (but that doesn't stop many folks from bathing au natural).

The Elwha River is a popular destination for river-runners, with Class II whitewater conditions. Check with the Park Service for current flow conditions and precautions if you decide to run it yourself. **Olympic Raft and Guide Service,** tel. (360) 452-1443, has scenic two-hour trips down the Elwha River ($39 adults, $35 kids), plus sea kayaking in Lake Crescent, Lake Aldwell, and Freshwater Bay.

Take the Elwha River Trail for two miles to **Humes Ranch,** built in 1889 by Grant Humes, who made his living leading wilderness expeditions and by hunting and trapping game. Today his cabin is on the National Register of Historic Places.

A number of hiking trails head into the backcountry from the Elwha area, and a variety of short and long hikes are available, including an across-the-park route that follows the Elwha Trail to Low Divide and then drops down to Quinault Lake on the North Quinault Trail, a distance of 44 miles.

Elwha Ranch B&B, tel. (360) 457-6540, is a country home overlooking above the Elwha River valley. The two guest rooms have private baths, a deck, and full breakfasts. A full breakfast is served, and kids are accepted. $90-95 s or d.

Lake Crescent

According to Native American legend, Mount Storm King once became so fed up with the fighting between the Clallams and Quileutes that he broke a rock off his head and threw it down at the warring tribes. The scientific view of the lake's origin isn't much different; it's attributed to ancient landslides that divided a glacial lake into two large sections (Lake Crescent and Lake Sutherland), sending water from Lake Crescent out the Lyre River. Today, freshwater Lake Crescent, 624 feet deep and 8.5 miles long, is famous for its Beardslee trout, a subspecies that is large (some are in the 12-14 pound range) and a hard fighter when hooked. Swimming, boating, camping, picnicking, and, of course, fishing are popular lake activities. The lake has an impressive mountain-rimmed setting. The Park Service's **Storm King Ranger Station,** tel. (360) 928-3380, is staffed during the summer months.

Fairholm Campground ($10; open year-round), on the west end of Lake Crescent, has summertime naturalist programs on some evenings. The Forest Service's **Klahowya Campground,** nine miles west of Lake Crescent on Hwy. 101, has sites for $12; open May to mid-October.

The lake has two concession-operated lodges around its perimeter. Built in 1916, **Lake Crescent Lodge,** tel. (360) 928-3211, is a cozy place with a comfortable feeling from decades of guests, including President Franklin D. Roosevelt, who stayed here in 1937. Sit on the porch for fine views of the mountains and Lake Crescent, or lounge in front of the big fireplace on a cool evening. The lodge has all sorts of accommodations, including lodge rooms (bath down the hall), cottages (some with fireplaces), and modern motel units. Rates are $65-138 s or d. Open late April to late October. The lodge has a restaurant and gift shop and rents rowboats.

Log Cabin Resort, tel. (360) 928-3325, at the northeast end of the lake, is three miles from Hwy. 101 on E. Beach Road. Rates are $48-103 s or d for very rustic cabins, motel rooms, and waterfront A-frame chalets. Many of the buildings have stood here since the 1920s. In addition to accommodations, the resort also has meals, rowboat, paddleboat, canoe, and kayak rentals, a gift shop, grocery store, RV and tent sites. Open April-October.

East of Crescent Lake is the smaller Sutherland Lake, a popular place to swim. **Lake Sutherland Lodge B&B,** tel. (360) 928-2111 or (888) 231-1444, is a modern log home with a covered deck facing the lake. The four guest rooms have private or shared baths and a full breakfast is served; $65-90 s or d. Park RVs along Lake Sutherland at **Shadow Mt. RV Park,** tel. (360) 928-3043.

Fairholm General Store, tel. (360) 928-3020, on the west end of Lake Crescent, is open April-Sept., and has tent sites and RV hookups, plus motorboats, rowboats, and canoes for rent. They also serve meals in the cafe; eat al fresco on a deck overlooking the lake.

Hiking: From the ranger station, follow the **Marymere Falls Trail** three-quarters of a mile for a spectacular view of this 90-foot falls. Not a lot of water, but quite impressive nevertheless. Return via the Crescent Lake Lodge Trail for a two-mile loop hike.

The **Mt. Storm King Trail** splits off from the Marymere Trail and climbs more than 3,000 feet in a bit over a mile with fine views across the lake. The path ends before the summit, and the Park Service recommends against continuing to the top due to hazardous conditions.

A four-mile hike starting at Lyre River Rd. or North Shore Rd. at opposite ends of Lake Crescent, the **Spruce Railroad Trail** follows the tracks of the 1918 Spruce Railroad, built to supply spruce for WW I aircraft. The war was over before the railroad was completed, however, and the spruce was no longer needed. Two tunnels (closed) and depressions from the railroad ties remain. Besides a taste of local history, the almost-level hike provides a view of Lake Crescent.

The nonprofit **Olympic Park Institute** offers excellent hands-on field seminars covering such diverse topics as Makah basketry, ecology of the forest canopy, and wolf biology. Seminars last 2-5 days, and some may be taken for college credit. They also have an Elderhostel. Headquarters for the institute is the historic Rosemary Inn, near Lake Crescent Lodge. Students stay in nearby cabins, and meals are served family style at the inn. For information and registration, call (360) 928-3720 or (800) 775-3720.

Sol Duc Hot Springs

About 30 miles west of Port Angeles and 12 miles south of Hwy. 101, Sol Duc (pronounced "SOLE duck") hot springs. Bask in the 99-105° F mineral water piped into three large outdoor pools. A fourth freshwater pool is also on the site. The springs ($6.50 adults, $5.50 seniors) are open daily 9 a.m.-9 p.m. mid-May through Sept. (till 8 p.m. in Sept.); and Sat.-Sun. 9 a.m.-8 p.m. April to mid-May, and October. Massage is also available.

In addition to the springs, **Sol Duc Hot Springs Resort,** tel. (360) 327-3583, has a restaurant, grocery store, and gift shop, plus cabins (some with kitchenettes) for $87-97 s or d. Two-night minimum on holidays. Open mid-May through September. A campground with RV hookups is also available.

The springs were long known to the Native peoples who first lived here, and white settlers were attracted to the area as a place of healing. By 1912, the area had an elegant hotel, theater, bowling alley, a 100-bed sanitorium, plus immaculately landscaped grounds with a golf course, tennis courts, and croquet grounds. A fire, begun by a defective flue, brought this to a crashing halt four years later. As the hotel burned to the ground, a short circuit caused the player organ to begin playing Beethoven's "Funeral March." Today's resort is considerably more modest.

Pitch a tent at the Park Service's **Sol Duc Campground** ($12); open all year, but sometimes closed in the winter months. Between July and Labor Day, park naturalists offer evening programs in the amphitheater some evenings.

Hiking: Several trails head up the Sol Duc Valley. A favorite is the one-mile **Sol Duc River Trail,** which passes through enormous western hemlocks and Douglas firs to Sol Duc Falls, one of the state's best-known waterfalls. A footbridge crosses the deep gorge cut by the river. From here, you can climb another three miles (one-way) to **Deer Lake,** bordered by trees. For variety, return to the campground from Sol Duc Falls on the **Lovers Lane Trail,** a three-mile path along the south side of the river.

A fine loop trip for backpackers (wilderness permit required) is to head up the Sol Duc River Trail to Seven Lakes Basin, then uphill to the summit of Bogachiel Peak and back out for a roundtrip of 22 miles.

Hoh Rain Forest

One of the park's most famous sights is also one of its most remote. The Hoh (pronounced "hoe") Rain Forest sits at the end of a paved 19 mile road that heads east from Hwy. 101 14 miles south of Forks. The **Hoh Rain Forest Visitor Center,** tel. (360) 374-6925, offers interpretive exhibits and summertime guided walks and campfire programs. Open daily 9 a.m.-7 p.m. in July and August, and daily 9 a.m.-4 p.m. most of the rest of the year. (The center may be unstaffed some of the year.) Stop by for brochures, information, books,

and educational exhibits on the life of the forest and the climate. It rains a *lot* here; 140 inches of rain per year keep this forest perpetually green and damp under towering conifers over 200 feet tall and up to 10 feet wide. The driest months are July and August. Not far away from the visitor center, the **Hoh Rain Forest Campground** has forested campsites for $10; open year-round. Be sure to bring food with you; there are no restaurants. Five miles up the Hoh Rain Forest Rd. is **Peak 6 Adventure Store,** tel. (360) 374-5254, selling all sorts of camping and climbing gear and clothes. The owners are friendly and knowledgeable about local trails, and prices are reasonable. Open daily in summer. They also rent mountain bikes and lead bike tours of the area.

Three short interpretive trails lead through the lush spikemoss-draped forests behind the visitor center. Lacy ferns carpet the forest floor, and some even survive in the tops of the bigleaf and vine maples. A paved wheelchair-accessible mini-trail is directly behind the center, and the **Hall of Mosses Trail** offers an easy three-quarter-mile loop. **Spruce Nature Trail** covers a 1.25-mile loop that crosses a crystalline spring-fed creek and then touches on the muddy glacially fed Hoh River. More adventurous folks can head out the **Hoh River Trail,** an 18-mile path that ends at Blue Glacier and is used to climb Mt. Olympus (see "Hiking and Mountaineering," below, for details). Hikers heading into the wilderness need to pick up permits at the visitor center or the Wilderness Information Center in Port Angeles.

Quinault Valley and the Eastside

Beautiful Lake Quinault on the southwest corner of Olympic National Park features a diversity of trails, accommodations, and other attractions. For details on this fascinating and very popular area, see **Lake Quinault.**

See **Lake Cushman** for details on the **Staircase** area on the southeast corner of the park, where trails and a popular campground are located at the upper end of Lake Cushman. Also see **Doeswallips Recreation Area** for access from the Dosewallips River area, and **Quilcene** for access via the Buckhorn Wilderness.

OLYMPIC COAST SIGHTS

Washington's rocky and essentially undeveloped Olympic coast is truly a national gem, and in 1994 it was declared the **Olympic Coast National Marine Sanctuary,** a designation that helps protect the shore and ocean from development. The coast contains rich fishing grounds, more species of whales, dolphins, and porpoises than anywhere else on earth, some of the largest seabird colonies in the Lower 48, and an unparalleled beauty that attracts painters, photographers, and anyone with a sense of wonder. The shore is dotted with seastacks, cliff-rimmed beaches, and forested hills.

To preserve the natural habitat, automobile access to the park's Pacific Ocean beaches is severely limited, but the picturesque cliffs and sea stacks are worth the effort to get there. Be prepared for soggy, windy weather; 100 inches of annual rainfall combine with sometimes violent winds for less-than-pleasant hiking weather, although thanks to the warming effect of the Japanese Current that flows past the Olympic coast, the temperatures are mild year-round. Only rarely does the thermometer drop below 40° F.

Park Service offices have a helpful *Olympic Coastal Strip* handout with a map and dos and don'ts for backcountry users. The Olympic coastline can be dangerous to hikers. Two "watchout" situations are attempting to round headlands and getting caught by incoming tides, and being struck by floating logs in the surf. Note that The Hoh and Quillayute Rivers are too deep to ford at any time, and that other creeks and rivers may be difficult to cross, particularly at high tide or when runoff is strong. Always take a tide chart and use caution. This is, after all, the wilderness.

Point of Arches and Shi Shi Beach

Near the north park boundary, **Point of Arches** is a testimony to the relentless pounding of the Pacific where, with a force of two tons per square inch, the ocean carves giant arches out of ancient rock. The Arches, legendary children of Destruction Island and Tatoosh Island, were pushed from Mother Tatoosh's canoe when she deserted her husband because, she said, "You'd probably grow up just like your father!" The bluffs above neighboring Shi Shi (pronounced "shy-shy") Beach provide a vantage point for watching the spring and fall gray whale migrations; the best viewing season is March-May. This stretch of coastline features some of the finest beaches and tidepools anywhere on the Washington coast; you might even find remains of a shipwreck still visible. Shi Shi Beach and Point of Arches are currently only accessible from the south (Ozette) end. Conflicts over access and rights of way have led to closures from the Neah Bay side. Call the Park Service at (360) 452-0330 for the latest on access.

Ozette Lake Area

Located in the northwest corner of the coastal strip, eight-mile-long Lake Ozette is the third largest natural lake in Washington. In the 19th century this area was crowded with 130 homesteaders scratching out a living, but they gradually gave up and moved away. A 21-mile paved road heads southwest from Sekiu, ending at the **Ozette Ranger Station,** tel. (360) 963-2725, on the north end of the lake. The ranger station is open daily in the summer, but in the winter there are no set hours. This area has one of the most popular overnight hikes along the Olympic coast, and summer weekends attract outdoor enthusiasts. Parking costs $2 per day.

Because of overcrowding and resource damage, the Park Service has instituted a **quota system** for overnight hiking in the Ozette area between Memorial Day weekend and Labor Day. (There are no restrictions on day-use, however.) Make reservations at the Wilderness Information Center in Port Angeles, tel. (360) 452-0300. If you don't have a permit, you might try arriving early to grab one of the 18 campsites accessible by car, but if those are gone, you'll have to drive all the way back to a private campground in Sekiu. The busiest times are weekends in July and August.

The small **Ozette Campground** has camping ($10) year-round, but get here early to be sure of a space (no reservations). The lake is a popular place for boats, canoes, and kayaks, but take care since winds can create treacherous wave action at times. The free **Erickson's Bay** boat-in campground is halfway down the lake on the west side. Good fishing for largemouth bass, cutthroat trout, kokanee, and other fish.

Two trails head to the coast from the ranger station. One leads southwest to **Sand Point,** three miles away; the other three miles northwest to **Cape Alva**—the westernmost point in the Lower 48. By hiking the beach connecting the two, you can create a triangular loop trip of 9.3 miles. You can also continue south on the beach for 2.3 miles to the **Norwegian Memorial,** a tribute to the victims of a 1903 shipwreck. There is much to explore in the Cape Alva area: fascinating tidepools, cannonball shaped rocks, an anchor from one of the ships that ran aground here, and even an occasional Japanese glass ball. This is probably the best place to see wildlife in Olympic National Park, with bald eagles in the air, deer along the beach, sea lions and seals in the water, and migrating gray whales in fall and spring. This area contains the largest population of sea otters in the Lower 48; look for them in the kelp beds off Sand Point. The Wedding Rocks area between Cape Alva and Sand Point is well known for its petroglyphs, which were carved by the original inhabitants of this land at an unknown time. Pick up a handout describing the petroglyphs from the ranger station.

The famous Makah village site is just a short distance from where the Cape Alva trail meets the beach. During the 1970s, archaeologists from Washington State University uncovered a wealth of ancient artifacts. The dig is now closed and buried, but many of the items found are displayed in the Makah Cultural Center at Neah Bay. It was only early in this century that the last Makah peoples moved away—not because they wanted to, but because the state insisted that their children attend schools, and the closest one was at Neah Bay.

The Lost Resort, tel. (360) 963-2899 or (800) 950-2899, has a general store, deli, camping supplies, showers, and private campsites next to the lake.

Rialto Beach Area

This is one of the most popular entry points for the coastal strip of Olympic National Park. Rialto Beach is on the north side of the Quillayute River, just west of the Mora campground and ranger station. The one-and-a-half-mile beach is popular with folks out for a stroll or day hike, but continue northward and the crowds thin out as

Rialto Beach

DON PITCHER

the country becomes a jumble of sea stacks—remnants of the ancient coast. Hole in the Wall is one of the most interesting of these. This treacherous stretch of shore has claimed many lives, as memorials to Chilean and Norwegian sailors attest. The 21 long and remote miles between Rialto Beach and the Ozette Ranger Station feature abundant wildlife—including bald eagles, harbor seals, shorebirds, and migrating whales at different times of the year. The resident raccoons are here year-round, so hang your food in a hard-sided container!

On the south side of the Quillayute River is the village of La Push (later in this chapter), with access to many more miles of Olympic shoreline. A very popular day hike from the La Push area is **Second Beach,** an easy three-quarter-mile trail that starts just south of La Push, followed by a mile and a half of beach, tidepools, and sea stacks, including a pointed one called Quillayute Needle. You can camp at a couple of points in the trees, making this some of the most accessible beach camping in the state.

Park at Third Beach, just south of the Second Beach trailhead, for a challenging hike all the way down to **Oil City,** 17 miles away on the north side of the Hoh River. Be sure to carry a tide chart. Oil City has neither oil nor is it a city. Three different exploration parties came here in search of oil—attracted by crude seeping from the ground just north of here. During the 1930s, 11 exploratory wells were drilled and a town was platted, but there simply wasn't enough oil to justify development. A part-paved, part-gravel road leads 11 miles from Hwy. 101 to the Oil City trailhead.

Pitch a tent at **Mora Campground** ($10; open year-round), where summertime naturalist programs and nature walks are also offered. RVers can park at nearby Ocean Park Resort and Three Rivers Resort (see **La Push**).

Clallam Transit, tel. (360) 452-4511 or (800) 858-3747, provides daily bus service to La Push from Port Angeles and Forks. Hikers can catch the bus as far as the turnoff to Rialto Beach, and walk or hitch the final three miles.

Hoh River to Queets River

The southern end of Olympic National Park's coastal strip is the most accessible, with Hwy. 101 running right along the bluff for more than a dozen miles. Short trails lead down to the water at half a dozen points, and at the southern end one finds the town (of sorts) called Kalaloch, with a comfortable lodge, two Park Service campgrounds, and other facilities. See **Kalaloch** for a description of this area. Beach camping is not allowed along this stretch of the coast.

HIKING AND MOUNTAINEERING

Wilderness Hikes

Backcountry users should request a copy of the *Olympic Wilderness Trip Planner* from the Wilderness Information Center (WIC) in Port Angeles, tel. (360) 452-0300. **Wilderness use permits** ($5 for the permit, plus $2 pp/night) are required for backcountry camping; pick one up at the WIC or the ranger station nearest your point of departure. Because of overuse, summer quotas are in effect and reservations are required for overnight hikes in the Ozette, Flapjack Lakes, Hoh, Grand and Badger Valleys, Lake Constance, and Sol Duc areas.

The only way to cross the central portion of Olympic National Park is on foot; auto roads barely penetrate it. More than 600 miles of hiking trails can be found within the park, covering the park's virgin forest core, its matchless beaches, and its alpine peaks. Shorter day hikes and loop trips are described in appropriate parts of this chapter. For complete information on backcountry hiking in the park, see the *Olympic Mountains Trail Guide* by Robert L. Wood (Seattle: The Mountaineers) or *Hiking Olympic National Park* by Erik Molvar (Helena: Falcon Press).

It's always a good idea to hang your food—raccoons can be a real problem, especially along the coast. Because of excellent public bus systems on roads surrounding the park, long one-way hikes are possible; and you may be able to catch the bus back to your starting point. Call **West Jefferson Transit,** tel. (800) 436-3950, or **Grays Harbor Transit,** tel. (800) 562-9730, for route information.

For a south-to-north (or vice-versa) 44-mile hike, start at the North Fork Ranger Station near Lake Quinault. The **North Fork Trail** follows the North Fork Quinault River for 16.5 miles to Low Divide, then it joins the **Elwha River Trail** terminating at Lake Mills near Elwha (just west of Port Angeles). You'll be hiking in reverse the route of James Halbold Christie, leader of the Seattle Press expedition across the then-unexplored Olympic Peninsula. It took Christie and his party six months and one black bear to complete the route in 1890; it should take you only four days and a packful of gorp.

For a 24-mile one-way, relatively level hike, start at the end of South Shore Rd. on the south side of the park, follow the east fork of the Quinault River for 13 miles, passing Enchanted Valley Ranger Station and Anderson Pass, then travel alongside the Dosewallips River to the Dosewallips Ranger Station and campground.

Climbing

Climbing the glacier-clad 7,965-foot **Mt. Olympus** is a 44-mile roundtrip. From the Hoh Ranger Station—the closest and most popular departure point—hike 12 flat miles along the Hoh River Trail, then another five steep ones to the Olympus base camp, Glacier Meadows. Crossing Blue Glacier and the Snow Dome requires rope, ice ax, crampons, and mountaineering skills; a hard hat is advised because of rock falls near the summit. Inexperienced climbers should go with a professional guide service. The eight-mile climb from Glacier Meadows to the summit takes about 10 hours. The best months for climbing are late June through early September, the driest months in the park; prior to that time mud and washouts may slow you down. *A Climber's Guide to the Olympic Mountains,* published by The Mountaineers, gives detailed information on this and other climbs in the park. This book, other trail guides, and quadrangle maps can be obtained from The Northwest Interpretive Association in Port Angeles, tel. (360) 452-4501 ext. 239.

OTHER OUTDOOR ACTIVITIES

Naturalist Programs

Guided walks and campfire programs are held frequently throughout the summer at Heart O' the Hills, Hoh, Kalaloch, Mora, and Sol Duc campgrounds July-Labor Day. Check the campground bulletin board for times and topics.

Olympic Park Institute, tel. (360) 928-3720 or (800) 775-3720, a nonprofit educational organization, offers field seminars for naturalists, photographers, and anyone interested in the ecology or geography of the park. See **Lake Crescent** for details.

Summer Recreation

The clear turquoise waters of Lake Crescent are open to fishing and boating; boats and canoes can be rented from Lake Crescent Lodge, Fairholm General Store, and Log Cabin Resort. Bottom fishing is popular in the Strait of Juan de Fuca and along the coast; no license is necessary within park limits, though salmon and steelhead catch record cards are required, available from sporting goods stores.

Both **Olympic Raft Adventures,** tel. (360) 452-1443 or (888) 452-1443, and **Chinook Expeditions,** tel. (800) 241-3451, lead float trips down the Elwha, Hoh, and Queets rivers.

Lake Quinault Outfitters, tel. (360) 452-8742 or (888) 452-9635, offers horseback rides and overnight trips into the park from the south end of Lake Mills near Elwha.

Winter Sports

Ski rentals, two rope tows, Poma lift, and cross-country ski trails provide Nordic and Alpine skiing at Hurricane Ridge ski area when the snow is deep enough. Nonskiers can enjoy the sights via a naturalist-led snowshoe walk ($2 donation for snowshoes). Snow-tubing is another popular winter activity at the Ridge. Weather permitting, the road is plowed and the lodge and ski facilities are open for holiday and weekend day-use only from late December to late March.

ACCOMMODATIONS AND FOOD

Within Olympic National Park are a number of concessionaire-operated lodging places: Lake Crescent Lodge and Log Cabin Resort at Lake Crescent, Sol Duc Hot Springs Resort at the springs, and Kalaloch Lodge on the southwestern edge of the park. Kalaloch Lodge is open year-round, but the others are open spring through early fall. All of these also serve three meals a day. See above for descriptions and rates for each of these. In addition, dozens of other places are available in surrounding towns such as Port Angeles, Sequim, Forks, La Push, Quinault, Quilcene, Brinnon, and Hoodsport.

CAMPING

Park Service Sites

Seventeen park campgrounds offer camping on a first-come, first-served basis for $8-12 a night. No showers or laundry facilities are available at any campground; if you really miss bathing, Sequim Bay State Park, Bogachiel State Park, and Dosewallips State Park have showers you can use, or head to one of the nearby RV parks. Although lacking trailer hookups, some campgrounds do have trailer dumping stations. The camping limit is 14 days. Specific campground information is described for each part of the park.

Other Campgrounds

Other campgrounds around the park borders include 24 on Olympic National Forest land, a dozen Dept. of Natural Resources campgrounds, and five state parks. Fees range from free to $13 a night. See appropriate sections for descriptions of these campgrounds. Full RV hookups are available at **Log Cabin Resort** on Lake Crescent, tel. (360) 928-3325, and **Sol Duc Hot Springs Resort**, tel. (360) 327-3583. Additional private RV parks are in towns surrounding the park.

INFORMATION AND SERVICES

For detailed information on camping, hiking, and accommodations within the park, stop by or call the **Olympic National Park Visitor Center,** about one mile from Hwy. 101 on Race St. in Port Angeles, tel. (360) 452-0330. The visitor center is open throughout the year, but the hours are dependent upon the park budget and season. In the past they have been open daily 8:30 a.m.-6 p.m. Memorial Day to Labor Day, and daily 8:30 a.m.-5 p.m. the rest of the year. Get complete and up-to-date info from the park's Web page: www.nps.gov/olym.

The **Wilderness Information Center** (WIC) behind the visitor center, has backcountry trail info, trip planning tips, tide charts, and more. They also issue wilderness permits for backcountry camping ($5 for the permit, plus $2 pp/night). The WIC is open daily from late spring to early autumn.

Other places for park information are: **Hoh Rain Forest Visitor Center,** on the east side, tel. (360) 374-6925; **Hurricane Ridge Visitor Center; Storm King Ranger Station** on Lake Crescent, tel. (360) 928-3380; plus ranger stations at Quinault Lake, Fairholm, Elwha, Kalaloch, Ozette, Staircase, Sol Duc, and Mora. The Park Service and Forest Service jointly operate information offices in Hoodsport and Forks.

The most up-to-date topographic maps of the Olympic Peninsula are produced by **Custom Correct Maps** produced by Little River Enterprises. They're available in park visitor centers or by calling (360) 457-5667.

TRANSPORTATION

Public buses operate throughout the Olympic Peninsula, making it easy to reach towns surrounding the park for a minimal fare. **Clallam Transit,** tel. (360) 452-4511 or (800) 858-3747, covers the northern end, including Port Angeles, Forks, Neah Bay, La Push, and Lake Crescent. Connect with **Jefferson Transit,** tel. (360) 385-4777 or (800) 773-7788, in Sequim for Port Townsend and other east Jefferson County points; or with **West Jefferson Transit,** tel. (800) 436-3950, in Forks for free transportation south to Kalaloch, Queets, and Lake Quinault. At Lake Quinault, catch **Grays Harbor Transit,** tel. (800) 562-9730, in Quinault for points to the south and east.

Olympic Bus Lines, tel. (360) 452-3858 or (800) 550-3858, provides backpacker trailhead shuttles throughout Olympic National Park, and also offers a variety of day tours in the summer, including to Hurricane Ridge, Hoh Rain Forest, and a "see-it-all" park tour.

WEST END AND PACIFIC COAST

JOYCE

Joyce is the easternmost in a series of small towns on the Strait of Juan de Fuca that cater primarily to commercial and recreational fishermen. Accommodations and restaurants here and in neighboring fishing towns are no-frills enterprises. The town's centerpiece is the **Joyce General Store,** with everything you might need—from pipe fittings to frozen chicken. In business since 1911 and owned by the same family for more than four decades, it started out with the same false front, oiled wood floors, beaded ceiling, and fixtures. This is said to be the oldest continuously operated store in the state. Also in Joyce are two cafes, a tavern, and a couple of other small businesses.

Housed in a former railroad station, the **Joyce Museum,** tel. (360) 928-3568, has relics from the town's early days, logging and railroad equipment, photos, and driftwood carvings. Open weekends only June-August.

The local bash is **Joyce Daze** on the first weekend of August, with a parade, salmon bake, arts and crafts show, and the main event, a wild blackberry pie contest. Call (360) 928-3821 for details.

West of Joyce, Hwy. 112 winds through the tree farms and along the coast before cutting inland up the Pysht River Valley. Watch out for the speeding logging trucks on this stretch. Learn about private forestry practices in a visit to the 26,000-acre **Pysht Tree Farm,** tel. (360) 963-2382 or (800) 998-2382. The tree farm is east of Clallam Bay near milepost 29.

Campgrounds

The county-run **Salt Creek County Park** three miles east of Joyce off Hwy. 112, tel. (360) 928-3441, has camping ($10), a beach, picnic areas, hiking trails, playfields, showers, and a marine sanctuary. This was the site of Fort Hayden during WW II, and the concrete gun emplacements are still visible, though the 45-foot-long guns are long gone.

The Department of Natural Resources maintains the free but primitive **Lyre River Recreation Area** five miles west of Joyce; open year-round. It's right on the river and only a few steps from the Strait of Juan de Fuca. RVers can stay at **Lyre River Park,** five miles west of Joyce, tel. (360) 928-3436, or **Whiskey Creek Beach,** three miles west of Joyce, tel. (360) 928-3489. Cabins are available at the latter. **Carol's Crescent Beach,** 3456 Crescent Beach Rd., tel. (360) 928-3344, has RV and tent sites, and the use of a half-mile of beach.

CLALLAM BAY AND SEKIU

The twin towns of Clallam Bay and Sekiu (SEE-kyoo) are just a mile apart on the Strait of Juan de Fuca approximately 50 miles west of Port Angeles and offer the basic services but not much else. The bay has been the site of a salmon cannery, a sawmill town, and a leather-tanning factory, but of late the bay and Sekiu are best known for fishing, both commercial and charters. With the decline of salmon in recent years, the fishing has focused more on bottom fish, particularly halibut. The area is also popular with scuba divers, and a prison in Clallam Bay provides guaranteed jobs. The land near here is privately owned and managed for timber production. Enormous clearcuts stare down the rugged slopes and logging trucks roll past every few minutes, hauling more former trees to the mill.

Motels

Local lodging places are all in Sekiu. **Curley's Resort,** tel. (360) 963-2281 or (800) 542-9680, has nice motel units ($38 s or d) and cabins with kitchenettes ($45-48 d), as well as RV hookups, boat and kayak rentals, a dive shop, and even whalewatching trips through their **Puffin Charters.** Another good place is **Van Riper's Resort,** tel. (360) 963-2334, with a variety of lodging options for $50-135 s or d. **Herb's Motel and Charters,** tel. (360) 963-2346, has motel rooms for $40-85 s or d. **Bay Motel,** tel. (360) 963-2444, charges $40-70 s or d for its rooms with kitchenettes.

Straitside Resort, tel. (360) 963-2100, has five basic units and two well-maintained older cabins, all with kitchenettes for $55-85 s or d.

Winter Summer Inn B&B, tel. (360) 963-2264, has decks overlooking the Clallam River and the Strait of Juan de Fuca, and two rooms with private baths and full breakfasts for $65-75 s or d. A separate studio apartment (no breakfast) is $85 s or d.

Parks and Campgrounds

The beaches beyond Slip Point Lighthouse, on the east end of the bay, are great for beachcombing and exploring the tidepools, and the area east of here is famous for its marine fossils. County parks in the Clallam Bay area are **Clallam Bay Spit,** a 33-acre waterfront park for day-use only, and **Pillar Point County Park,** just east of Clallam Bay. The latter is a four-acre park with a boat launch and campsites ($10); open mid-May to mid-September. Call (360) 963-2301 for details.

RVers can park at **Curley's Resort** (described above); **Sam's Trailer RV Park,** in Clallam Bay, tel. (360) 963-2402; **Coho RV Park,** tel. (360) 963-2333; and **Tretteviks RV Park,** eight miles west of Sekiu, tel. (360) 963-2688, which has the standard RV hookups and tent spaces, plus an attractive sandy beach.

Other Practicalities

Groceries and meals can be found in Clallam Bay. The local festival is **Sekiu/Clallam Bay Fun Days,** held the second weekend in July, with live music, rowboat races, arts and crafts, and a big fireworks show. Also popular is a July Fourth **Halibut Derby.** Get info from the **Clallam Bay/Sekiu Chamber of Commerce,** tel. (360) 963-2339, or www.northolympic.com/cbs.

NEAH BAY

Heading west from Sekiu on Hwy. 112, you begin to realize that you really are reaching the end of the line. This is one of the most dramatic shoreline drives in Washington—the narrow road winds along cliff faces and past extraordinary views. The only radio stations to be found are from Canada, and the ocean is up-close and personal the entire time. At the end of the road,

72 miles from Port Angeles, Neah Bay sits on the 44-square-mile **Makah Indian Reservation** in virtual isolation, at the northwesternmost point of the contiguous United States. Anyone who has spent time in a remote Alaskan village will feel right at home in Neah Bay.

For many years, Neah Bay was a center for salmon fishing, attracting both commercial fishermen and vacationing anglers. As with other settlements on the Olympic Peninsula, the decline of salmon stocks and the resulting lack of a sport-fishing season have had a devastating effect. Once-thriving motels now stand abandoned, and the village has a gritty down-in-the-dumps feeling. Buildings are of unpainted or peeling plywood, and abandoned cars litter the yards. The fishing is still good for bottom fish, and a few charter boats now target halibut, ling cod, red snapper, and black sea bass. The town also has a small U.S. Coast Guard base and an impressive new marina.

In 1998—after a 70-year hiatus—the Makah people again started hunting migrating gray whales, with a maximum of five taken each year for food. The hunt has created intense controversy, with tribal authorities viewing it as a means to revive cultural traditions, while environmentalists fear that it could lead to similar claims from Norway, Russia, and Japan that will result in many more whales being killed in the name of traditional use.

Makah Cultural Center

In 1970 tidal erosion unearthed old Ozette Indian homes that had been destroyed by a mudslide some 500 years earlier. The slide entombed and preserved the material, and 11 years of excavations by archaeologists from Washington State University unearthed one of the richest finds in North America. Many of the thousands of artifacts discovered are now on display in the $2 million Makah Cultural and Research Center, tel. (360) 645-2711, at Neah Bay. This is the finest collection of Northwest Coast Indian artifacts from pre-contact times, with an extraordinary range of material, including beautifully carved seal clubs, spears, bentwood boxes, combs, paddles, bows and arrows, clothing, woven baskets, whale bones, and much more. Not on display—it is too fragile—but visible in photos, is an intricate plaid blanket woven from

© MOON PUBLICATIONS, INC.

woodpecker feathers, dog hair, cattail fluff, and cedar bark. A re-created 15th-century longhouse is the museum's centerpiece, showing how the people lived in the abundance of the land. Outside, a modern longhouse is sometimes used for basketry and carving demonstrations.

The museum is open daily 10 a.m.-5 p.m. from Memorial Day to September 15; closed the rest of the year. An hour-long video about Neah Bay and the archaeological dig is shown daily at 11 a.m. and 2 p.m. The small gift shop sells local baskets and beadwork. You can also obtain local information here. Admission costs $4 adults, $3 seniors and students, free for kids under six.

Other Sights

The setting for Neah Bay is simply spectacular, with rocky Waadah Island just offshore, connected to land by a two-mile-long breakwater. A totem pole stands in the little grassy park across from the BP station, and one often sees bald eagles around town, especially in the spring.

The **Cape Loop Rd.** provides an interesting drive or mountain bike ride to the tip of Cape Flattery. The narrow dirt road is not for RVs. Pick up a route map at the museum, or head west from town to the Makah Tribal Center, and then turn right to the cape (left will take you to Hobuck Beach and a fish hatchery). About eight miles from town, you'll come to one of the few unlogged areas remaining on the cape, and the new **Cape Flattery Trail.** This fine boardwalk path leads downhill three-quarters of a mile to the rocky shoreline, with views of Tatoosh Island and **Cape Flattery Lighthouse,** built in 1858. Most folks return to Neah Bay the same way they come out, but mountain bikers and four-wheelers will enjoy the very rough road that leads back eastward around the cape to Neah Bay, passing a small waterfall with sculpted pools large enough to sit in on a warm summer day, and several miles later a dump that has to be one of the worst in the state of Washington (but a good place to look for ravens and eagles) Total length of this loop is approximately 16 miles.

On the southwest side of the Makah Indian Reservation are two attractive day-use beaches facing Mukkaw Bay: Hobuck Beach and Sooes

Beach. Just south of here is Shi Shi Beach within Olympic National Park, a favorite place for hikers. No access to Shi Shi from this end.

Motels

Neah Bay lodging can leave much to be desired. The "resorts" are mostly shoestring operations dependent upon fishermen and hunters who don't mind ancient furnishings and marginally clean rooms. The nicest in-town motel is **The Cape Motel,** tel. (360) 645-2250, with rooms for $40-75 s or d, including kitchenettes. RV and tent spaces are available. The friendly **Silver Salmon Resort,** tel. (360) 963-2688, has basic motel units (some with kitchenettes) for $39-44 s or d; it's very popular with anglers.

If you want to get away from town, **Hilden's Motel,** three miles east on Bowman Beach, tel. (360) 645-2306, has five units for $45-55 s or $55-65 d. All have full kitchens and sit right on the water with rocky islets just offshore. This is a fine place to watch the surfbirds or scan the horizon for seals. **Chito Beach Resort,** tel. (360) 963-2581, is a new place with attractive cabins and cottages with kitchens; $70-100 s or d. They're right on the water 10 miles east of Neah Bay.

Campgrounds

Most local motels also have RV parks (of a sort) and allow tents for a fee. More RV parking four miles east of town at **Snow Creek Resort,** tel. (360) 645-2284. A better bet is **Tretteviks RV Park,** 10 miles east of town, tel. (360) 963-2688, with grassy sites and a sandy beach.

Food and Crafts

Get burgers and similar fare at **Makah Maiden,** tel. (360) 645-2508. **JJ's Pizza & Bakery** has pizzas and sweets. **Washburn's General Store,** tel. (360) 645-2211, sells groceries and has a deli with fresh sandwiches and espresso (this is Washington after all), plus a small gift shop selling Indian jewelry, baskets, carvings, and knitted items. **Raven's Corner Gifts & Indian Arts** sells local crafts and T-shirts with Makah designs.

Events

Makah Days is the town's big annual festival, celebrating the day the reservation first raised the American flag in 1913. Held on the weekend closest to August 26, the three-day festival is

TACOMA PUBLIC LIBRARY

Charley Swan dressed to impress for Neah Bay's Makah Days

highlighted by dances, a parade, fireworks show, salmon bake, canoe races, and bone games (Indian gambling). Also popular is the **Chito Beach Bluegrass Jamboree** in mid-June.

Information and Transportation

The Makah Museum has local information. **Clallam Transit,** tel. (360) 452-4511 or (800) 858-3747, provides daily bus service to Neah Bay and throughout the northern Olympic Peninsula. **Pennco,** tel. (360) 452-5104 or (888) 673-6626, offers door-to-door van service around the Olympic Peninsula. For guided tours of the Neah Bay area, contact **Cape Flattery Tours,** tel. (360) 645-2395.

FORKS AND VICINITY

The westernmost incorporated city in the Lower 48, Forks is the economic center and logging capital of the western Olympic Peninsula—a big handle for this town of 3,300 with one main drag. Since the spotted-owl controversy began, logging in this area has been severely curtailed on Forest Service lands, and Forks went into something of a depression as loggers searched for alternate means of earning a living. In recent years the town has diversified, emphasizing the clean air, remote location, and abundance of recreational possibilities within a few miles in any direction. For travelers, the town's big selling point is its proximity to the west side of Olympic National Park and Pacific coast beaches. Also nearby is a modern University of Washington natural resources research facility.

Sights

The **Forks Timber Museum,** tel. (360) 374-9663, has historical exhibits that include a steam donkey, a logging camp bunkhouse, old logging equipment, and various pioneer implements. The real surprise is a large 150-year-old Indian canoe that was discovered by loggers in 1990. Out front is a memorial to loggers killed in the woods and a replica of a fire lookout tower. Open daily 10 a.m.-4 p.m. mid-April through October; no charge.

The tiny crossroads settlement called **Sappho,** 13 miles north of Forks, is where you'll find the **Solduc Salmon Hatchery.** An interpretive center describes how hatcheries work.

Bogachiel State Park

Six miles south of Forks on Hwy. 101, Bogachiel (Indian for Muddy Waters) State Park encompasses 123 acres on the usually clear Bogachiel River. Enjoy the short nature trail through a rain forest, or swim, paddle, or fish in the river—famous for its summer and winter steelhead, salmon, and trout. The park has campsites ($10 tents, $15 RVs) and is open year-round; tel. (360) 374-6356.

Accommodations

Forks has an abundance of B&Bs and motels. Budget travelers will want to check out the quirky **Rain Forest Hostel,** tel. (360) 374-2270. The hostel is out in the sticks 23 miles south of Forks on Hwy. 101, and has two dorm rooms with bunk beds, a family room, and a trailer outside for couples. Closed 10 a.m.-5 p.m., lights out at 11, and no booze allowed. Rates are $10 pp, and $5 kids. Those without vehicles can catch the West Jefferson Transit bus.

Bed and Breakfasts

The Forks area has many B&Bs offering comfortable accommodations. Unless otherwise noted, all B&Bs listed below serve a full breakfast and do not allow young children. They are listed by price (more or less).

Miller Tree Inn, 654 E. Division, tel. (360) 374-6806, has seven guest rooms (private or shared baths) in a beautiful three-story 1914 homestead set on a shady lot on the edge of town. The back deck has a large hot tub; $45-80 s or $60-95 d.

Stay at **Fisherman's Widow B&B,** 31 Huckleberry Lane, tel. (360) 374-5693, for $55-65 s or d, including a continental breakfast. The two guest rooms have private baths.

Bear Creek Homestead B&B, 2094 Bear Cr. Rd., tel. (360) 327-3699, has two units that share a bath; $75 s or d. A hot tub is outside.

Mill Creek Inn B&B, 1061 S. Forks Ave., tel. (360) 374-5873, charges $60 s or d, for two guest rooms in a comfortable older home.

Sol Duc Guest House, tel. (360) 327-3373, has a home in Beaver (10 miles north) for $65 s or d, including a kitchen and continental breakfast.

Misty Valley Inn, tel. (360) 374-9389, sits on a ridge two miles north of Forks. The spacious home includes dramatic views, a baby grand piano, and rhododendron gardens. The four guest rooms have shared or private baths; $65-85 s or d.

Three miles west of town near the Solduc River, **Brightwater House B&B,** tel. (360) 374-5453, is a good place for the fly-fishing crowd. Two guest rooms share a bath in this contemporary home with a deck; $70-85 s or d.

Shadynook Cottage B&B, 41 Ash Ave., tel. (360) 374-5497, has two cottage units with kitchens and a continental breakfast; $75 for up to four.

River Inn B&B, tel. (360) 374-6526, is three miles south of town on the Bogachiel River, with three guest rooms, shared baths, a deck, and jacuzzi. $75-85 s or d.

Huckleberry Lodge B&B, 1171 Big Pine Way, tel. (888) 822-6008, has five comfortably appointed rooms with private baths, plus a hot tub, sauna, and pool table. They also have a separate cabin with kitchen. Kids are accepted; $75-110 s or d.

Eagle Point Inn B&B, tel. (360) 327-3236, 10 miles north in Beaver, is a beautiful custom-built log home on a bend of the Sol Duc River with a hot tub, fireplace, three comfortable guest rooms, and private baths; $85 s or d.

Motels

Several Forks motels offer standard accommodations. **Town Motel,** 1080 S. Forks Ave., tel. (360) 374-6231 or (800) 742-2429, is a friendly and clean place with kitchenettes available, but no phones; $31 s or $44 d. **Olympic Suites,** 800 Olympic Dr. (1.5 miles north of Forks), tel. (360) 374-5400 or (800) 262-3433, charges $45-65 s or d for one- and two-bedroom suites with kitchens.

Bear Creek Motel, 15 miles northeast in the town of Beaver, tel. (360) 327-3660, has rooms for $47-80 s or d; RV hookups too. **Pacific Inn Motel,** 352 S. Forks Ave., tel. (360) 374-9400 or (800) 235-7344, has rooms for $48 s or $53 d. The **Forks Motel,** 432 Forks Ave., tel. (360) 374-6243 or (800) 544-3416, has an outdoor pool and rooms for $48-70 s or $53-75 d. Located at 100 Fern Hill Rd., tel. (360) 374-4055 or (888) 433-9376, **Dew Drop Inn,** is Forks' newest motel; $54 s or 60 d.

Campgrounds

Camp at **Bogachiel State Park,** four miles south on Hwy. 101 (see above), or at the Park Service's **Mora Campground** ($10; open year-round), 14 miles west of Forks, which offers summertime naturalist programs and nature walks. Dispersed camping (pullouts off the road) is allowed on Forest Service lands throughout Olympic National Forest. Park RVs at **Forks 101 RV Park,** 901 S. Forks Ave., tel. (360) 374-5073 or (800) 962-9964. Camp for free at Rayonier's **Tumbling Rapids Park,** 11 miles northeast of Forks along Hwy. 101, tel. (360) 374-6565.

Food

Meet the loggers over coffee and donuts at **Pay & Save Coffee Shop,** 314 Forks Ave. S, tel. (360) 374-6769, with friendly waitresses and dependably good food three meals a day. Also popular is **Rain Drop Cafe,** 111 Forks Ave. S, tel. (360) 374-6612, with live music on weekends. **The In Place,** 320 S. Forks Ave., tel.

(360)0 374-4004, is a good lunch spot, with deli sandwiches and great mushroom bacon burgers. They also serve pasta, steak, and seafood dinners.

A mile north of Forks at the La Push road junction on Hwy. 101, the **Smoke House Restaurant,** tel. (360) 374-6258, is open daily for lunch and dinner with wonderful prime rib and a full menu of other all-American faves.

Get good Mexican lunches and dinners at **El Burnito's,** 90 N. Forks Ave., tel. (360) 374-5414, and fairly authentic Chinese food at **Golden Gate Restaurant,** 80 W. A St., tel. (360) 374-5579. **Pacific Pizza,** 870 Forks Ave. S, tel. (360) 374-2626, has the best local pizzas and pasta.

The **Forks Farmers Market** takes place in the Thriftway parking lot Fri.-Sat. 10 a.m.-3 p.m. mid-May to mid-Oct.; tel. (360) 374-6623.

Events

Fork's **Fourth of July** is actually a three-day festival of fun that includes an art show, pancake breakfast, parades, a loggers show, frog jump, demolition derby, dancing, and fireworks.

Information and Services

Get local info on the south end of town at the helpful **Forks Chamber of Commerce Visitor Center,** 1411 S. Forks Ave., tel. (360) 374-2531 or (800) 443-6757; www.forkswa.com. Open daily 9 a.m.-5 p.m. in summer, and daily 10 a.m.-4 p.m. the rest of the year. The museum is right next door.

The **Olympic National Forest and Park Recreation Information Office** is housed in the new transportation building at 551 Forks Ave. N, tel. (360) 374-7566. Stop here for recreation information, maps, and handouts, and to take a look at the big 3-D model of the Olympic Peninsula. Open daily 8:30 a.m.-12:30 p.m. and 1:30-5:30 p.m. in the summer; same hours, but Mon.-Fri. only the rest of the year.

Transportation

Local buses all stop at the new transportation building in Forks. **Clallam Transit,** tel. (360) 452-4511 or (800) 858-3747, provides daily service north to Port Angeles and Neah Bay, and west to La Push. Catch the free **West Jefferson Transit** bus, tel. (800) 436-3950, south from Forks to Kalaloch, Queets, and Lake Quinault. At Lake

Quinault, join the Grays Harbor Transit system for points south and east. **Pennco,** tel. (360) 452-5104 or (888) 673-6626, offers door-to-door van service around the Olympic Peninsula.

LA PUSH AREA

A 14 mile road heads west from Forks through the Bogachiel/Quillayute River Valley. Nearly all this land has been logged at least once, so be prepared for typical Olympic Peninsula clearcut vistas. The road ends at La Push, a small village bordering the Pacific Ocean on the south side of the Quillayute River, and the center of the **Quileute Indian Reservation.** The name La Push was derived from the French "la bouche," meaning "mouth," a reference to the river mouth here. It is an attractive little town with a fantastic beach for surfing and kayaking in the summer or watching storm waves in the winter. Locals have a small fleet of fishing and crabbing boats, a seafood plant, a fish hatchery, and a resort offering simple shoreside accommodations and camping.

Sights
The main attraction at La Push is simply the setting: James Island and other rocky points sit just offshore, and waves break against First Beach. The small **Quileute Tribe Museum,** housed in the Tribal Center office, has a few artifacts and is open Mon.-Thurs. 8 a.m.-3 p.m., and Friday 2-4 p.m. Ask here for local folks who sell beadwork and other handicrafts, and about ocean and river tours in traditional cedar canoes.

Mora Rd. branches off from La Push Rd. three miles east of La Push and provides access to **Rialto Beach** within Olympic National Park. It's pretty easy to tell you've entered public land; instead of clearcuts, you'll find tall old-growth trees. The Mora Campground is here, and the beach is a favorite picnicking area and starting point for hikers heading north along the wild Olympic coast. The town of La Push is just across the wide river mouth to the south.

Accommodations
Ocean Park Resort, right on the beach, has very basic cabins (some with kitchens), two motels, tent sites, and RV hookups. Cabins are

$74-142 and can sleep four to six people; motel rooms are $59-74 s or d. Rundown bring-your-sleeping-bag "camper cabins" sleep six for $44. The same folks run **Shoreline Resort,** with old cabins for $48-63 s or d. No phones, maid service, or TVs in any of the rooms or cabins, but you don't come here to watch *Star Trek* reruns. Two-night minimum. The water is very hard; bring in your own for drinking purposes. Make reservations up to a year in advance if you plan to visit in mid-summer. For details, call (360) 374-5267 or (800) 487-1267.

Three Rivers Resort, tel. (360) 374-5300, at the intersection of La Push and Mora Roads (halfway between Forks and La Push), has cabins for $35-45 s or d and an RV park. They also offer guided fishing trips, horseback rides, and float trips.

Manitou Lodge, tel. (360) 374-6295, is a modern country lodge on 10 acres of forested land (surrounded by clearcuts) off Mora Road. Seven luxurious guest rooms with private baths are $65-90 s or d, including a full breakfast. Book up to six months ahead for summer weekends. A gift shop here sells quality Indian baskets, woodcarvings, and beadwork.

Olson's Resort, 3243 Mora Rd., tel. (360) 374-3142, has space for up to five in a cozy and quiet cabin with kitchen just 2.5 miles from Rialto Beach; $45-65 s or d.

Campgrounds
Olympic National Park's **Mora Campground** ($10; open year-round) is a pretty in-the-trees place to pitch a tent. Check with the ranger station here for summertime naturalist programs and nature walks. **Ocean Park Resort,** tel. (360) 374-5267 or (800) 487-1267; **Lonesome Creek RV Park,** tel. (360) 374-4338; and **Three Rivers Resort,** tel. (360) 374-5300, all have tent and RV camping.

Food and Events
There are no restaurants in La Push, but you can get locally famous burgers and other fast food east of town at Three Rivers Resort, tel. (360) 374-5300.

The unannounced **Surf Frolic Festival** in January attracts surfers and kayakers, but the big event is **Quileute Days** in mid-July, with an Indian tug-of-war, bone games, a fish bake, canoe races, and fireworks.

Information and Transportation

The Olympic National Park's **Mora Ranger Station,** tel. (360) 374-5460, next to the Mora Campground, is usually staffed daily June-Aug., but the rest of the year it's catch-as-catch-can. Stop by for a tide chart and information on hiking along the coast. They offer daily beach walks and short guided hikes, and campfire programs on Fri.-Sun. nights at the amphitheater.

Clallam Transit, tel. (360) 452-4511 or (800) 858-3747, provides daily bus service to La Push and other parts of the Olympic Peninsula, transporting you south as far as Lake Quinault, and north to Port Angeles and Neah Bay.

HOH RIVER AREA

Heading south from Forks on Hwy. 101, you pass through the heart of the Olympics and get a taste of the economic importance of logging and how it has changed the landscape. Despite reductions in the amount of timber cut in recent years on Forest Service lands, you're bound to meet a constant parade of trucks laden with heavy loads of logs from private land and Indian reservations.

Fourteen miles south of Forks is the turnoff to the world-famous **Hoh River Rain Forest,** located at the end of the paved 19 mile Upper Hoh Road. The road follows the river through a beautiful valley with a mix of second-growth stands and DNR clearcuts. Once you enter the park, old-growth stands dominate. Several trails, a campground, and visitor center are located here (see **Olympic National Park** for details on this not-to-be-missed attraction).

Accommodations

Hoh River Resort, 15 miles south of Forks on Hwy. 101, tel. (360) 374-5566, has roadside very rustic cabins (bring your own bedding) with kitchenettes for $40 s or d. Tent and RV spaces are also here. **Hoh Humm Ranch,** 20 miles south of Forks on Hwy. 101, tel. (360) 374-5337, is certainly one of the more unique lodging places, with five guest rooms in mobile homes (shared bath) for $35-65 s or d, including a full breakfast. The ranch raises a zoo's worth of critters: llamas, strange breeds of cattle, goats, sheep, ducks, geese, rhea birds, and Asian Sika deer. For in-

expensive lodging check out the **Rain Forest Hostel,** described in "Forks and Vicinity," above.

Campgrounds

The Park Service's **Hoh Rain Forest Campground,** 19 miles east from Hwy. 101 at the end of the road, is open year-round with in-the-trees camping for $10. The visitor center has evening naturalist programs in the summer.

The Dept. of Natural Resources has five small free, year-round campgrounds near the Hoh River: **Hoh Oxbow Campground,** located directly across from a horrific clearcut near milepost 176; **Cottonwood Campground,** two miles west on Oil City Rd.; **Willoughby Creek Campground,** 3.5 miles east on Hoh Rain Forest Rd.; **Minnie Peterson Campground,** 4.5 miles east on Hoh Rain Forest Rd.; and **South Fork Hoh Campground,** 6.5 miles east on Hoh Mainline Rd. (on the way to the correction center). Willoughby Creek is right on the river, but has just three sites.

THE COASTAL STRIP

Commercialization is minimal from Neah Bay to Grays Harbor because the coast itself is protected nearly all the way down, first by the coastal strip of Olympic National Park, and then by the Quinault Indian Reservation, which was closed to non-Indians in the early 1960s. Not many Washingtonians complain about this lack of development; it suits most just fine and they are proud of the wild coast, a place where you can hike and camp without seeing or hearing any kind of motor vehicle.

When the highway emerges on the coastline south of Forks, you will quickly become aware that the northern half of Washington's coastline—from the state's northwest corner at Neah Bay to the Quinault Indian Reservation—is a picture of how the Pacific coast looks in brochures and calendar photos: pristine beaches, pounding waves, trees sculpted by relentless sea breezes.

West Jefferson Transit, tel. (800) 436-3950, provides free daily bus service to Kalaloch and Queets, and makes flag stops elsewhere on Hwy. 101. Service continues south as far as Lake Quinault, and north to Forks where you can transfer to Clallam Transit buses.

Ruby Beach Area

Highway 101 rejoins the coast at Ruby Beach, just south of the mouth of the Hoh River. A very popular trail leads down to beautiful sandy shoreline dotted with red pebbles (garnets, not rubies), with piles of driftwood and the flat top of **Destruction Island** several miles offshore. The island is capped by a 94-foot lighthouse.

The tiny, 400-acre **Hoh Indian Reservation** is a couple miles north of Ruby Beach at the mouth of the Hoh River. A three-mile road leads to the tribal center building, tel. (360) 374-6582. Stop here to ask about locally made cedar bark baskets, but be ready to pay upwards of $200. The village is a trashed, badly littered place, but the ocean views are impressive. On the north side of the river is the area called Oil City, accessible via a partly gravel 11 mile road off Hwy. 101.

South of Ruby Beach, the highway cruises along the bluff, with five more trails dropping to shoreline beaches, creatively named Beach 1, Beach 2, Beach 3, and etcetera. A massive western red cedar tree stands just off the highway near Beach 6.

Kalaloch

The place called Kalaloch has a campground, gas station/country store, and the **Kalaloch Lodge,** tel. (360) 962-2271, operated as a park concessionaire. The lodge consists of three different types of facilities: the main lodge (built in 1953), cabins of various types, and the Seacrest House Motel. No TVs in the rooms, but the sitting room has one for those who can't miss their soaps. Some of the cabins have kitchens and offer waterside views. Summer rates are $72-215, and there's a two-night minimum on weekends. Make reservations far ahead for the nicest rooms or the bluff cabins; some places are reserved 11 months ahead of time for July and August. The lodge also has a cafe, gift shop, and lounge.

Across from the lodge is the Park Service's **Kalaloch Visitor Information Center,** tel. (360) 962-2283, where you'll find natural history books, maps, pamphlets, and tide charts for beach walking. Open daily June-Sept., with variable hours the rest of the year.

The Park Service's **Kalaloch Campground** ($12; open year-round) sits on a bluff overlooking the beach. During the summer, attend camp-

fire programs, or join a tide pool walk at Beach 4. The primitive **South Beach Campground** is on the southern edge of the park three miles south of Kalaloch and costs $8; open summers only. These are the only two campgrounds on the dozen miles of Pacific shoreline between Queets and the Hoh Indian Reservation. Others wanting to camp should head up the Queets River (see below) or to campgrounds on the Hoh River (described above).

Queets River Area

South of Kalaloch, Hwy. 101 crosses the **Quinault Indian Reservation** where you get to see what clearcuts really look like. A narrow corridor of Olympic National Park extends along the Queets River, protecting a strip of old-growth timber bordered by cutover DNR and private lands. The gravel Queets River Rd. (well marked) follows the river eastward from Hwy. 101, ending 14 miles later at **Queets Campground.** This free, primitive campground has no running water, but it is open year-round. A seasonal ranger station is also here. The **Queets Loop Trail** departs the campground for an easy three-mile walk through second-growth forests and fields where elk are often seen. Another route, the **Queets Trail,** is more challenging. It requires the fording of Queets River near the campground—wait till late summer or fall for this hike, and use caution—and then continues along the river for 15 miles, passing through magnificent old-growth stands of Sitka spruce. Not for beginners, but an impressive hike.

The Department of Natural Resources has additional free campsites approximately 14 miles up Hoh-Clearwater Mainline Road. The turnoff is at milepost 147 on Hwy. 101 (three miles west of the Queets River Rd. turnoff).

Both **Olympic Raft Adventures,** tel. (360) 452-1443 or (888) 452-1443, and **Chinook Expeditions,** tel. (800) 241-3451, lead relaxing float trips down the Queets River each spring.

The Quinault Indian Reservation beaches, from just south of Queets almost to Moclips, have been closed to the public since 1969. However, you can arrange for an escorted tour of Point Grenville or Cape Elizabeth, two good birding spots, by calling (360) 276-8211.

QUINAULT LAKE AREA

Surrounded by steep mountains and dense rain forest, Lake Quinault is bordered on the northwest by Olympic National Park and on the southeast by Olympic National Forest; the lake itself and land to the southeast are part of the Quinault Indian Reservation and subject to Quinault regulations. Located at the southwestern edge of Olympic National Park, Lake Quinault is a hub of outdoor activity during the summer months. This very scenic tree-rimmed lake is surrounded by cozy lodges, and hiking trails provide a chance for even total couch potatoes to get a taste of the rain forest that once covered vast stretches of the Olympic Peninsula.

The Quinault Rain Forest is one of three major rain forests that survive on the Peninsula; here the annual average rainfall is 167 inches, resulting in enormous trees, lush vegetation, and moss-carpeted buildings. If you arrive in the rainy winter months, bring your heavy rain gear and rubber boots, not just a nylon poncho and running shoes. If you're prepared, a hike in the rain provides a great chance to see this soggy and verdant place at its truest. July and August are the driest months, but even then it rains an average of three inches. Typical Decembers see 22 inches of precipitation.

Day Hikes
The Quinault area is a hiker's paradise, with trails for all abilities snaking through a diversity of

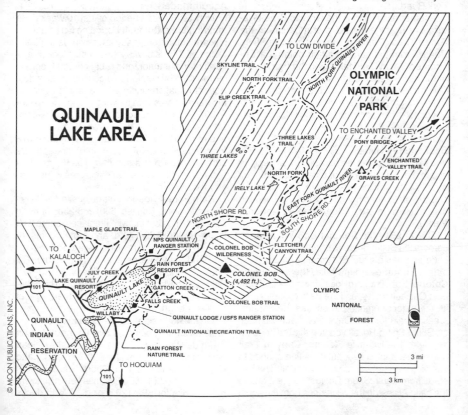

terrain. Note, however, that the Forest Service now charges a trailhead parking fee of $3 per day; or purchase an annual Trail Park Pass ($25) that covers most national forests in Washington. The 10-mile **Quinault National Recreation Trail System,** accessible from Willaby and Falls Creek Campgrounds and Lake Quinault Lodge, provides several loop trail hiking opportunities along the lakeshore and into the rain forest. Easier still is the half-mile **Quinault Rain Forest Nature Trail,** where informative signs explain the natural features. A good hike for those traveling with small children begins at North Fork Campground, following the Three Lakes Trail for the first mile to **Irely Lake.** The half-mile **Maple Glade Rain Forest Trail** begins at the Park Service's Quinault Visitor Center on North Fork Road.

Another easy jaunt is the **Graves Creek Nature Trail,** a one-mile loop that begins at the Graves Creek Campground on the South Shore Road. From the same starting point, the **Enchanted Valley Trail** takes you through a wonderful rain forest along the South Fork of the Quinault River. Day hikers often go as far as Pony Bridge, 2.5 miles each way, but more ambitious folks can continue to Dosewallips, a one-way distance of 28 miles.

Backcountry Hikes

You'll find two across-the-park hikes that begin or end in the Quinault area, one heading northeast over to Dosewallips (see "Day Hikes," above), and the other heading north over Low Divide to the Lake Elwha area. (See **Olympic National Park.**)

The 11,961-acre **Colonel Bob Wilderness** borders the South Shore Rd. just east of Quinault Lake and has a couple of popular backcountry paths. For an overnight hike, the seven-mile **Colonel Bob Trail** provides views of Mt. Olympus, Quinault Valley, and the Pacific Ocean from its 4,492-foot summit and passes through impressive rain forests. Drive past Lake Quinault on South Shore Rd. till you see the trailhead on the right. The two-mile **Fletcher Canyon Trail** doesn't get a lot of use, but it's a fine chance to see virgin timber and a pretty waterfall. The trail starts from South Shore Rd. just before it enters the park. Access to the wilderness from the south side is via Forest Rd. 2204, northeast from the town of Humptulips. If you enter from this remote area, be sure to visit the beautiful Campbell Tree Campground (free) and to check out the **West Fork Humptulips River Trail** that departs from the campground.

A 21-mile loop begins near the North Fork Campground, heads up the **Three Lakes Trail** for seven miles to three shallow alpine lakes, and then turns down the **Elip Creek Trail** for four miles before catching the **North Fork Trail** back through dense rain forests to your starting point. An added advantage of this loop is the chance to see the world's largest Alaska cedar, located just off the trail approximately a mile east of Three Lakes.

Accommodations

Built in 1926 over a period of just 10 weeks, the rambling **Lake Quinault Lodge** occupies a magnificent setting of grassy lawns bordering Lake Quinault. This is how a lodge should look, with a darkly regal interior, and a big central fireplace surrounded by comfortable couches and tables. Accommodations include a variety of rooms in the main lodge and in newer buildings nearby for $100-270 s or d, including an indoor pool, sauna, and jacuzzi. Some of the rooms have kitchenettes. Call (360) 288-2900 or (800) 562-6672 for reservations. Call two months ahead to be sure of space in mid-summer. The lodge offers two-hour tours of the Quinault area, plus seasonal canoe and boat rentals.

Rain Forest Resort Village, just a short way up South Shore Rd., tel. (360) 288-2535 or (800) 255-6936, has cabins with fireplaces (some with kitchens) for $120-170 d, and motel rooms for $85-90 d. The resort also has a good restaurant and lounge, a general store, laundry, RV hookups, and canoe rentals. The world's largest Sitka spruce is on the resort grounds. This thousand-year-old behemoth is more than 19 feet in diameter and 191 feet tall.

On the north side of Lake Quinault are several small lodging places. **Lake Quinault Inn,** in Amanda Park, tel. (360) 288-2714, has clean and comfortable rooms for $59-99 s or d. **Lake Quinault Resort,** 314 N. Shore Rd., tel. (360) 288-2362 or (800) 650-2362, has very nice townhouse units for $99-129 s or d, all with decks and beach access, and some with kitchenettes. Across the road, a trail leads to the world's largest western red cedar—63 feet in circumference and 159 feet tall. Families may want to rent **Eagle's Nest,** tel. (360) 288-2633, a three-bedroom home along the north shore of the lake.

Amanda Park Motel, is right on the Quinault River in Amanda Park, tel. (360) 288-2237, with rooms for $50-65 s or d.

Campgrounds
Choose from seven different public campgrounds in the Quinault Lake area. The Forest Service maintains three campgrounds on the south shore of Lake Quinault: **Falls Creek** ($13; open late May to mid-September); **Gatton Creek** ($10; no water; open late May to mid-September); and **Willaby** ($13; open mid-April to mid-November). Willaby is the nicest of these and has a boat ramp. Olympic National Park campgrounds are more scattered, and all three are open year-round. **July Creek** ($10) is a walk-in campground on the north shore of the lake. **Graves Creek** ($10) is near the end of the South Shore Rd., 15 miles from the Hwy. 101 turnoff. The free **North Fork Campground** is at the end of the North Shore Rd. and does not have running water. Not recommended for RVs.

Park RVs at the private **Rain Forest Village Resort** on the South Shore Rd., tel. (360) 288-2535 or (800) 255-6936, the only campground with showers. More RV parking at **Amanda Park Motel,** tel. (360) 288-2237, on the west end of the lake.

Food
Get groceries at the **Mercantile,** just up the road from Quinault Lodge. Their snack bar sells pizzas, burgers, milkshakes, espresso, and sandwiches. Quite good meals ($14-18 entrees) are available at **Quinault Lodge,** tel. (360) 288-2571, and just up the road at **Rain Forest Resort,** tel. (360) 288-2535. The tiny village of Amanda Park on the west end of the lake along Hwy. 101 has a fine old country store with narrow aisles and sloping wooden floors.

Information and Services
The Forest Service's **Quinault Ranger District Office,** tel. (360) 288-2525, next door to Quinault Lodge on the south side of the lake, is open daily 8 a.m.-4:30 p.m. from Labor Day to Memorial Day, and Mon.-Fri. 8 a.m.-4:30 p.m. the rest of the year. They have informative handouts and offer guided nature walks and talks at the lodge in the summer.

The Olympic National Park **Quinault River Ranger Station** is 5.5 miles up North Fork Rd. and open daily 9 a.m.-5 p.m. June to Labor Day (funding dependent), and intermittently the rest of the year. Stop by for brochures, maps, and information on the park. The area around the station is a good place to see Roosevelt elk, especially in early summer and after September.

In Amanda Park along Hwy. 101, the small **Quinault Rain Forest Visitor Information Center** is open summers only. Not far away, you'll find the essentials: a motel, library, church, school, general store, gas station, post office, cafe, and liquor store.

Transportation
A paved road circles Lake Quinault, with side routes up both the East and North Fork of the Quinault River for a total of 31 scenic miles. This makes a great bike ride. One of the nicest sections is up South Shore Rd., which passes scenic **Merriman Falls** and continues through towering old growth forests to Graves Creek Campground.

West Jefferson Transit, tel. (800) 436-3950, provides free daily bus service between Forks and the Amanda Park. Continue southward from Lake Quinault on **Grays Harbor Transit,** tel. (360) 532-2770 or (800) 562-9730, to Moclips, Ocean Shores, and Aberdeen.

Quinault to Grays Harbor
After Lake Quinault Hwy. 101 continues through the forests and clearcuts past through the minuscule settlements of **Neilton** and **Humptulips** before finally arriving at Hoquiam. Neilton has an old-fashioned country store and lots of "we support the timber industry" yard signs. Camping is available just west of here at **Humptulips Recreation Area** and at Rayonier's **Promised Land Park,** five miles north of town on Stevens Creek. Take a good country road (paved) off Hwy. 101 for the beach at Humptulips, or continue to Hoquiam and turn back west of Hwy. 109.

NORTH BEACH

Grays Harbor—one of just three deepwater ports on the West Coast—forms the southern border to the Olympic Peninsula. The northwestern part of the bay and the Pacific Coast north to the Quinault Indian Reservation is commonly called North Beach. Towns included in this 22-mile long stretch of beachfront are Moclips, Pacific Beach, Copalis Beach, Ocean City, and Ocean Shores.

The drive from Moclips south to Ocean Shores marks the transition from the timber-dominated lands of the Olympic Peninsula to beachside resorts. Between Moclips and Copalis Beach, Hwy. 109 winds along the crest of a steep bluff, with dramatic views of the coastline (and more than a few recent clearcuts in the other direction). From Copalis Beach southward to Ocean Shores, the country is far less interesting and the highway straightens out on the nearly level land. The broad sandy beaches are backed by grassy dunes and fronted by summer and retirement homes. The entire 22 miles of beach between Moclips and Ocean Shores is open to the public, with various vehicle entry points along the way. Check with the Ocean Shores Chamber of Commerce for a map of access points, seasons of use, and driving rules. (Forty percent of the beach is closed to vehicles between April 15 and Labor Day, when access is restricted to pedestrians only.)

Some commercial development has occurred along this stretch, but the only significant development is Ocean Shores. This resort/residential complex was developed as a summer resort area in the '60s and '70s and has never become as popular as its developers expected, in part because of the overcast, damp, windy weather, and in part because it lacks the offshore rugged beauty of, say, a Cannon Beach, Oregon. Still, it is one of the most popular resort areas on the Washington coast.

OCEAN SHORES TO TAHOLAH

MOCLIPS, PACIFIC BEACH, AND TAHOLAH

Two small settlements—Moclips and Pacific Beach—occupy the northern end of the North Beach region, with a handful of stores, lodging places, and cafes. Moclips is connected to Hwy. 101 by the 20-mile-long Moclips-Quinault Road. Ten of these miles are on a sometimes-rutted gravel road; nearly all of this time you'll be heading through clearcuts, logging slash, and scrubby trees. Early in this century, Moclips was home to a major destination resort, with a 285-room hotel and an end-of-the-line railway station for excursions trains from Seattle. The building was destroyed one violently stormy winter day in 1904 when ocean waves eroded away the cliff sending the hotel to the rocks below. It was never rebuilt.

The shabby and badly littered village of Taholah is situated on the south bank of the Quinault River mouth, nine miles north of Moclips. This is the main settlement on the **Quinault Indian Reservation.** Come here in the fall to watch the fishermen netting salmon in the river, and stop by the tribal headquarters, tel. (360) 276-8211, if you want to head out on the reservation or to request beach access. Taholah has no tourist facilities of any kind, though you might visit **Quinault Pride,** tel. (360) 276-4431 or (800) 821-8650, where smoked salmon and other seafood are processed. A spiderweb of logging roads covers the entire reservation, and the once grand forests here are long gone.

Lodging

Most local motels and cottages have kitchenettes. Local motels include the following. **Moclips Motel** in Moclips, tel. (360) 276-4228, charges $38-65 s or d. **Shoreline Motel** in Pacific Beach, tel. (360) 276-4433, has rooms with ocean views for $45 s or d. **Barnacle Motel** in Moclips, tel. (360) 276-4318, charges $48-65 s or d. **Sand Dollar Inn** in Pacific Beach, tel. (360) 276-4525, has suites for $55-75 s or d, and cottages with ocean views for $70-105 s or d. **Moonstone Beach Motel** in Moclips, tel. (360) 276-4346, charges $65-75 s or d for motel rooms, or $80 s or d for cabins near the beach.

Three resorts offer more elaborate lodging options. Book far ahead for **Sandpiper Resort,** 1.5 miles south of Pacific Beach, tel. (360) 276-4580, a fine family resort with ocean-view cottages, studios, and one, two, or three-room suites, but no TVs or phones; $55-105 s or d. Three-night minimum on weekends.

Ocean Crest Resort in Sunset Beach, Moclips, tel. (360) 276-4465 or (800) 684-8439, is another very nice beachside resort with an indoor pool, sauna, jacuzzi, exercise room. Some rooms have fireplaces and full kitchens; $58-129 s or d. **Hi Tide Ocean Beach Resort** in Moclips, tel. (360) 276-4142 or (800) 662-5477, has one-and two-bedroom suites with decks along the shore; $84-94s or d. Two-night minimum on weekends.

Campgrounds

Pacific Beach State Park, tel. (360) 289-3553, in Pacific Beach has surf fishing, clamming, and beachcombing with beachfront campsites. The nine-acre park is really little more than a parking area for RVs and has no protection from the wind. Open for day-use and camping late February to October, and on weekends and holidays the rest of the year. Call (800) 452-5687 for reservations ($6 extra).

Food and Transportation

For ocean-view dining, try the excellent **Ocean Crest Restaurant** at the resort in Moclips, tel. (360) 276-4465. Open for three meals, the varied dinner menu features Northwest specialties, steak, and seafood, with weekend entertainment in the lounge. Very good breakfasts too.

Grays Harbor Transit, tel. (360) 532-2770 or (800) 562-9730, has daily service throughout the county, including Ocean Shores to Taholah.

Events

The **Chief Taholah Day Celebration** in early July includes Indian arts and crafts, a powwow, salmon bake, canoe races, a parade, and games on the reservation. The **Kelper's Parade & Shake Rat Olympics** is Pacific Beach's festival, featuring two parades on Labor Day weekend. It's followed in mid-September by a **Sandcastle Sculpture Contest** that is open to everyone.

COPALIS BEACH AND OCEAN CITY

The dinky town of Copalis Beach has a cluster of older buildings on the Copalis River, along with RV parks, motels, and gift shops. Ocean City, three miles farther south, is a bit larger and has simple homes set in the trees. This decidedly unpretentious town contrasts sharply with its bigger and newer neighbor to the south, Ocean Shores; there's probably more character in a few of the buildings here than in all of Ocean Shores. No fancy hotels or restaurants here! The **Anderson Cabin,** on the east side of the highway, tel. (360) 289-3842, is open in the summer. Built of beach logs in the 1920s, the cabin contains period furnishings and a display on local author Norah Berg.

Copalis Beach and Ocean City are "Home of the Razor Clam." The State Dept. of Fisheries sponsors clam-digging clinics and beach walks throughout the summer at Ocean City State Park to better prepare you for the short, intense razor clam season; call (360) 249-4628.

State Parks

Just west of Copalis Beach, **Griffiths-Priday State Park** is a day-use facility for picnicking, kite flying, beachcombing, surf fishing, and bird-watching at the mouth of the Copalis River. The Copalis Spit is one of three snowy plover breeding grounds on the Washington coast. These birds—an endangered species—are very sensitive to human intrusion. To protect them, large areas of the beach north of the park entrance are closed to the public—from the high-tide mark to the dunes—between mid-March and late August. The restricted areas are marked on the map at the park entrance. A boardwalk leads to the beach where you can dig for razor clams below the tide line.

Accommodations

Most Ocean City and Copalis Beach lodging places have kitchenettes available. The following motels and small resorts are arranged by price: **North Beach Motel** in Ocean City, tel. (360) 289-4116 or (800) 640-8053, charges $30-55 s or d. **Linda's Low Tide Motel** in Copalis Beach, tel. (360) 289-3450, charges $32 s or $35 d for beachfront rooms. **West Winds Resort Motel** in Ocean City, tel. (360) 289-3448, charges $38-66 s or d for cabins and motel rooms. **Pacific Sands Resort** in Ocean City, tel. (360) 289-3588, has rooms for $40-56 s or d, including an outdoor pool. Rooms at **Echoes of the Sea Motel** in Copalis Beach, tel. (360) 289-3358, are $48-80 s or d. **Blue Pacific Motel** in Ocean City, tel. (360) 289-2262 or (800) 453-2262, has rooms for $42 s or $45 d. **Dunes RV Resort & Motel** in Copalis Beach, tel. (360) 289-3873, charges $48 s or d. **Iron Springs Resort** in Copalis Beach, tel. (360) 276-4230, has family cottages with ocean views, an indoor pool, and full kitchens for $66-104 s or d. Three-night minimum in summer. **Beachwood Resort** in Copalis Beach, tel. (360) 289-2177, costs $70-80 s or d, including an outdoor pool, hot tub, and sauna.

Campgrounds

Ocean City State Park has camping ($11 tents, $16 RVs; year-round) near the intersection of Highways 109 and 115. Call (800) 452-5687 for reservations ($6 extra).

Private RV parks in Copalis Beach and Ocean City include: **Western Horizons,** tel. (360) 289-0618; **Blue Pacific,** tel. (360) 289-2262; **Surf& Sand RV Park,** tel. (360) 289-2707 or (800) 867-2707; **Driftwood Acres,** tel. (360) 289-3484; **Dunes RV Resort,** tel. (360) 289-3873; **Echoes of the Sea,** tel. (360) 289-3358 or (800) 578-3246; **Ocean Mist Resort,** tel. (360) 289-3656; **Riverside RV Park,** tel. (360) 289-2111; **Rod's Beach Resort,** tel. (360) 289-2222; **Screamin' Eagle Campground,** tel. (360) 289-0223; **Silver Maple Trailer Park,** tel. (360) 289-0166; and **Sturgeon Trailer Harbor,** tel. (360) 289-2101.

Other Practicalities

The **Washington Coast Chamber of Commerce,** is a small Ocean City information center; tel. (360) 289-4552 or (800) 286-4552. Open Thurs.-Mon. 11 a.m.-5 p.m. summers; or Monday, Thursday, Friday, and Saturday 11 a.m.-5 p.m. and Sunday 10 a.m.-2 p.m., the rest of the year. No great local restaurants, but try **Copalis Beach Restaurant and Lounge,** tel. (360) 289-2240, for three meals a day.

Ocean City sponsors the area's big Fourth of July **Fire O'er the Water** fireworks and picnic, with live music, arts and crafts. In early August, Copalis Beach comes alive with **Copalis Days,** featuring a car parade, street dancing, and food booths. Head to Copalis Beach in mid-Sept. for a popular **Sandsculpture Contest** with contestants of all levels of ability.

Grays Harbor Transit, tel. (360) 532-2770 or (800) 562-9730, has daily service throughout the county.

OCEAN SHORES

The summer-home/retirement community of Ocean Shores (pop. 2,800) occupies the six-mile dune-covered peninsula at the north side of the entrance to Grays Harbor. It's an odd place out here so far from other developments, with a big gate that welcomes visitors, businesses strewn along a wide main drag, and homes on a network of 23 miles of canals. Some of these homes are elaborate contemporary structures, other lots simply have a concrete pad to park an RV, and many more feature for-sale signs. Many of the working folks live in trailer parks in nearby Ocean City. Two main roads head down

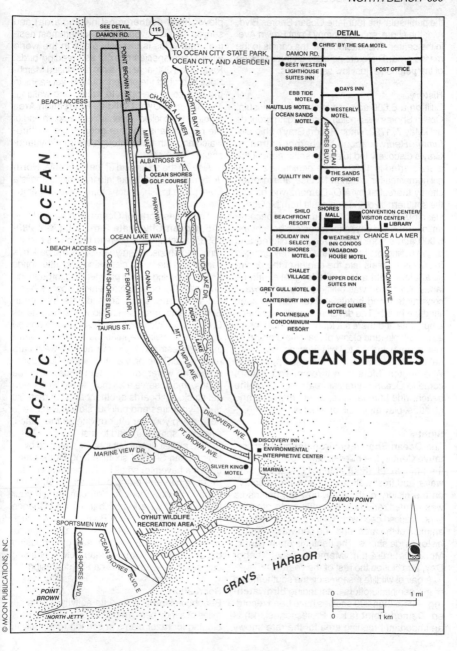

DETAIL

● CHRIS' BY THE SEA MOTEL

DAMON RD.

● BEST WESTERN
LIGHTHOUSE
SUITES INN

■ POST OFFICE

EBB TIDE
MOTEL
● DAYS INN

NAUTILUS MOTEL ●
● WESTERLY
MOTEL

OCEAN SANDS
MOTEL ●

SANDS RESORT ●

QUALITY INN ●
● THE SANDS
OFFSHORE

SHILO
BEACHFRONT
RESORT ●

SHORES
MALL

■ CONVENTION CENTER/
VISITOR CENTER

■ LIBRARY

HOLIDAY INN
SELECT ●
● WEATHERLY
INN CONDOS

OCEAN SHORES
MOTEL ●
● VAGABOND
HOUSE MOTEL

CHALET
VILLAGE ●
● UPPER DECK
SUITES INN

GREY GULL MOTEL ●

CANTERBURY INN ●
● GITCHE GUMEE
MOTEL

POLYNESIAN
CONDOMINIUM
RESORT ●

OCEAN
SHORES
BLVD

CHANCE A LA MER

POINT BROWN AVE.

OCEAN SHORES

SEE DETAIL
DAMON RD.

115

TO OCEAN CITY STATE PARK,
OCEAN CITY, AND ABERDEEN

POINT BROWN AVE

CHANCE A LA MER

NORTH BAY AVE.

BEACH ACCESS

MINARD

ALBATROSS ST.

OCEAN SHORES
GOLF COURSE

PARKWAY

OCEAN LAKE WAY

DUCK LAKE DR.

BEACH ACCESS

OCEAN SHORES BLVD.

PT. BROWN DR.

CANAL DR.

MT. OLYMPUS AVE.

DUCK
LAKE

TAURUS ST.

P A C I F I C   O C E A N

DISCOVERY AVE.

PT. BROWN AVE.

MARINE VIEW DR.

● DISCOVERY INN

■ ENVIRONMENTAL
INTERPRETIVE
CENTER

● SILVER KING
MOTEL

● MARINA

DAMON POINT

OYHUT WILDLIFE
RECREATION AREA

SPORTSMEN WAY

OCEAN SHORES BLVD.

OCEAN SHORES BLVD E.

G R A Y S   H A R B O R

POINT
BROWN

NORTH JETTY

© MOON PUBLICATIONS, INC.

0   1 mi

0   1 km

the peninsula: the four-lane Ocean Shores Blvd. near the shore, and the bumpy Point Brown Ave. in the center. The latter follows the canals to the marina area. There are no trees on the east side of the peninsula, just low sand dunes.

History

Built on a 6,000-acre, six-mile-long peninsula, Ocean Shores was Indian clam-digging grounds until May 7, 1792, when Robert Gray's ship *Columbia Rediviva* found the harbor entrance. Gray's discovery led to a slow settlement of the area, started in 1860 by the peninsula's original homesteader, Matthew McGee, and followed shortly thereafter by A.O. Damon, who bought the southern tip of the peninsula from McGee. It wasn't until 1970 that Ocean Shores became an incorporated city, after investors bought the 6,000 acres from Damon's grandchildren and began selling lots for $595 and up. They dredged freshwater canals into the center of the peninsula, along with a four-mile-long lake with islands. An airport was built, four-lane highways constructed, and hotels and restaurants soon lined the beach. The development still has many empty lots and there's a lot of beachfront property available (and plenty of real estate offices to sell the lots), but the town is growing as a destination and is now one of the most popular in Washington. More than three million visitors come to Ocean Shores annually to play on the beach, ride bumper cars, bikes, mopeds, and go carts, play mini-golf, or fly kites.

Sights

The **Ocean Shores Environmental Interpretative Center,** five miles south of town center, at the marina, tel. (360) 289-4617, features saltwater and freshwater aquariums and displays on the history of the area, how the peninsula was formed, and how it continues to grow as sand is added each year. Other exhibits detail the animals of the area, and you can watch natural history slide shows. The center is open Thurs.-Mon. 10 a.m.-4 p.m. Memorial Day to Labor Day, and closed the rest of the year.

A pair of wildlife reserves on the southern end of the peninsula offers outstanding **birdwatching**—more than 200 species have been recorded. **Damon Point** (a.k.a. Protection Island) is an important breeding area for the rare snowy plover (their northernmost nesting area) and semipalmated plovers (their southernmost nesting area). This is the only place in the world where both species coexist as breeding birds. Parts of the 300-acre preserve are closed March-Sept. to protect the plovers, but the wet sands in the tidal zone are open to fishing and walking. The 682-acre **Oyhut Wildlife Recreation Area** (sometimes spelled "Oyehut") at the south end of the peninsula is another good place for birdwatching, with trails through the marshy landscape.

Also on the south end of the peninsula, **North Jetty** reaches a mile out into the Pacific and is a great place to fish, watch storm waves, or enjoy the sunset.

Two miles north of Ocean Shores on Hwy. 115, **Ocean City State Park,** tel. (360) 289-3553, has campsites close to the town's restaurants and shops. Open year-round, the park has camping in the trees, picnicking, two little ponds for birdwatching, and a path leading through the dunes to the beach. No vehicle access here, but there are six access points in Ocean Shores—just head south along Ocean Shores Blvd. and look for the turnoffs. Signs are posted with beach driving regulations and safety warnings. Pedestrians have the right of way; cars must yield. Drive only on the higher hard sand, not in the water, on the clam beds, or in the dunes, and observe a 25 mph speed limit. If you get stuck, put boards or other hard, flat material under your tires and pull out slowly. Be sure to hose down your car after driving on the beach, since salt spray can lead to rust.

With all that ocean out there, it's easy to overlook Ocean Shores' six-mile-long **Duck Lake,** but it's a haven for small boats, canoes, anglers (trout, bass, and crappie are all here), swimmers, and water-skiers. You can launch your boat from City Park, at Albatross and Chance à la Mer, or Chinook Park Boat Launch on Duck Lake Drive. At the south end, the lake connects with a maze of canals that lead past housing developments. Pick up a map before heading out, since these channels can be confusing.

Recreation

Beachcombing is a favorite activity on the six miles of sandy beach along Ocean Shores, as is digging for razor clams in season (generally in

March and October). Check with the chamber of commerce for the regulations and where to buy a license. Rent boats and canoes from **Summer Sails,** tel. (360) 289-2884, located on the canal at the south end of Pt. Brown Avenue. Three local companies offer horseback rides along the shore: **Nan-Sea Stables,** tel. (360) 289-0194, **Rising Star Horse Rental,** tel. (360) 580-7754, and **Chenois Creek Horse Rentals,** tel. (360) 533-5591.

Ocean Shores is a great place for kite flying, with strong offshore winds much of the year. If you didn't bring your own, head to one of the three local kite shops: **Cutting Edge Kites,** 676 Ocean Shores Blvd. NW, tel. (360) 289-0667; **Cloud Nine Kite Shop,** 420 Damon Rd., tel. (360) 289-4578; and **Ocean Shores Kites,** Ocean Shore Mall, tel. (360) 289-4103.

At Canal and Albatross in Ocean Shores, **Ocean Shores Golf Course,** tel. (360) 289-3357, is an 18-hole championship course open to the public.

Olympic Outdoor, 773 Pt. Brown Ave. NW, tel. (360) 289-3736, rents mountain bikes, mopeds, and kayaks. You can also rent mopeds from **O.W.W. Inc.,** at the Shores Mall on Chance à la Mer, tel. (360) 289-3830.

Pacific Paradise Family Fun Center, 767 Minard Ave., tel. (360) 289-9537, has mini-golf, an entertainment center, bumper boats, and more fun options for kids.

Accommodations

Ocean Shores has more than two dozen motels, along with dozens more private home rentals. **Ocean Shores Reservations Bureau,** tel. (360) 289-2430 or (800) 562-8612, is very helpful and can make reservations at many of these motels. They also rent houses and condos in the $75-250 range. **Beach Front Vacation Rentals,** tel. (800) 544-8887 or (800) 577-4312, has many more condo and home rentals in the same price range. Other reservation services are: **Chris' by the Sea,** tel. (360) 289-3066 or (800) 446-5747, and **Ocean View Resort Homes,** tel. (360) 289-4416 or (800) 927-6394. Note that many places have a two-night minimum on weekends and July-August, and a three-night minimum on holidays. On holidays, the chamber of commerce keeps track of room availability; call them at (360) 289-0226 or (800) 762-3224.

Silver Waves B&B, 982 Point Brown Ave. SE, tel. (360) 289-2490 or (888) 257-0894, is a newly built B&B with two decks facing the Grand Canal. Four guest rooms and a separate cabin (kids okay here) all have private baths and a breakfast buffet; $65-130 d.

Campgrounds

Camp year-round at **Ocean City State Park,** two miles north of Ocean Shores. Both tent ($11) and RV ($16) sites are available, along with showers. Find more campsites at **Pacific Beach State Park,** 14 miles north in the town of Pacific Beach (see above). Call (800) 452-5687 for state park reservations ($6 extra). The nearest private RV parks are **Yesterday's RV Park,** 512 Damon Rd., tel. (360) 289-9227, and **Ocean Shores Marina RV Park,** 1070 Discovery Ave. SE, tel. (360) 289-0414 or (800) 742-0414. Many more RV parks are located in Ocean City and Copalis Beach.

Food

Our Place, 676 Ocean Shores Blvd. NW, tel. (360) 289-8763, is a tiny eatery with inexpensive but filling breakfasts and all-American lunches. Also popular for downhome breakfasts is **Jimmy D's Country Waffle & Steak House** on Point Brown Ave., tel. (360) 289-2018. **Flying Cats,** 114 E. Chance à la Mer NW, tel. (360) 289-2287, is the local espresso cafe, with delicious boysenberry cheesecake.

The Home Port Restaurant, 857 Pt. Brown Ave., tel. (360) 289-2600, serves three meals, including good breakfasts and specialties such as salmon, Dungeness crab, and steak and lobster dinners.

Find very good south-of-the-border meals at **Las Marachas Mexican Restaurant,** 729 Point Brown Ave. NW, tel. (360) 289-2054.

Mariah's tel. (360) 289-3315, at the Polynesian Resort, is the most upscale local restaurant, with seafood, steak, and pasta, along with a weekend breakfast buffet. The lounge has live music Friday and Saturday evenings. **Alec's by the Sea,** tel. (360) 289-4026, next to Dick's IGA, has lower prices and a big menu that includes burgers, fresh clams, salads, steaks, pasta, seafood, and chicken. **Galway Bay Irish Pub,** tel. (360) 289-2300, makes great clam chowder.

OCEAN SHORES MOTELS AND HOTELS

Accommodations are arranged from least to most expensive within each town. Many places in Ocean Shores have a two-night minimum stay on Friday and Saturday nights year-round, and all of July and August. Rates may be lower during the winter and on summer weekdays.

INEXPENSIVE

Vagabond House; 686 Ocean Shores Blvd. NW; tel. (360) 289-2350 or (800) 290-2899; $39-189 s or d; kitchenettes available, game room

Silver King Motel; 1070 Discovery Ave. SE (five miles south of town); tel. (360) 289-3386 or (800) 562-6001; $45-55 s or d; next to marina, condo motel, kitchenettes available

Gitche Gumee Motel; 648 Ocean Shores Blvd. NW; tel. (360) 289-3323 or (800) 448-2433; $50 s or d in condo motel, $75-85 s or d for one-bedroom townhouse; indoor and outdoor pools, saunas, kitchenettes, fireplaces

Ocean Shores Motel; 681 Ocean Shores Blvd. NW; tel. (360) 289-3351 or (800) 464-2526; $50-95 s or d; oceanfront location, kitchenettes and jacuzzi rooms available

Days Inn; 891 Ocean Shores Blvd. NW; tel. (360) 289-9570 or (800) 325-2525; $53-99 s or d; indoor pool, jacuzzi, continental breakfast

Discovery Inn; 1031 Discovery Ave. SE (five miles south); tel. (360) 289-3371 or (800) 882-8821; $54-80 s or d; condo motel on marina, outdoor pool, jacuzzi, playground, rowboat, game room, kitchenettes available, AAA approved

The Sands Offshore; 165 N.W. Barnacle St.; tel. (360) 289-2249 or (800) 562-9748; $58 s or d; kitchenettes available

Ocean Sands Motel; Ocean Shores Blvd.; tel. (360) 289-3585; $59 s or d; microwaves and fridges

MODERATE

Westerly Motel; 870 Ocean Shores Blvd. NW; tel. (360) 289-3711 or (800) 319-3711; $60-70 s or d; kitchenettes available

Chris' by the Sea Motel; 17 Chickiman Rd., tel. (360) 289-3066 or (800) 446-5747; $65 s or d; kitchenettes available, no phones in rooms

Polynesian Condominium Resort; 615 Ocean Shores Blvd. NW; tel. (360) 289-3361 or (800) 562-4836; $79-149 s or d for motel rooms, efficiencies, or suites; indoor pool, sauna, jacuzzi, fireplaces, balconies, ocean views, kitchenettes available, game room, two-night minimum stay in summer, AAA approved

Mike's Seafood, 830 Point Brown Ave. NE, tel. (360) 289-0532, has a stand selling fresh-cooked crab. Several places have fish and chips in town; a good one is **Flipper's Fish Bar,** 185 W. Chance à la Mer NW, tel. (360) 289-4676. Get homemade ice cream, fudge, and chocolates from **Murphy's Candy and Ice Cream** in the Shores Mall, tel. (360) 289-0927.

Events

Ocean Shores hosts an annual **Beachcombers Fun Fair** at the convention center in early March. See displays of glass floats and driftwood art, and sample the fresh seafood. Ocean Shores' annual **Festival of Colors,** held each May, is family fun with a sandcastle contest, arts and crafts bazaar, and kite festival. In late July, the leather-jacket crowd rolls into Ocean Shores for the **Harley Owners Group Sun & Surf Run,** an event that attracts 2,000 bikes and riders. It's followed in mid-October by the **American Kite Association Competition,** with displays at the convention center and colorful kites filling the air on the shore. The **Dixieland Jazz**

Canterbury Inn; 643 Ocean Shores Blvd. NW; tel. (360) 289-3317 or (800) 562-6678; $82-170 s or d; on the beach, large indoor pool, hot tub, private balconies, studios with kitchenettes, or one and two-bedroom suites with full kitchens and fireplaces, two-night minimum stay, AAA approved

EXPENSIVE

Chalet Village; 659 Ocean Shores Blvd. NW.; tel. (360) 289-4297 or (800) 303-4297; $85-95 s or d; A-frame duplex cabins with kitchens and fireplaces

Sands Resort; 801 Ocean Shores Blvd. NW; tel. (360) 289-2444 or (800) 841-4001; $85-105 s or d for motel rooms; $110-185 s or d for kitchenettes; ocean views, indoor and outdoor pools, game room, two jacuzzis, sauna

Grey Gull Motel; 651 Ocean Shores Blvd. SW; tel. (360) 289-3381 or (800) 562-9712; $98-129 s or d; efficiencies, one- and two-bedroom suites, or penthouses, ocean vistas, kitchens, fireplaces, outdoor pool, sauna, two-night minimum stay on summer weekends, AAA approved

Shilo Beachfront Resort; 707 Ocean Shores Blvd. NW; tel. (360) 289-4600 or (800) 222-2244; $99-199 s or d; very nice motel, all rooms face ocean, indoor pool, sauna, jacuzzi, steam room, fitness center, microwaves, fridges, wet bar, AAA approved

Nautilus Motel; 835 Ocean Shores Blvd. NW; tel. (360) 289-2722 or (800) 221-4541; $100-120 s or d; oceanfront condos, fireplaces, full kitchens, jacuzzi, AAA approved

Best Western Lighthouse Suites Inn; 491 Damon Rd.; tel. (360) 289-2311 or (800) 757-7873; $100-185 s or d; ocean views, indoor pool, jacuzzi, sauna, gas fireplaces, microwaves, fridges, video players, exercise room, continental breakfast, AAA approved

PREMIUM

Weatherly Inn Condos; 201 Ocean Shores Blvd. SW; tel. (360) 289-3088 or (800) 562-8612; $110-150 s or d; ocean front location, indoor pool, hot tub, sauna, fitness room, game room, full kitchens

Holiday Inn Express; 685 Ocean Shores Blvd.; tel. (360) 289-4900 or (888) 770-7878; $119-149 s or d; new motel, indoor pool, jacuzzi, complimentary breakfast, kitchenettes and jacuzzi suites available, AAA approved

Upper Deck Suites Inn; 668 Ocean Shores Blvd. NW; tel. (360) 289-4555; $125-165 s or d; new one- and two-bedroom suites with full kitchens, fireplaces, jacuzzi tubs, very nice

Quality Inn; 773 Ocean Shores Blvd. NW; tel. (360) 289-2040 or (800) 562-6373; $129-189 s or d; ocean front location, mini-golf, indoor pool, spa, game room, continental breakfast, microwaves and fridges, some rooms with ocean view balconies

Festival in early November features acts from all over the Northwest at the convention center and around town.

Shopping
Ocean Shores' **Shores Mall** has bike and moped rentals, a kite shop, bank, clothing store, and state liquor store on Chance à la Mer, just before the beach. In Homeport Plaza on Pt. Brown Ave., Ocean Shores' **Gallery Marjuli,** tel. (360) 289-2858, is open daily with art and gifts created by Northwest artists. **Tide Cre-** **ations Gift Shop,** tel. (360) 289-2550, near the marina on Pt. Brown Ave., has thousands of items, from kites and windsocks to fudge.

Information and Services
Get information from the helpful folks at **Ocean Shores Chamber of Commerce Visitor Information Center,** 120B W. Chance à la Mer, tel. (360) 289-2451 or (800) 762-3224. Open Mon.-Fri. 9 a.m.-5 p.m., and Sat.-Sun. 10 a.m.-4 p.m. year-round.

Transportation

Grays Harbor Transit, tel. (360) 532-2770 or (800) 562-9730, has daily bus service throughout the county, connecting Ocean Shores with Aberdeen, Lake Quinault, and Olympia. Ocean Shores has an airport, but no commercial service.

The **Westport-Ocean Shores Passenger Ferry,** *El Matador,* is a 74-foot passenger boat with service to Westport for $8 roundtrip; free for kids under five. Gray whales are often seen along the way. The ferry leaves six times a day and takes 20-40 minutes, with daily service mid-June to Labor Day, and weekend-only service mid-April through mid-June and in September. No service the rest of the year. The boat leaves from the marina; get tickets at the Marina Store, tel. (360) 289-0414.

GRAYS HARBOR AND VICINITY

Grays Harbor has long been a major center for the timber industry, and the surrounding country bears witness to this. Heading toward Aberdeen and Hoquiam from any direction leads you through mile after mile of tree farms, with second- or third-growth forests interspersed with newly logged hillsides. Logging and fishing have long been the primary focus of workers here, and remain so.

ABERDEEN AND HOQUIAM

Aberdeen and Hoquiam (HO-qwee-um) are twin cities on the easterly tip of Grays Harbor; Aberdeen is the larger of the two, with a population of 17,000, almost double the 9,000 of Hoquiam. The population is clustered along the eastern end of Grays Harbor where the rivers come into the harbor. The Hoquiam River separates Hoquiam from Aberdeen. The area could easily be called another Tri-Cities because a third town, Cosmopolis (pop. 1,400), is just across the Chehalis River from Aberdeen. These are not tourist towns, but a number of attractions are worth a visit.

With the recent reduction in timber harvesting and the poor salmon runs of late, the towns have fallen on hard times as timber industry workers are forced to retrain and go into other lines of work. The hard times show on these grim, working-class milltowns, but folks aren't giving up. Aberdeen has a downtown core of long-established businesses in solid brick buildings, the ubiquitous mega-marts on the outskirts, and a bevy of tidy but plain working-class homes. Downtown Hoquiam is smaller, with the Hoquiam River winding through. An **observation tower** at 8th St. Landing provides a view up the river.

History

Grays Harbor was discovered by, and named for, Capt. Robert Gray, an American en route to China to trade sea otter pelts for tea. On May 7, 1792, Gray sailed his ship, *Columbia Rediviva,* across the bar and into the harbor, had a look around, calling it a "safe harbor, well sheltered from the sea," and continued on his way. A few days later he discovered the mouth of the Columbia River, another major feature missed by Capt. James Vancouver, who had passed by a few weeks earlier.

The first European to settle in the area is believed to be William O'Leary in 1843, but the first real settlement began in 1859 when James Karr and his family arrived just ahead of a family of four brothers named Campbell. They used the local Chehalis Indians' name for the area; Hoquiam meant "hungry for wood" because they collected driftwood there for their fires. In another 10 years the site had grown enough to deserve a post office, and in 1873 the first school opened.

A plat for a city named Wishkah was filed on December 18, 1883, but few liked the name, so on February, 16, 1884, the plat was re-filed as Aberdeen in honor of the Aberdeen Packing Company of Ilwaco that had a plant on the Wishkah River near its junction with the Chehalis River. (The Scottish name means, fittingly enough, "where two rivers merge.") After a devastating fire destroyed Aberdeen's business district in 1903, the downtown was rebuilt using brick, and many of these buildings still stand.

From the beginning it was wood that kept the towns going. The area is rich with Douglas fir, cedar, hemlock, and spruce, and several of the major timber companies—notably Weyerhaeuser

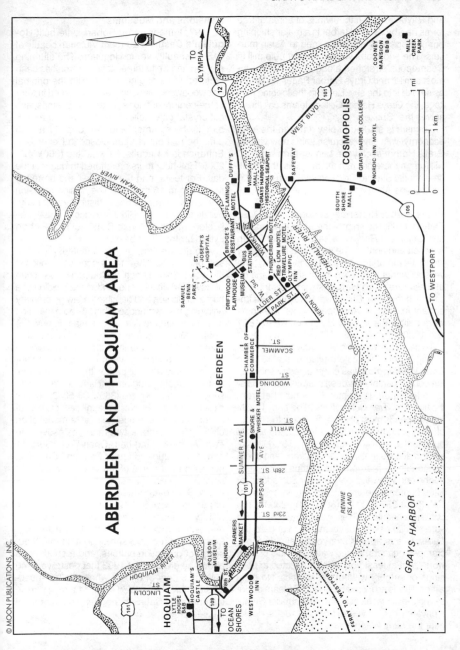

ABERDEEN AND HOQUIAM AREA

© MOON PUBLICATIONS, INC.

TO OLYMPIA

COSMOPOLIS

MILL CREEK PARK

COONEY MANSION

WEST BLVD.

GRAYS HARBOR COLLEGE

NORDIC INN MOTEL

SAFEWAY

SOUTH SHORE MALL

TO WESTPORT

WISHKAH RIVER

FLAMINGO MOTEL

DUFFY'S

WISHKAH MALL

GRAYS HARBOR HISTORICAL SEAPORT

ST. JOSEPH'S HOSPITAL

BRIDGE'S RESTAURANT

THUNDERBIRD MOTEL

RED LION MOTEL

TRAVELURE MOTEL

OLYMPIC INN

SAMUEL BENN PARK

DRIFTWOOD PLAYHOUSE

MUSEUM

BUS STATION

WISHKAH ST.

ALDER ST.

W. 3RD ST.

PARK ST.

HERON ST.

CHEHALIS RIVER

ABERDEEN

CHAMBER OF COMMERCE

SCAMMEL ST.

WOODING ST.

MYRTLE ST.

SUMNER AVE

SHORE & WHISKER MOTEL

SIMPSON AVE

28th ST

23rd ST

RENNIE ISLAND

GRAYS HARBOR

FERRY TO WESTPORT

HOQUIAM RIVER

HOQUIAM

LYTLE HOUSE B&B

HOQUIAM'S CASTLE

LINCOLN ST.

POLSON MUSEUM

FARMERS MARKET

8th ST. LANDING

WESTWOOD INN

TO OCEAN SHORES

1 mi

1 km

and Rayonier—own thousands of acres of tree farms nearby. Grays Harbor is a major shipping port for logs and lumber headed to Asian markets. The enormous Weyerhaeuser pulp mill in Cosmopolis stretches along Hwy. 101 for almost a mile, and Grays Harbor Paper still belches smoke into the sky. Befitting the logging heritage, the Grays Harbor College teams call themselves the "Chokers."

Tourism is starting to play a role in the local economy, with several cruise ships now visiting Grays Harbor each year. Longer-term "visitors" will form a more permanent job basis: the medium-security Stafford Creek Prison opens in 2000 just outside Aberdeen.

Grays Harbor Historical Seaport

Early in 1788, two ships—the *Lady Washington* and *Columbia Rediviva*—sailed around South America and north to the west coast of the new world. Commanded by Capt. Robert Gray, the vessels were the first American ships to land on these shores and were instrumental in later claims to this land. Shipbuilding was later an important industry in Aberdeen; some 130 ships were built in the shipyards here between 1887 and 1920.

To celebrate Washington's centennial in 1989, a magnificent full-scale replica of the 107-ton *Lady Washington* was constructed to serve as the central part of Aberdeen's Grays Harbor Historical Seaport. (You may recognize her from the film, *Star Trek Generations*.) The *Lady Washington* spends most of June-August at the mouth of the Wishram River. While in port, the ship is open for tours daily 10 a.m.-1 p.m. ($3 adults, $2 seniors and students, and $1 children), and offers outstanding three-hour sailing trips most afternoons and weekend evenings for $35 adults, or $20 children. The crew is entirely in costume. Call (360) 532-8611 or (800) 200-5239 for the current schedule and reservations (advised). Be sure to also ask about volunteering aboard the *Lady*. This is not for everyone—simple food, cramped quarters, limited water, and lots of hard work—but at least you aren't subjected to floggings or surgery without anesthetics. No grog either. This is an incredible chance to learn about sailing the old-fashioned way. The smaller *Sylvia*, a privately owned vessel from the 1880s, docks near the *Lady Washington*.

Mansions and Museums

In 1897, lumber baron Robert Lytle built **Hoquiam's Castle,** a 20-room Victorian beauty at 515 Chenault Ave. in Hoquiam. The stunning maroon and white three-story mansion has been restored to its original luster, with the original oak woodwork, and completely furnished in turn-of-the-century antiques, Tiffany-style lamps, and cut-crystal chandeliers. Open daily 10 a.m.-5 p.m. in the summer, and Sat.-Sun. 11 a.m.-5 p.m. the rest of the year, closed in December. Entrance is $4 adults, $1 kids, tel. (360) 533-2005. Half-hour tours are offered throughout the day. For tours, ring the doorbell and be ready to wait up to 15 minutes. The hillside mansion overlooks town and has a distinctive monkey-puzzle tree outside. Right next door is the equally elegant Lytle House B&B, built for Robert Lytle's brother (see below).

Another wealthy lumber magnate, Alex Polson, once owned the largest logging operation in the world, Polson Logging Company (now a part of Rayonier). In 1923 he funded the building of a home for his son and daughter-in-law on property adjoining his own house. This 26-room mansion at 1611 Riverside Ave. in Hoquiam is now the **Polson Museum.** Alex Polson's own home was razed after his death in 1939; his widow didn't want anyone else to live in it. The site of their home is now a small park with a rose garden, historic logging equipment, and a blacksmith shop. The museum, tel. (360) 533-5862, houses all sorts of memorabilia: a magnificent old grandfather clock, a fun model railroad, a model of an old logging camp, a two-man chainsaw, and even an old boxing bag. Open Wed.-Sun. 11 a.m.-4 p.m. June to Labor Day, and Sat.-Sun. noon-4 p.m. the rest of the year; $2 adults, $1 students, 50 cents for children.

The **Aberdeen Museum of History,** 117 E. 3rd St., tel. (360) 533-1976, has exhibits of local history including a turn-of-the-century kitchen and bedroom, pioneer church, blacksmith shop, four antique fire trucks, a dugout canoe, thousands of pro-union buttons, and a short video about the great fire of 1903 that destroyed 140 buildings. Lots of offbeat what-was-that-used-for stuff here. Open Wed.-Sun. 11 a.m.-4 p.m. in summer, and Sat.-Sun. noon-4 p.m. the rest of the year; free.

Wildlife Refuge

Due west of Hoquiam off Hwy. 109, **Grays Harbor National Wildlife Refuge,** tel. (360) 533-5228, is a 500-acre wetland in the northeast corner of Grays Harbor Estuary. This is one of the most important staging areas for shorebirds in North America, attracting up to a million birds each spring. The two dozen shorebird species that visit the basin include the western sandpiper, dunlin, short- and long-billed dowitcher, and red knot; other birds seen here are the peregrine falcon, northern harrier, and red-tailed hawk. A one-mile path leads to the viewing areas, but bring your boots since it's often muddy. The best viewing time is one hour before and one hour after high tide.

Bed and Breakfasts

Built in 1900, **Lytle House B&B** 509 Chenault in Hoquiam, tel. (360) 533-2320 or (800) 677-2320, is a gorgeous three-story Queen Ann mansion next door to Hoquiam's Castle. Inside are four parlors, and eight guest rooms with antiques, shared or private baths. A full breakfast is served; $65 s or $75-145 d. No young kids.

Cooney Mansion B&B, 1705 5th St. in Cosmopolis, tel. (360) 533-0602 or (800) 411-6462, was built in 1908 by lumber baron Neil Cooney, and sits adjacent to woods on a dead-end street. Outside is a rose garden and sundeck. This 10,000-square-foot B&B has eight antique-decorated guest rooms, private baths, a jacuzzi, sauna, exercise room, and fireplace; $60-145 s or $70-165 d.

The **Aberdeen Mansion Inn B&B,** 807 N. M St. in Aberdeen, tel. (360) 533-7079 or (888) 533-7079, is another lumber-baron mansion from the turn of the century. The inn features a magnificent entry hall, five guest rooms with private baths, and full breakfasts. The attractively landscaped grounds cover an acre; $95 s or d.

A Harbor View B&B, 113 W. 11th St., tel. (360) 533-7996, is a spacious turn-of-the-century duplex with two guest rooms sharing a bath, and full breakfasts; $65-75 s or d. No kids under 12.

Motels

The following motels are arranged by price. Two places with budget rates are: **Snore & Whisker Motel,** 3031 Simpson Ave. in Hoquiam, tel. (360) 532-5060, for $35 s or d; and **Travelure Motel,** 623 W. Wishkah in Aberdeen, tel. (360) 532-3280, for $37 s, $45 d. **Central Park Motel,** tel. (360) 533-1210 or (800) 927-1210, is out in the country five miles east of Aberdeen; $35-45 s or d. Rooms are $40 s or d at **Towne Motel,** 712 E. Wishkah St. in Aberdeen, tel. (360) 533-2340. They also have a hot tub.

Thunderbird Motel, 410 W. Wishkah St. in Aberdeen, tel. (360) 532-3153, charges $46 s or $55 d, including fridges and a hot tub. **Olympic Inn,** 616 W. Heron St. in Aberdeen, tel. (360) 533-4200 or (800) 562-8618, has large rooms for $50-74 s, $55-78 d. **Red Lion Inn,** 521 W. Wishkah in Aberdeen, tel. (360) 532-5210 or (800) 547-8010, charges $77-92 s or d, including a continental breakfast buffet. Spacious rooms are $79 at **Westwood Inn,** 910 Simpson Ave. in Hoquiam, tel. (360) 532-8161 or (800) 562-0994.

Campgrounds and RV Parks

Campsites ($11 tents, $16 RVs) are available at **Lake Sylvia State Park** near Montesano (see below), approximately 12 miles east of Aberdeen. Open late March through September. Call (360) 249-3621 for information. Park RVs at **Arctic Park,** 893 Hwy. 101 in Aberdeen, tel. (360) 533-4470.

Food

In business since 1945, **Duffy's** is the local family restaurant, featuring a varied, inexpensive-to-moderate seafood and steak menu and great blackberry pies. There are three Duffy's in an incredibly small area: 1605 Simpson Ave., tel. (360) 532-3842, in Aberdeen; 1212 E. Wishkah St., tel. (360) 538-0606, in Aberdeen; and 825 Simpson Ave., tel. (360) 532-1519 in Hoquiam.

Aberdeen's **Breakwater Seafood,** 306 S. F St., tel. (360) 532-5693, is a seafood market/restaurant with good chowder and fresh fish and chips to eat in or take out. In Hoquiam, the **Levee Street Restaurant,** 709 Levee St., tel. (360) 532-1959, serves fine seafood sautés, fettuccine, prime rib, and steaks with a European flair and a river view.

At 112 N. G St. in Aberdeen, **Bridge's,** tel. (360) 532-6563, has prime rib, steak, and seafood dinners, including razor clams. The atmosphere is elegant but not stuffy; open for lunch and dinner daily plus Sunday brunch. **Billy's Bar**

& Grill, a restored saloon at 322 E. Heron in Aberdeen, tel. (360) 533-7144, serves delicious and reasonably priced steaks, seafood, and burgers.

Parma in Aberdeen at 116 W. Heron St., tel. (360) 532-3166, is open for dinner with fresh homemade pasta, veal cordon bleu, delicious breads, and homemade desserts. Very good. More Italian food and the best local pizzas are at **Casa Mia Pizza,** 2936 Simpson Ave. in Hoquiam, tel. (360) 533-2010.

The **Grays Harbor Farmers Market,** tel. (360) 532-7896, takes place at Hoquiam's Levee Park, on the river on Hwy. 101 N. Open Tuesday and Thurs.-Sat. 9 a.m.-6 p.m. year-round.

Recreation

At E. 9th and N. I Streets, Aberdeen's **Samuel Benn Park** has rose and rhododendron gardens, tennis courts, playground, and picnic facilities. **Lake Aberdeen** at the east entrance to town has swimming and nonmotorized boating and play equipment. For an indoor pool, head to the **Hoquiam Aquatic Center,** 717 K St., tel. (360) 533-3474. **NorthWest Experiences,** 409 E. Market St. in Aberdeen, tel. (360) 532-9176, has sea kayak rentals and trips.

The **Grays Harbor Gulls** play professional baseball May-Aug. at Hoquiam's Olympic Stadium, one of the few surviving wooden stadiums in the country. Call (360) 532-4488 for tickets.

Events and Entertainment

Kick the year off with a fun time at Aberdeen's **Dixieland Jazz Festival** held on Presidents Day weekend in mid-February. The **Grays Harbor Shorebird Festival** in late April—the peak of the migration—includes birding field trips and workshops. In early May the city's **Grays Harbor Discovery Days Celebration** attracts longboats from throughout the Northwest for rowing and sailing races.

Hoquiam's **Loggers Playday,** held the second weekend in September, is an opportunity for sedentary executives to see what real work is all about. After kicking off the event with a parade and salmon barbecue, loggers compete in ax-throwing, log-chopping, tree-climbing, and more. Evening brings a big fireworks show.

The **Driftwood Players,** a community theatrical company, puts on several plays a year at Driftwood Playhouse, 120 E. 3rd in Aberdeen, tel. (360) 538-1213.

Information and Transportation

The **Grays Harbor Chamber of Commerce and Visitor Center,** 506 Duffy St. in Aberdeen, tel. (360) 532-1924 or (800) 321-1924, is open daily 9 a.m.-5 p.m. all year.

Aberdeen and Hoquiam are well served by **Grays Harbor Transit,** tel. (360) 532-2770 or (800) 562-9730. Buses take you throughout the county seven days a week, including Lake Quinault, Westport, Ocean Shores, and even east to Olympia. **Pacific Transit System,** tel. (360) 875-9418 or (800) 875-9418, provides bus service southward to Raymond, Long Beach, and Astoria, Oregon.

MONTESANO

The cozy town of Montesano (mon-te-SAY-no; pop. 3,600) occupies the juncture of the Chehalis, Satsop, and Wynoochee Rivers. The town has tidy brick buildings and the hilltop Grays Harbor County Courthouse, built in 1910 of marble and granite. Not far away is the nation's first tree farm, established by Weyerhaeuser in 1941. **Chehalis Valley Historical Museum,** 703 W. Pioneer Ave., tel. (360) 249-5800, houses historical logging equipment and turn-of-the-century photos in what was originally a 1906 church. Open Sat.-Sun. noon-4 p.m. all year; no charge.

Lake Sylvia State Park

About a mile north of Montesano off Hwy. 12, Lake Sylvia State Park encompasses 233 acres around this narrow but scenic reservoir. The lake was created by a dam built in 1909 to supply water and power and is a popular place to swim, canoe, or fish. Two miles of trails circle the lake and connect with two more miles of trail in adjacent Chapin Collins Memorial Forest. Be sure to check out the four-foot wooden ball, carved by loggers from a spruce log and used for log rolling until it became waterlogged and sank. The ball was rediscovered in 1974 when the lake level was lowered and is now on display. The park is open late March through September; tel. (360) 249-3621.

Accommodations

Local motels are: **Monte Square Motel,** 528 1/2 S. 1st St., tel. (360) 249-4424, with rooms for $35 s or $40 d; and **Palm Tree Motel,** 822 Pioneer E, tel. (360) 249-3931, charging $35 s or d.

Abel House B&B, 117 Fleet St. S, tel. (360) 249-6002 or (800) 235-2235, is an historic 1908 home with five guest rooms, Tiffany chandeliers, and attractive grounds. A full breakfast is served; $65-85 s or d.

Campgrounds

Lake Sylvia State Park (see above) has wooded campsites ($11) along the shore and RV hookups ($16); open late March to September. Call (800) 452-5687 for reservations ($6 extra). **Lake Wynoochee,** approximately 35 miles north of Montesano, is a popular summertime fishing, hiking, and swimming area within Olympic National Forest. Pitch a tent at **Coho Campground** for $10, and hike the scenic 12-mile Wynoochee Lake Shore Trail.

Food

For breakfasts and lunches, the small **Savory Faire,** 135 S. Main St., tel. (360) 249-3701, is hard to beat, with a menu that includes omelettes, from-scratch soups, fresh salads, sandwiches, plus fresh-baked breads, pastries, and espresso to go. Also try **Bee Hive Restaurant,** on the corner of Main and Pioneer, tel. (360) 249-4131, for all-American meals and homemade pies.

Other Practicalities

The **Festival of Lights** in December includes a big lighted parade that features everything from logging trucks to cement mixers. **Grays Harbor Transit,** tel. (360) 532-2770 or (800) 562-9730, has daily bus service throughout the county, including Lake Quinault, Westport, Ocean Shores, and east to Olympia.

ELMA AND McCLEARY

The small town of Elma (pop. 3,000) has a wide main street, several old-timey murals, and the now-required espresso shops. Just west of here area the cooling towers of the never-completed Satsop Nuclear Power Plant. The **Satsop**

Methodist Church, built in 1872, is visible three miles west of Elma along Hwy. 410.

McCleary (pop. 1,500) has a Simpson Co. door manufacturing plant, a small museum, several eating places, and a fascinating old hotel. **Vance Creek County Park,** just west of Elma, has nature trails, jogging paths, and swimming in two small lakes. McCleary's **Carnell House Museum,** 314 2nd St., is open Sat.-Sun. noon-4 p.m., Memorial Day through Labor Day only. Inside are historic photos and a collection of farming, logging, and household equipment from the past.

Lodging and Food

The **Grays Harbor Hostel,** 6 Ginny Ln. (near the fairgrounds) in Elma, tel. (360) 482-3119, is a sprawling ranch house situated on eight acres of land. The spotless facilities include an outdoor jacuzzi, two common rooms, a kitchen, and storage rooms. Blankets and pillows are available, and there's even a three-hole golf course. Shared rooms go for $10-12 pp, and the private room is $20 d. Open all year, but closed daily 9 a.m.-5 p.m. Tent space is available for cyclists.

Built in 1912 and on the National Historic Register, the **Old McCleary Hotel** was originally the home of Henry McCleary, for whom the town is named. Today it is owned by Penny Challstedt, who has kept the place as something of a museum, with the original furniture, brass beds, unusual toilets, dark paneling, and Victorian wallpaper. Don't expect a TV or fax machine here. The three-story hotel is located at 42 Summit Rd., tel. (360) 495-3678; rooms are $45-55 s or d. The owner also serves family-style meals, but these are mainly for wedding receptions. Otherwise, try **Sharon's Rose Garden,** a mom-and-pop restaurant.

Campgrounds

Follow the signs for 12 miles north of Elma to **Schafer State Park** on the Satsop River. Originally a park for Schafer Logging Company employees, today it has public campsites ($10 tents, $15 RVs), riverside picnic areas, and a fine collection of mossy trees. Good fishing for steelhead (late winter) and sea-run cutthroat (summers) in the East Fork of the Satsop River. The park is open April-September.

*Old McCleary Hotel,
McCleary, WA*

DON PITCHER

Weyerhaeuser's **Swinging Bridge Park** is about 10 miles from Elma in the middle of nowhere, forking left off the road to Schafer; here you'll find free camping with a five-day limit, free firewood, and secluded picnic and play areas. Park RVs at **Elma RV Park,** Hwy. 12 and 30 S, tel. (360) 482-4053, or **Travel Inn Resort & Campground,** 801 E. Main in Elma, tel. (360) 482-3877.

Other Practicalities

Elma is home to the county fairgrounds, where you can take in an indoor pro rodeo in late March, horse racing in late July, the old-fash-ioned **Grays Harbor County Fair** in mid-August, and Saturday night auto racing April-September. The **McCleary Bear Festival** in mid-July offers two parades, entertainment, arts and crafts, and food booths. In mid-September, Elma has a **Wild Blackberry Festival** with a pie contest, car show, arts and crafts, and parade.

Get local information from the **Elma Chamber of Commerce,** tel. (360) 482-3055.

Grays Harbor Transit, tel. (360) 532-2770 or (800) 562-9730, provides daily bus service throughout the county—from Ocean Shores to Olympia.

SOUTH BEACH/CRANBERRY COAST

The section of coastline between Westport and North Cove is known as both "South Beach" and the "Cranberry Coast"; the former because it is the southern entrance to Grays Harbor, the latter because of the bogs east near Grayland that produce much of the state's cranberry crop. The area is especially popular for sportfishing but also offers long beaches, good surfing, and reasonably priced lodging. The beaches are favorites of post-storm beachcombers who still turn up an occasional glass ball from old Japanese fishing floats.

WESTPORT

Westport (pop. 2,000), the principal South Beach city, once called itself "The Salmon Capital of the World," and charter services and commercial fishing and crabbing boats still line the waterfront. This is one of the most active ports in Washington, and chainsmoking fishermen drive beat-up old pickups through town. The town also has a crab cannery and several seafood markets, plus the expected waterfront shops offering kitschy gifts, saltwater taffy, and kites. Ragged-at-the-edges Westport is quite unlike its upscale cross-bay twin, Ocean Shores.

Sights

At 2201 Westhaven Dr. in Westport, the **Westport Maritime Museum,** tel. (360) 268-0078, is housed in a magnificent old Coast Guard station built in 1939. Capped by six gables and a watchtower with a widow's walk, the building was used until 1974, when newer quarters were completed just down the road. Inside are photographs of the early Aberdeen-Westport plank road, cranberry and logging industry exhibits, and Coast Guard memorabilia. Out front in glass cases are gray whale, minke whale, sea lion, and porpoise skeletons. Also on the grounds is a new building housing the massive lens from the Destruction Island Lighthouse. Built in 1888, it was replaced in 1995 by an automated light. On weekends March-May, the museum offers talks about whales and whalewatching; also check

out the interesting video on fish trapping. Open daily 10 a.m.-4 p.m. June-Sept.; Wed.-Sun. noon-4 p.m. the rest of the year. $1 adults, 50 cents for kids.

Housed inside a tacky gift shop, the private **Westport Aquarium,** 321 Harbor St., tel. (360) 268-0471, open daily April-Dec., offers large display tanks holding octopus, sharks, bottom fish, and anemones, plus a chance to feed the performing seals. Entrance is $2 adults, $1 ages 5-16, and free for kids under four.

Head to the three-quarter-mile **South Jetty** at the end of State Park Access Rd. for a chance to fish, look for birds and marine mammals, or watch the winter storms roll in. Use care on the slippery rocks. The road passes Half Moon Bay, popular with scuba divers. A tall **observation tower** on the east end of Nettie Rose Dr. in town provides a fine vantage point to view freighter activity, scenery, sunsets, or an occasional whale, and a lower **ramp tower** on the east end of Nettie Rose looks into the marina. In front of this is a small memorial to fishermen lost at sea.

Parks and Viewpoints

Open for day-use only, **Westhaven State Park,** on Hwy. 105 just north of Westport, is popular with rockhounds, beachcombers, and divers. Surfers and sea kayakers find some of the most consistent waves in Washington. The jetty was built here to increase the velocity of the seagoing water, collected from six rivers flowing into Grays Harbor. Prior to the construction of the jetty, deposits of sediment mandated annual channel dredging. The jetty worked—the channel hasn't required dredging since 1942.

Westport Light State Park, about a mile south of Westhaven off Hwy. 105 (continue straight when 105 goes left), is another day-use park good for kite flying, rockhounding, and fishing for ocean perch, but no camping. A paved, mile-long **Dune Interpretive Trail** wanders through the dunes, providing several observation platforms that overlook the water. There's vehicular beach access here, but the sand is considerably softer than at other driveable beaches; be careful if you don't have 4WD. Check with

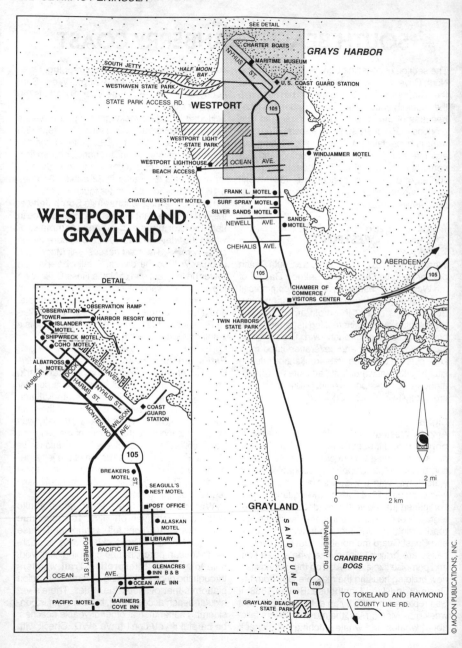

SEE DETAIL

CHARTER BOATS

GRAYS HARBOR

MARITIME MUSEUM

NYHUS ST.

SOUTH JETTY

HALF MOON BAY

U.S. COAST GUARD STATION

WESTHAVEN STATE PARK

STATE PARK ACCESS RD.

WESTPORT

105

WESTPORT LIGHT STATE PARK

OCEAN AVE.

WINDJAMMER MOTEL

WESTPORT LIGHTHOUSE

BEACH ACCESS

FRANK L. MOTEL

CHATEAU WESTPORT MOTEL

SURF SPRAY MOTEL

SILVER SANDS MOTEL

WESTPORT AND GRAYLAND

NEWELL AVE.

SANDS MOTEL

CHEHALIS AVE.

105

TO ABERDEEN

105

CHAMBER OF COMMERCE / VISITORS CENTER

DETAIL

TWIN HARBORS STATE PARK

OBSERVATION RAMP

OBSERVATION TOWER

HARBOR RESORT MOTEL

ISLANDER MOTEL

SHIPWRECK MOTEL

COHO MOTEL

ALBATROSS MOTEL

DOCK

WESTHAVEN ST.

HARBOR

HARMS ST.

NYHUS ST.

WILSON

COAST GUARD STATION

MONTESANO

AVE.

105

BREAKERS MOTEL

SEAGULL'S NEST MOTEL

ST.

POST OFFICE

GRAYLAND

ALASKAN MOTEL

LIBRARY

SAND DUNES

CRANBERRY RD.

PACIFIC AVE.

FORREST ST.

OCEAN AVE.

GLENACRES INN B & B

OCEAN AVE. INN

CRANBERRY BOGS

PACIFIC MOTEL

MARINERS COVE INN

105

GRAYLAND BEACH STATE PARK

TO TOKELAND AND RAYMOND COUNTY LINE RD.

0   2 mi

0   2 km

the park for regulations on beach driving, since some sections are closed part or all of the year. The classic **lighthouse** inside the park—tallest on the West Coast—was built in 1898 and is visible from an observation platform on Ocean Avenue. The building is closed to the public, but tours may be offered by the museum. The lighthouse originally stood much closer to the water, but the accretion of sand has pushed the beachfront seaward.

On Hwy. 105, two miles south of Westport, **Twin Harbors State Park** has campsites, a three-quarter-mile sand dune nature trail, picnic areas, and a playground. This is one of the most popular ocean-side campgrounds, especially when razor clam harvesting is allowed (usually March and October). Twin Harbors is open for day-use all year.

Fishing

Even the casual visitor to Westport will see that this is a major sport and commercial fishing port. The harbor is packed with vessels of all dimensions, and charter operators line the marina. You don't have to charter a boat to go fishing; the whole stretch from Westport to North Cove is popular for surf fishing. The rock jetty near Westhaven State Park (see above) is a good spot for catching salmon, rockfish, ling cod, surf perch, and crabs. In September and October, a coho salmon run returns to the marina area (the young are raised in pens here, so this is "home"). Clamming is seasonal and requires a license; see the chamber of commerce for a copy of the regulations. The 1,000-foot-long **Westport Fishing Pier,** off the end of Float 20 at the Westport Marina, is another landlubber fishing option.

Offshore rocks and reefs are feeding grounds for salmon, bottom fish, halibut, and even albacore tuna; take a charter boat to find the best spots, not to mention having your fish cleaned and ready to cook by the time you get back to shore. The charter services all charge about the same amount, so when you call for reservations be sure to check whether the price includes bait and tackle, cleaning, sales tax, etc., to see if your "bargain" is really a good deal. Note, however, that most departures are at the frightfully early hour of 6 a.m., with a return around 3:30 p.m. Be sure to take along your seasickness pills. Some companies also offer overnight trips

that head far offshore in search of tuna. Wander along Westhaven Dr. to check out the various charter companies, or get a listing of boats from the visitors center. Expect to pay around $125 pp for halibut charters, $325 for tuna, or $60-70 pp for coho salmon or bottom fishing.

Whalewatching

Many of the charter operators provide whalewatching trips March-May, when the gray whales are heading north from their winter quarters off Baja California. Get a list from the visitor center. Expect to pay $20-30 for a three-hour trip. You may also spot whales from the jetty or from the Westport viewing towers. The passenger ferry to Ocean Shores is an inexpensive way to watch for the whales that periodically wander into Grays Harbor. The Maritime Museum offers weekend whalewatching seminars, films, and workshops in season.

Other Recreation

Surfers can check out the waves at Westhaven State Park, one of the most popular surfing beaches in the state. Rent surfboards and wetsuits from the **Surf Shop,** 207 Montesano, tel. (360) 268-0992, or **Catalyst Surf Shop & Espresso,** 105 N. Montesano St., tel. (360) 268-9283.

Both **Cachalot Kites,** 2511 Westhaven Dr., tel. (360) 268-0323 or (800) 356-0323, and **Pic a Patch Kite Shop,** 2511 Westhaven Dr., tel. (360) 268-0323, have kites and windsocks of every description.

Accommodations

Accommodations here are fairly simple. Many have kitchenettes, but only a few offer jacuzzis or pools. As one owner told me in her broken English, "no pool; big giant ocean out there!" Contact the chamber of commerce for a list of rental homes in the Westport area.

Built in 1898 and surrounded by tall evergreens, **Glenacres Inn B&B,** 222 N. Montesano St., tel. (360) 268-9391, is the most interesting place to stay in Westport. The B&B has eight guest rooms with private baths for $59-72 s or d, including a full breakfast. Four separate cottages are $45-170 and can sleep up to eight. A gazebo encloses the hot tub.

Campgrounds
Camp two miles south of town at the very popular **Twin Harbors State Park** for $11 ($16 RVs). Some campsites are just steps away from the beach, and showers are available. The campground is open late February-October. For reservations ($6 extra), call (800) 452-5687. Addi-

tional camping is available at Grayland Beach State Park (see below).
  Westport is jam-packed with RV parks catering to the fishing crowd. The better ones include **Coho Charters RV Park,** 2501 N. Nyhus St., tel. (360) 268-0111 or (800) 572-0177; **Kila Hana Camperland,** 931 S. Forrest Ave., tel. (360)

WESTPORT MOTELS

Accommodations are arranged from least to most expensive within each town. Rates may be considerably lower during the winter months. Bed and breakfasts are described in the text.

INEXPENSIVE

Windjammer Motel; 461 E. Pacific Ave.; tel. (360) 268-9351; $35-45 s, $45-50 d; kitchenettes available; AAA approved

Frank L. Motel; 725 S. Montesano St.; tel. (360) 268-9200; $40 s or d, two-room apartments $110 d; kitchenettes available, jacuzzi

Surf Spray Motel; 949 S. Montesano St.; tel. (360) 268-9149; $42-46 s or d; full kitchens

Orca Motel; 221 E. Dock St.; tel. (360) 268-5010; $42-72 s or d; fridges, kitchenettes available

Albatross Motel; 200 E. Dock St.; tel. (360) 268-9233; $44 s, $48-64 d; kitchenettes available

Mariners Cove Inn; 303 Ocean Ave.; tel. (360) 268-0531; $44-50 s or d; newer motel, kitchenettes available, AAA approved

Alaskan Motel; 708 N. 1st St.; tel. (360) 268-9133; $45 s or d for kitchenettes; $75 for cottages

Sands Motel; 1416 S. Montesano St.; tel. (360) 268-0091; $45-55 s or d; kitchenettes available

Shipwreck Motel; 2653 Nyhus St., tel. (360) 268-9151 or (888) 225-2313; $45-120 s or d; kitchenettes $70 s or d; distinctive '60s-era round motel

Silver Sands Motel; 1001 S. Montesano St.; tel. (360) 268-9029; $48 s or d

Ocean Avenue Inn; 275 W. Ocean Ave.; tel. (360) 268-9278 or (888) 692-5262; $49 s or d; kitchenettes available, clean and friendly

Seagull's Nest Motel; 830 N. Montesano St.; tel. (360) 268-9711 or (888) 613-9078; $49-69 s or d; large rooms with fridges, kitchenettes available

Pacific Motel; 330 S. Forrest Ave.; tel. (360) 268-9325; $54 s or d; outdoor pool, kitchenettes available

Breakers Motel; 971 Montesano St.; tel. (360) 268-0848; $54-72 s or d; kitchenettes available

Coho Motel; 2501 N. Nyhus; tel. (360) 268-0111 or (800) 572-0177; $59-70 s or d; AAA approved

MODERATE

Harbor Resort Motel; 871 Neddie Rose Dr.; tel. (360) 268-0169; $65 s or d in rooms with kitchens; $110 for up to five in cottages

Islander Motel; Westhaven and Nettie Rose; tel. (360) 268-9166 or (800) 322-1740; $65 s, $73-80 d; kitchenette suites $98 d; outdoor pool

Chateau Westport Motel; 710 Hancock; tel. (360) 268-9101 or (800) 255-9101; $67-72 s or d; ocean views, indoor pool, jacuzzi, continental breakfast, balconies, fireplaces, kitchenettes available, AAA approved

268-9528 or (800) 262-9528; and **Pacific Aire RV Resort,** tel. (360) 268-0207.

Food

Because of the early morning departure of fishing charters, several local cafes are already open when the clock strikes five in the morning. Local smokers hang out at two very popular but nothing-special cafes: **Rich's Family Diner,** 203 S. Montesano, tel. (360) 268-0545, and **Inn of the Westwind,** 2119 N. Nyhus, tel. (360) 268-0677. **The Bakery Cottage,** 389 W. Ocean Ave., tel. (360) 268-1100, has lighter breakfasts and lunches. Another recommended lunch place with a salad bar and good seafood is **Barbara's by the Sea,** across from the marina; tel. (360) 268-1329. Get chili or clam chowder in a bread bowl, and good sandwiches at **Coley's Seafood & Sub Shop,** 2300 N. Westhaven Dr., tel. (360) 268-9000.

Anthony's, 260 E. Dock St., tel. (360) 268-1609, has a fine cross-nationality menu that includes pasta, fish and chips, pizza, and Greek dishes. **Las Marachas Mexican Restaurant,** 202 W. Ocean Ave., tel. (360) 268-6272, makes good enchiladas, tostadas, and chimichangas.

You'll find a "surf and turf" menu that includes oysters, halibut, and prawns, along with steaks and pasta at **Sourdough Lil's,** 301 E. Dock St., tel. (360) 268-9700, and **King's LeDomaine,** 105 Wilson St., tel. (360) 268-0312.

Buy freshly shucked oysters to go from **Brady's Oysters,** 3714 Oyster Place E, tel. (360) 268-0077. They were the first to grow oysters on suspended lines, a method that many claim produces a more delicately flavored oyster. You can often buy ultra-fresh fish from commercial fishermen at the marina, and fresh-cooked crab at **Strong's Seafood,** 1863 S. Montesano, tel. (360) 268-5083.

Events

Westport's **World Class Crab Races & Feed** in mid-April is not a good time to be a crab; the races are followed by a big crab feed. Live music too, but they don't make the crabs play the instruments. The **Blessing of the Fleet,** held annually in May, includes a memorial service for people lost at sea and demonstrations of Coast Guard sea-air rescues. Held in early July, the two-day **Festival of the Wind** has contests for the youngest and oldest kite flyers, best crash event, longest train of kites, and more. In August, an **International Nautical Chain Saw Carving Contest** (no it is not done underwater), and the **Brady's Oyster Feed** both come early in the month. Mid-August has the **Longboard Classic Surf Festival,** attracting top longboard surfers from throughout the Northwest.

A very popular event—it's been going on for more than 50 years—is the **Westport Seafood Festival** on Labor Day weekend. Taste fresh salmon, oysters, crab, and all sorts of other fresh-from-the-sea foods, with musical accompaniment.

Information and Services

At 2985 N. Montesano St. in Westport, the **Westport-Grayland Chamber of Commerce Visitors Center,** tel. (360) 268-9422 or (800) 345-6223, is open Mon.-Fri. 9 a.m.-5 p.m. all year, plus Sat.-Sun. 10 a.m.-3 p.m. May-September. Stop by for maps, brochures, and festival and tour information.

Transportation

Grays Harbor Transit, tel. (360) 532-2770 or (800) 562-9730, provides daily bus service throughout the county, including Grayland, Aberdeen, Lake Quinault, Ocean Shores, and even to Olympia.

The **Westport-Ocean Shores Passenger Ferry,** *El Matador* is a passenger ferry that runs between Ocean Shores and Westport for $8 roundtrip; free for kids under five. The ferry leaves six times a day, with daily service mid-June to Labor Day, and weekend-only service early May to mid-June and in September. No service the rest of the year. The ferry departs from Float 10 at the Westport marina, tel. (360) 268-0047.

GRAYLAND

Grayland is a frumpy, old fashioned little place with simple accommodations and a ragged appearance. It's the sort of place where the local gallery sells sea shells, pottery, and paintings from the school of sawblade art. Locals complain of the influx of wealthy Californians buying up the land, punching taxes to the sky, and pinching struggling local businesses.

The **Ocean Spray Cranberry** processing plant is east of Westport in Markham, tel. (360) 648-2512; no tours. Elk are often seen across the highway from the Ocean Spray plant at the **Johns River Wildlife Area** in the winter and spring. Look for cranberry bogs south of Grayland off Cranberry and Larkin roads.

A mile south of Grayland on Hwy. 105, **Grayland Beach State Park** has 7,450 feet of ocean frontage, a self-guided nature trail through huckleberry, Sitka spruce, and lodgepole pine, and 200 acres for picnicking and camping. This is a popular place to dig for clams.

The **Beach Shop,** 2191 Hwy. 105, tel. (360) 267-7691, rents boogie boards and mountain bikes.

Accommodations

For the nicest rooms in town, stay at **Walsh Motel,** 1593 Hwy. 105, tel. (360) 267-2191, a modern on-the-beach motel with rooms for $38-102 s or d. **Ocean Gate Resort,** 1939 Hwy. 105 S, tel. (360) 267-1956 or (800) 473-1956, has basic older cottages near the beach for $35-45 s or d. **Grayland Motel & Cottages,** 2013 Hwy. 105, tel. (360) 267-2395 or (800) 292-0845, charges $42-72 s or d. **Western Shores Motel and RV Park,** 2193 Hwy. 105, tel. (360) 267-6115, has rooms for $40-50 s or d. **Surf Motel & Cottages,** 2029 Hwy. 105, tel. (360) 267-2244, charges $39 s or d in motel rooms, and $56 for up to four in cottages with kitchenettes. **Grayland B&B,** 1678 Hwy. 105, tel. (360) 267-6026, has two bedrooms with a shared bath in a two-story home built in the 1930s. Kids are okay; $100 s or d.

Campgrounds

A mile south of Grayland on Hwy. 105, **Grayland Beach State Park** has camping ($11) and RV hookups ($16), plus showers; open year-round. For reservations ($6 extra), call (800) 452-5687. Additional camping is available at Twin Harbors State Park (see **Westport**).

Park RVs at the well-maintained **Kenanna RV Park,** 2959 S. Hwy. 105, tel. (360) 267-3515 or (800) 867-3515; or **Ocean Gate Resort,** 1939 Hwy. 105 S, tel. (360) 267-1956 or (800) 473-1956.

Events

The third weekend of March, Grayland-area artists display their driftwood and shell creations at the town's **Beachcombers Driftwood Show.** The **Fourth of July** means a big fireworks display over Booming Bay, and a fun run, arts and crafts, and food booths in Grayland. Early October brings the **Cranberry Harvest Festival** with bog tours, a cranberry cookoff, parade, and dancing.

Information and Transportation

The small **Cranberry Coast Chamber of Commerce,** next to Grandma's Treasure Chest store, has local flyers; tel. (360) 267-2003 or (800) 473-6018. **Grays Harbor Transit,** tel. (360) 532-2770 or (800) 562-9730, provides daily bus service throughout the county, including Westport, Aberdeen, Lake Quinault, and Ocean Shores.

NORTH COVE AND TOKELAND

The town of North Cove occupies the northern edge of the entrance to Willapa Harbor and was once considerably larger. Over the years the sea has been winning the war with the land, pulling a lighthouse, life-saving station, canneries, homes, hotels, and schools over the retreating cliff. The shore is now more than two miles back from its position a century ago, a rate unparalleled elsewhere on the Pacific Coast. Although the rate of erosion has slowed, there's often something ready to go over the edge at the aptly named **Washaway Beach** in North Cove.

Protruding into the north end of Willapa Bay off Hwy. 105, tiny Tokeland (pop. 200) is the site of a number of turn-of-the-century homes and commercial buildings and a marina and public dock (a favorite place for recreational crabbing). The waterfront community—protected by a long rock wall fronting the ocean—attracts retirees, summer visitors, and anglers. Today it is also home to the **Shoalwater Bay Bingo and Casino,** tel. (360) 267-6083, located at the Hwy. 105 turnoff to Tokeland. Warning: the Tokeland area is known as a favorite cop hangout, and the 25 mph speed limit is strictly enforced!

Practicalities

A focal point for Tokeland is the wonderfully old fashioned **Tokeland Hotel,** Kindred Rd. and Hotel Rd., tel. (360) 267-7006. Built as a home in 1885, it became an inn in 1899 and is now on the

National Register. The hotel and town are named for Chief Toke, whose daughter married a worker at the life-saving station here. Together they built a home that was later turned into the Tokeland Hotel. Now on the National Register of Historic Places, it's said to be the oldest resort hotel in Washington, and the spacious front lawn, brick fireplace, and jigsaw puzzles provide an air of relaxation. The restored hotel has upstairs rooms with bath down the hall for $55 s or $65 d; reserve several weeks ahead for summer weekend stays. A full breakfast is included—served downstairs in the open dining room overlooking Willapa Bay. The restaurant also serves lunch and dinner, specializing in very reasonably priced seafood ($10-15 entrees).

More Tokeland lodging at **Tradewinds on the Bay Motel,** 4305 Pomeroy Ave., tel. (360) 267-7500, with an outdoor pool, and kitchenette rooms for $65-75 s or d. This is a quiet on-the-water location.

Get fresh-cooked crab and other seafood at **Nelson Crab, Inc.,** tel. (360) 267-2911. The Shoalwater Bay Tribe has a small reservation and tribal offices at Tokeland (Willapa Bay was originally called Shoalwater Bay).

Park RVs at **Bayshore RV Park,** 2941 Kindred Ave., tel. (360) 267-2625; or **Willapa RV Park,** 3230 Front St., tel. (360) 267-7710.

Tokeland has a small but fun **Fourth of July Parade** that winds through town.

SOUTHWESTERN WASHINGTON AND COLUMBIA GORGE

WILLAPA BAY

East and south from Tokeland, Washington's coastline wraps around Willapa Bay, a 25-mile-long inlet protected by the Long Beach Peninsula. It is believed to be the cleanest and least developed estuary on the West Coast of the Lower 48 states. Locals posit that these waters produce the best-tasting oysters in the nation (a claim disputed by folks in Grays Harbor and Shelton). Highways 105 and 101 skirt Willapa's scenic marshy shoreline, and tree farms carpet the surrounding hills. This is timber country. A handful of small settlements—notably Raymond and South Bend—offer accommodations, meals, and a few attractions.

RAYMOND

Raymond (pop. 2,900), on the Willapa River just east of the bay, began as a booming milltown,

with 20 lumber mills processing Pacific Coast trees. Thanks to years of tree farming, loggers still harvest these hills to feed two mills, including a state-of-the-art Weyerhaeuser plant.

Highway 101 continues north from Raymond to Aberdeen, past a patchwork of Weyerhaeuser tree farms and clearcuts. The winding road can be a traffic nightmare of logging trucks, poking RVs, and too-few passing lanes. The cops are often out in force here, so don't even think about going over the speed limit.

Sights

Not a lot to see in Raymond, but do stop by the **Dennis Company,** a big, old fashioned dry goods store at 146 5th St., tel. (360) 942-2427. In addition to hardware, clothing, and sporting goods, the store has many historic photos. A big mural—said to be the largest in Washington—covers one wall of the building and depicts the early days of logging. Across the street is a display of antique logging and farm equipment. You may also want to visit the **Edwards Flower Garden and Tree Farm,** 1736 Ocean, tel. (360) 942-3622, covering 150 acres of hill country between Raymond and South Bend. The attractively landscaped area includes five trout ponds with ducks and geese and 10 acres of flowering shrubs and trees. Hikers and cyclists will enjoy the 3.5-mile **Rails to Trails** paved path that follows the river from Raymond to South Bend. Along the way, look for the historic *Krestine,* a majestic, 100-foot sailing ship that plied the North Sea waters for many years.

Accommodations

Maunu's Mountcastle Motel, 524 3rd St., tel. (360) 942-5571, has rooms for $36-40 s or $44 d. Kitchenettes are available. **Brackett's Log Cottage B&B** on Hunt Club Rd., tel. (360) 942-6111 or (800) 942-6113, has two cottages on a 60-acre tree farm four miles east of town. An extended continental breakfast is served; $55 s or d.

Timberland RV Park at Park and Crescent, tel. (360) 942-3325, has RV hookups.

Food

For spicy fast food, stop by **Willapa Willy's Chili,** 524 N. 3rd St., tel. (360) 942-3438, where the owner, Everett "Tiny" McVey uses five different types of peppers. The chili is so hot that even he won't eat it; gives him the hiccups he claims. The chili/hot dog/burger stand is also home to the **Raymond Chamber of Commerce,** tel. (360) 942-5419, open same hours as the chili stand: daily 11 a.m.-9 p.m. or so.

For sit-down meals and pizza, head to **The Barge Restaurant,** 160 Laurel St., tel. (360) 942-5100, or **Raymond Cafe,** 216 N. 3rd St., tel. (360) 942-3408.

The **Public Market on the Willapa,** tel. (360) 942-2679, takes place at Riverfront Park on Sat.-Sun. 10 a.m.-3 p.m. from mid-June through September.

Events

Raymond's main event is the **Willapa Harbor Festival,** held the first weekend of August, where you'll find a parade, logging show, car show, crafts fair, music, pancake breakfast, and a fire department barbecue. The **Willapa Harbor Play-**

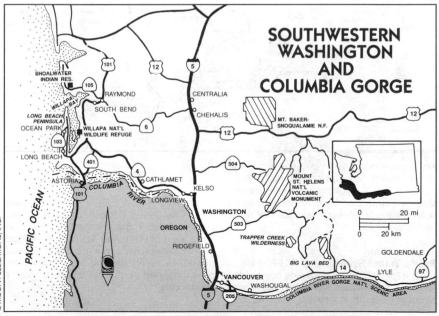

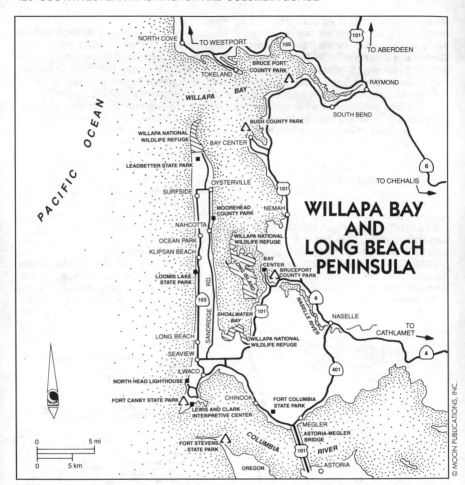

WILLAPA BAY AND LONG BEACH PENINSULA

ers perform theatrical productions during the winter months. Menlo, six miles east of Raymond on Hwy. 6, sponsors the annual **Pacific County Fair,** a four-day event in late August with all the usual 4-H contests, carnival rides, and sweet treats.

Transportation
Pacific Transit System, tel. (360) 875-9418 or (800) 875-9418, has county-wide bus service Mon.-Sat., and connects with Grays Harbor Transit buses in Aberdeen for points eastward.

SOUTH BEND

South Bend (pop. 1,600), the town that calls itself "The Oyster Capital of the West," occupies a bend in the Willapa River just four miles west of Raymond. It's a rough-edged blue-collar seaport with a mix of abandoned downtown storefronts and flourishing enterprises capped by the out-of-place county courthouse.

History

Founded in 1869, South Bend started out as a sawmill town; when the Northern Pacific Railroad extended a spur to South Bend in the late 1880s, it became "the Baltimore of the Pacific." Victorian homes, churches, and an ornate glass-domed courthouse attest to the prosperity of the times. The Panic of 1893 put an end to South Bend's grandiose logging plans, while the Willapa Bay oysters that had brought great sums of wealth to a few shrewd businessmen were just about farmed out.

Aquaculture had its start in the early 1900s, when 95 carloads of Chesapeake oysters were "planted" in the bay. Oyster-processing plants flourished until 1919, when a mysterious pestilence wiped out the crop. In 1924, the Japanese oyster was introduced; they began spawning faster than they could be harvested. When the Great Depression finished off South Bend's lumber business, the oyster plants were still going strong—as they are today. The largest oyster processing plant in the nation—Coast Oyster Company—is located here. South Bend's other contribution to the state is Helen Davis; she composed the state song, "Washington, My Home."

Sights

Follow the signs up the hill to the **Pacific County Courthouse,** built in 1910 and covered by an immense, multicolored stained-glass dome over mosaic-tile flooring. This "gilded palace of reckless extravagance" as it was called, was built at the then-extravagant cost of $132,000, but not everything is as it appears: the marble columns are actually concrete painted to look like marble. A county jail inmate painted the columns and created the decorative panels inside. The courthouse's parklike grounds—complete with a stocked duck pond—offer views of Weyerhaeuser-shaved hills and the town below. South Bend's raucous battle for the county seat led local citizens to ransack the Oysterville courthouse in 1893, thus "liberating" the county records.

Also in South Bend, the **Pacific County Museum,** tel. (360) 875-5224, has an impressive collection of Indian and pioneer artifacts and historic photos at 1008 W. Robert Bush Drive. Open daily 11 a.m.-4 p.m. in the summer. Pick up the brochure describing South Bend's many historic buildings at the museum. A mural on the side of the museum depicts the harbor at the turn of the century.

Willie Keil's Grave

Three miles east of Raymond along Hwy. 6 is Willie Keil's Grave, a testimony to a father's devotion to his son. The elder Keil was founder and titular head of a Christian communal organization called the Bethelites, in honor of the town they founded in northern Missouri. They became very wealthy on the community-owned farms and town, and when the great migration over the Oregon Trail occurred, the Bethelites decided to establish a branch of their belief and business empire at the opposite end of the Oregon Trail. Nineteen-year-old Willie Keil was excited about the trip, but as the departure date neared, he fell ill with malaria. In his final delirium he imagined himself at the head of the wagon train going across the continent.

Willie's brokenhearted dad promised the boy he *would* lead a wagon train west; when Willie died in Bethel, in 1855, his father put the body in a lead-lined, whiskey-filled casket and carried his remains to Washington in honor of his pledge. Willie was buried on the little knoll where the park stands today. After a short time in the area, the Bethelites gave up on the Willapa Bay site and moved south of Portland to found Aurora.

Accommodations

H & H Motel on E. Water at Pennsylvania, tel. (360) 875-5523, has rooms for $34 s or $43 d, some with kitchenettes. **Sequest Motel,** 801 W. 1st St., tel. (360) 875-5349, has rooms with kitchenettes for $35-60 s or d.

The nicest local place is **Maring's Courthouse Hill B&B,** W. 2nd St., tel. (360) 875-6519 or (800) 875-6519. Built in 1892, this hillside home was originally a church. It has three guest rooms for $60 s or $65 d with private bath, full breakfast, and friendly hosts.

The Russell House B&B, 902 E. Water St., tel. (360) 875-5608 or (888) 484-6907, is a beautiful antique-filled Victorian mansion with views of Willapa Bay. The four guest rooms have private or shared baths, a full breakfast is served, and kids are accepted. Rates $60-70 s or $65-75 d.

Campgrounds

Camp at **Bruceport County Park,** five miles south of town on Hwy. 101, tel. (360) 875-6611; open year-round. Park RVs at **Gypsy RV Park,** 524 Central, tel. (360) 875-5165, or H & H Motel.

Food

The Boondocks Restaurant, 1015 W. Robert Bush Dr., tel. (360) 875-5155 or (800) 875-5158, is *the* place to eat in South Bend. The specialty, not surprisingly, is oysters, and for breakfast (served anytime) you'll get "hangtown fry," fresh pan-fried Willapa oysters. Also featured are seafood quiche, pastas, veal, and fresh fish.
Gardner's Restaurant, 702 W. Robert Bush Dr., tel. (360) 875-5154, emphasizes fresh pasta and seafood and homemade desserts. **H & H Cafe** on E. Water at Pennsylvania, tel. (360) 875-5523, is a good place to meet the locals over homemade pie and coffee.

Get fresh oysters in South Bend at **Coast Oyster,** tel. (360) 875-5557, **E.H. Bendiksen Co.,** tel. (360) 875-6632, and **East Point Seafood Co.,** tel. (360) 875-5507.

Festivals

South Bend's Memorial Day weekend **Oyster Stampede,** tel. (360) 875-5608, includes oyster shucking and eating contests, wine tasting, art shows, plus country music and dancing. Summer ends with the **Come and Play on Labor Day** festival that includes a big parade, salmon barbecue, art and crafts fair, softball tournament, carnival, dances, and fireworks; tel. (360) 875-5231.

Fifteen miles east of Raymond, the ghost town of Frances comes to life twice each year for Swiss festivals: **Schwingfest** in early July, a tribute to Switzerland's national sport, wrestling, and autumn's **Oktoberfest,** with beer, polka music, and lots of bratwurst.

Information and Transportation

An info stand next to Boondocks has maps and other information on the Willapa Bay area, or call the chamber of commerce at (360) 875-5231.

The **Pacific Transit System,** tel. (360) 875-9418 or (800) 875-9418, has county-wide bus service, plus buses to Astoria, Oregon and connections in Aberdeen for points north and east.

SOUTH TO LONG BEACH

Highway 101 curves along scenic Willapa Bay from South Bend en route to the Long Beach Peninsula in the southwest corner of Washington. The country is a ragged mix of forest and farms—similar to Maine—with tree farm signs proclaiming the date the forest was last harvested and planted. It's a place for trailer homes, pickup trucks, and woodstoves.

Bay Center

This historic fishing town has a New England feel, with simple frame homes and a wonderful Willapa Bay setting. It is still home to productive oyster beds, as evidenced by the enormous piles of shells and the cluster of shoreside oyster plants, several of which offer fresh oysters for sale. Camping and great views across the bay are available nearby at **Bush Pioneer Park,** open summers only. Park RVs at **Bay Center KOA,** tel. (360) 875-6344 or (800) 562-7810. **Blue Heron Motel,** tel. (360) 875-5130, has lodging for $35 s or $40-55 d. The restaurant here specializes (not surprisingly) in fresh oysters and other seafood.

Willapa National Wildlife Refuge

The 12,000-acre Willapa National Wildlife Refuge encompasses all of Long Island, plus the northern tip of the Long Beach Peninsula and freshwater marshes on the south end of Willapa Bay, which provide important feeding grounds for migrating geese, ducks, and shorebirds.

Long Island

Part of Willapa National Wildlife Refuge, 5,000-acre Long Island can be reached only by boat from launch areas at refuge headquarters (nine miles west of Naselle and 12 miles north of Ilwaco on Hwy. 101, tel. (360) 484-3482), Nahcotta, or points on the Long Beach Peninsula. Before heading to the island, get a map and more information from refuge headquarters. The island has five primitive campgrounds that often fill up on summer weekends (bring your own water; no reservations), but getting there can be tough due to tidal fluctuations—during low tide, you can practically walk out to it. No motorized travel is permitted. Like the rest of this cutover corner of the state, much of Long Island has been repeatedly logged and is still being cut. Because of its remote location, a small 247-acre stand of cedars managed to avoid Weyerhaeuser's chainsaws long enough to be purchased by the refuge. This is one of the few old-growth forests remaining in southwest Washington. A three-quarter mile trail passes through part of this wonderful old grove, with enormous cedars and a lush rainforest floor; some of the trees are over a thousand years old. The muddy tide flats and rich salt grass marshes around Long Island are important resting and feeding areas for migratory waterfowl. You don't have to get out to the island to enjoy the wildlife; there are numerous turnouts along Highways 105 and 101 where you can pull off and watch herds of elk or black-tailed deer.

LONG BEACH PENINSULA

The Long Beach Peninsula is a 28-mile-long strip of sand and fun off the southwesternmost corner of Washington. Locals call it the "World's Longest Beach," though you're bound to hear disagreement from folks in Australia and New Zealand. Be that as it may, this is one *very* long stretch of sand, and a favorite getaway for folks from Seattle and Portland.

Ask most Puget Sounders who frequent the Long Beach Peninsula what they think about it, and you'll probably get the same protective response Washingtonians have about their state when talking to Californians and North Dakotans: they love it and don't want it to change. The towns on this peninsula have a lived-in look to them, and many of the houses are so sand-peppered and rain-washed that they look as though a designer talked everyone into the weathered-home look. The peninsula is the kind of place where you'll find rubber boots and heavy raingear on almost every porch—it rains over 70 inches a year here, so be ready to get wet even in the summer—and somewhere in every house is a glass float from a Japanese fishing net and a piece of driftwood.

The peninsula begins at the Astoria-Megler bridge, and the first town is Chinook, although technically it isn't on the peninsula. Ilwaco is next, then comes Seaview, the town of Long Beach, Klipsan Beach, and Ocean Park on the Pacific Ocean side. On the Willapa Bay side are Nahcotta and Oysterville.

The town of Long Beach has the only walkable downtown area on the coast, with little shops and the typical souvenir joints—like a *real* beach town. At the north end of the peninsula, things are drastically different, with beautifully restored turn-of-the-century homes in Oysterville, and an

Long Beach

ARCHIE SATTERFIELD

isolated natural area at Leadbetter Point. In recent years, a controversy has brewed over development on the sand dunes that line Long Beach. Real estate interests, speculators, and conservative politicians are pushing to open them to wholesale development; environmentalists have attempted to block this encroachment. So far, things are at a stalemate, but look for massive changes if the developers get their way.

FORT CANBY STATE PARK

Located 2.5 miles southwest of Ilwaco, Fort Canby State Park, tel. (360) 642-3078, is the peninsula's most scenic state park, and a place packed with history. In this 1,882-acre facility you'll find a museum dedicated to Lewis and Clark, historic lighthouses, dramatic vistas across the mouth of the Columbia River, old-growth forests, white beaches, famous fishing, excellent campsites ($11 tents; $18 RVs), and turn-of-the-century military fortifications.

The park is located on Cape Disappointment—Washington's southernmost point. The name originated in 1788, when British fur trader John Meares was searching for the fabled Northwest Passage. He had heard tales of an enormous river near here from a Spaniard, Bruno Heceta, who had noted it in 1775. Meares failed to find the river (which he hoped would lead to the fabled Northwest Passage), hence the cape's disappointing name. The mighty river is surprisingly easy to miss from the sea; Capt. George Vancouver also sailed past. The river wasn't officially "discovered" until 1792 when an American, Capt. Robert Gray, sailed his *Columbia Rediviva* into the treacherous river mouth.

More than 230 ships were wrecked or sunk on the Columbia bar before jetties were constructed to control the sand. The longest of these—North Jetty—reaches a half-mile out from the end of the cape and is a very popular place to fish for salmon, rock cod, perch, and sea bass. Although the jetties succeeded in stabilizing the shifting Columbia bar, they also caused sand dunes to accumulate north of here and worsened an undertow that makes for dangerous swimming conditions.

History

Fort Canby holds an important place in history, for on this hill Meriwether Lewis and William Clark stood in November of 1805; they had finally "reached the great Pacific Ocean which we been so long anxious to See." Because game proved scarce and this side of the Columbia lacked protection from winter storms, they crossed the river to build a winter camp called Fort Clatsop near present-day Astoria, Oregon.

The commanding presence and strategic location of Cape Disappointment made it a vital fort location for the new Oregon Territory. The initial cannons arrived in 1862, and the fort itself was later named for Major General Edward Canby, killed in California's Modoc Indian War. During the two world wars, the fort served as a command post for underwater mines placed at the mouth of the Columbia. The fort never fired its guns at enemy ships, but in 1942, a Japanese submarine fired on—and missed—Fort Stevens, across the river in Oregon. After WW II, Fort Canby was decommissioned, becoming a state park in 1957. Many of the old bunkers and gun emplacements remain, making for interesting explorations.

Lewis and Clark Interpretive Center

This fascinating museum is one of the must-see places on Long Beach Peninsula. Open daily 10 a.m.-5 p.m. year-round, the interpretive center, tel. (360) 642-3029, is an excellent introduction to the 1804-06 expedition led by William Clark and Meriwether Lewis. A ramp leads you to a lower level where you can watch a 20-minute slide show (shown every half-hour), and then back up to the second floor again. Along the way you pass fascinating exhibits detailing their trip up the Missouri River, over the Rockies, and then down the Columbia River. You'll learn about the various participants, the unusual air gun they used to impress the Indians, how they constructed dugout canoes, and the everyday experiences in their winter camp at Fort Clatsop.

The ramp emerges in a large room with expansive windows fronting on Cape Disappointment Lighthouse, the Columbia River, and the mighty Pacific. You're certain to see ships plying the waters offshore or moving upriver. Turn around to find displays detailing the "Graveyard of the Pacific" on the bar at the mouth of the

Columbia; more than 230 ships (along with hundreds of smaller boats) have gone down in these treacherous waters, killing over 700 people. You'll learn about early rescue methods, and how they have advanced to the sophisticated helicopter rescues of today. The Coast Guard still operates a major rescue station at Point Disappointment, as well as a **Motor Lifeboat School** that trains seafarers to handle boats under extreme weather conditions and in dangerous seas. This is the only such school in the United States.

Lighthouses and Trails
You can see the mouth of the Columbia by turning right at the concession area and driving to the road's end; park here and walk through the sand to the lookout atop North Jetty. **Cape Disappointment Lighthouse** is the Northwest's oldest, built in 1856; follow the quarter-mile trail from the interpretive center or a steep quarter-mile path from the Coast Guard Station. (This was intended to be the first lighthouse on the Pacific Coast, but a storm wrecked the ship loaded with lighthouse materials just as it was coming in to the Columbia River, so construction was delayed for three years.) Great vistas from here across the mouth of the Columbia; look for an old wrecked ship along the south jetty. Deer are common sights near the lighthouse, especially around dusk.

DON PITCHER

the North Head Lighthouse

North Head Lighthouse was built in 1898 and stands above Dead Man's Hollow, named for the sailors of the ill-fated *Vandelia,* which sank here in 1853. The lighthouse is no longer used; today marine lanterns shine out instead from North Head. The lighthouse is a short walk through the trees from the upper parking lot, or a two-mile hike from McKenzie Head (just west of the campground). Lighthouse tours ($1) are given daily during the summer; call (360) 642-3078 for details. To the south are the dunes and driftwood piles of **Benson Beach** (no vehicles allowed), with Long Beach pointing its finger northward. **West Wind Trail** leads a mile north from the lighthouse through the old growth forests to Beards Hollow. From there you can continue along the beach all the way to the town of Long Beach, four miles away.

North Head is a favorite place to watch for migrating **gray whales** heading north March-May or south late December to early February. It's also an awe-inspiring place during winter storms when waves pound hard against the rocks below.

Tiny **Waikiki Beach** is a favorite local spot for picnics and swimming in the summer (but no lifeguard). The beach received its name when a Hawaiian sailor's body washed ashore here after his ship was wrecked in a failed attempt to cross the Columbia River bar in 1811. You can follow a trail uphill from Waikiki to the Lewis and Clark Interpretive Center, and then on to Cape Disappointment Lighthouse.

For a taste of old-growth forests, take the 1.5-mile **Coastal Forest Trail** that begins at the boat ramp along Baker Bay. This is a very enjoyable loop hike.

ILWACO

Historic Ilwaco (ill-WOK-o; pop. 900) is a charter, sports, and commercial fishing town on the south end of the Long Beach Peninsula, with docks on protected Baker Bay. The town was named for a Chinook leader, Chief Elowahka Jim. Walk around town to find five murals on the sides of local businesses, and some wonderful old buildings. Ilwaco's old Fire Station No. 1 on Lake St. contains the "Mankiller," an 1846 hand pumper that was the first fire-fighting apparatus of its

a good day's catch at Ilwaco

STATE OF WASHINGTON TOURISM DIVISION

kind in Washington Territory. You can view the Mankiller through a window when the building isn't open. Just north of Ilwaco is a pullout along scenic Black Lake; paddle boats are available for rent here in the summer; tel. (360) 642-3003.

Visit the excellent **Ilwaco Heritage Museum** at 115 S.E. Lake St., tel. (360) 642-3446, for a look into Pacific Coast history via models, Indian exhibits, and photographs of early settlers' fishing, oystering, and logging methods, along with Cape Disappointment shipwrecks and rescues. Of particular interest is a detailed scale model of the Columbia River estuary, and a display on the *Sector*, a 26-foot boat that Gérard D'Aboville rowed from Japan to Ilwaco in 1991. The museum is open Mon.-Sat. 9 a.m.-5 p.m., Sunday noon-4 p.m. in the summer; and Mon.-Sat. 9 a.m.-4 p.m. in the winter. Entrance costs $2 adults, $2.50 seniors, $1 children under 12, and $5 families.

Washington State Parks conducts tours ($1) of historic **Colbert House** at the corner of Spruce and Quaker Streets, daily in the summer. Call (360) 642-3078 for details.

SEAVIEW

Seaview grew up around a small beach resort established in 1881 by Jonathon L. Stout. Today, it is home to a number of restaurants, motels, and B&Bs, as well as the Long Beach Peninsula Visitors Bureau at the junction of Highways 101 and 103 (Pacific Highway).

Although the same sort of developments are creeping into Seaview as in its rowdy make-a-buck neighbor to the north, Long Beach, the settlement is best known as home to the historic Shelburne Inn. A number of antique shops line the highway, and not far away is the **Charles Mulvey Studio,** 46th Pl. at L St., tel. (360) 642-2189, selling works by this well-known but formulaic watercolorist.

LONG BEACH

Long Beach (pop. 1,400) comprises the commercial core of the peninsula, with all the typical beachfront services, including kitschy gift shops, fish and chips takeouts, real estate offices, kite stores, salt-water taffy shops, mini-strip malls, RV parks, motels, and bumper boat, go-kart, and mini-golf amusement parks. Not everything is tacky, but don't come here expecting a classy, romantic experience; this is a family fun-for-all place. In the summer Long Beach hums with traffic and the ringing of cash registers; in winter it slows to a quieter pace but is still popular as a weekend getaway.

History

The first whites to arrive in Long Beach were the Lewis and Clark party, who traveled through this area of sand dunes and pine trees in late 1805, stopping long enough for William Clark to carve his name on a tree; it's the westernmost

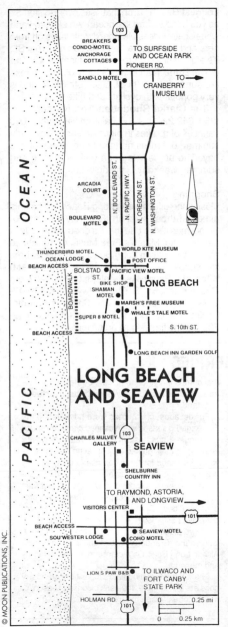

point reached by the expedition. A life-size bronze statue of the explorers can be found in downtown Long Beach. The town did not come into existence until 1880, when Henry Harrison Tinker—an adventurer from Maine—settled here and gradually attracted summer visitors from Portland, Oregon, and other cities.

World Kite Museum

Befitting its beachside location, Long Beach is home to the World Kite Museum and H of Fame. Inside, you'll learn the history of kites and how they were used during wartime and in developing airplanes. Also here are kites from around the globe, a re-created Japanese kite artist workshop, and a gift shop. Located near the corner of 3rd St. NW and Pacific Hwy., tel. (360) 642-4020, the museum is open daily 11 a.m.-5 p.m. June-Aug.; Fri.-Mon. 11 a.m.-5 p.m. Sept.-Oct.; and Sat.-Sun. 11 a.m.-5 p.m. the rest of the year. Admission is $1.50 adults, $1 children or seniors, and $4 families. The museum offers kite-making workshops the first Saturday of the month May-August.

Marsh's Free Museum

It may be campy, but you definitely don't want to miss Marsh's Free Museum, a huge souvenir shop in downtown Long Beach, tel. (360) 642-2188. Inside is a delightful collection of the tasteless and bizarre, much of it from old amusement parks, traveling shows, and attics. You'll find an impressive collection of glass fishing balls, the world's largest frying pan, a vampire bat skeleton, an old bottle with a human tapeworm, a gruesome photo of a 1920 triple hanging, and a two-headed calf. Drop a nickel for a flapper-era peep show, pay a dime to test your passion factor on the "throne of love," or search the jam-packed shelves for a stupid postcard, goofy T-shirt, cheap trinket, or bright seashell. Oh, and you won't want to miss "Jake the Alligator Man," stuck in a back corner inside a glass aquarium; he once starred in that arbiter of tabloid discernment, the *Weekly World News.* If you like junk, you'll rate this as Washington's finest gift shop!

Cranberries

Around 600 acres of cranberries are grown in the Long Beach Peninsula area, and you're bound to see them growing along Hwy. 101 as you approach the peninsula. Cranberries were originally called "crane berries" by early settlers who thought the blossoms resembled cranes' heads. Ocean Spray Cranberries, Inc. has a processing plant on Sandridge Rd. in Long Beach, and a second one in Westport. **Anna Lena's Pantry,** at the light in Long Beach, tel. (360) 642-8948 or (800) 272-6237, sells locally made cranberry products.

On Pioneer Rd. about a mile northeast of Long Beach, is the **Cranberry Museum & Gift Shop,** tel. (360) 642-4938, open Fri.-Sun. 10 a.m.-3 p.m. May through mid-December; no charge. Operated jointly by the University of Washington and the Pacific Coast Cranberry Research Foundation, the museum shows old and new ways of growing and harvesting cranberries. Visitors can walk the adjacent 10-acre demonstration cranberry bog at any time to learn about this unique crop. Try to time your visit for June, the peak bloom season, or October, to see the harvest.

Other Sights

Several fine murals grace the sides of buildings in Long Beach. One of the peninsula's most photographed local spots is the **"World's**

Longest Beach" arch that rises over Bolsted St. as you head toward the ocean. An elevated and wheelchair-accessible **boardwalk** takes off from here and continues a half-mile south to 10th St.; it's a great place for romantic sunset strolls. The gravel **Dune Trail** extends for two miles across the dunes from 17th St. S to 16th St. N, and is very popular with cyclists and hikers.

The **Clarke Rhododendron Nursery,** tel. (360) 642-2241, is a visual treat with over 1,000 varieties of rhodies in bloom in spring and early summer, 6.5 miles north of Long Beach on the bay. The nursery is open daily in spring and summer, weekdays fall and winter.

Shopping

Most of the gift shops in Long Beach sell trinkets aimed at those with an IQ barely topping 70. Sometimes it's so bad that it's good, especially at the delightful Marsh's Free Museum, described above. Downtown Long Beach is home to three kite shops; the best and oldest is **Long Beach Kites,** 104 Pacific Hwy., tel. (360) 642-2202, but **Ocean Kites,** 511 S. Pacific Hwy., tel. (360) 642-2229, is also well worth a visit. **Campiche Studio,** 3100 S. Pacific Way in Seaview, tel. (360) 642-2264, is the finest local art gallery.

CRANBERRIES

Cranberries are one of two native American fruits (the other being the blueberry) grown in wetlands. The berries originated on the East Coast, and Massachusetts still leads in cranberry production, but they now are also raised in New Jersey, Wisconsin, Oregon, and Washington, as well as British Columbia and other Canadian provinces. They were introduced to Washington in 1883, and the state now produces 8,000 tons of cranberries annually, four percent of the nation's total output. Nearly all of the 130 cranberry farms in the state are family-run operations with an average of just 11 acres each.

Cranberries grow on perennial vines in acidic peat bogs and are named for the flowers that resemble the head and bill of a crane. The traditional way to harvest cranberries has been to flood the fields, causing the berries to float to the surface for harvesting. This is still done on some bogs, but most in Washington use dry-harvesting equipment

that combs the vines to pull the berries. (The Furford picker, used for harvesting, was invented in Grayland.)

For decades, cranberries were relegated to the Thanksgiving season when canned cranberry sauce is a required purchase. In recent years, however, cranberries have gained a bit of caché with the public, and demand for them has risen rapidly as they are used in various foods and drinks. Dried cranberries are especially popular, with more flavor than raisins (and a much higher price). The primary producer is Ocean Spray Cranberries, a farmers cooperative best known for their juice cocktails. They have two plants in southeast Washington: at Grayland on the "Cranberry Coast" and in Long Beach. Also in Long Beach is a cranberry research facility and museum.

The most interesting times to visit the cranberry bogs are in mid-June, the peak blooming season, or mid-October, to see the harvest.

OCEAN PARK

Once the Pacific Hwy. (a.k.a. Hwy. 103) exits the north end of hectic Long Beach you are suddenly in an almost flat landscape of lodgepole pine trees and scattered summer and retirement homes. You can't see the ocean or Willapa Bay from here, but there are access points all along the way, including at Klipsan Beach. After 11 miles of this, the highway widens into Ocean Park (pop. 1,400), a place that is considerably more sedate than Long Beach, but nevertheless a popular summer retreat.

Established in 1883 as a Methodist church camp and revival center—and a place to escape the booze and wildness of nearby Oysterville—Ocean Park was transformed into a summer refuge after construction of the narrow-gauge "Clamshell Railroad" in the late 1880s. The church camp remains, but gone are the laws prohibiting saloons. Today, Ocean Park consists of a cluster of shops and businesses lining the highway, surrounded by a spread of summer homes. Nearby **Surfside** is a residential area north of Ocean Park with a couple of businesses, a golf course, and a median age that probably approaches 72.

Sights

The **Wreckage,** on the south side of 256th just west of Hwy. 103, is a unique house constructed in 1912 from logs salvaged after a storm broke apart a raft of logs being towed off the coast. It's on the National Register of Historic Places. **Wiegardt Studio Gallery,** 2607 Bay Ave., tel. (360) 665-5976, contains the watercolor works of Eric Wiegardt, one of several respected local artists. **Shoalwater Cove Gallery,** 25712 Sandridge Rd., tel. (360) 665-4382, has beautifully detailed pastels by Marie Powell.

Loomis Lake State Park, south of Klipsan Beach, has picnic tables on the ocean, not the lake; the real Loomis Lake is about a quarter mile north. No camping here.

NAHCOTTA

Named for Chinook Indian leader, Chief Nahcati, tiny Nahcotta (nah-COT-ah) consists of a smattering of businesses—mainly oyster farms and canneries—along quiet Willapa Bay. Established in 1889, the town was the northern terminus of the narrow-gauge Ilwaco Railroad and Navigation Co. (alias the "Clamshell Railroad") that ran up Long Beach Peninsula. Its dock was used to ship oysters south to San Francisco. In 1915 a fire destroyed much of the business district, and it was never entirely rebuilt. The railroad ran until 1930, when cars and ferries ushered in a new era. Nahcotta is the center for the oyster industry on the peninsula, an industry that contributes more than $20 million to the economy and leaves enormous piles of whitened shells along the shore.

Intrepretive signs next to the Nahcotta's Willapa Bay Field Station explain local ecology and the lives of shellfish. The oyster beds are closed to the public, but you can purchase fresh oysters and other seafood at **Wiegart Brothers Oyster Co., Bendiksen's East Point Seafood Co.,** or the smaller **Hilton's Coast Oyster Company.** Also in Nahcotta is the respected Ark Restaurant (see below).

Across from Bendiksen's is tiny **Willapa Bay Interpretive Center,** tel. (360) 665-4547, open Fri.-Sun. 10 a.m.-3 p.m., late May to mid-October, with exhibits on the oyster industry and the natural history of Willapa Bay.

OYSTERVILLE

Approximately 16 miles north of Long Beach and just off Hwy. 103 is the somnambulant settlement of Oysterville. It was not always thus; for many years this was one of the busiest places in southwestern Washington.

History

Following the discovery of gold in California, San Franciscans had both gold and a yen to spend it on good food, especially fresh oysters. With oysters selling for up to $50 a plate, the demand led men to search far and wide for new sources. In 1854, Chief Nahcati (the source of the name Nahcotta) showed R.H. Espy and I.A. Clark the rich oyster beds of Willapa Bay. Sensing a profit, they quickly built the new town of Oysterville on the site, and within a scant few months another 500 boomers had arrived.

The rowdy town grew to become the county seat within two years, and even had a college for a brief period, before overharvesting and winter freezes made the oysters scarce in the late 1880s. With the loss of oysters and the money and jobs they attracted, the Oysterville's economy collapsed, and county voters decided to move the Pacific County seat to the logging town of South Bend. Oysterville charged ballot box stuffing by railroad workers in South Bend and sued to overturn the vote.

A bitter legal battle ensued that threatened to keep the matter tied up in the courts for years, so a group of South Bend men decided to force the issue. On a Sunday morning in February of 1893, some 85 men crossed to Oysterville abroad two steamships. They first stopped for liquid reinforcement at a local saloon. Then, finding most everyone in church, the mob proceeded to plunder the county courthouse, stealing (or legally removing, depending upon who is telling the story) all the records and furniture. After returning to South Bend with the booty, they sent a bill to Oysterville for services rendered in the process of moving the county records! The county seat has been in South Bend ever since, but the bill was never paid.

Oysterville Today
The loss of the county courthouse sounded the death knell for Oysterville, and over the decades that followed, many homes and three entire streets were swallowed by the bay as storms eroded the shoreline. It wasn't until the 1930s with the introduction of a new species of oyster—this time from Japan—that the beds again became productive. Today, you can stop at **Oysterville Sea Farms,** tel. (360) 665-6585, for fresh or smoked oysters and clams.

A number of homes constructed during the town's heyday have been restored and are now part of the Oysterville National Historic District. For a self-guided walking tour map, visit the beautiful white and red **Oysterville Baptist Church,** built in 1892. On Sunday afternoons in summer the church comes alive with vespers programs featuring an ecumenical mix of secular and religious music. No need to dress up for these informal services. Not far away is the old **Oysterville School,** constructed in 1908. The historic **Espy House** is especially notable. Built in 1854 by the cofounder of Oysterville, this big white house with gingerbread ornamentation has a classic country feel. The **cemetery** contains the grave of Chief Nahcati, who first brought the oyster beds to the attention of the whites.

Leadbetter Point State Park
The northern tip of Long Beach Peninsula is capped by two publicly owned natural areas, Leadbetter Point State Park, and a portion of the Willapa National Wildlife Refuge (see above). Leadbetter has a 1.5 mile trail through the evergreen forest, connecting both parking lots. From the north lot, you can enter Willapa and walk through stunted lodgepole pine forests to beach-grass-covered sand dunes along the Pacific Ocean, or head down to the shore of Willapa Bay for a beach walk. The northern end of Willapa National Wildlife Refuge is closed to all entry April-Aug. to protect the threatened snowy plover that nests on the dunes here. This area is also a very important sanctuary for waterfowl, particularly during spring and fall migrations. Birdwatchers will see thousands (and sometimes hundreds of thousands) of black brant, Canada geese, dunlin, plovers, sandpipers, and other birds in the marshes and beaches during these times. No fires or camping allowed.

PENINSULA ACCOMMODATIONS

Lodging can be hard to come by on summer weekends, especially during the big festivals. Many rooms are booked a year ahead for Memorial Day weekend, the International Kite Festival in August, and Labor Day weekend. It's a good idea to reserve two to four weeks ahead for other summer weekends. The visitors bureau, tel. (360) 642-2400 or (800) 451-2542, tries to keep track of who has space. They also have a listing of several dozen vacation houses and cabins available for longer periods of time.

Budget travelers will want to check out the excellent **youth hostel** located at historic Fort Columbia in Chinook (11 miles east; see **Lower Columbia River**), tel. (360) 777-8755. It's open Mar.-Oct. only.

Unusual Lodging
If you're looking for standard motel accommodations, there are plenty of places along the peninsula, but if you want a friendly place with a

funky sense of nostalgia, character, and charm, look no farther than Seaview's **Sou'wester Lodge,** 38th Pl., tel. (360) 642-2542. Here, literary owners Leonard and Miriam Atkins have created a rustic and offbeat haven for those who appreciate a place with simple comfort rather than ostentatiousness. The accommodations include "Bed and Make Your Own Damn Breakfast" rooms in the stately three-story lodge built in 1892 as a summer estate by Henry Winslow Corbett, a wealthy timber baron, banker, and U.S. Senator from Oregon. Outside are weathered beach cottages furnished in "early Salvation Army" decor, and even a hodgepodge of 1950s-era trailers. Artists and writers often "book in" for months at a time, relaxing in this cozy and informal lodge. On many Saturday nights, the sitting room comes to life with lectures, concerts, or poetry. You're likely to find everything from chamber music to discussions on sufism. Rates are $60-110 d in the lodge, $40-95 d in trailers (sleep up to six), $82 d in cabins with kitchens; tent and RV spaces are also available.

Seaview's acclaimed **Shelburne Inn** is an elegant 1896 Victorian building at 4415 Pacific Way, tel. (360) 642-2442 or (800) 466-1896. The oldest continuously used lodging place in Washington, the inn is packed with tasteful antiques, stained glass windows (from an old English church), and original artwork. No televisions. A full country breakfast is included; for many, it's the highlight of their stay. The inn is, however, located just a few feet from busy Pacific Hwy., and roadside rooms can be quite noisy. Also beware of the ghost who is rumored to wander the third floor some nights. Rates are $99-165 s or $105-170 d.

Folks in search of a quiet night along the beach will love the 10 new cottages at **Blackwood Beach Cottages,** 20711 Pacific Way in Ocean Park, tel. (360) 665-6356 or (888) 376-6356. Very well maintained, and just steps from the ocean; $80-139 s or d. No kids.

One of the most distinctive local lodging places is at Fort Canby State Park where you can rent the historic three-bedroom **North Head Lighthouse keeper's house** for $200 a night (two-night minimum). The house sleeps six, and has excellent views of the lighthouse and the mouth of the Columbia River. Call (360) 642-3078 for reservations.

Bed and Breakfasts

Unless otherwise noted, all B&Bs listed below serve a full breakfast, and do not allow young children. They are listed alphabetically.

Boreas B&B, 607 N. Boulevard St. in Ocean View, tel. (360) 642-8069 or (888) 642-8069, is a quiet and cozy 1920s beachfront home with an enclosed sundeck and jacuzzi. The four guest rooms have shared or private baths; kids are accepted. $95-125 s or d.

The modern Victorian-style **Caswell's on the Bay B&B,** 25204 Sandridge Rd. in Ocean Park, tel. (360) 665-6535, offers friendly, spacious, and comfortable accommodations facing Willapa Bay. This is a very quiet and relaxing place on a three-acre spread. Five guest rooms are furnished with antiques and private baths; $95-150 s or d.

Chick-a-dee Inn at Ilwaco, 120 Williams St. NE in Ilwaco, tel. (360) 642-8686 or (888) 244-2523, has 10 guest rooms in a beautifully restored 1928 Presbyterian church; $86 s or d.

Coast Watch B&B in Ocean Park, tel. (360) 665-6774, has two ocean view suites, each with a private entry and bath; $85 s or $95 d.

Newly built **DoveShire B&B,** 21914 Pacific Hwy., tel. (360) 665-3017 or (888) 553-2320, has four guest suites with private baths and TVs. A buffet breakfast is served; $100 s or d.

Edgewood Inn; 112 8th St. NE, Long Beach; tel. (360) 642-8227 or (800) 460-7196; is a turn-of-the-century bungalow with three guest rooms and a suite. Kids are welcome; $71-90 s or $79-99 d. Two-night minimum in summer.

Kola House B&B, 211 Pearl Ave. in Ilwaco, tel. (360) 642-2819, is a restored 1891 boardinghouse. The B&B has a sauna, fireplace, pool table, and five guest rooms with private baths; $60-70 s or $65-75 d.

Land's End B&B three miles north of Long Beach, tel. (360) 642-8268, is an elegant ocean view home with antiques and a grand piano. Two guest rooms have private baths; $105-120 s or d.

The Lion's Paw B&B Inn, 3310 Hwy. 101 in Seaview, tel. (360) 642-2481 or (800) 972-1046, is a lovingly restored 1911 home featuring a stone fireplace, sun porch, and hot tub. The four guest rooms have private or shared baths, and kids are welcome. $80-100 s or d.

LONG BEACH AREA MOTELS AND COTTAGES

Accommodations are arranged from least to most expensive. Winter rates at many motels are often 20-40% cheaper. See the text for descriptions of local B&Bs and the hostel at Fort Columbia.

INEXPENSIVE

Sands Motel; Long Beach; tel. (360) 642-2100; $33-50 s or d; cabins with kitchens

Coho Motel; 3707 Pacific Hwy., Seaview; tel. (360) 642-2531 or (800) 681-8153; $40-70 s or d; kitchenettes available

Heidi's Inn; 126 Spruce St., Ilwaco; tel. (360) 642-2387 or (800) 576-1032; $42-48 s or d; jacuzzi, kitchenettes available

Sand-Lo Motel; Long Beach; tel. (360) 642-2600 or (800) 676-2601; $42-65 s or d

Motel 101 Haciendas; Spruce at Brumbach, Ilwaco; tel. (360) 642-8459; $45-50 s or d, kitchenettes available

Our Place at the Beach; Long Beach; tel. (360) 642-3793 or (800) 538-5107; $45-54 s or d; fridges, jacuzzi, sauna, ocean view, kitchenettes available, AAA approved

Arcadia Court; 401 N. Boulevard St., Long Beach; tel. (360) 642-2613; $45-89 s or d; kitchens available

Thunderbird Motel; 201 N. Boulevard St., Long Beach; tel. (360) 642-5700; $47 s or d; kitchenettes available, indoor pool

Westgate Motel; 20803 Pacific Hwy., Ocean Park; tel. (360) 665-4211; $48-65 s or d; cabins with kitchens, game room, ocean view

Long Beach Inn Garden Golf; 1200 Pacific Hwy. S, Long Beach; tel. (360) 642-3500 or (800) 789-2287; $49-89 s or d in motel rooms, $59-79 s or d cottages with kitchenettes

Anthony's Cabins; 1310 Pacific Hwy. N, Long Beach; tel. (360) 642-2802 or (888) 787-2754; $50-70 s or d; studio and one-bedroom with kitchens

Seaview Motel; Seaview; tel. (360) 642-2450; $50-80 s or d in motel rooms or cabins with kitchenettes

MODERATE

Sou'wester Lodge; 38th Pl., Seaview; tel. (360) 642-2542; $60-110 d in the lodge, $40-95 d in trailers (sleep up to six), $82 d in cabins with kitchens; tent and RV spaces are also available; see text for full description

Ocean Lodge I & II; 101 N. Boulevard St., Long Beach; tel. (360) 642-5400; $75-90 s or d in motel, $50-80 for cabins (sleep up to eight); jacuzzi, outdoor pool, sauna, ocean view, kitchens available

Lighthouse Motel; 2.5 miles north of Long Beach; tel. (360) 642-3622 or (877) 220-7555; $55-69 s or d for older studios; $99-139 for new one or two-bedroom condos; sundecks and kitchens in all units

---

A three-story Victorian home along Willapa Bay, **Our House in Nahcotta B&B,** tel. (360) 665-6667, has a spacious two-room suite with private bath. Kids accepted; $75 s or $95 d.

Scandinavian Gardens Inn, 1610 California St. in Long Beach, tel. (360) 642-8807 or (800) 988-9277, is a quiet hideaway featuring a gourmet Scandinavian breakfast plus a sauna and jacuzzi. Four guest rooms have private baths; $85-140 s or d.

Whalebone House, 2101 Bay Ave. in Ocean Park, tel. (360) 665-5371 or (888) 298-3330, is a beautiful 1889 Victorian farmhouse with four guest rooms, private baths, an enclosed sunporch, and a flower-filled yard; $85-99 s or d.

Campgrounds
One of the most popular places to camp in Washington, **Fort Canby State Park** (described

Chautauqua Lodge; Long Beach; tel. (360) 642-4401 or (800) 869-8401; $55-100 s or d; indoor pool, jacuzzi, kitchenettes available, ocean views

Whale's Tale Motel; Long Beach; tel. (360) 642-3455 or (800) 559-4253; $60 s or d; one- and two-bedroom suites with kitchens, sauna, jacuzzi, fitness center

Anchorage Cottages; 2209 N. Boulevard St., Long Beach; tel. (360) 642-2351 or (800) 642-2351; $60-85 s or d; apartments with kitchens, ocean view, AAA approved

Edgewater Inn; 409 10th St., Long Beach; tel. (360) 642-2311 or (800) 561-2456; $64-89 s or d; controversial in-the-dunes location, AAA approved

Pacific View Motel; Long Beach; tel. (360) 642-2415 or (800) 238-0859; $64-100 s or d in cabins (some sleep six) with kitchens

Sunset View Resort; 25517 Park Ave., Ocean Park; tel. (360) 642-4494 or (800) 272-9199; $65 s or d in motel, $99-185 for studios, one- and two-bedroom suites with kitchens and fireplaces; family oriented place, hot tubs, sauna, tennis, volleyball, basketball

Shakti Cove Cottages, 1204 253rd Pl., Ocean Park, tel. (360) 665-4000, $65-75 s or d, comfortable historic cottages with kitchenettes

Boulevard Motel; Long Beach; tel. (360) 642-2434; $70-75 s or d in motel units with kitchens, $80-85 s or d in cabins with kitchens; indoor pool

Moby Dick Hotel; Nahcotta; tel. (360) 665-4543; $70-95 s or d; restored 1930s hotel, sauna, full breakfast

Boardwalk Cottages; 800 S. Boulevard St., Long Beach; tel. (360) 642-2305 or (800) 569-3804; $71-82 s or d; comfortable one or two bedroom cottages, some with kitchenettes, private decks, jacuzzi, AAA approved

The Breakers Condo-Motel; one mile north of Long Beach; tel. (360) 642-4414 or (800) 288-8890; $74 s or d in motel rooms, $141-186 for up to four in one or two bedroom suites with kitchens; indoor pool, sauna, jacuzzi, ocean view

Super 8 Motel; Long Beach; tel. (360) 642-8988 or (888) 478-3297 $79 s or d; AAA approved

Harbor Lights Motel; Ilwaco; tel. (360) 642-3196; $69 s or d

Klipsan Beach Cottages; Ocean Park; tel. (360) 665-4888; $70-150 s or d; comfortable older cottages with kitchens, ocean views, beautiful place

Ocean Park Resort; 259th and R St., Ocean Park; tel. (360) 642-4585 or (800) 835-4634; $71-81 s or d; kitchens available, outdoor pool, rec room, jacuzzi, Saturday pancake breakfast, AAA approved

Shaman Motel; 115 3rd St. SW, Long Beach; tel. (360) 642-3714 or (800) 753-3750; $79-84 s or d; outdoor pool, kitchens available, two-night minimum stay on weekends, AAA approved

Blackwood Beach Cottages; 20711 Pacific Way in Ocean Park; $80-139 s or d; tel. (360) 665-6356 or (888) 376-6356; see text for full description

Shelburne Inn; 4415 Pacific Way, Seaview; tel. (360) 642-2442 or (800) 466-1896; $99-165 s, $105-170 d; see text for full description

above) has tent sites ($11) and RV sites ($16), plus coin-operated showers. The campground—within a few yards of beautiful Benson Beach—is open all year. The park also rents cabins and yurts for $35/night for four people. Call (800) 452-5687 for campsite, cabin, or yurt reservations ($6 extra). It's illegal to camp on the sand along Long Beach, but county parks with camp-ing can be found in Naselle (22 miles east), Bay Center (30 miles northeast), and Bruceport (32 miles northeast). Bruceport has RV hookups, but is closed in winter. County park rates are $10 for tents, and $5 for bike camping.

RVers will find more than 20 different parking lot/campgrounds along the Long Beach Peninsula. Get a complete listing at the visitor center, or just drive along Pacific Hwy. till one looks acceptable. Two on-the-ocean RV parks are **Anderson's RV Park** 3.5 miles north of Long Beach, tel. (360) 642-2231 or (800) 645-6795, and **Westgate Motel and Trailer Court** in Ocean Park, tel. (360) 665-4211. A well-maintained and friendly place is **Driftwood RV Park,** 1512 N. Pacific Hwy., tel. (360) 642-2711.

PENINSULA FOOD

The Long Beach Peninsula is blessed with restaurants of all types, including some of the most innovative purveyors of Northwest cuisine in Washington.

Breakfast
Two Seaview restaurants vie for the breakfast crowds. **Laurie's Homestead Breakfast House,** 4214 Pacific Hwy., tel. (360) 642-7171, has a seven-page breakfast menu and very good food. Open daily 6:30 a.m.-1 p.m. Across the street is **Cheri Walker's 42nd St. Cafe,** tel. (360) 642-2323, with traditional American breakfasts, lunches, and dinners. The restaurant features iron-skillet fried chicken, pot roast, steaks, and seafood, with homemade bread and jam, all served in heaping helpings.

American Food
Popular with old-timers is **Chuck's Restaurant,** N. 19th at Pacific Hwy. in Long Beach, tel. (360) 642-2721, with all-American meals, including excellent chicken fried steak with gravy. **Bubba's Pizza,** 115 S. Pacific Hwy. in Long Beach, tel. (360) 642-8700, makes thick and cheesy handthrown pizzas, with a variety of unusual toppings. Pasta and sub sandwiches are also here. **Doogar's Seafood & Grill,** 900 Pacific Ave. S. in Long Beach, tel. (360) 642-4224, is a bit formulaic, but brags about its homemade clam chowder and fish and chips. **The Dunes Restaurant** 1507 Bay Ave. in Ocean Park, tel. (360) 665-6677, has fresh fish, clam chowder, and Saturday night prime rib.

For creative and distinctive seafood, steak, and pasta, you won't go wrong with a visit to **Max's Bar & Grill,** 111 S. Pacific Hwy. in Long Beach, tel. (360) 642-5600. Everything is very fresh, and prices are moderate.

Get fresh seafood at **P&K Crab & Seafood Market** in Ocean Park, tel. (360) 665-6800 or (800) 519-3518.

Gourmet Meals
Some of the best food on the peninsula can be found at the **Shoalwater Restaurant,** 4415 Pacific Hwy., tel. (360) 642-4142, in the Shelburne Inn. Dinners include Northwest seafood and game enhanced by in-season vegetables and berries, Northwest wines, and homemade breads, pastries, and desserts. Open in summer for Sunday brunch, and daily for lunch and dinner; reservations are required. Across the hall is **Heron and Beaver Pub** with microbrewed beers and light meals from the same kitchen.

The Ark Restaurant, tel. (360) 665-4133, is another local legend, located in Nahcotta, 12 miles north of Long Beach. The rustic building overlooks Willapa Bay, the source of oysters for which the restaurant is justly famous.

Bakeries, Sweets, and Espresso
Cottage Bakery, in downtown Long Beach, tel. (360) 642-4441, has cabinets filled with sticky-sweet old-fashioned pastries. It's a favorite place for a coffee and dessert while watching the people stroll by.

My Mom's Pie Kitchen, 12th and Pacific Hwy. in Long Beach, tel. (360) 642-2342, will cut you a big slice of one of their delicious homemade pies, or try the fresh crab quiche or creamy clam chowder. My Mom's trailer house location is vintage Long Beach kitsch.

In business since 1892, Long Beach's **Milton York Restaurant,** tel. (360) 642-2352, is America's oldest continuously operating candy company in the same location. The real standout here is great homemade ice cream.

PENINSULA EVENTS AND ENTERTAINMENT

Events
In April, come to Long Beach for the **Ragtime Rhodie Dixieland Jazz Festival.** Then comes Ocean Park's **Garlic Festival,** held the third weekend of June, which features garlic shucking and garlic eating contests, plus all sorts of garlicky meals. Bring a couple of bottles of Listerine along. Long Beach hosts the annual Fourth of

July **Fireworks on the Beach,** and Ocean Park has a popular **Street Fair** the same weekend. Then comes **Sandsations Sand Sculptures** at the end of the month.

The year's biggest event, the **Washington State International Kite Festival,** lasts the entire third week of August and draws well over 200,000 spectators and participants. This is the largest kite festival in the western hemisphere, and every day brings a different contest, ending with Sunday's grand finale in which the sky teems with upwards of 4,000 kites of all sorts. The world record for keeping a kite aloft (over 180 hours) was set here in 1982.

Ocean Park hosts an enormously popular classic car show, the **Rod Run to the End of the World,** on Labor Day weekend that ends with a 15-mile-long parade. The annual **Cranberrian Fair,** held in Ilwaco in mid-October, celebrates more than a century of coastal cranberry farming. Bog tours give you the chance to see the flooded fields with thousands of floating berries awaiting harvest. It's followed the third weekend of October by **Water Music Festival** with chamber music concerts all over the peninsula.

Nightlife
Every Saturday all summer long, you'll find free concerts in Long Beach's downtown gazebo. Seaview's **Sou'wester Lodge,** tel. (360) 642-2542, often has concerts, lectures, or poetry on Saturday nights. During the summer and fall, **Nick's West** has country or rock bands on the weekends.

PENINSULA RECREATION

Fishing and Boating
Ilwaco is home to the peninsula's fishing fleet, with charter boats leaving daily for deep-sea rockfish, flounder, sole, and ling cod, migrating albacore tuna, sturgeon, and salmon. Recent years have seen curtailment of the salmon season due to poor returns. Stop by the visitors center for a complete listing of local charter operators, along with info on razor clam seasons and harvesting.

Other Recreation
Contrary to expectations, the 28 miles of sandy beach on Long Beach Peninsula are not safe for swimming. Not only are there dangerous undertows and riptides, but rogue waves can occur, and there are no lifeguards. Every year waders or swimmers get trapped in these bitterly cold waters; sometimes the accidents end in tragedy. Locals and visitors looking for a chance to swim generally head to Waikiki Beach in Fort Canby State Park, or to local motel swimming pools. Dunes Bible Camp in Ocean Park, tel. (360) 665-5542, has a large outdoor pool open to the public.

Rent mountain bikes from **Long Beach Bike Shop,** tel. (360) 642-7000, located on Oregon Ave. at 2nd St.; they have a second summertime rental outlet on the Ilwaco waterfront.

Horse enthusiasts can rent horses for guided beach rides from **Skipper's Equestrian Center,** behind the Long Beach go-kart track, tel. (360) 642-3676; or **Back Country Wilderness Outfitters,** on 10th St. S in Long Beach, tel. (360) 642-2576.

Two local golf courses are open to the public: **Peninsula Golf Course** in Long Beach, tel. (360) 642-2828, and **Surfside Golf Course,** north of Ocean Park, tel. (360) 665-4148.

PENINSULA INFORMATION

Long Beach is the place to go to do your laundry, buy groceries, or get your car washed. Get information at the **Long Beach Peninsula Visitors Bureau** at the junction of Highways 101 and 103, tel. (360) 642-2400 or (800) 451-2542, www.visitors@funbeach.com, open Mon.-Sat. 9 a.m.-5 p.m. and Sunday 9 a.m.-4 p.m., in summer; and Mon.-Sat. 9 a.m.-4 p.m. the rest of the year. Call Long Beach Info-Line, tel. (800) 835-8846, for a recording of current activities, festivals, fun things to do, B&Bs, and more.

The two local **public libraries** are in Ilwaco at 158 1st Ave. N, tel. (360) 642-3908, and in Ocean Park at 1308 256th Pl., tel. (360) 665-4184.

PENINSULA TRANSPORTATION

Getting Around
The Long Beach Peninsula is divided by two parallel main roads: Highway 103, going through the commercial centers on the ocean side, and

Sandridge Road, passing the largely residential sections on the bay side. The roads intersect at Oysterville, where only one road continues to Leadbetter Point.

Pacific Transit System, tel. (360) 642-9418 or (800) 642-9418, has county-wide bus service Mon.-Sat., and dial-a-ride service in certain areas. The system connects with Grays Harbor Transit buses in Aberdeen, and also crosses the bridge to Astoria, Oregon. There is no Greyhound service, and the nearest airport with commercial service is in Astoria.

Beach Driving
Approximately 15 miles of Long Beach are open to driving during the summer, but stay on the hard-packed sand, away from the car-eating soft sand and rich clam beds along the water's edge. The sand dunes are off limits to all vehicles. The maximum speed is 25 mph, and it *is* enforced. If you decide to drive the beach, be sure to wash the salt spray off your car immediately to prevent later rust problems. Check at the visitors center for a current description of areas open and closed to beach driving.

LOWER COLUMBIA RIVER

The stretch of river from the ocean to Bonneville Dam is the only part of the river still subject to the ebb and flow of the tides. The tidal force is so strong in the river that tugs pulling log booms upstream must tie up when the current and the tide are flowing in the same direction. From the mouth of the Willamette River on down, the Columbia has a distinct saltwater ambience to it. Seagoing ships steam back and forth in the 40-foot-deep channel, loading and unloading in Portland, Kalama, Longview, and Astoria. Seagulls wheel overhead with their rusty-hinge cries, and fishing boats share the waterway with the ships and tugs.

Chinook
Although it's hard to believe this today, the somnolent fishing settlement of Chinook was once one of the richest towns per capita anywhere in America. Built on an old Indian village site, Chinook prospered in the 1880s from fish traps that crowded Baker Bay. In a single day, one man is said to have hauled in some 12,000 pounds of salmon, netting a then-unheard-of $500 profit. After the fish traps were outlawed early in this century, the town went into decline, but many of the wealthy fishermen's regal old homes still stand. The port in Chinook is still home to a small fleet of commercial fishing boats. Just east of town are the carved wooden statues of Lewis and Clark; the explorers camped here in late November 1805 on their way to the Pacific Ocean.

Chinook's claim to gastronomic fame is the **Sanctuary Restaurant,** tel. (360) 777-8380.

Housed in a turn-of-the-century church, the restaurant features fresh seafood and Scandinavian specialties prepared in unusual ways. The desserts are a special treat. Open Wed.-Sunday for dinner only.

Also in Chinook is the private **Sea Resources Hatchery,** tel. (360) 777-8229, where you can watch high school students raising salmon at the state's oldest hatchery, opened in 1893 (though it was closed from 1935 to 1969). Hours are daily 9 a.m.-5 p.m. Come here in September to see the adult salmon return from the ocean.

Local RV parks are **Chris' RV Park,** tel. (360) 777-8475; **Rivers End RV Park,** tel. (360) 777-8317; and **Mulch's Sundown RV Park,** tel. (360) 777-8713.

Fort Columbia State Park
Two miles southeast of Chinook on Hwy. 101, Fort Columbia State Park is a National Historic Site built in the late 1890s. It, along with Fort Canby and Fort Stephens (in Oregon) formed a triad of military bases guarding the mouth of the Columbia. Fort Columbia remained in use through WW II, but never engaged in battle. It still has 30 of the original buildings, along with various concrete batteries and two rapid firing six-inch guns that face out over the mouth of the Columbia. (The original guns were removed after WW II, and these were moved here from an old fort in Newfoundland, Canada, in 1994.) A couple of delightful trails wind through the steep country along the river.

An **interpretive center** in the enlisted men's barracks features two floors' worth of history, with displays on the Indian inhabitants, exploration, commercial fishing, and the military presence here. Upstairs are the bunks of enlisted men. The lives of military families are revealed in a second museum—furnished with period pieces—located in the old **Commander's House.** Hike up Scarborough Hill behind the fort for a view of the Columbia River or walk down to the riverside cliffs to see why this made such an easily defended spot. The fort is open daily 10 a.m.-5 p.m. April-Sept. only; call (360) 642-3028 for more information.

On the grounds is the **Hostel International Fort Columbia,** tel. (360) 777-8755. Located in the old post hospital, this is a friendly and popular place for budget travelers. If you don't want to camp out and can't afford to pay the high lodging rates on Long Beach Peninsula, this is an outstanding option. Besides the enjoyable historic structure, you get a big warm kitchen and the chance to watch dramatic sunsets from the cliffs along the Columbia River. Dorm spaces go for $10-13 per person. The one private room rents for $26-32 d. Reservations are advised during mid-summer, especially on weekends; they are imperative if you want the "couples" room. The hostel is open April-Sept. only.

Travelers can also rent the **Steward's House** at Fort Columbia for $125 per night (two-night minimum in summer). This quaint and historic two-bedroom home sleeps four, and has an excellent view of the Columbia River. Call (360) 642-3078 for reservations.

Astoria-Megler Bridge

Completed in 1966, this 4.4-mile bridge is—according to the *Guiness Book of Records*—the longest continuous-truss span bridge in North America. If you don't know what a continuous-truss span is, take a look at the bridge. It looks like one to me, but they could have just as well called it a discontinuous truss and I'd believe it. Anyway, it's a long, tall bridge with a corkscrew approach into Astoria on the Oregon side. The toll that was collected here for almost three decades was discontinued at the end of 1993, so you won't be charged for a sidetrip into Oregon. By the way, the pilings visible on sandbars near the middle of the river once housed horse stalls. The horses were used to drag fishing nets to catch salmon; the process was known as "horse-seining."

Astoria, Oregon, has all sorts of interesting sights, good restaurants, and a number of motels; for specifics, see *Oregon Handbook* by Stuart Warren and Ted Long Ishikawa. Historical enthusiasts shouldn't miss **Fort Clatsop,** the winter encampment site of the Lewis and Clark expedition, where a reconstructed fort features buckskin-clad park rangers and demonstrations all summer long.

Back on the Washington side you'll find the small **Megler Visitor Information Center,** tel. (360) 777-8388, overlooking the river a mile east of the Astoria Bridge on Hwy. 401. Open daily 9 a.m.-5 p.m. May-Sept.; and Friday 11 a.m.-4 p.m., Saturday 9 a.m.-4 p.m., and Sunday 10 a.m.-4 p.m. in fall and spring; closed Dec.-February.

Naselle Area

East of the Astoria-Megler bridge, Hwy. 401 continues along the river for another three miles, passing the old **St. Mary McGowan Church**—built in 1904 and still in use—and the pilings that once supported a U.S. Customs and Detention Center. Early in this century, thousands of Chinese immigrants entered the country here and were forced to remain 30 days in quarantine before being allowed to look for work. Immediately after this, the highway turns inland and north to connect with Hwy. 4 at the weather-beaten little town of **Naselle.** This is lumbering country, and an abundance of "We support the timber industry" lawn signs and cutover forests all around are evidence of this support. The town's Finnish heritage comes to the fore in the **Finnish-American Folk Festival** in July on even-numbered years. It features folk art, crafts, music, and of course, Finnish food. Lodging is available at **Hunter's Inn,** tel. (360) 484-9215 for $30-48 s or d; **Naselle Village Inn Motel,** tel. (360) 484-3111 for $50 s or d; and **Sleepy Hollow Motel,** tel. (360) 484-3232 for $35-40 s or d. Local events include the **Grays River Covered Bridge Festival** in early August with music and dancing, wagon rides, food and crafts, and a beer garden, plus the **Harvest Festival** in early October.

A gravel road leads seven miles uphill to **Radar Ridge,** which offers impressive vistas of the entire region. The road passes two lakes where you can hike and camp for free. Approximately two miles east of Naselle along Hwy. 4 is the pocket-sized **Salmon Creek Park,** a clump of old-growth forest surrounded by clearcuts and waiting-to-be-logged second-growth land. Camp here for free under the big trees along Salmon Creek.

Grays River Area
East of Naselle, the sinuous Grays River (no, it doesn't flow into Grays Harbor) cuts a wide swath, with bucolic farms and fields on both sides and timber country climbing the hillsides. A few miles east on Hwy. 4 brings you to the country store-post office town of **Rosburg.** Here you can turn south on Hwy. 403 and follow Grays River down to the broad Grays Bay. Out on the open river are the remains of three cannery towns; Cottardi, Altoona, and, farther upriver on a dirt road, Pillar Rock. The dormitories housed workers, often Chinese brought in and treated as indentured servants.

Follow the signs from Rosburg to the only covered bridge in Washington still in use. The 158-foot-long **Grays River Covered Bridge,** on the National Register, was built in 1905 and covered five years later. The bridge was carefully restored in 1989 and is now a National Historic Landmark. A **Grays River Covered Bridge Festival** is held at the local Grange each August, and includes a parade, crafts booths, music, and a logging contest.

From here on east to Skamokawa you pass through timber company land. This corner of the state has almost no public timber holdings, and it's easy to see what happens when pure economics rules how the land is managed. Money and jobs always yell louder than preserving the environment.

Skamokawa
After a detour away from the Columbia at Grays River, Hwy. 4 rejoins the river at Skamokawa (ska-MOCK-away), and then follows it all the way to Longview. Quiet and picturesque Skamokawa is a delightful place to stop for a few hours or overnight. The word comes from a Wahkiakum tribal chief whose name meant "Smoke on the water," a reference to the dense fog that frequently drapes the Columbia River mouth. The town's most notable building is **Redmen Hall,** located on a steep bluff overlooking

the creek and river. The 1894 schoolhouse was taken over by the Redmen, a fraternal organization that died out in the 1950s. The restored hall is now the **River Life Interpretive Center,** tel. (360) 795-3007, open Sunday 1-4 p.m. and Wed.-Sat. noon-4 p.m. The center features historical photos, artifacts, and regional displays. Be sure to stop here and climb the belfry for extraordinary views over the Columbia River estuary.

Right in the center of town is the beautifully restored **Skamokawa Inn,** tel. (360) 795-8300 or (888) 920-2777, where you'll find a general store, post office, and cafe. Lodging costs $70-90 d including a full breakfast, or $190 for a two-bedroom apartment with kitchen in the adjacent Lott House. Also here is the **Paddle Sports & Outdoor Center,** offering canoe, kayak, and bike rentals.

Skamokawa Vista Park, tel. (360) 795-8605, has tent and RV sites and showers. Besides camping, the park also has a boat ramp and a sandy beach for swimmers, but no lifeguard. This park is a good place to watch ships crossing the treacherous Columbia River Bar; the busiest time is an hour before or an hour after low tide. When conditions are rough, you'll see enormous swells and waves breaking over these sandbars. Skamokawa is also home to the **Wahkiakum County Fairgrounds.**

Columbian White-Tailed Deer Refuge
Just west of Cathlamet is the 4,400-acre **Julia Butler Hansen National Wildlife Refuge,** established in 1972 to protect the few remaining Columbian white-tailed deer. The subspecies became endangered by the sort of habitat loss readily visible all around here—logging and agricultural development. The population rebounded from a low of just 230 animals to 900, but a devastating 1996 flood killed almost half the population again. They can be seen on the refuge, on nearby Puget Island, and on the Oregon shore near Westport. Brooks Slough Rd. and Steamboat Slough Rd. circle the refuge, offering a chance to see the small deer sharing grazing rights with dairy cattle and numerous birds, including bald eagles. To protect the deer from disturbance, hiking is prohibited, but you may see them from a blind located at a highway pullout. The refuge is named for the first woman to

chair a congressional appropriations subcommittee. For information on the refuge, call (360) 795-3915.

Cathlamet

Cathlamet (cath-LA-met), with a population of about 600, is the largest town between Longview-Kelso and the Pacific Ocean, and a great place to stop for a taste of history. It was built on the side of a steep hill overlooking Puget Island, and was a favorite haunt of Ulysses S. Grant when he was a lieutenant stationed at Fort Vancouver before the Civil War.

Before WW II this area was one of the most remote in America; many emigrants never bothered to learn English because they had little use for it, and their children born along the Columbia still speak with Scandinavian and Finnish accents. Today, Cathlamet is a quiet burg with a cluster of businesses along the mighty Columbia.

The small **Wahkiakum Museum**, tel. (360) 795-3954, contains photos and exhibits on early logging practices and is open Tues.-Sun. 11 a.m.-4 p.m. June-Sept., and Thurs.-Sun. 1-4 p.m. the rest of the year. Admission is $1 adults, 50 cents for kids. Next door is Strong Park and Waterfront Trail. In the park is an unusual geared steam locomotive that hauled logs up steep grades from 1923 to 1958. There's a "fine" view of the local sewage treatment plant from here. Also in town is Pioneer Church and an old cemetery with the graves of early settlers and Chief Wahkiakum. Meals are available at **Ranch House Restaurant.** Two salmon hatcheries— Beaver Creek Hatchery and Elokomin Hatchery are up Schoonover Rd. north of Cathlamet.

The Cathlamet area has several good places to stay. **Nassa Point Motel,** three miles east of town on Hwy. 4, tel. (360) 795-3941, charges $35 s or $40 d with kitchenettes. **Country Keeper B&B,** 61 Main St., tel. (360) 795-3030 or (800) 551-1691, is a beautiful two-story 1907 mansion that is now an elegant small inn. It has four rooms, two of which have private baths. Rates are $65-85s or $75-95 d, full breakfast included; no kids under eight.

The local **farmers market** takes place in Cathlamet Saturday 9 a.m.-1 p.m. early June-Oct.; tel. (360) 849-4769.

Puget Island

As you drive east along the Columbia on Hwy. 4, the lower river is marked by a series of islands, many little more than sandbars with a fringe of willows and grass. Most are named, but only one is inhabited: Puget Island, which is between Cathlamet and the Oregon side. It is connected to the Washington side by a bridge across the narrow channel, and to Oregon by a small ferry, the *Wahkiakum.* The ferry runs daily 5 a.m.-10 p.m. and costs $3 for cars, 50 cents for passengers.

Puget Island was settled by dairy farmers from Switzerland who built high levees to protect their rich farmland, and by fishermen from the Scandinavian countries. Some of the best commercial fishing boats used on the Columbia River were built on Puget Island. Over the years many of the boats were taken to Bristol Bay, Alaska, where they can still be found. The 27 miles of almost-level roads make for great bike riding. Stay at **Redfern Farm B&B,** 277 Cross Dike Rd., tel. (360) 849-4108, where the two guest rooms have a private bath and jacuzzi. A full breakfast is served. No young children; $55 s or d.

East to Longview

East of Cathlamet, Hwy. 4 hugs the Columbia River for 20 scenic miles, passing through undeveloped land. Tall cottonwood trees line the riverbanks; high rocky cliffs and Douglas fir trees line the slopes above the highway. For an interesting side trip, follow the signs to **Abernathy National Fish Hatchery.**

There's a small historical museum in **Stella** with local artifacts and photos. A turn-of-the-century blacksmith shop is open by appointment; call (360) 423-8663. Not much else to Stella, and nothing in the way of businesses. Camp ($10), swim, or sunbathe on the sandy beach at **County Line Park,** four miles west of Stella, tel. (360) 577-3030.

LONGVIEW AND KELSO VICINITY

Longview (pop. 33,000) and Kelso (pop. 12,000) are twin cities sandwiched between I-5 and the Columbia River, approximately 40 miles north of Portland. The Cowlitz River separates the two, with the older town of Kelso on the east side, and Longview right across two busy bridges. Longview was a planned city; the main streets head out like wheel spokes from the civic center. The main drag through both cities is Hwy. 4, a heavily trafficked route that seems to be perpetually jammed with vehicles.

LONGVIEW

History

The Lewis and Clark expedition camped at the mouth of the Cowlitz River in 1805 near the site of present-day Longview, and the first white settlers arrived in 1849 to establish a place they called "Monticello." On November 25, 1852, a group of settlers met in the "Monticello Convention" to petition the formation of a new territory north of the Columbia River. Within weeks the U.S. Congress had approved the creation of Washington Territory. In 1854 the Territorial government established Cowlitz County and made Monticello its seat. Unfortunately, Monticello sat on a peninsula surrounded by the Columbia and Cowlitz Rivers, and it flooded seasonally. In the winter of 1866-67 it was almost washed away, so the townsite was abandoned and the county seat moved across the Cowlitz River onto higher ground upriver in Kalama.

It wasn't until the 1920s that the city experienced its first growth spurt. Engineers from the

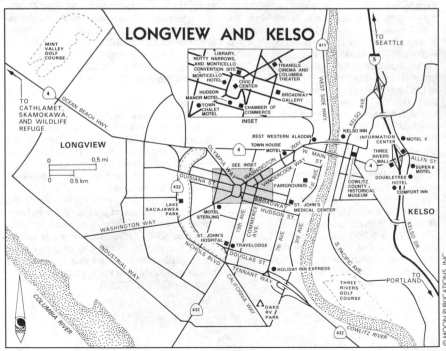

Long-Bell Lumber Company sought a new supply for timber as their resources were running out in Texas and Louisiana. Southwest Washington had an abundant supply of old-growth timber and, from a logging viewpoint, Longview's location on a major river with deep-water frontage and rail lines was ideal. They bought 70,000 acres of timber and started cutting.

Lumber baron and multimillionaire R.A. Long founded the city in 1923, and Longview became the first planned city in the Pacific Northwest, designed by nationally known planners working with stringent zoning requirements and an eye toward the aesthetic. Unfortunately, the planners also created a traffic nightmare, with a rabbit warren of confusing streets that meet at odd angles. Be prepared to get lost sometime in your visit to Longview. Longview's original mill is gone, but the city is home to several big plants, including a Reynolds Metals aluminum plant, a hydrogen peroxide plant, the Longview Fibre pulp mill, and Weyerhaeuser's state-of-the-art Norpac newsprint recycling plant. Visitors to the area will immediately notice the acrid "eau de pulp mill" stench from these plants along the Columbia River.

Parks

Longview's early planning is revealed by the beautiful **Lake Sacajawea Park,** a 110-acre greenbelt that bisects the city along Nichols Blvd. with a string of serene lakes surrounded by grassy hillsides, shady trees, and a gravel jogging/cycling path.

R.A. Long Park (a.k.a. Civic Center) is a grassy green in the city's core, at the intersection of Olympia and Washington Ways. Surrounding the green are many of the city's oldest buildings, including the wonderful red brick **Public Library** donated by the town's founder and finished in 1926. Featured attractions on the library grounds are the Nutty Narrows bridge and giant squirrel statue, an old logging locomotive, and a rose garden. The **Monticello Hotel,** built in 1923 and still the town's most elegant building, faces R.A. Long Park from 17th Avenue.

A small park at 18th, Maple, and Olympia in Longview marks the **Monticello Convention Site,** where Washington residents met to petition the government to separate Washington Territory from Oregon.

Nutty Narrows

Just up Olympia Way from the Civic Center, the Nutty Narrows is the world's only skybridge for squirrels. Builder and developer Amos J. Peters built it in 1963 to save the critters as they attempted to cross the busy street. Peters is honored for his effort with a many-times-greater-than-life-size squirrel sculpture between the library and skybridge.

Bed and Breakfasts

Built in 1924, the Victorian-style **Rutherglen Mansion B&B,** 420 Rutherglen Rd., tel. (360)

DIANNE BOULERICE LYONS

Lake Sacajawea Park

425-5816, has two guest rooms with private baths. A continental breakfast is served, and kids are accepted; $80 s or d. The restaurant downstairs serves dinners nightly except Sunday.

Misty Mountain Llamas B&B, 1033 Stella Rd., tel. (360) 577-4772, is a custom-built country home on a five-acre llama ranch. The two bedrooms share a bath, and a hearty breakfast is served. $80 s or $85-90 d.

Motels

Motel accommodations in Longview are listed by price. **Longview Budget Inn Longview,** 1808 Hemlock, tel. (360) 423-6980, has rooms for $30 s or $36 d. **Town Chalet Motel,** 1822 Washington Way, tel. (360) 423-2020, has rooms for $34 s or $38 d. **Town House Motel,** 744 Washington Way in Longview, tel. (360) 423-7200, charges $34-38 s or $40-45 d, and has an outdoor pool. **Travelodge,** 838 15th Ave., tel. (360) 423-6460 or (800) 578-7878, charges $35-40s or $41-46 d. **Hudson Manor Motel,** 1616 Hudson in Longview, tel. (360) 425-1100, has rooms for $38 s or $48 d. **Holiday Inn Express,** 723 7th Ave., tel. (360) 414-1000 or (800) 465-4329, has an indoor pool, jacuzzi, and continental breakfast; $67 s or d. **Monticello Motel,** 17th and Larch, tel. (360) 425-9900, has a jacuzzi; rooms are $68-75 s or d.

Campgrounds

The closest public camping spaces are at **Lewis and Clark State Park,** 10 miles north on I-5 and six miles east on Hwy. 504. Camp for $10 (no hookups) April-September. Nearby RV parks include **Deluxe Trailer Court,** 1112 Tennant Way, tel. (360) 425-4147, and **Oaks RV Park,** 636 California Way, tel. (360) 425-2708.

Food

Stuffy's Restaurant, 418 Long Ave., tel. (360) 423-6356, *the* place for breakfast, features an extensive menu, friendly family service, and enormous servings. **Commerce Cafe,** Commerce and Broadway, tel. (360) 577-0115 has a popular champagne Sunday brunch.

Get sandwiches and other lunch fare at **Country Folks Deli,** 1323 Commerce Ave., tel. (360) 425-3837. The enormous sweet rolls here should best be moved with a forklift. A few doors away at the corner of Broadway and Commerce is the

Mercantile Building, where you'll find **The Merk Deli,** a good place for an espresso. Pick up a book at the **Benevolent Bookworm** (across the street) and plunk yourself down at a courtyard table to read.

Henri's Restaurant, 4545 Ocean Beach Hwy., tel. (360) 425-7970, is a very popular spot for the "power-lunch" business crowd. Specializing in moderately priced salmon or steak dinners and an impressive wine collection, it's open weekdays for lunch, Mon.-Sat. for dinner.

La Playa, 1310 Ocean Beach Hwy., tel. (360) 425-1660, has the best Mexican food in the area.

The **Cowlitz Community Farmers Market,** tel. (360) 425-1297, held Tuesday and Saturday 8 a.m.-1 p.m. April-Oct. at 7th and Washington, has fruits, flowers, fresh vegetables, honey, bedding plants, berries, and more.

Recreation

Swim in the local YMCA pool at 15th and Douglas, tel. (360) 423-4770, or play a round of golf at **Mint Valley,** 4002 Pennsylvania in Longview, tel. (360) 577-3395. If you have a canoe, the Cowlitz River from Castle Rock to Longview is a fine 16-mile float. The current can be strong and sandbars are visible at low water, but there are no major obstructions along the way. Windsurfers flock to the Columbia River west and south of Longview, where wind conditions are often perfect for intermediate-level boarders.

Events

In late June, the **Cowlitz River Canoe Race** is a fast 14-mile river run that starts in Castle Rock and pulls out at Kelso. The Independence Day **Go 4th Celebration** is said to be one of the largest in the country, with a parade, logging show, rubber duck race, concession stands, and a big fireworks show. In mid-July, the **Summer Arts Festival** attracts artisans from throughout the Lower Columbia. Held at the fairgrounds in late July or early August, the **Cowlitz County Fair** has exhibits and entertainment, including the PRCA Thunder Mountain Rodeo; tel. (360) 577-3121. In late August, the **Unique Tin Weekend** features old cars, street cruising, and dancing at the fairgrounds.

Arts and Entertainment

The **Columbia Theatre,** 1231 Vandercook Way, tel. (360) 423-1011, a legacy from the prosperous 1920s, hosts local theater and dance groups as well as national acts. The **Southwest Washington Symphony** gives performances there Nov.-April; tel. (360) 425-5346. During July and August music lovers head to Lake Sacajawea for free Sunday **concerts in the park** featuring everything from tuba fests to country-western bands.

Stop by **Broadway Gallery,** 1418 Commerce Ave., tel. (360) 577-0544, to see an outstanding collection of southwestern Washington art produced by more than 30 area artists, including jewelry, pottery, watercolors, weaving, baskets, sculpture, and more.

Information

For information on the town, contact the **Longview Chamber of Commerce,** near the Civic Center at 1563 Olympia Way, tel. (360) 423-8400; open Mon.-Fri. 9 a.m.-5 p.m. See **Kelso** for local transportation options.

KELSO

Kelso is much older than Longview. It got its start in the 1840s when the Hudson's Bay Co. grazed cattle nearby and used Cowlitz and Columbia River ports to export beef from the wharves here. Settlement began in 1847, when Peter Crawford donated land on the Cowlitz River for the town of Crawford. It was renamed Kelso in 1884 after the founder's Scottish birthplace (now officially a sister city). Kelso was incorporated in 1889, became county seat in 1923, and has since been an important logging, milling, and fishing town. Kelso is called "The Smelt Capital of the World" in honor of the abundant winter run of these fish up the Cowlitz River. The first Cowlitz County cannery was built in 1886, and the smelt industry is still a dominant force in Kelso's economy as tons of fish are shipped annually to Asia. Also important is the boat-building company, Tollycraft, and a Foster's Farm chicken processing plant.

Cowlitz County Historical Museum

Visit the Cowlitz County Historical Museum, 405 Allen St. in Kelso, to see well presented Chinook and Cowlitz Indian artifacts, a cabin from 1884, historic photos from the heyday of log-

ging, and changing exhibits. Open Sunday 1-5 p.m., and Tues.-Sat. 9 a.m.-5 p.m. year-round; tel. (360) 577-3119. No charge.

Accommodations and Camping

Motel accommodations in Kelso are arranged below by price. **Kelso Budget Inn,** 505 N. Pacific, tel. (360) 636-4610, has rooms for $35-40 s or $41-45 d. **Motel 6,** 106 Minor Rd. in Kelso, tel. (360) 425-3229 or (800) 440-6000, has an outdoor pool, and rooms for $44 s or $50 d. Rooms at **Super 8 Motel,** 250 Kelso Dr., tel. (360) 423-8880 or (800) 800-8000, are $56 s or $62 d, with an indoor pool.

Best Western Aladdin Motor Inn, 310 Long Ave., tel. (360) 425-9660 or (800) 764-7378, charges $65-69 s or $73-85 d, including an indoor pool, jacuzzi, exercise facility, microwaves, and fridges. **Comfort Inn,** 440 Three Rivers Dr., tel. (360) 425-4600 or (800) 221-2222, has an outdoor pool and continental breakfast; $69 s or $74 d. **Doubletree Hotel,** 510 Kelso Dr., tel. (360) 636-4400 or (800) 636-4400, has an outdoor pool, children's pool, and jacuzzi; $75-95 s or $80-105 d.

Longfellow House B&B; 203 Williams-Finney Rd. in Kelso, tel. (360) 423-4545, has a bedroom in a small home. A full breakfast is served, and kids are accepted; $84 s or $89 d.

Brookhollow RV Park, 2506 Allen St., tel.(360) 577-6474 or (800) 867-0453, has campsites and RV hookups.

Food

Hilander Restaurant, 1509 Allen St., tel. (360) 423-1500, is a real surprise. Located in—of all places—the bowling alley, it has great strawberry waffles and big omelettes for breakfast, a salad bar, homemade soups, and tasty halibut fish and chips. **Yan's Chinese Restaurant,** 300 Long Ave. W, tel. (360) 425-3815, has reasonable prices and serves up ample portions.

For pizza, head to **Izzy's Pizza Restaurant,** at Three Rivers Mall, tel. (360) 578-1626. Also in Kelso, **Peter's Restaurant,** 310 S. Pacific, tel. (360) 423-9620, specializes in steaks in an 1890s atmosphere highlighted by a solid marble bar, antique lamps, and stained glass.

Events

On the last Sunday of August, the **Three Rivers Air Show** attracts stunt pilots, hang gliders, hot air balloons, military aircraft, and private planes of all types. The **Kelso Highlander Festival,** held the second weekend of September each year, features a parade, wine festival, art show, rubber duck race, Scottish bagpipe music, dancing, and food at Tam O'Shanter Park.

Recreation
Swim at the Kelso high school pool, 1904 Allen St., tel. (360) 577-2442. Golfers should head to the eight-hole **Three Rivers Golf Course,** 2222 S. River Rd., tel. (360) 423-4653.

Shopping
For a shopping mall frenzy, the impressive **Three Rivers Mall,** just off I-5 at Longview/Kelso exit 39 has The Bon Marché, JCPenney, Emporium, Sears, Target, and scores of smaller specialty shops.

Information
The **Kelso Tourist Information Center,** tel. (360) 577-8058, just east of the I-5 entrance ramp at 105 Minor Rd., provides local info and houses a small exhibit for those who may have missed the *real* Mount St. Helens visitor centers closer to the mountain. This one has a 15-foot model of the volcano and Toutle River valley, plus photos and exhibits of the 1980 eruption. Open daily 9 a.m.-5 p.m. May-Oct., and Wed.-Sun. 9 a.m.-5 p.m. the rest of the year. Find them on the Web at www.tdn.com/kelso.

Transportation
Community Urban Bus Service, 254 Oregon Way, provides local service in the Kelso-Longview area Mon.-Sat.; call (360) 577-3399 for schedule information. **Greyhound,** tel. (360) 423-7380 or (800) 231-2222, has cross-country bus connections from the train station in Kelso.

Blue Star Airporter, tel. (800) 247-2272, has shuttle van service between Longview/Kelso and Portland International Airport. **Aeronautics Unlimited,** tel. (360) 414-5960, offers scenic flights over Mt. St. Helens from the Longview/Kelso airport.

Amtrak trains head north from Kelso to Centralia, Olympia, Tacoma, Seattle, and points beyond, and south to Vancouver, Portland, and California. Service is four times a day; call (800) 872-7245 for details.

CASTLE ROCK

Castle Rock (pop. 2,200) lies just west of I-5 along the Cowlitz River. The town is named for a 150-foot-high rocky knob that can be climbed by an easy-to-find path. The town was hit hard by the eruption of Mt. St. Helens in 1980, when mud flows turned the Cowlitz into a raging torrent that washed out bridges and damaged or destroyed more than 200 homes. In town is a memorial to Harry Truman, the old-timer who died at his Spirit Lake home when the volcano erupted and buried the lake in hundreds of feet of debris. (Mt. St. Helens sights are described in the Cascades chapter.)

Sights and Information
The **Castle Rock Exhibit Hall and Visitor Information Center** at 147 Front Ave. NW, tel. (360) 274-6603, details the town and its connection to the Cowlitz River, the importance of the timber industry to the economy, and the impact of the 1980 eruption of Mt. St. Helens. Open daily 9 a.m.-6 p.m. in summer, and Wed.-Sat. 10 a.m.-2 p.m. the rest of the year. No charge.

Accommodations
7 West Motel, 864 Walsh Ave. NE, tel. (360) 274-7526, has the cheapest rooms in Castle Rock: $38 s or $45 d. **Timberland Inn & Suites,** 206 Spirit Lake Hwy., tel. (360) 274-6002, has rooms for $60 s or $65 d. The **Mount St. Helens Motel,** 227 Spirit Lake Hwy., tel. (360) 274-7721, charges $48 s or d.

At 3201 Spirit Lake Hwy. in Silver Lake, **Silver Lake Motel and Resort,** tel. (360) 274-6141, has motel rooms, rustic two-bedroom cabins with full kitchens ($55-80 d), and RV and tent sites. They also rent fishing boats. Rooms are $75 d, with a balcony over the water and full kitchens.

Five miles up from I-5, the spacious and newly built **Blue Heron Inn B&B,** tel. (360) 274-9595, has seven guest rooms all with private baths. A full breakfast and dinner are served; $115 s or $145 d. No kids under six.

BG's B&B, 405 Hall Road in Silver Lake, tel. (360) 274-8573, has six guest rooms with shared baths. Children are accepted, and a full breakfast is served; $65-80 s or d.

Campgrounds

Camp amid tall trees at **Seaquest State Park,** six miles east of Castle Rock on Silver Lake; $10 tents, $15 RVs. Call (800) 452-5687 for reservations ($6 extra). Private RV parks in the Castle Rock area include **Mount St. Helens RV Park,** 167 Schaffran Rd., tel. (360) 274-8522; **Cedars RV Park,** in Castle Rock, tel. (360) 274-5136; and **Toutle RV Park,** in Toutle, tel. (360) 274-6208.

Food and Events

Waldo's Restaurant, 51 Cowlitz St., has the best local meals, but several other places offer quick eats.

The **Castle Rock Fair** on the fourth weekend of July is the big annual event, with a parade, stage shows, games, and carnival. The Mount St. Helens Motorcycle Club sponsors **Pro-Am TT Motorcycle Races** all summer at Castle Rock racetrack. Bicyclists come here for the **Tour de Blast** race in June, and the **Seattle to Portland** bike race each July.

LEWIS RIVER VALLEY

The Lewis River and its tributaries drain the southern side of Mt. St. Helens and the eastern slopes of Mt. Adams, cutting through the farm-and-forest country of northern Clark County. A number of towns and parks dot the lowland areas, separated by a confusing grid of roads. This is rural Washington, a great place to enjoy a drive or bike ride on a country route.

KALAMA

Interstate 5 slices through the center of Kalama (pop. 1,200), leaving the main part of town with its abundance of antique shops to the east, while to the west lie enormous piles of logs at a sawmill, a massive steel coating plant and other industrial facilities, a grain export facility, and the harbor. Right across the Columbia River on the Oregon side is the now defunct Trojan Nuclear Plant, owned by Portland General Electric. It closed abruptly in 1993 when cracks were discovered in thousands of the vital heat-exchange tubes; it's expected to cost an astounding $1 billion to decommission.

The section of the Columbia River near Kalama has in recent years become a favorite of windsurfers. The wind is generally not as strong here as upriver in the Columbia Gorge, so this area is more popular with intermediate-level boarders.

Sights

Kalama is well known for its many antique shops, the biggest collection in southwest Washington.

More than 100 dealers are spread through several large antique malls, the largest being the **Hendrickson Mall.**

The world's tallest single-tree totem, the 149-foot **totem pole,** carved by Chief Don Lelooska, stands along the river on the west side of the freeway. A mile-long paved path follows the Kalama River near here.

Practicalities

Stay at **Columbia Inn Motel,** 602 N.E. Frontage Rd., tel. (360) 673-2855, for $39 s or $45 d; kitchenettes are available.

Pitch a tent along the Kalama River at the city-run **Louis Rasmussen RV Park,** tel. (360) 673-2626, or the private **Camp Kalama RV Park,** 5055 N. Meeker Dr., tel. (360) 673-2456.

The **Kalama Community Fair** on the third weekend of July includes a parade, barbecue, talent show, and FFA exhibits.

WOODLAND AND VICINITY

Woodland (pop. 2,600) acts as the southern gateway to Mt. St. Helens, with Hwy. 503 heading northeast to the volcano. The area was first settled in the 1840s, and the town was incorporated in 1906. Today it is home to a plant where Fleetwood prefab homes are constructed.

Sights

There isn't a lot to the town of Woodland, but be sure to follow the signs to **Hulda Klager Lilac Gardens,** tel. (360) 225-8996, where you'll dis-

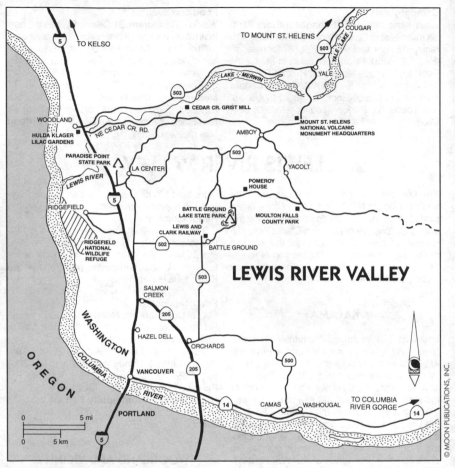

cover an 1889 farmhouse surrounded by three acres of grounds filled with colorful flowers and trees of all descriptions. Hulda Klager began hybridizing lilacs in 1903, and developed more than 250 new varieties, including 10 that can be found in the gardens here. The gardens are open year-round and lilac starts (rooted lilac cuttings) are available weekdays, but the lovely Victorian-era home is open only for Lilac Week (the week preceding Mothers Day). Entrance to the gardens is $1. The gardens sit near **Horseshoe Lake,** formerly part of the Lewis River. It was created in 1940 when the

river was rerouted to construct what is now I-5. The lake is a popular place to fish for trout and largemouth bass.

Another nearby sight is the **Highland Lutheran Church,** built in 1883 and used for years by the Scandinavian community in this part of Washington. Now on the National Register of Historic Places, the beautiful old church sits against a backdrop of pastures and second-growth forests; it's still used for special services. The church is five miles east of Woodland near the corner of N.E. 389th St. and N.E. 41st Avenue.

Grist Mill

The **Cedar Creek Grist Mill,** 10 miles east of Woodland off N.E. Cedar Creek Rd., is one of the few 19th century water-powered grist mills remaining in the Northwest. Built in 1876, it has been carefully restored, with water fed in by a 650-foot log flume. Volunteers grind wheat here Saturday 1-4 p.m. and Sunday 2-4 p.m. Upstairs is a small museum detailing the reconstruction process. Donation. Call (360) 225-9552 for details.

Lodging

There are half-a-dozen lodging choices in the Woodland area. Cheapest is **Lakeside Motel,** 785 Lakeshore Dr., tel. (360) 225-8240, with rooms for $38-40 s or d. A step up is **Scandia Motel,** 1123 Hoffman St., tel. (360) 225-8006, where rooms are $38 s or $40 d, including an outdoor jacuzzi. **Hansen's Motel,** 1215 Pacific, tel. (360) 225-7018 or (888) 225-7018, charges $32 s or $36 d.

Stay at **Lewis River Inn,** 1100 Lewis River Rd., tel. (360) 225-6257 or (800) 543-4344, for $44-54 s or $50-60 d. It's located along the river, with balconies offering a view from the more expensive rooms. **Woodlander Inn,** 1500 Atlantic St., tel. (360) 225-6548 or (800) 444-9667, is the nicest around, with quality rooms for $47-51 s or $51-55 d, including an indoor pool and jacuzzi.

Grandma's House B&B, 4551 Old Lewis River Rd., tel. (360) 225-7002, is eight miles east of Woodland on Hwy. 503 in a 1917 farmhouse overlooking the Lewis River. The three guest rooms come with a full breakfast for $39 s or $55 d.

Located right along the riverbanks, **Lewis River B&B,** 2339 Lewis River Rd., tel. (360) 225-8630 or (800) 517-3200, is a modern place with seven guest rooms, all with private baths and luxurious furnishings. A full breakfast is served, and guests enjoy the big deck facing the river; $80-130 s or d. No kids.

Campgrounds

Five miles southeast of Woodland and just off I-5, **Paradise Point State Park,** tel. (360) 263-2350, has fishing, boating, and swimming in the East Fork Lewis River, a two-mile hiking trail, and camping ($10, no hookups). Open for day-use and camping April-Sept., plus weekends and holidays the rest of the year. Because of its location right along I-5, this isn't a particularly quiet place to spend a night, but at least the highway makes for easy access. Call (800) 452-5687 for reservations ($6 extra).

More camping is available at **Woodland Special Campground** in dense forests three miles east of Woodland on N.W. 389th St., run by the Dept. of Natural Resources. Free, and open mid-May to mid-Oct.; tel. (800) 527-3305.

Local private RV parks are: **Columbia Riverfront RV Park,** 1881 Dike Rd., tel. (360) 225-8051; **Woodland Shores RV Park,** 109 A St., tel. (360) 225-2222 or (800) 481-2224; and **Lewis River RV Park,** 3125 Lewis River Rd., tel. (360) 225-9556.

Other Practicalities

Oak Tree Restaurant 1020 Atlantic, tel. (360) 887-8661, is a very popular place for steaks. **Planter's Day** is billed as the state's oldest continuously running festival. The four-day event celebrates the building of dikes to prevent flooding of Woodland and includes a carnival, fun run, pancake breakfast, firemen's barbecue, frog jumping contest, and car show.

A small trailer at Lakeshore Dr. and Goerig St. houses the **Woodland Chamber of Commerce Information Center,** tel. (360) 225-9552; open daily 8 a.m.-4 p.m. year-round, and Fri.-Mon. till 7 p.m. April-October.

LA CENTER

La Center (pop. 1,000) was established in the 1850s as a supply post for nearby settlers. This was the farthest up the East Fork of the Lewis River that boats could travel, and the remains of one of these boats, the sternwheeler *Leona,* sits just west of the bridge in La Center. The town is the only place in this part of Washington where poker and blackjack gambling are legal in several small casinos.

Built in 1903, the **Inn at La Center,** 305 W. 5th St., tel. (360) 263-5863, has two guest rooms that share a bath. A continental breakfast is served; $60-70 s or d. No kids.

Salishan Vineyards, North Fork Rd. in La Center, tel. (360) 263-2713, is a small family-owned winery that produces award-winning pinot noirs and dry rieslings. Open for tours and tastings Sat.-Sun. 1-5 p.m. May-Dec., or by appointment.

COUGAR

The hamlet of Cougar is a 32-mile scenic climb into the hills east of Woodland on Hwy. 503. The narrow road cuts through second-growth forests, with periodic glimpses of Lake Merwin and Yale Lake—reservoirs that were created by dams on the Lewis River. Anglers may want to stop at the Merwin and Speelyai fish hatcheries, while picnickers and swimmers may want to stop at Yale Park Recreation Area on Yale Lake. The highway also passes through the tiny burg of **Ariel**, along the Cowlitz River, believed to be the approximate landing place of the 1971 skyjacker known as D.B. Cooper, who demanded $200,000 before jumping from a Northwest Airlines jet. Some of the money was found many years later along the banks of the Columbia River.

In addition to Cooper's jump, Cougar serves as a jumping off point (so to speak) for access to the southern and eastern sides of Mount St. Helens National Volcanic Monument. Climbers register at Jack's Store; see **Mount St. Helens National Volcanic Monument** for specifics on the climb. The **Mount St. Helens National Volcanic Monument Headquarters**, tel. (360) 247-3900, is out in the boonies on Hwy. 503, three miles north of Amboy and seven miles north of the town of Yacolt. Much of this area was consumed in the 1902 Yacolt Burn that killed 38 people and burned 238,000 acres of timber.

Lodging

Stay at the comfortable **Monfort's B&B,** 132 Cougar Rd., tel. (360) 238-5229, with two guest rooms, private baths, and full breakfasts; $75-85 s or d. Kids okay. **Lone Fir Resort,** 16806 Lewis River Rd., tel. (360) 238-5210, has motel rooms and a cabin in a wooded location for $38-50 s or d, including an outdoor pool. RV spaces are also available here. See **Mount St. Helens National Volcanic Monument** for camping and other recreational options in the area around Cougar.

RIDGEFIELD

Ridgefield (pop. 1,800) is just west of I-5 and south of Woodland along the Columbia River. The town is a surprising throwback to America's past, with tall shade trees lining the quiet streets, and a sense of history that is quickly disappearing elsewhere in Washington. Built in 1850, **Lancaster House** is one of the oldest structures in the state. Also of interest is **Ridgefield Hardware,** one of the few old-time hardware stores remaining in Washington.

The **Ridgefield National Wildlife Refuge,** tel. (360) 887-4106, a mile north of town, has 5,150 acres of fields, woodlands, and marshes. In winter, up to 10,000 geese and 40,000 ducks land here. Hiking and fishing are permitted—the two-mile "Oaks to Wetlands Wildlife Trail" is popular with all ages. Parts of the refuge are closed October through mid-April.

Campgrounds

The closest public campgrounds are at Paradise Point State Park near La Center (described above) and Battle Ground Lake State Park (described below). The privately run **Big Fir Campground,** tel. (360) 887-8970 or (800) 532-4397, is a mile east of Ridgefield, with wooded campsites and RV hookups.

Events

Ridgefield's **Fourth of July** celebration features an old-fashioned parade, a pet parade, arts and crafts displays, music, and a big community breakfast and salmon bake. The **Clark County Fair** in early August is the fifth largest in the nation, held at the fairgrounds in Ridgefield; call (360) 573-1921 for a schedule of fair events. The fair attracts big name entertainers and always includes agricultural exhibits, a carnival, horse shows, art exhibits, and all the other events you'd expect.

BATTLE GROUND

Battle Ground (pop. 7,000) is a nondescript settlement strewn along a lengthy Main Street with the now-standard strip malls. The town's name came from a battle that never took place. During the conflict between Klickitat Indians and white settlers in 1855, a tribal chief was accidentally killed. Soldiers from nearby Fort Vancouver allowed a traditional burial, but when they returned to the fort without forcing the Indians to come with them, their officers chastised them for not provoking a battle on the "battle ground." The name stuck, even though the battle never actually occurred.

Parks

Battle Ground Lake State Park is a popular summer getaway three miles northeast of Battle Ground on N.E. 244th Street. Covering just 280 acres, the park features a sandy beach that attract swimmers, along with a snack bar and lakeside campground ($11, no RV hookups). Hikers and horseback riders will enjoy the many trails that circle this small, cold spring-fed lake in a caldera. The park is open year-round. Call (360) 687-4621 for details or (800) 452-5687 for reservations ($6 extra).

Lewisville County Park covers 154 forested acres just north of Battle Ground along the East Fork of the Lewis River. This exceptionally pretty place has rustic shelters and other structures built by the Works Progress Administration in the 1930s, and is a great place for a picnic in the trees or a weekend walk. No camping at Lewisville Park. Parking fees are charged in the summer.

Moulton Falls County Park, tel. (360) 699-2467, is 10 miles northwest of Battle Ground on N.E. Lucia Falls Rd. and was an historic meeting place for Indians in the area. A swinging footbridge over Big Tree Creek offers fine views of Moulton Falls, and trails lead three miles through the forest. No camping. **Lucia Falls Park,** tel. (360) 696-8171, is a small private park along the East Fork of the Lewis River, with walking trails and picknicking spots.

Living History Museum

Several miles northeast of Battle Ground is the **Pomeroy Living History Farm,** 20902 N.E. Lucia Falls Rd., tel. (360) 686-3537, where visitors are given a glimpse into Clark County's rural lifestyle of the 1920s. Located in the beautiful Lewis River Valley with its fill of classic farmsteads and second-growth forests, Pomeroy includes a working blacksmith shop, herb garden, and historic log home, all in the same family for five generations. Open Saturday 11 a.m.-4 p.m., and Sunday 1 p.m.-4 p.m. on the first full weekend of each month, June-October. Admission is $3.50 adults, $2 kids ages 3-11. The farm and house are on the National Register of Historic Places. A very popular **Pumpkin Festival** is held here each October.

Practicalities

No local lodging places, and Battle Ground's food scene is limited. A couple of good places are **Dante's Ristorante, 15 Main St. E, tel. (360) 687-4373, with nightly Italian dinner specials; and** Pete's Sports Barn and Schnitzel Haus, 705 SE 1st, tel. (360) 687-2699, for authentic German food and microbrews, plus big screen TVs. The big local festival is **Summer Fest,** featuring hot air balloons, pancake breakfasts, a parade, carnival, food booths, root beer float garden, and a street dance on the third weekend of July.

Get local information at the **Battle Ground Chamber of Commerce,** 912 E. Main, tel. (360) 687-1510. They're open Mon.-Fri. 9 a.m.-4:30 p.m. all year. If you're in the market for antiques, check out the high quality antique shops around Battle Ground. **C-TRAN,** tel. (360) 695-0123, has local bus connections to Vancouver.

VANCOUVER

A two-time winner of the All-America City Award, Vancouver has a population of 126,000 supported by wood products, electronics, food processing, and the neighboring Portland economy, where many of Clark County's 300,000 residents are employed. Besides serving as a Portland suburb and Washington's I-5 gateway city, Vancouver enjoys a colorful history, kept alive by the Fort Vancouver National Historic Site and Officers' Row. Vancouver is also a gateway to recreational opportunities at nearby Mt. St. Helens and the Columbia River.

The name, honoring Capt. George Vancouver, who explored the Columbia River in 1792, came from the Hudson's Bay post named Fort Vancouver. While the city was still part of the Oregon Ter-

ritory, the Oregon Territorial Legislature named it Columbia City. However in 1855 the Legislature changed it back to its original name, creating a situation that will always cause confusion. Locals point out that Vancouver, British Columbia, is a Johnny-come-lately city and if any name should be changed, it should be the Canadian one. That prospect is very doubtful. To help avoid confusion, the city is often referred to as Vancouver, U.S.A.

HISTORY

Fort Vancouver

The United States and Great Britain had been unable to come to terms on the ownership of

© MOON PUBLICATIONS, INC.

Oregon Country, a fur- and lumber-rich land that included the Northwest Coast of North America. In 1818, the two powers had agreed to share the land until an agreement could be reached, but seven years later the British-owned Hudson's Bay Company moved its headquarters from Fort George, at the mouth of the Columbia, to Fort Vancouver, 100 miles inland, in hopes of solidifying the British claim to the region.

Fort Vancouver became the Pacific Northwest's commercial and cultural center for fur trading from Utah to Hawaii; shops, fields, pastures, and mills made the fort a self-sufficient, bustling pioneer community. By the 1840s it was the "New York" of the Northwest and was home to a widely diverse set of workers, including many "Kanakas" from the Hawaiian Islands. The blacksmith shop employed eight men full-time to manufacture more than 50,000 beaver traps, plus countless knives, axes, and other tools of the trade. Other important work included maintaining 2,500 acres of farms and orchards outside the fort itself.

The American Years

Droves of pioneering Americans were drawn to Oregon's fertile Willamette Valley farmland in the 1840s, leading to the division of the territory along the 49th parallel in 1846—a boundary that put Britain's Fort Vancouver squarely on American soil. By 1860 all of Fort Vancouver was in the hands of the U.S. Army—which proceeded to carry off anything of value. Decay and fire had destroyed all of the remaining structures by 1866. The Army built new buildings on the slope behind the fort at **Vancouver Barracks,** including grand officers' quarters and not-so-grand barracks and other facilities for those of lower rank. Several of these lesser buildings are still used by the Army.

The city of Vancouver initially served as the Washington state capital, but legislators feared it was too close to Oregon and might come under their sway, so moved the seat of government to Olympia. During WW II, Vancouver's Kaiser Shipyards employed 38,000 people (including activist and musician Woodie Guthrie) in the building of more than 140 ships for the war effort. The shipyard closed after the war.

SIGHTS

Fort Vancouver National Historic Site

Beginning in 1948, archaeologists recovered more than a million artifacts, leading to the accurate reconstruction of six of Fort Vancouver's 27 buildings on the original location as they were in 1845, now preserved as a national historic site. The buildings are surrounded by a tall wooden stockade and guarded by a three-story tower (bastion) that was originally built in 1845 as protection from American settlers and to salute arriving ships with its eight three-pound cannons. The fort was a peaceful place, however, and the occupants never had to hide in fear. Other reconstructed buildings include a blacksmith's shop, bakery, Indian trade shop, storage house, and the elegant residence of Dr. John McLoughlin, the chief factor who looked so fearsome with his hard stare and great head of white hair, but who was one of the most generous men in those

Fort Vancouver National Historic Site

pioneer years. Although McLoughlin had been charged with keeping the American settlers out of the market, he quickly realized that trade was far more practical. When the land was officially declared American soil, he resigned, became an American citizen, and moved to Oregon City where he was hailed as the "Father of Oregon."

Historic Fort Vancouver is open daily 9 a.m.-5 p.m. March-Oct., and daily 9 a.m.-4 p.m. the rest of the year (closed Thanksgiving, Christmas, and New Year's). Amazingly detailed guided tours are given by Park Service rangers hourly 9 a.m.-4 p.m. The tour includes a visit to the fully restored home of chief factor John McLoughlin, along with a visit to the working blacksmith shop (open Thurs.-Mon.) where you will learn how the Hudson's Bay Co. produced beaver traps and other goods. Today the shop is used to train apprentices to create iron pieces for National Park Service historic facilities across the nation. Also of interest during the tour are the kitchen and carpentry shop (both with living history activities all summer), the bake house, and the fur store, housing displays on the fur trade in one section and ongoing archaeological research in the other half. The fort's period gardens are interesting to view, and gardeners will be happy to tell you of the crops that were—and are—grown here.

A block north of the fort at 1511 E. Evergreen Blvd. is the **visitor center** (same hours as the fort), where you can watch a 15-minute orientation video and view displays on the fort along with artifacts found during the excavations.

From downtown, catch the free shuttle bus to Fort Vancouver, or drive east for a half mile on E. Evergreen Boulevard. A $2 entrance fee ($4 for families; kids under 17 free) is charged May-Oct., free the rest of the year. Call (360) 696-7655 or (800) 832-3599 for details on the fort. See "Events and Entertainment," below, for several of the fort's seasonal activities.

Officers' Row

The only fully restored collection of officers' homes in the nation is at Vancouver's lovingly restored Officers' Row National Historic District. They occupy one side of a tree-draped street and are used by local businesses; opposite is spacious **Central Park**—a favorite place for locals to relax on a sunny day. Less impressive old Army barracks lie just west of the central park in various stages of repair. A free shuttle bus connects Officers' Row with downtown.

The two most famous buildings on Officers' Row are the Marshall House and Grant House, named for their onetime residents Gen. George C. Marshall and President Ulysses S. Grant. Other famous residents included Phillip Sheridan, Benjamin Bonneville, and Omar Bradley; presidents Rutherford B. Hayes and Franklin D. Roosevelt attended receptions here.

The **Marshall House,** 1313 Officers' Row, tel. (360) 693-3103, is open for free tours and has videotapes describing the fort and Officers' Row. The building is very popular for weddings and other events, so it is often closed to the public on weekends. Hours are Mon.-Fri. 9 a.m.-5 p.m., and on wedding-less weekends. Named for the man who authored the famous postwar Marshall Plan, it was George C. Marshall's home during his time as commanding officer at Vancouver Barracks from 1936 to 1938.

Built in 1849, the **Grant House Folk Art Center & Cafe,** 1101 Officers' Row, tel. (360) 694-5252, features changing exhibitions of folk art from throughout the Northwest. Grant was stationed at the fort as a quartermaster in the 1850s and visited this building many times, but he did not actually live here, since it was home to the fort's commanding officer at the time.

More History

The **Clark County Historical Museum,** 1511 Main St., tel. (360) 695-4681, is open Tues.-Sun. 1-5 p.m. Free exhibits include an 1890 country store, a 1900 doctor's office, Indian artifacts, and a railroad exhibit.

The **Covington House,** 4201 Main St., tel. (360) 695-6750, is one of the state's oldest log cabins. Built in 1848, it housed the area's first school. Open to the public Tuesday and Thursday 10 a.m.-4 p.m. June-Aug.; free. Another interesting building is the **St. James Church** at 12th and Washington Streets. Built in 1885, this was the first Gothic Revival style church in Washington and is home to the state's oldest Catholic congregation.

Exhibits at **Pearson Air Museum,** 1105 E. 5th St. (near Fort Vancouver), include two aircraft hangers filled with planes and exhibits, including a fully restored Curtiss Jenny and a Ryan PT-22.

Admission is $4 adults, $3 seniors, $1.50 ages 6-18, free for under age six; tel. (360) 694-7026. Hours are Tues.-Sun. 10-5 p.m. The adjacent Pearson Airfield is one of the oldest operating fields in the nation; its first landing was a dirigible that floated over from Portland in 1905, and the first plane arrived seven years later. This was also where the Russian trans-polar flight ended in 1937.

At the **Vancouver Fire Department Museum,** 900 W. Evergreen Blvd., tel. (360) 696-8166, visitors will find a restored 1934 fire engine and a collection of historic photos. Tours are given Mon.-Fri. 8 a.m.-5 p.m.

City Parks

The wide, paved **Columbia River Waterfront Trail** follows the shore eastward for 3.5 miles from downtown to Tidewater Cove. It's a wonderful place for a sunset stroll or bike ride.

Old Apple Tree Park, along the river just east of I-5, honors what is believed to be the oldest apple tree in the Northwest. The tree was planted in 1826, when Fort Vancouver was a Hudson's Bay Co. trading center, and it still bears small green apples each summer.

Marine Park occupies the site of the Kaiser Shipyards, where more than 140 ships were hurriedly constructed during WW II by "Rosie the Riveter." Today you can climb a three-story **riverside tower** next to Kaiser Center for dramatic views of Vancouver and Portland. Also in the park is the new **Water Resources Education Center,** 4600 S.E. Columbia Way, tel. (360) 696-8478; open Mon.-Sat. 9 a.m.-5 p.m.; free. The center houses hands-on exhibits, a video theater, and a 350-gallon aquarium filled with Columbia River creatures. Not far away is the **Chkalov Monument,** commemorating the Soviet transpolar flight of 1937, when three Russian aviators were the first to cross over the pole to America.

Shady **Esther Short Park,** at W. 6th and Esther, contains the historic Slocum House (see "The Arts," below), along with a Victorian rose garden, 1917 steam locomotive, playground, and a monument to pioneer women. It is named for the wife of an early settler who jumped another settler's claim and later murdered two of his supporters. Despite this (or perhaps because of it), Short's children gained legal title to the land.

Vancouver Lake Park, three miles west of downtown, is a local hot spot for both windsurfers and fishermen. The nearly 300-acre strip of land offers picnicking, swimming, and fishing, plus grassy and shady areas. It is also home to one of the largest great blue heron rookeries in the region, and bald eagles can be found roosting in the trees during the winter months. A favorite summer swimming beach (with lifeguards) is in a small lake at **Salmon Creek Park,** off N.W. 117th Street.

ACCOMMODATIONS AND CAMPGROUNDS

Dozens more motels and a hostel are available just across the river in Portland, Oregon. More distinctive accommodations can be found at **Vintage Inn B&B,** 310 W. 11th St., tel. (360) 693-6635 or (888) 693-6635, a 1903 craftsman style home furnished like a living museum. The four guest rooms share a bath, and a full breakfast is served. Kids are accepted; $75-85 s or d.

Campgrounds

The closest public campgrounds are **Paradise Point State Park,** 16 miles north on I-5 near Woodland, tel. (360) 263-2350, and **Battle Ground Lake State Park,** 20 miles northeast of town in Battle Ground, tel. (360) 687-4621.

Nearby private campgrounds include: **Jantzen Beach RV Park,** tel. (503) 289-7626 or (800) 443-7248, on Hayden Island, just south of Vancouver on I-5; **Vancouver RV Park,** 7603 N.E. 13th Ave., tel. (360) 695-1158; and **99 RV Park,** 1913 N.E. Leichner Rd. in Salmon Creek, tel. (360) 573-0351.

FOOD

Ask someone from Vancouver where to eat, and half the time you'll be steered across the bridge to Portland, where the abundance of great restaurants rivals Seattle's. But Vancouver does quite well for itself, with a number of quality restaurants covering the spectrum of tastes.

Breakfast and Lunch

One place wins hands-down on the Vancouver breakfast front: **Dulin's Village Cafe,** 1905

VANCOUVER MOTELS AND HOTELS

Accommodations are arranged from least to most expensive. Rates may be lower during the winter months.

BUDGET

Value Motel; 708 N.E. 78th St.; tel. (360) 574-2345; $21 s, $22 d shared bath and no phone; $34 s or d private bath and phone; marginal neighborhood, see rooms first

INEXPENSIVE

Fort Motel; 500 E. 13th St.; tel. (360) 694-3327; $37 s, $44 d

Sunnyside Motel; 12200 N.E. Hwy. 99, Salmon Creek; tel. (360) 573-4141; $38 s, $42 d; kitchenettes available

Riverside Motel; 4400 Lewis and Clark Hwy.; tel. (360) 693-3677; $38 s, $45 d

Vancouver Lodge; 601 Broadway; tel. (360) 693-3668; $42 s, $46 d; fridges and microwaves

Guest House Motel; 11504 N.E. 2nd St.; tel. (360) 254-4511; $45 s, $50 d

Salmon Creek Motel; 11901 N.E. Hwy. 99, Salmon Creek; tel. (360) 573-0751; $45-48 s, $50-56 d; kitchenettes available, AAA approved

Rodeway Inn Cascade Park; 221 N.E. Chkalov Dr.; tel. (360) 256-7044 or (800) 426-5110; $50-55 s, $55-60 d; indoor pool, jacuzzi, continental breakfast, airport shuttle, AAA approved

Travelodge; 11506 N.E. 3rd St.; tel. (360) 254-4000 or (888) 254-3900; $53 s, $57 d; indoor pool, jacuzzi, microwaves, fridges, continental breakfast, exercise facility, AAA approved

MODERATE

Best Western Ferryman's Inn; 7901 N.E. 6th Ave.; tel. (360) 574-2151 or (800) 528-1234; $54-59 s, $63-68 d; outdoor pool, jacuzzi, kitchenettes available, continental breakfast, AAA approved

Comfort Inn; 13207 N.E. 20th Ave., Salmon Creek; tel. (360) 574-6000 or (800) 221-2222; $55-60 s, $65-70 d; indoor pool, jacuzzi, exercise facility, continental breakfast, free airport shuttle, AAA approved

---

Main St., tel. (360) 737-9907, with great home fries, omelettes, and whole wheat pancakes. They're also popular at lunch with the downtown crowd.

Travelers can pretend they're in Seattle with an espresso and croissant at **Java House,** 210 W. Evergreen Blvd., tel. (360) 737-2925; or **Paradise Cafe,** 1304 Main St., tel. (360) 696-1612. Paradise also has a deli with fresh sandwiches. Another can't-go-wrong downtown lunch spot is **Andrew's Restaurant,** 611 W. 11th St., tel. (360) 693-3252.

American
The Holland Restaurant, on the corner of Main and McLoughlin, tel. (360) 694-7842, has been around since the 1930s and still serves reasonable all-American fare. It has a good salad and soup bar. Enjoy entrees of prime rib, seafood, steak, and chicken in a railroad diner car at **The Crossing,** 900 W. 7th St., tel. (360) 695-3374. **Clancy's Family Restaurant,** 9901 N.E. 7th Ave., tel. (360) 573-3474, has justly famous fish and chips, but also cranks out chicken fried steaks, burgers, and Mexican meals.

Italian and Pizza
Cafe Augustino's, 1109 Washington St., tel. (360) 750-1272, has Italian and continental cuisine, along with an extensive wine list. **Little Italy's Trattoria,** 901 Washington St., tel. (360) 737-2363, is another good place for Italian food and pizzas. Two recommended local pizza places are **Izzy's,** 1503 N.E. 78th St., tel. (360)

Holiday Inn Express; 9107 N.E. Vancouver Mall Dr., Orchards; tel. (360) 253-5000 or (800) 465-4329; $65 s, $70 d; indoor pool, jacuzzi, continental breakfast, AAA approved

Shilo Inn Downtown; 401 E. 13th St.; tel. (360) 696-0411 or (800) 222-2244; $65-99 s or d; outdoor pool, jacuzzi, sauna, continental breakfast, airport shuttle, AAA approved

Shilo Inn—Hazel Dell; 13206 N.E. Hwy. 99, Salmon Creek; tel. (360) 573-0511 or (800) 222-2244; $69-89 s or d; indoor pool, jacuzzi, steam room, sauna, continental breakfast, kitchenettes available, airport shuttle, AAA approved

Quality Inn; 7001 N.E. Hwy. 99; tel. (360) 696-0516 or (888) 696-0516; $70 s or d; outdoor pool, jacuzzi, continental breakfast, kitchenettes available, AAA approved

Comfort Suites; 4714 N.E. 94th Ave., Orchards; tel. (360) 253-3100 or (800) 221-2222; $71 s, $76 d; indoor pool, jacuzzi, continental breakfast, AAA approved

Phoenix Inn; 12712 S.E. 2nd Circle; tel. (360) 891-9777 or (888) 988-8100; $77 s, $77-82 d; indoor pool, jacuzzi, continental breakfast buffet, microwaves, fridges, AAA approved

EXPENSIVE

Doubletree Hotel at the Quay; 100 Columbia St.; tel. (360) 694-8341 or (800) 733-5466; $90 s, $100 d; overlooks Columbia River, outdoor pool, airport shuttle, AAA approved

Heathman Lodge; 7801 N.E. Greenwood Dr.; tel. (360) 254-3100 or (888) 475-3100; $109-119 s or d; new motel with spacious rooms, indoor pool, jacuzzi, sauna, exercise facility, microwaves, continental breakfast, AAA approved

PREMIUM

Residence Inn by Marriott; 8005 N.E. Parkway Dr., Orchards; tel. (360) 253-4800 or (800) 331-3131; $105-125 s, $125 d; apartment-style rooms with kitchens and fireplaces, outdoor pool, jacuzzi, continental breakfast, evening dessert, free newspaper, airport shuttle, AAA approved

Homewood Suites Hotel; 701 S.E. Columbia Shores Blvd.; tel. (360) 750-1100 or (800) 225-5466; $115 s or d; luxurious business hotel, suites with kitchens, outdoor pool, jacuzzi, fitness center, breakfast buffet, AAA approved

---

573-2962, or 7615 E. Mill Plain Blvd., tel. (360) 693-3228, with a big salad bar, and **Bortolami's Pizzaria,** 9901 N.E. 7th Ave., tel. (360) 574-2598, for the gourmet variety and a choice of microbrews on tap. Great pizza by the slice and sub sandwiches from **New York Richies,** 8086 E. Mill Plain Blvd., tel. (360) 696-4001.

Other International
For south-of-the border meals served north of the border, head to **Casa Grande,** 2014 Main, tel. (360) 694-7031; with a big choice of vegetarian entrees, or **Salsa Mexican Restaurant,** 5406A E. 4th Plain Blvd., tel. (360) 693-3102. **Phoenicia Restaurant,** 14415 S.E. Mill Plain Blvd., tel. (360) 253-4789, has distinctive Lebanese meals.

For an authentic taste of Asia, head to **Thai Little Home,** 3214 E. 4th Plain Blvd., tel. (360) 693-4061, for Thai cooking; **Oriental Fast Bowl,** 905 Main St., tel. (360) 737-2730, for quick Japanese meals; or **Fa Fa Gourmet Restaurant,** 11712 N.E. 4th Plain Blvd. (Orchards), tel. (360) 260-1378, for surprisingly good Chinese meals.

Eats with a View
Several waterside restaurants are popular for sunny lunches and sunset dinners on the patio. Enjoy the Columbia River view from **Beaches Restaurant & Bar,** 1919 S.E. Columbia River Dr., tel. (360) 699-1592, a fun place with tasty appetizers, a diverse menu, and a hopping bar. Also facing the river are **Who-Song and Larry's**

Cantina, 111 E. Columbia Way, tel. (360) 695-1198, where the singing waiters are a local phenomenon; and The Chart House, 101 E. Columbia Way, tel. (360) 693-9211, with steak, seafood, prime rib, an oyster bar, and a good wine list.

Northwest Cuisine and Beyond

Enjoy delicious homemade lunches and dinners (pastas, salads, soups, and seafood) in an elegant historic setting at Sheldon's Cafe at the Grant House, 1101 Officers' Row, tel. (360) 699-1213. Also open for Sunday brunch.

Hidden House was built in 1885 for a prominent Vancouver citizen, Lowell M. Hidden. Hidden House Restaurant, 100 W. 13th St., tel. (360) 696-2847, still retains the original brick exterior, stained glass, shutters, and woodwork—but now it offers an eclectic and rather pricey lunch and dinner menu that changes throughout the year. The family continues to manufacture the bricks found in many local homes and businesses at Hidden Brick Co. on Kauffman Avenue.

Brewpubs

Hazel Dell Brew Pub, 8513 N.E. Hwy. 99, tel. (360) 576-0996, serves pub meals, including fish and chips, burgers, and pasta in a lively, noisy setting to accompany their 10 different brewed-on-the-premises beers. McMenamins of the Columbia Brew Pub, tel. (360) 699-1521, is next to the river on Hidden Way just east of Marine Park.

Bakeries, Produce, and Markets

MaMa's Bake Shop, 5411 Mill Plain Blvd., tel. (360) 735-7555, is more than a bakery. The cafe has many kinds of pancakes for breakfast, Italian cuisine for dinner, and wonderful desserts all the time.

The Vancouver Farmers Market, tel. (360) 737-8298, takes place at 5th and Broadway Streets on Saturday 9 a.m.-3 p.m., April-Oct.; tel. (360) 737-8298. It's a great place to look for local produce, herbs, arts and crafts, baked goods, and entertainment.

Nature's Marketplace, 8024 E. Mill Plain Blvd., tel. (306) 695-8878, is a standout upscale grocery store, with organic (and nonorganic) produce, their own cooking school, and a cafe/deli

that makes healthy fast food, including pizzas, sandwiches, stirfrys, burgers, and pastas.

EVENTS AND ENTERTAINMENT

Festivals

Fort Vancouver Days, the big July Fourth weekend celebration, has historic tours of the fort, a chili cook-off, golf tournament, rodeo, jazz concert, food, crafts, and the largest fireworks display west of the Mississippi. Call (360) 693-5481 for details of this year's activities.

In July, the Fort Vancouver Brigade Encampment fills the fort with trappers and traders dressed in 1840 period costumes. There are tepees, baking and cooking demonstrations, tomahawk throwing, and other demonstrations. Call (360) 696-7655.

In early October, don't miss the Fort Vancouver Candlelight Tours with interpreters dressed in 1840s period clothing. The Christmas Parade of Boats is a favorite event, with decorated vessels plying the Columbia and Willamette Rivers on the second and third weeks of December. You'll also find Officers' Row decorated with traditional evergreens for the holidays, plus concerts and carriage rides to get you in the spirit of the holidays.

The Arts

At 400 W. Evergreen Blvd., the Columbia Arts Center offers a year-round schedule of theatrical productions, dance troops, art shows, and concerts in a 1911 church. For information, call (360) 693-0350.

Listed on the National Register of Historic Homes, the 60-seat Slocum House Theater was built in 1867 and moved to Esther Short Park at W. 6th and Esther in 1966. The theater stages productions year-round; call (360) 694-8383 for tickets. Free Six to Sunset summer concerts take place in the Waterworks Park amphitheater on the corner of 4th Plain Blvd. and Ft. Vancouver Way.

Since hopping Portland is just a short drive away, you won't find a lot on Vancouver's live music scene. To see who has something going on in town, take a gander at the Friday entertainment section of the Portland newspaper.

SHOPPING

The two-level **Vancouver Mall** has over 115 shops, restaurants, and services, including five major department stores—JCPenney, Nordstrom, Mervyn's, Sears, and Meier & Frank—at the junction of I-205 and Hwy. 500. One of the largest malls in the Portland/Vancouver area is the jazzy **Jantzen Beach Center** on Hayden Island in the Columbia River. Included is a big **REI** store, where you'll find quality outdoors gear and all sorts of special events. And while you're crossing the bridge, keep going to downtown Portland, where you'll find **Powell's,** one of the largest and best bookstores this side of the Mississippi.

INFORMATION AND SERVICES

For maps or other information, visit the **Washington State Visitor Information Center** at 404 E. 15th St. (left off the I-5 Mill Plains exit 1D), tel. (360) 694-2588 or (800) 377-7084. Open Mon.-Fri. 8 a.m.-5 p.m., and Sat.-Sun. 8:30 a.m.-5 p.m. all year, and on the Web at www.vancouverusa.com.

The **Gifford Pinchot National Forest Supervisor's Office** is in Vancouver at 10600 N.E. 51st Circle (Orchards), tel. (360) 891-5000. Open Mon.-Fri. 8 a.m.-4:30 p.m. Stop by for details on Mt. St. Helens and other nearby outdoor attractions, or call (360) 891-5009 for recorded recreation info. Ask here for directions to the **Wind River Canopy Crane,** a 245-foot research crane that allows scientists access to treetops. It's one of just two in the world. By the way, Pinchot is pronounced "PINCH-oh"; Gifford Pinchot was the founder of the U.S. Forest Service.

Swim at the indoor pool at **Marshall Community Center,** 1009 E. McLoughlin Blvd., tel. (360) 693-7946.

For the full scoop on Vancouver's big sister city of Portland, see *Oregon Handbook* by Stuart Warren and Ted Long Ishikawa (Moon Publications).

TRANSPORTATION

The local transit system is **C-TRAN,** tel. (360) 695-0123, which provides daily service throughout Clark County as well as to downtown Portland. Free shuttle buses operate downtown and to Officers' Row at Fort Vancouver.

For cross-country trips, contact **Greyhound,** 615 Main St., tel. (360) 696-0186 or (800) 231-2222.

Amtrak trains stop at a classic early 1900s depot at the foot of W. 11th St., with daily connections north and south on the Coast Starlight, and eastward up the Columbia River aboard the Empire Builder. Call (360) 694-7307 or (800) 872-7245 for specifics.

For air service, head south across the Columbia River to **Portland International Airport.**

THE COLUMBIA GORGE

This stretch of the Columbia River is one of the truly special places for both Washington and Oregon. No matter the season, no matter the weather conditions, the gorge is always beautiful. And you have a choice of highway types. The Oregon side has I-94 roaring along its full length at river level for the gotta-get-there crowd, and the restored Columbia River Highway that was carved from the mountains à la roads in Switzerland. Across on the Washington side (which is where we're supposed to be, anyway) is Hwy. 14, a combination country road and highway that tends to follow the contours of the land rather than burrowing and bulldozing along a surveyor's line. On the western end, the Lewis and Clark Highway (Hwy. 14) winds through maple and Douglas fir forests punctuated by periodic vistas into the river valley far below.

The only sea level route through the Cascades, the Columbia has been an important migration route for centuries. Driving this route is a geology, meteorology, and botany course combined with a drive through great beauty. The scenery takes a dramatic turn, from the green forested hills of the western section to the dry basaltic and barren hills of the eastern half. In a distance of just 40 miles—from Cascade Locks to The Dalles—average annual rainfall changes by 40 inches! The gorge has its own climate, and temperature extremes on the east side range from zero or less in winter to 110° F of dry heat in summer. This often means the gorge has one set of conditions while over the hill is another kind of weather. It isn't unusual to descend into the gorge and into a gale because this narrow gap is the only place weather systems can get through the mountains rather than over them. Sometimes in the winter a sudden Arctic blast comes down the gorge to create an ice storm, which is locally called a "silver thaw."

The gorge between Hwy. 97 and I-5 is heavily traveled on both sides of the river, but the area from Hwy. 97 at Maryhill Museum east to Paterson is the least traveled stretch of the gorge and signs alert you to its lack of facilities. The description below follows the river up from Vancouver to McNary Dam, where the highway heads away from the river and north to the Tri-Cities area.

For more on the equally interesting Oregon side of the gorge, including such famous sights as Vista House and Multnomah Falls, see **Oregon Handbook** by Stuart Warren and Ted Long Ishikawa (Moon Publications). Another good source for information is the **Columbia Gorge Visitors Association,** in The Dalles at tel. (800) 984-6743, or on the Web at www.gorge.net/crgva.

HISTORY

When Capt. George Vancouver's 1792 expedition sailed up the Northwest coast, they must have been napping as they passed the Columbia River—George never saw it. That same year, American trading captain Robert Gray discovered this great river on his journey to become the first American to sail around the world. Gray claimed the river and its huge drainage area for the U.S., naming the river after his ship, the *Columbia Rediviva,* "Columbus lives again." After Gray's discovery, Vancouver sent William Broughton out to explore the upriver territory; Broughton asserted that Gray hadn't found the true channel, and claimed the river for England. Canadian traders searched western Canada for the Columbia's source. Finally, in 1811, David Thompson found it and canoed to the confluence of the Snake and Columbia where he erected a sign, stating, in part, "Know thereby that this country is claimed by Great Britain." The conflicting claims weren't settled until the U.S.-Canada boundary treaty of 1846.

Lewis and Clark Expedition
The most famous Columbia River explorers were Meriwether Lewis and William Clark. Selected by

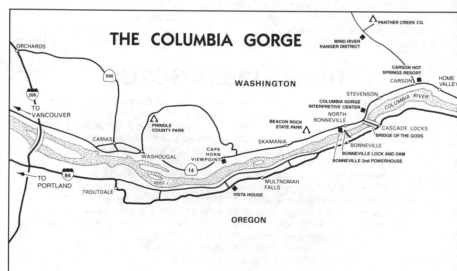

Thomas Jefferson in 1803 to lead an expedition from St. Louis to the Pacific Coast, they were to keep extensive logs of the flora, fauna, and geography of this unknown territory, and to establish friendly relations with the area's Indians. The 28 members of the expedition, accompanied by an Army detachment, set out on May 13, 1804 in several canoes and a 55-foot barge powered by 22 oars and men towing it along the bank. When they ran out of river, the party of 28 got horses from the Indians and headed for the mountains, where they nearly starved to death. The Plateau Indians helped them find the Columbia River, where they built canoes and paddled downstream, arriving at Fort Clatsop on the Pacific Coast in late November 1805. Upon his arrival, Clark wrote in his journal: "I beheld the grandest and most pleasing prospects which my eyes ever surveyed . . . a boundless ocean . . . raging with immense waves and breaking with great force from the rocks."

Northwesterners won't be surprised to hear that Lewis and Clark recorded 31 consecutive days of rain during their visit to the Northwest! In March 1806, the party headed home. After a two-year absence, many had given them up for dead, but only one member of the party died en route, apparently of a ruptured appendix.

The Great Migration
Following the Lewis and Clark expedition, American interest in the "Oregon Country" began to rise, led first by fur trappers, and then by missionaries. The turning point came in 1843, when the Applegate Wagon Train left Independence, Missouri, with 1,000 people, 120 wagons, and 5,000 head of livestock. It was the largest wagon train ever assembled. Under the leadership of Dr. Marcus Whitman—a missionary who had come west in 1836, and guided by mountain man Bill Sublette, they made it all the way to the Columbia and Willamette Rivers by September. It had taken six long months to travel the 2,000 miles, but they had shown that the "Oregon Trail" route was feasible. The gates of history had been cracked open, and they could never be closed again. Soon, the trickle westward turned into a flood tide.

Americans emigrated west for a number of reasons: for the free and productive lands in Oregon and California, to escape a severe economic depression in the East, to get out of the crowded and polluted cities, to find religious freedom in Utah, to search for gold in the mountains of California, or simply to join in a great adventure in a new and undiscovered land. Most travelers tried to depart Independence or St. Joseph, Missouri, in the spring, leaving as soon as the grass

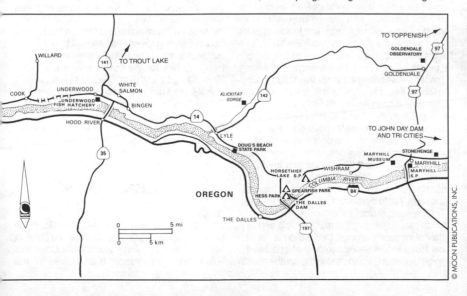

© MOON PUBLICATIONS, INC.

Columbia Gorge

DIANNE BOUERICE LYONS

would support their stock. Typically, each evening found the emigrant just 15 miles farther down the trail, and it generally took five or six months to travel from Missouri to Oregon or California. They had to be over the mountains before the first snows of winter struck, and those who erred—such as the infamous Donner Party of 1846—paid a high price.

Perhaps a tenth of the people who set out on the Oregon Trail never made it to their destination. Many died from diseases such as cholera, or from accidents and drownings; others were killed by early winter storms and Indian attacks. Few of the graves are marked. By 1870, perhaps 350,000 people had traveled the Oregon Trail by wagon train, stagecoach, horseback, and foot—over one percent of the nation's population at that time. It was the greatest peacetime migration in America's history.

The Columbia River Gorge lay near the end of the journey for emigrants heading west on the Oregon Trail, the last major obstacle along the way. The narrow confines of the gorge forced them to dismantle their wagons and load them onto log rafts to float down the gorge as far as the Cascades, which they portaged before continuing by raft to the area of present-day Portland. Treacherous rapids, strong currents, and high winds caused the death of many people almost in sight of the promised land. Completion of the Barlow Road in 1846—a toll route that avoided the gorge by heading south around the south shoulder

of Mt. Hood—provided a difficult but safer alternative path to the Willamette Valley. It cost pioneers an exorbitant $5 a wagon and 10 cents a head for cattle and livestock to use the road.

The Gorge Today
In 1986, President Reagan signed into law a measure that established the **Columbia River Gorge National Scenic Area,** encompassing 292,000 acres on both sides of the river from Washougal to Maryhill. The national scenic area is managed jointly by the U.S. Forest Service, the states of Washington and Oregon, and the six local counties involved in an attempt to protect the rich scenic and recreational values of the gorge. Headquarters for the scenic area are in Hood River, Oregon; call (541) 386-2333 for details.

A fee of $3 per vehicle per day is charged at all Forest Service trailheads in the scenic area. A better option is to purchase an annual Trail Park Pass ($25) that is valid for most national forest trailheads in Washington and Oregon. Get one from any Forest Service office.

TRANSPORTATION

By Car
While the trip along Highway 14 does offer some beautiful Gorge scenery, by the time you arrive at Maryhill Museum you'll realize this Columbia River trek is a lot longer than it looks on the

map—especially if your destination is Tri-Cities, more than 200 miles from Camas. The crowds at Maryhill probably have less to do with art appreciation than with sore fannies. This is truly a remote part of the state, so stock up on Cokes, chips, or whatever gets you through the drive.

Scenic Cruises

Take a cruise on the Columbia, with views of steep basalt cliffs and stops at Cascade Locks, Bonneville Dam, and Stevenson, aboard the sternwheeler *Columbia Gorge,* tel. (503) 223-3928. Their standard two-hour cruises ($13) start at Oregon's Cascade Locks, just across the river on the Bridge of the Gods, and are available daily from mid-June to mid-October.

Cruise West, tel. (800) 888-9378, takes you on up the Columbia aboard three small cruise ships. These 1,000-mile trips leave from Portland and head upriver through locks all the way to the Idaho border and back. Seven-night trips start at $925 pp, all inclusive, and are offered April, May, September, and October.

Special Expeditions' twin ships *Sea Bird* and *Sea Lion* make weeklong cruises on the river, departing Portland in the spring and fall. For information call (800) 762-0003. The cost is $2,100-3,280 pp double occupancy.

Train Service

Amtrak, tel. (800) 872-7245, has service up the Columbia Gorge, departing from Portland or Vancouver and stopping at Bingen/White Salmon and Wishram before continuing to Pasco, Spokane, and points east.

By Bus

Bus service to these parts is close to nonexistent: Vancouver's **C-TRAN,** tel. (360) 695-0123, will get you as far east as Camas and Washougal. Cross over to the Oregon side for Greyhound bus service along I-84. **Columbia River Gorge Tours,** tel. (800) 886-4416, leaves Portland or Vancouver on day tours of the Columbia River Gorge by van or helicopter.

CAMAS AND WASHOUGAL AREA

It's pretty easy to see—and smell—what makes Camas (pop. 8,800) tick; the enormous James River Corporation paper mill dominates the center of town. Established in 1883 to provide newsprint for the Portland newspaper, *The Oregonian,* the mill was the first to operate in Washington Territory. Tours of the paper mill are offered in the summer; call (360) 834-8118, and bring your face mask. Camas itself is an attractive town right along the Columbia, with big trees lining the main route.

The town of Washougal (pop. 7,300), just a couple miles east of Camas on Hwy. 14, was the first place settled by American pioneers in what would become Washington. David C. Parker and his family arrived here in 1844 and built a small dock on the river. Thirty eight years earlier, the Lewis and Clark Expedition had camped near here on their return trip up the Columbia River.

Washougal's claim to fame is the **Pendleton Woolen Mill,** in operation since 1912 and still producing their acclaimed woolen products. The mill at 17th and A streets is open for hour-long guided tours (no cameras) Mon.-Fri. at 9, 10, and 11 a.m. and 1:30 p.m.; tel. (360) 835-2131 or (800) 568-2480. An outlet store here sells seconds and overstocked items.

Sights and Recreation

The **Two Rivers Heritage Museum,** Front and 16th Streets in Washougal, tel. (360) 835-8742, has local historical artifacts and photos; open Tues.-Sat. 11 a.m.-3 p.m. all year. Entrance is $2 adults, $1 seniors, 50 cents ages 6-18, free for under six, and $5 for families. A fine walking path along the Columbia River levee leaves from Steamboat Landing Park in Washougal.

The **Rocket City Neon Museum,** 1554 N.E. 3rd Ave. in Camas, tel. (360) 834-6366, is one of the more unusual museums in Washington, with hundreds of neon signs, some more than 50 years old.

On Hwy. 14 between Washougal and North Bonneville, the **Cape Horn Viewpoint** provides a good spot for photographing the dramatic west entrance to the Gorge and for viewing massive Beacon Rock. For a short and scenic side trip, take Cape Horn Dr. downhill to the river, through overhanging maples and Douglas fir trees.

Raft the class-II and III Washougal River with **Renegade River Rafters,** tel. (509) 427-7248 or (360) 837-3470. They offer three- to four-hour trips for $60 including lunch, as well as kayak and overnight river trips.

Practicalities

Stay at **Economy Lodge Motel,** 544 6th St. in Washougal, tel. (360) 835-8591, for $44 s or $56 d, including an outdoor pool;

Publisher's Cafe, 2131 B St. in Washougal, tel. (360) 835-7637, is the standout on the restaurant scene, attracting folks from Portland for "nostalgic cuisine" such as roast pork loin, homemade soups and breads, and fresh-baked lemon meringue pies. Nothing fake here, just great home cooking for lunch and dinner. Also of note is **2nd Ave. Diner,** 3519 S.E. 2nd Ave. in Camas, tel. (360) 835-7752, with 1950s-style burgers and thick shakes.

Camas Days in late July includes a parade, street dance, live entertainment, craft and food booths, and a carnival.

Find the **Camas-Washougal Chamber of Commerce** at 422 N.E. 4th Ave. in Camas, tel. (360) 834-2472. Open Mon.-Fri. 9 a.m.-5 p.m. all year. Camas also has a summer-only outdoor **swimming pool** at 120 N.E. 17th, tel. (360) 834-2382.

BEACON ROCK STATE PARK

Beacon Rock State Park, tel. (509) 427-8265, is 35 miles east of Vancouver on Hwy. 14, and just west of the little town of North Bonneville. The core of an ancient volcano, 848-foot-high Beacon Rock is the largest such monolith in North America and the second largest in the world (after Gibraltar). The rock was named by Lewis and Clark in 1805. It was a "beacon" informing river travelers that there were no further obstructions in the river from here to the Pacific Ocean, 150 miles away! Henry J. Biddle bought the rock in 1915 to preserve it and spent two years blazing the 4,500-foot trail to the summit; his heirs donated the rock to the state in 1935.

Hike Biddle's steep one-mile trail for spectacular views of the Gorge; the trail boasts a 15% grade, but handrails make the hiking both easier and safer. This and other trails provide 14 miles of hiking in the park. Advanced climbers only may attempt to climb on the south side of the rock, but it is closed part of the year to protect nesting hawks; register at the trailhead. The main part of the park is north of the highway, and old roads are perfect for mountain biking and horseback riding. A four-mile trail switchbacks to the 1,200-foot summit of **Hamilton Mountain,** passing the very scenic Rodney Falls. Fishermen can launch their boats from the boat ramp to catch Columbia River white sturgeon, and campers can stay in the densely forested sites (no RV hookups) for $10. The campground is open April-October. A smaller state park campground below the noisy railroad tracks along the river is open all year, but you'll need to take showers at the nearby private Beacon Rock RV Park, tel. (360) 427-8473.

BONNEVILLE DAM AREA

Bonneville Dam snakes across the Columbia in three sections, connecting dot-to-dot between the shorelines and Bradford and Cascades Islands. This was the site of the famous Columbia River Cascades that made travel down the river so treacherous for Oregon Trail emigrants. An Army base, **Fort Cascades,** was constructed on the Washington side of the Cascades in the early 1850s, and remained in use until 1861, after the Indians of the region had been forcibly moved onto reservations. A small settlement grew up around the Cascades, providing a railroad portage until the opening of the Cascades Canal and Locks in 1896 made it possible for ships to pass freely around the falls. Today the old Fort Cascades site has an interesting 1.5 mile loop path with interpretive signs describing the area's rich history.

Bonneville Dam

The original Bonneville dam and power plant were built here between 1933 and 1937; a second plant was added on the Washington shore that opened in 1981. Together they produce over a million kilowatts of power that feed into a grid for the Northwest and California.

Visit the **Bonneville Second Powerhouse** visitor center, on the Washington side of the Bonneville Dam, to see the inner workings of the powerhouse (including a peek inside a spinning turbine), and informative displays. You'll feel dwarfed by the enormity of the river, dam, and surrounding hills. Windows offer a chance to watch coho, sockeye, and king salmon, along with steelhead, shad, lamprey, and other fish as they head upstream each summer and fall. Only a quarter of the salmon that historically negotiated the Columbia River to spawn still do so. Massive dams such as these, upstream developments, changing ocean currents, and overfishing have all contributed to their decline. The visitor center, tel. (509) 427-4281, is open daily 8 a.m.-6 p.m. in summer, and daily 9 a.m.-5 p.m. the rest of the year.

Cross "The Bridge of the Gods" (75 cents toll) into Oregon and visit the original **Bonneville Lock and Dam,** a popular tourist spot with continuous presentations, exhibits, and another fisheye view of the Columbia's inhabitants as they head up the fishpass. The **Bradford Island Visitor Center** here has hourly movies and dam tours in the summer; in the winter they offer movies on request but no tours. You can also watch migrating fish at the fish ladder on Bradford Island. Open daily 9 a.m.-5 p.m. all year, tel. (541) 374-8820. The adjacent **Bonneville Fish Hatchery** has informative displays and ponds filled with fat rainbow trout and a half-dozen massive white sturgeon looking quite unhappy in their small pool. Just across I-84 is the trail to scenic Wahclella Falls, one of many waterfalls that line the Oregon side of the Columbia River. Stop by the locks to watch ships and barges heading through or to watch Indian fishermen dipnetting salmon from rickety wooden platforms in the summer.

Bridge of the Gods

According to Indian legend, a stone arch once spanned the river at the Cascades, allowing people to move freely across the river. There are different versions of the tale, but each of them involves two brothers feuding over a beautiful young woman. The Great Spirit had built the bridge to promote peace in the land, and when he saw the fighting, he shook the ground and caused the stone bridge to collapse. An old woman tried in vain to stop the fighting, and the Great Spirit rewarded her by making her young again. The various participants became the still-feuding volcanic peaks that dot this region and periodically hurl rocks at one another—Mt.

Adams and Mt. Hood are the brothers, Squaw Mountain is the young woman they fought over, and Mt. St. Helens is the old woman turned young maiden.

Interestingly, geologists believe that the Cascades were indeed a crossing point at one time. Approximately 750 years ago a great earthquake triggered the collapse of a mountain on the Washington side of the river, blocking the Columbia River and creating a 270-foot high dam that held the water back for several years. Eventually, water topped the dam and washed most of the landslide away, but it left behind the rocky islands that created the Cascades. The turbulent water that in this stretch made for treacherous river travel until the creation of the Cascade Locks in 1896. You can see these locks, no longer in use, at **Cascade Locks Marine Park,** on the Oregon side of the river. A small museum here relates Columbia River history and includes the Northwest's first steam locomotive.

In 1926, the modern version of the legendary rock span was constructed at the site of the former Cascade Rapids. The "Bridge of the Gods" had to be raised 44 feet following construction of the Bonneville Dam in 1938. Today it provides a link across the Columbia to the Oregon side of Bonneville Dam (described above) and to the town of Cascade Locks, where you can catch the sternwheeler *Columbia Gorge* for a two-hour cruise up the river (see "Transportation," above). The **Pacific Crest National Scenic Trail** crosses the Columbia River along the Bridge of the Gods, heading north from here through Indian Heaven, Mt. Adams, and Goat Rocks wilderness areas—some of Washington's most scenic and middle-of-nowhere real estate—on its way to the Canadian border.

STEVENSON

The small town of Stevenson (pop. 1,150) has been the governmental seat for Skamania County since 1893—when the county records were stolen from nearby Cascades, transforming Stevenson overnight into the new county seat—but is only now starting to come into its own, with a sparkling new museum, one of the fanciest lodges in Washington, and hordes of summertime windsurfers. Over in **Rock Creek Park,** on the west side of town, you'll find a Corliss steam engine and an old Spokane, Portland, and Seattle Railway caboose.

Columbia Gorge Interpretive Center

Located a mile west of Stevenson, this award-winning museum looks across Rock Creek Cove to the mighty Columbia River. The interior of the main room is built around a tall simulated basalt cliff, with its crevices filled by Indian and pioneer artifacts. Wander through the museum to discover the area's rich human and natural history. Step into the theater to take a visual trip through the cataclysmic events that created the gorge. Museum exhibits include a 37-foot high fishwheel, a restored Corliss steam engine that once powered a sawmill, and Indian artifacts. Another section introduces you to the spiritual side of the Columbia Gorge. A Russian refugee and member of the Imperial family, Baron Eugene Fersen, claimed that the Gorge was a spiritual vortex. His objets d'art and furniture are housed here, along with the world's largest collection of rosaries—nearly 4,000—gathered from around the world and fashioned from a variety of materials. Special exhibits change frequently, and a museum store features the works of local artisans. Located at 990 S.W. Rock Creek Dr., the museum is open daily 10 a.m.-5 p.m. all year (except Thanksgiving, Christmas, and New Year's). Admission is $6 adults, $5 seniors, $4 ages 6-12, and free for kids under six. Call (509) 427-8211 or (800) 991-2338 for more information.

Lodging

The **Skamania Lodge,** 1131 S.W. Skamania Lodge Dr., tel. (509) 427-7700 or (800) 221-7117—the finest luxury resort in the gorge—has an indoor pool, sauna, jacuzzis, fitness center, tennis courts, 18-hole golf course, hiking trails, and convention facilities. Although newly built, the lodge has a classic feeling, and its tall windows face the Columbia River. Inside is a small Forest Service **information center** and bookshop, tel. (509) 427-2528, open daily 9 a.m.-5 p.m. year-round. They also have guest speakers each spring and fall. Rates are $145-255 s or d.

The Timbers, tel. (509) 427-5656, has modern log cabins along the Columbia River near Stevenson. No phones or TVs, but each has a kitchen, back deck, and access to the hot tub; $125-215 d.

Econo Lodge, tel. (509) 427-5628 or (800) 424-4777, has standard rooms for $45-55 s or $50-60 d.

Campgrounds

Camp west of town at **Beacon Rock State Park,** tel. (509) 427-8265, for $10 (described above, no RV hookups).

Park RVs at **Lewis & Clark RV Park** in North Bonneville, tel. (509) 427-5982; **NW Guide Service** in Skamania, tel. (509) 427-4625; or **Beacon Rock RV Park** in Skamania, tel. (509) 427-8473.

Food

The Crossing Cafe, tel. (509) 427-8097, has homemade soups, deli sandwiches, and various lunch specials. This is a good place to meet hard-core "boardheads;" the shop may be closed when the windsurfing is great. Get very good brewpub fare and microbrews on tap at the friendly and smoke-free **Big River Grill,** tel. (509) 427-4888. They brew their own beer on the premises, and always have a good mix of old standbys such as steaks, pork chops, and meatloaf, along with lighter fare such as pasta primavera and chicken Caesar salads. **El Rio,** tel. (509) 427-4479, has authentic Mexican cuisine to eat in or carry out; open summers only.

Skamania Lodge, described above, serves gourmet Northwest cuisine three meals a day in an elaborate and busy setting. Be ready to drop $40 or more for dinner; reservations recommended. Their Sunday brunch is especially popular.

Recreation

Rent sailboards, kayaks, canoes, snowshoes, climbing gear, and mountain bikes from **Waterwalker,** tel. (509) 427-2727. They also offer sailboard lessons most summer afternoons. Skamania Lodge, tel. (509) 427-7700 or (800) 221-7117, also rents mountain bikes.

Events

July Fourth brings the usual fireworks, picnics, and concessions to Skamania County; the best way to see the fireworks is aboard the sternwheeler *Columbia Gorge,* (described above) which offers a special tour. In late July, the **Columbia Gorge Bluegrass Festival** brings footstompin' music and plenty of food all day long at the Rock Creek Fairgrounds. The annual **Skamania County Fair and Timber Carnival,** held the fourth weekend in August, offers entertainment, a parade, timber contests, exhibits, and food.

Information

The **Stevenson Chamber of Commerce and Visitor Information Center,** 167 N.W. 2nd, tel. (509) 427-8911 or (800) 989-9178, is the place to go for the scoop on Stevenson. Hours are daily 8 a.m.-5 p.m. in the summer; and Mon.-Fri. 8 a.m.-5 p.m. in the winter.

CARSON AREA

Just a few miles east of Stevenson is minuscule Carson, known for its hot springs and as an entry point into Gifford Pinchot National Forest. The drive north from Carson to the east side of Mt. St. Helens provides ample photographic and recreational opportunities.

Carson Hot Springs

Historic Carson Hot Springs Resort, tel. (509) 427-8292 or (800) 607-3678, has been drawing visitors to its 126° F natural mineral baths since the springs were discovered in 1876. At that time, the baths were seen as a cure for everything from arthritis to kidney disorders. The St. Martin Hotel was built here in 1897 to replace the tents that had accommodated the droves of guests; cabins were added in the 1920s. Today you can stay in the same aging and rather funky lodgings—and enjoy the same relaxing bath plus a massage—with no TVs or radios to distract. The resort attracts visitors from all over the globe. Hot mineral baths ($10), one-hour massages ($40), and facials ($32) are all available. The restaurant serves three old-fashioned meals daily. Both the hotel rooms ($43 d) and basic cabins ($60 d), have 1950s-vintage furnishings in shoddy condition. Somewhat nicer is the hot tub suite ($80 d). Reserve early if you plan to stay at Carson Hot Springs on a weekend.

Hiking

Several day-hikes are possible nearby, including the Bob Kuse Memorial Trail to the 1,000-foot summit of **Wind Mountain,** a three mile hike that provides dramatic views over the Columbia Gorge. The trailhead is a mile up Wind Mountain Rd. on the east side.

For a good view of the area's peaks, take a short hike to the top of **Little Huckleberry Mountain,** best hiked mid-July to October. Take Forest Service Rd. 66 (along the east edge of the lava bed) to the 49 trailhead; climb the steep grade for 2.5 miles to the summit and a refreshing berry break.

A fee of $3 per vehicle per day is charged at all National Forest trailheads. A better bet is the $25 annual Trail Park Pass that can be used on most Washington national forests. Get one from the Forest Service office near Carson.

Lava Beds

The **Big Lava Bed Geologic Area** encompasses 12,500 acres of lava beds (remains of an ancient volcano). In the north section of the beds, the crater—now covered by trees—rises 800 feet. Inside, the walls slope down almost to lava-bed level and a small meadow covers the bottom of the bowl. Another visually interesting feature is the 100-foot-deep trough or sink of unknown geologic origin, northeast of the crater. When exploring the lava beds, be sure to bring your own water; by mid-June all the creeks are dry. Be careful in your wanderings since there are no trails or landmarks to follow. Get here by heading north up Cook-Underwood Rd. from the town of Cook, eight miles east of Carson on Hwy. 14. It turns into South Prairie Rd. (Forest Rd. 66) after several miles and continues to the lava beds, approximately 14 miles up. The road follows the east side of the lava for the next 10 miles or so.

Lodging and Camping

Carson Hot Springs Resort is described above. **Wind River Motel,** tel. (509) 427-7777, has cottages with kitchens for $45-65 s or d.

Several Forest Service campgrounds are north of Carson off Wind River Road. Closest is **Panther Creek Campground,** nine miles up Wind River Rd., and 1.5 miles up Forest Service Rd. 6517. The campground is open mid-

May to mid-November. **Beaver Campground** is 12 miles up Wind River Rd.; open mid-April through October. **Paradise Creek Campground** is 21 miles up Wind River Rd., and another six miles on Forest Rd. 30; it's open mid-May to mid-November. All three of these charge $13; make reservations ($9 extra) by calling (877) 444-6777.

More camping is available at **Big Cedars County Park** north of Willard on Oklahoma Rd. and **Home Valley County Park,** tel. (509) 427-9478. RVers can park at **Carson Hot Springs Resort,** tel. (509) 427-8292; **Bigfoot RV Park,** tel. (509) 427-4441; **Wind River Motel,** tel. (509) 427-7777; or **Valley Grocery** in Home Valley, tel. (509) 427-5300.

Events and Information

Bigfoot Daze on the fourth weekend of August features talks on Bigfoot, live entertainment and other activities.

The Gifford Pinchot National Forest's **Wind River Ranger Station** office is north of Carson, with information on local hikes, including the nearby Pacific Crest Trail. Open Mon.-Fri. 8 a.m.-4:30 p.m. all year; tel. (509) 427-3200.

WHITE SALMON AND BINGEN AREA

Continuing eastward from Carson and Home Valley, the highway passes the trailhead ($3 parking fee) for **Dog Mountain Trail,** a rugged, switchback-filled 3.5 mile climb to the summit of this 2,900-foot peak. This is a good chance to stretch your legs and enjoy wildflower-filled meadows in spring. Beyond here Hwy. 14 parallels an old log flume. For decades the Broughton Lumber Co. timbered in the mountains north of here, sending their logs to the riverside mill on this nine-mile flume. The mill has been closed for several years, and the old flume is slowly rotting away. Between the don't-blink-or-you'll-miss-them places called Cook and Underwood, the Lewis and Clark Highway cuts through five short tunnels and the landscape begins to open up, with fewer trees. Often, you'll find the weather changing simultaneously, as the wet west side of the Cascades gives way to the drier east. After awhile you pass the **Little**

White Salmon/Willard National Fish Hatchery (13 miles east of Stevenson) and the **Spring Creek National Fish Hatchery** (two miles west of the Hood River Bridge); both are open Mon.-Fri. 7:30 a.m.-4 p.m., plus weekends in the winter months.

The toll bridge (50 cents) to Hood River, Oregon is just west of Bingen. Here you'll find the **Mount Adams Chamber of Commerce Visitor Center,** tel. (509) 493-3630; www.gorge.net/mtadamschamber. They're open daily 8 a.m.-5 p.m. June-Sept.; and Mon.-Fri. 8 a.m.-5 p.m. the rest of the year.

The attractive little town of Bingen (pop. 700) straddles Hwy. 14; its twin, White Salmon (pop. 1,900), is just a mile and a half up the hill. Bingen has a big SDS Lumber Company sawmill and plywood factory, while White Salmon has several Bavarian-style buildings, and a 14-bell **glockenspiel** that plays hourly 8 a.m.-8 p.m. By the way, White Salmon is named for the white fungus growth that shows up on returning chinook salmon! East of these two towns, the road continues past barren cliffs along the river's edge and through the flyspeck called **Lyle.** See the Cascades chapter for details on two towns to the north: Trout Lake and Glenwood.

Sights

The **Gorge Heritage Museum,** 202 E. Humbolt in Bingen, tel. (509) 493-3228, has local historical items, Indian artifacts, historic photos, and even an old permanent wave machine that could pass for an electric chair, all housed in a building that was built as a Congregational church in 1911. Open Wed.-Sun. 12:30-4:30 p.m. from late May through September.

Founded in 1975, **Mont Elise Vineyards** in Bingen, tel. (509) 493-3001, is one of the oldest family-run wineries in the state. This is a friendly and funky operation located in a 19th-century building with wines not available outside the area. They produce gewürztraminer, pinot noir blanc, gamay beaujolais, and pinot noir, along with a sparkling wine. Open for tastings daily noon-5 p.m. in the summer, and Fri.-Sun. noon-5 p.m. the rest of the year. The vineyards are just three miles north of here.

Eleven miles north of White Salmon, the family-run **Wind River Cellars** produces white riesling, chardonnay, gewürztraminer, and pinot noir blanc. All are pure varietals, not blends. The winery is open daily 11 a.m.-5 p.m. in the summer, and weekends 11 a.m.-5 p.m. in the winter; call (509) 493-2324 for information. There's a stunning view of Mt. Hood from the winery.

Klickitat River Rafting

The Klickitat Gorge, just north of Lyle, is a strikingly scenic area accented by rope bridges, where you can often see local Indians fishing with dip nets. The Klickitat River is one of the more remote rivers in Washington, quite unlike many of the Cascade rivers that are paralleled by roads the entire way. Rated class III-IV, the river drops through a narrow, pine-forested canyon with high rock walls on either side. Most rafting takes place in May and June, with runs covering 15 river miles. Expect to pay $60-75 for an all-day excursion. Contact one of the following for details: **AAA Rafting,** tel. (800) 866-7238; **All Rivers Adventures,** tel. (800) 743-5628; **Blue Sky Outfitters,** tel. (800) 228-7238; **Northern Wilderness River Riders, Inc.,** tel. (800) 448-7238; and **River Recreation,** tel. (800) 464-5899. AAA Rafting is the only local company.

White Salmon River Rafting

The White Salmon River—a National Wild and Scenic River—offers a fairly short but intense and exciting eight-mile whitewater trip. The river cuts through a 150-foot-deep gorge, requiring rafts to be dropped into the river by a cable system. This class III-IV river is generally run May-Aug., with the highest water in May. (The class-V rated Husum Falls is always portaged, except by experts.) Expect to pay $50-75 for a half-day excursion (more for the treacherous upper White Salmon). Contact one of the following for details: **AAA Rafting,** tel. (800) 866-7238; **All Rivers Adventures,** tel. (800) 743-5628; **Blue Sky Outfitters,** tel. (800) 228-7238; **North Cascades River Expeditions,** tel. (800) 634-8433; **Northern Wilderness River Riders, Inc.,** tel. (800) 448-7238; **River Recreation,** tel. (800) 464-5899; **Phil's White Water Adventure,** tel. (800) 366-2004; and **Wildwater River Tours,** tel. (800) 522-9453. Phil's White Water Adventure and AAA Rafting are the local companies.

Accommodations

Built in 1860, **Bingen Haus B&B,** tel. (509) 493-4888, has seven antique-filled guest rooms with shared baths, plus an outdoor hot tub. A full breakfast is served, and kids are welcome. Reasonably priced at just $40 s or $65 d.

Another place with a long history is **Inn of the White Salmon,** in White Salmon, tel. (509) 493-2335 or (800) 972-5226. This European-style hotel features antique-furnished rooms, a fireplace, jacuzzi, and delicious gourmet breakfasts for $75 s or $89-115 d.

City Center Motel in Bingen, tel. (509) 493-2445, is a plain older motel with rooms for $32-42 s or d, and kitchenettes for $42-52 d.

The **Bingen School Inn,** Humboldt and Cedar Streets, tel. (509) 493-3363, is certainly the most unusual local place to stay. This rambling wooden grade school built in 1938 has been transformed into a very popular place for young windsurfers and mountain climbers. Don't expect the cleanest conditions here, but what would you expect from a bunch of sweaty windsurfers? Managed something like a hostel, the school attracts travelers from all over the globe. Both dorm beds ($11 pp) and private rooms ($29 d) are available, along with a weight room, climbing wall, and kitchen area. You can rent mountain bikes or sailboards, and they also offer windsurfing shuttle services. Reservations recommended in mid-summer.

Food

The **Inn of the White Salmon,** tel. (509) 493-2335, has locally famous country breakfasts, but phone ahead for reservations. For a lighter start on the day, **Loafers Old World Bakery** in White Salmon, is a favorite place for espresso and pastries, along with delicious breads (especially the cheesy onion bread) and homemade soups.

White Salmon's **Wild Mushroom Grill,** tel. (509) 493-8566, is a cozy and intimate place for a gourmet lunch or dinner ($14-20 entrees), with a menu that changes all the time. Great desserts too.

Fidel's, tel. (509) 493-1017, serves very good Mexican food and big margaritas in Bingen. Large helpings, so arrive hungry.

Mother's Marketplace in Bingen, tel. (509) 493-1700, sells organic produce and natural foods, and has a vegetarian deli with good sandwiches, soups, and pizzas.

Events

White Salmon's **May Fest** on the third weekend of May includes a parade, food, entertainment, and a fun run. Bingen's **Huckleberry Festival** on the second weekend of September includes food, crafts, live music, and a beer garden.

Recreation

North Western Lake Riding Stables, tel. (509) 493-2965, has horseback rides near White Salmon. Rent mountain bikes from **Sunset Cycles** in White Salmon, tel. (509) 493-3117.

Information and Transportation

Get regional info from the **Mount Adams Chamber of Commerce** next to the toll bridge just west of Bingen, tel. (509) 493-3630. Hours are daily 8 a.m.-5 p.m. June-Sept.; and Mon.-Fri. 8 a.m.-5 p.m. the rest of the year. Find them on the Web at www.gorge.net/mtadamschamber.

The Bingen **Amtrak** station is located at 800 N.W. 6th, tel. (509) 248-1146 or (800) 872-7245. Service is daily, heading west to Vancouver and Portland, and east to Wishram, Pasco, Spokane, and then all the way to Chicago.

THE DALLES AREA

A transformation begins east of the Lyle area as the country opens up into rolling dry hills of grass and rock. In this desolate place the rumble of long freight trains and the sounds of tugs pushing barges upriver are never too far away. Look across the river to Oregon's busy I-84 and be glad you're on the less-hurried side of the river.

The Dalles Dam

"The Dalles" is from the French "La Grand Dalle de la Columbia," meaning "flagstone," a reference to the basaltic rocks lining the narrows. This was the most dangerous point in the river for early navigators because it was a virtual staircase of rapids called Celiclo Falls. Most Oregon Trail travelers opted to portage around the rapids at The Dalles. For centuries the falls were a major fishing spot for Indians who caught salmon as they headed upstream to spawn. When Lewis and Clark visited this area in 1805, they reported a village of 21 large wooden houses and called the place a "great emporium . . . where all the neighboring nations assemble." The dam at The Dalles was completed in 1957, covering forever this famous old falls, along with countless cultural sites, and ending forever a way of life. Some salmon still make it up this far, and Indian fishing platforms can be found on both sides of the river.

Cross over the 1.5-mile-long dam into Oregon via Hwy. 197 to see The Dalles Dam and the adjacent city of the same name. Free tour trains leave the **Dalles Dam Visitors Center** tel. (541) 296-9533, on guided half-hour explorations of the dam, displays on Lewis and Clark, petroglyphs recovered before the dam was completed, and the fish ladders. The center is open daily 10 a.m.-5 p.m., mid-June to early Sept., and Wed.-Sun. 10:30 a.m.-4 p.m. mid-April to mid-June and in September. Closed Oct.-May. In the nearby city of The Dalles, Oregon, you'll find the **Fort Dalles Museum,** tel. (541) 296-4547, with a number of 1850s structures, plus the impressive **Columbia Gorge Discovery Center,** tel. (541) 296-8600.

Camp for free in undeveloped **Hess Park** or **Spearfish Park** on the Washington side of the Dalles Bridge. **Columbia Hills RV Park,** tel. (509) 767-2277, has camping spaces just north of the bridge.

Doug's Beach State Park

This tiny park is basically a staging area for the throngs of windsurfers who come here all summer long to play on the Columbia River. This is not a place for beginners since the swells can reach six to eight feet at times. No water or camping, but it does have outhouses. The park is located 2.5 miles east of the town of Lyle along Hwy. 14, and seven miles west of Horsethief Lake State Park.

Horsethief Lake State Park

Located two miles east of Hwy. 197 on Hwy. 14, Horsethief Lake State Park has good trout and bass fishing from your boat or one of the park's rentals, with two boat launches—one on the lake, one on the river. Nearby is 500-foot-high Horsethief Butte, a favorite of rock climbers. The park is surrounded by Indian petroglyphs on natural rock formations, including the famous *Tsagaglalal* (She Who Watches) petroglyph.

WINDSURFING

Because the Columbia is the only major break in the Cascade Range, it acts as an 80-mile-long wind tunnel. The wind blowing through the Columbia Gorge provides some of the best windsurfing conditions in the nation. In 1991, a windsurfer set the national speed record, 47.4 miles per hour. This place isn't for beginners. Gusty winds, large waves, a strong current, and frigid water make the Gorge challenging for even experienced sailors, and the constant parade of tugs and barges adds more hazards. Winds average 16 mph between March and mid-October, but most windsurfers prefer to come in July and August when the water is warmer and the current is slower.

The most protected waters in the Gorge are at **Vancouver Lake** near Vancouver, and at **Horsethief Lake** near the Dalles bridge, but here strong winds may make it difficult for the beginner to return to the upwind launch area. A good place to learn windsurfing is The Dalles Riverfront Park, just across the river in Oregon, where you can take lessons and rent equipment in a relatively protected location. Board rentals are also available in Stevenson and Bingen, Washington, and Hood River, Oregon. If you just want to watch, the best place is near the Spring Creek Fish Hatchery three miles west of Bingen, where you may see upwards of 300 boarders on a windy August day.

Several good places for intermediate level boarders are near Stevenson, Home Valley, Bingen, and Avery Park (east of Horsethief Lake). The last of these is especially good because it has a long straight stretch of river that gets nicely formed waves.

Expert-level conditions can be found at Swell City, four miles west of the Bingen Marina; the Fish Hatchery, 3.5 miles west of White Salmon; Doug's Beach, 2.5 miles east of Lyle; Maryhill State Park, where the river is less than a half mile wide; and the east end of the river near Roosevelt Park. Experts head to The Wall, 1.5 miles east of Maryhill State Park. For information on the sport, contact the **Columbia Gorge Windsurfing Association**, 202 Oak St., Suite 150, Hood River, Oregon, tel. (541) 386-9225; www.gorge.net/windsurf/cgwa. The **RE/MAX Windsurfing Race Series** features board contests in the Gorge all summer long; tel. (541) 386-9463.

More than 50 sites provide access on both sides of the Columbia River; see local shops for details. For up-to-date windsurfing conditions listen to radio stations 104.5 FM and 105.5 FM, or check with windsurfing shops in Hood River, Oregon—the center of the winsurfing universe. On the Web, head to www.windance.com for live Gorge cameras and weather updates. One company (Windsight, tel. 800-695-9703) even offers a paging service listing current conditions! Showers are available at Lyle Merc or the Bingen School Inn.

Legend has it that this carved rock represents a woman who was once a tribal chief, and who still sees all that goes on through her stone eyes. Because of vandalism, the rock art site is only open for hour-long tours Friday and Saturday at 10 a.m. April-October. Make reservations by calling (509) 767-1159. A small campground at Horsethief has out-in-the-open sites for $10 (no RV hookups); open April-October.

Transportation
Amtrak trains stop at the little settlement of Wishram, nine miles east of the Dalles dam. Service is daily, heading west to Bingen, Vancouver, and Portland, and east to Pasco, Spokane, and continuing all the way to Chicago. Call (800) 872-7245 for more information.

GOLDENDALE AREA

Highway 97 heads north from the Columbia to the rather plain little town of Goldendale (pop. 3,300), 10 miles away, passing cattle ranches and fields of dryland wheat along the way. The horizon is dominated by the snowcapped summits of Mt. Hood to the south and Mt. Adams, Mt. St. Helens, and Mt. Rainier to the west. North of Goldendale, Hwy. 97 climbs through ponderosa pine forests as it reaches 3,107-foot **Satus Pass,** before descending into the scenic and lonely Yakama Indian Reservation, and finally the town of Toppenish in Yakima Valley, 50 miles away. Goldendale began when the first farmers and loggers settled here in 1879 and has grown slowly over the decades since.

Presby Mansion

Goldendale's 20-room Presby Mansion, 127 W. Broadway, tel. (509) 773-4303, is the home of **Klickitat County Historical Museum.** Built in 1903, this magnificent white-clapboard mansion is filled with pioneer furniture, historic photos, and other exhibits. It's open daily 9 a.m.-5 p.m. April-Oct., and admission costs $3 adults, $1 ages 6-12, free for children under age six.

Goldendale Observatory State Park

Head a mile north of town and uphill through open ponderosa pine forests to Goldendale Observatory State Park, tel. (509) 773-3141, where you'll find one of the nation's largest telescopes open to public viewing, a 24.5-inch reflecting Cassegrain. Also here are several smaller portable telescopes. Take a tour and enjoy free audiovisual programs, displays, and demonstrations Wed.-Sun. 2-5 p.m. and 8 p.m.-midnight April-Sept.; winter hours are Saturday 1-5 p.m. and 7-9 p.m. and Sunday 1-5 p.m. The observatory is a gathering place for amateur astronomers, and facilities include a kitchenette, restroom, and all-purpose room. Group camping only here. In the day this is a good place to view Mt. Adams.

Brooks Memorial State Park

Camp at Brooks Memorial State Park, tel. (509) 773-4611, 15 miles north of Goldendale on Hwy. 97. Tent ($10) and RV ($15) sites on 700 forested acres are available year-round. Enjoy the nine miles of hiking trails through the cool ponderosa pine forests and good trout fishing in the Klickitat River, and cross-country skiing in winter. An environmental learning center here is used mainly by school groups.

Accommodations and Camping

The Victorian House B&B, 415 E. Broadway, tel. (509) 773-5338 or (888) 426-7281, is a 1910 home with four nicely furnished second-floor bedrooms sharing a bath. Children are accepted; $50 s or $55 d with a continental breakfast.

Timberframe Country Inn, 223 Golden Pine, tel. (509) 773-0060 or (800) 861-8408, has two guest rooms in a distinctive Gorman-style home on five acres of land. A full country breakfast is served; $95-125 s or d. No kids.

Barchris Motel, 128 N. Academy, tel. (509) 773-4325, is an older place with bargain-price rooms, each with kitchenettes: $35 s or $38 d. **Far Vue Motel,** 808 E. Simcoe Dr., tel. (509) 773-5881 or (800) 358-5881, has rooms for $49 s or $57 d, including an outdoor pool. They also have parking for RVs. Another good place to stay is **Ponderosa Motel,** 775 E. Broadway St., tel. (509) 773-5842, where rooms are $38 s or $45 d.

Park campers at **Sunset RV Park,** 821 Simcoe Dr., tel. (509) 773-3111.

Other Practicalities

Try **The Homestead Restaurant** 808 Simcoe Dr., tel. (509) 773-6006, for standard family meals.

Goldendale Community Days in early July features arts and crafts, ethnic food, a flea market, antique auction, beer garden, and parade. The **Klickitat County Fair and Rodeo** is held annually in Goldendale over Labor Day weekend, and includes a carnival, parade, and exhibitions.

For local information, stop by **Goldendale Chamber of Commerce,** on 903 E. Broadway, tel. (509) 773-3400. Open daily 9 a.m.-3 p.m. June-Sept., and Mon.-Fri. 9 a.m.-3 p.m. the rest of the year. Swim in the **outdoor pool** at Community Park during the summer months.

MARYHILL AND VICINITY

There isn't much left of the settlement known as Maryhill, near the intersection of Highways 14 and 97, but several sights make this remote area well worth a visit, particularly the famous Maryhill Museum.

The **Cascade Cliffs Winery,** just west of the town of Wishram, tel. (509) 767-1100, is a small family winery that produces red wines, including merlot, petite sirah, and nebbiolo. Open Fri.-Sun. 11 a.m.-5 p.m. April-November.

Just down the hill from Stonehenge are fruit orchards surrounding the small settlement of Maryhill with its New England-style white church and old steam engine. Not much remains of Sam Hill's grandiose dreams of a Quaker community. The **Maryhill Fruit Stand** and **Gunkel Orchards** sell some of the finest fresh peaches, apricots, cherries, and other fresh fruits that you'll ever taste. Camp or park RVs along the river at **Peach Beach Campark,** tel. (509) 773-4698.

Maryhill Museum

The eccentric collection exhibited here veers all over the spectrum, with everything from Indian rock art to neon sculptures. On the entry level, you'll find a gift shop, a room describing the life of Sam Hill, and items donated by Queen Marie of Romania: collections of Russian Orthodox icons and her intricately carved throne and elaborate coronation gown. Also on this floor are miniature French fashion mannequins outfitted by the finest couturiers of post-WW II Paris, and donated by Alma Spreckels. (Postwar Europe had such severe shortages of fabric that designers were forced to display their creations on dolls.) Upstairs are special exhibitions, works by American painters, and other pieces. The lower level is the largest space, with a wing devoted to the sculptures and drawings of Auguste Rodin, two small rooms filled with intricate chess sets from all over the world, and a separate wing with Native American works—basketry, beaded dresses, Inuit carvings, and rock art. The lower level also has a collection of pieces by contemporary artists, and a small cafe with a pleasant patio where you can watch the peacocks roaming the spacious grounds and enjoy the Columbia River vistas that brought Sam Hill here. See the special topic "Castle Nowhere" for more on the life and times of Sam Hill, the founder of this remote but extraordinary museum overlooking the Columbia River.

Maryhill Museum, tel. (509) 773-3733, is open daily 9 a.m.-5 p.m. March 15-Nov. 15; closed the rest of the year. Admission is $5 adults, $4.50 seniors, $1.50 ages 6-16, and free for kids under six.

Stonehenge

Three miles east of Maryhill is another oddity. On a hilltop surrounded by open grass and sage sits a poured concrete replica of England's Stonehenge, but with all the rocks neatly in place rather than scattered around. This is another of Sam Hill's monumental creations, this time in memory of the 13 Skamania County men who died in WW I. It was built between 1918 and 1930 in the mistaken belief that the original Stonehenge had been used for human sacrifice. It is believed to be the nation's first WW I memorial. The ashes of Sam Hill himself are in an urn just down the slope from Stonehenge. The monument is open daily 7 a.m.-10 p.m.

Maryhill State Park

This popular park is five miles east of the Maryhill Museum and right along the Columbia River near the intersection of Highways 14 and 97. Maryhill State Park offers Columbia River access for boating, windsurfing, and fishing, plus full-hookup campsites ($16) and showers. Open year-round. Call (509) 773-5007 for details, or

Stonehenge replica, near Maryhill

(800) 452-5687 for reservations ($6 extra). A **Travel Information Center** here has Columbia Gorge and Washington state info seasonally.

EAST TO TRI-CITIES

The stretch of Hwy. 14 between Maryhill and McNary Dam is some of the most desolate country to be found in Washington. Dry grassy hills provide grazing land for cattle, and a few scattered old farmsteads are slowly returning to the land. The land is bisected by tall power lines marching like misshapen insects over the landscape. Not much traffic here, so tune in to the Spanish-language radio station, KDNA (FM 92) for music.

Two podunk settlements—**Roosevelt** and **Paterson**—are the only places on this side of the river. Roosevelt's claim to fame (or infamy) is Roosevelt Regional Landfill—said to be the nation's most technologically advanced—where

Rabanco brings trash from Everett and other Snohomish County cities by railcar. They dump 75,000 rail containers of garbage here each year, and the methane gas produced provides most of Klickitat County's electrical needs. It's the second biggest employer in the county. Tours (!) are available; call (800) 275-5641. The town of Paterson is known for its expansive vineyards and several wineries.

John Day Lock and Dam

The John Day Lock and Dam, 24 miles upriver from The Dalles and a half-dozen miles east of Stonehenge, gave birth to Lake Umatilla and produces enough electricity for two cities the size of Seattle. Here you'll find one of the largest single-lift locks in the world, hefting vessels 113 feet. At the dam on Oregon's I-84, enjoy the fish-viewing room, visitor's gallery, and Giles French Park, which has a boat launch, a picnic area, and fishing.

CASTLE NOWHERE

The Northwest has no Hearst Castles or Winchester Mystery Houses, no Death Valley Scotties. In that favorite tourist catagory of eccentric mansions, the Northwest offers only the **Maryhill Museum of Art,** a place whose evolution from barren hillside to empty palatial home to museum took 26 years.

The museum—jokingly called "Castle Nowhere"—stands in isolated splendor on a bleak, sagebrush-strewn section of desert along the Columbia River, 100 miles east of Portland and Vancouver and 60 miles south of Yakima. This was just the setting that the Seattle attorney and entrepreneur Sam Hill wanted when he was searching for a homesite early in this century. Forced to be the primary breadwinner for his family at age 10, Hill grew up fast. He later went on to the finest schools before becoming an attorney and gaining a strong reputation for his lawsuits against the Great Northern Railway, run by James J. Hill (no relation). James Hill was so impressed that he decided to put Sam Hill on his payroll to have him as an ally rather than an adversary. Sam would later marry the railway magnate's daughter, Mary Hill. Although many of his later ventures failed, he

went on to form the "Good Roads" program and was a major force behind the creation of the Columbia River Highway, the coastal highway (101), and what would become today's I-5.

Maryhill

Hill's most extravagent venture was an attempt to establish a utopian Quaker town "where the rain of the west and the sunshine of the east meet." He purchased 7,000 acres of treeless terrain on the north side of the Columbia River south of Goldendale, and in 1914, began building his concrete palace, which was to be the farm's centerpiece. He named the spread Maryhill, after his wife, daughter, and mother-in-law, all three named Mary Hill. Hill attempted to interest Quakers—who shared his pacifist philosophy—to invest in his community. He built them a meeting hall and a few other facilities as enticement, but the Quakers declined; they wanted no part of that sun- and wind-blasted countryside. His wife refused to live in this God-forsaken place, taking the children and returning to Minnesota, and all the buildings he constructed for the utopian town were destroyed in a fire in 1958. The man-

A good portion of this power is used in the enormous Columbia Aluminum Corporation plant that stretches for two-thirds of a mile next to the dam. Camp for free at undeveloped **Cliffs Park** approximately three miles off the highway on John Day Road.

Bickleton

For a pleasant side trip, drive north from Roosevelt to the farming town of Bickleton, with a friendly cafe on one side of the street and a tavern on the other. The town has something of a Clint Eastwood western look to it with a few Victorian homes, some no longer occupied. But it does have another kind of home, hundreds of them, that are seasonally occupied: Bickleton is the **bluebird capital of the world.** It has blue and white houses for bluebirds on fence posts, on mailboxes, on trees, and virtually everywhere you look. There's even one in front of the community church, a mirror-image (although considerably smaller) of the church. The bluebird housing project started in the 1960s when Jess and Elva Brinkerhoff built one, then another and another, and soon it was a community project. When the birds leave for the winter, the 700 houses are taken down, cleaned, and painted if they need it, and everyone has the pleasure of watching for the first arrivals each spring. Spring is the best time to view the bluebirds, but you're likely to see them all summer long.

In Cleveland Park, four miles west of town, is a delightful old **carousel** with 24 wooden horses and a musical calliope. Built at the turn of the century, the carousel has been here since 1928 and is a rare type that moves around a track. It only operates for a two-day period each summer: during the **Alder Creek Pioneer Picnic and Rodeo** in mid-June. This is the oldest rodeo in the state of Washington.

For another piece of history, visit **Bluebird Inn,** said to be Washington's oldest tavern. Built

---

sion was built with two garages big enough for 48 automobiles, along with a sweeping ramp entrance that allowed vehicles to drive right into the mansion to drop off passengers.

About three miles upriver from the museum, just east of Hwy 97, Hill built a concrete replica of England's Stonehenge, as it might have looked when intact, and dedicated it to the Klickitat County soldiers who died in WW I. Hill also built the Peace Arch that marks the U.S.-Canadian border at Blaine, Washington.

The WW I years saw the mansion incomplete and bereft of inhabitants. After the war, President Herbert Hoover appointed Hill to a commission to help with Europe's reconstruction. There he met the three women who were responsible for Maryhill becoming a museum: Loie Fuller, a modern-dance pioneer at the Folies Bergere; Alma Spreckles of a prominant California sugar family; and Queen Marie of Romania, whose country Hill aided during the recovery period.

Fuller was particularly enthusiastic about the project and introduced Hill to members of the Parisian artistic community. Hill soon bought the large Auguste Rodin collection of sculptures and drawings.

When the 1926 dedication of the still-unfinished museum neared, Queen Marie agreed to come to New York and cross America by train to attend the ceremonies—the first visit of any European royalty to this country. She brought along a large collection of furniture, jewelry, clothing, and religious objects to be donated to the museum. Today her collection is one of the museum's largest.

Hill died in 1931. He was interred just below the Stonehenge monument, overlooking the river. At the time of Hill's death, the museum still wasn't complete. Alma Spreckles took over the project, donating many pieces from her extensive art collection and seeing to it that the museum was finished and opened in 1940. On that occasion *Time* magazine called it "the loneliest museum in the world."

Sam Hill's original 7,000 acre spread remains intact. Most of the land is leased to ranchers and farmers. Adjoining the Stonehenge monument is the Maryhill State Park, featuring a swimming area, boat launch onto the Columbia, picnic areas, and 50 overnight campsites with restrooms and hot showers.

Only in the past decade or so has the museum enjoyed much popularity or prominance; weekend travelers have begun driving farther to the remote site, and the curators have lined up respected exhibits.

in 1892, it has a classic turn-of-the-century Brunswick pool table with leather pockets, along with other local artifacts.

The **Whoop-N-Holler Ranch Museum** on East Rd. between Bickleton and Roosevelt, tel. (509) 896-2344, contains a lifetime of collecting by Lawrence and Ada Whitmore. Two large buildings are filled with Model T Fords and other antique cars, a horse-drawn hearse on sled runners, local historical items, and family heirlooms (including an electrified lunch box to heat your food). This is one of the largest collections of antique and classic cars in the state and is open daily 10 a.m.-4 p.m. April-Sept.; $3.

Winery

Founded in 1962, and now one of Washington's largest wine producers, **Columbia Crest Winery,** tel. (509) 875-2061, sits on a high hill just north of Paterson with a commanding view across the Columbia River and adjacent vineyards. Much of the winery is below ground, making it easier to maintain cool temperatures throughout the year. The tasting room is open daily 10 a.m.-4:30 p.m. Bring your chewing tobacco; Columbia Crest (like its sister wineries Chateau Ste. Michelle and Snoqualmie Winery) is owned by U.S. Tobacco Company.

Crow Butte State Park

Located at the site of a camping place for the Lewis and Clark Expedition, this 1,312-acre park sits along a virtually unpopulated stretch of highway halfway between the nowhere towns of Roosevelt and Paterson. It offers boating, swimming, fishing, and water-skiing, with tent ($10) and RV sites ($15) and coin-operated showers. The campground is open daily late March to late

October, plus winter weekends. Call (800) 452-5687 for reservations ($6 extra). Crow Butte State Park covers half of an island created when the John Day Dam backed up the river to form Lake Umatilla; the other half is within **Umatilla National Wildlife Refuge,** which straddles both sides of the Columbia. A three-quarter-mile trail leads to the top of Crow Butte (671 feet), with views across the Columbia to Mt. Hood when the weather permits; keep your eyes open for rattlesnakes.

The Umatilla National Wildlife Refuge has an overlook a few miles east of Crow Butte where you can peer across the river below and pick up a brochure describing the refuge and its abundant waterfowl. For more on the refuge, call their office in Umatilla, Oregon, at (541) 922-3232.

McNary Dam

By the time you reach the McNary Dam area, the land has opened into an almost-level desert of sage and grass, broken only by center-pivot irrigation systems. The Columbia River's McNary Lock and Dam, 30 miles south of Pasco in Umatilla, Oregon, creates 61-mile-long Lake Wallula, which reaches up past the Tri-Cities to Ice Harbor Dam. The McNary Dam, tel. (509) 922-3211, completed in 1953, is open daily 8 a.m.-5 p.m. April-Sept. and offers hourly guided tours of the facility and fishpass.

The **McNary National Wildlife Refuge,** next to McNary Dam, has a mile-long hiking trail popular with birdwatchers. Area species include hawks, golden and bald eagles, and prairie falcons.

For descriptions of the country east of here— including the Tri-Cities—see the South-central Washington and Eastern Washington chapters.

THE CASCADE RANGE

INTRODUCTION

The Cascade Range is Washington's great divide. In addition to creating almost opposite climates on either side of the state, the mountains also serve as a political and psychological barrier between east and west, resulting in what seems like two states within one. Many historians have said the founding fathers erred in creating the state, and that they should have drawn the state border along the crest of the Cascades. Perhaps—but that would have robbed the state of much of its cultural and geographical richness.

The two halves of the state are different not only in appearance but also in other less-obvious ways. Speaking very generally, western Washington is urban-oriented, with an emphasis on commerce and manufacturing, while eastern Washington is mainly rural and agricultural.

Crossing the Cascade passes in winter—an adventure many Washingtonians prefer to forgo—is an experience that thousands of avid skiers tolerate to reach the slopes. They simply learn to live with the snow-tire and chain requirements, snow-packed and icy roads, and occasional pass closures.

In summer, the Cascades take on a more benign image and become a popular destination for all manner of travelers, who have a wide variety of places and experiences from which to choose. Millions of acres have been set aside for recreation. The North Cascades and Mount Rainier National Parks, Mount St. Helens National Volcanic Monument, the areas around Mt. Baker and Mt. Adams, along with numerous wilderness areas and wildlife refuges—all constitute the backbone of Washington's outdoor recreation.

This long chapter roughly follows the Cascade Range from Mt. Baker at the north all the way to the Mt. Adams area near the state's southern border, following the main highways over the passes, and visiting the sights, backcountry trails, and settlements en route.

Geology and Climate

The Cascade Range is about 25 million years old, but the range's volcanoes in Washington—

Mount Baker from Table Mountain

DIANNE BOUERICE LYONS

Adams, St. Helens, Rainier, Glacier Peak, and Baker—plus another 15 or so in Oregon and California, are less than a million years old. Although none can be declared totally dead, only two have erupted in this century: Northern California's Mt. Lassen in 1914, and Mt. St. Helens in 1980. Not long before Mt. St. Helens came to life in such a violent manner, Mt. Baker began heating up and sent out clouds of steam and melted some of its glaciers, but Mt. St. Helens stole the show in 1980.

The only break in the Cascade Range is the Columbia Gorge (see previous chapter), which lets the Columbia River flow through and also permits an exchange of air between east and west that is impossible elsewhere along the range. Because it is the only such corridor for hundreds of miles, the resulting winds are strong and almost constant—and thus provide some of the country's best windsurfing conditions.

The rest of the range continues uninterrupted, shielding the interior from storms coming off the ocean and resulting in two vastly different climates: wet on the west side, dry on the east. This weather variation is caused by what is commonly called the rain-shadow effect: incoming storms dump most of their rain and snow on the western side of the ridge as the air is forced up and over the mountain range, leaving the back side drier.

MOUNT BAKER AND VICINITY

Mount Baker, the northernmost of the Cascade volcanoes, towers dramatically over the surrounding hills. At 10,778 feet, it is bathed in glaciers and snowfields and serves as a scenic backdrop for Bellingham and Vancouver, B.C. Besides improving the scenery, the Mt. Baker area offers up a wealth of recreational activities, from skiing to hiking to whitewater rafting. Much of this land lies within the Mt. Baker Wilderness and National Recreation Area. Bordering them to the east is North Cascades National Park, another favorite of those who love the outdoors.

The Natural World

The four "life zones" on the mountain, from sea-level forest to alpine meadows, have a wide variety of wildlife, including coyotes, black bear, black-tailed deer, porcupines, elk, marmots, and mountain goats. Forest birds include grouse, gray jays, ptarmigan, and a large winter population of bald eagles on the Skagit (rhymes with "gadget") and Nooksack Rivers. All five species of Pacific salmon spawn in the rivers, and the insect population is well represented by three of its least popular members, the mosquito, black fly, and no-see-um.

HISTORY

Discovered in 1792 by Captain Vancouver's first mate, Joseph Baker, Mt. Baker had been known for centuries to local Indians as "Koma Kulshan," meaning "Broken One," a reference to an early eruption that blew out part of its summit. Like other Cascade volcanoes, Baker is asleep, but not dead. In 1843 it awoke from its slumber, spewing vast amounts of smoke and ash for the next 16 years, and causing a major forest fire on the east shore of Baker Lake. The mountain lay dormant from 1884 to 1975, when it again began to release steam, leading seismologists to believe it would erupt, but it was upstaged in a grand manner in 1980 by Mt. St. Helens. Since that time the mountain continues to vent steam periodically, with small clouds frequently visible over the summit. There is little evidence of a return to life—but this could change at any time.

Mount Baker has been a source for year-round recreation since 1868, when librarian-turned-mountaineer Edmund Coleman and his party climbed to the summit after two failed attempts. Either poor planners or extremely conscious of pack weight, the entire climbing party shared one plate and spoon and ate only bacon, bread, and tea during the 10-day ascent. By 1911, the mountain had become an integral part of the Mt. Baker marathon, a 118-mile roundtrip between Bellingham and the summit using any mode of transportation in addition to at least 24 miles on foot. The marathons were discontinued two years later after one competitor fell into a crevasse, though he lived to tell about it. More recently the race has been revived as the 85-mile long **Ski to Sea Marathon,** where teams begin by skiing down Mt. Baker, and relays of bike riders, paddlers in canoes, and runners complete the course to Puget Sound.

SIGHTS

Mt. Baker Highway
Highway 542 is the primary access road to Mt. Baker, a 62-mile drive from Bellingham, through the little towns of **Nugents Corner, Deming, Kendall, Maple Falls,** and **Glacier,** and then

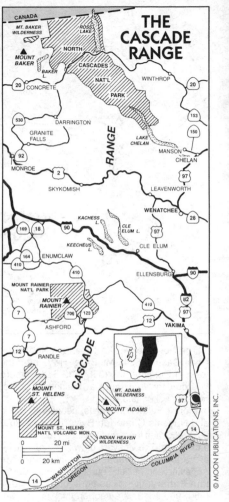

all the way to the end of the road at Heather Meadows. **North Fork Brewery** in Deming, tel. (360) 599-2337, has brewed-on-the-premises beer and a menu centered around handthrown pizzas. Not much to these settlements, but you may want to stop by for the **Deming Logging Show** in mid-June, and the **Everson-Nooksack Summer Festival** on the second weekend in July.

© MOON PUBLICATIONS, INC.

The Nooksack Indian Tribe runs **Nooksack River Casino,** 5048 Mt. Baker Hwy. (near the town of Deming), tel. (360) 592-5472, where you can try your hand at blackjack, craps, roulette, poker, and keno.

Mount Baker Vineyards, between Deming and Nugents Corner on Hwy. 542, tel. (360) 592-2300, has tours and tastings Wed.-Sun. 11 a.m.-5 p.m. The vineyard grows several unusual varieties of grapes, including Madeline Angevine and Müller-Thurgau. **Cloudy Mountain Pottery,** five miles north of Kendall, tel. (360) 988-8645, is a cooperative gallery with pottery by local artisans.

Nooksack Valley

Highway 542 climbs along the beautiful Nooksack River Valley, gently at first, then in a series of steep switchbacks as you approach the terminus near the mountain. The road enters Mt. Baker-Snoqualmie National Forest just east of Glacier, where you'll find the Glacier Public Service Center (described below), along with a handful of businesses. East from here to the end, the road is officially a National Forest Scenic Byway. Enjoy the finest views of Mt. Baker at the end of paved Glacier Creek Rd. (Forest Rd. 39), which begins just east of Glacier and heads south for seven miles to a parking lot and trailhead at an elevation of almost 2,900 feet.

East of Glacier, the highway cruises through a wonderful stand of 700-year-old Douglas firs. Seven miles east of Glacier is the turnoff to impressive **Nooksack Falls,** one mile away along a gravel side road. As you wend your way eastward from here, you'll find periodic views down the valley. The road passes columnar volcanic rock just below the **Mt. Baker Ski Area,** where you can purchase snacks on summer weekends or full meals in the winter, and then circles around famous **Picture Lake.** Join the crowd for a photo of Mt. Shuksan rising behind the mirrored waters of this small lake. It's one of Kodak's favorite places in America.

Heather Meadows Area

The highway ends at 5,200-foot **Artist Point** in Austin Pass, 23 miles east of Glacier, and the only alpine area in the North Cascades accessible by car. The surrounding area—Heather Meadows—delivers up incredible vistas, enjoyable picnic sites, and a multitude of hiking trails to explore in late summer. The stone-walled **Heather Meadows Visitor Center,** built by the CCC in 1940, offers up local information and is open daily 10 a.m.-4:30 p.m. July-September.

Heather Meadows, stuck between Mounts Baker and Shuksan, has been drawing tourists since the first lodge was built here in 1927 (it burned to the ground four years later). The lakes, meadows, and rock formations surrounded by snowcapped peaks were the setting for Clark Gable's *Call of the Wild* and Robert DeNiro's *The Deer Hunter.*

The road to Picture Lake is kept plowed all winter, but the last five miles from here to Artist Point close with the first snows—generally mid to late October—and usually don't open till late July. Because of the short season, the months of August and September are busy beyond belief, especially on weekends. Try to visit on a weekday instead.

The Forest Service has instituted a $5 per-vehicle charge for parking at Heather Meadows. Annual passes are $15, or use the annual Trail Park Pass ($25), also valid at other Washington national forest trailheads.

RECREATION

River Rafting

The Nooksack River emerges from Nooksack Glacier, high up Mt. Shuksan, and drops over

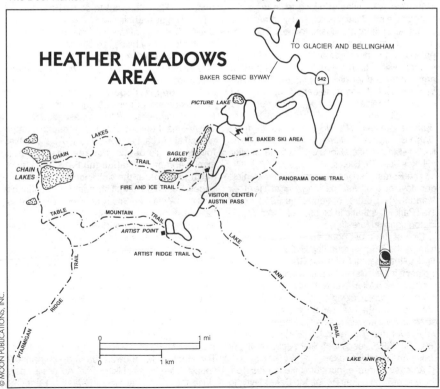

HEATHER MEADOWS AREA

© MOON PUBLICATIONS, INC.

Nooksack Falls before entering a wild gorge. After four miles of class II-III whitewater, the silt-laden waters emerge into the lower river delta, providing fine views of Mt. Baker and the chance to observe bald eagles and other wildlife. Several rafting companies offer eight-mile whitewater trips down the Nooksack from Glacier to Deming June-August. Expect to pay $55-65 per person with the following rafting companies: **Blue Sky Outfitters,** tel. (800) 228-7238; **Alpine Adventures,** tel. (800) 723-8386; **Northern Wilderness River Riders,** tel. (800) 448-7238; and **River Recreation,** tel. (800) 464-5899.

A more leisurely summertime float—extremely popular with inner tubers and families—is the South Fork of the Nooksack River from Acme to Van Zandt.

Hiking Trails

More than 200 miles of hiking trails meander through the Mt. Baker district, and, fortunately for hikers, all of them are closed to motorized vehicles. The variety of trails is great: both backpackers and one-milers alike can find striking scenery within their reach. Wilderness permits are not needed for hiking within the Mt. Baker Wilderness, but be sure to get one at the Glacier Public Service Center if you will be entering North Cascades National Park from the Mt. Baker area. See *100 Hikes in Washington's North Cascades: National Park Region* (Seattle: The Mountaineers) for a complete description of hikes near Mt. Baker.

The Forest Service charges $3 per vehicle per day for trailhead parking ($5 at Heather Meadows). A better option is the $25 annual Trail Park Pass that can be used on most Washington national forests.

One of the most popular—and overused—hikes is the 3.5-mile roundtrip **Heliotrope Ridge Trail** to the edge of **Coleman Glacier,** the starting point for Mt. Baker summit climbs. (Don't attempt to climb Mt. Baker without previous climbing experience; accidents and even deaths are not uncommon.) The trail begins from Rd. 39 off Mt. Baker Hwy. and gains 1,500 feet along the way. **Mountain Madness,** tel. (206) 937-8389 or (800) 328-5925, leads technical climbs of Mount Baker and nearby peaks.

An easy four-mile roundtrip hike leaves from the end of Twin Lakes Rd. off Mt. Baker Hwy. to a lookout atop **Winchester Mountain,** with excellent views of Mt. Baker, Mt. Shuksan, and the North Cascades.

Popular with equestrians and hikers alike is the six-mile roundtrip **Skyline Divide** trail, beginning 13 miles up Rd. 37 and providing ample Baker views and wildflower meadows.

Loop Trips

Only a few loop trails are suitable for overnight trips; most Mt. Baker trails are walk-in-walk-out propositions. Still, the scenery here is good enough to see twice. One loop trip, perhaps too short for the more robust, starts across from Nooksack Falls, seven miles east of Glacier, for a 4.5-mile hike to **Excelsior Pass,** gaining a tortuous 3,800 feet en route. It then follows the **High Divide Trail** for four miles, with spectacular views of Baker and Shuksan, and returns to Rd. 3060 via **Welcome Pass** for 1.8 miles. The descent is via 67 demented switchbacks. Sections of this loop make popular, albeit difficult, day hikes. To stretch it out, travel north for three miles past the Excelsior Pass/High Divide junction to **Damfino Lakes** and Forest Rd. 31.

The **Copper Ridge-Chilliwack Loop Trail** is an extremely popular 35-mile trek into Mount Baker Wilderness and North Cascades National Park that begins from the Hannegan Campground at the east end of Forest Rd. 32. The first four miles are gentle, but after that the trail climbs abruptly to **Hannegan Pass,** then back down to a fork at the entrance to North Cascades National Park. The right fork continues east over Whatcom Pass and eventually to Ross Lake. Take the left fork instead, and climb along the spine of **Copper Ridge** with vistas across the top of the Cascades. From here, the trail drops into Indian Creek, where you join the Chilliwack Trail for the return trip along Chilliwack River. A cable car provides a crossing over the river. This trail is best hiked from late July through September. Wilderness permits are required for this hike; get them at the Glacier Public Service Center.

Heather Meadows Hikes

The Heather Meadows area is an immensely popular late-summer hiking area. Access is easy, since the Mt. Baker Hwy. (Hwy. 542) ends at

4,700-foot Austin Pass, with trails branching out in all directions for all levels of ability. Easiest is the **Artist Ridge Trail,** a mile-long loop with interpretive signs and views all the way to Mt. Rainier on clear days. The first 200 feet are wheelchair-accessible. Another easy path, **Fire and Ice Trail,** is paved to an overlook above Bagley Lakes.

Starting at Austin Pass near the end of Mt. Baker Hwy., the four-mile one-way hike to **Lake Ann,** one of the Cascades' most beautiful high-country lakes, is a very popular route with day-hikers and the major approach trail to 9,127-foot Mt. Shuksan. Lake Ann Trail is often covered by snow till late summer.

From the end of Hwy. 542 at Artist Point, follow the steep 2.5-mile trail up lava cliffs to the appropriately named, flat-topped **Table Mountain.** Incredible views of Mt. Baker and Mt. Shuksan from here.

The 5.5-mile **Chain Lakes Trail** begins at the end of the road, traverses Table Mountain, and passes a series of alpine lakes. Beyond this, the trail climbs over Herrmann Saddle, enters the Bagley Lakes basin, and ends near the Mt. Baker Ski Area. For a return loop, take the **Wild Goose Trail** back to Artist Point.

Skiing

Mt. Baker Ski Resort is open from early November through April—the longest ski and snowboarding season in the state. The snow here is considered the best in Washington. Eight chair lifts (two of these are quads) put 1,500 vertical feet of slope underfoot, from machine-groomed intermediate runs to open powder bowls. Other facilities include a big day lodge, child care, ski school, rentals, restaurant, and bar. Weekend lift tickets are $30 adults, $22 seniors and ages 7-15. For a ski report, call (360) 671-0211 from Bellingham, or (206) 634-0200 from Seattle; the business office is (360) 734-6771.

ACCOMMODATIONS

Accommodations near Mt. Baker are mostly in the form of cabins, B&Bs, and condos; the closest are in the town of Glacier, 15 miles below Mt. Baker Ski Area. Note that many places require a two-night minimum on weekends, and have higher rates around Christmas and New Year's. Call well ahead for weekend reservations during the ski season.

Bed and Breakfasts

Three places in Maple Falls offer B&B accommodations. **Yodeler Inn,** 7485 Mt. Baker Hwy., tel. (360) 599-2222 or (800) 642-9033, is a countrified B&B, built by an early settler in 1917. The inn's five guest rooms and a cottage have private or shared baths and a hot tub; rates are $65-75 s or d.

Country Hill B&B, 9512 Silver Lake Rd. in Maple Falls, tel. (360) 599-1049, has lakeside accommodations that include a three-room suite and a cabin with a kitchen and fireplace; $85-90 s or d, including a continental breakfast.

Thurston House B&B, tel. (360) 599-2261, features a lakefront location with rowboat and jacuzzi. Their suite sleeps four, and the cabin sleeps up to eight and has a kitchen. Rates are $65 d with a full breakfast. RV hookups are available.

Cabin Country B&B in Glacier, tel. (360) 599-2903, has two upstairs bedrooms that share a bath. A full breakfast is served, and you can relax in the outdoor hot tub; $75 s or d.

Mt. Baker B&B, 9447 Mt. Baker Hwy., tel. (360) 599-2299, is a modern chalet a half-mile west of Glacier. A full breakfast is served, and guests can enjoy the hot tub; $70 s or d.

Glacier Guest Suite, 8040 Mt. Baker Hwy., tel. (360) 599-2927, is part of a 100-acre farmstead. This new log cabin overlooks Nooksack River Valley with views of Mt. Baker, and has a kitchenette and fireplace. A continental breakfast is served; $95 s or d.

Cabins and Inns

Two reservation services represent a wide variety of local vacation cabins, homes, and suites: **Mt. Baker Lodging,** tel. (360) 599-2453 or (800) 709-7669, and **Mount Baker Chalet,** tel. (360) 599-2405 or (800) 258-2405.

Snowline Inn, 10433 Mt. Baker Hwy., tel. (360) 599-2788 or (800) 228-0119, is the closest lodging to Mt. Baker—one mile east of Glacier—with condos containing kitchenettes for $65-75 for up to four in the summer, $10 more in winter. **Glacier Creek Motel,** in Glacier, tel. (360) 599-2991 or (800) 719-1414, has motel rooms

($40 s or $42 d) and small creekside cabins ($60 s or d) accommodating up to six people. They also have an outdoor hot tub, and an espresso shop.

The Logs, 9002 Mt. Baker Hwy., tel. (360) 599-2711, has five cozy cabins with fireplaces, kitchens, and a swimming pool along the Nooksack River for $85 s or d. **The Guest House** 5723 Schornbush Rd. near Deming, tel. (360) 592-2343, has a country cottage with kitchenette for $50 d.

Campgrounds

Camp at one of three Forest Service campgrounds ($10) in the Mt. Baker area. **Douglas Fir Campground,** two miles east of Glacier on Mt. Baker Hwy., is situated in a beautiful old-growth forest along the Nooksack River, and is open all winter. **Silver Fir Campground,** 13 miles east of Glacier, is open mid-May to mid-September. Make reservations ($9 extra) by calling (877) 444-6777. **Hannegan Campground,** 17 miles east of Glacier and right next to the Mount Baker Wilderness on Forest Rd. 32, is a primitive campground with no running water and no fees; open mid-May to mid-September.

The 411-acre **Silver Lake County Park,** three miles north of Maple Falls, has a beautiful day lodge/information center, year-round camping and RV hookups, showers, swimming, plus boat rentals; call (360) 599-2776 for reservations. **Hutchinson Creek Campground,** on Mosquito Creek Rd. near Acme, has free camping, but no water. More free camping at **Nooksack City Park.** Dispersed camping is free on Forest Service land below milepost 52; just find a good off-the-road place to camp.

Park RVs at **Mt. Baker RV Park,** next door to Snowline Inn, tel. (360) 599-1908 or (888) 250-7077. Campers and hikers can take **showers** at the Texaco minimart near the intersection of Highways 9 and 542.

FOOD

If you love fresh homemade pasta, don't miss **Milano's** in Glacier, tel. (360) 599-2863. The prices are reasonable, and the atmosphere is friendly and light-hearted. Milano's also has a deli for lunchtime sandwiches, and Tuesday night pizzas.

For fine dining after a tiring romp in the woods, the **Innisfree Restaurant,** tel. (360) 599-2373, serves Northwest regional foods in an elegant setting. The emphasis is on organic produce, Washington-grown lamb and chicken, and a fresh menu that changes with the seasons. On the pricey side, but outstanding quality.

The **Chandelier Restaurant** in Glacier, tel. (360) 599-2233, is popular for family dining, pizzas, and noteworthy desserts. The bar features rock, country, or blues bands on winter weekends. Stop by to watch games on the big-screen TV.

The **Deming Tavern,** in Deming, tel. (360) 592-5282, has locally famous steaks and a big choice of brews.

INFORMATION AND TRANSPORTATION

The **Glacier Public Service Center** in the town of Glacier is the place to go for information on Mt. Baker and surrounding areas. They also issue backcountry permits, and have summertime interpretive talks and walks. Located in a stone building built by the CCC in 1938, the center is open daily 8:30 a.m.-4:30 p.m. from mid-June to mid-September, with reduced hours the rest of the year. Call (360) 599-2714 for more information.

Heather Meadows Visitor Center, at the end of Mt. Baker Hwy., is open daily 10 a.m.-5 p.m. July-Sept. and has a variety of interpretive activities on late summer weekends. The **Mt. Baker Ranger District** office is in Sedro-Woolley, tel. (360) 856-5700.

THE MOUNTAIN LOOP: GRANITE FALLS TO DARRINGTON

The scenic Mountain Loop Highway, one of the state's most popular weekend drives, connects Granite Falls to Darrington via a 55 mile long road. From Granite Falls, the road is paved for the first 22 miles as it follows the South Fork of the Stillaguamish River to its headwaters at Barlow Pass, entering the Mt. Baker-Snoqualmie National Forest near Verlot. Numerous campgrounds and hiking trails offer diversions along the way, and access to three fabulous swaths of wild mountain country: Boulder River Wilderness, Henry M. Jackson Wilderness, and Glacier Peak Wilderness. North of Barlow Pass, the road turns to gravel and becomes narrow and winding as it drops along the Sauk River. It remains gravel for 14 miles; the last seven miles to Darrington are paved. West of Darrington, the Mountain Loop Road passes through a wide valley bisected by the North Fork of the Stillaguamish River and filled with hay piles, beehives, horses, sheep, chickens, hogs, big red barns, cut-your-own Christmas tree farms, lumber mills, clearcuts, and regenerating stands of trees. Openings provide glimpses of the snowy peaks that cap the Cascade Range.

History

Parts of today's Mountain Loop Hwy. overlay trails that were used for centuries by the Indians who first inhabited these lands. The 1889 discovery of gold and silver in the Monte Cristo area (see below) led to a mad rush of miners and others attempting to get rich quick. To transport the (assumed) mineral wealth, a railroad was constructed from Monte Cristo over Barlow Pass, down the canyon created by the South Fork of the Stillaguamish River, through the new town of Granite Falls, and on to Everett, where the ore would be refined. Funded by an East-Coast syndicate with financial backing from John D. Rockefeller, the railroad was poorly designed and subject to repeated flooding. These floods, combined with a financial depression in the 1890s, forced the mine owners to sell out to Rockefeller in 1899, and even he was compelled to give up when the ore petered out a few years later.

With cessation of mining, the Monte Cristo area began attracting tourists, and the trains turned to offering weekend excursions into the mountains. Business flourished in the 1920s, and hotels were added in Silverton and near Big Four Mountain to cater to the wealthy—the latter even featured a nine-hole golf course. All this came to a screeching halt following the stock market crash of 1929. The railroad shut down in 1936, and the old railroad grade became an automobile road. Two years later, the CCC began construction of a narrow mountain route north from Barlow Pass to Darrington, completing the final link in today's Mountain Loop Highway.

Weather

The Darrington area is an anomaly in the Cascades. Whereas the Seattle area receives 30-40 inches of rain per year, Darrington gets an average of 80 inches, while Monte Cristo gets over 140 inches, creating a dense rainforest much like those of the Olympics. The low elevation here means questionable snowfall, though cross-country skiing and snowmobiling are popular area activities.

It is imperative to carry adequate clothing while hiking in this part of the Cascades, even if you're out on a short hike. The weather changes rapidly sometimes, and nearly every summer someone dies of hypothermia a short distance from his or her car.

The highway and logging roads are popular snowmobile routes in winter, but that portion of the road over 2,361-foot Barlow Pass is blocked by snow beyond Elliot Creek on the north side and Deer Creek on the south side from mid-November to mid-April.

HIKING TRAILS

More than 300 miles of trails lie within the Darrington Ranger District. Due to budget cuts, many of these are maintained by volunteers, so do your part to keep them clean. Parking-area theft is a major problem in this isolated area, so

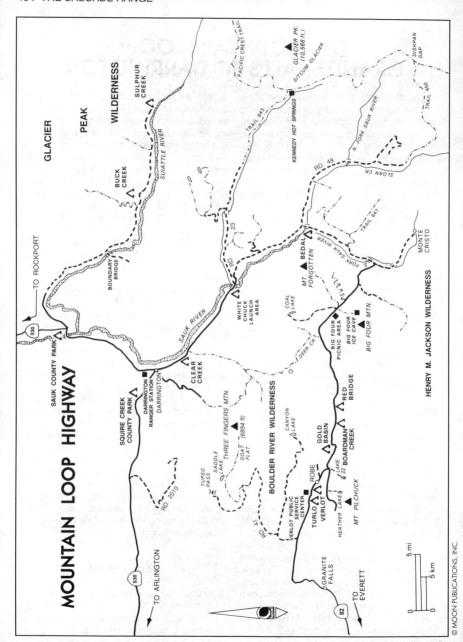

© MOON PUBLICATIONS, INC.

don't assume your valuables are safe in the trunk. Leave them at home or carry them with you. Report all thefts to a ranger station or the county sheriff. The following hiking trails are listed in a roughly northeastward progression from Verlot to Darrington along the Mountain Loop Highway.

Mt. Pilchuck State Park
The 5,324-foot Mt. Pilchuck offers a challenging day hike, with dramatic 360-degree views of the Cascades and Puget Sound from the summit. Get to the trailhead by heading a mile east of Verlot Public Service Center and turning onto Forest Rd. 42. Follow it seven miles uphill to the park entrance at an abandoned ski area. Allow five hours for the six-mile roundtrip hike, and be prepared for a 2,300-foot gain in elevation and some boulder-hopping at the end; the hike is best in late summer. Drinking water is scarce along the trail, so take plenty with you. Mountain climbers practice their techniques on the rugged northeast side of Mt. Pilchuck; be sure to sign the climbers' register at the Verlot Public Service Center before doing so.

Other Verlot Area Hikes
The subalpine forests and meadows are as much the attractions as the clear mountain lake on the four-mile roundtrip hike to **Heather Lake.** To reach the trailhead, take Forest Rd. 42 for 1.5 miles, then hike up an old logging road before reaching the forest and then open meadows. Allow three hours; elevation gain is 1,100 feet. Because of its easy access, Heather Lake is a very popular day-hiking spot on summer weekends.

Late spring is a good time to hike the 2.7 miles to **Lake 22** (trail No. 702) to see the numerous waterfalls along the way in their most turbulent state. The trail, starting two miles east of the Verlot Ranger Station, also passes through an old-growth western red cedar forest on the way to the mountain lake. Allow four hours for the 1,400-foot elevation gain; no camping is allowed in the area.

Boulder River Wilderness
Established in 1984, the 49,000-acre Boulder River Wilderness occupies the low range of mountains between Verlot and Darrington. A handful of trails provide access to the wilderness from various sides, but travel off these paths can be a challenge in this rugged and oft-brushy terrain. The main attraction is Three Fingers, a 6,850-foot peak offering outstanding alpine vistas.

The 6.7-mile one-way trail to **Tin Pan Gap** and **Three Fingers Mountain** is a popular overnight hike. From Verlot, go west on Mountain Loop Hwy. for four miles, then head north on Forest Rd. 41, following it 18 miles to the trailhead at Tupso Pass. The trail climbs through dense forest for 2.5 miles to four-acre Saddle Lake; continue for another 2.3 miles through meadows to Goat Flat, an oft-crowded camping spot. Use only a campstove; fire rings leave near-permanent scars in these fragile meadows. The trail reaches Tin Pan Gap after about six miles; from here, the hike becomes a technical climb (not for the inexperienced) over Three Fingers Glacier and a scramble to the top of Three Fingers Mountain and the old fire lookout.

Ice Cave
The **Big Four Ice Cave** (trail No. 723) is a favorite two-mile roundtrip hike, starting 26 miles from Granite Falls at the Big Four Picnic Area. The hike begins on boardwalks over a beaver-created marsh, then heads through a dense forest and across the South Fork of the Stillaguamish River to the ice caves and a view of 6,135-foot Big Four Mountain. The caves—created when water channels under a small glacier—are generally exposed in late July and are visible through October. Admire them from afar; the caves are very dangerous to enter because tons of ice may separate from the ceiling at any time, as happened in the summer of 1993 when the roof caved in on a young man but, miraculously, didn't kill him. In winter and spring the snowfield is susceptible to avalanches.

Mount Forgotten Meadows
A full-day hike to an alpine meadow starts 26 miles from Granite Falls and heads up 6,005-foot **Mt. Forgotten** for an eight-mile roundtrip hike. Take the Mountain Loop Hwy. 15 miles east from the Verlot Public Service Center, then go north on Perry Creek Rd. (No. 4063) for a mile to the Perry Creek trailhead. The trail climbs

past waterfalls at about two miles, heading through an old-growth forest for another 1.7 miles to the first meadow. Allow seven hours to reach the meadows at 5,200 feet, an elevation gain of 3,100 feet. The trail continues through meadows to Mt. Forgotten's climbing route (for experienced alpine climbers only).

Monte Cristo Area

See "Recreation" in the Stevens Pass and Skykomish Valley section for details on the magnificent alpine-topped 103,591-acre **Henry M. Jackson Wilderness Area,** accessible from several trailheads on the eastern end of the Mountain Loop. The most popular hiking paths here center around the fascinating old mining town of Monte Cristo. In the 1890s, gold and silver strikes lured 2,000 people to this boomtown, but the ore turned out to be of poor quality, and within 20 years Monte Cristo had become a ghost town. The fireplace and foundation of the

The Darrington area is popular with hikers and backpackers.

TACOMA/PIERCE COUNTY VISITOR AND CONVENTION BUREAU

Big Four Inn—a luxurious turn-of-the-century resort that burned to the ground in 1949—stand as mute reminders of the town's earlier glory. During the Depression, the railroad to Monte Cristo was replaced by the Mountain Loop Highway. Today, the townsite and abandoned mines around Monte Cristo remain privately owned.

Get here by driving 20 miles east from Verlot to Barlow Pass, where the four-mile side road to Monte Cristo begins. Floods in 1980 and 1990 left it impassable to cars, but it remains a popular place for mountain bikers and hikers in the summer, and cross-country skiers and snowmobilers in the winter. Check at the Forest Service offices in Darrington or Verlot for current road and bridge conditions. The Forest Service's free **Monte Cristo Campground** offers a pleasant overnighting spot near the ghost town.

Glacier Basin Trail (No. 719) is a popular two-mile hiking route from Monte Cristo into nearby high country. The trail follows an old railroad grade for the first half-mile, then climbs steeply past Glacier Falls, around Mystery Hill, and into gorgeous Glacier Basin, gaining 1,300 feet in elevation. The route passes all sorts of rusting mining equipment, pieces of the cable tramway, and old mine shafts on the way. Bring your stove, since no campfires are allowed in the high country, and avoid camping on the fragile meadow areas. Good campsites can be found at Ray's Knoll and Mystery Ridge.

Another very steep hike (trail No. 708; 4.4 miles each way) climbs over **Poodle Dog Pass** from Monte Cristo. This trail leaves from the townsite, ascends to Silver Lake, and then on to an open ridge offering panoramic views of the surrounding mountains.

Glacier Peak Wilderness

Covering 576,865 acres—35 miles long by 20 miles wide—massive Glacier Peak Wilderness is one of Washington's largest stretches of wilderness landscape. Its dominant geologic feature, Glacier Peak, is the fourth highest mountain in the state, reaching 10,541 feet. A dormant volcano, Glacier Peak last erupted some 12,000 years ago; today its summit is almost encircled by glaciers. In the Glacier Peak Wilderness, you're likely to see deer, blue grouse, and marmots, plus an occasional lynx, mountain goat, and cougar. Deep snow buries much of the wilderness high country till late June, and some trails are not free of snow until mid-July.

More than 450 miles of backcountry trails provide diverse hiking opportunities in the wilderness, with access from all sides, including the Marblemount, plus the Lake Chelan, Stehekin, and Entiat River areas. The western side of the wilderness reaches almost to the Mountain Loop Hwy., with access via several Forest Service spur roads. The ultimate hiking experience, the **Pacific Crest Trail,** cuts right through the heart of Glacier Peak Wilderness, following the ridges for 60 miles of ascending and descending paths. For a complete description of hiking trails in the wilderness, see *100 Hikes in Washington's North Cascades: Glacier Peak Region,* by Ira Spring and Harvey Manning (Seattle: The Mountaineers).

The most popular path in the wilderness is the seven-mile-long **White Chuck Trail** (No. 643). This trail begins at the end of Forest Rd. 23, near the Sulphur Creek Campground, and follows the White Chuck River along a fairly gentle route for the first five miles, passing ancient groves of trees along the way. A short detour 4.2 miles in takes hikers to **Kennedy Hot Springs,** where the warm (not hot) natural pool is a favorite soaking spot for day-hikers. More adventurous folks continue up White Chuck Trail to its junction with the Pacific Crest Trail, or follow side trails into other parts of the wilderness. Mountaineers heading up the glaciers of Glacier Peak often use White Chuck Trail to reach the base of the mountain, scrambling to the timberline and following the Sitkum Glacier to the summit. Consult a North Cascades climbing guidebook for a detailed description of the route. In spring, call (360) 527-6677 for avalanche information.

The Pacific Crest Trail is accessible from the west side at various points off the Mountain Loop Highway. One of the best of these is the **North Fork Sauk Trail** (No. 649), an 8.4-mile path offering a gentle riverside route through a magnificent old-growth cedar forest, before relentlessly switchbacking upwards to the Pacific Crest Trail, gaining 3,900 feet en route. An excellent loop hike (26 miles roundtrip) is to continue south on the PCT to its junction with the **Pilot Ridge Trail** (No. 652), and then follow that trail back downhill past alpine lakes to its junction with the

North Fork Sauk Trail. The Pilot Ridge Trail offers hikers vistas of Glacier Peak and Mt. Rainier, but be sure to carry plenty of water, since portions of this loop hike lack water sources. Get to the North Fork Sauk trailhead by driving east from the Verlot Public Service Center for 27 miles (or south from Darrington for 20 miles), and turning east onto Sloan Creek Rd. 49 near the Bedal Campground. The trailhead is located 6.6 miles up, where the road crosses Sloan Creek.

Darrington Area Trails

Several short paths provide fun day hikes in the Darrington area. **Old Sauk Trail** (No. 728) is an easy three-mile stroll that departs from Clear Creek Campground, four miles south of Darrington. The trail parallels the Sauk River, passing riverside alder stands and moss-covered cedar stumps. Salmon and steelhead spawn in Murphy Creek at the southern end of the Old Sauk Trail.

A three-mile path, **Beaver Lake Trail** (No. 629), starts across from White Chuck Campground, 10 miles south of Darrington. The trail sits atop an old railroad grade and crosses beaver ponds where you're likely to see ducks and herons. It continues through a beautiful stand of old-growth cedar trees at the upper end before looping back to the Mountain Loop Highway. Both of these are also good for mountain bikes.

Another hike through virgin timber is the **Boulder River Trail** (No. 734). Get here by heading 8.2 miles west from Darrington, turn south onto French Creek Rd. 2010, branch right after a mile, and then follow it another 2.8 miles to the trailhead. In addition to thick old-growth forests, this four-mile trail passes a delightful series of Boulder River waterfalls and cascades.

OTHER RECREATION

Whitewater Trips

The **Sauk River,** a National Wild and Scenic River that rises in the Henry M. Jackson Wilderness and joins the Skagit River near Rockport, offers a combination of fast and complex rapids, fantastic mountain scenery, and plenty of wildlife. Trips generally start 10 miles upriver and end in Darrington, with lots of class III-IV whitewater along the way. The primary season is May to mid-August. This whitewater trip is offered by **North Cascades River Expeditions,** tel. (800) 634-8433, and **Orion Expeditions,** tel. (800) 553-7466.

The **Suiattle River** (soo-AT-ul) starts in the Glacier Peak Wilderness and meets the Sauk River north of Darrington. This is a good whitewater river for families and folks starting out, with great mountain scenery and lots of small rapids along the 13 miles of river. Because of its glacial origins, the Suiattle has a milky, silt-laden appearance and braided channels. The main season for river-running is June to early September. Companies offering whitewater floats down the Suiattle are: **All Rivers Adventures,** tel. (800) 743-5628; **Blue Sky Outfitters,** tel. (800) 228-7238; **North Cascades River Expeditions,** tel. (800) 634-8433; and **Northern Wilderness River Riders,** tel. (800) 448-7238.

On Your Own

Experienced, do-it-yourself river runners will enjoy the challenges of the Sauk and Suiattle Rivers. The Suiattle is the tamer of the two, rated class II-III from Boundary Bridge to the Sauk River; it's not navigable within the national forest due to logjams, hidden stumps, and debris. Put in at Boundary bridge. The Sauk River ranges from class I to V; from the White Chuck launch area to Clear Creek it's a IV or V, with difficult rapids through narrow passages. From Bedal to White Chuck, the river is classified as a class III-IV, and below Clear Creek it ranges from class I to III. North of Darrington, the river is considerably calmer and is popular for canoeing.

Canoeing and Fishing

The Darrington District boasts a large number of small lakes, some of which provide excellent fishing. Check at the ranger station or public service center for a list of lakes and suggestions on the best ones for boating, fishing, or paddling.

Paddlers and rafters will enjoy exploring six-acre **Coal Lake,** a subalpine lake at 3,600 feet elevation. Go east on the Mountain Loop Hwy. for 15 miles from the Verlot Public Service Center, then go north on Coal Lake Rd. 4060 for 4.5 miles to the trailhead. Carry your boat for about

50 feet to the lake, where you'll find a limited number of campsites that fill up very quickly.

Another lake with easy canoe and raft access is five-acre **Canyon Lake.** From the Verlot Public Service Center, drive four miles on the Mountain Loop Hwy. to Rd. 41; turn right, continuing for two miles to Green Mt. Rd. 4110. Turn right again (heading east now), driving almost 1.4 miles to Rd. 4111; follow this road for 10.75 miles to the trailhead on the left side of the road. Carry your boat along the 50-foot trail to Canyon Lake, surrounded by trees and a few campsites; fair fishing.

Cross-Country Skiing

Skiers and snowshoers can count on solitude when exploring the Darrington District; most roads aren't plowed and snowfall is unpredictable at this low elevation. Any existing snow here is often wet and difficult to ski through. Still determined? Take these routes as suggestions; if the roads themselves aren't snow-covered, keep driving along the route until you come to some that are.

From Hwy. 530 on the way to Darrington, go south on **French Creek Rd. 2010** to the snowline, and then ski uphill from there. The road takes you through dense forest and switchbacks for great views and a fast downhill trip back. Or, from the Darrington Ranger Station, drive north on Hwy. 530 for 6.5 miles to **Suiattle River Rd. 26;** follow it till you hit snow, and then ski up the road and along the river. Fine views of Glacier Peak along the way.

On the Granite Falls side, the **Big Four** area is very popular with skiers, snowshoers, snowmobilers, and winter hikers; take the Mountain Loop Hwy. 23 miles from Granite Falls to the end of the maintained road at Deer Creek Rd. 4052. Ski two miles from the parking area to Big Four Picnic Area, following the South Fork of the Stillaguamish River; continue another mile to the snowfield near the Big Four Ice Cave. The avalanche danger here is severe; don't travel beyond the edge of the clearing—it's the force of avalanches that created and maintains that clearing! Allow 3-5 hours roundtrip; suitable for beginning skiers.

A more challenging route is the **Deer Creek/Kelcema Lake Ski Route** that follows Deer Creek Road uphill to Kelcema Lake, a distance of 4.6 miles, with an elevation gain of 1,600 feet. Allow 5-7 hours for the roundtrip, and avoid it during periods of high avalanche danger. Get here by heading 12 miles east from the Verlot Public Service Center to the end of snow plowing and the start of the ski route. No snowmobiles are allowed here.

Another popular cross-country ski route (for advanced skiers only) begins at the Deer Creek parking area and continues 11 miles to the old mining town of Monte Cristo, gaining 1,275 feet in elevation en route. This is best done as an overnight trip due to its length; be sure to check on avalanche conditions before heading out.

CAMPING

The Forest Service operates 16 campgrounds ($6-12) along the Mountain Loop. Reserve any of these ($9 extra) by calling (877) 444-6777. Campgrounds are generally open Memorial Day to mid-September (or longer). Free dispersed camping is allowed on Forest Service lands away from the campgrounds.

From Granite Falls, neighboring **Turlo** and **Verlot** campgrounds are near the Verlot Service Center, while **Gold Basin Campground** is 2.4 miles east of the service center. Gold Basin also features an amphitheater where Saturday night campfire programs are presented in the summer. Across the road is a short wheelchair-accessible interpretive trail. Continuing on from Verlot these include: **Boardman Creek Campground** (open all year), six miles east; and **Red Bridge Campground**, seven miles east.

From Darrington, Forest Service campsites include: **Clear Creek Campground,** four miles south, and **Bedal Campground,** 18 miles south, both open year-round. A mile east of Bedal Campground on Forest Rd. 49 is a quarter-mile path to the base of spectacular **North Fork Sauk Falls,** where the river plunges 45 feet.

From Darrington via Suiattle River Rd. No. 26, **Buck Creek Campground,** 22 miles northeast of town, features a quiet riverside setting in an old-growth forest. **Sulphur Creek Campground,** 28 miles from Darrington (near the end of Suiattle River Rd.), is just a mile away from the Glacier Peak Wilderness and is open year-round. A short trail leads from the campground along

Sulphur Creek to colorful pools containing rather odoriferous hydrogen sulfide gas. See **Darrington** for other camping options.

INFORMATION

Get detailed camping, hiking, and historical information at the Mt. Baker-Snoqualmie National Forest's **Verlot Public Service Center,** tel. (360) 691-7791, located 11 miles east of Granite Falls; open daily 8 a.m.-4:30 p.m. June-Labor Day, and Thurs.-Mon. 8 a.m.-4:30 p.m. in the spring and fall; closed in winter. The buildings at Verlot were built by the CCC between 1933 and 1942. The **Darrington Ranger District,** 1405 Emmens St. in Darrington, tel. (360) 436-1155, is open Mon.-Fri. 8 a.m.-4:30 p.m. year-round.

GRANITE FALLS

Granite Falls (pop. 1,100) sits at the southwest end of the Mountain Loop Hwy. with Pilchuck Mountain offering a dramatic backdrop. The town began in 1889 as construction headquarters for the railroad route to the mines at Monte Cristo, and grew up as a waystation and center for logging and farming in the area. Because of its location at the base of the Cascades, the town provides a jumping-off point for hikers, campers, cross-country skiers, and snowmobilers exploring the Mt. Baker-Snoqualmie National Forest. Granite Falls is a tobacco-chewing, pickup truck, beer gut, ballcap-and-jeans sort of place, where you'll find live music at the Corner Tavern on summer weekends, and a rough-at-the-edges feel every day of the week. The older houses are accentuated by mossy roofs, while the false-fronted buildings of downtown show their heritage with pride. This conservative, country feel is in the process of changing, as the first wave of new housing development rolls in, and as the first neon "Espresso" signs start flashing.

Sights
The **Granite Falls Museum** (open Sunday 1-4 p.m. during the summer; closed winters) houses local memorabilia; check out the cross-section from an enormous 1,200-year-old Douglas fir tree in the front.

Just east of town is the **Granite Falls Fish Ladder,** the world's longest vertical baffle fish ladder when it was built in 1954. Stop here to marvel at the raging South Fork of the Stillaguamish River as it roils over the falls (actually more of a giant rapids) for which the town was named. Salmon swim up a 240-foot tunnel dug through the granite.

Practicalities

Walk down the main drag to find several places with standard American fare, including **Ike's Diner,** tel. (360) 691-6636, where the Formica and burger atmosphere is straight from the '50s. Good chicken burgers and fries.

Mountain View Inn, 10 miles east of town in the rustic Robe Valley, tel. (360) 691-6668, has rooms for $40 s or d.

The **Granite Falls Farmers Marketplace,** tel. (360) 691-6173, comes to town Sunday noon-4 p.m. late June-September.

Pick up a handful of local brochures at **Granite Falls Town Hall,** tel. (360) 691-6441. Local events include the **Show 'N Shine Festival** on the first weekend of August, and **Railroad Days** on the first weekend of October.

Community Transit, tel. (360) 778-2185 or (800) 562-1375, has daily bus service throughout Snohomish County.

DARRINGTON

Darrington (pop. 1,100), in the foothills of the Cascades northeast of Everett, was home to the Sauk and Suiattle Indians until white miners in search of gold and silver arrived in the late 1800s and early 1900s. Though some deposits were found, the real money in this area was in logging. Swedish, Irish, Welsh, and Norwegian loggers, plus a very large group from North Carolina, Georgia, and Tennessee, founded a community that still reflects its ethnic origins, especially the North Carolinians, who take great pride in their Tarheel heritage and mountain music.

Darrington, backdropped to the southwest by the 6,563-foot summit of Whitehorse Mountain, is located in a low pass separating the Sauk River from the North Fork of the Stillaguamish River. A collection of old buildings occupies the streets. Prominent among these is the **Trafton School,** a two-story white clapboard structure built in 1907. The town has a run-down feel, as if it were just waiting to be discovered by the next wave of outmigrating Seattleites in search of a peaceful place to escape the city life. With a setting like this, that shouldn't take long.

Accommodations

Darrington's **Stagecoach Inn,** 1100 Seaman St., tel. (360) 436-1776 or (800) 428-1776, is an attractive, small motel with rooms offering mountain views for $59-69 s or d.

Out in the country 11 miles west of Darrington is **Mt. Higgins House B&B,** tel. (360) 435-8703 or (888) 296-3777, a beautiful modern home with a trout pond and gorgeous mountain views. The two guest rooms have private baths, and a buffet breakfast is included; $85-105 s or d. No kids.

Food

Most of Darrington's eateries offer pretty standard American fare, but **Country Coffee and Deli,** 1015 Sauk Ave., tel. (360) 436-0213, cranks out tasty homemade soups and sandwiches. **Back Woods Cafe,** 45700 Hwy. 530, tel. (360) 436-1845, is the only real "sit-down" place in Darrington. Stop at the **Whitehorse Store,** five miles west of Darrington, for old fashioned ice-cream cones.

Campgrounds

The closest Forest Service campground is the **Clear Creek Campground** ($12; reserve by calling 800-444-6777), four miles south of town on Forest Rd. 20. **Squire Creek County Park,** tel. (360) 435-3441, offers year-round camping ($10 tents; $15 RVs) amid old-growth Douglas fir and cedar trees four miles west of Darrington on Hwy. 530. The park is also home to the largest cottonwood tree in Washington.

Sauk River County Park, seven miles north of Darrington on Sauk Valley Rd., has more campsites. No charge and no drinking water.

Events

The last weekend in June brings the **Timber Bowl Rodeo** to the rodeo grounds four miles west of town. Darrington's three-day **Bluegrass Festival and Street Fair** in mid-July is one of the most popular musical events in the Puget Sound Basin, in part because the area has developed some of the best bluegrass musicians outside Kentucky and Tennessee. Darrington also hosts the **National Archery Tournament** every third year; next time is 2000.

Information and Transportation
For up-to-date information on trail conditions, campgrounds, fishing, and other outdoor activi-

ties contact the **Darrington Ranger Station,** a half-mile north of town, tel. (360) 436-1155. Across the street from the Darrington Ranger Station is **Nels Bruseth Memorial Garden,** with several Sauk cedar canoes on display.

Community Transit, tel. (360) 778-2185 or (800) 562-1375, has daily service throughout Snohomish County.

NORTH CASCADES HIGHWAY

The North Cascades Highway—State Highway 20—begins in the Skagit River Valley, and follows this drainage to 5,477-foot Washington Pass, before descending into Methow Valley on the east side of the Cascade Range. Along the way, the road passes several small towns— Sedro-Woolley, Concrete, Rockport, and Marblemount—but after this you enter North Cascades National Park and Okanogan National Forest lands. This is magnificent mountain country, with numerous pullouts for viewing the striking scenery and a multitude of recreation options—campgrounds, visitors centers, and access to many other hiking paths, including the Pacific Crest Trail. Because of this, Hwy. 20 is one of the most popular and scenic drives in Washington. But don't plan on just driving through; bring your hiking boots, map, and a flexible schedule to really experience the North Cascades. Highway 20 is also a popular cycling route in the summer months, providing an official Bikecentennial route across rural America from Anacortes, Washington, to Bangor, Maine. This description of the North Cascades Highway starts on the eastern end at Sedro-Woolley and follows the road over the mountains into the Methow Valley.

History
The earliest white men to explore the North Cascades were Alexander Ross and his party, who crossed today's southern park boundary at Cascade Pass in 1814. In 1859, Henry Custer, working as an assistant of reconnaissances for the International Boundary Commission, traversed the region and commented: "Nowhere do the mountain masses and peaks present such strange, fantastic, dauntless and startling outlines as here. . . . [It] must be seen, it cannot be

described." From 1880 to 1910, prospectors struck gold, platinum, lead, and zinc, but mountain travel was too difficult to justify the modest return.

On the west side of the mountains, the potential of the Skagit River wasn't harnessed until 1924, when the first of three dams was built by Seattle City Light. This rugged area was preserved as the North Cascades National Park Service Complex in 1968, incorporating Ross Lake and Lake Chelan National Recreation Areas that were created as buffers to the park.

The North Cascades Scenic Highway (Highway 20) was originally commissioned in 1893, when state legislators set aside $20,000 for the completion of the Cascade Wagon Route. Over the decades that followed, sections of the road were gradually completed, and by 1968—the year the national park was established—a rough dirt road crossed the summit. The highway finally opened in 1972, some 79 years after the first shovel of dirt had been dug.

Climate
Summer weather on the west side of the North Cascades is cooler and wetter than the eastern portion, which is protected by the rain-shadow effect. The east side of the range gets quite hot in the summer and is almost always dry. One of the major attractions of the Methow Valley for Puget Sounders is the usually sunny weather, the cold Colorado-style winters and the hot, dry summers that make a perfect antidote to the damp, often overcast Puget Sound weather.

Driving Highway 20
No gas stations, restaurants, or other facilities (except restrooms at Washington Pass) are found along the 75 miles of Hwy. 20 between

Ross Dam and Mazama, so fill up when you leave I-5 (Sedro-Woolley is cheapest if you get lots of miles per tank). No bus service goes along this route either; the closest you'll get is Mount Vernon on the west and Pateros and Okanogan on the east.

The middle section of Hwy. 20 closes for the winter after the first major snowfall because of avalanche danger. It is usually gated in late November and doesn't open again until late April, sometimes nearly June, depending on the amount of snow. In mid-winter, snow depths can exceed 15 feet at the summit. Parts of the highway remain open to snowmobile traffic from Colonial Creek Campground on the west side to Early Winters Campground near Mazama. Lower-elevation hiking trails, such as those along Ross Lake, are generally accessible from April through mid-October; at higher elevations, trails are open from mid-July through September.

Cascade Loop Trips

Highway 20 joins Hwy. 153 at Twisp, Hwy. 97 near Pateros, and Hwy. 2 near Wenatchee to form the northwest portion of the "Cascade Loop." This 400-mile scenic drive winds through the North Cascades, past Lake Chelan, through Leavenworth on its approach to Stevens Pass, and returns to western Washington and Whidbey Island. You'll find free *Cascade Loop* booklets at visitors centers along the way, or call the Cascade Loop Association in Wenatchee, tel. (509) 662-3888, for a copy, or check www.cascade-loop.com on the Web.

A similar promotional highway route has been organized and is called the "North Cascades Loop." It follows the same route over Hwy. 20, continues on to the twin towns of Omak and Okanogan, turns north on Hwy. 97 and goes across into British Columbia's Okanagan (note that Canada and the U.S. spell the word differently), then heads west on the Trans-Canada Highway to the Vancouver area. Look for free *International Loop* booklets at visitors centers.

North Cascades Institute

The nonprofit North Cascades Institute offers a wide spectrum of classes, lectures, kayak trips, whalewatching cruises, birdwatching safaris, photography training, and even poetry workshops. You'll find something going almost all the time between April and December. For more information, contact the North Cascades Institute, 2105 Hwy. 20 in Sedro-Woolley, tel. (360) 856-5700, ext. 209; on the Web at www.ncascades.org/nci.

SEDRO-WOOLLEY

The riverside town of Sedro-Woolley (pop. 7,600) is a place in transition. The decline of the logging industry in recent years has hit hard, forcing the town to look elsewhere for an economic base. It remains a commercial center for the farmlands that surround it, while becoming an outfitting town for adventurers on their way east into North Cascades National Park. This odd amalgam is reflected in two downtown buildings. One is home to a gun association (the U.S. Practical Shooting Association); the other houses an organic foods company (Cascadian Farm).

History

Settlement of land at the mouth of the Skagit River began as early as 1863, but a huge natural logjam prevented any upriver development until it was dynamited apart in 1879. After this, sternwheelers could move up and down the river, opening the country to mining and logging. Five years later, Mortimer Cook opened a general store in a riverside town he named "Bug"—for the mosquitoes that tormented him in the summer. Cook later succumbed to local pressure and changed the name to Sedro, a corruption of "cedra," the Spanish word for the cedar trees that once covered this area. About the same time, P.A. Woolley built a sawmill a few miles away that became the economic basis of a small but thriving community. The towns were so close together it was difficult to determine their borders, so in 1898 they agreed to join forces while retaining both names. Hence the only hyphenated town name in Washington, and one of just two in America.

After a pair of devastating turn-of-the-century fires, the town was rebuilt using bricks. As a major logging settlement, Sedro-Woolley attracted many of its residents from North Carolina, a heritage that is still evident today. By early in this century, the town was home to 17 lumber mills, a steel foundry, and a big state hospital.

Very little of these remain. An effort is now underway to re-create Sedro-Woolley's 1920s-era downtown with old-style lamps and restored brick buildings.

Sights
Sedro-Woolley Museum, 727 Murdock St., tel. (360) 855-2390, contains local memorabilia and old logging and farming equipment, and is open Saturday 9 a.m.-4 p.m., and Sunday 1:30-4:30 p.m. year-round. While here, pick up a walking tour of historic sight around town, including a steam donkey from 1913. Seven of the historic logging pictures by famed turn-of-the-century documentary photographer Darius Kinsey have been turned into murals on downtown buildings.

Though dwarfed by the nearby mountain lakes in the national park, **Clear Lake** has swimming beaches, boating, and fishing just three miles south of town.

North from Sedro-Woolley
Highway 9 north from Sedro-Woolley leads through quiet Nooksack Valley with its aging dairy barns, big bales of hay, and comfortable homesteads. A series of podunk towns form wide spots in the road: **Wickersham, Acme, Clipper, Van Zandt, Deming, Nugents Corner,** and **Nooksack.** A favorite tubing float trip is down the warm South Fork of the Nooksack River from Saxon to Van Zandt. On hot August weekends several thousand folks join in the fun, creating traffic congestion and conflicts with spawning salmon.

Everybody stops at the turn-of-the-century **Everybody's Store** in Van Zandt, tel. (360) 592-2297, where the shelves are filled with all manner of supplies: delicious baked goods, ice-cream cones, wool caps, 40 kinds of cheese, Indonesian batiks, and organic produce from the backyard garden. The deli here makes great sandwiches.

Woolly Prairie Buffalo Co., tel. (360) 856-0310 or (800) 524-7660, just north of Sedro-Woolley, offers summertime hay rides where you can learn about bison.

Accommodations and Camping
Three Rivers Motel, 210 Ball St., tel. (360) 855-2626 or (800) 221-5122, has comfortable lodging for $58-88 s or d, including an outdoor pool, jacuzzi, and continental breakfast. **Skagit Motel,** 1977 Hwy. 20, tel. (360) 856-6001, charges $32-37 s, $42-47 d.

Riverfront RV Park on McDonald Ave., tel. (360) 855-1661, has tent ($5) and RV ($10) sites on the banks of the Skagit River.

Food
Timbers Restaurant, tel. (360) 856-4460, is a locals favorite, with prime rib, pasta, and seafood in a cheerful interior. **Ferry St. Grill & Bar,** 208 Ferry St., tel. (360) 855-2210, has a wide range of meals, from big breakfasts to ribs and salmon for dinner. Get authentic Greek food at **Rhodes Pizza & Pasta,** 617 Metcalf St., tel. (360) 855-2313. The belly dancers entertain on Friday nights. **Hal's Drive-In,** 321 State St., tel. (360) 855-0868, is a longtime favorite, with burgers, shakes, corn dogs, and onion rings.

Events
The Fourth of July brings the weeklong **Loggerodeo** to Sedro-Woolley—an annual event for more than 65 years—with logging contests, parades, a rodeo, street dance, bed race, carnival, vintage car show, crafts fair, and big fireworks display. In mid-May the town carves out a niche for itself with **Woodfest,** a celebration of woodcarving and woodworking from klutzy chainsaw art to intricately carved works. **Founders' Day** in mid-September includes a pancake breakfast, animal parade, and children's games.

Information and Services
On Hwy. 20, just west of Sedro-Woolley, you'll find the **Mt. Baker Ranger Station/North Cascades National Park Service Complex,** tel. (360) 856-5700, with a North Cascades relief map, books and brochures for sale, and information on road conditions. It's open daily 8 a.m.-4:30 p.m. in the summer (till 6 p.m. on Friday), and Mon.-Fri. 8 a.m.-4:30 p.m. in winter.

The **Sedro-Woolley Chamber of Commerce,** downtown at 714B Metcalf, tel. (360) 855-1841 or (888) 225-8365, is open Mon.-Fri. 9:30 a.m.-5 p.m., and Sat. 9:30 a.m.-1 p.m. The city also has a summer-only **Information Caboose** in Harry Osborne Park at the junction of Hwy. 20 and W. Ferry St., tel. (360) 855-0974.

Free **Skagit Transit** buses connect Sedro-Woolley with other towns in Skagit County; call (360) 757-4443 for details.

BAKER LAKE

Nine-mile-long Baker Lake was created by the Upper Dam on the Baker River; the Lower Baker Dam created Lake Shannon, just off Hwy. 20 near Concrete. Baker Lake is very popular with campers, swimmers, motor boaters, and water-skiers, despite the enormous stumps that lurk just below the water's surface. To get there, take Baker Lake-Grandy Lake Rd. north from Hwy. 20. Get to 100-foot-high **Rainbow Falls** by driving 20 miles out Baker Lake Rd., and then another five miles up Forest Rd. 1130. The name comes from the rainbow that appears at the base on sunny days.

Campgrounds

Puget Sound Energy maintains the **Kulshan Campground** near Upper Baker Dam; $5. Free camping (no running water) at **Grandy Lake County Park,** four miles northeast of Hwy. 20 on Baker Lake Highway. Farther up Baker Lake Rd. are the **Horseshoe Cove, Panorama Point, Shannon Creek, Boulder Creek,** and **Park Creek** Forest Service campgrounds ($7-12). No drinking water at Boulder Creek or Park Creek. All of these can be reserved ($9 extra) by calling (877) 444-6777. A boat-in or hike-in campground at Maple Grove is also available. The campgrounds are usually open mid-May to mid-October; call (360) 856-5700 for details.

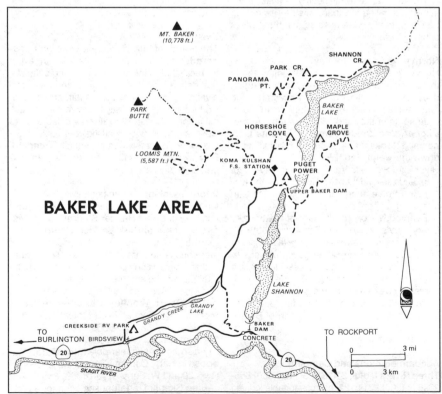

BAKER LAKE AREA

Rasar State Park

Washington's newest state park, Rasar opened in 1997 on a quiet 128-acre site along the Skagit River. It's a great place for a riverside picnic, and bald eagles are visible early in the year. Several trails lead through the tall second-growth forests, and year-round camping is available for $10 tents or $15 RVs; no reservations. The park is just off Hwy. 20 along Cape Horn Rd. near Concrete.

Baker Lake Resort

Six miles past the Forest Service's Koma Kulshan Guard Station on the west shore, Baker Lake Resort has a dozen rustic cabins with full kitchens, camping and RV sites, boat rentals, a store, and restaurant. There's a two night minimum on weekend, and the resort is open only from mid-April through October. Call (888) 711-3033 for reservations.

Hiking Trails

A fee of $3 per vehicle per day is charged at Forest Service trailheads. A better option is the $25 annual Trail Park Pass that can be used on most Washington national forests. Get one from any Forest Service office.

The easiest hike around is the half-mile wheelchair-accessible **Shadow of the Sentinels Trail** that winds through an old-growth Douglas fir stand. It begins a mile beyond the Koma Kulshan guard station.

An excellent, gentle rain-forest hike is up the **Baker River.** To reach the trailhead for this six-mile roundtrip hike, drive north on Baker Lake-Grandy Lake Rd. for 14 miles to the Komo Kulshan Guard Station. Follow the Forest Service road for 11.5 miles, then left a mile, then right on the first side road for half a mile to the start of Trail 606. This level, low-elevation trail affords views of glaciers and beaver ponds on the way to Sulphur Creek, the turnaround point. Because of its low elevation, the trail is snow-free from early spring to late fall.

Another Baker Lake hike takes you to **Park Butte,** a 5,450-foot summit with incredible views of Mt. Baker glaciers. This summer-only trek is seven miles roundtrip, but with an elevation gain of over 2,200 feet it'll take a good part of the day to complete. Go north for 12.5 miles on Baker Lake-Grandy Lake Rd., then turn left on Loomis-Nooksack Rd. 12 for 3.5 miles, then turn right onto Rd. 13 for five miles to the road's end. The trail is west of the road, crossing Sulphur Creek before the switchbacks begin.

CONCRETE

East from Sedro-Woolley, Hwy. 20 skirts the Skagit River, climbing easily toward the first Cascade foothills. The landscape is farms, fields, and forests, with the serrated summit of Sauk Mountain to the east. Clearcut hillsides, second (or third) growth forests, and closed lumber mills offer contrasting versions of the logging heritage.

The fading town of Concrete (pop. 700) was home for many years to the largest cement plant in the state, and the source for cement used in building Grand Coulee Dam, as well as the Ross and Diablo dams. Although environmental regulations closed the outdated, dusty plant in 1968, the prosaic town name remains. (It could have been worse; the town's original name was Cement City.) The town burned several times in the early part of this century, and was finally rebuilt, using concrete, of course. The 5,537-foot summit of Sauk Mountain rises straight behind Main St.; see **Rockport** for access to the top. Today, the rundown town creeps along on a mix of tourism and timber. All that remains of the cement industry are the aging silos on the west end of town, a scattering of other buildings, and the quarry near Lake Shannon.

Sights

There aren't a lot of in-town attractions; your best bet is to pick a Main St. bench and sit with the locals a spell. Of minor interest is Superior St., with its unique under-the-high-school access to the airport. Eagles are visible along the Skagit River in winter, and elk herds can be seen just west of town in winter and spring.

Camp Seven Logger's Museum ($2) is a small private collection of logging-era flotsam and jetsam on Railroad Avenue. Open weekends in the summer; tel. (360) 853-7185.

Just east of town is the **Henry Thompson Bridge** over the Baker River. When completed in 1918, it was the longest single-span cement

Ross Dam

DIANNE BOULERICE LYONS

bridge in the world. A quarter mile east of this is the **Puget Sound Energy Visitors Center.** Check out the unusual fish elevator nearby, used to help get returning salmon around the Baker Dam; see the salmon here between June and December. **Sauk Mountain Pottery,** three miles east of Concrete, is worth a visit for wood-fired stoneware and porcelain.

Lodging and Food

Located just west of town, **North Cascade Inn,** tel. (360) 853-8870, has rooms for $45 s or $50 d. **Eagles Nest Motel** on the east end of Concrete, tel. (360) 853-8662, charges $45 s or $48 d, and has space for tents and RVs.

Cascade Mountain Inn B&B, tel. (360) 826-4333, is five miles west of Concrete. Most of the five guest rooms have views of Sauk Mountain, and each has a private bath; $120 s or d. No kids.

Located on the 700-acre working cattle ranch, **Ovenell's Heritage Inn B&B,** 4442 Concrete Sauk Valley Rd., tel. (360) 853-8494, is a 1915 ranch house with four guest rooms. A full breakfast is served; $105-115 s or d. No kids.

Baker St. Bar & Grill, 92 Baker St., tel. (360) 853-7002, has the best local meals, including seafood, steaks, burgers, and salads.

Visit Concrete's **Saturday Market,** where produce, crafts, baked goods, and art are offered for sale 9 a.m.-4 p.m. every Saturday mid-May through August.

Events

The **Upper Skagit Bald Eagle Festival** celebrates the hundreds of eagles that gather along the Skagit River in late January. Festivities include music, an arts and crafts show, and naturalist presentations in Concrete, Marblemount, and Rockport. Other local events include the **Concrete Fly-Inn** on the third weekend in May, attracting pilots from around the Northwest, the **River Raft Challenge Race,** held the fourth Saturday in July, and **Good Olde Days,** on the third weekend in August.

Information and Services

The **Concrete Chamber of Commerce** office, tel. (360) 853-8400, open weekdays, is right off Hwy. 20 in the Community Center. Catch the **Sockeye Express** trolley here ($2) for a 45-minute historical tour of town on weekends and holidays in the summer. **Skagit Transit,** tel. (360) 757-4433, offers free daily bus service throughout the county, from Anacortes to Concrete.

ROCKPORT

There isn't much to the tiny settlement called Rockport (pop. 150), but two pleasant parks offer a break from the highway, and bald eagles congregate along the Skagit River here. The **Bald Eagle Interpretive Center** is inside the fire hall, tel. (360) 853-7614; open Fri.-Sat. 10 a.m.-4 p.m. and Sunday noon-4 p.m.

Practicalities

Rockport Country Store has something you don't see every day, a "self-kicking machine." Great for masochists. **Cascadian Farm Roadside Stand,** tel. (360) 853-8173, sells organic strawberries, blueberries, and raspberries, along with sweet corn and other produce from the cooperative's gardens. They also offer homemade ice cream, espresso, and wonderful fresh berry shortcakes. Open May-October.

Howard Miller Steelhead Park tel. (360) 853-8808, is a small county park with big grassy lawns right along the river. Tent sites are $12, Adirondack shelters and RV hookups cost $16. In the park you'll find Chief Campbell's old dugout canoe and a log cabin built in the early 1880s. The old **Rockport Ferry,** last used in 1961, sits along the river. Right across the street is **Pleasant View Inn Tavern,** with live music on summer weekends.

Rockport State Park

As you drive east from Concrete on Hwy. 20, the clearcuts are recent and hideous in places. There are very few old growth trees remaining on private land anywhere in the area, and it isn't till you reach Rockport State Park, about 10 miles east of Baker Lake, that you realize what has been lost. Covering 457 acres, the park has five miles of wooded hiking trails, Skagit River steelhead fishing, and camping at tent sites with Adirondack shelters ($10) and RV sites ($15) beneath incredible 250-foot high old-growth Douglas fir trees. The campground is open mid-April through October and has showers. The paved and wheelchair-accessible **Skagit View Trail** leads right down to the riverbank, providing a great place to look for bald eagles in the winter.

Immediately west of the park is the start of **Sauk Mountain Rd.,** a 7.5 mile gravel road that takes you to a trailhead most of the way up this 5,537-foot peak. A steep, switchback-filled trail begins at the parking lot, climbing another 1.5 miles to the summit, where you're treated to views of the northern Cascades and the Skagit and Sauk River Valleys.

BALD EAGLE VIEWING AND WHITEWATER RAFTING

The Skagit River is one of the best places in the Lower 48 to watch wintering bald eagles, with over 300 birds stopping by for a salmon feast on their journey south from Alaska and Canada. Just east of Rockport, the Nature Conservancy's 1,500-acre **Skagit River Bald Eagle Natural Area,** tel. (206) 343-4344, is a haven for these birds; they arrive in October and feast on Skagit River salmon through March. Eagles are visible from Hwy. 20 pullouts all along the Skagit River Valley, but the best way to see them is on a scenic float trip down the river. You're likely to see at least 50 of these majestic birds perched in trees along the nine-mile float from Marblemount to Rockport. To protect the eagles, this stretch of the river is voluntarily closed to all boats 5-11 a.m. from late Dec.-February.

Float Trips

A number of companies offer scenic bald eagle float trips Dec.-Feb., when the population is at a peak. The river is so gentle that wetsuits are not necessary; just wear warm winter clothing. Expect to pay $50-75 for the three and a half hour float. One of the oldest and best companies is **Chinook Expeditions,** tel. (800) 241-3451. Other companies with similar trips are: **Alpine Adventures,** tel. (800) 723-8386; **Blue Sky Outfitters,** tel. (800) 228-7238; **North Cascades River Expeditions,** tel. (800) 634-8433; **Northern Wilderness River Riders,** tel. (800) 448-7238; **Orion Expeditions,** tel. (800) 553-7466; **Osprey Rafting,** tel. (800) 743-6269; **River Recreation,** tel. (800) 464-5899; and **Wildwater River Tours,** tel. (800) 522-9453.

Whitewater Trips

In the summer, you can float eight miles of the upper Skagit River through North Cascades National Park, where the water is a bit rougher, but nothing over class III. It's a good beginning river for whitewater enthusiasts. The following companies have upper Skagit trips: Alpine Adventures, Orion Expeditions, Osprey Rafting, and Wildwater River Tours; see above for phone numbers.

MARBLEMOUNT

Entering Marblemount from the west, signs warn "Last Gas for 69 Miles" and, more importantly, "Last Tavern for 89 Miles." The little town is a good place to stock up on these—and other—essentials, and to get information and back-country permits for North Cascades National Park. A small museum features displays on the area's logging history. This pretty country settlement is surrounded by open fields and big-leaf maple trees (brilliant yellow in the fall), and is split by two rivers: the Skagit and the Cascade. Among the big-leaf maples is quaint **Wildwood Chapel,** covering barely enough space for a minister and the couple to be married. The chapel was built here in 1977 and has been used for weddings and countless I-was-there photos.

The **Marblemount Fish Hatchery,** a mile southeast of town on Fish Hatchery Rd., rears and releases thousands of king, silver, and chum salmon each year.

Accommodations and Food

Halfway between Rockport and Marblemount is **Totem Trails Motel,** tel. (360) 873-4535, with rooms for $50-55 s or d. Right across the road is **Wilderness Village RV Park,** tel. (360) 873-2571, offering tent and RV sites. The public laundromat here has **showers.**

Log House Inn, tel. (360) 873-4311, has additional lodging ($30-35 d with shared bath); it was built in 1890 as a roadhouse for workers who were attempting to build a road over the mountains. The road they began was not completed until the 1972 opening of Hwy. 20.

A Cab in the Woods, three miles west of Marblemount, tel. (360) 873-4106, has clean, modern cabins with full kitchens for $75 s or d. Friendly folks, too.

Salmonberry Way B&B, is a turn-of-the-century Victorian home 2.5 miles west of Marblemount, tel. (360) 873-4016. Inside are two comfortable guest rooms with shared baths for $45-55 s or d, including a continental breakfast. Kids are accepted.

Clark's Skagit River Cabins, three miles west of Marblemount, tel. (360) 873-2250 or (800) 273-2606, has cute rustic cabins for $52-

109 s or d, space for tents and RVs, and showers. Also here is **The Eatery Restaurant** with all-American meals. Be sure to check out the curious handsewn flag made in 1890. Rabbit lovers will have a hopping time here; dozens of bunnies are all over the big green grounds.

Buffalo Run Restaurant, tel. (360) 873-2461, makes the best—and most reasonable—meals in the area. The home-baked breads, berry pies, hearty soups, and fresh-from-the-garden organic greens are special treats.

Backcountry Permits

Follow the signs to the National Park Service's **Wilderness Information Center in Marble-mount;** open Sun.-Thurs. 7 a.m.-6 p.m., and Fri.-Sat. 7 a.m.-8 p.m. in July and August, with reduced hours in June and the first half of September. The rest of the year, it's catch as catch can. Get backcountry permits here for the park. Because there are no advance reservations, weekend campers arrive early to get permits for the most popular sites, especially Cascade Pass, Hidden Lake, MonogramS Lake, Ross Lake, and Thornton Lakes. If you're willing to accept alternate destinations, you should be able to get into the backcountry under most circumstances. Behind the Wilderness Office is a greenhouse used to grow plants to revegetate damaged backcountry areas.

NEWHALEM AND EASTWARD

Heading east from Marblemount, Hwy. 20 enters North Cascades National Park after five miles, then passes Goodell Creek and Newhalem Campgrounds, the turnoff to North Cascades Visitor Center, and **Skagit General Store** in Newhalem.

The little settlement of Newhalem is a quiet company town with only one focus, producing electricity for Seattle at nearby Gorge, Diablo, and Ross Dams. The parklike grounds are surrounded by trim clapboard homes occupied by employees of Seattle City Light. In the town park find **Old Number Six,** a 1928 Baldwin steam locomotive that hauled passengers and supplies to the Skagit River dams; today it's a favorite of kids. The small **Seattle City Light Visitor Center** here makes a good bathroom stop.

Over the Top

East of Newhalem, Hwy. 20 begins a serious climb into the forested Cascades, and quickly passes a chain of three dams and reservoirs—Gorge, Diablo, and Ross—that constitute the centerpiece of Ross Lake National Recreation Area (a part of North Cascades National Park). Tours of Diablo Dam and Lake are a popular attraction here. Be sure to stop at the Forge Creek Falls overlook near milepost 123 for views of the creek plunging into the gorge below. Colo-

nial Creek Campground is along the highway near Diablo Lake, and a mile east is an overlook where you can peer down on the emerald green lake waters and across to the jagged summits of Pyramid Peak and Colonial Peak.

Continuing eastward, the highway climbs along Granite Creek before topping two passes—4,855-foot Rainy Pass and 5,447-foot Washington Pass. A short paved trail leads from Washington Pass to over-the-highway viewpoints of 7,720-foot Liberty Bell—the symbol of the North Cascades

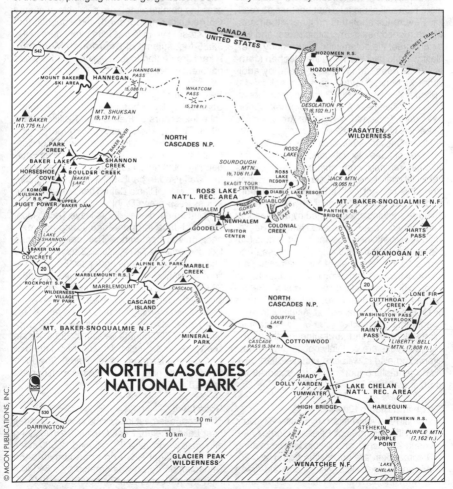

© MOON PUBLICATIONS, INC.

Highway—and Early Winters Spires. Beyond this, the highway spirals downward to Methow Valley and the town of Winthrop, 30 miles to the east and 3,600 feet lower.

NORTH CASCADES NATIONAL PARK

The half-million-acre North Cascades National Park is one of the wildest in the Lower 48, and an outdoor lover's paradise. It has 318 glaciers—more than half of the total number outside Alaska. Few roads spoil this pristine wilderness, where rugged peaks, mountain lakes, and waterfalls greet the determined backcountry hiker. Nearly all the park lies within the **Stephen Mather Wilderness,** and it is surrounded by additional wilderness buffers covering well over a million acres: Liberty Bell Primitive Area, Noisy-Diobsud Wilderness Area, Glacier Peak Wilderness Area, Pasayten Wilderness Area, and Mt. Baker Wilderness Area.

North Cascades National Park is actually a complex of three distinct units: the park itself is split into northern and southern units by Ross Lake National Recreation Area (Hwy. 20 passes along this corridor), while the southern end includes Lake Chelan National Recreation Area. All three sections are managed by the National Park Service, but Ross Lake National Recreation Area contains dams and power plants that are operated by Seattle City Light; these three plants supply nearly all of Seattle's electrical needs. If this isn't confusing enough, look at the maps to find that east-side portions of Mt. Baker-Snoqualmie National Forest are administered by Okanogan National Forest. Actually, to most visitors these distinctions are of little meaning; this is all public land, and although the dams and reservoirs are certainly not natural, almost everything else is wild and undeveloped, providing fantastic opportunities for explorations afoot and afloat.

Gorge and Diablo Lakes

Two small reservoirs created by Seattle City Light dams on the upper Skagit River are Gorge Lake, covering 210 acres, and Diablo Lake, covering 910 acres; both are accessible from Hwy. 20. Diablo and Gorge Lakes get their emerald-green color from fine sediments in the glacial runoff.

The **Gorge Powerhouse** observation lobby is open daily 8 a.m.-4 p.m. May-Sept. and is accessed by a cable suspension footbridge. Continue beyond the power plant to **Ladder Creek Falls and Rock Gardens.** The colorful flower gardens were first planted here in the 1920s and form a delightful setting for the adjacent falls. At night both are lit up.

A mile off Hwy. 20 is the tiny company town of **Diablo,** the home of Diablo Powerplant and the Skagit Tour Center. A half-dozen free campsites (no potable water) are available at nearby **Gorge Lake Campground,** and a popular (but very steep) five-mile trail leads from here to the 5,985-foot summit of **Sourdough Mountain.** Hikers are treated to lush alpine meadows and panoramic views.

Seattle City Light Tours

Seattle City Light has been offering regularly scheduled tours of their Skagit facilities since 1928. Today, a four-hour guided tour begins with a slide presentation at the Skagit Tour Center in Diablo, followed by a 558-foot ride up Sourdough Mountain on an antique incline railway that was used to haul supplies during the construction of the Diablo Dam. Then, enjoy a cruise across deep-green Diablo Lake and back to an all-you-can-eat dinner. Tours leave Thurs.-Mon. from mid-June through August, and on weekends only in September. The total cost of the tour and dinner is $25 adults, $22 seniors, $12.50 ages 6-11, free for kids under six. For reservations (strongly recommended), call (206) 684-3030 in Seattle, or, from late June to Labor Day, stop by the Skagit Tour Center in Diablo.

A quicker 90-minute tour is also given twice a day Thurs.-Mon. from mid-June to early September. This 90-minute version includes a slide show, ride on the incline lift, and tour of the Diablo Powerhouse (sorry, no boat ride); $5 adults, free for kids under age 12. No reservations are needed.

Ross Lake

The second-largest lake in the North Cascades after Lake Chelan, Ross Lake is 24 miles long and up to two miles wide, covering 12,000 acres from the Skagit River up to and beyond the Canadian border. It was created by a 540-foot high hydroelectric dam completed in 1949 by

Seattle City Light. Fortunately, efforts to enlarge the dam were thwarted in the 1980s by environmentalists and the government of British Columbia. You can see the reservoir from the Ross Lake overlook at milepost 135 on Hwy. 20 or area hiking trails (see below), but the only vehicle access and motorboat launch is at the lake's north end, via a 39-mile gravel road from Canada. This means that Ross Lake is more of a canoeing and kayaking lake than other reservoirs in the Cascades. The glacier-fed waters of Ross Lake are too cold for swimming.

Although you can't drive to **Ross Lake Resort,** tel. (206) 386-4437, you can catch the **Seattle City Light boat** ($10 roundtrip) that leaves the parking lot across Diablo Dam daily at 8:30 a.m. and 3 p.m. The tug takes you to the end of Diablo Lake, where a truck ($5 roundtrip) carries you on to Ross Lake. This is one of the most unique lodging places in Washington; everything here is literally on the water, with cabins and bunkhouses built on log floats. Visitors can stay in modern cabins for $90 s or d, rustic 1950s-era cabins for $60 s or d, a 10-person bunkhouse for $115, or brand new nineperson cabins for $160. Enjoy fantastic views up the lake to 8,300-foot Mt. Hozomeen at the Canadian border. You can rent motorboats, kayaks, or canoes here, but there are no telephones, groceries, or food service. The lodge is open mid-June through October.

Ross Lake has water-side campsites and half-a-dozen trailheads that provide access into adjacent North Cascades National Park. Ross Lake Resort runs a **water taxi** service to these, along with boat tours and portages from Diablo Lake for small boats and canoes. The water taxi fares are by the boat load (it can hold six), not per person, so it's best if you can coordinate your travel with other folks to save money. Call (206) 386-4437 for specifics. These water taxi trips are a fun way to reach the backcountry, but be sure to pick up backcountry permits from the Wilderness Information Center in Marblemount before heading out to camp along Ross Lake or hike in the backcountry.

Campgrounds

Park Service campgrounds accessible by car on the North Cascades Hwy. include **Goodell Creek** ($7; open year-round), **Newhalem Creek** ($10; open mid-May to mid-October), and **Colonial Creek** ($10; open mid-May to mid-October). All are on a first-come, first-served basis, with no reservations. Brave the 39-mile gravel road from Canada and camp at the free **Hozomeen Campground** at the north end of Ross Lake, from mid-May through October. A handful of free campsites (no potable water) are available at **Gorge Lake Campground** near the town of Diablo. Enjoy summer naturalist activities at the Colonial Creek and Newhalem Creek campgrounds.

Along Cascade River Rd. southeast of Marblemount, stay at **Marble Creek Campground** ($7; open year-round, no drinking water) can be reserved ($9 extra) by calling (877) 444-6777. The free **Mineral Park Campground** is also open year-round. On the east side of Washington Pass, you can camp at the very popular **Lone Fir, Klipchuck,** and **Early Winters** campgrounds managed by the Forest Service.

Day Hikes

More than 300 miles of maintained trails provide ample opportunities to explore North Cascades National Park. Short hikes—some are wheelchair accessible—abound around Colonial Creek Campground and Newhalem; pick up flyers describing these and others at the visitor centers. Trails below 3,000 feet are generally open by mid-April or May; higher up, you may meet snow in July, so be prepared.

Some of the park's most spectacular scenery can be seen at **Cascade Pass.** Drive to the trailhead at the end of Cascade River Rd., a 23-mile mostly gravel road from Marblemount. The first two miles of the seven-mile roundtrip hike climb steadily through forest and meadows to the 5,400-foot pass at 3.7 miles. Allow about five hours for this hike.

Backcountry Treks

A free **backcountry permit** is required for all overnight trips into the park, a policy meant to reduce overcrowding and preserve the fragile alpine environment. Pick one up from the Wilderness Information Center in Marblemount or from information or ranger stations in Newhalem, Hozomeen, Sedro-Woolley, Winthrop, Twisp, Chelan, or Stehekin. Some areas fill up on summer weekends, so you may need to go with another option. The North Cascades are among the most rugged mountains in the Lower 48, so plan accordingly: lots of wool clothing, extra food, a waterproof tarp, and a flexible schedule for waiting out storms or resting feet and muscles sore from all the ups and downs.

From June to November, enjoy the 31-mile trip from the East Bank Trailhead (milepost 138) to Hozomeen along Ross Lake's **East Bank Trail.** The trailhead is on Hwy. 20, eight miles east of the Colonial Creek Campground at the Panther Creek bridge. The trail leads through low forest and along the lakeshore for 18 miles, at which point you have the option of continuing to Hozomeen or taking a side trip up 6,102-foot **Desolation Peak.** The roundtrip up the peak is nine miles, almost straight up, with an elevation gain of 4,400 feet; you'll be rewarded with views of Mt. Baker, Mt. Shuksan, Jack Mountain, and The Pickets. To get right to the peak, skip the first 18 miles of hiking by taking the water taxi to the Desolation Peak trailhead; stay overnight at Lightning Creek Campground, since you probably won't return in time to catch the boat. Beat Generation fans will want to make this pilgrimage to spend time as one of their own did: Jack Kerouac spent the summer of 1955 as a fire lookout here.

The **Pacific Crest Trail** enters the park from the south from Glacier Peak Wilderness Area (see **The Mountain Loop,**), crossing Hwy. 20 at Rainy Pass and heading north through the Liberty Bell Roadless Area (see below) and the Pasayten Wilderness Area (see below) to the Canadian border.

If you can set up a vehicle shuttle or are willing to hitchhike, an excellent long hike begins at the Colonial Creek Campground, climbs over 6,100-foot **Park Pass** via Thunder Creek and Park Creek trails, and ends at Flat Creek Campground, a total hike of 27 miles. From here, you can catch the shuttle bus to Stehekin, and then ride the *Lady of the Lake II* down Lake Chelan to the town of Chelan. An alternative ending would be to hike (or catch the shuttle bus) four miles up the Stehekin Valley Rd., and follow **Cascade Pass Trail** over this 5,400-foot pass to the end of Cascade River Rd. (23 miles south of Marblemount).

If you don't mind a long uphill slog, **Easy Pass** makes a fine overnight hike. The trailhead is six miles west of Rainy Pass on Hwy. 20 (46 miles east of Marblemount), and the misnamed Easy Pass Trail climbs steadily for 3.7 miles to this 6,500-foot summit, where you enter North Cascades National Park. The magnificent vista includes knife-edged mountains and active glaciers. From here, you can continue deeper into the wilderness on **Fisher Creek Trail.** Easy Pass Trail is usually open from late July to late September.

Additional hiking trails leading into the park are described in **Mount Baker and Vicinity, Baker Lake, Liberty Bell Roadless Area, Harts Pass Area,** and **Stehekin.** For more detailed descriptions of these and many other North Cascade hikes, see Ira Spring and Harvey Manning's *100 Hikes in Washington's North Cascades: National Park Region,* published by The Mountaineers in Seattle.

Pack Trips

Early Winters Outfitters, tel. (509) 996-2659 or (800) 737-8750, has horse pack trips of all types throughout the northern Cascades. If you're traveling with young children, your best bet may be **Back Country Burro Treks,** tel. (509) 996-3369. The outfitters will supply you with a burro for the child and will pack all of your camping equipment and meet you at a designated campsite.

Information and a View

The elaborate **North Cascades Visitor Center,** tel. (206) 386-4495, is 14 miles east of Marblemount and a half-mile south of Hwy. 20 in Newhalem. Inside are natural history exhibits, a large relief model of the region, a theater with slide shows, movies, and other presentations, and a gift shop. The visitor center is open daily 9 a.m.-5 p.m. from April through mid-November (till 6 p.m. in July and August), and weekends only 9 a.m.-4:30 p.m. the rest of the year. Ask at the center about borrowing one of the free audiotapes that describe the region's rich natural and human history. Daily naturalist walks are offered during the summer, with weekend talks in the winter months.

Immediately behind the center is a guaranteed-to-please 330-foot saunter to a view of the precipitous **Picket Range.** This is a great place to take in the view and to enjoy the sounds of bird calls. The path is wheelchair accessible.

Other helpful public information centers are the Wilderness Information Center in Marblemount (described above), and the Methow Valley Visitor Center in Winthrop (described below).

LIBERTY BELL ROADLESS AREA

The 141,000-acre Liberty Bell Roadless Area adjoins Hwy. 20 at Washington Pass and includes a long stretch of the Pacific Crest Trail, as well as some of the finest rock climbing in the Cascades. An outstanding day hike takes you past two forest-rimmed lakes and over **Maple Pass.** The trail begins right along Hwy. 20, from the south parking lot at Rainy Pass (30 miles west of Winthrop). An almost-level paved trail (wheelchair accessible) leads a mile to **Rainy Lake,** with interpretive signs along the way. The cirque lake is backed by high cliffs with plummeting waterfalls. From here, you can continue up a steeper trail to Maple Pass, and then loop back past **Lake Ann** (good fishing for cutthroat trout) before returning to the parking area, a total distance of approximately six miles. No camping is allowed anywhere along this very popular route.

Also popular is an easy trail to **Blue Lake** that leads two miles through subalpine meadows to the emerald waters of this mountain lake. Surrounding it are a trio of spectacular summits:

Liberty Bell Mountain, Whistler Mountain, and Cutthroat Peak. The Blue Lake trailhead is a half-mile west of Washington Pass.

PASAYTEN WILDERNESS

One of the largest wilderness areas in Washington, the Pasayten (pa-SAY-tin) Wilderness covers 530,000 acres of mountain country. Its northern edge is the U.S.-Canadian border, while to the south it extends almost to Methow Valley. The country contains deep canyons, mountains topping 7,500 feet, and an abundance of wildlife that includes a few gray wolves and grizzly bears.

Hiking
The Pasayten Wilderness contains more than 600 miles of trails; see *100 Hikes in Washington's North Cascades: National Park Region* by Ira Spring and Harvey Manning (Seattle: The Mountaineers) for details. An enjoyable short hike is the 12-mile long **Billy Goat Loop Trail.** To get here, drive nine miles north from Winthrop on West Chewuch Rd., and turn left onto Eightmile Creek Road. Continue another 17 miles to the trailhead at the end of the road. The trail climbs through evergreen forests and then over Billy Goat Pass before dropping into the narrow Drake Creek Valley. From here, it circles back around the other side of Billy Goat Mountain,

DIANNE BOUERICE LYONS

Liberty Bell at Washington Pass in the North Cascades

and over Eightmile Pass, before returning you to the starting point.

The trailhead for a longer loop hike (approximately 30 miles) is 20 miles west of Mazama at the second switchback above Harts Pass on the way to Slate Peak (see **Harts Pass Area**). Follow the **Buckskin Ridge Trail** (No. 498) from here through high meadows and past Silver Lake to Silver Pass and Buckskin Ridge (7,300 feet), before descending to the Pasayten River. Here you catch trail No. 478 and follow it upriver through old-growth forests to trail No. 498, which takes you back to your starting point. See the Green Trails maps or talk with folks at the Winthrop Forest Service office before heading up this interesting but challenging route.

Four-Legged Treks

Several companies provide horse pack trips into the Pasayten, including: **Early Winters Outfitters,** tel. (509) 996-2659 or (800) 737-8750; **North Cascade Outfitters,** tel. (509) 997-1015; **Back Country Burro Treks,** tel. (509) 996-3369; **North Cascade Safari,** tel. (509) 996-2350; and **Sawtooth Outfitters,** tel. (509) 923-2548. **Pasayten Llama Packing,** tel. (509) 996-2326, leads llama trips into the wilderness.

METHOW VALLEY

Scenic Methow Valley is a land of contrasts. To the west are the massive, glacially carved summits of the Cascades, with dense Douglas fir forests carpeting their lower flanks, but as you enter the valley, the forests are replaced by irrigated pastures surrounded by rounded hills covered with sage, grass, and scattered pines. Highway 20 follows the Methow River, with tall bankside cottonwoods providing a shady screen from the hot summer sun.

In recent years the Methow (pronounced "MET-how") has become a haven for mountain bikers, river-rafters, and cross-country skiers. There are excellent lodges and restaurants, and a comfortably relaxed country atmosphere. Unfortunately, there's an alarming amount of new development taking place as ranchettes replace real ranches and fancy inns sprout up along the riverbanks. Some places are downright ugly, and as they spread across the valley, its quiet country flavor is being replaced by a Disneyland-ish version of the West. These same schlocky developments threaten other much-loved places in the West: Jackson Hole, Sedona, and Park City.

The bustling town of Winthrop is the center of activity in Methow Valley, with its made-over Western theme. Thirteen miles northwest of here is minuscule Mazama (the name means "mountain goat" in Greek); 11 miles south is the ranching town called Twisp. The valley is accessible from all sides during the summer, but Hwy. 20 closes from late November through April (or longer). Point your browser to www.methow.com for up-to-date info on the Methow Valley area.

Harts Pass Area

After the discovery of gold and silver near Harts Pass in 1893, prospectors hurriedly built a road from Methow Valley to the mines. The precious metals petered out, but in the 1940s, fear of a Japanese invasion led the military to flatten the top of the Slate Peak and erect an early warning station, supplied in winter via dogsled. The site was later used for a Cold War radar station.

Today, a gravel road leads 19 miles from Mazama past the 2,000-foot slopes of glacially carved **Goat Wall,** and on to Harts Pass (6,197 feet), where it crosses the Pacific Crest Trail (PCT). The road splits at the pass. Turn left (south) for nine downhill miles to the ghost towns of Barron and Chancellor—once home to 2,000 miners. Turn right (north) for three steep miles to **Slate Peak Lookout.** When you park here, you're at the highest point you can drive to in Washington: 7,440 feet. A short walk leads to the lookout tower; be ready for spectacular 360-degree views of the entire Cascade Range. Harts Pass Rd. is steep and narrow; RVs and trailers are prohibited. It's a great, but tiring, mountain bike ride. The road is not plowed beyond Lost River in the winter. Near Harts Pass, you can camp at two free Forest Service campgrounds with gorgeous alpine settings: **Meadows** and **Harts Pass.** They are usually open mid-July to late September; no potable water.

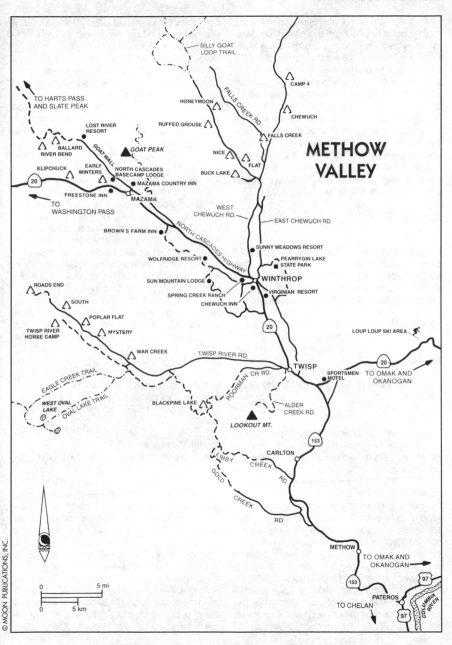

© MOON PUBLICATIONS, INC.

This high alpine country offers some of the most popular day-hiking in this part of the state. **Windy Pass Trail** begins 1.5 miles up Slate Peak Rd. from Harts Pass and follows the PCT for 3.5 miles to Windy Pass. The hike begins at 6,800 feet with little additional elevation gain but offers striking views of peaks and meadows all along the route. A second fun hike with little change in elevation begins at Harts Pass and proceeds along the PCT south to **Grasshopper Pass.** The roundtrip distance is 11 miles, and the route follows the crest of the mountains to beautiful meadows at Grasshopper Pass. Because of the high elevation, these trails are often covered with snow until late July.

WINTHROP

Located near the junction of the Methow and Chewuch (CHEE-wuk) Rivers, Winthrop began as a mining settlement, settled into middle age as a ranching town, and has reemerged as a tourist mecca. Home to just 375 year-round residents, Winthrop greets over 600,000 visitors annually. Winthrop's Main Street buildings have been remodeled with an Old West theme to reflect the town's 1890s mining boom—and to encourage hungry, tired Hwy. 20 drivers to stop for a meal, gas, and souvenirs. Winthrop also hosts annual festivals and rodeos that reflect the Western mood.

History
The Methow Valley was originally part of the Moses Indian Reservation, but when members of the Moses-Columbia tribe refused to be placed on land away from their home along the Columbia River, the government opened the valley to homesteaders. The first white settlers reached the site of present-day Winthrop in the 1880s, lured by gold fever. The town itself goes back to 1891, when an easterner named Guy Waring opened Methow Trading Company. A devastating fire two years later nearly destroyed the new town and forced Waring to return East to recoup his losses and get East Coast financing. After returning, Waring incorporated the town in 1897 and named it in honor of John Winthrop, the colonial governor of Massachusetts (another version says it was for Theodore Winthrop, an

early Washington settler killed in the Civil War). Waring stayed in business for almost half a century, and at one time owned every building on the main street except the town hall. One of Waring's Harvard classmates, Owen Wister, came to visit and used some of his friend's experiences in his famous novel, *The Virginian*—considered the first Western novel. (This is the Washington version; folks in Medicine Bow, Wyoming, say it was inspired by their townfolks, and they seem to have a stronger point. A hero has many fathers.)

After the collapse of mining in the area, Winthrop headed toward oblivion; even the founder went bankrupt and moved back East. But then, as the North Cascades Highway was being completed in the late 1960s, the citizens of Winthrop began looking for a way to pull themselves out of the doldrums. The successful transformation of nearby Leavenworth into a Bavarian theme town inspired locals to do their own makeover into a Hollywoodesque Old West town. A local benefactor, Kathryn Wagner, widow of a sawmill owner, put up matching funds, and Leavenworth architects brought in their design expertise. By the time the first carloads of tourists crossed Washington Pass in 1972, Winthrop had covered its concrete buildings with false fronts, laid down wooden sidewalks, and added Old West signs and hitching posts. Today the shops are crowded with trendy gear, trinkets, upscale foods, books, and, of course, espresso. Warning: Gas prices here are some of the highest in the state of Washington. Tank-up elsewhere!

Shafer Museum
Winthrop's Shafer Museum on Castle Ave., tel. (509) 996-2817, is housed in an 1897 log home (alias "The Castle") built by the town's founder, Guy Waring. Displays include pioneer farming and mining tools, bicycles, furniture, an impressive rifle collection, and other relics from the early days in the Methow Valley. Outside, you'll find a town's worth of buildings, including a general store, print shop, homestead cabin, schoolhouse, and assay office, plus old wagons, mining equipment, and aging farm implements. The 1923 Rickenbacker automobile here is one of just 80 still in existence. Shafer Museum is open daily 10 a.m.-5 p.m. late May to September, closed the rest of the year; donations appreciated.

Other Sights

Walk down Riverside ("Main Street") to find all sorts of Western shops, some with authentic arts and crafts, most with junk. **White Buck Trading Co.,** tel. (509) 996-3500, is named for a big white buck displayed inside. It was shot in 1953. The **White Buck Museum** in the rear of the store contains more stuffed critters and a collection of trivial items from the past, including—of all things—the first dial phone in Chicago. The charge is $2 adults, $1.50 seniors, and $1 ages 7-18. **Last Trading Post,** tel. (509) 996-2103, is packed with Old West Americana, from antiques to painted cattle skulls. Downstairs is a museum of sorts, with historic flotsam and jetsam, plus various Indian artifacts.

The Forest Service's **North Cascade Smoke-jumper Base,** tel. (509) 997-2031, halfway between Winthrop and Twisp along Hwy. 20, is open for tours daily 8 a.m.-5 p.m. during the fire season (June-Sept.). It was here in the fall of 1939 that the first experimental parachute jumps were held to determine the safety and effectiveness of reaching remote mountain forest fires from the air. The first fires were successfully attacked by smoke jumpers from this base the following summer. Today, the "birthplace of smoke jumping" has historical photos, but it is also a very active center during the peak of fire season and home to an elite group of firefighters. Other smoke jump bases are in Alaska, California, Idaho, and Oregon.

The **Winthrop National Fish Hatchery,** a mile south of town, tel. (509) 996-2424, raises 1.5 million spring chinook salmon and 750,000 trout annually in large, covered raceways. Open daily 8 a.m.-4 p.m.

Lodging

Visitors should reserve well ahead for summer weekends. Many of these lodging places are just southeast of Winthrop along the Methow River, and most of these are recently completed, sterile structures with little charm. If you plan to stay at one of the cross-country ski lodges over the hectic Christmas-New Year's holiday, you'll find some places full six months in advance. Contact **Methow Valley Central Reservations,** tel. (509) 996-2148 or (800) 422-3048, for reservations at most of the places on the chart or other vacation rental cabins, guesthouses, and apartments. They're open Mon.-Fri. 9 a.m.-5 p.m.

Atop a 5,000-foot peak with 360-degree views into the North Cascades and the Methow Valley is **Sun Mountain Lodge,** one of the premier destination resorts in Washington. Owned by the Haub family of Germany—who also own the A&P grocery chain—Sun Mountain has almost every amenity you could want, from fly-fishing lessons and children's programs to the largest string of saddle horses in the region.

Another very nice place is **Mazama Country Inn,** with comfortable guest rooms in a delightful country setting. **Spring Creek Ranch** is a great option for families: a grand, fully equipped country home that sleeps up to 10 people, with a separate modern cabin that sleeps four.

Bed and Breakfasts

A large three-story home, **Fly Rod Ranch B&B,** 464 Rendezvous Rd., tel. (509) 996-2784, is five miles out of town on Rendezvous Road. The owner teaches fly-fishing classes, and has a two-acre trout pond. Inside, three luxurious rooms and a suite have private or shared baths. A gourmet breakfast is served; $65-85 s or d. No kids.

Lost River Bess' B&B, 98 Lost River Rd., Winthrop, tel. (509) 996-2457, has two large bedrooms, sundecks, and a full breakfast; $65 s or $75 d.

Chokecherry Inn B&B; Mazama; tel. (509) 996-2049; is a comfortable newer home with two guest rooms, private baths, a jacuzzi, and a full breakfast. They are right on the Methow River; $75 s or d.

Dammann's B&B, a half-mile southeast of Winthrop on Hwy. 20, tel. (509) 996-2484, has two antique-filled guest rooms with private baths along Methow River. A continental breakfast is served; $52 s or d.

Campgrounds

Pearrygin Lake State Park, five miles north of Winthrop, has lakeside campsites that are open mid-April through October for $11 tents, $16 RVs. Call (509) 996-2370 for information, or (800) 452-5687 for reservations ($6 extra).

The Forest Service maintains a dozen campgrounds ($6-8) within 25 miles of Winthrop, and

METHOW VALLEY MOTELS AND HOTELS

Accommodations are arranged from least to most expensive. Rates may be lower during the winter months. See the text for descriptions of Methow Valley B&Bs and lodging places in Twisp.

INEXPENSIVE

The Farm House Inn; three-quarter mile southeast of Winthrop on Hwy. 20; tel. (509) 996-2191 or (888) 996-2525; $39-75 s or d; jacuzzi

Winthrop Inn, one mile southeast of Winthrop on Hwy. 20; tel. (509) 996-2217 or (800) 444-1972; $50-60 s, $65-75 d; Methow River location, outdoor pool, jacuzzi, full breakfast, AAA approved

Lost River Resort; 672 Lost River Rd., Mazama; tel. (509) 996-2537 or (800) 996-2537; $50-65 s or d; rustic cabins with wood stoves and kitchens

RiverRun Inn; 27 Rader Rd.; tel. (509) 996-2173 or (800) 757-2709; $52-89 s or d; indoor pool, jacuzzi, riverside location, microwaves and fridges, continental breakfast, AAA approved

Duck Brand Hotel; downtown Winthrop; tel. (509) 996-2192 or (800) 996-2192; $55-65 s or d; balconies

Virginian Resort; three-quarter mile southeast of Winthrop on Hwy. 20; tel. (509) 996-2535 or (800) 854-2834; $55-75 s or d; outdoor pool, jacuzzi, cabins with kitchenettes, AAA approved

MODERATE

North Cascades Basecamp; 255 Lost River Rd., Mazama; tel. (509) 996-2334; $60 s or $80 d with breakfast, $80 s or $120 d with three meals; hot tub, shared bath

Chewuch Inn; 223 White Ave., Winthrop; tel. (509) 996-3107 or (800) 747-3107; $60-75 s or d in motel, $85-95 in cabins with kitchenettes; full breakfast, AAA approved

Winthrop Mt. View Chalets; two miles southeast of Winthrop on Hwy. 20; tel. (509) 996-3113 or (800) 527-3113; $63 s or d; tiny cabins with kitchenettes, AAA approved

Trail's End Motel; downtown Winthrop; tel. (509) 996-2303; $63-71 s or d; sauna

Chewack River Guest Ranch; 508 E Chewuch Rd.; tel. (509) 996-2497; $65 s or d; jacuzzi, country setting

Winthrop Inn; one mile southeast of Winthrop on Hwy. 20; tel. (509) 996-2217 or (800) 444-1972; $65 s, $70 d; riverside location, jacuzzi, outdoor pool, fridges and microwaves, continental breakfast

Sunny Meadows Golf & 4 Seasons Resort; three miles north of Winthrop; tel. (509) 996-3103; $65-80 s or d; country location along Chewuch River, rooms and housekeeping apartments, golf course access, fly-fishing ponds, ice skating, continental breakfast

most other areas are open to free dispersed camping (with the exception of the Hwy. 20 corridor). Closest are the campgrounds up West Chewuch Rd.: **Falls Creek, Nice, Flat,** and **Buck Lake.** Falls Creek has the added attraction of a beautiful falls just a quarter mile hike away, while quiet Buck Lake has ducks and cattails. Three other often-full Forest Service campgrounds are west of Winthrop along Hwy. 20: **Early Winters, Klipchuck** (very quiet spot), and **Lone Fir.** Most of these campgrounds are open June-September. Get more information from the Winthrop Ranger District office, tel. (509) 996-2266.

Private RV parks include: **Big Twin Lake Campground,** tel. (509) 996-2650; **Derry's Resort,** tel. (509) 996-2322; **Methow KOA,** tel. (509) 996-2258 or (800) 562-2158; **Rocking Horse Ranch** near Mazama, tel. (509) 996-2768; and **Pine Near RV Park,** tel. (509) 996-2391.

Best Western Cascade Inn; 960 Hwy. 20; tel. (509) 996-3100 or (800) 528-1234; $65-80 s, $70-95 d; outdoor pool, jacuzzi, continental breakfast, AAA approved

WolfRidge Resort; five miles west of Winthrop; tel. (509) 996-2828 or (800) 237-2388; $69-84 for hotel rooms; $108-164 for suites and two-bedroom units with kitchens; modern log townhouses along river, outdoor pool, jacuzzi, rec room

Riverside Lodge; 281 Riverside Ave.; tel. (509) 996-3940; $75-85 s or d; riverside location, hot tub, fridges and microwaves

Brown's Farm Inn; eight miles west of Winthrop on Wolf Creek Rd.; tel. (509) 996-2571; $75-120 s or d; country location, three cabins (one sleeps 10) with kitchenettes

Mazama Country Inn; Mazama; tel. (509) 996-2681 or (800) 843-7951; $80-95 s or d in summer (no meals), $165-175 d in winter with three meals; rustic mountain lodge, jacuzzi, sauna, children welcome in summer, no kids under 13 in winter

EXPENSIVE

Hotel Rio Vista; 285 Riverside (half-mile south of Winthrop); tel. (509) 996-3535 or (800) 398-0911; $85 s or d; jacuzzi, decks overlooking Methow River, nice rooms, AAA approved

Mazama Ranch House; Mazama; tel. (509) 996-2040; $85-90; cabins or ranch house rooms with kitchenettes and woodstove, jacuzzi, horse facilities

Aspen Loft; four miles east of Mazama; tel. (509) 996-2110; $100 s or d; popular cross-country ski lodging, fireplace, full kitchen

PREMIUM

Freestone Inn & Early Winters Cabins; 17798 Hwy. 20, Mazama; tel. (509) 996-2752 or (800) 639-3809; $120-200 s or d; elaborate new lodge or restored historic cabins with kitchens

Sun Mountain Lodge; nine miles southwest of Winthrop; tel. (509) 996-2211 or (800) 572-0493; $140-350 s or d; mountaintop location, lodge or cabin rooms with view, swimming pool, exercise room, three jacuzzis, two-night minimum stay on weekends, AAA four diamond resort

LUXURY

River's Edge Resort; 115 Riverside Ave.; tel. (509) 996-8000 or (800) 937-6621; $200 d; two-bedroom cabins, kitchens, hot tubs

Spring Creek Ranch; 491 Twin Lakes Rd.; tel. (509) 996-2495; $220 for up to 10 people in a large 1929 refurbished house with antique furnishings, $160 for up to four in a new cabin with fireplace

Food

Because of its compact size, it's easy to find a place to eat in Winthrop; just walk the two-block downtown to see what looks good. For casual dining in a cluttered and funky atmosphere, downtown's **Duck Brand Hotel & Cantina,** tel. (509) 996-2192, serves outstanding, artfully presented, and moderately priced Mexican and American food. There's an outside deck for sunny days. Breakfasts are a real treat: huge piles of potatoes come with the meals, and monstrous cinnamon rolls sit temptingly on the bakery counter.

Housed in the Emporium Building, **Boulder Creek Deli,** tel. (509) 996-3990, makes very good sandwiches and salads for lunch. Get a lunchtime slice of pizza to go from **Grubstake & Co.,** tel. (509) 996-2375; Starbucks espresso here too. Come back at dinner for a full menu of steak, chicken, or pasta dishes.

The Virginian, at the motel of the same name just south of Winthrop on Hwy. 20, tel. (509)

996-2536, serves steak, chicken, pasta, and other dinners.

Coffee fiends will be pleased to note the presence of at least nine espresso spots in town (that's one for every 40 permanent residents!). **Mazama Store** in Mazama, tel. (509) 996-2855, is another very good place for lunch, serving sandwiches, salads, pastas, and espresso. One of the most popular places on a summer afternoon is **Sheri's Sweet Shoppe** at the downtown corner, tel. (509) 996-3834, with homemade ice cream, chocolates, and carmels.

The small **Winthrop Brewing Company,** tel. (509) 996-3174, has a riverside deck and beer garden. They usually have at least four freshly brewed ales on tap and a creative dinner menu, along with an outdoor barbecue in the summer.

For pizza, snacks, sandwiches, and ribs, the over-21 crowd will enjoy **3 Fingered Jack's Saloon,** also downtown. Good food, but smoke drifts into the restaurant from the adjacent bar.

Sun Mountain Dining Room, in Sun Mountain Resort, tel. (509) 996-2211 or (800) 572-0493, is the most famous local restaurant. The menu leans toward Northwest cuisine—including an award-winning smoked duckling in plum sauce—with stellar prices to match.

Events

The second weekend of May marks the start of Winthrop's festival season with **49ers Days,** featuring a parade, horsepacking demonstrations, a chili cookoff, dance, and baseball tournament. This is followed by Memorial Day weekend's popular **Winthrop Rodeo Days.**

The three-day long **Winthrop Rhythm and Blues Festival** in mid-July has quickly become a major blues event, attracting more than 5,000 fans to hear such acts as Charlie Musselwhite, BB King, or John Hammond. (And if you like the blues, be sure to tune in to the eclectic "Methow Community Radio," KVLR at 106.3 FM.) The **Methow Music Festival** brings nationally known classical performers to Mazama each August; call (888) 463-8469 for details.

Summer ends the way it begins, with the big **Labor Day Rodeo.** The **Antique Auto Rally** in mid-September features more than 60 old vehicles and is followed in early October by the **Methow Valley Mountain Bike Festival,** which brings over 500 participants for races, hill climbs, and group rides. Winthrop's **Octoberfest** includes a festival with vendors, dancing, and the obligatory beer garden. The Methow Valley Sport Trails Association has a series of ski races, triathalons, and foot races throughout the year; contact them at (800) 682-5787 for details.

Entertainment

Both **The Winthrop Palace** and **3-Fingered Jack's Saloon** usually have rock or R&B bands on summer weekends. **Winthrop Brewing Company,** tel. (509) 996-3174, has Friday night jam sessions.

a Winthrop street

DON PITCHER

Mountain Biking

Winthrop is a summer mecca for cyclists, with an incredible range of trails and country roads spreading through the valley and into the surrounding mountains. There are routes for every ability level. Pick up descriptions of local routes at the Forest Service visitor center, or call the **Methow Valley Sports Trail Association** at (509) 996-3287 or (800) 682-5787 for information and maps to more than a hundred miles of mountain biking and hiking trails; they become cross-country ski paths in winter. Approximately seven miles of trails are wheelchair accessible. Mountain bikes can be rented from **Mazama Store,** tel. (509) 996-2855, and **Winthrop Mountain Sports,** tel. (509) 996-2886 or (800) 719-3826.

River Rafting

The Methow River is a favorite of whitewater enthusiasts, with many access points and a wide range of conditions, from easy float trips to class III-IV whitewater. Rafters generally float the river from early May till early July, when the river is running hard from spring runoff but the air is warm and dry. The sections below Winthrop grow progressively more difficult as you follow the Methow to the Columbia, 17 miles down river. Black Canyon is the pinnacle, with roller-coaster waves and wild action as the river plunges through dozens of rapids.

Expect to pay $45-75 for day trips, more for the overnight adventures offered by several companies. Wetsuits can be rented from most companies. **Osprey Rafting** in Twisp, tel. (509) 997-4116 or (800) 743-6269, is the only local company doing river trips on the Methow. Other companies are: **All Rivers Adventures,** tel. (800) 743-5628; **Alpine Adventures,** tel. (800) 723-8386; **Blue Sky Outfitters,** tel. (800) 228-7238; **North Cascades River Expeditions,** tel. (800) 634-8433; **Northern Wilderness River Riders,** tel. (800) 448-7238; **Orion Expeditions,** tel. (800) 553-7466; **River Recreation,** tel. (800) 464-5899; and **Wildwater River Tours,** tel. (800) 522-9453.

Other Summer Activities

A multitude of hiking trails surround the Methow Valley. For horseback rides and pack trips, contact: **Early Winters Outfitters,** tel. (509) 996-2659 or (800) 737-8750; **Rocking Horse Ranch,** tel. (509) 996-2768; **Chewack River Riding Stables,** tel. (509) 996-2497; or **North Cascade Outfitters,** tel. (509) 997-1015.

The 578-acre **Pearrygin Lake State Park,** five miles north of Winthrop, offers a sandy beach for swimming, plus fishing, camping, a boat launch, store, and boat rentals. This small spring-fed, glacially carved lake is a delightful break from the dry summer hills of sage and pine that surround it.

Winthrop's **Bear Creek Golf Course,** tel. (509) 996-2284, is a nine-hole course. **Morning Glory Balloon Tours,** tel. (509) 997-1700, has hot air balloon flights year-round in Methow Valley.

The mountains around Methow Valley are becoming increasingly popular with rock climbers. **Mazama Moutaineering,** 42 Lost River Rd. in Mazama, tel. (509) 996-3802, teaches one- to seven-day classes and guides rock climbing, backcountry skiing and snowboarding, and mountain biking.

Winthrop Mountain Sports, tel. (509) 996-2886 or (800) 719-3826, rents bikes, skis, backpacks, snowshoes, and sleeping bags.

Cross-Country Skiing

In winter, when Methow Valley often has two or three feet of powdery snow on the ground and sunshine in the sky, outdoor recreation changes from hiking, biking, and river-running to cross-country skiing. The nonprofit **Methow Valley Sports Trail Association** (MVSTA) maintains four sets of interconnected cross-country ski trails throughout the valley. They groom 175 km of trails—second longest in America—setting tracks for both classical and skate skis. Fees are $13 for one day or $30 for three days. Call MVSTA at (509) 996-3287 or (800) 682-5787 for trail conditions, maps, and ski passes.

The MVSTA's ski trail systems connect to several local lodges, making it possible to walk outside and ski right from your door. A public warming hut is located at WolfRidge Resort, and several of the lodges welcome skiers with hot drinks. A van service provides transport to trailheads throughout the valley; call (509) 996-8294 for specifics.

Backcountry skiers will be very interested in the hut-to-hut skiing opportunities on the MVSTA-maintained Rendezvous Trail system. A series of five fully equipped cabins (each sleeps eight; $25 pp/night) are located 7-12 km apart in the mountains north of Winthrop. Call **Rendezvous Outfitters,** tel. (509) 996-2148 or (800) 422-3048, for details.

Rent skis and get cross-country lessons from: **Sun Mountain Resort,** tel. (509) 996-2211 or (800) 572-0493; **Mazama Country Inn,** tel. (509) 996-2681 or (800) 843-7951; **Jack's Hut at the Wilson Ranch,** tel. (509) 996-2752; and **Winthrop Mountain Sports,** tel. (509) 996-2886 or (800) 719-3826.

Downhill Skiing

The nearest place for alpine skiers and snowboarders is **Loup Loup Ski Bowl,** tel. (509) 826-2720, a small family place 12 miles east of Twisp on Hwy. 20. Loup Loup has a new quad chairlift, two Pomas, a rope tow, and a vertical drop of 1,240 feet. Shredders will have fun on the halfpipe. Ski lessons, ski and snowboard rentals, and groomed cross-country tracks are here, along with a snack bar. Lift rates are $18 on weekends, $16 on Wednesday, and just $12 on Friday.

For those with the bucks, **North Cascade Heli-Skiing,** tel. (509) 996-3272 or (800) 494-4354, will take downhillers into untracked powder or provide drop-offs for backcountry telemark skiers.

Other Winter Sports

Malamute Express, tel. (509) 997-6402, has drive-your-own-team dogsled rides in the Twisp River area. Public **ice skating** ponds are available at Sun Mountain Resort and North Cascade Base Camp. Mazama Country Inn, tel. (509) 996-2681 or (800) 843-7951, offers hourlong **sleigh rides.** Snowmobile rentals are available from several local shops.

Information and Services

Local information is available at several Winthrop locales. The downtown **Chamber of Commerce Information Station,** tel. (509) 996-2125 or (888) 463-8469, is open daily 10 a.m.-5 p.m. from mid-April through September, and some weekends the rest of the year. On the Web at www.methow.com.

The **Methow Valley Visitors Center** is near the can't-miss-it red barn just west of town, tel. (509) 996-4000. It's open daily 9 a.m.-5 p.m. from mid-May to mid-October only. Get booklets on mountain biking, scenic drives, and day hikes here. The Methow Valley has no bus service of any kind, and there is no scheduled air service. The nearest commercial airport is in Wenatchee.

TWISP

The name Twisp is believed to have originated from an Indian word, "Twasp-tsp," an onomatopoeic sound based upon the noise made by yellow jacket wasps. Established in 1898, Twisp grew up on a diet of precious metals from the now-defunct Alder Mine, but then suffered through a string of disasters. A devastating 1924 fire destroyed all but a few of the town's buildings, and a 1948 flood rampaged through, carrying more buildings downstream. This was followed in 1968 by a bitter freeze (temperatures dropped to -48° F!) that wiped out local apple orchards.

Today, Twisp (pop. 900) is experiencing a spillover effect from nearby Winthrop. It's still a minor ranching and logging center, but the town also has a couple of interesting antique shops, a beautiful B&B, a great brewpub, and several good restaurants. And yes, you can get espresso here.

Accommodations

Built in 1910, the lovingly restored old **Methow Valley Inn B&B,** 234 2nd E. Ave., tel. (509) 997-2253, is one of the few structures to survive the fire of 1924. It's a friendly and homey place, with seven guest rooms (four with private baths), and a full breakfast; $79-89 s or d. No kids.

Other local places offer more standard accommodations. **Sportsmen Motel,** three miles east of Twisp on Hwy. 20, tel. (509) 997-2911, is a friendly small place with rooms for $35 s or $40 d, most with kitchens. **Blue Spruce Motel,** tel. (509) 997-8852, charges $34 s or $37-42 d, with kitchenettes for $45-50 d. **Idle-A-While Motel,** tel. (509) 997-3222, has rooms for $45-57 s or $51-63 d, including a jacuzzi and sauna.

Campgrounds

A half-dozen Forest Service campgrounds are west of town out Twisp River Road. Closest is **War Creek Campground,** 15 miles out, $8; open late May to early September. RV parking is available at **River Bend RV Park,** two miles north of Twisp on Hwy. 20, tel. (509) 997-3500.

Food

Head to **Glover St. Cafe,** tel. (509) 997-1323, for the finest local breakfasts and lunches, including Mexican and vegetarian specials. Next door is the **Confluence Art Gallery,** which displays changing exhibits of local artists. **Hometown Pizza,** tel. (509) 997-2100, makes some of the best pizzas in Methow Valley.

    Cinnamon Twisp Bakery, tel. (509) 997-5030, has wonderful fresh breads, organic coffees, and healthy foods. Get organic produce at **Glover Street Market,** or come to town on Saturday 9 a.m.-noon mid-April to mid-Oct. for Twisp's **Farmers Market.**

    Methow Valley Brewing Co., 209 E. 2nd Ave., tel. (509) 997-6822, is a fine addition to the local scene, with great beer and food, including nightly specials. They also feature decadent homemade desserts and live music some weekends.

Hiking

To visit a working fire tower with mountain vistas in all directions, take the Alder Creek Rd. southwest from Twisp to Lookout Mountain. At the end of the road a trail leads 1.3 miles to **Lookout Mountain Lookout.**

    Twisp River Rd., west of town, provides access to the north side of the 145,667-acre **Lake Chelan-Sawtooth Wilderness,** with a dozen different paths taking off from the valley. A fine loop trip of approximately 15 miles begins just southwest of War Creek Campground on Forest Rd. 4420. The **Eagle Creek Trail** starts at an elevation of 3,000 feet and climbs steadily through Douglas fir forests and meadows, reaching 7,280-foot Eagle Pass after seven miles. Here it meets the **Summit Trail,** with connections to the Stehekin end of Lake Chelan or to other points in the wilderness. To continue the loop hike, follow it south a mile to **Oval Creek Trail.** This path leads back down to the trailhead, passing beautiful West Oval Lake on the way; a two-mile detour climbs to two additional cirque lakes.

    A fee is now charged for camping or trailhead parking on Okanogan National Forest land in the Winthrop and Twisp area. These passes cost $5 per night, or $25 annually for a region-wide Trail Park Pass.

Events

The annual **Freeze Yer Buns Run** takes place in late January and features a 10-km run with a Hawaiian vacation to the winner. In late June the **Twisp Show 'N' Shine** brings classic and antique cars to town.

Information and Services

The **Twisp Visitor Information Center,** tel. (509) 997-2926, downtown in the old grade school, is open Mon.-Fri. 8 a.m.-5 p.m. Interesting historical school photos line the walls. Twisp's summer-only outdoor **swimming pool** is on the northeast edge of town; tel. (509) 997-5441.

    The Forest Service's **Twisp Ranger District** office is at 502 Glover St., tel. (509) 997-2131. It is open Mon.-Fri. 7:45 a.m.-4:30 p.m. all year.

METHOW AND PATEROS

Scenic Drives

East of Twisp the highway splits; Hwy. 20 continues east to Okanogan and Omak, and Hwy. 153 turns south along the Methow River. Highway 20 offers a chance to cruise past old farms and ranches with aging wooden barns, horses grazing in the pastures, and hay piles draped with sky-blue tarps. The road then climbs into Ponderosa pine forests with openings of sage, before topping out in the western larch forests of Okanogan National Forest. These larch trees are especially pretty in the fall when the needles turn a vivid yellow. Near the summit of Loup Loup Pass is Loup Loup Ski Bowl.

    Highway 153 is another gorgeous drive, with the cottonwood-lined Methow River bottom surrounded by ranches, and rolling hills covered with sage and Ponderosa and lodgepole pines. It leads to the small towns of Methow and Pateros. Nothing of note at Methow, but you can camp at **Lightning Pine RV Park,** tel. (509) 923-2572.

Pateros

Five miles south of Methow, at the junction of Highways 97 and 153, is Pateros (pop. 600). The town has more to it, including popular Alta Lake State Park, and access to the Lake Pateros (the dammed-up Columbia River). Pateros was moved here during construction of Wells Dam, just a few miles downstream on the Columbia. The surrounding country is crowded with fruit orchards and apple processing plants. For a taste, stop at **Rest Awhile Fruit Stand** just north of town, tel. (509) 923-2256. In addition to fruit, they also sell fresh baked breads and pies, plus espresso coffee. You can also pick your own fruit in their orchard (one of the few places around that lets you do this).

Pateros itself consists of a few stores and a pretty waterfront park; it's a popular place to stop and fish or play in the reservoir. Be sure to look up into the hills above town to one of the state's more unusual art installations—15,000 colorful reflectors covering two old water towers.

Accommodations

Stay at **Amy's Manor B&B,** five miles north of Pateros on Hwy. 153, tel. (509) 923-2334 or (888) 923-2334, a charming 170-acre estate with spectacular views across the Methow River. The three guest rooms have private baths, and a full breakfast is served; $65 s or $80 d. No kids.

Valley View B&B, tel. (509) 923-9636, five miles from Pateros, is a contemporary home with huge picture windows overlooking the Columbia River. Three guest rooms have shared or private baths; $80 s or d with a full breakfast. Kids okay.

Lodging is also available at modern **Lake Pateros Motor Inn,** tel. (509) 923-2203 or (800) 444-1985, for $61 s or $65 d. The motel has an outdoor pool and dock on Lake Pateros.

Alta Lake Golf Resort, two miles from Pateros, tel. (509) 923-2359, has rooms (some with kitchenettes) for $52-78 s or d. An outdoor pool is here, along with an 18-hole golf course.

Whistlin' Pine Resort/Sawtooth Outfitters, off Hwy. 153 on the south end of Alta Lake, tel.

(509) 923-2548, is a popular spot for horseback riding and fishing. Rustic cabins ($30 d) and tent sites ($13 d) are also available.

Recreation and Campgrounds

Right in the town of Pateros is **Peninsula Park,** a verdant green stretch along Lake Pateros. Here are picnic areas, swimming, water skiing, RV parking, and showers. Sprinklers keep tenters away.

Popular with the summer crowd is **Alta Lake State Park,** tel. (509) 923-2473, two miles southwest of Pateros off Hwy. 153. Fish for rainbow trout, swim in the clear waters, or just enjoy the east-of-the-mountains sunshine. A mile-long trail takes you 900 feet higher to a scenic plateau overlooking the Columbia River Valley. The campground has tent sites ($10) and RV hookups ($15), and is open April-Oct., plus weekends and holidays the rest of the year. In winter, the park is a favorite of cross-country skiers and snowmobilers.

Events

The popular and tasty **Apple Pie Jamboree** hits Pateros the third weekend of July and includes a parade, street dance, arts and crafts fair, and fireworks. But people really come for the big pie feed, featuring 500 volunteer-baked apple pies with homemade ice cream. The **Pateros Hydro Classic** in mid-August is another big attraction, with inboard hydroplane boats topping 150 mph.

South to Chelan

Highway 97 south from Pateros is a busy thoroughfare paralleling the reservoir all the way to Chelan, 17 miles away. **Wells Dam,** seven miles south of Pateros, has a vista viewpoint where you can look across the blue lake to the surrounding rocky, arid landscape of grass and sage. The dam sits in a narrow canyon, and one of the old turbines is also at the vista point, along with a rock covered by Indian pictographs. Wells Dam visitors center is open daily 8 a.m.-6 p.m. and includes a fish-viewing area and salmon hatchery.

CHELAN AND VICINITY

Lake Chelan (sha-LAN) occupies a long, glacially carved valley on the eastern edge of the Cascades. The town of Chelan (pop. 3,200) sits on the southeast shore of the lake; Manson is seven miles northwest, and tiny Stehekin 55 miles away on the north shore. Stehekin is the only town on the Washington mainland that cannot be reached by road.

Lake Chelan is one of Washington's favorite summer playgrounds, offering resort accommodations, fine restaurants, water-skiing, swimming, and boating, but also delivering magnificent wilderness country just a boat ride away. Over the years the Chelan area has developed into a resort community that has—so far—managed to retain its small-town charm. It's still a genuine town with real orchardists, farmers, wilderness outfitters, and forest and park rangers standing in line with you in the grocery checkout line. Your children can meet and play with the children of residents and visitors from all over the world. Few other small towns in Washington have such a wide cross-section of people.

The vast majority of the Lake Chelan watershed is in public ownership and not open to major development (unless Newt Gingrich gets elected president), but such is not the case on the privately held portions. Here, the lake's popularity may prove its undoing. Tacky developments of all sorts are packing the shoreline between Chelan and Manson, as timeshare condos, elaborate resorts, ranch-style homes, retirement villas, and summer cottages crowd up the hillsides and through the apple orchards. The first orchard in the area—at Wapato Point— is now the site of the elaborate Wapato Point Resort. The area is still magnificent, but one wonders how long till all the orchards are replaced by urban sprawl, and the pristine lakeshore becomes yet another housing development.

Climate

These statistics will tell you why Chelan is so popular in Puget Sound: an average of only 24 days per year register temperatures below 32°, and 33 days are above 90°. Rainfall occurs less than nine days in an average year, and snow, sleet, or hail in excess of an inch falls on 31 days per year. The lake never freezes. The most telling statistic is this: although no official records are kept on the number of sunny days, it is roughly 300 days per year.

The Lake

Ice Age glaciers carved the deep trough that forms Lake Chelan. At its deepest point, the glacier- and stream-fed lake dips down 1,486 feet, or 450 feet below sea level. The only two deeper lakes in America are Oregon's Crater Lake (1,962 feet) and California and Nevada's Lake Tahoe (1,645 feet). Lake Chelan is 55 miles long, but seldom more than two miles wide. A dam built here in 1927 to increase electrical production raised the lake's level by 24 feet and increased its length by a mile. Water flows from the dam through a tunnel to a power plant at Chelan Falls, four miles away and 390 feet lower. Because of this hydroelectric project, the gorge cut by the Chelan River is now dry much of the year, and the lake level fluctuates 10-18 feet through the season.

Apple Land

Most visitors to Lake Chelan tend to think of it in terms of recreational opportunities, but in agricultural circles, the shores of the lake are much better known for something else: the finest apples in the world. This isn't a slogan created by the local community; Chelan apples are known all over the world for their excellent taste, long shelf life, and vivid colors.

Gross income from the apple industry is in the $100 million-per-year range, and upwards of 10,000 acres are devoted to apple orchards. Most of these are relatively small, averaging 30 acres or less. Annual production is in the range of 8 million boxes. The most popular apples are red delicious and golden delicious, followed by the reddish-yellow galas and the pinkish-red fujis, an apple developed in Japan.

Nobody is quite sure why Chelan apples are so much better than those grown only a few miles away. Some believe it is due to the soil,

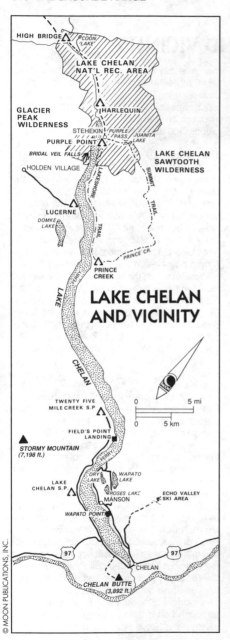

LAKE CHELAN AND VICINITY

which was created by the retreating glaciers that carved the valley. Also, the lake helps moderate the air temperature, keeping the valley above freezing during most of the winter, and cooling things down in the summer. This keeps the apples from being damaged by the heat, helping create a crisper and juicier apple that remains fresh longer in storage. Some also believe that the lake water used to irrigate the orchards contributes to the quality because it is colder than irrigation water used elsewhere.

Although apples are the major crop grown around the lake, some soft fruits are also grown. Scattered among the apple orchards are smaller plots of cherries, pears, apricots, and peaches.

SIGHTS

In Town

Visit the **Lake Chelan Museum** at Woodin Ave. and Emerson St. in Chelan, tel. (509) 682-5644, to see displays of pioneer and Native American relics, and a big collection of colorful applebox labels. Open daily 1-4 p.m. June-Sept., and by appointment the rest of the year; no charge.

The most interesting building in Chelan is **St. Andrew's Episcopal Church,** a charming log structure completed in 1899. The architect remains in dispute, though there is evidence that it may have been Stanford White, the designer of New York's Madison Square Garden. A carillon rings out the hours daily from the church, located on Woodin Avenue. Also of interest downtown is the **Ruby Theater,** built in 1913.

Scenic Drives

On the north shore of Lake Chelan, drive the 12-mile scenic loop from downtown Manson along the shore of Lake Chelan, up into apple orchards and past smaller lakes in the foothills, with striking views all along the way. From Manson, drive west on Lakeshore Dr. and Summit Blvd., north on Loop Ave. and Manson Blvd., east on Wapato Lake Rd., then south on the Chelan-Manson Hwy. back to Manson.

Another scenic drive is on the south shore of the lake; follow Hwy. 97 to the **Chelan Butte Lookout** sign across the street from the Park Lake Motel. The road curves upward for seven miles, with pullouts for photos of the lake and

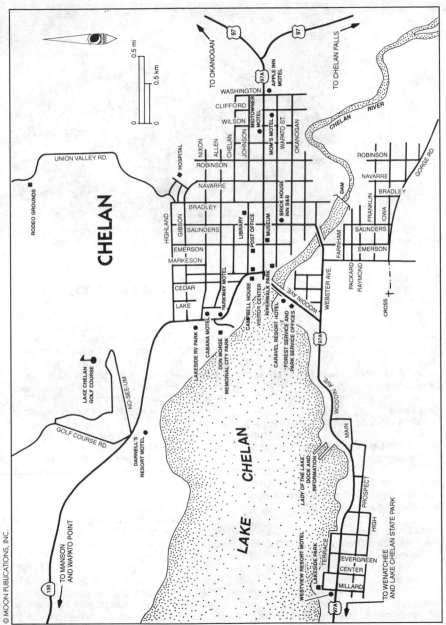

© MOON PUBLICATIONS, INC.

a street in Chelan

DON PITCHER

surrounding hills, the Columbia River almost directly below, the wheat fields of eastern Washington, and acres of apple orchards. The 3,892-foot butte is also one of the state's best launching pads for hang gliders.

Stormy Mountain has views across Lake Chelan, into the North Cascades, and over into the arid wheat country. You reach it by driving up Lake Chelan's South Shore Rd. to its end at Twenty-Five Mile Creek State Park, then take Forest Service Rd. 2805 to its end at Windy Camp. The view here is wonderful; a half-mile hike to the summit of 7,198-foot Stormy Mountain is even better.

State Parks

Two state parks provide camping (see below) and other attractions along the south shore of Lake Chelan. **Lake Chelan State Park** is right on the lake, nine miles west of Chelan, with an underwater park, a boat launch, and concession stand. **Twenty-five Mile Creek State Park,** 18 miles northwest of Chelan, has a swimming pool for campers and a boat launch.

Apple Tours

Both **Trout Blue Chelan,** tel. (509) 682-4541, and **Beebe Orchard Company,** tel. (509) 682-2526, give free tours of their huge apple warehouses and packing sheds on the road to Chelan Falls. Call ahead to schedule a tour. Trout/Blue Chelan doesn't offer tours during the hectic Sept.-Oct. harvest period. **Sunshine Fruit Market,** just

west of town at the junction of Hwy. 97A and South Lakeshore, tel. (509) 682-5695, has a roadside fruit stand open daily in the summer.

ACCOMMODATIONS

Make mid-summer reservations as early as possible; many of the rooms book up six months ahead of time for weekends in July and August. Winter rates are often 30% lower than the listed summer rates. In addition to the places listed below, the Chelan area has many private vacation homes available; see the Lake Chelan Chamber of Commerce for a complete list. The chamber also keeps track of motel availability in the summer.

Bed and Breakfasts

Unless otherwise noted, all B&Bs listed below serve a full breakfast and do not allow young children.

Relax in Victorian splendor at the romantic **Mary Kay's Whaley Mansion B&B,** 415 3rd St., tel. (509) 682-5735 or (800) 729-2408, an elegantly restored 1911 home. It has six guest rooms with private baths; $115-135 s or d. Two-night minimum on weekends

Built in 1902, **A Quail's Roost Inn,** 121 E. Highland, tel. (509) 682-2892 or (800) 681-2892, is one of Chelan's oldest homes, with a distinctively Victorian design, period antiques, a wraparound porch, and commanding views of the town and valley. The three guest rooms have private baths; $79-104 d. Kids by arrangement. Two-night minimum on summer weekends.

The **Brick House Inn,** Wapato and Saunders Streets, tel. (509) 682-2233 or (800) 799-2332, is a 1910 home with six bedrooms, shared baths, and a wrap-around porch. A continental breakfast is served on weekends; $68-87 d.

The Inn Above the Lake B&B, 914 Cone Rd., tel. (509) 682-3184, is a large contemporary home with great views. Three guest rooms have private baths, a sauna, hot tub, pool table, and outdoor pool; $115 s or d.

Another modern place with lakeshore views and hospitable owners is **Captain's Quarters,** 283 Minneapolis Beach Rd. (five miles west of Chelan), tel. (509) 682-5886 or (888) 977-1748. The three two-room suites have private entrances and two include jacuzzi suites. Enjoy breakfast on the deck overlooking Lake Chelan; $95-115 s or $115-135 d.

Apple Country B&B, 5220 Manson Blvd. in Manson, tel. (509) 687-3982, is a 1930 ranch house with two guest rooms that share a bath; $65 s or $70 d. Open May-September.

Holden Village B&B, tel. (509) 687-9695, is a newer home 25 miles west of Chelan, with mountain and lake vistas. Many folks stay here en route to Holden Village; the boat stops at nearby Fields Point. It has six guest rooms with shared baths and a full breakfast. Rates are $33 s or $45 d in private rooms, or $19 pp in the small dorm.

Resorts

The oldest and best-established resort on Lake Chelan, **Campbell's Resort,** 104 W. Woodin Ave.; tel. (509) 682-2561 or (800) 553-8225, is right in town and offers 150 rooms, plus two pools, hot tubs, boat moorage, and a 1,200-foot sandy beach. Campbell's is also a popular convention facility; $138-150 s or $148-160 d.

Darnell's Resort Motel, 901 Spader Bay Rd., tel. (509) 682-2015 or (800) 967-8149, features luxury family accommodations with a private beach, heated pool, hot tub, sauna, exercise room, lighted tennis courts, putting greens, rowboats, bicycles, moorage, and kids' play area. Rates are $144-159 for up to four; a four-night minimum is required in mid-summer.

The **Westview Resort Hotel,** 2312 W. Woodin Ave., tel. (509) 682-4396 or (800) 468-2781, is around the bend from the main part of town and features views back across the lake to Chelan and the Cascades. It also includes an outdoor pool, jacuzzi, and decks with lake views, kitchenettes available; $103 s or d.

Kelly's Resort, tel. (509) 687-3220, is a friendly and quiet family resort 13 miles west of Chelan. Shoreside cottages have kitchens, fireplaces, boat moorage, and lake swimming. $120-140 s or d for cottages in the woods; $150-170 s or d for lakeside units.

Caravel Resort Motel; 322 W. Woodin Ave.; tel. (509) 682-2582 or (800) 962-8723; is a large, impersonal resort right in town with an outdoor pool and jacuzzi; $107-143 s or d.

Watson's Harverene Resort; 10 miles west of Chelan; tel. (509) 687-3720 or (800) 687-3720; is a quiet family place with beachfront cottages available on a weekly basis ($1,050), including a private beach, outdoor pool, and hot tub.

Motels

Three places offer inexpensive and well-maintained motels. The cheapest is **Parkway Motel,** 402 N. Manson Rd., tel. (509) 682-2822, where rooms are just $40 s or d; kitchenettes cost $65 d. **Mom's Montlake Motel,** 823 Wapato St., tel. (509) 682-5715, $48 s or d, is a friendly and clean little place off the main drag for $58 s or d; open March-October. Another fine bargain place is **Apple Inn Motel,** 1002 E. Woodin Ave., tel. (509) 682-4044, with a jacuzzi and outdoor pool. Rates are $55 s or d, and kitchenettes are available.

Chelan Country Lodge, 531 E. Woodin Ave., tel. (509) 682-8474 or (800) 373-8474, has rooms for $79 s or $89 d, including microwaves and fridges. **Midtowner Motel,** 721 E. Woodin Ave., tel. (509) 682-4051, charges $60 s or d, and has an outdoor pool, jacuzzi, sauna, and kitchenettes. Find an outdoor pool and kitchenettes at **Cabana Motel,** 420 Manson Road, tel. (509) 682-2233, where rooms are $68-83 s or d. **Mountain View Lodge,** 25 Wapato Point Pkwy,. Manson, tel. (509) 687-9505 or (800) 967-8105, charges $87-115 s or d, including an outdoor pool and jacuzzi. Kitchenettes are available. **Wapato Point Village Inn,** at Wapato Point in Manson, tel. (509) 687-2500 or (800) 771-5300, is a new motel. All rooms have microwaves and fridges; $95 s or d.

Condos
The Chelan and Manson areas have many condo units for rent by the day or week. Some of these, such as Peterson's, are massive shoreside developments with dozens of units. For specifics, contact one of the following companies: **Chelan Vacation Rentals,** tel. (509) 682-4011 or (800) 356-9756; **Lake Chelan Shores Resort,** tel. (509) 682-4531; **Peterson's Waterfront,** tel. (509) 682-4002; and **Resort Vacation Rentals,** tel. (509) 687-9549 or (888) 687-9549.

Campgrounds
Right in town, the **City of Chelan Lakeshore RV Park,** tel. (509) 682-5031, has both tent sites ($22) and RV spaces ($27), along with showers, public swimming, and picnic areas. Rates are lower in the off-season; open all year.

Lake Chelan State Park, tel. (509) 687-3710, is 12 miles up-lake from Chelan along the south shore and offers swimming, tent sites ($11), and RV sites ($16). Call (509) 687-3710 for information, or (800) 452-5687 for reservations ($6 extra). The park is open daily April-Oct., and on weekends and holidays the rest of the year. This is the largest and most popular park in the area, with a swimming beach, boat ramp, docks, and summertime campfire programs.

Twenty-Five Mile Creek State Park, tel. (509) 687-3610, open May-Sept., has tent sites for $11 and RV hookups for $16. Call (800) 452-5687 for reservations ($6 extra). This pleasant, wooded park is 22 miles west of Chelan at the end of S. Lakeshore Dr., and 10 miles beyond Lake Chelan State Park. It's a favorite place for boaters who use the launch ramp here and purchase supplies at the marina store. The Forest Service's primitive and free **Ramona Creek Campground** is just three miles uphill from Twenty-Five Mile Creek State Park.

Tiny **Daroga State Park,** tel. (509) 664-6381, is 22 miles southeast of Chelan on the east bank of the Columbia River and just off Hwy. 97. Be ready for towering high-voltage power lines right next to the campground. Tent and RV sites here are $15 ($7 for bikes); open late March to late

October. More camping is available at **Wapato Lake Campground** near Manson; sites with electricity are $16 for tents and RVs. Call the Manson Parks office at (509) 687-6037 for reservations. **Kamei Resort,** tel. (509) 687-3690, also has RV and tent spaces.

The shore of Lake Chelan is dotted with 14 boat-in campgrounds, accessible by private boat or from the *Lady of the Lake II;* see the Forest Service office for specifics. Several other campgrounds are on the road system, including Antilon Lake Campground, north of Manson.

Beebe Bridge Park sits along the Columbia River across from the town of Chelan Falls, and has tent and RV sites for $15, along with showers, a swimming area, and play fields. Open mid-April through Oct.; tel. (509) 663-8121.

FOOD AND ENTERTAINMENT

Chelan has a large number of restaurants from which to choose. They tend to change quite frequently, and new owners or chefs can dramatically improve (or worsen) the reputation, so ask around to see who's hot, or simply take a look inside to see what looks interesting.

Breakfast and Lunch
Apple Cup Cafe is a family-type place with very good breakfasts (great cheese blintzes) in a Denny's-like setting. Head to **Latte Da Coffee Stop Cafe,** 303 E. Wapato Ave., tel. (509) 682-4196, for the best local espressos, plus light breakfasts and lunches in a cozy atmosphere. **Dagwoods,** 246 W. Manson Way, tel. (509) 682-8630, features stir fry and vegetarian dishes, along with soda fountain specials for lunch or dinner.

Dinner
Peter B's Bar & Grill, 116 E. Woodin Ave., tel. (509) 682-1031, sits right along the Chelan River, with a diverse menu of steaks, burgers, pastas, chicken, and seafood. Good food, reasonable prices, and a busy, convivial atmosphere. **Cactus Jack Grill & Saloon,** 502 E. Woodin, tel. (509) 682-2013, is a good place for light meals and coffees, along with prime rib, chicken, and pasta.

Goochi's, 104 E. Woodin Ave., tel. (509) 682-2436, is a noisy, happening place with an old cherry wood back bar that delivers lots of microbrews on tap. The trendy but tasty menu features gourmet burgers, fresh seafood, chicken, pastas, and homemade soups. Goochi's has comedy, blues, and rock acts on throughout the week in summer.

Built in 1930, the **Campbell House,** 104 W. Woodin Ave., tel. (509) 682-2561, is the old standby, offering elegant dining and a continental menu specializing in Angus steaks and fresh seafood; prices are moderate to expensive. Reservations highly recommended in the summer. The patio is very popular on summer evenings.

For the best pizzas around—including a spicy chicken garlic version—head to **Uncle Tim's Pizzaria** in Manson, tel. (509) 687-3035.

Produce and Bakeries
Golden Florins General Store, 125 E. Woodin Ave. tel. (509) 682-5535, doesn't appear like much outside, but step inside to find a spacious natural-foods store with a big selection of organic produce and other goods.

For the finest local pastries and breads, monster cinnamon rolls, and good deli sandwiches and espresso, head to **Village Bake Shop** in Manson, tel. (509) 687-3774. Not far away is **Laura's,** tel. (509) 687-6105, where the homemade pies are famous hereabouts.

The **Chelan Valley Farmers Market,** tel. (509) 682-4641, comes to town mid-June to mid-October on Saturday 8:30-noon. It's held on Johnson St. next to the chamber of commerce office.

EVENTS

The year begins with **Lake Chelan Winterfest,** featuring fireworks, a cross-country ski race, snow-sculpting contest, snowmobile events, Christmas tree bonfire, chili cookoff, and splash in the lake for the really bold. The nine-day **Lake Chelan Bach Feste** comes to town each July with concerts in the new Performing Arts Center, and in local churches and parks. The **Apple Blossom Festival** is held the second weekend in May in Manson, with a parade, car shows, and a chicken-noodle dinner (!) at the American Legion Hall. It's been happening here for over 75 years. The third weekend of May brings a **Chinook Salmon Derby** with $5,000 for the biggest fish. Arts and crafts, a carnival, live music, and food fill the streets on the fourth weekend of June, for the annual **Taste of Chelan Street Fair.** Manson's **Fourth of July** brings fireworks, an arts and crafts fair, a sparerib barbecue, and a watermelon-seed-spitting contest. See a popular PRCA rodeo and watch the crowning of the rodeo queen at **Lake Chelan Western Days** the fourth weekend in July.

SPORTS AND RECREATION

Hiking
The entire Chelan Valley is user-friendly for walkers and runners because the heaviest vehicle traffic is limited to the main routes—Hwy. 97A, the Chelan-Manson Hwy., and the south shore route. Several day hikes are available in the 25-Mile Creek area; for a complete description of hiking trails around the lake, stop by the Chelan District office at 428 W. Woodin Avenue. Trails out of Stehekin are described below.

If you're just out for a walk and want to enjoy the scenery, one of the nicest is **Riverwalk Park.** It runs a mile along the Chelan River from the Woodin Ave. bridge to the next bridge downstream and just above the dam. The park has restrooms, a picnic area, and boat launch.

A steep but brief climb is up the cross-topped hill overlooking town, nearby apple orchards, and the lake. The path begins at the intersection of S. Saunders St. and E. Iowa Avenue.

Hang Gliding and Paragliding
Chelan has an international reputation as an excellent place to hang glide or paraglide. The best place for launching (or watching) is the summit of 3,892-foot Chelan Butte where the hot winds blowing in from the Columbia River Basin give enormous lift. The flying is so good, in fact, that it isn't unusual for a hang glider to launch there and go nonstop to Spokane or into Idaho. They can also be launched to the west over the town and lake with a choice of several landing sites along the lake shore.

Golf
The **Chelan Municipal Golf Course,** tel. (509) 682-5421, has one of the most beautiful settings

of any course in the region, overlooking the lake. A small "executive" course, **Ma-8 Golf Course,** tel. (509) 687-6338, is southeast of Manson near Mill Bay Casino, and the acclaimed **Desert Canyon Resort** is halfway between Lake Chelan and Wenatchee, tel. (509) 682-2697 or (800) 258-4173.

Swimming

The lower end of Lake Chelan is lined with sandy beaches just right for swimming in the clean, cool waters. By late summer the water at the lower end of the lake is a bearable 70° F. Most public parks have popular swimming beaches, including Lake Chelan State Park, Chelan City Park, and the newer parks built by Chelan County—Manson Bay Park, Old Mill Park, Chelan Riverwalk Park, Chelan Falls Park, and Beebe Bridge Park. Up-lake beyond Manson and Lake Chelan State Park, the beaches become fewer due to the steep terrain. Swimming is possible in the Stehekin area, but with the water seldom above 50°, few people are found in the lake by choice. The lake never freezes.

Fishing

Lake Chelan is a very popular fishing spot, with kokanee salmon, chinook salmon, lake trout, rainbow trout, cutthroat trout, smallmouth bass, and burbot. Fish get big in these waters, with lake trout and chinook salmon averaging 6-10 pounds; a 24-pound lake trout was caught in the lake. Nearby, on the Columbia River and in mountain lakes, you will find smallmouth bass, rainbow, cutthroat, brown and eastern brook trout, and other game fish. The chamber of commerce has a brochure with fishing tips for Lake Chelan.

Boats and Jet Skis

Whatever kind of boating activity you like, you'll find it at Lake Chelan; sightseeing by boat, sailboarding, water-skiing, jet-skiing, kayaking, canoeing, rowing, and paddleboating are all popular. You'll also see sailboards and sailboats of all sizes. You can bring your own craft or rent jet skis, sailboats, canoes, and water-ski boats from several local companies, including **Chelan Boat Rentals,** 1210 W. Woodin, tel. (509) 682-4444; **Lakeland Marine Services,** 3414 Wapito Lake Rd., tel. (509) 687-3504; **Reed Shoreline Corp.,**

15 Hale St. in Manson, tel. (509) 687-1302 or (888) 558-7333; and **Ship 'n Shore Boat Rentals,** 1230 W. Woodin, tel. (509) 682-5125. **Chelan Parasailing,** tel. (509) 687-7245, brings this resort sport to Lake Chelan in the summer.

Play Parks

Slidewaters at Lake Chelan, 102 Waterslide Dr., tel. (509) 682-5751, one of Chelan's most popular places for children, is a short walk from the downtown area. Ten waterslides overlook the town and lake, plus kiddie slides, a 60-person hot tub, swimming, inner tube ride, picnic area, video arcade, gift shop, and concession stand. Open daily in summer.

Lakeshore Bumper Boats in **Don Morse Memorial City Park,** tel. (509) 793-2126, open daily 10 a.m.-10 p.m. Memorial Day to Labor Day, is the floating equivalent of bumper cars; very popular with kids. Paddle boats, miniature golf, and go-carts can also be found in Don Morse Park.

Bicycling

The popularity of mountain biking has made the Lake Chelan area a particular favorite with bike riders. All sorts of scenic loop trips are possible, covering a wide diversity of terrain. Both highways that go up-lake from Chelan are popular, as are several roads with lighter traffic such as the Manson Loop, the Echo Ridge cross-country ski trails, and numerous Forest Service roads and trails that are open to mountain bikes. Check with the Chelan Ranger District for information and maps on roads and trails.

Winter Sports

The Lake Chelan Valley is a heavily skied area. In Echo Valley, 12 miles northwest of Chelan, **Echo Valley Ski Area** tel. (509) 682-4002, has day and night downhill skiing on 3,000-foot Echo Mountain, served by three rope tows and a Poma lift; open Saturday and Sunday. Lift tickets cost just $15. Other facilities here include ice-skating and snowmobile trails. Get to Echo Valley aboard the free Link buses connecting Chelan with Manson; ski racks are on all the buses.

The **Echo Ridge** area contains 27 km of groomed cross-country ski trails ($5) for every level of ability. Vistas from the summit are extraordinary, encompassing Lake Chelan, the Cascades, and the Columbia River Valley. These are maintained by the Lake Chelan Nordic Ski Club, and are used as mountain bike paths in the summer. Other Chelan-area Nordic ski trails include five km of groomed runs at **Lake Chelan Golf Course** ($3), and another five km of groomed trails plus plenty of backcountry touring at Stehekin (described below). Get ski trail maps from the chamber of commerce.

Rent cross-country and downhill equipment from **Lake Chelan Sports,** 137 E. Woodin Ave., tel. (509) 682-2629, or **Lakeland Ski** in Manson, tel. (509) 687-2629.

Snowmobilers will enjoy the 125 miles of trails on both sides of Lake Chelan, accessible from three Sno-Parks. For information contact the Lake Chelan Ranger Station, tel. (509) 682-2576.

Ice-skaters will find outdoor rinks at Don Morse Memorial Park in Chelan, Echo Valley Ski Area, and Roses, Wapato, and Dry Lakes in Manson.

Gambling
Located on land owned by the Colville Tribe and staffed in part by workers who commute all the way from the reservation, **Mill Bay Casino,** tel. (509) 687-2102 or (800) 648-2946, is a mile southeast of Manson. The buildings house smoke-filled rooms with folks playing blackjack, craps, keno, roulette, poker, or yanking the handles on the slot machines.

SHOPPING

In addition to the restaurants and markets, Chelan and Manson have a number of interesting specialty shops. **The Harvest Tree,** 109 E. Woodin, tel. (800) 568-6062, offers baskets of apples, some with additional foods such as trail mix, Aplets, Cotlets, and honey.

Three local galleries are well worth a visit: **The Gallery at Allisons** also in Manson, tel. (509) 687-3534; **Sunburst Gallery,** 215 E. Woodin Ave., tel. (509) 682-8708; and **Wapato Studio and Fine Art,** 108 E. Woodin Ave. in Chelan, tel. (509) 682-2423. The last of these has works by the famed sculptor Rich Beyer and oils by Rod Weagant.

Out in the orchards near Manson sits **Bee's Antiques,** with a huge warehouse filled with beautifully restored (and pricey) antiques. It's one of the best known antique stores in Washington but doesn't advertise and has an unlisted phone; ask in town for directions.

INFORMATION AND SERVICES

For maps or other information, contact the **Lake Chelan Chamber of Commerce,** 102 E. Johnson, tel. (509) 682-3503 or (800) 424-3526. Hours are Mon.-Sat. 9 a.m.-6 p.m. and Sunday 10 a.m.-4 p.m. June-Aug.; daily with reduced hours in the spring and fall; and Mon.-Fri. 9 a.m.-5 p.m., Saturday 10 a.m.-4 p.m. Nov.-March. Their Web address is www.lakechelan.com.

The combined Forest Service/National Park Service, **Chelan Ranger District Office,** 428 W. Woodin, tel. (509) 682-2576, dispenses information on all forms of outdoor recreation, including many places to camp, picnic, or just have a look around. The office is open Mon.-Fri. 7:45 a.m.-4:30 p.m. all year, plus Sat.-Sun. 7:45 a.m.-4:30 p.m. from late June to early September.

TRANSPORTATION AND TOURS

See **Stehekin** for info on the ever-popular scenic boat and plane trips up Lake Chelan.

Bus Service
Link, tel. (509) 662-1155 or (800) 851-5465, is one of several free bus systems in Washington, funded by local taxes. Bus routes cover Chelan and Douglas Counties, including the towns of Chelan, Manson, Wenatchee, and Leavenworth. You can put your skis on the bus in Chelan and ride to Wenatchee, then change to Route 40 and ski at Mission Ridge. Or put your bicycle on the special racks and ride anywhere one-way and pedal back. Buses operate Mon.-Friday.

No long distance bus service operates to Chelan, but you can catch the Link bus to Wenatchee for connections to Northwest Trailways and Amtrak.

Air Service
Chelan Airways, tel. (509) 682-5065, offers daily seaplane service to Stehekin, Domke Lake, and other up-lake destinations, plus sightseeing flights over Lake Chelan and Stehekin Valley. The nearest airport with air service to larger cities is in Wenatchee.

STEHEKIN

Stehekin (ste-HEE-kin) sits at the northwest end of Lake Chelan and can be reached only by boat, floatplane, or foot; thousands of visitors take the boat trip "up-lake" from Chelan for lunch or an overnight stay at one of Stehekin's resorts. The town is also a launching point for treks into the heart of North Cascades National Park, or beyond into Lake Chelan-Sawtooth Wilderness and Glacier Peak Wilderness.

The word "Stehekin"—an Indian term meaning "the way through"—seems to fit this mountain gateway well. The town began in the late 1880s when prospectors came here in search of gold and silver. They found the minerals, but not in sufficient quantity to establish a large mine, and Stehekin has never been connected to the outside world by road. Today it is home to fewer than 100 permanent residents, but has all the basics, including a post office, grocery store, restaurant, and grade school. A summer-only outdoor supply shop and bakery are also in town.

Holden Village
Like Stehekin, the old copper and gold mining town of Holden is off the main road system. The *Lady of the Lake* stops at Lucerne, and a bus takes you 12 miles uphill to Holden. The mine closed in 1957, but the historic buildings remain, now run as a friendly Lutheran retreat that is especially popular with families. There are classes of all sorts, plus sessions on theology, the environment, and interpersonal issues. It's a spectacular mountain-rimmed setting, and many fine trails surround Holden, becoming ski trails in winter. You don't have to be religious or a member of any church to stay here. Guests stay in simple but comfortable lodges, and three healthy meals are included in the rate of $48 pp/per night or $226 pp/per week. A sauna, jacuzzi, pool room, bowling alley, and snack bar are also

in the village. The Lake Chelan Boat Company's vessels stop here daily. Call (509) 687-3644, or write to: Registrar, Holden Village, Chelan, WA 98816 for more information.

Hiking
The Stehekin area is a favorite of hikers of all levels—trails wander in all directions. The shuttle buses (described below) make it easy to get to the trailheads or back to Stehekin. Keep your eyes open when you walk since the area has a fair number of rattlesnakes.

A short three-quarter-mile-long loop hike— the **Imus Creek Nature Trail**—begins behind the visitor center and climbs a nearby hill overlooking the lake. Spectacular **Rainbow Falls**— a towering cataract of water that plummets 312 feet—is just off the road amid tall western red cedar trees. Get there by walking (or catching the shuttle) 3.5 miles up the road.

Take the shuttle to High Bridge for a beautiful day hike to **Coon Lake.** The 1.2-mile trail leads uphill to this scenic lake, with excellent views of Agnes Mountain and good birdwatching. Those with more energy can continue another seven miles to the 8,122-foot summit of **McGregor Mountain,** a tortuous climb up countless switchbacks.

An easy, albeit not especially challenging hike is the **Lakeshore Trail** that connects Stehekin with Moore Point, seven miles away. Or, continue to Prince Creek Campground, 17 miles to the southeast, where you can flag down the *Lady of the Lake II* (described below) for a return to Chelan. The campground is also a great departure point for a fine day hike up **Prince Creek Trail.** The route switchbacks through pine forests and then follows the creek into the high country around Cub Lake (a good place to camp). You'll discover dramatic vistas of the high Cascades from here. The Prince Creek Trail can also be used as part of a 38-mile loop trip that leaves Prince Creek Campground, climbs to the **Summit Trail,** and follows it along the ridge before dropping down to Stehekin. This hike features lots of ups and downs through forests and alpine meadows, and striking views of surrounding mountains. Much of the Summit Trail passes through the **Lake Chelan-Sawtooth Wilderness** with side trails leading north into the Twisp River drainage (see **North Cascades National**

Park for longer hikes over Cascade Pass and Park Pass).

Additional boat-accessible hikes start from Holden Village (described above), providing access to the Glacier Peak Wilderness. One of the most popular is the **Hart/Lyman Lakes Trail** (No. 1256). From Holden it follows Railroad Creek for 3.5 miles to Hart Lake before switchbacking up to Crown Point Falls and Lyman Lake and on to Cloudy Pass (10.5 miles), where it meets the Pacific Crest Trail. This trail gets a lot of use in mid-summer so don't expect solitude, and bears can be a problem in campsites along Railroad Creek. Showers and campsites are available in Holden Village.

Other Recreation

The center for outdoor recreation options is the **Courtney Log Office,** 150 yards past the post office along the lake. Here you can set up wagon and horseback rides, as well as week-long guided hikes, through **Cascade Corrals** tel. (509) 682-7742. Book an easy raft trip down the Stehekin River ($40 adults or $30 kids) through Stehekin Valley Ranch, or rent mountain bikes from **Discovery Bikes,** tel. (509) 686-3014. Discovery also offers a guided ranch breakfast ride each morning. North Cascades Stehekin Lodge rents bikes too.

Accommodations

Stehekin is a wonderful place to relax and enjoy the wilderness splendor without interference from TVs or phones. As with all places in the Lake Chelan area, advance reservations are a must in the summer. **North Cascades Stehekin Lodge,** tel. (509) 682-4494, has lodge rooms and housekeeping units for $77-93 s or d. Amenities include a restaurant, bar, bike and boat rentals, a marina, gas, and groceries. During the winter, the Park Service and North Cascades Stehekin Lodge jointly maintain 19 km of free **cross-country ski trails.** Rent skis in Chelan or bring your own. The lodge has snowshoes for rent.

At **Stehekin Valley Ranch,** tel. (509) 682-4677 or (800) 536-0745, nine miles up from Stehekin, your lodging, three hearty meals, and local transportation are included in the price of your cabin: $60 pp for adults, less for kids. Most are primitive tent cabins with no running water or electricity, and kerosene lamps for light. Showers are nearby. They also have three nicer cabins with private baths for $70 per person. The ranch is open mid-June to early October.

Several other Stehekin area houses and cabins are also available for rent by the day or week. These include: **Silver Bay Inn at Stehekin,** tel. (509) 682-2212 or (800) 555-7781; **Stehekin Log Cabin,** tel. (509) 682-4677, **Stehekin House,** tel. (509) 884-1730; **Stehekin Cedar Home,** Box 14, Stehekin, WA 98852; **Rustic Retreat,** Box 84, Stehekin; and **Flick Creek House,** tel. (509) 884-1730.

Campgrounds

Purple Point Campground is just a third of a mile from the boat landing in Stehekin. Campers can also ride the shuttle bus from Stehekin to **Harlequin, Bullion, High Bridge, Tumwater, Dolly Varden, Shady, Bridge Creek, Park Creek,** and **Flat Creek** campgrounds along the Stehekin River. **Weaver Point Campground,** is a very popular boat-access campground at the north end of the lake across from Stehekin. The old Weaver homestead here was the site where *The Courage of Lassie* was filmed in 1944, starring none other than Elizabeth Taylor (and Lassie, of course). All of these campgrounds are free; obtain a camping permit at Golden West Lodge Information Center. All boat-access campgrounds on Lake Chelan do not require a camping permit, but they do require a dock site pass of $5 per day or $40 for a season pass.

Food

Stehekin Valley Ranch Restaurant, tel. (509) 682-4677, is open June-Sept. with a menu that includes steaks, burgers, salad bar, and homemade desserts—all of which will taste pretty good after a week of backcountry travel or a long day in the saddle. Reservations are required. The restaurant is nine miles up the valley from Stehekin, but free transportation is provided. Two miles up from the boat dock is **Stehekin Pastry Company,** which offers delicious baked goods, ice cream, and espresso; open summers only. Another restaurant—open all year—is inside **North Cascades Stehekin Lodge,** tel. (509) 682-4494, just a short walk from the dock.

Information and Services

The National Park Service-run **Golden West Visitor Center,** (360) 856-5700, ext. 340, then ext. 14, in Stehekin is the place to go for information on hiking and camping in the area. Talks and evening programs are offered during the summer. Golden West is open daily 8:30 a.m.-5 p.m. mid-May to mid-Sept., with reduced hours in spring and fall. The ranger station is open Mon.-Fri. 8-4:30 year-round. Nearby are **The House That Jack Built,** selling locally made crafts, and **McGregor Mt. Outdoor Supply.** The only public phone in the Stehekin area is next to the coin-operated laundry and shower facility, 200 yards uplake from the Stehekin landing.

Boat Access

A longtime favorite of visitors to Lake Chelan is the 55-mile voyage from Chelan or Manson to Stehekin. **Lake Chelan Boat Company** has been operating boats along this route for more than 65 years and now runs three vessels: the 350-passenger *Lady of the Lake II,* which takes fours hours to reach Stehekin, the 65-foot-long *Lady Express,* which gets there in two hours, and a high speed catamaran, the *Lady Cat,* that takes just one hour. Food is available on all three boats, and onboard Forest Service interpreters give talks on the human and natural history of the area. Service is year-round, but only the *Lady Express* operates Nov.-April, and only the *Lady of the Lake II* operates May and October. (No winter boat service on Tuesday and Thursday.)

In addition to Chelan and Manson, the boats stop at Field's Point (accessible by car along the south shore), Lucerne (access to Holden), and Stehekin. The *Lady II* also makes flag stops at any Forest Service campsite upon request during the summer season. Service changes through the year; pick up a copy of the schedule at visitors centers or from the Lake Chelan Boat Company, tel. (509) 682-2224, at 1319 W. Woodin Ave. on the southwest end of Chelan. Find them on the Web at www.ladyofthelake.com. A separate service provides weekly barge trips up the lake carrying vehicles, fuel, groceries, and supplies to Stehekin. Roundtrip fares are $22 for the *Lady of the Lake II,* $41 for the *Lady Express,* and $79 for the *Lady Cat.* The *Lady Cat* makes two roundtrips daily, and the other boats each make one roundtrip daily. Mix and match the boat

schedules for day trips to Stehekin. You can also carry bikes, canoes, or kayaks aboard the boats for an extra charge.

Air Access

Chelan Airways, tel. (509) 682-5555, offers daily seaplane service to Stehekin and sightseeing flights over the Stehekin Valley. Or, fly one-way and take a boat in the other direction.

Shuttle Buses

The National Park Service and Stehekin Adventure Company combine to offer daily van or bus transportation from the dock at Stehekin to Flat Creek, 20 miles into the mountains. This service is offered from late May through mid-October and costs $5 one-way to High Bridge, or $10 one-way to Flat Creek. Both buses carry backpacks, and the Stehekin Adventure bus also carries bikes. Contact the Park Service's Golden West Visitor Center in Stehekin for details or reservations; tel. (360) 856-5700, ext. 340, then 14, or stop by their visitors centers in Stehekin or Chelan. Reservations are not needed for the larger Stehekin Adventures buses. Passengers on both services are given a narrated tour along the way, and you can get on or off at any point along the route.

Bus Tours

In the summer **North Cascades Stehekin Lodge,** tel. (509) 682-4494 offers daily trips to Rainbow Falls. Their bus meets the *Lady Express* and *Lady of the Lake II* boats when they arrive in Stehekin and provides a narrated 45-minute tour for $6. They also offer $20 bus tours that include a picnic lunch at High Bridge and a visit to Rainbow Falls and Buckner Orchard (said to be the largest common red delicious orchard surviving in the U.S.).

ENTIAT AREA

Heading south from Chelan on Hwy. 97A, you pass through the center of the large Tyee Complex Fire of 1994, with extensive areas of charred timber. After several miles of this, the highway enters a tunnel and then descends to the Columbia (or the dammed version thereof) through hills draped in sage and grass.

Entiat

The town of Entiat (ANN-ee-at; pop. 500) sits along Lake Entiat, that portion of the Columbia River that backs up behind massive Rocky Reach Dam 10 miles downriver. This is orchard country; stop at a local fruit stand for fresh apples, cherries, apricots, peaches, or pears in season.

For information on the area, head to the Wenatchee National Forest **Entiat Ranger Station,** tel. (509) 784-1511. Camping and RV places ($16) are available along the lake at **Entiat City Park;** open April to mid-Nov.; call (509) 784-1500 or (800) 736-8428 for reservations (recommended in mid-summer). Near the city park, the **Entiat Historical Museum,** tel. (509) 784-1832 contains local memorabilia in an 1895 farmhouse. Open summers only, Sunday 10 a.m.-2 p.m., and Saturday 10 a.m.-4 p.m.

Link, tel. (509) 662-1155 or (800) 851-5465, has free daily bus service throughout Chelan and Douglas Counties, including Entiat, Chelan, Wenatchee, and Leavenworth.

Entiat River Valley

South of Entiat, Hwy. 97A hugs the shore of the lake, passing rugged rocky slopes. Orchards edge the east shoreline. A mile south of Entiat is the turnoff to **Entiat River Rd.,** which leads to **Entiat National Fish Hatchery,** tel. (509) 784-1131, and eventually to the Entiat trailhead for the Glacier Peak Wilderness. Along the way are seven Forest Service campgrounds ($5-10; open May-October); closest is the free **Pine Flat Campground,** 14 miles up, and located along the Mad River. Hiking trails lead up to mountain lakes above here. Also of note is **Silver Falls,** 30 miles up the road. A campground is here, along with a 1.5-mile loop trail to this 150-foot waterfall. Get supplies at the small store in the tiny settlement of **Ardenvoir,** nine miles up. The Forest Service charges trailhead parking fees ($3/day or $25 for an annual Trail Park Pass) in the Entiat River Valley.

CASHMERE

Tucked between strip-mall Wenatchee and Bavarian-mall Leavenworth, tiny Cashmere (pop. 2,300) has long featured a Colonial American theme on its buildings. Highway 2 between Leavenworth and Cashmere is lined with fruit orchards (visit in late April to enjoy the trees in bloom), and the dry climate helps produce the finest D'Anjou pears in America. A half-dozen fruit stands sell fresh apples, pears, cherries, apricots, peaches, plums, and berries in season. Because of this fruit production, Cashmere was a logical place to establish a business that produces a confection made from fruit juices, walnuts, and powdered sugar—the treats known as Aplets and Cotlets.

SIGHTS

Candy Town

If you have a sweet tooth, be certain to stop at **Liberty Orchards,** 117 Mission St., tel. (509) 782-2191, the home of Aplets and Cotlets. These all-natural confections are made of fruit juices (apple, grape, and apricot) and walnuts, and are coated with powdered sugar and corn starch. Tours take 15 minutes or so and end back in the gift shop where you can sample a number of different candies and purchase gift boxes and various knickknacks. The original sweets were developed by two Armenian immigrants, Mark Balaban and Armen Tertsagian, who had established fruit orchards in the Cashmere area. Unable to sell all the fruit they produced, they decided to mix apple juice and walnuts to make a Middle Eastern confection called locum. More than 75 years have passed, but the candy is still made in Cashmere (two million pounds a year), and the company president is a grandson of the original owners. Old standbys such as Aplets and Cotlets are still around, along with several dozen other varieties, from chocolate passion fruit to sugar-free, nut-free versions. Tour hours are Mon.-Fri. 8 a.m.-5:30 p.m., Sat.-Sun. 10 a.m.-4 p.m., April-Dec.; Mon.-Fri. 8:30 a.m.-4:30 p.m. Jan.-March. On weekends you aren't likely to see a lot of activity in the plant during a tour, but the free samples make any stop worthwhile. Call (800) 888-5696 for a mail-order catalog of gift boxes.

Chelan County Historical Museum

Considered one of the top pioneer villages in the country, the Chelan County Historical Museum, 600 Cottage Ave., tel. (509) 782-3230, has restored and furnished 20 of the oldest buildings in Chelan County to create an authentic Old West atmosphere. A blacksmith shop, railroad passenger car, school, gold mine, mission building, hotel, and assay office are part of the Pioneer Village; there's also a large waterwheel that lifted water out of the Wenatchee River to irrigate the orchards. The large main museum building houses an extraordinary collection of Native American artifacts—baskets, prehistoric antler carvings, beaded clothing, medicines, pipes, and more—along with natural history and pioneer exhibits. Hours are Tues.-Sun. 9:30 a.m.-5 p.m.; closed Nov.-March. Admission is $3 adults, $2 seniors and students, $1 ages 5-12, and families $5.

PRACTICALITIES

Accommodations and Camping

Cashmere has two comfortable places. **Cashmere Country Inn,** 5801 Pioneer, tel. (509) 782-4212 or (800) 291-9144, is a pretty 1907 farmhouse with five guest rooms, all with private baths. Ouside, find flower gardens and a pool and hot tub. A generous country breakfast is served, two night minimum on weekends, no kids. $75-80 s or d. **Village Inn Motel,** 229 Cottage Ave., tel. (509) 782-3522 or (800) 793-3522; has rooms for $48-55 s or $50-60 d.

Camping ($12) and RV spaces ($17) with showers are available at **Wenatchee River County Park,** just west of town, tel. (509) 662-2525. Open April to late October; no reservations.

Food

Among Cashmere's more elegant eateries is **The Pewter Pot,** 124 Cottage Ave., tel. (509) 782-2036, a colonial-style restaurant featuring fresh-baked bread, locally grown produce, and from-scratch cooking, including traditional English dinners and tea and scones in the afternoon. Be sure to save space for the marionberry pie. More tasty baked goods across the street at **Sure to Rise Bakery,** tel. (509) 782-2424.

For pasta, steak, fish, and Greek specialties, head to the attractive **Siraco's Restaurant,** 106 Cottage Ave., tel. (509) 782-3444. This is also the place to go for breakfast in Cashmere.

Events

Celebrated the first week in July, the highlight of **Founder's Days** is the "Stillman Miller Hill Climb," inspired by an early resident who claimed he could pour himself a beer in the local tavern, run up Numbers Hill, and be back before the head settled. Whether or not he actually made it is anybody's guess, but the concept was so appealing that runners are still trying it today. Other events include a parade, barbecue, arts and crafts show, and street dance.

Cashmere is also home to the **Chelan County Fair,** held the second week in September, highlighted by rodeos, musical entertainment, a carnival, and exhibits. The first weekend in October brings **Cashmere Apple Days;** apple bin races, an apple-pie-baking contest, music, dancing, and staged shoot-outs are all part of the fun.

Transportation

Catch a free **Link** bus, tel. (800) 851-5465, for connections from Cashmere to other parts of Chelan and Douglas counties, including Leavenworth, Wenatchee, and Lake Chelan. **Cascade Helitours,** tel. (509) 548-4759, provides scenic helicopter flights over the Cascades out of Cashmere.

LEAVENWORTH

One of the most distinctive towns in the Pacific Northwest, Leavenworth has a scant 2,000 residents but manages to attract more than a million visitors per year.

The attraction? A fanciful Bavarian village, complete with authentic architecture, hand-carved benches, and flower-bedecked streets, all backdropped by peaks of the Cascades. Add in the female clerks in Bavarian dirndl dresses and waiters in lederhosen, and the town gets a bit hokey at times, but it is certainly unique in America. With almost 100 lodging places and dozens of restaurants and shops, it's pretty clear that people love this place.

HISTORY

Although preceded by prospectors and Hudson's Bay fur traders, the first Anglo settlers in the Leavenworth area didn't arrive until the late 1880s, with the news that the Great Northern Railway planned to lay tracks through the valley. The resulting population "boom" brought Leavenworth (originally called Icicle) about 300 people by the turn of the century. They were mostly railroad men or lumberjacks employed by the Lamb-Davis Lumber Co., operators of one of the state's largest sawmills. The after-hours rowdiness of these laborers gave little Leavenworth a rather unrefined reputation that took years to live down. Even so, by the early 1920s a wave of families bought tracts of land to grow "Wenatchee Big Red" apples.

When the railroad moved its switching yard from Leavenworth to Wenatchee, and the sawmill closed its doors after logging all its waterfront land, these family-based fruit farms provided much of the town's income. But by the 1960s, it was clear that Leavenworth needed more than apples to survive. With help from the University of Washington, a committee on tourism was formed to brainstorm, and it suggested a fall festival and a major remodeling job.

Suggestions for the town's new motif ranged from a Gay '90s theme to a Western town, but with the impressive mountain backdrop, an alpine village seemed the best answer. One of the first proponents was Ted Price, owner of a Swiss Bavarian-style cafe in Coles Corner. (The building, now Squirrel Tree Inn, still stands 14 miles northwest of Leavenworth.) The town's

Leavenworth's Bavarian Village is a popular tourist attraction.

DON PITCHER

LEAVENWORTH

SKI BOWL

HAUS ROHRBACH PENSION

CHUMSTICK HWY

BAYERN ON THE RIVER

U. S. FOREST SERVICE

BINDLESTIFF'S RIVERSIDE CABINS

PINE VILLAGE KOA

RIVER'S EDGE LODGE

EVERGREEN INN

CHALET RV PARK

TO WENATCHEE

FRONT ST.

COMMERCIAL ST.

MAIN ST.

DIVISION ST.

13th ST.

9th ST.

CHAMBER OF COMMERCE / VISITOR CENTER

SEE DETAIL

COMMERCIAL ST.

HAUS LORELEI B&B

WENATCHEE RIVER

BOSCH GARTEN B&B

LINDERHOF MOTOR INN

ENZIAN MOTOR INN

TYROLEAN RITZ HOTEL

MTN. HOME RD.

DER RITTERHOF MOTOR INN

SAFEWAY

GREYHOUND STOP

TO SEATTLE

W. COMMERCIAL ST.

E. LEAVENWORTH RD.

DYE RD.

MOUNTAIN HOME LODGE

RUN OF THE RIVER B & B

DETAIL

ALPEN INN HOTEL

ICICLE RIVER

RODEWAY INN

ALL SEASONS RIVER INN

ICICLE RD.

TO HATCHERY AND CAMPGROUNDS

0   0.25 mi

0   0.25 km

DETAIL:

2

LIBRARY

POOL

CITY PARK

INNSBRUCKER INN

THE BREWERY

9th ST.

FRONT ST.

8th ST.

GINGERBREAD FACTORY

DANISH BAKERY

BLACKBIRD LODGE

PENSION ANNA

OBERTAL MOTOR INN

COMMERCIAL

MRS. ANDERSON'S LODGING HOUSE

LORRAINE'S EDEL HAUS

HOSPITAL

WATERFRONT PARK

© MOON PUBLICATIONS, INC.

renovation was financed with private funds and backed by local bankers. It quickly earned national recognition for the attention to detail, aggressive promotion, and bootstraps efforts. Many of the buildings were designed by Karl Heinz Ulbricht, who had fled East Germany in the 1950s, and who insisted upon authenticity and quality construction. By the late '60s, the Bavarian theme had taken hold; it now covers almost every commercial building in town. Tourism has transformed a going-nowhere place into one of the premier success stories in community improvement.

More than 85,000 acres around Leavenworth were burned in a series of 1994 fires, but the town itself escaped almost unscathed. The burned areas—varying from conspicuously blackened swatches to patchy ground fires—are visible for miles along Hwy. 2 as you head over the Cascades from Leavenworth, up the Icicle Canyon drainage, and along Hwy. 97 north of Blewett Pass.

SIGHTS

The Bavarian Village

Start your tour of the Bavarian Village in the heart of town—on Front Street, where there's plenty of on-street parking. Shops, restaurants, taverns, and hotels are squeezed side by side, all beautifully decorated with carved wood, flower boxes, and murals—even the automated teller machine is surrounded by a painted alpine scene.

Trinket and gewgaw places are spread throughout town—shops with plastic Santas, inane T-shirts, and made-in-Taiwan Bavarian figurines—but fortunately, Leavenworth also has more than its share of distinctive, great-for-browsing places. **A Matter of Taste,** 647 Front St., tel. (509) 548-6949 or (800) 497-3995, lets you savor all sorts of unusual treats, from "Ass Kickin' Chicken Wing Sauce" to coffee jelly. Just above their entrance is the town **glockenspiel,** with carved dancers who clog on the hour. Another "glock" lives above the entrance to **The Cuckoo Clock,** 725 Front St., tel. (509) 548-4857, with dancers coming out of the closet (so to speak) every half-hour. Inside are tall grandfather clocks priced over $5,000, weird and wacky timepieces, and more than a few Bavarian cuckoo clocks. The **Emerald Fox Gallery,** 715 Front St., tel. (509) 548-9088 or (800) 530-9088, has a beautiful collection of glass art and jewelry. Upstairs at 723 Front St. is **Jubilee Global Gifts,** tel. (509) 548-3508, with handmade gifts from all over the planet—but nothing from Germany.

A few doors down (and past the Danish Bakery, if you can make it beyond their luscious pastries without being enticed inside) is **Nusskracker Haus,** 735 Front St., tel. (509) 548-7014, showcasing imported collectibles and hundreds of German nutcrackers. For an even more impressive collection, head upstairs to the **Nutcracker Museum,** tel. (509) 548-4708 or (800) 892-3989, where over 2,000 different kinds of nutcrackers are displayed. Open daily 2-5 p.m. May-Oct., and weekends the rest of the year; $2.50 adults, $1 ages 5-16. Its enough to drive Tchaikovsky nuts.

Next comes **Der Marketplatz,** 801 Front St., tel. (509) 548-7422, which has an extraordinary stein collection for beer drinkers, European crystal, Hummel figurines, and even Bavarian polka CDs. Continue down the block and down the basement stairs to **Die Musik Box,** 837 Front St., tel. (509) 548-6152 or (800) 288-5883, where 5,000 intricate music boxes from around the globe create a chorus of whimsical sounds.

Be sure to also visit **The Train Store,** 636 Front St., tel. (509) 546-5018 or (800) 546-5018. Inside the Train Store you're likely to meet railroad artist H.L. "Scotty" Scott, III whose intricate pen and ink drawings and prints line the walls. Work your way back through the side streets and onto Commercial Street for more shops; you'll even find a shop selling Australian imports.

Front St. Park, sandwiched between Hwy. 2 and the shops of Front St., is a relaxing, sunny spot for a picnic lunch or noontime break in the central gazebo. It's also the place to see street dances, art exhibits, and other public events, or to stop at the public restrooms. Across Hwy. 2 is the Chamber of Commerce Visitor Center, and the city hall/library building.

Waterfront Park, on the cottonwood-shaded banks of the Wenatchee River off 8th and Commercial Streets, has walkways over and around the river, benches for a respite from shopping, and views of the peaks surrounding Icicle Canyon. You can cross-country ski from here to the golf course during the winter.

Fish Hatchery and Interpretive Trail
The **Leavenworth National Fish Hatchery,** two miles out Icicle Rd., tel. (509) 548-7641, cranks out some 2.5 million salmon each year. Built in 1939-40, the hatchery was the largest such facility in the world when completed. Water for the hatchery comes from Icicle Creek, the Wenatchee River, deep wells, and a half-mile tunnel from Snow Lakes in the Alpine Lakes Wilderness. Stop by to watch the steelhead trout and chinook salmon in the raceways (favorite spots for dive-bombing belted kingfishers), or step inside to see displays and educational videos. Exhibits reveal how Columbia River dams and development have devastated natural salmon and steelhead runs and how the hatchery attempts to mitigate some of the damage. The real attraction here is an "outdoor aquarium" where you can watch rainbow trout in the eye-level concrete "stream." The hatchery is open daily 8 a.m.-4 p.m. all year.

Icicle Creek Interpretive Trail provides a mile-long circular path from the hatchery. Pick up one of the informative trail brochures before heading out to see various sites along the creek, including a wildlife viewing blind. Keep your eyes open for the resident ospreys.

Nearby State Parks
Twenty-three miles north of Leavenworth on Hwy. 207, **Lake Wenatchee State Park** is a popular year-round recreation area, with cross-country skiing in winter, plus swimming, fishing, and canoeing in summer. The spectacular Lake Wenatchee waterfront is set against a backdrop of majestic snow-covered peaks. Other facilities include boat rentals, weekend interpretive programs, and wooded campsites (no hookups). Summer camping is $11 per site; a number of sites are plowed for winter camping. Horseback rides are available summers from **Icicle Outfitters and Guides,** tel. (509) 784-1145 or (800) 497-3912.

Eight miles east of Leavenworth on Hwy. 2 is **Peshastin Pinnacles State Park.** This 35-acre park provides public access to a popular rock-climbing mecca. There are routes for all ranges of ability here, and nonclimbers can stop to photograph the dramatic pinnacles, walk the short trails, or watch more daring folks. No camping.

Blewett Pass

Highway 97 heads south from the Leavenworth area, connecting Hwy. 2 with I-90. The road climbs 21 miles to 4,102-foot Blewett Pass, a popular area for hiking, skiing, and snowmobiling. **Blewett Pass Interpretive Trail** offers a three-mile loop through high-country forests. Several nearby Forest Service campgrounds (Bonanza, Tronsen, Swauk, and Mineral Springs) have campsites for $8 or less. For more adventure, take the slightly shorter, but significantly steeper, sinuous, and serpentine old highway over Blewett Pass.

The **Swauk Forest Discovery Trail** is an easy three-mile path at the summit of Swauk/Blewett Pass. The trail passes through both old-growth forests and clearcuts, and educational signs are scattered along the way.

Blue Creek Rd. (Rd. 9738) leads from the Mineral Springs area west approximately seven miles to an old fire lookout on Red Top Mountain, providing vistas in all directions. This is a popular area to search for blue agates and geodes (a.k.a "thunder eggs"). Also nearby is **Mineral Springs Resort,** tel. (509) 857-2361, which has

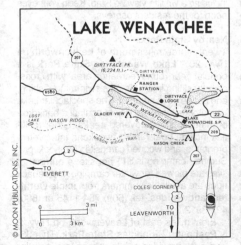

RV spaces and good meals. Come winter, this area is very popular with snowmobilers and cross-country skiers. Sno-Parks at Swauk Campground and Pipe Creek provide skier-only access to many miles of cross-country trails. For details, contact the Forest Service's Cle Elum Ranger Stations, tel. (509) 674-4411.

The Forest Service charges $3 per vehicle per day for trailhead parking, or $25 for an annual Trail Park Pass valid on most Washington national forests.

SUMMER RECREATION

River Runnin'

The rivers of the central Cascades support many rafting outfitters, but the Wenatchee is easily the most popular river in the state. Above Leavenworth, the Wenatchee drops through rugged Tumwater Canyon, with several class VI stretches before calming down to more manageable class III rapids below town. Leavenworth is the most common put-in point, and whitewater trips cover 16-24 miles, depending upon the take-out spot. Conditions change through the year; high spring runoff creates excellent whitewater conditions from April to mid-July (and often longer). Gentler float trips begin at Lake Wenatchee and cover the stretch of easy water before the river enters Tumwater Canyon near Tumwater Campground (the take-out point). These are especially popular when flow levels drop during August and September. Inner tubers often float down slower parts of the Icicle and Wenatchee Rivers to Blackbird Island near Leavenworth's Waterfront Park. Rent inner tubes at **Leavenworth Sports Center,** Hwy. 2 at Icicle Rd., tel. (509) 548-7864, or rent kayaks and canoes at Lake Wenatchee from **Osprey Rafting,** tel. (800) 743-6269, or **Leavenworth Outfitters,** tel. (509) 763-3733 or (800) 347-7934.

For half-day rafting excursions, expect to pay $65-80 for whitewater trips, $40-65 for scenic float trips. Most companies include guides, wetsuits, booties, meals, and shuttle bus service. Contact one of the following companies for more info, or look for their brochures in the visitors center: **All Rivers Adventures,** tel. (800) 743-5628; **Alpine Whitewater** (a locally based company), tel. (800) 723-8386; **Alpine Adventures,** tel. (800) 723-8386; **Blue Sky Outfitters,** tel. (800) 228-7238; **Enchanted Water Tours,** tel. (800) 723-8987; **Leavenworth Outfitters,** tel. (800) 347-7934; **Northern Wilderness River Riders, Inc.,** tel. (800) 448-7238; **Orion River Expeditions,** tel. (800) 553-7466; **Osprey Rafting,** tel. (800) 743-6269; **River Recreation,** tel. (800) 464-5899; and **Wildwater River Tours,** tel. (800) 522-9453.

Mountain Biking

Cyclists love the back roads around Leavenworth, including an almost-level seven-mile loop through Icicle Valley. A more adventurous ride climbs the dirt road up Tumwater Mountain, just north of town, and offers vistas into Tumwater Canyon and the Wenatchee Valley far below. Stop by the local Forest Service offices for descriptions of other mountain biking trails. Rent mountain bikes from **Leavenworth Ski & Sports,** Hwy. 2 at Icicle Rd., tel. (509) 548-7864, or **Der Sportsman,** 837 Front St., tel. (509) 548-5623.

Hiking

The Forest Service now charges a fee for trailhead access and overnight camping in many parts of Wenatchee National Forest. You can either get a $25 for an annual Trail Park Pass, or pay $3 per vehicle per day.

The Alpine Lakes Wilderness Area, one of the most popular and scenic hiking destinations in Washington, lies just a few miles west of Leavenworth (**Stevens Pass and Skykomish Valley** for details). Stop by the Wenatchee National Forest's **Leavenworth Ranger District,** 600 Sherbourne, tel. (509) 548-6977, for a brochure on nearby day hikes and a detailed trail guide to longer treks.

The **Lake Wenatchee** area at the north end of Hwy. 207 has an extensive system of hiking trails. Popular with hikers and photographers is the **Dirtyface Trail,** a steep 4.5-mile one-way hike from the Lake Wenatchee Ranger Station to the Dirtyface Lookout at 6,000 feet with views of the lake and surrounding scenery. Backpackers may want to try the **Nason Ridge Trail,** a 22-mile one-way scenic trail along the length of the Nason Ridge, starting at South Shore Rd. off Hwy. 207. A number of other one-day or longer hikes start from various points along a compli-

cated network of numbered forest roads; your best bet is to check at the ranger station for detailed maps and printed trail descriptions. This is black bear country; hikers and campers should use standard bear precautions.

The upper Chiwawa River drainage north of Lake Wenatchee is one of the most popular access points for the Glacier Peak Wilderness. Several trails take off near the end of this road, including the heavily used **Phelps Creek Trail,** which follows the creek for five miles to mountain-rimmed Spider Meadows inside the wilderness.

Equine Expeditions and Excursions

During the summer months, **Eagle Creek Ranch**—a 580-acre ranch surrounded by Wenatchee National Forest—offers a number of pack trips to nearby wilderness areas, along with horseback rides, wagon rides, and barbecue dinners. For more info, call (509) 548-7798 or (800) 221-7433. The same activities also take place at **Mountain Spring Lodge** in Plain, tel. (509) 763-3483 or (800) 858-2276. **Icicle Outfitters and Guides,** tel. (509) 784-1145 or (800) 497-3912, provides guided all-day rides into the Cascades, and an assortment of pack trips.

For hay rides and barbecues, contact **Red-Tail Canyon Farm,** a working draft horse farm at 11780 Freund Canyon Rd., tel. (509) 548-4512 or (800) 678-4512. For something even easier, hop on one of the **horse-drawn carriages** that roll through Leavenworth all summer long; call (509) 548-6825 for info.

Swimming and More

The city's outdoor **swimming pool,** 500 Hwy. 2, tel. (509) 548-4142, is open mid-June through August. Other options are the Wenatchee River at Waterfront Park or Lake Wenatchee State Park. **Club West,** 10421 Titus Rd., tel. (509) 548-4028, has saunas, a jacuzzi, racquetball courts, a weight room, and other facilities open to the public for a fee. **Icicle Junction,** 565 Hwy. 2, tel. (888) 462-4242, is the local fun park, with mini-golf, bumperboat rides, video games, and a miniature train.

The two local golf courses are **Leavenworth Golf Club,** out Icicle Rd. along the Wenatchee River, tel. (509) 548-7267, and **Kahler Glen Golf Course,** near Lake Wenatchee, tel. (509) 763-3785.

WINTER RECREATION

Cross-Country Skiing

Leavenworth, a popular spot with cross-coun-try ski enthusiasts, offers 25 km of groomed trails within minutes of downtown. Three ski areas are maintained by the Leavenworth Win-ter Sports Club with both classical and skate-skiing lanes. The most accessible of these—**Waterfront Park**—is just a block from down-town, and covers eight kilometers along the Wenatchee River. These connect with the **Leavenworth Golf Course Trail. Icicle River Trail,** one mile from Leavenworth on Icicle Rd., has eight km of level tracks at the mouth of Icicle Canyon, through meadows and forests above the fish hatchery. **Ski Hill Trail** has a five-km track, with two km lighted for night ski-ing (till 9 p.m.) that roll over the hills adjacent to the downhill ski area. Here you get the added benefit of a lodge and weekend food service. The club also often grooms trails up the last several miles of Icicle River Rd., on an un-plowed stretch. Trail fees are $7 per day for adults, kids under five free. For more informa-tion, contact the **Leavenworth Winter Sports Club,** tel. (509) 548-5115. Rent cross-coun-try and skate skis at **Der Sportsman,** 837 Front St., tel. (509) 548-5623, or **Leavenworth Ski & Sports,** Hwy. 2 at Icicle Rd., tel. (509) 548-7864.

Lake Wenatchee State Park, 23 miles north-west of Leavenworth, has 10 km of maintained free trails in the park and on surrounding land, but you'll need a Sno-Park permit to park here; pick one up in Leavenworth. Cross-country ski lessons and rentals are available nearby at **Leav-enworth Outfitters,** tel. (509) 763-3733 or (800) 347-7934, next to Parkside Grocery; or rent skis from another Lake Wenatchee place, **Cougar Inn,** tel. (509) 763-3354.

Contact the Leavenworth Ranger District of-fice, tel. (509) 548-6977, for more skiing options (ungroomed wilderness trails and logging roads) around Blewett Pass in Wenatchee National Forest. Skiers need a Sno-Park permit to park here. The Lake Wenatchee Ranger District, tel. (509) 763-3103, has details on cross-country trails near the lake.

Backcountry Skiing

For overnight cross-country skiing (17 miles of ski trails), snowshoeing, and snowboarding, plus some of the finest Telemark skiing in the high Cascades, stay in rustic-luxury at **Scottish Lakes Backcountry Cabins,** tel. (509) 884-2000 or (800) 909-9916. Eight cozy cabins ($40 d) come equipped with woodstoves, mattresses, propane stoves, kerosene lamps, and cooking utensils. From the parking area near Coles Corner (16 miles northwest of Leavenworth), the cabins are eight and a half miles and 3,000 feet higher in el-evation. Most folks choose to ride up and back aboard their 12-passenger Sno-Cat or snowmo-bile, but they will haul your gear (extra charge) if you have the energy to ski up and back your-self. The cabins are on private timber company land adjacent to 5,000-foot McCue Ridge in the Alpine Lakes Wilderness and are generally open Thanksgiving through April, plus mid-October to mid-November for fall hikers. Recommended.

Downhill Skiing

Leavenworth has its own tiny ski area, **Leaven-worth Ski Hill,** with two rope tows providing up-hill transportation for the handful of runs. There's also a snowboard half-pipe. The ski season here is generally shorter than at the bigger areas be-cause of the lower elevation; call (509) 548-5115 for conditions.

Two larger ski areas are close by: **Stevens Pass,** 35 miles to the west on Hwy. 2 (see **Stevens Pass and Skykomish Valley**), and **Mission Ridge,** 35 miles in the other direction near Wenatchee (see **Wenatchee**). Mission Ridge is a favorite of locals because of the dry snow and less crowded slopes.

Sleigh Rides

Sleigh rides are available from three local places in winter. **Red-Tail Canyon Farm,** 11780 Freund Canyon Rd., tel. (509) 548-4512 or (800) 678-4512, has champion Belgian draft horses that pull you through scenic Red-Tail Canyon. **Eagle Creek Ranch,** tel. (509) 548-7798 or (800) 221-7433, offers sleigh rides over the meadows and through the woods surrounding the ranch, two miles north of town off Hwy. 209. **Mountain Springs Lodge,** 14 miles north of Leavenworth, tel. (509) 763-2713 or (800) 858-2276, has a similar service.

Dogsled and Snowmobile Tours
See the Cascades and the Leavenworth valley from a unique perspective aboard a dogsled from **Enchanted Mountain Tours,** tel. (509) 763-2975, or **Alaska Dreamin Sled Dog Company,** tel. (509) 763-8017. **Mountain Spring Lodge** runs snowmobile tours out of Plain; call (509) 763-3483 or (800) 858-2276 for reservations and prices.

ACCOMMODATIONS

As a favorite vacation spot in both winter and summer, Leavenworth is jam-packed with accommodations options. Because of their popularity, prices are high, and you'll have a tough time finding anything under $60 d a night. Leavenworth has no hostel, so travelers on a tight budget should consider staying in nearby Wenatchee or camping out. Prices at many motels and B&Bs rise on Friday and Saturday nights, and many places require a two-night minimum for weekends (especially festival weekends). If you're arriving on a weekend or in the peak summer or winter holiday seasons, try to book your lodging as soon as possible, since rooms fill up early. Crowding is not nearly as much of a problem on weekdays, especially in the winter.

Finding a Place to Stay
The **Leavenworth Chamber of Commerce,** tel. (509) 548-5807, has brochures describing local lodging places and keeps a listing of those that have space. **Bedfinders,** tel. (509) 548-5800 or (800) 323-2920 (www.bedfinders.com), provides free reservation assistance 24 hours a day for Leavenworth B&B's, cabins, condos, and vacation homes. **Destination Leavenworth,** tel. (509) 548-5802 or (800) 962-7359, has a similar service.

I have not listed the many cabins, rental houses, and condos available on a short- or long-term basis in the Leavenworth area. See the chamber of commerce for a listing, or contact Bedfinders or Destination Leavenworth.

At the low end, you won't go wrong at **Mrs. Anderson's Lodging House,** where a pair of small but comfortable rooms (one has a balcony) are available for less than $40, including a light breakfast. Head to **Enzian Inn** for one of the most authentically furnished local places; the owner even plays an alpenhorn from the top floor each morning! Another notable place is **Mountain Home Lodge.** This is particularly popular in the winter when they groom 40 miles of private cross-country trails. Winter guests who stay here also get three excellent meals.

Bed and Breakfasts
Unless otherwise noted, all B&Bs listed below serve a full breakfast, and do not allow young children. They are arranged by price.

Das Wisenhaus, 8089 Icicle Rd., tel. (509) 548-6746 or (800) 448-1293, is a new house with three guest rooms, private baths, and a continental breakfast; $55 s or $70 d.

Mt. Valley Vista B&B, 8695 Larson Rd. in Peshastin (four miles east of Leavenworth), tel. (509) 548-5301, charges $65-75 s or d. This contemporary home has panoramic views and four guest rooms with shared baths.

Vienna Woods B&B 12842 Prowell Rd., tel. (509) 548-7843, is an elegant home on two wooded acres in Icicle Valley. The three large guest rooms have private baths, and kids are accepted; $65-115 s or $75-125 d.

Phippen's B&B, 10285 Ski Hill Dr., tel. (509) 548-7755 or (800) 666-9806, has an outdoor pool and hot tub. The three guest rooms have private baths. $70-80 s or $80-90 d.

Bosch Garten B&B, 9846 Dye Rd., tel. (509) 548-6900 or (800) 535-0069, is a new home with tall windows facing the mountains and three guest rooms (private baths). The attractive grounds include a Japanese-style garden with an enclosed hot tub. $75 s or $98 d.

Leirvangen B&B, 7586 Icicle Rd., tel. (509) 548-5165, has big windows facing the Cascades and three rooms with private baths. A Norwegian smorgasbord breakfast is served; $75-90 s or d.

Moonlight & Roses B&B, 12590 Spring St., tel. (509) 548-6766, has two bedrooms that share a bath; $85-95 s or d.

Run of the River, 9308 E. Leavenworth Rd., tel. (509) 548-7171 or (800) 288-6491, is one of the finest local B&Bs, a luxurious log home along Icicle Creek with a flower-filled yard, plus an outside deck and jacuzzi. The six guest rooms have private baths; $85-135 s or d. Two-night minimum on weekends.

LEAVENWORTH AREA MOTELS AND LODGES

Included below are lodging places in Leavenworth, Peshastin, and Lake Wenatchee, arranged from least to most expensive. Many of these require a two-night minimum stay on festival weekends. Rates may be lower during the winter months and on weekdays. Bed and breakfasts are described in the text.

INEXPENSIVE

Mrs. Anderson's Lodging House; 917 Commercial St.; tel. (509) 548-6984 or (800) 253-8990; $39-70 s or d; historic lodging house, nine guest rooms (seven with private and two with shared bath), light breakfast

Squirrel Tree Motel; Coles Corner (16 miles NW of Leavenworth); tel. (509) 763-3157; $50 s or d

Valley Cottage Motel; 8912 Motel Rd., Dryden (five miles east of Leavenworth); tel. (509) 548-5731; $50-60 d without kitchens, $60-70 d with kitchens; cute one and two bedroom older cottages

River's Edge Lodge; 8401 Hwy. 2 (four miles east of town); tel. (509) 548-7612 or (800) 451-5285; $57-77 s or d; along Wenatchee River, outdoor pool, hot tub, kitchenettes, two night minimum stay, AAA approved

Bindlestiff's Riverside Cabins; 11798 Hwy. 2; tel. (509) 548-5015; $58-69 s or d in cabins; continental breakfast, wooded setting along Wenatchee River

MODERATE

Evergreen Inn; 1117 Front St.; tel. (509) 548-5515 or (800) 327-7212; $60-120 s or d; jacuzzi, continental breakfast, kitchenettes available, AAA approved

Obertal Village Motor Inn; 922 Commercial St.; tel. (509) 548-5204 or (800) 537-9382; $63 s or d; jacuzzi, AAA approved

Alpen Inn Motel; 405 Hwy. 2; tel. (509) 548-4326 or (800) 423-9380; $63 s, $68 d; outdoor pool, jacuzzi, continental breakfast, kitchenettes available, AAA approved

Innsbrucker Inn; 703 Hwy. 2; tel. (509) 548-5401; $65-95 s or d

Tyrolean Ritz Hotel; 633 Front St.; tel. (509) 548-5455 or (800) 854-6365; $68 s, $68-130 d; European-style hotel, fridges, AAA approved

Rodeway Inn; 185 Hwy. 2; tel. (509) 548-7992 or (800) 693-1225; $69 s or d; indoor pool, jacuzzi, continental breakfast, AAA approved

Wedge Mountain Inn; 7335 Hwy. 2, Peshastin (five miles east of Leavenworth); tel. (509) 548-6694 or (800) 666-9664; $69 s or d; outdoor pool, two night minimum stay

Bayern on the River; 1505 Alpensee Strausse; tel. (509) 548-5875 or (800) 873-3960 (U.S.) or (800) 255-3151 (Canada); $69-77 s or d; outdoor pool, jacuzzi, balconies, kitchenettes $98 d

Der Ritterhof Motor Inn; 190 Hwy. 2; tel. (509) 548-5845 or (800) 255-5845; $70 s, $76 d; outdoor pool, jacuzzis, putting green, kitchenettes available, AAA approved

Haus Lorelei B&B, 347 Division St., tel. (509) 548-5726 or (800) 514-8868, is a gorgeous 1903 guest house on a two-acre spread along the Wenatchee River. Inside are 10 guest rooms with private baths; outside is a hot tub along the river. A full German breakfast is served and children are welcome; $89-99 s or d. Two-night minimum on weekends.

Autumn Pond B&B, 10388 Titus Rd., tel. (509) 548-4482 or (800) 222-9661, sits along a pond on three acres of land and has a hot tub and six guest rooms with private baths; $89 s or d.

Tamarack Timbers, 7680 Icicle Rd., tel. (509) 548-4049, is a new elegant log home that was featured in *Log Home Magazine.* The three guest rooms have private baths, and guests will enjoy the hot tub; $95 s or d.

Featherwind's Farm B&B, 17033 River Rd., tel. (509) 763-2011, is a newly built old-fash-

Leavenworth Village Inn; 1016 Commercial; tel. (509) 548-6620 or (800) 343-8198; $70-85 s or d; continental breakfast, AAA approved

Linderhof Motor Inn; 690 Hwy. 2; tel. (509) 548-5283 or (800) 828-5680; $70-100 s or d; outdoor pool, jacuzzi, continental breakfast, kitchenettes available, AAA approved

Hotel Pension Anna; 926 Commercial St.; tel. (509) 548-6273 or (800) 509-2662; $70-155 s, $80-175 d; continental breakfast, jacuzzi, authentic Austrian decor, AAA approved

Haus Rohrbach Pension; 12882 Ranger Rd.; tel. (509) 548-7074 or (800) 548-4477; $75-160 s or d; 10-room hotel, outdoor pool, jacuzzi, full breakfast, AAA approved

Abendblume Inn; 12570 Ranger Rd.; tel. (509) 548-4059 or (800) 669-7634; $77-159 s or d; luxurious seven-room inn, jacuzzi, fireplaces, grand piano, Austrian breakfast, two-night minimum stay on weekends, AAA approved

Blackbird Lodge; 309 8th St.; tel. (509) 548-5800 or (800) 446-0240; $79-98 s or d; jacuzzi, fireplaces, continental breakfast, AAA approved

Lorraine's Edel Haus; 320 9th St.; tel. (509) 548-4412 or (800) 487-3335; $80-105 s or d; three rooms over the Edel House Restaurant, and a separate cottage, jacuzzi

EXPENSIVE

Enzian Motor Inn; 590 Hwy. 2; tel. (509) 548-5269 or (800) 223-8511; $80-170 s, $90-175 d; authentic Bavarian craftsmanship and furnishings, large indoor and outdoor pools, jacuzzis, exercise facility, buffet breakfast, AAA approved

AlpenRose Inn; 500 Alpine Pl.; tel. (509) 548-3000 or (800) 582-2474; $85-150 s or d; outdoor pool, jacuzzi, fireplaces, exercise room, full breakfast, fireplaces, AAA approved

Pine River Ranch; 19668 Hwy. 207, Lake Wenatchee; tel. (509) 763-3959 or (800) 669-3877; $89-145 s or d; jacuzzis, fireplaces, mountain views, AAA approved

Best Western Icicle Inn; 505 W. Hwy. 2; tel. (509) 548-7000 or (800) 558-2438; $89-169 s, $95-169 d; outdoor pool, jacuzzi, exercise room, continental breakfast, AAA approved

Mountain Home Lodge; Mt. Home Rd. (three miles E of Leavenworth); tel. (509) 548-7077 or (800) 414-2378; $92-172 s, $100-180 d in summer including a full breakfast, outdoor pool, jacuzzi, tennis, two night minimum stay, no kids; $250-330 d in winter includes three gourmet meals and cross-country skis, snowshoes, and toboggans

LUXURY

Mountain Springs Lodge; 19115 Chiwawa Loop Rd. (18 miles NW of Leavenworth); tel. (509) 763-2713 or (800) 858-2276; $195 d for cabins with kitchens and private hot tubs, $175 d for suites with fireplaces, kitchenettes and spa tubs, two night minimum stay on weekends; horseback, wagon, or sleigh rides available

ioned home on farmland near Lake Wenatchee. Inside are three guest rooms with private baths; outside, find an outdoor pool and jacuzzi. $95-125 s or d.

All Seasons River Inn, 8751 Icicle Rd., tel. (509) 548-1425 or (800) 254-0555, has antique-furnished rooms (some with fireplaces) in a large contemporary home. Breakfast is served on the riverfront deck; $95-130 s or $100-135 d. Two-night minimum on weekends.

Bavarian Meadows B&B, 11097 Eagle Creek Rd., tel. (509) 548-5331 or (800) 996-9399, is a small guest house with an outdoor hot tub; $125 s or d.

Campgrounds

Wenatchee National Forest campgrounds near Leavenworth are generally open May to late October and charge $7-11. Get there very early on summer weekends or all the spaces may be gone! The closest is **Eightmile Campground,** eight miles up Icicle Rd.; six more Forest Service campgrounds are spread within 20 miles of Leavenworth along this road. The 1994 Rat Creek Fire burned through much of this country, so be ready for blackened trees in some campgrounds.

Another very popular Forest Service tenting spot, **Tumwater Campground** is 10 miles northwest from Leavenworth along Hwy. 2. Farther afield (16 miles northwest) is Lake Wenatchee, where you can pitch a tent at the Forest Service's **Nason Creek** and **Glacier View** Campgrounds. Four more Forest Service campgrounds lie northwest of the lake.

Lake Wenatchee State Park at the east end of the lake has 197 oft-filled campsites for $11 ($16 RVs) including showers. It's open from early April to late October. Call (509) 763-3101 for information, or (800) 452-5687 for reservations ($6 extra), required in the summer. Showers are also available at **Oxbow Trading Post** in Cole Corner (16 miles northwest of Leavenworth). See **Cashmere** above for other camping options.

Eighteen miles southeast of Leavenworth along Hwy. 97 is the Forest Service's free but tiny **Bonanza Campground;** no potable water.

Hikers and campers will find hot showers and washing machines at **Die Wascherei,** 1317 Front St. (behind Dan's Food Market). Open daily 7 a.m.-9:30 p.m.

RV Parks

Several RV parks (summer only) can be found around Leavenworth: **Pine Village KOA,** 11401 River Bend Dr., tel. (509) 548-7709 or (800) 562-5709; **Chalet RV Park,** 9825 Duncan Rd., tel. (509) 548-4578 or (800) 477-2697; **Icicle River RV Park,** 7305 Icicle Rd., tel. (509) 548-5420; and **Blu-Shastin RV Park,** 3300 Hwy. 97 (11 miles southeast of Leavenworth), tel. (509) 548-4184.

FOOD

Leavenworth village has a number of restaurants, all very Bavarian from the outside, but often more diverse on the inside; even the local McDonald's features pseudo-German architecture (but no bratwurst or *leberkäse*).

Breakfast

Two local places are popular for breakfast. **Sandy's Waffle & Dinner Haus,** 894 Hwy. 2, tel. (509) 548-6779, is crowded most every morning and has all the old breakfast standbys. The **Renaissance Cafe,** 217 8th St., tel. (509) 548-6121, strays a bit, with huevos rancheros, pancakes, or omelettes, plus a lunchtime menu of salads, wraps, and salads.

Mittagessen (Lunch)

Leavenworth has many lunchtime choices, from simple bratwurst and burger stands like the **Bavarian Bar-B-Que & Sausage Haus** with outside tables on the corner of 8th and Commercial, to delectable soup, sandwich, salad, and sausage places like **Rumpelstilzchen's,** 1133 Hwy. 2, tel. (509) 548-4663. **The Gingerbread Factory,** 828 Commercial St., tel. (509) 548-6592 or (800) 296-7097, is famous for its wonderful soft gingerbread cookies and houses; try the amusingly decorated cookies even if you aren't generally a gingerbread fanatic. The lunchtime deli here is a locals' favorite for salads, sandwiches, and espresso. Also recommended is **Uncle Uli's Pub Restaurant,** 9th and Front, tel. (509) 548-7262, where the lunch menu includes soups, salads, great sandwiches, and at least one pasta. For the best lunchtime location and upscale eats, head to **Bouliana,** 633 Front St., tel. (509) 548-2127, where the patio sits right on the Wenatchee River.

Bavarian Eats

Several eateries dish out the dense, meaty German fare one expects to find. You'll get the real thing at **Andreas Keller,** 829 Front St., tel. (509) 548-6000, including *leberkäse,* knackwurst, and **kassler kottlets.** Be sure to order the big Bavarian-style pretzels—quite unlike the standard shopping-mall variety—with your brew. **King Ludwig's Gasthaus,** 921 Front St., tel. (509) 548-6625, features German and Hungarian dishes, along with more standard American faves. **Gustav's,** 617 Hwy. 2, tel. (509) 548-4509, has additional Germanic fare but is best known for the great hamburgers, including an Ortega Mexican burger. For excellent gourmet Austrian meals ($16-21 entrees) head to **Restaurant Österrieich,** 633A Front St., tel. (509) 548-4031. On summer days, get a simple "bier garten" menu at picnic tables overlooking the river.

The Un-Bavarians

Ask the locals their favorite dinner place, and you're likely to hear **Lorraine's Edel Haus Inn,** 320 9th St., tel. (509) 548-4412. Their menu changes every month or so, but always includes a good choice of flavorful Northwest and "new German" cuisine, fish, pasta, and luscious desserts served in an elegant interior, or outside on the garden patio. Dinner entrees are $9-19.

Katzenjammer's, 221 8th St., tel. (509) 548-5826, is the place for a romantic evening with a dinner of Alaskan king crab or prime rib, but don't come here if you're on a tight budget. **Los Camperos,** 300 8th St., tel. (509) 548-3314, has tasty and reasonably priced Mexican favorites. A good spot for pizzas is **Leavenworth Pizza Co.** at 894 Hwy. 2, tel. (509) 548-7766.

The local brewpub, **Leavenworth Brewery Restaurant & Pub,** 636 Front St., tel. (509) 548-4545, has tours and tastings starting at 2 p.m. daily. It's a very popular place for music on weekends; pretty good pub grub too.

If you're headed up to Lake Wenatchee, try **Cougar Inn Resort,** 23379 Hwy. 207, tel. (509) 763-3353, for a scrumptious Friday night prime rib and seafood buffet or a Sunday champagne brunch with stunning lake and mountain views to boot; call (509) 763-3354 for reservations. The food is worth the drive. On the way to Cougar Inn is **Beaver Hill Cafe,** 18630 Hwy. 209, tel. (509) 763-3072, with excellent homemade breads and delicious breakfasts.

A **Leavenworth Farmers Market** takes place Tuesday 9 a.m.-1 p.m. June-Oct. next to the swimming pool.

Bakeries and Espresso

Leavenworth's bakeshops provide something for all tastes. The earth-bound deli at **The Gingerbread Factory,** (described above), is a can't-miss stop, with great baked specialties and sandwiches. **Berti's Backstube** in the Obertal Mall at 220 9th St., tel. (509) 548-4001, bakes traditional German breads, pretzels, cakes, and tortes. **The Danish Bakery,** 731 Front St., tel. (509) 548-7514, sells fresh soft pretzels and outstanding Danish pastries and cookies. Out of the way and near the fish hatchery is **Homefires Bakery,** 13013 Bayne Rd., tel. (509) 548-7362, where delicious sourdough breads, pies, and cinnamon rolls emerge from a German brick oven. Homefires is a popular stopping place for hikers and cyclists. Closed Tuesday and Wednesday. A bright hangout place for espresso, frozen yogurt, and fresh pastries is **Leavenworth Coffee Roaster,** 220 Hwy. 2, tel. (509) 548-1428. **The Corner Store,** 703 Front St., tel. (509) 548-7216, offers sweets, healthy sandwiches, and espresso coffees.

EVENTS AND ENTERTAINMENT

Festivals

Leavenworth always finds something to celebrate—festivals and fairs circle the calendar.

Leavenworth, the festival capital of the state

Contact the chamber of commerce at (509) 548-5807 for details on all of these. January brings **Bavarian Ice Fest** and its snowshoe and cross-country ski races, dogsled pulls, a tug of war, and fireworks in mid-month. Smaller festivals fill the months until the big **Maifest,** held on Mother's Day weekend, when costumed Bavarian dancers circle the Maypole, and concerts, a parade, and Saturday night street dance are accompanied by oompa music from the bandstand and the chiming of bells from the Marlin Handbell Ringers. Another fun Maifest event is the authentic traditional Bavarian farm wedding. This weekend also marks the start of **Art in the Park,** during which area artists display their talents every weekend May-Oct. in Front St. Park.

Other summer festivals are **Craftfair** in early June, and two popular mid-June events, **The International Folk Dance Festival** and **Kinderfest. Leavenworth International Accordion Celebration** in early August brings concerts, workshops, and fun competition for all ages. The **Washington State Autumn Leaf Festival,** takes place the last weekend of September and the first weekend of October, starts with a grand parade featuring dozens of marching bands, and includes daily polka music in the gazebo, Saturday night polka dances, a pancake feed, flea market, and food booths.

Christmas is Leavenworth's most festive holiday. The **Christmas Lighting Festival** is held the first and second Saturday in December when all the Christmas lights go on simultaneously at dusk and Mr. and Mrs. Claus appear in their house in the park while Scrooge wanders curmudgeonly around. Caroling, sleigh rides, concerts, and food booths add to the holiday festivities. (Cynics call this one a nonevent, since they switch on the lights the first weekend, then turn them off in time to do it again the following Friday. Besides, the lights stay lit till February, so there's no need to hurry up to see them.)

Music and Theater

Leavenworth's **Icicle Creek Music Center** has a series of diverse musical performances, including jazz, chamber music, bluegrass, symphonies, and string quartets. These are held at Sleeping Lady Retreat & Conference Center, 7375 Icicle Rd.; call (509) 548-6344 or (800) 574-2123 for details.

The **Leavenworth Summer Theatre,** tel. (509) 548-4607, presents very popular all-ages musical productions of such classics as *Sound of Music, Carousel,* or *Heidi* at the Ski Hill outdoor stage.

On a less sophisticated level, accordion-playing musicians and polka-dancin' fools can be found weekend evenings at **Andreas Keller,** 829 Front St. (downstairs), tel. (509) 548-6000, and **King Ludwig's Gasthaus,** 921 Front St., tel. (509) 548-6625. **Leavenworth Brewery,** 636 Front St., tel. (509) 548-4545, is the place for Saturday night blues music, and the **Community Coffeehouse** at the Adler, 633 Front St., has live music and poetry most Friday nights in a no-smoking, no-alcohol setting.

INFORMATION AND SERVICES

For maps, brochures, and additional information, stop by the **Leavenworth Chamber of Commerce Visitor Center,** 894 Hwy. 2 (the Clocktower Building), tel. (509) 548-5807. They're open Mon.-Sat. 8:30 a.m.-6 p.m. and Sunday 10 a.m.-4 p.m. year-round, and on the Web at www.leavenworth.org.

The Wenatchee National Forest **Leavenworth Ranger District,** 600 Sherbourne St., tel. (509) 548-4067, is open daily 7:45 a.m.-4:30 p.m. mid-June to mid-October, and Mon.-Fri. 7:45 a.m.-4:30 p.m. the rest of the year.

The **public library,** tel. (509) 548-7923, sits right across from Front St. Park and features a periodicals room with a fireplace and stunning mountain vistas.

TRANSPORTATION AND TOURS

By Car

Driving to Leavenworth in the winter over Stevens Pass has been described as "driving through a Christmas card." Rocky, snow-covered peaks surround the highway as you approach the 4,061-foot pass; then, closer to Leavenworth, the Wenatchee River rushes alongside the road through high, rocky walls and areas burned in the 1994 forest fires. The trip from Seattle is about 125 miles. From late fall to early spring, call (888) 766-4636 for the Department of

Transportation's **Mountain Pass Report.** Have your chains ready! As an alternate route, take I-90 over Snoqualmie Pass to Hwy. 97 north over Sauk Pass; these passes are generally drier and snow-free earlier than Stevens.

Buses and Tours

Free local buses connect Leavenworth with other parts of Chelan and Douglas Counties, including Lake Wenatchee, Cashmere, Wenatchee, and the popular tourist destinations of Lake Chelan and the Mission Ridge Ski Area. Buses run Mon.-Sat., and can carry bikes in the summer or skis in the winter; contact **Link,** tel. (800) 851-5465, for details.

Northwest Trailways, tel. (800) 366-6975, stops in Leavenworth at the Park & Ride near Safeway, with service east to Spokane, and west to Everett. The nearest commercial airport and Amtrak station are in Wenatchee, approximately 30 miles east of Leavenworth.

Totem Tours, tel. (206) 661-9079 or (800) 845-7291, has tours ($35) from Seattle to the International Folk Dance Festival, the Autumn Leaf Festival, and the Christmas Lighting Festival.

STEVENS PASS AND SKYKOMISH VALLEY

US Highway 2 is one of the state's most beautiful drives, and the western end of a transcontinental two-lane route that runs eastward all the way to Maine. Heading west from Leavenworth, the highway enters spectacular Tumwater Canyon, with the roiling Wenatchee River—a popular rafting and kayaking waterway—as a guide into the mountains. The road eventually tops out at 4,061-foot **Stevens Pass,** named for John F. Stevens, the chief locating engineer for the Great Northern Railway that was pushed through here in 1892. (Stevens is perhaps better known as the builder of the Panama Canal.)

At Stevens Pass you'll find popular downhill and cross-country ski areas, and a jumping off point for the **Pacific Crest Trail.** Serious backpackers can hook up with the Pacific Crest Trail and hike clear up to Canada or down to Mexico if they like—or, more likely, just hike a short chunk of the trail. Two wilderness areas on either side of the pass—Henry M. Jackson Wilderness and Alpine Lakes Wilderness—contain striking natural features, from glaciers and alpine meadows to dense forests intersected by clear, clean rivers. Much of the area's beauty can be seen through your car windows and from short roadside paths, but hundreds of miles of hiking trails let you experience its splendor at close range.

On the western side of the pass, Hwy. 2 drops quickly—2,000 feet in 14 miles to the little town of Skykomish. As you switchback down from the summit, the Burlington Northern railroad tracks emerge from seven-mile-long **Cascade Railroad Tunnel,** one of the longest in the western hemisphere. The drive downhill takes you past rugged snow-covered peaks, plunging waterfalls, popular campgrounds, fishing holes in the Skykomish River, and nature trails to explore along the way. Finally, the grade lessens in the wide Skykomish Valley (alias "Sky Valley"), as the highway slips through a chain of small towns before emerging into the flat farmland and spreading suburbia near Monroe.

RECREATION

The Forest Service now charges a fee for trailhead access throughout the Cascades, including access to wilderness areas. You can either pay $25 for an annual **Trail Park Pass** (available at Forest Service offices), or $3 per vehicle per day.

Alpine Lakes Wilderness Area

The spectacular Alpine Lakes Wilderness covers 393,000 acres of high Cascades country, a diverse landscape ranging in elevation from 1,000-foot valleys to towering 9,000-foot mountain spires. Much of the area—hence the name—is high alpine country filled with some 700 crystalline lakes, ponds, and tarns.

Because of its proximity to Seattle, an abundance of short and long hiking possibilities, and the dramatic alpine-and-lake scenery, this is one of the most heavily used wild places in Washington. In some ways, Alpine Lakes Wilderness is being loved to death by those who come to escape city life, but find instead crowded back-country sites and abused trails. Avoid the crowds by coming here in mid-week rather than on weekends. To alleviate crowding, the Forest Service has instituted a wilderness permit system that limits the number of hikers in Enchantment area near Leavenworth. The policy is still evolving, so call the Alpine Lakes Wilderness info hotline at (206) 775-9702 or (800) 627-0062 before heading out. Find them on the Web at www.washington.edu/trails/alpine. Permits are required throughout the wilderness June 15 to October 15. In most areas of the wilderness, free, self-issued permits can be obtained at the trailheads. In the Enchantments, permits ($3 pp/day) are required for overnight camping, and they may be obtained anytime after March 1. Mid-summer weekends fill up fast, so apply early by calling the Leavenworth Ranger Station at (509) 548-6977. Day use is free in the Enchantments, but you'll need to fill out a permit at the trailhead.

The following hikes are a tiny sample of those available. For a more complete description, pick up a copy of *100 Hikes in Washington's Alpine Lakes,* by Vicky Spring, Ira Spring, and Harvey Manning (Seattle: The Mountaineers). Forest Service offices have detailed information on individual trails within the wilderness, or stop by the Outdoor Recreation Information Center at the Seattle REI store.

Heading south from Hwy. 2, the **Pacific Crest Trail** climbs past the downhill ski area and Lake Susan June before reaching Josephine Lake on the wilderness boundary (4.5 miles from the highway). From here, you enter a web of trails that covers the high alpine land, opening up many loop-trip possibilities. Two fun and very popular trails (wilderness permits required) begin from the Foss River Rd. (Forest Rd. 68; two miles east of Skykomish). One of these, the **Necklace Valley Trail** (No. 1062) starts up an old narrow-gauge railroad bed before entering a tight canyon and ascending quickly to a cluster of lakes in upper Necklace Valley. The one-way length is seven and a half miles, with a gain of 3,140 feet in elevation. A second excellent short hike is to follow **West Fork Foss River Trail** to Trout Lake, and then on to a chain of half-a-dozen jewel-like lakes. The one-way distance is seven miles, with an elevation gain of

2,900 feet. Deception Creek Trail, another access path off Hwy. 2, is described below under "Waterfalls."

Many very popular trails lead into the Enchantment portion of the wilderness, including the seven-mile **Snow Lake Trail,** which starts from Icicle Rd. out of Leavenworth. Backpackers often use Snow Lake as a base area and day hike into the rugged and spectacular **Enchantment Lakes.**

Henry M. Jackson Wilderness Area

This 103,591-acre mountain wilderness is accessible from the Stevens Pass, Skykomish, Lake Wenatchee, and Darrington areas; see Forest Service maps for specifics. It was named for a longtime U.S. Senator from Washington, Henry M. Jackson, who was instrumental in helping establish wilderness areas throughout the West. The glacier-carved landscape has a Swiss-Alps quality: numerous alpine lakes, prominent knife-edged ridges, and deep U-shaped valleys. Dozens of backcountry hikes are possible, and ambitious backpackers could continue on into the adjacent Glacier Peak Wilderness Area. The Pacific Crest Trail passes through the center of Henry M. Jackson Wilderness before crossing Hwy. 2 and continuing on southward into the Alpine Lakes Wilderness.

An interesting and very scenic 18-mile loop trek can be made by following the Beckler River Rd. (Forest Rd. 65) from the town of Skykomish to Jack Pass, and continuing another mile to Forest Rd. 63. Turn right here, and proceed to the trailhead at the end of the road. The **North Fork Trail** (No. 1051) climbs into high mountain country from here, through masses of hillside wildflowers in mid-summer, eventually emerging into the alpine after five miles or so. It meets the Pacific Crest Trail at Dishpan Gap. Turn right and follow the PCT past Lake Sally and then back around 6,368-foot Skykomish Peak to the Pass Creek Trail, which will take you back to your starting point. Another option is to turn left at Dishpan Gap and follow **Bald Eagle Mt. Trail** (No. 650) back to trail No. 1050, which leads back to the road.

See *100 Hikes in Washington's North Cascades: Glacier Peak Region,* by Ira Spring and Harvey Manning (Seattle: The Mountaineers) for detailed descriptions of these and other interesting hikes. Contact the **Skykomish Ranger Station** at (360) 677-2414 for current conditions, use restrictions, and trail descriptions.

Downhill Skiing
About halfway between Skykomish and Lake Wenatchee is **Stevens Pass Ski Area,** a major downhill area that is popular with Seattleites. It has a base elevation of 3,821 feet and a summit elevation of 5,845 feet; its 10 lifts serve 1,125 acres of beginner through expert terrain. Call (206) 634-1645 for snow conditions; or check www.stevenspass.com. Stevens Pass is generally open mid-November through late April, offering night skiing, ski and snowboard rentals and lessons, a ski shop, restaurant, cafeteria, and cocktail lounges. Many different ski and snowboard schools operate out of Stevens Pass; contact the ski area for a listing. A tubing and sledding area is adjacent to the ski hill.

Weekend lift tickets cost $35 adults, $24 kids, and $26 seniors, with bargain rates on weekdays. Lodging is not available at Stevens Pass, although RVs can park in the lot (no hookups). The nearest overnight accommodations are in Skykomish (16 miles west) and Leavenworth (35 miles east).

Cross-Country Skiing
Stevens Pass Nordic Center, tel. (360) 973-2441, is five miles east of the Stevens Pass downhill area and costs $7.50 adults, $6.50 children or seniors. Classical and skating skis can be rented here, and a snack bar has hot food. It is open Fri.-Sun. and on winter holidays. There are 30 km of groomed trails, most of which follow closely along the very noisy overhead power lines. The main route climbs uphill for 7.5 km, gaining over 700 feet along the way.

Raft Trips
The Skykomish River is an extremely popular rafting place during the peak snowmelt period from mid-March to mid-July. The upper portion of the "Sky" from Skykomish to Baring and the South Fork from Skykomish to Index are *not* for beginners. The famous "Boulder Drop" section is class IV+ water, and there are many other deep plunges and vertical drops of class IV. The various commercial rafting companies recommend that anyone running the upper Skykomish have previous rafting experience and be in good physical condition. Trips are available on most early summer weekends, with fewer weekday runs. Some companies restrict Skykomish rafting to those at least 16 years old.

Based in Index, **Chinook Expeditions** runs excellent float and whitewater trips, including a six-day Cascade loop trip that includes runs down the Skagit, Skykomish, Methow, and Wenatchee rivers. Call (800) 241-3451 for current Skykomish River conditions and reservations. Chinook also offers Skykomish trips in the winter months when conditions are fast and wild. **Wave Trek,** tel. (206) 793-1705 or (800) 543-7971, is an Index-based rafting and kayaking company with trips down both the main fork of the Sky, and the wild North Fork. They also teach multiday kayaking classes for those who want to take a bigger step into river running. Other rafting outfitters waiting to take you down the Sky are: **Alpine Adventures,** tel. (800) 723-8386; **Blue Sky Outfitters,** tel. (800) 228-7238; **North Cascades River Expeditions,** tel. (800) 634-8433; **Orion River Expeditions,** tel. (800) 553-7466; **River Recreation,** tel. (800) 464-5899; and **Wildwater River Tours,** tel. (800) 522-9453.

For a do-it-yourself trip, the lower Skykomish is a peaceful river to raft or kayak, with a few small, generally avoidable rapids above Sultan. It's rated class II+ from Big Eddy State Park (a.k.a. Sky River State Scenic Park; two miles east of Gold Bar where Hwy. 2 cross the river) to Sultan, and class I from Sultan to Monroe.

Waterfalls
The Highway 2 planners must have loved waterfalls: several raging falls are right along the roadside. Easternmost of these is **Deception Falls,** right along the highway approximately seven miles west of Stevens Pass. A short paved path crosses the Tye River and continues to a cascading torrent of water, but much more interesting is the half-mile nature trail that drops down along the river. Educational plaques describe the forest and river, and lead to two more impressive cataracts, both backdropped by the deep green rainforest. Some of this is second growth timber, while other parts were never logged. The lowest falls is the biggest surprise, but I'll let you discover it for yourself. **Deception Creek Trail** starts on the south side of Hwy.

2 and provides a delicious old-growth forest hike. The trail climbs 10 miles (gaining almost 2,500 feet along the way) to Deception Pass in the Alpine Lakes Wilderness Area, where you can join up with the Pacific Crest Trail.

About one and a half miles farther west, **Alpine Falls** drops 50 feet into the Tye River below; park on the south side of the highway and follow the can't-miss path. **Bridal Veil Falls,** a quarter mile east of the Index junction, vary with the season; summer brings two distinctive "veils," while winter freezes the falls into a glistening sheet of ice. The highest falls of all—265-foot Wallace Falls—is described below under the town of Index. Scenic **Eagle Falls** on the South Fork Skykomish River is a favorite place for summertime swimmers who play in the big jade-green plunge pool. Be careful if you join in the fun since there are more falls just downstream. The falls are 11 miles west of Skykomish and right along Hwy. 2.

PRACTICALITIES

Campgrounds
Four Forest Service campgrounds provide in-the-woods lodging options in the Skykomish vicinity. Two of these—**Beckler River** and **Money Creek**—are open late May through September and cost $12. Make reservations ($9 extra) by calling (877) 444-6777. Beckler River is two miles north of Skykomish on Forest Rd. 65. Money Creek is four miles west of Skykomish and right along Hwy. 2. The more primitive places—Troublesome Creek and San Juan Campgrounds—are described below under "Over Jack Pass."

Transportation
Stevens Pass is often a challenge to traverse and is sometimes closed by winter storms. If you're heading up to ski at Stevens Pass or continuing east to Leavenworth or Wenatchee, be sure to call (206) 368-4499 or (888) 766-4636 for the Department of Transportation's **Mountain Pass Report.** Their Web page, www.traffic .wsdot.wa.gov/sno-info, also has live cameras showing current conditions at Stevens Pass. For avalanche and mountain weather information in the winter, call (206) 526-6677.

Northwestern Trailways, tel. (800) 366-6975, stops at Stevens Pass and Skykomish Junction, with service east to Spokane and west to Everett and Seattle.

SKY VALLEY

As you head down from the Cascades into Skykomish ("Sky") Valley, several towns pop up along Hwy. 2, each a little larger than the last, till you reach the edge of Seattle's sprawl at fast-growing Monroe.

Skykomish
The historic railroad town of Skykomish (pop. 250; pronounced "sky-KOH-mish") is primarily a resting point on the way into or out of the mountains. There's a cafe with respectable food, a motel and hotel, gas station, and Forest Service office, but not much else. **Sky River Inn,** tel. (360) 677-2261 or (800) 367-8194, has comfortable rooms for $56-68 s or $59-71 d. This is a popular stopping point for weekend skiers in the winter, so it's a good idea to reserve ahead at those times. Basic lodging can be found at the historic **Skykomish Hotel and Restaurant,** tel. (360) 677-2477, where old fashioned bath-down-the-hall rooms go for $40 s or $45 d. The hotel was constructed in 1905, and the back room was very popular with card-playing railroad crews. The old **depot** still stands next to the tracks, but Amtrak doesn't stop on its way through.

Skykomish Ranger Station, tel. (360) 677-2414, has recreation and topographic maps, books, and current information on trails and campgrounds. The ranger station is open daily 8 a.m.-4:30 p.m. Memorial Day to Labor Day, and Mon.-Fri. 8 a.m.-4:30 p.m. the rest of the year.

The **Maloney-Sobieski Mountain Road** provides views of Glacier Peak and deep valleys. To get there, head east from the ranger station for a half mile, then turn left onto Foss River Rd. 68. Drive about 5.5 miles to the intersection of Roads 68 and 6840; go right onto 6840. When you reach the next fork, stay to the right onto 6846 until the next fork; then go left to Sobieski Mountain or right to Maloney Mountain, with spectacular views on either route.

Community Transit, tel. (360) 778-2185 or (800) 562-1375, has daily bus service to Skykomish and the rest of Snohomish County.

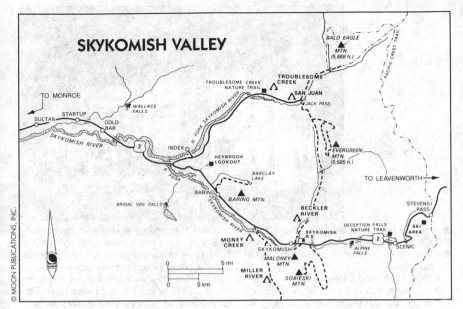

SKYKOMISH VALLEY

© MOON PUBLICATIONS, INC.

Over Jack Pass

For a fascinating 26-mile side trip away from busy Hwy. 2, head up Beckler River Rd., which starts a half-mile east of Skykomish. The road (Forest Rd. 65) climbs 13 miles up—the last five are dusty gravel—along the river into Mt. Baker-Snoqualmie National Forest before switchbacking over Jack Pass and down the Galena Road. A forest lookout tower atop **Evergreen Mountain** can be reached via a 1.5-mile one-way hike from the end of Evergreen Mountain Rd. 6554. The road takes off to the right (east) from the Beckler River Rd. just before you reach Jack Pass. The trail gains 1,300 feet in elevation, but on a clear day the 360-degree view includes Glacier Peak and Mt. Rainier. Regrettably, this trail is open to off-road vehicles. The lookout tower is available for rent; call (360) 677-2414 for details.

Privately owned Garland Hot Springs (near Jack Pass) has a few old buildings and a caretaker who shoos away stray tourists. A mile down Galena Rd. is **San Juan Campground** ($7; no running water). Two miles farther downhill is **Troublesome Creek Campground** ($12), reservable ($9 extra) by calling (877) 444-6777. Also here is **Troublesome Creek Nature Trail**, a delightful half-mile path through rainforest and canyon. Beyond the campgrounds, Galena Rd. parallels the North Fork Skykomish River for 10 miles—paved the entire way—ending at Hwy. 2 near the town of Index. You can also camp for free anywhere on Forest Service land. Just look for the side roads heading into the woods.

Index

Tiny Index (pop. 150) lies a mile off Hwy. 2 and just across the clear waters of the Skykomish River. This quaint old mining, logging, and quarrying camp has tidy homes, a delightful old lodge, and an almost-encircling Cascade Range backdrop that features Mt. Index. Plenty of hiking, rock climbing, steelhead fishing, and mountain biking options in the area. The granite quarry (closed in the 1930s) was the source of stones for the steps to the state capitol in Olympia.

Directly behind town rises **Index Town Wall**, a 400-foot granite cliff that's a favorite of Seattle-area rock climbers. It was recently purchased by the state to be run as a small state park, and trails and restrooms are planned. A steep path leads much of the way up the slope for those who aren't climbers; ask at the Bush House for

Skykomish Hotel

DON PITCHER

directions. **Wave Trek,** tel. (360) 793-1705 or (800) 543-7971, is an Index-based company that teaches beginner-level climbing classes at the Index Wall.

Pickett Historical Museum, tel. (360) 793-1534, is housed in one of the little clapboard structures that dot Index. Entrance is $1 for adults or 50 cents for kids. Open Sat.-Sun. noon-3 p.m., Memorial Day through September only; pick up a brochure here that indexes Index's historic buildings. Lee Pickett's extraordinary collection of photographs from the early part of this century make up the centerpiece of the museum. (He was the official photographer for the Great Northern Railway.) Also of note is **Redman Hall,** built in 1903.

Index General Store, tel. (360) 793-0693, is one of the finest old-time general stores left in the state, selling everything from gardening supplies to espresso. Their home-baked goods are especially noteworthy, and the friendliness is legendary. **Index Tavern,** tel. (360) 793-0584, has live music, dart boards and a pool table inside, and a beer garden overlooking the Skykomish River. Each August they host the nation's largest outdoor dart contest.

A don't-miss-it place is the beautifully restored **Bush House Country Inn,** 300 5th St., tel. (360) 793-2312 or (800) 428-2874. Several U.S. presidents stayed at Bush House in the early days, including Teddy Roosevelt (but not George Bush). Built in 1898, the hotel has nine guest rooms with shared or private baths ($59-80 s or d). A

continental breakfast is served in the garden-side dining room with a stone fireplace. The restaurant makes a romantic back-from-the-slopes stopping place. Good food from a diverse menu, including blackberry cobbler with ice cream for dessert. Outside is a fragrant rose garden. Reserve ahead for weekends (especially in ski season), or come on a weekday to avoid the crowds.

Another beautiful and historic place is **A Stone's Throw B&B,** tel. (360) 793-0100. Only one room is available ($75 s or $90 d) in this 1912 home, but you get the entire upper floor to yourself, including a bath and private jacuzzi; full breakfast.

A Rivers Edge Country Cottage, tel. (360) 793-0392, is a new cottage (sleeps four) with a kitchen, full breakfast, and spa in the courtyard. Kids are accepted. $80 d.

Index has a popular **Easter Sunday Pancake Breakfast,** but the town's big shindig comes on **Memorial Day Weekend** with ballgames, a goofy relay fun run, and a popular spaghetti feed. Of course, the town's **Fourth of July** has the all-American standards: a parade, crafts fair, live music, a rubber duck derby, and fireworks echoing off the surrounding mountains.

For a short day hike near Index, try the one-mile one-way hike from Hwy. 2 just east of town to **Heybrook Lookout.** This Forest Service fire tower provides views of Mt. Index, Baring Mountain, and the Skykomish Valley. Slightly longer (2.2 miles one-way) but with little elevation gain is the **Barclay Lake Trail,** which follows the course of Barclay Creek to the lake with a nice view of Baring Mountain. To get to the trailhead, take Barclay Creek Rd. 6024 for four miles.

Transportation: Community Transit, tel. (360) 778-2185 or (800) 562-1375, has daily bus service to Index and other parts of Snohomish County.

Wallace Falls State Park

Located two miles northeast of Gold Bar, this 678-acre park is famous for its towering 265-foot cataract (visible from Hwy. 2). The park is open daily in the summer, and Wed.-Sun. from October to mid-April. A half-dozen gorgeously situated walk-in tent sites are available ($10; no showers), but the main attraction is the falls. Two routes lead to Wallace Falls, an easy path along an old railroad grade that's open to mountain bikes, and a steeper route (Woody Trail) that follows closer to the river. The two trails join for the last mile and a half, with several viewpoints along the way, including one atop the falls. The hike to the falls is six miles roundtrip via Woody Trail and eight miles roundtrip via the old railroad grade. Along the way, you gain almost 1,400 feet in elevation. Call (360) 793-0420 for park information.

Startup and Gold Bar

Located in an old church, the **Parallax Gallery,** tel. (360) 793-9588, in minuscule Startup has an interesting collection of fine art, ceramics, and jewelry by local artists. They also serve espresso. The small **Gold Bar Museum** is open summers Sat.-Sun. noon-3 p.m.

For an interesting drive or mountain bike ride, head up Kellogg Lake Rd. out of Startup and follow it four miles to Sultan Basin Road. Turn right and continue uphill along Olney Creek to Spada Lake (Everett's water source; no swimming or motorboating). The last part of the road is gravel and can be dusty in the summer, but the fine mountain and river vistas make this a pleasant trip.

Just west of Gold Bar (pop. 1,200) is the turnoff to **Skykomish State Salmon Hatchery,** a small operation of interest to anglers.

Community Transit, tel. (360) 778-2185 or (800) 562-1375, has daily bus service to Gold Bar and Startup, along with other parts of Snohomish County.

Sultan

Sultan (pop. 2,800) is home to the **Sultan Summer Shindig** the second weekend of July, with a parade, games, food booths, as well as arts and crafts displays. You'll also find live music at Sultan River Park on summer Sundays. The town itself doesn't have much to offer, though you may want to take a look at the tiny wayside chapel two miles west of town. The clean and friendly **Dutch Cup Motel,** tel. (360) 793-2215 or (800) 844-0488, charges $51 s or $59 d, and has kitchenettes in some rooms. This is the Sultan's de facto chamber of commerce. The **Sultan Farmers Market,** tel. (360) 793-2565, is held in River Park May-Sept. on Saturday 9 a.m.-2 p.m. For something different, camp north of town at **Lake Bronson Family Nudist Park,** tel. (360) 793-0286. This 320-acre resort includes a lodge, lake, sauna, hot tub, cafe, campsites, RV park, and more.

Community Transit, tel. (360) 778-2185 or (800) 562-1375, has daily bus service to Sultan and other parts of Snohomish County.

MONROE

Located just 30 commuter-miles from Seattle and 50 weekend-miles from downhill skiing at Stevens Pass, the town of Monroe (pop. 8,000) is a booming bedroom community of condos, tract houses, and more-established residences. A local promotional brochure brags about Monroe's "thoughtful planning" that makes it such a great place to live. But first impressions—especially if you're coming from the relatively undeveloped Cascades or the pretty town of Snohomish—are a bit different. Highway 2 through Monroe is a sickening chain of strip malls, fast food joints, and neon signs. God help them if they hadn't had any "thoughtful planning!" Despite this, there is at least one redeeming quality that attracts visitors to Monroe: the state fair.

The small **Monroe Historical Society Museum,** 207 E. Main St., tel. (360) 794-7056, is open Saturday 11 a.m.-3 p.m. April through Labor Day, and houses local memorabilia and videos from old-timers. Also of interest is the open farmland that surrounds Monroe (at least till the "thoughtful planning" spreads out more), and pleasant backcountry roads that are great for bike riding. To the south are **U-pick farms** for strawberries, raspberries, and blueberries, and farm stands offering fresh produce. Horse owners especially like the mild climate here, making Monroe a regional center for horse training and breeding.

Evergreen State Fairgrounds

On the west end of Monroe sits the enormous Evergreen State Fair complex, which features a raceway, outdoor arena, exhibit halls, and a 3,000-seat indoor Equestrian Park—one of the finest on the West Coast. The fairgrounds are the site of major equestrian shows all year long, including the **Washington Hunter/Jumper Spring Nationals** in April, the **Pacific Northwest Quarter Horse Shows** in May and September, along with a diversity of other events: medieval tournaments in January, a big craft show in April, an antique car show in May, and a Christmas crafts fair in December.

The biggest month is August, when the calendar is packed with activities, including an **Old Time Threshing Bee,** and the ever-popular **Evergreen State Fair,** the largest fair in Washington. Besides all the usual fair activities—agricultural displays, live entertainment, food and craft booths, and carnival rides—there's a fun run, parade, and all sorts of other activities. The fair lasts for 11 days, from the last full week in August through Labor Day weekend. For details on upcoming events, call the fairgrounds at (360) 794-7832 for a recording of upcoming events, or (360) 794-4344 to speak to a real person.

Also at the fairgrounds is the **Evergreen Speedway,** tel. (360) 794-7711, where you can watch NASCAR auto racing, demolition derbies (biggest of all is on the Fourth of July), and other contests of bravado late March to mid-September.

Lodging

Frog Crossing B&B, 306 S. Lewis, tel. (360) 794-7622, is a 1910 home with two guest rooms that are rented together, a private entrance, and full breakfast. Kids okay; $50-75 s or d.

The nicest local motel is **Best Western Baron Inn,** 19233 Hwy. 2, tel. (360) 794-3111 or (800) 238-7234, where rooms are $58-88 s or $64-94 d, including an outdoor pool, jacuzzi, exercise room, and continental breakfast. **Fairground Inn Motel,** 18950 Hwy. 2, tel. (360) 794-5401, charges $50 s or d, including an indoor hot tub. **Monroe Motel,** 20310 Old Owen Rd., tel. (360) 794-6751, has older motel rooms for $40 s or $44 d.

Campgrounds

The closest public campsites ($10 tents, $15 RVs) are two county parks: **Flowing Lake Park,** 10 miles north of Monroe, tel. (360) 568-2274, open year-round (no water in the winter months); and **Lake Roesiger Park,** 12 miles north of Monroe, tel. (360) 568-5836, open mid-May through September. Both of these parks have popular swimming beaches, and Flowing Lake has ranger-led nature hikes, along with Saturday-night amphitheater programs in the summer. Park RVs ($10) or pitch tents ($5) during events at **Evergreen State Fairgrounds;** call (360) 794-4344 for reservations. Other nearby public camping can be found eight miles east in Snohomish, and at Forest Service sites near Skykomish (described above).

Food

Although the scent of deep-fry cookers often pervades Monroe's air, several local places go beyond this greasy menu. Start the day at **Monroe Cafe,** 19837 Hwy. 2, tel. (360) 794-6940, where breakfast is served all day. **Fiddler's Bluff Coffee Company,** 102 W. Main St., tel. (360) 805-9450, is a good place to get an espresso or ice cream cone. **Sky River Bakery,** 117 W. Main, tel. (360) 794-7434, serves Starbucks coffee and fresh-baked goodies.

You'll find very good seafood at **Sailfish Bar & Grill,** 104 N. Lewis, tel. (360) 794-4056. The same building houses the classy **Twin Rivers Brewery.** And, of course, there's always McDonald's, Burger King, Domino's, KFC, Skippers, or Taco Time if you just want to eat and escape Monroe as fast as possible.

Information and Transportation

The **Monroe Chamber of Commerce,** 211 E. Main St., tel. (360) 794-5488, is open Mon.-Fri. 9:30 a.m.-4 p.m.

Community Transit, tel. (360) 778-2185 or (800) 562-1375, has daily bus service from Monroe to other parts of Snohomish County.

SNOQUALMIE VALLEY AND SNOQUALMIE PASS

When most Washington residents hear "Snoqualmie," they think first of Snoqualmie Pass and its ski areas, then Snoqualmie Falls, which looked so ominous in the credits to the 1980s TV show, *Twin Peaks*. The small town of Snoqualmie is usually an afterthought, unless you live there or have come to appreciate the great restaurants and beautiful scenery of the area. Snoqualmie Pass is the easiest way through the Cascades in winter: it has both the widest highway (I-5) and lowest elevation of any of the mountain passes. The ski areas at the summit bring a lot of vehicular traffic through the region.

SNOQUALMIE

The quaint little town of Snoqualmie (pop. 1,500), with about two blocks of civilization on either side of the tracks, has a number of attractions worth a look, including nearby Snoqualmie Falls. As you approach the town, dozens of aging train engines and railcars in varying states of repair crowd the railroad tracks.

The restored Snoqualmie Depot—built in 1890—contains the small **Northwest Railway Museum,** with a ticket office for the **Snoqualmie Valley Railroad.** These diesel trains operate through the Snoqualmie Valley to North Bend (a slow 40-minute ride that covers seven miles roundtrip). Trains depart the Snoqualmie and North Bend depots on weekends late May-Oct., and the ticket office is open Thurs.-Mon. 10 a.m.-5 p.m. Fares are $6 adults, $5 seniors, $4 ages 3-12, and free for kids under three. Call (425) 746-4025 for details. You can depart from either town, and layover before catching a later train. Reservations are not needed. They also have special Santa trains at Christmas.

Winery

The **Snoqualmie Winery,** 37444 S.E. Winery Rd. in Snoqualmie (take a right off the Snoqualmie Falls exit from I-90), tel. (425) 888-4000, produces several varieties of wine, including Johannesburg riesling, merlot, and muscat canelli. Besides the usual gift shop, this one has a big picnic area with panoramic views of the Cascades and Snoqualmie Valley. Open for tours and tastings daily 10 a.m.-4:30 p.m. The winery is owned by U.S. Tobacco Company. Taste wines from a variety of small wineries at **Northwest Cellars,** 8050 Railroad Ave., tel. (425) 888-6176 or (800) 947-3701. Open Thurs.-Tuesday.

Snoqualmie Falls

Located a mile north of the town of Snoqualmie, the 270-foot tall Snoqualmie Falls—a hundred feet higher than Niagara—has been awe-inspiring since the last ice age. As Washington's most famous waterfall, Snoqualmie attracts 1.5 million visitors annually. Unfortunately, the falls also attracted the attention of civil engineers in the 1890s as a potential source of electricity. Puget Sound Energy excavated a 1,215-foot tunnel through the rock to divert water into the world's first totally underground generating facility, with an above-ground plant added later. Visitors don't come to see the power plant, and in fact, most may not even know it exists since the only obvious evidence from below is water pouring from a hole at the base of the falls. The falls still run, but because of this diversion they do so at a vastly reduced level from the natural flow.

Stop at Snoqualmie Falls for a picnic lunch, or to stand in awe on the viewing platform as the noisy river plummets to the rocks far below. A steep half-mile **River Trail** leads downhill to the second power plant where you can view the falls from below. While you're standing here, think how much more powerful these falls were before over 90% of the water was siphoned off into power plants. You can check today's water flow in cubic feet per second inside the nearby Salish Lodge. The Snoqualmie Falls Preservation Project, 4759 15th Ave. NE, Seattle, tel. (206) 528-2421, is an environmental group attempting to restore Snoqualmie Falls to its original majesty, and to prevent Puget Sound Energy from expanding its power plants even more.

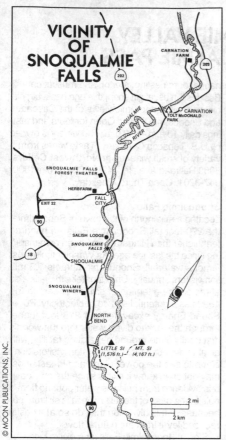

VICINITY OF SNOQUALMIE FALLS

CARNATION FARM

202

203

SNOQUALMIE RIVER

CARNATION
TOLT McDONALD
PARK

SNOQUALMIE FALLS
FOREST THEATER

HERBFARM

EXIT 22

FALL CITY

90

SALISH LODGE
SNOQUALMIE
FALLS

18

SNOQUALMIE

SNOQUALMIE
WINERY

NORTH
BEND

LITTLE SI
(1,576 ft.)

MT. SI
(4,167 ft.)

90

0   2 mi
0   2 km

© MOON PUBLICATIONS, INC.

A mile north of the falls, Hwy. 202 passes **Tokul Creek State Fish Hatchery,** tel. (425) 222-5464, where trout and steelhead are raised. Open daily.

Accommodations

The **Salish Lodge,** tel. (425) 888-2556 or (800) 826-6124, atop Snoqualmie Falls, is easily the most luxurious hotel in the area, featuring a fireplace, jacuzzi, and honor bar in every room, plus a balcony in most. Also here is a fully equipped exercise room, sauna and steam room, hydrotherapy pools, tanning booths, massage rooms, library, and one of the finest restaurants in the area. A great place for a honeymoon or a

getaway weekend; rooms are budget priced (if your last name is Gates) at $199-320 s or d.

For more homey accommodations in a country setting, stay at **The Old Honey Farm Country Inn,** 8910 384th Ave. SE, tel. (425) 888-9399, where guest rooms go for $75-125 s or d.

Food

The **Salish Lodge Restaurant,** tel. (425) 888-2556, atop Snoqualmie Falls has been in operation (under various names) since 1916. The dinner menu features seafood and game entrees ($25-35 each). Their farm-style four-course Sunday brunch remains a regional favorite. The homey lodge atmosphere, with overstuffed chairs surrounding a warm fire in the lounge, is worth the price of admission. Reservations are virtually required, especially if you want a window seat.

Theater

Set amongst towering evergreens at the foot of the falls, the **Snoqualmie Falls Forest Theater** has stage performances and dinners Fri.-Sun. in July and August. This is the only outdoor dinner theater in Washington. For current productions and ticket information call (425) 222-7044.

Transportation and Tours

Seattle's **Metro** buses serve Snoqualmie Falls, Snoqualmie, and North Bend; call (206) 447-4800 for a schedule. Rent bikes from **The Bike Rack,** 115 Newton, tel. (360) 888-4886.

FALL CITY, CARNATION, AND DUVALL

The attractive little riverside town of Fall City is three miles northwest of Snoqualmie Falls, and six miles south of the even smaller settlement of Carnation. Highway 202 ties the towns together. The road is narrow, with tight corners, and is posted at 30 miles an hour all the way through Carnation. Exceed this at your own risk; the cops are always out in force here! Continue another nine miles north from Carnation on Hwy. 203 through dairy farming land (rich with eau de manure) to the quaint town of Duvall, where older places survive next to trendy espresso and book shops.

Tolt McDonald Park, just west of Carnation at the confluence of the Tolt and Snoqualmie Rivers, is a pleasant place to relax or pitch a tent. Open late March to October.

Carnation Farm

Carnation Farm is owned and operated by the Carnation milk-and-ice-cream, dog- and cat-food people. The farm was purchased in 1910 by E.A. Stuart, the founder of Carnation Company, as a place to improve milk production. Many champion cows (defined by their ability to produce milk, not their speed on the track), have been raised here, and one—Segis Pietertje Prospect—even merited a statue on the grounds. The farm still raises 360 Holstein cows that are milked twice a day. Free, self-guided tours include "The Birth of a Calf" video, the milking carousel, maternity barn, and the petting area in "Frisky Acres" with Labrador retrievers and cats. Bring your picnic lunch to enjoy in the flower gardens. Carnation Farm, tel. (425) 788-1511, is open Saturday 10 a.m.-3 p.m. Labor Day through September.

Herbfarm

More than a 20 years ago, Lola Zimmerman put out a few pots of her home-grown herbs at a roadside stand. Today, The Herbfarm boasts over 600 kinds of live herb plants (including 27 varieties of thyme!), and over 300 classes in everything from folk herbalism to herbal soap-making. Pick up an herbal flea collar, beer bread mix, live plants, books, herbal deodorant, or gourmet coffees at the farm's country store. Tours of the 17 herb gardens are given on summer weekends at 1 p.m. Open Mon.-Fri. 10 a.m.-5 p.m., and Sat.-Sun. 9 a.m.-6 p.m. April-Sept., and daily 10 a.m.-5 p.m. the rest of the year. The Herbfarm's famed restaurant burned to the ground in 1996, but is expected to reopen in late 1999. Call (425) 784-2222 or (800) 866-4372 for the latest. The Herbfarm is located at 32804 Issaquah-Fall City Rd. in Fall City.

Food

Stop at the historic Falls City's **Colonial Inn,** tel. (425) 222-5191, built in 1920, for a cup of coffee and a slice of pie. North of town, the road follows the river past a mix of old farmsteads, timbered lands, and rural homes. In the middle of this is **Remlinger Farms,** 32610 N.E. 32nd in Carnation, tel. (425) 333-4135, with pick-your-own berries, pumpkins, and other produce in season.

Accommodations and Campgrounds

Stay at **River Inn Snoqualmie Valley,** 4548 Tolt River Rd. in Carnation, tel. (425) 333-4262, where the five rooms go for $65-225 d. These luxurious accommodations include an indoor pool, sauna, steam room, and soaking tub, plus a beach along the Tolt River and an abundance of wild birds.

Located on five wooded acres, **Windsong Farm B&B,** 515 286th Ave. SE, tel. (425) 222-4734, is a charming modern farmhouse with a single guest room. A full breakfast is served; $95 s or $120 d. The B&B is a favorite of birders.

The privately run **Snoqualmie River Campground,** 34807 S.E. 44th Pl. in Fall City, tel. (425) 222-5545, has RV and tent spaces.

Events and Transportation

On weekends in July and August, the **Camlann Medieval Village** takes place three miles north of Carnation, with knights in armor, minstrels, dramatic productions, plus crafts and food, all in a wooded setting. Call (425) 788-1945 for details. The Herbfarm, tel. (425) 784-2222, has a number of popular annual events, including the big **Northwest Microbrewery Festival** on Father's Day weekend in mid-June, and the **Garlic Festival** in August.

Metro buses serve Fall City, Snoqualmie, and North Bend; call (425) 447-4800 or (800) 542-7876 for a schedule.

NORTH BEND

Located at the foot of Mt. Si, the settlement of North Bend (pop. 2,600) is the last Snoqualmie River town before I-90 climbs into the Cascade Range. Nothing special here, although a few buildings carry a Swiss theme, and several others are recognizable from the old *Twin Peaks* television series. North Bend is fast becoming yet another in a string of bedroom communities, with new condos being added all the time. Nintendo Corporation has a big plant here, and a collection of some 35 factory outlet stores can be found just off I-90's exit 31.

Sights

The **Snoqualmie Valley Museum,** 320 North Bend Blvd. S, tel. (425) 888-3200, has permanent displays of Indian artifacts and pioneer and logging history, and a small gift shop. Open Thurs.-Sun. 1-5 p.m. April-Oct., and the first two weeks of December; donation.

Snoqualmie Valley Railroad, tel. (425) 746-4025, operates steam trains through the Snoqualmie Valley; see the town of Snoqualmie (above) for details on these popular rides.

Mount Si Bonsai, 43321 S.E. Mt. Si Rd., tel. (425) 888-0350, features a collection of these miniature trees.

The 113-mile-long **Iron Horse State Park** starts from Olallie State Park and follows a gentle old railroad grade over Snoqualmie Pass and down to all the way to the Columbia River, 113 miles later. See **Cle Elum** for details on this popular hiking, horseback riding, biking, and ski trail.

Mount Si and Little Si

The 4,167-foot-tall Mt. Si (named for an early settler, Josiah "Si" Merrit) is one of the most climbed mountains in the state—10,000 people a year take the eight-hour roundtrip hike. It's not just the length of the hike that's tough, but the elevation gain of 3,100 feet that keeps you puffing. Be prepared for lots of switchbacks! The views west to Mt. Rainier, Puget Sound, Seattle, and the Olympics, however, are worth the effort. To reach the trailhead, turn left on 432nd SE (Mt. Si Rd.) about a mile from the east edge of North Bend. After you cross the Middle Fork of the Snoqualmie River, go right at the first intersection then drive two and a half miles to the parking lot, trailhead, and picnic area. The trail is generally snow-free April to November. Avoid the crowds by getting an early morning start.

An easier alternative to Mt. Si is Little Si, offering views across Snoqualmie Valley. The trail is two and half miles each way. Get to the trailhead by following North Bend Way a half mile southeast from the Forest Service Ranger Station to Mt. Si Rd.; then turn left and go a half mile to a bridge. Park at the gravel lot here across the bridge, and walk downhill to the signed trailhead just past the fifth house on the right.

Twin Falls

Just a short distance from busy I-90, at **Olallie State Park,** the South Fork of the Snoqualmie River drops 300 feet over a stunning series of cataracts. The park is accessible from exit 34 (five miles east of North Bend); after exiting, turn right on Edgewick Rd., and then left onto S.E. 159th St.; continue a half mile to the park. A 1.3-mile path leads to Twin Falls, and from there, you can cross a footbridge and continue uphill another 1.6 miles to a second trailhead near exit 38. Day-use only, and no mountain bikes or horses allowed on the trails. Olallie State Park continues eastward along the river above Twin Falls, with several good fishing holes.

Accommodations

North Bend Motel, 322 E. North Bend Way, tel. (425) 888-1121, has rooms for $38-42 s, $40-45 d, including a jacuzzi. Three miles east of town, the **Edgewick Inn,** 14600 468th Ave. SE, tel. (425) 888-9000, has modern rooms for $55 s or d, including a jacuzzi. Rooms cost $42 s or d at **Sunset Motel,** 227 W. North Bend Way, tel. (425) 888-0381. Kitchenettes are available here, and at **Nor'West Motel & RV Park,** 45810 S.E. North Bend Way, tel. (425) 888-1939, where rooms are $47-89 s or d.

The Roaring River at North Bend B&B, 46715 S.E. 129th St., tel. (425) 888-4834 or (877) 627-4647, offers views of the Middle Fork of the Snoqualmie River. The four rooms all have private entrances, baths, and decks. A breakfast basket is delivered to your door; $85-150 d. No kids.

Campgrounds

The closest public camping is the Forest Service's **Tinkham Campground,** 10 miles east on I-90 at exit 42. Sites are $12; open May-September. Another seven miles east on I-90 is **Denny Creek Campground,** which has the same rates and season. Park RVs (no tents) in town at **Nor'West Motel & RV Park,** 45810 S.E. North Bend Way, tel. (425) 888-1939.

Food

George's Bakery, 127 W. North Bend Way, tel. (425) 888-0632, is a favorite local gathering place that serves sweets, fresh-baked breads, sandwiches, and salads. Get pizzas at **Anthony's**

New York Pizza, 480 E. North Bend Way, tel. (425) 831-6836.

The standout place in North Bend is **Giuliano Restorante Italiano,** 101 W. North Bend Way, tel. (360) 888-5700, with a romantic atmosphere and food that includes a variety of reasonably priced homemade pastas. Delicious desserts too.

Information and Services

The **North Bend Ranger Station,** a half mile east of town, tel. (425) 888-1421, has Forest Service information on local trails, mountain bike routes, and campgrounds. Open Mon.-Fri. 8 a.m.-4:30 p.m., plus Saturday in summer. The **Upper Snoqualmie Valley Chamber of Commerce,** tel. (425) 888-4440, has a small visitor center on the west end of town that dispenses maps, brochures, and other information.

Transportation

Seattle's **Metro** buses serve North Bend and surrounding communities; call (206) 447-4800 or (800) 542-7876 for a schedule. **Greyhound,** tel. (800) 231-2222, stops in North Bend at the corner of 219 Main Ave. S, with connections throughout the nation.

SNOQUALMIE PASS

Skiing the Summit

Located 53 miles from downtown Seattle, and right along I-90, Snoqualmie Pass is Washington's oldest and largest downhill ski area, with four separate areas now managed by Booth Creek Ski Holdings, one of the largest ski operators in the nation. Major changes have taken place here in the last few years, and another $30 million in improvements are in the works. The complex is now called **The Summit at Snoqualmie,** and includes: **Alpental, Summit West, Summit Central,** and **Summit East.** Together they encompass 22 chair lifts, two half-pipes, and 65 runs, and are connected together by a free weekend shuttle bus. All told, Snoqualmie Pass's ski areas cover more than 1,900 skiable acres and constitute the largest night skiing area in the world. The summit elevation is 3,675-5,400 feet, with a base of 3,000 feet, for a vertical drop reaching up to 2,200 feet.

You can ski at all four hills on the same lift ticket; weekend rates are $32 for adults, and $22 for ages 7-11, with lower prices on weekdays. The nearby **Summit Nordic Center** has 55 km of groomed and tracked trails, and **Snowflake Tubing and Snowplay Area** rents inner tubes ($5) and offers lighted rope tows ($8) for kids of all ages. Summit at Snoqualmie services include ski shops, equipment rentals, ski schools, day lodges, food service, child care, and bus service to the area. For rates, operating hours, snow conditions, and general info on all four places, call (206) 236-1600. Find them on the Web at www.summitatsnoqualmie .com.

Come summer, the **Ski Acres Mountain Bike & Hiking Center,** tel. (206) 409-0459, has mountain bike rentals and tours along parts of the 113-mile Iron Horse Trail. The route—an old railroad grade—is all downhill from here. They also have a shuttle service ($8) to bring you back uphill. See **Cle Elum** for details on this popular hiking, horseback riding, biking, and ski trail.

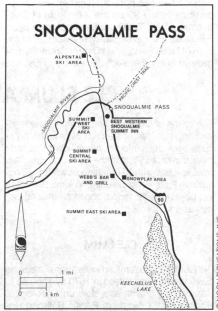

Accommodations

The **Best Western Snoqualmie Summit Inn,** tel. (425) 434-6300 or (800) 557-7829, has an indoor pool, jacuzzi, sauna, and a restaurant. Rates are $85-99 s or d.

Valley High Mountain Lodge, tel. (425) 432-1409, has 16 beds in a large chalet-style home right on the slopes, with a kitchen and two fireplaces. Rates are $250 in summer, $300 in winter, and $350 on holidays.

Frantzian Mt. Hideaway, tel. (425) 434-6270, has a private apartment (sleeps six) with a deck and kitchen. Breakfast is provided, and kids are welcome; $55-75 s or d. Lodging is also available at **Wardholm West B&B,** tel. (425) 434-6540, where the six rooms are $50-80 s or d with a shared or private bath.

Murphy Mountain Retreat, tel. (425) 434-6613, has a two-bedroom unit with private entrance, full kitchen, gas fireplace, and make-your-own breakfast. $100 d to $160 for six people.

Camping

RV parking is permitted at the summit parking lots, but no hookups are available. The Forest Service has two popular summertime campgrounds near I-90 on the west side of Snoqualmie Pass. **Tinkham Campground** is on Forest Rd. 55, approximately 12 miles east of the town of North Bend, while **Denny Creek Campground** is another six miles east and just two miles west of Snoqualmie Pass. Both are open mid-May to mid-September and cost $12. Reservations are $9 extra; call (877) 444-6777.

Food

Atop Snoqualmie Pass, **Family Pancake House** at the Summit Inn serves meals, and **Traveler's Rest** has inexpensive sandwiches, burgers, light meals, and groceries. Food is also available at all four ski areas in the winter.

Information and Transportation

Snoqualmie Pass is a popular entry point for the Alpine Lakes Wilderness (described above). **Snoqualmie Pass Visitor Center,** tel. (425) 434-6111, has information and issues wilderness permits. Open Thurs.-Sun. 8:30 a.m.-4:45 p.m. summers only.

Although Snoqualmie Pass is generally the easiest way to traverse the Cascades, it does get snowy and sometimes closes during heavy storms. Call (888) 766-4636 for the Department of Transportation's **Mountain Pass Report,** or check their Web page, www.traffic.wsdot.wa.gov/sno-info, for a webcam showing current conditions at Snoqualmie Pass.

The **I-90 Ski Bus,** tel. (206) 232-8210, provides service from Seattle, Bellevue, and Issaquah between January and early March.

CLE ELUM AND VICINITY

The towns of Cle Elum and Roslyn provide interesting side trips or starting points for hiking or horseback treks into the magnificent Cascade mountain country just to the north and west. Access is easy, with I-90 cutting down from Snoqualmie Pass along the upper Yakima River Valley, passing fields, farms, and stream-laced valleys as you descend.

CLE ELUM

Cle Elum (KLEE-elum), an Indian name meaning "Swift Water," was settled in 1870 by Thomas L. Gamble, but growth was slow until geologists working for the Northern Pacific Railroad discovered coal in 1884. A forest fire in the late 1880s wiped out a large part of the mining town, but additional coal veins discovered in 1889 gave Cle Elum four quite prosperous years. Today the town is a jumping-off point for hiking, fishing, and other recreational activities in the Wenatchee National Forest.

Museums

Cle Elum was the last place in America to use a manually operated switchboard, and the last to institute the touch-tone dial system. The old phone building was transformed into the **Cle Elum Historical Telephone Museum** 221 E. 1st St., tel. (509) 674-5702. Inside this surprisingly well-done little museum are switchboard exhibits, photographs of early Cle Elum, and other memorabilia. Open Tues.-Fri. 9 a.m.-4 p.m., Sat.-Mon. noon-4 p.m., from Memorial Day to Labor Day, and by appointment the rest of the year; $1. For something different, try the "coal" candy sold here.

The spacious **Carpenter Museum,** 302 W. 3rd St., tel. (509) 674-5702, was built in 1914 by a prosperous local banker, Frank Carpenter. His granddaughter donated it, along with much of the original furnishings (including Tiffany lamps, an oak dining table with 11 leaves, and a beautifully carved rosewood chair), to the local historical society. The museum is open Sat.-Sun. noon-4 p.m. between Memorial Day and Labor Day; $2 adults, $1.50 seniors, and $1 kids.

Iron Horse State Park

This is Washington's most unusual state park, a 113-mile long trail that starts near North Bend, crosses the Cascades, and continues all the way to the Columbia River. The route extends along property once belonging to the Milwaukee, St. Paul and Pacific Railroad; they ran electric trains from 1912 until their bankruptcy in 1980. Open to hikers, skiers, mountain bikers, and horseback riders, but closed to motorized vehicles, the trail begins at Olallie State Park (I-90 Exit 34), climbs up the west slope of the Cascades to Snoqualmie Pass, and then descends past Cle Elum and Ellensburg (there is a short gap near here) before ending near Vantage along the Columbia River. The gravel trail is gentle, with a maximum two percent grade. It crosses 30 substantial trestles, and goes through four tunnels, including the 2.3-mile Snoqualmie Pass tunnel; bring flashlights and warm clothes. No overnight camping is allowed. Trailhead access points can be found near many I-90 exits along the way, including Olallie State Park, Snoqualmie Pass, Easton, South Cle Elum and Thorp. Iron Horse State Park actually extends all

the way across eastern Washington to the Idaho border, but access to the eastern section requires a special permit. Call (509) 656-2230 for more park information.

Lake Easton State Park

About 15 miles west of Cle Elum just off I-90, Lake Easton State Park encompasses 247 forested acres on the west and north sides of Lake Easton and is a popular camping spot (if you can ignore the traffic noise). The mile-long reservoir is good for swimming, boating, trout fishing, and water-skiing; hiking, cross-country skiing, and snowmobiling are popular dryland sports. Kids enjoy the big-toy playground. The water level changes through the year in this reservoir, and it is drained each winter to provide irrigation water for eastern Washington farms.

Recreation

The **Cle Elum Ranger District** office of the Wenatchee National Forest has information on more than 750 miles of hiking trails. Stop by their office at the west end of 2nd St., tel. (509) 674-4411, for maps, a detailed trail guidebook, and camping, cross-country skiing, and snowmobiling information. The office is open Mon.-Fri. 7:45 a.m.-5 p.m. and Sat. 8 a.m.-2 p.m. year-round.

Take Hwy. 903 from Cle Elum northwest to Cle Elum Lake; a number of forest roads leave it for backcountry hiking trails, including access to the south end of Alpine Lakes Wilderness Area (see **Stevens Pass and Skykomish Valley**). From the north end of the lake, take forest roads 4308 and 4312 to the Thorp Creek trailhead for a 3.1-mile hike to tiny **Thorp Lake** and **Kachess Ridge**.

A six-mile one-way hike on Trail 1307 leaves Salmon la Sac Campground and follows a ridge to an excellent view atop **Jolly Mountain**.

For horseback trips into the backcountry, contact **Three Queens Outfitter/Guide Service**, tel. (509) 674-5647, and **High Country Outfitters**, tel. (425) 392-0111 or (888) 235-0111. See **Leavenworth** for information on Blewett Pass, a popular hiking and cross-country skiing destination halfway between Cle Elum and Leavenworth. More cross-country skiing at **Cabin Creek Nordic Ski Area**, at exit 63 off I-90, and west of Lake Easton State Park.

Two local ranches offer horse rides: **Hidden Valley's Pony Express**, tel. (509) 857-2087, and **Unionville Ranch**, tel. (509) 857-2235.

Accommodations

Now a B&B on the National Historic Register, the restored **Moore House**, 526 Marie Ave., tel. (509) 674-5939 or (800) 228-9246, was built in 1909 by the Chicago, Milwaukee, Pacific, and St. Paul Railroads to serve the men who worked on some of the most treacherous mountain tracks in the country. The 10 rooms ($58-115 s or d) feature train toys and memorabilia and historic photographs. A jacuzzi on the deck makes a nice place to relax. Beds are on the short side in these small rooms, so tall folks may feel cramped. Iron Horse State Park Trail is just a few feet from here, making this a great place for cross-country skiers or cyclists. Outside, the railroad theme continues with two cabooses that have been transformed into cozy quarters for up to five people ($105-115 d). These are a good option for families or couples looking for privacy. Two-night minimum on holiday weekends.

Hidden Valley Guest Ranch, off Hwy. 97, is the state's oldest dude ranch. Here you can indulge your cowboy fantasies while still enjoying cabins, a pool and hot tub, and someone else's cooking. You don't have to be an overnight guest to join the horseback rides ($33). In winter, the ranch is generally open for cross-country skiing; call ahead to check on conditions. Cabins begin at $200 per person for two nights, including delicious ranch-style meals. Call (509) 857-2344 or (800) 526-9269 for more information.

Cle Elum's other accommodations are listed by price. Two budget place have kitchenettes: **Bonita Motel**, 906 E. 1st St., tel. (509) 674-2380, where rooms are $27 s or $34 d; and **Astor Inn**, 521 E. 1st St., tel. (509) 674-2551, where rooms cost $30 s or $35 d. **Cedars Motel**, 1001 E. 1st St., tel. (509) 674-5535, charges $32 s or $42 d; and **Chalet Motel**, 800 E. 1st St., tel. (509) 674-2320, has rooms for $35-50 s or d.

Wind Blew Inn Motel, Hwy. 97 at I-90 exit 85, tel. (509) 674-2294, charges $36 s or $38 d, including a continental breakfast. **Timber Lodge Inn**, 301 W. 1st St., tel. (509) 674-5966, has a jacuzzi and continental breakfast; $42-49 s or $47-53 d. **Stewart Lodge**, 805 W. 1st St., tel. (509) 674-4548, has an outdoor pool and jacuzzi, and rooms for $43-56 s or $48-56 d. **Cascade Mountain Inn;** 906 E. 1st, tel. (509) 674-2380 or (888) 674-3975, is a new place with rooms for $45 s or $50 d, including a continental breakfast.

Campgrounds

The Forest Service maintains 20 campgrounds in the Cle Elum area. The most popular places charge $6-10 a night, but those with more primitive facilities are free. Closest is **Wish Poosh Campground,** eight miles northwest of town on the eastern shore of Cle Elum Lake. Continue up Salmon la Sac Rd. to three more campgrounds: **Cle Elum River, Red Mountain,** and **Salmon la Sac.** More camping is available at **Kachess Lake** (pronounced "ka-CHEES"), approximately 27 miles east of Cle Elum. This beautiful blue-green lake also offers swimming, boating, picnicking, and a nature trail through old-growth forests. Make reservations ($9 extra) for Kachess and Salmon la Sac campgrounds by calling (877) 444-6777. More campgrounds are northeast of town on Hwy. 97 over Blewett Pass en route to Leavenworth.

About 15 miles west of Cle Elum and just off I-90, **Lake Easton State Park** has additional camping ($11 tents, $16 RVs), along with showers. Open late April to mid-October. Call (509) 656-2230 for details or (800) 452-5687 for reservations ($6 extra).

Sun Country Golf Resort, six miles west of Cle Elum, tel. (509) 674-2226, has an RV park and a nine-hole golf course. More RV parking at **Whispering Pines RV Park,** 100 Whispering Pines Dr., tel. (509) 674-7278.

Food

Get cinnamon rolls and espresso for the road, or a crusty loaf of Dutch crunch bread fresh from the brick oven (in use since 1906) at **Cle Elum Bakery,** 501 E. 1st St., tel. (509) 674-2233. **Cottage Cafe** is a truck stop that is popular for breakfast.

MaMa Vallone's Steak House and Inn, 302 W. 1st St., tel. (509) 674-5174, serves a large selection of steaks as well as Italian dishes made with homemade pasta. A country buffet is offered on Sunday. **El Caporal,** 107 W. 1st St., tel. (509) 674-4284, has quite good Mexican meals and margaritas.

Other Practicalities

Cle Elum's big event is **Pioneer Days** on the Fourth of July, which features a street fair, parade, softball and bocci ball tournaments, and races.

For local information, stop by the city office at Penn and 3rd, open Mon.-Fri. 8 a.m.-4 p.m. **Kittias County Connector** has bus service to Ellensburg, Thorp, Roslyn, and Vantage; tel. (509) 674-2251.

ROSLYN

Located almost at road's end on Hwy. 903, the little town of Roslyn (pop. 900) has always been a favorite of Washingtonians. it contains the largest collection of cemeteries in the state, but is best known as the place where the television series *Northern Exposure* was filmed.

History

When large coal deposits were discovered in this area, the Northern Pacific Railroad bought up all the land and opened a mine in 1886. The town that grew up around the mine (and other nearby coal mines) was named by Logan M. Bullitt, general manager of the Northern Pacific Coal Co., in honor of Roslyn, New York, the hometown of his sweetheart. The coal mines attracted many European immigrants—Slavs, Italians, Austrians, Croatians, Germans, Italians, Scots, Swedes, Hungarians—who brought interesting customs with them, including the Central European method of proposing marriage. The man wishing to propose gathered his friends to accompany him to his beloved's house, where on bended knee he proposed. If she rejected him, he bought a keg of beer in which to drown his sorrow in their company. If she accepted, his friends had to pay the wedding expenses. This variety of nationalities and religions, plus various fraternal lodges in Roslyn, led to each group having its own cemetery along 5th St. on the edge of town. Today there are 26 small cemeteries spread over 15 acres here.

At its peak in 1910, some 4,000 people lived in Roslyn. The mines that produced more than a million tons of coal were deadly; an 1892 explosion killed 45 men, and another in 1909 killed another 10 men. Eventually, competition from cheaper coal, and the conversion of train engines from coal to diesel fuel, led to the closing of

Roslyn's mines. The last coal mine shut its doors in 1963, and it wasn't till the arrival of the *Northern Exposure* crew that things really started to change in this sleepy burg. Although the show was canceled in 1995, the town still attracts visitors looking for familiar sights. Amazingly, Roslyn has become a commuter town for folks who work in Seattle; two vanpools do the commute daily! Many of Roslyn's other homes are used as weekend getaways.

Sights and Tours
Roslyn's main attractions are its old-West false-fronted buildings, many of which appeared in *Northern Exposure,* including the famous Roslyn's Cafe sign. Fans of the TV show will recognize at least a dozen different locations where the program was filmed, from the doctor's office to the dump. **Central Sundries,** tel. (509) 649-2210, was the location of "Ruth-Anne's General Store." The **Brick Tavern,** across the street, is the oldest licensed tavern in Washington. It opened in 1889 and is famous for the 23-foot long running water spittoon that still washes away patrons' tobacco juice.

The **Roslyn Museum,** next to the Roslyn Cafe, houses an interesting collection of historic photos, coal mining equipment, and other items from Roslyn's past. Open summer weekends; $1.

Accommodations
The Last Resort, five miles west of town at Lake Cle Elum, tel. (509) 649-2222, has the least expensive rooms, just $45 s or d. In town, **Little Roslyn Inn,** tel. (509) 649-2936, isn't much more: $48 s or d, including a kitchen, piano, and sundeck.

Coal Country Inn B&B, tel. (509) 649-3222 or (800) 543-2566, is a 19th-century rooming house where three rooms share a bath. A full breakfast is served; $57 s or $62 d. **Hummingbird Inn B&B,** tel. (509) 649-2758, charges $65-75 d, including a full breakfast.

Roslyn's Harry's Inn B&B, tel. (509) 649-2551, has three guest rooms with fireplaces and kitchenettes. A continental breakfast is served; $65-75 s or d.

Roslyn B&B, tel. (509) 649-2463, is an 1889 home with three guest rooms, private baths, plus an outside deck and flower gardens where a full breakfast is served; $75 s or d. Friendly owner too.

Mountain Rose Lodge B&B, tel. (509) 649-2569, sits on the shore of Lake Cle Elum, five miles west of Roslyn. The three guest rooms are $85 d.

Two century-old houses (one with seven bedrooms, and the other with 10 rooms) are available for families or groups through **Roslyn Inns,** tel. (509) 649-2936. The cost is $180 and $260 respectively.

Food and Drink
For such a small town, Roslyn has surprisingly good food. Very good breakfasts at **Roslyn Cafe,** (509) 649-2763, best known for its colorful mural (altered to say "Roslyn's" for the television show). Another good breakfast option is **Pennsylvania Station,** tel. (509) 649-2756.

If you've got a penchant for perfectly prepared pizzas, don't miss **Village Pizza,** tel. (509) 649-2992, where the staff is friendly and the topping choices range all over the map. **Pioneer Restaurant and Sody-Licious Lounge** has steaks, fresh seafood, and desserts, along with a big screen TV and live music on weekends.

Roslyn Bakery, tel. (509) 649-2521, is a friendly place with excellent fresh European-style breads, pastries, and bagels. Open May to Thanksgiving.

For more than 80 years, people have been coming to **Carek's Meat Market** to purchase fresh and smoked meats. Today, folks make the pilgrimage all the way from Seattle for their Polish sausages, beef jerky, and pepperoni.

The **Brick Tavern,** tel. (509) 649-2643, features live music and dancing on weekends and is famous for its running water spittoon. **Roslyn Brewing Company,** tel. (509) 649-2232, brews two fine beers, and is open for tours on weekends noon-6 p.m.

Other Practicalities
Roslyn's **Wing Ding Parade** on Labor Day always includes an amusing parade, performers, plus a street fair. More strangeness at the **Manly Man Festival** in late June, including a Spam cookoff, the crowning of the Spam queen, and street vendors. **Moosefest** in mid-July brings back stars from *Northern Exposure* for a parade, dinner, theater, and live music. One of the town's biggest events is the **Run to Roslyn,** which attracts 500 antique cars each August.

Roslyn Bike & Ski, 101 N. 2nd, tel. (509) 649-3423, rents mountain bikes. **Kittias County Connector** has bus service to Ellensburg, Thorp, Cle Elum, and Vantage; tel. (509) 674-2251.

MOUNT RAINIER NATIONAL PARK

Washington's tallest and best-known peak, the perennially snowcapped Mt. Rainier, towers over surrounding Cascade summits. To the residents of Puget Sound, it is simply "The Mountain," and its presence is so dominant that even the state's best-known beer is named Rainier. (Beer connoisseurs may view this as an insult to the mountain, however.) With 300 miles of hiking trails covering terrain from the lowland forests all the way to the ice-topped summit at 14,411 feet, Mt. Rainier is a recreational paradise. More than two million people visit Mount Rainier National Park annually, viewing towering waterfalls from the winding mountain roads, strolling through flower-filled mountain meadows at Paradise, camping beneath old-growth Douglas fir forests, climbing the mountain's glacier-clad slopes, listening to the bugling of elk on a fall evening, and skiing backcountry trails in the winter.

HISTORY

Although various tribes of Indians made seasonal fishing, hunting, and berry-picking forays into the foothills around Mt. Rainier, they apparently avoided the mountain itself, either in reverence for the great mountain, or because of its severe weather. The Klickitat Indians who lived near present-day Ashford called the peak "Ta-ho-ma," a word that probably simply means "The Mountain," or "Snowiest Peak." The city of Tacoma gained its name from the mountain that rises so tall behind it. Unfortunately, the Indian name for the peak itself was supplanted by an English name. In 1792, Capt. George Vancouver named it after his friend, Rear Admiral Peter Rainier. Thus Rainier—a minor character in British naval history—lives on in an American mountain that he never even saw. It would be almost like naming the nation's tallest peak after a minor president who had nothing to do with it. (Oops, they already did that with a mountain called Denali and a president named McKinley.)

First to the Top

It is said that the Native American inhabitants of the area viewed "Tahoma" as a sacred ground, inhabited by a vengeful deity who didn't welcome visitors. Although there are stories that an Indian guide led two white men to the summit as early as 1855, the men's names are long forgotten. Hazard Stevens, the Union's youngest Civil War general, was determined to be the first to (officially) reach Rainier's summit. So in 1870 he began assembling his climbing party. An un-

STATE OF WASHINGTON TOURISM DIVISION

The Klickitat called Mt. Rainier "Tahoma."

employed miner, Philomon Beecher Van Trump, and landscape artist Edward T. Coleman would accompany him to the summit; James Longmire, a local farmer, would guide them as far as Bear Prairie, at 2,630 feet. But the group needed someone with expertise. They found it in Sluiskin, a nomad Indian who had taken up residence at Bear Prairie, and whose grandfather, going against Indian tradition, had once attempted a summit climb—without success.

The first day out after Bear Prairie, Coleman turned back. He'd found himself in a precarious position on a precipice where he could go neither forward nor back with his 40-pound pack; so he chucked it, along with most of the party's food. Stevens, Van Trump, and Sluiskin continued.

As the climbers progressed, Sluiskin began losing his nerve. Stevens wrote about him in an article for *Atlantic Monthly* in 1876:

Takhoma, he said, was an enchanted mountain, inhabited by an evil spirit who dwelt in a fiery lake on its summit. No human being could ascend it or even attempt its ascent and survive . . . at first, indeed, the way was easy . . . but above [the broad snow fields] the rash adventurer would be compelled to climb up steeps of loose, rolling rocks, which would turn beneath his feet and cast him headlong into the deep abyss below. . . . Moreover, a furious tempest continually swept the crown of the mountain, and the luckless adventurer, even if he wonderfully escaped the perils below, would be torn from the mountain and whirled through the air by this fearful blast.

Begging off, Sluiskin promised to wait three days for the climbers to return; then he'd go to Olympia to tell their friends they were dead.

Sluiskin's description of the mountain wasn't far from the truth. Stevens wrote,

Our course . . . brought us first to the southwest peak. This is a long, exceedingly sharp, narrow ridge springing out from the main dome for a mile into mid-air. The ridge affords not over ten or twelve feet of foothold on top, and the

sides descend almost vertically. . . . The wind blew so violently that we were obliged to brace ourselves with our Alpine staffs and use great caution to guard against being swept off the ridge.

After reaching the true summit of the mountain, Stevens and Van Trump found a volcanic steam cave where they huddled for warmth. In spite of the rotten-egg stench of the sulfuric steam, they spent the night. The next day the two men returned to Sluiskin, who was *really* surprised to see them, and expressed his deep admiration for the men who had conquered Takhoma: "Strong men," he said; "stout hearts." The first woman to top the summit was a schoolteacher named Fay Fuller, who climbed the mountain in 1890.

Creating a Park

In 1883, James Longmire—who had guided climbers to the base of Mt. Rainier for many years—discovered a mineral springs near the Nisqually River and staked a mining claim on the site. Longmire recognized the land for its true value—as a place to enjoy the wild beauty and grand mountain views. His Longmire Springs Resort was built in 1906 on what is now national park land in the park's oldest developed area: Longmire.

Mount Rainier became the nation's fifth national park in 1899, due in large part to pressure from a prominent group of Northern Pacific Railroad stockholders who not only appreciated the beauty of the mountain, but also saw money to be made in the proposition. The railroad had earlier been given alternating square-mile chunks of land in a checkerboard pattern as part of the federal government's incentive to promote building a transcontinental railroad. To allow the park to be created, the company exchanged land around Mt. Rainier—most of which happened to lack trees—for federal government parcels—that just happened to contain commercially valuable timber. The Northern Pacific Railroad then proceeded to log their new land while simultaneously hauling visitors to the new park that they helped create. Not a bad business deal! The awesome beauty of this sleeping volcano has been drawing visitors ever since. Some 228,400 acres (97%) of the park was declared the Mount Rainier Wilderness Area in 1988.

GEOLOGY AND CLIMATE

Building a Mountain

The volcanic summit of Mt. Rainier—fifth highest in the Lower 48 states—was created over a period of many millennia. Around a million years ago, lava began flowing through a weak spot in the earth's crust. A series of massive lava flows and sometimes-explosive eruptions created the volcanic cone of Mt. Rainier, scraping the clouds at more than 16,000 feet high. Around 5,700 years ago, something happened—perhaps an earthquake—that triggered an enormous collapse of one side of the mountain. More than a half cubic mile of debris (the Osceola Mudflow) roared down the White River valley in a mudflow that reached almost to Puget Sound. The collapse knocked nearly 2,000 feet off the summit of Mt. Rainier, and the mud and debris inundated areas where the cities of Enumclaw, Buckley, Puyallup, and Kent are now located. Additional large mudflows have continued to occur every 500 to 1,000 years, and geologists say that they may well return without warning, engulfing cities in their path. Smaller mudflows have occurred in this century, including one in 1947 that created a "ghost forest" of trees along Kautz Creek.

Today's Mt. Rainier actually consists of three primary summits, with the highest, Columbia Crest, forming the rim of a relatively recent lava cone. The other two, Liberty Cap and Point Success, remain from the older cone that once reached to 16,000 feet. The volcano has been relatively quiet for the past 2,500 years, but an eruption approximately 150 years ago released a plume of pumice, and steam explosions in the 1960s and '70s show that the mountain is still very much alive. The danger of a catastrophic eruption is not out of the question, but geologists warn that devastating mudflows are a more obvious danger to the mountain's neighbors.

Glaciation

While forces from within the earth have created massive Mt. Rainier, the forces from above have worked to wear it down. Glaciers—created when more snow falls than melts off—have proven one of the most important of these erosional processes. After a period of several years and under the weight of additional snow, the accumulated snow crystals change into ice. Gravity pulls this ice slowly downhill, creating what is essentially a frozen river that grinds against whatever lies in the way, plucking loose rocks and soil and polishing hard bedrock. This debris moves slowly down the glacier as if on a conveyer belt, eventually reaching its terminus.

During the last ice age, which ended around 10,000 years ago, the glaciers flowing out from Rainier stretched for up to 40 miles into lowland valleys, while smaller glaciers filled the mountain cirques. Since that time, several thousand years of warming was followed by a period of cooling—the Little Ice Age—that caused the glaciers to expand. Geologists say that we are still in that cooler period, although a long warming trend (accentuated by human activities in this century) has caused Mt. Rainier's glaciers to retreat considerably since the 1930s.

Spreading out from Mt. Rainier are some 40 glaciers, 25 that have names. Together, they represent the largest single-peak glacial system in the U.S. outside Alaska. (They probably wouldn't even rank in Alaska's top 50, however.) The largest of these, **Emmons Glacier,** heads down the northeast side and is visible from Sunrise, while Paradise Visitor Center showcases the **Nisqually Glacier.**

Climate

Because of its incredible height, Rainier creates its own weather by interrupting the air flow around it and causing wet air blowing off the Pacific Ocean to release its moisture. This produces massive amounts of snowfall on the western slopes of the mountain; a world-record 1,122 inches (more than 93 feet!) fell at Paradise in 1971-72. The mountain's height also accounts for its lenticular clouds—the upside-down-saucer-shaped clouds that obscure or hover just above the summit on otherwise clear days.

Although it can rain or snow any month of the year on Rainier, most of the precipitation arrives between October and early May, and nearly all of this falls as snow at the higher elevations. July and August are the driest and sunniest months. At Paradise (5,400 feet in elevation), the snowpack often tops 15 feet by late March, remaining on the ground until early July. Down the mountain at Longmire (2,761 feet in elevation), snow

MOUNT RAINIER NATIONAL PARK

averages four feet deep in mid-winter and is generally gone after early May.

Throughout most of the park, temperatures are not much different from those around Puget Sound; the nasty summer heat will sometimes follow you right up to Paradise, although generally the higher elevations enjoy cooler temperatures. The average summer day at Longmire is in the 70s, with nights dipping into the high 40s. Temperatures at Paradise are commonly around 10° cooler than this during the summer. Spring and fall are the times to be careful; rain at Longmire can very often translate to snow at Paradise. But fall weather also means fewer people and the brilliant yellow and red leaves of cottonwoods, vine maples, bigleaf maples, Sitka mountain ash, and blueberry bushes.

SIGHTS

Driving through Mount Rainier National Park provides numerous sightseeing and photographic opportunities; the surrounding mountains, waterfalls, forests, and canyons alone justify the trip. Several easily accessible places are especially noteworthy and are highlights of many travelers' journeys in Washington. The following descriptive tour begins in the southwest corner of the park and follows the main roads to the northeast corner.

Longmire Area
Longmire is seven miles from the Nisqually entrance in the southwest corner of the park. Named for James Longmire, whose Longmire Springs Resort first attracted large numbers of

travelers to the park, Longmire is home to the National Park Inn (housed in an old Longmire Mineral Springs Resort building), and the **Longmire Museum,** one of the oldest national park museums in existence. The small museum—located in the original park headquarters—contains displays on the park's natural history, along with exhibits of Indian basketry, a small totem pole, and photos from the early days of the park. It is open daily year-round 9 a.m.-4 p.m., with additional summertime hours. Nearby is a small transportation history museum inside the historic **Longmire Gas Station.**

Several nearby hiking trails cover the gamut, from easy strolls through the woods to steep mountain climbs. The **Wilderness Information Center** at Longmire, tel. (360) 569-2211, ext. 3317, can provide you with all the options. It's

open daily from early June through September. Less than a mile in length, the **Trail of the Shadows** takes you on a stroll around the meadow where Longmire's resort stood, with views of the mountain. A longer loop hike continues from here up Rampart Ridge to a majestic view over the Nisqually River far below, and then joins the Wonderland Trail. Follow this back to Longmire for a total distance of five miles.

More adventurous hikers can climb the many switchbacks to the summit of 5,958-foot **Eagle Peak,** a distance of seven miles roundtrip. The route passes through a wide range of vegetation, from dense old-growth stands along the Nisqually River to flowery alpine meadows offering extraordinary vistas across to Mt. Rainier. The mountain-encircling Wonderland Trail (see below) also passes through Longmire, making

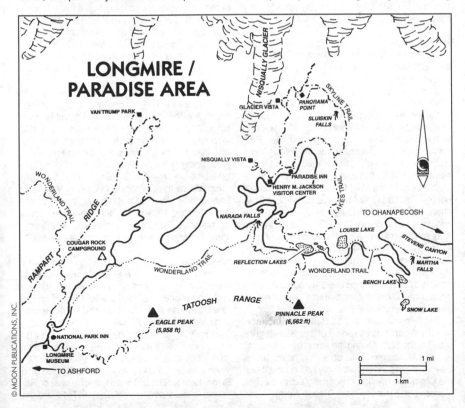

LONGMIRE / PARADISE AREA

© MOON PUBLICATIONS, INC.

Longmire's mineral
springs resort

this is a favorite starting point for backcountry hikes of varying lengths.

Paradise Area

The 13-mile drive from Longmire to Paradise is a delightful climb through tall evergreen forests where periodic openings provide down-valley and up-mountain vistas. Three miles before you reach Paradise is a pullout overlooking **Narada Falls,** where a steep trail leads to the plunge pool at its base. At an elevation of 5,400 feet, and with views across to the nearby mountain, Paradise Valley is appropriately named. When Virinda Longmire first visited this gorgeous area in the summer of 1885, the abundant wildflowers created a colorful contrast to the snowy summit of Mt. Rainier. "This must be what paradise is like!" she exclaimed, and thousands of tourists have concurred ever since. Get here in late July and August to see the peak of the floral display (and to join the throngs of fellow visitors who jam the parking lots and mountain trails on weekends.) Paradise is easily the most popular place in the park, with an abundance of short and long hiking trails, grand scenery, and ample winter recreation opportunities.

The flying saucer-shaped **Henry M. Jackson Visitor Center** at Paradise offers 360-degree views of the park. During the summer, naturalists lead walks and give talks on a daily basis, and a 20-minute video is shown every half-hour. Check the information desk for upcoming activities. The visitor center is open daily 9 a.m.-7 p.m. in the summer, with reduced daily hours in the spring and fall. It is open weekends and holidays only October 15 to early May. Call (360) 569-2211, ext. 2328, for specifics. Built in 1917, Paradise Inn offers mountain-vista accommodations (described below) and meals mid-May through September only.

A spider web of trails spins out over the subalpine forests and high-country meadows at Paradise; see the visitors center for a detailed map. Easiest is the **Nisqually Vista Trail,** a 1.2-mile loop hike that leads through flamboyantly floral high country meadows west of the visitor center. Almost everyone in decent physical condition takes the oft-crowded **Skyline Trail,** a five-mile romp above the timberline to Glacier Vista and Panorama Point. Needless to say, the views are extraordinary. Be sure to carry water and to stay on the path. Far too many folks wander off, creating damage to the meadows that takes years to restore.

Heading east from Paradise toward Stevens Canyon, the road passes **Reflection Lakes,** where on a calm and clear day the mirror-like surface reflects Mt. Rainier. The **Pinnacle Peak Trail** starts at the Reflection Lakes parking lot; hike this one-and-a-half-mile trail to the saddle between Pinnacle and Plummer Peaks for Mt. Rainier vistas. You'll gain 1,100 feet in elevation along the way.

An easier trail takes you uphill to **Bench and Snow Lakes.** The trailhead is a mile east of Reflection Lakes on Stevens Canyon Rd., and the path goes 1.25 miles each way, through late-summer meadows filled with bear grass and flowers.

Stevens Canyon/Ohanapecosh Area

East of Paradise, the road passes 100-foot-high **Martha Falls** and cuts across the slopes of Stevens Canyon as it follows Stevens Creek downhill. At **Box Canyon** a short trail leads to a footbridge spanning the deep but narrow gorge created by the Muddy Fork of the Cowlitz River. By the time you reach the junction with Hwy. 123, the road is deep within old-growth forests of Douglas fir and western hemlock at an elevation of just 2,200 feet.

The **Ohanapecosh Visitor Center** is open daily 9 a.m.-6 p.m. late June through September, and daily 9 a.m.-5 p.m. late May to mid-June and in early October. It is closed mid-October to late May. Call (360) 569-2211, ext. 2352, for specifics. Rangers lead two-hour walks several times a week during the summer months; see the information desk for specifics.

The **Grove of the Patriarchs Trail** starts just west of the Stevens Canyon entrance station and covers 1.5 miles of virgin forest terrain. This easy loop trail circles an island in the crystalline Ohanapecosh (oh-HAH-na-pee-kahsh) River, passing thousand-year-old Douglas firs, western hemlocks, and western red cedars that tower over a verdant fern-filled understory.

A longer hike, the **Silver Falls Trail**, follows the river in a three-mile loop that takes you to the 75-foot cataract of Silver Falls, passing a sidetrail to the site of Ohanapecosh Hot Springs Resort along the way. The resort was a popular Roaring-'20s vacation place, but the badly dilapidated building was closed in the 1960s and torn down by the Park Service. It's illegal to enter the shallow springs here, and there are no pools anyway. The trail begins at the Ohanapecosh Campground.

The **Shriner Peak Trail** starts from Hwy. 123, three and a half miles north of the Stevens Canyon entrance; park on the west side of the road about a half mile from the Panther Creek bridge. This eight-mile hike—about five hours roundtrip—is almost completely devoid of shade and ends up at a lookout/ranger station at Shriner Peak (5,846 feet).

Cayuse Pass

North from Ohanapecosh, Hwy. 123 follows the Ohanapecosh River and Chinook Creek upstream, reaching 4,694 feet at Cayuse Pass, 11 miles from the Stevens Canyon entrance station. Here the road meets Hwy. 410, which continues north past the White River entrance and east over Chinook Pass (see **Vicinity of Mount Rainier**), where Tipsoo Lake creates a picture-postcard image. Yakima is another 64 miles to the east.

Sunrise Area

The Sunrise area occupies a high subalpine plateau showcasing the northeast side of Mt. Rainier. Getting here is half the fun; a long series of switchbacks takes you 11 miles up from Hwy. 410, past the White River entrance station and through tall evergreen forests along the river before finally emerging into subalpine meadows offering all-encompassing vistas. Because of the rain-shadow effect, this side of Mt. Rainier gets far less precipitation than the western side, and the vegetation reflects this: grasses, sedges, and even whitebark pine are common here. The Sunrise area is also home to large numbers of elk during the summer and fall. Elk are not native to the park but were brought here from Yellowstone and other parts of the West between 1903 and 1933; around 1,500 of them now inhabit the park.

Located at 6,400 feet, the log cabin **Sunrise Visitor Center,** tel. (360) 569-2211, ext. 2357, is open daily 9 a.m.-6 p.m. July to early September; closed the rest of the year. It houses natural history displays and has viewing telescopes where you can check out Mt. Rainier's glaciers, including massive Emmons Glacier, largest in the Lower 48. The interpretive staff leads nature walks on a daily basis; stop by the information desk for times and destinations. Not far away is **Sunrise Lodge** with food and gifts, but no lodging. Open July-Sept. only.

Many trails head out from the Sunrise area, including sections of the Wonderland Trail and shorter hikes to nearby lakes and mountains. The **White River Hiker Information Center** at the entrance station has backcountry and climbing permits, along with maps and other information. The center is open daily late May through September. **Shadow Lake Trail** is one of the most popular of these, a three-mile jaunt that departs from Sunrise parking lot, drops to a rim overlooking the White River Valley, and then follows that ridge to Shadow Lake. Return via Frozen Lake and Sourdough Ridge.

To get to **Mt. Fremont Lookout** from the Sunrise parking lot, follow the trails to Sourdough Ridge and Frozen Lake, then branch off to the north. The mountain is 7,181 feet high, a gain of 1,200 feet. This well-marked six-mile path takes about three hours roundtrip.

For **Dege Peak,** start between Sunshine Point and the Sunrise parking area; this one-mile trail climbs 7,006-foot Dege Peak in the Sourdough Mountains.

Carbon River Area

Because of its location in the far northwest corner of the park, this part of Mount Rainier National Park sees considerably less visitation than others. The region is named for the coal deposits that once attracted miners, but it is best known today for its magnificent temperate rainforest. Access is via Hwy. 165 south from Buckley; a gravel road continues past the Carbon River Ranger Station to Ipsut Creek Campground, six miles inside the park. A second gravel road enters the park south of here and climbs to Mowich Lake, located in a high glacial cirque. Get information at the **Wilkeson Caboose** in the town of Wilkeson, tel. (360) 829-5127.

Take the quarter-mile **Carbon River Rain Forest Trail** for a quick taste of Mt. Rainier's only true rain forest. The **Carbon Glacier** extends northwest from Mt. Rainier, reaching just 1,100 feet in elevation at its terminus, the lowest of any glacier in the U.S. outside Alaska. A section of the Wonderland Trail leads from Ipsut Creek Campground to the snout of the glacier, three and a half miles each way. Watch out for rocks falling off the glacier.

From Mowich Lake, hike the three-mile trail past pretty Eunice Lake and on to the historic **Tolmie Peak** fire lookout at 5,939 feet in elevation.

BACKCOUNTRY HIKING

Rainier's hiking season is quite short: most trails are snow-free only from mid-July to mid-October,

though trails at the lower elevations may open earlier and remain snow-free later in the year. It's always advisable to dress for *all* seasons when hiking in the Cascades, carrying cotton, wool, and rain gear. About 300 miles of hiking trails crisscross the park, many miles of which are suitable for day hikes. More than a dozen of the most popular of these are described above; drop by one of the hiking or visitors centers upon your arrival for up-to-date trail info. The park has a helpful *Wilderness Trip Planner* available by mail; get a copy, along with other information, by calling the park's backcountry desk at (360) 569-2211, ext. 3317. *50 Hikes in Mount Rainier National Park,* by Ira Spring and Harvey Manning (Seattle: The Mountaineers), is a detailed guide to the park's many backcountry trails. A number of companies lead guided hikes in the park, including REI Adventures, tel. (800) 622-2236; contact the park for other concessionaires with similar services.

Backcountry Regulations

Backcountry permits are required for all overnight trips in the park throughout the year and are available for $10 for the group, plus $5 pp (or $40 pp total for an annual pass). Get them from the wilderness information centers and ranger stations in Longmire, White River, Wilkeson, Ohanapecosh, and Paradise. Permits are available up to 24 hours before you depart. If you're heading into a popular area on a busy weekend, your first choice may be full. Sunday-Thursday nights are far less crowded, so head out on these days if possible.

Fires are not allowed in the backcountry, so bring a stove along. Be sure to filter or otherwise treat any drinking water, since the protozoan *Giardia* and other harmful micro-organisms may be present. Always practice no-trace camping and haul out any garbage. Hikers in backcountry meadows should stay on the trails at all times; plants here have only a brief growing season, and damaged areas take a long time to recover. Pets are not allowed on any park trails.

There are three types of backcountry camps within the park. "Trailside camps" are located every 3-7 miles along backcountry trails, including the mountain-circling Wonderland Trail. Trailside camps all contain a nearby water source and pit toilet, and five people (in two tents) are allowed at an individual campsite. The vast majority of hikers use these established campsites. If you choose to camp away from these, you'll need to stay at "crosscountry camps," sites located a quarter-mile away from the trail and other camps and at least 100 feet from water sources. "Alpine camps" are in areas above 6,000 feet, and have their own rules; see the hiker information centers for details.

Wonderland Trail

The Wonderland Trail is a backpacker's dream: 93 miles of mountain passes, forests, streams, and alpine meadows that completely encircle the mountain. The trail has lots of ups and downs, including 3,500-foot changes in elevation in several stretches of the route. Allow 10 days to two weeks for the entire trip. Food (but not fuel) can be cached at ranger stations along the way by mailing packages to yourself; contact the Park Service at (360) 569-2211 for addresses and other specifics.

You can start your Wonderland hike almost anywhere—Mowich Lake, Longmire, White River, Box Canyon—but Ipsut Creek may be the best choice, since you'd be hitting the only showers in the park at Paradise about halfway through. A wide range of shorter one-way and loop hikes are also possible along the Wonderland Trail.

Also for marathon packers, the **Pacific Crest Trail** touches the east edge of the park at Tipsoo Lake on Hwy. 410, continuing north to British Columbia and south to Mexico. (See **Vicinity of Mount Rainier.**)

Other Trails

The **Mother Mountain Loop** is a rewarding one- or two-night trip in the northwest section of the park. Begin at the Ipsut Creek Campground, follow the Wonderland Trail up the Carbon River, and then turn onto the **Spray Park Trail.** The trail approaches Cataract Falls (a quick side trip), and crosses Marmot Creek. Camping is permitted about one mile below Seattle Park in Cataract Valley with a permit. Hike across a permanent snowfield into Spray Park (where avalanche lilies carpet the meadows late in the summer), and continue to Mowich Lake, turning northeast to follow the Wonderland Trail down Ipsut Creek and back to your starting point. It's about 16 miles roundtrip.

Another good overnighter, though not a circular route, is **Indian Bar.** This hike starts at Box Canyon on Stevens Canyon Rd., crosses Nickel Creek, then turns left to follow the Cowlitz Divide. At Indian Bar, the Ohanapecosh River divides a meadow; the shelter is on the west side, just above Wauhaukaupauken Falls. Return by the same route for a total of 15 miles.

Gobbler's Knob is a fire lookout (5,500 feet) that can be reached from Round Pass on Westside Rd., near the Nisqually entrance. This two-and-half-mile trail passes Lake George. Westside Rd. is closed at Fish Creek, three miles up, due to recurring floods that have washed out the road, so you may need to wade across (sometimes this is not safe). The area is always prone to floods and mudflows. Bikes are allowed on the road (but not off the road) beyond here, but be sure to get current conditions from the Park Service before heading up. The lookout is also accessible from outside the park via the tiny Glacier View Wilderness (see **Vicinity of Mount Rainier**).

CLIMBING

Because of its many glaciers and rocky faces, Mt. Rainier has long been one of the premier training peaks for American climbers. More than 4,500 people reach Mt. Rainier's summit every year—of some 9,000 who attempt it. Two days are usually required for the trek: the first day involves a four- to five-hour hike over trails and snowfields to Camp Muir, the south-side base camp at 10,000 feet, or Camp Schurman, on the northeast side, at 9,500 feet. The second day starts early (about 2 a.m.) for the summit climb and the return to the Paradise starting point. Reservations are not accepted for the high camps, so be prepared to camp outside: Muir's 25-person capacity is frequently filled, and Schurman has no public shelter—your only luxury is a pit toilet.

All climbers must be in top physical condition before heading out, and experience in glacier travel is highly recommended. Rainier is a difficult climb, and before heading up, you need to undertake a rigorous conditioning program. Above the high camps climbers are roped, using ice axes and crampons to inch their way over glaciers to the summit. All climbers must register and get a **climbing card** (a backcountry permit is not needed) at a hiker information center, visitor center, or ranger station before their climb. Solo climbers need the park superintendent's approval. To offset increasing costs (and decreasing support from Congress), the Park Service has instituted a $15 pp fee for all climbers heading above 10,000 feet on the mountain, or $25 pp for an annual pass to climb.

Guided Climbs
Even inexperienced climbers can conquer the mountain if they are in excellent physical condition. **Rainier Mountaineering, Inc.**—founded in part by famed mountain climber Louis Whittaker in 1968—offers guided treks up Mt. Rainier, along with snow- and ice-climbing seminars for climbers of all skill levels. The guides—including some of the most experienced in America—operate from the Guide House at Paradise (open daily in the summer). Rates are $90 for their one-day snow- and ice-climbing school (no reservations necessary), or $465 for a three-day summit climb package (one day of instruction plus the two-day climb). RMI also offers crevasse rescue seminars, private lessons, and six-day winter mountaineering seminars ($885). Some of the required equipment—including boots, crampons, ice ax, and pack—is available for rent at the Guide House in Paradise. RMI's climbing programs operate from late May to late September. For a brochure, call RMI in Paradise at (360) 569-2227 during the summer, or in Tacoma at (253) 627-6242 during the winter (October to mid-May).

In recent years, several other guide companies have been leading climbs up Mt. Rainier via the Emmons Glacier route, but this may change. Contact the park for the current status, and a list of other guide operations.

OTHER SUMMER RECREATION

Fishing is generally disappointing at Rainier; the fish, if you get any, are small. Or, as the Park Service notes, "angler's success is often less than anticipated." Park waters are not stocked—the trout and char are native, so restrictions are plentiful, and barbless hooks are recommended. No fishing license is required. Stop at any ranger station for current info on limits, fishing season, and closures. The park's lakes and ponds are ice-free from July to October; rivers, streams, and beaver ponds from late-May through late-October.

Nonmotorized **boating** is allowed on all park lakes except Frozen Lake, Reflection Lakes, Ghost Lake, and Tipsoo Lake; canoes are a great way to view the wildlife.

Horses are allowed on 100 miles of park trails; contact the Park Service for a horse trail map.

Cyclists find Mt. Rainier's roads to be steep, winding, and narrow—a prescription for trouble due to the heavy automobile traffic. Use extreme caution when cycling in the park since RVers have a reputation for not always knowing the width of their vehicles. None of the backcountry trails in the park are open to mountain bikes, although nearby Forest Service land has hundreds of miles of such trails.

WINTER RECREATION

Cross-Country Skiing
Mount Rainier is famous for its abundant backcountry, where the snow seems to reach out forever, and the Telemark skiing is unmatched in Washington. Many beginners head to the Paradise parking lot to ski up the unplowed road, or out the trails to Nisqually Vista, Narada Falls, or Reflection Lake. None of these are groomed, but it generally doesn't take long for other folks to set down tracks in the new snow. The area gets an incredible 630 inches of snow in a typical year!

The east-side roads provide other skiing options, including, of course, the groomed slopes at Crystal Mountain Ski Area, just a few miles outside the park's northeast corner. For a quieter experience, the Ohanapecosh area is a good bet. Park near the ranger station and ski up the roads toward Cayuse Pass or Box Canyon if you are ambitious, but be sure to check about avalanche dangers before heading up. Easier skiing can be found in the unplowed Ohanapecosh Campground loops.

Rent skis, avalanche beacons, snowshoes, and other winter gear from the Longmire store, tel. (360) 526-2411. They also provide ski lessons and tours. Ski rentals are not available at

Paradise. If you plan to overnight in the back-country be sure to get a permit before heading out; they are required year-round (but free in winter). Call (425) 526-6677 for current avalanche conditions, or talk with Park Service folks in Longmire before heading up the hill.

Other Snow Play
Facilities are open for winter sports at Paradise from December to April. The park constructs a supervised snow play area here·in early December; no snow sliding is allowed before that time to protect the vegetation. The area is very popular place for inner tubes, saucers, or other soft sliding toys, but no wooden toboggans or sleds with metal runners. Bring your own, since they are not available for rent.

Ranger-led **Snowshoe walks** are offered at the Paradise Visitor Center on winter weekends and holidays. Rent snowshoes for just $1.

ACCOMMODATIONS AND CAMPING

Inns
There are two inns within the park itself; both are run by the park concessionaire, Mount Rainier Guest Services, tel. (360) 569-2275, or on the Web at www.guestservices.com/rainier. The **National Park Inn** at Longmire is open daily year-round. This inn has a central stone fireplace, and decent rooms for $66-91 s or d with shared or private baths. Built in 1917, **Paradise Inn** is an imposing wooden lodge with high ceilings, stone fireplaces, and unsurpassed mountain views from its elevation of 5,400 feet. The lodge is open daily from late May through September; rooms (nothing fancy here) are $69-98 s or d with shared or private baths.

A broad spectrum of accommodations outside the park are described below; see the towns of Ashford, Enumclaw, Eatonville, Elbe, and Morton.

Campgrounds
Mount Rainier National Park has 600 drive-in campsites around the park, all with running water and flush or pit toilets, but no RV hookups. Coin-op showers are available at the Paradise Visitor Center when it is open, but you'll need to head to Ashford or other towns for laundry facilities.

Gathering firewood is prohibited in the park, but it can be purchased at the Cougar Rock and Ohanapecosh Campgrounds, as well as the Longmire General Store.

The park's five campgrounds are: **Sunshine Point Campground,** located just inside the southwest entrance at Nisqually ($10; open year-round); **Cougar Rock Campground,** two and a half miles northeast of Longmire ($12, or $14 with reservations; open late May to mid-October); **Ohanapecosh Campground,** near the southeast entrance on Hwy. 123 ($12, or $14 with reservations; open late May to mid-October); **White River Campground,** on the east side in the Sunrise area ($10; open late June to late September); and **Ipsut Creek Campground,** at the end of the Carbon River Rd. in the northwest corner ($10; open late May to late September; free walk-in use only in the winter, but no water). The free **Mowich Lake Campground** in the northwest corner of the park is open mid-July to mid-November, and has walk-in sites. Reservations are *required* July 1 to Labor Day for the Ohanapecosh and Cougar Rock campgrounds; call (877) 444-6777. Camping is not permitted in the Paradise area or along park roads in the summer, but winter camping is allowed at Paradise once the snow depth tops five feet. Get permits and details on locating your camp from the visitor center.

FOOD

Longmire has a sit-down restaurant inside the **National Park Inn,** tel. (360) 569-2411, which is open year-round. The dining room at **Paradise Inn,** tel. (360) 569-2413, serves three meals a day and a big Sunday brunch during its season of operation from late May through September. For something less formal, the **Henry M. Jackson Visitor Center** at Paradise contains a snack bar with typical fast food; open daily May to early October, and on weekends and holidays the rest of the year.

The cafeteria at **Sunrise Lodge** operates only between late June and early September. Limited groceries are available year-round at Longmire General Store and during the summer at Sunrise. For food outside park limits, see the towns of Greenwater, Ashford, Elbe, Eatonville, Packwood, Randle, Morton, and Mossyrock.

INFORMATION AND SERVICES

Getting In
Entrance to Mount Rainier National Park is $10 per vehicle, and $5 per person for folks arriving by foot and on bikes, motorcycles, buses, or horses. Your entrance fee is good for seven days. If you plan to visit several parks, get a $50 Golden Eagle Pass that lets you in all of the nation's national parks for a year. Seniors over age 62 can pay a one-time fee of $10 for a Golden Age Passport that lets them in all national parks. No charge for disabled visitors or kids under 17.

Information
Information and assorted publications are available at visitor centers in Longmire, Paradise, Ohanapecosh, and Sunrise, and from the various entrance stations. The park's quarterly newspaper, *Tahoma,* is packed with up-to-date details on park activities, camping, hiking, climbing, and facilities. Get a copy in advance of your visit, along with a park map and other brochures, by calling the Park Service at (360) 569-2211. The **Northwest Interpretive Association** has a mail-order catalog of publications and topographic maps; call (360) 569-2211, ext. 3320. Park headquarters are located nine miles outside the park in Ashford's Tahoma Woods area, tel. (360) 569-2211. Find them on the Web at www.nps.gov/mora.

Services
Gift shops are found at Sunrise, Paradise, and Longmire. Camping supplies are limited in the park; it's better to bring yours in from the outside. Climbing supplies—including boots, crampons, ice axes, and packs—can be rented from the RMI Guide House at Paradise, or Summit Haus in Ashford.

Park **post offices** are in Paradise Inn (summers) and Longmire's National Park Inn (all year). Short on cash? The closest ATM is located in Ashford at Ashford Valley Grocery.

Interpretive Programs
The National Park Service schedules nature walks, campfire programs, and children's activities from July to late September. Program schedules are posted at visitor centers and campgrounds, as well as in the park newspaper, *Tahoma.* Come winter, naturalists offer snowshoe walks at Paradise.

TRANSPORTATION AND TOURS

In 1911, the first automobile to reach Mount Rainier National Park carried president William H. Taft aboard. Since then, the car has become the primary means of transportation to the park, with many visitors following the roads along the park's southern and eastern margins. Gasoline is not available inside the park, so be sure to fill your tank in surrounding towns.

Winter Roads
Winter snow closes most of Mt. Rainier's roads, with the exception of the section between the Nisqually entrance and Paradise. This road closes each night and reopens in the morning after the plows have cleared any new-fallen snow. Chains are frequently required and should always be carried. The road between Paradise and Ohanapecosh is generally open Memorial Day to early November, while Hwy. 123 and 410 over Cayuse Pass usually opens in late April and remains open till the first heavy snowfall (November). Chinook Pass is open from early June to sometime in November, and the road to Sunrise generally opens by the first of July and closes once the snow gets too deep, frequently in early October. Early snows can close any of these, so be sure to call ahead at (360) 569-2211 to see which roads are open. The Longmire store sells tire chains.

Bus Tours
Rainier Shuttles, tel. (360) 569-2331, has bus connections from SeaTac to Paradise ($34) via Eatonville and Ashford. **Mt. Rainier Shuttle Service,** tel. (360) 569-0851, offers a similar service, plus trailhead drop-offs and custom trips.

Gray Line, tel. (206) 626-5208 or (800) 426-7532, leads hurried day trips to the park from Seattle ($45 adults, $23 kids), along with overnight trips that include a stay at Paradise Inn for $135. **Scenic Bound Tours,** tel. (206) 433-6907 or (888) 293-1404, has even more rushed tours that depart Seattle and take you to both Mt. St. Helens and Mt. Rainier in one day for $65.

VICINITY OF MOUNT RAINIER

WILDERNESS AREAS

Half-a-dozen wilderness areas cover more than 356,000 acres of mountainous Forest Service terrain in the Mt. Rainier Area. The largest of these—Norse Peak, William O. Douglas, and Goat Rocks Wilderness Areas—form an almost continuous reach of wild country along the crest of the southern Cascades, broken only by Hwy. 410 near Chinook Pass and Hwy. 12 at White Pass.

Before heading out to the wilderness areas below, check with a local ranger station, or purchase the *Washington's Backcountry Access Guide* (Seattle: The Mountaineers), for details on regulations in each area. Find it online at www.mountaineers.org.

A fee of $3 per vehicle per day is charged at all Forest Service trailheads. A better option is the $25 annual **Trail Park Pass** that can be used on most Washington national forests. Buy one at any Forest Service office.

Norse Peak Wilderness

This 50,923-acre wilderness reaches north from Hwy. 410 and just west of the Crystal Mountain Ski Area and covers rocky ridges, steep valleys, and forests of Douglas fir, western red cedar, and western hemlock. The **Pacific Crest Trail** climbs across the backbone of these ridges for approximately 27 miles from Gov-

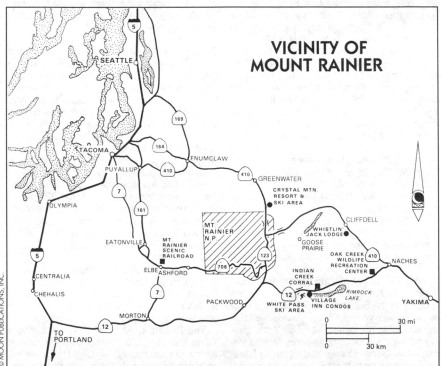

VICINITY OF MOUNT RAINIER

ernment Meadow (accessible via Forest Rd. 70) on the north end, to Hwy. 410 near Chinook Pass on the south end. Along the way it cruises over high ridges, including two that top 6,400 feet; a popular side path leads to the summit of 6,856-foot Norse Peak for extraordinary views across to Mt. Rainier. The **Fifes Peaks** area on the east side of the wilderness is popular with rock climbers, but the rock can be weak in places. Some of the easiest access to the Pacific Crest Trail comes from near the Crystal Mountain Ski Area. Several paths leave from this area, including the **Silver Creek Trail** (No. 1192) and **Bullion Basin Trail** (No. 1156), both of which reach the PCT in a bit over two miles of hiking.

For a short hike with excellent views of Mt. Rainier, head 32 miles east from Enumclaw on Hwy. 410 to Corral Pass Rd. (No. 7174), and follow it seven miles to a parking area just before the Corral Pass Campground. From here, the appropriately named **Rainier View Trail** climbs for a mile to a 6,080-foot ridge overlooking the mountain. This is a popular camping place, but carry water since none is available at the ridge. The trail continues beyond this, connecting with the Castle Mountain Trail, 2.2 miles from your starting point. An additional five miles of hiking brings you to the Pacific Crest Trail near Martinson Gap. Check with the Forest Service for the condition of Castle Mountain Trail; at last check it was difficult to follow.

William O. Douglas Wilderness

Covering 167,195 acres, the William O. Douglas Wilderness is a delightful slice of wild mountain country that includes hundreds of small lakes, more than 250 miles of trails, and grand ridges that offer panoramic views. The wilderness is named for the Supreme Court Justice whose environmental stands helped create areas such as this, and who spent considerable time hiking in these mountains.

William O. Douglas Wilderness is accessible via Hwy. 410 on the north side, Hwy. 12 on the south, and the Bumping River Rd. in the center, along with various Forest Service roads on the east side. Bumping Lake Rd. leads past eight Forest Service campgrounds, the little settlement of Goose Prairie, and Bumping Lake. Boats can be rented and RV spaces are available at **Bumping Lake Marina,** tel. (509) 575-0417, and **Goose Prairie Inn,** tel. (509) 837-3767, has a restaurant and cabin rentals (but these are generally only available in the fall and winter).

The **Pacific Crest Trail** heads through the southwest side of the wilderness for 14 miles; access it from Highways 12 and 410 on either end. Within the wilderness, the PCT passes many small lakes, marshes, tarns, and meadows, topping out on a 5,740-foot ridge where you can enjoy the mountain spectacle.

For an interesting loop trip that includes a section of the PCT, take Bumping River Rd. past Bumping Lake, and turn onto Rd. 18 to its end where the **Bumping Lake Trail** (No. 971) climbs the headwaters of the Bumping River to Fish Lake. Here you turn north on the PCT, follow it to the **American Ridge Trail** (No. 958), and then two miles to the **Swamp Lake Trail** (No. 970), where you turn again to reach your starting point. The roundtrip distance is approximately 27 miles for this loop hike.

A long one-way trek is the **American Ridge Trail** (No. 958), which starts just off Hwy. 410 and eventually meets the PCT after coursing over 27 miles of forests, ridges, and mountaintops, including 7,473-foot Goat Peak. At the PCT, you can turn north to connect back with Hwy. 410, but you'll need to catch a ride back to your starting point or set up a vehicle shuttle.

Goat Rocks Wilderness

At 105,633 acres, Goat Rocks Wilderness occupies a long stretch of rocky volcanic peaks, alpine meadows, and open mountain country. The wilderness sits just south of Hwy. 12 (William O. Douglas Wilderness is on the north side of this route) and is also accessible from the southeast side via Forest Rd. 21, along with a myriad of other logging roads on the northeast and northwest margins.

A new backcountry permit system is being discussed for Goat Rocks Wilderness; call **Cowlitz Valley Ranger Station** in Randle, tel. (360) 497-1100 for details. They can also provide details on snow levels and trail conditions.

The **Pacific Crest Trail** (PCT) intersects White Pass as it continues north to Chinook Pass and south through the Goat Rocks Wilderness, on its long path to Canada and Mexico.

The PCT follows the crest of the Cascades for 36 miles through the Goat Rocks Wilderness, passing through some alpine meadows but generally following rough terrain 4,200 to 7,500 feet in elevation. The two miles between Elk Pass and Packwood Glacier are the most hazardous, but the scenery here is also the most spectacular. The trail is usually snow-free from late July to mid-September, but even in late August you can expect to cross snowfields up to a half mile across, so bring your ice ax and warm clothing—several hikers have died from hypothermia on these exposed ridges.

For a fine, but oft-crowded 13-mile loop trip, begin at the Berry Patch trailhead near Chambers Lake Campground at the end of Forest Rd. 2150 on the southwest side of the wilderness. The **Snowgrass Trail** (No. 96) climbs past high meadows near Snowgrass Flat, well known for its summertime wildflowers; no camping here. From here, you can connect in with the PCT, and follow **Lily Basin Trail** (No. 86) along the ridge, and then return via exposed **Goat Ridge Trail** (No. 95) to your starting point.

Tatoosh Wilderness

This 15,800-acre wilderness abuts the southeast flank of Mount Rainier National Park and is one of the few remaining parcels of unlogged Forest Service land for miles. The nine-mile **Tatoosh Trail** (No. 161) is a strenuous forest and alpine hike but has outstanding views, especially if you take the side route to the 6,310-foot mountain that was formerly topped by Tatoosh Lookout. Another enjoyable side trail leads a half-mile to Tatoosh Lakes. Get to the trailhead by turning off Hwy. 12 at the Packwood Ranger Station and following Forest Rd. 52 to Rd. 5270, which takes you to the trailhead, a distance of 11 miles from the Ranger Station.

A new backcountry permit system is being discussed for Tatoosh Wilderness; call **Cowlitz Valley Ranger Station** in Randle, tel. (360) 497-1100, for details.

Glacier View Wilderness

Tiny Glacier View Wilderness covers just a bit over 3,000 acres on the southwest side of Mount Rainier National Park near the town of Ashford. The **Puyallup Trail** (No. 248) ascends from Forest Rd. 59 for two and a half miles to the park boundary, continuing eastward an equal distance to the park's Westside Road. A side route climbs 5,485-foot **Gobbler's Knob** for a grand view of Mt. Rainier.

A new backcountry permit system is being discussed for Glacier View Wilderness; call **Cowlitz Valley Ranger Station** in Randle, tel. (360) 497-1100, for details.

Clearwater Wilderness

This 14,300-acre wilderness occupies an oddly shaped parcel of unlogged land near the northern edge of Mount Rainier National Park. Much of the surrounding lands have been clearcut. Access is from Forest Service roads off Hwy. 410 along the West Fork White River and from the Carbon River Rd. area. The **Carbon Trail** (No. 1179) cuts across this small wilderness for 9.4 miles, with a mile-long spur to the summit of 6,089-foot Bearhead Mountain, which provides views across the alpine meadows to still-wild Mt. Rainier and the heavily logged slopes of adjacent private and Forest Service lands. Get to the eastern end of Carbon Trail by following Forest Rd. 74 from Hwy. 410, and turning up Rd. 7450 to its end at the trailhead. From the west, take the Carbon River Rd. from Wilkenson, and turn up Rd. 7810 to its end beyond Copley Lake at the trailhead.

CHINOOK PASS

The highest of the Cascade mountain passes, Chinook Pass rises more than a mile above sea level (5,440 feet) on Hwy. 410. This is a fair-weather route, closed in winter and often dusted with snow as late as June. Just west of the pass, the highway enters Mount Rainier National Park, passing **Tipsoo Lake,** one of the most beautiful and easily accessed Cascade alpine lakes. Enjoy a picnic lunch here against a striking Mt. Rainier backdrop. More adventurous folks will enjoy the **Naches Peak Loop,** a three-and-a-half-mile hike that skirts the lakeshore and then circles this mountain. Part of this loop follows the Pacific Crest Trail.

Boulder Cave is up a forest road just west of the little settlement of Cliffdell on Hwy. 410. Take a flashlight to explore this tunnel-like cavern.

Cliffdell to Naches

Whistlin' Jack Lodge, 25 miles northwest of Naches (Na-CHEEZ) on Hwy. 410, tel. (509) 658-2433 or (800) 827-2299, is on the sunny side of the mountains, with just 15 inches of precipitation annually and over 300 days of sunshine. Open year-round, the lodge includes a motel, cabins, restaurant, lounge with live music on weekends, gas, and groceries. Rooms cost $90 s or d for motel units, $140-220 d for cabins with kitchens (some with private hot tubs). The restaurant is also noteworthy.

Squaw Rock Resort, 20 miles northwest of Naches on Hwy. 410, tel. (509) 658-2926, has cabins for $75-85 d with fireplaces and kitchens, and motel units for $60-65 d; amenities include a heated pool, hot tub, restaurant, store, and public showers.

The Cozy Cat B&B, 17 miles west of Naches on Hwy. 410, tel. (509) 658-2953, has two guest rooms with private baths for $55 s or $65 d, including a light breakfast. The location is close to a small pond and offers fine mountain vistas.

Apple Country Inn B&B, tel. (509) 965-0344, is a remodeled 1911 farm house and working ranch. Two guest rooms have private baths, a continental breakfast is served, and kids are okay; $75 s or d.

Campgrounds

Get regional camping and hiking info from the **Naches Ranger District,** tel. (509) 653-2205. The Forest Service has many popular campgrounds along Hwy. 410 between Enumclaw and Naches, including **The Dalles Campground,** located 26 miles southeast of Enumclaw and five miles from the northern edge of Mount Rainier National Park. The short and easy **Dalles River Trail** leaves from the campground and follows the White River. The main attraction here is a Douglas fir tree that reaches almost 10 feet in diameter. **Silver Springs Campground** is near the turnoff to Crystal Mountain Resort on Hwy. 410. Both of these are open mid-May to mid-October, cost $12, and can be reserved ($9 extra) by calling (877) 444-6777. More than a dozen other Forest Service campgrounds can be found just off Hwy. 410 between the park and the town of Naches; some are free, others charge $7-12. These are only available on a first-come, first-camp basis.

WHITE PASS

Highway 12 between Yakima and Mt. Rainier traverses 4,500-foot White Pass. The route climbs westward along the Tieton River through heavily forested areas with a few clear views of Rainier along the way.

White Pass Ski Area

Located off Hwy. 12 about 55 miles west of Yakima, and 12 miles southeast of Mount Rainier National Park, White Pass Ski Area offers a 1,500-foot vertical drop and 650 acres of skiing, served by five chairlifts (including a high-speed quad chair), a Poma, and rope tow. The base elevation is 4,500 feet. Amenities include a ski and snowboard lessons and rentals, child care, cafeteria, and bar. Weekend rates are $33 adults, $21 kids and seniors, with lower midweek rates. Call (509) 672-3100 for more information or the snow report.

Practicalities

Near the ski area, **White Pass Village Inn,** tel. (509) 672-3131, has condos of various sizes (studio units are $80-85 d in winter), including a winter-only heated outdoor pool. Nearby, find a store, gas station, and the **Summit House Restaurant,** tel. (509) 672-3111.

Eight miles east of White Pass Ski Area on Hwy. 12, **Indian Creek Corral** offers one-hour to three-day horseback rides in the summer, and hikers can take advantage of their drop-camp service. Call (509) 925-2062 for more info.

Rimrock Lake Area

Traveling along Hwy. 12, you can't miss **Rimrock Lake,** just a few miles east of White Pass. This massive blue-green lake was created in 1927 by what was then one of the largest earth-filled dams in the country. Today Rimrock is popular with anglers in search of good-sized silvers mid-May to late June, and with boaters, swimmers, and campers.

On the lake, **Twelve West,** tel. (509) 672-2460, has RV hookups, a marina, and a fine restaurant serving three meals daily. Open year-round. **The Cove Resort,** tel. (509) 672-2470, two miles to the east, also has an RV park, marina, and a restaurant on Rimrock Lake. Open mid-April to mid-October.

Silver Beach Resort, 40350 Hwy. 12, tel. (509) 672-2500, has rustic cabins with kitchenettes for $60 (sleeps four), RV hookups, and a boat dock. **Trout Lodge,** 27090 Hwy. 12 , tel. (509) 672-2211, has a four-unit motel ($35 s, $45 d), store, and restaurant. **Game Ridge Motel,** tel. (509) 672-2212 or (800) 301-9354, has additional motel rooms and cabins (some with kitchenettes and private hot tubs) for $43-95 s or d. It's right along the Tieton River, with a striking mountain backdrop, an outdoor pool, and jacuzzi.

Tieton River Rafting
The Tieton River is one of the more challenging rivers in Washington, dropping 50 feet per mile from Rimrock Dam to the confluence of the Tieton and Naches River, 20 miles downriver. The river is rated class III (intermediate), and the terrain begins high in the mountains and descends through basalt canyons into the dry valley on the east side of the Cascades. It is best late in the season; most rafting companies run it in September, though you'll find folks out there Aug.-October. Trip lengths vary between the companies. Expect to pay $60-75 for a half-day excursion, depending upon the number in your group and the company. Contact one of the following for more info: **All Rivers Adventures,** tel. (800) 743-5628; **Alpine Adventures,** (800) 723-8386; **Alpine Whitewater,** tel. (800) 926-7238; **Blue Sky Outfitters,** tel. (800) 228-7238; **Downstream River Runners,** tel. (800) 234-4644; **North Cascades River Expeditions,** tel. (800) 634-8433; **River Riders, Inc.,** tel. (800) 448-7238; **Orion Expeditions,** tel. (800) 553-7466; **Osprey Rafting,** tel. (800) 743-6269; **River Recreation,** tel. (800) 464-5899; and **Wildwater River Tours,** tel. (800) 522-9453.

Elk and Bighorn Sheep
During most winters, the large White Pass elk population and a small herd of bighorn sheep are fed at the **Oak Creek Wildlife Recreation Area,** two miles west of the intersection of Highways 410 and 12, and 17 miles west of Yakima. Best times to see them are early morning or late afternoon when the animals are most active. Call (509) 575-2740 for more info.

CRYSTAL MOUNTAIN AND GREENWATER

Crystal Mountain Ski Area
This year-round resort on Hwy. 410, just outside the north Mount Rainier National Park boundary, has winter Nordic and alpine skiing, plus hiking, fishing, swimming, tennis, horseback riding, and chairlift sightseeing rides from July to early September. Many folks consider this Washington's finest skiing and snowboarding, with a wide diversity of runs and state-of-the-art snow grooming. The ski resort boasts 3,100 vertical feet, 10 lifts (including two high-speed six-passenger chairs) serving 1,300 acres, plus 1,000 acres of backcountry trails. With a top elevation of 7,002 feet—highest in the state—you'll have a fantastic view of nearby Mt. Rainier on clear days.

Adult lift rates are $35. Other services at Crystal Mountain include rentals, ski and snowboard schools, day care, and lots of food and lodging options. Access to a hot tub, fitness room, sauna, and showers costs $5. For more info on the resort, call (360) 663-2265, or get snow conditions at (888) 754-6199. Summer visitors can ride the chairlift to the Summit Restaurant (see below) for $10.

Crystal Mountain is 76 miles from Seattle. The **Crystal Mountain Express,** tel. (800) 665-2122, provides bus service on from Seattle, Bellevue, and Tacoma on weekends and holidays from late Dec.-February. The cost is $49 roundtrip transport, including an all-day lift ticket.

Hiking and River Running
Several popular hiking trails lead from the Crystal Mountain area to the **Pacific Crest Trail** in the nearby Norse Peak Wilderness Area. Another favorite is the **Crystal Mountain Trail** (No. 1163), a 12-mile loop hike (or mountain bike ride) that follows the ridge along Crystal Mountain. The lazy way to do this is to ride the chairlift to Summit House and hike down.

Lodging
Crystal Mountain Lodging Suites, tel. (360) 663-2558 or (888) 668-4368, has one- and two-bedroom condos within walking distance of the lifts for $145-230 on winter weekends. Save

considerably on weekdays, in summer, or with ski package deals. All condos have kitchens; some have fireplaces and an outdoor heated pool.

Crystal Mountain Hotels, tel. (360) 663-2262 or (888) 754-6400, has rooms at the Village Inn, Alpine Inn, and Quicksilver Lodge near the base of the mountain. Winter weekend rates are $70-125 s or d for motel rooms, or $40 d in a room with bunkbeds and shared bath. Crystal Mountain Hotels are open early November-April only. **RV hookups** are available year-round in the resort parking lot.

Alta Crystal Resort, tel. (360) 663-2556 or (800) 277-6475, is two miles north of Mt. Rainier on Hwy. 410. It includes a central lodge, one- and two-bedroom condo units with kitchens and fireplaces ($119-169 d), and a luxurious honeymoon cabin ($179 d). Outside is a hot tub and swimming pool, plus hiking/skiing trails. Kids love the nightly bonfires in the summer.

Food

Food of all types is available at on-the-mountain and base eateries. The **Summit House,** tel. (360) 663-2300, accessible only by chairlift, is the highest restaurant in the state and offers a phenomenal view of Mt. Rainier; watch for climbers approaching the summit. Open for lunch and dinner, the Summit House is a favorite place to watch the sunset over Mt. Rainier. Reservations are strongly recommended on weekends.

In Greenwater, the **Naches Tavern,** tel. (360) 663-2267, is a cozy country place with a friendly atmosphere and good food served in large quantities.

ASHFORD

Ashford is your last chance for food, lodging, and gas before you enter Mount Rainier National Park. Rather than being a "last resort," some of the hotels, cabins, and restaurants here are as good or better than park facilities. Established in 1891, Ashford began as an end-of-the-line town where tourists stepped off the Tacoma Eastern Railroad cars to enter the park.

For incredible views of Mt. Rainier, head north from Ashford on Copper Creek Rd. (Forest Rd. 59). The road also provides access to the Glacier View Wilderness. Unfortunately, there's also a lot of deforested land around here, including an enormous gouge cut from the hills just south of Ashford and right next to the national park.

Mount Tahoma Trails

Halfway between Elbe and Ashford is Mt. Tahoma Trails, featuring 75 miles of groomed cross-country skiing in the winter, and mountain biking, horseback riding, and hiking on the trails in the summer. A series of three huts and a yurt provide overnight accommodations for six people (up to 12 in some of these), making it possible to

timberland near Ashford

ski or hike from hut to hut. No charge to stay in the huts, but a $25 pp/night damage deposit is required in advance, and you'll need a Sno-Park permit to park your vehicle. Get maps and current conditions from Whittakers, tel. (360) 569-2451.

Accommodations

Ashford has quite a few comfortable cabins, B&Bs, and lodges. Because of their popularity, reserve space at least two weeks ahead for midsummer. At the budget end, **Whittaker's Bunkhouse,** 30205 Hwy. 706 E, tel. (360) 569-2439, is a well-maintained facility popular with the climbing and hiking crowd. Built in 1912 as a logger's bunkhouse, it was renovated in 1990, but the floors are still pockmarked by the corked boots from loggers who once stayed here. Warm up in the hot tub, or head to the espresso shop for a cup of java. Dorm rooms are $25 pp, and private rooms cost $65-90 s or d.

Another unique and recommended place is **Wellspring,** two miles east of Ashford; tel. (360) 569-2514, which offers attractive log cabin lodging, a hot tub, and two rooms with their own wood-fired saunas; $85-95 s or d. A continental breakfast is served. The sauna and hot tub, plus massage therapy, are also available on an hourly basis for folks not staying here.

Alexander's Country Inn 37515 Hwy. 706 E (a mile west of the park entrance), tel. (360) 569-2300 or (800) 654-7615, occupies the top end of the lodging spectrum. Constructed in 1912 (with more recent additions), the inn was visited by presidents Theodore Roosevelt and William Howard Taft early in this century, was closed for many years, and has been lovingly restored to its original beauty, with antique furnishings, fireplaces, stained-glass windows, and the modern addition of a jacuzzi; $89 s or d with shared bath; $135 s or d with private bath. A full breakfast is served.

Jasmer's B&B and Cabins, 30005 Hwy. 706 E, tel. (360) 569-2682, has rooms in a guest house for $45-95, including a continental breakfast, or $80-165 in six-person cabins with kitchens (some with hot tubs); two-night minimum in the cabins.

Growly Bear B&B, 37311 Hwy. 706 E, tel. (360) 569-2339 or (800) 700-2339, $70 s or $80-105 s or d, is an 1890 home with two guest rooms (private or shared bath), and full breakfasts.

A classic old 1910 home, **Mountain Meadows Inn B&B,** 28912 Hwy. 706 E, tel. (360) 569-2788, $85 s or $95-110 d, has six guest rooms with private baths and a lovely country setting. Outside is a sauna, fishing pond, and nature trails. A full breakfast is served.

Hershey Homestead, 33514 Mt. Tahoma Canyon Rd., tel. (360) 569-2897, has two cottages with full kitchens; $135 for a family of five in the larger one, or $115 for three in the smaller. A continental breakfast is served.

Lodges and Cabins

Nisqually Lodge, 31609 Hwy. 706 E; tel. (360) 569-8804 or (888) 674-3554, has large motel rooms, a jacuzzi, and continental breakfast for $67-77 s or d.

Three miles from the park entrance is **Stormking Cabin and Spa,** tel. (360) 569-2964, a luxurious new cabin with a woodstove, private hot tub on a covered deck, and distinctive greenhouse shower. It's very popular with honeymooners, and the owner also offers massages. No kids; $95 d. Hot tub rentals are available by the hour when the cabin isn't in use.

Mounthaven at Mt. Rainier 38210 Hwy. 706 E, tel. (360) 569-2594 or (800) 456-9380, has a dozen cabins with kitchenettes, fireplaces or stoves; $59-125 s or d. Two-night minimum on weekends.

Rainier Overland Lodge, 31811 Hwy. 706 E, tel. (360) 569-0851, rents two cabins with kitchens for $105 s or d, or stay in motel accommodations for $65-85 s or d.

The Cabinette, Ashford, tel. (360) 569-2954, $80-90 d, includes two small luxurious cabins with a hot tub, kitchenettes, and fireplaces. No kids.

Close to the park entrance at 38624 Hwy. 706 E, **Mt. Rainier Country Cabins,** tel. (360) 569-2355 or (800) 678-3942, has cabins with kitchenettes and fireplaces for $80 s or d. Also near the park entrance, **Gateway Inn Motel,** 38820 Hwy. 706 E, tel. (360) 569-2506, charges $70 d for rustic log cabins with fireplaces.

The Lodge Near Mt. Rainier, 38608 Hwy. 706 E, tel. (360) 569-2312, has cabins with kitchens and fireplaces for $59-79 s or d. Larger groups (up to 16 people) can rent the lodges or chalet for $275-375/day.

Just a mile from the park entrance, **The Cabin at Berry** tel. (360) 569-2858, has two rustic cottages with full kitchens for $65 s or d.

Campgrounds

The closest public campsites ($10; open year-round) are just inside the southwest entrance to Mount Rainier National Park at **Sunshine Point Campground.**

Park RVs at **Mounthaven at Cedar Park,** 38210 Hwy. 706 E, tel. (360) 569-2594, and **Ashford Valley Store,** tel. (360) 569-2560. **Highlander Tavern and Laundry,** tel. 569-2953, offers an unusual mix: suds on tap, suds in the laundromat, and showers to suds up after a backcountry trip.

Food

The finest food (priced accordingly) in the Mt. Rainier area is served at **Alexander's Country Inn,** tel. (360) 569-2300, where specialties include salmon, fresh trout (catch your own from the backyard pond), home-baked bread, and famous wild blackberry pie. They also offer a large wine list.

Rainier Overland Lodge, 31811 Hwy. 706, tel. (360) 569-0851, serves big family style breakfasts, a good chicken BLT sandwich, and a choice of all-American faves. Get espresso coffees and sweets at **Whittaker's Bunkhouse,** 30205 Hwy. 706 E, tel. (360) 569-2439.

For pizza, sandwiches, nachos, and over 60 beers and wines, head to **Wild Berry Restaurant,** 37720 Hwy. 706 E, tel. (360) 569-2628. It's open every day and has an imaginative menu of chicken crepes, pizzas, and, of course, blackberry pie. Don't come here in a hurry.

Information and Services

Call **Mt. Rainier Business Association,** tel. (360) 569-0910, for local brochures. After a weekend of hiking in the park, head to **Well-spring,** tel. (360) 569-2514, for a relaxing massage, sauna, and hot tub. **Stormking Cabin and Spa,** tel. (360) 569-2964, offers massage and hot tub rental when their cabin isn't rented.

Summit Haus next to Whittaker's, tel. (360) 569-2142, sells and rents a wide range of camping and outdoor clothing and gear. Summits Adventure Travel leads treks all over the world, from hiking trips in the Italian Dolomites to mountaineering expeditions in the Andes. Call (360) 569-2992 for details.

ELBE

Fourteen miles from Mount Rainier National Park, Elbe is a wide spot in the road and a pleasant place to enjoy the foothill sights with a dose of railroad memorabilia. Visitors can eat dinner aboard the Cascadian Dinner Train, spend a night in a caboose at Hobo Inn, or peek inside Elbe's **Evangelische Lutherische Kirche,** a tiny white clapboard church measuring just 18 by 24 feet.

Mount Rainier Scenic Railroad

One way to view the area west of Mt. Rainier is from the Mt. Rainier Scenic Railroad, tel. (360) 569-2588 or (888) 783-2611. The vintage steam train leaves Elbe Station for a 14-mile, 90-minute ride over bridges and through forests, with live music accompanying the impressive views. The train runs weekends Memorial Day through September, and daily from June 15 through Labor Day. Fares are $10.50 adults, $9.50 seniors, $8.50 ages 12-17, and $7.50 kids under 12.

DON PITCHER

A more luxurious option is the **Cascadian Dinner Train** that leaves the Elbe station and cruises over 40 miles of country. The prime rib, salmon, or chicken dinner is served to you by waiters in tuxedos, and you can enjoy the view from the observation car. Dinner trains run April-Nov. on either Saturday or Sunday; call (360) 569-2588 or (888) 773-4637 for reservations and more information. Fare is $65 for this four-hour journey into the past.

Accommodations and Campgrounds
Stay at the quiet **Eagles Nest Motel,** two miles west of Elbe near Alder Lake, tel. (360) 569-2533, where rooms are $48 s or d. Kitchenettes are available, along with RV hookups. For something more unique, stay right in town at **Hobo Inn,** tel. (360) 569-2500, Elbe's train going nowhere. Stay in one of the eight cabooses—some date back to 1916—that have been completely reconditioned, with beds and bathrooms added, for $70-85 s or d; one even features a jacuzzi. Make reservations a month ahead in the summer to be assured of your own caboose.

The local Lions Club manages campsites at **Mineral Lake,** three miles south of Elbe. The lake is famous for its exceptional trout fishing, including rainbows and German brown trout (some to 10 pounds). Cabins ($55-100 for up to eight) and RV spaces are available at **Mineral Lake Resort,** tel. (360) 492-5367. Pontoon and rowboats are also available for rent.

Food
In addition to caboose lodging, **Hobo Inn,** tel. (360) 569-2500, has a restaurant and lounge where you can enjoy dinner in dining cars from a bygone era. Be sure to try the enormous and tasty scaleburgers and fries. See above for another train-dining option, the Cascadian Dinner Train.

EATONVILLE

Rural Eatonville (pop. 1,500) is located in farming and logging country in the foothills west of Mt. Rainier and boasts of its many horses—Pierce County is said to have more horses per capita than anywhere else in America. Mount Rainier is just 25 miles away, and the sleazy developments of Puyallup have not yet spread to this little town. In recent years, Eatonville has gained a number of artists and craftspeople, and several small galleries dot downtown.

Northwest Trek Wildlife Park
One of the region's biggest attractions is Northwest Trek Wildlife Park. Located on Hwy. 161 near Eatonville, this 600-acre wildlife park is a refuge for grizzly and black bears, wolves, mountain goats, moose, bighorn sheep, elk, and even a herd of bison. A tram transports visitors on a six-mile, hour-long tour of the park; also available are five miles of nature trails. Join in a park-sponsored weekend festival, salmon bake, or photo tour. The park opens daily Feb.-Oct. at 9:30 a.m. (closing times vary); open weekends only the rest of the year. The trams leave hourly beginning at 10 a.m. Admission costs $8.25 adults, $7.75 seniors, $5.75 ages 5-17, $3.75 ages 3-4, free for tots under three. For details, call (360) 832-6116 or (800) 433-8735.

Pioneer Farm Museum and Ohop Indian Village
Three miles north of Eatonville, between Highways 7 and 161, is the Pioneer Farm Museum and Ohop Indian Village. Here you can experience what pioneer life was really like as you grind grain, churn butter, and milk a cow. Ninety-minute guided tours are available daily 11 a.m.-4 p.m. in the summer, with reduced hours in the spring and fall. Closed Thanksgiving through February. Admission is $5.50 adults, $4.50 seniors and kids. The farm is also home to a replica Indian village where you can learn about traditional hunting and fishing, tool making, and Native foods. Hour-long tours of the Indian village are available only on summer weekends at 1 and 2:30 p.m. and cost an additional $5 adults and $4 kids. A trading post sells old-fashioned candy, trinkets, books, and rabbit skins. Call (360) 832-6300 for details on the farm and Indian village.

Pack Experimental Forest
Pack Experimental Forest is on University of Washington land just west of Eatonville. The roads across Pack Forest are open weekdays only, but hiking trails are open daily. Call (360) 832-6534 for more information. Short hiking trails crisscross the forest, taking you through stands of trees of varying ages, including a 42-acre pre-

serve of old-growth Douglas fir, cedar, and hemlock—one of the few unlogged patches of trees remaining in this part of Washington. Clearcuts on private land line the roads throughout the Cascade foothills; only small bits of the public land have been saved from this onslaught. It doesn't take much to see that the whole spotted owl controversy comes down to arguing over the few parcels of old-growth forest that have somehow escaped.

Accommodations and Campgrounds

Stay at the spacious and modern **Mill Village Motel,** 210 Center St., tel. (360) 832-3200 or (800) 832-3248, for $53-57 s or d. Kitchenettes and RV parking are also available here.

Camp at **Alder Lake Park,** seven miles south of Eatonville, where both tent sites and RV spaces are available, along with showers. The seven-mile-long lake was created by a dam that produces hydroelectric power for Tacoma City Light. Reservations are advised for summer weekends; call (360) 569-2778. The lake also has a very popular sandy beach for sunbathing and swimming.

Nearby private RV parks include **Mill Village RV Park,** 220 Center St. E, tel. (360) 832-4279, and **Silver Lake Resort,** 33201 Spirit Lake Hwy., tel. (360) 274-6141.

Food

Ohop Valley Bakery, 212 N. Washington Ave., tel. (30) 832-7795, bakes delicious breads and other pastries in a wood-fired oven. Get espresso here too.

Eat good Mexican food at **Puerto Vallarta,** 220 Center St., tel. (360) 832-4033. **Between the Bread** 311 Center St., tel. (360) 832-3777, is a small place with homemade breads and tasty breakfasts, plus gourmet steak, veal, salmon, pork, and vegetarian entrees nightly.

The **Eatonville Farmers Market** takes place at Washington and Center Streets from May to early October on Saturday 10 a.m.-4 p.m., and features fresh produce, flowers, and local crafts.

Events and Information

Local events of note include the **Fourth of July** with all the fun of a small-town festival, and the very popular **Eatonville Arts Festival,** held the first weekend of August.

The **Eatonville Visitor Information Center,** 220 Center St., tel. (360) 832-4000, is open Mon.-Fri. 9 a.m.-5 p.m., and Saturday 10 a.m.-2 p.m. Take a shower at the laundromat next door.

PACKWOOD

There isn't a lot to Packwood, just a stretch of businesses scattered along the highway, but be sure to stop at the old library, set in a grove of Douglas fir trees—some of the few big ones remaining in these parts. The town runs on the Packwood Lumber Co. mill west of town, and you're likely to meet loaded logging trucks rolling in from all directions. It also gets by with a dose of Mt. Rainier tourism for good measure; Packwood motels offer fairly reasonable accommodations near the southern edge of the national park.

The small and virtually unknown **Packwood State Park** lies just northwest of town along Skate Creek. This park has tall trees and decent fishing, but no facilities. Access is via Forest Rd. 52 across the Cowlitz River.

Accommodations

Hotel Packwood is a renovated 1912 hotel with a big veranda at 104 Main St., tel. (360) 494-5431. Cozy and friendly, this is a good place to step back in time; $25-30 s or d with bath down the hall, or $38 s or d with private bath. President Theodore Roosevelt once slept in what is now the Roosevelt Suite.

Packwood's other lodging places are listed below by price. The **Woodland Motel,** tel. (360) 494-6766, has a handful of simple rooms out in the country five miles west of Packwood for just $25-35 s or $38-42 d. **Tatoosh Motel,** 12880 Hwy. 12, tel. (360) 494-6710, has homey cabins (some with kitchenettes) and a jacuzzi for $38-85 s or d. Stay at **Mountain View Lodge & Motel,** 13163 Hwy. 12, tel. (360) 494-5555, for $31-70 s or $34-73 d, including an outdoor pool and jacuzzi.

Peter's Inn, 13059 Hwy. 12, tel. (360) 494-4000, charges $43-53 s or d. **Timberline Village Resort** four miles east of Packwood, tel. (360) 494-9224, has rooms for $46-73 s or d. Rooms at **Crest Trail Lodge,** 12729 Hwy. 12, tel. (360) 494-4944 or (800) 477-5339, are $53 s or d, including a jacuzzi and continental breakfast. **Cowlitz River Lodge,** 13069 Hwy. 12, tel. (360) 494-4444 or (888) 881-0371, has an outdoor jacuzzi and continental breakfast for $50-60 s or d. Another good place is **Inn of Packwood,** 12032 Hwy. 12, tel. (360) 494-5500, with an outdoor pool and jacuzzi; $53 s or $60 d.

Camping
The closest Forest Service camping can be found at **La Wis Wis Campground,** seven miles northeast of town on Hwy. 12. Also fairly close is the free **Summit Creek Campground,** 12 miles north of town, and just east of the Hwy. 12 and Hwy. 123 junction on Forest Rd. 2160. No trailers here. Park RVs at **Packwood RV Park,** tel. (360) 494-5145.

Food
Eat at **Club Cafe,** where the food can be inconsistent, but when it's good, it's stellar. **Peters Inn** has good breakfasts, seafood in season, steaks and prime rib, and homemade pies.

Other Practicalities
Little Cayuse Ranch, 121 Baker Rd., tel. (360) 494-6608, has guided hour-long horseback rides during the summer.

Get information on nearby Gifford Pinchot National Forest from **Packwood Work Center,** 13068 Hwy. 12, tel. (360) 494-0600.

RANDLE

Randle is another in a string of logging towns along Hwy. 12, with scalped nearby hills as a reminder of what makes the economy tick. The town acts as an access point to the east side of Mount St. Helens National Volcanic Monument, with Forest Rd. 25 cutting south to the Spirit Lake/Windy Ridge area. It's also an entry point for travelers continuing north to Mount Rainier National Park.

Accommodations
Several local places provide accommodations. **Tall Timber Motel,** one mile east of Randle on Hwy. 12, tel. (360) 497-2991, has rooms for $30-40 s or d. **Mt. Adams Inn,** 9514 Hwy. 12, Randle, tel. (360) 497-7007, charges $40 s or d, including

an exercise room. **Woodland Motel,** 11890 Hwy. 12, tel. (360) 494-6766, costs $40 s or $50 d. **Medici Motel,** is out in the country three miles south of Randle, tel. (360) 497-7700, with rooms for $45 s or d. **Randle Motel,** 9780 Hwy. 12, tel. (360) 497-5346, charges $35-45 s or d.

The most unusual nearby lodging is the Forest Service's **Burley Mountain Fire Lookout** which is rented Nov.-May for $20/night. It sleeps four; call (360) 497-1100 for reservations and directions.

Camping
Public campsites can be found south of town on the Gifford Pinchot National Forest, along the east side of Mt. St. Helens. Nearest is **Iron Creek Campground,** 12 miles south on Forest Rd. 25, ($11; open mid-May to late October). Make reservations ($9 extra) by calling (877) 444-6777. Campfire programs are given at Iron Creek Friday and Saturday evenings in the summer. **Tower Rock Campground** is six miles east of Iron Creek on Rd. 76; $11; open mid-May to late September.

Randle's private RV parks are: **Maple Grove RV Park,** tel. (360) 497-7680; **Shady Firs Campground,** 107 Young Rd., tel. (360) 497-6108; and **Tower Rock U-Fish RV Park,** 137 Cispus Rd., tel. (360) 497-7680.

Other Practicalities
Big Bottom Bar & Grill, tel. (360) 497-9982, is a fun place for lunch or dinner with great service and dependably good all-American steaks and burgers. Open till 2 a.m. most nights.

Randle's **Cowlitz Valley Ranger Station,** three miles east of town, tel. (360) 497-1100, is open daily 8 a.m.-4:30 p.m. from late May through September, and Mon.-Fri. 8 a.m.-4:30 p.m. the rest of the year. The office has detailed information on local hiking and mountain biking trails.

MORTON

Logged slopes frame the Cascades foothills town of Morton (pop. 1,100). It's a place where red-suspendered men drive aging pickups with anti-environmentalist bumperstickers, and where half the downtown storefronts are empty. Hard times have come to the timber industry.

The **Old Settlers Museum** has local exhibits; stop by city hall for access to the museum. Three miles west of Morton on Short Rd. is a fine binocular-view of the crater opening and lava dome.

Accommodations and Camping

For something quite out of the ordinary, the historic **St. Helens Manor House B&B,** six miles east of Morton on Riffe Lake, tel. (360) 498-5243 or (800) 551-3290, has four guest rooms with private or shared baths and serves a gourmet breakfast. The 1910 three-story home is said to be haunted by two female ghosts that slam doors, appear in hallways, and toy with the security system. $65-75 s or d. No kids.

Other local places are more standard. **Evergreen Motel,** Main and Front, tel. (360) 496-5407, has budget prices: $29-35 s or d. **Stiltner Motel;** just north of town on Hwy. 7, tel. (360) 496-5103, charges $30-35 s or d for basic cabins with kitchenettes. Stay at **Roy's Motel & RV Park,** 161 N. 2nd St., tel. (360) 496-5000, for $48-58 s or d. **The Seasons Motel;** 200 Westlake; tel. (360) 496-6835; is a good place, with rooms for $55 s or d, including a continental breakfast. Five miles north of town, **Resort of the Mountains,** tel. (360) 496-5885, has condo-style apartments with fireplaces and full kitchens. They also have RV hookups and a natural-food store.

Camp or park RVs at **Backstrom Park** along the Tilton River, tel. (360) 496-3361.

Other Practicalities

The **Wheel Cafe,** tel. (360) 496-3240, has steaks, seafood, a salad bar, and chicken and sandwiches to go, plus a lounge. A mile west of Morton, the **Roadhouse Inn,** tel. (360) 496-5029, is strictly sit-down, serving steak and seafood dinners plus breakfast and lunch.

The **Morton Loggers Jubilee,** held the second weekend in August, is one of the largest timber carnivals in Washington. In addition to the standard ax throwing, log rolling, and other contests, you'll discover a riding lawnmower race, parades, barbecues, and dancing, along with an arts and crafts fair.

The **Morton Chamber of Commerce,** tel. (360) 496-6086, has a summer-only log cabin visitor center at 2nd and Westlake.

MOSSYROCK AND VICINITY

Mossyrock (pop. 450) occupies farming country along the Cowlitz River northwest of Mt. St. Helens and east of Chehalis. The primary crops raised here are tulips, blueberries, and Christmas trees. Two dams have created nearby Riffe and Mayfield Lakes, ironically named for the towns they inundated.

Sights

A pullout four miles east of Mossyrock leads to a viewpoint offering a glimpse—on clear days—of Mt. St. Helens, 24 miles to the south. The

Jackson House

DON PITCHER

Cowlitz Salmon Hatchery is on the Cowlitz River just below the Mayfield Lake dam, providing a good chance to watch salmon returning up a fish ladder in the spring and fall. Get there by following the signs from the Hwy. 12 turnoff, nine miles west of Mossyrock.

Mayfield Lake County Park, off Hwy. 12 just west of Mossyrock, has a campground (open May-Sept. only; tel. 360-985-2364), swimming beach, boat launch, small picnic area, and playground. Follow Hwy. 12 east to Mossyrock and the **Mayfield Dam;** there's a nice roadside viewpoint about three miles east of Mossyrock.

Marys Corner to Toledo

Twenty miles west of Mossyrock on Hwy. 12 and just three miles east from I-5 is the crossroads called Marys Corner. Just south of the intersection on Jackson Hwy. is the **John R. Jackson House,** a log cabin built in 1845 that was a popular stopping place for Oregon Trail travelers. Jackson was one of the first American settlers north of the Columbia River, and this building served as the first U.S. District Court in what would become the state of Washington. Just north of Marys Center on Jackson Rd. is a monument to John Jackson's wife, Matilda. (Technically, this five-acre plot of land is **Matilda N. Jackson State Park.**)

Two miles south of Marys Corner, the road passes **Lewis and Clark State Park,** tel. (360) 864-2643. This wonderful 528-acre parcel represents one of the few remaining stands of old-growth forest in this part of Washington. Several short trails provide loop hikes through the tall Douglas fir, western red cedar, western hemlock, and grand fir trees. The west side of Lewis and Clark State Park emphasizes horseback use. Camp beneath the forest for $10 (no hookups) April-September. Underlying the park and surrounding areas are caverns that were created by cooling lava from Mount Rainier. El Paso Natural Gas stores natural gas in these massive underground vaults.

Four miles beyond the park is **St. Francis Xavier Mission,** founded in 1838 by French Catholic missionaries from the Winnipeg area. The first priest here, Father Francis Blanchet, was so intent upon converting the Indians that he devised a system of lines, dots, and other designs to explain the intricacies of Catholicism. The end result was a six-foot-long parchment called the "Catholic Ladder," a replica of which stands outside the church. The red brick church was built in 1932; the first three versions of this church were destroyed by fire.

The self-explanatory **Cowlitz Prairie Steam Threshing and Antique Gas Engine Show** takes place in Toledo in late August; tel. (360) 864-4917.

Accommodations

Lake Mayfield Motel, west of Mossyrock, tel. (360) 985-2484, has rooms for $40 s or d. Seven miles west of Mossyrock in Salkum, **The Shepherd's Inn B&B,** tel. (360) 985-2434 or (800) 985-2434, is an attractive, quiet, country home with five guest rooms (shared or private baths) for $65-80 d, including an indoor jacuzzi and full breakfast. Cozy and clean rooms are also available at Salkum's **White Spot Motel,** tel. (360) 985-2737, for just $30-32 s or d.

The Farm B&B near Toledo, tel. (360) 864-4200, is a delightful new place with five guest rooms, all with private baths. The real treat here is breakfast, prepared by owner Michel Paulin, an accomplished French chef; $75 s or $85 d. Kids are accepted.

Campgrounds

To reach **Mossyrock Park,** turn south at the Mossyrock flashing light and follow the signs three miles east. Here you'll find campsites, picnic tables, and boat launches on the green-blue Riffe Lake. The 24-mile-long lake was created in 1968; it was named Riffe Lake to honor the settlement of Riffe, founded in 1898 and now covered by about 225 feet of water.

If you turn north at the Mossyrock light you'll eventually get to **Ike Kinswa State Park,** about three miles off the highway. This 454-acre park is open year-round for trout fishing on Mayfield Lake, with swimming, picnicking, and lakeside campsites ($11) and RV sites ($16). In the winter, look for bald eagles on the trees along the shore. Call (360) 983-3402 for more info, or (800) 452-5687 for reservations ($6 extra fee).

Private RV parks in the area include **Lake Mayfield Resort,** 350 Hadlaller Rd., Silver Creek, tel. (360) 985-2357; **Barrier Dam Campground** 273 Fuller Rd. in Salkum, tel. (360) 985-2495; and **Mountain Road RV Park,** 262 Mossyrock Rd. W, tel. (360) 983-3094.

MOUNT ST. HELENS
NATIONAL VOLCANIC MONUMENT

The 1980 explosion of Mt. St. Helens transformed a quiet and beautiful landscape into a moonscape of devastation. Today plants and animals are returning to the land as it recovers, but the immensity of the eruption continues to overwhelm and astound visitors. Mount St. Helens has become one of Washington's must-see sights, and a fine set of visitor facilities, access roads, and trails now offer ample opportunities to learn about the power of this active volcano.

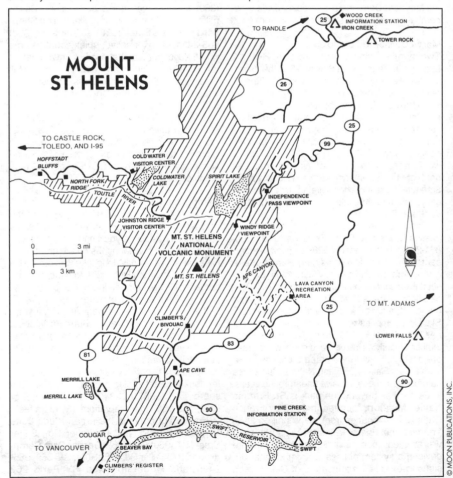

THE SLEEPING DRAGON AWAKES

Prior to May 18, 1980, Mt. St. Helens had the most perfectly shaped cone in the Pacific Northwest volcanic chain. The mountain was named by Capt. George Vancouver in 1792 for Baron St. Helens, the British Ambassador to Spain. Often called "the ice-cream cone in the sky," and compared constantly with Japan's Mt. Fuji, 9,677-foot Mt. St. Helens was viewed as a sleeping beauty, popular with hikers, climbers, and other outdoor adventurers. It was silent for as long as any of them could remember—the volcano had been dormant for 123 years.

The Eruption

On March 20, 1980, Mt. St. Helens began to rumble. By March 30, steam was rising from two brand-new craters, which had merged by April 4 into one huge crater measuring 1,700 feet across. Seven weeks of minor earthquakes followed.

At 8:32 a.m. on May 18, 1980, Mt. St. Helens blew her top in an eruption that had the explosive power of several atomic bombs. The eruption was triggered by an earthquake measuring 5.1 on the Richter scale that sent a massive avalanche of rock, snow, and ice down the mountain's north slope at 200 mph, filling Spirit Lake—whose surface was instantly raised by 200 feet—and cresting over a 1,200-foot ridge. A second debris avalanche blasted down the North Fork of the Toutle River, and additional flows sent muddy water, rocks, and logs down the river, destroying bridges and homes along the way.

The landslide allowed pressure inside the volcano to escape explosively in an eruption that blew 1,312 feet (8.8 *billion* cubic yards) off the volcano's summit. A lateral blast shot northeast at 670 miles an hour, searing surrounding forests and flattening them up to 15 miles away. Temperatures 15 miles away reached an incredible 572° F, and the blast was followed by a plume of ash that rose 16 miles into the atmosphere. This explosion, along with the intense heat, landslides, and falling trees, killed 57 people within the blast zone, and destroyed more than 220 homes and 17 miles of railroad. The wildlife death toll was upward of 5,000 black-tailed deer, 1,500 Roosevelt elk, 200 black bear, and millions of birds and fish; the economic loss included 4.5 billion board feet of usable timber on 96,000 acres.

The damage wasn't limited to the area of the blast itself; 60,000 acres not destroyed by the blast were covered with more than eight inches of ash. Six hours after the eruption, river water at Castle Rock, 40 miles downstream, was over 100° F, and towns in eastern Washington—150 miles away—were coated with up to three inches of ash, clogging carburetors and shrouding the towns in thick darkness at noon. Traces of ash were detected as far away as mid-Montana, Vancouver, B.C., and Denver.

After the Explosion

For six years following the blast, Mt. St. Helens experienced 21 additional eruptions, mostly dome-building eruptions and irregular spurts of activity. The steaming lava dome inside the crater grew 1,000 feet, but has been fairly quiet of late. Geologists have scaled back their monitoring, but the crater itself remains off limits, and even scientists don't venture in for long.

In 1982, the 110,000-acre **Mount St. Helens National Volcanic Monument** was created, and the area has been gradually opened to visitors as roads, bridges, visitors centers, and trails are built. The government still keeps parts of it off-limits to serve as a natural laboratory for scientists. They have learned one basic fact so far: nature heals itself more quickly than anyone expected. Plant and animal life is returning quite rapidly considering the extent of the destruction.

The Forest Service has imposed stringent regulations on activity within the National Monument, both to protect visitors from potential hazards and to protect the area as a natural laboratory of ecological change. These rules include that visitors stay away from certain areas and not venture off trails; they are stringently enforced. A minimum $100 fine awaits those who travel off-trail; see the visitors centers for specifics.

VISITING MOUNT ST. HELENS

Roads approach Mt. St. Helens from the east and west sides, offering dramatic views into its center, while more adventurous visitors can climb to the summit from the south side. The vast majority of visitors arrive from the west, turning off I-

5 and following Spirit Lake Highway 54 miles past a series of visitors centers and ending at Johnston Ridge, where you can peer into the volcano's crater. Be sure to fill your gas tank before you start out on any of the Mt. St. Helens access roads; gas stations are few and far between, especially on the east side. Specific access routes are described below from the east, south, and west. From the north side you are limited to distant views from a roadside pull-out near Mossyrock Dam.

All visitors to the monument (including those visiting the more remote east side) must purchase a **visitor pass.** These are good for three days and cost $8 pp, $4 for seniors or disabled persons, or free for under age 16. Get them from any of the visitor centers. The Park Service's annual Golden Eagle pass gets you in for free.

Campgrounds

Specific campgrounds are described below for each side of Mt. St. Helens. Dispersed camping is allowed only outside the restricted areas around the volcano. No camping is permitted within the upper North Fork of the Toutle River drainage, around Coldwater Lake and Spirit Lake, or around the volcano itself; check with the Forest Service for specifics.

Information

Call (360) 274-4038 for recorded road and other visitor information. For more general area information, visit the small travel information building just west of I-5 at exit 49 in Castle Rock, or stop at any of the visitors centers on the Spirit Lake Highway. Closest to I-5 is **Spirit Lake Visitor Center,** just five miles east of the interstate on Hwy. 504. The ranger stations and work centers can also help; they're located in Packwood, tel. (360) 494-0600; Randle, tel. (360) 497-1100; and Wind River, tel. (360) 427-3200.

The **Mount St. Helens Volcanic Headquarters,** tel. (360) 247-3900, is three miles north of Amboy on Hwy. 503. Call them for brochures and the latest on conditions at Mt. St. Helens, including the status of volcanic activity and any trail closures.

Tours

Mount St. Helens Adventure Tours, tel. (360) 274-6542, has four-hour van tours from Castle

Rock to the various sights along the Spirit Lake Memorial Highway. The company is run by the owners of Spirit Lake Lodge, which was destroyed in the eruption, and offers a personalized version of the events of 1980 that goes beyond the canned bus tours.

Scenic Bound Tours, tel. (360) 433-6907 or (888) 293-1404, leads day trips to both Mt. Rainier and Mt. St. Helens from Seattle for $65 per person.

Scenic Flights

Several aviation companies offer scenic flights over Mt. St. Helens, affording passengers a view of the crater and lava dome that you can't get otherwise. **Aeronautics Unlimited,** tel. (360) 414-5960, offers scenic flights from the Longview/Kelso airport. Helicopter overflights of the volcano are provided by **Hillsboro Helicopters,** tel. (360) 274-7750 or (800) 752-8439, from Hoffstadt Bluffs; and **Pacific Air Tours,** tel. (360) 274-9330 or (888) 274-9330, from Toutle.

WEST SIDE ACCESS

The west side of Mt. St. Helens offers the quickest access and has some of the finest views and the most developed facilities. Nearly 900,000 visitors take this route each year. With five elaborate visitors centers, and a wide new paved road reaching the center of the monument, this is the place most folks view the volcano. The main access route to the west side is Hwy. 504, the **Spirit Lake Memorial Highway.** Starting from the town of Castle Rock (exit 49 from I-5), Hwy. 504 offers a 54-mile scenic climb right to the heart of the volcanic destruction that resulted from the 1980 eruption. A secondary access is Hwy. 505, which cuts east from I-5 at the tiny town of **Toledo** (exit 60) and joins Hwy. 504 after 16 miles near the town of **Toutle** (TOOT-ul). The description below follows Spirit Lake Memorial Hwy. from I-5 to its terminus inside the national monument.

Silver Lake Visitor Center

Your first stop should be the comprehensive Silver Lake Visitor Center, tel. (360) 274-2100, just five miles from I-5 on Hwy. 504, where the focus is on the eruption and its impacts. The center-

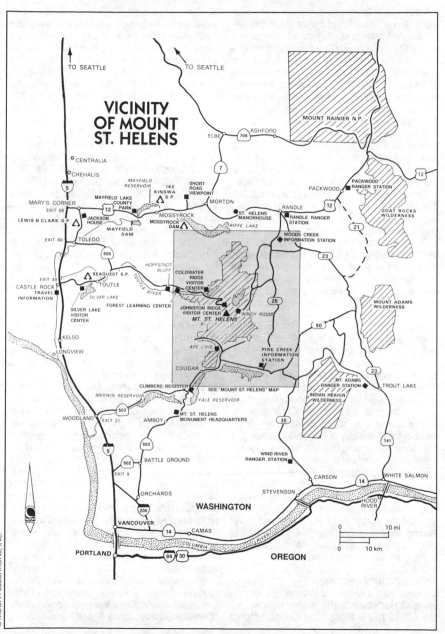

piece is a walk-in volcano that reveals the geological forces at work, but the other exhibits are equally well-done, including models comparing the 1980 eruption with other volcanic eruptions (this was puny compared to the eruption that created Crater Lake), descriptions of the buildup to the eruption and images of the volcano in action, a working seismograph to see the latest shakers, and newspaper front pages from 1980. The mountain is 30 miles from here, but can be seen—on a clear day—through the spotting scopes outside. An extraordinary 10-minute slide show and a 22-minute movie alternate every half-hour throughout the day. Silver Lake Visitor Center is open daily 9 a.m.-6 p.m. May-Sept., and daily 9 a.m.-5 p.m. the rest of the year. In addition to maps, books, and current trail and road information, the center offers interpretive programs on a daily basis throughout the year.

Seaquest State Park is right next to the visitors center, within a beautiful stand of gigantic old-growth Douglas firs and hemlocks. Camping is available here year-round (see below). Silver Lake is one of the best bass fishing lakes in the state, and a public boat ramp is a mile east of the park.

As you continue east on Hwy. 504 from Silver Lake, the road slips past the ugly collection of trailers and homes called **Toutle** at the juncture of the South and North Fork of the Toutle River, and then up along the North Fork into the mountains. Much of the route is on private timberland, with Weyerhaeuser tree plantations lining both sides of the road. You may want to stop at the Army Corps of Engineers' 184-foot-high **sediment retention dam,** built in 1989, to see the muddy water spewing out and to pick up tourist trinkets and T-shirts at a nearby gift shop. A few miles west, signs point to the famous buried A-frame, another place to purchase souvenirs and one of the casualties of the mudflows created by the eruption. Hopefully, the next eruption will take out the corny "Big Foot" statue out front! **Pacific Air Tours,** tel. (360) 274-9330 or (888) 274-9330, has Toutle River Valley helicopter flights from the A-frame in the summer.

Hoffstadt Bluffs and Creek

Continue east through the Weyerhaeuser tree farms to **Hoffstadt Bluffs Visitor Center,** tel. (360) 274-7755 or (800) 752-8439, at milepost

27. Owned by Cowlitz County, this timber-frame building houses two gift shops and a restaurant that serves three meals a day. Eat inside and enjoy the picture-window panorama, or outside on the patio overlooking the North Touttle Valley and Mt. St. Helens. A picnic area is also available, along with telescopes to watch the several hundred elk below and the mountain above. Despite the name, this really isn't a visitors center, so head elsewhere for information on the volcano. The center is open daily 9 a.m.-10 p.m. in the summer, or Mon.-Thurs. 10 a.m.-4 p.m., and Fri.-Sun. 10 a.m.-8 p.m. the rest of the year.

Hillsboro Helicopters, tel. (360) 274-7750 or (800) 752-8439, has scenic helicopter flights from Hoffstadt Bluffs, and **Mount St. Helens Wagon Tours,** tel. (360) 748-9591, has horse-drawn wagon tours across the mud flows in the Hoffstadt Bluffs area.

From here eastward, Spirit Lake Memorial Hwy. climbs steadily uphill, with wide shoulders for bikes and numerous turnouts to take in the scenery. RVers should park at Hoffstadt Bluffs and those towing trailers should leave them there, since the road has some seven percent grades ahead.

Next stop is the **Hoffstadt Creek Bridge,** one of 14 bridges that had to be reconstructed on Hwy. 504 after the eruption. The new bridge rises 370 feet above the canyon, and stands near the edge of the blast zone—an incredible 14.8 miles from the crater. Everything from here on was killed by the heat of the explosion. Also, from here on you can see a sharp contrast between what private companies did after the eruption and what took place on Forest Service land. Weyerhaeuser salvage-logged its lands and immediately replanted millions of trees. With fertilization, the new stands are coming back surprisingly fast; some trees are already 40 feet tall! As a public agency, the Forest Service had a rather different mandate, and no logging or replanting took place within the national volcanic monument. Instead, the area has become a natural laboratory where scientists can study the recovery process, and where visitors can marvel at the power of nature. (Salvage logging and replanting were, however, done on Forest Service lands outside the monument boundaries.) Today the upper Toutle River Valley is home to over 500 Roosevelt elk, many of which are visible by hiking two miles down Rd. 3100 near the Hoffstadt Creek Bridge. Despite harsh conditions, the elk survive on the nutritious grasses and clover that were planted in the mudflow following the eruption.

North Fork Ridge

The **Forest Learning Center,** tel. (360) 414-3439, near milepost 33 on North Fork Ridge highlights some of the differences between public management and that of Weyerhaeuser Company (while providing a public relations boost for the timber industry). The center sits on a 2,700-foot-high bluff over the North Fork of the Toutle River and is open daily 10 a.m.-7 p.m. May-Oct. (closed winters); no charge. The emphasis here is on Weyerhaeuser's salvage and recovery efforts after the eruption. Elaborate exhibits take you through a diorama of the forest prior to the 1980 eruption, an "eruption chamber" where a you-are-there multimedia program surrounds you, and then past additional exhibits extolling the salvage, reforestation, and recovery efforts, plus the benefits of private forestry practices and conservation. The Forest Learning Center is especially popular with families; kids can climb aboard a toy helicopter or play in the seven-foot-high rubber volcano outside. Telescopes provide a chance to watch elk in the valley below, and a one-mile trail descends into the valley. Other facilities include a gift shop and picnic area.

Be sure to stop at the **Elk Rock Viewpoint,** at the entrance to the Mount St. Helens National Monument, for magnificent views of the crater to the south and the deep river valley below, filled with a 700-foot-deep layer of rock, ash, and debris. Also look below for Roosevelt elk.

Coldwater Ridge Visitor Center

Located 45 miles east of I-5, the Forest Service's Coldwater Ridge Visitor Center, tel. (360) 274-2131, peers directly into the volcano's gaping crater mouth, just eight miles to the southeast. Also visible are the debris-filled Toutle River Valley and Coldwater Lake—formed when the eruption sent a massive landslide across Coldwater Creek. The emphasis here is on the long recovery process after the eruption, a process that can be seen from the spacious glass-enclosed foyer. This high-tech multi-million-dollar facility features computer animation of how the area is expected to change over the next two centuries, an amusing exhibit in which a ranger mannequin explains the recovery to mannequins representing visitors, and educational exhibits of all sorts. A multimedia program provides a stunning introduction to the recovery process. A gift shop sells books, maps, and brochures, and the cafe has light meals and espresso. Coldwater Lake Visitor Center is open daily 9 a.m.-6 p.m. May-Sept., and daily 9 a.m.-5 p.m. the rest of the year. Interpretive walks and talks are given on a daily basis throughout the year; check the bulletin board for today's activities around Coldwater Lake.

One unfortunate side effect of the razzle-dazzle show at Coldwater is that it may give visitors the sense of having visited Mt. St. Helens without having actually experienced the land. You really need to get away from the computer animations and out onto the trails to appreciate the immense power of this volcano. An easy way to begin is the quarter-mile **Winds of Change Interpretive Trail,** just outside the visitor center. For another short hike, head two miles downhill to five-mile-long Coldwater Lake, where the quarter-mile **Birth of a Lake Trail** takes you by boardwalk past the debris avalanche left behind by the eruption. The lake is well-known for excellent rainbow and cutthroat trout fishing, with a minimum size of 16 inches for keepers. Rafts or float tubes are recommended to lessen the damage from bankside anglers, and gasoline-powered motorboats are prohibited. No camping, and be sure to stay on the trails (or risk a $100 fine).

Johnston Ridge Visitor Center

Spirit Lake Memorial Hwy. ends eight miles uphill from Coldwater Lake at the 4,300-foot level and the Johnston Ridge Visitor Center, tel. (360) 274-2140. This facility emphasizes the geology of Mt. St. Helens and ongoing scientific research work, and is named for Dr. David Johnston, the geologist who was working here in 1980 when the volcano erupted. His last radio transmission, sent out as the mountain gave way, still haunts anyone who hears it: "Vancouver, Vancouver, this is it!" This new visitor facility peers directly into the lava dome—just three miles away—that formed after the eruption (encased in clouds 200 days each year). The center is open daily 10 a.m.-6 p.m. mid-May through September, and daily 10 a.m.-4 p.m. the rest of the year. Step inside to find a large model of the volcano that shows how the eruption progressed, along with geological monitoring equipment and displays on the landscape both before and after the explosion. The highlight is a 16-minute film that recreates the eruption in gripping, wide-screen detail. A half-mile **Eruption Trail** loops past a marker commemorating the 57 people who were killed by the 1980 blast.

West Side Hiking

For a spectacular hike with commanding views into Spirit Lake, begin at the Johnston Ridge Observatory and follow **Boundary Trail** four miles to Harry's Ridge. For an overnight hike, continue along this path to the summit of Mount Margaret, and down before returning via the five-and-a-half-mile **Lakes Trail.** You can camp at several small high country lakes here (permit required). This is a research area, and scientists are attempting to keep human impacts to a minimum, so hikers need to stick within 10 feet of the trails.

West Side Campgrounds

There are no developed campsites within Mount St. Helens National Volcanic Monument, but camping is available across from the Silver Lake Visitor Center at **Seaquest State Park,** with both tent sites ($10) and RV hookup sites ($15) available year-round. Call (800) 452-5687 for reservations ($6 extra fee). Camping is prohibited along the Spirit Lake Memorial Hwy. inside the monument boundaries.

Eco Park at Mount St. Helens, tel. (360) 274-6542, has summertime basic cabins ($48), wall-tent lodging ($30), and RV hookups in a remote area on the northeast side. Located on private land, these are the only accommodations inside the volcano's blast zone.

EAST SIDE ACCESS

Unlike the west side, where a wide, new highway passes four visitor centers that seem to compete with each other to see which one can offer the most wows per minute, visitors to Mt. St. Helens' eastern flanks will discover narrow, wind-

ing one-lane routes, simple information stations, and more basic facilities. This is the wild side of the mountain, where the crowds are less and you're allowed to draw your own conclusions without being inundated with flashy multimedia shows and elaborate computer animations. Information, maps, and monument passes ($8) are available at the **Woods Creek Information Station,** approximately seven miles south of Randle, and the **Pine Creek Information Station,** on the east end of Swift Reservoir (20 miles east of Cougar).

The east side of Mt. St. Helens is accessed by Forest Rd. 25, which heads south from the town of Randle. This paved, but steep one-lane road (with turnouts) continues all the way to Pine Creek Ranger Station on Swift Creek Reservoir, south of the mountain. It is closed due to snow from late October to Memorial Day weekend and is not recommended for trailers or RVs. For easier driving, drop off your trailer at the Woods Creek Information Station or Iron Creek Picnic Site on Forest Service Rd. 25 if traveling from the north, or at the Pine Creek Information Station if you're coming from the south.

To Windy Ridge

Forest Roads 25, 26, and 99 provide access to the east side of Mt. St. Helens. The primary destination on the east side is Windy Ridge, where you can see Spirit Lake and a magnificent up-close view of the volcano. Take Roads 25 and 99 to reach the viewpoint. Forest Rd. 26 turns south from Iron Creek Campground and leads to **Quartz Creek Big Trees** area, where a half-mile path takes you through old-growth Douglas firs that escaped the eruption. Just a mile away is the edge of the zone where trees were flattened in the blast (trees in this area were salvaged after the eruption). From here on, everything was destroyed by the force of the eruption. Road 26 is blocked south of here due to washouts.

At **Ryan Lake** another short trail provides views of the lake filled with downed trees. This area is usually accessible year-round, with open, flat areas for cross-country skiing. **Meta Lake**—at the junction of Forest Roads 26 and 99—has a paved trail and the famous **Miner's Car,** destroyed in the blast. Three people had driven here the night before the volcano gave way on

May 18, 1980, and were killed in a nearby cabin by the superheated explosion. Meta Lake is coming back surprisingly fast from the destruction, in part because ice and snow protected fish and other animals from the heat. Nature walks are offered here daily during the summer months. The Norway Pass Trailhead (see "East Side Hiking Trails," below) is just a mile north of Meta Lake; a water pump is also here.

Windy Ridge stands at the end of Rd. 99, 4,000 feet above sea level and 34 miles southwest of Randle. It is just five miles from the crater itself. Climb the 361 steps for an incredible view into the volcano, across the devastated pumice plain, and over the log-choked Spirit Lake. Forest Service interpretive personnel are here daily May-Oct., providing frequent talks about the volcano from the amphitheater.

East Side Campgrounds
Iron Creek Campground ($11) is located in a stand of old-growth trees along the Cispus River 12 miles south of Randle on Forest Rd. 25 and is open mid-May to late October. Saturday evening campfire programs are provided at Iron Creek in the summer. **Tower Rock Campground,** six miles east of Iron Creek on Rd. 76, is open mid-May to late September and has sites for $11. Make reservations for both of these ($9 extra) by calling (877) 444-6777.

East Side Hiking Trails
The **Woods Creek Watchable Wildlife Trail,** an easy one-and-a-half-mile path through mixed forests, a meadow, and past several beaver ponds, leaves from the Woods Creek Information Station. Two other easy walks are the quarter-mile **Iron Creek Old-Growth Trail** and the one-and-a-half-mile **Iron Creek Campground Trail,** both of which depart from Iron Creek Campground and offer treks though tall stands of cedar and Douglas fir. Also nearby—at the end of a quarter-mile path—is beautiful 60-foot **Iron Creek Falls.**

For something more strenuous, follow the two-and-a-half-mile **Norway Pass Trail** (No. 1) through blown-down forests to the 4,500-foot pass, gaining 900 feet in elevation along the way. You can continue beyond to the Coldwater Lake area, return the same way you came, or return to Independence Pass along Rd. 99 via **In-dependence Pass Trail** (No. 227), with extraordinary views over Spirit Lake. The roundtrip distance for this is six miles.

Harmony Trail drops 570 feet in just a mile, offering the only legal access to the shore of Spirit Lake. Most living things were killed when pyroclastic flows filled it in 1980, causing water temperatures to reach almost 100° F. The trailhead is halfway between the Independence Pass trailhead and Windy Ridge.

At Windy Ridge you can hike the six-mile **Truman Trail** (No. 207) for up-close-and-personal views of the lava dome inside the crater, and to connect with the round-the-mountain **Loowit Trail** (No. 216). A spur of this (216 E) leads to the Loowit Falls, where 100° F water pours out of the crater (no swimming).

East Side Information
Get information on Mt. St. Helens at the Forest Service's **Woods Creek Information Station,** six miles south of Randle on Forest Rd. 25. Open daily 9 a.m.-5 p.m., mid-May through September, they even offer drive-through service! **Cowlitz Valley Ranger Station,** three miles east of Randle on Hwy. 12, tel. (360) 497-1100, is open daily 8 a.m.-4:30 p.m. Memorial Day through September, and weekdays the rest of the year. **Pine Creek Information Station,** 17 miles east of Cougar on Forest Rd. 90 (and 45 miles south of Randle) has information for the southeast side of St. Helens. Open daily 9 a.m.-6 p.m. mid-May through September. Just a mile southeast of the info station is **Eagles Cliff General Store,** tel. (360) 238-5335, a classic country store offering everything from junk food to cross-country ski rentals.

SOUTH SIDE ACCESS

The south side of Mt. St. Helens was not impacted nearly as much by the 1980 eruption and is best known as the access route to climb the summit, for Ape Cave, and for various hiking trails, including the Loowit System that circles the mountain.

Ape Cave
This 12,810-foot lava tube is one of the longest such caves in the nation, and one of the most

popular visitor attractions at Mt. St. Helens. The cave is 10 miles northeast of Cougar at the junction of Forest Roads 83 and 90 and is open all the time. From the entrance a staircase leads down to a chamber where the route splits. The downhill arm ends after an easy three-quarter-mile walk, while the uphill route is more difficult and rocky, continuing one and a half miles to an exit where an above-ground trail leads back to the starting point. Forest Service interpreters lead half-hour tours of Ape Cave twice a day in the summer. Be sure to bring drinking water and two flashlights and extra batteries (or rent a lantern for $2). Wear hiking boots, gloves, and warm clothes (the air is a steady 42° F all year). A small visitors center at Ape Cave can provide assistance, publications, and lantern rentals daily 10 a.m.-5:30 p.m., Memorial Day through September. A monument pass ($8 pp) is required for access to the cave. The road is plowed to the Trail of Two Forests, a half mile away, in the winter.

Climbing Mount St. Helens

Mount St. Helens is the second most climbed peak on the planet, exceeded only by Japan's Mt. Fuji. With 16,000 people making the pilgrimage each year up Mt. St. Helens, you're bound to have company on your trip to the top.

All climbing routes up Mt. St. Helens are from the south side of the peak, and a permit is required for travel above the 4,800-foot level. These cost $15 pp April-Oct.; free the rest of the year. From May 15 through October, 100 permits are issued per day on a first-come basis, with up to 60 of these available by advance reservation. The rest of the year, permits are required ($15 pp), but there are no limits. Make reservations as early as possible after February 1, since most summer weekends are reserved by late March. Pay for and pick up your permits from Jack's Store, tel. (360) 231-4276, 23 miles east of Woodland on Hwy. 503. The other 40 permits are issued on a first-come basis starting at 6 p.m. each evening for the next day's climb. Stop by Jack's Store to purchase these. These confusing rules may change, so check with the monument before planning a climb; call (360) 750-3961 for a recorded message, or (360) 247-3900 for a real person. You'll need to sign in at Jack's Store both before and after the climb.

The climb begins past the entrance to Ape Cave. Follow Forest Rd. 83 a mile beyond the cave, then turn left on Rd. 8100 for another mile, and finally right on Rd. 830 for the final three miles to Climbers Bivouac at an elevation of 3,750 feet. Even though the climb is not technically difficult, don't underestimate the steep slopes and severe weather. The first stretch ascends through the forest at a gradual pace, but above the 4,800-foot level the pole-marked route is a scramble over boulderfields, volcanic pumice, ash, and snowfields (often present till mid-July). The crater itself is off limits to the general public because steam explosions can create extremely dangerous conditions. Avoid the edge of the crater when snow tops the peak, since you may be stepping on a cornice that could give way.

Watch the weather reports before heading up the mountain; it can snow at any time of year, and low clouds can drastically reduce visibility. Call (503) 243-7575 for the latest weather forecast. Climbing boots, sunscreen, and plenty of water are requirements (no water is available on the route or at Climbers Bivouac), and you need to start early—say 7 a.m.—to have enough time to get up and back before nightfall. Most folks take around eight hours for the nine-mile (roundtrip) trek. Take an ice ax when snow is present, along with plenty of warm clothes and rain gear. Gaiters will help keep the snow and ash out of your boots. Primitive camping is available in the woods at the trailhead. Some climbers prefer to get a head start the night before, camping three miles up at the 4,800-foot level where you'll find a composting toilet. Camping is not allowed above this point.

Other South Side Hiking Trails

A very easy path is the **Trail of Two Forests,** a brief boardwalk that takes you past the molds left when trees were immersed in lava flows 2,000 years ago. You can even crawl through two of these ancient impressions. The trail is right across from Ape Cave on Rd. 8303.

One of the most interesting hikes on the south end of Mt. St. Helens is the 2.5-mile **Lava Canyon Trail** that drops 1,400 feet along the Muddy River. This canyon was scoured out by a mudflow during the 1980 eruption, revealing sharp cliffs and five tall waterfalls. Although the upper end is wheelchair-accessible, the lower part crosses a long suspension bridge and then descends a cliff face by a steel ladder. Great for the adventurous, not fun if you have a case of acrophobia. Get to the trail by following Forest Rd. 83 nine miles (paved the entire way) beyond Ape Cave to the trailhead.

The **Loowit System** (No. 216) is a difficult 29-mile trail that circles Mt. St. Helens and is accessible from trailheads on all sides of the mountain. Plan on three days to get all the way around, and be prepared for lots of up-and-down hiking and faint trails in places. Camping is available at various points along the way, but contact the Forest Service for specifics since some areas are off limits.

For an enjoyable loop hike, head to the end of Forest Rd. 8123 on the southwest side of the mountain and the start of **Sheep Canyon Trail** (No. 240). This path climbs through old-growth forests and drainages that were ravaged by volcanic mudflows and into a flower-filled alpine meadow along the Loowit Trail before returning downhill on the Toutle Trail (No. 238), which connects to the Sheep Canyon Trail and your starting point. Total distance is approximately seven miles.

The **Lewis River Trail** (No. 31) follows along this beautiful river from the Curly Creek Falls to Lower Falls (a fun swimming hole), a distance of more than 10 miles. Between Curly Creek Falls and Lower Falls on Rd. 99 is **Big Creek Falls,** plummeting 125 feet into a pool that makes a popular place for a summer dip. Above Lower Falls, you can follow the road to a series of roadside falls, including the very scenic Middle Falls and Upper Falls.

South Side Campgrounds

The Forest Service's **Lower Falls Campground** is a fine camping place, with views of three large falls along the Lewis River and a hiking trail that heads downriver for 10 miles. The campground ($12) is 15 miles east of the Pine Creek Information Station on Forest Rd. 90 and is open mid-May to mid-October. Make reservations ($9 extra) by calling (877) 444-6777.

Several other non-Forest Service public campgrounds provide camping on the south side of Mt. St. Helens. Near the town of Cougar, **Cougar Campground** and **Beaver Bay Campground** offer tent camping and showers on the Yale Reservoir along Forest Rd. 90. Go north on Rd. 8100 to **Merrill Lake Campground,** a free Department of Natural Resources camping area, or head east on Rd. 90 to **Swift Campground** just south of the Pine Creek Information Station; reserve a spot by calling Pacific Power and Light, tel. (503) 464-5035. They also have very popular summer-only campgrounds at **Cresap Bay Park,** seven miles north of Amboy on Hwy. 503, and **Saddle Dam Park,** near the Yale Lake dam on Frasier Road. Cresap Bay and Swift Campgrounds have campfire programs on Friday and Saturday nights June-August. For RV hookups head to **Volcano View Campground** just south of Yale on Hwy. 503, tel. (360) 231-4329, or **Cougar RV Park,** in Cougar, tel. (360) 238-5224.

Winter Sports

Forest Service Rd. 83's two Sno-Parks offer a wide area for winter activities, including cross-country skiing, snowshoeing, and snowmobiling. Most popular is the **Marble Mountain Sno-Park,** located seven miles east of Cougar on Forest Rd. 90, and another six miles up Rd. 83. Get a Sno-Park permit and ski trail maps at Cougar area stores. A large log **warming shelter** is open here in the winter months, and includes a woodstove. Rent it as a summertime cabin for $40 per night; call the Forest Service at (360) 247-3900 for reservations.

South Side Information

The **Mount St. Helens Volcanic Headquarters** is located at 42218 N.E. Yale Bridge Rd. (three miles north of Amboy on Hwy. 503) and is open Mon.-Fri. 7:30 a.m.-5 p.m. year-round; call (360) 247-3900 for information. The Forest Service's **Pine Creek Information Station,** 17 miles east of Cougar on Forest Rd. 90, also has information. Open daily 9 a.m.-6 p.m. from mid-June through September.

MOUNT ADAMS AND VICINITY

If it stood alone, 12,276-foot Mt. Adams would be a prime recreation site, silhouetted on license plates and key chains. But from a Seattle viewpoint, Adams is geographically behind and below its attention-getting neighbors: Mt. Rainier, a heavily used national park, and Mt. St. Helens, a rumbling national volcanic monument. The distance from main towns and roads make Mt. Adams an isolated, relatively unpopulated mountain. Those willing to venture out onto remote forest roads will find trails, unusual geologic formations, and scenic areas; if your goal is to escape civilization, this is the place to do it.

Geology
Like its more active neighbors, Mt. Adams is of volcanic origins, but unlike its neighbors, the mountain is believed to have been formed by a congregation of volcanic cones instead of a single large one. The mountain has been relatively quiescent for probably 10,000 years, and large glaciers crown its summit, including the Klickitat Glacier, second biggest of all Cascadian glaciers.

SIGHTS

Viewpoints
Approaching Trout Lake from the south on Hwy. 141, the **Indian Sacred Viewpoint** provides a spectacular view of Mt. Adams. For a closer look, take Forest Service Rd. 23—the main Mt. Adams access road—about eight miles north from Trout Lake. Just before the pavement gives way to gravel, you'll have a fine view of the mountain to the east.

Gular Ice Cave
Ancient volcanic activity formed this 650-foot-long, four-section lava tube cave, which during pioneer times supplied ice for the towns of The Dalles and Hood River. Accessible from Ice Caves Campground, six miles west of Trout Lake, the cave entrance is a collapsed sink, 15 feet across and 14 feet deep, connected to three other collapsed sinks by passageways. Wear warm clothing and sturdy boots, and bring at least two dependable flashlights. A helmet is also a good idea. Contact the Forest Service for details on the cave.

PRACTICALITIES

Campgrounds
The Mount Adams Ranger District has 17 developed campgrounds on the south side of Mt. Adams. Most are free, but there is an $11 fee at the larger campgrounds, including **Moss Creek** and **Peterson Prairie.** The historic **Peterson Prairie Guard Station,** west of Trout Lake, can be rented ($35 d) Dec.-April and is popular with skiers, snowshoers, and snowmobilers. Contact the Mount Adams Ranger Station in Trout Lake, tel. (509) 395-3400, for reservations.

Other Forest Service campgrounds line Forest Rd. 23, the route that connects the town of Randle with the northwest side of Mt. Adams. These are managed by the Cowlitz Valley Ranger District in Randle, tel. (360) 497-1100, and range from free to $9 a night. Closest to the Mount Adams Wilderness Area are Council Lake, Olallie Lake, Takhalakh Lake, and Horseshoe Lake campgrounds. Takhalakh Lake Campground affords a fine view of Mt. Adams.

Getting There
There are two ways to approach Mt. Adams: from Seattle, take I-5 south to I-205 near Vancouver, then follow I-205 to Hwy. 14 and head east. At Underwood, take Hwy. 141 north to Trout Lake. An alternative is to take I-5 south past Chehalis, then east on Hwy. 12 to Randle and take the **Randle Road** (Forest Service Rd. 23) south for 56 miles to Trout Lake. This isolated road is definitely the scenic route, and the entire length is paved. Approaching from the east, you can drive down Hwy. 97 to Goldendale and west on Hwy. 142 to Klickitat and take the Glenwood-Trout Lake Rd., or follow Hwy. 14 from Maryhill to Underwood and drive north. The roads into the Mt. Adams area are closed each winter due to heavy snowfall.

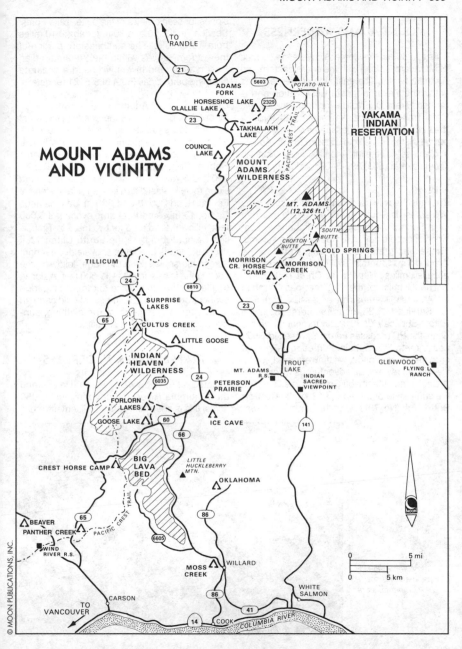

MOUNT ADAMS AND VICINITY

MOUNT ADAMS WILDERNESS

This 42,280-acre wilderness covers the summit of Mt. Adams, along with the entire eastern and northern flanks. The east side of the peak lies within the Yakama Indian Reservation and is termed "Tract D." Trails—including the Pacific Crest Trail—provide a semicircular path through the heart of the wilderness. A new backcountry permit system is being discussed for Mt. Adams Wilderness; call the Mt. Adams Ranger District in Trout Lake at (509) 395-3400 for details.

Hiking

The most heavily used trail in the Mount Adams Wilderness is **South Climb,** a 2.2-mile trail from Cold Springs Campground to timberline, from where climbers depart for routes to the summit. Those who prefer to stay low can follow the **Around the Mountain Trail** (No. 9) northwest for about six miles to the **Pacific Crest Trail** (PCT).

The 21 miles of the PCT that pass through Mt. Adams Wilderness are accessible from Forest Service Rd. 23, near its intersection with Forest Service Rd. 8810, on the south; on the north, the PCT crosses Forest Service Rd. 5603 near Potato Hill. Subalpine meadows, glacial streams, dense forest, wildflowers, and scenic viewpoints reward the adventurous hiker.

Beginning at Morrison Creek Horse Camp on the south side of Mt. Adams, 2.7-mile **Crofton Butte Trail** (No. 73) follows the mountain's lower slopes for scenic views of the butte. Take Forest Service Roads 80 and 8040 for about 10 miles from Trout Lake. The southeastern portion of the wilderness lies within the Yakama Indian Reservation, and hikers will need a separate camping permit; call (509) 865-5121 for details.

Climbing Mount Adams

Mount Adams is one of the easiest Northwest volcanic peaks to climb; in fact, it's often used as a first climb by area mountaineering clubs. Before you begin, be sure to register with the Mt. Adams Ranger Station in Trout Lake, tel. (509) 395-2501. Use quotas may be in effect. The south slope route is least difficult: it begins at the end of Forest Roads 8040 and 500 at Cold Springs Camp, 13 miles north at an elevation of 6,000 feet; follow the old road for two miles to Timberline Camp. From here the **South Climb Trail** (No. 183) leads to a large snowfield. Bear right across the snowfield to the ridge, following the ridge to the false summit at 11,500 feet. A zigzag trail leads through pumice to the summit, for a six-hour one-way trip. Climbers should carry an ice ax, rope, crampons, warm clothing, sunglasses, and other basic supplies.

TRAPPER CREEK WILDERNESS

Located halfway between Mt. St. Helens and the Columbia River and covering just 6,050 acres, this is one of the smaller wilderness areas

Mount Adams is popular among novice mountaineers.

DIANNE BOULERICE LYONS

in Washington. It is also one of the few places where the forests have been spared from logging in this part of the state. Several trails provide access; longest is the **Observation Trail** (No. 132), which takes you through dense old-growth stands of timber, across a ridge, and to a spur trail that edges up 4,207-foot Observation Peak for panoramic views. From here, you can continue down to the junction with **Trapper Creek Trail** (No. 192), which takes you back along this pretty creek to your starting point. This loop hike is approximately 12 miles long. A new backcountry permit system is being discussed for Trapper Creek Wilderness; call the Mt. Adams Ranger District in Trout Lake at (509) 395-3400 for details.

INDIAN HEAVEN WILDERNESS

The 20,960-acre Indian Heaven Wilderness offers miles of little-used hiking trails; you won't find Mt. Rainier's crowds here because the average day-hiker isn't willing to drive this far into the woods on beat-up forest roads. The wilderness covers a high plateau that is split through by the Pacific Crest Trail and pockmarked with small ponds, evergreen forests, meadows, and mosquitoes. It is located due west of Trout Lake and north of Carson. A new backcountry permit system is being discussed for Indian Heaven Wilderness; call the Mt. Adams Ranger District in Trout Lake at (509) 395-3400 for details.

Hiking Trails
Thomas Lake Trail is a well-used 3.3-mile path that starts on the west side of the wilderness from Forest Rd. 65, and passes Dee, Thomas, Naha, Umtux, and Sahalee Tyee lakes before intersecting with the Pacific Crest Trail near Blue Lake. Head north on the main road from Carson, then turn right onto Forest Service Rd. 65 for about 17 miles to the trailhead.

The Pacific Crest Trail traverses Indian Heaven Wilderness from south to north: start at Crest Horse Camp, just south of the wilderness boundary on Forest Rd. 60 (right off Forest Service Rd. 65); the trail passes lakes, meadows, and forest for 17 miles through the wilderness area, then connects with Forest Service Rd. 24 near Surprise Lakes on the north side.

TROUT LAKE AND GLENWOOD

Trout Lake is a tiny agricultural settlement with dairy and horse farms (along with a llama ranch), found approximately 30 miles north of the Columbia Gorge town of White Salmon. The world's largest D'Anjou pear orchard (Mt. Adams Orchards) is just a few miles south of here on the way to White Salmon. Trout Lake is the main access point for the Mt. Adams area, but has minimal services—a pair of restaurants, a grocery store, and gas station. For more dining variety and other services, head south to the Columbia River or east to Goldendale.

The town does have the Forest Service's **Mt. Adams Ranger Station,** tel. (509) 395-3400, where you can get maps, camping information, and current trail conditions. Mountain climbers must register here to climb Mt. Adams. They're open Mon.-Fri. 8 a.m.-4:30 p.m. all year. Just east of Trout Lake is a magnificent view of Mt. Adams, with a foreground of ripening huckleberry bushes in late August.

The equally small town of Glenwood is approximately 10 miles east of Trout Lake and six miles north of **Conboy Lake National Wildlife Refuge,** tel. (509) 364-3410. This 5,800-acre refuge provides a feeding and resting area for thousands of geese, ducks, and swans during their spring and fall migrations. It's the only place in Washington where sandhill cranes nest. A two-mile loop hike makes for a nice shoreline and forest hike, with the chance to view the waterfowl. Call (509) 364-3410 for more information.

Lodging and Food
Trout Lake Country Inn, 15 Guler Rd., tel. (509) 395-2894, has five guest rooms in an historic turn-of-the-century inn. Rates are $65-85 s or d, including a full breakfast and shared or private baths. Kids are accepted. The restaurant here serves lunch and dinner, and a comedic dinner theater takes place in the summer.

The Farm B&B, 490 Sunnyside Rd. in Trout Lake, tel. (509) 395-2488, is a classic three-story farmhouse constructed in 1890. Two cozy guest rooms share a bath, kids are accepted, and a full farm breakfast is served. Rates are $75-85 s or d. More basic rooms are available for mountain climbers at $65 d including breakfast. Also in Trout Lake is **Serenity's,** tel. (509)

395-2500 or (800) 276-7993, where cabins with kitchenettes go for $90-125 d; two-night minimum. The restaurant here serves prime rib to die for.

Glenwood's 80-acre **Flying L Ranch,** tel. (509) 364-3488 or (888) 682-3267, sits in a secluded valley on the eastern slope of the Cascades, with a spectacular skyline dominated by Mt. Adams. The lodge is a favorite place for family reunions and other groups, but also has cabins for $70-140 d including a full breakfast. Guests enjoy the hot tub and one-mile hiking trail.

Trout Lake has a popular **Saturday market** in July and August, with fresh produce, arts and crafts, and baked treats.

Trout Lake's **Elk Meadows RV Park,** tel. (509) 395-2400, has spaces for tents and RVs.

Llama Ranch B&B, four miles south of Trout Lake, tel. (509) 395-2786 or (800) 800-5262, is a 100-acre ranch where they raise 70 llamas. The seven guest rooms (two with private baths) for $79-99 d. Guests can take the llamas for a walk after enjoying the full country breakfast. Kids accepted.

Events and Transportation
The main local events are Glenwood's **Ketchum Kalf Rodeo** on the third weekend of July, and **Trout Lake Fair and Dairy Show** on the first weekend of August. In mid-July, the **Trout Lake Festival of the Arts** attracts local artisans of all types.

Woodruff Aviation, tel. (509) 395-2938, has flightseeing tours of Mt. St. Helens from the Trout Lake airport.

SOUTH-CENTRAL WASHINGTON

WENATCHEE

Driving east on Highway 2 from the damp Puget Sound area, the transition to the "dry side of the mountains" is abrupt. The heavily forested, snow-capped Cascades give way to bone-dry hills, blanketed by snow in winter and covered only by dry brown grass in summer. You'll experience few of Puget Sound's mostly cloudy days here: Wenatchee gets over 300 sunny days and only 10-15 inches of rain per year. The warm, sunny days, cool nights, and volcanic ash soil combine to provide ideal apple-growing conditions. The area also grows pears, cherries, peaches, and other fruits.

The city of Wenatchee (pop. 24,000) faces its twin, East Wenatchee (pop. 4,000), across the Columbia River, teaming up to form a major population center smack-dab in the middle of Washington's apple orchards. Downtown Wenatchee is a prosperous place with an abundance of fine shops, museums, and restaurants, plus a fun riverside path and many great places to explore nearby. Unfortunately, Wenatchee's positive aspects are partially offset by the ugliness of rampant development. The main thoroughfare—Wenatchee Ave.—is the standard mix of shopping and cars, with all the big mega-marts strewn along both sides as you exit town to the north. It's sad to see the rich agricultural land around the twin Wenatchees being swallowed up by shopping malls, roads, and housing developments.

HISTORY

The name Wenatchee comes from Wa-Nat-hee, an Indian word that means "water flowing out." Philip Miller was Wenatchee's pioneer apple grower and one of the first white settlers. In 1872, Miller took squatter's rights on a parcel of land in the Wenatchee Valley and planted a handful of apple seedlings. The trees flourished, and when the railroad came to Wenatchee in 1892, Miller drove in the silver pike to link the

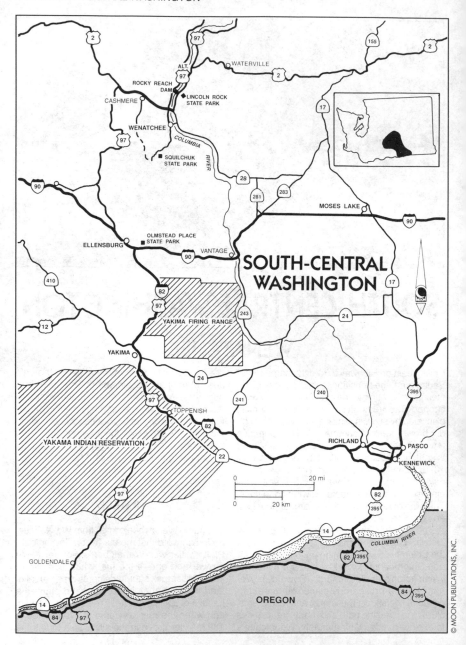

SOUTH-CENTRAL
WASHINGTON

last rails—and to help determine Wenatchee's economic future. Miller's ranch shipped its first full carload of apples to Seattle in 1901. Irrigation projects, beginning with the Highline Canal in 1904, brought much-needed water to this arid region and helped the apple industry blossom. Today, an average of 30,000 carloads of apples are shipped from the Wenatchee Valley every year. The local economy of Wenatchee is still heavily based in agriculture and food processing, but a huge Alcoa aluminum plant, an underground gold mine, and the many retail businesses are also major employers.

SIGHTS

Ohme Gardens

Located just north of Wenatchee on a bluff overlooking the Wenatchee Valley, Ohme Gardens is a testimony to over 50 years of watering and weed-pulling by the Ohme family. Their hard work transformed a barren hillside of sagebrush into one of America's most highly acclaimed gardens. Originally created for their personal use, the patch of green was eventually purchased by the state. Now covering nine acres, the gardens resemble natural alpine scenery: evergreens, grass, ponds, and waterfalls blend with the existing rock—a cool reprieve from the scorching Wenatchee sunshine. A lookout from the gardens' highest point provides broad views of the valley, Cascades, and Columbia River. The gardens are near the junction of Highways 2 and 97, just north of Wenatchee, tel. (509) 662-5785. Open April 15-Oct. 15, daily 9 a.m.-7 p.m. in the summer, or daily 9 a.m.-6 p.m. in spring and fall. Admission is $5 adults, $3 ages 7-18, free for kids under seven. Steep drop-offs in some sections make this a hazardous place for toddlers.

Rocky Reach Dam

Although this looks like just another large Columbia River dam, Rocky Reach is actually one of the most unusual and interesting visitor attractions in Washington. The 4,800-foot-long dam, seven miles north of Wenatchee on Hwy. 97A, was built across the Columbia between 1956 and 1962, with additions completed in 1971. Picnic tables and elaborately landscaped areas cover 18 acres of grounds (including a floral U.S. flag composed of red, white, and blue petunias), while a visitor center sells snacks and gifts and offers summertime guided tours. A variety of films and videos are shown upon request in the theater. The visitor center and exhibit galleries are open daily 8 a.m.-8 p.m. from Memorial Day to Labor Day, daily 8 a.m.-4 p.m. in the spring and fall, and closed January to mid-February. Call (509) 663-7522 for details.

Be sure to visit the fish-viewing room where you can watch salmon and steelhead heading upriver from mid-April to mid-November. They are also visible in the fish ladder outside. Enter the powerhouse where you can view the enormous gantry crane and 11 generators producing 1.3 million kilowatts, enough to supply power for all of Seattle. Nearly a quarter of this energy goes to power an enormous Alcoa aluminum plant in Wenatchee.

The dam's real treat is a long—and I do mean long—**Gallery of the Columbia** filled with an astounding collection of educational exhibits. Here you will learn about the channeled scablands, explore Indian artifacts (including a unique steatite pipe enclosed in a carved wood case), learn about early explorers and settlers, and follow the development of the region. Be sure to check out the Waterville Tramway exhibit; this ingenious device was used early in this century to transport wheat to steamers on the Columbia River and simultaneously haul coal and other supplies 9,200-feet uphill to the settlement. An extensive **Gallery of Electricity** relates the history of electricity in displays and photos, and allows visitors to generate their own power. All told, these exhibits are enough to keep history and science buffs occupied for several hours.

North Central Washington Museum

Wenatchee's North Central Washington Museum, 127 S. Mission St., tel. (509) 664-3340, is one of the finest museums in the state, a surprisingly large collection spread over two floors and two connected buildings. The main level takes you on a tour of turn-of-the-century Wenatchee, past a restored 1917 Oldsmobile sedan and the Liberty Theater pipe organ (1919), used for occasional performances with silent films in the performance center, and an exhibit on Clyde Edward Pangborn, who made the first nonstop

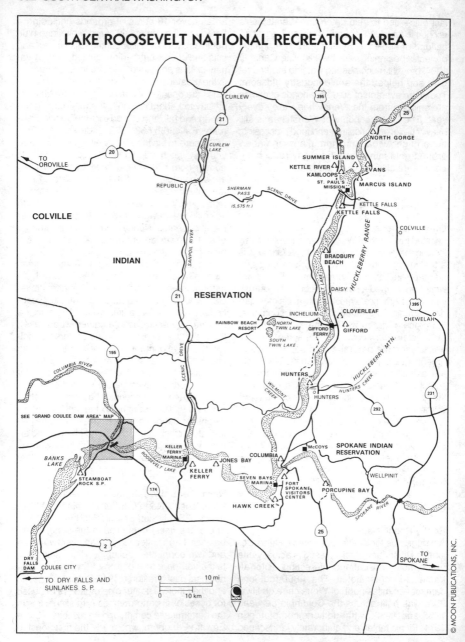

LAKE ROOSEVELT NATIONAL RECREATION AREA

trans-Pacific flight. He left Japan on October 3, 1931, and landed in Wenatchee 41 hours later, at an airfield that now bears his name. Upstairs, you'll discover an impressive model railroad that chugs through a Cascades mountain setting, historic photos, and Indian petroglyphs from the site of Rock Island Dam (the others are under water). Across the skybridge is an art gallery with changing exhibits, a delightful collection of miniatures (including the world's smallest belt), and even a 1916 bathroom. Head down the stairs to apple industry exhibits and videos, and an ingenious 1920s-era apple sorter.

The museum is open Mon.-Fri. 10 a.m.-4 p.m., Sat.-Sun. 1-4 p.m. (closed January weekends and holidays). Admission is $3 adults, $1 ages 6-12, free for kids under five, $5 for families, free on Monday. While here, pick up a walking tour brochure describing Wenatchee's historic downtown buildings.

Kids will love the **Children's Discovery Museum** at 233 N. Wenatchee Ave., open Wednesday, Thursday, and Saturday 10 a.m.-3 p.m. Inside are all sorts of interactive exhibits to educate and entertain. Call (509) 665-0941 for details.

Apples
At 2900 Euclid Ave., the **Washington State Apple Commission Visitor Center,** tel. (509) 663-9600, has a video and displays about the apple industry, along with apples and apple juice samples. Open Mon.-Fri. 8 a.m.-5 p.m., Saturday 9 a.m.-5 p.m., and Sunday 11 a.m.-4 p.m. May-Dec.; Mon.-Fri. 8 a.m.-5 p.m. the rest of the year. While here, you'll learn that Washington produces 10 billion apples each year, over half of the nation's apples and three times as many apples as its nearest competitor, New York. Most apples are picked mid-September to mid-October, so get here before this to see the heavily laden fruit trees.

Parks
The **Apple Capital Recreation Loop Trail** is a paved 11-mile path that makes for a wonderful riverfront stroll, bike ride, or run. Several parks provide picnic and play areas along the way. The trail follows both sides of the Columbia River, connecting a series of parks, including Wenatchee Confluence State Park with hiking trails and good birdwatching, Riverfront Park (with an

ice arena and miniature steam train, tel. 509-884-0494), and Walla Walla Point Park (with a swimming beach).

On the south end, the trail crosses the river on a footbridge to East Wenatchee. One path heads north through Porter's Pond Nature Area and back over the Odabashian Bridge, and a second continues south to tiny **View Point Park,** a great place to watch sunsets. Two miles farther south is **Rock Island Hydro Park,** another riverside park with paths, a boat ramp, a swimming area, and other recreation.

Waterville
Approximately 25 miles northeast of Wenatchee is the small farming town of Waterville (pop. 1,100) with wide streets and all-American homes. It is the county seat for Douglas County and the highest incorporated town in Washington. The 10-mile drive from Orondo (on the banks of the Columbia) gains 2,000 feet in elevation, climbing up a steep canyon before emerging onto the flat farming plateau around Waterville. Several beau-

Ohme Gardens

tiful old buildings are here, including the **Douglas County Courthouse,** the 1916 **St. Joseph's Catholic Church,** and the classy three-story **Waterville Historic Hotel,** tel. (509) 745-8695. Built in 1903, the hotel has been lovingly restored to its authentic beauty and is now on the National Register of Historic Places. Inside are original and other antique furnishings. Rates are $42-82 s or $48-88 s or d with private or shared baths; including some deluxe suites. This is great place to step back in time in style.

Waterville is also home to the **Douglas County Historical Museum,** tel. (509) 745-8435, where the collection includes a 73-pound meteorite, a two-headed calf, and the old Winthrop post office. Open Tues.-Sun. 11 a.m.-5 p.m. Memorial Day to mid-Oct.; donation. Ask here about tours of nearby wheat farms.

Local events include **Waterville Days** in mid-July, and the **North Central Washington Fair** in late August. A large outdoor pool is in the city park. **Badger Mountain** six miles south of Waterville, is a small area with three rope tows and a 1,500-foot drop—a family place for downhill and cross-country skiing and snowboarding. **Link** has free bus service from Waterville to the rest of Douglas and Chelan counties, tel. (800) 851-5465.

ACCOMMODATIONS

Motels
The Wenatchee Area Chamber of Commerce, tel. (800) 572-7753, keeps track of room availability and can transfer you to local motels and B&Bs that are chamber members. Many of the motels also offer ski package deals in the winter.

Bed and Breakfasts
Set on a 10-acre riverside spread, **Warm Springs Inn,** 1611 Love Ln., tel. (509) 662-8365 or (800) 543-3645, is an enormous 1917 plantation-style mansion. The three guest rooms and suite all have private baths and full breakfasts; $75-105 s or d. This is a very popular wedding locale.

Cherub Inn B&B, 410 N. Miller, tel. (509) 662-6011, is a 1930 English Tudor home in downtown Wenatchee with four guest rooms, shared baths, a grand piano, and full breakfast; $85 d. Kids okay.

Rimrock Inn B&B, 1354 Pitcher Canyon Rd., tel. (509) 664-5113 or (888) 664-5113, has quiet accommodations three miles south of Wenatchee. The three guest rooms have private baths, there's a hot tub, and a full breakfast is served; $70 d; no young kids.

Campgrounds
Wenatchee Confluence State Park, tel. (509) 664-6373, sits at the confluence of the Wenatchee and Columbia Rivers, just north of town, and has a bike- and footbridge across the Wenatchee to marshes on the south side. Camp at the park in an open grassy field (hot in the summer). Tent sites are $11, RV hookups $16, including showers; open year-round. Call (800) 452-5687 for reservations ($6 extra).

Wenatchee River County Park, six miles west of Wenatchee on Hwy. 2, has playgrounds, picnic areas, and camping for tents ($15) and RVs ($18). The park is open April-Oct.; call (509) 662-2525 for reservations.

Lincoln Rock State Park—named for a geologic feature across the river that some say resembles President Lincoln's profile—is seven miles north of East Wenatchee on Hwy. 2. The day-use area has a swimming beach on the Columbia River, boat moorage, and tennis courts. The park has tent sites ($11) and RV spaces ($16), and is open mid-March through October. Interpretive programs are offered at the amphitheater on summer evenings. Call (509) 884-8702 for information, or (800) 452-5687 for reservations ($6 extra).

FOOD

Breakfast and Bakeries
Start the day with delicious breakfasts and espresso at **Wild Huckleberry Bakery & Breakfast House,** 302 S. Mission, tel. (509) 665-6692. Also popular for breakfast is **Prospector Pies Restaurant & Bakery,** 731 N. Wenatchee Ave., tel. (509) 662-1118. If you're just looking for a cup of java, the ubiquitous **Starbucks,** 10 Grant Rd. in East Wenatchee, tel. (509) 884-1924, will certainly fill the cup. Great Mexican pastries at **La Espiga Panaderia,** 818 S. Wenatchee Ave., tel. (509) 664-7254. **Edible Art Bakery,** 104 11th St.

WENATCHEE AREA MOTELS AND HOTELS

Accommodations are arranged from least to most expensive. Rates may be lower during the winter months. See the text for descriptions of local B&Bs.

INEXPENSIVE

Lyle's Motel; 924 N. Wenatchee Ave.; tel. (509) 663-5155 or (800) 582-3788; $34 s, $40 d; outdoor pool, jacuzzi, kitchenettes available

Welcome Inn; 232 N. Wenatchee Ave.; tel. (509) 663-7121 or (800) 561-8856; $37 s, $40 d; outdoor pool, microwaves, fridges

Holiday Lodge; 610 N. Wenatchee Ave.; tel. (509) 663-8167 or (800) 722-0852; $40-60 s, $45-65 d; outdoor pool, jacuzzi, sauna, AAA approved

Avenue Motel; 720 N. Wenatchee Ave.; tel. (509) 663-7161 or (800) 733-8981; $47 s or d; outdoor pool, jacuzzi, kitchenettes available, AAA approved

Travelodge; 1004 N. Wenatchee Ave.; tel. (509) 662-8165 or (800) 578-7878; $48 s, $53 d; outdoor pool, jacuzzi, sauna, continental breakfast, kitchenettes available, AAA approved

Starlite Motel; 1640 N. Wenatchee Ave.; tel. (509) 663-8115; $49-59 s or d; outdoor pool, sauna, kitchenettes

Vagabond Inn; 700 N. Wenatchee Ave.; tel. (509) 663-8133 or (800) 522-1555; $50 s or d; continental breakfast, AAA approved

Chieftain Motel; 1005 N. Wenatchee Ave.; tel. (509) 663-8141 or (800) 572-4456; $53-62 s or d; outdoor pool, jacuzzi

MODERATE

Rivers Inn; 580 Valley Mall Pkwy. in E. Wenatchee; tel. (509) 884-1474 or (800) 922-3199; $47 s, $62 d; outdoor pool, jacuzzi

Orchard Inn; 1401 N. Miller; tel. (509) 662-3443 or (800) 368-4571; $56 s, $61 d; outdoor pool, jacuzzi, AAA approved

Comfort Inn; 815 N. Wenatchee Ave.; tel. (509) 662-1700 or (800) 228-5150; $57-75 s, $65-83 d; indoor pool, exercise room, continental breakfast, AAA approved

Cedars Inn; 80 9th St. NE in East Wenatchee; tel. (509) 886-8000; $61-76 s, $67-82 d; indoor pool, jacuzzi, continental breakfast, microwaves and fridges, AAA approved

Holiday Inn Express; 1921 N. Wenatchee Ave.; tel. (509) 663-6355 or (800) 465-4329; $69-79 s or d; indoor pool, continental breakfast, AAA approved

Best Western Heritage Inn; 1905 N. Wenatchee Ave.; tel. (509) 664-6565 or (800) 528-1234; $70-89 s, $75-99 d; indoor pool, jacuzzi, sauna, exercise room, continental breakfast, AAA approved

Doubletree Hotel; 1225 N. Wenatchee Ave.; tel. (509) 663-0711 or (800) 547-8010; $79-89 s or d; outdoor pool, jacuzzi, airport shuttle, AAA approved

EXPENSIVE

WestCoast Wenatchee Center Hotel; 201 N. Wenatchee Ave.; tel. (509) 662-1234 or (800) 426-0670; $87-97 s, $95-105 d; indoor and outdoor pools, jacuzzi, exercise room, airport shuttle, AAA approved

NE in East Wenatchee, tel. (509) 884-0542, creates tasty pecan nut rolls, cookies, scones, and other treats.

Lunches and Delis

Located in an old brick-walled pub, **McGlinn's Public House,** 111 Orondo, tel. (509) 663-9073, has plenty of microbrews on tap, plus burgers, salads, and wood-fired pizzas for a light dinner. Friendly, popular, and smoke free, with live jazz on weekends. Excellent lunches and dinners also at **Lemolo Cafe & Deli,** 114 N. Wenatchee Ave., tel. (509) 664-6576. They offer deli sandwiches, soups, salads, and distinctive stoneoven pizzas. The place gets packed at lunch.

Palouse Juice & Java, 119 Palouse St., tel. (509) 665-3262, is a tiny shop with organic fruit and veggie juices, soups, salads, and other healthy fare. **Bonzetti's Fresh Pasta,** 406 N. Mission, tel. (509) 663-5460, is an Italian take-out deli with gourmet pastas and salads, along with a good selection of wines.

All-American

Stop by for a malt, banana split, or sundae from the old fashioned soda fountain at **Bellmore's Owl Drug,** 39 S. Wenatchee Ave., tel. (509) 662-7133, in business since 1894. **EZ's Burger Deluxe,** 1950 N. Wenatchee Ave., tel. (509) 663-1957, has the best local hamburgers, or head to **Bob's Classic Bar & Grill,** 110 2nd St., tel. (509) 663-3954, where the noisy, smokey crowd enjoys burgers served in a flashy '50s decor. **The Cottage Inn,** tel. (509) 663-4435, has been serving chicken, steak, and seafood at the 134 Easy St. location since 1940. Open for dinner only Tues.-Saturday.

For the best local pizzas—made with a distinctively spicy sauce—head to **Abby's Legendary Pizza,** 5th and Western, tel. (509) 662-2226, or 702 Grant Rd. in East Wenatchee, tel. (509) 884-7211.

Fine Dining

The **John Horan House Restaurant,** 2 Horan Rd., tel. (509) 663-0018, serves steak, seafood, and other fine meals in an elegant farmhouse built in 1899 by John Horan, one of the valley's "Apple Kings." Open daily for dinner only, and lunch on Sunday; reservations advised.

It's a bit pricey, but the **Roaster & Ale House** at WestCoast Wenatchee Center, 201 N. Wenatchee Ave., tel. (509) 662-1234, serves three dependably good meals a day, including a fine Caesar's salad at lunch. The location—atop the WestCoast Wenatchee Center Hotel—affords great sunset vistas. Get here for happy hour to sample some of the 21 draught beers.

International Restaurants

Visconti's Italian Restaurant, 1737 N. Wenatchee, tel. (509) 662-5013, serves quite good Northern Italian food in a white-linen setting. Prices are fairly reasonable. Another fine Italian place over in East Wenatchee is **Garlini's Italian Restaurant,** 810 Valley Mall Pkwy. E, tel. (509) 884-1707.

Get authentic Mexican meals at **El Abuelo,** 601 S. Mission, tel. (509) 662-7331, or a couple of blocks away at **La Fuente's** 816 S. Mission, tel. (509) 664-1910; or stop by one of the vans scattered around town for cheap and meaty tacos.

A personal favorite is tiny **Cuc Tran Cafe,** 7 N. Wenatchee Ave., tel. (509) 663-6281, where the Vietnamese food is as good as it gets, especially the Saturday-only pho ga noodle soup. Recommended. Get authentic Thai cookery at **The Thai Restaurant,** 1211 N. Mission, tel. (509) 662-8077. **Wok-About Grill,** 110 N. Wenatchee Ave., tel. (509) 662-1154, has a Mongolian barbecue with a big grill in the center of the room and quick service. This is a good way to fill up without spending much.

Fresh Produce

The Wenatchee area is filled with fruit stands selling fresh apples, apricots, cherries, peaches, and pears in season. **Stemilt Growers** is a large local apple, cherry, and pear grower with tours (call 509-663-1451) and a retail shop at 524 S. Columbia St., tel. (509) 663-7848. The **Wenatchee Valley Farmers Market** takes place Thursday 4-8 p.m. June-Oct. in front of the Convention Center on Wenatchee Ave., and on Wednesday and Saturday 7 a.m.-1 p.m. in Riverfront Park; tel. (509) 884-6412.

EVENTS AND ENTERTAINMENT

Events

Ridge to River Relay consists of six different competitions, with teams competing over a 35-mile course that includes cross-country and downhill skiing, running, cycling, and canoeing. It attracts 2,000 participants each year and is held the third Sunday in April. Call (509) 662-8799 for details.

The self-proclaimed "Apple Capital of the World" is the only proper place to hold the annual **Apple Blossom Festival**, tel. (509) 662-3616, going strong since 1919. This 10-day event starts the last weekend of April and is highlighted by a youth parade and the Apple Blossom Parade on the first Saturday in May; other festivities include carnivals, a "Classy Chassis" auto parade, hydroplane races, pancake breakfast, arts and crafts fair, and lots more.

The **Wenatchee Youth Circus**, tel. (509) 662-0722, perhaps the best amateur youth circus in America, opens in July in Wenatchee, and then heads all over the Pacific Northwest in summer. The **Festival of Trees** takes place Thanksgiving weekend, with 25 elaborately decorated Christmas trees, a gingerbread village, parade, visits with Santa, and all sorts of entertainment.

Music and the Arts

Join the **Fun at the Fountain** series in downtown Wenatchee for live music and entertainment Wednesday at noon June-August. Wenatchee has two new downtown theaters: the 150-seat **Riverside Playhouse Theatre** with in-the-round seating, and the 500-seat **Seafirst Performing Arts Theatre** for concerts and performances.

Nightlife

Wenatchee Roaster & Ale House, 201 N. Wenatchee Ave., tel. (509) 662-1234, has live pop music most nights. **Grizzley's Lounge**, 1225 N. Wenatchee Ave., tel. (509) 663-0711, has rock and alternative bands, while **McGlinn's Ale House & Espresso Bar**, 111 Orondo, tel. (509) 663-9073, features live jazz on Wednesday. **TJ Cooper's Lounge**, 27 S. Chelan, tel. (509) 663-1227, is the place for C&W dancing. For pool tables and sports on the big-screen TV, head to **Mickey O'Reilly's Sports Bar &** **Grill**, 560 Valley Mall Pkwy. in East Wenatchee, tel. (509) 884-6299. The outside deck fronting the river is popular with the lunch crowd.

SPORTS AND RECREATION

See "Parks" above for info on the very popular Apple Capital Recreation Loop Trail.

Swimming

Swim at the roped-off area in **Wenatchee Confluence State Park;** the **Wenatchee swimming pool**, 220 Fuller, tel. (509) 664-3397; the **YMCA**, 217 Orondo, tel. (509) 662-2109; or at the covered pool at **Eastmont County Park** in East Wenatchee, tel. (509) 884-3113.

Skiing

Just 12 miles from Wenatchee, **Mission Ridge Ski Area** is the area's largest and Washington's east-side secret, with drier snow and more sun than other Cascade ski areas. It has 35 runs (plus a snowboard half-pipe) spread across 2,000 acres, and a base elevation of 4,570 feet. At the base, you'll find a restaurant, lounge, ski and snowboard rental shop, ski school, and child care facility. Midway Cafe is halfway up the mountain. Mission Ridge is generally open Thanksgiving to early April, and weekend tickets cost $33 adults, or $18 for students and seniors. Kids under seven ski free. Mission Ridge does not publicize its snow depth because it is often considerably lower than elsewhere in the Cascades, but the snow is often of better quality than in places where the base is deeper. To check on conditions, call (509) 626-5208 or (800) 374-1693. A SkiLink bus (tel. 800-851-5465) means that you can reach Mission Ridge from Wenatchee, Leavenworth, or Chelan absolutely free. Ski racks are attached to the side of the bus.

Golf

Golfers will enjoy playing at four local courses: **Kahler Glen Golf Course,** three and a half miles north off Hwy. 2, tel. (509) 763-4025; **Three Lakes Golf Course,** on W. Malaga Rd. off the Wenatchee-Malaga Hwy., tel. (509) 663-5448; **Rock Island Golf Course,** in Rock Island, tel. (509) 884-2806; and the new **Desert Canyon Golf Course,** north of E. Wenatchee, tel. (800) 258-4173.

Other Sports

Skate at **Riverfront Park Ice Arena,** at the base of 5th St., tel. (509) 664-3392; skate rentals are available. **Wenatchee Valley Raceway,** tel. (509) 884-8592, on Fancher Heights above E. Wenatchee has auto racing on Sunday nights all summer.

All Rivers Adventures, tel. (800) 743-5628, and **Alpine Adventures,** tel. (800) 926-7238, lead whitewater and float trips down the Wenatchee River. Ever wanted to learn to fly like a bird? **Air Play Paragliding School,** tel. (509) 782-5543, offers tandem rides for novices, along with lessons and rentals.

Boarders will be happy to find one of Washington's best **skateboard parks** at 220 Fuller Street. Rent mountain bikes to enjoy the loop trail from **The Second Wind,** 85 N.E. 9th St. in E. Wenatchee, tel. (509) 884-0821. Rent jet skis from **RSI Sports,** 334 N. Keller, tel. (509) 669-4779 or (800) 786-2637.

SHOPPING

The Wenatchee area has several big malls, including **Wenatchee Valley Mall** in East Wenatchee, and **Valley North Mall,** Miller St. in North Wenatchee. Downtown has a big choice of boutiques, including a number of fine-art galleries and a quilt shop. Skiers and other outdoors enthusiasts will want to visit **Asplund's,** a sporting goods store at 1544 N. Wenatchee Ave., tel. (509) 662-6539. They also offer rentals of snowshoes, snowboards, and cross-country ski equipment. The **Victorian Village,** at 611 S. Mission, is a collection of small shops and restaurants. And if you just want something cheap, head up Wenatchee Ave. to find all the major discount chains, including Kmart and Wal-Mart.

INFORMATION AND SERVICES

For maps, brochures, or specific information on the Wenatchee area, contact the **Wenatchee Area Chamber of Commerce,** 2 S. Chelan Ave., tel. (509) 662-2116 or (800) 572-7753. Open Mon.-Fri. 8 a.m.-5 p.m. year-round; on the Web at www.wenatchee.org. While here, pick up a brochure describing the imaginative sculptures that are found downtown.

The **East Wenatchee Chamber of Commerce** is located at 44 Rock Island Rd., tel. (509) 884-2514 or (800) 245-3922. Get camping and hiking info from the **Wenatchee National Forest** headquarters at 215 Melody Ln. (junction of Highways 2 and 97), tel. (509) 662-4335.

TRANSPORTATION

Buses and Trains

Columbia Station at Wenatchee and Kittitas is Wenatchee's downtown intermodal center. Amtrak trains, Link buses, and Northwest Trailways all stop here, providing convenient connections for travelers.

Link, tel. (509) 662-1155 or (800) 851-5465, has free (!) bus service throughout Chelan and Douglas counties, including Wenatchee, Chelan, Leavenworth, and to Mission Ridge Ski Area. The buses also carry bicycles. **Northwestern Trailways,** tel. (800) 366-6975, offers bus service east to Spokane and west to Everett and Seattle.

Amtrak's Empire Builder serves Wenatchee, with daily service east to Spokane and Chicago, and west to Seattle. For reservations and information call (800) 872-7245.

Air

Wenatchee's airport, **Pangborn Field,** was named in honor of Clyde Pangborn, a pilot who piled up aviation record after record in the '20s and '30s. Pangborn's most notable feat was accomplished on October 6, 1931, when he and Hugh Herndon completed the first nonstop flight over the Pacific Ocean, landing at the Wenatchee airport—minus the landing gear they had intentionally dropped when excess weight threatened to shorten their flight. The trip was an eventful one—the pair was charged with spying and held in Tokyo for several weeks before being released with a hefty fine; then, while crossing the Pacific, icy wings and an empty gas tank nearly ended the flight prematurely.

Today, **Horizon Air,** tel. (800) 547-9308, flies into Pangborn Field from Seattle.

ELLENSBURG

One of Washington's best-known Western towns, Ellensburg is famous for its Labor Day weekend rodeo that attracts thousands of spectators and top rodeo talent from across the country. It is also home to the Western Art Association, which has an annual show and convention of the top Western artists, and to the Clymer Museum, devoted to the Western art of John Clymer. Yet the town isn't particularly Western in appearance; the Western clothing stores, tack shops, and country-western bars that you might expect in a rodeo town just aren't there. Instead you'll find an old, quiet college town of fewer than 14,000 with progress squeezing in on an historic city center. Ellensburg sits near the geographic center of the state, serving as commercial center for the small mining towns and cattle ranches surrounding it. Besides the rodeo, Ellensburg has something found nowhere else in the world: the beautiful "Ellensburg Blue" agate, fashioned at local jewelry stores into earrings, necklaces, and rings.

Driving toward Ellensburg from Puget Sound, the change in weather and geography is dramatic. From Seattle to Snoqualmie Pass, you'll pass forested hills and snow-covered peaks, often under a thick cloud cover. By the time you're 20 miles west of Ellensburg, the clouds have thinned out, the temperature rises in the summer and falls in the winter, and the landscape flattens to low rolling hills dotted with bushes and an occasional tree. Out here the summers are sunnier and hotter—nearly every motel has a pool—but the winters are harsh, with snow and bitter cold that the Puget Sound region rarely sees. You'll also note that in the Ellensburg area most trees have a permanent eastward tilt from the almost constant wind that blows down from the Cascades.

HISTORY

From the beginning, the Kittitas Valley has been blessed with an abundance of fish and wildlife. Indians from the otherwise hostile Nez Percé, Yakima, and Wenatchee tribes tolerated each others' presence as they hunted and fished the area peaceably. White settlers first arrived in the Ellensburg area in 1867. By 1870, Jack Splawn and Ben Burch had built the town's first store, "Robber's Roost," and the town took on the store's name until a few years later, when John Shoudy bought the store and platted the town, naming it for his wife, Mary Ellen.

Ellensburg's population grew rapidly in the late 1880s, when the Northern Pacific Railroad finished its line through town to Puget Sound. Ellensburg was a contender for the state capital seat until a fire in July 1889 destroyed its new commercial center and 200 homes; but the town fought back, rebuilding the community in brick before the year was out. One of the first colleges in the state, Central Washington University (originally called the Normal School), was established here in 1891, and Ellensburg later became the county seat. Since then, the town hasn't seen a great deal of growth, but it remains the hub of the central Washington cattle business and commercial center of the mining and agricultural region.

SIGHTS

Museums

At E. 3rd and Pine Streets, the **Kittitas County Museum**, tel. (509) 925-3778, has Native American artifacts and displays of pioneer tools, photographs of early Ellensburg, and an impressive collection of petrified wood and gemstones, including a six-pound Ellensburg Blue agate. The museum is housed in the 1889 Cadwell Building, a two-story brick structure with horseshoe-shaped windows. Open Tues.-Sat. 10 a.m.-4 p.m. May-Aug., and Tues.-Sat. 11 a.m.-3 p.m. the rest of the year; $1.

The **Clymer Museum,** 416 N. Pearl, tel. (509) 962-6416, honors John Ford Clymer, who was born in Ellensburg in 1907 and went on to fame for his illustrations in *Field and Stream* and more than 80 *Saturday Evening Post* covers. His most enduring works, however, are his carefully researched paintings of the Old West. Clymer died

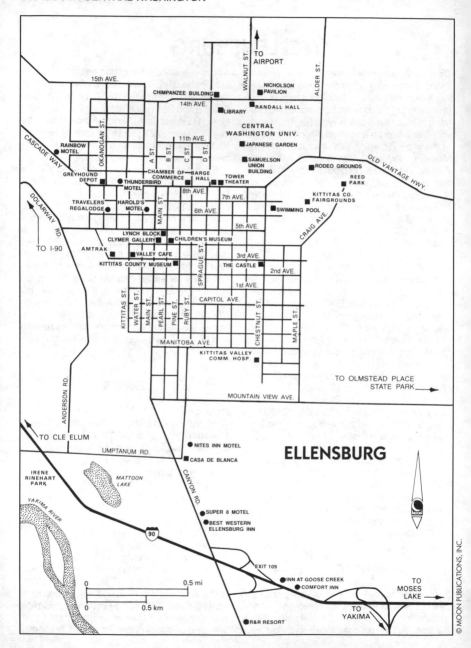

ELLENSBURG

© MOON PUBLICATIONS, INC.

in 1989 in Jackson Hole, Wyoming (another state that claims him as theirs). At the museum, you can watch a video on Clymer's life and view dozens of his cover art designs, along with a number of his Western paintings. A separate gallery here exhibits changing displays of contemporary artwork, and a gift shop has local crafts and books. The museum is open Mon.-Fri. 10 a.m.-5 p.m., Sat.-Sun. noon-5 p.m. year-round; admission is $3 adults, $2 seniors, students, and kids, and $7 families; free for kids under six. Free admission on Wednesday.

The **Children's Activity Museum,** 400 N. Main, tel. (509) 925-6789, is a hands-on museum for kids, with new exhibits monthly. Closed Tuesday; $2.50 per person.

Historic Buildings
Pick up a map at the museum or chamber of commerce for a self-guided tour of 31 Victorian-era buildings, most located within a five-block area between 6th and 3rd Avenues and Main and Pearl Streets. The **Davidson Building** at 4th and Pearl is probably the first you'll notice because of its proud tower and ornate windows. Next door, the 1889 **Stewart Building** now houses the Gallery One. **Lynch Block,** at 5th and Pearl, is the only remaining structure that survived the 1889 fire; when it was built, its front windows were the largest in central Washington. Travel down to 3rd and Chestnut to see **The Castle,** optimistically built in 1888 to be the governor's mansion when Ellensburg entered the contest for state capital; it's lost much of its elegance since, and it now houses apartments.

Thorp Mill, tel. (509) 964-9640, in the town of Thorp (eight miles northwest of Ellensburg) is a restored 1883 flour mill with the Northwest's most complete display of milling equipment. The mill was used to grind flour and cornmeal until 1946 and is now a National Historic Landmark. An interpretive slide show is provided. Open Wed.-Sun. 1-4 p.m., Memorial Day through September.

Offbeat Sights
The park bench on 4th and Pearl has a friendly *Ellensburg Bull,* complete with strategically placed hat and blue balls. It was created by noted sculptor Richard Beyer. An amusing gunslinger sculpture by Dan Klennerd guards the corner of 5th and Pearl. Also in town is **Dick & Jane's Spot,** at 101 N. Pearl, an odd collection of cast-off items that never cease to bring a smile.

Central Washington University
In existence since 1891, the 350-acre Central Washington University campus makes a fine place for a stroll. For tours of the campus, call the Admissions Office at (509) 963-3001. A **Japanese Garden** near the center of campus is open year-round and contains interesting Japanese lanterns and grounds landscaped with dozens of types of plants, including cherry trees donated by the Japanese Consulate General. Central Washington University's **Sarah Spurgeon Art Gallery,** tel. (509) 963-2665, has regional artists' and students' work displayed in Randall Hall. Built in 1893-94, four-story **Barge Hall,** 8th and D at Central Washington University, is the oldest building on campus. The center of student life is the **Samuelson Union Building,** where visitors can shop for books at the largest bookstore in the area and eat at the cafeteria for the cheapest meals in town. Another building worth a visit is **Lind Hall,** which contains a huge relief map of the state of Washington and a two-story pendulum. The **CWU Library** houses more than 350,000 volumes. **Nicholson Pavilion** contains a gymnasium, fieldhouse, and other facilities beneath a unique cable-supported roof built to withstand earthquakes.

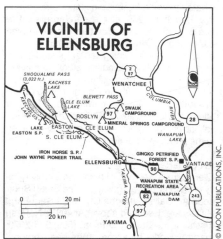

VICINITY OF ELLENSBURG

© MOON PUBLICATIONS, INC.

DON PITCHER

Ellensburg Bull, Ellensburg

The CWU's **Chimpanzee & Human Communication Institute,** tel. (509) 963-2244, is where the world famous sign language chimps live. Begun in 1966, this research project now has five chimpanzees that use American Sign Language to communicate with humans and each other. It is a training center for students, a research center for scientists studying primate communication, and a visitor education facility. Visitors can attend fascinating hour-long **Chimposiums** on Saturday mornings and Sunday afternoons for $10 adults, $7.50 students. Reservations are recommended; the center is not open to the public at other times.

Art Galleries

Ellensburg is crowded with antique stores, quality gift shops, and art galleries. The Sarah Spurgeon Art Gallery and the Clymer Museum and Gallery are described above. At 408¹/₂ N. Pearl (upstairs), the **Gallery One,** tel. (509) 925-2670, features works by some of the best regional artists in the 1889 G.R. Stewart Building. **Fairchild's,** 109 E. 6th Ave., tel. (509) 925-2326, is a print and gift shop located in an attractive Victorian home built in 1885.

Parks

Four miles southeast of Ellensburg on Ferguson Rd., see one of the first Kittitas Valley farms at **Olmstead Place State Park,** tel. (509) 925-1943. The log cabin dates back to 1875; you can tour the eight buildings filled with old farming equipment, including a granary, dairy barn, and wagon shed, open Sat.-Sun. noon-4 p.m. Memorial Day to Labor Day, or the rest of the year by appointment. The three-quarter mile **Altapes Creek Trail** leads from the red barn to the Seaton Cabin Schoolhouse, originally located farther away in a meadow; the kids didn't trudge miles through blizzards—they rode horseback.

Irene Rinehart Park, on the Yakima River off Umptanum Rd., is a welcome relief from the relentless summer sunshine. You can cool your toes in the swift green river, take a walk along shaded paths, or enjoy a riverside picnic. **Reed Park** at the end of Craig Ave. has a small shaded green for reading and relaxing, plus superb views of the county below and the snow-covered Stuart Range to the northwest.

ACCOMMODATIONS

Lodging can be very hard to come by during the Ellensburg Rodeo in early September, the Western Art show in May, and the Gorge Concerts on summer weekends. The Chamber of Commerce, tel. (509) 925-3137, keeps track of who has space. Reservations should be made far in advance for these times, and before mid-January for the rodeo. Also be forewarned that rates may be considerably higher than those listed during the rodeo. Central Washington University opens its residence halls and other facilities for lodging during the rodeo; call (800) 752-4379 for details.

Bed and Breakfasts

Located right across the street from CWU, **Campus View Inn,** 706 N. Anderson, tel. (509) 933-2345, offers cozy B&B accommodations in a grand home built in 1910. The five guest rooms have private baths, and a full breakfast is served; $60-74 s or $65-79 d.

Built in 1912, **Wren's Nest B&B**, 300 E. Manitoba Ave., tel. (509) 925-9061, is another comfortable in-town home with a big front porch, three guest rooms, shared baths, and a generous breakfast; $80-90 s or d. No kids.

Murphy's Country B&B, 2830 Thorp Hwy. S, tel. (509) 925-7986, is a 1915 antique-furnished country home with two large guest rooms and private baths. A full breakfast is served, and kids are accepted, $60 s or $70 d.

Leslie's Lazy B&B, tel. (509) 968-3829, is out in the country seven miles south of town. Two guest rooms have private baths, and a full breakfast is served; $80 d. No kids.

Circle H Holiday Ranch, tel. (509) 964-2000, has country cabins 15 miles west of Ellensburg. These are $85 pp (double occupancy) with three meals in the summer, or $125 d with breakfast in the winter. Two-night minimum; horseback rides $15/hour.

Carriage House B&B, 140 Rosebriar Ln., tel. (509) 925-2108, is a new two-bedroom cottage with jacuzzi, sauna, and full kitchen. A make-your-own-breakfast is provided; $125 for up to five people. The cottage is in the country three miles north of town. Kids will enjoy the playground; adults will like the flower gardens.

Motels

Accommodations are arranged from least to most expensive. **Travelers RegaLodge**, 300 W. 6th Ave., tel. (509) 925-2547 or (800) 523-4972, charges $33 s or $40 d, including an indoor pool, fridges, and microwaves. **Nites Inn Motel**, 1200 S. Ruby, tel. (509) 962-9600, has park-like grounds and microwaves and fridges in all rooms; $38 s or $41 d. **I-90 Inn Motel**, 1390 Dolarway Rd. (Exit 106 off I-90), tel. (509) 925-9844, has rooms for $38 s or $42 d. **Harold's Motel**, 601 N. Water, tel. (509) 925-4141, charges $42-50 s or d, and has an outdoor pool and a quiet location. **Thunderbird Motel**, 403 W. 8th, tel. (509) 962-9856 or (800) 843-3492, charges $38 s or $43 d, with an outdoor pool. **Rainbow Motel**, 1025 Cascade Way, tel. (509) 925-3544, has standard rooms for $40-85 s or d; kitchenettes available.

R&R Resort, 901 Berry Rd., tel. (509) 933-1500 or (888) 889-9870, is a new motel with an indoor pool, jacuzzi, fitness center, and continental breakfast; $55 s or d. **Super 8 Motel**, 1500 Canyon Rd., tel. (509) 962-6888 or (800) 800-8000, charges $56 s or $62-68 d, with an indoor pool and jacuzzi. **Best Western Ellensburg Inn**, 1700 Canyon Rd., tel. (509) 925-9801 or (800) 321-8791, has an indoor pool, sauna, and jacuzzis; $62-67 s or $67-72 d.

The newly built **Comfort Inn**, 1722 Canyon Rd. (509) 925-7037 or (800) 221-2222, features an indoor pool, jacuzzi, and continental breakfast for $76-96 s or d.

The **Inn at Goose Creek**, 1720 Canyon Rd., tel. (509) 925-6831 or (800) 533-0822, is a unique lodge where the 10 rooms all have different motifs. Each includes a fridge and spa tub, and a continental breakfast is served; $89 s or d.

Campgrounds

The nearest public campground is 27 miles east at **Wanapum State Recreation Area** (see under "Wanapum Lake Area" in the Columbia Basin section). RV spaces are available at the **Kittitas County Fairgrounds** during the summer months; call (800) 637-2444 for details. More camping and RV spaces at **KOA** in West Ellensburg, tel. (509) 925-9319 or (800) 562-7616, **R&R Resort**, 901 Berry Rd., tel. (509) 933-1500 or (888) 889-9870; and **Yakima River RV Park**, 791 Ringer Loop, tel. (509) 925-4734.

FOOD

The Valley Cafe, 103 W. 3rd Ave., tel. (509) 925-3050, is a European-style bistro where you won't go wrong any meal of the day. Their breakfasts include all the standards, exceptionally well prepared. Stop for lunch at **Valley Take-Out** next door for sandwiches, distinctive salads, espresso, and tempting cheesecakes. Then come back to the cafe for an evening dinner of Ellensburg lamb, seafood, chicken, or pasta. The attractive brick building was built in the 1930s.

Billy Mac's Juice Bar, 115 W. 4th Ave., tel. (509) 962-6620, has tasty juice drinks and smoothies, vegetarian sandwiches, and lunch specials.

Frazzini's Pizza Place, 716 E. 8th Ave., tel. (509) 925-9855, has quick food: pizzas, nachos, chicken hot wings, and a salad bar. More all-

American food—notably prime rib on Friday and Saturday—at **The Blue Grouse,** 1401 N. Dolarway, tel. (509) 925-4808.

Fine Dining

For an elegant night out on the town, **The Pub Minglewood,** 1889 Davidson Bldg., 402 N. Pearl St., tel. (509) 962-2260, features Italian pastas, fresh fish, the famous Ellensburg lamb (the lamb kebabs are especially good), and great desserts. Open for dinner only; closed Sunday.

Casa de Blanca, Canyon and Ruby Roads, tel. (509) 925-1693, has Mexican specialties and moderately priced steak and prime rib. For Americanized Chinese food, including inexpensive lunch specials, try **China Inn,** 116 W. 3rd Ave., tel. (509) 925-4140.

Baked Goods and Produce

Get fresh baked breads, soups, salads, and unusual sweets at **Sweet Memories,** 319 N. Pearl, tel. (509) 925-4783. Housed in a 1920s gas station, **D&M Coffee Company,** 408 S. Main, tel. (509) 962-6333, is a great place for fresh-roasted coffee beans and a cup of espresso.

The **Kittitas County Farmers Market** brings fresh produce, baked goods, and arts and crafts to the corner of 5th and Anderson on Saturday 9 a.m.-1 p.m. May-Oct.; tel. (509) 925-1776.

SPORTS AND RECREATION

On the Water

Swim at the **Ellensburg City Pool,** 815 E. 6th Ave., tel. (509) 962-7211, where you'll also find a sauna, fitness center, and jacuzzi.

The **Yakima River** is a favorite place for floaters during the summer, and a great place to cool off when temperatures top 100° F. Much of the 40-mile stretch between Cle Elum and Roza Dam is a relaxing float, but you need to watch for dangerous sweepers and logs in the water. For specific put-in points and hazardous areas, check with the chamber of commerce visitors center. The most popular run is the 15 miles from Teanaway Bridge (below Cle Elum) to the diversion dam; it generally takes five to six hours.

Rent rafts and kayaks for a do-it-yourself float in Thorp from **Rill Adventures,** tel. (509) 964-

2520, or **River Raft Rentals** in Thorp, tel. (509) 964-2145. They can also provide an equipment delivery service. The river is a popular fly-fishing place for the many large rainbow trout, and several local guide companies will take you out for a spin of the reel.

On Land

The Ellensburg area has an abundance of enjoyable backcountry roads for bike riding, along with more strenuous trips into the Cascades to the west. **Mountain High Sports,** 105 E. 4th Ave., tel. (509) 925-2626, rents mountain bikes, rollerblades, tents, climbing shoes, skis, backpacks, and other outdoor gear.

For horseback rides, contact **Happy Trails Horseback Riding Ranch,** tel. (509) 925-9428, or **Rock 'N' Tomahawk Ranch,** tel. (509) 962-2403.

Rockhounding

Kittitas County is the only place on earth that you'll find the "Ellensburg Blue" agate. Most finds are made on private or leased land northwest of Ellensburg (you'll need permission to hunt there), but you can check Dry Creek, on Hwy. 97, or Horse Canyon Road. Here are the rules: no digging—surface hunting only; respect property lines and fences; and don't bother the cows. If you come up empty handed, Ellensburg stores sell the uncut stones as well as jewelry.

Elk Watching

Winter visitors to the Ellensburg area can watch around 750 elk at the feeding station in Joe Watt Canyon, 15 miles west of town. The elk are fed hay by the Washington Dept. of Wildlife. Get here by heading west on I-90 to exit 102, then across the freeway and uphill a quarter mile. Turn right on Old Thorp Cemetery Rd. and follow it to Joe Watt Canyon Rd. where you turn left and continue a mile to the elk feeding site.

OTHER PRACTICALITIES

Events and Entertainment

Visit the **National Western Art Show and Auction,** tel. (509) 962-2934, the third weekend in May, for Western paintings. More than 200 artists display their works. Auctions give you a chance to purchase your favorites, but the highlight for many is the "Quick Draw," when about a dozen artists each create a work of art in 45 minutes.

The **Whisky Dick Triathlon,** held annually in July, consists of a one-mile swim, 26-mile bicycle ride, and eight-mile run—not impossible, even though the swim is in the 60° F Columbia River and the bike leg climbs 1,900 feet in the first 12 miles. At least the running leg is on level ground! For info, call (509) 925-3137.

Labor Day weekend's **Ellensburg Rodeo** is one of the top rodeos in the nation, attracting cowboys from all over with a $100,000 purse. The rodeo has been around since 1923 and features calf roping, wild horse races, cliff races, Brahma bull riding, and wild cow milking during this four-day event. It's held in conjunction with the carnival, parade, exhibits, and top-notch country entertainment of the **Kittitas County Fair** at the fairgrounds at the east end of 6th Avenue. Rodeo tickets include admission to the fair; order up to a year advance by calling (509) 962-7831 or (800) 637-2444. Nearly all the tickets are gone for the weekend events by early August.

Held in mid-September at Olmstead Place State Park, the **Threshing Bee** gives city slickers an opportunity to see blacksmithing, plowing, and steam and gas threshing. A big country breakfast is served in the morning, and an antique tractor pull contest is a highlight. Call (509) 925-3137 for details.

Pearl's on Pearl, 311 N. Pearl, tel. (509) 962-8899, has live blues and jazz music on weekends in a smoke-free atmosphere.

Information and Transportation

The **Ellensburg Chamber of Commerce** is located at 801 S. Ruby No. 2, tel. (509) 925-3137 or (888) 925-2204, and is open Mon.-Fri. 8 a.m.-5 p.m. year-round.

Kittias County Connector has bus service in Ellensburg, and to Thorp, Cle Elum, Roslyn, and Vantage; tel. (509) 933-2287. **Greyhound,** tel. (509) 925-1177 or (800) 231-2222, can get you out of town from their 801 Okanogan depot. The nearest commercial airport is in Yakima.

YAKIMA

Yakima (pop. 63,000; pronounced "YAK-a-ma") is one of the largest cities in Central Washington and the commercial hub of the Yakima Valley. The population includes a rapidly growing Hispanic community; by the turn of the century they are expected to represent more than half of the Yakima County population. Immediately north of Yakima is the Biblically named town of **Selah,** home to 5,700 people. Like neighboring Yakima, Selah is an agricultural center with fruit warehouses, strips of shopping malls, and fast food joints. Seven miles north is the Army's **Yakima Training Center,** the premier training and weapons firing area in the Northwest (though some Seattle neighborhoods run a close second on the weapons firing claim). It covers more than 261,000 acres. **Union Gap** (pop. 3,100) is home to the biggest local shopping center, Valley Mall. **Wapato** (pop. 3,900) is a dozen miles southeast of Yakima in the middle of apple and other orchards and filled with huge fruit processing warehouses.

Yakima, a far cry weatherwise from its neighbors to the west, averages 300 sunny days per year with just eight inches of precipitation. Summer temperatures on the dry side of the mountains generally run 10 or more degrees higher than in Puget Sound cities, explaining why virtually every motel, no matter how cheap, has a pool. Despite the dry, brown hills surrounding the city, Yakima's suburbs are green, due to the constant chit-chit-chit of lawn sprinklers.

The Yakima Valley's volcanic soil is twice as productive as ordinary soil—teamed with irrigation and a 200-day growing season, it's hard to beat. The county ranks first in the nation in apples, winter pears, fruit trees, hops, and mint, with pears, grapes, cherries, peaches, and apricots as major crops. The largest local employers include many of the major fruit companies, including Tree Top, Del Monte, and Snokist.

HISTORY

Yakima-area Indians defended their ground, preventing any permanent white settlement here until the end of the 1855-57 Indian War. With

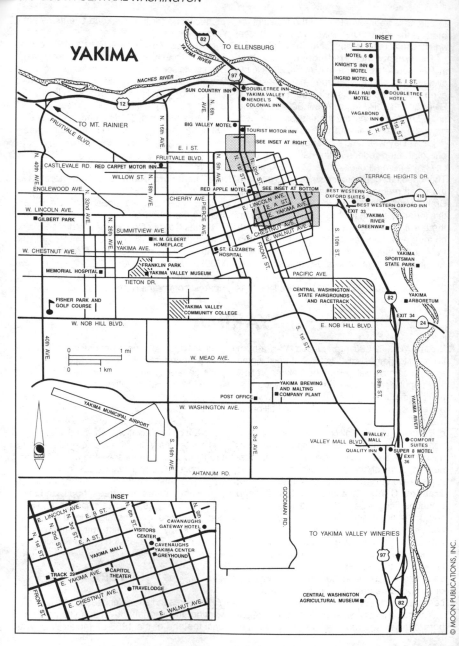

the Indians' acceptance of the Yakama Reservation in 1858, pioneer cattlemen settled in the valley—farmers weren't interested in this arid region. In 1861, Fielding M. Thorpe and his wife Margaret became Yakima's first homesteaders. Dry soil was the area's biggest drawback, so in the 1860s Sebastian Lauber and Joseph and Charles Schamo built an irrigation ditch to shift some of the Yakima River's water into town, paving the way for agriculture.

In 1870, John W. Beck planted 50 apple trees and 50 peach trees in the region's first orchards, marking the end of the cattle era and the start of a major fruit industry.

Moving Yakima

With a population of 400, "Yakima City" was incorporated in 1883. The Northern Pacific Railroad had a problem acquiring land from some of the property owners, so they built their Yakima Valley station four miles north of town, offering to move the buildings at the railroad's expense, plus free land. Since the railroad couldn't come to the city, most townspeople put their houses on skids and rollers and moved the city to the railroad—in time to meet the first train pulling into town on December 14, 1884. The new town was officially called "North Yakima," but in 1919, representatives from North Yakima persuaded the state to amend the charter of Yakima City, forcing it to adopt the new name of Union Gap. Thus the original Yakima City lost its name to the upstart.

SIGHTS

Historical Sights

The North Front St. Historical District boasts some of Yakima's oldest buildings, including the 1898 Lund Building, which once housed a saloon and brothel (now the Greystone Restaurant) directly across from the Northern Pacific Railroad depot.

Three miles northwest of Yakima on Hwy. 12 you'll find the mysterious **Indian Painted Rocks,** a state historical site. Although the pictographs were partially destroyed by an early irrigation flume, some remain at Naches Highway and Powerhouse Road. The cliffs nearby are popular with local rock climbers.

DIANNE BOUERICE LYONS

view from Umtanum Ridge midway between Yakima and Ellensburg

The **Ahtanum Mission,** east of Yakima along Ahtanum Creek, was built in 1852 by Oblate priests. Though it burned down during the Yakama Indian wars of the 1850s, the church was rebuilt in 1869 and is still used. You can visit the mission and surrounding park for a small fee.

Museums

Start your visit to Yakima at the unusually spacious (50,000 square feet) and complete **Yakima Valley Museum,** 2105 Tieton Dr., tel. (509) 248-0747. This is one of the finest large museums in Washington, with an extraordinary collection of Yakama Indian clothing, beadwork, basketry, and artifacts, a replica of Chief Justice William O. Douglas's office (Douglas was a Yakima native son), and one of the best collections of horse-drawn vehicles west of the Mississippi. The display on the Oregon Trail is particularly notable, as are the exhibits on the Yakima Valley's fruit tree industry and a **Children's Underground** hands-on exploratorium downstairs. The museum is open Mon.-Fri. 10 a.m.-5 p.m. and Sat.-Sun. noon-5 p.m. year-round; admission is $3 adults, $1.50 students and seniors, $7 families, free under age five. They also have a gift shop with a fine collection of history books.

A block away from the museum is the **H. M. Gilbert Homeplace,** 2109 W. Yakima Ave., tel. (509) 248-0747, built in 1898 amidst 20 acres of sagebrush. Horace M. Gilbert was a farmer, land developer, and one of the pioneers in the irrigation of the Yakima Valley. You can tour his early Yakima Valley farm home on Friday 1-4 p.m. April-Dec., and 1-4 p.m. on the first Sunday of each month for $2.50.

The **Yakima Electric Railway Museum,** 306 W. Pine St., tel. (509) 575-1700, was built in 1910 and is home to the local trolleys that connect Yakima and Selah. Inside are interpretive displays on the history of the trolleys. Open when the trolleys are running: weekends May-October.

Union Gap's **Central Washington Agricultural Museum,** tel. (509) 457-8735, displays tractors, pea pickers, threshers, wagons, balers, and other early Yakima Valley farm equipment on 15 acres in Fulbright Park. The collection is spread over more than a dozen buildings arranged in a semicircle around a working windmill. A Burlington-Northern boxcar houses railroad memorabilia, and the Magness Room is a special treat, packed with more than 3,000 antique hand tools. The same building houses a small Grange museum and library. Most folks view this as a drive-through museum, taking their vehicles past the many open-sided buildings and stopping at those of interest. The main collection is open at any time, and the Magness Room is open daily 9 a.m.-5 p.m. A popular threshing bee is held here each August.

Wine and Beer

If you're a wine lover, visit **The Wine Cellar,** 25 N. Front St., tel. (509) 248-3590, for a good selection of Yakima Valley and other wines; the shop always has a few bottles open for tasting. (See **Yakima Valley** for details on local wineries.)

In a region known for its wineries, it's easy for beer drinkers to feel left out—but there's a place here for you too! The **Yakima Brewing and Malting Co.,** 1803 Presson Place, tel. (509) 575-

1900, became the nation's first microbrewery when investors got a taste of Bert Grant's home-brew in 1981. Grant's Scottish Ale launched the brewery and remains the flagship product, but they now also produce half-a-dozen others from locally grown Cascade hops. They continue to maintain a reputation for brewing some of the finest beers anywhere, in large part due to the meticulous control by Bert Grant and his refusal to let the business grow too large. Make reservations for their informative brewery tours as far ahead as possible. Or stop by **Grant's Brewery Pub,** at 32 N. Front St. in the historic train depot, for a taste of their best.

Scenic Drives

Driving on I-82 between Ellensburg and Yakima, you'll realize that Central Washington isn't the flat desert wasteland that it's sometimes made out to be—a desert wasteland, maybe, but not flat. As the road snakes up treeless ridges over 2,000 feet high, the brown hills in the distance look as if they're covered with velvet; up close, sagebrush dots the brown grass (in an imitation of a scruffy three-day beard). Pull in at the Viewpoint sign for broad vistas of green valley farmland below and the snowcapped Stuart Range to the north. Along the way, you'll cross the largest single concrete span bridge in North America. The **Fred Redmon Memorial Bridge** twin spans are 1,336 feet long and 330 feet high. Pull into the rest stop at the south end of the bridge for a striking view of the summits of Mt. Adams and Mt. Rainier.

The **Jacob Durr Wagon Road** (a.k.a. Wenas Rd.) was the only route linking Yakima and Ellensburg in the 1880s; today it's surely the most scenic, climbing over Umtanum Ridge for a 360-degree view of the Cascades and Yakima Valley. Drive north from Selah on N. Wenas Ave., which becomes Wenas Rd., the old Durr Wagon Road. The more standard route northward—I-90—also offers excellent vistas from the **Manatash Ridge Viewpoint** into the lush Kittitas Valley, with the Wenatchee Mountains rising behind the town of Ellensburg.

On the Water

At **Eschbach Park,** five miles past the fish hatchery on the Old Naches Hwy., rent a tube or kayak and take a lazy float down the Naches River.

The day-use, 168-acre county park offers boating, swimming, picnicking, and play areas. Call (509) 574-2435 for details.

Many locals also float, water-ski, or fish (trophy-sized rainbows; catch-and-release fishing only) in the beautiful 27-mile **Yakima River Canyon** between Ellensburg and Yakima. The river is paralleled by State Hwy. 821, with several boat ramps and picnic sites along the route. Call (509) 665-2100 for more info on this fun float.

Parks

The **Yakima River Greenway** encompasses 3,600 acres east of the city, connecting Selah, Yakima, and Union Gap along a seven-mile biking and walking path; almost half of this is paved.

The **Yakima Area Arboretum**, I-90 and Nob Hill Blvd., tel. (509) 248-7337, is a 70-acre park with a Japanese garden and bird sanctuary, and a small interpretive center, gift shop, and library. Open Tues.-Fri. 9 a.m.-5 p.m., Saturday 9 a.m.-4 p.m.

Randall Park, south of Nob Hill Blvd. on S. 48th Ave., has a picnic area, nature trails, duck pond, and creek on 38 grassy acres. **Franklin Park,** behind the museum at Tieton Dr. and 20th Ave., has tennis courts, a swimming pool, and grassy hills for romping or winter sledding.

Across the Yakima River from Union Gap, **Moxee Bog,** a spring-fed preserve, is home to a rare breed of monarch butterfly that feeds on the violets that grow here. Birders will want to visit the **Boise Cascade Bird Sanctuary** in the Wenas Valley, five miles west of Selah on Wean Road. Over 100 species of birds have been sighted in the 40-acre sanctuary.

Cowiche Canyon is a scenic and remote rocky canyon just a few minutes west of Naches. An almost-level trail follows the old railroad route along and across Cowiche Creek as it winds past distinctive rock formations, some that resemble the Easter Island faces. The canyon is managed by Cowiche Canyon Conservancy, tel. (509) 966-8608, which produces a brochure on the three-mile trail.

ACCOMMODATIONS

Most of Yakima's motels can be found along the Hwy. 97 corridor through town (1st Street). Several cheaper places on the south end of Union Gap are not included, but may be acceptable if you're desperate enough.

Bed and Breakfasts

A Touch of Europe B&B, 220 N. 16th Ave., tel. (509) 454-9775, is a classic Queen Anne Victorian built in 1889. The home sits on an acre of shady grounds and has three elegantly furnished guest rooms. A delicious European breakfast is served (the owners are from Germany); $65-110 s or d. No kids.

Birchfield Manor B&B, 2018 Birchfield Rd., tel. (509) 452-1960 or (800) 375-3420, is the biggest local B&B, with 11 luxurious rooms in two buildings, one from 1910, and the other just a few years old. All rooms have private baths with jacuzzi tubs, and some contain gas fireplaces and private decks. The spacious parklike grounds contain a swimming pool. Breakfasts are memorable, and Thurs.-Sat. dinners in the restaurant here are some of the finest around ($22-34 for full dinners). Lodging is $125-195 d.

Cherry Hill Manor, 81 Mapleway Rd. in Selah, tel. (509) 697-8686 or (800) 927-2689, is a new Tudor-style home with four guest rooms, private baths, and full breakfasts; $125 s or d. Kids accepted. **Orchard Inn B&B,** 1207 Pecks Canyon Dr., tel. (509) 966-1283, is a contemporary home surrounded by cherry trees. Inside are three guest rooms with private baths, private entrance, and full breakfasts; $80 s or d. Kids okay.

Located in the old Wiley City Hotel, **Mystery Manor,** 3109 S. Wiley Rd., tel. (509) 966-9971, calls itself a "who done it" B&B. Guests can attend a mystery dinner theater downstairs on the first Saturday of each month. Facilities include an indoor pool, four guest rooms, and full breakfasts; $55-65. Kids welcome.

Campgrounds

About a mile east of town off I-82, **Yakima Sportsman State Park** has a stocked pond for kids to fish—adults can try their luck in the nearby Yakima River—plus tent ($11) and RV sites ($16) along the greenbelt; a great spot to escape the summer heat. Coin-operated showers are available; open year-round. Call (800) 452-5687 for reservations ($6 extra). **Boise Cascade Bird Sanctuary** in the Wenas Valley, five miles west of Selah on Wean Rd., also has a campground.

YAKIMA AREA MOTELS AND HOTELS

Lodging places are arranged from least to most expensive. Rates may be lower during the winter months. See the text for local B&Bs.

BUDGET

Knight's Inn Motel; 1022 N. 1st St.; tel. (509) 453-5615; $27 s, $29 d

INEXPENSIVE

Bali Hai Motel; 710 N. 1st St.; tel. (509) 452-7178; $28 s, $35 d; outdoor pool

Tourist Motor Inn; 1223 N. 1st St.; tel. (509) 452-6551; $35-70 s or d; outdoor pool, continental breakfast, kitchenettes available

Ingrid Motel; 803 N. 1st St.; tel. (509) 248-9120; $36 s, $38 d; kitchenettes available

Red Carpet Motor Inn; 1608 Fruitvale Blvd.; tel. (509) 457-1131; $37 s, $41 d; outdoor pool, sauna, kitchenettes available, AAA approved

Motel 6; 1104 N. 1st St.; tel. (509) 891-6161 or (800) 466-8356; $39 s, $45 d; outdoor pool

Nendel's Colonial Inn; 1405 N. 1st St.; tel. (509) 453-8981 or (800) 547-0106; $39 s, $45 d; indoor pool, two jacuzzis, continental breakfast

Red Apple Motel; 416 N. 1st St.; tel. (509) 248-7150 or (888) 248-7150; $43 s, $48-55 d; apple-shaped outdoor pool

Travelodge; 110 S. Naches Ave.; tel. (509) 453-7151 or (800) 255-3050; $45, $51-57 d; outdoor pool

Vagabond Inn, 510 N. 1st St.; tel. (509) 457-6155 or (800) 446-6900; $47 s or d; outdoor pool, continental breakfast, AAA approved

Sun Country Inn; 1700 N. 1st St.; tel. (509) 248-5650 or (800) 559-3675; $52 s, $57 d; outdoor pool, sauna, kitchenettes available, continental breakfast, AAA approved

Days Inn; 2408 Rudkin Rd., Union Gap; tel. (509) 248-9700 or (800) 348-9701; $54 s, $57 d; outdoor pool, continental breakfast

---

Yakima area RV parks include: **Circle H RV Ranch,** 1107 S. 18th St., tel. (509) 457-3683; **KOA Kampground,** 1500 Keyes Rd., tel. (509) 248-5882 or (800) 562-5773; **Stagecoach RV Park,** northwest of Yakima at Wenas Lake, tel. (509) 697-5431 (no tent spaces here); **Woodland Park,** 2008 N. 1st St., tel. (509) 453-9353; **Wenas Lake Resort,** tel. (509) 697-7670; and **Trailer Inns,** 1610 N. 1st St., tel. (509) 452-9561 or (800) 659-4784.

FOOD AND DRINK

Breakfast and Lunch
Get a big, hearty home-cooked breakfast or lunch at **Elton Young's Restaurant,** 810 N. 5th Ave., tel. (509) 457-6027. **Settler's Inn,** 1406 N. 1st St., tel. (509) 453-9060, is a family place with good breakfasts and outstanding pies. Come back at dinner for chicken fried steaks.

A popular coffee shop (meet the cops and lawyers here) is **City Espresso/Country Charm,** 25 N. Front St., tel. (509) 248-2483. Get espresso and bagels from **Some Bagels & Great Coffee,** 1006 S. 3rd Ave., tel. (509) 575-0747, or head to the local Starbucks and SBC outlets.

Mel's Diner, 314 N. 1st St., tel. (509) 248-5382, is the local greasy spoon; popular for breakfast and lunch. Also of note is **Jack-Son's Sports Bar,** 432 S. 48th Ave., tel. (509) 966-4340, a fun place with burgers, sandwiches, and a big screen TV.

901 Pasta, 910 Summitview Ave., tel. (509) 457-4949, is a good place for deli sandwiches.

MODERATE

Quality Inn; 12 Valley Mall Blvd., Union Gap; tel. (509) 248-6924 or (800) 228-5151; $54-59 s, $61-71 d; outdoor pool, continental breakfast, jacuzzi

Super 8 Motel; 2605 Rudkin Rd.; Union Gap; tel. (509) 248-8880 or (800) 800-8000; $55-65 s; indoor pool

Comfort Suites; I-82 and Valley Mall Blvd.; tel. (509) 249-1900 or (800) 228-5150; $55-65 s, $65 -75 d; all-suites motel, indoor pool, jacuzzi, microwaves and fridges, exercise room, continental breakfast

Best Western Oxford Inn; 1603 Terrace Heights Dr.; tel. (509) 457-4444 or (800) 521-3050; $55-72 s, $65-75 d; on the river, outdoor pool, jacuzzi, exercise facilities, kitchenettes available, airport shuttle, AAA approved

Cavanaughs at Yakima Center; 607 E. Yakima Ave.; tel. (509) 248-5900 or (800) 843-4667; $57-77 s, $57-87 d; two pools, airport shuttle, local calls 50 cents, AAA approved

Big Valley Motel; 1504 N. 1st St.; tel. (509) 248-3393 or (800) 248-3360; $58 s, $60 d; outdoor pool

Peppertree Inn; 1614 N. 1st St., tel. (509) 453-8898 or (800) 834-1649; $60-64 s or d; new motel, indoor pool, fitness facility, microwaves and fridges, continental breakfast, AAA approved

Doubletree Hotel; 818 N. 1st St.; tel. (509) 453-0391 or (800) 222-8733; $66-80 s, $76-89 d; outdoor pool, fitness center

Holiday Inn Express; 1001 E. A St.; tel. (509) 249-1000 or (800) 465-4329; $68 s, $76 d; new motel, indoor pool, jacuzzi, fitness room, continental breakfast

EXPENSIVE

Best Western Oxford Suites; 1701 Terrace Heights Dr.; tel. (509) 457-9000 or (800) 528-1234; $72-139 s, $79-146 d; indoor pool, fridges and microwaves, continental breakfast, evening reception, river views, AAA approved

Cavenaughs Gateway Hotel; 9 N. 9th St.; tel. (509) 452-6511 or (800) 325-4000; $75-85 s, $85-95 d; outdoor pool, jacuzzi, kitchenettes available, local calls 50 cents, airport shuttle

Doubletree Inn—Yakima Valley; 1507 N. 1st St.; tel. (509) 248-7850 or (800) 547-8010; $81-99 s or d; two pools, jacuzzi, airport shuttle, AAA approved

American
Miner's Drive-In, 2415 S. 1st St., tel. (509) 457-8194, cranks out monster burgers and delicious onion rings. **Marti's Restaurant,** 1601 Terrace Heights Rd., tel. (509) 248-2062, has an outside patio overlooking the Yakima River; popular for Sunday brunches. Dinners include everything from steak to seafood to pizza. More all-American steak and seafood at **Restaurant at the Airport,** tel. (509) 248-4710, located—where else—but the airport.

Gourmet Restaurants
One of Yakima's finest eating places is **Birchfield Manor,** tel. (509) 452-1960, a restored 1910 farmhouse two miles east of the city on Birchfield Rd. that also serves as a luxurious B&B. Formal dinners (around $30) are served Thurs.-Sat., complemented by a vast selection of Yakima Valley wines. The innovative cuisine changes seasonally, but they always have a perfect filet mignon.

In the historic district, **The Greystone Restaurant,** 5 N. Front St., tel. (509) 248-9801, has moderately priced Northwest cuisine, fresh seafood, and homemade pasta in an elegant atmosphere; open for dinner only Tues.-Saturday.

The best local pizzas are at **Mr. C's Pizza & Spaghetti House,** 12 S. 3rd Ave., tel. (509) 453-2765.

International Food
For gourmet (but pricey) Italian food and Northwest specialties, visit **Gasparetti's,** 1013 N. 1st St., tel. (509) 248-0628; open for dinner only

Tues.-Saturday. The pastas are all freshly made, and desserts are a real treat.

Despite the name, **Deli de Pasta,** 7 N. Front St., tel. (509) 453-0571, isn't a deli but does offer wonderful fresh pastas such as smoked salmon ravioli and garlic tiger shrimp. Dinner entrees are $13-22.

Santiago's Gourmet Restaurant, 111 E. Yakima Ave., tel. (509) 453-1644, is a lively and very popular Mexican restaurant with all the standards and excellent daily specials. **El Pastor,** 315 W. Walnut, tel. (509) 453-5159, is a small place with inexpensive and delicious Mexican dishes. **Tequila's,** Yakima Ave. and N. 1st St., serves Mexican dishes for lunch and dinner daily in two restored 1920s railroad cars; enjoy a beer and appetizers on their sunny patio. Find lots more *tortillerías* and *panaderías* on south 1st St. heading toward Union Gap.

For Cantonese and American cuisine, try the **Golden Wheel,** 9 S. 1st St., tel. (509) 457-8400, or **Golden Moon Restaurant,** 1527 Summitview Ave., tel. (509) 575-7563. Get authentic Japanese food, including fresh sushi, at **Ichiban,** 1107 Tieton Dr., tel. (509) 248-2585. Also recommended is **Keoki's Oriental Restaurant,** 2107 W. Lincoln Ave., tel. (509) 453-2401, where the cooking takes place at your table.

New Thai Restaurant, 4808 Tieton Dr., tel. (509) 966-9730, has a pleasant atmosphere and authentic Thai cuisine.

Brewpub

Visit **Grant's Brewery Pub** in the historic train depot at 32 N. Front St., tel. (509) 575-2922, where you'll find at least five different brews on tap at all times, plus tasty pub grub. No smoking.

Bakeries and Produce

Located next to the Wine Celler, **Pain au Levain,** 25 N. Front St., tel. (509) 453-7848, bakes the best breads in town, and creates tasty light lunches. **Pulse Foods,** 4315 Main St. in Union Gap, tel. (509) 452-5386, has earthy fresh breads and health foods.

Fresh fruit and vegetable stands and U-pick places can be found throughout the Yakima Valley; get a complete listing—and check out the informative exhibits—at **Washington's Fruit Place Visitor Center,** 105 S. 18th St., Suite 103, tel. (509) 576-3090, or just head down High-

ways 97 and 22 till something looks interesting. Right on the west edge of town is **Johnson Orchards,** 4906 Summitview Ave., tel. (509) 966-7479. **Donald Fruit & Mercantile,** in Wapato, tel. (509) 877-3115, is a working orchard with produce (a dozen kinds of peaches at various times of the summer) and gourmet foods and gifts. Don't miss their fresh peach sundaes. Many other places offer fresh fruits and veggies throughout the summer months, including the **Selah Farmers Market** at 110 W. Naches Ave. on Saturday 9 a.m.-2 p.m. from mid-June to early November; tel. (509) 697-4059.

SPORTS AND RECREATION

Cycling and Swimming

The Yakima Valley farming country makes for great back-roads cycling, with a multitude of possible loop trips. Rent mountain and tandem bikes, and rafts, kayaks, and canoes from **Richies River Rentals,** tel. (509) 453-2112. They also offer a river shuttle service for folks floating the Yakima River. (See **Ellensburg** for raft trips down the Upper Yakima.) **Sagebrush Cycles,** 1406½ Fruitvale Blvd., tel. (509) 248-5393, also rents bikes. Get a map of local cycling routes from the visitor center.

Yakima contains four outdoor public pools open in the summer, including the **Franklin Park** pool with a spiral water slide. A big indoor pool at **Lions Park** is open all year. Call (509) 575-6020 for details. The **YMCA,** 5 N. Naches Ave., tel. (509) 248-1202, has a complete sports facility with gyms, handball courts, an indoor jogging track, exercise equipment, and indoor pool.

Golf

Yakima has four public golf courses: **Suntides,** 2215 Pence, tel. (509) 966-9065; **Fisher Park Golf Course,** tel. (509) 575-6075; **Apple Tree Golf Course,** tel. (509) 966-5877; and **Westwood Golf Course,** tel. (509) 966-0890.

Spectator Sports

The **Yakima Valley SunDome** at the fairgrounds is home for the Yakima SunKings basketball team, along with various sporting and concert events all year. **Yakima County Stadium** is nearby and is home to the Yakima Bears, tel.

(509) 457-5151, professional baseball team (a class A affiliate of the L.A. Dodgers). The Yakima Reds play professional soccer here.

ARTS AND ENTERTAINMENT

Music
Every Tuesday evening in July and August, you'll find free **Something for Everyone Concerts** at Robertson Amphitheater in Sarg Hubbard Park, with country, folk, Mexican, blues, and jazz music. The **Yakima Community Band** has free concerts on Wednesday evenings from mid-July to mid-August in Randall Park. The **Yakima Symphony Orchestra,** tel. (509) 248-1414, performs at the Capitol Theater Oct.-April.

The smoke-free **Grant's Pub Brewery,** 32 N. Front St., tel. (509) 575-2922, has live jazz and blues on weekends and occasional folk groups. For live music or comedy, try lounges in the Cavanaughs or DoubleTree hotels, and **Premier Pub,** 5625 Summitview Ave., tel. (509) 965-9757. Hear C&W tunes at **Country Connection,** 115 E. Naches Ave., Selah, tel. (509) 697-5533. **McGuire's Irish Pub,** 4807 Tieton Dr., tel. (509) 966-7440, serves good pub grub and has Guinness on tap.

Theater and Galleries
The historic **Capitol Theater** at 19 S. 3rd St., tel. (509) 575-6267, first opened its doors in 1920 featuring vaudeville and feature films. Today the beautifully restored and elegant theater hosts a full schedule of musical, theatrical, and Broadway productions. Yakima's **Country Drive-In,** 4309 W. Nob Hill, tel. (509) 966-5340, is one of the few left in Washington.

Several downtown art galleries offer high quality works. Two of the best are **Simon Edwards Gallery,** 811 W. Yakima Ave., tel. (509) 453-7723; and **New Horizons Art Gallery,** 1320 S. 16th Avenue.

EVENTS

Selah's **Community Days** starts the summer off with a festival that's been going strong for over 75 years. Held the third weekend of May, it includes a parade, beauty pageant, pancake feed, danc-

ing, bingo, golf tournament, and local entertainment. The **Union Gap Kite Festival** in mid-June attracts kite enthusiasts from all over the region. It's followed by a big **Fourth of July** celebration, and the **Yakima Air Fair,** one of the larger air shows in this part of Washington—all sorts of aircraft converge on the Yakima airport.

The most popular local event is the **Central Washington State Fair,** held in late September, which features a PRCA championship rodeo, carnival, country music, and agricultural displays. It attracts well over 300,000 visitors each year. The **Washington State Pioneer Power Show** on the third weekend of August features an old-time threshing bee and working displays of farm equipment at the Central Washington Agricultural Museum.

The **Yakima Speedway,** tel. (509) 248-0647, 1600 Pacific Ave., has NASCAR racing every Saturday night April to early October. More cars at the **Vintages Northwest Nationals** car show and rod run held the first weekend in August. It's the largest gathering of vintage cars in the Northwest.

Labor Day weekend means the **Wapato Harvest Festival** with a small-town parade, carnival rides, food and concession booths, and musical entertainment.

The **Great Yakima Duck Race** is a popular raffle event where hundreds of rubber duckies float down the Yakima River in early October. Top prize is $20,000, so it pays to plunk down $5 for a duck.

SHOPPING

Usually the giant shopping malls are found in suburbia, but Yakima's biggest shopping center is in the heart of downtown: the **Yakima Mall** has over 75 shops including The Bon Marché, Nordstrom, JCPenney, and Mervyn's. At Yakima Ave. and N. 1st, a trainful of 22 old railroad cars and pseudo-Victorian buildings house the **Track 29 Shopping Mall** where you'll find gift shops and eateries. Many more places—including the largest collection of antique pedal cars on the West Coast—can be found in antique shops inside the adjacent **Yesterday's Village.** Just over the line into Union Gap, **Valley Mall** on S. 1st St. has 44 stores including Sears, Lamonts, and PayLess.

INFORMATION AND SERVICES

For maps, brochures, and current festival information, contact the **Yakima Valley Visitors and Convention Bureau,** 10 N. 8th St., tel. (509) 575-3010 or (800) 221-0751. Hours are Mon.-Fri. 8 a.m.-5 p.m. all year, plus Sat.-Sun. 9 a.m.-4 p.m. May-October. If they're closed, stop next door at Cavanaugh's for brochures, or check the Web at www.yakimanet.com.

TRANSPORTATION

By Air
The **Yakima Municipal Airport** off Washington Ave. is the largest in the area, served by **Horizon Airlines,** tel. (800) 547-9308, and **United Express,** tel. (509) 457-3368 or (800) 241-6522. **Noland-Decoto Flying Service,** tel. (509) 248-1370, offers flightseeing trips.

By Trolley
Ride the Yakima Trolley Line's restored trolley cars on the two-hour ride through orchards, over the Naches River to the town of Selah and back. The trolleys were first brought to Yakima in 1930 and operated till 1947. Service returned in 1989 when the original cars were leased from a railroad museum in Snoqualmie. The two trolley cars depart several times a day on weekends from the Yakima Electric Railway Museum at 306 W. Pine St., late April to Labor Day. Fares are $4 adults, $3.50 seniors, $2.50 kids, or $12 for the whole brood; call (509) 575-1700 for information.

By Bus
Yakima Transit, tel. (509) 575-6175, serves the Yakima area, including the municipal airport, with Mon.-Sat. service. For local tours, contact **Accent! Tours,** tel. (509) 575-3949 or (800) 735-0428; or **Travel Tramps** for more individualized tours, tel. (509) 965-2719.

To get out of town or across the country, hop aboard **Greyhound** from its station at 602 E. Yakima Ave., tel. (509) 457-5131 or (800) 231-2222.

TOPPENISH

Located 18 miles southeast of Yakima, Toppenish (TOP-pen-ish; pop. 8,000) has a comfortable Western flavor and an unusual mix of cultures that is approximately 65% Hispanic and 20% Indian. The prosperous center of town is made even more attractive by an outdoor mural program that has resulted in more than 50 wall murals of superior quality.

The town name comes from the Indian word "Thappahn-ish," which means, more or less, "People of the trail that comes from the foot of the hills." Its name was committed to maps, again more or less, by Capt. George McClellan when he wandered through in 1853. He spelled it "Sahpenis," which was written on maps as "Toppenish."

Yakama Indian Reservation
Toppenish is the home of the Yakama Indian Agency and the commercial center for the 1.37 million-acre Yakama Indian Reservation. (Note: The tribal council decided in 1994 that the correct spelling for their tribe is "Yakama," rather than "Yakima," hence the spelling differences. And no, Dan Quayle had nothing to do with the change.) The reservation reaches from Grandview on the east to the slopes of 12,276-foot Mt. Adams and is home to approximately 5,000 Native people from 14 different tribes and bands, along with another 20,000 non-Indians. It was established by the 1855 Walla Walla Treaty and originally covered much of central Washington before other sections were ceded to the U.S. government. As part of the 1855 treaty, the Yakimas were given $51.28 per person for 18 million acres of their land! Today, employment on the reservation comes mainly in farming, lumber, cattle ranching, and a new casino. The westernmost edge of the reservation includes land within the Mt. Adams Wilderness, and a permit is required for camping, fishing, or hunting; call (509) 865-5121 for details.

Rosalie Harry and Annie May of the Yakama tribe

SIGHTS

Yakama Nation Cultural Center

This impressive center, tel. (509) 865-2800, features a museum that tells the story of the Yakama Nation from its beginnings to the present, a library specializing in Indian books, a theater that presents first-run movies and stage productions, a restaurant, and an RV park. The museum is centered around a 76-foot-tall tepee-shaped building and contains fine dioramas on the sad history of the Yakama peoples. History is presented from a Yakama perspective, emphasizing how their land was stolen and divided up, how Indian children were sent off to boarding schools to destroy their heritage, and how their Celilo Falls fishing grounds near the present-day Dalles Dam were destroyed by the damming of the Columbia River. Especially interesting are the time ball—used to record events and to recount stories—and the huge winter lodge and sweathouse in the center. A visit to this outstanding museum is an eye-opening experience, revealing what happens when a people's culture is ripped away from them and they are dumped into a new system.

The museum's library contains the collection of 10,000 books from **Nipo Stongheart,** who began his show-business career with Buffalo Bill's Wild West Show at the age of 11 and went on to star in many Hollywood Westerns. Born in White Swan, Nipo was the grandson of a Hudson's Bay Company trader and was given an honorary Yakama tribal membership in 1950. He died in 1966 and is buried on the reservation.

The museum is open Mon.-Sat. 9 a.m.-5 p.m. and Sunday 9 a.m.-4 p.m. all year; admission costs $4 adults, $2 seniors and students, 75 cents for children under seven, or $10 for the family.

Murals

The more than 50 murals covering Toppenish walls are a very popular attraction, and the chamber of commerce produces a free guide describing the various scenes. **Old Timers Plaza** downtown is bordered by two long murals and has an old wagon, along with a bronze sculpture of an Indian woman gathering hops. For a rolling visit past the murals, take one of the wagon tours offered by **Toppenish Mural Tours,** tel. (509) 865-4515, that leave from the depot area.

Toppenish Museum

This surprising small museum is upstairs in the library building at 1 S. Elm St., tel. (509) 865-4510. Inside is the extraordinary Estelle Reel Meyer collection of Native American basketry and beadwork, including a war bonnet of eagle feathers found on the battlefield of Custer's last stand. (One of the first women to hold a federal job, she collected these pieces during her travels as Superintendent of Indian Affairs from 1898 to 1910.) Also here are exhibits on the cattle industry in the valley, a quilt filled with local brands, and such oddities as an egg sorter, a curtain stretcher, and gold pans. Open Tues.-Thurs. 1:30-4 p.m., and Fri.-Sat. 2-4 p.m. Admission is $1.50 adults, 50 cents for children.

American Hop Museum

Hops—a vital bittering ingredient in the production of beer and ale—have been grown in America for almost 400 years, and in the Northwest since the 1860s. Today, Yakima Valley is one of the major hop-growing regions in the world, accounting for 75% of the total U.S. production. Despite its importance to beer drinkers, few people know what hops are, let alone have ever seen hop vines.

This fine little museum is the only one of its kind, offering a glimpse into how hops are grown, harvested, and used in making beer. A hop har-

vest mural graces an outside wall, and hop vines have been planted out front. The museum is located at 22 S. B St., tel. (509) 865-4677, and is open daily 11 a.m.-4 p.m. May-Sept.; donation. (By the way, did you know that hops and marijuana come from the same plant family?)

Yakima Valley Rail and Steam Museum

The restored railroad depot houses this minor downtown Toppenish museum. Inside are rail and steam artifacts, a restored telegraph office, and gift shop. A steam locomotive in the rail yard is in the initial stages of restoration. The museum is open Sat.-Sun. 10 a.m.-5 p.m. May-November; $2 adults, $1 kids and seniors, and $5 for families.

Several times late summer the volunteer-run **Toppenish, Simcoe and Western Railroad** offers three-hour excursions through the country between the nearby towns of Harrah and Wes-

McCLELLAN SUCCEEDS AT FAILURE

Anyone who thinks military blundering began this century would be well advised to study the careers of several Union Army generals just before and during the Civil War. A good place to start would be with the career of George Brinton McClellan.

The Secretary of War at that time was Jefferson Davis, who would soon become President of the Confederacy. But for the time being he was in a responsible job in Franklin Pierce's cabinet. When Millard Fillmore was leaving the presidency, one of his last acts was to create the Washington Territory, and when Pierce came into office, one of his first official acts was to appoint Major Isaac Ingalls Stevens the governor of the territory. He instructed Stevens to go overland to his new post all the while surveying a railroad route from the Great Lakes to Puget Sound. Stevens left with 240 soldiers, engineers, and naturalists. He and his crew explored a wide swath of the countryside, some 400 miles wide, and more than 2,000 miles long.

Jefferson Davis didn't like this activity because he didn't want a railroad built across the northern part of the country for fear it would interfere with his plan for a confederacy of southern slave states. Davis tried to stop Stevens, but the little soldier and statesman would have none of it. He wanted the railroad, and he opposed slavery.

Davis came up with an alternate plan: he would prove there was no practical route for a railroad through the Cascades. Davis didn't dare try to disprove the routes through the Rockies because this range was too familiar to too many people. But the Cascades were *terra incognito* to most Americans. Davis sent McClellan out to explore the Cascades while Stevens was occupied with the Rockies. McClellan was told to report directly to Davis, in spite of his being under Stevens' jurisdiction. McClellan proved to be good at not finding things, and in his report wrote, "There is nothing to be seen but mountain piled upon mountain, rugged and impassable."

He reached Fort Vancouver on June 27, 1853, where he found Captain Ulysses S. Grant busy working in his potato patch. McClellan was disgusted to see an officer doing such menial labor, and he took an instant dislike to Grant. (The dislike lasted into the Civil War, when McClellan arrested Grant after his victory at Fort Donelson, a battle that had turned the direction of the war.) It took McClellan three weeks to assemble 66 men, 73 saddle horses, 100 pack horses, and 46 mules. On July 18 he finally left Fort Vancouver on his quest not to find the passes. They traveled 1.75 miles, set up camp, and sat there for three days before moving on.

When they struck out again, they went six miles this time before setting up camp, and this hectic

ley, providing a panoramic view of the orchards, hop fields, and farms of Yakima Valley; call (509) 865-1911 for details.

Toppenish National Wildlife Refuge

More than 250 species of birds have been sighted on this refuge located five miles south on Hwy. 97, then south a half mile on Pump House Road. It has an interpretive center and nature trail. For information call (509) 865-2405.

Fort Simcoe State Park

Head 27 miles west from Toppenish through the heart of the Yakama Indian Reservation to peaceful Fort Simcoe State Park. The drive takes you through fields of grapes and hops, past fast-growing Heritage College, past the rundown town of White Swan and Indian burial grounds with decorated gravesites, to the fort site.

Fort Simcoe was erected by the Army in 1856 as a base for military operations against nearby Indians but was abandoned just three years later. It then served as a Bureau of Indian Affairs school and Indian Agency headquarters until becoming a state park in 1953. (The land is under a 99-year lease from the Yakama Nation.) Two blockhouses and a barracks have been reconstructed, and five of the original buildings have been restored and furnished, including the New England-style commanding officer's house, three captain's quarters, and a log blockhouse. Tour the buildings and the brick interpretive center with artifacts and old photos, then enjoy a picnic lunch on the parklike grounds. The grounds are open daily till dusk; the museum and interpretive center are open Wed.-Sun. 9 a.m.-4 p.m., April-Oct.; tel. (509) 874-2372. No camping at Fort Simcoe.

---

pace took them 25 miles in seven days. For the rest of July and into August McClellan averaged a little more than three miles a day when normal travelers would have averaged around 25 miles a day. The historian Robert Cantwell estimated that if the people crossing the plains on the Oregon Trail had traveled at that pace, it would have taken them six years, instead of five months, to get to the Oregon Country.

McClellan was just doing his job, and it took careful planning to avoid all the 11 passes the Indians used to cross the mountains. It was well known that the Hudson's Bay Company routinely drove cattle through Snoqualmie Pass. When it appeared they might stumble onto a route, Mcclellan would swing wide to avoid it. Thus, rather than going along the west side of Mt. Adams, he led his party east so they could go around the southern side, and swing down south so that they ended up at Goose Lake, out on the plains. McClellan took his party farther east, and by the time they reached about where the town of Yakima would later be built, they were out of food, in part because McClellan had only three hunters to supply 66 men. They were in luck because a Catholic mission had been there several years and McClellan and his men almost swept the priests' cupboards bare. They also bought some cattle from the Indians who lived around the mission, and the next several days were spent butchering the cattle and jerking the meat to preserve it for the rest of the trip.

It took them 11 days to get ready, and by now it was almost September. McClellan divided his force and instructed one group to head north toward Canada in search of a route up there, while two other groups were sent back to the Columbia River. He sent still another group over Naches Pass, which McClellan knew existed but also knew it was too dangerous for a railroad. After dividing his party into so many pieces, that left him and his personal escort to explore the Cascades for a pass, and that apparently was what the exercise was all about: he wanted to not find the passes without too many witnesses. He passed by every route across the Cascades, and went as far north as Stevens Pass. He went by Chinook Pass, Stampede Pass, White Pass, Cowlitz Pass, Carleton Pass, Hart's Pass, Cascade Pass, Cispus Pass, and Twisp Pass. He thus determined that only two routes went through the mountains: the Thompson River far up in Canada, and the Columbia.

Governor Stevens was infuriated at McClellan's report and sent Abiel Tinkham over Snoqualmie Pass in the dead of winter. Tinkham snowshoed across the pass, then turned around and snowshoed back home.

McClellan went on to become a total failure as a general in the Civil War. Stevens was killed in the war, and Grant, of course, came into his own late in the war and won it for the Union. It wasn't long before several railroads went through the Cascades at several places, and trails were followed by wagon roads, then highways. None of these routes bear the name of McClellan.

PRACTICALITIES

Accommodations

The nicest and newest local place is **Toppenish Inn Motel,** 515 S. Elm St., tel. (509) 865-7444 or (800) 222-3161, which features an indoor pool, jacuzzi, exercise room, fridges, microwaves, and continental breakfast. Rates are $58 s or $63 d. **Oxbow Motor Inn,** 511 S. Elm, tel. (509) 865-5800, has standard rooms for $36 s or $39-44 d. **El Corral Motel,** 61731 Hwy. 97, tel. (509) 865-2365, charges $36-39 s or d.

Camping

The **Yakama Nation Resort RV Park,** next to the Cultural Center, tel. (509) 865-2000 or (800) 874-3087, has parking spaces for RVs ($18), plus 14 very popular tepees ($30; sleeps five), a tent-camping area ($12), outdoor pool, hot tub, and other facilities.

Food

Toppenish's strong Hispanic culture is evidenced in the plethora of Mexican restaurants, clothing stores, and "se habla español" signs. **Taqueria Mexicana,** 105 S. Alder St., tel. (509) 865-7116, has the best

---

THE RAWHIDE RAILROAD

Pioneers used rawhide for a variety of things, but Dr. Dorsey Syng Baker was probably the only one to use it instead of metal on railroad rails. Dr. Baker was born in Iowa in 1823, and, after becoming a doctor, followed the overland migration to Oregon in 1848. The following year he headed south to the California gold rush, and made some money on it, although he never explained how to historians. A few years later he was back in the Northwest with a hardware store in Portland and a flour mill in Oakland, Oregon. In 1861 the gold rush in Idaho got him interested in that part of the country and he went into the outfitting business in Walla Walla.

But his true genius came into its own when he got interested in the transportation business. He joined forces with two other men and built the steamboat *Spray* and ran it on the Columbia River between Lewiston and Celilo Falls, which until then had been the end of the line for river traffic. So the good doctor did something about it: He built a mile-long tramway around the falls, and before long he was meeting a schedule between Portland and Lewiston and towns between.

As he became better acquainted in the area, he saw that a railroad was needed to connect the Columbia River to the rich farmlands around Walla Walla. At that time, there wasn't a railroad anywhere in the Northwest. In the spring of 1871 Dr. Baker made up his mind to build that railroad, and placed an order for two small, narrow-gauge locomotives along with 100 pairs of car wheels and 1,000 plug hats.

He laid out 32 miles of roadbed between Wallula and Walla Walla and signed a contract with a logger for timber to make the track. The logging contractor took his men up the Yakima River for the logs and was going to float them down the river to Wallula, but the season was dry and the log drive failed. Dr. Baker pressed ahead with his plans as though nothing had happened. He built a sawmill, and then following spring another logger showed up claiming he could deliver the logs. This one did, and when spring thaw came, Dr. Baker's men began laying square ties to support the six-by-six timbers that would be the rails.

Soon the locomotives, wheels, and plug hats arrived on the river, and it was at Celilo Falls that the plug hats came into their own: Dr. Baker knew the Indians loved hats, and he used them as pay for the Indians whose help he needed to unload the locomotives and muscle them onto the tramway and onto the *Spray* for the rest of the trip. When they reached Wallula, the locomotives were dragged onto the rails built for them, and Dr. Baker had a railroad. Cars to go on the sets of wheels were built from lumber milled at his sawmill, and the railroad inched its way eastward across the prairies.

Then it became obvious, after several split and worn-out rails, that some kind of protection was needed for them. And it is here that the story of the rawhide-covered rails enters history. How much was used, and how long it was used, is not known, but it couldn't have been long because Dr. Baker placed an order for strap iron, an inch and a half wide with pre-drilled holes for nails. The rawhide strips worked reasonably well, according to the folklore that grew up around the railroad, but some said Dr. Baker was plagued by wolves eating the rawhide.

One passenger in the 1870s, John M. Murphy, wrote of the railroad in his book, *Rambles in North-Western America From the Pacific Ocean to the*

south-of-the-border meals in town. **Los Murales,** 202 W. 1st, tel. (509) 865-7555, specializes in northern Mexican lunches and dinners, along with steaks and seafood. For authentic Mexican pastries, stop by **El Porvenir Panaderia,** 209 S. Toppenish, tel. (509) 865-7900. For a rather different type of ethnic food, **Lotus Restaurant,** 901 W. 1st Ave., tel. (509) 865-4552, is the place to go for the best Chinese food in the area.

The **Yakama Nation Cultural Center** has a popular restaurant with a large salad bar, salmon, buffalo, and Indian fry bread. The Sunday brunch is very popular.

For a homemade breakfast with the locals, head to **Sue's Pioneer Kitchen,** 227 S. Toppenish Ave., tel. (509) 865-3201. You'll discover the best burgers around, along with floats, shakes, and cold drinks, at the old-fashioned soda fountain in **Gibbon's Pharmacy,** 117 S. Toppenish Ave., tel. (509) 865-2722. Enjoy a hearty charbroiled steak or barbecue ribs dinner at **Cattlemen's Restaurant,** 2 S. Division St., tel. (509) 865-1800. More American food at **The Branding Iron,** at Highways 22 and 97, where the plate-sized cinnamon rolls are said to be the biggest in the civilized world. Live music on weekends, too.

Rocky Mountains. Murphy saw the whole operation—the tiny train, the rails that looked like they had been gnawed, the rattle-trap cars and the man who collected his $2 and was "the president, secretary, conductor, and brakeman of the road." He was a little nervous about the journey from Wallula to Walla Walla and decided he would be safer on a flatcar than in the coach. He was "placed on some iron in an open truck and told to cling to the sides, and to be careful not to stand on the wooden floor if I cared anything about my limbs." So he stood in the hot sun waiting for the train to depart the station. To his astonishment, the conductor told the engineer to go ahead without him, that he had a few things to do and he would catch up with them. The engineer nodded and put the train into motion "The miserable little engine gave a grunt or two, several wheezy puffs, a cat-like scream, and finally the car attached to it got under way" until it reached its top speed of about two miles an hour. Soon the conductor came strolling along the track, passed all the cars and slowed to chat with the engineer. He walked the whole six miles.

"Before I had proceeded half a mile, I saw why I was not permitted to stand on the floor of the truck," Murphy wrote. "For a piece of hoop-iron, which covered the wooden rails in some places, curled into what is called a 'snake head' and pushed through the wood with such force that it nearly stopped the train." The 15-mile trip took Murphy seven hours. At the station, which was a "rude board shanty," Murphy found a ride into town on a farmer's wagon and agreed to drive the team while sitting beside the owner, who slept all the way into town. He wrote that he came to regret his decision to drive the wagon because every driver he met had something to say about his attire.

"The badinage was, as a rule, so original and

witty that I had several good laughs at my own expense; and I found after awhile that the chaff was richly merited, as my black broadcloth coat was one mass of burnt holes in the back, and my silk hat looked like a sieve."

Another story, perhaps a bit of exaggeration, involved the day a train jumped the track. A man walking along the road that paralleled the railroad stopped to help. When the train was back to normal on the track, the engineer offered the man a ride.

"No, thank you," he replied. "I'm in a hurry."

One of the continuing problems for the Bonanza Line was cattle wandering onto the track and being killed or injured by the train. Dr. Baker came up with a novel solution. He built a small platform on the front of the engine, and then trained a dog to ride on the platform. When the engineer blasted the whistle, the dog would leap off and run ahead and clear the track of cattle. When his duty was done, the dog would lie down on the track and wait for the second locomotive so he could ride on it. One day the dog fell asleep and was run over. Dr. Baker decided then that a mechanical cowcatcher used by trains throughout the world was in order.

Passengers became accustomed to the unusual while riding Dr. Baker's train. Engineers and firemen stopped at bridges and creeks to refill the boiler, and since oil for the bearings was expensive and sometimes hard to find, the crewmen carried buckets of hog lard to use instead, which added an olfactory treat to riders. It was unique in at least one other aspect: Dr. Baker always paid dividends to its stockholders, and the railroad was never in debt. It ran until 1877, when Dr. Baker sold six-sevenths interest to the Oregon Railway & Navigation Company, and two years later the railroad was converted to standard gauge so it could be absorbed into the whole system.

Events

The **Speely-Mi Arts & Craft Trade Fair** in mid-March brings exhibitions of Native artisans to the Cultural Center. Each year on the first Saturday in June, Toppenish sponsors a **Mural-in-a-Day** program in which more than two dozen artists complete a wall-sized mural in a day's work. The chamber of commerce simultaneously sponsors an arts and crafts and food fair. Call (509) 865-6516 for details.

Treaty Days in early June celebrates the signing of the Treaty of 1855 between the U.S. government and the Yakama Indian Nation and features an all-Indian rodeo, pow wow, and parade.

The Fourth of July weekend brings a frenzy of activity to Toppenish: the **Pow Wow & Rodeo,** tel. (509) 865-5313. This event has something for everyone—a carnival, nightly rodeos, Indian dancing, fireworks, a Wild West Parade featuring cowboys, cowgirls, and Indians in full regalia, an antique power show, and arts and crafts booths. Various **Mexican rodeos** are held in Toppenish most summer weekends, and the second weekend of June brings the **All-Indian Rodeo and Pow Wow** to nearby White Swan. Another big pow wow is held in White Swan in mid September.

The last weekend in August attracts some 100 top Northwest artists who display their art at the **Toppenish Western Art Show.** An auction takes place Friday and Saturday nights.

Shopping

Toppenish is filled with antique, craft, and gift shops. For authentic Indian arts and crafts, visit the gift shop at Yakama Nation Cultural Center. **The Amish Connection,** tel. (509) 865-5300, has handcrafted Amish furniture, dolls, quilts, and other items. A few doors away is **Kraff's,** tel. (509) 865-3000, the largest retailer of Pendleton blankets in the United States. **Inter Tribal Trading Post,** tel. (509) 865-7775, creates beautiful coats and clothing, including ones made from Pendleton blankets. For Mexican clothing, including ponchos, leather jackets, skirts, hats, and more, visit **Reflexion de Mexico,** on the corner of Hwy. 97 and Fort Rd., tel. (509) 865-7888. Bored with shopping? **Legends Casino** on Fort Rd., tel. (509) 865-8800, has gambling of all sorts.

Information and Services

For information, head to the very helpful **Toppenish Chamber of Commerce,** 11 S. Toppenish Ave., tel. (509) 865-3262. Open daily 10 a.m.-4 p.m. April-October (till 5 p.m. in mid-summer), and Mon.-Sat. 11 a.m.-3 p.m. the rest of the year. Catch **Greyhound** buses at 602 W. 1st, tel. (509) 865-3773 or (800) 231-2222. Swim at Toppenish's big 50-meter **outdoor pool** in the summer.

YAKIMA VALLEY

While Toppenish is virtually a world—or a nation—apart, the rest of the Yakima Valley blends together to form a single conceptual region, basing its reputation, if not its economy, on the wineries that line the Yakima River. Interstate 82 cuts across the north side of the valley, with the older Hwy. 22 following a parallel route on the south side. Other than Toppenish (described above), several small towns dot the route between Yakima and the Tri-Cities; largest are Zillah, Granger, Sunnyside, Grandview, and Prosser.

ZILLAH

Zillah (pop. 2,300) was named for Zillah Oakes, the 17-year-old daughter of the president of the Northern Pacific Railroad, by one of the first settlers in the area; apparently he was infatuated with her. Or maybe he just wanted to curry favor with the owner of the railroad.

Sights
Certainly the strangest local sight is the **Teapot Dome** gas station located just south of I-82. This tiny station consists of a one-room teapot-shaped structure with a concrete handle on one side and a metal spout on the other. Built in 1922 as a protest over the Teapot Dome scandal that sent President Harding's interior secretary to prison, the station is now a National Historic Site. Fill up at the nation's oldest working gas station; it's been owned by the same family for more than 70 years. Zillah's **Seventh Day Adventist Church** at 202 5th St. was built in 1910 and has intricate stained glass windows and unusual twin steeples. **Zillah Oakes Winery** has a wine shop and tasting room near I-82 exit 52.

Lodging and Food
Comfort Inn, 911 Vintage Valley Pkwy., tel. (509) 829-3399 or (800) 501-5433, $65 s or $69 d, has an indoor pool, jacuzzi, exercise room, and continental breakfast.

For Mexican food, steer your steers toward **El Ranchito,** just south of Zillah, tel. (509) 829-5880. In business since 1950, this is fast Mexican food at its meaty best, with no pretense. Order at the counter and wait for your order to arrive on a paper plate. Satisfaction guaranteed, but get here early since they close at 7 p.m. most nights. Another fine Mexican eatery is **El Porton,** tel. (509) 829-9100, at exit 52. Good food, great service, and a big selection of seafood and vegetarian offerings.

Teapot Dome
gas station, Zillah

DON PITCHER

Another very popular Zillah restaurant is **Squeeze Inn,** 611 1st Ave., tel. (509) 829-6226, where the breakfasts bring out the coffee klatch crowd, and the dinners of steak, prime rib, and seafood attract folks from all over the valley. Shrimp cocktails come with all dinners. Squeeze Inn has been in the same family since 1932. **Doc's Pizza,** 505 1st Ave. in Zillah, tel. (509) 829-6259, makes some of the Valley's best pizzas. Their antique bathtub salad bar is unusual, to put it mildly.

Rocky Mountain Chocolate Factory at exit 52 in Zillah, tel. (509) 829-3330 or (800) 454-7623, makes all sorts of chocolate goodies, including fudge, macadamia clusters, truffles, and another 75 or so varieties of candy.

Events and Information

Zillah' s **Community Days** in mid-May features a pancake breakfast, craft fair, parade, and contests. For local information, head to the **Zillah Chamber of Commerce,** 119 1st Ave., tel. (509) 829-5055.

GRANGER

The farming town of Granger (pop. 2,000) sits along the north side of the Yakima River and just a few miles east of Zillah. Granger is home to the first nonprofit Spanish-language radio station in Washington, KDNA. Seventeen dinosaurs welcome you to Granger's "Jurassic Pond," including aptosaurus in the water. Get a good view of the surrounding country from **Cherry Hill,** just east of town; Stewart Vineyards has a tasting room here. Visit **Worden's Lamp House** on Main St., tel. (800) 541-1103, for more than 80 types of Tiffany-style stained-glass lamps, many of which are made here.

Located in the wine country east of Granger, **Outlook Inn B&B,** 1320 Independence Rd. in Outlook, tel. (509) 837-7651, has three guest rooms and a deck overlooking the vineyards. Tefft Cellers Winery is right next door. A full breakfast is served; $45-75. No kids.

Granger's **Cherry Festival** in early May includes music, dancing, a fishing derby, and a Mexican fiesta.

SUNNYSIDE

Sunnyside (pop. 12,000) is near the center of Yakima Valley's grape-, hop-, and fruit-producing region. On the west end of town are several large feedlots that add a rather pungent odor to the air. Because of all the farm jobs, the town has a strong Hispanic presence; plenty of good Mexican food here!

Sunnyside Museum, 704 S. 4th St., tel. (509) 837-6010, has Native American artifacts, pioneer items, and ice age fossils; open Fri.-Sun. 1:30-4:30 p.m. all year. Entrance is 50 cents for adults, free for kids. Nearby is the **Ben Snipes Cabin,** built in 1859. Snipes—the "Northwest cattle king"—introduced cattle into Yakima Valley, raising them for gold mining camps in British Columbia, Colville, and Idaho.

Lodging

For classic lodging, stay at **Von Hellstrum Inn B&B,** 51 Branden Rd., tel. (509) 839-2505 (800) 222-8652, located in a hilltop 1908 home overlooking the Yakima Valley. The four antique-furnished guest rooms have private baths, and a full breakfast is served; $65 s or $70 d.

For in-town accommodations, **Sunnyside Inn B&B,** 800 E. Edison, tel. (800) 839-5557, has eight luxurious and spacious rooms with private baths (most with jacuzzi tubs) in two attractive older homes. A hearty breakfast is served, and kids are accepted; $59-89 s or d.

Travelodge, 408 Yakima Valley Hwy., tel. (509) 837-4721 or (800) 578-7878, charges $48 s or $51-55 d and has an outdoor pool, jacuzzi, and continental breakfast.

Food

The **Tillicum Restaurant,** tel. (509) 837-7222, 410 Hwy. 12, serves only Yakima Valley wines with their steak and prime rib dinners. For Sichuan and Mandarin cooking, try **China Grove,** 325 Hwy. 12, tel. (509) 839-3663. Eat authentic Mexican food for reasonable prices at **La Fogata Mexican Restaurant,** 1204 Yakima Valley Hwy., tel. (509) 839-9019.

Sunnyside's big Darigold cheese factory—one of the largest cheese plants in the nation—has tours, fun exhibits (including flying cows), and videos, plus fresh ice cream, cheeses, sandwiches, and gifts. Find the **Darigold Dairy Fair** at 400 Alexander Rd., tel. (509) 837-4321. **Snipes Mountain Microbrewery & Restaurant,** 905 Yakima Valley Hwy., tel. (509) 837-2739, is hard to miss. It's the huge new log building near the center of town, with a brewery behind glass and a diverse menu that includes everything from wood-fired pizzas to seafood satays. Very popular, with a lively atmosphere, good food, and no smoking.

Events

Cinco de Mayo Fiesta Days are a major celebration time for Sunnyside, with art, music, food, and dancing. In early December, the **Country Christmas Lighted Farm Implement Parade** features lit-up tractors, farm machinery, and horse-drawn carriages and wagons.

Information and Services

For local information, visit the **Sunnyside Chamber of Commerce,** 812 E. Edison Ave., tel. (509) 837-5939 or (800) 457-8089. Sunnyside has a beautiful 50-meter outdoor **swimming pool** with a water slide in the town park. The **Greyhound** bus depot is at 13th St. and Hwy. 12, tel. (509) 837-5344 or (800) 231-2222.

GRANDVIEW

Grandview (pop. 7,900) is another in a chain of small agricultural settlements in Yakima Valley. The **Ray E. Powell Museum,** tel. (509) 882-2070, is next to the town library at 313 S. Division St., and contains Indian artifacts, pioneer items, antique clocks and guns, and a turn-of-the-century Kiblinger car, one of just two in existence. Open Tues.-Fri. and Sunday 2-4 p.m. March-October. The distinctive circular **Marble Ranch Barn** 1.5 miles south of town is on the National Register of Historic Places.

Lodging

Grandview Motel, 522 E. Wine Country Rd., tel. (509) 882-1323, has rooms for $35-43 s or d with outdoor pool. **Apple Valley Motel,** Hwy. 12, tel. (509) 882-3003, also has an outdoor pool; $32 s or d.

Cozy Rose Inn B&B, 1220 Forsell Rd., tel. (509) 882-4669, has two contemporary homes in the country between Grandview and Sunnyside. Four guest suites have private baths, fireplaces, and kitchenettes. A full breakfast is delivered to your door; $98 d. Kids accepted. Guests will enjoy taking the llamas for a walk.

Other Practicalities

Housed in a grand 1914 home, **Dykstra House Restaurant,** 114 Birch Ave., tel. (509) 882-2082, serves elegant lunches Tues.-Sat. and dinners on Friday and Saturday. The menu changes to match what's fresh that day, but always includes delicious homemade breads and desserts. Expensive, and reservations are required.

The **Grandview Grape Stomp** is one of the stranger events in Yakima Valley; contestants see who can squeeze out the most juice using traditional foot-power. It attracts big-footed competitors from all over the Northwest.

The **Grandview Chamber of Commerce** is in the old depot at 103 W. 5th, tel. (509) 882-2100.

PROSSER

When you enter the small and prosperous town of Prosser (pop. 4,800), you're greeted by a sign proclaiming it, "A pleasant place with pleasant people." Hard to argue about this, especially after a saunter through Prosser's clean streets and busy downtown. It's one of the prettiest spots in this part of Washington, and is the center of government for Benton County. Much of this prosperity comes from agriculture, with not only the many Yakima Valley wineries, but also the enormous Twin City Foods plant in town (they process Tater Tots, hash browns, and other frozen potato products here).

Sights

In Prosser City Park, the **Benton County Historical Museum,** tel. (509) 786-3842, is open Tues.-Sat. 10 a.m.-4 p.m. and Sunday 1-5 p.m.; admission is $2 adults, $1 kids. Curator Nez Thompson has been here for over 30 years and will be happy to show you the 1867 Chickering Square grand piano (used for Mother's Day concerts), the collection of old gowns, a handcarved replica of a Holt combine pulled by 26 horses, and historical photographs. The brick and stone **Benton County Courthouse** on Market St. was built in 1926 and is on the National Register of Historic Places.

Be sure to stop at the **Chukar Cherries** on the west end of town to taste the dried cherries, chocolate-covered berries, and other delicious sweets. They also have branch stores in Seattle, Issaquah, Pasco, and Vancouver, B.C., plus a mail-order business; call (800) 624-9544 for a catalog.

Storyland, tel. (509) 786-6900, is a miniature golf place with an amusing fairy tale collection of creatures. Open daily April-September.

Accommodations
Prosser Motel, 1206 Wine Country Rd., tel. (509) 786-2555, has rooms for $30 s or $35 d. **The Barn Motor Inn,** 490 Wine Country Rd., tel. (509) 786-2121, has an outdoor pool and rooms for $40 s or $46 d. Park RVs here too. **Best Western Prosser Inn,** 225 Merlot Dr., tel. (509) 786-7977 or (800) 688-2192, has an outdoor pool, jacuzzi, fridges, continental breakfast; $56-62 s or $59-65 d.

Located along the Yakima River, **Wine Country Inn B&B,** 1106 Wine Country Rd., tel. (509) 786-2855, has four guest rooms (two with private baths), and serves a full breakfast; $65-75 s or d.

Food
The Barn Restaurant, on the west end of town, tel. (509) 786-2121, is one of the best local restaurants for steak and seafood; munch the great appetizers while watching sports on the big-screen TV. Another local favorite is **The Blue Goose,** 306 7th St., tel. (509) 786-1774, which features a menu that includes prime rib, pastas, and seafood. Come here for a breakfast omelette.

The **Prosser Farmers Market** takes place Saturday 8 a.m.-12:30 p.m. June-Sept. in the city park; tel. (509) 786-3600.

Events and Information
Dog lovers will enjoy Prosser's **National Championship Chucker Field Trials** on the last weekend in March. It attracts English pointers and shorthairs from all over the country. The **Prosser Wine & Food Fair** on the second Saturday of August is the largest outdoor wine and food show in the state, attracting thousands of people for a chance to sample wine, beer, and food. The event usually sells out, so order advance tickets by calling (509) 786-3177. It's only open to people over age 21.

The **Prosser Balloon Rally and Harvest Festival** on the last weekend of September attracts balloon enthusiasts for morning launches, nighttime lighted balloons, and arts and crafts exhibits.

The **Prosser Chamber of Commerce** is located in the old railroad depot at 611 6th St., tel. (509) 786-3177. Open Mon.-Fri. 10 a.m.-4 p.m.

YAKIMA VALLEY WINERIES

The Yakima and Columbia valleys comprise the premier wine-growing regions in Washington and have helped make it the second largest producer of fine wine grapes in America. Yakima Valley is located along the same latitude as France's Burgundy and Bordeaux regions, and the dry climate, sunny weather, and ample irrigation waters make for ideal growing conditions. The wineries along the Yakima River provide more than a day's touring; all of these wineries have tasting rooms and picnic facilities.

Events
In mid-February, visit the valley for a **Celebration of Chocolates and Red Wine** during which the various wineries provide chocolate sweets to match their reds. The biggest annual wine event is the **Yakima Valley Spring Barrel Tasting** in late April when the wineries pour samples of their new releases straight from the barrel and offer tours, hors d'oeuvres, and educational exhibits. All 25 wineries are open 10 a.m.-5 p.m. during this three-day event. Call (800) 258-7270 for details.

The season winds down with **Thanksgiving in Yakima Valley Wine Country,** featuring food and wine tasting at most local wineries. This is a fine way to taste a variety of gourmet foods and to get recipe ideas.

Wine Tour
Stop by the local visitor centers for a map of 27 local wineries, or request a copy from the **Yaki-**

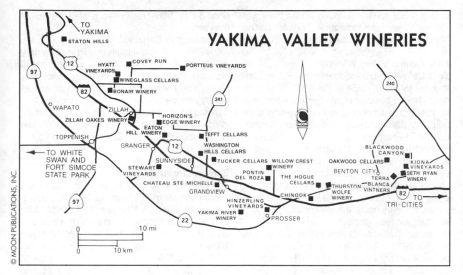

ma Valley Wine Growers Association, tel. (800) 258-7270. The following tour is based upon their brochure.

From Yakima, your first stop will be **Staton Hills,** 71 Gangl Rd. in Wapato, tel. (509) 877-2112, open for tastings daily 11 a.m.-5:30 p.m. in the summer, and noon-5 p.m. Nov.-February. You'll get a fine view of the Yakima Valley from their hilltop location. Next comes **Zillah Oakes Winery,** 1001 Vintage Valley Parkway in Zillah, tel. (509) 829-6690; open for tastings daily 10 a.m.-5 p.m. This is actually just a tasting room for Zillah Oakes wines, along with those from Paul Thomas Winery, Columbia Winery, and Covey Run Vintners.

Bonair Winery, 500 S. Bonair Rd. in Zillah, tel. (509) 829-6027 or (800) 882-8939, is a small, family-run place specializing in chardonnay, riesling, and cabernet sauvignon and is open daily 10 a.m.-5 p.m. summers, and Sat.-Sun. 10 a.m.-4:30 p.m. winters. They sell most of their production from the winery.

Another small family place is **Hyatt Vineyards Winery,** 2020 Gilbert Rd. in Zillah, tel. (509) 829-6333, featuring merlot and cabernet sauvignon, plus very sweet ice wine; open daily 11 a.m.-5 p.m. April-Oct., daily 11 a.m.-4:30 p.m. winters, and closed January. **Wineglass Cellars,** 260 N. Bonair Rd., tel. (509) 829-3011,

produces chardonnay and several reds; open for tastings Fri.-Sun. 11 a.m.-5 p.m. (closed December-February).

West Yakima Valley Wineries

Covey Run Winery, at 1500 Vintage Rd. in Zillah, tel. (509) 829-6235, is one of the area's big-name wineries and was the first major Washington winery to use only Yakima Valley grapes. Most of their production is white wine, primarily riesling. The mezzanine tasting room affords a nice vineyard view; open daily 10 a.m.-5 p.m.

Portteus Vineyards, 5201 Highland Dr. in Zillah, tel. (509) 829-6970, is famous for red wines, including cabernet. Washington's first zinfandel was produced here; open daily noon-5 p.m. in summer; call for winter hours.

Also in Zillah, at 4530 E. Zillah Dr., **Horizon's Edge Winery,** tel. (509) 829-6401, has dramatic views across the valley. Releases include sparkling wines and merlots. The tasting room is open daily 10 a.m.-5 p.m. in the summer and fall, call ahead at other times of the year. **Eaton Hill Winery,** 530 Gurley Rd. in Granger, tel. (509) 854-2508, is a small family operation with a variety of wines; open for tastings Fri.-Wed. 10 a.m.-5 p.m. in summer, and Mon.-Fri. noon-4 p.m. winters.

A longtime local favorite, **Stewart Vineyards,** tel. (509) 854-1882, is at 1711 Cherry Hill Rd. in

Granger. Get panoramic views across the lower Yakima Valley from their deck. Open for tasting Mon.-Sat. 10 a.m.-5 p.m. and Sunday noon-5 p.m.

East Yakima Valley Wineries

Tefft Cellars, 1320 Independence Rd. in Outlook, tel. (509) 837-7651 or (888) 303-7651, produces limited bottlings of late harvest wines, Italian varietals, champagne, and port. Tasting room hours are daily noon-5 p.m.; call ahead December to mid-February.

Washington Hills Cellars, 111 E. Lincoln Ave. in Sunnyside, tel. (509) 839-9463, is in the old Carnation Dairy building and has a retail shop and picnic area; open for tours and tasting daily 10 a.m.-5:30 p.m. They produce a wide variety of wines under the Bridgman, Apex, and Washington Hills labels.

Tucker Cellars, 70 Ray Rd. in Sunnyside, tel. (509) 837-8701, is a family winery that produces a variety of wines. The tasting room is open daily 9 a.m.-5 p.m. summers, and daily 10 a.m.-4:30 p.m. winters. An adjacent market sells fresh fruit and produce.

Washington's oldest winery, **Chateau Ste. Michelle,** tel. (509) 882-3928, no longer offers tours or tasting at their Grandview facility; visit their Woodinville winery instead.

Pontin del Roza, 35502 N. Hinzerling Rd. in Prosser, tel. (509) 786-4449, produces pinot gris, merlot, chardonnay, and cabernet sauvignon; open daily 10 a.m.-5 p.m. **Willow Crest Winery,** 135701 Snipes Rd. in Prosser, tel. (509) 786-7999, is a new winery housed in a renovated farmhouse; open Sat.-Sun. 10 a.m.-5 p.m.

Also in Prosser at 143302 North River Rd., **Yakima River Winery,** tel. (509) 786-2805, was started in 1978 and produces wines ranging from barrel-aged reds to semi-dry whites to ports. The tasting room is open daily 10 a.m.-5 p.m. in summer; call for winter hours.

Founded in 1976, **Hinzerling Vineyards,** 1520 Sheridan in Prosser, tel. (509) 786-2163 or (800) 727-6702, specializes in estate-grown cabernet and ports. Tastings are usually held in the wine cellar, Mon.-Sat. 11 a.m.-5 p.m. and Sunday 11 a.m.-4 p.m. March-Dec.; call for winter hours.

Chinook Wines, Wine Country Rd. in Prosser, tel. (509) 786-2725, offers sauvignon blanc, chardonnay, semillon, or merlot. Open Sat.-Sun.

noon-5 p.m. May-December, closed the rest of the year.

The Hogue Cellars, Wine Country Rd., tel. (509) 786-4557, is the big-name Prosser winery (and third largest in Washington), with a range of products, from rieslings to merlot to a very nice blush wine. Their tasting room, gift shop, and art gallery are open daily 10 a.m.-5 p.m.

Just a short distance from Hogue is the small, family-run **Thurston Wolfe Winery** at 3800 Lee Rd., tel. (509) 786-3313. Open Fri.-Sun. 11 a.m.-5 p.m.

Benton City Area Wineries

The quiet small town of Benton City provides a sharp contrast to the bustling Tri-Cities, just a few miles to the east. Stop here for fresh produce at **Dee's Fruit Stand,** or just enjoy the lush valley with vineyards and fruit trees. **Seth Ryan Winery,** 35306 Sunset Rd. in Benton City, tel. (509) 588-6780, produces small quantities of riesling, gewürztraminer, merlot, cabernet, and chardonnays; open Sat.-Sun. 11 a.m.-6 p.m. (winter Sat.-Sun. noon-5 p.m.).

Oakwood Cellars, 40504 N. Demoss Rd. in Benton City, tel. (509) 588-5332, has chardonnay, merlot, muscat, and lemberger; open Sat.-Sun. noon-5 p.m. in summer, by appointment at other times.

Kiona Vineyards, 44612 N. Sunset NE in Benton City, tel. (509) 588-6716, sits on Red Mountain with a nice tasting-room view of the vineyards. Kiona produces a full range of varietal wines; open daily noon-5 p.m.

One of the most interesting and personable wineries is Benton City's **Blackwood Canyon,** Rte. 2, Box 2169H, tel. (509) 588-6249, open daily 10 a.m.-6 p.m. The winery sits at the end of a rough gravel road in the middle of the vineyards, and the tasting room is just a counter in their warehouse. The chardonnays, cabernets, and late-harvest wines are quite distinctive. **Hedges Cellars,** 53511 N. Sunset Rd. in Benton City, tel. (800) 859-9463, is open by appointment only, or sample their wines at their Issaquah tasting room.

Located on Red Mountain, **Terra Blanca,** 34715 N. DeMoss Rd. in Benton City, tel. (509) 588-6082, is one of Washington's newest wineries. The tasting room is open Mon.-Fri. noon-6 p.m. and Sat.-Sun. 11 a.m.-6 p.m.

TRI-CITIES

The Tri-Cities comprise three adjacent cities: Kennewick faces its poorer cousin Pasco across the Columbia River, and the "Atomic City" of Richland is seven miles to the west near the entrance to the massive Hanford Site. Together, these three make up the fifth-largest metropolitan area in the state (over 100,000 people). They have prospered in recent years from the cleanup of the nearby Hanford Site, and in the late 1990s the area was booming from the billions of federal dollars being dumped into the economy. Besides Hanford, the Tri-Cities are famous for their hydroplane race, held annually in July, and their wineries, at the southeast end of the fruitful Yakima Valley. The area is also becoming something of a retirement destination, in part because of the dry and sunny weather.

The Setting
The Tri-Cities are located in Pasco Basin on the Columbia Plateau, a desert land at the confluence of the Yakima, Snake, and Columbia Rivers. Columbia and Snake River dams provide water recreation, electrical power, and water for agriculture. Upstream from Richland is the last free-flowing segment of the Columbia River in Washington—the "Hanford Reach." It is under study for possible Wild and Scenic River status, but given the current political climate that status seems unlikely any time soon.

Farms cover 1.3 million acres—400,000 of them irrigated—in Benton and Franklin Counties; potatoes, wheat, apples, grapes, alfalfa, strawberries, asparagus, corn, and hops are the big money producers here. Much of this production is shipped from the port facilities in the Tri-Cities to the Pacific Rim.

The Cities
Kennewick, at 49,000 residents, is the largest and fastest growing of the Tri-Cities. With its pleasant downtown surrounded by wide, shady streets with quiet older homes, Kennewick could double for any Midwestern town. Unfortunately, Clearwater Ave.—the main business thoroughfare—is a typical stretch of fast food joints, car repair shops, and strip malls with the standard jumble of glaring neon signs vying for attention. The giant Columbia Center Mall is the largest in this part of the state.

Richland—with 36,000 people it's the second most populous of the Tri-Cities—has an attractive older downtown right along the river, and several fine city parks, but an unsightly sprawl of enormous homes belonging to the elite spreads to the south along Columbia Drive. This is the "Atomic City," and it grew up as a secret settlement during the 1940s, with the nearby Hanford Site as an ominous neighbor. In 1949, *Time* magazine proclaimed Richland "an atomic age utopia." During WW II, only government workers could live here, but the buildings were returned to private hands in 1958. The Richland high school's sports teams are still called "The Bombers."

Pasco has 25,000 residents and contrasts sharply with its prosperous neighbors. It is separated from Kennewick by a pair of bridges across the Columbia: the **10th Ave. bridge** is notable for its distinctive girder-span design; the Hwy. 395 bridge is better known as the "Blue Bridge." Pasco—the Franklin County seat—is a working-class town with thrift stores, run-down businesses, and a seedy, hard-times feeling. You won't find the elaborate shopping malls of Kennewick here. Pasco's redeeming attribute is a plethora of fine Mexican bakeries *(panaderías),* shops *(tiendas),* taco vans, and close to a dozen Mexican restaurants.

Weather
The Tri-Cities endure weather extremes that western Washingtonians never see. Plenty of below-zero days have been recorded here, as well as summer temperatures soaring over 100 bone-dry degrees; fortunately, a fairly constant breeze makes the heat almost tolerable (of course, the breeze can also stir up dust). The area receives an average annual precipitation of just six inches, scattered between 225 sunny days. Most of the rain occurs November-April, and snow is not uncommon in the winter months, though it rarely exceeds six inches on the ground.

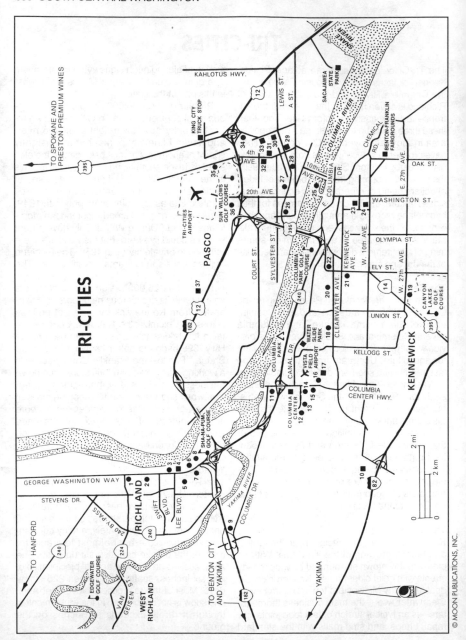

© MOON PUBLICATIONS, INC.

TRI-CITIES

1. Best Western Tower Inn
2. Bali Hai Motel
3. Doubletree Hotel/Hanford House
4. CREHST Museum
5. Nendel's Inn
6. Hampton Inn
7. Vagabond Inn
8. Shilo Motel
9. Bookwalter Winery
10. Badger Mt. Winery
11. Motel 6
12. Fairfield Inn
13. Comfort Inn
14. Silver Cloud Inn
15. Cavanaugh's at Columbia Center
16. Super 8 Motel
17. Tri-Cities Visitors Center
18. Clearwater Inn
19. Best Western Kennewick
20. Shaniko Suites Motel
21. Nendel's Inn
22. Tapadera Inn
23. east Benton County Historical Museum
24. Kennewick General Hospital
25. Quality Inn
26. Goal Post Motor Inn
27. Vineyard Inn
28. Trimark Motel
29. Farmer's Market
30. Washington State Railroads Museum
31. Franklin County Museum
32. Court House
33. Transportation Depot
34. Motel 6
35. Starlite Motel
36. Doubletree Hotel
37. Gordon Brothers Cellars

HISTORY

The Lewis and Clark expedition arrived at the confluence of the Columbia and Snake Rivers in 1805. The first permanent settlers arrived in 1861 to raise cattle on these wide-open plains. The Northern Pacific Railway platted the twin towns of Pasco and Kennewick on either side of the Columbia River railroad bridge and advertised for settlers with flyers that proclaimed this stark, dusty place as the "lordly plain of the Columbia." Settlers moved in, and Pasco eventually became the hub of the rail traffic in the region, as well as the county seat. (The name came from Cerro de Pasco in Peru. Apparently a construction engineer for the Northern Pacific Railway had helped build an Andes railroad there and contrasted the beautiful high mountain country with this then-desolate spot as something of a joke.)

Incorporated in 1891, Pasco became a major transportation center. The airport—built in 1910—was the first one west of the Mississippi; the first U.S. airmail service operated out of Tri-Cities Regional Airport by what would later become United Airlines; and Pasco became a significant upriver terminal for Columbia River steamboat and barge traffic.

Franklin County irrigation projects began in the 1890s, when schemes were developed to pump water from the Snake River onto the dry fields. Kennewick grew into a small agricultural center following the opening of the Northern Pacific Irrigation Company Canal in 1903, and then prospered from the massive Columbia Basin Irrigation Project that now irrigates over 500,000 acres. But the big story in Tri-Cities is not agriculture, but nuclear weapons (see the special topic "A Nuclear Legacy"). The development of the massive Hanford Site just north of Richland brought well-paying jobs and a high-tech status to the area. Today it is the site of the nation's largest cleanup, a multi-billion-dollar effort that helped fuel a boom in growth during the 1990s.

SIGHTS

Museums
The **Columbia River Exhibition of History, Science, and Technology** (CREHST) shows a split personality, with agricultural displays on one side, and nuclear exhibits on the other. The nuke stuff is more interesting (and frightening). Visitors can pretend they're Homer Simpson, using a "hot cell" manipulator arm to pick up (and drop) various items. Oops. Also here are scale models of the reactors, samples of radioactive waste containment tanks, and a Geiger counter to check your radiation level. The mu-

A NUCLEAR LEGACY

Cruise around the Tri-Cities and you'll find Atomic Ale Brewpub & Eatery, Atomic Body Shop, Atomic Laundry, Atomic Foods (now that's scary!), and Atomic Health Center (even scarier). The local high school team's name is the "Bombers," with an atomic mushroom cloud as their emblem. There's a reason for this—the 560-square-mile Hanford Site just north of Richland, the source of much of the plutonium in America's nuclear arsenal, and now one of the most toxic places on earth.

The Buildup

With the start of WW II, the U.S. began a frenzied race to develop an atomic bomb. The first controlled nuclear chain reaction experiments were conducted in late 1942, and within a few months the government had selected the Hanford site for its plutonium production plant. The location seemed perfect: remote enough so that accidents would not immediately kill thousands of people, but still near railroads, an abundant source of water for cooling, and hydroelectric power for energy. The original residents were evacuated from the towns of Hanford, White Bluffs, and Richland, and a flood of some 51,000 workers took their place. The secret government city of Richmond was open only to Hanford construction workers and scientists; only they could live there, and they were permitted to live nowhere else. The entire "Manhattan Project" was done with such secrecy that few of the construction workers knew what they were building, and even Vice President Harry S. Truman didn't know of the project till after Roosevelt's death. Three plutonium production reactors were quickly constructed along the banks of the Columbia River, providing the concentrated nuclear material for the bomb that destroyed Nagasaki, Japan (the Hiroshima bomb used uranium manufactured in Oak Ridge, Tennessee), just 28 months after construction began.

The Cold War

The end of WW II saw a new threat on the horizon, the Soviet Union. Fearful over the rapid expansion of communism into Eastern Europe and China, the U.S. embarked on a massive nuclear warhead buildup based upon Eisenhower's policy of "massive retaliation." Hanford became the center of fuel fabrication, chemical processing, and nuclear waste management and research during the Cold War, and by 1964 had grown to include nine plutonium production reactors. Production began to slow after this, and by 1971 only one plant was still making plutonium for nuclear weapons. It was finally shut down in 1988; a plutonium-uranium extraction plant was closed two years later. The experimental Fast Flux Test Facility is in "cold standby" as the Federal government ponders the prospect of using this $5 billion facility as a source of tritium for medical research. The Hanford Site is also still home to a Washington Public Power Supply System (WPPSS) nuclear plant.

Toxic Soup

After the closing of the last plutonium reactor, the environmental problems that had been hidden in secrecy for more than 45 years began to surface. The worst disasters emerged from the early years of operation, when the hazards were not as well understood, and when the pressure to build nuclear bombs as quickly as possible meant lax safety measures. Military leaders were also fearful of telling workers the truth, lest they refuse to work, so they calmed them with promises that everything was fine. The officer who oversaw the Manhattan Project, Gen. Leslie Groves, noted that: "Leaks are bound to occur; people are bound to talk . . . but the less the better and the less disclosure there will be to unauthorized persons." Secrecy was more important than safety, and it wasn't until the 1980s that documents detailing the radioactive hazards were finally released.

The production of plutonium 239 creates many unwanted byproducts, and in more than four decades of production, Hanford left behind 54 million gallons of radioactive chemical waste. At first, the waste was simply dumped onto the land; when radioactive swamps began to form, it was pumped into the ground, and later it was stored in 177 large underground tanks (at least 66 of which leaked). Not surprisingly, this highly concentrated plume of radioactive and other toxic contaminants spread underground into the water table and continues today to seep into the Columbia River. In addition, airborne radioactive iodine collected on plants where they were eaten by people and cattle (and people who drank milk from cows). More than 685,000 curies of radioactive iodine 131 spewed from the separation plants in just the first three years of operation, causing thousands of people to be exposed to potentially lethal doses of radiation. Ongoing studies are trying to determine what happened to these people and others who were exposed, but there are many stories of entire "downwind" families stricken by mysterious cancers, of a high incidence of multiple sclerosis, stillborn babies, immune-system disorders, and brain tumors.

Another legacy of plutonium production was contamination of the Columbia River. Water from the river was used to cool the nuclear plants, and between 1958 and 1964 so much heat and radioactivity were being dumped into the Columbia that the Grand Coulee Dam had to release massive quantities of water to keep the river from becoming dangerously hot as it flowed past Hanford. Heavily contaminated fish and shellfish began showing up at the Columbia's mouth, and there was concern for public safety since both Pasco and Kennewick drinking water supplies came from the river downstream of the nuclear plants. Fortunately, the radionuclide levels in river water have dropped to background levels since the closure of the plants.

The Cleanup

In 1994, the U.S. Dept. of Energy, the Washington State Dept. of Ecology, and the U.S. Environmental Protection Agency signed a "Tri-Party Agreement" to spend the next 30 years in the largest and most complex waste cleanup ever. The Department of Energy is in charge of the project and is spending close to $1 billion a year in that effort. Sometimes the task must seem hopeless. Hanford is considered the worst hazardous waste mess anywhere in the nation, the sort of place that makes most other sites pale by comparison. The easiest places at Hanford have been cleaned up in the last few years, but the real problems remain, particularly the toxic stew of radioactive waste that sits in underground tanks or has escaped into the ground (we're talking groundwater contamination covering hundreds of square miles). The tanks were meant to be temporary, but there is little chance that this waste will be removed for decades to come, since no other storage options exist. And then there are the nuclear reactors with their miles of contaminated pipes and other materials, the plutonium/uranium solution sitting in tanks at an old processing plant, other buildings with large quantities of highly carcinogenic PCBs, and boiling

pools filled with cesium and strontium capsules. You get the picture, Hanford's an environmental nightmare, and even politicians are starting to suggest that it will never be entirely cleaned up. Critics talk of the potential for explosions that could spew radiation into the air, and leaking storage tanks polluting local water supplies. Supporters of Hanford say the amount of radiation received by Tri-Cities residents from the plant is far less than what Spokane residents receive from natural sources such as radon gas.

One surprising effect of the shutdown of Hanford and subsequent cleanup has been that it actually spawned economic growth in the Tri-Cities. Billions of Federal dollars have flowed into the region, providing employment for more than 19,000 engineers, spill experts, construction workers, and others. With an eventual price tag of at least $30 billion (and possibly $100 billion), the environmental cleanup has proven to be a far bigger project than the reactors ever were. Because of all the research needs, there are more Ph.D.s per capita in Kennewick than any other town in the western U.S.

workers checking radioactive solid waste placed in drums

WESTINGHOUSE HANFORD COMPANY

seum is located along the river next to popular **Howard Amon Park** at 95 Lee Blvd. in Richland; open Mon.-Sat. 10 a.m.-5 p.m. and Sunday noon-5 p.m.; $3.50 adults, $2.75 seniors, $2.50 children. Call (509) 943-9000 for more info.

Just a few steps from CREHST is **Three Rivers Children's Museum**, 650 George Washington Way, tel. (509)946-5437, with fun hands-on science exhibits for kids. Open Mon.-Sat. 10 a.m.-5 p.m. and Sunday noon-5 p.m.; $2.50 for adults or kids.

Kennewick's **East Benton County Historical Museum**, 205 Keewaydin Dr., tel. (509) 582-7704, has exhibits from pioneer days in the Tri-Cities area; free. Open daily 1-4 p.m. Memorial Day to Labor Day, and Tues.-Sat. noon-4 p.m. the rest of the year; $2 adults, 50 cents for seniors and kids.

At 305 N. 4th Ave. in Pasco, the **Franklin County Museum**, tel. (509) 547-3714, depicts early Native American culture, railroad and aviation history, pioneer life, and agriculture. It's open Tues.-Fri. 1-5 p.m. and Saturday 10 a.m.-5 p.m. year-round; donation.

The **Washington State Railroads Historical Society Museum,** has a new museum at 122 N. Tacoma Ave. in Pasco, with additional exhibits across the street in the old Amtrak station. Outside are several old locomotives, a 1912 Pullman car, cabooses, and other railcars. The museum is open Saturday 9 a.m.-3 p.m.; tel. (509) 543-4159.

City Parks

Columbia Park forms a 609-acre border along the south shore of the Columbia River (Lake Wallula) in Kennewick, with four boat ramps for fishing and water-skiing, an 18-hole golf course, tennis courts, a picnic area, nature trails, and campsites. One of the main attractions is a six-mile paved path that's a favorite of cyclists, rollerbladers, joggers, and lovers out for a riverside stroll.

In 1996, a college student stumbled upon a skull along the riverbank, and a full skeleton was later found. Initial research showed **Kennewick Man** to be 9,200 years old, but—amazingly—with Caucasian features. This discovery created a firestorm of media attention and years of legal wrangles. Local Indian tribes wanted the bones reburied; anthropologists wanted further study; and proponents of the Viking explorers even joined in the court battle. Check with local mu-

seums for the latest on this unusual story. The archaeological site is not marked.

Volunteer Park in downtown Pasco is an attractive, shady place, perfect for a picnic lunch. An old Northern Pacific Steam engine sits in the park across from the impressive, white-domed **County Courthouse** on 4th St., built in 1913. Richland's **General Leslie R. Groves Park** forms a scenic five-mile-long border along the Columbia River.

Nuke Plants

No, you can't visit the decommissioned plutonium facilities on the Hanford Site; though you might find a job walking around in one of those space suits cleaning up 45 years of nuclear waste. Instead, head to the **Plant 2 Visitors Center,** tel. (509) 372-5860 run by Washington Public Power Supply System (WPPSS; commonly called "Whoops") at their plant approximately 10 miles north of Richland on Route 4. The center is open Thurs.-Fri. 11 a.m.-4 p.m., and Sat.-Sun. noon-5 p.m. Inside, you can watch a video about the power plant, learn the wonders of nuclear power, and see how uranium is mined and processed. Great fun for the whole family; be sure to ask what they do with all the radioactive waste the plant produces and how they're going to make sure it's still safe for the next 10,000 years or so.

Ice Harbor Dam and Lake Sacajawea

Nine miles east of Pasco on the Snake River, Ice Harbor Lock and Dam is the first of four dams on the Lower Snake, with one of the highest single-lift locks in the world, rising 103 feet. Take a self-guided tour, watch the fish climb the ladders, or stop by the visitors center, open daily 9 a.m.-5 p.m. April-October. The Ice Harbor Dam creates Lake Sacajawea, accessible for fishing, water-skiing, or swimming at **Levey Park** on the Pasco-Kahlotus Rd. on the lake's west side, **Charbonneau Park**, and **Fishhook Park** off Hwy. 124 on the east side. Charbonneau and Fishhook also have campsites (fee charged).

Lake Wallula

McNary Dam, 30 miles south of Pasco, backs up the Columbia River to form the 64-mile-long Lake Wallula. Slack water extends to Richland on the Columbia River and to the Ice Harbor Dam on the Snake River, creating ideal conditions for the popular hydroplane races each July. Five miles east of Kennewick off Finley Rd., **Two Rivers County Park** is open daily for boating, swimming, and picnicking along the Columbia River/Lake Wallula.

Sacajawea State Park

Two miles east of Pasco off Hwy. 12, Sacajawea State Park sits at the confluence of the Snake and Columbia Rivers at the site where Lewis and Clark camped in 1805 on their way to the Pacific Ocean. You can fish, water-ski, and picnic here Wed.-Sun. April-Sept.; no camping. An **interpretive center** contains exhibits on Sacajawea—the Shoshoni girl who acted as interpreter for the Lewis and Clark party—plus information about the expedition, videos, and Indian artifacts.

Juniper Dunes Wilderness

This 7,140-acre parcel of BLM wilderness is 16 miles northeast of Pasco on Pasco-Kahlotus Road. It contains the six largest remaining western juniper groves in Washington, along with sand dunes that top 120 feet high and are up to 1,200 feet long. Access is only through private land, so you'll need to get the permission of local ranchers to reach the dunes, and you may need a 4WD vehicle for the last several miles of road. Call (509) 536-1200 for details. There are no trails or drinking water, and summer temperatures often exceed 100° F, so come prepared. The best time to visit is in the spring and fall when temperatures are more moderate. Overnight camping is possible, but permits are recommended from the BLM.

Wineries

Most of the 35 or so wineries in southeast Washington are covered in "Yakima Valley Wineries," above. The Tri-Cities area has a handful of its own, including **Preston Premium Wines,** tel. (509) 545-1990, one of the area's biggest, five miles north of Pasco off Hwy. 395. Established in the early 1970s, Preston is the state's largest family-owned and -operated winery. They are especially known for their chardonnays and rieslings, and the parklike grounds are great for a picnic. The tasting room is open daily 10 a.m.-5:30 p.m. Preston has frequent events throughout the year, including a kite festival in early May and a chili cook-off in mid-September.

Gordon Brothers Cellars, tel. (509) 547-6331, has a new production and tasting room at 5960 Burden Blvd. in Pasco. They primarily grow grapes for other wineries, but also produce a number of varieties. **Barnard Griffin,** 878 Tulip Ln. in Richland, tel. (509) 627-0266, produces dry table wines; open for tasting daily 10 a.m.-6 p.m. Also in Pasco is the newly opened **Claar Cellars,** 1081 Glenwood Rd., tel. (509) 266-4449, with chardonnay, late harvest riesling, cabernet sauvignon, and merlot. Their tasting room is open Mon.-Fri. 10 a.m.-2 p.m., and Sat.-Sun. 11 a.m.-5 p.m.; call for winter hours.

Bookwalter Winery, 710 S. Windmill Rd. in Richland, tel. (509) 627-5000, makes a full range of varietal wines; open daily 10 a.m.-5 p.m. **Badger Mountain Winery,** 1106 S. Jurupa in Kennewick, tel. (800) 643-9463, is one of the first certified organic vineyards making estate wines; open for tastings daily 10 a.m.-5 p.m.

ACCOMMODATIONS

It's a good idea to book ahead, especially during July when the hydroplane races attract throngs of visitors from across the Northwest.

Bed and Breakfasts

Casablanca B&B is a large modern home at 94806 E. Granada Court in Kennewick, tel. (509) 627-0676 or (888) 627-0676. Stay in one of the three guest rooms with private baths, and enjoy the English-style garden, terrace overlooking Badger Canyon, and hot tub. A continental breakfast is served, and kids are accepted; $65-85 s or d. Horseback rides are also available.

Red Mountain B&B, 12911 E. Hwy. 224 in Benton City, tel. (509) 588-1900, is a new Cape Cod-style home with three guest rooms, private baths, and a central fireplace. A full breakfast is served; $65-75 s, $70-80 s or d. No kids.

A turn-of-the-century farmhouse on 10 shady acres near the Yakima River, **Palmer Farm B&B,** 42901 N. River Rd. in Benton City, tel. (509) 588-4011 or (800) 635-3131, has four rooms, shared baths, and a full breakfast; $70-75 s or d. No kids.

Campgrounds

Columbia Park, tel. (509) 783-3711, two miles west of Kennewick on Hwy. 240, has campsites

TRI-CITIES MOTELS AND HOTELS

Accommodations are arranged from least to most expensive. Rates may be lower during the winter months. See the text for local B&Bs.

BUDGET

Goal Post Motor Inn; 2724 W. Lewis St. in Pasco; tel. (509) 547-7322; $26 s, $30 d; outdoor pool, kitchenettes

Trimark Motel; 720 W. Lewis St. in downtown Pasco; tel. (509) 547-7766; $29 s, $33 d; well maintained and clean, outdoor pool

Airport Motel; 2532 N. 4th St. in Pasco; tel. (509) 545-1460; $30 s, $33 d; kitchenettes available

INEXPENSIVE

Columbia Motor Inn; 1133 W. Columbia Dr. in Kennewick; tel. (509) 586-4739; $32 s, $36 d

Motel 6; 1520 N. Oregon St. in Pasco; tel. (509) 546-2010 or (800) 466-8356; $32 s, $38 d; outdoor pool

Green Gable Motel; 515 W. Columbia Dr. in Kennewick; tel. (509) 582-5811; $35 s, $38 d; fridges

Starlite Motel; 2634 N. 4th Ave. in Pasco; tel. (509) 547-7531; $35 s, $40 d; airport transport, kitchenettes, next to noisy railroad tracks

Vagabond Inn; 515 George Washington Way in Richland; tel. (509) 946-6117 or (800) 446-6900; $36-45 s, $40-45 d; outdoor pool, AAA approved

Tapadera Inn; 300 N. Ely; tel. (509) 783-6191; $36-46 s, $44-54 d; outdoor pool, AAA approved

Bali Hi Motel; 1201 George Washington Way in Richland; tel. (509) 943-3101; $37 s, $41-43 d; outdoor pool, sun deck, fridges

Motel 6; 1751 Fowler St. in Kennewick; tel. (509) 783-1250 or (800) 466-8356; $37 s, $43 d; new motel, outdoor pool

King City Truck Stop; 2100 E. Hillsboro Rd. in Pasco; tel. (509) 547-3475; $39 s, $44 d

Nendel's Inn; 615 Jadwin Ave. in Richland; tel. (509) 943-4611 or (800) 547-0106; $39 s, $44 d; outdoor pool, continental breakfast, airport shuttle, AAA approved

Nendel's Inn; 2811 W. 2nd in Kennewick; tel. (509) 735-9511 or (800) 547-0106; $43-47 s, $48-52 d; outdoor pool, kitchenettes available, continental breakfast, airport shuttle, AAA approved

Shaniko Suites Motel; 321 N. Johnson in Kennewick; tel. (509) 735-6385; $45 s, $50 d; outdoor pool, kitchenettes, AAA approved

Vineyard Inn; 1800 W. Lewis in Pasco; tel. (509) 547-0791 or (800) 824-5457; $45-50 s or d; indoor pool, jacuzzi, sauna, continental breakfast, kitchenettes available, airport shuttle

---

($7) and RV spaces ($11). Open all year. More camping at **Hood Park,** on the Snake River near its confluence with the Columbia, four miles southeast of Pasco; open May to mid-September. **Charbonneau Park,** 14 miles northeast of Pasco on Lake Sacajawea (Snake River), tel. (509) 547-7781, has campsites that are open April-October. Farther away are campsites at **Fishhook Park,** 23 miles northeast of Pasco on Lake Sacajawea; open May to mid-September.

Private RV parks in the Tri-Cities area include **Columbia Mobile Village,** 4901 W. Clearwater Ave. in Kennewick, tel. (509) 783-3314; **Desert Gold RV Park,** 611 Columbia Dr. SE in Richland, tel. (509) 627-1000; **Green Tree RV Park,** 2200 N. 4th in Pasco, tel. (509) 547-6220; **Maxey's Mobile Home Park,** 3708 W. Clearwater Ave. in Kennewick, tel. (509) 783-6411; **Village at Canyon Lakes RV Park,** tel. (509) 586-5633 or (800) 722-5762; and **Trailer City**

Comfort Inn; 7801 W. Quinault in Kennewick; tel. (509) 783-8396 or (800) 221-2222; $47-59 s, $52-69 d; indoor pool, jacuzzi, continental breakfast, AAA approved

Clearwater Inn; 5616 W. Clearwater Ave. in Kennewick; tel. (509) 735-2242; $50 s, $55 d; continental breakfast, AAA approved

Super 8 Motel; 626 N. Columbia Center Blvd. in Kennewick; tel. (509) 736-6888 or (800) 800-8000; $50 s, $56 d; indoor pool, jacuzzi, AAA approved

Sleep Inn; 9930 Bedford St.; tel. (509) 545-9554 or (800) 753-3746; $55-60 s or d; indoor pool, jacuzzi, airport shuttle, exercise facility, continental breakfast, kitchenettes available

Fairfield Inn by Marriott; 7809 W. Quinault Ave. in Kennewick; tel. (509) 783-2164 or (800) 228-2800; $59 s or d; new motel, indoor pool, jacuzzi, continental breakfast, AAA approved

MODERATE

Silver Cloud Inn; 7901 W. Quinault Ave. in Kennewick; tel. (509) 735-6100 or (800) 205-6938; $58-72 s, $68-82 d; indoor and outdoor pools, jacuzzi, exercise room, continental breakfast, AAA approved

Ramada Inn on Clover Island; Kennewick; tel. (509) 586-0541 or (800) 272-6232; $60-105 s, $70-115 d; outdoor pool, jacuzzi, sauna, exercise room, riverside location, airport shuttle, AAA approved

Best Western Kennewick; 4001 W. 27th Ave. in Kennewick; tel. (509) 586-1332 or (800) 528-1234; $62-92 s, $68-92 d; new motel, indoor pool, fitness room, sauna, continental breakfast

Hampton Inn; 486 Bradley Blvd.; tel. (509) 943-4400 or (800) 426-7866; $64-74 s, $74-84 d; new hotel, indoor pool, jacuzzi, continental breakfast, fridges and microwaves in rooms, AAA approved

Shilo Inn; 50 Comstock in Richland; tel. (509) 946-4661 or (800) 222-2244; $69-99 s or d; outdoor pool, jacuzzi, kitchenettes, tennis courts, airport shuttle, AAA approved

EXPENSIVE

Doubletree Hotel Hanford House; 802 George Washington Way in Richland; tel. (509) 946-7611 or (800) 733-5466; $74-93 s, $85-102 d; outdoor pool, jacuzzi, boat dock, very nice riverside lodging, airport transport, AAA approved

Holiday Inn Express; 4220 W. 27th Pl. in Kennewick; tel. (509) 736-3326 or (800) 465-4329; $79-99 s, $89-99 d; indoor pool, jacuzzi, sauna, continental breakfast, kitchenettes available, AAA approved

Cavanaugh's at Columbia Center; 1101 N. Columbia Center Blvd. in Kennewick; tel. (509) 783-0611 or (800) 843-4667; $80 s, $90 d; outdoor pool, jacuzzi, airport shuttle, local calls 50 cents, AAA approved

Best Western Tower Inn; 1515 George Washington Way in Richland; tel. (509) 946-4121 or (800) 528-1234; $89-109 s or d; indoor pool, jacuzzi, saunas, recreation area, airport transportation, AAA approved

Doubletree Hotel; 2525 N. 20th Ave. in Pasco; tel. (509) 547-0701 or (800) 733-5466; $90-95 s, $100-105 d; two outdoor pools, jacuzzi, exercise room, airport shuttle, AAA approved

---

Park, 7120 W. Bonnie Ave. in Kennewick, tel. (509) 783-2513.

FOOD

Start your day at **Blackberry's Restaurant,** 329 N. Kellogg in Kennewick, tel. (509) 735-7253, for the best local breakfasts. **Bagelby's,** 5200 W. Clearwater Ave. in Kennewick, tel. (509) 735-2161, is a great place for espresso and the best

local bagels, lunches, and smoothies. The ubiquitous **Starbucks** has dependably good coffee at three local shops, including 2801 W. Clearwater Ave. in Kennewick, tel. (509) 735-9464.

For seafood, steak, prime rib, and pasta with outside riverside seating, head to **Cedars Pier 1,** 7 Clover Island (next to the Quality Inn), tel. (509) 582-2143. **Bruce's Steak and Lobster House,** 131 Vista Way in Kennewick, tel. (509) 783-8213, serves lunch and dinner daily.

Mexican Food

Because of the large number of agricultural workers from Mexico and other points south, the Tri-Cities have an abundance of Mexican restaurants. The finest of these is probably **Casa Chapala,** 107 E. Columbia Dr. in Kennewick, tel. (509) 586-4224, with authentic Mexican food and ultra-fresh tortillas. They also have restaurants in Pasco and Richland. Also good are two Richland Mexican restaurants: **Isla Bonita,** 1520 Jadwin Ave., tel. (509) 946-3383; and **Las Margaritas,** 627 Jadwin Ave., tel. (509) 946-7755.

The big Mexican grocery store is **Mitiendita Mexicana,** 106 10th Ave. in Pasco, with the popular **Panaderia la Reyna** bakery right next door. An even bigger Mexican bakery is **Panaderia Colima** out 4th Ave.; if you don't speak Spanish, you may be the only one here who doesn't.

More International Eats

Chez Chaz Bistro, 5011 W. Clearwater Ave. in Kennewick, tel. (509) 735-2138, is a very popular lunch emporium with sandwiches, quiche, and other fare. **Pasta Mama's** manufactures pasta and sauces shipped all over the United States. They're available locally at **Taste of America,** 701 George Washington Way in Richland, tel. (509) 946-4142.

Emerald of Siam, 1134 Jadwin Ave. in Richland, tel. (509) 946-9328, creates authentic and delicious Thai food and has an inexpensive lunch buffet weekdays. **Bangkok Restaurant,** 8300 Gage Blvd. in Kennewick, tel. (509) 735-7631, is also popular for Thai cooking.

Mandarin House, 1035 Lee Blvd. in Richland, tel. (509) 943-6843, has the best local Chinese food.

Located in an cozy old railroad dining car, **Monterosso's Italian Restaurant,** 1026 Lee Blvd. in Richland, tel. (509) 946-4525, has classic Italian cuisine and nightly seafood specials. Entrees are $9-23; reservations recommended.

Fine Dining

The **Blue Moon,** 21 W. Canal Dr., Kennewick, tel. (509) 582-6598, is one of the best (and most expensive) restaurants in the region. The seven-course prix-fixe menu features seafood, lamb, pork, chicken, and more, and the wines are all local; open weekends for dinner only. Reservations required.

Another fine local establishment is **Green Gage Plum Restaurant,** 3892 W. Van Giesen in West Richland, tel. (509) 967-2424, where the menu emphasizes pasta and seafood, and the pastries are homemade.

Pubs and Breweries

Maybe it really is something in the water (as Olympia Beer claims), but for some reason the Tri-Cities have become a center of beer brewing, with two brewpubs and three other small breweries. Located at 1015 Lee Blvd. in Richland, tel. (509) 946-5465, **Atomic Ale Brewpub & Eatery** is the oldest of the lot (from way back in 1997). Their beers include the appropriately named Plutonium Porter, Atomic Amber, and Half-Life Hefeweisen, and the menu centers around distinctive pizzas cooked in a wood-fired oven, though they also have steaks, seafood, and bratwurst. No smoking.

Rattlesnake Mountain Brewing Co., 1250 Columbia Center Blvd. in Richland, tel. (509) 783-5747, is one of the nicer local places and also features outside dining along the Columbia River with a wide-ranging and reasonably priced menu.

Next to the Pasco Farmers Market, **Ice Harbor Brewing Co.,** 415 W. Columbia St., tel. (509) 545-0927, brews a number of ales, and has tasting and tours. Two other small breweries have tasting and tours in the Port of Benton industrial park: **Whitstran Brewing Company,** tel. (509) 786-3883, and **Cirque Brewery,** tel. (509) 786-2337.

Produce and Treats

Visit the **Pasco Farmer's Market,** 4th Ave. and Columbia St., tel. (509) 545-0738 for local produce, sausages, fresh breads, arts, and crafts on Wednesday and Saturday 8 a.m.-noon May-November. This is the largest open-air farmers market in Washington. The **Kennewick Farmers Market,** tel. (509) 586-3101, is held on Flag Plaza at the corner of Kennewick Ave. and Benton St. on Wednesday and Saturday 8 a.m.-noon, June-October.

Adam's Place Country Gourmet, Route 11 in Pasco, tel. (509) 582-8564, is located in an apple orchard and makes all sorts of sweet confections, even chocolate-covered pizzas.

Country Mercantile 232 Crestloch Rd. (10 miles north of Pasco), tel. (509) 545-2192, has a produce market and ice cream parlor, along with "agricultural entertainment" that includes a seasonal cornfield maze, petting zoo, and pumpkin patch. Great fun for families.

EVENTS AND ENTERTAINMENT

Events

Start your summer with the **Tri-Cities à la Carte Festival,** an early May celebration of food, wine, beer, art, and music. The festival season kicks into high gear for the **Cinco de Mayo** Mexican festivities in Pasco. The **Tri-Cities Wineries Barrel Tasting** in early June is a favorite introduction to local wineries.

Richland's **Sunfest** is a summer-long series of weekend activities that feature international food, music, and dancing. Sunfest events include the **Tri-Cities Children's Festival** in mid-June, **Ye Merrie Greenwood Renaissance Faire** in late June, and the **Sidewalk Art Show** in late July— southeast Washington's largest arts and crafts show.

The Tri-Cities' biggest event is the annual **unlimited hydroplane races** on the Columbia River, the highlight of the late-July **Columbia Cup with Wings.** Originally called the "Atomic Cup," the races have been going on for more than three decades. The action centers around Columbia Park in Kennewick, but you can also watch from the Pasco side if you don't mind the sun in your face; get to the park early on Friday or Saturday to take a pit tour before the races. The "wings" part of the title comes from the big air show that takes place at the same time. Call (509) 547-2203 for details.

Kennewick hosts the **County Fair and Rodeo** every August, with top entertainers performing at the fairgrounds at 1500 S. Oak Street. More music, arts, food, and dancing at the **Fiery Foods Festival** on the weekend after Labor Day. November brings the **Tri-Cities Wine Festival** to Kennewick, featuring 60 different wineries. December's big event is the **Christmas Lights Boat Parade,** when decorated boats cruise down the Columbia.

Nightclubs

Rattlesnake Mountain Brewing Co., 1250 Columbia Center Blvd. in Richland, tel. (509) 837-2739, has live jazz or blues. Several other places offer live music and comedy: **Cavanaugh's at Columbia Center,** 1101 N. Columbia Center Blvd. in Kennewick, tel. (509) 783-0611, and **Tower Inn,** in Richland, tel. (509) 946-4121, have live music or comedy. **The Cowboy Club** 109 W. Kennewick Ave., tel. (509) 586-9292, has C&W music and a big dance floor. More country tunes at the Doubletree Hotel's **Grizzly Bar,** 2525 N. 20th Ave. in Pasco, tel. (509) 547-0701.

THE ARTS

Art Galleries

In the Tri-Cities area, Richland comes out ahead in art galleries; perhaps it's a reflection of the highbrow tastes of all the local Ph.D.s. Visit the **Allied Arts Gallery,** 89 Lee Blvd., tel. (509) 943-9815, and see paintings, pottery, and weavings by local artists. Also in town are **Alexander's Art Gallery,** 1507 George Washington Way, tel. (509) 946-6802, and **Anvil Studio & Gallery,** 1955 Birch Ave., tel. (509) 946-6735. At 135 Vista Way in Kennewick, **Beaux Art Gallery,** tel. (509) 783-4549, has stained glass, pottery, paintings, and crafts.

Music and Dance

For those of classical taste, call for scheduled events staged by the **Mid-Columbia Symphony,** tel. (509) 735-7356, in existence for more than 50 years, or the **Mid-Columbia Regional Ballet,** 1405 Goethals, Richland, tel. (509) 946-1531.

SPORTS AND RECREATION

Spectator Sports

The Tri-Cities are home to two professional teams: The **Tri-City Posse,** tel. (509) 547-6773, plays AA professional baseball, while the **Tri-City Americans,** tel. (509) 783-9999, plays hockey in the Western Hockey League.

Cycling

Riverfront bike paths link Pasco city parks. Kennewick's **Columbia Park** has a popular six-mile paved, nearly level path. Rent bikes from **Kennewick Schwinn,** 3101 W. Clearwater Ave. in Kennewick, tel. (509) 735-8525.

Swimming and Boating

With all this heat and unrelenting sunshine, you'll need a place to cool off. The city of Pasco has two public **swimming pools,** and other public pools can be found in Kennewick and Richland. The **YMCA** is at 19 N. Cascade in Kennewick, tel. (509) 586-0015.

Take your swimsuit to **Oasis Waterworks,** 6321 W. Canal Dr. in Kennewick, tel. (509) 735-8442, and try their 10 water slides, a "rolling rapids river ride," 5,000-square-foot swimming pool, shaded picnic area, 100-person hot tub, and more. Open daily in the summer.

Rent boats and jet skis at **Columbia Park Marina,** 1776 Columbia Dr. SE in Richland, tel. (509) 736-1493, and jet skis from **TLC Sports,** 2527 W. Kennewick in Kennewick, tel. (509) 783-2290.

Racing

The favorite local racing events are the hydroplane races during the Columbia Cup with Wings (see "Events," above). Watch auto racing on Saturday nights in the summer at **Tri-City Raceway,** two miles west of West Richland, tel. (509) 967-3851. At Kennewick's Benton-Franklin Fairgrounds on E. 10th Ave., **Sundowns Horseracing Track,** tel. (509) 582-5434, has quarterhorse racing in spring and fall. Off-road enthusiasts will enjoy **Horn Rapids Off-Road Vehicle Park,** tel. (509) 967-5814, off Hwy. 240 in Richland. Open all year.

Golf

Golfers will find eight 18-hole public courses in the Tri-Cities area, including Pasco's **Sun Willows Golf Course,** 2335 N. 20th, tel. (509) 545-3440; Kennewick's **Columbia Park Golf Course** at Columbia Park, tel. (509) 586-4069; **Columbia Point Golf Course,** 225 Columbia Pt. Dr. in Richland, tel. (509) 946-0710; **Canyon Lakes Golf Course,** 3700 Canyon Lakes Dr., tel. (509) 582-3736; **Meadow Springs Country Club Golf Course,** 700 Country Club Place in Richland, tel. (509) 627-2234; **Tri-Cities Country Club,** 314 N. Underwood, tel. (509) 783-6014; West Richland's **West Richland Municipal Golf Course,** 4000 Fallon Dr., tel. (509) 967-2165; and Richland's **Horn Rapids,** tel. (509) 375-4714.

SHOPPING

Columbia Center in Kennewick is the Tri-Cities's largest shopping mall, with 100 stores including The Bon Marché, Lamonts, Sears, and JCPenney. Not far from here are practically every known mega-store: Kmart, Best, Target, ad nauseam. For something a bit less hectic, head to **Pasco Village Marketplace,** on the corner of 4th and Lewis in Pasco, where various shops sell arts and crafts, clothing, gourmet food, imported textiles, jewelry, and more.

INFORMATION AND TRANSPORTATION

Pick up all the current maps and information you need from the **Tri-Cities Visitor and Convention Bureau,** housed in the Vista Airport building at the end of Grandridge Blvd. in Kennewick, tel. (509) 735-8486 or (800) 254-5824. Open Mon.-Fri. 8:30 a.m.-5 p.m. year-round, and on the Web at www.triconvis.com.

Buses and Trains

Public transport comes together at the new **Transportation Depot** at 535 N. 1st Ave. in Pasco. Here you can catch a local bus from **Ben Franklin Transit,** tel. (509) 735-5100, for service to the three cities and airport Mon.-Saturday. **Greyhound,** tel. (509) 547-3151 or (800) 231-2222, also stops here, as does **Amtrak,** whose Empire Builder provides daily service east to Spokane, Minneapolis, and Chicago, and west to Portland. Call (509) 545-1554 or (800) 872-7245 for Amtrak info.

By Air

Departing from the Tri-Cities Airport in Pasco—the first airport west of the Mississippi—are **Horizon Air,** tel. (800) 547-9308, **Delta Air Lines,** (800) 221-1212, and **United Express,** tel. (800) 241-6522. The Richland airport is a popular place for skydiving; call **Richland Skysports,** tel. (509) 946-3483 for details. **Kennewick Aircraft Services,** tel. (509) 735-2875, offers flightseeing trips in the Tri-Cities area.

Tours

River City Tours, tel. (509) 735-6722, leads a range of tours around the Tri-Cities area, including boat trips, winery tours, and farm visits. **Columbia River Journeys,** tel. (509) 943-0231, runs jet-boat trips to Hanford Reach, the last free-flowing segment of the lower Columbia River.

EASTERN WASHINGTON

When you cross the Columbia River on I-90 headed toward Spokane, you are entering the northernmost reaches of the Great American Desert, which runs through portions of eastern Washington, Oregon, Nevada, and California, and down into Arizona and Mexico. It ends with the trees of the Spokane area and the Okanogan Highlands. The Columbia River, in its huge S-shaped turn across the state, helps define the desert's northern and western boundaries.

Despite open country that alternately freezes in the winter and sears in the summer, scarce rainfall, and precious few year-round streams, this basaltic desert has always had several small, scattered natural lakes. Their numbers increased dramatically when the enormous Columbia Basin Irrigation Project created Lake Roosevelt, Moses Lake, and Banks Lake, and raised the water table to create hundreds of small ponds. Much of the region receives less than 10 inches of rain a year and sees 300-plus days of sunshine. Wind can sometimes be a problem, especially in the spring when blinding dust storms can arise.

Geology

Probably the most exciting event in eastern Washington history was witnessed by no one: the **Spokane Flood,** which occurred 18,000-20,000 years ago. As the last ice age came to an end, the glaciers melted and water backed up behind the ice-dammed Clark Fork River in the great basin where Missoula, Montana, now stands. The ice-and-earthen dam created an enormous lake covering more than 3,000 square miles—larger than Puget Sound—and marks from its shoreline can still be seen along the mountains above the basin.

As the ice dam melted, the great pressure from the backed-up water caused it to suddenly collapse, sending an unimaginable rush of water over all of eastern Washington, flattening the landscape, gouging out coulees, washing away soil, and emptying the great lake in as little as two days. It is said to have been the greatest flood ever recorded on the planet. Evidence of the flood is shown on the landscape between Spokane and the Columbia River around the Tri-Cities area, a region known as the **Channeled Scablands.** Most protruding rocks and mesas

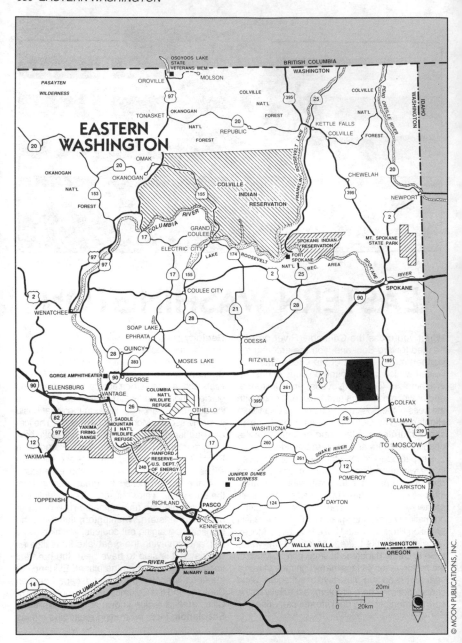

fishermen in Banks Lake

are ship-shaped, all pointing in a northeasterly direction, and there's no evidence that the erosion process was caused by streams, the normal source of such erosion. The prevailing geological theory is that there may have been many of these floods (see the special topic "The Catastrophist")

COLUMBIA BASIN

MOSES LAKE AND POTHOLES RESERVOIR

Two large reservoirs center around the small city of Moses Lake: Potholes Reservoir south of I-90, and Moses Lake north of I-90. Built as part of the massive Columbia Basin Project, the reservoirs provide irrigation water to thousands of acres of surrounding land. Though eastern Washington is best known for its wheat production, the Columbia Basin leads the country in potato production per acre, with alfalfa and corn as its other major crops.

You would expect that two large bodies of water in such a hot and arid climate would be surrounded by time-share condos and RV parks. They probably would be if they were in a more populated part of the state, but in lonely central Washington the lakes are often just a pit stop on the way to somewhere else, except for fishermen who come for trout, perch, and the sunshine. Although a lot of the area remains in its natural state of basaltic outcroppings, sand, and sagebrush, irrigation water is being used on more and more land in this area, and it is losing its desert look.

Potholes Reservoir

When Columbia River water was pumped onto the fields, reclamation engineers didn't know exactly what to expect from the water—whether it would stand and create lakes, or flow underground. It did both. The irrigation water in the Moses Lake area and farther north toward Grand Coulee generally seeps southward—following the natural slope of the land—and collects in Potholes Reservoir behind O'Sullivan Dam.

The **O'Sullivan Dam,** on Hwy. 17 at the south end of Potholes Reservoir (halfway between Moses Lake and Othello), is one of the largest earth-filled dams in the nation. The reservoir collects overflow from irrigated lands to the north, transferring the water into the Potholes East Canal and feeding farms to the south. South of the dam are more than 50 seep lakes included within Columbia National Wildlife Refuge (see **Othello**). In the winter, Potholes Reservoir is a major resting place for waterfowl—thousands of ducks are visible. The area has a number of in-

THE CATASTROPHIST

It is much easier to understand the Channeled Scabland when you fly over it in a small plane. This geological oddity is a series of dry channels that run south-southwest out of the Spokane area, then fan out toward the Columbia River in the Tri-Cities area. Geologists always assumed the channels were created over a period of centuries by normal erosion. Then a University of Chicago professor named J. Harlen Bretz became interested in the area while visiting Spokane in the early 1920s.

He got the idea from a topographic map and soon formulated the theory that the Channeled Scabland was not created by glacial activity and normal water erosion. Instead, he believed it was created by one or more catastrophic floods that originated from a vast lake dammed by earth and ice in the valley where Missoula, Montana, stands.

Bretz found more and more evidence to support his theory. He found lap marks high on the cliffs around Missoula, and erratics (boulders found far from their place of origin) high on the mountainsides along the Columbia River Gorge. He believed the flood occurred as the Ice Age waned and snow and ice melt went over the top of an earth and ice dam that might have been as high as 2,000 feet. When it broke, it released a 3,000-square mile lake that contained half the volume of Lake Michigan, which is 500 cubic miles of water.

The catastrophic flood Bretz envisioned headed due west from Missoula across the Idaho Panhandle, down the Spokane Valley, where the natural contour of the land turned it south and west. He believed the Palouse River originally flowed down the Washtucna Coulee where the towns of Washtucna and Kahlotus are now and emptied into the Snake River about 70 miles further downstream from its present confluence at Lyons Ferry. Bretz also believed that the first floods ponded in the Pasco basin and formed what he called Lake Lewis, and eventually filled the Yakima, Walla Walla, and Snake River valleys, and finally bore into the Columbia River at Wallula Gap. He theorized that the floods came through the gap up to 800 feet deep and at 1.66 cubic miles of water an hour for two or three weeks, or 190 times the greatest Columbia River flood on record.

The floods scoured the sides of the Columbia Gorge up to 1,000 feet, and carried boulders embedded in ice that were stranded on the mountainsides and up valleys. When the waters hit the Willamette River, they headed upriver as far as Eugene and formed a temporary lake that covered up to 3,000 square miles.

This sounded pretty wild to his colleagues and went completely against the grain; nearly all geologic theory evolved in the 19th century and was based in part on religion which held strictly to the version of Creation given in the Bible. When the Ivy Leaguers heard of Bretz's theory, some referred to his school, the University of Chicago, as "that Western trade school."

They picked on the wrong man. Bretz was tenacious and enjoyed a good academic brawl. For several summers he worked in eastern Washington, gathering more ammunition for the battle. One by one he gained converts to his cause, especially from those who actually toured the area with him and geologists already there.

It took 42 years for Bretz to be vindicated. In 1965 when the International Geophysical Year was held in Denver, Bretz couldn't attend because of health problems, but he was well represented by a band of disciples who were determined that their point of view at least be seriously considered by on-site examination.

They arranged a trip across the west by chartered bus through the Rockies and into Montana, then down the course of the floods. At Missoula a Bretz believer began lecturing on what they were seeing from the bus windows and at specific stops. This continued all along the flood route. Finally, when the group stopped at a site near Kahlotus all the pieces of Bretz' theory fell into place: dry cataracts, the rerouting of the Palouse River, the stream beds that haven't had running water in them in centuries, the ripple marks on canyon and coulee walls.

On that day most of his most outspoken opponents began back-pedaling, and it was on that day that the group sent Bretz a dramatic telegram of congratulations. It ended with these words:

"We are all catastrophists."

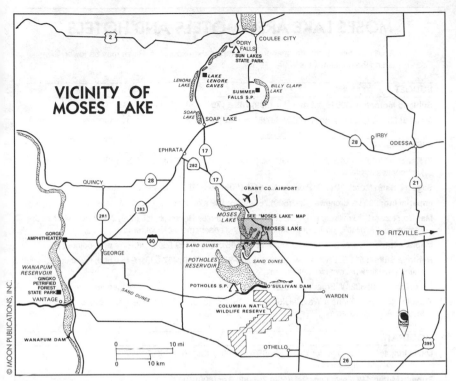

VICINITY OF MOSES LAKE

© MOON PUBLICATIONS, INC.

teresting rock formations, including striking columnar basalt formations in the Crab Creek Marsh area.

Parks

Located at the southwest end of O'Sullivan Dam, **Potholes State Park** is a popular spot for launching a boat to catch the reservoir's trout, walleye, and perch. Water-skiers, picnickers, and swimmers also enjoy the sunny east-of-the-mountains weather at this 2,500-acre park. The park offers summertime slide shows and nature hikes. Tent ($11) and RV sites ($16) are available year-round. Call (509) 765-7271 for information, and (800) 452-5687 for reservations ($6 extra).

The city-run **Cascade Park** on Valley Rd. on Moses Lake, offers swimming, boating, water-ski-ing, showers, plus camping and RV hookups. Open mid-April through mid-October. Call (509) 766-9240 for reservations.

Moses Lake State Park, immediately north of I-90 (take exit 175), has swimming, fishing for trout, crappie, and catfish, a grassy picnic area, and a snack bar—but no camping. In the winter, this is a favorite ice-skating spot.

Cascade Water Rentals, tel. 766-7075, has jet skis, canoes, and fishing boats for rent at Cascade Marina.

Sand Dunes

Hike, slide, or ride your off-road vehicle on over 3,000 acres of sand dunes south of the city of Moses Lake. Go four miles south on Division St., then follow the signs—and six miles of gravel road—to the ORV park. Camping is permitted here, but there are no facilities.

MOSES LAKE AREA MOTELS AND HOTELS

Accommodations are arranged from least to most expensive. Rates may be lower during the winter months.

BUDGET

Sunland Motor Inn; 309 E. 3rd Ave.; tel. (509) 765-1170 or (800) 220-4403; $33-38 s or d

Motel 6; 2822 Wapato Dr.; tel. (509) 766-0250 or (800) 466-8356; $33 s, $39 d; outdoor pool

INEXPENSIVE

El Rancho Motel; 1214 S. Pioneer Way; tel. (509) 765-9173 or (800) 341-8000; $33-55 s, $36-55 d; kitchenettes available

Sage 'N' Sand Motel; 1011 S. Pioneer Way; tel. (509) 765-1755; $36-45 s or d; outdoor pool

Imperial Inn; 905 W. Broadway; tel. (509) 765-8626; $39 s or d; outdoor pool, kitchenettes

Mar Don Resort; 16 miles south of Moses Lake on Potholes Reservoir; tel. (509) 346-2651; $40 s or d; kitchenettes available, no TV or phones, swimming beach, marina, boat rentals

Maples Motel; 1006 W. 3rd Ave.; tel. (509) 765-5665 or (800) 359-5605; $40-50 s or d; outdoor pool

Heritage Suites; 511 S. Division St.; tel. (509) 765-7707 or (800) 457-0271; $45 s or d; townhouse suites with kitchens, two-night minimum

Lakeside Motel; 802 W. Broadway Ave.; tel. (509) 765-8651; $50-75 s or d; kitchenettes available

Travelodge; 316 S. Pioneer Way; tel. (509) 765-8631 or (800) 255-3050; $59 s or d; outdoor pool, jacuzzi, AAA approved

MODERATE

Oasis Inn; 466 Melva Lane; tel. (509) 765-8636 or (800) 456-0708; $60-70 s or d; kitchenettes, jacuzzi, sauna, continental breakfast

Super 8 Motel; 449 Melva Lane; tel. (509) 765-8886 or (800) 800-8000; $64 s, $69 d; outdoor pool

Shilo Inn; 1819 E. Kittleson Rd.; tel. (509) 765-9317 or (800) 222-2244; $65-95 s or d; indoor pool, jacuzzi, sauna, steam room, exercise facility, airport shuttle, kitchenettes available, AAA approved

Holiday Inn Express; 1735 E. Kittleson; tel. (509) 766-2000 or (800) 465-4329; $68-90 s, $75-105 d; indoor pool, jacuzzi, kitchenettes, continental breakfast, fitness center, AAA approved

EXPENSIVE

Best Western Hallmark Inn; 3000 Marina Dr.; tel. (509) 765-9211 or (800) 235-4255; $81-107 s, $97-107 d; outdoor pool, jacuzzi, exercise facility, fridges, tennis courts, AAA approved

MOSES LAKE (THE CITY)

The bustling small city of Moses Lake (pop. 11,700) is a growing desert settlement with all the usual trappings of American "progress": Wal-Mart, Kmart, fast-food chains, strip malls, and developments spreading across the landscape. It isn't especially attractive but will do as a stop-ping point. The main attractions here are nearby Moses Lake and Potholes Reservoir, along with the immensely popular summertime concerts at the Gorge Amphitheater near George on the Columbia River. Like most of eastern Washington, the Moses Lake area gets little rainfall—about eight inches a year—and some of the state's highest summer temperatures.

History

Moses Lake is named for Chief Moses of the Sinkiuse tribe. Early white settlers came on the promises of developers and the Northern Pacific Railroad but found a hardscrabble existence in this desert country. One wrote of it being "100 miles to town, 20 miles to water, six inches to hell!" Two major government developments changed this. The first was the construction of Grand Coulee Dam in the 1930s, and more importantly, the completion of the Columbia Basin Irrigation Project in 1952. This brought large quantities of cheap water to the region and transformed it into some of the most productive fields in Washington. During WW II, a major army air base was developed on the flat lands near Moses Lake; eventually this became Larson Air Force Base. It closed in 1966, but the citizens of Moses Lake turned it into a training center for Boeing where the pilots and crews of various international airlines—most notably Japan Air Lines—flight test new planes. Visitors to the area are likely to see jumbo jets circling slowly overhead, practicing maneuvers (look out below!).

Sights

Eighteen-mile-long Moses Lake is two miles west of town and a popular attraction for boaters and anglers. **Adam East Museum and Art Center,** 122 W. 3rd Ave., tel. (509) 766-9395, displays fossils from prehistoric animals, geological specimens, old photos, a fine collection of Indian pipes and pottery, and changing art exhibits. Open Tues.-Sat. 11 a.m.-5 p.m. all year; free. **Monty Holm's House of Poverty and Mon Road Railroad,** 228 S. Commerce, tel. (509) 765-6342, contains things Monty has collected over the years, including entire trains, gasoline engines, antique cars, fire engines, and just plain stuff. The yard out front is packed with vehicles of all types, from sheepwagons to a steam engine. Free admission; open Mon.-Fri. 8 a.m.-3:45 p.m. summers only. Armed forces buffs may want to check out the small **Schiffner Military and Police Museum,** 4840 Westshore Dr., tel. (509) 765-6374, with over a hundred uniforms on display. Open by appointment.

Accommodations

If you're coming to one of the popular summertime concerts at the Gorge Amphitheater, be sure to reserve at least two weeks ahead of time; things sometimes fill up all the way to Wenatchee. The chamber of commerce keeps track of who has space; call (800) 992-6234.

Carriage House B&B, 2801 W. Peninsula Dr., tel. (509) 766-7466 or (800) 761-7466, is a new Victorian-style home with four guest rooms, private baths, a jacuzzi, and full breakfast on weekends; $95-130 s or d.

Campgrounds and RV Parks

The city-run **Cascade Park,** on Valley Rd. and Cascade Valley along Moses Lake, has camping ($15) and RV hookups ($18); open mid-April through mid-September. Call (509) 766-9240 for reservations ($5 extra). **Potholes State Park** at the west end of O'Sullivan Dam, tel. (509) 765-7271, has tent sites ($11) and RV spaces ($16). Open year-round. Call (800) 452-5687 for reservations ($6 extra).

The local RV parks are: **Big Sun Resort,** 2300 W. Marina Dr., tel. (509) 765-8294; **Suncrest Resort,** 303 Hansen Rd., tel. (509) 765-0355; and **Willows RV Park,** two and a half miles south of I-90 exit 179 off Hwy. 17, tel. (509) 765-7531.

Food

Michael's on the Lake, 910 W. Broadway Ave., tel. (509) 765-1611, is a good place for breakfast, with a choice of dining inside or on the deck overlooking Moses Lake. For lunchtime sandwiches and salads, head to **Johanathan's,** 4075 Road NE, tel. (509) 765-8699. **Thai Cuisine,** 601 S. Pioneer Way, tel. (509) 766-1489, has an inexpensive lunch buffet.

Kiyoji's Sapporo International, 440 Melva Ln., tel. (509) 765-9314, makes delicious steaks and teriyaki. For Chinese cooking in a range of styles, head to **Eddie's Restaurant,** 801 N. Stratford Rd., tel. (509) 765-5334. **Inca Mexican Restaurant,** 404 E. 3rd, tel. (509) 766-2426, and **Mexico Bakery,** 225 E. 3rd Ave., tel. (509) 765-1829, offer authentic south-of-the-border fare.

Chico's Pizza in Vista Village Shopping Center, tel. (509) 765-4589, makes distinctive and dense pizzas with unusual toppings. For steaks and pastas in an upscale setting, try **Cade's** at the Best Western Hallmark Inn, 3000 Marina Dr., tel. (509) 765-9211.

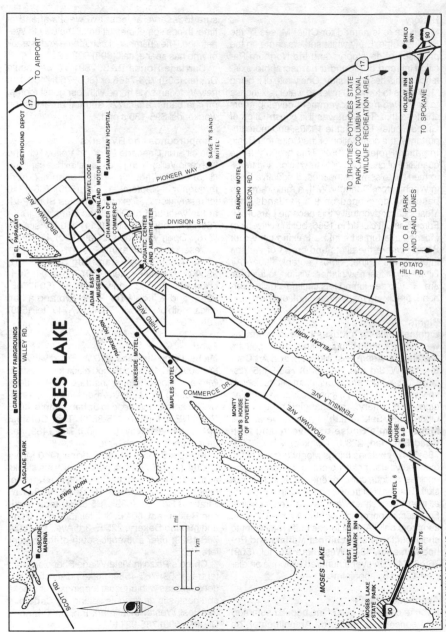

© MOON PUBLICATIONS, INC.

The **Columbia Basin Farmers Market,** tel. (509) 765-4902, takes place downtown Saturdays 7:30 a.m.-1 p.m. June-October.

Live Music

See **Quincy and George** for the extremely popular **Gorge Amphitheater,** where major concerts take place all summer long. McCosh Park Amphitheater along Moses Lake is the home to the free **Centennial Concert** series with a range of styles. The concerts are held on Saturday July-September. Past performers have included such groups as The Platters, Glenn Yarbrough, and Ranch Romance. For information call (800) 992-6234.

Several local bars have live music on weekends: **Best Western Hallmark Inn,** 3000 Marina Dr., tel. (509) 765-9211; **The Porterhouse,** 217 N. Elder, tel. (509) 766-0308; **Michael's on the Lake,** 910 W. Broadway, tel. (509) 765-1611; and **El Papagayo,** Hwy. 17 and Stratford Rd., tel. (509) 765-1265.

Events

The Memorial Day weekend **Spring Festival** features a carnival, arts and crafts displays, a torchlight boat parade, antique cars, fireworks, ATV races, and a 10-km run; call (509) 765-8248 for specifics. A popular rodeo is the highlight of the **Grant County Fair,** held the third week of August at the fairgrounds just north of town off Hwy. 17. For information, call (509) 765-3581.

Recreation

Moses Lake Family Aquatic Center in McCosh Park at 4th and Dogwood, tel. (509) 766-9246, has an Olympic-size outdoor swimming pool, two 200-foot water slides, a tube slide, sand volleyball courts, concession stands, and lots of fun places for kids to play. It's open mid-May through mid-Sept., and costs $3 adults, $2 kids.

Play golf in the sunshine at: **Sage Hills Golf Course,** 12 miles south of Moses Lake on Hwy. 17, tel. (509) 349-7794; **South Campus Golf Course,** 1475 E. Nelson Rd., tel. (509) 766-1228; and **Potholes Golf Course,** 6897 O'Sullivan Dam SE, tel. (509) 346-2447.

Information and Services

For local information, contact the **Moses Lake Chamber of Commerce,** 324 S. Pioneer Way,

tel. (509) 765-7888 or (800) 992-6234; open Mon.-Fri. 8 a.m.-noon and 1-4 p.m. You can get Western duds at **Skeen's Western Wear,** 305 E. 3rd Ave., tel. (509) 765-7522.

Transportation

Both **Greyhound,** tel. (509) 765-6441 or (800) 231-2222, and **Northwestern Trailways,** tel. (800) 366-3830, have bus service throughout the Northwest from Shilo Inn at 1819 E. Kittleson Road. **Horizon Air,** tel. (800) 547-9308, offers scheduled passenger service to Seattle from Grant County Airport (one of the longest civilian runways west of the Mississippi), north of town off Randolph Road. The nearest **Amtrak** station is in Ephrata.

QUINCY AND GEORGE

The almost-flat Quincy Valley is a study in contrasts: although receiving just eight inches of rainfall, it contains some of the most productive farms in Washington, producing potatoes, apples, wheat, alfalfa, corn, and many other vegetable crops. This is possible because of the West Canal that feeds water from the Columbia River via Banks Lake to irrigate these fields. The valley was first settled in the late 19th century; it struggled along until 1951 when irrigation waters first reached here. Today the town of Quincy contains 4,000 people and is the primary agricultural center in the area. It has frozen food processing plants, massive apple warehouses, a diatomaceous earth chemical plant, and even a still to extract mint flavoring. Good views across Quincy Valley, from the top of **Monument Hill,** north of town.

Over in George (pop. 400), **White Heron Cellars,** tel. (509) 785-5521, has tours and tastings Thurs.-Sun. noon-5 p.m. This isn't your standard hoity-toity winery. Located in an old gas station, they advertise "three different grades of wine guaranteed to increase the mileage of any meal, while providing motor protection & lubrication." For a look at one of the more unusual geologic features in the area, take exit 143 (six miles southwest of George) from I-90, and follow Old Vantage Rd. west down Frenchman Coulee to the basaltic rock **Pillars,** a favorite rock-climbing spot.

Gorge Amphitheater

Located 14 miles southwest of Quincy and seven miles northwest of George, the Gorge Amphitheater, tel. (509) 255-3600, is a natural amphitheater in the basaltic bluffs overlooking the Columbia River. Operated by MCA Concerts Northwest, the amphitheater is home each summer to Saturday concerts by internationally known musicians that attract upwards of 15,000 people. Get tickets from TicketMaster, tel. (509) 735-0500. These shows mean packed motels as far away as Wenatchee and Moses Lake, so reserve ahead. Camping and RV spaces are available on adjacent grounds, and a full range of food services are offered.

Practicalities

There are three places to stay in Quincy: **Traditional Inns,** tel. (509) 787-3525, where rooms go for $57 s or $65 d; **Sundowner Motel,** tel. (509) 787-3587, for $39 s or 45 d ($55 s or d during Gorge concerts); and **Villager Inn Motel,** 711 2nd Ave. SW, tel. (509) 787-3515, for $54 s or d. All of these have kitchenettes, and the Villager has RV parking.

Eight miles west of Quincy off Hwy. 28, **Crescent Bar Resort,** tel. (509) 787-1511, on Wanapum Reservoir offers a restaurant, condos and camping, plus a wide choice of recreation, from swimming to golf. Eight local places offer private camping and RV parks, including at the Gorge Amphitheatre, tel. (800) 738-5531.

Get local information from the **Quincy Valley Chamber of Commerce,** 119 F St. SE, tel. (509) 787-2140, or from the seasonal **George Visitor Center,** tel. (509) 787-3831. The **library** is located at 108 B St. SW. An outdoor **swimming pool** is also in Quincy at Jaycee Municipal Park. Quincy is served by **Northwestern Trailways,** tel. (800) 366-6975, with service east to Spokane and west to Everett.

Events

Other than the amphitheater concerts, the main local event is **Farmer Consumer Awareness Day** on the second Saturday of September in Quincy. It includes a fun run, parade, food booths, exhibits, live music, and guided tours of local food processing plants.

The tiny town of George is known for its **George, Washington** celebration on the Fourth of July (pretty obvious where the town name originated). Each year, locals bake the "world's largest cherry pie," and light the fireworks when evening comes. More nighttime fun at Christmas when local farmers put lights on their rotating pivot-irrigation lines. Look for them along I-90 east of George.

WANAPUM LAKE AREA

Gingko Petrified Forest State Park

Fifteen to 20 million years ago, this part of Washington was first covered by lush forests and then by molten lava that poured out of fissures in the earth's crust. Logs that had washed into nearby lakes were preserved intact by the lava cover; water eventually leaked through to the logs, and the silica in the groundwater replaced the natural structure of the wood. The tremendous erosion during the last ice age exposed 259 species of petrified trees in this area, including the prehistoric gingko, a "living fossil" that still grows in Japan and has been planted in city parks throughout America.

An **interpretive center,** tel. (509) 856-2700, just north of the town of Vantage (exit 136 of I-90) houses displays on the geologic history of the area and a slide show about gingkoes. Outside are large pieces of petrified wood and several Indian petroglyphs. The center is open daily 10 a.m.-6 p.m. from mid-May to mid-September.

For a beautiful country drive, head west from the interpretive center along the Vantage Hwy. that connects Vantage to Ellensburg. This is the back way, and makes a good bike ride (narrow shoulders, alas). Sagebrush, rugged land, cattle, and ranches give this a Western appeal. Tune in the AM radio for cowboy or Mexican music to fit the mood. Two miles west on Vantage Hwy. are several interpretive trails that lead uphill past more samples of various petrified tree species beneath wire cages. A two-and-a-half-mile trail leads across the dry, windblown hills past an assortment of scrappy wildflowers, sagebrush, and broad views. Watch for bald eagles, hawks, deer, elk, coyote, and a variety of lizards and snakes, including the poisonous northern Pacific rattlesnake.

Camping is available at **Wanapum State Recreation Area,** four and a half miles south of the Gingko Visitor Center. All sites have complete hookups and cost $16; open April-Oct., plus weekends and holidays the rest of the year. Call (800) 452-5687 for reservations ($6 extra).

Wanapum and Priest Rapids Dams

Wanapum Dam was named for the Wanapum Indians, a peaceful and religious tribe that lived along the river between present-day Pasco and Vantage. The last Indian peoples to live in traditional tule mat longhouses, the Wanapum refused to leave their ancestral home along the Columbia. Finally, in the early 1950s, four men—the last full-blooded Wanapum—agreed to allow a dam at the site. They had been forced from their land south of here when Hanford Atomic Works began in the 1930s. (Lewis and Clark found 2,500 Wanapum in the region, but introduced diseases devastated the tribe.) Following this agreement, Grant County built the Wanapum and Priest Rapids Dams here and added the **Wanapum Dam Heritage Center,** tel. (509) 754-3541. Open Mon.-Fri. 8 a.m.-4:30 p.m., Sat.-Sun. 9 a.m.-5 p.m., the center houses a collection of artifacts and other Wanapum materials, a replica of the steamship *Columbia,* and exhibits on the development of the Columbia River Basin and the building of the dams. Watch a slide show on the Wanapum people, and check out the 29-foot long dugout canoe they once used. A stone object here is of particular interest; some archaeologists theorize that it served as a calendar, while others say it was used to record songs and dance ceremonies. Tours are available on weekdays.

One of the major attractions at the Wanapum Dam is a fish ladder and fish viewing room where you can watch salmon, steelhead, and other fish heading upstream April-November. An artificial spawning channel and hatchery downstream from Priest Rapids Dam provide a chance for salmon to spawn; their original spawning creeks were nearly all destroyed when the dams were built. Nearby is a dramatic vista point overlooking the Columbia River.

Priest Rapids Dam is 12 miles downriver from Wanapum Dam, at the site of seven now-inundated rapids. It was here in 1811 that fur trappers saw Wanapum Indian spiritual leaders performing ceremonies.

OTHELLO

Othello (pop. 4,700) is about 20 miles south of Moses Lake and 46 miles north of the Tri-Cities area. Named for the Shakespearean play, Othello began as a stop along the Milwaukee Railroad early in this century but did not come into its own until the 1950s, when water from the Columbia River—50 miles to the north—reached the area in irrigation canals. Earlier farming and ranching efforts failed due to the desert conditions, and it took the massive Columbia Basin Project of the New Deal to transform this land by the building of Grand Coulee Dam, Banks Lake, and a series of three canals to send water into the Columbia Basin deserts.

Today, Othello is surrounded by pool-table flat agricultural fields with giant circular irrigation systems fed by water from the Columbia River. These farms grow potatoes and other vegetables, as well as a wide variety of fruits. With two major processing plants, Othello lays claims to the potato processing capital of the world. Also in town is a plant that makes Seneca apple juice.

Columbia National Wildlife Refuge

The Columbia National Wildlife Refuge covers 23,000 acres of scenic desert land between Moses Lake and the Othello area. The refuge contains a rugged jumble of cliffs, wide open sagebrush grasslands, eroded canyons, and a scattering of more than 50 lakes and ponds created by rising groundwater due to irrigation. Most impressive of all are the **Drumheller Channels,** just south of

Canada goose

Potholes Reservoir. They are visible from a viewpoint along McManamon Rd., approximately nine miles northwest of Othello. The refuge is home to more than 100,000 birds each fall and is a vital winter resting area for mallards and Canada geese. Although the refuge is closed to public entry during the peak season (to protect the birds), it is open for birdwatching, hiking, camping, and fishing in the spring and summer. Several short trails lead through; stop by the headquarters at 44 S. 8th St. in Othello, tel. (509) 488-2668, for maps and other specifics.

Sights

Built in 1912, **The Old Hotel,** 33 E. Larch St., tel. (509) 488-5936, is now a combination arts and crafts gallery and restaurant. Stop here at lunch for sandwiches and homemade soups. The **Othello Chamber of Commerce** is also inside, tel. (509) 488-2683 or (800) 684-2556; open Mon.-Sat. 9 a.m.-5 p.m. all year.

Othello Community Museum at 3rd and Larch Streets is open June-Oct. on Saturday only 1-5 p.m. Inside this 1908 Presbyterian church—the oldest building in town—are exhibits on the area's irrigation, railroad history, the "day the lights went out" after the eruption of Mt. St. Helens, and the usual pioneer items.

Hunter Hill Vineyards, 2752 W. McManamon Rd., tel. (509) 346-2736, is open for tours and tastings daily 11 a.m.-5:30 p.m. Located nine miles northwest of Othello, the winery overlooks Columbia National Wildlife Refuge.

Accommodations and Campgrounds

Cabana Motel, 655 E. Windsor, tel. (509) 488-2605 or (800) 442-4581, has an outdoor pool, jacuzzi, and kitchenettes; $30-66 s or d. It also has RV parking. The **Lincoln Inn Best Western,** 1020 E. Cedar St., tel. (509) 488-5671 nor (800) 528-1234, has an outdoor pool and kitchenettes for $35-55 s or $40-60 d.

Campsites are available in **Scooteney Park,** tel. (509) 234-0527, 11 miles south along Hwy. 17 for $8 (no hookups), and at **Soda Lake Campground,** 20 miles north of town within Columbia National Wildlife Refuge.

Food

Like many other eastern Washington farming centers, Othello has a large number of migrant workers and a growing community of immigrants from Mexico and Central America. Because of this, you'll find a tortilla factory and several authentic Mexican restaurants, including **El Caporal Restaurant,** 1244 E. Main, tel. (509) 488-0487, and the recommended **Casa Mexican,** 1224 E. Main, tel. (509) 488-6163. Each Saturday 8 a.m.-noon from mid-May to mid-Oct., you'll find a **farmers market** in Pioneer Park on Main St. and 4th Ave., with fresh fruits and veggies, honey, baked goods, and local crafts.

Events and Recreation

A popular new event is **Sandhill Crane Fest** the third Saturday of March, with workshops and field trips to view these majestic birds on the nearby wildlife refuge. Othello's main event is the **Adams County Fair and Rodeo,** held in mid-September at the fairgrounds two miles south of town. Come here for country music, PRCA rodeos, arts and crafts displays, a livestock auction, parade, carnival, food booths, demolition derby, and the crowning of Miss Othello Rodeo. The **Fourth of July Sun Faire** includes arts and crafts, a children's parade, sports tournaments, and evening fireworks.

Othello has an outdoor **swimming pool,** as well as the **Othello Golf Club,** tel. (509) 488-2376, three miles south of town.

ODESSA

Odessa is a tiny agricultural and retirement center of fewer than 1,000 folks. Wheat is the primary crop grown here. Like neighboring Ritzville, Odessa was settled by Volga Germans in the late 19th century, and 80% are still of that heritage. The wide main street (1st Ave.) passes neat small homes of brick and wood, along with a handful of German-style buildings, including city hall. Odessa gets blazing hot in the summer.

Geology

Much of the land surrounding Odessa is raw, rough-edged desert, the heart of two cataclysmic geologic episodes. The first was a series of 150 volcanic eruptions starting 17 million years ago that covered much of the Northwest in lava up to three miles thick, followed by the ice ages that led to massive Columbia River floods. These floods carved enormous gouges in the basalt, creating the dry coulees prominent in eastern Washington. The Odessa area has dozens of shallow craters of varying sizes; some reach 2,000 feet across. There are as many theories on their origin as there are geologists who have studied these odd features.

To tour the Channeled Scablands around Odessa, stop by the information booth and pick up a detailed brochure. The tour takes you west of town along the bizarre formations of Crab Creek, past the ghost town of Irby, and on to the fascinating region around **Lakeview Ranch** on BLM land. Nearby are a series of large craters to explore, a picnic area, a few primitive campsites, and shady trees. Keep your eyes open for rattlesnakes, however.

Sights

The **Odessa Historisches Museum** on the west edge of town has exhibits on the Germans from

---

A HOME FOR VOLGA GERMANS

One of Washington's most interesting migrations was that of the Volga Germans to the wheat country, particularly in the dryland area around Odessa and Ritzville. The Volga Germans had a history of migration that went back a century when their ancestors were lured to Russia from Germany. Russia's Empress Catherine II, like all of Russia's royalty in the 18th and 19th centuries, was German. She was born and reared in Germany, but when she ascended to the throne, she became fluent in Russian and wanted Russia to mature and develop.

The Volga River valley had some of Russia's richest soil, but it was hardly tilled because few people lived there, partially due to the frequent attacks by Turks only a short distance south. So Catherine II decided to colonize the area with a people she knew from her childhood: the poor, often displaced German farmers. She brought in an estimated 27,000 farmers who proved themselves industrious, perhaps to a fault because their presence was resented by many Russians from the start. Half a century later, the dislike of the immigrants grew into hostility as the Slavophile movement gained momentum. This movement was originated in the Volga area by misguided intellectuals, and it stressed the superiority of the Orthodox church over all others, especially the German's Lutheran Church, and the superiority of the Slavic people in general.

Almost coincidental with this unrest was the emergence of an American industrialist named Henry Villard, who began as a journalist and became a major railroad and land entrepreneur with a special interest in the rich farming land of eastern Washington. He was reared in Germany and was educated there before coming to America, so he saw the connection between European immigrants and the building of America more clearly than most railroad men.

Villard at one time had more than 900 agents traveling around Europe handing out pamphlets urging people to come to America and take his trains and his steamships to eastern Washington where they could buy land from Villard for between $5 and $10 an acre at seven percent interest.

An estimated 100,000 Volga Germans sold everything they owned and bought tickets to America. Many of them stopped first in the Great Plains states of Kansas, Nebraska, and the Dakotas, but many of those had to give up and move on to Washington because of blizzards, droughts, locusts, hail, windstorms, and the other weather conditions that have always plagued farmers there. To their pleasant surprise, when they came to Washington they found that Villard's claim of having the "best wheat, farming, and grazing lands in the world" weren't exaggerated.

While some settled in the rich Palouse Country, the largest number went into what is now called the dryland area. One of the first towns established was Ritzville, named for its founder, Philip Ritz, who came up from Walla Walla after amassing a fortune as a farmer and businessman. Ritz hired some Volga Germans to work on his farm and quickly learned to value their industriousness and sense of community. He began encouraging others to come to the area, and today most of the names on mailboxes and in the telephone directory date back to the time when Philip Ritz encouraged and assisted these newcomers.

It wasn't easy at first, because almost none of the Volga Germans had any money. Most arrived in America with little more than their clothing, and had left the Great Plains with not much more than that. Many had to live in dugouts in the Great Plains the first year or two, and many did so again on their arrival in the Ritzville area. But this didn't last long, and today the third and fourth generation of the Volga Germans are among Washington's most successful farmers.

Russia who settled the area, and a replica of a barn from early Odessa. Open by appointment; call (509) 982-2539. Nine miles west of Odessa off Hwy. 28 is the ghost town of **Irby,** where the 90-year-old Irby Hotel stands surrounded by desolate desert country. Immediately north of here are rich Palouse soils—prime wheat-growing areas—that escaped the massive floods of the ice ages. South of town are several Hutterite colonies; for tours, call **Schoonover Farms** at (509) 982-2257.

Practicalities

Lodging is available at **Odessa Motel,** tel. (509) 982-2412, where rooms go for $38-45 s or d. The **Odessa Tourist Park** on the corner of 1st Ave. and 2nd St. has free camping. For a taste of the area's German heritage, visit **Voise Sausage,** 7 S. 1st St., tel. (509) 982-2956, where the sausage, brautwurst, bologna are all made on the premises. More handmade goods across the street at **The Quilt Crossing,** tel. (509) 982-2194.

Get information from a kiosk in Record Square at 3 W. 1st Ave., or call the **Odessa Chamber of Commerce,** tel. (509) 982-0049. **Odessa Golf Course,** tel. (509) 982-0093, is a nine-hole course on the west end of town and has space for RV hookups. Odessa also has an aquatic center in Reiman Park with an outdoor **swimming pool,** water slide, and jacuzzi; open summers.

Events

Odessa's Germanic heritage comes out in **Deutschesfest,** on the third weekend of September. The festival includes a parade, homemade German food, arts and crafts, a carnival, and fun run, but the main attraction is a *biergarten* with polka music from the Oom Pas and Mas band. Deutschesfest attracts retired folks by the busloads, and more than 700 RVs fill the athletic field. Other Odessa events include a quilt show in late April, and a Christmas arts and crafts festival.

EPHRATA

Ephrata (ee-FRAY-ta) is a tidy town of 5,600 set amidst a sprinkling of trees and surrounded by miles of flat and desolate desertscape with short grasses and sage, alternating with irrigated fields of verdant crops. The town stretches for over a mile along Basin St. and is headquarters to the Columbia Basin Reclamation Project, the irrigation arm of the Grand Coulee Dam project. Few towns in Washington were more desolate than Ephrata before the irrigation project arrived in the 1950s. The name comes from the Biblical village where Christ was born, Bethlehem Ephratah, and supposedly originated when a traveler on the Great Northern Railway stopped here and found a prospering orchard irrigated by a spring. It reminded him of the Holy Land, and the name stuck. ("Ephratah" means "fertile region.")

Grant County Historical Museum and Pioneer Village

Ephrata is home to an outstanding collection of Indian and pioneer artifacts, clothing, tools, diaries, documents, and relics at Grant County Historical Museum and Pioneer Village, 742 N. Basin St., tel. (509) 754-3334. One of the finest historical collections in Washington, this museum covers almost four acres of downtown. The 30-building pioneer village includes a saloon, dress shop, barbershop, watch repair shop, Catholic church, jail, printing office, blacksmith, and even a house built from polished petrified wood. The buildings are both original structures and reproductions.

In the crowded main museum, be sure to find the 1895 Rockaway carriage, a beautifully refurbished glass-enclosed carriage used by the local postmaster who also happened to be a Scottish nobleman, Lord Thomas Blythe. An aimless young man, Blythe was sent to America by his father in an attempt to force him into maturity; it obviously worked, because Thomas Blythe went on to become a highly successful cattle rancher. Also surprising are the live snakes that occupy a back room, including a northern Pacific rattlesnake. Downstairs is an amusing collection of carved wooden creatures.

The museum and pioneer village are open Monday, Tuesday, and Thurs.-Sat. 10 a.m.-5 p.m. and Sunday 1-4 p.m. (closed Wednesday), May-Sept. only. Guided tours are available until 4 p.m. Entrance costs $2 adults, $1.50 ages 6-15, and free for kids under six.

Demonstrations of pioneer crafts are given during both the **Living Museum** on the second weekend of June and **Pioneer Day,** the last weekend of September. During these events, Pioneer Village comes alive with costumed participants in every building—from apple pressing to wool spinning—and cowboy poetry. Kids get to make their own horseshoes at the blacksmith shop.

Accommodations

Travelodge, 31 Basin St. SW, tel. (509) 754-4651 or (800) 255-3050, has rooms for $45-70 s, $55-70 d, and a heated pool. **Lariat Motel,** 1639 Basin SW, tel. (509) 754-2437, has rooms for $40 s or $45 d. **Columbia Motel,** 1257 Basin SW, tel. (509) 754-5226, charges $52 s or d for rooms with kitchenettes.

Ivy Chapel Inn B&B, 164 D St. SW, tel. (509) 754-0629, was originally a Presbyterian Church, but is now a distinctive and friendly B&B. The ivy-covered red brick building contains six guest rooms with private baths and a full breakfast; no kids under 14. $75 s or d.

No public campsites nearby, but travelers can pitch tents or park RVs at **Stars and Stripes RV Park,** 5707 Hwy. 28 W, tel. (509) 787-1062, or **Oasis RV Park,** a mile south of town, tel. (509) 754-5102. The latter is noteworthy for its big shade trees, swimming pool, and mini-golf. The city park next to Oasis has a popular fishing pond.

Other Practicalities

Downtown Ephrata is no bustling commercial hub, but you can get sandwiches and pies from **The Country Deli,** 245 Basin St. NW, tel. (509) 754-3143; pizzas from **Guido's Pizzeria,** 1070 Basin St. NW, tel. (509) 754-0354; and Greek meals from **Kafe Athens,** 459 Basin NW, tel. (509) 754-2839.

Ephrata's annual **Sage and Sun Festival,** held the second weekend of June, features a parade, arts and crafts, antique cars, and a carnival. The popular Living Museum, and Pioneer Day are described above.

For local information, contact the **Ephrata Chamber of Commerce,** 90 Alder St. NW, tel. (509) 754-4656. Open Mon.-Fri. 9 a.m.-4 p.m. all year. The city has an outdoor **swimming pool** on the south end of town.

Amtrak, tel. (800) 872-7245, provides service west to Wenatchee, Everett, Edmonds, and Seattle, and east to Spokane and Chicago. The Amtrak depot is on 1st Street. **Northwestern Trailways,** tel. (800) 366-6975, stops in front of the Chamber of Commerce, with daily bus service east to Spokane and west to Everett and Seattle.

SOAP LAKE

Located five miles northeast of Ephrata, Soap Lake is a small body of salty, highly alkaline water surrounded by the deserts of the Columbia Basin. The town of Soap Lake (pop. 1,300) occupies the south shore of the lake, and has long been a place for "taking the cure" for such ailments as psoriasis and arthritis. Other folks come to soak in the warm sunshine; it shines 310 days a year over Soap Lake, and only rains eight inches annually.

History

Though you'd never suspect it today, Soap Lake was once a bustling resort area surrounding the Soap Lake Sanitorium, a health retreat that capitalized on the lake's legendary medicinal qualities. The Tsincayuse Indians sent their sick to soak in the *smokiam* or "healing waters"; early white explorers called it Soap Lake because its 17 natural minerals and oils give the water a soft soapy feel and create a suds-like foam on windy days. The only other place on earth with similar water is said to be Baden Baden, Germany.

In the early 1900s, great crowds of people from around the country came here to drink and bathe in the alkaline water to cure joint, skin, digestive, and circulatory ailments. Most of the visitors weren't too sick: they found time for drinking, dancing, and general hell-raising, leading the local newspaper to admonish them to "be more careful" about remembering their swimsuits! The drought and Depression of 1933 brought an end to the revelry, turning Soap Lake into a curiosity in the midst of a desolate region. It has been making a comeback, though, and the chamber of commerce actively promotes the curative powers of the lake's water with testimonials from satisfied customers ("After only nine days, the pain has gone, and I feel like a new person . . ."). John's Thrift on Hwy. 17 sells soaps and other products made from the lake waters, and the mineral-rich water is piped into several motels for your convenience.

East Beach has play equipment, lake access, and restrooms; the Soap Lake Chamber of Commerce is also here if you need maps or directions. **West Beach** is on the other side of town. One warning: Swim in loose-fitting suits to avoid chafing that can be aggravated by the highly alkaline water. Also be careful to rinse off at the showers and to put on sunscreen after bathing since the minerals in the water act to increase tanning and burning.

Lodging

The spacious log **Notaras Lodge,** 231 Main St., tel. (509) 246-0462, features imaginative rooms named after the slightly famous and decorated with their belongings, such as the Norma Zimmer room, named for the old Lawrence Welk Show's "Champagne Lady." Rooms cost $58 s or $65 d; the more expensive units feature in-room whirlpools with Soap Lake water piped in, bathroom phones, skylights, and balconies. Also ask about massages and a one-night pass to the local members-only club.

The Inn at Soap Lake, 226 Main Ave. E, tel. (509) 246-1132, was built in 1905 from rounded river stones. Rooms are nicely furnished with antiques and have kitchenettes and mineral water soaking tubs; $50 s or $55 d, including a continental breakfast. Canoe and paddleboat rentals are available here.

Several places offer cheaper, if more standard, lodging in Soap Lake. **Lake Motel,** 322 Daisy St., tel. (509) 246-1903, has an outdoor pool, jacuzzi, sauna, mineral water baths, and kitchenettes; $25 s or $32 d. **Royal View Motel,** near East Beach, tel. (509) 246-1831, has rooms with kitchenettes for $45 s or d. **Tolo Vista Lodge,** 22 Daisy N., tel. (509) 246-1512, rents cozy log cabins with kitchens for $50-55 s or d. All of these also have Soap Lake on tap. **Tumwata Lodge,** 340 W. Main, tel. (509) 246-1416, has a heated pool, mineral baths, and private beach, but no phones. Cabins go for $45-60 s or d.

Campgrounds

Smokiam Campground, tel. (509) 246-1211, has waterfront camping for $7 tents or $10 RVs; open April-October. This is actually just a gravel lot sandwiched between the lake and the highway. More RV sites at **Soap Lake Trailer Court,** 510 5th St. SE, tel. (509) 246-0211, and **Robbies RV Park,** tel. (509) 246-0906. **Soap Lake Resort,** tel. (509) 246-1103, at the north end of the lake, has RV camping, an outdoor pool, jacuzzi, sauna, and swimming beach.

Other Practicalities

Don's Steak House, 14 Canna St. across from Notaras Lodge, tel. (509) 246-1217, specializes in delicious steak, seafood, and Greek dishes; open daily for dinner.

Several local events attract out-of-towners to Soap Lake. The **Greek Festival** in June kicks things off with a parade, auction, food, folk dancing, belly dancing, and even country and western music (Greek C&W?). The town has a big fireworks show and parade on the **Fourth of July,** and a popular **Great Canoe Race** the second weekend of July. The latter covers almost 18 miles of paddling and portaging, and ends with a sprint across Soap Lake to the finish line. The second weekend of August brings the **Soap Lake Rod Run & Pig Feed,** an odd combination that includes a fun run, pig barbecue, and classic car show.

The summer-only **Soap Lake Chamber of Commerce** is right along the lake in a small building, tel. (509) 246-1821. Next door is East Beach, a favorite swimming, picnic, and camping area.

GRAND COULEE DAM AND VICINITY

If you've been driving through the desert country of central Washington, Grand Coulee Dam comes as quite a surprise. Instead of barren sage, grass, and rock, you're suddenly in a cluster of small towns with lush green lawns and split-level suburban homes. This oasis in the desert is the result of one of the largest construction projects ever undertaken. The Grand Coulee is a 50-mile-long gorge carved by the Columbia River during the ice ages, when glaciers forced the river south of its current path. Much of the carving took place during the cataclysmic Spokane Floods thousands of years ago. By the way, the word "coulee" means dry ravine.

The dam is surrounded by a confusing cluster of towns with similar names. Electric City and Grand Coulee are south of the dam, Coulee Dam and Elmer City are north of the dam. All but Elmer City have services. Coulee City sits adjacent to Dry Falls Dam on Banks Lake, 30 miles south of Grand Coulee Dam. All four towns are described below.

GRAND COULEE DAM

Massive Grand Coulee Dam is the main destination for travelers in this part of Washington. The dam and surrounding facilities serve a variety of functions, including irrigation, power production, and flood control. Twice as high as Niagara Falls and nearly a mile long, the dam is one of the world's greatest producers of electricity, generating an incredible 22,000 megawatts of energy annually for cities in several states. Only Guri Dam in Venezuela and Itaipu Dam between Paraguay and Brazil generate more electricity. The dam stands 550 feet above bedrock—taller than the Washington Monument—with a 1,650-foot-wide spillway. The 12 million cubic yards of concrete and steel that it contains are enough to build a six-foot sidewalk around the equator (assuming, of course, that you could build a sidewalk around the equator even if you wanted to do so).

On the slope just west of the dam are gigantic pipes through which water is pumped 280 feet uphill into Banks Lake during periods of high flow. This water then feeds into a series of canals to irrigate a half-million acres of farmland in the Columbia Basin Project. In periods of high energy demand, the pumps become generators as water is released from Banks Lake back down these pipes.

History

For years, the Columbia Basin was recognized as an area of rich soils but low rainfall. Pressure built to harness the Columbia River—second largest in America—as a source of irrigation water, and to provide cheap power for the growing Pacific Northwest. Under the urging of President Franklin D. Roosevelt, Congress appropriated $60 million to build this massive project, the linchpin in the Columbia Basin Project. The construction of Grand Coulee Dam, at that time "the biggest thing built by the hand of man," employed thousands of workers during the Great Depression. Work began in 1933, as massive amounts of dirt were removed to get to bedrock. Temporary coffer dams were constructed to shift the river while excavation of the riverbed took place, and the first concrete was poured in 1935. Gradually the workers completed a foundation across the riverbed and began pouring concrete. The dam was finally completed late in 1941, and the third power plant was added in the 1970s. Today, Grand Coulee is one of 11 major dams along the Columbia River within Washington; there are some 200 dams within the entire Columbia River drainage.

Although rumors still abound of men buried alive in the concrete of Grand Coulee Dam, such was not the case. The work was dangerous, however, and 77 men were killed from drownings, blasting, or vehicle accidents. Another four men died during completion of the third power plant.

Unfortunately, the "eighth wonder of the world," as it is sometimes still called, inundated rich salmon fishing grounds that had been used by Native Americans for at least 9,000 years. It

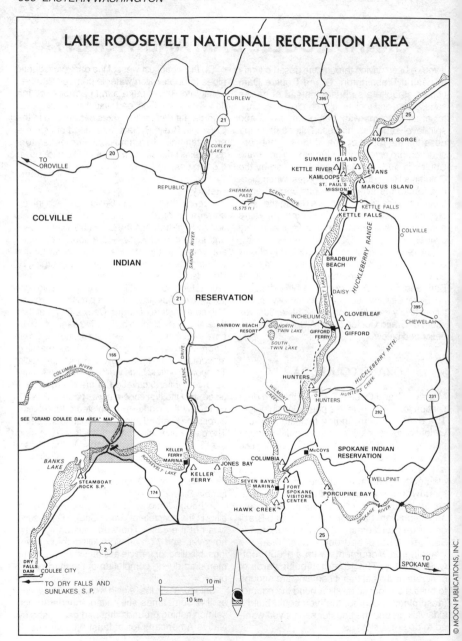

LAKE ROOSEVELT NATIONAL RECREATION AREA

© MOON PUBLICATIONS, INC.

wasn't until 1994—after 43 years of contentious litigation—that the U.S. Congress finally agreed to pay the Colville Tribe $53 million (plus additional annual payments of $15 million) as compensation for the loss of this way of life.

Tours and Information

Start your visit with a stop at the Bureau of Reclamation's **Visitor Arrival Center,** just north of the dam on Hwy. 155, tel. (509) 633-9265. It's open daily 8:30 a.m.-9:30 p.m. (till 11 p.m. in mid-summer) from Memorial Day through September, and daily 9 a.m.-5 p.m. the rest of the year (closed Thanksgiving, Christmas, and New Year's). Self-guided tours of the dam are available throughout the year when the center is open, and documentary movies are shown in the auditorium all day. The Visitor Arrival Center also houses one of the world's most advanced computer-controlled laser projection systems, used for spectacular summer shows. A gift shop sells books about the dam and local natural history.

Half-hour guided tours of the third power plant take place every half-hour between 10 a.m. and 6 p.m. in the summer, and four times a day in the winter. A highlight of the dam tour is riding the glass incline elevator to the face of the power plant for a spectacular view of the spillway from an outside balcony. An artifact room displays the Native American tools and arrowheads uncovered during the construction of the dam, along with agate stones.

Laser Light Show

Each summer evening brings a most unusual and immensely popular event to Grand Coulee Dam: an elaborate high-tech laser light show that paints 300-foot figures on the face of the dam and tells the history of the Columbia River, of the Indian people who first lived here, and of the dam and how it transformed the desert land. (You *won't* hear how the dam helped devastate the Columbia's salmon runs.) Created in 1989, this program packs the house, even though the "house" can sit on surrounding hillsides or in their vehicles. Best vantage points are from the Visitor Arrival Center, from the parking lot just below here, from the park at the east end of the bridge in Coulee Dam, and from Crown Point Vista (farther away, but overlooking the entire area). If you're planning to park at the visitor center, get there an hour early to be sure of a spot, especially on weekends. Thousands of other folks are looking for the same vista point.

These free 36-minute laser shows are offered from Memorial Day weekend through the end of September, with show time at 10 p.m. from Memorial Day through July, at 9:30 p.m. in August, and at 8:30 p.m. in September. If you're too far away to hear the broadcast sound from the speakers, tune to 89.9 FM or 1490 AM for nightly broadcasts of the music and story. It's all done in an entertaining and patriotic way, ending in a Neil Diamond song. Perfect for a Republican convention.

Grand Coulee is one of 14 dams on the Columbia River.

Sports and Recreation

Enormous **Franklin D. Roosevelt Lake**—stretching more than 150 miles from the dam almost to the Canadian border—is popular with boaters, water-skiers, swimmers, anglers, and campers. **Banks Lake** (see **Coulee City, Banks Lake, and Wilbur**) and the parks to the southwest of the dam—in the coulee formed by the Columbia River during the last ice age—are also scenic summer playgrounds.

The dry, sunny climate is perfect for lake activities; summer temperatures range from the mid-70s to 100° F, with evenings cooling off to the 50s or 60s. The area is a popular winter recreation spot as well, with cross-country skiers, ice fishermen, and snowmobilers enjoying the off-season, along with the many bald eagles that winter here before heading north to British Columbia for the spring. You won't be the only one around if you visit in the summer; more than 1.8 million folks pass through the area each year.

Hiking Trails

Several local paths provide a chance to get away from the dam and explore. The **Candy Point Trail** was first built by the CCC in the 1930s, and their hand-laid stone is still in evidence. The path begins from a trailhead 300 feet down the hill behind the Coulee Dam Credit Union in the town of Coulee Dam and climbs steeply to Crown Point overlook, then over Candy Point, before returning to the river near Coulee Dam City Hall.

The **Down River Trail** is a gentle six-and-a-half-mile path along the river north from the bridge with several tree-lined rest areas. A less developed trail heads south from the dam to the towns of Grand Coulee and Electric City. More hiking can be found at nearby Steamboat Rock State Park (described below).

LAKE ROOSEVELT

Much of Franklin D. Roosevelt Lake—from Grand Coulee Dam to just below the town of Northport—has been designated the sprawling **Lake Roosevelt National Recreation Area.** It is a favorite boating, water-skiing, fishing, camping, and swimming destination. The reservoir backs up not just the Columbia River waters, but also

parts of the Spokane, Kettle, Colville, and Sanpoil Rivers. At more than 150 miles long, it is said to be the second largest human-created lake in the world.

Campgrounds

Campers can stay at one of 35 campgrounds (10 of these are accessible only by boat) that line both sides of Lake Roosevelt and the Spokane River arm. None of the campgrounds offer hookups; all of them have restrooms (but no showers or RV hookups); and all but the most primitive have running water. A $10 fee is charged at Evans, Fort Spokane, Gifford, Hunters, Keller Ferry, Kettle Falls, Marcus Island, Porcupine Bay, and Spring Canyon; the rest are free. Summer **campfire programs** are offered Friday and Saturday evenings at Evans, Fort Spokane, Spring Canyon, Kettle Falls, Keller Ferry, and Porcupine Bay campgrounds. Most campgrounds are open year-round; Porcupine Bay is open May-October. There is a 14-day camping limit.

Houseboat Rentals

One of the best ways to explore the reaches of Lake Roosevelt is aboard a rented houseboat. Swimming and fishing are just outside your bedroom window; no noisy neighbors to contend with; and you'll see parts of the lake you just can't reach by car. Each houseboat is at least 46 feet long and comes equipped with a kitchen, bath, sleeping areas for up to 13, swim slide and ladder, gas grill, and more. You can also rent 18-foot ski boats or 14-foot fishing boats to take along. Weekend rates in the summer (two nights and three days) are steep, $1,100-1,800; save money by renting in the off-season or for longer periods. For more information, contact **Lake Roosevelt Resort and Marina,** tel. (509) 738-6121 or (800) 635-7585; or **Roosevelt Recreational Enterprises,** tel. (509) 633-0136 or (800) 648-5253; and **Dakota Columbia Houseboat Adventures,** tel. (509) 835-5647 or (800) 816-2431.

Swimming

No lifeguards on the lake, but popular swimming beaches are found at **Spring Canyon** and **Keller Ferry** in lower Lake Roosevelt, and at **Fort Spokane** and **Porcupine Bay** on the Spokane

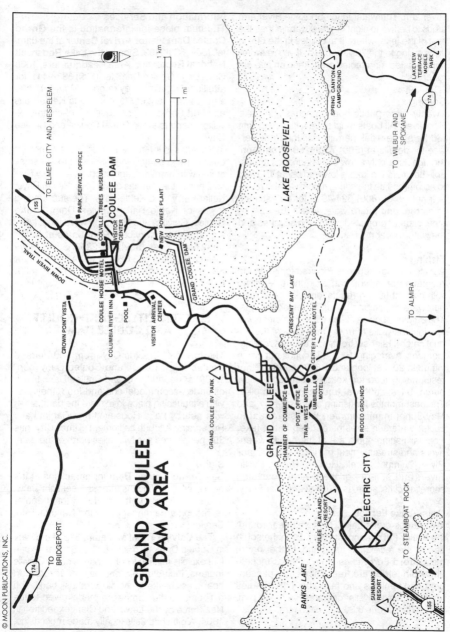

© MOON PUBLICATIONS, INC.

GRAND COULEE
DAM AREA

1 km
1 mi
0
0

TO BRIDGEPORT
174

TO ELMER CITY AND NESPELEM
155

DOWN RIVER TRAIL

PARK SERVICE OFFICE
COLVILLE TRIBES MUSEUM
VISITOR CENTER
COULEE DAM
NEW POWER PLANT
GRAND COULEE DAM
COULEE HOUSE MOTEL
COLUMBIA RIVER INN
POOL
VISITOR ARRIVAL CENTER
CROWN POINT VISTA

LAKE ROOSEVELT

SPRING CANYON CAMPGROUND
LAKEVIEW TERRACE MOBILE PARK
174
TO WILBUR AND SPOKANE

CRESCENT BAY LAKE
CENTER LODGE MOTEL
TO ALMIRA

GRAND COULEE RV PARK
GRAND COULEE
CHAMBER OF COMMERCE
POST OFFICE
TRAIL WEST MOTEL
UMBRELLA MOTEL
RODEO GROUNDS

ELECTRIC CITY
COULEE PLAYLAND RESORT
BANKS LAKE
SUNBANKS RESORT
155

TO STEAMBOAT ROCK

River arm. The water in the Spokane River arm tends to be five to eight degrees warmer than the rest of the lake, where it averages in the 60s in June, rising to the 70s in August. If you're swimming outside a protected area, keep an eye out for boats!

Boating

Twenty-three public boat launches line Lake Roosevelt. All boats must have a launch permit ($6 for a one-week permit); call the Park Service for details at (509) 738-6266. From April through June only a few of the launches are usable because the lake is lowered about 100 feet to accommodate the spring runoff. Call the reservoir hotline at (800) 824-4916 for an estimate of current and future water levels. Be sure to steer clear of protected swimming beaches and the waters near the dam.

Fishing

A state fishing license is required to fish in the recreation area; you can pick one up—along with current fishing regulations—at most area hardware or sporting goods stores or marinas. The 30 plus species of fish inhabiting these waters include walleye (more than 90% of the annual catch), rainbow trout, and enormous white sturgeon, averaging 100-300 pounds but growing up to 20 feet long and 1,800 pounds. Other residents include the kokanee salmon, yellow perch, bass, cutthroat trout, perch, and pike. The best months for fishing are Sept.-Nov. and May-June; in midsummer, the fish retreat to cooler waters in streams or deep in the lake. Popular fishing spots are at the points where rivers and streams meet the lake—the Sanpoil River, Wilmont Creek, Hunters Creek, Kettle River, and others—or the waters near high shoreline cliffs, such as those near Keller Ferry.

Cross-Lake Ferries

Two ferries cross Lake Roosevelt year-round: the **Keller Ferry** connects Hwy. 21 in the south part of the recreation area, and, farther north, the **Gifford Ferry** joins Hwy. 25 near Inchelium. Both ferries are free. They carry passengers and vehicles and take about 15 minutes for the crossing. Keller operates 6 a.m.-11 p.m. daily; Gifford runs 6:30 a.m.-9:30 p.m.

Information and Services

The best place for information is the **Grand Coulee Dam Visitor Arrival Center** at the dam, tel. (509) 633-9193. Stop by the **Lake Roosevelt National Recreation Area Headquarters,** 1008 Crest Dr. in Coulee Dam, tel. (509) 633-9441, for additional details. They're open Mon.-Fri. 7:30 a.m.-4 p.m. Ranger stations are in Kettle Falls and Fort Spokane, and chamber of commerce visitors centers are in Grand Coulee and Coulee City.

Services in the recreation area are generally open June to early September. There are small stores with groceries and supplies at Daisy Station, and in the marinas at McCoys, Seven Bays, Keller Ferry, and Kettle Falls. The surrounding towns of Kettle Falls, Coulee Dam, Grand Coulee, Colville, and Northport have food, lodging, and other services. Rent boats at Keller Ferry Marina, tel. (509) 647-2253; Seven Bays Marina, tel. (509) 633-0201 or (800) 648-5253, or Kettle Falls Marina, tel. (509) 738-6121 or (800) 635-7585.

ELECTRIC CITY, GRAND COULEE, AND COULEE DAM

The towns of Electric City (pop. 900), Grand Coulee (pop. 1,000), and Coulee Dam (pop. 1,100) surround the Grand Coulee Dam. In addition to accommodations and food, they provide a launching place to explore the dam, along with nearby Lake Roosevelt and Banks Lake Reservoirs. A fourth settlement, **Elmer City,** has 300 people and sits two miles north of the dam.

Sights

See **Grand Coulee Dam** for attractions at the dam itself, including the famous laser light show, and **Lake Roosevelt** for info on this popular recreation area managed by the National Park Service.

The **Colville Tribal Museum,** 512 Mead Way in Coulee Dam, tel. (509) 633-0751, has excellent exhibits relating to all 12 bands of the Colville Indians, including old photos, cedar root and bear grass baskets, fine old cornhusk bags, and a Thomas Jefferson peace medal given to the Nez Percé by the Lewis and Clark expedition in 1804. A gift shop sells locally made moccasins, beaded goods, turquoise jewelry, baskets, and blankets. The museum is open Mon.-Sat. 10 a.m.-6 p.m. April-Dec.; closed the rest of the year. No charge. **Rainbow Gallery,** 215 Main in Grand Coulee, also has Indian beadwork and art.

The famous **Gehrke Windmills** can be found at Bicentennial Park in the town of Grand Coulee. These amusing, brightly colored pieces of folk art were created by the late Emil Gehrke from scraps of iron.

One of the best views of the dam is from **Crown Point Vista,** on a bluff 626 feet above the river, and two miles west of the Grand Coulee on Hwy. 174.

Lodging

Lodging is mostly unpretentious in the Coulee area. Advance reservations are a good idea for the busy summer weekends; one or two months ahead should get you weekend lodging at the better motels. Winter rates can really plummet; places charging $50 d in summer can be had for $30 d in the off season. Call the **Grand Coulee Dam Area Chamber of Commerce** at (509) 633-3074 or (800) 268-5332 to see who has space.

Gold House Inn B&B, 411 Partello in Grand Coulee, tel. (509) 633-3276 or (800) 835-9369, has eight guest rooms with private baths and full breakfasts. Kids welcome; $50-90 s or d.

Another interesting place (great breakfasts too) is the historic **Four Winds Guest House B&B,** 301 Lincoln St. in Coulee Dam, tel. (509) 633-3146 or (800) 786-3146. Most of their 10 guest rooms have shared baths. No kids under eight. $62-74 s or d.

Coulee House Motel, overlooking the dam at 110 Roosevelt Way in Coulee Dam, tel. (509) 633-1101 or (800) 715-7767, has very nice facilities that include an outdoor pool, jacuzzi, sauna, and exercise room. Kitchenettes are available. Rooms are $50-60 s or d. **Columbia River Inn,** 10 Lincoln St. in Coulee Dam, tel. (509) 633-2100 or (800) 633-6421, is another very nice place, with an outdoor pool and hot tub. The rooms provide views of the laser light show each summer evening; $49-75 s or d. **Sky Deck Motel,** tel. (509) 633-0290, is an attractive motel along Banks Lake in Electric City, with an outdoor pool and jacuzzi; $60-70 s or d.

Other local lodging places include: **Center Lodge Motel,** Spokane Way in Grand Coulee, tel. (509) 633-0770, $39-70 s or d; **Trail West Motel,** 108 Spokane Way in Grand Coulee, tel. (509) 633-3155, with an outdoor pool and rooms for $39 s or $47 d; and **Umbrella Motel,** 404 Spokane Way in Grand Coulee, tel. (509) 633-1691, with clean older rooms for $25 s or $30 d.

Campgrounds and RV Parks

The Park Service operates campgrounds (no showers or RV hookups) all along Lake Roosevelt (see **Lake Roosevelt** for specifics). Closest to the dam is **Spring Canyon,** three miles east of the town of Grand Coulee; $10, open year-round, no reservations. Saturday evening campfire programs are held here during the summer. Eight miles southwest of the dam on Hwy. 155, **Steamboat Rock State Park** has tent ($11), and RV sites ($16). It is open all year. Call (800) 452-5687 for reservations ($6 extra).

Private RV parks in the area include: **Banks Lake Golf & Country Club,** two miles south of Electric City on Hwy. 155, tel. (509) 633-0163; **Coulee Playland Resort,** on Banks Lake in Electric City, tel. (509) 633-2671; **Grand Coulee RV Park,** Hwy. 174 east, tel. (509) 633-0750; **King's Court RV Park,** Hwy. 174 east of Grand Coulee, tel. (509) 633-0103 or (800) 759-2608; **Lakeview Terrace Mobile Park,** four miles east of Grand Coulee on Hwy. 174, tel. (509) 633-2169; and **Sunbanks Resort,** on Banks Lake just south of Electric City, tel. (509) 633-3786.

Food

The Coulee Dam area is not for gourmands, but you will find good food, generous portions, and friendly service. **Emily's New Flo's Cafe,** 316 Spokane Way in Grand Coulee, tel. (509) 633-3216, has a strange name and is somewhat smokey, but serves big solid American breakfasts and lunches for a reasonable price. A great place to meet the locals.

Tee Pee Drive In, in Grand Coulee, tel. (509) 633-2111, makes the best local burgers in a straight-from-the'60s setting. Go back a decade more in time for the **Rock 'N Robin,** with its Elvis-era decor and car hop service. In addition to the standard burgers, sandwiches, and shakes, they also serve a very '90s drink: espresso. A very popular summertime hands-on lunch and dinner place is **BBQ in the Park** in Coulee Dam, tel. (509) 633-1230, with tasty grilled pork, chicken, or steelhead seven days a week.

R & A Cafe, 514 Birch St. in Coulee Dam, tel. (509) 633-2233, serves generous portions of family-style home cooking for breakfast and lunch. **La Presa Mexican Restaurant,** in Coulee Dam, tel. (509) 633-3173, has authentic Mexican meals.

Events and Entertainment

The second weekend in May, the **Colorama Festival** brings a rodeo, parade, flea market, and carnival to the Coulee Dam area. Also in mid-May, the **Sunbanks Blues Festival** includes three full days of live blues acts; tel. (509) 633-3786. The **Memorial Day Festival** features arts and crafts, music, food, a fun run, and the grand opening of the laser light show followed by a big fireworks display off the top of the dam. This festival attracts some 75,000 visitors; call (800) 268-5332 for details. More fireworks from the dam, along with arts and crafts, food, and entertainment on the **Fourth of July.** Mid-August brings the nationally known **Golden Over the Dam Run,** with five-km and 10-km races; call (800) 268-5332 for details.

Throw away your cash in the slots and on the blackjack tables at **Coulee Dam Casino** in Coulee Dam, tel. (800) 556-7492.

Sports and Recreation

The Park Service has free guided canoe trips around **Crescent Bay Lake** behind the town of Grand Coulee. These 90-minute paddles take place June-Aug., and offer a good opportunity to see wildlife; call (509) 633-9444 for specifics. Canoes, paddles, and life jackets are provided.

No lifeguards, but popular swimming places are Spring Canyon Campground along Lake Roosevelt, and Steamboat Rock State Park, eight miles south on Banks Lake. **Sunbanks Resort,** tel. (509) 633-3786, rents jet skis on Banks Lake. About a mile south of Electric City on Grand Coulee Airport Rd., **Banks Lake Golf and Country Club** is a nine-hole public course, tel. (509) 633-0163.

Information and Services

For information on the surrounding area, contact the **Grand Coulee Dam Area Chamber of Commerce,** 306 Midway in Grand Coulee, tel. (509) 633-3074 or (800) 268-5332. Hours are Mon.-Sat. 8 a.m.-8 p.m. in the summer, and Mon.-Fri. 8 a.m.-5 p.m. in the winter. A summer-only **visitor center,** tel. (509) 632-5713, is located in Mason City Park (just uphill from the grocery store) in Coulee City. The Bureau of Reclamation's big **Visitor Arrival Center** is just north of the dam on Hwy. 155, tel. 633-9265.

COULEE CITY, BANKS LAKE, AND WILBUR

Coulee City

The somnolent town of Coulee City (pop. 600) sits on the eastern edge of Dry Falls Dam, the dam that creates Banks Lake. It's home to the PRCA **Last Stand Rodeo** held on Memorial Day weekend for over 45 years.

Accommodations: Most Coulee City accommodations are on the dowdy side—fine for hunters and fishermen, but not so great for people who want more than a bed and shower. **Main Stay B&B,** tel. (509) 632-5687, is a contemporary home with two guest rooms with private baths and a continental breakfast; kids are welcome. $35 s or $50 d. **Sun Lakes Park Resort,** seven miles south of Coulee City, tel. (509) 632-5291, has cabins (some sleep seven) for $61-94, including an outdoor pool. Kitchenettes are available, rowboat rentals, open mid-April to mid-October. **Ala Cozy Motel,** tel. (509) 632-5703, charges $40 s or $45-50 d, including an outdoor pool. Kitchenettes are available. **Blue Top Motel,** tel. (509) 632-5596, charges $35-38 s or d; kitchenettes available.

Camping: Camp in town at **Coulee City Community Park;** $9 tents, $12 RVs. They also have a good swimming beach here. **Sun Lakes State Park** is seven miles southwest of Coulee City on Hwy. 17; $11 tents, $16 RVs. Call (800) 452-5687 for reservations ($6 extra). Park RVs at **Coulee Lodge Resort,** tel. (509) 632-5565, six miles south along Blue Lake. They also have cabins and boat rentals; open April-September.

Food: Branding Iron Saloon has an antique bar, pool tables, and good pub grub, including the best burgers in town.

Steamboat Rock
State Park

DIANNE BOULERICE LYONS

Banks Lake

Banks Lake, which lies outside Lake Roosevelt National Recreation Area on the southwest side of the dam, is a 27-mile-long, clear-blue beauty surrounded by the deep sides of the coulee. In the early '50s, the coulee was dammed on both ends and filled with water from the Columbia. To get here, the water must be pumped 280 feet uphill from Lake Roosevelt through enormous pipes visible on the north side of Grand Coulee Dam. As well as being a popular recreational alternative to Lake Roosevelt for fishermen and water-skiers, water from Banks Lake irrigates over a half-million acres of farmland stretching south to the Oregon border. RVs and tenters often camp for free in roadside access points along the lakeshore.

Steamboat Rock State Park

Eight miles south of Grand Coulee on Hwy. 155, Steamboat Rock State Park has campsites ($11 tents; $16 RVs), swimming, good fishing, play equipment, and an underwater park on Banks Lake. The park is open all year. Call (509) 633-1304 for more information, or (800) 452-5687 for reservations ($6 extra).

Steamboat Rock, an island in the Columbia River during the last ice age, is now a scenic volcanic butte rising 700 feet above Banks Lake. You can hike a mile to the top of the butte for a panoramic view, and then explore the 640 acres on the flat top. The trail starts near the north

campground. Bring repellent to combat the vicious mosquitoes. Winter sports are also popular here, from ice fishing to snowmobiling and cross-country skiing.

Wilbur

The nothing wheat town of Wilbur (pop. 900) is 28 miles northeast of Coulee City and 19 miles southeast of the Grand Coulee Dam. The **Wilbur Museum** contains historic photos, displays of items from the past, and a collection of gems and minerals. Be sure to check out items from Samuel Wilbur Condon, the town founder who died in 1895 after a gun battle over a woman who refused to marry him. The museum is open Saturday 2-4 p.m. June-August.

Settle in at **Settle Inn Motel,** tel. (509) 647-5812, where rooms with kitchenettes go for $30-36 d. **Eight Bar B Motel,** tel. (509) 647-2400, has an outdoor pool and rooms for $30-65 d. Camping is available in the Park Service campground at Kellers Crossing 14 miles north of Wilbur, or in town at **Crescent Oaks RV Park,** tel. (509) 647-5608, and **Bell's RV Park,** tel. (509) 647-5888. Wilbur also has a big outdoor swimming pool open in the summer. The annual event for Wilbur is **Wild Goose Bill Days** on the third weekend of May, featuring a small-town parade, fun run, craft and food booths, dancing, and a barbecue in the park.

LOWER GRAND COULEE AREA

Sun Lakes State Park and Dry Falls

Sun Lakes State Park, seven miles southwest of Coulee City on Hwy. 17, is famous for its "dry falls." The main part of Sun Lakes Park boasts 3,300 acres with year-round camping ($11 tents, $16 RVs) along Park Lake, plus horse trails, boating, swimming, and rainbow trout fishing. Call (800) 452-5687 for reservations ($6 extra). Concessions offer snacks, fishing supplies, horse rentals, and groceries. At least 10 smaller lakes pockmark the park; they are ancient plunge pools from a stupendous waterfall that once raged through here. A road leads east from Park Lake along the basalt cliff walls lining Meadow Creek to Deep Lake, and hiking trails provide access to other parts of this fascinating park.

Four miles north of the main park entrance along Hwy. 17 is **Dry Falls Interpretive Center,** tel. (509) 632-5583, open Wed.-Sun. 10 a.m.-6 p.m. from mid-May to mid-September. The center describes the incredible geologic history of this area; outside, the cliff-edge viewpoints reveal a cluster of lakes bordered by green plants set against stark basalt cliffs. There is a certain strange beauty about this place, especially at dusk. A steep path leads a half mile down from the overlook to Dry Falls Lake. Look around the 400-foot cliff face and you may find the entrance to a small cave.

The Columbia River ran through this ancient volcanic landscape for eons, but during the ice ages that began a million years ago, glaciers forced the river to change course through the now-dry canyons called coulees. The ice also dammed the Columbia River in northern Idaho, creating an enormous body of water, Lake Missoula. When this ice dam burst around 17,000 years ago, a 2,000-foot high wall of water rushed downstream, carving the land in a way that is almost beyond imagination. Today's Dry Falls was once the mightiest waterfall on the planet, reaching 400 feet high and over three miles across! This massive rush of water—at an estimated 386 million cubic feet per second, its volume was 10 times that of the combined flow of all rivers on earth—probably lasted but a few days or weeks but was repeated many times, as glaciers advanced and blocked the river, and as the

ice dam broke again. The ripple marks left by the flood are up to 35 feet high and 350 feet apart. Over time, the periodic floods (geologists refer to these as the **Spokane Floods**) eroded the lip of the falls for a distance of almost 20 miles. Below this lip is Lower Grand Coulee, a deep 50-mile-long gorge that held the Columbia River during the ice ages. To get an idea of the magnitude of the flood, imagine this 900-foot deep, three-mile wide canyon filled with rushing water! After the glaciers retreated, the river returned to its old channel, leaving behind the dry coulees.

Lake Lenore Caves

Approximately nine miles south of Sun Lakes State Park, Hwy. 17 passes a series of four shallow caves, located high up the coulee cliffs. A trail leads from an information sign to several of these rock openings, which were created by the erosive action of floods that swept through the canyon during the ice ages. The caves were occupied by nomadic prehistoric peoples. Across the highway is a sign describing the Lahontan cutthroat trout that have been planted in the creek here.

Summer Falls State Park

Nine miles south of Coulee City on Pinto Ridge Rd., Summer Falls State Park is an appropriately named park since the falls created by the irrigation project exist only in the summer when irrigation water is needed. (The water reaches here from Banks Lake via an irrigation canal.) This is a cool spot for a picnic or fishing, but no camping, and sirens warn of sudden flow increases that make it very dangerous to swim.

COLVILLE INDIAN RESERVATION

The Colville Indian Reservation covers more than 1.4 million acres of forested mountains, rolling rangeland, and rich farms in the Okanogan Highlands and Valley. They also have hunting, fishing, and mineral rights to an equal area to the north that was originally included in the reservation but was later opened to settlement.

The Indian peoples on the Colville subsist on income from various tribal businesses: a sawmill, grocery stores, fish hatchery, wood treatment plant, houseboat rentals, marina, and prosperous casinos in Okanogan, Coulee Dam, and Manson. The reservation has a population of 8,000 people; tribal headquarters are just south of Nespelem. The Colville Tribal Museum is located in Grand Coulee. Anglers will need to purchase special reservation permits from stores in nearby towns; call (509) 634-8845. Camping on the reservation also requires a permit; call (509) 634-4711.

History

The Colville Reservation is home to 12 different tribes—Southern Okanogan, Lakes, Colville, San Poil, Nespelem, Methow, Entiat, Chelan, Wenatchi, Moses/Columbia, Palus, and Nez Percé—all shoehorned together by President Grant's executive order of 1872. The reservation was greatly reduced in 1886, when the Moses-Columbia tribe refused to be placed on land west of the Okanogan River—away from their home along the Columbia River—and these lands were opened to settlement by non-Indians. The tribes' traditional lands once reached from the Cascades to the Rockies, and from southern British Columbia to Oregon. The tribes have some similarities in language and cultural background, but many people still retain a clear tribal identity. Ironically, the term Colville comes from Fort Colville, named for Andrew Colville. a London financier who never even reached America!

Scenic Drives

Two very scenic country drives are Hwy. 21 between Keller and Republic, and Bridge Creek/ Twin Lakes Rd. connecting Inchelium to Hwy. 21. The latter of these climbs west from Inchelium into remote hills covered with ponderosa pine and other evergreens, and past **Rainbow Beach Resort,** tel. (509) 722-5901, which offers cabins, tent and RV sites, boat rentals, and a store on mile-wide North Twin Lake. West of the lake, the narrow, winding road climbs through rounded mountains dense with trees but sliced by periodic clearcuts. It eventually descends from the trees into rolling hills covered in grass and sage as you reach the Nespelem area.

St. Mary's Mission

This Jesuit mission was founded in 1896 by Father Steven DeRouge to bring Catholicism to the Okanogan and Chelan Indians. DeRouge's presence met stiff resistance until he saved an Indian child who had fallen into the swift waters of Omak Creek. This act of mercy led Indian leaders to change their minds, and Chief Smitkin provided land to construct the mission. It began as a log cabin and gradually grew until two fires destroyed nearly everything early in this century.

A new church was completed in 1915, with local settlers and Indians cooperating in the building of the altar; the side altars were shipped around the Horn from France. Today the mission contains a mix of old and new buildings, including the Paschal Sherman Indian School, now run by the Colville tribe, not the Jesuits. Up the hill behind the church is an old graveyard decorated with a thicket of wooden crosses and even a carved wooden burro. The surrounding rocky, dry hills are covered with grass and sage.

To reach the mission, take Hwy. 155 east of Omak for four miles, then go 1.5 miles south. Open daily; tel. (509) 826-2097. The **Sunflower Festival** takes place in late May, with Indian food and games.

Inchelium

The free **Gifford Ferry** crosses Lake Roosevelt between Gifford and Inchelium, operating daily between 6:30 a.m. and 9:30 p.m. Hardly anything to the village of Inchelium, other than the Seem-Uss-Spooss Restaurant (the word means "What's in your heart?"), where you can snack on an Indian taco. **Hartmans Log Cabin Resort,** tel. (509) 722-3543, has cabin and motel units, plus RV hookups.

Nespelem Area

Chief Joseph, leader of the Nez Percé Indians during the famous retreat of 1877 (see the special topic "The Nez Percé War"), is buried in Nespelem (nes-PEEL-em). He, along with 150 other tribal members, was exiled here in 1884. The cemetery is on the north end of town; follow 10th St. uphill to reach it. The **Chief Joseph grave** is a simple white obelisk with a few offerings and bandannas decorating a nearby tree; the monument notes that Hin-Mah-Too-Yah-Lat-Kekt ("Thunder Rolling in the Mountains") died here

September 21, 1904. He was approximately 60 years old. The nearby land is not greatly changed from the day of his passing: wide open spaces of rolling grassy hills.

South of Nespelem is the **Colville Indian Agency,** tel. (509) 634-8835, headquarters for the reservation. Stop here for information on the reservation and the names of local artisans. Local beadwork is sold in the nearby **Trading Post Store.** Out front is the **Skolaskin Church,** built in 1874 at the behest of Chief Skolaskin, renowned for predicting a large earthquake in 1872 that caused a rock slide that briefly halted the flow of the Columbia. The log building was the first church on the Colville Reservation.

Events

Across the highway from the tribal offices is the Nespelem Community Center and a powwow circle that comes to life during the **4th of July Nespelem Powwow and All-Indian Rodeo,** a 10-day event with Indian dance competitions— some involving full regalia—along with drumming, "stick" gambling, and delicious Indian fry bread. The compound is bordered with dozens of tepees during the festivities. Do not enter the dance circle or take photos without asking. Another powwow is held in Nespelem in late September.

CHIEF JOSEPH DAM AREA

Chief Joseph Dam

Though overshadowed by the Grand Coulee to the east, the Chief Joseph Dam boasts a 2,000-foot-long powerhouse—largest in the world— and reaches over a mile across the Columbia River. It is the second biggest producer of hydropower in the nation (after Grand Coulee), supplying the electrical needs of 1.5 million people throughout the West. The dam was built in the 1950s, with a major addition in the 1970s. Water backed up behind the dam forms Rufus Woods Lake. The dam itself was named for Chief Joseph, famous leader of the Nez Percé Indians in the 1870s, who is buried on the nearby Colville Indian Reservation (see above). One has to wonder how he would respond to having a dam named in his "honor." In late summer you may see Indians from the area fishing below

the dam; unfortunately, no fish ladder was built around this massive dam, so all salmon runs above this point were wiped out.

You'll find vantage points of the dam from both sides of the river. A **visitors center,** tel. (509) 686-5501, open daily 9 a.m.-6 p.m. all year, is located near the center of the dam and is accessible from the north bank. From here you can peer through windows across the lineup of 27 massive generators and feel the rumble as they spin. A slide show describes the dam, and exhibits reveal the history of the region with an emphasis on hydropower. Most of the time it's a strange and sterile place with surveillance cameras watching your every move. In the summer, park rangers lead free hour-long tours of the dam at 10 a.m. and 2 p.m. A big wall map shows the 200 dams that block the Columbia River at points all along its basin. Outside, be sure to visit the trunnion bridge where you get an up-close view of the massive spillway gates.

Bridgeport

The town of Bridgeport (pop. 1,600) sits just west of Chief Joseph Dam. **The Y Motel,** tel. (509) 686-2002, has rooms for $35-55 s or d, including an outdoor pool and jacuzzi. They also operate a restaurant and lounge and have RV parking. There's a public **swimming pool** at Berryman Park. A **farmers market** comes to town Friday 9 a.m.-2 p.m. mid-June to early October; tel. (509) 686-3875. The big local event is **Bridgeport Daze,** with a parade, crafts market, barbecue, horseshoe tournament, and fun run on the first Saturday in June.

The land east of Bridgeport is not unlike Nevada or Utah, an arid plateau of grass and sage interrupted by scattered volcanic boulders deposited by glaciers during the ice ages, with the sky dominating the land. As you approach Grand Coulee Dam, the road is accompanied by long sets of electrical towers radiating outward to supply energy for the Northwest.

Bridgeport State Park

Three miles northeast of Bridgeport on Rufus Woods Lake, Bridgeport State Park offers boating, fishing, swimming, campsites ($11 tents, $16 RVs), and showers. The 750-acre park is an oasis of cottonwood and aspen trees surrounded by dark, beehive-shaped volcanic formations.

THE NEZ PERCÉ WAR

In 1877, the federal government tried to force the Nez Percé Indians under Chief White Bird and Chief Joseph onto a reservation so that white ranchers could have their lands in Washington's Blue Mountains and Oregon's Wallowa Valley. The Indians stubbornly refused, and tensions quickly mounted. A few drunk young men killed four whites, and subsequent raids led to the deaths of at least 14 more. The Army retaliated, but was turned back by the Nez Percé. Rather than face government reinforcements, more than 1,000 Nez Percé began an 1,800-mile flight in a desperate bid to reach Canada. A series of running battles followed as the Indians managed to confound the inept Army using their geographic knowledge and battle skills.

East of the newly established Yellowstone National Park in Wyoming, the Indians plotted a masterful escape from two columns of Army forces, feinting a move down the Shoshone River and then heading north along a route that left their pursuers gasping in amazement-straight up the narrow Clarks Fork Canyon, "where rocks on each side came so near together that two horses abreast could hardly pass." Finally, less than 40 miles from the international border with Canada, the Army caught up with the Nez Percé, and after a fierce battle, the tribe was forced to surrender (although 300 did make good their escape).

Chief Joseph's haunting words at the surrender still echo through the years: "Hear me, my chiefs, I am tired; my heart is sick and sad. From where the sun now stands, I will fight no more forever." Despite promises that they would be allowed to return home, the Nez Percé were hustled onto remote reservations in Oklahoma, Kansas, South Dakota, and Washington, while whites remained on their rich ancestral lands. Chief Joseph spent the rest of his life on the Washington's Colville Reservation and died in 1904, reportedly of a broken heart.

Keep your eyes open for rattlesnakes. The park is open April-Oct. and includes the nine-hole **Lakewood Golf Course** within its boundaries. During the summer, Army Corps of Engineers rangers give Saturday night campfire programs; call (509) 686-5501 for details.

Fort Okanogan State Park

Nine miles north of Bridgeport on Hwy. 17 near the intersection with Hwy. 97, Fort Okanogan State Park is open daily 10 a.m.-6 p.m. from mid-May to mid-September (no camping, alas). Enjoy a picnic lunch on the grassy lawn overlooking Lake Pateros and step inside the **interpretive center,** filled with interesting artifacts, displays, and dioramas of this historic fort.

Beneath the waters of Lake Pateros lies the site of Fort Okanogan, an historic fur-trading post established near the juncture of the Okanogan and Columbia Rivers. Begun in July of 1811 by David Thompson and other trappers working for John Jacob Astor's Pacific Fur Company, this was the first place to hoist the American flag in what would become Washington. The business proved lucrative at first; Okanogan Indians were given trade items worth $160 in exchange for pelts that brought $10,000 in the East! Despite this, supply problems, stiff competition, and the threat of war with England forced Astor to sell his operation to Canadian interests. In 1821, the fort joined the vast Hudson's Bay Company holdings, operating as a major shipping point for buffalo hides down the Columbia River. Hudson's Bay continued to operate the fort until 1860, when an influx of settlers and the waning fur trade led them to pull out. The fort sites were excavated by archaeologists in the 1950s and early '60s, prior to completion of Wells Dam. The old fort location—as with many historic and cultural sites—is now buried beneath a Columbia River reservoir. So history becomes a collection of artifacts in a small museum.

Brewster

The town of Brewster (pop. 1,600) sits right on Lake Pateros (Columbia River), a couple miles west from the mouth of Okanogan River. This is a rich agricultural area, with expansive apple, pear, and cherry orchards on the flats near the river mouth, plus additional orchards lining Hwy. 97 southwest of town. The region is also crowded with fruit processing plants. Stay at the appropriately named and modern **Apple Avenue**

Motel, tel. (509) 689-3000, for $53 s or $61 d. Cheaper digs (but the same owners) at **Brewster Motel,** 806 Bridge St., tel. (509) 689-2625, where rooms go for $45 s or $55 d. RV spaces are also available here. **Columbia Cove RV Park** has tent and RV spaces in town. Head to **Rock Gardens Park,** halfway between Brewster and Bridgeport on Hwy. 173, for more camping.

Because of an abundance of Spanish-speaking farm workers, Brewster is gaining a distinctly south-of-the-border flavor. **La Milpa Grocery** has fresh corn tortillas and delicious Mexican pastries made in their bakery across the street.

Mi Casita Restaurant, 702 Jay Ave., tel. (509) 689-2071, has excellent Mexican food, including homemade sopapillas, but you're more likely to meet other patrons speaking Spanish at the less pretentious **Alicia's Mexican Food** on Main Street. If this isn't enough, try one of three local taco wagons.

The main local event is **Bonanza Days,** held the third weekend of June, with hydroplane races, street dancing, and three-on-three basketball. In addition to swimming in Lake Pateros, Brewster has an outdoor **swimming pool** in the grassy city park along the lake.

OMAK AND OKANOGAN

Omak and Okanogan (oh-ka-NO-gan), the valley's largest cities, are strung along the west bank of the Okanogan River, separated only by name. The Colville Indian Reservation comes down to the river on the opposite bank, with Hwy. 97 following that side of the river.

Nestled between the east and west sections of the Okanogan National Forest, the twin towns serve as the commercial hub for a sparsely populated area dominated by apple orchards along the river valleys, plus logging, cattle grazing, and recreation in the national forest. Okanogan (pop. 2,400), the older of the two towns, serves as the county seat, while thriving Omak (pop. 4,000) is the place for groceries, gas, and other necessities. Omak is home to the state's first Wal-Mart (there are plenty more now). Both Omak and Okanogan are plain-vanilla, conservative, rough-at-the-edges towns, but recent years have seen an influx of migrant workers from south of the border, and a growing Hispanic influence.

The two towns have had a low-level feud ever since, and despite their proximity, local voters have steadfastly refused to combine operations. Because of this, Omak and Okanogan have separate schools, city governments, and services.

Omak was chartered in 1910, but was slow to develop until the Biles-Coleman Lumber Company built a sawmill in 1922; it eventually became today's Omak Wood Products. You can't miss the plume of white smoke billowing into the air at their lumber and plywood mill. Recent years have seen less timber harvesting on nearby Okanogan National Forest due to the spotted owl and salmon controversies, but Omak still runs on timber. The native-owned Colville Precision Pine Mill uses timber from the adjacent Colville Reservation.

Both town names are from native words. Okanogan is derived from the Salish Indian term, *Ocanuckane,* meaning "rendezvous," while Omak comes from the word *Omache,* meaning "good medicine."

HISTORY

The city of Okanogan came about shortly after this region was opened to non-Indian settlers in 1886. Frank Cummings built a trading post at the mouth of Salmon Creek, and the town grew up around him. Omak was established in 1907 when Dr. J.I. Pogue, a disgruntled resident of Okanogan (they refused to name the town after him), moved north to found his own settlement.

SIGHTS

The **Okanogan County Historical Museum,** 1410 2nd N in Okanogan, tel. (509) 422-4272, is open daily 11 a.m.-5 p.m. from mid-May to mid-September; donation. Inside are displays depicting pioneer life in the county; outside find a replica of an Old West village, along with a replica of the old firehall.

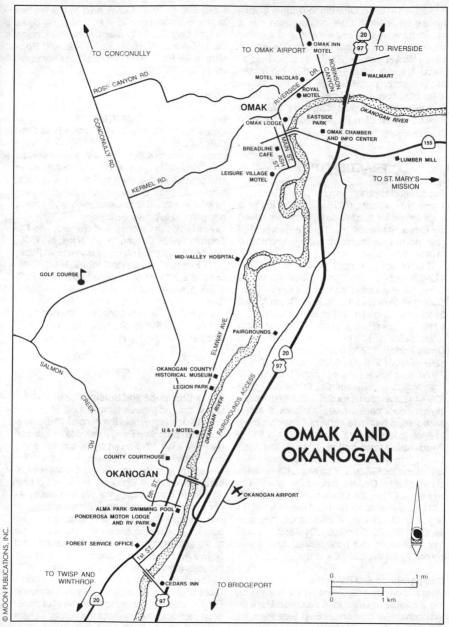

TO CONCONULLY

ROSS CANYON RD.

TO OMAK AIRPORT

OMAK INN
MOTEL

20
97

TO RIVERSIDE

ROBINSON CANYON

WALMART

MOTEL NICOLAS

RIVERSIDE DR.

ROYAL
MOTEL

OKANOGAN RIVER

CONCONULLY RD.

OMAK

EASTSIDE
PARK

OMAK LODGE

OMAK CHAMBER
AND INFO CENTER

MAIN ST.

155

BREADLINE
CAFE

ASH ST.

LUMBER MILL

KERMEL RD.

LEISURE VILLAGE
MOTEL

TO ST. MARY'S
MISSION

MID-VALLEY HOSPITAL

GOLF COURSE

ELMWAY AVE.

FAIRGROUNDS

SALMON

20
97

OKANOGAN COUNTY
HISTORICAL MUSEUM

FAIRGROUNDS ACCESS

LEGION PARK

OKANOGAN RIVER

CREEK

U & I MOTEL

RD.

COUNTY COURTHOUSE

**OMAK AND
OKANOGAN**

OKANOGAN

5th ST.

OKANOGAN AIRPORT

ALMA PARK SWIMMING POOL

PONDEROSA MOTOR LODGE
AND RV PARK

FOREST SERVICE OFFICE

1st ST.

© MOON PUBLICATIONS, INC.

TO TWISP AND
WINTHROP

20

CEDARS INN

97

TO BRIDGEPORT

0   1 mi

0   1 km

Built in 1915, the **Okanogan County Courthouse** on 3rd and Oak in Okanogan has a Mediterranean-style red-tile roof and a gothic castle-like exterior. A **mural** on the side of Main Street Market features a painting of the Suicide Race. A walking trail—marked by big horseshoes denoting past Suicide Race winners—leads from downtown Omak to East Side Park. Five miles east of Omak is **St. Mary's Mission** (see **Colville Indian Reservation** for more on this interesting historical place).

PRACTICALITIES

Accommodations

There are no nearby B&Bs. Be sure to make reservations far in advance if you plan to attend the Omak Stampede and Suicide Race in August. Accommodations are arranged from least to most expensive.

U & I Motel, 838 2nd N, Okanogan, tel. (509) 422-2920, is a clean little place along the Okanogan River with rooms for $28 s or $35 d including microwaves and fridges. **Royal Motel,** 514 E. Riverside Dr. in Omak, tel. (509) 826-5715, is a clean older place with reasonable rates: $29 s or $34 d. The newly remodeled **Omak Lodge,** 122 N. Main in Omak, tel. (509) 826-0400 or (888) 700-6625, charges $32 s or $36 d, and has an outdoor pool. **Leisure Village Motel,** 630 Okoma Dr., Omak, tel. (509) 826-4442, has rooms for $36 s or $40 d, including an indoor pool, jacuzzi, and sauna. **Motel Nicholas,** a half-mile north of Omak on Hwy. 215, tel. (509) 826-4611, charges $37 s or $42 d. **Ponderosa Motor Lodge,** 1034 S. 2nd Ave., Okanogan, tel. (509) 422-0400, is a nice place with rooms for $37-39 s or $40-42 d. Kitchenettes are available. **Cedars Inn,** at the junction of Highways 97 and 20, Okanogan, tel. (509) 422-6431, has an outdoor pool and rooms for $50 s or $55 d. **Omak Inn,** 912 Koala Dr. in Omak, tel. (509) 826-3822 or (800) 204-4800, is a new motel with an indoor pool, jacuzzi, and fitness center. Rates are $55-69 s or d.

Campgrounds and RV Parks

Riverside camping ($10) and RV hookups ($12) are available at Okanogan's **Legion Park** on the north end of town and at **East Side Park,** tel. (509) 826-1170, in Omak next to the visitors center. Both are open all year. Private RV parks include **Log Cabin Trailer Court,** 509 Okoma Dr. in Omak, tel. (509) 826-4462, and **Ponderosa RV Park,** 1034 2nd Ave. S in Okanogan, tel. (509) 422-0400.

Food

Get the finest local breakfasts and killer cheeseburgers at **Our Place Cafe,** 19 E. Apple in Omak, tel. (509) 826-4811. Omak's **Breadline Cafe,** 102 S. Ash St., tel. (509) 826-5836, is *the* place for lunch in the area, with soups, salads, sandwiches, and espresso. The restaurant is also popular for breakfast and dinner. The decor in this old soda pop bottling warehouse is of funky mismatched chairs and tables, aging signs, and painted exposed beams.

For Mexican lunches and dinners, head to **Tequila's,** 635 Okoma Dr. in Omak, tel. (509) 826-5417. Get good pizzas at **Hometown Pizza,** 2237 Elmway in Okanogan, tel. (509) 422-0744. **Leonel's** 5 N. Main in Omak, tel. (509) 826-3380, has a varied menu that includes steaks, Italian, and even French dishes.

Legion Park in Okanogan has a **farmers market** June to mid-Oct.; open Tuesday 4-6 p.m. and Saturday 9 a.m.-noon; tel. (509) 422-4128

EVENTS

Omak Stampede and Suicide Race

Omak is world-famous for its annual Stampede and Suicide Race, held the second weekend in August at East Side Park. Festivities include two parades, a big Western art show, carnival, and a major professional rodeo. During the week of the Stampede, a major attraction is the **Indian Encampment** in East Side Park. Hundreds of Indians come from all over the West to live in tepees, take part in traditional dance contests, or play the stick games—a form of gambling. (Be sure to request permission before taking photos at the encampment.) The **Omak Western and Native Art Show** runs during the stampede, and includes a quick-draw and salmon barbecue.

The main event features four chaotic horse races down a steep slope, across the Okanogan River, and into the crowded arena. Most of the 20 or so participants come from the nearby Colville

Indian Reservation, and this is a tradition that has gone on for more than 60 years. The dangerous downhill section often creates pileups that injure both riders and horses, sometimes leading to the death of the horse. This has led to vocal opposition from animal-rights organizations. Locals defend the race as a part of Indian and Western traditions. A shuttle bus provides service between Omak and Okanogan during the Stampede. Tickets for the Stampede are available in advance by calling (509) 826-1002 or (800) 933-6625.

Other Events

Okanogan Days on the first weekend of May features a parade, music, and airport fly-in. The **Okanogan County Fair** at the fairgrounds in Omak brings more rodeo action, horse racing, a livestock auction, and musical entertainment in early September. Another popular Omak event is the **Cowboy Poetry Jubilee** in mid-March.

OTHER PRACTICALITIES

The Omak Performing Arts Center is the site of all sorts of events through the year, including concerts by **Okanogan Valley Orchestra and Chorus.** The **Breadline Cafe,** 102 S. Ash in Omak, tel. (509) 826-5836, has folk, jazz, rock, or R&B most nights. For country music head to **Cariboo Inn,** 233 Queen St. in Okanogan, tel. (509) 422-6109, or **The Western Restaurant,** 1930 N. 2nd Ave. in Okanogan, tel. (509) 422-3499. Empty your wallet in the slot machines at **Okanogan Bingo & Casino,** on Hwy. 97, tel. (800) 559-4643.

Recreation

Swim at the Olympic-size outdoor pools in Omak's East Side Park, or in Okanogan's Alma Park. The Okanogan River is a popular place for tubing in the summer months. **The Bike Shop,** 137 S. 2nd Ave. in Okanogan, tel. (509) 422-0710, rents bikes. Play golf at the **Okanogan Valley Golf Club,** just west of town, tel. (509) 826-9902.

Loup Loup Ski Bowl, between Okanogan and Twisp on Hwy. 20, has Alpine skiing on a 1,250-foot vertical drop. (See **Methow Valley** for specifics.)

Information and Services

The **Omak Visitor Information Center,** 401 Omak Ave., tel. (509) 826-1880 or (800) 225-6625, has a ton of local info, along with videos on the Suicide Race. Open Mon.-Fri. 9 a.m.-5 p.m., Saturday 10 a.m.-4 p.m., and Sunday 11 a.m.-2 p.m. Memorial Day to mid-Oct.; Mon.-Fri. 9 a.m.-5 p.m. the rest of the year. Okanogan has a summer-only **visitor information center** in Legion Park on the north end of town, tel. (509) 422-9882. The Okanogan National Forest **Supervisors Office,** 1240 S. 2nd Ave. in Okanogan, tel. (509) 826-3275, has hiking and camping information for the Okanogan highland country. It's open Mon.-Fri. 7:45 a.m.-4:30 p.m. all year. I can't vouch for their hair-trimming ability, but **Wak N' Yak Beauty Salon** in Okanogan wins first prize in the name-freak category.

Looking for local transportation? Try hitchhiking. The Omak/Okanogan area has neither bus service nor commercial air service of any kind!

OKANOGAN VALLEY

Okanogan Valley is a dry area surrounded by mountains, with 28 inches of annual snowfall and a sizzling hot, dry summer. Major irrigation projects make this an ideal place to grow apples, pears, peaches, and cherries. The valley served as a major route to British Columbia's Cariboo gold fields in 1857-58, and in later years the 800-mile "Cariboo Trail" was used by cowboys to drive beef from the Yakima Valley to the mining towns. The old trail is now Highway 97, a busy north-south route along the wide Okanogan Valley. The highway cuts through most of the major towns—Okanogan, Omak, Tonasket, and Oroville—before entering Canada at a 24-hour border station. East of the valley are the Okanogan Highlands, a low range of mountains and hills covered with forests and rangeland. The highlands are essentially unpeopled, with a few small towns; only Republic is large enough to have all the services.

CONCONULLY

The pretty little burg of Conconully (pop. 170) is 22 miles northwest of Omak, and sits at an elevation of 2,300 feet, making for summertime temperatures that are much cooler than in the steamy Okanogan Valley. Conconully (derived from the Okanogan Indian word for "money hole," a reference to the valuable beaver pelts found here) has a couple of stores and restaurants, along with several popular lakeside resorts.

Conconully sits between the natural Conconully Lake and the unnatural Conconully Reservoir. Built in 1910, the latter was the first Bureau of Reclamation irrigation project in America. The **Outhouse Race** in January is one of those wacky events that attracts folks to Conconully from around the region. The town also has a fun **Fourth of July** parade and street fair.

Accommodations and Food

There are three comfortable resorts around Conconully: **Conconully Lake Resort,** tel. (509) 826-0813 or (800) 850-0813, with cottages for $30-50; **Liar's Cove Resort,** tel. (509) 826-1288, with cabins for $40-45; and **Shady Pines Resort,** tel. (509) 826-2287, with cabins for $55-65. Other lodging can be found at **Jack's RV Park & Motel,** tel. (509) 826-0132 or (800) 893-5668, for $62 s or d; **Maple Flats RV Park and Resort,** tel. (509) 826-4231 or (800) 683-1180, with apartments for $45 d; **Kozy Kabins & RV Park,** tel. (509) 826-6780 or (888) 502-2246, for $35-42 d; and **Conconully Motel,** tel. (509) 826-1610, for $35 d. **Gibson's North Fork Lodge,** tel. (509) 826-1475 or (800) 555-1690, has large new cabins ($45-55 for up to six).

Food

Several of Conconully's resorts have restaurants. Get good steaks and ribs from **Trails End Steak House,** tel. (509) 826-4893. **Salmon Creek Inn,** tel. (509) 826-1037, is well-known for Mexican meals, but also makes burgers, pizzas, and other fare.

Campgrounds

Five free Forest Service campgrounds are within nine miles of Conconully; closest is **Cottonwood Campground,** just two miles out Forest Rd. 38. The others are **Sugarloaf, Oriole, Kerr, and Salmon Meadows.** Many of the above lodging places also have tent and RV sites, as does Conconully State Park, below.

Conconully State Park

This cozy state park sits along the shore of Conconully Reservoir and contains a log cabin and a sod-roofed replica of the first Okanogan County courthouse; Conconully was the county seat from 1889 to 1914. The reservoir is a popular place for boating, fishing, and swimming. Trees surround spacious grassy lawns that make fine picnicking spots; take the half-mile nature trail for a relaxing stroll. Campsites are $10 (no RV hookups); open mid-April through October, and on weekends and holidays the rest of the year. Call (509) 826-7408 for more information.

RIVERSIDE

Just eight miles north of Omak, the little settlement of Riverside (pop. 250) is a cool and quiet place to relax along the Okanogan River. This was the head of upriver navigation until the railroad rolled through this area in 1914.

The main attraction here is **Detro's Triangle L Western Store,** tel. (509) 826-2200, where you'll find an amazing selection of Western gear: saddles, Indian jewelry, ranch clothes, fancy belt buckles, cowboy boots, and fashionable Western wear. Be sure to also keep your eyes open for the fun collection of whirligigs filling a yard on the west side of town.

Hidden Hills Resort, one mile from Fish Lake on Fish Lake Rd., tel. (509) 486-1895 or (800) 468-1890, has fine country lodging in an 1890s-era lodge. Rates are $75-105 s or d, including breakfast. Camp at **Margie's Riverside RV Park,** tel. (509) 826-5810, or **Glenwood RV-Park,** tel. (509) 826-5228. **Molly's Cafe** serves breakfast and lunch, with homemade pies, breads, and cinnamon rolls.

North of Riverside, Hwy. 97 heads away from the river through dry sage and grassy hills topped by open stands of ponderosa pine, before dropping back to the Okanogan River near Tonasket. From Tonasket all the way to Oroville both sides of the highway are crowded with irrigated apple orchards, laden with fruit by late summer. Old wooden barns in varying states of repair decorate the back roads.

TONASKET

This town of a thousand folks was named for the Okanogan Chief To-nas-ket, the first successful Indian cattleman in this part of Washington and a strong supporter of peace with whites. The town of Tonasket (TAWN-a-sket) is a minor timber, cattle, and apple orchard center.

Accommodations

The **Red Apple Inn** at Hwy. 97 and 1st, tel. (509) 486-2119, charges $35-44 s or $45-48 d. **Junction Motel,** 23 6th St., tel. (509) 486-4500, has rooms for $44-66 s or d. They also have a laundromat with showers. **Park RVs** in the lot next to the visitors information center on the north end of town for $10; showers are available at Junction Motel.

Three resorts lie northwest of Tonasket near the tiny settlement of **Loomis: Spectacle Lake Resort,** 12 miles northwest on Loomis Hwy., tel. (509) 223-3433, has $25 rustic cabins, $45 motel rooms, and a three-bedroom house for $105; and **Spectacle Falls Resort,** another mile northwest on Loomis Hwy., tel. (509) 223-4141, has mobile home units (!) that sleep four for $50-60. RV hookups are also available. **Rainbow Resort,** 14 miles northwest on Loomis Hwy., tel. (509) 223-3700, has more RV and tent sites.

Food

Okanogan River Coop 21 W. 4th, tel. (509) 486-4188, sells natural foods, local organic produce, bulk foods, sandwiches, and coffees. Picnic tables next to the store make a nice place to munch. This is the center for the counterculture crowd in the area. Beyond this, you can try **Don's Drive-In** for burgers, or **Hometown Pizza** for hometown pizzas.

Be sure to stop for fresh apples and other fruits at one of the several fruit stands between Tonasket and Oroville. The **Tonasket Farmers Market,** (509) 486-1328, comes to Triangle Park Friday 3-6 p.m. June-October.

Events

Tonasket Founders Day Rodeo the first weekend of June includes a big PRCA-sanctioned rodeo, parade, fun run, and cowboy breakfast, followed later that month by the **Tonasket Bluegrass Festival.** The main event of the summer is the **Sagebrush Logger's Tourney** with all sorts of logging contests on the last weekend of August. In late May or early June, a **Friendship Pony Express Ride** takes place between Tonasket and Princeton, B.C.

Skiing

About 12 miles northeast of Tonasket, **Sitzmark,** tel. (509) 488-3323, is a family place with a 680-foot vertical drop served by a chair, poma, and rope tow, plus six km of groomed cross-country trails; open Wed.-Sun. and holidays. The area generally opens just after Christmas and charges $15-18. Call (509) 486-2700 for information; the snow can be marginal at times. Nearby is the

Havillah Lutheran Church, built in 1910 and still in use. **Highland Park Sno-Park,** 10 miles northeast of Tonasket, has 12 km of groomed cross-country trails.

Information and Services

Get local facts at the tiny **Tonasket Visitor Information Center,** on the north end of town, tel. (509) 486-2154. Ask here about tours of local apple warehouses. The **Tonasket Ranger Station,** tel. (509) 486-2186, is open Mon.-Fri. 7:45 a.m.-4:30 p.m. all year. Stop here for a guide to local hiking trails. During the summer, hop in the water at the outdoor **swimming pool** in History Park next to the river.

Highland Stage Company, tel. (509) 486-4699, has two- and four-day stagecoach rides over the Okanogan Highlands.

OROVILLE

Oroville (pop. 1,500) lies four miles south of the Canadian border on Hwy. 97, near the south shore of Lake Osoyoos, in a region of orchards and pine-topped hills. It was first settled in 1858, shortly after gold was discovered in British Columbia's Cariboo region, and its name was based on the Spanish word for gold, "oro." The "Cariboo Trail" passed right through town, and this became the last chance to get American supplies before crossing the border. Today, the town survives on a sawmill, cross-border traffic, and fruit orchards. The local economy has recently been in the doldroms, hurt by the weak Canadian dollar.

Apple trees grew well here, and orchards are still a prominent feature in the valley; some 10,000 acres of farmland are irrigated along the Okanogan River from Oroville to Tonasket. An old irrigation flume follows the highway north from Oroville to the border. Local farmers have diversified in recent years, also planting nectarines, pears, apricots, peaches, and cherries. (By the way, the Okanogan River is called the Okanagan River once it crosses into Canada, another of the strange spelling quirks that pop up throughout this region.)

Sights

A mile north of Oroville on Hwy. 97, **Osoyoos Lake State Veterans Memorial Park** offers fishing, swimming, water-skiing, and concessions on a natural lake shared with our Canadian neighbors. The east side of Osoyoos Lake has apple and pear trees planted in the early 1860s by Hiram F. "Okanogan" Smith, the first permanent white resident of the area. Smith brought his trees in from Fort Hope, British Columbia, by backpack. Several of the 135-plus year old trees are still bearing fruit.

Palmer Lake, 18 miles west of Oroville, a popular spot with fishermen, is managed by the Bureau of Land Management; a boat launch and picnic area are at the south end of the lake.

The **Old Depot Museum** documents local history and includes considerable railroad memorabilia. Open Tuesday and Thursday 10 a.m.-4 p.m. in the summer.

Accommodations and Campgrounds

Camaray Motel, tel. (509) 476-3684, has comfortable rooms, an outdoor pool, and kitchenettes for $33 s or $39 d. **Red Apple Inn,** Hwy. 97 and 18th, tel. (509) 476-3694, has rooms for $33 s or $45 d, including an outdoor pool and riverfront picnic area.

Visit **Sun Cove Resort** on two-mile-long Wannacut Lake (11 miles southwest of Oroville) for a delightful family retreat with cozy cabins ($60 d), hiking, swimming, and fishing, plus tent and RV spaces; a swimming pool; boat, kayak, and canoe rentals; and guided horse-trail rides. Open April-Oct.; call (509) 476-2223. More RV slots can be found at **Orchard RV Park, Eisen's RV Park,** or the parking lot at **Prince's Center.** Much better is **Osoyoos Lake State Veterans Memorial Park,** tel. (509) 476-3321, a mile north of town, with tent sites for $11 (no RV hookups). Open April-Oct., plus weekends and holidays the rest of the year. The campground is often full all summer long; make advance reservations ($6 extra) by calling (800) 452-5687.

Food

The dining options in Oroville are not especially noteworthy. Start out with a cup of java at **Espresso Expressions,** on Main and Appleway. **Hometown Pizza,** 1315 Main St., tel. (509) 476-2410, makes quite good sandwiches, pasta, and pizza, plus steaks on weekends.

Oroville is home to the huge **Prince's Center** grocery store, very popular with Canadians in search of lower prices. Get fresh local fruits and juices from the cooler at **Golddigger Apples,** 1220 Ironwood, tel. (509) 476-3646. Oroville also has a **Farmers Market** in the city park on Saturday 8-10 a.m. May-August.

Other Practicalities

The second weekend of May means **Oroville May Festival,** a two-day party featuring a pa-rade, pancake breakfast, Maypole dancing, bass tournament, arts and crafts, and basketball. **Fao's** 1412 Main, tel. (509) 476-4142, has live music most weekends.

The **Washington State Information Center,** tel. (509) 476-2739, is along Hwy. 97 on the north end of town and is open daily 8 a.m.-6 p.m. May-August, and daily with reduced hours the rest of the year.

OKANOGAN HIGHLANDS

Okanogan National Forest

The 1.7-million acre Okanogan National Forest reaches from the Methow Valley to the Canadian border and offers a plethora of recreational activities, including 1,600 miles of hiking trails, dozens of campgrounds, and hundreds of miles of cross-country skiing and mountain biking trails. Included within these boundaries are vast reaches of ponderosa pine, Douglas fir, and western larch forests, plus numerous peaks topping 7,000 feet. Two wilderness areas, Pasayten and Lake Chelan-Sawtooth are found within the forest boundaries. Forest headquarters is in Okanogan at 1240 S. 2nd Ave., tel. (509) 422-2704; stop here for backcountry permits, maps, or other information. Ranger district offices are located in Tonasket, tel. (509) 486-2186, Twisp, tel. (509) 997-2131, and Winthrop, (509) 996-2266.

Molson

The Oroville-Toroda Creek Rd. cuts east from Oroville to Chesaw, climbing a canyon and emerging into open rolling grass hills with caps of western larch, Douglas fir, and ponderosa pine. Scattered ranch houses dot these hills. After eight miles, a side road leads five miles north to Molson, Washington's best known almost-ghost town, a delightful place in a wildly remote setting. Only a handful of folks still live here, surrounded by pieces of the past and the expansive land.

In the early 1900s, Molson became a major shipping point along the Great Northern Railroad, providing supplies for ranchers and miners, and sending their production to market. A spat over land—a local farmer claimed the town was entirely on his property—forced everyone to move a half-mile north, leaving behind the buildings of Old Molson. New Molson declined when the railroad stopped running in the late '20s.

Old Molson town consists of eight weathered log and clapboard structures from early in this century, including a false-fronted bank, shingle mill, homestead cabin, and assay office. Inside are collections of antiques and historic photos from the area; outside are old wagons, threshers, and fascinating aging farm equipment. The site is open April-December.

The **Molson Museum** is housed in a three-story brick schoolhouse a quarter mile up the road. Inside, find antique hand tools, historic photos, and a collection of artifacts from the area's rich mining history. The museum is open daily 10 a.m.-5 p.m. from Memorial Day to Labor Day. Volunteers serve cookies and tea and will tell you about the area's rich past.

Chesaw

Tiny Chesaw consists of something like 30 people in a smattering of homes, along with a store, cafe, and abandoned old buildings. The town was named for Joe "Chee-saw," a Chinese settler who, with his Indian wife, constructed a cabin along Meyers Creek in the 1880s. An influx of gold miners and prospectors led to establishment of a town around this cabin. Today Chesaw is in the center of summer homes, recreational cabins, and ranches. The town also has a very popular **Chesaw Rodeo** and fireworks on July 4th weekend.

Be sure to stop in the false-fronted **Chesaw Tavern,** where the ceiling is carpeted with dollar bills, the signs are pro-logging, and the beer is always cold. Hang around awhile and you're bound to meet "Chesaw Charlie," a former accountant who gave up the city life, grew a long white beard, rides around on a burro, and formed the "Church of the Utterly Indifferent." He'll be happy to perform marriage ceremonies.

Chesaw Vicinity

Four Forest Service campgrounds—**Beth Lake, Lost Lake, Bonaparte,** and **Beaver Lake**—are located south of Chesaw on the back way to Wauconda. They are open mid-May to mid-September and cost $5-7. **Big Tree Botanical Area** is a mile northeast of Lost Lake Campground (seven miles south of Chesaw) and includes enormous western larch (tamarack) trees. A short interpretive trail leads through the forest.

East of Chesaw, quiet country roads take you along bucolic Toroda Creek and Kettle River lined with tall riparian forests and populated by

hunters each fall. The land is marked with country homes and farmsteads, irrigated pastures, hilltop pine trees, open meadows, and grazing cattle. It's a fantastic place for bike riding, especially in the fall when leaves turn a brilliant yellow. During Prohibition, this part of Washington was a major center for smuggling Canadian liquor across the border.

Stop at **Kettle River Pottery,** tel. (509) 779-4695, for fine handmade pieces (some of their work is in the Smithsonian), or take a break by cutting north to see the Ranald MacDonald grave.

Ranald MacDonald Grave

Hidden away in this remote corner of Washington, and just two miles south of the Canadian border station at **Ferry** (open 9 a.m.-5 p.m. daily), is a hillside Indian cemetery overlooking the narrow Kettle River Valley. A monument marks the grave of Ranald MacDonald, an explorer who helped change history. MacDonald was born in 1824 at a Hudson's Bay Company fur-trading post near Astoria. His parents were Princess Raven—daughter of a Chinook Indian Chief—and the Scottish-American pioneer Archibald MacDonald. In Fort Vancouver, the young man became fascinated with Japan—a nation closed to all foreigners—and learned the language from a pair of sailors. While sailing off the coast of Japan in 1848, he intentionally capsized his sailboat. After making it to shore, he was taken prisoner but eventually gained acceptance by the Japanese people and was allowed to travel and teach English. He was "rescued" from Japan a year later, and continued his travels around the globe to Asia, Europe, as well as gold mining settlements in Australia and Alaska, before returning to Fort Colvile in Washington. MacDonald died in 1894, in the arms of his favorite niece; his last words were "Sayonara, Sayonara."

Ranald MacDonald's real heritage was as the first foreigner to teach English to the Japanese and the first to promote ties with the United States. One of his students, Monyama Einsouke, served as interpreter for Commander Matthew Perry's vital trip to Japan in 1854. Although Ranald MacDonald is virtually unknown in America, he is revered in Japan, and pilgrims occasionally come to this remote grave site to pay homage. A memorial to him now stands on Rishiri Island, Japan—the place he came ashore.

East of here is the **Danville Port of Entry,** where a single building is occupied by both U.S. and Canadian customs agents. It is open 8 a.m. to midnight every day.

CURLEW

Another podunk town surrounded by grand country is Curlew, approximately 20 miles north of Republic on Hwy. 21 and 10 miles from the Canadian border. Canadian radio stations dominate the airwaves in this part of Washington; tune in for a different perspective on the world, and a change of pace from Rush Limbaugh's incessant whining south of the border.

Sights

The pretty little **St. Patrick Mission Church** (1906) stands on the north end of town, and a genuine **country store** (1902) lures you inside to poke around. Get an espresso—this *is* still Washington after all—at the art shop, check out the Marlin parked in front of the funky secondhand shop, or step into the saloon for a meal or brew (one of the three bars and a liquor store in tiny Curlew!).

The **Hotel Ansorge Museum,** tel. (509) 779-4955, is a big corner hotel built in 1903 and filled with original furnishings. The building is on the National Register of Historic Places and is open weekends 1-5 p.m., with free tours. Henry Ford once spent a night here; his signature can still be seen in the 1917 register. Also in the building are a country store and cafe. Chief Tonasket (c. 1822-1891), for whom the town of Tonasket is named, is buried just north of Curlew on Vulcan Mountain Road. A house he built stands nearby.

Practicalities

Dine on big steaks, prime rib, and sweet desserts at **Riverside Bar & Grill,** tel. (509) 779-4813, Curlew's best eatery. Open for dinners only. It's a popular resting place for travelers. Stay at **Blue Cougar Motel and Bar,** or stop by for live bands on weekends. A few miles south of Curlew is **Malo General Store,** built in 1903 and packed with everything you might need.

Curlew Lake State Park

Located on the eastern shore of Curlew Lake, and 12 miles south of Curlew (nine miles north of Republic), this pretty little park has attractive shady campsites ($10 tents, $16 RVs) and good fishing and swimming. The park, tel. (509) 775-3592, is open April-October. Private resorts along the lake include: **Black Beach Resort,** tel. (509) 775-3989; **Tiffany's Resort,** tel. (509) 775-3152; **Pine Point Resort,** tel. (509) 775-3643; and **Wolfgang's Riverview Inn,** tel. (509) 779-4252.

Auto and Truck Museum

Four miles south of Curlew is the surprising Auto and Truck Museum, tel. (509) 779-4987, open daily 2-6 p.m. May-Sept., or by appointment; donation. A commodious aluminum building houses dozens of old vehicles, including a beautifully restored 1928 Ford Phaeton owned by

Walter Brennen (and used in several movies), a 1925 Howard Cooper (built in Spokane, and one of four in existence), and the smallest legal car ever built—the Orange Peel. All sorts of other oddities add to this wonderful collection—maintained by local car buffs—the only such museum in Washington. Even more amazing is that all the cars still run.

WAUCONDA

The drive east from Tonasket on Hwy. 20 follows Bonaparte Creek past old ranches into a beautiful valley bordered by wooded mountains. It's a great drive with little traffic, and one of the few places in Washington without the uglification that rapid development brings. Wauconda— about halfway between Tonasket and Republic—is literally a blink-and-you-missed-it town, with just a couple of buildings clustered around the combination restaurant, general store, video shop, gas station, and post office. Join the locals at a table in the small dining room overlooking the valley below. Surprisingly good food is served three meals a day, including burgers, shakes, steaks, prime rib, and even Chinese meals on weekends. Well worth the drive! Call (509) 486-4010 for hours.

Bonaparte Lake Resort, tel. (509) 486-2828, has rustic cabins for $23-38 d. Get to the lake by heading three miles west from Wauconda on

Hwy. 20, and then six miles north on Forest Rd. 32. Bring your own linen, towels, and kitchen utensils. The restaurant here makes the finest steaks in the area.

REPUBLIC

Backdropped by forested hillsides, Republic (pop. 1,000) is one of the few real mining and logging towns remaining in Washington, with an active gold mine run by Echo Bay Mining. Gold has been mined in the area almost continuously since John Welty discovered it on Granite Creek on February 20, 1896, attracting an influx of miners. Eureka Gulch and the surrounding countryside proved to contain some of the richest gold ore in the world. The Republic Mine produced $300,000 worth of gold in its first year, and the local paper reported that in May, "Large quantities of whiskey, flour, and other necessities arrived during the week." By the summer of 1898, Republic was one of the largest towns in eastern Washington. Things have calmed down a bit, but it is still the only incorporated town in Ferry County.

Today mining, along with a busy Vaagen Bros. Lumber mill, are the town's largest employers, but tourism is growing because of the hiking, camping, fishing, and hunting opportunities in the Okanogan Highlands. In the last few years downtown has undergone something of a re-

kids at Boot Hill Fossil Site, Republic

DON PITCHER

naissance, with a new motel and other buildings adapting the Old West look. Despite the changes, Republic remains an unpretentious blue-collar town with a split personality. Many folks are of the don't-tread-on-my-logging-rights school, but the community also has a post-hippie greenie crowd. This is reflected in the two radio stations you'll hear in town; one is C&W; on the other you'll hear an eclectic mix.

Stonerose Interpretive Center

A popular place for visitors is the Stonerose Interpretive Center, named for a 50-million-year-old fossil of an extinct rose found at a nearby rockpit. Many other plants, fish, and insects have been found here; they were deposited in an ancient lakebed. Stonerose, tel. (509) 775-2295, is open Tues.-Sat. 10 a.m.-5 p.m., May-October. It has displays of fossils found at the site, and literature on fossils.

Also in the same building is the **Republic Historical Center** with old photos lining the walls and a fine small gift shop selling local arts and crafts.

The public is invited to dig fossils at the **Boot Hill Fossil Site** on the northern edge of town ($2.50 per person or $5 for families), but you must get permission through the Stonerose Center and can only keep three fossils. Hammers and chisels may be rented here ($3).

Accommodations

Triangle J Ranch, 423 Old Kettle Falls Rd., tel. (509) 775-3933, is a friendly and well-maintained private hostel with dorm accommodations for $11 pp, plus a hot tub, outdoor pool, and kitchen. Call ahead to be sure of a place in mid-summer. Campsites ($8) are always available.

Northern Inn, 852 S. Clark, tel. (509) 775-3371 or (888) 801-1068, is an attractive new place with clean and comfortable rooms for $40 s or $44 d. Kitchenettes are also available. **Klondike Motel,** 150 N. Clark Ave., tel. (509) 775-3555, charges $38-40 s, $40-44 d, and has kitchenettes available. The **Frontier Inn,** 979 S. Clark Ave., tel. (509) 775-3361, charges $36 s, $39 d, and has a sauna and jacuzzi.

K-Diamond-K Ranch, tel. (509) 775-3536, is a friendly, family owned cattle ranch on 30,000 acres where guests go on horseback rides and hikes or just enjoy being outdoors. Stay in four large rooms with shared bath, and savor three hearty meals a day.

Campgrounds and RV Parks

Camp at **Ferry County Fairgrounds,** three and a half miles east of town on Hwy. 20. Showers are available; open summers only. More RV sites at Cottonwood Motel and **Miller RV Park,** 584 W. Curlew Lake Rd., tel. (509) 775-1039. The nearest Forest Service sites are approximately 15 miles southwest of town: **Ferry Lake Campground** and **Swan Lake Campground;** both open May-September. There are groomed **cross-country ski trails** here during the winter months. Closer camping can be found at **Curlew Lake State Park,** nine miles north.

Food

One place stands out on the Republic eating scene, **Ferry County Co-op,** 34 N. Clark Ave., tel. (509) 775-3754, a counterculture store with an earthy bakery and a surprisingly good serve-yourself deli. Come here for a filling buffet breakfast or lunch, or to stock up on groceries and the latest environmental news.

The **Republic Drug Store** at 6th and Clark has a genuine old-fashioned corner drug store; they've been in business since 1904. Another historic building houses **Carla's Cafe** 644 S. Clark Ave., tel. (509) 775-2096, where the menu includes the standard American faves: steaks, burgers, fried chicken, pork chops, and roast turkey sandwiches. **The Other Place,** 645 S. Clark Ave., tel. (509) 775-2907, has the best local breakfasts. A few doors away is **Back Alley Pizza,** tel. (509) 775-3500, the local pizza joint. Good Mexican meals in a fun setting at **Esther's Restaurant,** 90 N. Clark, tel.(509) 775-2088.

Events

Prospector's Days, held the second weekend of June, is the main local event, with a parade, golf tournament, crafts show, pancake feed, rodeo, stock car races, and even a cattle drive. Republic's **Fourth of July** festivities include a big picnic in the park.

The **Ferry County Fair** is held on the fairgrounds three and a half miles east of Republic on Labor Day weekend. This is one of the oldest fairs in the state, begun in the early 1900s as a chance to race horses. Today it includes 4-H demonstrations, livestock auctions, a parade, live entertainment, and, of course, horse racing.

Recreation

The Colville National Forest **Republic Ranger District** office is at 180 N. Jefferson, tel. (509) 775-3305. They have detailed brochures on hiking and mountain biking routes in the area, including the popular **Lakes Area Mt. Bike Loop** south of town and the Sherman Pass area to the east. Ask here about the "Mystery Man Trees" on North Namankin Creek, images of a man emblazoned on trees.

For an easy and very scenic walk, take the half-mile hike to **Nine Mile Falls.** The trailhead is southeast of Republic; get directions from the Forest Service.

Information

Republic's **Visitor Center** is next to the Stonerose Center (see above), and is open Tues.-Sat. 10 a.m.-4 p.m. mid-April through Oct.; tel. (509) 775-3387. Call ahead for tours of Republic's **Vaagen Bros. Lumber Mill,** tel. (509) 775-3774.

OVER SHERMAN PASS

From Republic, Hwy. 20 climbs easily into Colville National Forest through mixed forests of western larch (these turn a brilliant yellow each fall), Douglas fir, ponderosa pine, lodgepole pine, and aspen. The ascent tops out at **Sherman Pass,** the state's highest at 5,575 feet. In spite of the elevation, you won't see dramatic snowcapped peaks, just thousands of acres of forested hills. A 10-minute hike leads to fine views of lands to the east. Stop here for a pleasant picnic among the larch trees.

Hiking

At the pass, a side road leads to a trailhead for the **Kettle Crest Trail,** an excellent 30-mile-long hike that cuts north over the summit of the Kettle River Range. The area is popular with back-country skiers in the winter.

Two miles up the Kettle Crest Trail is a spur to the top of 6,782-foot Columbia Mountain. Take this path—**Columbia Mountain Trail**—for a wonderful short (but steep) climb to the summit where you'll find a decrepit CCC lookout cabin and wide-angle vistas. It's a bit over five miles roundtrip from the trailhead to the top of the mountain, making a fine chance to stretch your legs and enjoy the quiet, forested land and the ravens playing in the thermals. Water is available from a spring along the trail. Get additional information on these trails at the Forest Service office in Republic. .

THE NORTHEAST CORNER

Washington's northeast corner, north of Spokane and east of Lake Roosevelt, is dominated by Stevens and Pend Oreille (pon-der-RAY) Counties. (Pend Oreille is French for "pendant" or "earring," and is believed to have originated from French trappers who used the term for the earring-wearing Indians of this area.) The region is a paradise of good fishing in lakes and rivers, all-season recreation from swimming to snow-skiing, an abundance of wildlife, and very few people.

This uninhabited forest land gives wildlife photographers plenty of opportunities: the Pend Oreille River attracts ospreys, ducks, cranes, and geese, plus bighorn sheep, bears, cougars, elk, and an occasional moose or grizzly. This corner of the state isn't on the way to anywhere else in Washington, so only a determination to escape civilization or a strong exploratory drive brings visitors out here.

Several small towns serve the area: Kettle Falls, Colville, Chewelah, Ione, Metaline Falls, and Newport. They are unpretentious and friendly places and, although all have overnight accommodations and places to eat, most things of interest to visitors are out in the forests and along the rivers and lakes. Except for a bus that connects Colville with Spokane, there are no buses, trains, or planes servicing this part of Washington.

Politically, the northeast corner is Washington's outback. In many places the only radio voices you'll hear are right-wing talk shows, religious broadcasts, or country-western tunes. Stevens County Commissioner J.D. Anderson was recently quoted in newspapers as strongly defending the firearms and militias, noting that: "when the government fears the people there is liberty." Odd definition of liberty. But the remote and undeveloped beauty of this corner of the state also makes it popular with organic farmers, retirees, and escape-the-rat-race telecommuters, not to mention marijuana growers.

Rivers and Lakes

Pend Oreille River is one of just two rivers in North America that flow northward; it enters

Canada north of Metaline Falls before circling back south to join the Columbia River near the town of Boundary. Small lakes are scattered throughout northeast Washington. Many are encircled by summer cabins, modest year-round homes, or low-budget resorts and RV parks. As is common in eastern Washington, the natural features here aren't played up or exploited to the degree they would be on the more crowded, beach-hungry East Coast or other more populous areas of the country; yours is likely to be the only boat on the lake. With this serenity comes a corresponding lack of services, so keep the fuel tank and ice chest full.

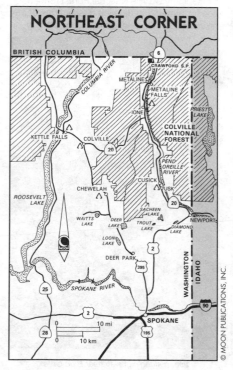

COLVILLE NATIONAL FOREST

Colville National Forest spreads over 1.1 million acres in half-a-dozen scattered puzzle pieces, reaching from Metaline Falls to Wauconda, 67 air-miles away. Abutting it on both sides are additional public lands: Okanogan National Forest to the west and Kaniksu National Forest reaching eastward into Idaho. The eastern portions of the Colville are capped by the Selkirk Mountains, one of the last places in the Lower 48 where grizzlies survive. The forests are a true mixture of evergreen and deciduous species, with grand fir, subalpine fir, lodgepole pine, aspen, Douglas fir, western white pine, western red cedar, western larch, birch, and cottonwood trees.

Hiking and Campgrounds

Contact any Colville National Forest ranger station for a map and detailed descriptions of day hikes and longer treks. This is bear country, so

make noise, store your food safely, and don't be too proud to choose another route if you encounter bears, bear tracks, or droppings.

Abercrombie Mountain Trail is a three-mile one-way hike to a ridge top with panoramic views of the Pend Oreille and Columbia River Valleys from 7,300 feet. From Colville, take Aladdin Hwy. north for 23 miles to Deep Creek Rd., turn north onto Deep Creek Rd. for seven miles, then turn right on Silver Creek Rd. 4720 to the junction with Rd. 7078. Take 7078 north to Rd. 300, then follow it to the road's end where the trail begins. Most of the three miles is wooded, crossing several streams and huckleberry bushes on the way to the ridge. This trail is also popular with hunters because of the abundant deer—so look conspicuous!

In addition to the many hiking trails, the Forest Service maintains 27 campgrounds on the Colville. A number of Colville National Forest campgrounds and hiking trails are described elsewhere in this chapter.

Information

For more specific information on hiking, camping, and other recreational activities in the Colville National Forest, contact **Colville National Forest Headquarters**, 765 S. Main, tel. (509) 684-7000. District offices are in Colville, Kettle Falls, Sullivan Lake, and Newport.

KETTLE FALLS

As you enter Kettle Falls, you're greeted by a sign proclaiming "Welcome to Kettle Falls—Home of 1,381 friendly people and one grouch." Ask around town and you'll find that the grouch is elected each year by the local citizenry, with each vote costing 25 cents. Using the vote-early, vote-often method, it's possible to buy the election for a particularly deserving individual each year. (All the "election" proceeds go to promoting the town.)

Kettle Falls runs on a spectrum of businesses, including a large Boise Cascade lumber mill and two other wood products mills, orchards, and tourism, especially at nearby Lake Roosevelt. A large wood-fired power plant produces electricity near Kettle Falls, burning wood waste and chips.

aspen along highway near Blue Creek

DON PITCHER

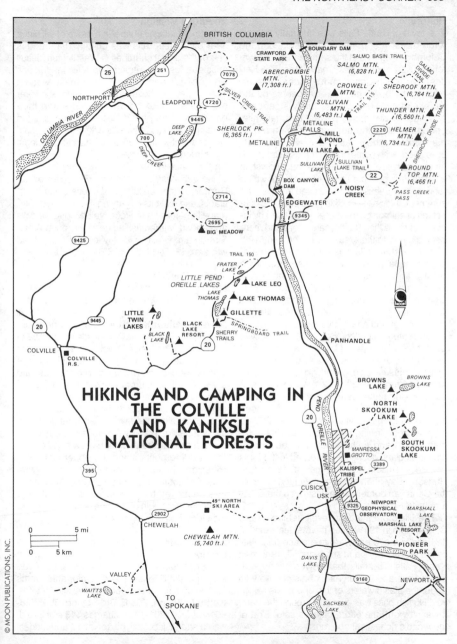

BRITISH COLUMBIA

CRAWFORD STATE PARK
BOUNDARY DAM
SALMO BASIN TRAIL

25
251
7078

ABERCROMBIE MTN.

SALMO MTN. (6,828 ft.)

SALMO DIVIDE TRAIL

NORTHPORT

SILVER CREEK TRAIL

LEADPOINT
4720

▲ (7,308 ft.)

CROWELL MTN.

SHEDROOF MTN. (6,764 ft.)

9445

SULLIVAN MTN. (6,483 ft.)

TRAIL 515

THUNDER MTN. (6,560 ft.)

DEEP LAKE

700

DEEP CREEK

SHERLOCK PK. (6,365 ft.)

METALINE FALLS

MILL POND

METALINE

SULLIVAN LAKE

2220

HELMER MTN. (6,734 ft.)

SHEDROOF DIVIDE TRAIL

COLUMBIA RIVER

SULLIVAN LAKE

SULLIVAN LAKE TRAIL

ROUND TOP MTN. (6,466 ft.)

9425

2714

BOX CANYON DAM

22

NOISY CREEK

PASS CREEK PASS

IONE

EDGEWATER

9345

2695

BIG MEADOW

TRAIL 150

FRATER LAKE

LITTLE PEND OREILLE LAKES

LAKE LEO

LAKE THOMAS

LAKE THOMAS

20

9445

LITTLE TWIN LAKES

BLACK LAKE RESORT

GILLETTE

SPRINGBOARD TRAIL

BLACK LAKE

SHERRY TRAILS

20

PANHANDLE

COLVILLE

COLVILLE R.S.

HIKING AND CAMPING IN THE COLVILLE AND KANIKSU NATIONAL FORESTS

BROWNS LAKE

BROWNS LAKE

NORTH SKOOKUM LAKE

20

SOUTH SKOOKUM LAKE

PEND OREILLE RIVER

MANRESSA GROTTO

3389

KALISPEL TRIBE

395

CUSICK

USK

NEWPORT GEOPHYSICAL OBSERVATORY

9325

MARSHALL LAKE

2902

49° NORTH SKI AREA

MARSHALL LAKE RESORT

CHEWELAH

PIONEER PARK

CHEWELAH MTN. (5,740 ft.)

DAVIS LAKE

VALLEY

9160

NEWPORT

WAITTS LAKE

TO SPOKANE

SACHEEN LAKE

0   5 mi
0   5 km

© MOON PUBLICATIONS, INC.

History

The town of Kettle Falls was originally located three miles west of the current site along the Columbia River falls of the same name. The waterfalls were named *Les Chaudieres* (The Kettles) by French-Canadian fur traders in reference to the bowl-shaped rocks carved by the water's force. They were actually a series of cascades that dropped 33 feet in a half mile, enough to slow the upstream salmon movement, making them easier to catch in baskets or to spear with poles. When the fish were running, a man could catch over a thousand fish in a single day, providing a major source of winter food for the various tribes that used the site. The summer fishing site—said to have been the richest run of salmon on the planet—was used by Indians for more than 9,000 years. More and more people came to the area, and by the early 19th century, Kettle Falls was a summer home for over a thousand people from the surrounding region. It was a natural site for a trading post.

The Hudson's Bay Company established **Fort Colvile** here in 1826. (Note that the fort name was spelled "Colvile," in contrast to the city, National Forest, Indian reservation, and other regional features spelled "Colville.") Fort Colvile grew rapidly into a small town, with barns, a windmill, coal kilns, and a water-powered grist mill. Farmers here supplied food for other Hudson's Bay forts along the Columbia River, and traders purchased and shipped furs from throughout the region; in 1840 they processed 18,000 furs. The arrival of missionaries—who emphasized farming rather than traditional Indian ways—and a shift away from beaver fur hats in England during the 1840s led to the fort's demise. It remained in existence until 1871 when Hudson's Bay abandoned all their land south of the Canadian border. A fire destroyed the structure in 1910.

The filling of Lake Roosevelt behind Grand Coulee Dam in 1941 forced the residents of Kettle Falls to move eastward to a place originally called Meyers Falls and subsequently renamed Kettle Falls. The falls themselves, along with the fort site and 9,000 years of history, now lie under the placid waters of this enormous reservoir. No fish pass was ever built around the dam; it wasn't worth the effort, officials said. End of the world's richest salmon run.

St. Paul's Mission

This small Catholic chapel in a grove of tall pines near old Kettle Falls was built in 1847, and is one of the oldest churches in Washington. Jesuit missionaries held services here for the Indians who often fished for salmon in these waters. The chapel was closed 1858-62 when gold fever brought an influx of white settlers and their booze, but it reopened for the summer salmon runs in the 1870s, after which it fell into disrepair. Reconstructed in 1939 using hand-hewn logs, the structure was turned over to the National Park Service in 1974.

Not far away is the **Kettle Falls Historical Center,** a small building that houses murals, artifacts, and exhibits portraying the old ways of Indian life before Lake Roosevelt flooded the falls and ended salmon fishing here. It is open Wed.-Sun. 11 a.m.-5 p.m. mid-May to mid-Sept. (closed winters); $2. Call (509) 738-6964 for details.

Meyers Falls

Meyers Falls—the oldest continually used source of industrial power in the Pacific Northwest—has a small log building that houses the small **Meyers Falls Interpretive Center** where historic photos line the walls. Outside is a replica of the 16-foot high water wheel that operated here for many decades, along with the original stone wheels used to grind the grain. The cascades are a few feet distant, dropping 20 feet into a pretty plunge pool below a small dam that has been producing electrical power here since 1903. Prior to its completion, the falls turned three gristmills, the first built in 1826 by the Hudson's Bay Company. It milled wheat, oats, barley, and corn for their trading posts along the upper Columbia River and is said to have produced the first patented flour in the United States. The old mill was destroyed by a fire in 1916. The falls are located a mile south of town on Juniper St.; follow the signs from the highway.

Accommodations

Grandview Inn Motel, 978 Hwy. 395, tel. (509) 738-6733, has a delightful woodsy location overlooking Lake Roosevelt and comfortable rooms for $30-40 s or d; some rooms have kitchenettes. **Kettle Falls Inn,** 205 E. 3rd St., tel. (509) 738-6514 or (800) 701-1927, charges $43 s or $46 d, with a sauna, jaccuzzi, microwaves, and fridges.

Blue Moose Cabin Rentals, five miles west of Kettle Falls, tel. (509) 738-6950, has three new cabins with kitchenettes; $40 s or d. **The Lake House,** eight miles northeast of Kettle Falls, tel. (509) 684-5132, is a spacious country home with two bedrooms, a full kitchen, hot tub, and canoe. No kids; $95 d.

The most elaborate local place to stay is **My Parent's Estate B&B,** tel. (509) 738-6220, a mile east of Kettle Falls. Set on 49 acres of land, it began in 1869 as the St. Regis Mission, and is today a luxurious country inn containing three rooms with private baths ($75 s or d) and a honeymoon suite ($100 d). No children.

Bull Hill Ranch and Resort is a working cattle ranch and dude ranch where you can ride horses, fish, swim, and take part in cattle drives (and soak in the jacuzzi afterwards). Call (509) 732-4355 for details. $105 s or d for three meals a day and horseback rides. Closed Dec.-April.

Campgrounds and RV Parks

The Park Service operates **Kettle Falls Campground,** tel. (509) 738-6266, in tall ponderosa pines along Lake Roosevelt. The campground is two miles south of Hwy. 395/20 on Boise Road. Open year-round; $10 (no RV hookups). Campfire programs take place most summer evenings; check at the Ranger Station for other offerings. No reservations, so get here early for summer holiday weekends. Take showers at the Chevron station on the west end of town.

Private RV parks around Kettle Falls include **Circle Up RV Park,** on Boise Rd. south of the Park Service office, tel. (509) 738-6617; **Grandview Inn and RV Park,** 978 Hwy. 395/20, tel. (509) 738-6733; **Whispering Pines RV Park,** tel. (509) 738-2593; and **Panorama RV Park,** 460 W. 6th St., tel. (509) 738-6831. **The Homeland,** tel. (509) 732-4367, has camping and RV hookups near the Canadian border, 45 miles north of Kettle Falls.

Food

Little Gallea, 270 W. 3rd, tel. (509) 738-6776, is the local breakfast and lunch joint with well-prepared and inexpensive American food in a smoke-filled room. For good steaks and seafood, stop by **Hudson Bay Co.,** three miles west of town on Hwy. 395/20.

More than a dozen local orchards produce cherries, apricots, peaches, pears, apples, and other fruits. Many of these operate fruit stands or have U-pick operations near the site of old Kettle Falls along Lake Roosevelt. Get a brochure from the chamber of commerce, or just head down Peachcrest Rd. till a place looks interesting. **China Bend Vineyards & Winery,** north of Kettle Falls near the town of Northport, tel. (800) 700-6123, has tastings of their organic wines and salsas. The grounds are gorgeous and right on the Columbia River. They also have a popular Fourth of July celebration here each summer.

Events and Entertainment

Town & Country Days is the big summer event in Kettle Falls, arriving the first weekend of June and featuring a parade, fun run, and local arts and crafts. This is also when the town grouch is chosen. The **Governor's Cup Walleye Tournament** on the third weekend of June is followed by the **Lake Roosevelt Regatta** on the second weekend of July.

Kettle Falls' **Woodland Theatre,** 120 W. 3rd Ave., tel. (509) 738-6626, features plays, concerts, and musicals throughout the year.

Recreation

The Park Service maintains a very popular campground, boat ramp, and swimming beach (no lifeguard) along the shore of Lake Roosevelt just south of Hwy. 395/20. There's an outdoor summer-only public **swimming pool** in the city park at the corner of Meyers and 7th Streets.

Fishing is a favorite activity in Lake Roosevelt. A net pen project near Kettle Falls produces rainbow trout, and the **Sherman Creek Hatchery,** four miles west of Kettle Falls, raises kokanee salmon for Lake Roosevelt. For the current lake elevation, call (800) 824-4916.

Lake Roosevelt is a feeding area for more than 200 **bald eagles** during the winter months, particularly the stretch from Kettle Falls south to Gifford Ferry. Best time to see these birds is late November to mid-February.

Information and Services

The **Kettle Falls Area Chamber of Commerce** is downtown along Hwy. 395/20, tel. (509) 738-2300. Hours are daily 1-3 p.m. in summer, and hit or miss the rest of the year.

The Park Service's **Kettle Falls Ranger Station** is at S. 1230 Boise Rd., tel. (509) 738-6266; stop by to view the displays of Indian artifacts and other items found at old Kettle Falls. Get Colville National Forest information at **Kettle Falls Ranger District,** 255 W. 11th St., tel. (509) 738-7700.

COLVILLE

Like many of its neighbors in this part of Washington, Colville (pop. 4,500) depends on timber, mining, farming, and tourism to survive. There are still three sawmills in Colville fed by timber from Colville National Forest and private lands. The town began as a U.S. Army post called Fort Colville (not to be confused with the older Fort Colvile run by Hudson's Bay Company). The fort was abandoned in the early 1880s, but the settlement survived to become today's Colville, the largest "city" in northeastern Washington. Downtown Colville is a prosperous slice of middle America, and the surrounding area shows even more evidence: a sparkling new high school on the edge of town and the only Wal-Mart in this corner of the state.

Sights

Stevens County Historical Museum 700 N. Wynne St., tel. (509) 684-5968, contains an extensive collection of items from Fort Colville and Fort Colvile, an along with Indian artifacts (a dugout canoe, headdresses, intricately woven baskets, and more), plus many historic photos. Be sure to ask the docents to play the old music box for you. Outside the museum you'll find spacious grounds containing the three-story **Keller House,** completed in 1912 and essentially unchanged today. Walk down the hill under tall walnut trees to a collection of farm machinery and old buildings, including a sawmill, farmstead cabin, schoolhouse, fire lookout, and trapper's cabin. The museum is open daily 10 a.m.-4 p.m. June-Aug., and daily 1-4 May and September; donation.

Accommodations

Downtown Motel, 369 S. Main, tel. (509) 684-2565, has very plain older rooms for $35 s or $40 d. **Colville Inn,** 915 S. Main, tel. (509) 684-2517 or (800) 680-2517, has a range of rooms

for $48-102 s or d, including an indoor pool, jacuzzi, and fitness center pass. **Comfort Inn** 166 N.E. Canning Dr., tel. (509) 684-2010 or (800) 228-5150, is a new motel with an indoor pool and jacuzzi, plus a continental breakfast for $54 s or $65 d.

Campgrounds

Tent and RV spaces are available at the **Northeast Washington Fairgrounds** on Columbia Street. Four Forest Service campgrounds (described below) are located in the **Little Pend Oreille Lakes Recreation Area,** 25 miles northeast of Colville along Hwy. 20. Several more remote campgrounds are free, including **Big Meadow Lake Campground** 27 miles northeast of Colville on Meadow Creek Road. Here you'll find three miles of hiking trails (partly handicapped-accessible), a replica of a homestead cabin, and a 35-foot wildlife-viewing tower where you may see moose, beavers, ospreys, or even black bears.

Food

Talk 'N' Coffee next to the chamber office at 119 E. Astor, tel. (509) 684-2373, is Colville's version of hip, with homemade scones and good espressos. Get a book with your espresso at **The Book Depot** 103 N. Main, tel. (509) 684-5562.

North Country Coop, 282 W. Astor, tel. (509) 684-6132, is a real surprise in this meat-and-potatoes town, offering fresh-baked breads, a serve-yourself deli for breakfast and lunch, and reasonably priced organic produce.

Head to **Angler's Grill,** tel. (509) 685-1308, for solid all-American cooking, or to **Rancho Chico** on S. Main for Mexican-style meals. **Cafe Italiano,** 153 W. 2nd St., tel. (509) 684-5957, is a cheery place with good pasta, chicken, veal, and seafood. **Barman's Country Store,** 230 S. Main. tel. (509) 684-9710, has an old-fashioned soda fountain with sandwiches and homemade ice cream floats.

Colville has **farmers markets,** tel. (509) 669-6438, on Wednesday 11 a.m.-6 p.m. May to mid-Oct. at the corner of Hawthorne and Elm, and Saturday 8:30 a.m.-1 p.m. at 3rd and Main.

Events and Entertainment

The **Colville Rodeo** comes to town in mid-June, with a parade and PRCA rodeo; tel. (509) 684-

4849. **Colville Rendezvous** on the first weekend of August features food, arts and crafts, egg tosses, entertainment, and various sporting contests. Early September brings the **Northeast Washington Fair** with a parade, animal judging, carnival, and live music. **Red Bull Steakhouse,** 542 S. Main, tel. (509) 684-6651, has bands most weekends.

Sports and Recreation
Swim at the outdoor swimming pool in City Park, or just hang out under the beautiful tall ponderosa pines and Douglas fir trees that cover the grassy lawns. Colville is one of the few places that still has a drive-in movie theater; it's three miles west of town. Golfers can putt around at **Colville Elks Golf Course,** tel. (509) 684-5508, a nine-hole course.

Information, Services, and Transportation
The **Colville Chamber of Commerce Visitor Information Center** 121 E. Astor, tel. (509) 684-5973, is open Mon.-Fri. 10 a.m.-noon and 1-4 p.m. Ask here for directions to the big "C" on Colville Mountain overlooking town.

For Forest Service info, visit contact **Colville Ranger District,** behind the Federal Building at 755 S. Main, tel. (509) 684-7000; open Mon.-Fri. 7:30 a.m.-4:30 p.m.

Borderline Stage, 127 E. Astor, tel. (509) 684-3950, has bus service connecting Colville with Spokane.

LITTLE PEND OREILLE LAKES RECREATION AREA

Heading east from Colville on Hwy. 20, the road cuts through beautiful mixed forests. Be sure to stop at **Crystal Falls,** 12 miles east of Colville, where the waters of Little Pend Oreille River drop over a 30-foot cascade. It's a fine place for a picnic beneath the trees.

Approximately 25 miles northeast of Colville on Hwy. 20 is a chain of eight glacially formed bodies of water: the Little Pend Oreille Lakes. These are a favorite getaway spot for folks from Spokane, offering more than 75 miles of multiuse trails open to hiking, motorcycles, mountain bikes, and horses. In winter, the Forest Service maintains 15 miles of groomed cross-country

ski trails here. The lakes themselves are popular for swimming, sailing, boating, fishing, and canoeing. The country around here is a beautiful mix of open meadows and dense forests with plenty of larch trees (bright yellow in the fall).

Beaver Lodge Resort is a fun family place on Lake Gillette, tel. (509) 684-5657, with comfortable cabins, tent and RV spaces, plus boat and canoe rentals. There's also a store, deli, and laundromat.

Campgrounds
You'll find four Forest Service campgrounds in the Little Pend Oreille Lakes area. **Lake Leo, Lake Thomas, Gillette,** and **Lake Gillette** Campgrounds are open Memorial Day to Labor Day (Lake Leo is open till the snow flies) and have an $8 fee. Make reservations for Gillette Campground ($9 extra) by calling (877) 444-6777.

Hiking and Cross-Country Skiing Trails
The Little Pend Oreille trail system has seven trails to satisfy all kinds of users. A popular 2.4-mile loop trail, **Springboard Trail** begins at the east end of the Gillette Campground. This self-guided interpretive trail relates the history of an early homesteader and leads to a viewing platform.

Sherry Trail is a set of three short loops that total four miles in length and begin at the trailhead just west of Lake Sherry. This hike or ski route passes through lodgepole pine and Douglas fir and provides views of the lake and Little Pend Oreille River.

Frater Lake Trail has three ski/hike loops—one three miles long, the other two—that start at Frater Lake on the east end of the recreation area. The shorter Tiger Loop cuts through Douglas fir close to the lake on gentle terrain. The longer and steeper Coyote Rock Loop crosses a stream and meadow and has a viewpoint from Coyote Rock. Across on the south side of Hwy. 20 is the 2.6-mile **Lake Leo Trail,** popular with beginning cross-country skiers because of its gentle terrain.

IONE

Ione (pop. 600) is a lumber and tourism town along the Pend Oreille River 35 miles north of Usk. Steamboats plied the Pend Oreille River in the 1880s; today nearby Box Canyon Dam backs up the river to create a popular place to water-ski and fish. The Vaagen Brothers sawmill is Ione's main employer.

Three miles north of Ione is **Box Canyon Dam,** the source of electrical power for much of the county. Stop at the visitors center for tours, tel. (509) 442-3232, open daily in summer; and weekdays in winter. The small pond here (complete with float) makes a great swimming hole and picnic area.

A few miles south of Ione is the crossroads called Tiger, where the **Tiger Historical Center** has a small collection of memorabilia, along with local crafts; open summer only.

Lodging
Plaza Motel, tel. (509) 442-3534, charges $35-40 s or d. The friendly and clean **Ione Motel and RV Park,** tel. (509) 442-3213, is right on the river, and has rooms for $40-85 s or d with microwaves and fridges. **Driscoll's B&B Inn,** tel. (509) 442-3442, is a beautiful three-story home along the river. The four guest rooms have private baths, and a full breakfast. No kids, and a two-night minimum on weekends; $100 s or d.

On Hwy. 20 between Cusick and Ione, **Outpost Resort,** tel. (509) 445-1317, has cabins, RV parking and tent sites, plus a restaurant, groceries, and boat launch. They also offer pontoon boat tours of the Pend Oreille River.

Box Canyon Resort, tel. (509) 676-8883 or (800) 676-8883, five miles north of Ione, has motel rooms for $40-55 s or $45-60 d. They also offer popular two-hour jet boat tours of the northern Pend Oreille River.

Campgrounds
The Forest Service's **Edgewater Campground** ($10; open mid-May through Sept.), sits across the Pend Oreille River and two miles north up Box Canyon-LeClerc Rd. (County Rd. 3669). RV hookups are available at Ione Motel.

Other Practicalities
The North Pend Oreille Valley Lions Club **Excursion Train** ($5) chugs between Ione and Metaline Falls, crossing Box Canyon Dam along the way. Trains leave Ione at 11 a.m., 1 p.m., and 3 p.m., with a stop in Metaline Falls before returning. They generally run six weekends each

summer from mid-June to mid-October. Call (509) 442-3397 for information and reservations.

Ione's **Down River Days** at the end of July features boat races, a parade, fun run, and street dance.

Get local information at **Reed's Shop & Save,** tel. (509) 442-3223, in the old depot. **Ione City Park** along the lake has a picnic area, boat launch, and outdoor swimming pool, open summers.

METALINE AND METALINE FALLS

The twin towns of Metaline and Metaline Falls—jointly home to 500 people—sit across the Pend Oreille River from each other and just 10 miles from Canada. Metaline began as a mining camp around 1865 and was named for the metals the miners found here; Metaline Falls came later as the site of a big cement plant (now closed). There's still lead and zinc mining going on north of Metaline. Metaline Falls is a delightful little burg with quiet streets and small frame homes with neatly trimmed lawns. Stop at **Metaline City Park** where the spacious lawns provide a place to picnic, toss a Frisbee, or just hang out by the water.

Crawford State Park
You can tour one of the largest limestone caves in the state, **Gardner Cave,** at Crawford State Park, 12 miles northwest of Metaline Falls off Hwy. 31. The cave is open late May to early September, with free guided tours Thurs.-Mon. between 10 a.m. and 4 p.m. Tours take you almost 500 feet into this 1,055-foot cavern, past fanciful (and fancifully named) stalactites, stalagmites, and columns. Dress warmly, it's always cold inside. Call (509) 446-4065 for more information. Camping is limited to 10 primitive campsites ($5). As you drive up to the cave, **mountain goats** are visible March to early June from a marked pullout along Flume Creek near the park; bring your binoculars.

Boundary Dam, just east of Gardner Cave, has a visitors center next to the 340-foot arched concrete dam that is jammed between two tall cliffs. Free tours of the dam and tunnels are given Thurs.-Mon. 10:30 a.m.-4:30 p.m. in the summer; call (509) 446-3073 for reservations. A deck 500 feet above the river provides impressive vistas. Magnificent **Peewee Falls** plunges

DON PITCHER

*Washington Hotel,
Metaline Falls*

200 feet into the south end of the reservoir; ask at the dam for directions.

Accommodations
Built in 1910, the historic **Washington Hotel,** tel. (509) 446-4415, is home to Lee McGowan, the local dynamo. Inside are 18 restored rooms ($35 s or d) with handmade quilts, rugs, book swap shelves, original "working-mans" furnishings, and bath down the hall. A studio and gallery include her works in progress. Be sure to ask about the "Santa's workshop" sculptures, a collection of 50 figures that are displayed around town each Christmas.

Mt. Linton Motel in Metaline Falls, tel. (509) 446-2238, has motel rooms with microwaves and fridges for $30-35 s or d. **Mt. Linton RV Park** in Metaline, tel. (509) 446-4553, has RV and tent spaces. Primitive camping is also available at nearby **Crawford State Park** (see above).

Food
Katie's Oven Bakery, tel. (509) 446-4806, at the Washington Hotel, is one of the anchors in this fascinating little town. Great breads, light breakfasts and lunches, and espresso in a cozy atmosphere. Everything is made from scratch. Get big juicy steaks at **Hoogy's Steak House & Lounge** in Metaline Falls, tel. (509) 446-3901.

Events
All summer long, the historic **Cutter Theatre** in Metaline Falls (an old school named for a famous Spokane architect, Kirtland Cutter) features live—and surprisingly good—summer weekend performances of comedic melodramas. Call (509) 446-4108 for ticket information. In the winter you'll find more plays, lectures, and concerts at the Cutter. For first-run films in a small town, head down the block to the **Showhouse.**

The North Pend Oreille Valley Lions Club **Excursion Train** ($5) rolls into Metaline Falls from Ione between mid-June and mid-October. Performances at the Cutter Theatre are often timed so you can see a play during your stop in Metaline Falls. Call (509) 442-3397 for train information and reservations.

In late August **Affair on Main Street** brings a downtown arts and crafts show. If you're in the region around Christmas, be sure to visit Metaline Falls for a display of 50 amusing **Christmas sculptures.**

Information
The **Metaline Falls Visitor Center** is open daily 10 a.m.-5 p.m. Memorial Day to Labor Day only; stop by the Washington Hotel at other times, or check www.povn.com/cutter.

SULLIVAN LAKE AREA

Four-mile-long Sullivan Lake anchors a large section of Forest Service land within Colville National Forest, providing outstanding camping and hiking opportunities. A feeding station at the south end of Sullivan Lake is a good place to look for **bighorn sheep** in the winter. Much of this country has been clearcut, but the Salmo-Priest Wilderness is here, along with Grassy Top Roadless Area. The Forest Service's **Sullivan Lake Ranger District** office, tel. (509) 446-7500, is at the north end of the lake.

Campgrounds

Four Forest Service campgrounds are along the shore of Sullivan Lake and nearby Mill Pond: **Sullivan Lake East, Sullivan Lake West, Mill Pond,** and **Noisy Creek.** All are open Memorial Day to Labor Day, and cost $10. Find good swimming beaches at Noisy Creek and the two Sullivan Lake campgrounds. All but Mill Pond can also be reserved ($9 extra) by calling (877) 444-6777.

Hiking

Sullivan Lake Trail is a four-mile one-way hike along the eastern shore of Sullivan Lake through forested areas, connecting Sullivan Lake Campground with Noisy Creek Campground. The clear blue lake is the main attraction, but watch for bighorn sheep, black bear, and white-tailed deer. A very nice hike, especially in the fall. For a short historical hike, head to **Mill Pond Historical Site,** where a wheelchair-accessible trail leads past displays on the 1910 hydroelectric project.

Salmo-Priest Wilderness

One of Washington's least-known wilderness areas, the 39,937-acre Salmo-Priest Wilderness sits in the northeastern-most corner of the state, bordering Idaho and Canada. Much of the surrounding land has been heavily logged, but this small corner reveals the land as it once was: dense old-growth western red cedar, Douglas fir, grand fir, and western larch forests at the middle elevations, and subalpine openings atop the mountains. This is not a place for beginners, but a number of trails provide hiking opportunities for the adventurous. The weather is fickle and often wet, so bring your rain gear. Best times to hike are mid-July to mid-August. No backcountry permits are required.

The Salmo-Priest Wilderness is home to a number of endangered animals, including grey wolves, grizzlies, and the last woodland caribou

in the lower 48 states; approximately 30 of them are here. In addition, the wilderness has a large black bear population. For your safety, pick up free food storage containers from the Sullivan Lake Forest Service office before heading out. And be sure you know how to stay safe in bear country!

A fine loop trip begins from the east end of Forest Rd. 2220 that leaves Forest Rd. 9345 just north of Sullivan Lake. The **Salmo Basin Trail** climbs up through virgin evergreen forests and crosses into Idaho (and almost into Canada) before joining the **Shedroof Divide Trail** near 7,572-foot Snowy Top (a rough but rewarding side trip). Follow Shedroof Divide Trail back across into Washington and its junction with **Salmo Divide Trail,** which will take you back to your starting point, a total distance of approximately 19 miles. Much of the trail is at 6,000 feet in elevation, so sea-level dwellers should expect to hike a little more slowly than usual.

USK, CUSICK, AND KALISPEL LANDS

Thirty-five miles south of Ione is the little settlement of Usk, home to the enormous Ponderay Valley Fibre newsprint factory; call (509) 445-1732 or (800) 638-4996 for tours. Usk is named for the town of Usk, England, and you can see "sister-town" photos inside the country store. The pilings visible all along the Pend Oreille River near here were used to corral logs as they floated downstream to local sawmills.

Cusick (pop. 240; pronounced "Q-sick") is just two miles north of here and is home to the county fairgrounds.

The Kalispel Tribe (approximately 200 people) own a small section of land along the east side of the Pend Oreille River; they originally lived on a three-million acre spread. The tribal lands were made official in 1934; this is one of the few non-reservation Indian homelands in the Lower 48.

Sights

Manresa Grotto is a 70-foot-wide cavern on Kalispel Tribal lands, right along LeClerc Creek Rd. and five miles north of the Pend Oreille River bridge at Usk. This spacious rock grotto was used by Father Jean Pierre DeSmet in the 1840s as a combination home and church to preach to local Indians. A stone alter and pews (of a sort) are still inside, and mass is held in mid-September every year. Osprey nest near here along the shore of the lake.

The Kalispel Tribal offices and the **Our Lady of Sorrows** church (built in 1914) are two miles south of here. Stop in to see who is making Indian crafts in the area. Also ask to see the enormous mounted buffalo head (in a back room); the herd of 100 buffalo is immediately south of the office. Behind here is the powwow grounds used for the Salish Fairs.

Practicalities

The **Hotel Usk,** tel. (509) 445-1526 or (888) 423-8084, is a delightful family-run hotel in tiny Usk, 16 miles north of Newport. Built around 1910, it served as a boardinghouse for many years and has been lovingly restored. The inn has 10 bath-down-the-hall rooms for $35-45 s or d. They also offer tent sites for cyclists.

Blueside Resort, 18 miles north of Cusick, tel. (509) 445-1327, is a nice family-oriented place with a motel ($36-38 s or d) and cabins ($44-60 s or d), along with tent camping and RV spots on the Pend Oreille River. Facilities include a boat ramp and dock, swimming pool, and store, but no TVs. This is the only place where boaters can buy fuel along the river.

Just south of Usk at the junction of Highways 211 and 20 is **Crossroads Cafe,** tel. (509) 445-1515, a large bar and all-American eatery with live music on weekends. The **Usk Bar & Grill** makes good burgers.

Events

The first weekend of August brings the unusual **Salish Fair** at the Kalispel powwow grounds. It includes a buffalo barbecue, arts and crafts, stick games (gambling), Indian war dancing, and a baseball tournament. Also enjoyable are the **Salish Barter Fairs** held here in August, where you can purchase or trade Indian crafts and other works. The **Pend Oreille County Fair & Rodeo** comes to Cusick in late August.

NEWPORT AND VICINITY

The town of Newport (pop. 1,800) is the Pend Oreille County seat and the largest settlement in these parts. It sits along the Pend Oreille River; the smaller Oldtown, Idaho, is on the other side of the bridge. The town was founded in Oldtown in 1889, but most everyone moved across the river when the Great Northern Railway built a depot on the Washington side three years later. Nothing particularly notable about Newport, but it is a pleasant old-fashioned town with an attractive and bustling main drag.

Sights

The **County Historical Society Museum,** tel. (509) 447-5388, sits in Centennial Plaza Park on the corner of Washington and 4th, with a 1909 Corliss steam engine and two historic cabins out front. Originally built as a train depot along the Idaho & Washington Northern Railroad, the museum now contains all sorts of obscure flotsam and jetsam, including a pencil collection. The museum (free) is open daily 10 a.m.-4 p.m. mid-May through September. Next door is another old depot, which was used for many years by the competing Great Northern Railway and now housing Plum Creek Timber Company. Just two miles east of Newport in Idaho is the **Albeni Falls Dam,** where tours are given daily in the summer; tel. (208) 437-3133.

Built in 1915, the **Pend Oreille County Courthouse** occupies the block at 4th St. and Warren Avenue. It is on the National Register of Historic Places.

Motels and Campgrounds

Your best local lodging option is **Golden Spur Motor Inn,** 924 W. Hwy. 2, tel. (509) 447-3823, with rooms for $40 s or $45 d.

Four Forest Service campgrounds are close to Newport: **Brown's Lake, South Skookum Lake, Pioneer Park,** and **Panhandle.** They charge $8 and are open Memorial Day to September. Pioneer Park Campground is a quick two miles north of town on LeClerc Rd.; cross the bridge over the Pend Oreille River, and turn left. Campsites are also available two miles east at the Priest River Recreation Area in Idaho.

Old American Campground, 701 N. Newport Ave., tel. (509) 447-3663, has tent and RV spaces. **Marshall Lake Resort,** seven miles north of Newport on Leclerc Rd., tel. (509) 447-4158, has campsites and RV hookups, boat and canoe rentals, and trails to hike.

Food and Drink

Golden China Restaurant, 924 W. Hwy. 2, tel. (509) 447-2735, has a wide range of Chinese meals, with lunch specials starting at $5. Many folks call this the best Chinese restaurant in northeast Washington. Good south-of-the-border fare at **Rancho Allegro,** 311 N. Washington, tel. (509) 447-0195. The best local burgers and steaks are over along the river in Oldtown at **Riverbank Restaurant,** tel. (208) 437-3926. **Pizza Factory,** 237 S. Washington, tel. (509) 447-5666, has gourmet pizzas, pasta, and calzones, plus microbrews on tap.

Kelly's Tavern, 324 W. 4th St., tel. (509) 447-3367, is Newport's oldest building (built in 1894) and has a back bar that came here via ship around South America, and by wagon to Newport. In a bygone era the saloon kept a black bear in a cage, ready to wrestle any patron foolish enough to try.

Owen's Grocery, on 4th and Washington has a deli and old-fashioned soda fountain with malts and banana splits. Get fresh produce and handicrafts at Newport's **Earth Market** on summer Saturdays 9 a.m.-1 p.m.

Recreation

The wheelchair-accessible **Pioneer Park Heritage Trail** begins at the Pioneer Park Campground and leads past interpretive signs that detail the life of the Kalispel tribe. **Lower Wolf Trail,** a short loop trail beginning from the north edge of town, passes through forest and wildflowers, affording views of Ashenfelder Bay. To reach it, turn north on Warren Ave. at its junction with Hwy. 20, continuing about a mile to the trailhead. The path is actually a series of short loops totaling 1.5 miles; half of them are wheelchair-accessible (but graveled).

The **Upper Wolf Trail System** consists of 2.5 miles of loop trails located just north of Newport off Laurel-Hurst Street. The trail system is popular with mountain bikers in the summer and cross-country skiers in winter.

A longer ski/bike/hike trail is the **Geophysical Trail System,** located approximately nine miles northwest of town on Indian Creek Road. In the winter, the Forest Service grooms six miles of trails. You'll need a Sno-Park permit to park here for skiing. The **Geophysical Observatory** was originally used for earthquake monitoring but

now serves to detect the detonation of nuclear weapons. It is one of three such sites in America. Closed to the public; the instruments are too sensitive!

Events

Start the summer at **American Heritage Days** in early May at the fairgrounds. Events include old-time demonstrations, Indian dancing, foods and crafts. The **Newport Rodeo** in late June includes a parade, carnival, cowboy breakfast, food and craft booths, and the main attraction, a PRCA-sanctioned rodeo. **Fourth of July** brings all the usual activities, including fireworks at Diamond Lake.

The annual **Poker Paddle,** held the third weekend in July, consists of a 40-mile canoe trip down the Pend Oreille River; participants collect poker cards at various stops along the two-day route. A crowd congregates at the finish to greet the paddlers and enjoy food and game booths. That same weekend, Newport has a popular **International Oldtime Fiddle Contest.**

Information

The museum at the old depot houses the **Newport Visitor Center,** tel. (509) 447-5812; open Mon.-Fri. 9 a.m.-noon all year. Stop by the **Newport Ranger District** office at 315 N. Warren Ave. (immediately north of town off Hwy. 20), tel. (509) 447-7300, for brochures on local trails and campgrounds. Ask here for directions to the **South Baldy Lookout** and the **Roosevelt Grove of Ancient Cedars.**

CHEWELAH AND VICINITY

Chewelah (pop. 2,200; pronounced "chew-WEE-lah") is a pretty little town with tidy brick stores lining the main thoroughfare, Park Street. Chewelah received its name from the Indian word for water snake. The region was first settled in 1845 when Jesuit missionaries established St. Regis Mission. It was later destroyed in a fire, but an Indian agency and various stores arrived, followed by an influx of miners. They discovered silver, copper, lead, and magnetite. The magnetite mines proved crucial during WW I, and a tramway was built (pieces are still visible south of town) to haul ore from the mines five miles to the Chewelah reduction plant. **Quartzite Mountain** rises just east of town, with steep cliff faces. Today, mining remains important to Chewelah, but so are logging, ranching, and tourism.

Sights

The small **Chewelah Museum,** E. 501 3rd St., tel. (509) 935-6091, is open daily 1-4 p.m. in the summer months. The historic **St. Mary of the Rosary** church is a beautiful old chapel topped by a copper dome and cross. Eight miles south of town right along Hwy. 231 is an exotic game farm with camels, zebras, and emu.

Accommodations and Campgrounds

New 49er Motel and RV Park, tel. (509) 935-8613, is a clean motel with an indoor pool and jacuzzi; $35 s or $40 d. Tent and RV sites are also available here, or camp for free at **City Park** on Park Street. The **Nordlig Motel,** 101 W. Grant St., tel. (509) 935-6704, is the best place in town, with a quiet off-street location, hot tub, and rooms for $44 s or $50 d. **Chewelah Creek Inn,** 414 Park St., (509) 935-8166, is a new creekside motel with rooms for $35-45 s or d, including an indoor pool and jacuzzi.

Love's Victorian B&B in Deer Park (20 miles south of Chewelah), (509) 276-6939 or (800) 929-2999, is a delightful country home built in 1886 with three antique-furnished guest rooms and hot tub. A full breakfast is served, and kids are welcome; $80-105 s or $85-110 d.

Lakeside Resorts

South of Chewelah are a number of popular recreation lakes lined by small summertime resorts. During July and August many of these places rent by the week only, so call ahead. Ten miles southwest of town off Hwy. 231 is Waitts Lake, a favorite getaway place for folks from Spokane. The largest rainbow trout caught in the state came from this lake; excellent fishing here for trout, perch, and bass. Three resorts have camping, cabins, and other facilities along the lake: **Silver Beach Resort,** tel. (509) 937-2811; **Waitt's Lake Resort,** tel. (509) 937-2400; and **Winona Beach Resort,** tel. (509) 937-2231.

Other nearby lakes with resorts include **Deer Lake Resort,** tel. (509) 233-2081; **Granite Point Park** at Loon Lake, tel. (509) 233-2100; **Shore Acres** at Loon Lake, tel. (509) 233-2474; **Jerry's**

Landing Resort at Eloika Lake, tel. (509) 292-2337; **Westbrook Resort** at Horseshoe Lake, tel. (509) 276-9221; and **Jump Off Joe Lake Resort,** tel. (509) 937-2133. The beautiful resort at Jump Off Joe Lake is especially noteworthy.

Food

Neighbor's Bakery serves breakfast, lunch, and espresso, plus decent pizzas. Try the **Parkside Restaurant,** next to the city park on Hwy. 395, for inexpensive sandwiches and light meals.

Polanski's Pizza, just south of downtown on Hwy. 395, tel. (509) 935-4443, has tasty pizzas, spaghetti, sandwiches, and chicken. Popular with smokers, so not great for families.

Sports and Recreation

Nine miles east of Chewelah, **49° North** has day and night skiing on 1,900 vertical feet of slope from four chairlifts. It's about an hour north of Spokane off Hwy. 395. Sixteen runs offer beginner through expert skiing; terrain is set aside for powder skiing on weekends. Weekend adult lift tickets are $28. Call (509) 935-6649 for information. Be sure to drive to the ski area from Hwy. 395 on the Chewelah (west) side; the road in from Hwy. 20 on the east is a narrow gravel logging road, impassable in winter and no fun the rest of the year.

Play golf at **Chewelah Golf & Country Club,** 2537 Sand Canyon Rd., tel. (509) 935-6807. Throw your money away at **Spokane Indian Bingo & Casino** two miles south of Chewelah; tel. (800) 322-2788.

Events

The big local event is a three-day celebration of the arts called **Chataqua Days,** held the second weekend of July, with acres of arts and crafts, musical entertainment, and food, plus a parade, dancing, and all sorts of other activities. It's a fun and funky affair, and one of the largest summer celebrations in the Pacific Northwest, attracting 50,000 visitors. Call (509) 935-8991 for details.

Information and Services

The **Chamber of Commerce Visitors Information Center,** 204B E. King St., tel. (509) 935-8991, is open Mon.-Fri. 11 a.m.-5:30 p.m. Chewelah also has a popular outdoor swimming pool. **Borderline Stage,** tel. (509) 684-3950, has bus service to Colville or Spokane.

HUCKLEBERRY MOUNTAIN/ SPOKANE RIVER AREA

For a beautiful country drive, head west from Chewelah along the paved road connecting the one-store towns of Bluecreek and Cedonia. It takes you through lush valleys with big old dairy barns in varying stages of disrepair, and over gentle Huckleberry Mountain, covered with forests of ponderosa pine and western larch.

Highway 25 is another delightful drive, following the shore of Lake Roosevelt from Northport all the way to Fort Spokane, 90 miles to the south. The dark blue lake waters contrast sharply with hills of pine and grass. Numerous campsites line this shore (see **Lake Roosevelt** for specifics). **Gifford Ferry** crosses the reservoir, taking you to the town of Inchelium on the Colville Indian Reservation. This free ferry runs 6:30 a.m.-9:30 p.m. every day. A few miles east of Gifford on Addy-Gifford Rd. is **Animal Adventures,** tel. (509) 738-6119, where Liv Kelly and her sons have a small zoo containing several captive-born animals, including lions, tigers, leopards, and wolves.

Spokane Indian Reservation

South of the tiny town called Fruitland, Hwy. 25 heads away from Lake Roosevelt and across the Spokane Indian Reservation to Fort Spokane and Davenport. **Wellpinit,** the only settlement on the reservation, has a community store, post office, and big high school with "Wellpinit Redskins" emblazoned on the front. The essentially undeveloped reservation is scenic, hilly land covered in open ponderosa pine, large sections of which have been logged.

Fort Spokane

From 1880 to 1898, the U.S. Army post at Fort Spokane served to keep the peace between the Indians on the Colville Reservation in the forested hills to the north and the white settlers on the grassy plains to the south. The fort was built at the confluence of the Spokane River and the Columbia River and had 45 buildings at its peak

in the 1890s. Those were peaceful years, in this area at least, so the soldiers practiced their drills and played a lot of baseball. They also drank more than a little, and many of the soldiers treated in the fort hospital were there because of bad whiskey or drunken brawls. The fort was closed at the outbreak of the Spanish-American War in 1898 and was later used as headquarters for the Colville Indian Agency and as a tuberculosis sanitorium. The grounds were abandoned in 1929 and transferred to the National Park Service in 1960, which has restored the remaining structures.

Take a walking tour through the grounds to see four of the original buildings, including an 1884 stable that housed the dozens of mules needed to haul supplies from the nearest railroad depot in Sprague. Trailside displays relate the fort's history, and the brick guardhouse (1892) has a **visitors center** open daily 9:30 a.m.-5:30 p.m. from mid-May to early September. Rangers in 19th-century costumes offer hour-long tours of the fort on Sunday mornings in the summer; call (509) 725-2715 for specifics.

The Park Service maintains a nearby swimming beach, campground ($10), and amphitheater for Saturday campfire programs from mid-June to early September. Across the river on reservation land you'll find the **Two Rivers Casino,** tel. (800) 722-4031, with roulette, craps, and blackjack; RV hookups are available. Nearby is a stand selling Indian tacos. Heading south toward Davenport, Hwy. 25 passes through an open landscape of rolling wheatfields with scattered old red barns and two-story white houses. Side roads off the highway provide access to **Seven Bays Marina** and **Porcupine Bay,** very popular camping, fishing, swimming, and boating areas within Lake Roosevelt National Recreation Area.

Long Lake Area

Long Lake Dam spans the Spokane River near the east edge of the Spokane Indian Reservation. The grounds here offer a pleasant picnic spot beneath ponderosa pines; free lakeside summer-only campsites are available at **Long Lake Camp,** five miles east on Long Lake Dam Road.

Approximately five miles east of the junction between Highways 291 and 231 are a couple of large boulders surrounded by a chain link fence. Behind the fence are several red-painted figures of unknown age, the **Long Lake petroglyphs.** Nothing special if you've seen the far more impressive petroglyphs of Utah and Wyoming, but worth a stop. East from here on Hwy. 291 the road follows the beautiful shore of Long Lake for quite a few miles, passing several small resorts and the podunk settlement called **Tumtum.** Forested hills climb up away from the blue lake waters. The road continues past Riverside State Park and then on to Spokane, 35 miles from the junction with Hwy. 231.

DAVENPORT

Located just 35 miles from bustling Spokane, Davenport (pop. 1,500) is the seat for Lincoln County and a minor farming and ranching center in this open land of cattle ranches and wheatfields. The brick county courthouse overlooks town, and a wide main street divides the business district.

Sights
Stop by the **Lincoln County Historical Museum,** at Park and 7th Streets, for local memorabilia and a fine collection of agricultural equipment in the back building. The strangest sight here is the death mask of the outlaw Harry Tracy, a member of the Hole-in-the-Wall gang who committed suicide after being cornered by lawmen nearby. The museum is open Mon.-Sat. 9 a.m.-5 p.m. May-Sept., plus Sunday 1-4 p.m. June-Aug., and also serves as the local visitors center; tel. (509) 725-7631 or (800) 326-8148. Birdwatchers will want to ask for directions to places where burrowing owls can be seen right in town.

Lodging
Black Bear Motel, 30 Logan, tel. (509) 725-7700, is an older motel with rooms for $36 s, $43 d, plus tent and RV spaces. **Davenport Motel,** 1205 Morgan, tel. (509) 725-7071, is an attractive place with rooms for $37-40 s or $41-44 d. Camping is available north of Davenport within Lake Roosevelt National Recreation Area (see **Lake Roosevelt** in the Grand Coulee Dam and Vicinity section).

Food
Eat at **Cottonwood Restaurant** for dinner, or **Ellie's,** tel. (509) 725-3354, for breakfast served any time of the day. **Old Pioneer Bakery,** tel. (509) 725-4281, has fresh baked breads and sweets, while **Paul's Lincoln County Pharmacy,** tel. (509) 725-7091, is home to a popular soda fountain (with espresso, of course). Twenty miles west of Davenport in the cowtown of Creston is **Deb's Cafe & Lounge** with charbroiled steaks, a big salad bar, and country and western bands every Saturday night. Inside are all sorts of memorabilia from Deb Cobenhaver, a famous bullrider in the 1950s.

Events
Pioneer Days on the third weekend of July is a favorite summer event for Davenport folks and includes parades, a football game, foot race, antique car show, arts and crafts booths, and various contests and games. Davenport is also home to the **Lincoln County Fair** in late August, including a bull-a-rama, salmon barbecue, C&W entertainment, and livestock show. In nearby Harrington, the big event is **Harrington Fall Festival,** held the last Saturday of Sept., and featuring a parade, games, and very popular beef barbecue.

SPOKANE

Spokane's population of 188,000 makes it the largest city between Seattle and Minneapolis and the second-largest city in Washington. Though Spokane is less than half as large as Seattle and has less of the latter's vertical and horizontal sprawl, the two cities have had much in common from their earliest days: both were leveled by great fires, after which both towns were rebuilt in brick; both cities attribute some of their early growth to outfitting gold and silver miners; both have impressive park systems designed by the same firm; and both cities hosted a world's fair. The legacy of that fair remains as Spokane's centerpiece: the 100-acre Riverfront Park.

Known as the "Lilac City" for its bountiful springtime blooms, Spokane has the same friendly, comfortable atmosphere of a small city in the Midwest. Located just 18 miles from the Idaho border, its tall downtown buildings and spreading suburbs seem an odd apparition among the undeveloped landscape of eastern Washington. The surrounding landscape is a mixture of rich agricultural lands, especially in the Palouse to the south, and piney hills as you head north toward the Selkirk Mountains. Slicing through it all is the Spokane River, or at least the dammed version; seven hydroelectric dams hold back the river waters between its origin in Coeur d'Alene Lake, Idaho, and its junction with the Columbia River near old Fort Spokane.

Spokane weather is much drier than cities east of the Cascades; it gets less than 17 inches of rain a year. Summers days frequently reach into the 80s, and winters are fairly mild, though it does snow.

HISTORY

The name Spokane comes from the Indian word "Spokan," meaning "Sun People." The area around Spokane Falls has been occupied for thousands of years and was a favorite place to fish for salmon each summer. The first white settlers came to this area around 1810—very early in Washington's history—when David Thompson built Spokan House, the first trading post in the state along the Spokan River. (The "e" in Spokane was added later.) The War of 1812 and turbulent times that followed led to abandonment of the post in 1826, and white settlers didn't return until 1838, when Elkanah Walker and Cushing Eels established a Protestant mission that lasted until 1847. Though Spokane County was created in 1859, including all of the land between the Columbia River and Rocky Mountains north of the Snake River, the first permanent settlers didn't arrive at "Spokane Falls" until 1872. The first real settler was James N. Glover, the "Father of Spokane" and a strong proponent of the region's benefits.

Early Years

By 1880, Spokane's population had grown to only 350, and the town competed hotly with neighboring Cheney for the county seat. Vote counters announced Spokane as the winner, but Cheney residents suspected the officials of lying about the results, so they came at night, kidnapped the election official and his records, and proclaimed Cheney the winner of the vote. Spokane's population grew dramatically by the next election—partly due to the arrival of the Northern Pacific Railway—and in 1886 the city had the votes it needed to win the county seat back.

Spokane experienced a tremendous boom following the discovery of fabulously rich silver, lead, and zinc deposits in the nearby Coeur d'Alene area: it grew from a population of 350 in 1880 to almost 20,000 by 1890. The Northern Pacific was the Northwest's first railroad, but its monopoly drove transportation prices sky-high; though eastern Washington was the cheapest place to grow wheat, the farmers paid the highest prices getting it to market. The city of Spokane was so determined to get a second railroad, they gave the land, free of charge, to the Great Northern Railroad Co. to be sure it would pass through town—and to loosen the Northern Pacific's grip on farmers.

As in Seattle and Ellensburg—and most cities in the pioneer West—a devastating fire ripped

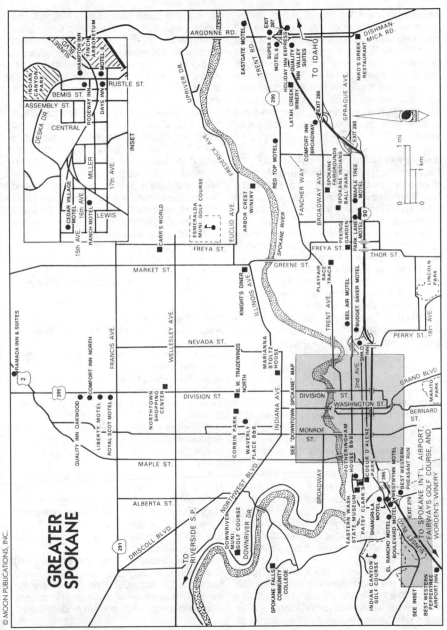

GREATER
SPOKANE

© MOON PUBLICATIONS, INC.

through Spokane. In the summer of 1889, the fire put an end to the all-wood construction that had previously been so popular in these forested regions, leaving 32 blocks in ruins. Henceforth, all downtown areas were rebuilt in brick. Though farming was a large part of the Spokane economy, the mining discoveries throughout the Northwest also sparked the city's economic growth. Several of Spokane's grand old homes belonged to those who made their fortunes from these mines.

World's Fair

The event that put Spokane on the map for most of the country was Expo '74, the city's World's Fair. The theme for the fair, "Celebrating Man's Fresh, New Environment," was a real problem for the developers, since the location chosen was Havermale Island in the middle of the polluted Spokane River, in a dirty, run-down section of town. Washington and Idaho combined their efforts to clean up the river, while grass and trees were planted and buildings torn down to prepare for the fair. The result was a world-class Expo that won international attention and served to gear up the country for the bicentennial celebration. Spokane is the smallest city to ever host a World's Fair.

SIGHTS

Riverfront Park

The site of Expo '74 has been preserved as a striking city park covering over 100 acres in downtown Spokane. Outdoors, stroll around the flower-bedecked paths, play on the rides, walk the suspension bridge over the upper falls to Canada Island, or take the gondola over dramatic **Spokane Falls,** illuminated at night. The most-photographed landmark is a tall riverside clock tower that was a part of the Great Northern Railroad depot for many years. Indoors, the five-story-high **IMAX Theater** features dazzling, sharp images and stereo sound; call (509) 625-6686 for a schedule.

Riverfront Park boasts the **Spokane Opera House,** home to the Spokane Symphony Orchestra. The **Pavilion** amusement park features rides for the daring and tamer attractions for young kids. Be sure to take a spin on the hand-

carved 1909 **Looff Carousel**—a National Historical Landmark—on the park's south side. Nearby is an amusing trash-eating mechanical goat. Kids of all ages enjoy the enormous red **Radio Flyer wagon** that doubles as a slide. Also check out the *Joys of Running Together* steel sculptures by David Govedare that race around the park borders.

Take a **gondola ride** over the Spokane River, park, and falls from the west side of the park, play miniature golf, pet the animals at the petting zoo, ride the park tour train, or try your maneuvers at the ice-skating rink. The park also includes a restaurant, picnic areas, and more. Bikes, rollerblades, strollers, and other wheeled devices can be rented from **Quinn's,** tel. (509) 456-6545, near the South Howard St. Bridge.

It's possible to buy individual tickets to the various rides and attractions, but your best bet is an all-inclusive park day pass for $11. Every weekend 10 a.m.-6 p.m. May-Sept., Riverfront Park hosts arts and crafts booths. Call (509) 456-4386 or (800) 336-7275 for more information on events at the park.

More Downtown Sights

A two-block section of **Wall St.** (between Riverside Ave. and Spokane Falls Blvd.) is blocked to cars and is a popular place to stroll and shop. Noontime concerts take place here on Friday all summer. Head to Crescent Court (Main and Wall) for a food court offering a range of quick meals. Hop aboard one of the frequent **trolleys** to cruise up Wall St. and along Spokane Falls Blvd., before circling the Riverfront Park area. **Skywalks** crisscross the Wall St. and other parts of downtown Spokane, linking 14 blocks above street level.

The **Children's Museum of Spokane,** at 110 N. Post St., tel. (509) 624-5437, features all sorts of fun exhibits to climb on, including a hydroelectric power station (hope they have the power turned off!). The center is open Tues.-Sat.10 a.m.-5 p.m., Sunday noon-5, and costs $4.50 for kids or adults.

Douglas Gallery, 120 N. Wall St., tel. (509) 624-4179, is an impressive private art gallery housed in an old bank building. You'll see the works of masters such as Monet and Rembrandt, along with a wide range of more modern pieces.

DOWNTOWN SPOKANE

Historical Buildings

You can't miss the **Spokane County Courthouse** on W. Broadway at Jefferson Street. Built in 1895 and modeled after a pair of French chateaux, the castle-like courthouse seems rather out of place in busy Spokane. Amazingly, this ornate masterpiece was designed by W.A. Ritchie, a 29-year-old man with no previous design experience; his architectural training came from a correspondence course.

Visit the magnificent sandstone **St. John's Cathedral,** 1125 S. Grand Blvd., tel. (509) 838-4277, to see an impressive example of gothic architecture, complete with stained-glass windows and stone carvings. Forty-nine-bell carillon concerts are held here Thursday at noon. Take a guided tour on Monday, Tuesday, Thursday, or Saturday noon-3 p.m.; admission is free.

Browne's Addition, on the city's west side along W. Pacific and W. 1st, boasts some of the city's finest homes from the 1890s; stroll through the tree-lined neighborhood and stop at **Patsy Clark's** (see "Food," below) for a drink at the grandest mansion on the block. Nearby you'll find the Cheney Cowles Museum and Campbell House, and the **Glover Mansion,** 321 W. 8th Ave., built in1888 for the "Father of Spokane." It's now on the National Register of

Riverfront Park

DON PITCHER

Historic Places, and serves dinners nightly, tel. (509) 459-0000.

Historical Museum

The Eastern Washington State Historical Society houses its extraordinary collection in two buildings at 2316 W. 1st Ave.: the Cheney Cowles Museum and the Campbell House. Both facilities are open Tues.-Sat. 10 a.m.-5 p.m., Sunday 1-5 p.m., and Wednesday evenings till 9 p.m.; tel. (509) 456-3931. Admission to the museum and Campbell House is $4 adults, $3 seniors, $2.50 ages 6-16, or $10 for families. Get in for half-price on Wednesday. Fascinating half-hour tours of the Campbell House are included in your museum entrance fee.

The **Cheney Cowles Museum** has regional artifacts from the prehistoric to the present, as well as changing contemporary and traditional exhibits in the Fine Arts Gallery. The collection spreads through a number of spacious rooms, with magnificent Indian basketry and other artifacts, exhibits on the fur trappers and early settlers, an electric car, and much more.

The **Campbell House,** built in 1898 by renowned Spokane architect Kirtland K. Cutter, is a restored Tudor revival style mansion from Spokane's turn-of-the-century "age of elegance." Amasa B. Campbell made his fortune in the mines of the Coeur d'Alene region and spared no expense on his home. His family lived here until 1924. The home is lavishly furnished with Persian carpets and period antiques. Be sure to

check out the basement-level gambling room and safe. Out back is a Japanese style fountain; the Spokane River rolls along directly behind the house.

Bing Crosby

One of America's best-known crooners, Bing Crosby grew up in Spokane and attended Gonzaga College as a pre-law student. (His real name was Harry Lillis Crosby; while still a child, he picked up the nickname from a comic-strip character.) Gonzaga claims that he "left school" just a semester short of his degree "to pursue his singing career," but he was actually kicked out for throwing a piano through a fourth floor window. Nevertheless, Crosby received an honorary doctorate from Gonzaga in 1937 (after he had become a star). Crosby gained fame in such films as *White Christmas* and *High Society,* and his performance in *Going My Way* won an Oscar in 1945. He went on to appear in or narrate 100 films. Bing died in 1979 at the age of 74 while playing golf in Spain; a posthumous biography by one of his sons was something less than flattering—to put it mildly.

The **Crosby Student Center** on the campus of Gonzaga University houses a collection of Bing Crosby gold records, trophies (the Oscar is actually a duplicate), awards, pipes, and other memorabilia. The building was Bing's gift to his alma mater, and the Crosbyana Room is open Mon.-Fri. 8:30 a.m.-4:30 p.m. in the summer, and daily till midnight during the school year. A bronze statue of Bing stands outside the student center, and his boyhood home is now the Gonzaga Alumni Association, across the street at 508 E. Sharp. More memorabilia here; also check out photos of Bing and his classmates inside the Administration Building. Bing Crosby souvenirs are sold in the student center; call (509) 328-4220, ext. 4279, for more information.

Other Collections
The **Fairchild Heritage Museum** at Fairchild Air Force Base (10 miles west of Spokane), tel. (509) 247-2100, is open Monday, Wednesday, Friday, and Saturday 10 a.m.-2 p.m.; free. A WW II Women's Air Corps Barracks houses exhibits detailing the base's history and the use of air power in the first and second world wars. Out front are eight historic aircraft, including a B-52D. By the way, Fairchild AFB has approximately 85 nuclear bombs in storage, just a few miles from Spokane.

Folks with a taste of the bizarre and tacky won't want to miss **Carr's World,** 5225 N. Freya, tel. (509) 489-8859 or (800) 350-6469. Open Sat.-Sun. 1-4 p.m.; $5. Inside are JFK's 1962 Lincoln Continental (not the one in which he was killed), Jackie Gleason's 1968 limo, and Elvis Presley's 1973 Lincoln. Other exhibits include a Chinese junk made from 27,500 matchsticks, plus a Cheyenne Indian chief mannequin atop a papier-mâché horse! Only in America.

Another small private museum is the **The Red Shed,** 13 miles north of Spokane on a working wheat farm. Here you'll find a red barn filled with old farm machinery, exhibits, and an impressive collection of ironstone dishes. Open by appointment; call (509) 466-2744.

Plants and Critters
Manito Park and Gardens, 4 W. 21st Ave., tel. (509) 625-6622, open daily 8 a.m.-dusk, contains immaculate old-fashioned floral and botanical displays, plus a duck pond that makes a delightful picnic spot. The park was created by the famous Olmsted Brothers, who also designed New York's Central Park. Features include the **Gaiser Conservatory,** which houses tropical plants and floral displays, a formal European-style garden with plantings that change with the seasons (May to early October), and the **Japanese Garden,** a tranquil place to relax. The last

of these is supported by Spokane's sister city, Nishinomiya, Japan. In addition to these, you'll find a rose garden with 150 varieties of roses, and a perennial garden containing native plants.

Stroll through the **John A. Finch Arboretum,** 3404 Woodland Blvd., to see 65 acres of maples, rhododendrons, and ornamental trees along Garden Springs Creek, or walk the interpretive trail. Open daily dawn to dark all year; free. Call (509) 625-6657 for more information. Unfortunately, the attractive setting is marred by the rush of I-90 traffic just a few feet to the south.

For a great view across Spokane, head to Cliff St. above the south side of Pioneer Park. This is a neighborhood with some of Spokane's most impressive homes. Not far away is the city's highest point in **Cliff Park** at 13th Ave. and Grove Street. The rock, a half-acre wide at the base, was once a volcanic island.

Cat Tales Endangered Species Conservation Park, 17020 N. Newport Hwy., tel. (509) 238-4126, has 30 rare or endangered big cats, including tigers, leopards, and pumas. Guided tours are offered; open daily 10 a.m.-6 p.m. April-Sept., and Wed.-Sun. 10 a.m.-4 p.m. the rest of the year. Admission is $5 adults, $4 seniors, and $3 kids under 12.

Riverside State Park
This delightful park six miles northwest of town has open ponderosa pine forests with a grassy understory. As the name suggests, it sits along the Spokane River. Access is from Nine Mile Rd. on the north side of the river or several convoluted routes along the south shore. The 7,655-acre park is a popular place for camping, hiking, horseback riding (guided horseback rides are offered by a concessionaire), birdwatching, kayaking (class III rapids), and even ORVing.

A favorite hiking destination is the **"Bowl and Pitcher"** area, where a trail leaves the campground and crosses a suspension bridge to connect with a network of enjoyable paths. These unusual volcanic formations stand along the fast-flowing river and are visible from a dramatic overlook; the resemblance to a bowl and pitcher is vague. Get here by heading northwest from town on Hwy. 291 (Nine Mile Rd.), and turning left onto Rifle Club Rd., then left again on Aubrey L. White Parkway after a half mile. The park entrance and the Bowl and Pitcher are on the right after 1.7 miles. Call (509) 456-3964 for more information.

Another feature of Riverside State Park is the **Spokane House Interpretive Center,** tel. (509) 466-4747, on the site of the first structure built by white men in the Pacific Northwest. Erected in 1810 by the Northwest Fur Company, this fur-trading post sat at the confluence of the Spokane and Little Spokane Rivers. After 16 years of use, the post was moved to a better site at Kettle Falls. No evidence remains of the trading post, but the interpretive center relates its history in a diorama, exhibits, and artifacts. It is located 12 miles northwest of Spokane on Hwy. 291, and a half mile north of the bridge (on the northeast bank); open Wed.-Sun. 9 a.m.-6 p.m. summers only, free.

Mt. Spokane State Park
This 16,000-acre park, 30 miles northeast of the city on Hwy. 206, encompasses 5,881-foot Mt. Spokane and 5,306-foot Mt. Kit Carson. Enjoy hiking, mountain biking, and camping in the summer, downhill or cross-country skiing (see below) in the winter. Bike rentals, RV parking, and horseback rides are available from the nearby Resort at Mt. Spokane, tel. (509) 238-9114. A narrow, winding road (no RVs) climbs to the summit of Mt. Spokane, where you can stop for a picnic at the CCC-built Vista House. The incredible 360-degree vista encompasses the entire region, including parts of Idaho, Montana, British Columbia, and Alberta. Dirt roads lead to other areas, and trails crisscross the park offering day hikes for all levels of ability.

Universities and Colleges
The Spokane area is home to four colleges and universities, along with two community colleges. Largest of these is Eastern Washington University in nearby Cheney (described below). Other area schools include the private Whitworth College, a branch of Washington State University, and the Community Colleges of Spokane.

One of 28 Jesuit colleges in the U.S., **Gonzaga University,** on Hamilton St. at Centennial Trail, is an independent liberal arts school with 5,000 students and a wide range of degree programs. The law school at Gonzaga is one of three in Washington. The school is best known as the alma mater of Bing Crosby (see above).

Also here is the **Jundt Art Center,** tel. (509) 328-4220, with changing exhibits, along with an extraordinary glass chandelier by Dale Chihuly.

Wineries
Although the Spokane area doesn't have vineyards, several local wineries produce wines from grapes grown in Yakima Valley and elsewhere. Most of these offer tours and free tastings. Enjoy a picnic with a bottle of award-winning wine at **Worden's Winery,** W. 7217 45th, tel. (509) 455-7835, located in a log cabin on the outskirts of Spokane. Open daily noon-5 p.m. for tours and tastings.

Washington's largest producer of Merlot wines, **Latah Creek Wine Cellars,** is off I-90 exit 289 at E. 13030 Indiana Ave., tel. (509) 926-0164. The attractive Spanish mission-style winery features tours, tastings, an art gallery, and a picnic courtyard and is open Mon.-Sat. 10 a.m.-5 p.m. and Sunday noon-5 p.m.,

Arbor Crest Wine Cellars, 4705 N. Fruithill Rd., tel. (509) 927-9894, also has a tasting room and gift shop open daily noon-5 p.m. The building, Cliff House, is a National Historic Site with a magnificent view and parklike grounds.

The small **Caterina Winery** is downtown in the historic Broadview Dairy Building at 905 N. Washington, tel. (509) 328-5069. Open for tours and tasting daily noon-5 p.m. **Knipprath Cellars,** 163 S. Lincoln St., tel. (509) 624-9132, is another downtown winery; open Tues.-Sun. 11:30 a.m.-5:30 p.m.

ACCOMMODATIONS

During major summer events such as Lilac Bloomsday Run, Lilac Festival, and Hoopfest, you should make lodging reservations well ahead of your visit to Spokane. Note that very heavy traffic on North Division may make for noise problems at motels in this area. The newly opened Kempis Executive Suites and Lusso European-style boutique hotels are especially noteworthy (and especially pricey).

Hostel
Brown Squirrel Hostel, 920 W 7th Ave., tel. (509) 838-5968, has a two dorms, a communal kitchen and TV room. No curfew, and the cost is

SPOKANE MOTELS AND HOTELS

Accommodations are arranged from least to most expensive. Rates at some lodging places are lower during the winter months. See the text for descriptions of local bed and breakfasts and the hostel.

BUDGET

Lantern Park Motel; Airway Heights; tel. (509) 244-3653; $24-30 s, $29-34 d; jacuzzi, kitchenettes available, see rooms first

Ranch Motel; 1609 S. Lewis; tel. (509) 456-8919; $25 s, $29 d; microwaves and fridges, see rooms first

Cedar Village Motel; 5415 W. Sunset; tel. (509) 624-2450; $28 s, $34 d; kitchenettes available, local calls 25 cents, quiet out-of-the-way location

Budget Saver Motel; 1234 E. Sprague; tel. (509) 534-0669; $29 s, $33 d; continental breakfast, kitchenettes available

Maple Tree Motel; 4824 E. Sprague; tel. (509) 535-5810; $30 s or d; kitchenettes available

Downtowner Motel; S. 165 Washington; tel. (509) 838-4411; $30 s, $33 d

INEXPENSIVE

El Rancho Motel; W. 3000 Sunset; tel. (509) 455-9400; $30 s, $37 d; outdoor pool, kitchenettes available

Boulevard Motel; 2905 W. Sunset; tel. (509) 747-1060; $31 s, $38 d; kitchenettes available

Shadows Motel & RV Park; 9025 N. Division; tel. (509) 467-6951; $33 s, $38 d; kitchenettes available, local calls 25 cents

Bel Air Motel 7; 1303 E. Sprague Ave.; tel. (509) 535-1677; $33-37 s, $37-39 d; AAA approved

Bell Motel; 9030 W. Sunset Hwy.; tel. (509) 624-0852 or (800) 223-1388; $34 s or d

Clinic Center Motel; 702 S. McClellan; tel. (509) 747-6081; $34-42 s or d; local calls 25 cents

Starlite Motel; 3809 S. Geiger Blvd.; tel. (509) 747-7186 or (800) 772-7186; $35 s, $40 d; kitchenettes available, local calls 25 cents

West Wynn Motel; 2701 W. Sunset; tel. (509) 747-3037; $37 s, $43 d; indoor pool, jacuzzi, sauna

Nendel's Valu Inn; 1420 W. 2nd Ave.; tel. (509) 838-2026 or (800) 246-6835; $38 s, $42-46 d; outdoor pool, kitchenettes available

Eastgate Motel; 10625 E. Trent; tel. (509) 922-4556; $40 s, $45-50 d; kitchenettes available

Liberty Motel; 6801 N. Division; tel. (509) 467-6000; $40-50 s or d

Shangri-La Motel; 2922 W. Government Way; tel. (509) 747-2066 or (800) 234-4941; $41 s, $43 d; outdoor pool, kitchenettes available, airport shuttle, AAA approved

Red Top Motel; 7212 E. Trent; tel. (509) 926-5728 or (800) 447-8202; $42 s, $45 d; outdoor pool, jacuzzi, kitchenettes available

Park Lane Motel and RV Park; 4412 E. Sprague; tel. (509) 535-1626 or (800) 533-1626; $43-58 s, $53-68 d; well-maintained family motel, kitchenettes available

Motel 6; 1508 S. Rustle St.; tel. (509) 459-6120 or (800) 466-8356; $44 s, $50 d; outdoor pool

Motel 6; 1919 N. Hutchinson Rd.; tel. (509) 926-5399 or (800) 466-8356; $44 s, $50 d

Towne Center Motor Inn; 901 W. 1st Ave.; tel. (509) 747-1041 or (800) 247-1041; $45 s, $50 d; continental breakfast, fridges

(continues on next page)

SPOKANE MOTELS AND HOTELS
(continued)

MODERATE

Trade Winds Motel; 907 W. 3rd Ave.; tel. (509) 838-2091 or (800) 586-5397; $46-60 s, $65 d; outdoor pool, jacuzzi, exercise room, pool table, continental breakfast, AAA approved

Days Inn Spokane Airport; 4212 W. Sunset Blvd.; tel. (509) 747-2021 or (800) 325-2525; $47 s $65 d; outdoor pool, tennis court, airport shuttle

Apple Tree Inn Motel; 9508 N. Division; tel. (509) 466-3020 or (800) 323-5796; $48 s, $50 d; outdoor pool, kitchen suites available, AAA approved

Super 8 Motel Spokane Valley; 2020 N. Argonne Rd.; tel. (509) 928-4888 or (800) 800-8000; $49 s, $57 d; airport shuttle, AAA approved

Rodeway Inn City Center; W. 827 1st Ave., tel. (509) 838-8271 or (800) 228-2000; $49-54 s, $54-67 d; outdoor pool, jacuzzi, sauna, exercise room, continental breakfast, kitchenettes available, AAA approved

Alpine Motel; 18815 E. Cataldo (10 miles east of Spokane); tel. (509) 928-2700; $50 s, $55 d; outdoor pool, AAA approved

Comfort Inn Broadway; 6309 E. Broadway; tel. (509) 535-7185 or (800) 228-5150; $52-67 s, $60-77 d; outdoor pool, jacuzzi, continental breakfast, kitchenettes available, AAA approved

Super 8 Motel West; 11102 W. Westbow; tel. (509) 838-8800 or (800) 800-8000; $55 s, $61 d; indoor pool, jacuzzi, AAA approved

Best Western Thunderbird Inn; 120 W. 3rd Ave.; tel. (509) 747-2011 or (800) 578-2473; $55-59 s, $69-74 d; outdoor pool, exercise room, jacuzzi, continental breakfast, AAA approved

Royal Scot Motel; 20 W. Houston Ave.; tel. (509) 467-6672 or (888) 467-7268; $55-60 s or d; outdoor pool

Best Western Trade Winds North; 3033 N. Division St.; tel. (509) 326-5500 or (800) 621-8593; $59-64 s, $69-73 d; indoor pool, jacuzzi, saunas, continental breakfast, AAA approved

Holiday Inn Express Valley; 9220 E. Mission; tel. (509) 927-7100 or (800) 465-4329; $59-69 sd, $67-77 d; indoor pool, jacuzzi, fitness center, business center, breakfast buffet, AAA approved

Howard Johnson Inn; 211 S. Division St.; tel. (509) 838-6630 or (800) 446-4656; $60 s, $70 d; AAA approved

Travelodge; 33 W. Spokane Falls Blvd.; tel. (509) 623-9727 or (800) 578-7878; $60-79 s, $70-79 d; airport shuttle, fitness center, business center, continental breakfast, AAA approved

Quality Inn Oakwood; 7919 N. Division St.; tel. (509) 467-4900 or (888) 535-4900; $62-79 s, $74-84 d; indoor pool, jacuzzi, exercise room, continental breakfast, AAA approved

Best Western Peppertree Airport Inn; 3711 S. Geiger Blvd.; tel. (509) 624-4655 or (800) 528-1234; $65-85 s, $75-115 d; new motel, indoor pool, jacuzzi, exercise room, microwaves and fridges, continental breakfast, airport shuttle, AAA approved

Shilo Inn; 923 E. 3rd; tel. (509) 535-9000 or (800) 222-2244; $65-99 s or d; indoor pool, fitness center, sauna, jacuzzi, breakfast buffet, airport shuttle, AAA approved

Cavanaughs Fourth Avenue; E. 110 4th Ave.; tel. (509) 838-6101 or (800) 843-4667; $66 s, $72 d; outdoor pool, airport shuttle, 50 cents for local calls, AAA approved

Hampton Inn; S. 2010 Assembly Rd.; tel. (509) 747-1100 or (800) 426-7866; $66-83 s, $76-93 d; indoor pool, jacuzzi, exercise room, continental breakfast buffet, airport shuttle, AAA approved

Comfort Inn Valley; 905 N. Sullivan Rd.; tel. (509) 924-3838 or (800) 228-5150; $66-95 s or d; outdoor pool, jacuzzi, kitchenettes available, continental breakfast

EXPENSIVE

Fairfield Inn by Marriott; 311 N. Riverpoint Blvd.; tel. (509) 747-9131 or (800) 228-2800; $67-77 s, $72-83 d; new motel, indoor pool, jacuzzi, continental breakfast, AAA approved

Country Inns & Suites; 3808 N. Sullivan Rd.; tel. (509) 893-0955 or (800) 456-4000; $69 s, $74 d; new motel, indoor pool, sauna, jacuzzi, continental breakfast, AAA approved

Best Western Pheasant Run; 12415 E. Mission; tel. (509) 926-7432 or (888) 297-1555; $69-125 s, $76-135 d; indoor pool, jacuzzi, sauna, exercise room, microwaves, continental breakfast

Doubletree Hotel Spokane Valley; 1100 N. Sullivan Rd. (I-90 exit 291); tel. (509) 924-9000 or (800) 222-8733; $72-90 s or d; outdoor pool, jacuzzi, airport shuttle, exercise room, kitchenettes available, AAA approved

Holiday Inn Express Downtown; 801 N. Division; tel. (509) 328-8505 or (800) 465-4329; $74 s or d; breakfast buffet, fitness center, business center

Comfort Inn North; 7111 N. Division; tel. (509) 467-7111 or (800) 228-5150; $75-130 s or d; outdoor pool, jacuzzi, continental breakfast, kitchenettes available

Ramada Inn & Suites; 9601 N. Newport Hwy.; tel. (509) 468-4201 or (800) 272-6232; $79 s, $84 d; indoor pool, jacuzzi, sauna, continental breakfast, AAA approved

Cavanaughs River Inn; 700 N. Division St.; tel. (509) 326-5577 or (800) 843-4667; $79-105 s, $89-115 d; two outdoor pools, wading pool, jacuzzi, sauna, airport shuttle, tennis courts, 50 cents for local calls, AAA approved

Ramada Inn; Spokane International Airport; tel. (509) 838-5211 or (800) 272-6232; $79 s, $87 d; indoor and outdoor pools, jacuzzi, exercise room, kitchenettes available, airport shuttle, AAA approved

Quality Inn Valley Suites; 8923 E. Mission; tel. (509) 928-5218 or (800) 777-7355; $79-300 s, $89-300 d; indoor pool, jacuzzi, sauna, fridges and microwaves, continental breakfast, exercise room, airport shuttle, AAA approved

Courtyard by Mariott; 401 N. Riverpoint Blvd.; tel. (509) 456-7600 or (800) 321-2211; $85-117 s or d; indoor pool, jacuzzi, exercise room, AAA approved

Ramada Limited; 123 S. Post; tel. (509) 838-8504 or (800) 272-6232; $89 s or d; continental breakfast, local calls 35 cents, airport shuttle

Doubletree Hotel Spokane City Center; 322 N. Spokane Falls Court; tel. (509) 455-9600 or (800) 222-8733; $94-104 s, $104-114 d; indoor pool, exercise room, sauna, jacuzzi, airport shuttle, AAA approved

PREMIUM

Cavanaughs Ridpath Hotel; 515 W. Sprague; tel. (509) 838-2711 or (800) 843-4667; $105-115 s, $115-125 d; outdoor pool, exercise facility, airport shuttle, 50 cents for local calls, AAA approved

Cavanaughs Inn at the Park; 303 W. North River Dr.; $109-119 s, $119-129 d; tel. (509) 326-8000 or (800) 843-4667; indoor and outdoor pools, wading pool, jacuzzis, sauna, exercise room, kitchenettes available, airport shuttle, 50 cents for local calls, AAA approved

LUXURY

Kempis Executive Suites; 326 W. 6th Ave.; tel. (509) 747-4321 or (888) 236-4321; $190-220 s or d; new hotel in a beautifully renovated 1906 building, antique furnishings, claw-foot tubs, suites with kitchens, business center, continental breakfast, concierge, exercise facilities, airport shuttle

WestCoast Hotel Lusso; North 1 Post; tel. (509) 747-9750 or (800) 426-0670; $220 s or d; luxurious boutique hotel in 1890 building, spacious rooms, continental breakfast, afternoon reception, fitness center, jacuzzi, valet parking, airport shuttle

just $12 per person. The hostel is closed 10 a.m.-4 p.m. Private rooms for couples are also available ($24 d), but not in summer. Reservations are advised in summer, but the hostel generally has space.

Bed and Breakfast

For referrals to Spokane's best B&Bs, call the **Spokane Bed & Breakfast Reservation Service,** tel. (509) 624-3776. Unless otherwise noted, all B&Bs listed below serve a full breakfast and do not allow young children.

Angelica's Mansion B&B, 1321 W. 9th Ave., tel. (509) 624-5598 or (800) 987-0053, is a graceful 1907 craftsman brick home on the National Register of Historic Places. The four guest rooms have private baths; $80-115 s or $85-125 d.

Cobblestone Bakery B&B Inn, 620 S. Washington, tel. (509) 624-9735, was built in 1900 and features two upstairs guest rooms, private baths, plus a big front porch and stained glass windows. Children are okay; $69-89 s or $79-99 d.

Built by Spokane's first mayor, **Fotheringham House B&B,** 2128 W. 2nd Ave., tel. (509) 838-1891, is a beautifully restored 1891 Victorian home in the historic Browne's Addition part of town. The home contains period furnishings, carved woodwork, and tin ceilings in the four guest rooms; $80-95 s or d.

Marianna Stoltz House, 427 E. Indiana, tel. (509) 483-4316 or (800) 978-6587, a classic American foursquare home built in 1908, stands on a tree-lined street near Gonzaga University. A wide veranda, spacious parlor, and antique furnishings add to the grace. The four antique-furnished guest rooms have private baths; $65-85 s or $75-95 d.

Oslo's B&B, 1821 E. 39th Ave., tel. (509) 838-3175, is a quiet contemporary home with two guest rooms, a large terrace and garden, plus a Norwegian owner and Norwegian-style breakfasts; $60-80 s or d.

Twickenham Cottage B&B, 2809 W. Summit Blvd., tel. (509) 326-2397, has two guest rooms with private baths; $80 s or d.

Waverly Place B&B, 709 W. Waverly Place, tel. (509) 328-1856, is a Victorian-era home on Corbin Park. Built in 1902, this gorgeous home features hardwood floors, gas chandeliers, and a wraparound porch, and an outdoor swimming pool. The four guest rooms have private or shared baths, and kids are welcome. A gourmet breakfast is served; $70-95 s or $75-105 d.

Campgrounds and RV Parks

The closest public campgrounds are in **Riverside State Park,** tel. (509) 456-3964, six miles northwest of town. Tent sites ($11; no RV hookups) are available year-round. **Mt. Spokane State Park,** tel. (509) 456-4169, 30 miles northeast of Spokane (described above), has tent sites for $10; open May-October.

Private RV parks include: **Alpine Motel RV Park,** 18815 E. Cataldo, tel. (509) 928-2700; **Alderwood RV Resort,** 14007 N. Newport Hwy., tel. (509) 467-5320 or (888) 847-0500; **Park Lane Motel & RV Park,** 4412 E. Sprague, tel. (509) 535-1626 or (800) 533-1626; **Yogi Bear's Camp Resort,** 7520 Thomas Mallen Rd., tel. (509) 747-9415 or (800) 494-7275; **Shadows Motel & RV Park,** 9025 N. Division, tel. (509) 467-6951; **KOA of Spokane,** 3025 N. Barker Rd. (I-90 exit 293), tel. (509) 924-4722 or (800) 562-3309; and **Trailer Inns,** 6021 E. 4th Ave., tel. (509) 535-1811 or (800) 659-4864.

FOOD AND DRINK

If you like good food, you're in for a treat in Spokane. Folks here eat out a *lot* and support a wide range of restaurants, from corner coffee shops to an elaborate mansion offering a gourmet menu. In addition to the places listed below, there are plenty of charming bistros that cater to the downtown lunch crowd. Walk around a bit and you're sure to come across something interesting.

Breakfast

For all-American breakfast "comfort food" served in an old railroad car, don't miss **Knight's Diner,** 2909 N. Market, tel. (509) 484-0015, a Spokane landmark for over 40 years. Sit at the long mahogany counter to watch the chef working a mountain of hash browns and catch the banter slung by the speedy waitresses. You'll find a cross-section of Spokane folks at this immensely popular, noisy, and hectic morning eatery any day of the week. A similar Spokane institution is **Frank's Diner,** 1516 W. 2nd, tel. (509) 455-

*Patsy Clark's
Restaurant*

DIANNE BOUERICE LYONS

7402, offering inexpensive breakfasts and other stick-to-the-ribs food in an antique railcar. **Cannon Street Grill,** 144 S. Cannon St., tel. (509) 456-8660, is an excellent local breakfast place. Good lunches too.

The **Milk Bottle Restaurant,** 802 W. Garland, tel. (509) 328-4540, has been around since 1932, and is locally famous for burgers, shakes, and homemade ice cream. The building's shape is easy to guess.

Light Meals and Coffee
Three Brothers Cafe, next to Auntie's Bookstore at 402 W. Main, tel. (509) 363-1055, serves a good homemade lunch of salads, pastas, healthy soups, and sandwiches. Another popular downtown sandwich and salad shop is **Domini Sandwiches,** 703 W. Sprague, tel. (509) 747-2324, in business for 90 years. This family-run place has a great chaotic atmosphere and huge sandwiches with thick slices of meat.

Also well worth a visit for pastas, sandwiches, salads, desserts, and espresso is **Lindaman's Gourmet-to-Go,** 1235 S. Grand Blvd., tel. (509) 838-3000. See also Huckleberry's, listed below under "Markets."

American Eats
In the Old Flour Mill near Riverfront Park, **Clinkerdagger's Restaurant,** 621 W. Mallon Ave., tel. (509) 328-5965, serves up a well-prepared menu that combines steaks, fresh seafood, and Northwest cuisine with a view of Spokane Falls.

The Onion, 302 W. Riverside, tel. (509) 624-9965, is a Spokane institution with fast and friendly service, a convivial atmosphere, and justly famous gourmet burgers, barbecue ribs, fajitas, and salads. Huckleberry milk shakes are another favorite, and beer drinkers will find plenty of offerings and a weekday happy hour. The location is within one of Spokane's classic old buildings, originally the St. Regis Hotel; many of its original furnishings are still present.

Calgary Steak House, 3040 E. Sprague, tel. (509) 535-7502, claims to make the best steaks in Spokane. If you just want a great inexpensive burger without the frills, head to **Dick's Hamburgers,** 10 E 3rd Ave., tel. (509) 747-2481. **Longhorn Barbecue,** in the valley at 7611 W. Sunset Hwy., tel. (509) 838-8372, is the place for beefy ribs, steaks, and good milkshakes. At the other end of the culinary spectrum is **Mizuna,** 214 N. Howard, tel. (509) 747-2004, with innovative vegetarian cuisine for lunch and dinner (plus Saturday and Sunday brunch).

Pizzas and Italian
For pizza, pastas, calzones, and desserts in a comfortable downtown setting, head to **Europa Pizzeria and Bakery,** 125 S. Wall St., tel. (509) 455-4051.

An Italian place with great specials, including a smoked salmon lasagna, is **Luiji's,** 113 N. Bernard, tel. (509) 624-5226. **Rock City,** W. 505 Riverside, tel. (509) 455-4400, is a very popular Italian eatery with calzones, pastas, unusual pizzas, and such specialties as chicken al forno and Jack Daniel's whiskey steak.

If you're just looking for a fast slice of New York-style pizza to go, drop by **David's Gourmet Pizza,** 4 N. Howard, tel. (509) 838-6982. The shop isn't much bigger than a breadbox but comes up with all sorts of distinctive pizzas.

Asian Food

Excellent Thai cooking (including several off-beat desserts) at **Thai Cafe,** 410 W. Sprague, tel. (509) 838-4783. A showy, Benihana-style Japanese steak, seafood, and sushi place is **Shogun Restaurant,** 821 E. 3rd Ave., tel. (509) 534-7777. Much smaller is the always-crowded sushi bar at **Suki Yaki,** 119 N. Bernard, tel. (509) 624-0022. Reservations advised.

Peking Garden, E. 3420 Sprague, tel. (509) 534-2525, is among the city's better Chinese restaurants—and inexpensive to boot. Try the big Mongolian barbecue where you select the food and watch them cook with flair (and flare).

Taste of India, 3110 N. Division St., tel. (509) 327-7313, has very good Indian food. Downtown's **Mustard Seed Cafe,** 245 W. Spokane Falls Blvd., tel. (509) 747-2689, is an airy place with a Japanese and Chinese menu of spring rolls, beef teriyaki, spicy Sichuan shrimp, and other items. Heavy on the grease at times.

More International Places

Enjoy delicious Greek food at **Niko's Greek and Middle Eastern Restaurant** downtown at 725 W. Riverside, tel. (509) 624-7444. In addition to traditional faves such as spanakopita, lamb dishes, and baklava, the restaurant has a number of Indian specialties. Fans of hearty German and Hungarian cooking will love **Restaurant Edelweis,** 218 N. Howard St., tel. (509) 459-6908. This is the real thing!

Luna, 5620 S Perry St., tel. (509) 448-2383, is a delightful and trendy little bistro with noteworthy meals, including Sunday brunch. The menu changes often. Make reservations to be sure of a table. **Marrakesh Restaurant,** W. 2008 Northwest Blvd., tel. (509) 328-9733, serves Middle Eastern meals, including five-course Moroccan feasts.

Mexican food is represented by **Azteca,** 200 W. Spokane Falls Blvd., tel. (509) 456-0350, and **Señor Guillermo's,** 7905 E. Trent, tel. (509) 924-4304, out in the Valley. **Chapala Mexican**

Food has four locations around town, all of them with very good south-of-the-border fare. Downtown, get tasty fast food from **Sonic Burritos,** 2622 E 29th Ave., tel. (509) 536-1170.

Seafood

Milford's Fish House, 719 N. Monroe St., tel. (509) 326-7251, is Spokane's favorite place for fresh seafood. Be sure to check the specials and fresh oysters. Excellent food, friendly service, and an attractive exposed-brick setting. Reservations are advised. **C.I. Shenanigan's Seafood Chophouse and Brewery,** 332 N. Spokane Falls Court, tel. (509) 455-6690, combines beer and seafood in a pleasant riverside location. The patio is especially popular on sunny afternoons.

Food with a View

Ankeny's, atop the Cavanaughs Ridpath Hotel at 515 W. Sprague Ave., tel. (509) 838-6311, and **Eagle's Nest,** atop Shilo Inn at 923 E. 3rd, tel. (509) 534-1551, both offer top-of-town dining with panoramic vistas across Spokane. **Windows of the Seasons Restaurant,** 303 W. North River Dr. at Cavanaughs Inn at the Park, tel. (509) 328-9526, sits along the Spokane River with more grand views. Stop by for a drink at sunset, but eat elsewhere, none of these have dinners worth a special trip. Clinkerdagger's and Shenanigan's (described above) also have nice views and more notable meals.

Pricey Eats

One of the most elegant mansions in the Northwest houses **Patsy Clark's,** 2208 W. 2nd St., tel. (509) 838-8300. Patsy came to America in 1870, made millions in the Anaconda copper mines, and commissioned an architect to build him a nice little home—and money was no object. The resulting structure features stained-glass windows from Tiffany's, Italian marble, carved wood from England, and an eight-foot-high grandfather clock. Enjoy a dinner of steak, ahi tuna, duck, or veal, or just have a drink from the extensive wine list and pick up the brochure for a self-guided tour of the lavish interior. If you sit down to eat, be prepared to drop $35 per person. Patsy's is the sort of place presidents dine (former President Bush did so), though critics are not always as kind. Open daily for dinner plus Sunday brunch; reservations required.

Bakeries and Coffee
Spokane town has several good bakeries, including **Great Harvest Bread Co.,** 816 W. Sprague, tel. (509) 624-9370, for whole grain breads, monstrous bagels, and sweets, and **Fitzbillies Bagel Bakery,** 1325 W. 1st Ave., tel. (509) 747-1834, for fresh bagels in a hang-out atmosphere. **4 Seasons Coffee,** 222 N. Howard St., tel. (509) 747-2315, is a great espresso and pastry shop, with a big brick-walled space and friendly service. **Rocket Bakery,** has four local locations, including 3315 N Argonne Rd., tel. (509) 927-2340. Good atmosphere, and great muffins, cookies, scones, and espresso.

Brewpubs
Birkebeiner's Brew Pub, W. 35 Main, tel. (509) 458-0854, serves up tangy, fresh-brewed suds in a smoke-free environment. Good pub grub too.

The food is nothing special, but **Ft. Spokane Brewery,** W. 401 Spokane Falls Blvd., tel. (509) 838-3809, has beer on tap and live blues music almost every night. **Bayou Brewing Company,** 1003 E. Trent, tel. (509) 484-4818, recreates the New Orleans French Quarter with a fun ambiance, Cajun and American cooking, and handcrafted beers—all in a no-smoking atmosphere.

Big Horn Brewery/RAM Family Restaurant, 908 N. Howard, tel. (509) 326-3745, is a combination sports bar and restaurant, with big screen TVs, pool tables, and great burgers. Service can be slow in this very popular eatery.

Markets
For upscale grocery shopping at its best, head to **Huckleberry's Fresh Market** 926 S. Monroe St., tel. (509) 624-1349, the largest organic market in the inland Northwest, and an excellent place to get produce, healthy foods, and wines. The first-rate deli features panini, soups, sandwiches, sushi, and baked goods, all to eat here or take away.

Spokane MarketPlace, tel. (509) 482-2627, is an outdoor market with fresh produce, seafood, ethnic specialties, flowers, pottery, and baked goods. Find the market every Sunday, Wednesday, Friday, and Saturday in the summer at 1202 W. 1st Avenue.

SHOPPING

Downtown, skywalks link 14 blocks of shopping and dining on two levels, including two shopping malls plus several large department stores. The **Flour Mill,** adjacent to the Riverfront Park at 621 W. Mallon, was the most modern mill west of the Mississippi when it was built in 1890; today the restored brick building is home to 17 shops, including galleries, restaurants, gifts, and candy stores. Several huge malls can be found on the outskirts of Spokane. For a sour taste of the new America, head out North Division to join the long traffic jam past ugly strip malls, shopping centers, and a clutter of neon signs.

One old-time shop worth a visit is **Indiana Harness & Saddlery Co.,** 3030 E. Sprague Ave., tel. (509) 535-3400, with Western wear, saddles, cowboy boots and hats, horse tack, and lots more. Another distinctive place is **Small Wonders,** 425 W. 1st, tel. (509) 458-4043, with a big selection of dollhouses and other miniature creations. Spokane has a number of high-quality antique shops, including **Schade Antique Mall** in a beautifully restored building at 528 E. Trent Ave., tel. (509) 624-0272. Also here are various artists and crafts workers.

RECREATION

Spokane is surrounded by a diversity of recreation opportunities. Located just 33 miles from Spokane is **Coeur d'Alene Lake,** one of the most beautiful in the mountain west with the world's longest floating boardwalk and an 18-hole shoreline golf course with a floating green. Immediately north of Spokane are the **Selkirk Mountains,** where you'll find all sorts of wild country and a string of small towns along the Pend Oreille River. To the south are the wide open spaces of the Palouse farmlands; to the west lies a massive desert in the Columbia Basin, along with famous Grand Coulee Dam.

Skiing
Thirty miles northeast of town on Hwy. 206 at Mt. Spokane State Park (see above), **Mt. Spokane Ski & Snowboard Park** offers alpine skiing and snowboarding, including five chair

lifts, and a 2,000-foot vertical drop. It's uncrowded and friendly, with a small-town atmosphere. Night skiing draws the crowds here, as does the dry snow and 360-degree view of the Cascade, Selkirk, and Rocky Mountains. Other features include ski and snowboard school and rentals, restaurant, and bar, but no child care. Lift tickets are reasonable: $25. Call (509) 238-2220 for more information, or (509) 443-1397 for the snow report. Bus transportation from Spokane is available on weekends. The **Resort at Mt. Spokane,** tel. (509) 238-9114, has lodging, food, and ski and snowmobile rentals near the park entrance.

Some 24 km of groomed **cross-country ski trails** are adjacent to the downhill area; get Sno-Park permits at local sporting goods stores before heading up to ski. The 10-km **Langlauf Cross-Country Ski Race** takes place here in early February; it's the biggest such race in the Northwest. Other nearby places with cross-country ski trails are **Downriver Golf Course,** tel. (509) 327-5259, **Indian Canyon Golf Course,** tel. (509) 747-5353; and **Hills Resort,** tel. (208) 443-2551 in Priest Lake, Idaho.

Other nearby ski areas include **49° North** near Chewelah, tel. (509) 935-6649, along with two Idaho resorts: **Schweitzer Mountain Resort,** tel. (800) 831-8810, and **Silver Mountain,** tel. (800) 204-6428.

Golf

Spokane is justly proud of its numerous public and private golf courses, and is considered one of the five best golfing cities in America. More than a dozen can be found in the area, including **Indian Canyon,** S. Assembly and West Dr., tel. (509) 747-5353—one of the top public courses in the U.S. and the site of many major golf tournaments. Spokane's newest course, **The Creek at Qualchan Golf Course,** 301 E. Meadow Ln., tel. (509) 448-9317, even boasts its own bird and wildlife sanctuary.

Other Adventures

Hikers and cyclists should be sure to check out the excellent **Spokane River Centennial Trail,** a nearly level paved path that extends 50 miles along the river from Coeur d'Alene, Idaho, to the confluence of the Spokane and Little Spokane Rivers in Riverside State Park.

Swim at one of more than half-a-dozen outdoor pools around Spokane; call (509) 625-6960 for details. The **YWCA,** W. 829 Broadway, tel. (509) 326-1190, has an indoor pool. More swimming at **Liberty Lake,** near the Idaho border. Contact **Wiley E. Waters White Water Rafting,** tel. (888) 502-1900, for nearby whitewater rafting opportunities on the Spokane River.

The local **REI** store, 1125 N. Monroe, tel. (509) 328-9900, has all sorts of classes and guides trips throughout the year. They also rent a range of camping and other outdoor gear. **Wild Walls,** 202 W. Sprague, tel. (509) 455-9596, has an indoor rock climbing wall with instruction and gear rentals.

Enjoy a trail ride with **Indian Canyon Riding Stable** at Indian Canyon Park, 4812 W. Canyon Dr., tel. (509) 624-4646. **Rockin' B Ranch,** tel. (509) 891-9016, has a chuckwagon barbecue and cowboy singing at Liberty Lake, near the Idaho border.

EVENTS

The **Lilac Bloomsday Run,** held the first Sunday in May, attracts over 60,000 runners with a downtown 12-km course. It's called the world's largest timed race; all competitors are given finishing times. At the same time, Spokane hosts one of America's largest fitness and running trade shows. Call (509) 838-1579 for more information. After Bloomsday, Spokane blossoms with two weeks of activity called the **Lilac Festival,** culminating in the Armed Forces Day Torchlight Parade on the third Saturday of May. The lilac garden at Manito Park is usually in full bloom for the festival; other events include entertainment, concerts, and an amateur golf tournament. Late May brings the **Spokane Dixieland Jazz Festival** with bands and dancing; tel. (509) 235-4401, and **ArtFest,** a kid-oriented hands-on event with arts, crafts, and food at the Cheney Cowles Museum.

Basketball players from all over the Western U.S. descend on Spokane for **Hoopfest** in late June, a weekend of three-on-three basketball games. More than 4,600 teams compete in this double-elimination tournament that spreads over 300 courts. In addition to the hoops, you'll find a food fair and other activities at Riverfront Park. Call (509) 624-2414 for more information.

On the fourth Saturday in July Spokane comes to life with the **Royal Fireworks Concert and Festival,** tel. (509) 326-3136, an extravaganza of food, entertainment, and an open air symphony concert at Riverfront Park. Fireworks follow the music. **Pig Out in the Park,** on the week before Labor Day, is four days of food, live music, and a beer garden in Riverfront Park. The **Spokane Interstate Fair,** tel. (509) 535-1766, held for nine days in mid-September at the fairgrounds at Broadway and Havana, features big name musical entertainment and a PRCA rodeo.

In late November, **Christmas Tree Elegance** features the lighting of an enormous metallic tree, a giant snowman, strolling carolers, carriage rides, and decorations.

Spokane Raceway Park has drag and stock car races on Saturday nights May-September. Call (509) 244-3663 for details.

ARTS AND ENTERTAINMENT

Nightlife

Spokane's surprisingly active club scene has spawned a number of national acts. You'll find something going on every night of the week, from garage band grunge to crowded poetry readings. Pick up a free copy of *The Inlander* newspaper for info on upcoming events.

Outback Jack's World Famous, 321 W. Sprague, tel. (509) 624-4549, is a spacious and popular bar featuring local and touring acts, plus a room filled with pool and foosball tables. Other clubs with live bands and DJs include: **Swackhammer's,** at Division and Lincoln, tel. (509) 467-5210; **Sunset Junction,** 1801 W. Sunset Blvd., tel. (509) 455-9131; and **Thudpucker's,** 43 W. Riverside, tel. (509) 747-5547. **The Rocket,** 152 S. Browne, tel. (509) 455-9210, has Friday night DJ dancing, and Saturday night rock bands. For Top 40, try **Ankeny's** atop the Ridpath Hotel at 515 W. Sprague, tel. (509) 838-6311.

Hang out with the college crowd at **Jack & Dan's Tavern,** 1226 N Hamilton St., (509) 487-6546. Owned by Carl Malone's dad, this is also a good place to meet SuperSonics players. Another very popular sports-and-boozing bar is **The Viking,** 1221 N. Stevens, tel. (509) 326-2942. On Sunday nights the scene shifts to **Mootsy's Tavern,** 406 W. Sprague, tel. (509) 838-1570, where the poetry readings often pack the house.

Ft. Spokane Brewery, W. 401 Spokane Falls Blvd., tel. (509) 838-3809, has live music almost every night, specializing in blues. **Birkebeiner's Brew Pub,** W. 35 Main, tel. (509) 458-0854, has live bands several times a week, and is one of the only local places where smoking is verboten. Good food too. **Bayou Brewing Company,** 1003 E. Trent, tel. (509) 484-4818, is the most packaged place in town, with a recreated New Orleans' atmosphere (created by movie

Spokane Opera House

set designers), fresh-brewed beers, Cajun cooking, pool tables, and dance bands or comedy acts nightly. This is *the* place to be on Fat Tuesday, and it's always smoke free. **O'Doherty's Irish Grille,** W. 525 Spokane Falls Blvd., tel. (509) 747-0322, often has live Irish music, and always has Guiness on draught. For jazz, head to **Hobart's,** in Cavanaughs Fourth Ave. at E. 110 4th Ave., tel. (509) 838-6101, or **Harry O's Bistro,** 508 E. 3rd, tel. (509) 458-2202.

Music and Theater

Riverfront Park sponsors concerts and other entertainment during the summer; call (509) 625-6685 or (800) 336-7275 for a schedule of upcoming events. Free **Summer Sizzle** noontime concerts take place Friday all summer on pedestrian-only Wall Street.

The **Spokane Symphony**—in existence for more than 50 years—presents classical, pops, and chamber concerts, plus *The Nutcracker* at the Spokane Opera House, 334 W. Spokane Falls Blvd., tel. (509) 624-1200. The opera house is also home to music, dance, and dramatic productions throughout the year, including a popular **Best of Broadway** series of musicals.

The **Spokane Civic Theater,** 1020 N. Howard, hosts performances from drama to comedy year-round; call (509) 325-2507 for schedule and ticket information. Get information on the **Spokane Interplayers Ensemble,** a resident professional theater group with seven productions each year, by calling (509) 455-7529.

Movies

Plenty of places to catch a flick in Spokane, including a new 20-plex theater downtown, but only the **Garland** 924 W. Garland, tel. (509) 327-1050, has films for just a buck.

Spectator Sports

The Northwest League's **Spokane Indians** play Class-A baseball at the Interstate Fairgrounds Stadium on Havana Street. The 10,000-seat stadium is the classiest ballpark in the league. Call (509) 535-2922 for ticket and schedule information. In the winter, the **Spokane Chiefs,** tel. (509) 535-7825, play tier-one ice hockey at Spokane Veterans Memorial Arena. Concerts,

ice shows, rodeos, circuses, and other major events also take place here. The professional **Spokane Shadow Soccer** team plays at Joe Albi Stadium; call (509) 535-8000 for details. From Aug.-Oct., take a chance on a horse at the **Playfair Race Course,** Altamont and Main Streets; call (509) 534-0505 for post times and prices.

INFORMATION AND SERVICES

Visit the **Spokane Regional Convention and Visitors Bureau** at 201 W. Main, tel. (509) 747-3230 or (800) 248-3230, for maps, brochures, and other information. Open Mon.-Fri. 8:30 a.m.-5 p.m., Saturday 8 a.m.-4 p.m., and Sunday 9 a.m.-2 p.m. May-Sept.; and Mon.-Fri. 8:30 a.m.-5 p.m. the rest of the year. Find them on the Web at www.spokane.areacvb.org.

Books

The main **public library** is located at 906 W. Main, tel. (509) 838-6757. Half-a-dozen branch libraries are scattered around town, not to mention the local colleges and university libraries.

Book lovers should be sure to stop by **Auntie's Bookstore,** 402 W. Main, tel. (509) 838-0206. This excellent and spacious store has frequent poetry and prose readings, along with a fun game and puzzle shop.

TRANSPORTATION AND TOURS

By Air

Spokane International Airport, just west of town, is served by several major airlines, including Delta, Horizon, Northwest, Southwest, and United, along with Central Mountain Air, tel. (800) 776-3000 for service to Calgary, Alberta.

By Train

Amtrak's Empire Builder has daily service to Spokane from Chicago and Minneapolis, continuing west to Ephrata, Wenatchee, Everett, Edmonds, and Seattle or southwest to Pasco, Wishram, Bingen, Vancouver, and Portland. Stop by their station at 221 W. 1st St. or call (509) 624-5144 or (800) 872-7245 for details.

By Bus
Spokane Transit serves downtown Spokane and the Cheney area; call (509) 328-7433 for routes and schedule information, or get a map from the visitors bureau. They offer a **trolley** (the Plaza Arena Shuttle) that circles the Riverfront Park area, with a side trip down Wall St.; rides are 25 cents.

Greyhound provides nationwide connections from their terminal at 221 W 1st Avenue. Call (509) 624-5251 or (800) 231-2222 for schedule and fares. **Northwestern Trailways,** tel. (509) 838-5262 or (800) 366-6975, also offer bus service from the same location. **Borderline Stage,** tel. (509) 684-3950, also stops here, with service to Colville.

PALOUSE COUNTRY

The Palouse is a broad area of low hills and wide open land; you'll see an occasional fringe of trees (particularly in the northern portion), but mostly these hills are nothing but soil—deep and rich. This soil is so rich and the climate so stable that the area, Whitman County particularly, is known as the best wheat-growing area in the world.

Early French fur traders called this area of green grassland *pelouse* (lawn). The name was soon given to the land, the Native Americans who lived here, and the river that runs through it. The Indians rode spotted horses that the white settlers dubbed palouse or palouse horses; "a palousey" eventually became "appaloosa." Today, the national headquarters of the Appaloosa Horse Club is a right across the Washington line in Moscow, Idaho.

Wheat Country
The Palouse begins just south of Spokane and runs south all the way to the Snake River and the Blue Mountains. It is bounded on the east by the Selkirk Mountains in western Idaho, and on the west by the Channeled Scablands. The soil in this area is all loess, meaning it was blown in over the centuries by the steady southwest wind. It is more than 100 feet deep in many places, and as you drive through this part of the state you'll notice that the wind has piled the soil up against the southern ends of buttes, especially in the Channeled Scabland area, while the northern ends are barren and blunt.

The Palouse Country (locals simply call it "the Palouse") is also set apart from the rest of eastern and central Washington by rainfall. The amount of rainfall increases as you travel east in Washington because of the gradual elevation gain.

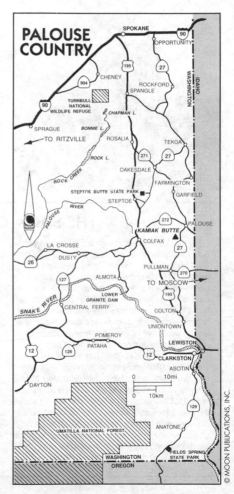

© MOON PUBLICATIONS, INC.

DON PITCHER

Wheat isn't the only crop in the region. Peas, soybeans, lawn-grass seed, rape, and a variety of other crops can be seen as you drive south from Spokane toward Pullman and Clarkston. Tourism is not a major factor in most of the small towns here, so expect lower prices for straightforward food, and motels that are plain, clean, and cheap.

Steptoe Butte State Park

Follow the signs from Hwy. 195 and drive to the top of Steptoe Butte State Park, about 50 miles south of Spokane, for panoramic views of the Palouse River farmland and Idaho's mountains to the east. The park has picnic areas, but no water or overnight facilities. Landscape photographers love Steptoe Butte because it serves as a 1,170-foot tripod for photos of the rolling hills of Washington and Idaho's Palouse Country. Almost a perfect pyramid—its original name was Pyramid Peak—it is also a popular place for kite flyers because of the almost-constant wind.

The peak has another distinction: it is the top of a quartzite mountain more than 600 million years old, part of the Selkirk Range rising above the 15 million-year-old basalt that covered the rest of the range. In geological vocabulary, any rem-

THE SAGA OF CASHUP

James Davis was an eccentric Englishman whose exploits made him one of Eastern Washington's most memorable characters. Davis was born in England in 1815. He and his brother, Sevier, decided to go to America in 1840. Unlike most immigrants, they did not travel steerage class. Davis brought with him a fine team of horses, an elegant surrey, a pair of hunting hounds and some expensive hunting rifles, and he wrote that he came to America "from choice and preference and not by accident of birth."

They first settled in Ohio. James married a local woman in 1844 and moved to Wisconsin where they lived for 22 years while they produced 11 children, all of whom survived and all but one of whom moved to Washington. The Davis clan set out across the plains for the Promised Land with the younger children riding in the covered wagon while the older ones walked almost all the way. They settled near McMinnville in Yamhill County, Oregon, but in 1872 James headed north alone across the Columbia

River into Whitman County, Washington Territory, for a homestead.

He found a site near Thornton he liked, staked it and returned for his family. When they arrived at the claim, they found it had been jumped, but Davis only shrugged and went a few miles west and found another he liked as well and staked it. He built a house that was part dugout. The walls were built of virgin bunch grass roots, and he used sacks of flour for the partition between rooms. They stayed there two years while they built up their herd of cattle to more than 100 head. Then he sold them to a man named Long who, it is said, drove them all the way to the market at St. Louis.

With the cash from the sale, Davis built a 10-room house, the first home in what is now St. John. Davis still wasn't satisfied. In 1875 he sold everything except his transportation and livestock, and with the children herding the cattle, they set off north. He thought they were going to British Columbia.

nant of an older formation protruding out of a newer formation now is called a "steptoe." The hill is named for Colonel Edward J. Steptoe, who was soundly defeated in the area in a running battle with the Cayuse Indians on May 17, 1858. It was only with the assistance of the Nez Percé Chief Timothy that Steptoe's men were able to escape down a narrow canyon through the middle of the Cayuse lines. A local storekeeper named James H. "Cashup" Davis (he insisted on "cash up front") built a hotel on the peak around the turn of the century, but it burned in 1911.

The state park has a day-use area at the foot of the peak with a well and picnic tables (open year-round). Several publicly and privately owned radio and television antennas bristle from the summit but don't interfere with the views from the road that corkscrews around and around to the summit. The best time to visit Steptoe Butte is early in the morning and late in the evening

---

After the first day on the trail, Mrs. Davis, Mary Ann, decided she had taken all of the wandering she was going to take.

"Stop the wagon, James!" she snapped. He stopped.

"We are staying here," she announced in words to that effect. "We are not going anywhere else. Enough is enough."

So they stayed. They were at a place called Cottonwood Springs, which now is called Cashup. Apparently he was a little tired of wandering around, too, because he gave up without a fight. They bought 1,600 acres for $2.60 an acre, and built another 10-room house and included a general store for good measure. It was also used as a roadhouse with a recreation hall and rooms upstairs for travelers. The Davis family lived next door in a smaller house.

Soon it became apparent that Mary Ann had good judgment for selecting a homesite because it was about halfway between Walla Walla and Spokane, a perfect stop for the stage coach. Davis built barns and corrals and a watering trough large enough for an entire string of freight horses to be watered at once. It was here he earned the nickname of Cashup because he was one of the few people in the area with real money, so he made all the deals he could by offering "cash up front" or simply "cashup" to people with no money in their pockets. As much as possible, he required cash payments for the goods in his store.

During all this time Davis had owned Steptoe Butte, then called Pyramid Peak, and had always been attracted to it. The Indian wars didn't last long, so the Davis family went back to their normal routine of farming and operating the stage stop and inn. They enjoyed the social aspects of the venture as much as the income it brought.

This came to a halt in 1883 when Northern Pacific built a line into the area, putting the stage coaches out of business. It was then that Davis put his next plan into effect: he had always thought the top of the butte would make a fine site for a hotel.

Davis spent around $10,000 building a road and then his two-story hotel on the 3,610-foot peak. He wrote a story for a local paper that told details on the structure. It was 60 feet square with the lower floor being a 40 by 60 foot hall that included a stage and dressing rooms. Also on that level was a kitchen and Davis's private reception room. The upper floor had an unspecified number of bedrooms plus a dance hall. On top was an observatory with a huge telescope strong enough to see Walla Walla on a clear day.

Davis didn't know it at the time, but Steptoe Butte, now named in honor of colonel Edward J. Steptoe, is a significant geological formation. It is the top of a quartzite mountain more than 600 million years old, part of the Selkirk Range, that stands above the basalt, only 15 million years old, that covered the rest of the range. In fact, all over the world similar formations of the remnant of an older formation protruding out of newer material are called "steptoes."

The hotel's popularity didn't last long and Davis lost a lot of money; the local population was too small to support such an extravagant establishment, and the steep roads weren't inviting. As business faded, so did Davis. Now in his 80s, he finally gave up and moved himself to the hotel while Mary Ann stayed in their house in Cashup, where she died in 1894. He told everyone he wanted to be buried on the peak, and even dug his own grave and left a shovel standing beside it. Death came on June 22, 1896. Unfortunately, his wish to be buried on the hill was not granted. He was buried in the community cemetery instead.

The hotel stood for another 15 years, but on March 11, 1911, two boys set fire to it, whether by accident or intent was never determined. Eventually the whole peak was sold at a sheriff's auction for $2,000. It was donated to the state to be used as a state park by the last owner, Virgil McCroskey.

when the low sunlight defines the rolling Palouse hills and you can see far into Idaho, south to the Blue Mountains of Washington and Oregon, west to the Cascade Range, and north past Spokane into Canada.

The park is east of Hwy. 195 on Hume Road. Follow the signs from the town of Steptoe if you're coming from Spokane; if you're driving north from Colfax and Pullman, the signs for the butte and Hume Rd. are a short distance south of Steptoe. For park information call (509) 549-3551.

Cheney

Just 13 miles southwest of Spokane, Cheney is home to **Eastern Washington University,** where 8,000 undergraduates and 1,600 graduate students study in over 100 majors, both on the 300-acre campus and by extension in downtown Spokane. The **Gallery of Art** here has changing exhibits throughout the school year, tel. (509) 359-6200.

The small **Cheney Historical Museum,** 614 3rd St., houses local memorabilia, and is open Tuesday and Saturday 1-3 p.m.; free. While here, pick up a brochure describing the town's many historical buildings.

Near Cheney are more than a dozen small recreation lakes, many with resorts. You can also park RVs or pitch tents at **Peaceful Pines Campground,** a mile southwest of Cheney on Hwy. 904, tel. (509) 235-4966. Several small resorts in the area have cabins, camping, RV parking, boat rentals, and fishing: **Williams Lake Resort,** tel. (509) 235-2391 or (800) 274-1540; **West Medical Lake Resort,** tel. (509) 299-3921; **Four Seasons Campground & Fishing Resort** on Sprague Lake, tel. (509) 257-2332; and **Rainbow Cove RV & Fishing Resort** on Clear Lake, tel. (509) 299-3717.

Cheney's mid-July **Rodeo Days** features bronc and bull riding, calf roping, and a parade at one of the largest amateur rodeos in the Northwest; tel. (509) 235-8480.

Turnbull National Wildlife Refuge

Just south of Cheney, 17,000-acre Turnbull National Wildlife Refuge, tel. (509) 235-4723, has miles of trails and roads for walking, cross-country skiing, horseback riding, mountain biking, or driving through the protected lake area. This refuge, unlike others in eastern Washington, is not open to hunting; this is strictly an observation-only area, and nature lovers will be rewarded with sightings of grebes, hawks, shorebirds, deer, coyote, owls, badgers, herons, and an occasional bald eagle or peregrine falcon. The refuge is open every day during daylight hours, and a $3 per vehicle fee is charged March-October.

Palouse

Seventeen miles north of Pullman on State Hwy. 27 is Palouse, where the local growth industry appears to be boarding up downtown windows. The small farm community of 900 is home to the **Boomerang Museum,** tel. (509) 878-1688, where you'll find a collection of old printing equipment. **Palouse Lions Park** has riverside campsites. The big local event is **Palouse Days Community Festival** on the third weekend of September.

Three-hundred-acre **Kamiak Butte County Park,** four miles southwest of Palouse along Hwy. 27, has camping and picnicking; tel. (509) 397-6238. A steep, one-mile hiking trail leads through evergreen forests to the top of this 3,641-foot butte, providing views of the Palouse Hills.

Garfield, Oaksdale, and Rosalia

Minuscule Garfield (pop. 500) is home to **New Morning Glass Studio,** 904 W. Main St., tel. (509) 635-1263 or (888) 303-1263, where you can watch as fine glass pieces are made. Open Saturday 9 a.m.-6 p.m. and Sunday 11 a.m.-6 p.m.

Just east of Oaksdale (pop. 350) is **Hanford Castle B&B** tel. (509) 285-4120, an imposing hilltop Victorian mansion built more than a century ago. On the grounds are a conservatory, an old fountain, and sweeping views of the surrounding wheat fields. The restored mansion features a full breakfast and rooms with private baths and antiques for just $45 s or $50 d.

The main event in Oaksdale is **Old Mill Days** on the third weekend of June, with a fun run, parade, fine arts show, and more. Over in nearby Rosalia, **Battle Days** comes the first weekend of June, with a rodeo, parade, fun run, and dancing.

Colfax

The town of Colfax (pop. 2,800) is county seat for Whitman County, one of the most productive wheat and barley producing counties in the nation. The town was named for Schuyler Colfax, vice president during the first administration of U.S. Grant. On Armistice Day in 1938, high school teams from Colfax and St. John met on a snowy football field; St. John won 14-0. Fifty years later the same players returned for a rematch, albeit in rather different physical condition; this time Colfax won 6-0. The **"Codger Bowl"** of 1988 is memorialized in an unusual 65-foot-high chainsaw-carved pole with the cartoonish faces of football players facing outwards from five columns. It is said to be the largest chainsaw sculpture in the world.

The **Perkins House** at 623 N. Perkins Ave., tel. (509) 397-3712, was built in 1884 by Colfax's first permanent resident, James Perkins. Inside this National Historic Site are household items from the late 19th century. Out back is a log cabin built in 1870. Stop here on the last Sunday in June for an ice cream social. Perkins House is open mid-April to mid-Oct. on Sunday and Thursday 1-4 p.m.

Get good steaks, pasta, and seafood, plus the "famous" vinegar pie at **Diana Lee's Grill & Bar,** tel. (509) 397-2770. **Siesta Motel,** tel. (509) 397-3417 has lodging for $31 s or $35 d. Swim during the summer months at the outdoor **swimming pool** in Schmuck Park.

Concrete River Festival on the second weekend of July includes a parade, car show, food fest, fun run, basketball tournament, and live music. The Palouse Empire Fairground near Colfax has rodeos, horse shows, and fairs all summer long, including **Palouse Empire Plowing Bee** in April, and **Palouse Empire Thrashing Bee** in September. In between is the **Colfax Jr. Rodeo** on Memorial Day weekend. The main event is the four-day **Palouse Empire Fair** beginning the weekend after Labor Day. It features a rodeo, demonstrations of antique harvesting equipment, a carnival, and all the standard country fair activities.

Northwestern Trailways, tel. (509) 397-4102 or (800) 366-3830, stops at 610 S. Main in Colfax.

PULLMAN

Pullman (pop. 25,000) is a typical small college town with an abundance of we-deliver pizza joints, sub-sandwich shops and beer-by-the-keg outlets. The prosperous downtown is an attractive, tidy place with red brick buildings and a wide range of shops. The diverse student body helps make Pullman a surprisingly open and culturally mixed small city. Surrounding Pullman are agricultural lands that make up the heart of the rich Palouse country and contribute to Pullman's reputation as "lentil capital of the world." (Despite this claim, much of the pea and lentil industry is actually based just across the border in Moscow, Idaho.) One minor drawback to Pullman is the city's convoluted layout that makes it easy to find yourself looping past the same buildings again.

History
Pullman was founded by Bolin Farr, who came from Missouri to settle at the confluence of Dry Fork Creek, Missouri Flat Creek, and the south fork of the Palouse in 1876. Thus, the town was first called "Three Forks." By 1881, it had grown—to a population of three. Hoping to attract financial aid from Chicago industrialist George Pullman (of Pullman sleeping-car fame), the citizens decided to name their "city" Pullman. It's still a matter of controversy whether he contributed anything, but the name stuck. A railroad branch extended to the town, the "crossroads of the Palouse," in 1883; by then Pullman had two stores, a hotel, a post office, and a blacksmith shop.

Following the common pattern of the West, two fires devastated the wooden downtown district in 1887 and again in 1890; structures were rebuilt in brick, and many of these buildings are still standing. In 1892, the Washington Agricultural College opened in Pullman. There were just 21 students that first semester, but the school would grow into Washington State University, and the central focal point for the city. Today, the local economy is dominated by academia; the university employs over 4,700 people.

WASHINGTON STATE UNIVERSITY

Washington State University has a student body of more than 17,000 distributed throughout one

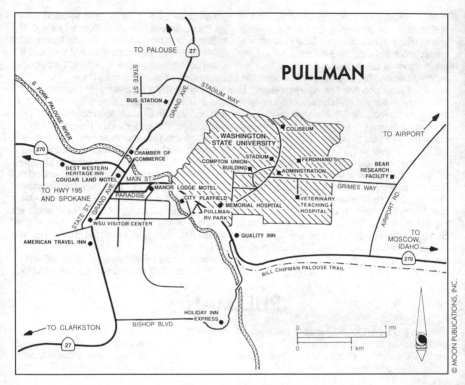

graduate school and seven undergraduate colleges offering more than 100 major fields of study. The school is well known as an agricultural research center, but facilities also include an Electron Microscopy Center, Nuclear Radiation Center, Water Research Center, and an International Marketing Program for Agricultural Commodities. Students live in 23 residence halls, in the community, or in 24 fraternities and 14 sororities.

WSU Visitor Center
Start your campus visit at the very helpful WSU Visitor Center in the historic train depot at the corner of State 270 and Grand Avenue. The center is open Mon.-Fri. 7 a.m.-4 p.m., plus some Saturdays (including game days and commencement). Football and other sports tickets are sold in the visitor center. For more info, call (509) 335-8633, or check their homepage: www.wsu.edu/visitor.

Public parking is available at a number of lots around campus; get a parking day-pass for $2 from the visitor center or on campus at the Public Safety Building.

Free **campus tours** depart the University Relations Office in Room 370 of the Lighty Student Service Building. These hour-long walking tours are offered at 1 p.m. Mon.-Fri. all year; call (509) 335-8633 for details.

CUB
The center of WSU student life is **Compton Union Building,** tel. (509) 335-9444, better known as the "CUB." Inside are all the standard student center stuff, including an information desk, eating places, a coffeehouse, billiards, bowling, a student art gallery, a convenience store, an outdoor recreation center, and even a hotel. The main campus library—**Holland Library**—is located next door. For a fine view of

the campus and surrounding Palouse landscape, head to the top of the Physical Sciences Building.

Ferdinand's Bar

The Food Quality Building is home to Ferdinand's, a soda fountain run by the university's agricultural school, and the most popular tourist attraction on campus. As part of its agricultural research work, the university has maintained a dairy herd for more than 70 years; today, most of the milk produced goes into cheeses and ice cream. The cheese is made at a state-of-the-art plant in the Food Quality Building, and you can watch the operation and a 10-minute cheesy video upstairs from Ferdinand's. The soda fountain has delicious ice cream and shakes, making this a popular stopping place for students and visitors. On football Saturdays, you may have to wait 45 minutes for a cone!

The most famous product at Ferdinand's is **"Cougar Gold,"** a delicious cheddar-like cheese that is only sold in hefty 30-ounce tin cans. This unique method of packaging came about in the 1930s, when researchers were looking for a way to protect cheese from contamination while being stored for long periods (the cheese still needs to be refrigerated). The cheeses are aged for up to a year to develop the proper flavor and texture. Technological advances have meant that plastic wrap now serves the same function, but Cougar Gold and other WSU Creamery cheeses still come in their distinctive tins.

Ferdinand's is open Mon.-Fri. 9:30 a.m.-4:30 p.m., and on special event weekends (such as home football games). You can also mail-order the cheeses by calling Ferdinand's at (509) 335-4014 or (800) 457-5442; they aren't cheap—around $12 a tin plus shipping.

Museum of Art

Although not impressive by Seattle standards, the Museum of Art in the Fine Arts Center houses Washington's finest arts exhibition space east of the Cascades, with changing exhibits throughout the year. Also here is a permanent collection of works by well-known 19th and 20th century American and European painters, from Goya to Warhol. Some of these works are always on display during the summer. The museum is open Tuesday 10 a.m.-10 p.m., Wed.-Fri. 10 a.m.-4 p.m., and Sat.-Sun. 1-5 p.m. Tours are available

by request. Call (509) 335-1910 for more information, or (509) 335-6607 for a recorded schedule of musical performances, art talks, and lectures. Student art galleries on campus can be found elsewhere in the Fine Arts Center and in the CUB. For more quality art, head downtown to the **Nica Gallery,** 246 E. Main, tel. (509) 334-1213.

Other Sights

The **Museum of Anthropology** on the first floor of College Hall, tel. (509) 335-3441, has traveling exhibits from all over the globe and Northwest Indian artifacts (mostly from Snake River sites now inundated by reservoirs). Certainly the most unusual items are the plaster casts of what are purportedly Sasquatch footprints. Open Mon.-Thurs. 9 a.m.-4 p.m., and Friday 9 a.m.-3 p.m.

My favorite WSU museum is the **Jacklin Collection** inside the Physical Sciences Building. Here you'll discover the largest petrified wood collection in the western states, many pieces of which have been beautifully polished. The collection is open weekdays 8 a.m.-5 p.m. In the entryway are several fun (and maybe even educational) science exhibits to play with.

Completed in 1996, WSU's **Veterinary Teaching Hospital** is a state-of-the art animal care facility covering three acres on the south side of campus. Call two days ahead for tours, tel. (509) 335-0711.

Connors Museum of Zoology (in the Science Building) claims the largest public collection of animals and birds in the Pacific Northwest; not all that interesting unless you enjoy stuffed critters in ancient glass cases. Open by appointment only is the **Drucker Collection of Oriental Art,** tel. (509) 335-3823, in White Hall. It includes oriental furniture, textiles, costumes, and art work. There's also an impressive **Nez Percé Music Archive** in Kimbrough Hall featuring tribal songs by historical Indian leaders, including the voice of Chief Joseph. (You can also hear the recordings in the Kemble A. Stout Music Listening Library on campus.)

In addition to the larger exhibits at WSU, visitors will discover a big herbarium collection in Heald Hall for botanists, fungi and insects in Johnson Hall, and even the Smith Soil Monolith Collection, donated by a pedagogical philanthropist. Get a brochure describing these and other on-campus collections at the visitor center.

Bear Research Facility
Don't miss the fenced-in bear research facility along Airport Rd. on the east edge of campus. Directed by Dr. Charles Robbins, the Bear Research, Education, and Conservation Program is an important facility for research on bruins from all over the world, particularly brown and black bears. This is the only place where adult grizzlies are housed for nutritional, physiological, and ecological research by graduate students and visiting scientists. The facility typically houses six grizzlies and four black bears, visible behind a stout fence. The resident bears were orphaned as cubs and would not have otherwise survived. In the winter, they hibernate in special temperature-controlled dens. Tours are available by reservation; call (509) 335-1119.

OTHER SIGHTS

Three Forks Pioneer Museum
Roger Rossebo likes to call his 17-building town on his wheat and pea farm near Pullman, "the Smithsonian of the Palouse." That isn't much of an exaggeration; although all the buildings are chock full of period furniture and decorations, Rossebo still has enough farming implements and other antiques in storage to furnish and decorate the small city he is assembling. The collection includes one of the first cabins built in the Palouse region, plus more than 15 other historic or recreated structures.

To reach Three Forks, go north from Pullman on Hwy. 27 one-half mile and turn left on Albion Road. Drive two miles and turn right at the Three Forks sign onto Anderson Rd., then drive 2.8 miles on the gravel road to the Rossebo farm and museum. Call ahead to make sure somebody is there; tel. (509) 332-3889. Admission is $2 adults, $1 students, and kids under 11 are free.

Parks
Lawson Gardens, on Derby St. near Dilke St., covers 11 acres of land and features a formal rose and flower garden with a reflecting pool and gazebo. On the west side of town, **Sunnyside Park** has hiking trails, picnic areas, tennis and basketball courts, and playgrounds; this is the site of Pullman's annual Fourth of July picnic

and fireworks. **Reaney Park** on Reaney Way and Gray Lane has a swimming pool, gazebo, and playground.

The paved **Bill Chipman Palouse Trail** follows a gentle old railroad grade for eight miles, connecting Pullman with Moscow, Idaho. It's a great place for rollerblading or bike riding. The trail starts next to Quality Inn at the intersection of Hwy. 270 and Bishop Boulevard. Rent rollerblades from **Sport Town** at Grand and Bishop, tel. 334-1813.

ACCOMMODATIONS AND CAMPING

Pullman has 10 motels and B&Bs, with an equal number in Moscow, Idaho, just eight miles to the east. If you're planning to be in town for WSU football games or graduation, reserve several months, and maybe a year, ahead of time. The busiest time is when the Applecup Game (against arch-rival University of Washington) comes to Pullman. Late folks end up staying in Clarkston and "commuting" to the game. The chamber of commerce keeps track of available accommodations; call them at (800) 365-6948.

Bed and Breakfasts and CUB
Pullman's nicest lodging is the turn-of-the-century **Ash Street House B&B,** N.E. 315 Ash St., tel. (509) 332-3638. The B&B has four guest rooms with shared baths and antique furnishings. Kids are allowed, and a full breakfast is served; $100 s or d. **Country B&B,** six miles south of Pullman, tel. (509) 334-4453, is a contemporary home with rooms for $40-100 s or d, including a continental breakfast. **Carstens B&B,** tel. (509) 332-6162, is a contemporary home four miles southwest of town amid the wheat and lentil fields. Two guest rooms share a bath, and a full breakfast is served. Kids are accepted, and a hot tub sits outside; $50-100 s or d.

The most unusual Pullman lodging place is the **Compton Union Building Hotel** (Cub Hotel) on the WSU campus. It's open only during the school year, and covers two floors in the Compton Union Building. Call (509) 334-9444 for details. Rates are $45 s or $60 d.

Motels

The following local motels are arranged by price. **Cougar Land Motel,** 120 W. Main, tel. (509) 334-3535 or (800) 334-3574, charges $32 s or $36 d, including access to the outdoor pool. **Manor Lodge Motel,** S.E. 445 Paradise, tel. (509) 334-2511, charges $39 s or $43 d. **American Travel Inn,** 515 S. Grand, tel. (509) 334-3500, has an outdoor pool and rooms for $40 s or $45 d. The **Best Western Heritage Inn,** 928 N.W. Olson St., tel. (509) 334-2555, has an indoor pool, jacuzzi, sauna, exercise room, and continental breakfast; $49-69 s or $59-139 d. **Quality Inn Paradise Creek,** S.E. 1050 Bishop, tel. (509) 332-0500 or (800) 669-3212, charges $59 s or $67 d. Facilities include an outdoor pool, sauna, jacuzzi, fitness center, and breakfast buffet. **Holiday Inn Express,** S.E. 1190 Bishop Blvd., tel. (509) 334-4437 or (800) 465-4329, has an indoor pool, jacuzzi, fitness center, and continental breakfast for $79 s or d.

Campgrounds

Campers can stay at the tiny city-run **Pullman RV Park** next to the city playfield at South and Riverview Streets ($12 RVs, $5 tents), April-Nov.; call (509) 334-4555 for reservations. **Kamiak Butte County Park,** 13 miles northeast of Pullman on Hwy. 27 has additional camping; tel. (509) 397-6238.

FOOD

Breakfast and Lunch

Get breakfast at the unpretentious **The Small Place,** 247 E. Main St., tel. (509) 334-1110, or a blast of espresso from **Starbuck's,** 1025 E. Main St., tel. (509) 332-8117. The cheapest eats are found on campus at the **Compton Union Building.** Here are five different eateries, including a cafeteria and a make-your-own-sandwich deli. Also be sure to check out the ever-popular **Ferdinand's Dairy Bar** at WSU (described above) for ice cream, milkshakes, and cheeses. **Dissmores IGA,** 1205 N. Grand Ave., tel. (509) 332-2918, has a good deli.

All-American

Pete's Bar & Grill, 1100 Bishop Blvd., tel. (509) 334-4200, serves inexpensive burgers, pasta, and chicken, and has a big salad bar. **Hilltop Restaurant,** Colfax Hwy., tel. (509) 334-2555, features a panoramic city view, decent steaks and a popular Sunday brunch. The best steaks anywhere around are across the border at **Lone Jack Steak Co.** in Potlatch, Idaho, tel. (208) 875-1421.

Ethnic

You won't go wrong at **Basilio's Italian Cafe,** 337 E. Main St., tel. (509) 334-7663, a big brick-walled space where you order at the counter and then wait for the surprisingly good pasta dishes. Quick service and reasonable too; entrees are all under $7. Very popular with students. The best local place for pizzas is **Sella's Calzones & Pizza,** 1115 E. Main St., tel. (509) 334-1895.

Enjoy authentic Mexican cuisine at **Nuevo Vallarta,** 1110 N. Grand Ave., tel. (509) 334-4689, and good Chinese food at **The Emerald,** 1140 N. Grand Ave., tel. (509) 334-5427.

Gourmet Fare

Swilly's Cafe, 200 Kamiaken, tel. (509) 334-3395, is a popular yuppified bistro with excellent lunches and dinners made from the freshest produce, baked goods, seafood, and meats. Riverside outdoor seating adds to the charm. Closed Sunday.

For fine French dining in an elegantly romantic setting, head to **Combray,** 215 Main, tel. (509) 334-9024. The menu changes seasonally and entrees are $18-28.

If you don't mind the drive, **Cafe Spudnik,** 215 S. Main in Moscow, Idaho, tel. (208) 882-9257, makes decidedly different (and very good) dishes such as salmon in pastry puff and gourmet pizzas. Nice atmosphere, and outdoor cafe seating during the summer.

From early June through October, Pullman's **Public Market** comes to the downtown High Street Mall Saturday 9 a.m.-1 p.m. This is a good place for fresh produce, entertainment, and crafts.

ENTERTAINMENT AND EVENTS

Events

Pullman's annual **Fourth of July** celebration actually covers three towns. It begins in Johnson, 10 miles south of Pullman, where a silly parade features the weirdest and wackiest floats and costumes. Then it's on to Albion, six miles north of Pullman, for a big potluck meal at Community Hall. In the afternoon, head back to Pullman for a barbecue, live music, and after-dark fireworks show.

Pullman's main event is the **National Lentil Festival,** in late August. It features a big parade, arts and crafts fair, live entertainment, a kids fishing derby, and a cookoff with such specialties as lentil pizza and lentil ice cream. Pack your bottle of Beano for this event! Call (800) 365-6948 for details.

The big **Holiday Arts and Crafts Show** comes to Beasley Coliseum in early November, and is followed by the **Downtown Holiday Celebration,** complete with carolers, Santa Claus, and a petting zoo on the first Saturday of December.

Performances
The 12,000-seat **Beasley Performing Arts Coliseum** at WSU stages events from rock concerts to comedy shows. For a schedule call (509) 335-1514; for tickets call (800) 325-7328. The university has theaters in Daggy Hall where you can attend Shakespearean plays, student productions, and a summer repertory season in June and July called **Summer Palace.** Call (509) 335-7236 for details. Many other musical recitals and theatrical performances take place on campus all year. Call (509) 335-8525 for upcoming events.

Established in 1969, the **Washington-Idaho Symphony,** puts on seven productions a year; tel. (208) 882-6555. You can also hear free **summer outdoor concerts** at Reaney Park on Wednesday evenings from the third weekend of June through July.

The **Lionel Hampton Jazz Festival** in nearby Moscow is one of the biggest area events. Held the third weekend in February, it features many of the greats in jazz. Call (800) 345-7402 for ticket info.

Nightlife
The best dancing and boozin' bars are in nearby Moscow, Idaho, but Pullman has a couple of options. **Rico's Tavern,** E. 200 Main St., tel. (509) 332-6566, is a great rockin' place with blues and jazz bands, imported beers, and homemade wine

coolers. **Butch's Den** in the CUB on campus has live music several nights a week.

Catch second-run flicks at the **Audian Theater,** 315 E. Main, for just $3, or on weekends at the CUB auditorium for $2.

SPORTS AND RECREATION

Outdoor Recreation Center
Located in the university's Compton Union Building, the Outdoor Recreation Center, tel. (509) 335-2651, offers excellent non-credit classes in kayaking, cross-country skiing, rock climbing, wilderness survival, backpacking, and other subjects. Most of these are open to the public for a fee. They also have a **climbing wall** in Bohler Gym, and rent a wide range of equipment to both students and the public, including backpacks, tents, rafts, canoes, skis, and snowboards.

Sports
The WSU Cougars field teams in football, basketball, baseball, gymnastics, and track and field; for a schedule of athletic events, call (509) 335-9626 or (800) 462-6847. The 40,000-seat Martin Stadium really rocks in even-numbered years when the Cougs play the arch-rival University of Washington Huskies.

Other Recreation
Swimmers will find two outdoor pools open in Reaney Park from mid-June to Labor Day, tel. (509) 334-4555, along with three more pools (one is Olympic-size) at the University, tel. (509) 335-9666. The university also has a nine-hole golf course and putting green open to the public.

INFORMATION AND SERVICES

The **Pullman Chamber of Commerce,** N. 415 Grand Ave., tel. (509) 334-3565 or (800) 365-6948, www.onvillage.com/pullmanchamber, is open Mon.-Fri. 9 a.m.-5 p.m. year-round. They have all sorts of local brochures, including a walking tour of historic buildings. By the way, although Pullman and Moscow, Idaho have different telephone area codes, it's a local call between the two cities, and you don't need to dial the area code.

For books, visit **Neill Public Library,** N. 210 Grand Ave., tel. (509) 334-4555, or one of the seven on-campus libraries at WSU. **Brused Books,** N. 105 Grand Ave., tel. (509) 334-7898, is a fun place to browse for used books.

TRANSPORTATION

Air Service
Horizon Airlines, tel. (800) 547-9308, has daily service between Moscow-Pullman Airport (in Pullman) and Spokane, Seattle, Boise, and Portland. **Inter-State Aviation,** tel. (509) 332-6596 or (800) 653-8420, offers flightseeing and air charter services.

Bus Service
Pullman Transit, tel. (509) 332-6535, provides local bus service throughout town Mon.-Saturday. **Wheatland Express Commuter Bus,** tel. (509) 334-2200 or (800) 334-2207, has Mon.-Sat. shuttle bus service between Pullman and Moscow, Idaho. Bikes are carried. **Link Transportation Services,** tel. (208) 882-1223 or (800) 359-4541, provides shuttle bus service from Pullman and Moscow to Spokane Airport, and local tours of the area. **Northwestern Trailways,** 1002 Nye St., tel. (509) 334-1412 or (800) 366-6975, has bus service north to Spokane, and south to Boise, Idaho.

PULLMAN VICINITY

Moscow
Although it's across the state line, the town of Moscow, Idaho, is a twin to Pullman. Moscow is just 10 miles away and has a number of attractions worth visiting: the **University of Idaho,** the **Appaloosa Museum and Heritage Center,** and many historic structures, including the **McConnell Mansion.** The country around here rises quickly into forested mountains, quite a change from the rolling grasslands of the Palouse. The weekly **farmers market** in downtown Moscow runs all summer long on Saturday 8 a.m.-noon. Call the **Moscow Chamber of Commerce** at (800) 380-1801 for more info.

Uniontown
Tiny Uniontown (pop. 400), a dozen miles south of Pullman, was first settled by German immigrants in the 1880s. Today, agriculture is the main support, as evidenced by the big grain elevator on the north side of town and the rolling farmland all around. Constructed in 1904, **St. Boniface Church** is Washington's oldest Catholic church.

The most distinctive feature—it's pretty hard to miss—is Steve Dahmen's old barn surrounded by a 600-foot fence of **iron wheels.** The wheels came from steam engines, threshing machines,

Churchyard Inn, Uniontown

DON PITCHER

hay rakes, tractors, wagons, and even sewing machines. Stop by to talk to the fence's friendly creator and to sign his guest book.

The Churchyard Inn B&B, tel. (509) 229-3200, contains seven guest rooms with private baths in a gorgeous brick 1905 inn listed on the National Register of Historic Places. The B&B was originally built as a parish and later served as a convent. No kids; $55-135 s or d.

Premier Alpaca Ranch & Guest Home, tel. (509) 229-3655, is a restored turn-of-the-century house with three guest rooms, plus an indoor lap pool. Guests will love to touch the alpacas. $50-90 s or d.

CLARKSTON AND VICINITY

Clarkston (pop. 7,000) lies in the very southeast corner of Washington along the Snake River, and right across the bridge from its larger neighbor, Lewiston, Idaho. The names reflect two famous explorers who traveled through here almost two centuries ago, Meriweather Lewis and William Clark. Clarkston is in the portion of eastern Washington often referred to as "The Banana Belt," because it has, as early Native Americans put it, "no wind, no snow." Some may take exception to the "no snow" part, but the climate is generally milder than that of other areas east of the Cascades. Clarkston is Washington's most inland seaport, more than 450 miles east of the Pacific via the Columbia River and its chief branch, the Snake.

History

On October 10, 1805, the Lewis and Clark expedition camped here en route to the Pacific. The region's first Anglo settlers were cattle ranchers, taking advantage of the nearly endless grazing lands. The Asotin Creek irrigation project of 1895 brought much-needed water to this parched region, and a wagon bridge built in 1896 between Clarkston (originally called Vineland) and Lewiston provided access to Lewiston's railroad. These projects, as well as dams constructed in the 1960s and '70s that turned the wild lower Snake into a navigable waterway, paved the way for agriculture, industry, and population growth. Unfortunately, these dams also destroyed magnificent stretches of wild river and buried countless archaeological sites.

Clarkston's first containerized shipment departed for Japan in 1975; today's primary exports are peas to Europe and paper products to Japan. Despite this, agriculture and forest products, not international shipping, are the mainstay of the city's economy. The largest (and stinkiest) local employer—by far—is Lewiston's **Potlatch Corporation.** Tours of the Potlatch Corporation's sawmill and paperboard plant are available Monday, Wednesday, and Friday; call (509) 799-1795 for reservations.

SIGHTS

See "River Rafting" below, for the biggest summertime attraction in the Clarkston area.

Scenic Drives

To reach Pullman and other points north, you need to cross into Lewiston, Idaho, and traverse the Clearwater River bridge. From here, you can follow the heavily trafficked Hwy. 95, which connects into Hwy. 195, or follow the **Old Spiral Highway** instead. The latter road switchbacks and corkscrews its way up a shorter and considerably more interesting route, with spectacular views into Washington, Idaho, and Oregon from the 2,750-foot summit. A less extraordinary, but still very scenic drive is along Hwy. 129 south from Clarkston to the Oregon border.

Asotin

The pretty little town of Asotin (as-O-tin) is six miles south of Clarkston along the Snake River. Visit the **Asotin County Historical Museum,** 3rd and Filmore, tel. (509) 243-4659, to see early artifacts and buildings and one of the largest collections of branding irons in existence. Open Mon.-Sat. 1-5 p.m. in summer, and Sat. 1-5 in winter; no charge. Ask here for directions to several Indian petroglyphs visible south of Asotin. Also in Asotin is the **Full Gospel Church.** Built in 1889, it is on the National Register of Historic Buildings and houses the original oak pump

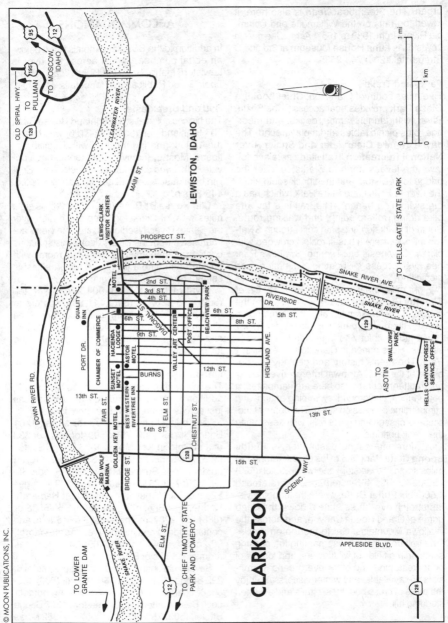

organ. The Steamboat *Jean* is also here; it towed log rafts on the Willamette and Columbia Rivers from 1938 to 1957. Across the river in Lewiston is **Luna House Museum** at 3rd and C Streets, tel. (208) 743-2535.

Parks and Trails

Five miles south of Clarkston, **Chief Looking Glass Park** provides boat access to the Snake River, with launch ramps, docks, and moorage, plus picnic tables and a playground. The paved 16-mile **Clearwater and Snake River National Recreation Trail** starts here and follows the levees north to Clarkston, over the bridge to Lewiston, and then back south along the river to Hells Gate State Park (which has a big swimming beach). The trail is a favorite bike riding, rollerblading, and walking route. South of Clarkston, the path cuts through **Swallows Park** where a basalt rock is crowded with cliff swallow nests each spring. Swallows Park has river access for boating, swimming, and picnicking.

Eight miles west of town on Hwy. 12, **Chief Timothy State Park** sits on Silcott Island in the middle of Lower Granite Lake (the dammed up Snake River). The park was named for a Nez Percé Indian chief who befriended early white settlers. He is buried in Clarkston's Beachview Park. The area's history and geology are depicted at the small **Alpowai Interpretive Center** (intermittent hours). Also here are campsites, a boat launch, playground, swimming beach, and summertime concession stand. The nearby landscape is of sage and grass hills, with trees along the creek bottoms.

A more interesting destination is **Fields Spring State Park,** 4.5 miles past Anatone (30 miles south of Clarkston) on Hwy. 129, tel. (509) 256-3332. This 445-acre park centers around 4,500-foot **Puffer Butte,** where the ridgetop vistas stretch over three states, down the deep gorge of Grand Ronde Canyon, and across the Wallowa Mountains. Get to the top on a mile-long trail from the day-use parking lot, passing summertime fields of wildflowers, and forests of ponderosa pine and other evergreens. Campsites are available, and winter visitors will enjoy the miles of cross-country ski trails and a lighted sledding hill.

ACCOMMODATIONS

In addition to the B&Bs and motels listed below, an equal number are just across the river in Lewiston, Idaho. See Don Root's *Idaho Handbook* (Moon Publications) for details.

Bed and Breakfasts

The historic colonial-style **Highland House B&B,** 707 Highland, tel. (509) 758-3126, was built in the 1890s, and is furnished with English antiques. Most of the five guest rooms have private baths, and a hot tub is available. A full English breakfast is served, and kids are accepted; $45-85 s or d.

Cliff House B&B, tel. (509) 758-1267, is eight miles west of Clarkston, atop a cliff high over the Snake River. Needless to say, the views are impressive from the B&B's deck. This spacious contemporary home has two guest rooms with private baths and a jacuzzi. A full breakfast is served; no kids; $70-75 s or d.

Swallowhaven B&B, 904 22nd Ave., tel. (509) 758-8357 or (800) 441-8357, caters to honeymooners. This turn-of-the-century home sits on an acre of land overlooking Clarkston, and has a guest room with a jacuzzi tub, and full breakfast; $100 d.

Motels

The following motels are arranged by price. In addition to these, nearly a dozen other places just across the border in Lewiston, Idaho.

Two budget places are: **Astor Motel,** 1261 Bridge St., tel. (509) 758-2509, for $26 s or $33 d; and **Golden Key Motel,** 1376 Bridge St., tel. (509) 758-5566, for $26 s or $30 d, including an outdoor pool. **Sunset Motel,** 1200 Bridge St., tel. (509) 758-2517 or (800) 845-5223, charges $28 s or $35 d, but is often filled. At **Hacienda Lodge,** 812 Bridge St., tel. (509) 758-5583 or (888) 567-2287, rooms are $28 s or $36 d, and contain fridges and microwaves. **Asotin Motel,** 90 2nd St. in Asotin, tel. (509) 243-4888, has rooms for $35 s or $40 d.

Several national chains are also here. **Motel 6,** 222 Bridge St., tel. (509) 758-1631 or (800) 466-8356, charges $38 s or $44 d with an outdoor pool. **Best Western RiverTree Inn,** 1257 Bridge St., tel. (509) 758-9551 or (800) 597-3621, has rooms for $59-89 s, $59-99 d, with amenities that include an outdoor pool, jacuzzi, sauna, exercise room, and continental breakfast. **Quality Inn,** 700 Port Dr., tel. (509) 758-9500 or (800) 228-5151, has an outdoor pool, and rooms for $60-79 s or d.

Campgrounds
The closest public campground lies across the bridge to Idaho and three miles south of Lewiston along the Snake River: **Hells Gate State Park,** tel. (208) 799-5015. Campsites with showers are $12 tents or $16 RVs; open all year. Eight miles west of town on Hwy. 12, **Chief Timothy State Park,** tel. (509) 758-9580, also has campsites ($11 tents, $16 RVs) with coin-operated showers. Open March to early December. Call (800) 452-5687 for reservations ($6 extra). **Fields Spring State Park,** tel. (509) 256-3332, 30 miles south of Clarkston on Hwy. 129, has campsites ($10) with showers and is open all year. Because it is at 4,000 feet in elevation, Fields Spring offers a cool break on hot summer days.

Park that land yacht at **Hillview RV Park,** 1224 Bridge St., tel. (509) 758-6299, or **Smith's RV Park,** 1398 Bridge St., tel. (509) 758-3544.

FOOD

For the best local breakfasts, cross over to Lewiston's **Waffles-N-More,** 1421 Main St., tel. (509) 743-5189. Or sit down for a coffee and big breakfast with the Clarkston locals at **Come Inn Cafe,** 508 Diagonal St., tel. (509) 758-2884. **Bridge Street Connection,** 1250 Bridge St., tel. (509) 758-3141, is a bit fancier.

Lewiston's bowling alley, **Strike & Spare Bar & Grill** at 244 Thain Rd., tel. (509) 743-8883, makes good sandwiches and burgers for lunch. Get reasonable family meals at **South Shore Landing** in the Quality Inn, 700 Port Dr., tel. (509) 758-9500.

If you're looking for something more exotic, **Bamboo Gardens,** 907 6th St., tel. (509) 758-8898, has Chinese food, and **El Sombrero,** 2315 Appleside Blvd. in Lewiston, tel. (509) 758-2416, has Mexican meals.

Fazzari's, 1281 Bridge St., tel. (509) 758-3386, features very good pizza, spaghetti, and sandwiches and is open daily for lunch and dinner. Another popular Italian place is **Tomato Brothers,** 200 Bridge St., tel. (509) 758-7902. **Rooster's Landing,** 1550 Port Dr., tel. (509) 751-0155, has a big patio right on the river, and a menu of steaks, seafood, burgers, and sandwiches.

OTHER PRACTICALITIES

Shopping
Meacham Mills, 1305 Main St. in Lewiston, tel. (208) 743-0505, is a unique family owned flour mill that uses stones to grind various types of grains. They also sell a variety of gourmet food products. The old Clarkston Airport hanger at 935 Port Way now houses a large **The Hanger Antique Emporium,** tel. (509) 758-0604, with some 100 dealers.

Events
The **Asotin County Fair,** held the last weekend in April, features a rodeo, parade, cowboy breakfast, and stock show and sale. Also in late April, Lewiston's **Dogwood Festival** celebrates spring's flowering dogwoods with concerts, art in the park, and historical walking tours. Several events in neighboring Lewiston complete the summer calendar: **Sunflower Days** in mid-August, **Hot August Nights** (concerts in the park and antique car show) in late August, **Lewiston Roundup Rodeo and Parade** in early September, and **Nez Percé County Fair** in late September. Mid-December's **Christmas on the Confluence** is a lighted boat parade on the Snake River. A lighted Christmas twilight parade takes place at the same time in Clarkston.

Music and Art
The best place for live country music is over in Lewiston: **The Corral,** 1618 Main St., tel. (509) 746-7353. **Tomfoolery,** 301 2nd St. in Lewiston, tel. (509) 746-2005, has rock and pop tunes.

The **Valley Art Center,** 842 6th St., tel. (509) 758-8331, features rotating exhibits and sales and also offers workshops and classes in all media.

Hells Canyon Recreation
Quite a few local companies offer float trips and jet-boat excursions through the deepest river

gorge in North America, the Snake River's **Hells Canyon,** separating Oregon and Idaho. The canyon lacks the steep cliffs of the Grand Canyon, but is nevertheless an extraordinary place. From the summit of He Devil Peak to the Snake River—five air miles distant—the terrain plummets more than 8,000 feet. (A Nez Percé Indian legend tells how their ancestors were threatened by seven devils. Using a very big stick, Coyote dug out the canyon, leaving the devils in what is now Idaho. Perhaps this could explain some of the right-wing militia mania that festers in parts of that state.)

Approximately 68 miles of the river—from Hells Canyon Dam in Oregon to the Washington border—is a National Wild and Scenic River. This is something of a miracle, since it represented a rare victory for conservationists over the electric power and agricultural interests that have managed to dam up lengthy portions of the Snake River. In 1964, a license was granted to build the High Mountain Sheep Dam in the middle of this undeveloped country. After years of litigation, congress finally voted to protect the river in 1975.

The Snake River features several class IV rapids (class V in high water), along with many class II and III rapids. In addition to the wild water of the canyon, along the way you'll see mysterious petroglyphs, an ancient lava flow, abundant wildlife, and rugged canyon scenery. Some outfitters use only inflatable rafts or dories, while the others use jet-powered boats. Most offer overnight trips as well as day trips.

For a complete list of commercial guides and outfitters, contact the Forest Service's **Hells Canyon Office,** three miles south of Clarkston on Hwy. 129, tel. (509) 758-0616. The office is open Mon.-Fri. 7:30-11:30 a.m. and 12:30-4:30 p.m. year-round, plus summer weekends. For a 24-hour recording of current river conditions and other info, call (509) 758-1957 or (800) 422-3143. The **Clarkston Chamber of Commerce,** 502 Bridge St., tel. (509) 758-7712 or (800) 933-2128, also has info on local river-running com-

panies. Expect to pay around $80 pp for the standard all-day canyon trip.

It is also possible to run the Snake River yourself if you have the equipment and skills, but you'll need to get permits for the summer season through a lottery system; contact the Hells Canyon office for their detailed "Floater's Guide."

Other Recreation

The outdoor public swimming pool in the Beachview Park at 2nd and Chestnut is open summers only; call (509) 758-1673 for hours. Several local parks offer Snake River swimming, and the Clearwater River—just over the Idaho border—is a popular summertime inner-tubing spot. Nearby reservoirs offer a variety of boating opportunities, including windsurfing, and the Snake River is famous for its rainbow trout, bass, steelhead, salmon, and monster sturgeon.

The local public putting-around place is **Quail Ridge Golf Course,** 1725 Swallow's Nest Loop, tel. (509) 758-8501.

Information

For maps or other information contact the **Clarkston Chamber of Commerce,** 502 Bridge St., tel. (509) 758-7712 or (800) 933-2128. Hours are Mon.-Fri. 9 a.m.-5 p.m. year-round. Lewiston's **chamber of commerce** is at 111 Main St., tel. (208) 743-3531 or (800) 473-3543. Although Clarkston and Lewiston have different area codes, it's a local call from Clarkston to Lewiston, and you don't need to include the area code for these calls.

Transportation

Horizon Airlines, tel. (800) 547-9308, has service from Lewiston Airport to Seattle, Spokane, Boise, and Portland. **Northwestern Trailways,** tel. (208) 746-8108 or (800) 366-3830, has bus connections north to Pullman and Spokane and south to Boise, Idaho from the bus stop at Don's Chevron in Lewiston.

SNAKE RIVER/BLUE MOUNTAINS COUNTRY

As you drive Highway 12 from Clarkston to Walla Walla, the country offers up a hilly palette of grassland, sage, and strip-cropped wheat fields. Harvesting these rolling fields requires special self-leveling combines. The wide, easy highway sails over an easy 2,785-foot pass at Alpowa Summit, and then drops slowly down to the town of Pomeroy on the western side. Not much development out here, just a few weathered homesteads set against the big land and the even larger sky. The Selkirk Mountains of Washington and Idaho are visible to the northeast, and the Blue Mountains of Washington and Oregon occupy the southern horizon.

Wilderness, and for the scoop on camping, hiking, and mountain-biking in the area. While here, pick up a map of the 70-mile **Kendall Skyline Drive.** The loop takes you through the Blue Mountains along rough but scenic forest roads.

The closest Forest Service campsite is **Alder Thicket Campground,** 18 miles south of Pomeroy on Forest Rd. 40. No charge (and no running water), and open till closed by snow in the fall. The Forest Service rents out three historic cabins for $25 a night: **Clearwater Lookout Cabin, Godman Guard Station,** and **Wenatchee Guard Station.** Contact the ranger station for details.

POMEROY

Thirty-one miles west of Clarkston is the farming town of Pomeroy (pop. 1,400), the county seat—and only real settlement—in Pomeroy County. It's also the only county seat to have been established by an act of congress. A bitter rift with neighboring Pataha City—now essentially a ghost town—was finally resolved when congress awarded the seat to Pomeroy in 1884. Today Pomeroy is an agricultural center with half-a-dozen big grain elevators in use (or disuse). Not far away is the world's largest producer of Kentucky bluegrass lawn seed, Dye Seed Ranch.

Practicalities
Pioneer Motel, 1201 Main St., tel. (509) 843-1559, has rooms for $35-40 s or d. Head to **Donna's Drive-In** for breakfast and burgers. The city park has an outdoor summer-only swimming pool. The **Garfield County Fair** comes to Pomeroy in mid-September. **Northwestern Stage Lines,** tel. (800) 366-6975, has bus connections from Pomeroy to other parts of the Northwest.

Recreation
The **Pomeroy Ranger Station** of Umatilla National Forest is on the west end of town at 120 Main St., tel. (509) 843-1891. Stop here for information on the nearby Wenaha-Tucannon

WENAHA-TUCANNON WILDERNESS

This 177,000-acre wilderness (pronounced "wen-NA-ha two-CAN-un") straddles the Washington and Oregon line within Umatilla (YOU-ma-til-la) National Forest. The wilderness is named for the two major rivers that cut through the Blue Mountains: the Wenaha and the Tucannon. The rugged terrain consists of deep canyons, narrow basaltic ridges, and mountains (2,000 to 6,400 feet in elevation) covered with lodgepole pine and other conifers. Some 200 miles of maintained trails cross the wilderness, with access from all sides, but the area is primarily used by elk hunters.

Hiking Trails
The **Mt. Misery Trail** (No. 3113) starts from the end of Diamond Peak Rd. (42 miles south of Pomeroy) off Forest Rd. 40, at an elevation of 5,900 feet. This 16-mile-long trail follows Horse Ridge for several miles, providing dramatic vistas into the wilderness and good camping spots with nearby springs. A number of loop trips of varying lengths are possible from this trail, or you can simply hike out as far as you want and return back down this relatively easy route. Snow is likely to cover the trails until mid-June.

A popular lower-elevation path is the five-mile-long **Panjab Trail** (No. 3127) that begins at the end of Forest Rd. 4713, approximately 60 miles south of Dayton. Starting at 2,900 feet in elevation, this path climbs 5.6 miles to the Indian Corral area at an elevation of 5,600 feet. It ends on a ridgetop offering breathtaking vistas, and from here you can continue deeper into the wilderness on several other trails. Because of the lower elevation, this trail is accessible earlier in the summer.

A fine day hike begins from the Teepee Campground, 32 miles south of Dayton at the end of Forest Rd. 4608. The **Oregon Butte Trail** (No. 3134) climbs for three miles into the wilderness—gaining 900 feet as you go—and ends at a fire lookout built in 1931. There's a good campsite on the ridge and a cold spring down the hill a short distance.

An access fee of $3 per vehicle per day is now charged for trailhead parking on the Umatilla, or pay $25 for an annual **Trail Park Pass** that can be used in most Washington national forests. For details on other hiking trails, see *100 Hikes in the Inland Northwest* by Rich Landers and Ida Rowe Dolphin (Seattle: The Mountaineers).

LOWER SNAKE RIVER AREA

Reservoir Recreation
The once-mighty Snake River through southeastern Washington is now just a series of placid reservoirs behind massive dams built in the 1960s and '70s. The lakes are popular with boaters, and locks make it possible for barge traffic to travel from the mouth of the Columbia all the way to Clarkston. Farthest east of these in Washington is Lower Granite Dam, which creates Lower Granite Lake. Downstream from here are the others: Little Goose Dam holding back Lake Bryan, Lower Monumental Dam creating Lake Herbert G. West, and Ice Harbor Dam creating Lake Sacajawea.

A number of parks and boat launches provide year-round recreation on these reservoirs. **Wawawai County Park** has camping ($7), picnic areas, a playground, rock climbing, and hiking trails; tel. (509) 397-6238. Get here by heading north from Clarkston on Hwy. 195 to tiny Colton, and turning left on Wawawai Road. Follow the road approximately 15 miles to the park; the last stretch is called Wawawai Grade Road.

Just south of the park, **Wawawai Landing** has a launch ramp and dock on Lower Granite Lake. **Lower Granite Dam** and reservoir are accessible by driving 25 miles north from Pomeroy. The dam has a visitors center and a fish ladder with underwater windows. The locks are a good place to watch barges loaded with wheat heading downriver for Portland.

Just west of this dam on Lake Bryan is **Boyer Park and Marina,** with launch ramps, moorage, docks, swimming beach and bathhouse, picnic area, and camping. Call (509) 397-3208 for details. **Central Ferry State Park,** tel. (509) 549-3551, on Hwy. 127 about 12 miles north of Dodge, features a swimming area with lifeguards, boat launches and docks, bass and catfish fishing, a picnic area, snack bar, showers, and camping in hookup sites ($10). The park is open mid-March to mid-November. Call (800) 452-5687 for reservations ($6 extra).

The **Lower Monumental Dam,** about six miles from Kahlotus on Devils Canyon Rd., has a visitors center, fish ladder, picnic area, and boat dock. Call (509) 547-7781 for details. **Windust Park,** three miles downstream of the dam on the north shore, has free primitive campsites (open all year), swimming, a picnic area, and boat launch facilities.

Little Goose Dam, tel. (509) 339-2233, the creator of Lake Bryan, is about a mile west of Starbuck on Hwy. 261. Facilities here include a boat dock, fish-viewing area, and visitors center.

For information on Ice Harbor Dam and Lake Sacajawea near the mouth of the Snake River, see **Tri-Cities.**

Starbuck
Not much here of note, other than the name—now better known as Washington's coffee company extraordinaire. The town was first incorporated in 1906 and has a grain elevator, a few houses, and a cafe, but no Starbucks Coffee. As might be expected in ranching country, Starbuck's big local event is the **Buck-Hi Rodeo** in mid-June. A Wyoming cowboy would feel right at home in the beautifully rugged sage-covered landscape around here. Cottonwood trees line the Tucannon River, and tumbleweeds pile against barbed wire fences. Stay along the river at **Starbuck Country B&B,** tel. (509) 399-2287, with three guest rooms, an outdoor pool, indoor

falls at Palouse Falls State Park

DON PITCHER

jacuzzi, game room, and full breakfast; $45-55 s or d. Kids accepted. Just north of Starbuck on Hwy. 261, the road descends to what was once the Snake River—now just a fat reservoir backed up behind the Lower Monumental Dam.

Lyons Ferry State Park
Located in remote and desolate country at the confluence of the Snake and Palouse Rivers, this popular park has fishing, swimming, and boating. It's eight miles northwest of Starbuck on Hwy. 261. The campground has out-in-the-sun tent sites ($10) and showers; open April to mid-November. Call (509) 646-3252 for more information.

In 1968, Washington State University researchers discovered human bones in what came to be known as the **Marmes Rockshelter.** Carbon-14 dating showed the bones to be at least 10,000 years old, making this one of the earliest known human occupation sites in North America. Unfortunately, the Lower Monumental Dam inundated both this important site and a Palouse Indian burial area; the graves were moved to a nearby hill. A three-quarter-mile trail leads from the campground to the new grave site.

The Army Corps of Engineers has free dispersed camping along the reservoir, approximately two miles north of Starbuck. Near the state park is **Lyons Ferry Hatchery,** tel. (509) 549-3551, where self-guided tours are available. **Lyons Ferry Marina,** tel. (509) 399-2001, has additional campsites, a launch ramp for the Snake River, and a small store. A towering **Union Pacific railroad trestle** spans the river nearby.

Palouse Falls State Park
About six miles north of Lyons Ferry and another two miles in along a gravel road is Palouse Falls, one of the most incredible waterfalls in Washington state. It's particularly impressive in the spring when the flow reaches its peak. Here, the Palouse River hurdles over a wide semicircle of volcanic rock into an enormous plunge pool almost 200 feet below. The dark basalt and dry sage-and-grass landscape seem stunned by the powerful roar of water in this remote place. On sunny days, you're likely to see a rainbow in the spray. Acrophobics should stay away from the cliff-top overlook that affords views of the pool far below.

The state park has picnic tables and on-the-lawn campsites ($7; open mid-March to early October). Primitive, unmaintained trails lead to the top of the falls and down into the gorge below. Watch your step if you take these steep and sometimes dangerous paths.

DAYTON

The landscape east of Dayton is a striped Pendleton blanket of undulating wheat-covered hills, scattered farms, and an over-arching sky. Home to some 2,500 people, the small farming town of Dayton has a Blue Mountains backdrop, a number of interesting historical buildings, and even a four-star restaurant. Lewis and Clark passed through the area in 1806, but the Cayuse Indians had long lived here, using present-day Main Street as a race track for their horses. The town was established in 1871 by Jesse Day (hence the Dayton name) and prospered as a crossroads town and agricultural center. The main business today is the Green Giant/Pillsbury plant where more than a third of the world's asparagus is canned. The plant also processes seed peas. The lazy Touchet (TWO-she) River flows right through town.

Depot Museum

Built in 1881 by the Oregon Railroad & Navigation Company, Dayton's train depot—oldest in the state—is now the town museum. The immaculate and beautifully restored wooden structure originally had quarters for the stationmaster upstairs, with passenger rooms below. The museum contains the original depot furnishings and woodstove downstairs, along with a fascinating collection of memorabilia that includes turn-of-the-century photos upstairs. The volunteer staff will be happy to offer tours of the museum. Admission is $1, and hours are Tues.-Sat. 9 a.m.-5 p.m. Call (509) 382-2026 for information.

Historic Buildings

Dayton's impressive **Columbia County Courthouse** was built in 1887, making it the oldest in the state of Washington. The recently restored Italianate-style courthouse features a tall central tower capped by wrought iron railings. It is one of more than 80 local buildings listed on the National Register of Historic Places. Pick up a walking tour brochure of the others from the museum, or just saunter down any of the tree-lined streets to enjoy the many turn-of-the-century Victorian homes (many of these remain unrestored).

Built in 1883, the **Bruce Memorial Museum** occupies a gorgeous, antique-filled Victorian home and carriage house in Waitsburg, 10 miles southwest of Dayton. Open Fri.-Sat. 1-4 p.m.; tel. (509) 337-6582.

Lewis and Clark Trail State Park

Five miles west of Dayton, this 37-acre park, tel. (509) 337-6457, is a choice stopping place for travelers. The best known travelers to camp here were the Lewis and Clark party as they were heading back east in 1806. The park's tall ponderosa pines and cooling waters of the Touchet River are a welcome break from the sizzling summer heat of the encircling wheat fields. A campground has space for tents and vehicles ($10; no hookups) and is open early May to mid-September; in the off-season you can camp in the day-use area. Coin-operated showers are available. There are always fish in the adjacent Touchet River, and you can walk the mile-long nature trail.

Accommodations

There are a surprising number of lodging choices in Dayton. Least expensive is **Dayton Motel,** 110 S. Pine St., tel. (509) 382-4503, for $34-65 s or d. **Blue Mountain Motel,** 414 W. Main St., tel. (509) 382-3040, charges $36 s or $40 d for its country-style rooms. The **Weinhard Hotel,** 235 E. Main St., tel. (509) 382-4032, offers the finest accommodations in town for $70-125 s or d. The building was built in 1890 by the nephew of Henry Weinhard, as in Henry Weinhard's Ale. Beautifully restored and furnished with antiques, the hotel exudes an elegance not expected in farming country.

The Purple House B&B, 415 E. Clay St., tel. (509) 382-3159 or (800) 486-2574, is in an historic home filled with Oriental rugs and antiques. It has four guest rooms with private or shared baths, a full breakfast, and an outdoor pool. Rates are $85-125 s or d in the house, or $125 d in the spacious carriage house.

Campgrounds

The closest public campsites are in Lewis and Clark Trail State Park, described above. The Umatilla National Forest's **Godman Campground** is 25 miles southeast of Dayton on Forest Rd. 26 at an elevation of 6,050 feet. No charge or running water, and it remains open till closed by snow. At the campground is a trailhead for the West Butte Creek Trail into Wenaha-Tucannon Wilderness Area (see above).

Food

Your best bet for start-the-day fare is **Panhandler's Pizza & Pasta,** 404 W. Main St., tel. (509) 382-4160. **Weinhard's Espresso Cafe,** at 235

E. Main St., tel. (509) 382-2091, also serves breakfast, but specializes in lunch, with soups, sandwiches (on homemade breads), pastries, espresso, and delicious cheesecakes. For more substantial meals (from sandwiches to steaks), try **Woodshed Bar & Grill,** 250 E. Main St., tel. (509) 382-2004.

Dayton's claim to fame is **Patit Creek Restaurant,** 725 E. Main St., tel. (509) 382-2625, the only four-star French restaurant east of the Cascades. The decor is simple, but the changing menu features regional dishes made from fresh local ingredients. Reservations strongly advised.

Events

The main local summer festival is **Dayton Days** on Memorial Day weekend, which includes three days of pari-mutuel horse racing, a rodeo, parade, arts and crafts displays, and dancing. There are more local activities—a parade, wine tasting, auction, and dancing—at **Festival at the Depot,** held the third weekend in July. The **Columbia County Fair** comes 'round on the second weekend in September and always includes big name country music, a rodeo, livestock auction, and demolition derby. On the second Sunday in October, the Dayton Historical Society sponsors a **Historic Homes Tour;** call (509) 382-2026 for details. On the day after Thanksgiving the town erupts in the **Christmas Kickoff,** with fireworks, hayrides, Santa, and caroling at the community tree.

Skiing

Ski Bluewood, 22 miles southeast of Dayton and 52 miles from Walla Walla, offers downhill skiing on 1,125 vertical feet in the Umatilla National Forest. It has the second highest base elevation in Washington (5,670 feet), and because Bluewood is over 300 miles from the coast, conditions here are generally drier than on most Washington slopes. The ski area has two triple chair lifts and a Poma. Slopes cover a spectrum from beginner through expert terrain. Adult rates are $26; call (509) 382-4725 for more information, or (509) 382-2877 for snow conditions.

Information, Services, and Transportation

The **Dayton Chamber of Commerce,** tel. (509) 382-4825 or (800) 882-6299, can be found inside the depot at 222 E. Commercial St., or on the Web at www.historicdayton.com. The town has an Olympic size outdoor **swimming pool** open summers in the city park, as well as a nine-hole **golf course.**

WALLA WALLA

As you drive toward Walla Walla from the east, Highway 12 takes you through mile after mile of gently rolling wheat fields growing out of the rich chocolate-brown soil. It's enough to make Midwest farmers drool. The strip-cropped patterns of plowed and fallow land look like cresting waves, with the Blue Mountains bordering the southeast horizon.

If you arrive in the pretty town of Walla Walla on a hot summer day, you'll probably wonder, at least momentarily, if you took a wrong turn somewhere and drove to New England. Walla Walla (30,000 people, plus another 7,000 in neighboring College Place) is an oasis in eastern Washington. Whereas many towns in this part of the state are hot and dry, Walla Walla is a refreshing change. Here, trees have been cultivated for decades and offer much-needed shade and visual relief from the sameness of the eastern Washington landscape; parks are cool and well cared for; old homes and commercial buildings add to the city's elegance. Walla Walla College, Whitman College, and Walla Walla Community College supply the youthful influence, while the big Washington State Penitentiary supplies the most jobs (including lots of inmate work at the prison license-plate factory). Kids will be happy to know that "Lincoln Logs" are made in Walla Walla.

Walla Walla has four distinct seasons, with an average of four days over 100° in summer, two winter days below zero, and about 20 inches of snow. There are nearly 300 sunny days most years. The Walla Walla Valley also enjoys a variation in height that much of eastern Washington lacks; the western end of town lies at 300 feet above sea level, while the Blue Mountain foothills to the east rise to 3,000 feet. The valley enjoys a long growing season with wheat, potatoes, asparagus, peas, alfalfa, grapes, and the

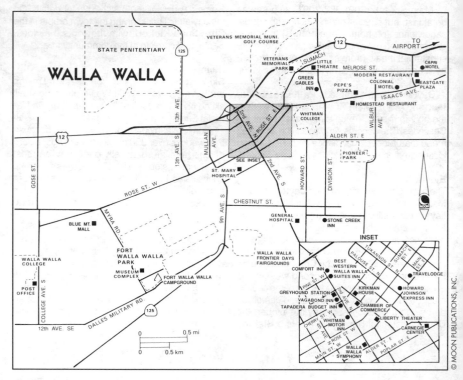

famous Walla Walla sweet onion the big money crops; livestock and dairy products are also significant parts of the economy.

HISTORY

In 1805, the Lewis and Clark party passed through the Indian hunting grounds at the confluence of the Columbia and Walla Walla Rivers, revealing this land to Anglo eyes for the first time. The first permanent white settler, and first to build a home anywhere in the Northwest, was Dr. Marcus Whitman, a medical missionary who arrived in 1836. His attempts to teach Christian principles to the Cayuse Indians met with little success, and the family was murdered by Cayuse Indians 11 years later (see the special topic "The Whitman Massacre"). After this incident, settlers were prevented from occupying these lands, and all Protestant missionaries were pulled out.

There was no further Anglo settlement in the Walla Walla area until after the Indians and whites agreed to the treaties laid out by the Great Council of Walla Walla in 1855. During this three-week gathering, Washington Territorial governor Isaac I. Stevens negotiated treaties between the U.S. and the Nez Percé, Cayuse, Umatilla, Yakama, and Wallawalla tribes. It was another four years before the U.S. Senate finally ratified these treaties, opening the land to settlement.

Steptoeville

In 1856, Col. Edward Steptoe built an army barracks—**Fort Walla Walla**—at Mill Creek to keep the peace. "Steptoeville" rose up around it and was later named Walla Walla, for the Indian word meaning "Many Waters." What had been a Nez Percé trail eventually turned into Walla Walla's Main Street. In 1859, the city was named the county seat—no small honor, since the county included half of Washington, all of Idaho, and parts of Montana. When gold was discovered in Idaho in the 1860s, prospectors came to Walla Walla for supplies, and the town prospered. Like a number of other Northwest cities, Walla Walla suffered a substantial loss when a series of fires swept through the wooden downtown area in the 1880s. Most of the oldest buildings still standing date back to the late 1880s, when the town was rebuilt in brick. Old Fort Walla Walla was finally abandoned by the army in 1910.

SIGHTS

Museums
Walla Walla has a surprising number of historic places to explore, including **Whitman Mission National Historic Site,** seven miles west of Walla Walla (see below).

Step back in time with a visit to the **Fort Walla Walla Museum Complex** at Fort Walla Walla Park on Myra Rd., tel. (509) 525-7703. This excellent museum features 15 original and re-created pioneer buildings. A large horse-era agricultural display—including a 33 mule-team combine—fills five buildings. Nearby in the trees is an old cemetery that contains the bodies of both Indians and cavalry soldiers. The museum is open Tues.-Sun. 10 a.m.-5 p.m. April-October. Admission is $4 adults, $3 seniors and students, $1 ages 6-12. Nearby is a short nature trail and campsites.

Visit the **Kirkman House,** a red brick mansion built in 1880 by entrepreneur William Kirkman, at 214 N. Colville. The ornate Italianate-style structure features a widow's walk and figurehead keystones and is on the National Register of Historic Places. Hours are Wed.-Sun. 1-4 p.m.; admission and tours cost $2 for adults, $1 for children under 13. Call (509) 529-4373 for more information.

Walking Tour
Pick up a brochure from the chamber of commerce, for a walking tour of the historic downtown area. Some of the sites you'll pass are the 1917 **Liberty Theatre,** built on the site of Steptoe's fort at W. Main and Colville, and the **Dacres**

Hotel, built in 1899 at W. Main and 4th. The **Reynolds-Day Building,** on Main between 1st and 2nd, was constructed in 1874. Washington's first State Constitutional Convention was held here in 1878. It's hard to miss the 10-story **Whitman Motor Inn,** built in 1928 at 2nd and W. Rose. President Dwight D. Eisenhower spent a night here in 1954 when he was in the area to dedicate nearby McNary Dam. The hotel is now closed. Another piece of trivial history: Founded in 1869, the **Baker Boyer Bank** is the oldest in Washington and one of the few independent banks left in the state. Their seven-story home office at the corner of Main and 2nd Streets was built in 1910 and was the town's first "skyscraper."

Colleges
Walla Walla College is located east of town in College Place. The quiet campus of this Seventh-Day Adventist school educates some 1,600 students and is particularly strong in business and engineering. Founded in 1859, **Whitman College** was the first higher education center in the West and is home to 1,300 students. One of the just two liberal arts and science colleges in the Pacific Northwest, the campus is just west of downtown Walla Walla. Despite being named for a missionary (Marcus Whitman), this private school is not connected with any religion. The tall clock tower, built in 1900, is on the National Register of Historic Places. Walla Walla is also home to a 2,200-student community college.

Big Trees and Parks
Walla Walla is famous for its tall, stately trees, a heritage from pioneer settlers who wanted a reminder of their eastern homes. A booklet, available at the chamber of commerce, describes some of the largest of these, including 25 different individuals that are the biggest in Washington. One of the trees, a 21-foot-in-circumference catalpa on the Whitman College campus, is the largest in America. The 47-acre **Pioneer Park** contains many more state record trees. Located on Alder St. at Division St., this well-kept city park was originally a cow pasture but now includes—in addition to marvelous forested areas—an aviary, rose garden, duck pond, swimming pool, gazebo, brass cannon, and picnic tables. The design for Pioneer Park came from

THE WHITMAN MASSACRE

Following the Lewis and Clark expedition of 1805-06, American interest in the "Oregon Country" began to rise exponentially. Some of the earliest to travel westward as settlers were missionaries seeking to convert the Indians to Christianity, and one of the first of these pioneers was a young medical missionary, Dr. Marcus Whitman. Whitman had been lured west in part by new reports (mostly fraudulent) that the northwest Indians were seeking men to teach them about the Bible. In 1835, he and another missionary, Samuel Parker, headed west to locate sites for Protestant missions in the Oregon Territory. Convinced of a need, Whitman hurried back, married Narcissa Prentiss, and recruited three other missionaries. By 1836, this small entourage was heading westward in covered wagons; it was the first time white women ventured across the continent overland.

The success of this trek helped establish the Oregon Trail as a way westward. Whitman played another crucial role in 1843 when he led the largest wagon train ever assembled—the almost 900 person Applegate Wagon Train—from Independence, Missouri, to the mouth of the Columbia River. This six-month trip fired the public's imag-

Narcissa Whitman

ination and helped open the gates to a flood of some 350,000 later emigrants. But this is not why he is remembered today, though it certainly had an impact on what followed.

The Mission

The Whitmans settled along the Walla Walla River in a spot the Cayuse Indians called Waiilatpu (wy-EE-la-poo), "Place of the Rye Grass." The home they built was the first permanent home whites had built in the Northwest, and their new daughter was the first white girl born west of the Rockies and north of California. Their new mission was intended to convert the Cayuse Indians, but these efforts met with minimal success; the Cayuse had little interest in religious worship, books, schooling, or farming. They did, however, appreciate Dr. Whitman's medical knowledge and assistance. Despite setbacks, the Whitmans persevered, and their mission became a vital Oregon Trail stopping point until 1844 when most emigrants shifted to a more southerly route. One day a wagon train arrived carrying the seven Sager children whose parents died on the way west; the Whitmans took them in as their own.

John C. Olmstead, creator of New York's Central Park. **Fort Walla Walla Park** is the largest city park and is home to more tall trees, along with the Fort Walla Walla Museum (described above). **Mountain View Cemetery,** on S. 2nd Ave. near Abbott Rd., is considered one of the most attractive in the state.

Grape Power

Walla Walla Valley is one of Washington state's four official viticultural appellations, and is best known for cabernet sauvignon, merlot, riesling, and chardonnay grapes. Nine small family-owned wineries are near Walla Walls. Visit **Woodward Canyon Winery,** tel. (509) 525-

4129, about 10 miles west of town in Lowden, for a taste of top-quality chardonnay and cabernet; open Mon.-Sat. 10 a.m.-5 p.m. and Sunday noon-5 p.m. **L'Ecole No. 41 Winery,** tel. (509) 525-0940, also in Lowden, specializes in semillon and merlot wines and is open daily 11 a.m.-4 p.m. The largest local winery, **Waterbrook Winery,** also in Lowden, tel. (509) 522-1918, is open daily 10:30 a.m.-4:30 p.m.

Other local wineries include: **Canoe Ridge Vineyard,** at 13th Ave. and W. Cherry St., tel. (509) 527-0885, open Mon.-Fri. 11 a.m.-4 p.m., Sat.-Sun. 11 a.m.-5 p.m.; and **Patrick M. Paul Vineyards,** 1554 School Ave., tel. (509) 526-0676, open Sat.-Sun. 1-4 p.m.

Historians have forever after argued over the attitude the Whitmans and other missionaries had toward the Indians, but most agree that they treated the Indians with courtesy. One basic fact remains: the missionaries of that era showed little respect for the natives' culture and beliefs, an attitude that led to suspicion and distrust. To compound matters, some Indians became ill from medicines the Whitmans gave them, while others ate some of the poisons Whitman used to keep coyotes away from his gardens.

End of a Dream

The Indians of Oregon Territory lived in relative peace with the emigrants, although there were scattered raids on wagon trains, along with thefts of equipment, horses, and cattle. But as the trickle of wagons turned to a westward deluge, and as settlers began to occupy their ancestral lands, an anger began to boil inside. The breaking point came in 1847 when a devastating measles epidemic—brought by the emigrants—swept through the region, killing fully half of the Cayuse. Doctor Whitman's medicines worked for whites, but not for the Indians, who had no natural resistance to the disease. Cayuse leaders feared that it was all a ruse, and that Whitman

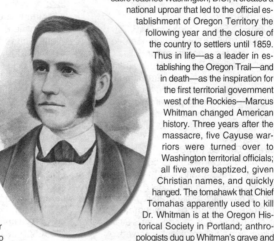

Dr. Marcus Whitman

was poisoning their people to make room for more Anglo settlers.

On November 29, 1847, a band of Cayuse Indians raided the mission, killing Marcus and Narcissa Whitman, two of the Sager children, and nine others. They then took 50 people captive; most of them were eventually ransomed for $500 worth of trade goods, but three more children died of measles while in captivity. The murders provoked a war between the Cayuse and emigrant settlers, and when news of the massacre reached Washington, D.C., it created a national uproar that led to the official establishment of Oregon Territory the following year and the closure of the country to settlers until 1859.

Thus in life—as a leader in establishing the Oregon Trail—and in death—as the inspiration for the first territorial government west of the Rockies—Marcus Whitman changed American history. Three years after the massacre, five Cayuse warriors were turned over to Washington territorial officials; all five were baptized, given Christian names, and quickly hanged. The tomahawk that Chief Tomahas apparently used to kill Dr. Whitman is at the Oregon Historical Society in Portland; anthropologists dug up Whitman's grave and matched the fracture in his skull to this tomahawk.

Two local wineries are open by appointment only: **Glen Fiona Winery,** tel. (509) 522-2566, and **Walla Walla Vintners,** tel. (509) 525-4724. **Leonetti Cellar,** tel. (509) 525-1428, is closed to the public, but their 1992 merlot gained a number four ranking in *Wine Spectator's* "Top 100 Wines of the World."

Onion Power

Although wheat is the most important crop in the Walla Walla area, onions are the town's claim to fame. The famous Walla Walla sweet onions were developed from Spanish and Italian varieties first brought here in the late 19th century. Careful experimentation by John Arbini in

the 1920s produced a sweet-tasting onion that quickly became a favorite of vegetable buyers. Their sweetness is illusory; actually these mild-flavored, juicy, large onions have almost no sugar, but only half the sulfur of other onions. And it's the sulfur that gives onions their strong bite and causes tears. Walla Walla sweets are best used raw or slightly cooked, in hamburgers, sandwiches, and salads. These onions are so mild that you can bite into one like an apple, and so soft they have to be harvested by hand. Unfortunately, they have a short three- to six-week shelf life and must be stored separately. This means you're likely to only see them in stores from mid-June to mid-August when they are at their best. Today, the "Walla Walla Sweet" label can only be put on onions grown within Walla Walla County in Washington and adjacent Umatilla County in northeastern Oregon. Contact the chamber of commerce at 29 E. Sumach, tel. (509) 525-0850 or (877) 998-4748, for a list of local shippers, along with a wonderful recipe for roasted Walla Walla Sweets.

ACCOMMODATIONS

Bed and Breakfasts

Built in 1883, **Stone Creek Inn B&B**, 720 Bryant, tel. (509) 529-8120, was once home to Washington's last territorial governor, Miles Conway Moore. A National Historic Site, this grand three-story Victorian mansion is surrounded by four acres of parklike grounds and has four antique-furnished guest rooms. A swimming pool (summers) and hot tub (winters) are available, and a full formal breakfast is served. No kids; $78-125 s or $95-125 d.

Green Gables Inn B&B, 922 Bonsella, tel. (509) 525-5501 or (888) 525-5501, is located in a beautiful 1909 craftsman mansion along a tree-lined street. The five guest rooms ($85-110 s or d) all have private baths and a mix of antique and modern furnishings. A separate carriage house ($160 for up to four people) is available for families, and a full breakfast is served.

Mill Creek Inn B&B, is on 22 acres of land seven miles east of Walla Walla, tel. (509) 522-1234. The turn-of the century farmstead is surrounded by three cottages with private baths and kitchens. A full breakfast is delivered to your door each morning, and kids are okay; $85-135 s, $100-150 d. The award-winning Glen Fiona Winery is on the premises.

Motels

A good choice for those on a tight budget is the inexpensive but clean **Tapadera Budget Inn**, 211 N. 2nd Ave., tel. (509) 529-2580 or (800) 722-8277; $33 s or $38 d. **Capri Motel**, 2003 Melrose, tel. (509) 525-1130, has rooms for $33 s or $42 d, including an outdoor pool. **Colonial Motel**, 2279 E. Isaacs, tel. (509) 529-1220, charges $35 s or $45 d. **City Center Motel**, 627 W. Main, tel. (509) 529-2660 or (800) 453-3160, has an outdoor pool; rooms are $39 s or $43 d.

Several of the national chains are in town. **Walla Walla Travelodge**, 421 E. Main St., tel. (509) 529-4940 or (800) 255-3050, is $46 s or $52 d, including an outdoor pool and jacuzzi. Rooms are $55 s or $60 d at **Vagabond Inn**, 305 N. 2nd Ave., tel. (509) 529-4410 or (800) 522-1555, including an outdoor pool. **Super 8 Motel**, 2315 Eastgate St. N, tel. (509) 525-8800 or (800) 800-8000, costs $49 s or $54 d, with an outdoor pool and jacuzzi. **Comfort Inn**, 520 N. 2nd Ave., tel. (509) 525-2522 or (800) 221-2222, charges $59-94 s or $65-99 d, and features an indoor pool, exercise room, jacuzzi, and continental breakfast. **Best Western Walla Walla Suites Inn**, 7 E. Oak St., tel. (509) 525-4700 or (800) 528-1234, charges $59-90 s or $69-100 d, including an indoor pool, jacuzzi, exercise room, fridges, microwaves, and continental breakfast. **Howard Johnson Express Inn**, 325 E. Main St., tel. (509) 529-4360 or (800) 446-4656, has an outdoor pool, continental breakfast, jacuzzi, sauna, exercise room; $70-73 s or $75-80 d.

Campgrounds

Fort Walla Walla Park, 1530 Dalles Military Rd., tel. (509) 525-3770, is a shady, city-run campground with showers. Tents $10; RVs $15. Nearby is a privately run place, **Four Seasons RV Resort**, 1440 Dalles Military Rd., tel. (509) 529-6072. More camping at **Lewis and Clark Trail State Park**, 26 miles northeast of Walla Walla.

FOOD

Breakfast and Lunch

Start your day at **Clarette's Restaurant**, 15 S. Touchet, tel. (509) 529-3430, for the best home-style breakfasts in Walla Walla. At lunchtime, your options increase considerably. **Merchants Ltd.**, 21 E. Main, tel. (509) 525-0900, is a great deli with a lunch buffet that includes homemade soups, fresh salads, and baked goods. You can also get charged up with an espresso here. Also of note for lunch is **Cookie Tree Bakery & Cafe**, 23 S. Spokane, tel. (509) 522-4826, with homemade breads and pastries. **Cyndra's Panini & Juice Bar**, 38 E. Main St., tel. (509) 529-7533, has organic juices, gazpacho, baked goods, and panini sandwiches. **Blue Mt. Tavern,** 2025 E. Isaacs Ave., tel. (509) 525-9941, serves excellent sandwiches for lunch, TV sports at night, and live music on weekends. No kids allowed.

American

Jacobi's Cafe, 416 N. Second, tel. (509) 525-2677, is housed in the old Northern Pacific Railroad depot and adjacent railroad dining car. The big menu includes steaks, Mexican food, and various kinds of seafood, soups, and sandwiches, but the students come for the microbrews, local wines, and espresso. The **Homestead Restaurant,** 1528 Isaacs, tel. (509) 522-0345, serves three meals daily from a varied menu that includes steaks, seafood, sautés, and vegetarian selections.

Although Walla Walla has all the standard fast-food eateries (out on Wilbur and Isaacs), you'd do far better visiting **The Ice Burg,** 616 W. Birch, tel. (509) 529-1793. This popular drive-in makes great hamburgers and wonderful banana shakes. **Mill Creek Brewpub,** 11 S. Palouse St., tel. (509) 522-2440, is a fun place with fresh-brewed beer on tap and pub grub from the kitchen.

International

The Walla Walla area has a rich Italian heritage. One example is **Pastime Cafe,** 215 W. Main, tel. (509) 525-0873, where the big old-time Italian meals—lasagna, ravioli, and spaghetti—are still cranked out, just as they have been since 1927. Much newer is **Paisano's,** 26 E. Main, tel. (509) 527-3511, where the northern Italian cuisine uses fresh ingredients and changes with the seasons. A bit pricey, but worth it.

For a pizza, stop by **Pepe's Pizza,** 1533 Isaacs, tel. (509) 529-2550. Another good place for pizza is **Lorenzo's,** 1415 Plaza Way, tel. (509) 529-6333, with an all-you-can-eat buffet.

Looking for big Mexican meals and great margaritas? Head to **El Sombrero's** at Oak and N. 2nd, tel. (509) 522-4984. The **Golden Horse,** 628 W. Main, tel. (509) 525-7008, specializes in authentic Cantonese cuisine.

Bakers and Grocers

Although Walla Walla has the big chain grocers, one place is more noteworthy: **Andy's Market,** 1117 S. College Ave., tel. (509) 529-1003, out in College Place. Because of the Seventh-Day Adventist college nearby, this large market is almost entirely vegetarian. You'll find a few frozen meat items (but no pork), lots of frozen and canned "vegemeat" products, bulk foods, and deliciously earthy breads. Closed Saturday and open Sunday. Not far away, at 166 N. College Ave., is **Rodger's Bakery,** tel. (509) 522-2738, with breads, bagels, breadsticks, and hot soups. **John's Wheatland Bakery,** 1828 E. Isaacs, tel. (509) 522-2253, is another excellent bake shop that uses fresh local ingredients.

EVENTS

A popular event with photographers is the **Walla Walla Balloon Stampede,** held in mid-May; after the 50 or so balloons go up, enjoy the arts and crafts displays and demonstrations. A big **Fourth of July** at Pioneer Park is followed by the **Walla Walla Sweet Onion Harvest Festival** a week later. Labor Day weekend brings the **Walla Walla Frontier Days Fair & Rodeo,** with horse racing, an evening rodeo, concerts, and educational exhibits. In mid-September, the **Fall Harvest and Community Festival** at Fort Walla Walla Museum provides a chance to learn about pioneer life.

ARTS AND ENTERTAINMENT

The **Walla Walla Symphony Orchestra,** 3 W. Alder, tel. (509) 529-8020, has been performing since 1907, and is the oldest continuous symphony west of the Mississippi. Founded in 1944, the **Walla Walla Little Theatre,** 1130 E. Sumach, tel. (509) 529-3683, is a community theater that produces four plays each season. **Harper Joy Theatre** at Whitman College, 345 Boyer, tel. (509) 527-5180, also stages several productions each year, and the local community college puts on **Outdoor Summer Theater** musical productions at Fort Walla Walla amphitheater each July.

Art buffs will want to visit the **Clyde and Mary Harris Gallery,** tel. (509) 527-2561, at Walla Walla College. Other galleries include the **Sheehan Gallery** at Whitman College, tel. (509) 527-5111; and **Carnegie Art Center,** 109 S. Palouse, tel. (509) 525-4270.

covered wagon at Whitman Mission National Historic Site

DON PITCHER

Blue Mt. Tavern, 2025 E. Isaacs Ave., tel. (509) 525-9941, is *the* place for blues and rock bands. **Merchants Ltd.,** 21 E. Main, tel. (509) 525-0900, also has live jazz or other music most weekends.

SPORTS AND RECREATION

For information on hiking and camping in the Blue Mountains of Umatilla National Forest (much of which lies in Oregon), visit the **Walla Walla Ranger Station** 1415 W. Rose St., tel. (509) 522-6290. The Wenaha-Tucannon Wilderness Area is described on under "Snake River/Blue Mountains Country."

Veteran's Memorial Golf Course, off Hwy. 12, is an 18-hole course open to the public; tel. (509) 527-4507. The closest winter downhill place is Ski Bluewood near Dayton.

Cycling

Enjoy the **bike path** from Cambridge Dr. to Rooks Park, or from 9th and Dalles Military Rd. to Myra Road. For a more adventurous ride, head out scenic Old Milton Highway south of town. It's especially pretty in the fall. Rent bikes from **The Bicycle Barn,** 1503 E. Isaacs, tel. (509) 529-7860.

Swimming

Outdoor summer-only **swimming pools** include one in Jefferson Park at 9th Ave. and Malcolm St., along with a 50-meter pool on Rees Ave. at Sumach Street. Call (509) 527-4527 for details. Indoor pools are at the YMCA, tel. (509) 525-8863; Whitman College, tel. (509) 527-5921; and Walla Walla College, tel. (509) 527-2396.

INFORMATION AND TRANSPORTATION

For local information, contact the **Walla Walla Chamber of Commerce,** 29 E. Sumach, tel. (509) 525-0850 or (877) 998-4748; www.bmi.net/ww-chamb. Hours are Mon.-Fri. 8:30 a.m.-5 p.m. all year, plus Saturday 8 a.m.-2 p.m. in the summer.

Valley Transit, tel. (509) 525-9140, serves the Walla Walla/College Place area Mon.-Saturday. The **Greyhound** depot is at 315 N. 2nd, tel. (509) 525-9313 or (800) 231-2222.

Horizon Air, tel. (800) 547-9308, has service to Seattle and Portland from **Walla Walla Regional Airport.**

WALLA WALLA AREA

West from Walla Walla lies farming country with a Midwestern look; this could just as well be Nebraska. There are two wineries in tiny Lowden, but not much else of interest to the traveler. Far to the southeast lie rolling tree-covered hills that rise into the Blue Mountains. A blanket of snow covers the summits till late summer.

Whitman Mission

You can get the whole story of Marcus and Narcissa Whitman's pioneer mission on the Oregon Trail at the **Whitman Mission National Historic Site,** seven miles west of Walla Walla on Hwy. 12, tel. (509) 522-6360. None of the original buildings remain, but you can walk the self-guiding trails to the mission site, grave, monument, and locations of the first house, blacksmith shop, and grist mill. Maintained by the National Park Service, the visitors center here is open daily 8 a.m.-6 p.m. mid-June to Labor Day, and daily 8 a.m.-4:30 the rest of the year (closed Thanksgiving, Christmas, and New Years). The grounds are open till dusk year-round. Admission is $2 adults, $4 families, and free for kids under 17. Cultural demonstrations—including adobe brick making, beadwork, moccasin making, and butter churning—take place on summer weekends

Inside the visitor center you'll find a diorama of the Whitman mission, plus artifacts found here and a fine exhibit about the Cayuse tribe and the sad end to the Whitman's work (see the special topic "The Whitman Massacre" for more on this story). Be sure to walk up the hill to the Whitman Memorial, a 27-foot-tall obelisk overlooking this lonely place. Come here on a late fall day with the clouds overhead, the brown grass at your feet, great blue herons on the shore of the pond, and a chill west wind to really appreciate the peaceful wildness that both the Cayuse and the Whitmans loved. A restored section of the Oregon Trail (used until 1844) passes right through the Whitman Mission site.

Fort Walla Walla

The tiny settlement of **Wallula** stands along the east shore of Lake Wallula, the Columbia River reservoir created by McNary Dam. Look for **Two Sisters,** twin basalt pillars that the Cayuse legends said were two sisters who had been turned to stone by Coyote. A plaque in Wallula commemorates one of the earliest garrisons in the Northwest. In 1818, the Northwest Fur Company established **Fort Nez Percé** at the junction of the Walla Walla and Columbia Rivers. The fort soon became a center for fur trade in the region. Fearing Indian attacks, the company built two strong outer walls and armed the men heavily; it was soon being called the "Gibraltar of the Columbia." In 1821, the British-owned Hudson's Bay Company took over the business, later renaming it Fort Walla Walla. The fears of Indian attacks intensified, and in 1856 the company abandoned the fort rather than risking destruction. The fort's commander ordered the black powder and shot balls be dumped into the Columbia River to keep them out of Cayuse hands. Shortly after his men abandoned the fort, Indian warriors burned it to the ground.

Two years later a new Fort Walla Walla rose, but this time as a U.S. Army military garrison farther up the river. This fort would eventually become the center around which the city of Walla Walla grew. The original fort site later grew into the town of Wallula, but in the late 1940s, construction began on the McNary Dam downstream along the Columbia River. After its completion, the old town and fort site were inundated, and the town's residents moved to higher ground.

BOOKLIST

DESCRIPTION AND TRAVEL

Begoun, Paula, Stephanie Bell, and Elizabeth Janda. *Best Places to Kiss in the Northwest.* Seattle: Beginning Press, 1995. A silly title and sappy sweet writing, but a fun guide to romantic hideaways, intimate restaurants, viewpoints, gardens, and more in Oregon, Washington, and British Columbia.

Bergman, Ann, and Rose Williamson. *Going Places: Family Getaways in the Pacific Northwest.* Seattle: Northwest Parent Publishing, Inc., 1995. A useful guide to family-friendly places, with tips on travel with kids.

Bergman, Ann, and Stephanie Dunnewind. *Out and About Seattle with the Kids.* Seattle: Northwest Parent Publishing, Inc., 1998. Family places around Seattle.

Brewster, David, and Stephanie Irving. *Northwest Best Places.* Seattle: Sasquatch, 1998. A thorough guide to restaurants and lodging, with a smattering of things to do, in Washington, Oregon, and British Columbia. Highly regarded for its honesty and accuracy, but primarily aimed at upscale places.

Chasan, Daniel Jack and John Doerper; photos by Bruce Hinds. *Washington.* Oakland, CA: Compass American Guides, 1998. An attractive photo-and-text guide to the state.

Holden, Ronald, and Glenda Holden. *Wine Country of Washington.* Holden Pacific, Inc., 1989. Detailed information on Washington wineries.

Irving, Stephanie. *Seattle Best Places.* Seattle: Sasquatch, 1996. A complete guide to restaurants, hotels, shopping, sights, and things to do in and around Seattle.

Irving, Stephanie, and Nancy Leson. *Northwest Cheap Sleeps.* Seattle: Sasquatch, 1995. A guide to budget lodging places and other attractions in Washington, Oregon, and British Columbia.

Johnston, Mandy. *Stepping Out in Seattle.* Medina, WA: JASI, 1998. Useful for singles and couples looking for a night on the town.

Jones, Phillip N., ed. *Columbia River Gorge: A Complete Guide.* Seattle: The Mountaineers, 1992. Complete information on hiking, climbing, windsurfing, bicycling, and other activities in the Gorge.

Litman, Todd, and Suzanne Kort. *Washington off the Beaten Path.* Old Saybrook, CT: The Globe Pequot Press, 1999. A tour of Washington's out-of-the-way and little-known places.

McFarlane, Marilyn. *Best Places to Stay in the Pacific Northwest.* New York: Houghton-Mifflin, 1998. There is more than one "best places" guide, and this one from the east coast does a fine job. Easy-to-use breakdowns by type of facility—destination resorts, island getaways, ski lodges—make vacation planning a breeze.

McRae, Bill, and Judy Jewell. *Pacific Northwest.* Oakland, CA: Lonely Planet, 1999. A regional guide to Oregon, Washington, and Idaho.

Robinson, Kathryn, and Stephanie Irving. *Seattle Cheap Eats.* Seattle: Sasquatch Books, 1998. Helpful reviews of more than 300 inexpensive restaurants, cafes, and dives around Seattle. A fine book for budget travelers in search of good eats.

Offline Restaurant Guide. Seattle: Sasquatch Books, 1997. The print version of Microsoft's useful online restaurant guide (www.seattle.sidewalk).

Seattle Access. New York: Access Press, 1997. The best overall guide to the city of Seattle, with up-to-date information and helpful maps. Easy to use.

Washington State Lodging & Travel Guide. Published annually, this very complete book lists nearly every lodging place in the state. Available from the Washington State Tourism Development Division, tel. (800) 544-1800, or visitors centers around the state.

Welke, Elton. *Places to go with Children around Puget Sound.* San Francisco: Chronicle Books, 1994. State parks, fish hatcheries, museums, and attractions that appeal to all ages.

Seattle Portland Restaurants. New York: Zagat Survey, 1997. Hundreds of survey-based restaurant reviews. Good price info, too.

HIKING AND CLIMBING

Adkison, Ron. *Hiking Washington.* Helena, Montana: Falcon Press Publishing Co., 1993. Seventy-five of Washington's most popular hikes, from Hurricane Ridge to Mt. Spokane, along with lesser-known trails in wilderness areas; maps included.

Beckey, Fred. *Cascade Alpine Guide: Climbing and High Routes.* Seattle: The Mountaineers, 1995. Four volumes of very detailed Cascade climbing routes, plus historical information and photos.

Burton, Joan. *Best Hikes with Children in Western Washington and the Cascades.* Seattle: The Mountaineers, 1998. Having kids doesn't have to mean the end of your days on the trail. A two-volume guide to short hikes, all featuring lakes, waterfalls, views, or other points of interest that will motivate kids of all ages.

Coates, Sally O'Neal. *Hot Showers, Soft Beds, and Dayhikes in the North Cascades.* Berkeley: Wilderness Press, 1997. A useful guide to short hikes and lodging in the north Cascades.

Hooper, David. *Exploring Washington's Wild Olympic Coast.* Seattle: The Mountaineers, 1993. A detailed (but not always accurate) guide to hiking the coastal strip of the northern Olympic Peninsula from Neah Bay to Queets.

Judd, Ron C., and Dan A. Nelson. *Pacific Northwest Hiking.* San Francisco: Foghorn Press, 1997. Useful descriptions of hundreds of trails throughout Washington and Oregon.

Landers, Rich, and Ida Rowe Dolphin. *100 Hikes in the Inland Northwest.* Seattle: The Mountaineers, 1987. Descriptions, photos, and maps of hikes in eastern Washington plus parts of Idaho, Montana, and Oregon.

Manning, Harvey and Penny Manning. *Walks & Hikes in the Foothills and Lowlands Around Puget Sound.* Seattle: The Mountaineers, 1995. Descriptions and photos of hikes from Bellingham around the sound to the Olympic Peninsula.

Molvar, Erik. *Hiking Olympic National Park* Helena: Falcon Press, 1996. A popular guide to the Olympics.

Spring, Ira, and Harvey Manning. *50 Hikes in Mount Rainier National Park.* Seattle: The Mountaineers, 1988. Maps, descriptions, and photos of 50 Mt. Rainier hikes.

Spring, Ira, and Harvey Manning. *100 Hikes in Washington's North Cascades: Glacier Peak Region.* Seattle: The Mountaineers, 1996. Lesser-known areas of Glacier Peak Wilderness from Darrington to Wenatchee and Lake Chelan; maps, photos, trail descriptions.

Spring, Ira, and Harvey Manning. *100 Hikes in Washington's North Cascades: National Park Region.* Seattle: The Mountaineers, 1994.

Spring, Ira, and Harvey Manning. *100 Hikes in Washington's South Cascades and Olympics.* Seattle: The Mountaineers, 1992.

Spring, Ira, and Harvey Manning. *Fifty-Five Hikes in Central Washington: Yakima, Pot Holes, Wenatchee, Grand Coulee, Columbia River, Snake River, Umtanum*. Seattle: The Mountaineers, 1997.

Spring, Vicky, Ira Spring, and Harvey Manning. *100 Hikes in Washington's Alpine Lakes*. Seattle: The Mountaineers, 1993.

Sterling, E.M. *Best Short Hikes in Washington's North Cascades and San Juan Islands*. Seattle: The Mountaineers, 1994.

Sterling, E.M. *Best Short Hikes in Washington's South Cascades and Olympics*. Seattle: The Mountaineers, 1995.

Whitney, Stephen R. *A Field Guide to the Cascades and Olympics*. Seattle: The Mountaineers, 1983.

Whitney, Stephen R. *Nature Walks In & Around Seattle*. Seattle: The Mountaineers, 1987. Short nature walks at 25 parks and natural areas between Redmond and Federal Way. Great for families, nature photographers, or a quick escape to the outdoors.

Wood, Robert L. *Olympic Mountains Trail Guide*. Seattle: The Mountaineers, 1991. Detailed trail descriptions, maps, and photos of national park and national forest trails on the Olympic Peninsula.

HISTORY

Bennett, Robert A. *Walla Walla: Portrait of a Western Town 1804-1899*. Walla Walla: Pioneer Press Books, 1980. Indians, treaties, trails, and Walla Walla's beginnings in Washington Territory days. The three-book series features excellent historical photos and drawings and informative, interesting text.

Bennett, Robert A. *Walla Walla: A Town Built to be a City 1900-1919*. Walla Walla: Pioneer Press Books, 1982. Early automobiles, aviation, Chinese community, street cars, and over

400 photos celebrating Walla Walla's turn-of-the-century growth spurt.

Bennett, Robert A. *Walla Walla: A Nice Place to Raise a Family 1920-1949*. Walla Walla: Pioneer Press Books, 1988. WW II, a new airport, the rise of the canning industry, and Walla Walla's emergence as a modern city.

Brewster, David, and David M. Buerge. *Washingtonians: A Biographical Portrait of the State*. Seattle: Sasquatch Books, 1988. Washington's history in a series of insightful biographies. Enjoyable reading.

Chevigny, Hector. *Russian America: The Great Alaskan Venture*. New York: The Viking Press. 1979. A very readable account of the Russian years. The complete story of Anna Petrovna is one of the saddest from the Northwest.

Cook, Warren L. *Flood Tide of Empire: Spain and the Pacific Northwest, 1543-1819*. New Haven: Yale University Press. 1973. This is a thorough book, perhaps best known for being the first to tell of Spanish efforts to stop the Lewis and Clark expedition.

Dodds, Gordon B. *The American Northwest: A History of Oregon and Washington*. Arlington Heights, Illinois: The Forum Press, Inc., 1986. A comprehensive history of the Northwest from 15,000 B.C. to the present, with emphasis on the people and their politics.

Kirk, Ruth, and Carmela Alexander. *Exploring Washington's Past: A Road Guide to History*. Seattle: University of Washington Press, 1996. A town-by-town description of hundreds of historical sights around the state.

Lambert, Dale A. *The Pacific Northwest: Past, Present, and Future*. Wenatchee, WA: Directed Media, Inc., 1985. A very readable, well-illustrated textbook on Pacific Northwest history.

LeWarne, Charles P. *Washington State*. Seattle: University of Washington Press, 1993. A detailed and profusely illustrated Washington history textbook covering pre-history through modern times.

LeWarne, Charles P. *Utopias on Puget Sound, 1885-1915.* Seattle: University of Washington Press. 1995. The history of five communal experiments: Home, Burley, Freeland, Equality, and Port Angeles.

Lewis, William S., and Naojiro Murakami. *Ranald MacDonald: The Narrative of His Life, 1824-1894.* Portland: Oregon Historical Society Press, 1990. The incredible story of a man almost unknown in America but revered in Japan. MacDonald was an adventurer whose daring exploits helped open Japan to the outside world.

McCoy, Keith. *The Mount Adams Country: Forgotten Corner of the Columbia River Gorge.* White Salmon, Washington: Pahto Publications, 1987. History of the Mt. Adams area from pre-Indians, Lewis and Clark, and early pioneers to modern-day climbers, the CCC, and Bigfoot. Interesting reading and numerous photographs assembled by a lifetime Mt. Adams-area resident.

Martinson, Arthur D. *Wilderness above the Sound: The Story of Mount Rainier National Park.* Niwot, CO: Rinehart, Roberts Publications, Inc., 1994. An enjoyable history covering the mountain's discovery, early ascents, and development of the national park, illustrated with lots of historical photos.

Ross, Alexander. *Adventures of the First Settlers on the Oregon or Columbia River, 1810-1813.* Lincoln: University of Nebraska Press, 1986. A reprint of Ross's original eyewitness account of John Jacob Astor's 1810 expedition from New York to the Columbia River aboard the Tonquin. Fascinating and lively, the book describes the fur-trade existence as it happened, based on Ross' original journal entries.

Ruby, Robert H., and John A. Brown. *A Guide to the Indian Tribes of the Pacific Northwest.* Norman, Oklahoma: University of Oklahoma Press, 1992. History, location, numbers, culture, and contemporary life of over 150 Indian tribes of the Pacific Northwest. An excellent reference tool.

Ruby, Robert H., and John A. Brown. *The Chinook Indians: Traders of the Lower Columbia River.* Norman, Oklahoma: University of Oklahoma Press, 1988. Comprehensive history of the relationship between whites and the Indians of the lower Columbia Valley, from fur trading to modern-day legal battles.

Ruby, Robert H., and John A. Brown. *Indians of the Pacific Northwest; A History.* Norman, Oklahoma: University of Oklahoma Press, 1988.

Schwantes, Carlos, et al. *Washington: Images of a State's Heritage.* Spokane: Melior Publications, 1988. A comprehensive pictorial history of the state, covering early Native American life through the eruption of Mt. St. Helens and Bill Gates' Microsoft. Rarely seen photos and historic drawings highlight the easily digestible text.

Scott, James W., and Ronald L. DeLorme. *Historical Atlas of Washington.* Norman, Oklahoma: University of Oklahoma Press, 1988. Very informative atlas depicting the many faces of Washington in map form, from the earliest explorers to the present day.

Seattle, Chief. *Who Can Sell the Air?* Summertown, TN: The Book Publishing Co. The words of Chief Seattle, including his legendary homage to the natural world.

Shepherd, Donald, and Robert F. Slatzer. *Bing Crosby: The Hollow Man.* New York: St. Martins Press, 1983. The contrasting life of an American family man and private jerk.

Swan, James G. *The Northwest Coast Or, Three Years' Residence in Washington Territory. 1857.* Seattle: University of Washington Press, 1992. A fascinating report of life on the frontier with both whites and Native Americans depicted.

Winthrop, Theodore. *Canoe and the Saddle.* Portland: Binfords & Mort. nd. The first book written (1863) about the Washington Territory. Out of print.

Wood, Robert L. *Across the Olympic Mountains; the Press Expedition, 1889-1890.* Seattle: The Mountaineers. 1989. The interesting story of the most famous early exploration of Olympic National Park.

NATURAL SCIENCES

Alt, David D., and Donald W. Hyndman. *Roadside Geology of Washington.* Missoula, MT: Mountain Press Publishing Co., 1986. A great book for anyone with an interest in geology, with easy-to-understand descriptions of how volcanoes, glaciers, floods, and other processes shaped the state's topography over the eons.

Angell, Tony, and Kenneth C. Balcomb III. *Marine Birds and Mammals of Puget Sound.* Seattle: University of Washington Press, 1982. Habits and habitats of western Washington birds and marine mammals.

Feeney, Stephanie. *The Northwest Gardeners' Resource Directory.* Everything you need to know about gardening in Washington, from hardiness zones to seed sources to display gardens.

Kozloff, Eugene N. *Plants and Animals of the Pacific Northwest.* Seattle: University of Washington Press, 1978. The most thorough, and illustrated, book of its kind.

Kozloff, Eugene N. *Seashore Life of the Northern Pacific Coast.* Seattle: University of Washington Press, 1983.

Mosher, Milton M., and Knut Lunnum. *Trees of Washington.* Pullman, WA: Washington State University Cooperative Extension, 1992. A 40-page guide to the state's trees, with distribution maps, identification keys, and lots of details.

OUTDOOR RECREATION

Kaysing, Bill. *Great Hot Springs of the West.* Santa Barbara, California: Capra Press, 1994. A complete guide to well-known and obscure hot springs from Washington to Colorado, complete with maps, facilities, and clothing requirements; plenty of photos.

Kirkendall, Tom. *Mountain Bike Adventures in Washington's North Cascades & Olympics.* Seattle: The Mountaineers, 1996.

Kirkendall, Tom, and Vicky Spring. *Cross-Country Ski Trails No. 1: Washington's North Cascades.* Seattle: The Mountaineers, 1989. Descriptions and photos of more than 80 ski trails.

Kirkendall, Tom, and Vicky Spring. *Cross-Country Ski Trails No. 2: Washington's South Cascades and Olympics.* Seattle: The Mountaineers, 1989. Descriptions and photos of more than 80 ski trails.

Lans, Ken (editor). *Washington's Backcountry Access Guide,* Seattle: The Mountaineers. An inexpensive annual booklet with detailed and up-to-date info on rules and regulations in Washington's wilderness areas.

Morava, Lillian B. *Camper's Guide to Washington Parks, Lakes, Forests, and Beaches.* Houston, TX: Gulf Publishing Co., 1994. The photos are amateurish, and the descriptions are basic, but the book includes some campgrounds missed by other books.

Mueller, Marge, and Ted Mueller. *North Puget Sound: Afoot & Afloat.* Seattle: The Mountaineers, 1995. Painstakingly detailed guide to North Puget Sound, from Point Roberts to Whidbey Island and west to Neah Bay, helpful to both boaters and landlubbers. Boat launches, parks, points of interest, plus photos and maps.

Mueller, Marge, and Ted Mueller. *The San Juan Islands: Afoot & Afloat.* Seattle: The Mountaineers, 1995. Thorough guide to "the big four" and numerous lesser islands in the San Juan chain. Boating, biking, sightseeing, and more, with maps and photos. Books by these prolific authors are always well written and very helpful.

Mueller, Marge, and Ted Mueller. *The San Juan Islands Essential Guide*. Seattle: The Mountaineers, 1994. Yet another in the in-depth series, this time with a nuts-and-bolts focus on lodging, restaurants, shopping, tours, and other activities in the San Juans.

Mueller, Marge, and Ted Mueller. *Washington's State Parks*. Seattle: Mountaineers, 1993. A very detailed guide to all of the state parks that shows each park's facilities, history, and activities.

Mueller, Marge, and Ted Mueller. *Exploring Washington's Wild Areas*. Seattle: Mountaineers, 1994. This book provides an overview of Washington's wilderness areas and national parks, with brief descriptions of hiking and climbing in each. An excellent introduction to these wild places. Nicely illustrated, too.

North, Douglass A. *Washington Whitewater I*. Seattle: The Mountaineers, 1992. Seventeen whitewater trips on the Cascades' most popular rivers for paddlers and rafters; every detail is covered, from put-ins and take-outs to camping, scenery, and special hazards.

Perry, John, and Jane Greverus Perry. *The Sierra Club Guide to the National Areas of Oregon and Washington*. San Francisco: Sierra Club Books, 1997. Features, activities, camping, boating, and more in national forests, parks, and beaches.

Stienstra, Tom. *Pacific Northwest Camping*. San Francisco: Foghorn Press, 1998. The complete guide to over 1,500 campgrounds, from boat-in island sites to RV parks, state parks to wilderness areas.

Washburne, Randel. *Kayaking Puget Sound, the San Juans, and the Gulf Islands*. Seattle: The Mountaineers, 1990. Destinations, routes, ratings, and launching info.

Williams, Chuck. *Mount St. Helens National Volcanic Monument*. Seattle: The Mountaineers, 1988. Great pocket guide for post-eruption hikers, sightseers, and skiers; photos, history, and detailed trail descriptions.

Woods, Erin, and Bill Woods. *Bicycling the Backroads*. Seattle: The Mountaineers, 1989-94. Three volumes—Around Puget Sound, of Northwest Washington, and of Southwest Washington—provide in-depth information on bike routes, terrain, elevation gain, and points of interest, plus explicit directions and plenty of maps.

INDEX

CAMPGROUNDS AND RV PARKS

CONSERVATION AND WILDERNESS AREAS

FAIRS

GARDENS

HIKING

LIGHTHOUSES

MUSIC FESTIVALS

NATIONAL PARKS, MONUMENTS, AND HISTORIC SITES

SCENIC DRIVES

UNUSUAL CLAIMS TO FAME

America's tallest chestnut tree: 147
Aurora Bridge Troll: 63
Baker Dam fish elevator: 496
bluebird capital of the world: 473
Brandy's Troll Haven: 359-360
Country Christmas Lighted Farm
  Implement Parade: 633
Ellensburg Bull: 611-612
53-foot-high Russian rocket: 63
"Galloping Gertie" suspension bridge: 256
giant Radio Flyer wagon: 708, 710
Grandview Grape Stomp: 633
longest continuous-truss span bridge: 437
Spam Cookoff/Spam Queen: 558
Stonehenge: 471
Teapot Dome gas station: 631
Toutle "Big Foot" statue: 588
Waiting for the Interurban artwork: 63
world's largest chainsaw sculpture: 727
world's largest king salmon barbecue: 214
world's largest single-tree totem: 445
world's longest beach arch: 428
world's longest vertical baffle fish ladder:
  490
world's only skybridge for squirrels: 441

WINES/WINERIES

ABOUT THE AUTHOR

Born in Atlanta, Georgia, Don Pitcher grew up all over the East Coast—from Florida to Maine—but moved west to attend college. After receiving a master's degree in fire ecology from the University of California at Berkeley, he worked seasonally for a variety of state and federal agencies. Over the years Don did all sorts of outdoor work: calling spotted owls in northern California, mapping grizzly habitat in the mountains of Wyoming, and doing a wide range of work in Alaska: building backcountry trails, running salmon weirs, conducting forest fire research, and working with brown bears.

Don's love of travel and the outdoors led him to write and photograph various guidebooks. In addition to this volume, he authored *Wyoming Handbook* and *Berkeley Inside/Out,* and co-authored *Alaska-Yukon Handbook.* He also photographed books on Wyoming and Alaska for Compass American Guides. Don Pitcher's photographs have appeared in a wide variety of books, calendars, magazines, and advertisements. He bases his travels around the world from his Anchorage, Alaska home, where he lives with his wife, Karen Shemet, and their child, Aziza Bali.

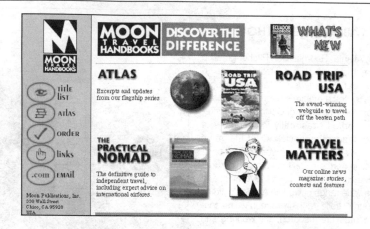

LOSE YOURSELF IN THE EXPERIENCE, NOT THE CROWD

For 25 years, Moon Travel Handbooks have been the guidebooks of choice for adventurous travelers. Our award-winning Handbook series provides focused, comprehensive coverage of distinct destinations all over the world. Each Handbook is like an entire bookcase of cultural insight and introductory information in one portable volume. Our goal at Moon is to give travelers all the background and practical information they'll need for an extraordinary travel experience.

The following pages include a complete list of Handbooks, covering North America and Hawaii, Mexico, Latin America and the Caribbean, and Asia and the Pacific. To purchase Moon Travel Handbooks, check your local bookstore or order by phone: (800) 345-5473 M-F 8 am.-5 p.m. PST or outside the U.S. phone: (530) 345-5473.

"An in-depth dunk into the land, the people and their history, arts, and politics."
—*Student Travels*

"I consider these books to be superior to Lonely Planet. When Moon produces a book it is more humorous, incisive, and off-beat."
—*Toronto Sun*

"Outdoor enthusiasts gravitate to the well-written Moon Travel Handbooks. In addition to politically correct historic and cultural features, the series focuses on flora, fauna and outdoor recreation. Maps and meticulous directions also are a trademark of Moon guides."
—*Houston Chronicle*

"Moon [Travel Handbooks] . . . bring a healthy respect to the places they investigate. Best of all, they provide a host of odd nuggets that give a place texture and prod the wary traveler from the beaten path. The finest are written with such care and insight they deserve listing as literature."
—*American Geographical Society*

"Moon Travel Handbooks offer in-depth historical essays and useful maps, enhanced by a sense of humor and a neat, compact format."
—*Swing*

"Perfect for the more adventurous, these are long on history, sightseeing and nitty-gritty information and very price-specific."
—*Columbus Dispatch*

"Moon guides manage to be comprehensive and countercultural at the same time . . . Handbooks are packed with maps, photographs, drawings, and sidebars that constitute a college-level introduction to each country's history, culture, people, and crafts."
—*National Geographic Traveler*

"Few travel guides do a better job helping travelers create their own itineraries than the Moon Travel Handbook series. The authors have a knack for homing in on the essentials."
—**Colorado Springs** *Gazette Telegraph*

MEXICO

"These books will delight the armchair traveler, aid the undecided person in selecting a destination, and guide the seasoned road warrior looking for lesser-known hideaways."

—*Mexican Meanderings* Newsletter

"From tourist traps to off-the-beaten track hideaways, these guides offer consistent, accurate details without pretension."

—*Foreign Service Journal*

Archaeological Mexico	**$19.95**
Andrew Coe	420 pages, 27 maps
Baja Handbook	**$16.95**
Joe Cummings	540 pages, 46 maps
Cabo Handbook	**$14.95**
Joe Cummings	270 pages, 17 maps
Cancún Handbook	**$14.95**
Chicki Mallan	240 pages, 25 maps
Colonial Mexico	**$18.95**
Chicki Mallan	400 pages, 38 maps
Mexico Handbook	**$21.95**
Joe Cummings and Chicki Mallan	1,200 pages, 201 maps
Northern Mexico Handbook	**$17.95**
Joe Cummings	610 pages, 69 maps
Pacific Mexico Handbook	**$17.95**
Bruce Whipperman	580 pages, 68 maps
Puerto Vallarta Handbook	**$14.95**
Bruce Whipperman	330 pages, 36 maps
Yucatán Handbook	**$16.95**
Chicki Mallan	400 pages, 52 maps

"Beyond question, the most comprehensive Mexican resources available for those who prefer deep travel to shallow tourism. But don't worry, the fiesta-fun stuff's all here too."

—*New York Daily News*

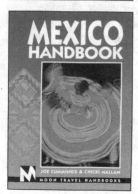

LATIN AMERICA
AND THE CARIBBEAN

"Solidly packed with practical information and full of significant cultural asides that will enlighten you on the whys and wherefores of things you might easily see but not easily grasp."

—-Boston Globe

Belize Handbook	**$15.95**
Chicki Mallan and Patti Lange	390 pages, 45 maps
Caribbean Vacations	**$18.95**
Karl Luntta	910 pages, 64 maps
Costa Rica Handbook	**$19.95**
Christopher P. Baker	780 pages, 73 maps
Cuba Handbook	**$19.95**
Christopher P. Baker	740 pages, 70 maps
Dominican Republic Handbook	**$15.95**
Gaylord Dold	420 pages, 24 maps
Ecuador Handbook	**$16.95**
Julian Smith	450 pages, 43 maps
Honduras Handbook	**$15.95**
Chris Humphrey	330 pages, 40 maps
Jamaica Handbook	**$15.95**
Karl Luntta	330 pages, 17 maps
Virgin Islands Handbook	**$13.95**
Karl Luntta	220 pages, 19 maps

NORTH AMERICA AND HAWAII

"These domestic guides convey the same sense of exoticism that their foreign counterparts do, making home-country travel seem like far-flung adventure."

—Sierra Magazine

Alaska-Yukon Handbook	**$17.95**
Deke Castleman and Don Pitcher	530 pages, 92 maps
Alberta and the Northwest Territories Handbook	**$18.95**
Andrew Hempstead	520 pages, 72 maps,
Arizona Handbook	**$18.95**
Bill Weir	600 pages, 40 maps
Atlantic Canada Handbook	**$18.95**
Mark Morris	460 pages, 61 maps
Big Island of Hawaii Handbook	**$15.95**
J.D. Bisignani	390 pages, 23 maps
Boston Handbook	**$13.95**
Jeff Perk	200 pages, 20 maps
British Columbia Handbook	**$16.95**
Jane King and Andrew Hempstead	430 pages, 69 maps

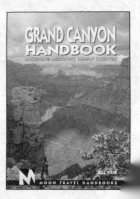

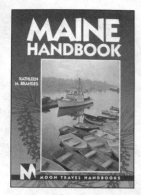

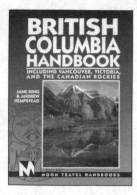

Canadian Rockies Handbook	**$14.95**
Andrew Hempstead	220 pages, 25 maps
Colorado Handbook	**$17.95**
Stephen Metzger	480 pages, 59 maps
Georgia Handbook	**$17.95**
Kap Stann	380 pages, 50 maps
Grand Canyon Handbook	**$14.95**
Bill Weir	220 pages, 9 maps
Hawaii Handbook	**$19.95**
J.D. Bisignani	1,030 pages, 90 maps
Honolulu-Waikiki Handbook	**$14.95**
J.D. Bisignani	400 pages, 20 maps
Idaho Handbook	**$18.95**
Don Root	610 pages, 42 maps
Kauai Handbook	**$15.95**
J.D. Bisignani	320 pages, 23 maps
Los Angeles Handbook	**$16.95**
Kim Weir	370 pages, 15 maps
Maine Handbook	**$18.95**
Kathleen M. Brandes	660 pages, 27 maps
Massachusetts Handbook	**$18.95**
Jeff Perk	600 pages, 23 maps
Maui Handbook	**$15.95**
J.D. Bisignani	420 pages, 35 maps
Michigan Handbook	**$15.95**
Tina Lassen	300 pages, 30 maps
Montana Handbook	**$17.95**
Judy Jewell and W.C. McRae	480 pages, 52 maps
Nevada Handbook	**$18.95**
Deke Castleman	530 pages, 40 maps
New Hampshire Handbook	**$18.95**
Steve Lantos	500 pages, 18 maps
New Mexico Handbook	**$15.95**
Stephen Metzger	360 pages, 47 maps
New York Handbook	**$19.95**
Christiane Bird	780 pages, 95 maps
New York City Handbook	**$13.95**
Christiane Bird	300 pages, 20 maps
North Carolina Handbook	**$14.95**
Rob Hirtz and Jenny Daughtry Hirtz	275 pages, 25 maps
Northern California Handbook	**$19.95**
Kim Weir	800 pages, 50 maps
Ohio Handbook	**$15.95**
David K. Wright	340 pages, 12 maps
Oregon Handbook	**$17.95**
Stuart Warren and Ted Long Ishikawa	588 pages, 34 maps

Pennsylvania Handbook	**$18.95**
Joanne Miller	448 pages, 40 maps
Road Trip USA	**$24.00**
Jamie Jensen	900 pages, 165 maps
Road Trip USA: Chicago Getaways	**$9.95**
	60 pages, 1 map
Road Trip USA: Seattle Getaways	**$9.95**
	60 pages, 1 map
Santa Fe-Taos Handbook	**$13.95**
Stephen Metzger	160 pages, 13 maps
South Carolina Handbook	**$14.95**
Mike Sigalas	250 pages, 20 map
Southern California Handbook	**$19.95**
Kim Weir	720 pages, 26 maps
Tennessee Handbook	**$17.95**
Jeff Bradley	530 pages, 44 maps
Texas Handbook	**$18.95**
Joe Cummings	690 pages, 70 maps
Utah Handbook	**$17.95**
Bill Weir and W.C. McRae	490 pages, 40 maps
Virginia Handbook	**$15.95**
Julian Smith	340 pages, 30 maps
Washington Handbook	**$19.95**
Don Pitcher	840 pages, 113 maps
Wisconsin Handbook	**$18.95**
Thomas Huhti	590 pages, 69 maps
Wyoming Handbook	**$17.95**
Don Pitcher	610 pages, 80 maps

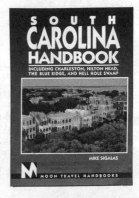

ASIA AND THE PACIFIC

"Scores of maps, detailed practical info down to business hours of small-town libraries. You can't beat the Asian titles for sheer heft. (The) series is sort of an American Lonely Planet, with better writing but fewer titles. (The) individual voice of researchers comes through."

—*Travel & Leisure*

Australia Handbook	**$21.95**
Marael Johnson, Andrew Hempstead, and Nadina Purdon	940 pages, 141 maps
Bali Handbook	**$19.95**
Bill Dalton	750 pages, 54 maps
Bangkok Handbook	**$13.95**
Michael Buckley	244 pages, 30 maps
Fiji Islands Handbook	**$14.95**
David Stanley	300 pages, 38 maps

Hong Kong Handbook	**$16.95**
Kerry Moran	378 pages, 49 maps
Indonesia Handbook	**$25.00**
Bill Dalton	1,380 pages, 249 maps
Micronesia Handbook	**$14.95**
Neil M. Levy	340 pages, 70 maps
Nepal Handbook	**$18.95**
Kerry Moran	490 pages, 51 maps
New Zealand Handbook	**$19.95**
Jane King	620 pages, 81 maps
Outback Australia Handbook	**$18.95**
Marael Johnson	450 pages, 57 maps
Philippines Handbook	**$17.95**
Peter Harper and Laurie Fullerton	670 pages, 116 maps
Singapore Handbook	**$15.95**
Carl Parkes	350 pages, 29 maps
South Korea Handbook	**$19.95**
Robert Nilsen	820 pages, 141 maps
South Pacific Handbook	**$22.95**
David Stanley	920 pages, 147 maps
Southeast Asia Handbook	**$21.95**
Carl Parkes	1,080 pages, 204 maps
Tahiti-Polynesia Handbook	**$15.95**
David Stanley	380 pages, 35 maps
Thailand Handbook	**$19.95**
Carl Parkes	860 pages, 142 maps
Vietnam, Cambodia & Laos Handbook	**$18.95**
Michael Buckley	760 pages, 116 maps

OTHER GREAT TITLES FROM MOON

"For hardy wanderers, few guides come more highly recommended than the Handbooks. They include good maps, steer clear of fluff and flackery, and offer plenty of money-saving tips. They also give you the kind of information that visitors to strange lands—on any budget—need to survive."

—*US News & World Report*

Moon Handbook	**$10.00**
Carl Koppeschaar	141 pages, 8 maps
The Practical Nomad: How to Travel Around the World	**$17.95**
Edward Hasbrouck	575 pages
Staying Healthy in Asia, Africa, and Latin America	**$11.95**
Dirk Schroeder	230 pages, 4 maps

MOONBELTS

Looking for comfort and a way to keep your most important articles safe while traveling? These were our own concerns and that is why we created the Moonbelt. Made of heavy-duty Cordura nylon, the Moonbelt offers maximum protection for your money and important papers. Designed for all-weather comfort, this pouch slips under your shirt or waistband, rendering it virtually undetectable and inaccessible to pickpockets. It features a one-inch high-test quick-release buckle so there's no fumbling for the strap nor repeated adjustments. This handy buckle opens and closes with a touch, but won't come undone until you want it to. Moonbelts accommodate traveler's checks, passport, cash, photos, etc. Measures 5 x 9 inches and fits waists up to 48″.

Available in black only. **US$8.95**
Sales tax (7.25%) for California residents
$1.50 for 1st Class shipping & handling.

To order, call (800) 345-5473
outside the US (530) 345-5473 or fax (530) 345-6751

Make checks or money orders payable to:
MOON TRAVEL HANDBOOKS
PO Box 3040, Chico, CA 95927-3040 U.S.A.
We accept Visa, MasterCard, or Discover.

 MOON TRAVEL HANDBOOKS

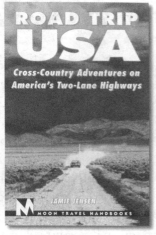

THE PRACTICAL NOMAD

✈ TAKE THE PLUNGE

"The greatest barriers to long-term travel by Americans are the disempowered feelings that leave them afraid to ask for the time off. Just do it."

✈ TAKE NOTHING FOR GRANTED

"Even 'What time is it?' is a highly politicized question in some areas, and the answer may depend on your informant's ethnicity and political allegiance as well as the proximity of the secret police."

✈ TAKE THIS BOOK

$17.95   576 pages

With experience helping thousands of his globetrotting clients plan their trips around the world, travel industry insider Edward Hasbrouck provides the secrets that can save readers money and valuable travel time.
An indispensable complement to destination-specific travel guides, *The Practical Nomad* includes:

airfare strategies

ticket discounts

long-term travel considerations

travel documents

border crossings

entry requirements

government offices

travel publications

Internet information resources

WHERE TO BUY MOON TRAVEL HANDBOOKS

BOOKSTORES AND LIBRARIES: Moon Travel Handbooks are distributed worldwide. Please contact our sales manager for a list of wholesalers and distributors in your area.

TRAVELERS: We would like to have Moon Travel Handbooks available throughout the world. Please ask your bookstore to write or call us for ordering information. If your bookstore will not order our guides for you, please contact us for a free catalog.

> **Moon Travel Handbooks**
> **P.O. Box 3040**
> **Chico, CA 95927-3040 U.S.A.**
> **tel.: (800) 345-5473, outside the U.S. (530) 345-5473**
> **fax: (530) 345-6751**
> **e-mail: travel@moon.com**

IMPORTANT ORDERING INFORMATION

PRICES: All prices are subject to change. We always ship the most current edition. We will let you know if there is a price increase on the book you order.

SHIPPING AND HANDLING OPTIONS: Domestic UPS or USPS first class (allow 10 working days for delivery): $4.50 for the first item, $1.00 for each additional item.

Moonbelt shipping is $1.50 for one, 50 cents for each additional belt.

UPS 2nd Day Air or Printed Airmail requires a special quote.

International Surface Bookrate 8-12 weeks delivery: $4.00 for the first item, $1.00 for each additional item. Note: We cannot guarantee international surface bookrate shipping. We recommend sending international orders via air mail, which requires a special quote.

FOREIGN ORDERS: Orders that originate outside the U.S.A. must be paid for with an international money order, a check in U.S. currency drawn on a major U.S. bank based in the U.S.A., or Visa, MasterCard, or Discover.

TELEPHONE ORDERS: We accept Visa, MasterCard, or Discover payments. Call in your order: (800) 345-5473, 8 a.m.-5 p.m. Pacific standard time. Outside the U.S. the number is (530) 345-5473.

INTERNET ORDERS: Visit our site at: www.moon.com

ORDER FORM

Prices are subject to change without notice. Be sure to call (800) 345-5473,
or (530) 345-5473 from outside the U.S. 8 a.m.–5 p.m. PST for current prices and editions.
(See important ordering information on preceding page.)

Name: _____Date: _____

Street: _____

City: _____Daytime Phone: _____

State or Country: _____Zip Code: _____

QUANTITY	TITLE	PRICE

Taxable Total_____

Sales Tax (7.25%) for California Residents_____

Shipping & Handling_____

TOTAL_____

Ship: ☐ UPS (no P.O. Boxes)   ☐ 1st class   ☐ International surface mail

Ship to: ☐ address above   ☐ other _____

_____

Make checks payable to: **MOON TRAVEL HANDBOOKS**, P.O. Box 3040, Chico, CA 95927-3040
U.S.A. We accept Visa, MasterCard, or Discover. **To Order**: Call in your Visa, MasterCard, or Discover number,
or send a written order with your Visa, MasterCard, or Discover number and expiration date clearly written.

Card Number: ☐ **Visa**   ☐ **MasterCard**   ☐ **Discover**

☐ ☐ ☐ ☐   ☐ ☐ ☐ ☐ ☐ ☐ ☐   ☐ ☐ ☐ ☐

Exact Name on Card: _____

Expiration date:_____

Signature: _____

U.S.~METRIC CONVERSION

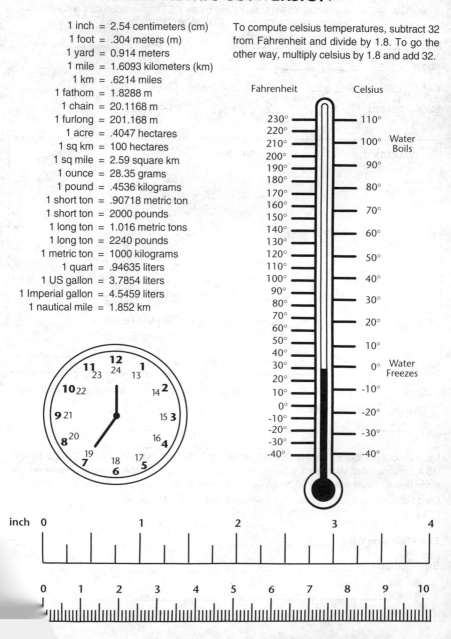

1 inch = 2.54 centimeters (cm)
1 foot = .304 meters (m)
1 yard = 0.914 meters
1 mile = 1.6093 kilometers (km)
1 km = .6214 miles
1 fathom = 1.8288 m
1 chain = 20.1168 m
1 furlong = 201.168 m
1 acre = .4047 hectares
1 sq km = 100 hectares
1 sq mile = 2.59 square km
1 ounce = 28.35 grams
1 pound = .4536 kilograms
1 short ton = .90718 metric ton
1 short ton = 2000 pounds
1 long ton = 1.016 metric tons
1 long ton = 2240 pounds
1 metric ton = 1000 kilograms
1 quart = .94635 liters
1 US gallon = 3.7854 liters
1 Imperial gallon = 4.5459 liters
1 nautical mile = 1.852 km

To compute celsius temperatures, subtract 32 from Fahrenheit and divide by 1.8. To go the other way, multiply celsius by 1.8 and add 32.

Fahrenheit | Celsius

230° — 110°
220°
210° — 100° Water Boils
200°
190° — 90°
180°
170° — 80°
160°
150° — 70°
140°
130° — 60°
120° — 50°
110°
100° — 40°
90°
80° — 30°
70°
60° — 20°
50°
40° — 10°
30°
20° — 0° Water Freezes
10°
0° — -10°
-10° — -20°
-20° — -30°
-30°
-40° — -40°

inch 0 — 1 — 2 — 3 — 4

0 1 2 3 4 5 6 7 8 9 10

IF YOU CAN'T AFFORD TO TRAVEL, JOIN THE CLUB

...AND SEE WASHINGTON STATE!

Traveling in the United States doesn't have to mean hotels that cost $200 a night. With a Hostelling International Membership Card, you can stay in great Washington cities for a fraction of the cost of a hotel—in Bellingham for just $15, Blaine for $14, Seattle for $18, or any one of the other 140+ HI hostels in the U.S. for less than the price of this book! Your HI Card will also get you all kinds of special discounts on everything from museum fees and restaurants, to special excursions and a variety of transportation. So if you're looking for a less expensive way to travel, join the club! Call 202/783-6161. Or check out our website at http://www.hiayh.org.

WASHINGTON HOSTELS INCLUDE:

- HI-BELLINGHAM 360/671-1750
- HI-BIRCH BAY 360/371-2180
- HI-FORT COLUMBIA/CHINOOK 360/777-8755
- HI-GRAYS HARBOR/ELMA 360/482-3119
- HI-FORT FLAGLER/MARROWSTONE ISLAND 360/385-1288
- HI-PORT TOWNSEND 360/385-0655
- HI-SEATTLE 260/622-5443
- HI-VASHON ISLAND RANCH HOSTEL 206/463-2592

HOSTELLING INTERNATIONAL
The new seal of approval of the International Youth Hostel Federation.

HOSTELLING INTERNATIONAL